MICROECONOMICS
An Advanced Treatise

SECOND EDITION

S.P.S. CHAUHAN

Visiting Professor of Economics
Lal Bahadur Shastri Institute of Management (LBSIM)
New Delhi
and
IBS Gurgoan, Haryana

PHI Learning Private Limited

Delhi-110092
2016

₹ 695.00

MICROECONOMICS: An Advanced Treatise, Second Edition
S.P.S. Chauhan

© 2016 by PHI Learning Private Limited, Delhi. All rights reserved. No part of this book may be reproduced in any form, by mimeograph or any other means, without permission in writing from the publisher.

ISBN-978-81-203-5222-3

The export rights of this book are vested solely with the publisher.

Second Printing (Second Edition) ...   .   June, 2016

Published by Asoke K. Ghosh, PHI Learning Private Limited, Rimjhim House, 111, Patparganj Industrial Estate, Delhi-110092 and Printed by Rajkamal Electric Press, Plot No. 2, Phase IV, HSIDC, Kundli-131028, Sonepat, Haryana.

Contents

Prelude to the Book   *xiii*
Preface   *xv*
Preface to the First Edition   *xvii*

1. Introduction to Economics   1–28

INTRODUCTION: NATURE AND SCOPE OF ECONOMICS   *1*
1.1   Economic Problems, Tools and Solutions   *3*
1.2   Tools of Analysis—Price-Mechanism and Production Possibility Curve (PPC)   *4*
1.3   Positive and Normative Economics   *17*
1.4   Classification of the Economic Systems   *18*
1.5   Microeconomics and Macroeconomics   *18*
Key Terms and Concepts   *20*
Exercises   *22*

2. Forces of Demand and Supply in Action: The Price Mechanism   29–99

INTRODUCTION   *29*
2.1   Meaning of Demand and the Law of Demand   *30*
2.2   Determinants of Demand   *32*
2.3   Reasons for Downward Slope of Demand Curve   *35*
2.4(A) Expansion of and Increase in Demand   *37*
2.4(B) Contraction of and Decrease in Demand   *38*
2.5   Market Demand Curve   *39*
2.6   Meaning of Supply and The Law of Supply   *40*
2.7   Determinants of Supply   *41*
2.8(A) Expansion of and Increase in Supply   *44*
2.8(B) Contraction of and Decrease in Supply   *45*
2.9   Market Supply Curve   *45*
2.10   Concept of Equilibrium   *46*
Key Terms and Concepts   *83*
Exercises   *86*
CASE STUDY: THE FAD THEORY OF FAMINES   *97*

3. Elasticity of Demand and Supply   100–131

INTRODUCTION   *100*
3.1   Elasticity of Demand   *101*
    3.1.1   Price Elasticity   *101*
    3.1.2   Income Elasticity   *101*
    3.1.3   Cross-Price Elasticity   *102*
    3.1.4   Types of Price Elasticity of Demand   *104*
    3.1.5   Relationship Between Price Elasticity of Demand and the Slope of the Demand Curve   *107*
    3.1.6   Degree of Price Elasticity   *112*
    3.1.7   Measurement of Price Elasticity of Demand   *113*
    3.1.8   Factors Affecting Price Elasticity of Demand   *114*
3.2   Elasticity of Supply   *115*
    3.2.1   Degrees of Price Elasticity of Supply   *118*
    3.2.2   Factors Influencing the Price Elasticity of Supply   *120*
3.3   Partial Price Elasticities   *121*
Key Terms and Concepts   *122*
Exercises   *124*

4. Approaches to Demand Analysis and Consumer Behaviour   132–256

INTRODUCTION   *132*
4.1   Theory of Demand—Cardinal Utility Approach   *133*
    4.1.1   Assumptions of Cardinal Utility Approach   *133*
    4.1.2   Consumer's Equilibrium   *134*
    4.1.3   Critique of the Cardinal Utility Approach   *136*
4.2   Theory of Demand–Ordinal Utility or Indifference Curve Approach   *137*
    4.2.1   Assumptions of Indifference Curve Approach to Demand   *137*
    4.2.2   Indifference Curves (ICs)   *138*
    4.2.3   Features of Indifference Curves   *146*
    4.2.4   Conditional Properties of the Indifference Curves   *150*
    4.2.5   Consumer's Equilibrium   *155*
    4.2.6   Is Tangency of the Budget Line to the Indifference Curve a Sufficient Condition for Optimality in Consumption?   *162*
4.3   Expansion Path   *165*
    4.3.1   Income Consumption Curve (ICC)   *166*
    4.3.2   Engel Curves   *169*
    4.3.3   Can Engel Curve for a Commodity be Partly Upward Rising, Partly Vertical and Partly Backward Bending?   *173*
    4.3.4   Price Consumption Curves (PCCs)   *174*
    4.3.5   Derivation of Demand Curve from PCC   *174*
    4.3.6   Special Cases of Substitutes, Complements and Discrete Goods   *181*
4.4   Price Effect and its Components—The Income and the Substitution Effects   *184*
    4.4.1   Splitting the Price Effect into Substitution and Income Effects when the Price of X Rises   *191*
4.5   Applications of Indifference Curves   *191*

4.6 The Composite Commodity Theorem 222
4.7 Critique of Indifference Curve Approach 224
4.8 The Revealed Preference Approach 225
    4.8.1 Derivation of Demand Under the Revealed Preference Theory 226
    4.8.2 The Weak and the Strong Axioms of the Revealed Preference Theory 226
Key Terms and Concepts 236
Exercises 239
CASE STUDY: THE FOOD STAMP PROGRAMME AND SOCIAL WELFARE 252

5. Production and Producer's Equilibrium 257–298

INTRODUCTION 257
5.1 Factors of Production 258
5.2 Production Function 259
5.3 Short-Run Production 261
5.4 Long-Run Production 264
    5.4.1 Causes of Increasing, Constant and Decreasing Returns to Scale 266
5.5 Isocost and Isoquant Curves 266
    5.5.1 Isocost Curves 266
    5.5.2 Isoquant Curves 267
    5.5.3 Properties of Isoquants 268
5.6 Producer's Equilibrium 269
    5.6.1 One Variable Factor Case 269
    5.6.2 Two Variable Factors Case 271
    5.6.3 Expansion Path 276
    5.6.4 Is Tangency of Isocost to Isoquant A Sufficient Condition for Optimality in Production? 278
5.7 Returns to Variable Proportions and Returns to Scale 278
5.8 Features of Cobb–Douglas Production Function and Elasticity of Factor Substitution 285
    5.8.1 Features of Cobb–Douglas Production Function 286
5.9 Economic and Non-Economic Regions of Production 287
5.10 Influence of Technical Progress on Position and Shape of an Isoquant 289
Key Terms and Concepts 290
Exercises 293

6. Cost and Revenue 299–353

INTRODUCTION 299
6.1 Classification of Costs 300
6.2 Cost Functions and Traditional Theory of Costs 303
    6.2.1 Relationships Among AC, AVC and MC in the Short-Run 309
    6.2.2 Long-run Cost Curves in the Traditional Theory 313
    6.2.3 Derivation of the Long-run Total Cost Curve for a Firm from its Expansion Path 316
6.3 Modern Theory of Costs 319

	6.4	Economies and Diseconomies of Scale	324

		6.4.1	Internal and External Economies	324
		6.4.2	Classification of Economies of Scale	329
		6.4.3	Economies of Scope	330
		6.4.4	Diseconomies of Scale	331

6.5 Revenue Curves 332
6.6 Linear Break-even Analysis 335
6.7 Non-Linear Break-even Analysis 338
Key Terms and Concepts 340
Exercises 343

7. Market Forms 354–377

INTRODUCTION 354
7.1 Assumptions of Perfect Competition 355
7.2 Fluctuations in Market Price and their Effect on the Price of a Competitive Firm 356
7.3 Monopoly and its Features 363
7.4 Forms and Features of Imperfect Market 368
7.5 Economic Efficiency of a Market 370
Key Terms and Concepts 371
Exercises 374

8. Price-output Decisions of a Firm Under Perfect Competition 378–406

INTRODUCTION 378
8.1 Price-output Decisions of a Competitive Firm in the Short-run 384
8.2 Price-output Decisions of a Competitive Firm in the Long-run 386
8.3 Dynamic Changes and Industry Equilibrium 389
8.4 Important Observations About a Competitive Firm 396
Key Terms and Concepts 402
Exercises 403

9. Price-output Decisions of a Monopoly 407–455

INTRODUCTION 407
9.1 Price-output Decisions of Monopoly in Short-Run 408
9.2 Price-output Decisions of Monopoly in Long-Run 410
9.3 Monopoly Power and its Sources 411
9.4 Social Cost of Monopoly Power 412
9.5 Supply Curve of a Monopoly 413
9.6 Price Discrimination 414
    9.6.1 The Objectives of Price Discrimination 417
    9.6.2 Degrees of Price Discrimination 418
    9.6.3 Effects of Price Discrimination 419
    9.6.4 Existence of Monopoly Through Price Discrimination 423
    9.6.5 Other Forms of Price Discrimination 423
9.7 Price-Output Decisions of a Monopoly Under Dynamic Changes 426
9.8 Multiplant Monopoly 437

9.9 Monopoly versus Competitive Firm *441*
9.10 Monopsony and Monopsony Power *442*
    9.10.1 Monopsony Power and Its Sources *444*
    9.10.2 Social Costs of Monopsony Power *445*
Key Terms and Concepts *446*
Exercises *448*

10. Price-output Decisions of Monopolistically Competitive Firms   456–469

INTRODUCTION *456*
10.1 Price-output Decisions of Monopolistically Competitive Firm in Short-run and Long-run *457*
10.2 Monopolistic Competition and Economic Efficiency *458*
10.3 Chamberlin's Large Group Models of Monopolistic Competition *459*
    10.3.1 Model I: Equilibrium with New Firms Entering the Industry *459*
    10.3.2 Model II: Equilibrium with Price Competition *460*
    10.3.3 Model III: Price Competition and Free Entry *462*
    10.3.4 Critique of Chamberlin's Models *464*
10.4 Comparison with Pure Competition *465*
Key Terms and Concepts *468*
Exercises *468*

11. Price-output Decisions under Oligopoly   470–534

INTRODUCTION *470*
11.1 Simultaneous Quantity Setting: The Cournot Model with Costless Production *472*
    11.1.1 Assumptions of Cournot's Model *472*
    11.1.2 The Model *472*
11.2 Reaction Curve Approach to Cournot's Model—With and Without the Assumptions of Costless Production and Identical Costs *475*
11.3 Simultaneous Price Setting with Homogeneous and Heterogeneous Products—Bertrand's Model *482*
11.4 Quantity Leadership—Stackelberg Model *489*
11.5 Chamberlin's Oligopoly Model (Small Group Model) *495*
11.6 The Kinked Demand Model of Sweezy *496*
    11.6.1 Equilibrium of Oligopolistic Firms Under Indirect Taxation *497*
    11.6.2 Critique of Sweezy's Model *499*
11.7 Cartels *499*
    11.7.1 Cartels Maximizing Joint Profits *499*
    11.7.2 Mathematical Presentation of Joint Profit-Maximizing Cartel *500*
    11.7.3 Market Sharing Cartels *503*
11.8 Price Leadership Models *505*
    11.8.1 Price Leadership by a Low-cost Firm *505*
    11.8.2 Mathematical Treatment of Price Leadership by Low-cost Firm *507*
    11.8.3 Price Leadership by a Dominant Firm *511*
    11.8.4 Mathematical Treatment of Price Leadership of the Dominant Firm *512*
    11.8.5 Barometric Price Leadership *515*

viii Contents

11.9 Critique of Price Leadership Models *515*
11.10 Contestable Market Theory *516*
11.11 Competition Versus Collusion (The Prisoners' Dilemma) *517*
11.12 Prisoners' Dilemma *519*
    11.12.1 Implications of the Prisoners' Dilemma *519*
Key Terms and Concepts *520*
Exercises *523*

12. Game Theory   535–589

INTRODUCTION *535*
12.1 Pay-off Matrix, Strategies and Equilibria Revisited *539*
12.2 Non-Zero-Sum Games Under Pure Strategies
[Nash Equilibrium in Pure Strategies] *540*
    12.2.1 Nash Equilibrium Has Two Limitations *541*
12.3 Non-Zero-Sum Games Under Mixed Strategies
[Nash Equilibrium in Mixed Strategies] *541*
    12.3.1 The Need for Mixed Strategies *541*
    12.3.2 Mixed Strategies and Nash Equilibrium *542*
12.4 Non-Zero-Sum Games Under Maximin/Minimax Criteria *547*
    12.4.1 Maximin Criteria *547*
    12.4.2 Minimax Criterion *549*
12.5 Non-Zero-Sum Games [Assorted Applications] *549*
    12.5.1 Application 12.1: Problem of the Couple [The Battle of Sexes] *549*
    12.5.2 Application 12.2: Matching Coins [Matching Pennies] *551*
    12.5.3 Application 12.3: Repeated Games *553*
    12.5.4 Application 12.4: Sequential Games—Benefit of First Mover *554*
    12.5.5 Application 12.5: Sequential Games—Product Choice *555*
    12.5.6 Application 12.6: Limit Pricing and Short- and Long-run Profits *557*
    12.5.7 Application 12.7: Cournot–Nash Equilibrium
[Simultaneous Quantity Setting] *559*
    12.5.8 Application 12.8: Bertrand–Nash Equilibrium
[Simultaneous Price Setting for Homogeneous Products] *564*
    12.5.9 Application 12.9: Bertrand–Nash Equilibrium
[Simultaneous Price Setting for Heterogeneous Products] *566*
    12.5.10 Application 12.10: Quantity Leadership [Stackelberg Model] *568*
12.6 Non-zero-sum Mixed Strategy Games of Incomplete/Imperfect
Information *573*
12.7 Zero-sum Games *577*
    12.7.1 Zero-sum Pure Strategy Games—Minimax-Maximin Principles *578*
    12.7.2 Zero-sum Pure Strategy Games—Dominant Strategy Principle *578*
    12.7.3 Zero-sum Mixed Strategy Games *580*
Key Terms and Concepts *583*
Exercises *585*

13. Sales Maximization   590–612

INTRODUCTION *590*
13.1 Baumol's Static Models *591*
    13.1.1 Model 1: Static Single Product Model without Advertising *592*

13.1.2 Model 2: Static Single Product Model with Advertising *595*
13.1.3 Model 3: Static Multi-Product Model without Advertising *600*
13.1.4 Model 4: Static Multi-Product Model with Advertising *600*
13.2 Baumol's Dynamic Model *602*
13.2.1 The Model *603*
Key Terms and Concepts *607*
Exercises *609*

14. Determination of Factor Prices   613–654

INTRODUCTION *613*
14.1 When both Factor and Product Markets are Competitive *615*
14.2 When Factor Market is Competitive but Product Market is Not *618*
14.3 When Product Market is Competitive but Factor Market is Not *619*
14.4 When None of the Two Markets is Competitive *620*
14.5 Pricing of Factors when a Firm Employs More than one Variable Factor *622*
14.6 Market Supply and Market Demand of Factors *625*
14.7 Concluding Remarks and Marginal Productivity Theory of Distribution *627*
14.8 Rental Element in Factor Pricing *639*
Key Terms and Concepts *646*
Exercises *649*

15. Investment Decisions and Capital Asset Pricing   655–684

INTRODUCTION *655*
15.1 Types of Interest Rates *656*
15.2 Concept of Discounting Rates and Determination of Present Value (PV) *658*
15.2.1 Sum of the Present Values of Future Income Streams *660*
15.2.2 Effective Yield *666*
15.3 Net Present Value Criterion for Capital Investment Decisions *668*
15.4 Investment Decisions of Consumers *672*
15.5 Intertemporal Production Decisions *675*
15.5.1 Price Behaviour of Using Depletable Resources in a Competitive Industry *676*
15.5.2 Price Behaviour of Using Depletable Resource by a Monopoly *677*
15.6 Decision Under Risk *677*
Key Terms and Concepts *679*
Exercises *681*

16. General Equilibrium and Economic Efficiency   685–715

Introduction *685*
16.1 Path to General Equilibrium *687*
16.2 General Equilibrium Analysis: Efficiency of Exchange, Efficiency of Production and Efficiency of Product-Mix *691*
16.3 Some Implications and Applications *698*

16.4 Market Failure and its Sources 711
Key Terms and Concepts 712
Exercises 714

17. Markets with Asymmetric Information 716–729

INTRODUCTION 716
17.1 Mechanism of Market Failure Due to Asymmetric Information: Low-Quality Goods Drive High Quality Goods Out of the Market 717
17.2 Common Consequences of Asymmetric Information 719
    17.2.1 Adverse Selection 719
    17.2.2 Adverse Pricing 719
    17.2.3 Adverse Setting of Interest Rates 720
17.3 Remedies to some Assorted Cases of Market Failure 721
17.4 Efficiency Wage Theory 725
Key Terms and Concepts 727
Exercises 728

18. Externalities and Public Goods 730–743

INTRODUCTION 730
18.1 Externalities and Market Failure 731
18.2 Remedy to Market Failure Caused by Negative and Positive Externalities 733
18.3 Public Goods 736
Key Terms and Concepts 739
Exercises 740

19. Linear Programming 744–784

INTRODUCTION 744
19.1 Constrained Maximization (Graphic Method) 747
19.2 Constrained Maximization (Algebraic Method) 747
19.3 Constrained Minimization (Graphic Method) 750
19.4 Constrained Minimization (Algebraic Method) 751
19.5 Assorted Applications 751
19.6 The Dual Problem 759
19.7 The Simplex Method 762
19.8 Problem of Degeneracy in Linear Programming 770
19.9 Special Cases 773
19.10 Sensitivity Analysis 778
Key Terms and Concepts 780
Exercises 781

20. Input–Output Analysis 785–815

INTRODUCTION 785
20.1 The Input–Output Model 787

20.2 Open and Closed Input–Output Models   *794*
    20.2.1 The Open Model   *794*
    20.2.2 The Closed Model   *800*
Key Terms and Concepts   *807*
Exercises   *809*

21. International Trade Factor Mobility and Comparative Advantage   816–850

INTRODUCTION   *816*
21.1 International versus Inter-Regional Trade   *818*
21.2 Theories of International Trade   *819*
    21.2.1 Mercantilist Doctrine   *819*
    21.2.2 Theory of Comparative Advantage   *819*
21.3 Modern Theory of International Trade   *825*
21.4 A Comparative Analysis of Classical and the Modern Theories   *830*
21.5 International or World Terms of Trade   *831*
    21.5.1 Terms of Trade and Offer Curves   *833*
    21.5.2 Applications of Offer Curves   *834*
    21.5.3 Economic Growth and Terms of Trade   *840*
21.6 Factor Mobility and Factor Price Equalization   *841*
    21.6.1 Samuelson's Factor Price Equalization Theorem   *841*
Key Terms and Concepts   *845*
Exercises   *849*

22. Decision Theory   851–870

INTRODUCTION   *851*
22.1 Decision under Certainty   *852*
22.2 Decisions under Risk   *854*
    22.2.1 Expected Monetary Value Method   *855*
    22.2.2 Incremental Analysis Method   *857*
    22.2.3 Marginal Analysis Method   *859*
    22.2.4 Decision Tree Analysis Approach   *861*
22.3 Decision Under Uncertainty   *865*
Key Terms and Concepts   *867*
Exercises   *868*

23. Estimation of Functions in Economics—The Basics of Economics   871–906

INTRODUCTION   *871*
23.1 Stages of Econometric Estimation   *873*
    23.1.1 Stage 1: Specification of Variables   *873*
    23.1.2 Stage 2: Assignment of Signs and Symbols to the Coefficients (Parameters)   *874*
    23.1.3 Stage 3: Formulation of Mathematical Model   *874*
    23.1.4 Stage 4: Estimation of Functions   *875*
    23.1.5 Stage 5: Testing of the Estimated Functions   *876*

23.2 OLS Estimation of Functions   876
   23.2.1 OLS—Estimation of Functions of One Explanatory (Simple Regression)   876
   23.2.2 OLS—Estimation of Functions of More than One Variable—Multiple Regression   884
23.3 Testing the Estimated Functions   886
   23.3.1 Test for Goodness of Fit—Coefficient of Determination   886
   23.3.2 Tests for Significance of the Parameter Estimates   888
23.4 Problems with Regression Analysis   894
   23.4.1 Specification of Mathematical Model   894
   23.4.2 Multicollinearity of Variables   895
   23.4.3 Identification Problem   895
23.5 Effect on R^2 of Additional Explanatory Variables   897
Key Terms and Concepts   900
Exercises   903

24. Pricing Policies in Practice   907–940

INTRODUCTION   907
24.1 A Brief Review of Pricing Policies   908
24.2 Transfer Pricing   912
   24.2.1 Transfer Pricing when the Downstream Division Uses One Intermediate Input   912
   24.2.2 Transfer Pricing when the Firm Needs Two or More Inputs for its Product   915
   24.2.3 Transfer Pricing when the Upstream Division is a Monopoly Supplier of Input to the Outside Market   926
24.3 Cartel Pricing   927
24.4 Bundling   930
   24.4.1 Bundling—Pure and Mixed   931
24.5 Two-part Tariff Pricing   933
24.6 Suggestions of Prominent Study Groups on Pricing Policies   935
Key Terms and Concepts   936
Exercises   937

Statistics Tables   941–954

Index   955–964

Prelude to the Book

—Professor (Dr.) Manab Adhikary

Prof. Adhikary, a PhD from Indiana University, USA (1974–78), is the proud recipient of several awards and honours like Fullbright Fellowship (USA) (1970–78), London School of Economics and Business Scholarship (UK) (1979–80), Ezepeca Trainers Honours (Iran–Zabakenar), Trainer's Award (Eastern Europe) (1987–88), Bangkok Economic Tourism (1995–96) Conference on Eco-tourism, Bangkok, International Conference for Global Business Management (1995) Florida, USA, Asian Development Bank (Japan) 2012 Conference on Banking and Finance in Developing Countries, Asian Trade and Transport. Communication Seminar at Funket, Bangkok (2013), IMF keynote address on IBRD (World Bank) and IMF Conference, Florida, USA. His PhD thesis has the privilege of being supervised by the Research Committee comprising Paul Samuelson, Milton Friedman, Simon Kuznets Junior and Joseph Bachelor at Indiana University. He is also privileged to have Prof. Amartya Sen, Transatlantic Professor at London, UK, US and India-Chancellor, Nalanda Global University as his guide and mentor since his Delhi School of Economics days.

The book, *Microeconomics: An Advanced Treatise* (PHI Learning) attracted my attention while on shelf of the library of the management institute, which I often visited as its Director Emeritus in New Delhi. I picked it up out of curiosity for the Bayesian Game flow chart on its title page. I could not resist turning to the chapter on "Game Theory" in the book and I found it worth my time.

Later, when I scanned through some of its other chapters in my leisure time, I was delighted at the organisation and treatment of the subject-matter by its author, Prof. S.P.S. Chauhan. I found chapter planning as well as the concepts and precepts, contents and contexts in its reference—all delivered in a highly logical manner. The author has displayed unique boldness in upholding the cause of scientific treatment of the subject-matter. All the traditional and contemporary approaches have failed miserably in balancing logic and economic rationality so well.

The book in question can serve as a comprehensive text for all—from beginners (actual readers) to the potential researchers. The concepts in it are interwoven so logically and explained so nicely through mathematical tools that the reader feels sailing smoothly from one to the other. Key concepts at the end of each chapter provide a quick review, while short and long answer questions and caselets with hints provide enough practice-material for the students. The work is so unique that I cannot restrain myself from calling it a pioneering work, which, I am sure, will provide a good learning for one-and-all.

I have the pleasure and privilege to report that the author has raised the subject from ground level and lifted it to the heights of its orbit. I wish the author to move from his planet to others in the solar system of economics and to supplement/complement his work in the process through treatments of disciplines of Macroeconomics, Linear, Non-linear and Goal Programming, Statistics, Decision Theories, and other behavioural models. In the final count, I wish the author moves from economic applications to non-economic ones, that is, from positive to normative sides as well, which in the modern world of materialism seem completely lost. Let the readers judge that Economics has no limits and no limitations.

Prof. (Dr.) Manab Adhikary
Ex-Dean, Faculty of Management Studies (FMS)
University of Delhi
Founder Director and Director Emeritus
New Delhi Institute of Management (NDIM), New Delhi

Preface

I have great pleasure in presenting the **Second Edition** duly revised and re-composed in accordance with the suggestions made from time to time by my students as well as faculties. To simplify conceptual explanation, mathematical treatment of the concepts has been shifted from the main text to the footnotes, wherever possible. Some readers felt wary of it as a part of the text, not because the sight disheartened them, but because they preferred to understand the textual development of the concepts for clarity as required from them by the course-contents they pursued. This has been the case, in particular, with the management trainees whose interest is confined to non-academic workable clarity of the concepts for their day-to-day references in decision-making. It is, therefore, believed to serve their interest as well as that of the academicians.

To serve the former, an extra attention has been paid to provide clarity of concepts using real world caselets, but not at the cost of academic pursuits.

The basics of the methodology of estimation of functional relationships through econometrics that occupied its place in an Appendix in the previous edition has now been developed into a comprehensive chapter (Chapter 23—Estimation of Functions in Economics: The Basics of Economics) for better understanding. The same is the case with the Appendix on 'pricing policies in practice'. The concept has now been treated in a self-sufficient chapter (Chapter 24—Pricing Policies in Practice). Both these appendices follow the same treatment as the rest of the chapters, that is, with 'key terms and concepts', short- and long-answer questions along with essay-type ones to serve the purpose of those taking competitive examinations. Hints, answers and solutions to the tricky exercises have also been provided, wherever necessary.

As suggested by Prof. (Dr.) Manab Adhikary, Ex-Dean, Faculty of Management Studies (FMS), Delhi School of Economics (DSE), University of Delhi, a chapter on 'Decision Theory' too appears as Chapter 22 with usual treatment and practice questions. His suggestion to ensure development of these chapters from the grass-root level to their existing applicative one, too, has been taken care of.

The book now comprises 24 chapters in all which will provide academic, managerial as well as research-oriented clarity.

Suggestions from faculties and readers are always welcome for the improvement of the book. I will try to accommodate them in subsequent editions.

I am deeply indebted to **Prof. (Dr.) Manab Adhikary**, Ex-Dean of Faculty of Management Studies (FMS), Delhi School of Economics, University of Delhi; who took pains to browse through the first edition from the beginning to its end thoroughly to make his suggestions and comments which have been a great source of inspiration to me for preparing the second edition.

Last, but not the least, let me thank all the faculties, readers and students who made valuable suggestions from time to time for the improvement of the book.

S.P.S. Chauhan

Preface to the First Edition

The text is meant for students of microeconomics pursuing academic and management courses at the undergraduate and the postgraduate levels of different universities and management institutions. It caters to the requirements of all those who wish to develop application-oriented skills in microeconomics. Due emphasis has, therefore, been laid on the analytical treatment and mathematical concepts of the discipline. For proper pursuance of the course, students are expected to be familiar with the tools of differential and integral calculus. The objective is to introduce the economic concepts in a scientific manner, more so, to develop the skills to apply these concepts to the real-world observations and problems.

Despite multiplicity of the reference books and long reading lists prescribed, it is commonly observed that microeconomics continues to be the most dreaded discipline among the students because of the following three main reasons. *First*, most of the texts available in the market are syllabus-oriented in their approach. They deal with the syllabus barely with an objective of introducing the concepts to the students rather than organizing and linking them together scientifically for a comprehensive analysis which is crucial for the application orientation of the young minds. *Second*, the student is expected to refer to a number of texts to collect and compile bits and pieces from each to form his own text to enable him to meet the requirements of the prescribed syllabus. This often turns out to be a jigsaw puzzle. Bits and pieces from different authors rarely fit into the slots to build up a meaningful discipline. As a result, the students give up the cause of application orientation and settle for that of examination orientation. The author is not averse to the multiplicity of reference books, but to that of collecting and compiling bits and pieces to form a comprehensive discipline.

The science of economics is an interesting discipline. In many ways, it is more interesting than even the physical sciences. While physical sciences deal with inanimate objects whose behaviour is deterministic, the science of economics deals with human behaviour which is probabilistic. In deterministic sciences, behaviour of the inanimate objects can be predicted with a fairly high degree of accuracy, but the same cannot be said of the probabilistic sciences such as economics. This is so due to the unpredictable nature of the human behaviour with which the science of economics deals. It is this uncertainty of human behaviour that makes business and policy decisions difficult and challenging. The use of quantitative methods and mathematical tools helps in the measurement of uncertainty and facilitates decision making in business and policy formulations. The study of economics has this singlemost objective at its core. This necessitates development of the discipline as a science. Jargon of words and verbosity contribute little to the science. They serve the purpose only of familiarizing the reader with the discipline.

This, along with the multiplicity of problems faced by the students in pursuance of the discipline, compelled the author to attempt to write this text. The subject matter has been scientifically organized so as to maintain a logical link between the different concepts. The readers may find the topics arranged in a sequence different from that in most of the texts available in the market. It would be worth the effort if it succeeds in building up the discipline in the minds of the students.

Each chapter ends with precise notes on key terms and concepts to facilitate a quick review of the chapter. This is followed by short and long answer questions of numerical and analytical nature to provide ample practice for examinations. Hints, answers and solutions are given at the end of the questions, wherever necessary.

The book has been built upon the contents of *Microeconomics: Theory and Applications* (Parts I and II) published by PHI Learning. This edition includes additional topics such as **Theory of Games, Linear Programming, Input–Output Analysis** and **Introduction to International Economics** to meet the requirements of the syllabi prescribed for the undergraduate and postgraduate courses in several Indian and foreign universities. In addition, the book also provides a comprehensive treatment of **Econometrics** and **Pricing Policies in Practice** in its appendices to suit the needs of the decision makers, whether associated with managerial decision making in the corporate world or pursuing management courses in various institutions in India or abroad.

Feedback from colleagues and students at the stage of doing the manuscript was quite encouraging. The same is solicited from the entire teaching fraternity and students community for further improvement of the text.

It is hoped that the students would find it interesting, and helpful, in achieving the desired targets of performance, not only in examinations but also in their endeavour to solve the real-life problems.

S.P.S. Chauhan

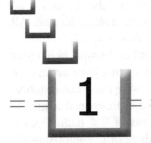

Introduction to Economics

CHAPTER OUTLINE

Introduction: Nature and Scope of Economics
- Economic Problems, Tools and Solutions
- Tools of Analysis—Price-Mechanism and Production Possibility Curve (PPC)
- Positive and Normative Economics
- Classification of Economic Systems
- Elementary Idea of Micro and Macro Economics
- Key Terms and Concepts
- Exercises

INTRODUCTION: NATURE AND SCOPE OF ECONOMICS

"Economics is a science which studies human behaviour as a relationship between ends and scarce means which have alternative uses"

—**Prof. L. Robbins**

Let there be three individuals — A, B and C. Each of them intends to buy a popular brand of car priced at ₹ 6 lakhs. Now assume that A, B and C possess, respectively, ₹ 8 lakhs, 6 lakhs and 4 lakhs. Evidently, A and B face no problem in buying the car. Both of them possess the required amount. It is only C who is not able to buy it. His resource (₹ 4 lakhs) falls short of his end (₹ 6 lakhs) by an amount of ₹ 2 lakhs. A problem, such as this is known as an *economic problem*. It arises whenever available resource falls short of the desired end. The gap between the two is known as the *resource-gap*. We can thus define an economic problem as the one arising from scarcity of the available resource in the face of the desired end. C can't buy the car unless he plugs the resource-gap. This requires raising the level of his resource to the level of his end. All the activities undertaken by C for the purpose are called his *economic activities*.

According to Prof. Robbins, economics is a science which studies human behaviour (i.e. activities) related to filling the gap between ends and scarce resources that have alternative uses. That is, the resources are not only scarce but also capable of alternative uses. For instance, suppose C drops the idea of buying the new car and decides to go for a pre-owned available to him for, say, ₹ 3 lakhs only. If he does so, he would have a surplus of ₹ 1 lakh. Does it mean C has no more problems now? Let us see. Suppose family members of C comprising his wife, a son and a daughter come to know of this surplus. Soon C is reminded of his pending promise of a diamond necklace to his wife, that of a motorcycle to his college-goer son and that of a sports bicycle to his figure-conscious daughter. Would the surplus realized eventually by C through an alternative use of the available resource, that is, buying a used car instead of a new one, suffice for all these needs of his family emerging one after another as soon as they smell of it? Most likely, it would not. This is so because human desires know no bounds. C's wife may choose a diamond necklace priced at ₹ 80,000; his son may settle for a motorcycle priced at ₹ 40,000 and his daughter may pick a sports bicycle that requires nothing short of ₹ 20,000! All this requires a sum of ₹ 1,40,000. C has only ₹ 1,00,000. He is again caught up in a resource-gap, though a little smaller one this time than that faced earlier. In all likelihood, no alternative use of the available resource can solve his economic problem.

Even A and B, seemingly facing no economic problem, have every chance to get caught up in the resource-gap soon. Prompted by their urge to maintain a social status higher than that of C, the two may decide to go for a costlier car priced at, say, ₹ 10 lakhs. They have thus every chance of working their way to the same economic problem which C is facing. Human desires being unlimited and resources being not only limited but also capable of alternative uses, it is difficult to find an individual who faces no economic problem.

The science of economics studies human activities directed at filling the gap between desired ends and scarce resources that have alternative uses. Scarcity of resource leads people to making choices amongst numerous alternatives. As a result they are compelled to prioritize their needs. Scarce resources cannot satisfy all their needs taken together. That is why some economists define economics as a *science of choice-making*.

Economics, thus, is a science that studies economic activities. An economic activity is a human activity that aims at filling the gap between ends and scarce resources that have alternative uses. Investment, production, distribution and consumption are the broad categories into which economic activities are commonly classified. Economics has nothing to do with human activities such as those of social, cultural, political or of religious nature unless such activities transform into economic activities seeking to solve the economic problems of the individuals involved.

Activities such as smuggling, robbery, stealing, etc. though helping those involved in raising their resource levels, fail to qualify as economic activities on the ground that they are against the law of the land in every country. The same is the fate of the activities undertaken against the prevailing social norms. Even those activities that fall within the legal and the social framework but have no *quid pro quo* associated fail to qualify as the economic activities. In the light of these discussions, a review of the definition of an economic activity is called for. We can therefore define an economic activity as *a human activity with a quid pro quo aiming, without violating the law of the land or the prevailing social norms, at filling the gap between ends and scarce resources that have alternative uses.*

1.1 ECONOMIC PROBLEMS, TOOLS AND SOLUTIONS

We have seen that an economic problem is the problem caused by scarcity of resources in the face of the desired ends. Solution to such problems essentially requires raising the resources to the level of desired ends. That, in turn, requires generation of at least that much income which is must for plugging the resource gap. Income generation, as we all know, is possible only through economic activities. Thus, one needs to produce either goods or services to raise his/her income level. This, however, involves a host of problems such as those discussed below. They are collectively called the *basic* or the *central problems*.

(a) What to produce and in what quantity?

To earn income to plug the resource-gap, one needs to produce either a tangible commodity or an intangible service as mentioned above. The basic question that one faces is what goods or services should one produce and in what quantities so that the gap may conveniently be filled? Individuals in the private sector choose production of such goods or services and in such quantities that command a high price in the market (i.e. goods and services enjoying a high demand). For them, *price mechanism* [refer to Section 1.2(i)] is a tool of analysis. On the contrary, public sector, striving for maximization of social welfare, resorts to the *principle of maximum social advantage* to decide the types and quantities of goods and services to be produced. While the private sector has the motive of profit maximization, the public sector has that of maximization of social welfare. The branch of economics that deals with the problem is *Theory of Price*.

(b) How to produce?

Having finalized the type and the quantity of the output to be produced, the next basic problem that arises is that of choice of technique of production. Should it be labour-intensive or capital-intensive? As for the private sector, it resorts to price mechanism again to finalize its choice of technique, while the public sector, once again, resorts to the principle of maximum social advantage for the purpose. Accordingly, the former picks up the cheaper of the two techniques while the latter, picks up one that maximizes employment. The former aims at minimization of production costs as a part of its strategy of profit-maximization while the latter, on the other hand, aims at maximizing employment as a part of its strategy of maximum social advantage and decides in favour of labour-intensive methods even though such methods may involve relatively higher costs than capital-intensive methods. The branch of economics that deals with this problem is *Theory of Production*.

(c) For whom to produce?

The problem implies who gets how much to consume. The answer to the question would depend on who has how much of income to buy the products. The private sector solves the problem through price mechanism. Who gets how much of income depends on who commands what price in the market (i.e. factor-market). The price is determined through price mechanism and every factor of production is paid the price it commands therein. In the public sector, on the contrary, factor prices are subject to government regulation keeping in view the principles of equity and social justice. The answer to the question in the public sector thus depends on who needs what to satisfy the minimum basic needs. The public sector, therefore, resorts to the principle of maximum social advantage to solve the problem. The branch of economics that deals with this problem is *Theory of Distribution*.

(d) Are the resources being fully utilized?

The problem of full-utilization of the resource is another one of the central importance. Its underutilization amounts to wastage of resource that has alternative uses. Thus, apart from its actual cost, there is yet another cost associated with the use of the resource. It is its *Opportunity Cost*.*

To investigate and analyze the problem, the tool employed is Production Possibility Curve (PPC) [refer to Section 1.2(ii)]. The branch of economics that deals with the problem is *Theory of Employment*.

(e) How efficient is the production?

Another central issue is the problem of inefficiency. Like underutilization of resources, inefficiencies in production and distribution have their own costs. The tool of analysis employed in this case too is the Production Possibility Curve (PPC) and the branch of economics dealing with the problem is *Welfare Economics*.

(f) Is the capacity to produce growing?

This relates to the problem of growth. Capacity to produce must grow year after year. Growth is essential for development and modernization. The tool of analysis is again the Production Possibility Curve (PPC) and the branch of economics that deals with the problem is the *Theory of Growth and Development*.

(g) Is the purchasing power of money constant or is it getting eroded through inflation?**

The problem relates to stability of prices. Fluctuating prices disrupt every calculation and every solution. The study of causes and consequences of price fluctuations has been gaining concern all over the world in recent time.

Problems (*a*), (*b*), (*c*) and (*e*) relate to resource allocation and distribution of income. They are commonly grouped under the broad category of Microeconomics. Problems (*d*), (*f*) and (*g*) are usually studied under the broad category of Macroeconomics.†

1.2 TOOLS OF ANALYSIS—PRICE-MECHANISM AND PRODUCTION POSSIBILITY CURVE (PPC)

Let us briefly introduce the tools of analysis, we have frequently referred to in our discussions on the central problems above:

---

*Opportunity cost of a resource refers to the cost of opportunity foregone for the sake of its current use. Transfer earning is yet another name given to it. It refers to income from the next best alternative use of the resource. For example, opportunity cost of a management graduate currently operating his/her own business refers to the salary he/she is entitled to while working as a manager in a firm owned by someone else.

** The growing concern among the economists about the problem of inflation prompted R.G. Lipsey and K.A. Chrystal to include it as the seventh basic economic problem. Refer to *An Introduction to Positive Economics,* 8th ELBS edition (1995), p. 6. The third edition of the same work (1971), pp. 51–58 contained only the first six problems.

†Lipsey, R.G., and Chrystal, K.A., *An Introduction to Positive Economics,* 8th ELBS edition (1995), p. 7.

(i) Price mechanism and its role in solving economic problems

It is a system of exchange which determines market price through market forces of demand and supply. Price so determined is called the *market clearing price* or simply the *market price*. Figure 1.1 demonstrates the functioning of the price mechanism.

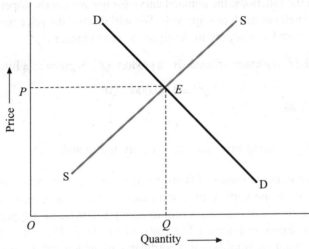

FIGURE 1.1 Price mechanism: DD, the demand curve, intersects SS, the supply curve, at E, the point of equilibrium.* Here, quantity demanded, Q^D, is equal to the quantity supplied, Q^S. The market-clearing price is OP and quantity transacted is OQ, so that $Q^D = Q^S = OQ$.

Demand refers to quantity of a product claimed by buyers at a given price, other things remaining unchanged. Demand equation, also known as *demand function*, refers to an algebraic relationship between quantity demanded of a product and its price, when all other factors remain unchanged. In general, it may be denoted as

$$Q = f(P)$$

If the function is linear, it takes the form,

$$Q = a - bP,$$

where, a and b are fixed parameters.

The relationship portrays the *Law of Demand* which states that, *other things remaining the same (ceteris paribus), more of a product is demanded at a lower price and less of it at a higher price.*

Supply refers to the quantity offered by sellers at a given price, other things remain unchanged *(ceteris paribus)*. Supply equation, also known as *supply function*, refers to an algebraic relationship between the quantity supplied of a product and its price, other things remaining unchanged. In general, it may be denoted as

$$Q = f(P)$$

---

* For details, please see Section 2.10.

If the function is linear, it takes the form,

$$Q = a + bP,$$

where, a and b are fixed parameters.

It portrays the *Law of Supply* which states that, *other things remaining unchanged* (*ceteris paribus*), *more of a product is offered for sale at a higher price and less of it at a lower price.*

As evident from the functions, the demand curve for normal goods slopes downwards, while, the supply curve for such goods slopes upwards. We will discuss the price mechanism along with its components of demand and supply in detail in the next chapter.

> **ILLUSTRATION 1.1:** Quantity demanded of a product, Q^D, is given as a function of price, P, as
>
> $$Q^D = 1,50,000 - 3P$$
>
> while its supply, Q^S, as
>
> $$Q^S = 7P$$
>
> Determine the market-clearing price and the quantity transacted.

Solution: The demand curve resulting from the demand equation, when plotted on the graph, with price represented on the vertical axis and quantity on the horizontal axis, is a downward sloping curve, DD, as shown in Figure 1.1 (not to scale). Likewise the supply curve is an upward sloping curve, SS, as shown in Figure 1.1 (again, not to scale). The point of intersection of the two, point E, is the point of equilibrium, coordinates of which can be read directly from the graph if drawn to scale or can be found by solving the two equations simultaneously as below. At point E,

$$Q^D = Q^S$$
$$\Rightarrow 1,50,000 - 3P = 7P$$
$$\Rightarrow 10P = 1,50,000$$
$$\Rightarrow P = 15,000$$

Substituting in either of the two equations, we have

$$Q^D = 1,05,000$$

and,

$$Q^S = 1,05,000$$

Thus, market-clearing price is ₹ 15,000 and quantity transacted is 1,05,000 units.

Assorted applications of price mechnism—consumer and producer surpluses

Price mechanism is said to be self-correcting in character. This is so because a self-adjustment process comes into play automatically to restore market price as soon as a destabilizing force attempts to distort it.* The self-adjustment process continues to operate even when the destabilizing force is introduced by state. Governments of welfare-states often intervene through taxation, subsidies, price floors and price ceilings to distort market price in public interest. They do so for the cause of equity and social justice. For instance, when consumer and producer surpluses move significantly away from the desired levels, government of a welfare-state intervenes in the free

---

*For working of the self-adjustment process, refer to Chapter 2.

play of price mechanism with a view to give an appropriate tilt in price movement. We will learn more about them in the subsequent chapters. Let us first discuss the two concepts—the consumer surplus and the producer surplus.

Consumer Surplus (CS) refers to excess of expenditures which consumers are willing to incur on a product, over and above their current levels so that they may not have to do without the desired level of consumption of the product. In other words, it is the excess of income which the consumers are willing to forego for a product rather than of remaining without it in the event of its scarcity. To demonstrate, suppose a consumer is currently having 10 units of a product at a price of ₹ 50 per unit. Income spent by him currently on the product is ₹ 500. Now suppose the same consumer is willing to pay as much as ₹ 80 per unit of the product in the event of its scarcity so that he/she may not have to do without it. Excess of income, which he/she is willing to forego for the purpose is ₹ 300 [(80 − 50) × 10]. This is what is known as the consumer surplus. In the system of given demand and supply of a product, consumers surplus may be defined by the area under the demand curve but above the horizontal line passing through the point of intersection of demand and supply (Figure 1.2).

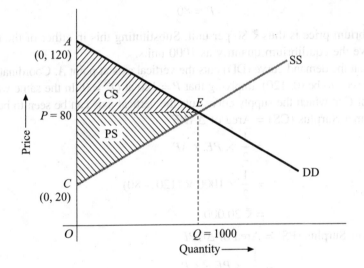

FIGURE 1.2 Consumer and producer surpluses (The triangular regions APE (CS) and CPE (PS) measure ₹ 20,000 and ₹ 30,000 respectively).

In the same way, *Producer Surplus* (PS) may be defined as the excess of revenue realized by the producers over and above that their supply schedule ensures. In the system of given demand and supply curves of a product, it is given by the area above the supply curve but below the horizontal line passing through the point of intersection of demand and supply (Figure 1.2).

Illustration 1.2 demonstrates the process of determining the two.

ILLUSTRATION 1.2: Equations of demand and supply of a product are

$$Q^D = 3000 - 25P \text{ (demand)}$$

and

$$Q^S = (50/3)P - 1000/3 \text{ (supply)}$$

Determine:

(i) Equilibrium price and quantity,
(ii) Consumer Surplus (CS), and
(iii) Producer Surplus (PS).

Solution: Demand and supply curves, when plotted, intersect at point E (Figure 1.2). At this point, $Q^D = Q^S$.

(i) Setting Q^D equal to Q^S, we have

$$3000 - 25P = (50/3)P - 1000/3$$

$$\Rightarrow \qquad P = 80$$

Equilibrium price is thus ₹ 80 per unit. Substituting this in either of the two equations, we have the equilibrium quantity as 1000 units.

Note that the demand curve (DD) cuts the vertical axis at point A. Coordinates of this point can be seen to be (0, 120), implying that $P = 120$ at $Q^D = 0$. In the same way, coordinates of point C at which the supply curve cuts the vertical axis can be seen to be (0, 20).

(ii) Consumer Surplus (CS) = Area of $\triangle APE$

$$= \frac{1}{2} \times PE \times AP$$

$$= \frac{1}{2} \times 1000 \times (120 - 80)$$

$$= ₹ 20,000$$

(iii) Producer Surplus (PS) = Area of $\triangle CPE$

$$= \frac{1}{2} \times PE \times CP$$

$$= \frac{1}{2} \times 1000 \times (80 - 20)$$

$$= ₹ 30,000$$

In general, if demand and supply functions were given as

$$P = f(Q), \text{ and}$$
$$P = g(Q)$$

respectively, CS and PS can be expressed through definite integrals as

Consumer Surplus (CS)* $= \left[\int_0^Q f(Q)\, dQ\right] - OP \times OQ$

Producer Surplus (PS)** $= OP \times OQ - \left[\int_0^Q g(Q)\, dQ\right]$

CS, in Illustration 1.2,

$$CS = \left[\int_0^Q f(Q)\, dQ\right] - OP \times OQ$$

$$= \left[\int_0^Q \left\{120 - \left(\frac{1}{25}\right)Q\right\} dQ\right] - (80 \times 1{,}000)$$

$$= \left[120\,Q - \left(\frac{1}{50}\right)Q^2\right]_{Q=0}^{Q=1{,}000} - 80{,}000$$

$$= \left[1{,}20{,}000 - \left(\frac{1}{50}\right) \times (1000)^2\right] - 80{,}000 = 20{,}000$$

(*Note:* $P = f(Q) = \{120 - (1/25)Q\}$; $F(Q)$, its integral, is $\{120\,Q - \{(1/50)Q^2\}$ and area of the rectangle $OQEP$ is equal to $OP \times OQ$, which is $80 \times 1{,}000$, for the data in Illustration 1.2)

PS, in Illustration 1.2,

$$PS = 80 \times 1{,}000 - \left[\int_0^Q \left\{20 + \left(\frac{3}{50}\right)Q\right\} dQ\right]$$

$$= 80{,}000 - \left[\left\{20Q + \left(\frac{3}{100}\right)Q^2\right\}\right]_{Q=0}^{Q=1{,}000} = 30{,}000$$

(*Note:* $P = g(Q) = \{20 + (3/50)Q\}$; $G(Q)$, its integral, is $\{20Q + \{(3/100)Q^2\}$ and area of the rectangle $OQEP$ is equal to $OP \times OQ$, which is 80×1000, for the data in Illustration 1.2)

---

*Consumer Surplus,

$\quad$ CS = Area of $\triangle APE$
$\quad\quad$ = Area of trapezium $OQEA$ − area of rectangle $OQEP$
$\quad\quad$ = Area under the demand curve ($OQEA$) − area ($OQEP$) below PE

$$= \left[\int_0^Q f(Q)\, dQ\right] - OP \times OQ$$

$$= [F(Q)]_0^Q - OP \times OQ$$

[$F(Q)$ = integral of $f(Q)$ with respect to Q]

**Producer Surplus, PS = Area of $\triangle CPE$
$\quad\quad$ = Area of rectangle $OQEP$ − area of trapezium $OQEC$
$\quad\quad$ = Area of rectangle $OQEP$ − area under the supply curve ($OQEC$)

$$= OP \times OQ - \left[\int_0^Q g(Q)\, dQ\right]$$

$$= OP \times OQ\,[GQ]_0^Q, \quad [G(Q) \equiv \text{integral of } g(Q) \text{ with respect to } Q]$$

Familiarity with techniques of integration and their application in determining the area under a curve come handy in explanation and calculation of CS and PS, whatever the nature of the demand and the supply functions. In the real world situations, these functions generally yield non-linear curves. Thus they are different from the first degree functions of Illustration 1.2. Reader is advised to work out CS and PS for the demand and supply situations of Q.31 to understand the utility of definite integral.

(ii) Production possibility curve (PPC) and its role in solving economic problems

Production Possibility Curve (PPC) is defined as the locus of various combinations of two goods that are possible to be produced with available technologies and resources under full and efficient utilization. Production Possibility Frontier (PPF) is the another name of the Production Possibility Curve (PPC).

To understand, let there be two goods — X and Y — which an economy can produce with available resources and technologies under full and efficient utilization. Let x denote the quantity of good X, say a consumer good and let y denote the quantity of good Y, say a capital good. With given technology and resources, suppose that the economy can produce the following combinations of these goods:

Quantity of $X(x)$	0	30	60	90	120	150
Quantity of $Y(y)$	100	95	88	75	50	30

Assuming full and efficient utilization of the available resources and technologies, the economy can produce 0 unit of good X with 100 units of good Y, or, 150 units of good X with 0 unit of good Y, or, any other combination in the table above.

Representing quantities of X on x-axis and those of Y on y-axis, plotting the combinations and joining them by means of a smooth curve, we get a curve as shown in Figure 1.3.

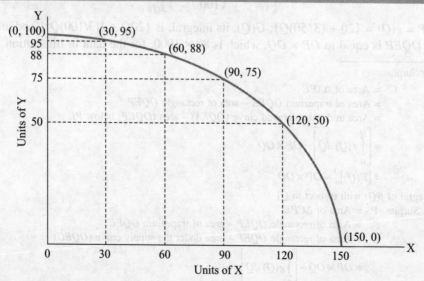

FIGURE 1.3 Production Possibility Curve (PPC), showing various combinations of two goods which are possible to be produced with given technology and resources being utilized at full employment and efficiency.

Every time, production of good X is increased by a given amount, production of good Y is foregone in successively increasing quantities. In other words, sacrifice of Y units for the sake of an additional unit of X has a rising tendency as we go down the curve from left to right. In the language of economics, the opportunity cost of producing an additional unit of X, called the *Marginal Opportunity Cost*, or more popularly, the *Marginal Rate of Product Transformation into X of Y*, written as $MRPT_{X,Y}$ has a rising trend. $MRPT_{X,Y}$ can be expressed as a ratio of quantity of Y foregone (Δy) to that of X gained (Δx) in exchange. It is the numerical value of $\Delta y/\Delta x$, that is, $MRPT_{X,Y} = |\Delta y/\Delta x|$. It can also be written as $(-\Delta y/\Delta x)$ or $(-dy/dx)$. Note that $\Delta y/\Delta x$ or dy/dx represents slope of the curve (PPC), while $MRPT_{X,Y}$ is the numerical value of the slope. While $MRPT_{X,Y}$ ($|\Delta y/\Delta x|$ or $|dy/dx|$) increases along the curve from left to right, the slope ($\Delta y/\Delta x$ or dy/dx) decreases along it in the same direction. The table below demonstrates calculations of the two for the data here and their variations along the curve from left to right.

TABLE 1.1 Production possibility schedule and $MRPT_{x,y}$

x:	0	30	60	90	120	150
y:	100	95	88	75	50	0
$\Delta y/\Delta x$:	—	−5/30	−7/30	−13/30	−25/30	−50/30
		(−0.17)	(−0.23)	(−0.43)	(−0.83)	(−1.67)
$MRPT_{X,Y} = |\Delta y/\Delta x|$:	—	0.17	0.23	0.43	0.83	1.67

Marginal Rate of Product Transformation into X of Y, thus, is

$$MRPT_{X,Y} = \frac{\text{Quantity of } Y \text{ foregone}}{\text{Quantity of } X \text{ gained}}$$

$$= |\Delta y/\Delta x|$$

$$= -(\Delta y/\Delta x)^*$$

The slope ($\Delta y/\Delta x$) decreases from -0.17 to -1.67 along the curve from left to right, but the $MRPT_{X,Y}$, the numerical value of the slope, increases from 0.17 to 1.67. Thus, the slope of the PPC (concave to origin, as in Figure 1.3) is a decreasing function of x while $MRTP_{X,Y}$ (Marginal Rate of Product Transformation into X and Y) is an increasing function of x. This is so due to the implicit assumption of diminishing returns to scale in production. In the event of constant returns to scale, the PPC is linear, sloping downwards. The slope of the PPC and its $MRPT_{X,Y}$ are both constant. Likewise, when production follows increasing returns to scale, the slope of the PPC (convex to origin) is an increasing function of x while $MRPT_{X,Y}$ is a decreasing function of x. Recall that dy/dx represents the slope of the curve while $|dy/dx|$ or the numerical value of the slope represents marginal rate of product transformation ($MRPT_{X,Y}$).

Applications of the PPCs to economic problem of Inefficiency, Unemployment or Growth

Any point on the PPC implies existence of full employment and full efficiency, but production of a combination below the PPC implies existence either of unemployment or of inefficiency or of both. Refer to point A in Figure 1.4.

---

*$\Delta y/\Delta x$ being negative, its numerical value (a positive number) is given by $|\Delta y/\Delta x|$ or by $(-\Delta y/\Delta x)$.

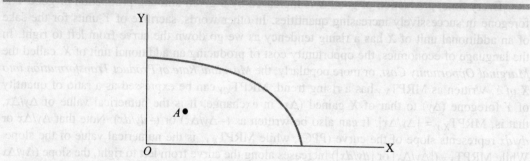

FIGURE 1.4 Existence of unemployment or of inefficiency or of both at a point A inside the PPC.

Given full employment, production at point A inside the PPC, implies existence of inefficiency at that point. Alternatively, given full efficiency, the combination produced at this point implies existence of unemployment. The problems of unemployment and inefficiency can, thus, be investigated with the help of these curves.

The PPCs help investigations into the problems of growth and development as well. In Figure 1.5, let FF be the production possibility curve for the year 2002 and let $F'F'$ be that for the year 2003. Since $F'F'$ is above FF at all levels of outputs of the two goods, it signifies growth of the national product. Growth in this figure is uniform for X and Y industries. When growth is confined only to X industry, the PPC blows out as in Figure 1.6; and when it is confined only to Y industry, it blows out as in Figure 1.7. If growth realized by the two industries is non-uniform, the PPC would blow out as in Figure 1.8.

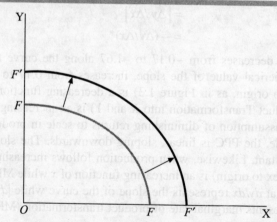

FIGURE 1.5 PPC blows out like a balloon in consequence to economic growth. Outward shift in PPC from FF to $F'F'$ is uniform indicating uniformity of growth of the two industries.

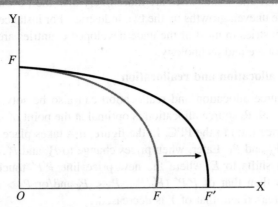

FIGURE 1.6 When growth is confined to X-industry, the PPC blows out, as in the figure, to the right. This shows that growth in Y-industry is almost stagnant while that in X-industry is rapid.

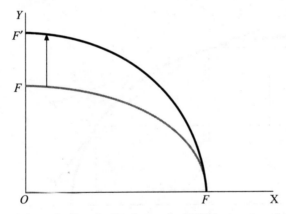

FIGURE 1.7 When growth is confined to the Y-industry, the PPC blows out as above. Growth of X-industry is almost stagnant.

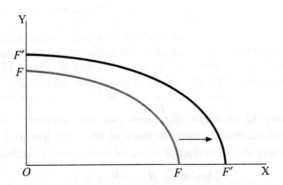

FIGURE 1.8 Both the industries show growth but X-industry shows higher growth than Y-industry.

Uneven growths in X and Y industries are more likely than their even growths. A number of factors contribute to the uneven growths in the two industries. For instance, growths in agriculture and manufacturing industries in most of the underdeveloped countries are uneven due to uneven availability of soil resource and technology.

Problem of resource allocation and reallocation

The problems of resource allocation and reallocation can also be solved with the help of the PPCs. Refer to Figure 1.9. Resource allocation is optimal at the point of tangency of the revenue line (also called the price line) to the PPC. In the figure, this takes place at point E when prices of the two goods are P_X and P_Y. Later, when prices change to P_X' and P_Y', the point of optimality of resource allocation shifts to E' where the new price line $P'P'$ touches the PPC. Slope of PP (P_X/P_Y) being less than that of $P'P'$ (P_X'/P_Y'), $P_X < P_X'$ and/or $P_Y > P_Y'$. This explains why production of X is increased and that of Y is decreased.

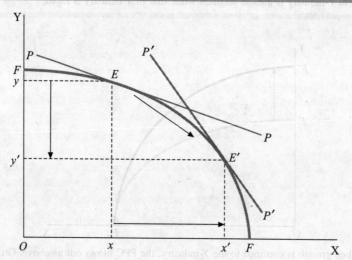

FIGURE 1.9 Problem of resource allocation and reallocation: In the figure PP is the revenue line, $R = x \cdot P_X + y \cdot P_Y$, where, x and y are the quantities of the two goods X and Y produced and sold at prices P_X and P_Y. With given resources and technologies under full and efficient utilization, various production possibilities are depicted by the PPC marked FF. Optimality of resource allocation requires maximization of revenue under the limited production possibilities. To serve the purpose, the revenue line must be tangential to the PPC. This takes place at point E, where slope of the revenue line (also called the price line), is equal to the slope of the PPC. Thus, point E is the point of optimal resource allocation. Changes in prices change the slope of the price line. If price of X rises and that of Y falls, the price line moves to $P'P'$ which touches the PPC at point E'. Production shifts from basket (x, y) to basket (x', y'). The movement from E to E' marks reallocation of resources.

Condition for optimality of resource allocation and reallocation: As mentioned already, optimality of resource allocation requires tangency of the price line to the PPC. The condition can be obtained by solving the following problem of constrained maximization:

$$\text{Maximize: } R = x \cdot P_x + y \cdot P_y$$
$$\text{Subject to: } C = f(x, y)$$

where, R = total revenue realized from the sale of x units of X at price P_X and y units of Y at price P_Y, while $\overline{C}$ is the given resource employed to produce various combinations of the two goods. $\overline{C} = f(x, y)$ is, therefore the equation of the PPC. Solving the problem, we have:

$$-\left(\frac{P_x}{P_y}\right) = -\left(\frac{f_x}{f_y}\right)^* \tag{1.1}$$

where, f_X and f_Y represent partial derivatives of $\overline{C} = f(x, y)$ with respect to X and Y. In other words, $-(P_x/P_y) \equiv$ slope of the price line, while $-(f_x/f_y) \equiv$ slope of the PPC.

For given production possibilities, it is not difficult to obtain the output mix that helps maximization of revenue through the condition given above. Illustration 1.3 demonstrates the mechanism of resource allocation and reallocation.

---

* To solve the problem of constrained maximization,

$$\text{Maximize: } R = x \cdot P_x + y \cdot P_y \tag{1}$$

$$\text{Subject to: } \overline{C} = f(x, y) \tag{2}$$

let us transform it into one of simple maximization through Lagrange's Method. For this, rewrite Eq. (2) as·

$$f(x, y) - \overline{C} = 0$$

Now multiply both of its sides by a positive constant λ, so that

$$\lambda \cdot [f(x, y) - \overline{C}] = 0 \tag{3}$$

Now, develop a composite function Φ, such that

$$\Phi = R - \lambda \cdot [f(x, y) - \overline{C}] \tag{4}$$

Equation 4 incorporates the constraint (2) and the objective function (1) through a positive number, λ, called Lagrange's Multiplier. The problem now is one of simple maximization of the composite function Φ, which involves variables x and y. Differentiating Φ partially with respect to x, y and λ and setting each partial derivative equal to zero, we have

$$\partial\Phi/\partial x = \partial R/\partial x - \lambda \cdot (\partial f/\partial x) = 0 \tag{5}$$

$$\partial\Phi/\partial y = \partial R/\partial y - \lambda \cdot (\partial f/\partial y) = 0 \tag{6}$$

and,
$$\partial\Phi/\partial\lambda = [f(x, y) - \overline{C}] = 0 \tag{7}$$

as the necessary conditions for maximization of Φ. Expressing $\partial R/\partial x = P_x$, and $\partial R/\partial y = P_y$, [from Eq. (1) and denoting

$$\partial f/\partial x = f_x,$$
$$\partial f/\partial y = f_y,$$

we have
$$\lambda = P_x/f_x$$

as also
$$\lambda = P_y/f_y$$

whence
$$P_x/P_y = f_x/f_y \tag{8}$$

or
$$-(P_x/P_y) = -(f_x/f_y) \tag{9}$$

In other words, slope of the revenue line must be equal to the slope of the PPC as a necessary condition for maximization of revenue under given resource constraint. The sufficient conditions for the purpose may be spelled out as

(i) $\partial^2\Phi/\partial x^2 < 0$ and $\partial^2\Phi/\partial y^2 < 0$; and

(ii) $(\partial^2\Phi/\partial x^2)(\partial^2\Phi/\partial y^2) > [\partial^2\Phi/\partial x\,\partial y\,]^2$

ILLUSTRATION 1.3: Quantities x and y of goods X and Y, that are possible to be produced with given resource and technology under full and efficient utilization, are related through the following equation:

$$12y = 36 - x^2$$

Find:
(i) the maximum of X and Y that is possible to be produced,
(ii) marginal rate of product transformation, $\text{MRPT}_{X,Y}$,
(iii) optimal level of product mix when $P_x = 12$ and $P_y = 24$,
(iv) optimal level of product mix when $P_x = 15$ and $P_y = 18$, and
(v) revenues generated in (iii) and (iv).

Solution:

(i) x is maximum when $y = 0$. Thus, maximum of x is 6. Likewise, y is maximum when $x = 0$. Maximum of y is thus 3.

(ii) $\text{MRPT}_{X,Y} = |dy/dx|$. Differentiating the given equation, we have

$$dy/dx = -2x/12$$
$$= -x/6$$

∴ $\text{MRPT}_{X,Y} = |dy/dx| = |-x/6| = x/6$

[Expressing the given function $\bar{C} = f(x, y)$, we have $\bar{C} = 36$, $f(x, y) = 12y + x^2$. Differentiating $f(x, y)$ partially with respect to x and y, we have

$$f_x = 2x \text{ and } f_y = 12$$

Hence, slope of the PPC,

$$dy/dx = -f_x/f_y = -x/6$$

$\text{MRPT}_{X,Y} = |-x/6| = x/6$]

(iii) For optimal product mix, slope of the revenue line = slope of the PPC. That is,

$$-(f_x/f_y) = -(P_x/P_y)$$

or $\quad -x/6 = -12/24$

∴ $\quad x = 3$

Then, $\quad y = (36 - 9)/12$
$\quad\quad\quad = 2.25$.

(iv) When $P_x = 15$, and $P_y = 18$, the optimal product mix is (5, 0.92).
(v) Revenues realized in (iii) and (iv) would work out as 90 and 91.5 respectively.

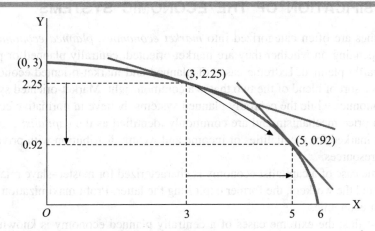

FIGURE 1.10 The original revenue line is $R = 12x + 24y$. After the change in market prices of the two goods, it changes to $R' = 15x + 18y$. Resources shift from production of (3, 2.25) to production of (5, 0.92).

1.3 POSITIVE AND NORMATIVE ECONOMICS

Economics, at times, is classified as *positive economics* and *normative economics*. Positive economics refers to that part of economic analysis in which solutions to basic economic problems recognize no considerations be they social or humanitarian. The entire analysis is based on *as is what is* and not on *what it should be*. Normative economics, on the other hand, refers to that part of economic analysis in which solutions to basic economic problems prioritize social and humanitarian considerations. The analysis is not based on *as is what is* but on *what it should be*. When production and consumption of liquor are allowed by the State for the sake of revenue generated by them, it is positive economics the State is indulging in; but, when the same are banned by the State on the grounds that they are injurious to human health, it is the normative economics the state is indulging in. In the former case, the State operates on the basis of *as is what is* but in the latter case, it operates on the basis of *what it should be*. In the former case, State's priority is its own interest of earning revenue while in the latter case, its priority is social welfare. When a government takes to production and distribution of goods and services of public utility at prices below the production cost incurring a heavy loss of revenue for itself in the process or when it provides free services of health and education or when it grants subsidy on certain production or when it decides to take over certain sick industries with an objective of retaining workers in their employment, it certainly believes in normative economics but if it allows things to proceed as they are with little or no respect for social or humanitarian considerations, it is surely indulging in positive economics. All market-oriented activities relate to positive economics while all welfare-oriented activities relate to normative economics. Generally, all market-oriented economies subscribe to positive economics while all centrally planned economies subscribe to normative economics.

Of the two, neither is perfect. In fact it is a judicious mix of the two that is considered ideal by economists. We will learn more about them in the next section.

1.4 CLASSIFICATION OF THE ECONOMIC SYSTEMS

World economies are often categorized into *market economies*, *planned economies* and *mixed economies*, depending on whether they are market-oriented, centrally planned or partly market-oriented and partly planned. Extreme cases of planned and market-oriented economies are rare nowadays. It is a sort of blend of the two that is a common sight. Market-oriented systems believe in positive economics while the centrally planned systems believe in normative economics. The former rely on price mechanism and are commonly identified as the *capitalist economies*. Such economies are marked for inequalities of income and wealth distribution with private ownership of productive resources.

The extreme case of a capitalist economy is characterized for master–slave relations between the capitalists and the workers, the former exploiting the latter. Profit maximization is yet another feature of such economies.

As against this, the extreme cases of a centrally planned economy is known for its social ownership of productive resources, central planning, much lesser inequalities of income and wealth and minimal role of price mechanism and the institution of money.

As stated earlier, the extreme cases of the two being rare nowadays, the detailed discussion on the two is only of academic interest and is spared for the scholars of the economic systems. Mixed economic systems combine what they call the good features of each and are common.

1.5 MICROECONOMICS AND MACROECONOMICS

We mentioned six different branches of economics while introducing the basic economic problems in Section 1.2. We also mentioned those ones that are studied under microeconomics and those ones that are studied under macroeconomics. In this section, let us discuss the nature, meaning, scope and inter-dependence of the two broad segments of economics.

Microeconomics refers to that branch of economics which studies economic problems of an individual person or of an individual firm. It provides microscopic view of an individual unit. For instance, the study of the economic problem faced by an individual when his income falls short of his expenditure or a similar study of an individual firm or producer provides the subject matter of microeconomics.

On the contrary, *macroeconomics* is a study of the economic problems faced by groups of individuals or of firms taken together. It is thus a study of aggregates. For instance, studies of national income and expenditure, or of the scarcity of income in the face of planned expenditure provide the subject matter for macroeconomics. From the viewpoint of the micro and macro classifications, the first three problems along with the fifth fall under microeconomics while the fourth, the sixth and seventh problems form the subject matter of macroeconomics. As one approaches to economic analysis, the two are more often complementary than competitive. Neither the behaviour of an individual entity reflect the behaviour of an entire group nor the behaviour of the group reflect that of an entity. An observation that a firm in electronic industry incurred heavy loss this year does not necessarily imply that all the firms in the industry incurred heavy losses and an observation that automobile industry in India is heading for huge profits need not imply that every automobile firm in it is heading for huge profits. Likewise, an observation that a particular mango tree in a forest has decayed does not necessarily imply that all the mango trees in it have decayed or the entire forest has decayed nor does an observation that forests cause rain need imply that every mango tree in them can cause rain individually. Indians are known for their hospitality all over the world but one particular Indian when tested for the attribute may test negative by letting his dog loose on the sight of visitors. Whatever is true of an individual need not be true of the community as a whole nor can one predict an individual's behaviour on the basis of the behaviour of a community in general. Even then practice of generalization of individual observation to draw inferences about the community or the group to which the individual belongs and that of deducing individual traits from the community traits are quite common. To crosscheck the validity of the inferences reached through generalization or through deduction, one needs to study the behaviour of the community in the former case and of the individual in the latter case. It is in this sense that micro and macro approaches complement each other.

Note that generalizations of individual traits to reflect community traits is known as the *inductive method* while deducing individual traits from the community traits is known as the *deductive method*.

To understand the true nature of micro and macro approaches to economic analysis, we compare their salient features in Table 1.2.

TABLE 1.2 Distinction between micro and macro branches of economics

Microeconomics	*Macroeconomics*
1. *Meaning:* Microeconomics may be defined as that branch of economics which studies the economic behaviour of the individual unit, may be a particular household or a particular firm. It is a study of one particular unit rather than of all the units combined together. For example, study of income and expenditure of an individual person or of an individual firm is microeconomic study. Microeconomics, thus, studies the behaviour of micro-variables.	1. *Meaning:* Macroeconomics may be defined as that branch of economics which studies the behaviour of not one particular unit, but of all the units taken together. It is a study in aggregates and is often referred to as *Aggregative Economics*. It is the study of the economic system as a whole. For example, study of overall production, overall saving, overall consumption and overall investment in the economy is macroeconomic study. It, thus, studies macro-variables.
2. *Methodology:* Microeconomics splits up the entire economy into smaller parts for the purpose of intensive study. This, sometimes, is referred to as the *Slicing Method* which forms the *Partial equilibrium* analysis based on the assumption of *ceteris paribus* (other things remaining unchanged).	2. *Methodology:* Macroeconomics deals with great averages and aggregates of the system rather than with particular units in it. Macroeconomics splits up the economy into *big lumps* for the purpose of study. This, sometimes, is referred to as the *Lumping Method* involving the analysis of *general equilibrium*.
3. *Domain:* Microeconomics covers the following: (i) *Theory of Product Pricing*, with its constituents of consumer's behaviour and the theory of production and costs. (ii) *Theory of Factor Pricing* with constituents of the theories of wages, rent, interest and profits. (iii) *Theory of Economic Welfare* in case of individual units and may not be true in case of aggregates. Microeconomic observations, thus, cannot be applied to the economy as a whole.	3. *Domain:* Macroeconomics covers the following: (i) *Theory of Income, Output and Employment*, with its constituents of the consumption function, the investment function and the theory of business cycles. (ii) *Theory of Prices* with its constituents of the theories of inflation, deflation and reflation. (iii) *Theory of Economic Growth* with long-term growth of income, output and employment. (iv) *Macro Theory of Distribution*.

(Contd.)

TABLE 1.2 Distinction between micro and macro branches of economics (*Contd.*)

Microeconomics	Macroeconomics
4. *Limitations*: Although microeconomic analysis is a very useful component of economics, yet, it has the following limitations: (i) It is true only in dealing with the relative shares of wages and profits in the total national income. For example, saving is a virtue for an individual but the same is not true for the community as a whole. (ii) Microeconomic analysis is based on certain assumptions such as the assumption of *ceteris paribus*, and that of full employment in the economy. In reality, neither of them exists. (iii) Microeconomic analysis throws no light on the functioning of the national economy.	4. *Limitations:* Although macroeconomics is gaining strength, yet there are certain pitfalls that need to be avoided in the interest of public policy. Some of them are as under: (i) Excessive generalization of the individual experience to the system as a whole. (ii) Excessive obsession of lumping the sectors together despite the fact that they are not of homogeneous character. (iii) The general tendency prevalent in the economy may not get transmitted in equal or proportionate measures to the constituent sectors. For instance, a general rise in prices may not affect the prices in the constituent sectors in the same measure. (iv) The study of the aggregates may reflect stagnation or saturation necessitating a change in economic policy while intersectoral comparisons may reveal positive symptoms of economic development. For instance, national income may appear stagnant while inequalities of income distribution may have declined significantly. The fact, however, signals economic development despite stagnation of national income.
5. *Pioneer:* Dr. Alfred Marshall's *magnum opus*, "*Principles of Economics*", published in 1890, is considered as a leading work on microeconomics.	5. *Pioneer:* John Maynard Keynes' work "General Theory of Employment, Interest and Money" published in 1936, is a leading work on macroeconomics.

KEY TERMS AND CONCEPTS

Central problems Also known as the basic problems, they refer to the economic problems one faces in the process of filling the resource gap. They are outlined below:

1. What to produce and in what quantity?
2. How to produce?
3. For whom to produce?
4. Are the resources being fully utilized? (Problem of unemployment)
5. How efficiently are production and distribution being carried out? (Problem of inefficiency)
6. Is the capacity to produce growing? (Problem of growth)
7. How are the prices rising? (Problem of Inflation)

Problems 1, 2, 3 and 5 refer to Microeconomics while problems 4, 6 and 7 to Macroeconomics.

Introduction to Economics

Consumption It is dissipation of utility in the process of satisfaction of human needs. It is the ultimate objective of production and all other human activities.

Consumer surplus (CS) It refers to excess of expenditures which consumers are willing to incur on a product, over and above their current levels, so that they may not have to do without the desired level of consumption of the product.

Deductive and inductive methods Drawing inferences about an individual person or firm from observations made about aggregates of them is the deductive method while generalization of observations made about an individual person or firm to reach inferences about their aggregates is the inductive method.

Economics It is a science that studies human behaviour as a relationship between ends and scarce resources that have alternative uses.
— L. Robbins.

Economic activity It is a human activity that aims at filling the resource-gap. Investment, production distribution and consumption are its broad categories.

Economic problem It is a problem of scarcity of resources in the face of desired ends. Apart from being scarce, resources have alternative uses as well. The problem therefore relates to making a choice amongst alternative uses of scarce resource and raising its level to the level of the desired ends.

Microeconomics A branch of economics which studies economic behaviour of an individual unit, such as, a person, a household or a firm. In other words, it is a science that deals with human activities directed at the individual level at filling the gap between ends and scarce resources that have alternative uses. Central problems 1, 2, 3 and 5 constitute its subject matter.

Market economy, planned economy and mixed economy Economies are often classified as market economies, planned economies or mixed economies depending on whether they are market oriented, centrally planned or partly market oriented and partly planned.

Macroeconomics A branch of economics which studies the economic behaviour not of one unit, but of all the units taken together. It is a study in aggregates and is often referred to as Aggregative Economics. In other words, it is a science that deals with group activities directed at filling its resource gap. Central problems 4, 6 and 7 constitute its subject matter.

Positive and normative economics Positive economics refers to that part of economic analysis in which solutions to basic economic problems recognize no considerations be they social or humanitarian. The entire analysis is based on 'as is what is' and not on 'what it should be'. Normative econonomics, on the other hand, refers to that part of economic analysis in which solutions to basic economic problems prioritize social and humanitarian considerations. The analysis is based on 'what it should be' and not on 'as is what is'.

Investment It is commitment of resources to acquisition and use of productive resources. Purchase of plant, machinery, equipment, etc. for production are a few examples of investment.

Marginal rate of product transformation Also known as the Marginal Opportunity Cost, the MRPT is defined as the rate of sacrifice of production of one of the two goods for the sake of the other. Symbolically,

$$\text{MRPT}_{X,Y} = \frac{\text{Quantity of good } Y \text{ foregone}}{\text{Quantity of good } X \text{ gained}}$$

$$= |\Delta y / \Delta x|$$

$$= -(\Delta y / \Delta x)$$

where

$\Delta y \equiv$ quantity of good Y foregone

$\Delta x \equiv$ increase in quantity of good X, in lieu of Δy foregone.

Opportunity cost Opportunity cost of a resource refers to the cost of opportunity foregone for the sake of its current use. Transfer earning is yet another name given to it. It refers to income from the next best alternative use of the resource. For example, opportunity cost of a management graduate currently operating his/her own business refers to the salary he/she is entitled to while working as a manager in a firm owned by some one else.

Price mechanism A system of exchange which determines market price through market forces of supply and demand.

Producer Surplus (PS) It may be defined as the excess of revenue realized by the producers over and above that their supply schedule ensures.

Production It is a creation or an addition of utility to basic inputs. The process of creation or addition of utility is called the *production-process*.

Production possibility curves (PPCs) Also known as production possibility frontiers, the PPCs refer to the loci of all the possible combinations of two types of goods that are possible to be produced with given resources and technologies under their full and efficient utilization.

Resource-gap It refers to the gap between desired ends and the scarce resources.

EXERCISES

A. Short Answer Questions

Define the following (1 through 15):
1. Economics
2. Economic activity
3. Price mechanism
4. Production possibility curve
5. Marginal rate of product transformation
6. Opportunity cost
7. Resource-gap
8. Positive economics
9. Normative economics
10. Market economy
11. Centrally planned economy
12. Inductive method of economic analysis
13. Deductive method of economic analysis
14. Consumer Surplus (CS)
15. Producers Surplus (PS)
16. Name any two central problems of an economy that can be solved with PPCs.
17. Is the marginal opportunity cost the same as the marginal rate of product transformation?
18. What do the following signify:
    (a) Movement from one point on the PPC to another.
    [**Ans.** Movement from one point on the PPC to another signifies resource reallocation. In other words, it means shifting resource from production of one combination on the PPC to another. Movement in the direction of the arrow from point E to F, as shown in Figure 1.11, signifies resource reallocation.]

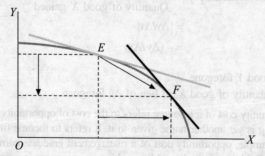

FIGURE 1.11 Movement from point E to F signifies resource reallocation.

(b) Movement from a point within the frontier to a point on the frontier.

[**Ans.** Movement from a point, A, in the interior of the PPC, to a point on it signifies movement either to full employment, given the level of efficiency or to attainment of full efficiency, given the level of resource utilization or both (Figure 1.12).]

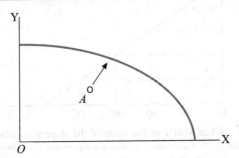

FIGURE 1.12 Movement from point A within the boundary to a point on the boundary indicates attainment of full employment or full efficiency or both.

(c) An outward shift in PPC

[**Ans.** An outward shift in PPC signifies economic growth. Please refer to Figure 1.5.]

(d) An inward shift in the PPC

[**Hint.** Reverse process of part (c).]

19. Define microeconomics.
20. Define macroeconomics.
21. Define market price.

    [**Ans.** Price determined by the interaction of market demand and market supply at a point of time is called the market price.]

22. What is normal price?

    [**Ans.** The normal price refers to the average price over a period of time. It shows a long run tendency of price.]

B. Long Answer Questions

23. "Economics is a science of choice-making." Explain the relationship between scarcity and choice in the light of this statement.
24. Explain any two of the central problems of an economy with particular reference to the branch of economics they relate to and the tools of analysis resorted to in their solution.
25. "PPC is concave to the Origin". Explain.
26. Would the PPC be concave to the origin when
    (a) the $MRPT_{X,Y}$ is constant along the PPC?
    (b) the $MRPT_{X,Y}$ be decreasing numerically (increasing in actual value) from left to right along the PPC? Give reasons in support of your answer.

    [**Ans.** (a) When $MRPT_{X,Y}$ = constant, so is dy/dx or $\Delta y/\Delta x$ along the curve. In other words, the slope of the PPC is constant, implying that the curve is a straight line with a negative slope, as shown in Figure 1.13(a).

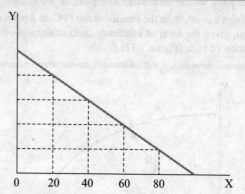

FIGURE 1.13(a) When MRPT or the value of the slope is constant, PPC is a straight line.

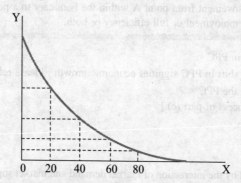

FIGURE 1.13(b) When MRPT or the value of the slope decreases from left to right, the PPC is convex to the origin.

(b) When MRPT decreases from left to right along the curve in numerical value (without the sign), the PPC is convex to the origin. The curve in Figure 1.13(a) shows the constant returns to scale while that in Figure 1.13(b) shows increasing returns to scale (for returns to scale, see Ch. 5 on *Theory of Production*).]

27. Define a production possibility curve with particular reference to the assumptions made. What would happen to the PPC in case any one of the assumptions be relaxed?

[**Ans.** There are four assumptions implicit in the concept of the PPC. These are:

1. Resources are fixed,
2. There exists full employment of resources,
3. There exists full efficiency in resource-utilization, and
4. There is no change in the available technology.

If any of these assumptions be relaxed (given up), production would not take place on the PPC. For instance, if the resources are not being fully utilized, other things remaining unchanged, production would take place in the region below the PPC rather than on it. The same is the case when efficiency is sub-optimal, other things remaining same. Again, if the assumption of "the technology remaining unchanged" be dropped, other things remaining unchanged, the PPC will shift upwards or downwards depending on whether the change is favourable or unfavourable. Another factor that shifts the PPC is growth resulting from the perfection of the man-machine system. As man gets used to the machine, he becomes an integral part of it and the output produced is higher despite no changes in any other parameter. The reader may support the answers with the help of suitable sketches.]

28. Explain the concept of the opportunity cost with the help of an illustration.

    [**Ans.** Opportunity cost refers to the cost of the opportunity foregone for the sake of the current opportunity. It is the cost of the next best alternative use of the resource that has been sacrificed for the sake of its current use. For instance, suppose a model, currently earning ₹ 10 lakh per month on an average from modeling, gets a break in movies entitling her to much higher monthly income. Evidently, she would give up modeling to join movies. Here, the opportunity cost of her career in the movies is ₹ 10 lakhs, her earning from the next best alternative use of her skills.]

29. An individual, A, is currently in a job, J_3, that pays him ₹ 10 lakhs per annum. Prior to this job, he was in a job J_2 which paid him ₹ 6 lakhs per annum and prior to J_2, he was in job J_1 which paid him ₹ 2 lakhs per annum. Calculate the opportunity costs of jobs J_2 and J_3. What was the opportunity cost of his initial job J_1?

    [**Ans.** 2 lakhs, 6 lakhs, Zero.]

30. Equations of demand and supply for a consumer good are as given below:

    $$Q^D = 100{,}000 - 4P$$
    $$Q^S = 6P$$

    where, P is the price, $Q^D \equiv$ quantity demanded,
    and, $Q^S \equiv$ quantity supplied.

    Sketch the curves and determine the market clearing price and the quantity transacted at the equilibrium.

    [**Ans.** $P = 10{,}000$; Quantity transacted = 60,000 units.]

31. Given that

    $$Q^D = 150{,}000/P, \text{ and}$$
    $$Q^S = 15P$$

    calculate price and quantity demanded in the equilibrium.

    [**Ans.** $P = 100$; $Q^D = 1{,}500$.]

32. Sketch the PPC for the data and calculate the $\text{MRPT}_{X,Y}$

Production Possibilities :	A	B	C	D	E
X :	0	10	20	30	40
Y :	20	15	10	5	0

    What is the maximum possible output of (a) X, and (b) Y?
    What is the likely reason for the MRPT to remain constant?

    [**Ans.** $\text{MRPT}_{X,Y} = 0.5$ throughout. (a) 40, (b) 20. Constant Returns to Scale in production.]

33. Sketch the data given below and calculate the Marginal Opportunity Cost at each point:

Production Possibilities :	A	B	C	D	E	F	G	H
X :	0	10	20	30	40	50	75	100
Y :	40	30	23	17	12	8	3	0

    What is the likely reason for its variation from left to right along the curve?

    [**Ans.** 1.0, 0.7, 0.6, 0.5, 0.4, 0.17, 0.075. Increasing Returns to Scale in production.]

34. Calculate the MRPT and sketch the data given below:

Production Possibilities :	A	B	C	D	E
X :	0	20	40	60	80
Y :	50	46	36	21	0

What is the likely reason for the MRPT to increase from left to right? What inference do you draw from your observations in Questions 32, 33 and 34?

[**Ans.** MRPT increases from left to right along the curve (Q. 34) due to the diminishing returns to scale. It is constant (Q. 32) under constant returns to scale and it decreases from left to right along the curve (Q. 33) under increasing returns to scale.

35. Bring out the main differences and similarities in the micro and the macro approaches of economics.
36. "An economy always produces on the PPC rather than anywhere else." Discuss.
   [**Hint.** Production at a point on the PPC implies full and efficient use of given resources and technology. Every economy aspires to be on the PPC, therefore, while a few succeed in approaching the PPC, a much larger number continue to produce inside it year after year due to their inability to utilize the existing resources fully and/or efficiently. Some of them fail even to tap a sizable part of their resources and remain much below the PPC. The reasons include non affordability of relevant technologies. Due to underdevelopment, they remain stuck up in the low-level-equilibrium-trap, that is, sustained low level of income. Due to low incomes, savings are low and so is the rate of capital formation and income generation. An external big-push, if available, may provide them the much needed break-through, but in its absence, year after year, they remain stuck up in the interior, much below the PPC. Low rate of capital formation is thus a big handicap. Not only the underground and the surface resource remains untapped or underutilized, but even their human resource remains unemployed/underemployed.

   As regards regions above the PPC, no economy can ever be there due to static conditions of resources endowment, technologies, employment and efficiencies.]
37. Does massive unemployment shift the PPC to the left? Explain.
   [**Ans.** In case of the massive unemployment, the economy would produce at a point inside the PPC. The PPC would remain unchanged. It represents a situation in which available resources and technologies are utilized fully and efficiently. Instead of shifting the PPC, massive unemployment pushes the economy off the PPC into the region below it.]
38. Do you think that the loss of life and the productive assets caused by calamities, whether natural or man-made, would result in a downward shift in the PPC? Give reasons in support.
   [**Ans.** Yes. The PPC would shift downwards if there is a decline in the volume of the productive resources, whether caused by an earthquake or by a bomb blast. The resources surviving the destruction may be put to their full use but the resources lost would adversely affect the volume of output, and hence, a downward shift in the PPC would result.]
39. Sketch the demand and supply curves of (Q. 30) again. What are your estimates of CS and PS?
   [**Ans.** CS = 450,000,000; PS = 300,000,000.]
40. Sketch the demand and supply curves of (Q. 31) again. What are your estimates of CS and PS? Assume that demand never falls below 500 units.

$$\text{Ans. } CS = \int_{Q=500}^{Q=1500} (150{,}000/Q)\, dQ - 100 \times 1500$$

$$= 150{,}000\,[\log_e 1500 - \log_e 500 - 1]$$

$$= 150{,}000\,[(\log_{10} 1500/\log_{10} e) - \log_{10} 500/\log_{10} e] - 150{,}000$$

$$= 150{,}000\,[3.1761/0.4343 - 2.6990/0.4343] - 150{,}000$$

$$= 150{,}000\,[1.0986] - 150{,}000$$

$$= ₹\,\mathbf{14790}$$

$$PS = 100 \times 1500 - \int_{Q=0}^{Q=1500} (1/15) Q\, dQ$$

$$= 150{,}000 - \left[(1/30)Q^2\right]_{Q=0}^{Q=1500}$$

$$= 150{,}000 - 75{,}000 = \mathbf{75{,}000}]$$

41. How can we use PPCs to demonstrate increasing, constant and decreasing returns to scale? Explain with the help of diagrams.

[**Ans.** Draw three PPCs – the *first*, concave to the origin, the *second*, linear sloping downwards, and the *third*, convex to the origin as in Figures 1.14(a), (b) and (c). Divide vertical axis into equal parts as shown. Going down the curve from left to right in (a) amounts to diminishing increments in quantities of X, each time production of Y is sacrificed by the same quantity. This shows diminishing returns in production. As opposed to this, the curve in (b) implies constant returns to scale as sacrifice of Y by the same amount each time leads to realization of same additional amount of X. In part (c), each time Y is sacrificed by the same quantity, realization of X follows an increasing trend, implying, increasing returns to scale. In (a), PPC is concave to origin, in (b), it is linear and in (c), it is convex to origin.]

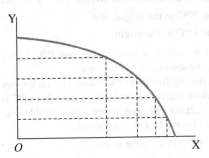

FIGURE 1.14(a)   PPC concave to the origin.   **FIGURE 1.14(b)**   PPC linear sloping downwards.

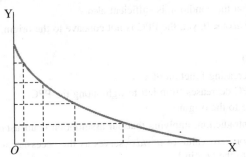

FIGURE 1.14(c)   PPC convex to the origin.

C. Essay Type Questions

42. Show how can PPCs be used to solve some of the central problems.
43. What is meant by the price mechanism? How can it be used to solve some of the central problems?
44. With the help of the price mechanism and the PPCs, show how can the problems of the resource allocation and reallocation be solved?
45. Quantities x and y of two goods X and Y that a firm can produce with efficient and full utilization of given resources and technology are related through the transformation curve:

$$y = 1000 - (x^2/250)$$

Current prices P_X and P_Y of goods X and Y are ₹ 100 and ₹ 50 per unit respectively. Determine the optimal product mix. How will your answer change if the prices of the two goods were to change to ₹ 120 and

₹ 40 per unit of X and Y respectively? Determine the revenues that will accrue to the firm in each case.

[**Ans.** (250, 750), (375, 437.5); 62,500, 62,500.]

46. Show that the necessary and sufficient condition for the production possibility curve to be concave to the origin is that the second order derivative of y with respect to x must be negative.

    [**Ans.** To show that the condition is necessary, refer to the schedule in Table 1.1 and also to its graphic presentation in Figure 1.3. Conclude from these that dy/dx is a decreasing function of x, that is, $d^2y/dx^2 < 0$ whenever the PPC is concave to the origin. Thus, if a PPC be concave to Origin, $d^2y/dx^2 < 0$

    To show that the condition is sufficient; show that $d^2y/dx^2 < 0 \Rightarrow$ concavity of the PPC to the origin. This can easily be done by the method of contradiction. There are two ways of doing this.

    (1) Suppose if possible that $d^2y/dx^2 \not< 0 \Rightarrow$ concavity of the PPC to the origin.

    Alternatively, (a) $d^2y/dx^2 = 0 \Rightarrow$ concavity of the PPC to the origin, and

    (b) $d^2y/dx^2 > 0 \Rightarrow$ concavity of the PPC to the origin.

    In the first case, $d^2y/dx^2 = 0 \Rightarrow dy/dx =$ constant, which in turn implies that PPC is linear. This leads to a contradiction, making our assumption unsustainable in this case.

    In the latter case, $d^2y/dx^2 > 0 \Rightarrow dy/dx$ is an increasing function of x, which in turn, implies that the slope of the curve increases from left to right along the curve implying in turn that PPC is convex to the Origin. This too leads to a contradiction, making our assumption unsustainable even in this case. Combining the results of the two cases, we observe that the statement,

    $$d^2y/dx^2 \not< 0 \Rightarrow \text{concavity of the PPC to the origin}$$

    is false, and hence

    $$d^2y/dx^2 < 0 \Rightarrow \text{concavity of the PPC to the origin.}$$

    This establishes that the condition is sufficient also.

    (2) Suppose, that $d^2y/dx^2 < 0$, yet, the PPC is not concave to the origin.

    But, $d^2y/dx^2 < 0$

    $\Rightarrow d(dy/dx)/dx < 0$

    $\Rightarrow (dy/dx)$ is a decreasing function of x

    $\Rightarrow$ Slope of the PPC decreases from left to right along the PPC.

    $\Rightarrow$ PPC is concave to the origin.

    This leads to a contradiction, implying that our assumption is unsustainable and hence false.

    Hence, negative non-zero value of d^2y/dx^2 serves as the necessary and sufficient condition for the concavity of PPC to the Origin.]

47. Without actually plotting, comment whether the following transformation curves lead to a PPC concave to the origin. Give reasons in support of your answers.

    (a) $12y = 36 - x^2$

    (b) $y = 1000 - (x^2/250)$

    (c) $16y = 220 - 20x - x^2$

    (d) $y = 100/x.$

    [**Ans.** Except (d), all other transformation curves lead to a PPC concave to origin. Just find d^2y/dx^2 in each case. If it is negative, PPC is concave to the origin.]

48. Distinguish between

    (a) Positive and normative economics.

    (b) Deductive and inductive methods of economic analysis.

    (c) Market economy and centrally planned economy.

    (d) Microeconomics and macroeconomics.

Forces of Demand and Supply in Action: The Price Mechanism

CHAPTER OUTLINE

Introduction
- Meaning of Demand and the Law of Demand
- Determinants of Demand
- Reasons for Downward Slope of Demand Curve
- Expansion of and Increase in Demand
- Contraction of and Decrease in Demand
- Market Demand Curve
- Meaning of Supply and the Law of Supply
- Determinants of Supply
- Expansion of and Increase in Supply
- Contraction of and Decrease in Supply
- Market Supply Curve
- Concept of Equilibrium
- Key Terms and Concepts
- Exercises
- Case Study: The Fad Theory of Famines

INTRODUCTION

In Chapter 1, we saw how the first three central problems, namely 'what', 'how' and 'for whom' to produce are solved through the price mechanism by market-oriented producers. That is, it is the price of the product offered by the market that helps them to decide what goods they should produce and in what quantities so that production may be profitable and may also remain so. In the same way, it is the market price that dictates the choice of technique for such producers. They decide in favour of the technique that is cheapest so that the production cost may be as low as possible. They engage those factors of production that cost them least. The objective is curtailment of production costs as a part of their strategy of profit maximization. Choice of products, choice of techniques and choice of factors of production, thus, all depend on price mechanism for the market-oriented producers.

We also had a fair idea of market price and the price mechanism in the last chapter. We noted that market price refers to the price prevailing in the market at a point of time and that the price mechanism is a system of exchange that determines the market price through market forces of demand and supply.

The forces of demand and supply are thus essential components of the price mechanism. In this chapter, we take them up in some detail so that the concept of price mechanism, briefly introduced in the previous chapter, may now be driven home fully.

2.1 MEANING OF DEMAND AND THE LAW OF DEMAND

A consumer's demand for a product represents his desire for it, provided such desire is supported by his willingness to pay for it as and when it is offered to him. One's desire for a luxury car cannot be treated as his/her demand for it unless he/she possesses the requisite purchasing power and is willing to exchange it for the car. In other words, the term *demand* implies an authentic claim on the product. If an individual does not possess requisite purchasing power, his desire for a product cannot pass as his demand for it. Likewise, if an individual possesses the purchasing power but at the last minute refuses to give effect to the transaction, whatever the reasons, his desire for it again cannot qualify as his demand for it. *Demand, therefore, is the desire for a product supported by requisite purchasing power and willingness to exchange it for the product as and when the same is offered for sale.*

An individual may be willing to buy the product under certain conditions:

1. *The price of the product remains unchanged at the time of purchase:* If it does not, the prospective buyer is likely to put off buying the product until the price settles down.

2. *The prices of the substitute goods remain unchanged:* For instance, suppose price of coffee falls in a local cafe. Its demand would go up only when price of its substitute, tea, remains unchanged. If tea also turns cheaper, demand for coffee may not register same increase as that it would when price of its substitute, tea, remains unchanged. Price of tea remaining unchanged, demand will shift from tea to coffee when price of coffee falls.

3. *The prices of the complementary goods remain unchanged:* A hike in price of petroleum affects demand for cars adversely despite car prices remaining unchanged. Here petroleum is a complementary good for cars. Hence, price of petroleum should remain unchanged along with that of the car itself so that the consumer may execute his decision to buy the car as soon as he is able to catch hold of the requisite amount of the purchasing power.

4. *Tastes, preferences, fashions, etc. in respect of the product remain unchanged:* Changes in any of these may lead to a change of mind of the perspective buyer. Having discussed the conditions that sustain the buyer's desire for the product, we are set to state the *Law of Demand.* "Other things remaining unchanged (ceteris paribus), more of a product is demanded at a lower price and less at a higher price."

The other things referred to here are:

1. Prices of related goods (substitutes and complements)
2. Income of consumers/buyers
3. Tastes, preferences and fashions.

The three are known as the *shift-factors* in respect of price–demand relationship (variation of demand with price). A change in any one of these results in a parallel shift in the demand curve.

Representing quantity demanded on the horizontal axis and the associated price on the vertical axis, we can portray the price–demand relationship as in Figures 2.1 and 2.2. The figures are drawn on the assumption that the good in question is a normal good for which quantity demanded varies inversely as the price. Tabular presentation of levels of demand and associated prices is called a *demand schedule* while the curve obtained on plotting the demand schedule on a graph, is called a *demand curve*. The mathematical relationship between quantity demanded and price, while the other things (shift factors) remain unchanged (*ceteris paribus*), is called a *demand function* or a *demand equation*. Functions such as the following express the inverse variation of demand with price:

1. $Q^D = a - bP$ (linear demand)
2. $Q^D = c/P$ (non-linear demand)

where, a, b and c are constants.

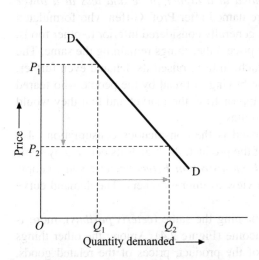
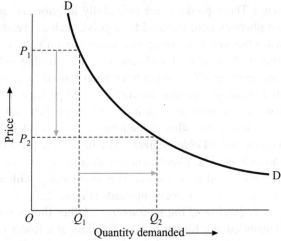

FIGURE 2.1 Linear demand: When price falls, quantity demanded rises, other things remaining same. The variation follows a linear trend resulting in linear demand as shown.

FIGURE 2.2 Non-linear demand: When a fall in price leads to a rise in demand, following a non-linear trend, the demand curve is a non-linear one or an exponential one as shown.

It is possible to portray variation of demand with income as *income–demand* while other things such as price, prices of related goods, tastes, preferences and fashions remain unchanged (Figure 2.4); or variation of demand for a product in relation to changes in price of a related good, a substitute or a complement, as *cross demand* while price of the product, income of the consumers, tastes, fashions and preferences remain unchanged (Figures 2.5 and 2.6, respectively). We will examine all these situations in the subsequent sections.

2.2 DETERMINANTS OF DEMAND

The factors that influence demand of a product can thus be enumerated as:
1. Price of the product
2. Income of the consumers
3. Prices of related goods
4. Tastes, Preferences, Fashions.

Collectively they are known as *determinants of demand.*

1. *Price of the product:* Other things remaining unchanged (*ceteris paribus*), more of a product is demanded at a lower price and less at a higher price. The relationship, as portrayed in Figures 2.1 and 2.2, is commonly referred to as the *Law of Demand.* So long as the product is a normal one, the demand curve would slope downwards from left to right as shown. If the product is a *Giffen good,* the variation of its demand with its price is direct. That is, *other things remaining unchanged, more of a product is demanded at a higher price and less at a lower price.* These products are essentially inferior and are named after Prof. Giffen who formulated the phenomenon. Demand for a good, such as bread, generally considered inferior to other foods, was observed to shoot up in response to a hike in its price, other things remaining the same. The hike in demand for bread raised its price further, which, in turn, raised its demand even further. The leverage effect might have been caused by panic buying of bread by the people who feared that bread, so essential for them, would perhaps disappear from the market and that they would have to do either without it or with its costlier substitutes.

Among the other deviations of the law of demand is the conspicuous consumption, also known as the **Veblen Effect**.* The higher the price of the product, the higher its demand by some individuals. The phenomenon is also known as the **Demonstration Effect** because some people buy more and more of a costlier commodity with a view to impress others. The demand curve in such cases too slopes upwards (Figure 2.3).

2. *Income of the consumers:* Other things remaining the same (*ceteris paribus*), more is demanded at a higher income and less at a lower income (Figure 2.4). Among the other things assumed here to remain unchanged are: the price of the product, prices of the related goods, tastes, fashions and preferences. If the product is an inferior one, less of it is demanded at higher incomes and more at lower incomes.

3. *Prices of related goods:* Related goods refer to substitutes and complements. Other things remaining the same (*ceteris paribus*), more of product A is demanded when price of product B,

---

*Veblen, Thorstein, Theory of Leisure Class (1899).

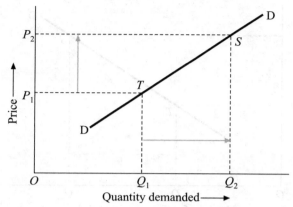

FIGURE 2.3 Demand curve for Giffen Goods: It portrays direct variation of demand with price, other things remaining same.

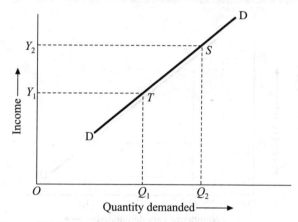

FIGURE 2.4 Income demand: Other things remaining same, more of a product is demanded at higher income and less at lower income.

a substitute, rises. For instance, when price of tea in a local café rises, price of coffee remaining unchanged, demand for coffee goes up. The opposite is the effect on the demand for coffee when price of tea falls, coffee price remaining unchanged. Figure 2.5 shows an upward rising curve of demand for coffee in response to a change in price of tea, coffee price remaining unchanged.

We can, likewise, analyze demand for complements. Let us take the example of petrol and car. When price of petrol rises, other things remaining unchanged, demand for cars falls. The same is the case with the demand of ink-pens when price of ink goes up. The demand curve for a complement slopes downwards in response to a change in the price of the related good, as shown in Figure 2.6.

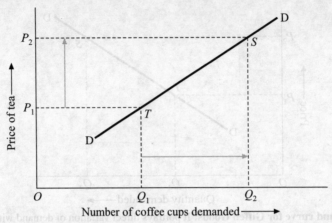

FIGURE 2.5 **Cross demand:** Demand for coffee rises in response to a rise in price of tea while price of coffee remains unchanged.

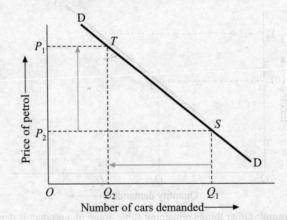

FIGURE 2.6 Cross demand for cars when petrol prices go up, other things remaining same.

4. *Tastes, preferences, fashions:* Changes in tastes, preferences and fashions affect demand significantly. For instance, people from rural areas prefer too much of sugar in sweets, while their urban counterparts prefer comparatively much less of it. Sweets with high sugar content command a low price while those with low sugar content, a high price. Urban people opt for sweets with low sugar content despite their high prices. Likewise, an old painting for an art-lover may be quite invaluable, but the same to those who have no eye for art means little. Any thing that disappears from the fashion scene, suffers a fall in its price and also in its demand at the same time. On the contrary, goods that catch up with the fashion, gain in price and also in demand. It is, however, difficult to measure the abstract factors such as tastes, preferences and fashions. As a result, it is not possible to represent them on a measuring rod nor is it possible to establish any relationship in quantitative terms with the other parameters. Thus, it is not possible to draw demand curves with such abstract things as independent variables.

2.3 REASONS FOR DOWNWARD SLOPE OF DEMAND CURVE

Demand curve, for normal goods, slopes downward from left to right as shown in Figures 2.1 and 2.2. That is, demand varies inversely as price, for normal goods. The relationship may take either of the following forms:

1. Additive inverse type, as depicted by the equation:

$$Q^D = a - bP,$$

where, a and b are fixed numbers; and

2. Multiplicative inverse type, as depicted by the equation:

$$Q^D = A/(BP),$$

where, A and B are fixed numbers.

The additive inverse type relationship yields a linear demand curve sloping downward as depicted in Figure 2.1 and the multiplicative inverse type relationship yields a non-linear demand, again sloping downward, as depicted in Figure 2.2. Whichever the case, demand curve for a normal good has a downward slope, which is a consequence of the inverse variation of demand with price. There are two explanations commonly provided for this:

(a) **The Law of Diminishing Marginal Utility:** Marginal utility refers to the change in total utility caused by consumption of an additional unit of a commodity. If the total utility derived from the first 3 apples is 50 units and that from the first four apples, 60 units; the marginal utility of the fourth apple is 10 units (60 – 50 = 10). The law of diminishing marginal utility states that *the additional utilities derived from the consumption of successive units of a commodity in one continuity depict a diminishing trend.* To demonstrate, suppose an individual sets himself to consume a bunch of bananas in one go and that utility is numerically measurable, as assumed by Alfred Marshall.

Let the total utilities after consumption of each banana be as given by Table 2.1.

TABLE 2.1 Schedule for total and marginal utilities

Number of bananas consumed :	1	2	3	4	5	6	7	8	9	10	11	12
Total utility :	20	38	54	68	80	90	98	104	108	110	110	108
Marginal utility :	20	18	16	14	12	10	8	6	4	2	0	–2

Total utility derived from the consumption of the first banana is 20 units, so is its marginal utility (MU). Total utility from first two bananas is 38 units, hence the marginal utility of the second banana is 18 units (38 – 20 = 18) and total utility from first three bananas is 54 units, hence the MU of the third banana is 16 units (54 – 38 = 16). Proceeding likewise, total utility from first 11 bananas is 110 units while that from first 10 bananas is also 110 units. The MU of eleventh banana is thus zero. Also, MU of the twelfth banana, likewise, is –2. Evidently, marginal utility of successive units of bananas follows a diminishing trend. It is as high as 20 for the first, 18 for the second, 16 for the third and so on until it falls to as low as 2 for the tenth, 0 for the eleventh and –2 for the twelfth. This implies that the eleventh and twelfth bananas should not be consumed by the consumer (Figure 2.7).

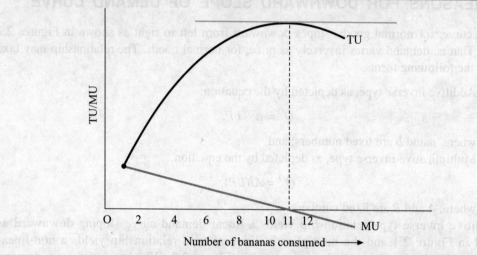

FIGURE 2.7 TU and MU schedules: While total utility increases to a maximum of 110 units with increasing consumption of bananas, the marginal utility diminishes each time an additional banana is consumed. It falls to zero for the 11th and to −2 for 12th. Even TU begins to decline after the consumption of 11th banana. The seller would have to lower the price, as more and more of them would be demanded only at successively reducing prices. This leads to an inverse relationship between price and demand and hence to a downward slope of the demand curve.

Consumer's keenness to have successive units of bananas follows a diminishing trend as consumption of the fruit increases unit by unit in one continuity. This is what explains the diminishing trend of marginal utility. If the consumer were to consume the successive units at intervals, his keenness for the fruit need not diminish with additional units. For the law of diminishing MU to operate, consumption must thus be indivisible. If consumer's keenness for a commodity follows an increasing trend, MU too would do the same, as observed in case of successive units of money or those of diamonds procured by an individual. A large number of ladies possess a never-diminishing fondness for diamonds and a large number of gents possess it for money but none of either consumes the cherished commodity the way he/she consumes bananas whether in one continuity or at intervals.

If the consumer were to buy bananas piece-by-piece and if the seller too were to charge for them on piece-by-piece basis, the seller would have to lower the price each time he tried to sell an additional piece to a consumer. In other words, more of them would be demanded at lower prices. This establishes the inverse relationship between price and quantity demanded, leading to a demand curve that slopes downwards from left to right for normal goods.

(b) **The Price Effect:**   The second explanation to the downward slope of the demand curve is provided by the price-effect. The price effect is split into two components:

1. *Income effect*:   When price of a product falls, the real income of the consumer rises. As a result, he consumes more of the product. A numerical illustration would drive the point home. Suppose a consumer has allocated a sum of ₹ 100 to buy chocolates, each priced at ₹ 10. The number of chocolates he can buy is 10. This implies that the consumer's income in terms of commodity bought is 10 chocolates, which is

called his/her real income. Consumer's income in monetary terms is ₹ 100, which is called his/her nominal income. Now suppose the price of chocolates falls to ₹ 5 each. The consumer's real income goes up to 20 chocolates while his nominal income remains unchanged. Thus, a fall in price leads to a rise in consumer's real income even though his/her nominal income remains unchanged. As a result, he buys more of the chocolates at a lower price. This leads to the inverse relationship between price and demand and hence to the downward slope of the demand curve.
2. *Substitution effect*: Under the substitution effect a consumer substitutes a costlier product by a cheaper one. When price of a product rises, some of the consumers, finding the product beyond their reach, settle for its cheaper substitutes, may be poorer in quality provided such substitutes exist. The rise in price, thus, boosts the demand of the substitutes, lowering that of the product in question. This again leads to an inverse relationship between price and demand and hence to a downward slope of the demand curve.

2.4(A) EXPANSION OF AND INCREASE IN DEMAND

Other things remaining the same, when more of a commodity is demanded at a lower price, the change in demand is known as an *expansion of demand*. It is also known as *movement along the demand curve* from left to right (Figure 2.8). *Increase in demand*, on the contrary, refers to an *outward shift* in demand curve caused by positive or favourable changes in any of the shift-factors while product price remains unchanged. The shift factors evidently include income of the consumers, prices of related goods, tastes, preferences, fashions, etc. For instance, when quantity demanded of a good increases in response to an increase in consumer's income, other things remaining unchanged, the change in demand is known as an *increase in demand*. In the same way, when price of a substitute rises or that of a complement falls or when consumers' tastes, preferences and fashions drift in favour of the product in question, while its own price remains unchanged, the change in demand is again known as an increase in it. Consider, for illustration, a situation in which consumers prefer a product not because it is cheaper or better, but because it is in fashion with its popularity among its consumers is high and rising. The demand curve shifts outwards each time its demand increases by virtue of 'keep up with the Joneses' or by what is called the ***bandwagon effect****, often referred to as an

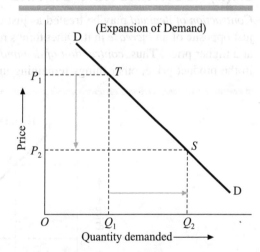

FIGURE 2.8 Expansion of demand or downward movement along the demand curve results in response to a fall in price of the product, other things remaining constant.

*****Bandwagon, Veblen and Snob Effects** were introduced by Harvey Liebenstein, "Bandwagon, Snob and Veblen Effects in the Theory of Consumers' Demand," *Quarterly Journal of Economics* 62 (Feb.1948); pp. 165–201.

example of *positive network externalities*. Such externalities always lead to an outward shift in the demand curve (Figure 2.9). In Figure 2.8, demand expands by Q_1Q_2 when product price falls, other things remaining same. In Figure 2.9, demand increases by Q_1Q_2 at the same price when consumer's income increases, other things remaining unchanged.

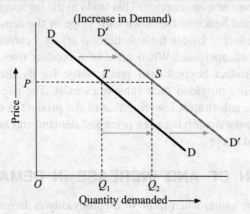

FIGURE 2.9 Increase in demand or an upward shift in demand results when more is demanded not because of a fall in product price but because of a favourable change in one of the other things (the shift factors) assumed fixed.

2.4(B) CONTRACTION OF AND DECREASE IN DEMAND

Contraction of demand may be treated as just opposite of its expansion, while a *decrease* in it as just opposite of an *increase* in it. Other things remaining unchanged, less of a product is demanded at a higher price. Thus, *contraction of demand* (Figure 2.10) is a fall in demand caused by a rise in the product price, other things remaining unchanged.

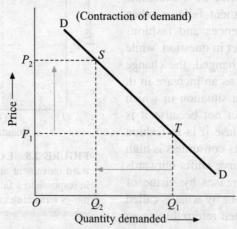

FIGURE 2.10 **Contraction of demand:** Other things remaining unchanged, less of a product is demanded at a higher price.

Decrease in demand, on the contrary, refers to an *inward shift* in the demand curve caused by the negative or unfavourable changes in any of the shift-factors while product price remains unchanged. The shift factors referred to here include income of the consumers, prices of the related goods, tastes, preferences, fashions, etc. For instance, when quantity demanded of a good decreases in response to a decrease in consumer's income, other things remaining unchanged, the change in demand is known as a *decrease in demand*. In the same way, when price of a substitute falls or that of a complement rises or when consumers' tastes, preferences or fashions drift away from the product in question while its own price remains unchanged, the change in demand is known as a *decrease* in it. As an illustration, consider a situation in which the proud rich reject a product not because it is costlier or inferior, but because its popularity among masses is high and on the rise. Their desire to prove them extraordinary leads them away from what the common people are doing. They would therefore prefer to go for the designer or exclusive products that remain rare during their use. The phenomenon is called the **snob effect*** and is often referred to as an example of *negative network externalities*. Such externalities lead to an inward shift in the demand curve (Figure 2.11).

In Figure 2.10, demand contracts by Q_1Q_2 in response to a rise in the product-price while in Figure 2.11, demand decreases by Q_1Q_2 at the same price due to a decrease in consumer's income.

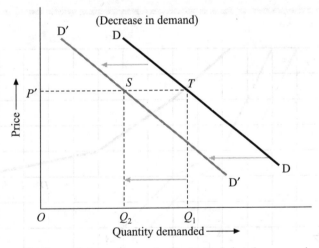

FIGURE 2.11 Decrease in demand: Less of a product is demanded at the same price due to a fall in any of the shift factors, say, income, other things remaining the same.

2.5 MARKET DEMAND CURVE

A number of people buy a product in the market at a given price. *Total demand of the product in the market at the given price is called the market demand.* To demonstrate, let there be three segments of consumers in the market. Call them segments A, B and C. Let the first, Segment A,

---

* **Bandwagon, Veblen and Snob Effects** were introduced by Harvey Liebenstein, "Bandwagon, Snob and Veblen Effects in the Theory of Consumers' Demand," *Quarterly Journal of Economics* 62 (Feb. 1948); pp. 165–201.

belong to the rich, the second, Segment B, to the middle income and the third, Segment C, to the low income people. Further, let there be five changes in the product price over the period of last one year. Also, let the number of units of the product demanded by each of the three segments at each of the five prices be as given in Table 2.2:

TABLE 2.2 Derivation of market demand schedule

Price	1200	1100	1000	900	800
No. of units demanded by the segments A :	40	60	80	120	160
B :	20	40	60	100	140
C :	10	20	40	60	80
Total demand :	70	120	180	280	380

We have plotted the demand schedules of the three segments as in Figure 2.12. On the same graph, we have plotted the total demand schedule as well to give the market demand.

In the process, we observe that the market demand curve is a horizontal summation of the demands of the individual segments. The technique is simple. It involves adding up the demands of the three segments at each price. Note that the market demand curve is flatter than any of the demand curves of the individual segments and that it is farthest from the origin.

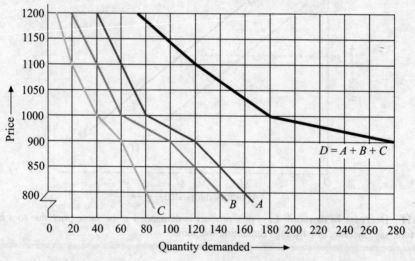

FIGURE 2.12 Derivation of market demand curve: Market Demand Curve, D, is a horizontal summation of the individual demand curves, A, B and C. It gives total demand of all the segments at each price, that is, $D = A + B + C$. Note that it is flatter than any of A, B or C. Also, it is farthest from the origin.

2.6 MEANING OF SUPPLY AND THE LAW OF SUPPLY

Supply refers to quantity of a product offered for sale at a given price at a given point of time. It should not be confused with stock of produced goods with the producers. In fact it is that quantity which is offered for sale at a particular price and at a particular point of time.

The law of supply states that, *other things remaining unchanged (ceteris paribus), more of a product is supplied at a higher price and less of it at a lower price.*

The relationship between quantities supplied and the prices* offered by the market is known as the *supply schedule*. Its graphical representation is called the *supply curve* (Figure 2.13). 'Other things remaining unchanged', include all the determinants of supply except the product price. We discuss the determinants of supply in the next section.

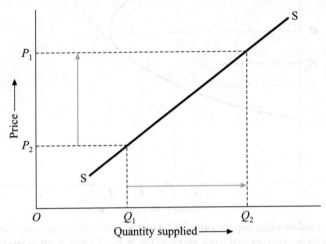

FIGURE 2.13 The law of supply: More is supplied at a higher price and less at a lower price, other things remaining unchanged.

2.7 DETERMINANTS OF SUPPLY

Price

The direct variation of supply with price, other things remaining unchanged, is known as the *law of supply*.

Figure 2.13 portrays the law. However, the law is not without exceptions. For example,

---

* A little discussion over price offered by the market for a product would not be out of order here. It is of common knowledge that product price, in general, is fixed by the producer and not by the market. This happens to be the case in general in all capitalist countries. Producers in these countries fix the price on the basis of the production cost incurred and the mark-up desired. Market can only accept or reject it through its buying behaviour. In respect of necessities, market has to accept whatever price producers fix. The question of rejection of price by the market arises only in respect of goods whose consumption can be deferred. It is only in case of agricultural products that the price is generally fixed by the market or the State, not by the producers. When a non-remunerative price is offered by the market for food grains at the harvest-time, a welfare oriented State generally resorts to its policy of intervention by fixing the *minimum support price* for each agricultural product so that the cultivators may get a fair deal. In respect of manufactures of mass consumption, prices are generally fixed by the producers rather than by the market. A welfare oriented State may administer such prices in public interest. Take petroleum products for example. Their prices are generally administered by government. The question of market fixing the price of a product arises only under consumer sovereignity, which in the modern world of aggressive marketing, is nothing more than a myth.

supply of hours of skilled work assumes negative slope at sufficiently high rates of hourly wages (Figure 2.14).

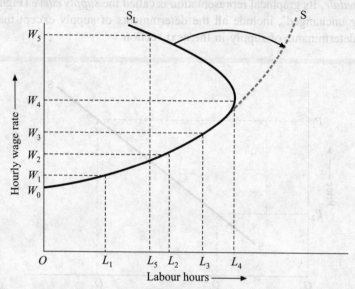

FIGURE 2.14 Backward bending supply curve of labour hours: When wage rate is low, say W_0, supply of labour hours is zero. That is, workers find work unrewarding at W_0. To lure them to work, employers raise the wage rate to W_1. As a result, OL_1 hours of work are supplied. But if employers need more hours of work from workers, they would have to raise the wage rate further to W_2 to get OL_2 hours of work. The supply of labour hours is maximum (OL_4 hours of work), when the wage rate is W_4. Now suppose the wage rate is further hiked to W_5 to attract more hours of work. Contrary to expectation, the supply of labour hours falls instead of rising. The reason for the unexpected response from the workers is that little work fetches them more income due to high rate of hourly wage. The workers begin to prefer leisure to labour in consequence. Up to a wage rate of W_4, supply of labour hours is increased due to the income effect but later it is decreased due to the leisure effect. As a result, the supply curve bends backwards beyond a wage rate of W_4. Market supply curve, due to free entry of skilled workers from regions of lower wage-rates, straightens the backward bend in the supply curve as shown in the figure by the broken segment.

Prices of related goods

Related goods include the substitutes and complements. If price offered by the market for substitute tea rises, other things including own price of coffee remaining unchanged, supply curve of coffee may undergo an upward to left shift (a decrease) in it taking cue from consumers' preference for tea, its close substitute. This will lead to a decrease in supply of coffee and an expansion of supply of tea. But, if prices of tea offered by the market register a fall, while those of coffee remaining same, the supply curve of coffee may undergo a downwards to right shift (an increase) in it taking cue from consumers' rejection of tea, its close substitute. This will lead to an increase in supply of coffee and a contraction of supply of tea. Opposite will the situation be when market offers a higher price for coffee, while other things including tea prices remaining unchanged or when market offers a lower price for coffee, while other things including tea prices remaining unchanged. In the former case, an expansion of supply of coffee and a decrease in supply of tea may result, while in the latter case, a contraction of supply of coffee and an increase in supply of tea may result.

Slightly different is the case with the supply of the complements. When price of ink offered by the market falls, other things including the prices of the ink-pens remaining the same, its own supply contracts and that of ink-pens decreases and when price of ink offered by the market rises, other things including the prices of the ink-pens remaining the same, its own supply expands and that of ink-pens increases.

The discussion above assumes that it is the market that determines the product price and the producers express their acceptance or rejection of the same by adjusting the volume of supply of the related products. As discussed in the footnote of the previous section, producers fix product prices and the market has to accept or reject them through its buying behaviour. Here, market indicates its willingness for a higher product price by exhausting its supply before the time and its willingness for a lower product price by allowing unsold stocks. Producers monitor the trends and adjust their supplies accordingly.

Cost of production

When production cost rises, given the market price of the product, its supply falls. Increasing costs, in the face of fixed market prices, reduce the producers' profit margin and compel them to switch over to production of goods that offer them higher profit margins. Alternatively, they have to mark-up the price which the market may or may not accept depending on whether it can afford it or not. The opposite will be the case when the production cost falls while market price is unchanged.

Change of technology

Under a better technology, production is often cheaper and better in quality. Under the circumstances, producers can afford to supply more at the same price or lower the price of the same supply. The opposite is the effect of technology deterioration.

Goal of production

Producers aim either at profit maximization or at sales maximization. Under sales maximization, supply is usually higher than under profit maximization. In the latter case producers control the supply with a view to maximize their profits while in the former case they do the opposite even if it amounts to reducing the price. Large-scale production under sales maximization helps them to cut costs on the one hand and to raise the total sales proceeds on the other. This helps the producers to slash prices without a fear of loss.

Strength or weakness of the infrastructure

Infrastructure refers to the means of transportation, communication, banking and insurance. A highly developed infrastructure boosts the supply while a weak infrastructure deters it.

Natural resources

Abundant natural resource helps production of the basic inputs. For instance, a sound agricultural base may help production of raw cotton and hence that of cloth in the textile industry. Likewise, underground deposits of minerals, metals and crude petroleum may curtail/boost the supply of a variety of goods.

Availability of time

Supply of products is generally fixed in the short period because it is not possible to increase the fixed factors of production in the short period. In the long run, the situation is, however, different.

Economic environment

Government policies of taxation and subsidies, business conditions, nature of competition among the firms in the market, availability of credit and finance, etc. also influence the supply of products quite a lot. Even social, political and religious factors have a great influence on supply.

2.8(A) EXPANSION OF AND INCREASE IN SUPPLY

Expansion of supply, like that of demand, refers to a movement along the supply curve. For instance, a rise in price, other things remaining the same, leads to a rise in supply [Figure 2.15(a)]. *Increase in supply*, on the other hand, refers to a downward to right shift in the supply curve, resulting from a favourable change in one of the shift factors. The shift factors, here, are the determinants of supply other than the price of the product offered by the market. For instance, an improvement in technology or adoption of an advanced technology leads to production and supply of higher quantity at the same price. Likewise, a fall in input prices also leads to production and supply of higher quantity at the same price. An increase in supply generally leads to a downward parallel shift in the supply curve [Figure 2.15(b)].

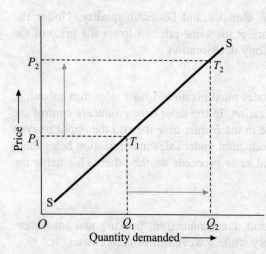

FIGURE 2.15(a) Expansion of supply: When product price rises from P_1 to P_2, supply expands from Q_1 to Q_2, other things remaining unchanged.

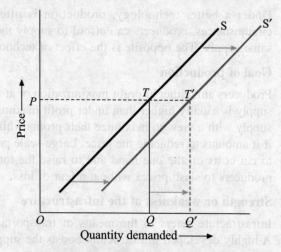

FIGURE 2.15(b) Increase in supply: When any of the shift factors change favourably, product price remaining unchanged, supply increases from Q to Q' at the same price P.

2.8(B) CONTRACTION OF AND DECREASE IN SUPPLY

Contraction of supply is just opposite of its expansion. A fall in price offered leads to a fall in supply. It results in a downward movement along the supply curve [Figure 2.16(a)].

On the other hand, *decrease in supply* is just opposite of an increase in it. An unfavourable change in one of the shift factors leads to an upward to left shift in the supply curve. As mentioned earlier, the shift factors refer to all the other determinants of supply except the price offered by the market for the product. For instance, a rise in input prices raises the production costs and hence lowers the supply despite no change in price offered for the product by the market [Figure 2.16(b)].

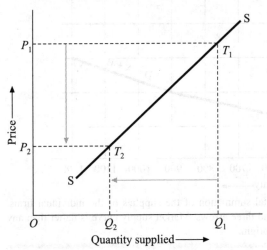

FIGURE 2.16(a) Contraction of supply: A fall in price from P_1 to P_2 contracts supply from Q_1 to Q_2, other things remaining unchanged.

FIGURE 2.16(b) Decrease in supply: An unfavourable change in any of the shift factors leads to an upward to left shift in supply. As a result, supply decreases from Q to Q'.

2.9 MARKET SUPPLY CURVE

Market supply refers to the aggregate supply of a product made by all the firms taken together at a given market price. The market supply curve is obtained by horizontal summation of the supply curves of individual firms. It follows the same process as that employed in derivation of market demand curve. To illustrate, let us construct a set of data as shown in Table 2.3.

TABLE 2.3 Derivation of market supply schedule

Price	Quantity supplied by firm A	Quantity supplied by firm B	Quantity supplied by firm C	Total supply of the three
10	100	150	200	450
20	200	300	400	900
30	300	400	500	1200

Quantities supplied by the three firms—A, B and C—at prices of ₹ 10, 20 and 30 per unit have been plotted as shown. Supply curves for them are marked with one, two and three arrows respectively. Total supply, D (A + B + C), made by the three firms at each price is also plotted as shown. Assuming that there are only these three firms in the market, the total supply as obtained above would give the *market supply curve*. It is clear that the market supply curve is flatter than any of the three supply curves and is the horizontal summation of the three (Figure 2.17).

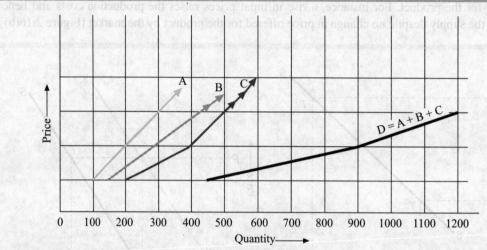

FIGURE 2.17 Market supply curve: It is a horizontal summation of the supplies of the individual firms. Individual supply curves are marked through one, two and three arrows. Market supply curve is flatter than any of the individual supply curves and is farthest from the origin.

2.10 CONCEPT OF EQUILIBRIUM

The term equilibrium refers to a state of balance. When a number of forces pull a body in different directions with the result that the body remains undisturbed, the forces are said to be in a state of balance or *equilibrium*.

The term 'equilibrium' has been derived from the Latin words, "acqui" meaning 'equal' and "libra" meaning 'balance'. Literally, it means 'equal balance'. The term has been borrowed from physics in which it was initially used to represent a balance between two or more opposing forces acting on an object in such a way that its position of rest remains undisturbed. Equilibrium in economic sense has, more or less, similar connotations. It implies a position of rest from which there is no tendency to drift. In words of Stigler*, "*An equilibrium is a position from which there is no net tendency to move, we say net tendency, to emphasize the fact that is not necessarily a state of sudden inertia but may instead represent the cancellation of power forces.*"

According to Scitovsky**, "*A market or an economy or any other group of persons and firms is in equilibrium when none of its members feels impelled to change his behaviour.*"

---

* G.J. Stigler, *The theory of price*, Macmillan, London, 1966, p. 28
** Tiber Scitovsky, *Welfare and Competition*, Unwin University Books, London 1971, p. 231.

Figure 2.18 below will drive the concept home. It shows existence of market equilibrium at the point *e*, where forces of demand and supply are in balance with each other. At this point, demand is equal to supply, that is, quantity demanded is equal to quantity supplied. Each one is *OQ*. It is called the *equilibrium quantity* and the corresponding price (*OP*), the *equilibrium price*.

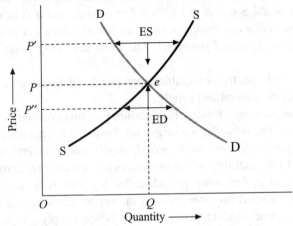

FIGURE 2.18 Market equilibrium: The demand curve (DD) intersects the supply curve (SS) at point *e*. Quantity demanded = *OQ* = Quantity supplied. *OQ* is, thus, the equilibrium quantity and the corresponding price *OP*, the equilibrium price. A price different from this creates either an excess supply (ES) or an excess demand (ED). ES initiates a downward pressure on price (as indicated by the downwardly pointing arrow), while ED initiates an upward pressure on price (as indicated by the upwardly pointing arrow). These pressures on price constitute the so called adjustment process which tends to restore the equilibrium. The process being automatic, it lends automatism to the price mechanism.

A price higher than the equilibrium price, sets up an excess supply initiating a downward pressure on price while a price lower than the equilibrium price, sets up an excess demand initiating an upward pressure on price. The excess supply tends to reduce price which begins to fall and continues to do so until the excess supply is wiped out. The excess demand tends to raise price which begins to rise and continues to do so until the excess demand is wiped out. The adjustment process made up of these downward and upward pressures is fully automatic. It comes into operation the moment market price drifts away from the equilibrium price. This lends the attribute of automatism to the price mechanism.

Equilibrium in economics, like that in physics, is thus a state of balance among opposing tendencies. Once reached, no agent has an incentive to deviate from it. Attainment and importance of equilibrium necessitates knowing it in all its manifestations.

Classification of equilibrium

In economic analysis, state of equilibrium is classified as:

1. Stable, unstable and neutral equilibria
2. Short-run and long-run equilibria
3. Static and dynamic equilibria
4. Unique and multiple equilibria
5. Partial and general equilibria
6. Marshallian and Walrasian equilibria

Let us briefly introduce each:

1. *Stable, unstable and neutral equilibria:* In the words of Prof. A.C. Pigou* "A system is in **stable equilibrium** position if, when any small disturbance takes place, forces come into play to re-establish the initial position; it is in **neutral equilibrium** if, when such a disturbance takes place, no re-establishing forces but also further disturbing forces are evoked so that the system remains at rest in the position to which it has moved; and it is in **unstable equilibrium** if, the small disturbance calls out further disturbing forces which act in a cumulative manner to drive the system from its initial position". The three are being explained in Figures 2.19, 2.20 and 2.21.

The equilibrium is stable, neutral or unstable depending on relative slopes, or more appropriately, relative price elasticities of demand and supply.

2. *Short-run and long-run equilibria:* Equilibrium is often classified as short-run equilibrium and long-run equilibrium. The classification originates due to the steepness of supply curves, which varies from period to period. In very short period, supply curve is vertical (perfectly inelastic) as supply is fixed due to the inability of the producers to increase productive factors to increase production. Supply curve in very short period, called the *very short period supply* (VSPS) is thus perfectly inelastic. In short run, steepness of the supply curve decreases as producers gain some time to increase some productive factors and hence supply. As a result, supply curve turns less steep (less than perfectly inelastic). It is called the *short period supply* (SPS).

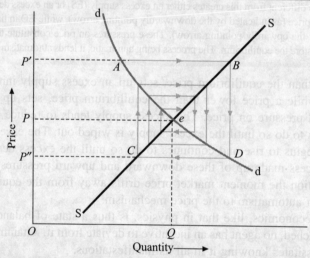

FIGURE 2.19 Stable equilibrium: Demand dd intersects supply SS at e. Equilibrium quantity is OQ and price, OP. Suppose some disturbance distorts price to OP'. This causes an excess supply (AB) which exerts a downward pressure on price. It falls to OP'', thereby creating an excess demand (CD). This initiates an upward pressure on price, which is somewhat weaker than the downward pressure built up by the excess supply (AB). This is because excess demand CD is less than excess supply AB. This in turn is due to the relative slopes, or more appropriately, relative price elasticities of demand and supply. After a number of such adjustments, the original price OP is restored. The adjustment process offsets the disturbance and makes the equilibrium stable.

---

* A.C. Pigou, *The Economics of Welfare*, Macmillan, London, 1952, pp. 794–795

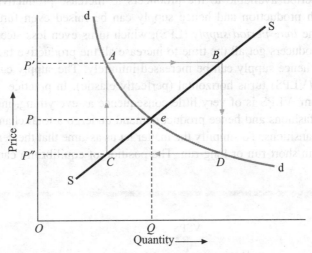

FIGURE 2.20 Neutral equilibrium: Demand dd intersects supply SS at *e*. Equilibrium quantity is *OQ* and price, *OP*. Suppose some disturbance distorts price to *OP′*. This causes an excess supply (*AB*) which exerts a downward pressure on price. It falls to *OP″*, thereby creating an excess demand (*CD*). This initiates an upward pressure on price which is equal to the downward pressure built up by excess supply (*AB*). This is because excess demand (*CD*) is equal to the excess supply (*AB*). This in turn is due to the relative slopes, or more appropriately, relative price elasticities of demand and supply. As a result, price rises back to *OP′*, sustaining the disturbance. The price thus fluctuates between *OP′* and *OP″*, never returning back to the equilibrium level.

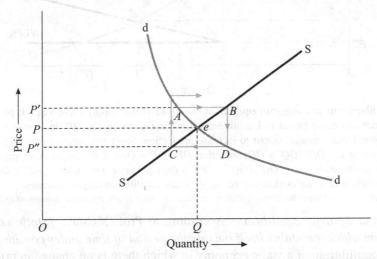

FIGURE 2.21 Unstable equilibrium: Demand dd intersects supply SS at *e*. Equilibrium quantity is *OQ* and price, *OP*. Now suppose an external disturbance distorts the price to *OP′*. This creates an excess supply *AB*, which exerts a downward pressure on price. As a result, it falls to *OP″*, creating thereby an excess demand (*CD*). This initiates an upward pressure on price. Since *CD* > *AB*, the upward pressure built up on price would raise it beyond *OP′*. The adjustment process not only sustains the disturbance but also imparts an additional impetus to it. The price deviates farther and farther away from the equilibrium level in each cycle. Equilibrium is therefore unstable.

In long-run, time period available to the producers to increase productive factors further is longer due to which production and hence supply can be raised even further. The supply in this case is called the *long period supply* (LPS), which turns even less steep (more elastic). In very long period, producers get all the time to increase all the productive factors with the result that production and hence supply can be increased infinitely. The supply curve, called the *very long period supply* (VLPS) turns horizontal (perfectly elastic). In practice, from the viewpoint of market equilibrium, VLPS is of very little consequence as everything, including consumers' tastes, preferences, fashions and hence product demand undergo a total change in the very long period due to such transitions. To simplify the matter let us assume that the demand curve remains unchanged whether in short-run or long-run. The position of equilibrium can be portrayed as in Figure 2.22.

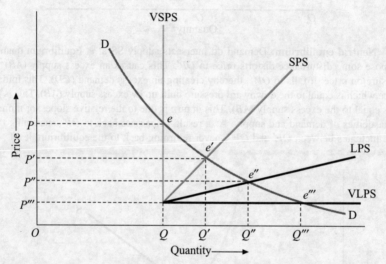

FIGURE 2.22 Short-run and long-run equilibria: In very short-run, supply curve VSPS is perfectly inelastic. It intersects the demand curve DD at e. Equilibrium output is OQ and price, OP. In short-run, producers can increase at least one factor, namely, labour to increase production. Short-run supply curve (SPS) cuts DD at e' where equilibrium output is OQ' ($OQ' > OQ$) and price, OP' ($OP' < OP$). In the long-run, supply curve LPS cuts DD at e'' where equilibrium output is OQ'' ($OQ'' > OQ' > OQ$) and price, OP'' ($OP'' < OP' < OP$). We observe that market price falls with a rise in elasticity of supply while equilibrium output increases.

3. *Static and dynamic equilibria:* According to Prof. Mehta*, *"Static equilibrium is that equilibrium which maintains itself outside the period of time under consideration."* It is related to the equilibrium of a static economy in which there is no change in prices, outputs, incomes, technology, tastes and consumers' preferences. It is based on the assumption that a state of bliss (equilibrium) once reached is relished by individuals, firms, industries, etc. so much so that they are reluctant to leave it. A ball rolling at a constant speed, a forest with fixed composition with decaying trees being replaced by new ones and an industry with all

---

* J.K. Mehta, *Advanced Economic Theory*, Macmillan Company of India Limited, 1971, p. 86.

the firms in it earning normal profits, are a few examples of the static equilibrium. The first two were given by Prof. Boulding.

Dynamic equilibrium, on the other hand, refers to the equilibrium in which nothing is assumed to remain unchanged be it price, output, incomes, tastes and preferences or technology. Participating individuals, firms and industries in equilibrium, face persistent threat to their equilibrium position from those in a state of disequilibrium. The position of equilibrium, thus, keeps changing at regular intervals. According to Prof. J.K. Mehta,"*when after a fixed period, the equilibrium state is disturbed, it is called dynamic equilibrium*". **Cobweb Theorem** is the best example, explained later in this section.

4. *Unique and multiple equilibria:* Equilibrium may be unique or non-unique depending on whether the demand and the supply curves intersect each other at one point or at more than one point. If they intersect at one point, the equilibrium is a unique one [Figure 2.23(a)] but if they intersect at more than one point, it is a non-unique or *multiple equilibrium* [Figure 2.23(b)].

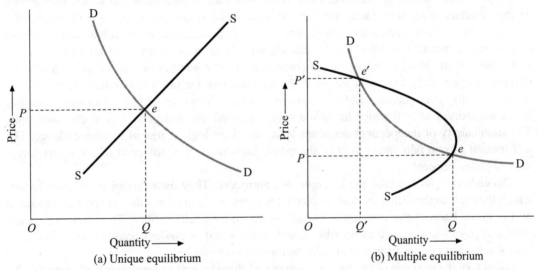

FIGURE 2.23 Equilibrium is unique [panel (a)] when demand and supply intersect each other at one point and it is multiple [panel (b)] when the two intersect each other at more than one point.

5. *Partial and general equilibria:* Equilibrium of a part of the system is called the *partial equilibrium*, while that of the entire system, the *general equilibrium*. To demonstrate, let us take a particular car manufacturer, say, Maruti Udyog Limited. To be more specific, let us focus on its economy model, Maruti 800. The manufacturer requires (i) engines from its engine division, (ii) chasis, body, rims, seats, etc. from its design division, (iii) tyres from the tyre manufacturers, (iv) airconditioners from AC manufacturers and (v) stereos from stereo manufacturers. Assuming that production and supply conditions of these five suppliers remain unchanged, the equilibrium price of Maruti 800 is ₹ 2,25,000 and equilibrium quantity of cars transacted is 12,00,000 per annum. This, evidently, is partial equilibrium because we are concerned with the quantity and price of just this brand under the assumption that the supply conditions of the components remain

unchanged and so do the demand and supply conditions of the competing brands. Now, suppose competing brands become cheaper or supplies of any or all of the five components Maruti 800 uses become scarce; would Maruti Udyog Limited still sell 12,00,000 cars per annum at a price of ₹ 2,25,000? Obviously not. Its price and quantity sold will both change, implying that a change in the equilibrium of the competitors' market or a change in the equilibrium of the components' market force changes in the equilibrium of the market of Maruti car. Simultaneous analysis of the equilibrium of Maruti car along with that of the equilibria of its competing brands as well as that of the equilibria of its components' markets may be treated as the general equilibrium in this example.

Partial equilibrium analysis was popularized by English economist, Marshall. It is based on restricted data. The role of *ceteris paribus* (other things remaining the same) is crucial for the partial equilibrium. Equilibria of individual markets such as product market and factor market each in isolation from the other under the assumption of *ceteris paribus* provide other examples of partial equilibrium.

General equilibrium, on the other hand, refers to a state of equilibrium in which all markets, be they product markets or factor markets, and all decision-making units, be they consumers, producers or factor-owners, are in simultaneous equilibrium. An economy consists of a number of markets operating side by side. We can classify these markets into two broad categories– *factor market* and *product market*. Each consists of a large number of buyers and sellers, each striving independently for his or her goal. Producers strive for profit maximization, consumers strive for utility maximization and factor owners, for maximization of factor incomes. Each has his or her individual goal which he or she strives to maximize independently at the same time. The simultaneity of independent decisions leads to a very high degree of interdependence. The self interest of one falls in the way of the other. Simultaneous equilibrium of all is certainly a very complex concept.

To elaborate further take the example of consumers. They own certain productive factors which they sell to the firms. Income so derived is spent by them on goods and services produced by the firms. Each of the consumers intends to maximize his/her utility. To achieve this, each strives to pay as low a price as possible to a firm for a unit of product bought and to charge as high a price as possible from a firm for a factor service provided.

Next take the example of producers. Each one of them intends to maximize his/her profits. To achieve this, each strives to pay as low a price as possible to a factor owner for a factor service utilized and to charge as high a price as possible from a consumer for a unit of product sold. Clearly, all of them cannot optimize their respective goals simultaneously. However, it is possible to reach a situation in which all of them can attain a certain steady state in which each one is able to get the best possible solution to his/her problem. This steady state is the general equilibrium.

Evidently the simultaneous solution of everybody's problem involves determination of prices and quantities of what buyers want to buy or sellers want to sell. This requires solution of millions of simultaneous equations involving prices and quantities of millions of products and factors. Note that there are as many markets as there are products and factors.

A simplified version of general equilibrium was developed by French economist Leon Walras* (1834–1910). Walras argued that all prices and quantities in all the markets are

---

*Leon Walras, Elements d' Economie politique pure (Lausanne, 1874). First translated in English by William Jaffe (Allen & Unwin, 1954).

determined simultaneously through their interaction with one another. He used a system of simultaneous equations to express prices and quantities of all the commodities and all the factors. There are as many markets as there are commodities and factors of production. In his model, each decision-maker acts as a buyer as well as a seller. In each market, there are three types of functions:

1. Demand equations,
2. Supply equations, and
3. Clearing-the-market equations.

To demonstrate, assume that an economy consists of two consumers, namely, A and B. They own two factors, namely, L and K, which they sell to two firms to produce two goods, namely, X and Y. This gives a $2 \times 2 \times 2$ general equilibrium model involving 18 equations – 4 of them representing consumers' demand for goods X and Y, 4 of them representing consumers' supply of L and K to the firms, 4 of them representing quantities of L and K demanded by firms, 2 of them representing quantities of X and Y supplied by firms, 2 of them representing the clearing-the-market equations of commodities and another 2 representing the clearing-the-market equations of factors. The 18 equations can be seen to involve 18 variables the values of which are determined by their simultaneous solution.

6. *Marshallian and Walrasian Equilibria:* Except for the multiple equilibria [Figure 2.23 (b)], the equilibria discussed so far involve demand and supply in their normal forms, i.e., demand sloping downwards and supply sloping upwards. What if either or both of them deviate from their normal behaviour? For example, demand curve slopes upwards for Giffen goods and supply curve of labour hours develops a negative slope beyond a certain rate of wage (W_4 in Figure 2.14). The adjustment process for equilibrium in such cases is better handled through the concepts of French economist Leon Walras and English economist Alfred Marshall. It would be appropriate to begin with their definitions, first. According to Walras, *equilibrium refers to the price that equates the quantity demanded to the quantity supplied* and according to Marshall, *equilibrium refers to the quantity that equates the demand price to the supply price*. Walrasian adjustment process operates through price movements while that of Marshall, through quantity movements. The two approaches are in agreement on stability or instability of equilibrium when demand and supply both demonstrate normal behaviour or when demand and suppy both deviate from their normal behaviour. However, the two approaches contradict each other on stability or instability of the equilibrium when only one of the two deviates from its normal behaviour. Let us classify various situations of demand and supply under the following four heads:

(i) When demand and supply both slope upwards (i.e., demand deviates from its normal behaviour)
(ii) When demand and supply both slope downwards (i.e., supply deviates from its normal behaviour)
(iii) When demand slopes upwards and supply downwards (i.e., both deviate from their normal behaviour)
(iv) When demand slopes downwards and supply upwards (i.e., both depict normal behaviour).

Let us discuss them in that order.

(i) **When demand and supply both slope upwards**

The upward slope of the supply curve is its normal behaviour but upward slope of the demand curve is a departure from its normal behaviour.

(a) **When demand curve is flatter (more elastic) than the supply curve:** Equilibrium is unstable in Walrasian sense, but stable in Marshallian sense (Figure 2.24)

(b) **When supply curve is flatter (more elastic) than the demand curve:** Walrasian equilibrium is stable while that of Marshall, unstable (Figure 2.25).

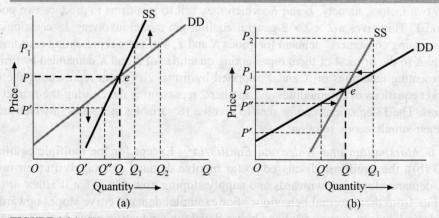

FIGURE 2.24 When demand and supply both slope upwards, as shown, equilibrium reached is *unstable* in Walrasian sense, but *stable* in Marshallian sense. Let the initial equilibrium price and quantity be OP and OQ, respectively.

Let us first see how *Walrasian process* of *price adjustment* [(panel (a)] works. Let the price distort to $OP_1(OP_1 > OP)$. Corresponding supply is OQ_1 while demand, OQ_2. A situation of excess demand ($= Q_1Q_2$) that arises would initiate an upward pressure on price pushing it farther above OP_1. This would push the system farther away from e. Further, let the price distort to $OP'(OP' < OP)$. This time, the situation that arises is of excess supply ($=Q'Q''$) initiating a downward pressure on price pushing it farther below OP'. This would push the system farther away from e. In each case, Walrasian price adjustment leads to an unstable eqilibrium.

Next, let us turn to *Marshallian process* [panel(b)] of *quantity adjustment*. To see, let the quantity at any point of time be set at $OQ'(OQ' < OQ)$. Corresponding demand price OP'' is higher than corresponding supply price $OP'(OP'' > OP')$. As a result, supply would rise above OQ' and the system would move towards e. Alternatively, let the quantity be set at OQ_1. This time corresponding supply price OP_2 is higher than corresponding demand price $OP_1(OP_2 > OP_1)$. As a result, supply would fall below OQ_1 and the system would move towards e. In each case, Marshallian quantity adjustment leads to a stable equilibrium.

Thus, when demand and supply both slope upwards with demand curve flatter (more elastic) then the supply curve, equilibrium is unstable in Walrasian price adjustment process while stable in Marshallian quantity adjustment process

(ii) **When demand and supply both slope downwards**

The downward slope of demand curve is its normal behaviour but downward slope of supply curve is a departure from its normal behaviour.

(a) **When demand curve is flatter (more elastic) than the supply curve:** Walrasian equilibrium is stable while that of Marshall, unstable (Figure 2.26).

(b) **When supply curve is flatter (more elastic) than the demand curve:** Walrasian equilibrium is unstable and that of Marshall, stable (Figure 2.27).

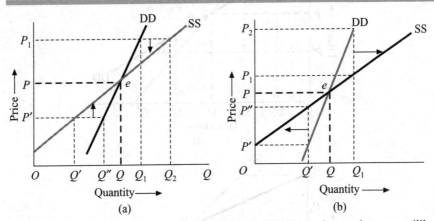

FIGURE 2.25 When demand and supply both slope upwards, as shown, equilibrium reached is *stable* in Walrasian sense, but *unstable* in Marshallian sense. Let the initial equilibrium price and quantity be OP and OQ, respectively. Let us first see how *Walrasian process of price adjustment* [(panel (a)] works. Let the price distort to $OP_1 (OP_1 > OP)$. Corresponding supply is OQ_2, while demand, OQ_1. A situation of excess supply ($=Q_1Q_2$) arises, which initiates a downward pressure on price pulling it down to OP. This would restore equilibrium at e.

Next, let the price distort to OP' ($OP' < OP$). This time, the situation that arises is that of excess demand ($=Q'Q''$) initiating an upward pressure on price pulling it up to OP. This would restore equilibrium at e. In each case, Walrasian price adjustment leads to a *stable* eqilibrium.

Now, let us turn to *Marshallian process* [panel(b)] of *quantity adjustment*. To see, let the quantity at any point of time be set at $OQ' (OQ' < OQ)$. Corresponding demand price OP' is lower than corresponding supply price $OP'' (OP' < OP'')$. As a result, supply would fall farther below OQ' and the system would move farther away from e. Alternatively, let the quantity be set at OQ_1. This time, corresponding supply price OP_1 is lower than corresponding demand price $OP_2 (OP_1 < OP_2)$. As a result, supply would rise farther above OQ_1 and the system would move farther away from e. In each case, Marshallian quantity adjustment leads to an *unstable* equilibrium.

Thus, when demand and supply both slope upwards with demand curve steeper (less elastic) then the supply curve, equilibrium is stable in Walrasian sense while unstable in Marshallian sense.

(iii) **When the demand curve slopes upwards while the supply curve, downwards**

In the first two cases, only one of the two curves deviated from the normal behaviour—in the first case, it was the demand curve that deviated from the normal behaviour and in the second case, it was the supply curve that deviated from its normal behaviour.

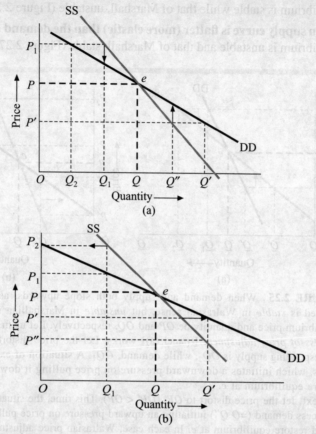

FIGURE 2.26 When demand and supply curves slope downwards with demand curve flatter (more elastic) than supply curve, the equilibrium reached is stable in Walrasian price adjustment process [panel (a)] and unstable in Marshallian quantity adjustment process [panel (b)]. To see, let us first consider *Walrasian process*. Let the initial price be set above the equilibrium level, say at OP_1. This causes an excess supply of Q_2Q_1, which initiates a downward pressure on price leading to a fall in it to the level of OP. This restores the equilibrium to point e. Next let the price get distorted below the level of equilibrium, say to OP'. An excess demand of $Q'Q''$ that arises, exerts an upward pressure on price which rises until it is equal to OP again. This restores equilibrium to point e. Equilibrium under Walrasian price adjustment process is, thus, a stable one.

As against this, in *Marshallian quantity adjustment process*, the equilibrium is unstable. To see, let the quantity supplied be set at OQ'. The corresponding demand price OP' is higher than the corresponding supply price OP'' ($OP' > OP''$). The adjustment process pulls the market farther away to right of the equilibrium point e. If the quantity supplied is set at OQ_1, the corresponding demand and supply prices are OP_1 and OP_2. Demand price OP_1 being lower than the supply price OP_2, the market drifts farther away to left of the equilibrium point e. The equilibrium in Marshallian sense is thus unstable.

Thus, equilibrium which is stable in Walrasian price adjustment process is unstable in Marshallian quantity adjustment process.

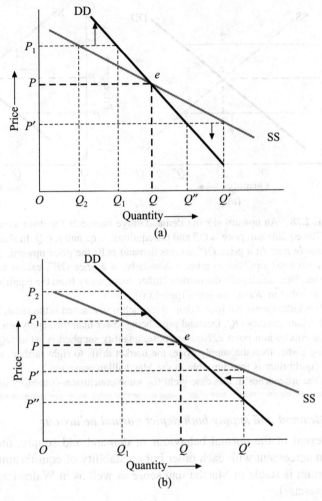

FIGURE 2.27 When supply and demand both slope downwards with demand curve steeper (less elastic) than the supply curve, equilibrium is *unstable* in *Walrasian sense* [panel (a)], but *stable* in *Marshallian sense* [panel (b)].

In *Walrasian sense*, a price set above the equilibrium level leads to excess demand causing a further hike in price and a drift farther away from the equilibrium point *e*. The same is the result when price set is below the equilibrium level at OP'. The excess supply caused lowers price and drifts the equilibrium farther away from point *e*.

In this case, we discuss the equilibrium for its stability when demand and supply both deviate from their normal behaviour. Figure 2.28 shows that the two approaches are in agreement with each other on instability of equilibrium, that is, the equilibrium is unstable in Marshallian sense as well as in Walrasian sense.

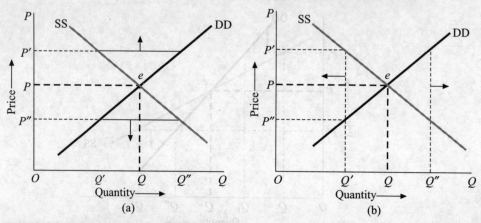

FIGURE 2.28 An upward sloping demand curve intersects the downward sloping supply curve at point e. The equilibrium price is OP and the equilibrium quantity, OQ. In *Walrasian sense*, equilibrium is an *unstable one*. At a price OP', excess demand pulls the price upward, driving the market farther up, away from the equilibrium point e. Similarly, at a price OP'', excess supply exerts a downward pressure on price which pulls the market farther down, away from the equilibrium point e. Equilibrium is, thus, unstable in Walrasian sense [panel (a)].

In *Marshallian sense* too [panel (b)], the conclusion reached is the same. Take quantity OQ', below the equilibrium quantity OQ. Demand price being lower than the supply price, the market drifts to the left of the equilibrium point e. Now suppose, quantity supplied is set at OQ'' instead. Demand price now being higher than the supply price, the market drifts to right farther away from the equilibrium point e. Equilibrium is thus unstable in the Marshallian sense too.

Both the approaches in this case yield the same conclusion–instability of equilibrium.

(iv) *When demand and supply both depict normal behaviour*

In the event of the normal behaviour of demand and supply, the two approaches are again in agreement with each other but on stability of equilibrium this time, that is, the equilibrium is stable in Marshallian sense as well as in Walrasian sense [Try the figure as an exercise].

Cobweb Theorem

The Cobweb Theorem provides the simplest form of a dynamic equilibrium. In it, supply of a product in the current period is guided by its price in the previous period. The best example of the Cobweb model is provided by the supply of agricultural products. Production and supply of corn in the current period is guided by its price of the previous period. If price of wheat in the previous year were high, its production and supply in the current year will also be high while its price, low. With a high price in mind, all the cultivators concentrate on production of wheat leading to a much higher supply of wheat than justified. The excess supply exerts a downward pressure on price, which falls in consequence. This prompts the cultivators to curtail production of wheat in the coming year with the result that the supply of wheat suffers next year. As obvious, price of wheat in the coming year would shoot up in consequence. Such supply lags often characterize industries where production is periodic (non-continuous), requiring a certain fixed time period for the production process to complete, and where, same output decisions are taken by all the producers independently. Producers never learn from their repetitive experiences of past frustrations and continue to be noseled by the previous year's price.

The Cobweb Theorem was developed by Henry Schultz, Jan Tinbergen and Arthur Hanai in 1930, but the name *Cobweb Theorem* was first suggested by Nicholas Kalder in 1934. The theorem* is based on the time lag concept, as explained above.

---

*Cobweb Theorem can be better understood mathematically. Quantity supplied in period T as a function of price in period $(T-1)$ may be given as

$$Q_T^S = f(P_{T-1}) \qquad (1)$$

Here, $Q_T^S \equiv$ quantity supplied in period T; $P_{T-1} \equiv$ price of the product in the period $T-1$
Let the demand and supply functions be given as

$$Q_t^D = a - bP_t \qquad (2)$$
$$Q_t^S = \alpha + \beta P_{t-1} \qquad (3)$$

Here, a, b, α and β are all positive constants. Note that demand is a function of the current price, P_t, while supply that of the previous year's price, P_{t-1}. Equilibrium, whether stable, unstable or neutral, requires quantity demanded and supplied to be same each; and price, whether current year's or previous year's, also to be same. Thus,

$$Q_t^D = Q_t^S \qquad (4)$$

and,
$$P_t = P_{t-1}$$
$$= \overline{P} \qquad (5)$$

at the point of equilibrium. From Equations 4, 3 & 2, we have

$$a - bP_t = \alpha + \beta P_{t-1} \qquad (6)$$

From Eqs. 5 and 6, we have

$$a - b\overline{P} = \alpha + \beta \overline{P} \qquad (7)$$

$$\overline{P} = \frac{(a - \alpha)}{(b + \beta)} \qquad (8)$$

From Eqs. 7 and 6, we have

$$b(\overline{P} - P_t) = \beta(P_{t-1} - \overline{P})$$
$$\Rightarrow -b(P_t - \overline{P}) = \beta(P_{t-1} - \overline{P})$$
$$\Rightarrow -bp_t = \beta p_{t-1} \qquad [\text{where, } p_t = (P_t - \overline{P}) \text{ and } p_{t-1} = (P_{t-1} - \overline{P})]$$
$$\Rightarrow p_t = -\frac{\beta}{b}(p_{t-1}) \qquad (9)$$

Equation 9 gives the first order *difference equation*. Its *complementary function* can be expressed as

$$p_t = p_0(-\beta/b)^t \qquad (10)$$
$$\Rightarrow (P_t - \overline{P}) = (P_0 - \overline{P}) \times (-\beta/b)^t \qquad [\text{Resubstituting for } p_t \text{ and } p_0]$$
$$\Rightarrow P_t = \overline{P} + (P_0 - \overline{P}) \times (-\beta/b)^t \qquad (11)$$

where, P_0 is the initial price.

(Contd.)

The term 'cobweb' is used to reflect the price-quantity variations that resemble a spider's cobweb. Economists have developed several cobweb models. We discuss below three standard ones for the sake of simplicity:

(a) Models with Damped Oscillations, also known as *convergent cobwebs*, leading to stable equilibrium.
(b) Models with Perpetual Oscillations, may be termed as *rectangular periphery cobwebs*, leading to neutrality of equilibrium.
(c) Models with Explosive Oscillations, also known as *divergent cobwebs*, leading to unstable equilibrium.

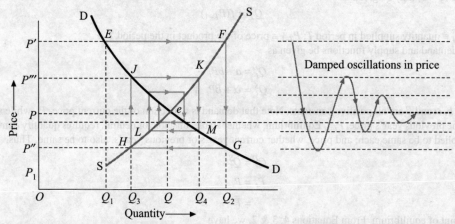

FIGURE 2.29 Convergent Cobweb: As evident, a stable equilibrium takes place at *e*. Equilibrium quantity is *OQ* and price, *OP*. The process of attaining it is explained here on the basis of lagged variation of supply to the previous year's price. To start, let the initial supply in Year 1 be OQ_1. Since, $OQ_1 < OQ$, buyers offer a price (*OP'*) higher than the equilibrium price (*OP*). This price provides an incentive to the producers to supply a matching quantity (OQ_2) in the following year, Year 2. As soon as they do so, an excess supply of the magnitude *EF* results, which exerts a downward pressure on price forcing it down to *OP"*. Producers had the last year's price *OP'* in mind and had supplied OQ_2 accordingly, but what they got was a lower price, *OP"* in Year 2. This prompts them to reduce supply to OQ_3 in Year 3. As soon as they do so, an excess demand by the magnitude *HG* results in Year 3 which exerts an upward pressure on price. It rises to *OP'''* in consequence. In Year 4, the price of Year 3 governs the supply which rises to OQ_4 leading to an excess supply worth *JK* in Year 4. Note that *JK* < *EF*. This depresses price as expected and creates an excess demand *LM* in Year 5. Again, *LM* < *HG*. This indicates that excess supply as well as excess demand both get damped in the subsequent years. The **lagged variations** in supply lead to **damped oscillations** which produce a **convergent cobweb** merging ultimately in the equilibrium point. The phenomenon owes its origin to the relative slopes, or more appropriately, to the relative price elasticities of demand and supply. It gives a **stable equilibrium** in the long-run.

Footnote (Contd.)

Equation 11 expresses price at time *t* in terms of equilibrium price $\bar{P}$, initial price P_0, slopes of demand (–*b*) and supply (*β*). The three possibilities that emerge can be summarized below:

(i) If *β* < *b*, i.e., if slope of the supply curve is less than the numerical value of the slope of the demand curve, the cobweb is a convergent one as in Figure 2.29, involving *damped oscillations* leading to *stability of equilibrium*. The interpretation follows from the fact that $P_t = \bar{P}$, the equilibrium price, as $(-\beta/b)^t \to 0$ when $t \to \infty$.

Figures 2.29, 2.30 and 2.31 demonstrate these models. Lagged variations of supply, based on the previous year's price, get adjusted only in the model of damped oscillations leading to a *convergent cobweb* (Figure 2.29), which yields a stable equilibrium in the long-run. The model of explosive oscillations leading to a *divergent cobweb* (Figure 2.30) results in an *unstable equilibrium* in the long-run. The model of perpetual oscillations leading to a *rectangular periphery* (Figure 2.31) results in a *neutral equilibrium* in the long-run implying sustained price fluctuations between the same price limits. The state of equilibrium–stable, unstable or neutral–depends on the relative slopes of the demand and the supply curves. You can try these curves with different slopes as an exercise.

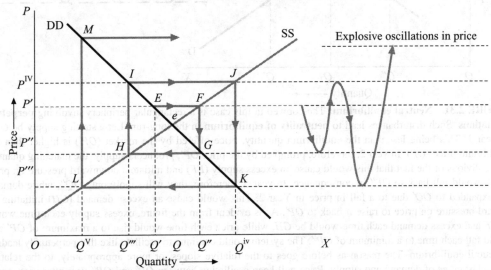

FIGURE 2.30 A **divergent cobweb** with explosive oscillations leads to an **unstable equilibrium** in the long-run. Let the initial equilibrium be at e. Further let the initial supply in Year 1 be OQ'. The corresponding price in Year 1 is OP'. Producers adjust their supply in Year 2 to this price and set it at OQ''. This causes an excess supply worth EF, which exerts a downward pressure on price which falls to OP'' in Year 2. The price governs the supply and sets it at OQ''' in Year 3. This creates an excess demand worth HG in Year 3 which exerts an upward pressure on price. The price rises to OP^{IV}. In Year 4, producers adjust their supply to this price and set it at OQ^{iv}. Previous year's price continues to govern the following year's supply in the form of lagged variations as explained above and also in Figure 2.29. The only difference is that excess supply and excess demand both in here have a rising trend. $IJ > EF$ and $KL > HG$. Price of the preceding year dictating the supply in the succeeding year, the adjustment process drifts the equilibrium farther and farther away from e, given the relative slopes, or more appropriately, the relative price elasticities of demand and supply as in the figure. Oscillations resulting here are termed as **explosive oscillations**. They lead to a **divergent cobweb** and an **unstable equilibrium**.

Footnote (Contd.)
 (ii) If $\beta = b$, i.e., if slope of the supply curve is equal to the numerical value of the slope of the demand curve, the cobweb is a rectangular periphery, as in Figure 2.31, involving *perpetual oscillations*, leading to *neutrality of equilibrium*. The interpretation follows from the fact that $P_t = \bar{P} \pm (P_0 - \bar{P})$, as $(-\beta/b)^t \to \pm 1$ when $t \to \infty$. That is, price at time t fluctuates between P_0 and $2\bar{P} - P_0$.
 (iii) If $\beta > b$, i.e., if slope of the supply curve is greater than the numerical value of the slope of the demand curve, the cobweb is a divergent one, as in Figure 2.30, involving *explosive oscillations* leading to *instability of equilibrium*. The interpretation follows from the fact that $P_t = \bar{P} \pm \infty$, as $(-\beta/b)^t \to \pm \infty$ when $t \to \infty$. That is, price at time t fluctuates infinitely above or below the equilibrium price, $\bar{P}$.

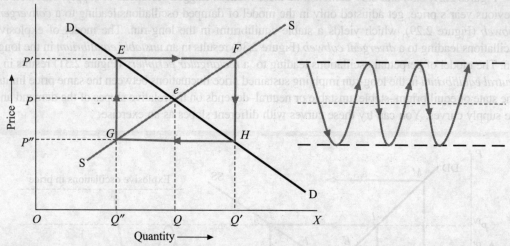

FIGURE 2.31 Neutral equilibrium: The cobweb in this case is a rectangular periphery involving **perpetual oscillations**. Such disturbances lead to **neutrality of equilibrium** in the long-run. Let a starting supply be OQ'' in Year 1. This being less than the equilibrium quantity, price offered by the market (OP') is higher than the equilibrium price (OP). In year 2, therefore, prompted by the price OP', producers supply the matching quantity OQ' oblivious of the fact that this would cause an excess supply (EF) and initiate a downward pressure on price which would fall back to OP'' in consequence. In year 3, therefore, they will supply only OQ'', while demand has expanded to OQ' due to a fall in price in Year 2. This would cause an excess demand (GH) initiating an upward pressure on price to raise it back to OP'. As is evident from the figure, excess supply each time would be EF and excess demand each time would be GH, while price each time would rise to a maximum of OP' and would fall each time to a minimum of OP''. The system would continue to oscillate like that perpetually leading to neutral equilibrium. The reason as before goes to the relative slopes, or more appropriately, to the relative price elasticities of demand and supply. Price will keep oscillating between OP' and OP'' year after year, never attaining the level of equilibrium at e.

Changes in Equilibrium

Equilibrium price prevailing at a point of time in the market is called the *market price*. It varies from time-to-time with changes in the position of equilibrium. Factors that change the position of

Note that:

(1) A *difference equation* expresses discrete changes in dependent variable with respect to discrete changes in the independent variable. For example, $Y_{t+1} - Y_t = 4$ or $\Delta Y_t = 4$ is a difference equation as it expresses a discrete change in the dependent variable Y in relation to a discrete change in the independent variable t. An equation, such as $dy/dt = 4$ is a differential equation as it expresses an infinitesimally small change in y in relation to an infinitesimally small change in t.

(2) The *complementary function* refers to the solution of the auxiliary form of a difference or differential equation. For instance, the auxiliary form of the differential equation $dy/dx + ay = b$ is $dy/dx + ay = 0$ and the solution of this auxiliary form is the complementary function.

(3) The expression for the complementary function can be obtained by the method of enumeration. From Eq. 9,

$$p_t = (-\beta/b)p_{t-1};\ p_{t-1} = (-\beta/b)p_{t-2};\ p_{t-2} = (-\beta/b)p_{t-3};\ \ldots \ldots;\ p_1 = (-\beta/b)p_0.$$

Expressing p_t in terms of p_0, we have, therefore,

$$p_t = (-\beta/b)^t p_0$$

equilibrium include shifts in the demand and supply curves. Most of these shifts are caused by the shift factors already discussed in this chapter. Other variations in market price arise from direct and indirect government interventions. The direct government intervention distorts the market price directly by pegging it up or down, while indirect government intervention tends to relocate equilibrium through shifts caused in demand or supply.

Changes in market price are also caused by changes in the existing market structure. Examples of such changes are many, but the important ones include rise or fall in monopoly power of the firms. We will study market structures and changes therein in Chapters 7, 8, 9, 10 and 11.

For the sake of simplicity of analysis, let us categorize the elements of change in the equilibrium position or market price under the following three heads:

(a) Shifts in demand,
(b) Shifts in supply, and
(c) Government regulations.

(a) **Shifts in demand** Such shifts are caused by shift factors, namely, changes in income of the consumers, changes in prices of the related goods and changes in tastes, preferences and fashions. A favourable change, shifts the demand curve upwards to right while an unfavourable one shifts it downwards to left. An increase or a decrease in population also leads to an upward or a downward shift in demand (Figures 2.32 and 2.33).

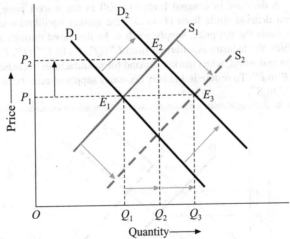

FIGURE 2.32 An increase in demand leads to a rise in the market price, other things remaining unchanged. When demand shifts from D_1 to D_2, the market equilibrium shifts from $E_1(Q_1, P_1)$ to $E_2(Q_2, P_2)$. To retain the old price, supply needs to be increased through a parallel shift in it from S_1 to S_2. This shifts the industry equilibrium from $E_2(Q_2, P_2)$ to $E_3(Q_3, P_1)$ in consequence. As an example from the real world, when market demand for food grains rises from D_1 to D_2, The market price rises from P_1 to P_2. To restore the price at P_1, government increases supply of food grains through the fair price shops so that the market supply curve may shift from S_1 to S_2.

(b) **Shifts in supply** The effect of an increase or decrease in supply (a downward or upward shift in it) on price–output decisions of the market can be explained on similar lines.

Increase/decrease in supply are caused by the shift factors as explained in Section 2.7. Figure 2.34 shows the effect of an increase in supply on the price–output decisions. The industry may resort to aggressive marketing to increase demand in order to retain the original level of price. When supply decreases, supply curve shifts upwards to left and market price rises in consequence. Figure 2.35 demonstrates the point.

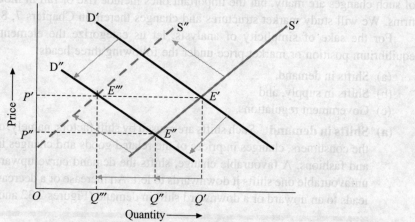

FIGURE 2.33 A decrease in demand leads to a fall in the market price, other things remaining unchanged. When demand shifts from D' to D", the market equilibrium shifts from $E'(Q', P')$ to $E''(Q'', P'')$. To retain the old price, supply needs to be decreased through a parallel shift in it from S' to S". This shifts the industry equilibrium from $E''(Q'', P')$ to $E'''(Q''', P')$ in consequence. As an example from the real world, when market demand for manufactures decreases from D' to D", market price falls from P' to P". To restore it, industry decreases supply of manufactures so that market supply may shift from S' to S".

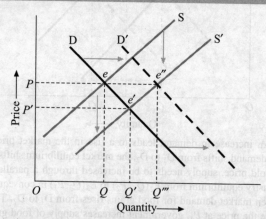

FIGURE 2.34 An increase in market supply shifts the curve from S to S'. In consequence, equilibrium shifts from e to e' with the result that market price falls from OP to OP'. To restore it, demand needs to be increased from D to D' so that price may be restored to the original level, OP at e''. This can be accomplished by aggressive marketing by the sellers.

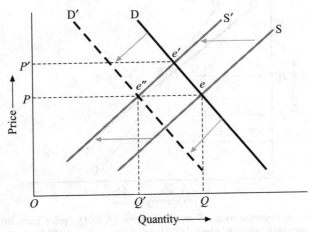

FIGURE 2.35 A decrease in market supply shifts the curve from S to S′. In consequence, equilibrium shifts from e to e' with the result that market price rises from OP to OP'. To restore it, demand needs to be decreased from D to D′ so that price may be restored to the original level, OP at e''. Government can accomplish this by decreasing the disposable income of the consumers through taxation or other suitable measures such as compulsory deposit schemes.

Some Assorted Applications of Demand and Supply Curves

(i) *Unplanned fluctuations in output lead to sharper fluctuations in price if demand is inelastic (steeper) than when it is elastic (flatter):*

Figure 2.36 explains the statement. Suppose unplanned fluctuations in output range from Q_1 to Q_2, while DD and D′D′ represent elastic and inelastic demands. Initial equilibrium (supply not shown) takes place at E_0 where price is P_0 and output, Q_0. If output drops to Q_1, price along the elastic demand curve (DD) would be P_1 while that along the inelastic demand curve (D′D′), P_1'. Since $P_1' > P_1$, price fluctuation (increase) is sharper along the inelastic demand D′D′ than along the elastic demand DD. In like manner, if output increases to Q_2, price fluctuation (fall) is again sharper along the inelastic (steeper) demand than along the elastic (flatter) one.

Thus, unplanned fluctuations in output lead to sharper fluctuations in price if demand is inelastic (steeper) than when it is elastic (flatter).

(ii) *When demand decreases, receipts from sale of output decrease whether supply is elastic (flatter) or inelastic (steeper), but fall in price is sharper when supply is inelastic (steeper) than when it is elastic (flatter)*

Figure 2.37 demonstrates the point. Receipts from sale decline in both the cases but fall in price is sharper in case of inelastic (steeper) supply than in case of more elastic (flatter) one.

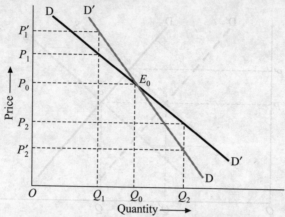

FIGURE 2.36 In response to a fall in output from Q_0 to Q_1, price rises from P_0 to P_1 along DD (more elastic demand) and to P_1' along D'D' (less elastic demand). P_1' being greater than P_1, price rise $(P_1' - P_0)$ is higher along inelastic (steeper) demand than that $(P_1 - P_0)$ along elastic (flatter) one. In the same way, if the output rises from Q_0 to Q_2, fall in price $(P_0 - P_2')$ is higher along the inelastic (steeper) demand than that $(P_0 - P_2)$ along the elastic (flatter) one.

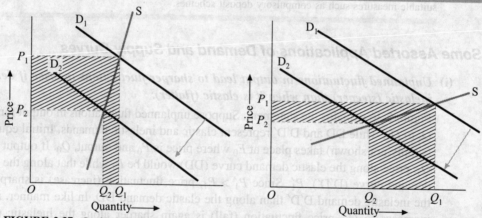

FIGURE 2.37 In the left panel, supply curve is less elastic (steeper) while in the right panel, it is more elastic (flatter). In response to a decrease (downward shift) in demand receipts from sale of the output decline in both the cases by the respective shaded regions; but fall in price is sharper in case of inelastic (steeper) supply than in case of elastic supply.

(iii) *Stabilizing quantity sold stabilizes income but stabilizing price does not*
Figure 2.38 explains the point.

If price is fixed at the equilibrium price, income of the producers can be stabilized only when fixed output (Q_0) is sold. Excess produce $(Q_2 - Q_0)$ is stored by a producers' organization or procured by government. Deficient produce $(Q_0 - Q_1)$ may be supplemented from the stocks so raised. In case price is allowed to fluctuate (no intervention from the government), income of the producers' can be stabilized provided the demand curve faced by the producers is a rectangular hyperbola. We examine the proposition in the next application.

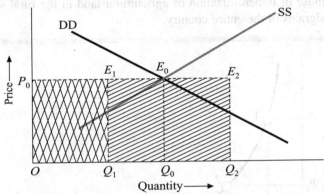

FIGURE 2.38 When price is fixed at P_0, income is $P_0 Q_1$ when Q_1 is sold, $P_0 Q_0$ when Q_0 is sold and it is $P_0 Q_2$ when Q_2 is sold. Thus, stabilizing price does not stabilize income as $P_0 Q_1 \neq P_0 Q_0 \neq P_0 Q_2$. But stabilization of quantity at Q_0 would lead to stabilization of income. When Q_2 is produced and Q_0 is sold, $(Q_2 - Q_0)$ is stored. Income received is $P_0 Q_0$. When Q_1 is produced and Q_0 is sold with $(Q_0 - Q_1)$ coming from the stocks of $(Q_2 - Q_0)$, income is again stabilized at $P_0 Q_0$.

(iv) *Income of the producers can be stabilized even when outputs fluctuate widely, provided that there is no regulatory intervention from government and that demand curve faced by the producers is a rectangular hyperbola (Figure 2.39)*

Every point on a rectangular hyperbola subtends a rectangle with the coordinate axes. Area of each of these rectangles is the same, as explained in Figure 2.39.

A number of applications of the tools of demand and supply befit the production conditions in agriculture. At the harvest time, market price of the corn is low; but at others, it is high. Cultivators, therefore, stand to suffer loss. This is likely to discourage them. Quitting cultivation, they might begin looking for alternative openings. No government can afford this. Intervention in the free-play of price mechanism becomes imperative, therefore. Let us see in part (c) how it works.

(c) **Government regulations**

(i) *Direct intervention through price floors*

In respect of the protected industries, government often resorts to *price floors* with a view to ensure a fair price to the producers. A *price floor,* also known at times as the *minimum support price,* is a price fixed by government to ensure the producers a fair return on production of essential products. It is always above the market clearing price and is maintained so through deliberate action. The excess supply resulting from it is purchased by government. Figure 2.40 demonstrates the mechanism.

During harvests, government of India procures foodgrains at the floor-price. This makes cultivation remunerative enough to sustain farmers' interest in it. Over 68% of the labour force in India derives its livelihood from agriculture. If they decide to move to the already overpopulated urban regions in search of greener pastures, which is a likelihood if cultivation fails to retain their interest, a host of problems would crop up for a welfare-oriented state like India. The most important ones among them include the problems of unemployment and overcrowding in the urban sector apart from those of underutilization of agricultural land in the rural sector and shortage of foodgrains in the entire country.

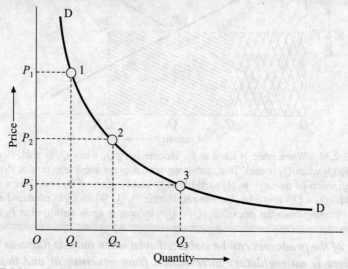

FIGURE 2.39 If the coordinates of a moving point on the rectangular hyperbola were (Q, P), the area of the rectangle subtended by the point on the two axes is $P \times Q$. Let it be denoted as α^2. By virtue of the property of a rectangular hyperbola, α^2 is a constant regardless of the location of the moving point (Q, P) on it. That is, in location 1, the point is (Q_1, P_1) and the area of the rectangle subtended by it is P_1Q_1; in location 2, the point is (Q_2, P_2) and the area of the rectangle subtended by it is P_2Q_2 and in location 3, the point is (Q_3, P_3) and the area of the rectangle subtended by it is P_3Q_3. By virtue of the property, $P_1Q_1 = P_2Q_2 = P_3Q_3 = \alpha^2$. To demonstrate, let $Q_1 = 10$ when P_1 is 40, Q_2 be 20 when P_2 is 20, and Q_3 be 40 when P_3 is 10. It can be seen that $\alpha^2 = 400$ as $P_1Q_1 = P_2Q_2 = P_3 Q_3 = 400$. Thus, if the producers enjoy the freedom to charge a higher price when output is low and a lower price when the output is high, as on a rectangular hyperbola, their income would be stable at α^2. It is a different issue whether the producers can be allowed to charge such an income stabilizing price by the government or not.

(ii) *Direct intervention through the price ceiling (price control and rationing)*
Rationing of essential commodities provides a good example of price ceiling. Rent control is yet another. Figure 2.41 demonstrates working of both. Ceiling price, also known as controlled price, is a price of essential products fixed by government to protect consumers against rising prices. It is always lower than the free market price. In case, government fails to supply excess demand of $(Q_2 - Q_1)$ from its buffer stocks at the ceiling price P_1, the policy would lead to emergence of a **black market**. The black marketeers purchase quantity Q_1 at price P_1 from the open market and sell the same at a price P_2 in the black market. In the process, they make a profit equal to $(P_2 - P_1) \times Q_1$ [Shaded rectangles 'C' and 'D' in Figure 2.41]. Triangular region A marks loss of *consumers' surplus* while B, that of *producers' surplus*. The two taken together $(A + B)$ mark loss of social welfare. To prevent this, government should refrain from implementing the policy unless it has sufficient buffer stocks to back it up, i.e. quantity $(Q_2 - Q_1)$ to meet the excess demand.

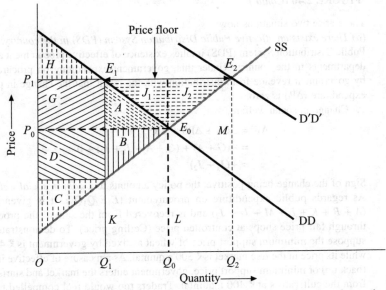

FIGURE 2.40 Price floor: Let the market clearing price of food grains at the harvest time be P_0, and the quantity transacted, Q_0. Now suppose government fixes a price floor at P_1 in execution of its policy of minimum support price. At P_1, supply of food grains is Q_2, while corresponding demand is only Q_1. This leads to an excess supply E_1E_2 equal to $(Q_2 - Q_1)$. Two possibilities emerge here:

(i) When government provides full back up to its price floor

In this case, quantity sold is Q_2, of which, Q_1 is bought by the traders and the rest, by the procurement department of the government. The price realized by the cultivators is P_1. This entails additional costs to the traders and additional public expenditure to the government on one hand and additional revenue to the cultivators on the other. To see how such costs and benefits affect social welfare, let us estimate changes caused in consumers and producers surpluses apart from changes caused in public expenditure/revenue. Change in social welfare (ΔW) is given by the sum of the changes in (i) consumers surplus, (ii) producer surplus, and (iii) public expenditure/revenue.

Before introduction of the price floor,

$$\text{Consumers Surplus (CS)} = H + G + A$$
$$\text{Producers Surplus (PS)} = B + D + C$$

After introduction of the price floor,

$$\text{Consumers Surplus (CS)} = H$$
$$\text{Producers Surplus (PS)} = D + C + G + A + B + J_1 + J_2$$

∴ Change in consumers surplus,

$$\Delta CS = H - (H + G + A)$$
$$= -(G + A), \text{ and}$$

Change in producers surplus,

$$\Delta PS = (D + C + G + A + B + J_1 + J_2) - (B + D + C)$$
$$= +(G + A + J_1 + J_2)$$

Loss of government revenue = Expenditure on procurement
= Area of the rectangle $E_1E_2Q_1Q_2$

(Contd.)

FIGURE 2.40 (Contd.)

There arise two situations now:

(a) There exists an effective Public Distribution System (PDS) in the country: An effective Public Distribution System (PDS) implies existence of effective procurement and distribution departments in the country. Under this, government expenditure on procurement is offset by government revenue from distribution with the result that the change in public revenue/expenditure (ΔR) is zero.

∴ Change in social welfare,

$$\Delta W = \Delta CS + \Delta PS + \Delta R$$
$$= -(G + A) + (G + A + J_1 + J_2) + 0$$
$$= +(J_1 + J_2)$$

Sign of the change being positive, the policy amounts to a *gain in social welfare*.

As regards public expenditure on procurement ($E_1E_2Q_1Q_2$), it is given by the region $(A + B + K + L + M + J_1 + J_2)$ and is recovered from the sale of the procured products through fair price shops at controlled price (Ceiling price). To demonstrate the working, suppose the minimum support price of wheat as fixed by government is ₹ 400 per quintal while its price in the free market is ₹ 300 a quintal. As a measure of effective implementation (back up) of minimum support price, government enters the market and starts buying wheat from the cultivators at ₹ 400 a quintal. Traders too would feel compelled to buy it at this price if the price they anticipate to fetch during the offseason is even higher, say, ₹ 600 a quintal. Their objective is profit. The objecting of government is to protect cultivators on one hand and common consumers on the other. While traders sell their merchandise at ₹ 600 a quintal later, government distributes the commodity so procured at the controlled price of say, ₹ 500 a quintal through its fair price shops. Government, thus, recovers the total cost of procurement (₹ 400 a quintal) and storage (₹ 100 a quintal). Procurement and distribution of essential commodities constitute the Public Distribution System (PDS) as practiced by welfare states like India. It raises social welfare by as much as $(J_1 + J_2)$.

(b) There exists only the procurement policy: As in US, government indulges in procurement at minimum support price, but it does not indulge in public distribution of the procured goods through fair price shops. Instead, it destroys the procured goods or dumps them into the oceans. In such cases, expenditure on procurement is not offset by revenue from distribution with the result that ΔR is negative, equal in magnitude to the area of the rectangle $E_1E_2Q_1Q_2$. The change in social welfare,

$$\Delta W = \Delta CS + \Delta PS + \Delta R$$
$$= -(G + A) + (G + A + J_1 + J_2) - [(A + B + J_1 + J_2 + K + L + M) - (K + L + M)]$$
$$= -(A + B)$$

Note that $(K + L + M)$ accrues to the cultivators by way of their production costs. Hence, loss of social welfare is limited to the region $(A + B)$. It is called the *deadweight loss*.

(ii) **When government decides against procurement but grants cash subsidy worth $(P_1 - P_0)$ to the cultivators**

In this case, quantity Q_0 is transacted at P_0 in the open market. Producers are compensated in cash the difference of P_1 over P_0 on each unit sold by them in the open market. Let us see the effect of this policy on the social welfare.

Before introduction of the price floor,

(Contd.)

FIGURE 2.40 (*Contd.*)

$$\text{Consumers Surplus (CS)} = H + G + A$$
$$\text{Producers Surplus (PS)} = B + D + C$$

After introduction of the price floor,

$$\text{Consumers Surplus (CS)} = H + G + A$$
$$\text{Producers Surplus (PS)} = D + C + G + A + B + J_1$$

Therefore, change in consumers' surplus,

$$\Delta CS = (H + G + A) - (H + G + A) = 0, \text{ and}$$

Change in producers' surplus,

$$\Delta PS = (D + C + G + A + B + J_1) - (B + D + C)$$
$$= +(G + A + J_1)$$

Loss of government revenue,

$$\Delta R = (G + A + J_1)$$

∴ Change in social welfare, $\Delta W = \Delta CS + \Delta PS + \Delta R$
$$= 0 + (G + A + J_1) - (G + A + J_1)$$
$$= 0$$

(Change in government revenue is negative.)

Thus, the policy of cash grant has cost government a revenue worth $(A + G + J_1)$. The same, if spent by government on productive activities, would have led to more output/income for the nation and hence more welfare. The same, if spent on public utilities, would have generated an equal amount of additional welfare directly. In either case, the policy of cash grant amounts to reallocation of welfare. Social welfare (total) remains same. If we compare the change in social welfare as in [(i)(a)], [(i)(b)] and (ii), we observe that [(i)(a)] increases social welfare, (ii) leaves the social welfare unaffected and [(i)(b)] causes a deadweight loss.

Government intervention in free play of price mechanism serves a number of welfare objectives. Firstly, it helps sustaining cultivators' interest in production of foodgrains by ensuring them a remunerative price (Figure 2.40) through the scheme of minimum support price (*floor-price*). Secondly, it helps government to protect the interest of the common consumer by providing the essentials such as foodgrains at controlled prices (*ceiling-prices*) during their scarcity (Figure 2.41). Government achieves both these goals through its Public Distribution System (PDS). Thirdly, it helps government to check the illegal trade practices of the intermediaries who exploit cultivators at the time of harvest and consumers at the time of lean supply of foodgrains. Stocks raised by the procurement department during harvests come handy in this regard.

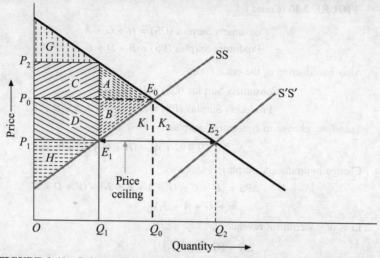

FIGURE 2.41 **Price ceiling:** Traders supply Q_0 at a price P_0, which is higher than the price P_1 masses can afford. To protect their interests, government introduces a price ceiling at P_1. At this price, traders supply Q_1 while consumers demand Q_2. This results in excess demand of $(Q_2 - Q_1)$, which, by all means, would exert an upward pressure on price to push it back to P_0 unless government meets it from its buffer stocks at P_1 through its fair price shops. Stocks raised through procurement or import come handy for the purpose. If government does not meet the excess demand, the policy of price ceiling would lead to emergence of a *black-market*. Profiteers would buy quantity Q_1 at the controlled price P_1 from the open market and would sell the same at a higher price P_2, in the black market earning a profit $[(P_2 - P_1) \times Q_1]$ in the process. It is shown by the shaded rectangles 'C' and 'D'. Regions 'A' and 'C' mark loss of consumers surplus while regions 'B' and 'D' mark that of producers surplus. Of these, C and D accrue to the black-marketers, while 'A' and 'B', to none. Taken together, A and B mark loss of social welfare (Deadweight Loss). Note that loss of region C of consumers' surplus and that of D of producer's surplus do not constitute the deadweight loss because they accrue to some members of the society (black-marketers).

In case government meets the excess demand from its buffer stocks, the consumers surplus would increase by the region $(D + B + K_1 + K_2)$, while the producers surplus would decrease by the region $(D + B)$. Net effect on social welfare would be an increase in it by the region $(K_1 + K_2)$. A systematic way of determining the effect of price ceiling on social welfare can be summarized as below:

(i) **When price ceiling is not backed up through distribution by the state**
Before introduction of price ceiling,

$$\text{Consumers Surplus (CS)} = A + C + G$$
$$\text{Producers Surplus (PS)} = B + D + H$$

After introduction of price ceiling,

$$\text{Consumers Surplus (CS)} = G$$
$$\text{Producers Surplus (PS)} = H$$

Income to the black-marketeers = $C + D$
Therefore, Change in CS,

$$\Delta\text{CS} = [G - (A + C + G)]$$
$$= -(A + C)$$

(Contd.)

FIGURE 2.41 (*Contd.*)

$$\text{Change in PS, } \Delta PS = [H - (B + D + H)]$$
$$= -(B + D)$$

∴ Change in social welfare,

$$\Delta W = \Delta CS + \Delta PS + \text{Income to the black-marketeers}$$
$$= -(A + C) - (B + D) + (C + D)$$
$$= -(A + B)$$

Change being negative, it is a loss of social welfare (deadweight loss)

(ii) **When price ceiling is backed up through distribution by the state**

Consumers Surplus (CS) = $D + B + K_1 + K_2 + G + C + A$

Producers Surplus (PS) = H

Therefore,

$$\Delta CS = (D + B + K_1 + K_2 + G + C + A) - (A + C + G)$$
$$= (D + B + K_1 + K_2)$$
$$\Delta PS = H - (B + D + H)$$
$$= -(B + D)$$

∴ Change in social welfare, $\Delta W = \Delta CS + \Delta PS$
$$= (D + B + K_1 + K_2) - (B + D)$$
$$= +(K_1 + K_2)$$

Change being positive, it is a gain in social welfare.

Thus, the policy of price ceiling duly backed up by public distribution system (PDS) increases social welfare.

(iii) *Indirect intervention through unit taxes and subsidies*

The government regulations of market price, as discussed above, provide examples of its direct *intervention* in the free play of price mechanism. In addition, government resorts to some indirect measures as well that influence the market price though indirectly. Such measures, called *indirect interventions,* include specific unit and percentage taxes and subsidies. While government levies indirect taxes on each unit produced or sold of some products, it grants subsidy on each unit produced and sold of certain other products.

An indirect tax is a levy on production or sale of goods and services. It generates revenue for government. When levied unitwise on a product, it is called a *specific unit tax,* or simply, a *unit tax* or *specific tax.* Under it, a fixed charge is made on production or sale of each unit. The levy causes a parallel shift in the supply curve upwards to its left [Figure 2.42(a)] when buyer's price is portrayed on the vertical axis or a parallel shift in the demand curve downward to its left when seller's price is portrayed on the vertical axis. In the former case, supply price of each unit increases by the amount of the tax while in the latter case, demand price of each unit decreases by the amount of the tax. When levied valuewise, the tax is a fixed percent of the product price and is called a *percent tax.* It causes a non-parallel shift in the supply curve upwards to its left when buyer's price is portrayed on the vertical axis [Figure 2.42(b)] or a non-parallel shift in the demand curve downward to its left when seller's price is portrayed on the vertical axis [Figure 2.42(c)]. Excise duty or specific excise is an example of a specific unit tax. Figure 2.42(a) demonstrates its effects on equilibrium price and quantity as also on the manner in which its burden is shared between the producers and consumers under the normal conditions of demand and supply.

As against an indirect tax, a subsidy is a grant of a part of the value of the product in favour of its producer. That way, it can be treated as a *negative indirect tax*. Its effect on the supply and demand curves can be viewed as exactly opposite of the effects of the indirect taxes [Figure 2.42(d)].

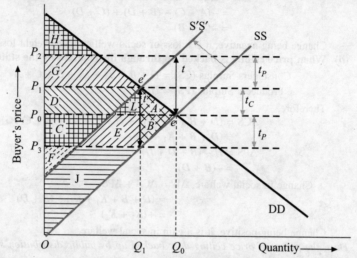

FIGURE 2.42(a)   Indirect tax: In the simple demand and supply framework, industry equilibrium takes place at e, where quantity Q_0 is transacted at price P_0. Levy of unit excise shifts the supply curve upwards to left by a vertical distance equivalent to its magnitude. The new supply curve, $S'S'$, intersects the demand curve at e' where quantity transacted is Q_1 at price P_1. At this level of sales, price realized by the producers after tax is P_3, which is lower than P_1 paid by the buyers by t, the amount of the tax levied so that $P_3 = P_1 - t$. As evident from the figure, a part of the tax, t_P, is borne by the producers and the rest, t_C, by the buyers/consumers so that $t_P + t_C = t$. The part t_C is said to have been shifted onto the consumers/buyers. Its magnitude depends on the relative slopes or the price elasticities of demand and supply (See Q. 50 of the exercises). Let us now investigate the effect of the levy on social welfare.

$$\Delta CS = [(H + G) - (H + G + D + L + A)]$$
$$= -(D + L + A)$$
$$\Delta PS = [(C + D + F) - (J + F + C + E + B)]$$
$$= D - (J + E + B)$$

Additional revenue realized by the government,

$$\Delta R = t \cdot OQ_1$$
$$= D + L + C + E$$
$$= (J + E + L)$$

[Rectangle $(D + L + C + E)$ and parallelogram $(J + E + L)$ have equal areas as the two share a common base and lie between same parallels.]

Change in social welfare, $\Delta W = \Delta CS + \Delta PS + \Delta R$
$$= -(D + L + A) + D - (J + E + B) + (J + E + L)$$
$$= -D - L - A + D - J - E - B + J + E + L$$
$$= -(A + B)$$

The sign of the change being negative, levy of the unit tax leads to a deadweight loss.

The levy of unit tax shifts the supply curve upwards to left [Figure 2.42(a)]. The shift implies vertical movement of each point on the supply curve by the magnitude 't' of the specific unit tax. Thus, if $P = mQ$ is the equation of the original supply curve, $P = mQ + t$ would be that of the post-tax supply curve. This shifts the equilibrium too in the same direction, that is, upward to left. Under normal conditions of demand and supply, a part of the unit-tax would be borne by the producers and the rest by the consumers. As a result, consumers get less at a higher price while producers realize a lower price for lower sales. In other words, unit tax may be used not only to generate revenue for the State but also to restrict consumption of any product.

As mentioned earlier, a **percent tax**, such as sales tax, is a certain percentage of the prevailing price. Its magnitude therefore varies with the product price, from one point on the supply/demand curve to another on it depending on whether it is the buyer's price portrayed on the vertical axis or the seller's price. When buyer's price is portrayed on the vertical axis, the post-tax supply price can be expressed as $[(100 + t)/(100)]$ of the pre-tax supply price. Also, the slope of the post-tax supply curve would change to $[(100 + t)/(100)]$ of the slope of the pre-tax supply curve. Shift in the supply curve is therefore pivotal, as shown in Figure 2.42 (b).

When seller's price is portrayed on the vertical axis, the post-tax demand price can be expressed as $[(100 - t)/100]$ of the pre-tax demand price, as shown in Figure. 2.42(c). The same is true of the slope of the post-tax demand curve, which is $[(100 - t)/100]$ of the pre-tax demand curve. From the left panel, it is clear that a buyer pays a higher price for a certain quantity or gets a lower quantity at a certain price in consequence. In the same way, from the right panel, it is clear that a seller receives a lower price for a given quantity or sells a lower quantity at a given price.

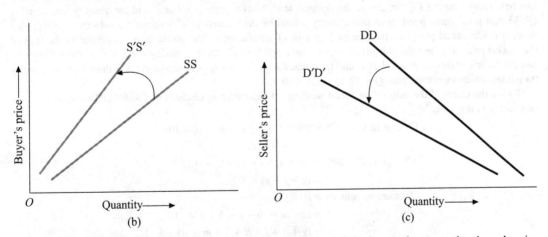

FIGURES 2.42(b) and (c) A per cent tax causes a non-parallel shift in the supply curve when buyer's price is portrayed on the vertical axis, as shown in panel (b). The slope of the new supply curve is $[(100 + t)/(100)]$ of the slope of the original supply curve, 't' being the tax rate as a per cent. A per cent unit tax causes a non-parallel shift in the demand curve when seller's price is portrayed on the vertical axis (panel c). The slope of the new demand curve is $[(100 - t)/(100)]$ of the slope of the original demand curve.

Grant of subsidy is another example of indirect intervention in the free play of price mechanism. It refers to grant of a fixed amount to the producer on each unit of the product transacted. For all practical purposes, it can be treated as a **negative specific tax**. Figure 2.42(d) demonstrates the effect of a subsidy on market price, quantity transacted and social welfare.

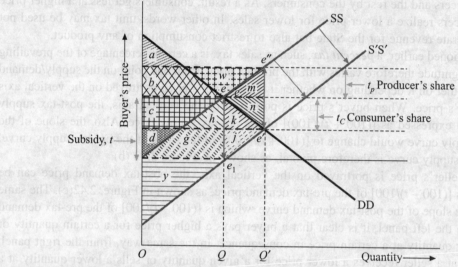

FIGURE 2.42(d) Demand (DD) intersects supply (SS) at e. Grant of a fixed amount of subsidy (t) by government leads to a parallel but downward to right shift in the supply curve as shown. This is done by taking a point e_1 vertically below the initial equilibrium, e, so that $ee_1 = t$, and then drawing S'S' parallel to SS through e_1. The new supply curve (S'S') intersects the demand at e'. Market price is set at e' and the quantity transacted is Q'. Market price corresponding to this quantity would be determined at e'' without the subsidy. Clearly, $e'e'' = ee_1 = t$. The actual price received on each unit of Q' transacted by the producer is thus equal to the sum of the market price at e' and the subsidy, t. It thus corresponds to e''. Of the subsidy, $e'e''$ or t, let the consumer's and producer's shares be denoted as t_C and t_P so that $t = e'e'' = t_C + t_P$. The reader can see the effect on quantity transacted which increases from Q to Q' in consequence.

To see the effect of the subsidy on social welfare, let us determine changes in CS, PS and compute the cost of subsidy to the state.

$$\text{Change in CS, } \Delta CS = [(h + k + c + b + a) - (a + b)]$$
$$= + (h + k + c)$$
$$\text{Change in PS, } \Delta PS = [(d + g + j + y) - (c + d)]$$
$$= (g + j + y) - c$$
$$\text{Amount of subsidy} = t(OQ')$$
$$= (b + w + m + c + h + k + n)$$
$$= (y + g + j + h + k + m + n)$$

[Rectangle $(b + w + m + c + h + k + n)$ has the same area as parallelogram $(y + g + j + h + k + m + n)$ by virtue of sharing same base, namely $e'e''$, and lying between same parallels, namely $e'e''$ and the vertical axis.]
Change in welfare,

$$\Delta W = \Delta CS + \Delta PS + \text{change in revenue (loss) caused by subsidy}$$
$$= (h + k + c) + (g + j + y) - c - (y + g + j + h + k + m + n)$$
$$= -(m + n).$$

Alternatively, $\Delta PS = b + w + c + d - c - d$ (Why?) $= + (b + w)$ and amount of subsidy $= (b + w + m + c + h + k + n)$. With $\Delta CS = + (h + k + c)$

Change in welfare, $\Delta W = \Delta CS + \Delta PS +$ change in revenue (loss) caused by subsidy.
$$= (h + k + c) + (b + w) - (b + w + m + c + h + k + n).$$
$$= -(m + n)$$

Thus, grant of subsidy amounts to a deadweight loss of social welfare.

Thus, State intervention in the free play of price mechanism leads to a loss of social welfare except in case of direct government intervention through the ceiling and floor prices duly backed up by the public distribution system (PDS).

Specific Examples of Government Regulations

We are in a position now to discuss some interesting cases of government regulations.

(1) Rent Control and its Implications: Rent control refers to fixation of *rent ceiling* by government. It is, therefore, a special case of price ceiling. With a view to keep rentals below the level of the free market rates, governments in many countries have enacted rent control legislation. Before we proceed any further, let us outline some implications of such legislation:

(a) There will be a shortage of rental accommodations. Quantity demanded at the controlled rent will exceed that supplied by $Q_2 - Q_1$ (Figure 2.41).

(b) Quantity of accommodation (Q_1) available under rent ceiling will be less than that (Q_0) available under the free market, i.e. $Q_1 < Q_0$ (Figure 2.41).

(c) A **black market** is likely to develop as owners of the dwellings require a lump-sum entry-fee (called *pagarhi* in India) from new tenants in lieu of the difference of the demand price P_2 over the controlled price P_1. The practice manifests itself in illicit eviction of old tenants so as to earn such entry fees from the new ones. Owners even force the tenants to enter into informal arrangements with them to secretly pay the difference, $(P_2 - P_1)$, in cash separately on monthly basis to avoid eviction. The practice is quite common in India. Landlords charge the market rate of rent from the tenants, but issue the receipt of the value of the controlled rent, P_1. As another variation, even the old tenants at times sublet a part or whole of the premise to others at the market rate of rent and pay only the controlled rate of rent to their landlords.

(d) Governments in many countries have enacted legislation for the security of the tenure of old tenants so that landlords may not force eviction on them through illegal harassment. Such legislation protects the existing tenants against illegal eviction and ensures them priority over the new tenants.

(e) Effective rent control, ultimately, leads to a shortage of housing, as the rental incomes of the landlords at controlled rates prove unattractive.

Let us now analyze effects of rent control in short- and long-run.

Rent control in short- and long-run

"Rent control causes housing shortages that worsen as the time passes"[*]

The statement implies that rent ceiling leads to curtailment of supply of housing in short-run and worsens it further in the long-run. Figure 2.43 explains the point. The short-run supply curve of

---

[*] R.G. Lipsey and K.A. Chrystal, *An Introduction to Positive Economics*, 8th ed., 1995, p. 115.

accommodation is inelastic (steeper, SS) while that of the long-run is elastic (flatter, LS). Both intersect the demand curve for housing at point E_0, where rent is r_0 and quantity of housing demanded and supplied, Q_0. Now suppose government fixes rent at r_C with the result that the quantity supplied falls from Q_0 to Q_1 while that demanded rises from Q_0 to Q_2. The magnitude of the excess demand so caused is $(Q_2 - Q_1)$. In the long-run, this, as explained in the figure, increases to $Q_2 - Q'_1$ in the event of government failure to supplement the supply of housing. *Thus, housing shortages worsen in the long-run due to the rent control policies of government.*

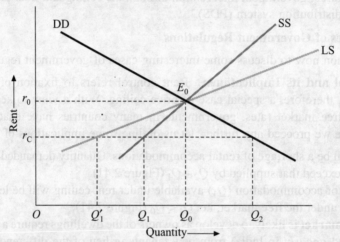

FIGURE 2.43 Short-run supply curve (SS) is inelastic. It intersects the demand curve DD at E_0 where demand for housing is equal to its supply (Q_0 each). The market clearing rent is r_0. Now suppose rent is controlled at r_C by government. In short-run, supply of housing drops to Q_1 while its demand rises to Q_2 with the result that an excess demand worth $(Q_2 - Q_1)$ emerges. If government fails to supplement the existing supply of Q_1 to the level of demand Q_2, an upward pressure on rent would develop, which if suppressed by government as a part of its rent control policy, would serve as a restraint on the suppliers of housing to further restrict the supply to Q'_1 in the long-run. Thus, rent control worsens the housing shortages in the long-run.

(2) Trade Protection versus Free Trade: A number of countries resort to protectionist policies to safeguard interests of the domestic industries against foreign competition. This is generally true in respect of the underdeveloped but developing countries. The world prices are usually lower than the domestic prices in these countries due to the smaller scale of operation of their industries. If trade is free (laissez faire), domestic consumers would resort to import of commodities from the rest of the world as the same proves cheaper to them. In consequence, domestic price would fall to the world level causing loss to the domestic industry. As a safeguard against this, governments of such countries resort to banning such imports or to levying tariff on them or even to fixing import quotas so that the domestic industry may be protected against foreign competition. Figure 2.44 explains how a ban on import works, Figure 2.45 explains how tariffs and quotas work as measures of partial protection and Figure 2.46 explains how tariff amounts to the effect of a ban on imports as a measure of full protection. The same figure shows the effects of a full protection of domestic industries through tariff on social welfare.

The discussions above would lead anybody to believe that underdeveloped but developing countries should never resort to trade protection. In fact, that is what the developed world always advises the underdeveloped world. But a little thought would reveal that free import proves fatal to the underdeveloped countries. It leads their domestic industries to their premature death. Most of them feel the compulsion to set a high price due to high costs of their small-scale operations. If forced to sell at P_W, which is what they would have to in the event of free trade (liberalization), substantial losses might force them to close down before reaching the level of production at which they may reap the same economies of large-scale production as the developed world does. If the domestic industries die a premature death, the country would have to rely solely on imports, to buy which, it would have no income. After all, income arises from production of goods and services only.

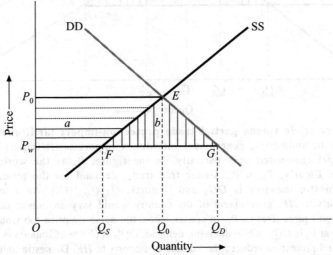

FIGURE 2.44 Free trade versus full trade protection: import ban—Let the economy be closed to foreign trade. Domestic demand DD would intersect domestic supply SS at E. Consumers would buy OQ_0 of the product at a price OP_0. Now, let it be opened to free trade. World price of the product is OP_W ($OP_W < OP_0$). Under free trade, at price OP_W, consumers would buy OQ_D, of which, OQ_S would be supplied by the domestic industry and the rest, 'FG', by the rest of the world. As a result, the domestic industry would suffer a loss of the producers surplus equal to the area of the trapezium $P_0 P_W F E$, marked in the figure as a. As regards, consumers, they would gain a surplus equal to the area of the trapezium $P_0 P_W G E$, which is equal to the sum of areas of trapezium $P_0 P_W F E$ (marked as 'a') and triangle EFG (marked as b). The net **gain in the social welfare,** therefore, is equal to the area of the triangle $EFG(b)$.

The loss of the producers surplus would discourage the domestic industry, which might decide to shutdown if failure to recover production costs persists. To prevent the premature closure of the domestic industry, a protectionist State may impose a ban on the import of the product in question and/or levy enough tariff on its import so that the import price rises at least to the level of the domestic price, OP_0. In either case, domestic price and domestic sales are both restored and so is the producers surplus. Whatever gain of surplus accrued to the consumers from import of the product, it would get automatically eliminated as soon as imports are eliminated. The net effect on social welfare is a loss of the region b, a **deadweight loss.** To see this, determine changes in consumers and producers surpluses caused by protectionist policies of State.

$$\Delta CS = - \text{area of trapezium } P_0 P_W GE \, (a + b), \text{ and}$$
$$\Delta PS = + \text{area of the trapezium } P_0 P_W FE \, (a).$$

The producers gain a but the consumers lose $a + b$. The net effect is loss of social welfare by the area of the triangle EFG (b). *In summary, free trade raises social welfare by the area of the triangle EFG while trade protection lowers it by the same.*

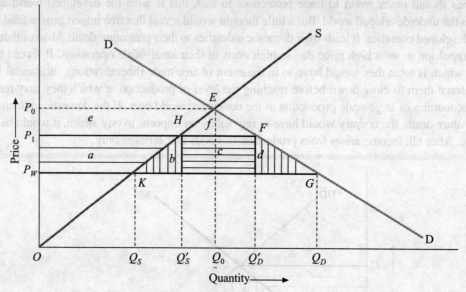

FIGURE 2.45 Free trade versus partial trade protection-import tariff/quotas: Under partial protection of domestic industries, government introduces import tariff/import quotas in such a way that imports get eliminated only partially. In the figure, P_W is the world price, while P_0, the domestic price. Clearly, $P_W < P_0$. Under free trade, demand for the product at P_W is OQ_D, supply by the domestic industry is OQ_S and imports, $Q_S Q_D$ (GK). As a measure of partial elimination of imports to HF, government of the country would levy an import tariff by the amount $(P_1 - P_W)$ so that import price rises to P_1. In consequence, the domestic price too would have to move to P_1. Domestic supply at P_1 is OQ'_S, while domestic demand, OQ'_D. Volume of imports is $Q'_S Q'_D$ (HF). Tariff as a measure of partial protection reduces the volume of imports to HF. Domestic industry gains sales by $Q_S Q'_S$ and a rise in price by $(P_1 - P_W)$. At the same time, government realizes a revenue equal to the area of the rectangle c. To see the net effect on social welfare, let us consider the following changes the levy has caused.

Change in consumers surplus, $\Delta CS = -(a + b + c + d)$, a decrease.

Change in producers surplus, $\Delta PS = + a$, an increase.

Change in government revenue, $\Delta R = + c$, an increase

$$\text{Change in social welfare} = \Delta CS + \Delta PS + \Delta R$$
$$= -(a + b + c + d) + a + c$$
$$= -(b + d), \text{ a decrease.}$$

This is **deadweight loss.**

Instead of import tariff, if an import quota be introduced to reduce imports to HF, the only difference it causes is in the government revenue which remains unchanged with the result that the deadweight loss caused is $-(b + d + c)$ instead of $-(b + d)$.

In absence of the partial protection, change in social welfare under free trade would have been $= a + b + c + d + e + f - a - e = +(b + c + d + f)$ which is a gain in social welfare.

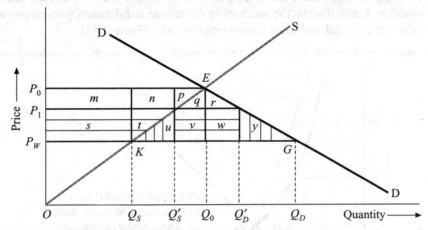

FIGURE 2.46 Free trade versus full trade protection: Effect of tariff as a measure of full protection of domestic industry is the same as the effect of a ban on imports. To see, suppose an economy is on free trade consuming a quantity OQ_D at a price P_W. Of this, it procures OQ_S from domestic industry and the rest, Q_SQ_D (KG), from the rest of the world. Domestic industry suffers a loss of $(P_0 - P_W)$ on each unit sold, apart from the loss of sales by Q_SQ_0. As a measure of its protection, the State may choose between import tariff and import ban. If it chooses tariff, it has to levy enough of it on each unit of import so that import price P_W rises to domestic price P_0. If it chooses import ban, as in Figure 2.44, it simply seals the border to restrict entry of products from the rest of the world. As a result, imports get eliminated and the economy consumes OQ_0 at P_0.

To examine the effects on social welfare, consider the following changes in CS and PS caused.

$$\Delta CS = -(m + n + p + q + r + s + t + u + v + w + y)$$
$$\Delta PS = +(s + t + m + n + p)$$
$$\Delta R = 0, \text{ as imports are zero.}$$

Change in social welfare,

$$\Delta W = \Delta CS + \Delta PS + \Delta R$$
$$= -(m + n + p + q + r + s + t + u + v + w + y) + (s + t + m + n + p) + 0$$
$$= -(q + r + u + v + w + y)$$
$$= -\text{Area } \Delta EKG.$$

The sign being negative, it is a deadweight loss. Thus, full protection through tariff leads to a deadweight loss equal in magnitude to the area of triangle EKG. Note that the same is the measure of the deadweight loss under import ban (Figure 2.44). Full protection through tariff, therefore, has the same effect as the import ban in every respect.

(3) Government Stabilization of Producers' Income under Fluctuating Outputs

In Figure 2.39, we saw how producers' income can be stabilized despite fluctuating outputs through a demand curve resembling a rectangular hyperbola. There we assumed no regulatory intervention in the free play of price mechanism. The situation becomes quite favourable when State itself attempts to stabilize cultivators' income. This, as stated earlier, a welfare-oriented State usually does to protect the interests not only of cultivators but of all the producers of the essential goods. In some cases, the State resorts to the grant of subsidy, while in others, it resorts to direct buying of essential goods from their producers at prices remunerative enough to sustain producers' interest in production of such goods. For instance, KHADI products are subsidized by government while foodgrains are procured by it from the cultivators at the minimum support price assured to them much before the sowing time of the crops. We have already discussed the effects of subsidies. Let us discuss the mechanism of income stabilization, particularly in respect of the producers of essential and mass consumption goods (Figure 2.47).

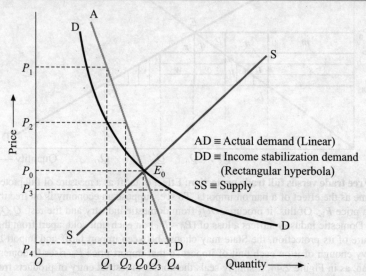

FIGURE 2.47 Let AD represent the actual demand curve for corn faced by cultivators. Further let SS be the supply curve of corn. SS intersects AD at the point E_0, where quantity of corn transacted is Q_0 at a price of P_0, yielding an income $P_0 \times Q_0$ for the cultivators. Let the income stabilizing demand curve, DD, a rectangular hyperbola, pass through E_0. The point E_0, thus, lies on all the three—DD, AD and SS. We have seen in Figure 2.39 that cultivators' income is stabilized at every point on DD and is numerically equal to the area of the rectangles subtended by each on the two axes. For example, the rectangle subtended by the point E_0 on the two axes is $E_0 Q_0 O P_0$ and its area is $OQ_0 \times OP_0$ or simply, $P_0 \times Q_0$. Now, suppose that the farm output fluctuates between Q_1 and Q_4. When output is Q_4, price would be as low as P_4 and cultivators income as low as $P_4 \times Q_4$ in the free market. Given the output Q_4, the income-stabilizing-price must correspond to DD and be P_3. Government, therefore, must ensure this price to the cultivators. This would necessitate procurement of $(Q_4 - Q_3)$ quantity to by government at P_3, since actual demand at this price is only Q_3. Thus, the part of Q_4 bought by the free market is Q_3, and the rest, bought by government, is $(Q_4 - Q_3)$. Cultivators earn an income $P_3 \times Q_4 = P_0 \times Q_0$ (all the rectangles subtended by the points of DD on the two axes have the same area). **Hence, when output exceeds the market demand, government must ensure a price higher than the market price so that it corresponds to the rectangular hyperbola; and, as a follow-up, must purchase the unsold supply to stabilize cultivators income.** When output is Q_1, the actual price is P_1 and income, $P_1 \times Q_1$, which is higher than the income required under the income stabilization. The government, therefore, must ensure a price P_2, lower than P_1, so that it corresponds to the rectangular hyperbola; and as a follow-up, must supply $(Q_2 - Q_1)$ at P_2 from their own sources (may be, from the stocks raised by them when farm-output exceeded market demand) to stabilize the cultivators' income. Thus, when output is Q_1, the market demand is Q_2 of which Q_1 is supplied by the cultivators and the rest, $(Q_2 - Q_1)$, by government. Producers income is stabilized at

$$P_2 \times Q_1 = P_0 \cdot Q_0 = Q_4 \cdot P_3.$$

Note that the actual demand at price P_2 is Q_2 and not Q_1. Government, therefore, must supplement the supply from their buffer stocks by an amount equal to $(Q_2 - Q_1)$. Thus, when output fluctuates and the government intends to stabilize the producers' income, they must let the prices corresponding to these outputs vary along the rectangular hyperbola and must buy or sell an amount equal to the horizontal distance between the actual demand and the hyperbolic demand.

KEY TERMS AND CONCEPTS

Cobweb theorem It is a form of dynamic equilibrium in which supply of a product in the current period depends on its price in the previous period. Equilibrium is stable when the cobweb is convergent, unstable when it is divergent and in neutral when it is a rectangular periphery.

Consumers' surplus Defined as excess expenditure consumers are willing to incur on a product rather than remain without it. Graphically, it is the area under the market demand curve that lies above the market price.

Deadweight loss Loss of consumers' and producers' surpluses that leaves no trace. It affects social welfare adversely. Its magnitude is equal to the sum of changes in consumers' surplus, producers' surplus and government revenue, if any, arising as a consequence of its direct/indirect intervention in the free play of price mechanism.

Demand It is desire for a product supported by purchasing power and willingness to purchase.

   Contraction of demand Movement along the demand curve from one point on it to its left in response to a rise in price, other things remaining unchanged.

   Decrease in demand A downward to left shift in demand curve in response to an unfavourable change in any of the other determinants assumed constant.

   Demand curve Locus of different combinations of quantities demanded and the corresponding prices.

   Reasons for downward slope of the demand curve Demand curve slopes downwards from left to right due to the law of diminishing marginal utility of the commodity and also due to the price effect which operates through its components of the income and the substitution effects.

   Demand equation The algebraic relationship between quantity demanded and the price of a product.

   Demand schedule Quantities of a product demanded over a given range of prices.

   Determinants of demand The factors such as the price of the product, income of the consumers, prices of the related goods, tastes, preferences and fashions that influence demand.

   Expansion of demand Movement along the demand curve from one point on it to another from left to right in response to a fall in price, other things remaining unchanged.

   Increase in demand An upward to right shift in demand curve in response to a favourable change in any of the other determinants assumed constant.

   Law of demand Other things remaining unchanged, more of a product is demanded at a lower price and less at a higher price.

   Market demand The horizontal summation of the individual demands to obtain the total demand of the market.

Income effect component of the price effect A fall in price leads to a rise in real income and a rise in it to a fall in the real income.

Income stabilization It refers to ensuring stable income to the producers of goods whose production fluctuates from time to time. Income stabilization can't be achieved without permitting variability in prices to the producers in a manner that the demand curve faced by the producers gets transformed into a rectangular hyperbola.

Market equilibrium A state of balance between the market forces of demand and supply.

Partial and general equilibria Partial equilibrium refers to the equilibrium of a part of the whole system. For example, equilibrium of a single product while prices of all the other products are assumed to remain unchanged during the period of such analysis. It is based on restricted data. The role of *ceteris paribus* (other things remaining the same) is crucial for the partial equilibrium analysis. General equilibrium, on the other hand, refers to the equilibrium of entire economy. It involves interdependence of all the market segments. For example, equilibrium of the product market along with that of the factor market and the money market is general equilibrium.

Per cent tax Also known as percentage tax, it is a commodity tax levied as a percentage of the price of the commodity. It causes non-parallel shifts in demand and supply curves. The demand curve undergoes a non-parallel and downward-to-left shift when seller's price is portrayed on the vertical axis while the supply curve undergoes a non-parallel and upward-to-left shift when buyer's price is portrayed on the vertical axis.

Price ceiling It refers to the controlled price. It is always below the market price so that necessities may be made available to the common people at an affordable price. To support the scheme, the state undertakes to supply the products at the controlled price through its fair price shops.

Price effect Effect of a change in price on the quantity demanded other things remaining unchanged. A price effect has two components—the income effect and the substitution effect.

Price floor It refers to the minimum support price. It is above the market price so that the producers of the essential goods may not suffer losses. To support the scheme, government itself purchases the excess supply at the price floor and stock it. It is from these stocks that it supplies goods at ceiling price through the fair price shops later during the scarcity of these goods.

Price ceiling and price floor are the two essential components of the Public Distribution System (PDS).

Producers' surplus Defined as excess receipt of producers from the sale over the supply prices. Graphically, it is the area above the market supply curve that lies below the market price.

Rent control It is a variant of price ceiling. It refers to the rentals fixed by government below the market rent. Rent controls in the long-run worsen the housing shortages if government fails to provide cheap accommodations to supplement the market supply of housing.

Shift factors All the determinants of demand other than price that are assumed to remain constant in the study of price-quantity relationship are called shift factors. If a change in any of the shift factors takes place, the demand curve undergoes a parallel shift.

Short- and long-run equilibria Equilibrium in short-run differs from that in long-run due to the elasticity of the supply curve which is low in short-run and high in long-run. Equilibrium price of a given quantity is higher in short-run than that in long-run. Alternately, quantity sold at a given price is lower in short-run than that in long-run.

Stable, unstable and neutral equilibria Stable equilibrium refers to that equilibrium in which small disturbances in the market price are rendered short lived by the adjustment process of price mechanism with the result that original equilibrium price is restored. As against this, unstable equilibrium refers to that equilibrium in which small disturbances in the market price get magnified to larger and larger disturbances by the adjustment process of price mechanism so that the market price deviates farther and farther away from the initial equilibrium. A neutral equilibrium is that equilibrium in which the disturbance in the market price gets perpetuated due to the neutrality of the adjustment process of price mechanism.

Static and dynamic equilibria Static equilibrium is related to the equilibrium of a static economy in which there are no changes or limited changes in prices, outputs, technology, incomes and consumers' tastes and preferences. It is based on the assumption that a state of bliss (equilibrium) once reached is relished by individuals, firms, industries, etc. so much so that they are reluctant to leave it. A ball rolling at a constant speed provides an example. Dynamic equilibrium refers to the equilibrium in which nothing is assumed to remain unchanged, whether it is price, output, incomes, or tastes or technology. Participating individuals, firms and industries which are in equilibrium, face persistent threat to their equilibrium position from those in a state of disequilibrium.

Substitution effect component of a price effect When price of a product rises, other things remaining unchanged, the demand for its substitutes rises even when their prices remain unchanged.

Supply Quantity of a product offered for sale at a price offered by the market at a certain point of time. It is only that part of the stock of goods produced which is offered for sale at a given price at a given point of time.

   Contraction in supply Movement along the supply curve from one point on it to another from right to left in response to a fall in price.

   Decrease in supply An upward to left shift in the supply curve in response to a change in any of the shift factors.

   Expansion of supply Movement along the supply curve from one point on it to another from left to right in response to a rise in price.

   Increase in supply A downward to right shift in supply curve in response to a change in any of the shift factors.

   Law of supply Other things remaining same, more is supplied at a higher price and less at a lower price.

   Determinants of supply: The following are the determinants of supply:
   1. Price of the product
   2. Prices of related goods
   3. Cost of production
   4. Change in technology
   5. Goal of production
   6. Natural resources
   7. Availability of time
   8. Economic environment
   9. Strength of the infrastructure.

   Market supply curve A horizontal summation of the supplies of the individual firms to get the total supply of the product in the market.

Unique and multiple equilibria When demand and supply curves cut each other at a single point, the equilibrium is said to be a unique equilibrium. In the opposite case, if the two intersect each other at more than one point, equilibrium is said to be a multiple equilibrium.

Unit tax Also known as unit excise or excise duty or specific unit tax, the unit tax is an indirect tax levied by government per unit of output produced. It is an indirect way of regulating production and consumption of certain goods. The tax causes a parallel and downward-to-left shift in the supply curve when buyer's price is portrayed on the vertical axis and a parallel and downward-to-left shift in the demand curve when seller's price is portrayed on the vertical axis.

Utility Property of a product, by virtue of which, it is capable of satisfying human needs. Utility is subjective. A book on economics has utility only for a student of economics. It may have no utility for a student of Biology. One man's mutton is another's poison.

   Marginal utility Change in total utility caused by consumption of an additional unit of a commodity.

   Law of diminishing marginal utility When a commodity is consumed unit by unit successively in a continuity, the marginal utilities derived from the additional units follow a declining trend. This is called the law of diminishing marginal utility.

   Total utility It is the sum of the utilities of all the goods in the consumer's basket. $TU = U_1 + U_2 + U_3 + \cdots + U_n$; given that the number of goods in the basket is n. The property is referred to as the additivity of utility. It was dropped in the later versions of the theory of the cardinal utility on the grounds that it implies independent utilities of various commodities in the basket*. Hicksian ordinal utility version stated total utility as a function of the quantities of various goods in the basket,

$$TU = f(X_1, X_2, X_3, \ldots, X_n)$$

---

*See J.R. Hicks and R.J. Allen, 'A Reconsideration of Theory of Value', *Economica* (1934). See also Hicks, *Value and Capital* (Oxford University Press, 1939).

Total utility of all the units of a single commodity is the sum total of the marginal utilities of the successive units of it consumed. Thus,

$$\text{Total Utility} = MU_1 + MU_2 + MU_3 + \cdots + MU_n$$

EXERCISES

A. Short Answer Questions

Define the following (1 through 30):

1. Utility
2. Concept of total utility
3. Law of diminishing marginal utility
4. Demand
5. Supply
6. Law of demand
7. Law of supply
8. Equilibrium
9. Market equilibrium
10. Cobweb theorem
11. Price floor
12. Ceiling price
13. Income stabilization
14. Consumers' surplus
15. Producers' surplus
16. Deadweight loss
17. Demand schedule
18. Demand equation
19. Assumptions of the law of supply
20. Determinants of demand
21. Determinants of supply
22. Factors that lead to a shift in the supply curve
23. Factors that lead to a shift in the demand curve
24. Implications of rent control
25. Factors that lead to a change in equilibrium
26. Assumptions of the law of demand
27. Condition of the market equilibrium
28. Bandwagon effect
29. Veblen effect
30. Snob effect

Distinguish between (31 through 38):

31. Stock and supply
32. Partial and general equilibria
33. Stable, unstable and neutral equilibria

34. Unique and multiple equilibria
35. Short-run and long-run equilibria
36. Static and dynamic equilibria
37. Marshallian and Walrasian equilibria
38. Unit tax and percent tax

B. Long Answer Questions

39. Distinguish between expansion of and increase in demand.
40. Distinguish between contraction of and decrease in demand.
41. What is the effect of a cost saving technical progress on the supply curve? Explain with the help of a sketch.
42. What is the effect of the levy of a unit excise on the supply curve of a product? Explain with the help of a sketch?
43. How would an increase in the price of wheat affect the supply curve of rice? Assume that the price of rice remains unchanged and that the farmer produces only wheat and rice.
44. If the number of firms in an industry increases from 100 to 150, what effect would it have on the market supply curve? Explain with the help of a sketch.
45. Given the demand and supply equations as $Q^D = 150{,}000 - 3P$ and $Q^S = 7P$, respectively, sketch the curves and hence or otherwise, calculate:
    (a) Consumers' surplus (CS).
    (b) Producers' surplus (PS).
    (c) Deadweight loss when unit tax of ₹ 5000 per unit is levied.
    How would your answers change if it is a unit subsidy of 5000 instead of a unit tax?
    [**Ans.** Consumers' surplus = ₹ 1,837,500,000; Producers' surplus = ₹ 787,500,000; Deadweight loss = 26,250,000. Refer to Figure 2.48(a).

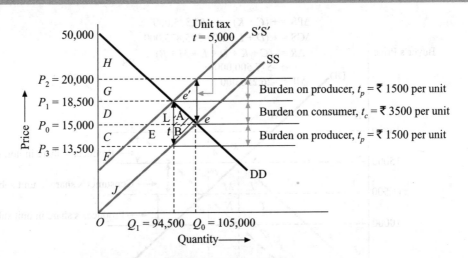

FIGURE 2.48(a) Effect of unit tax.

Solving the equations for price and quantity, we have $P = 15{,}000$ and $Q = 105{,}000$ units.

$$PS = C + E + B + F + J$$
$$= \frac{1}{2} \times 105{,}000 \times 15{,}000$$
$$= 787{,}500{,}000$$
$$CS = H + G + D + L + A$$
$$= \frac{1}{2} \times 105{,}000 \times 35{,}000$$
$$= 1{,}837{,}500{,}000.$$
$$\text{Change in CS} = -(D + L + A)$$
$$= -\frac{1}{2} \times (18500 - 15000) \times (105{,}000 + 94{,}500)$$
$$= -349{,}125{,}000.$$
$$\text{Change in PS} = (F + C + D) - (C + E + B + F + J)$$
$$= \frac{1}{2} \times (18500 - 5000) \times 94500 - 787{,}500{,}000$$
$$= -149{,}625{,}000$$
$$\text{Revenue raised} = D + L + C + E$$
$$= 5000 \times 94500$$
$$= 472{,}500{,}000$$
$$\text{Deadweight loss} = -349{,}125{,}000 - 149{,}625{,}000 + 472{,}500{,}000$$
$$= -26{,}250{,}000.$$

If it is a unit subsidy (Subsidy) of 5000 instead of unit tax, $\Delta CS = +385{,}875{,}000$; $\Delta PS = +165{,}375{,}000$; $\Delta R = -577{,}500{,}000$; $\Delta W = -26{,}250{,}000$ [See Figure 2.48(b)].

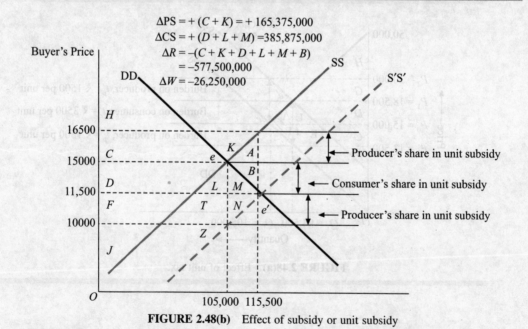

FIGURE 2.48(b) Effect of subsidy or unit subsidy

C. Essay Type Questions

46. In Figure 2.49, demand curve faced by the producers is given as

$$Q^D = 125 - 0.25P$$

For income stabilization, demand for the product must be a rectangular hyperbola such as one given by

$$Q^D = 1000/P$$

The output is known to fluctuate between 50 and 125 units. At present, it is 100 units and is being sold at a price of 100 per unit. Now, suppose government decides to stabilize price at 100 per unit.

(a) What policy mix would you recommend for the purpose?
(b) Does price stabilization lead to income stabilization as well?
(c) What policy mix would you recommed if the government were to stabilize income instead of stabilizing price?

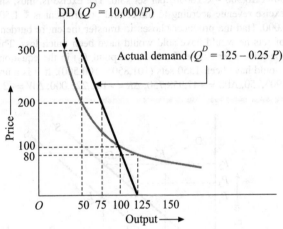

FIGURE 2.49 Policies of price and income stabilization by government when output varies between 50 and 125 (Q. 46).

[Ans. (a) When output is 50, price would rise to 300. To stabilize it at 100, government must supplement output by 50 units so that demand of 100 units at a price of 100 is satisfied. When output is 125 units, price would fall to 80. To restore it at 100, quantity transacted should be 100. Government must buy the surplus quantity for its stocks.

(b) The income at the output of 100 is 10,000. When output is 50 and price is stabilized at 100, income falls to 5,000 and when output is 125 and price 100, income rises to 12,500. Hence, price stabilization does not stabilize producers' income.

(c) To stabilize producers' income, government must ensure prices to vary along a rectangular hyperbola. When output is 50, government should fix the price at 200 and should supplement the supply by 25 units from their own stocks and when the output is 125, government should fix the price at 80 per unit and purchase 20 units for their own stocks. This would keep producers on the rectangular hyperbola.]

47. Demand for and supply of a popular brand of TV (Refer back to the illustration 1.1, Chapter 1) have been estimated to follow linear trends $Q^D = 150,000 - 3P$ and $Q^S = 7P$, respectively. The market price is ₹ 15,000 per TV and the number of the sets supplied and sold at this price is 105,000. Now suppose the

central excise department introduces an excise of ₹ 1500 on each set. How would this affect the sales and the market price of TVs? Would the producer succeed in shifting the entire burden of excise on the consumers? What revenue would the levy of excise raise for the central government?
How would your answers change if it is a unit subsidy of 1500 instead of a unit tax?

[**Ans.** The demand and the supply curves intersect at point E_1 (Figure 2.50) which is the point of equilibrium. At this point,

$$Q^D = Q^S = 105{,}000$$

and price, $P = 15{,}000$

Excise, $t = 1500$

Price with excise = ₹ $(15{,}000 + 1{,}500) = 16{,}500$

This would shift the supply curve above to the left by a vertical distance equivalent to the change in price, as shown in the figure. It is clear from the discussion that the burden of excise is being shared between the producers and the consumers. Consumers bear ₹ 1050 (16050 – 15000) of it while the producer bears the rest, ₹ 450 (₹ 16,500 – ₹ 16050) per set sold. The excise is, thus, shared between them in the ratio of 7:3. The excise revenue accruing to the central government is ₹ 1,500 × 101,850, which works out at ₹ 152,775,000. Had the producer chosen to transfer the entire burden of excise onto the consumers, the number of sets he would have sold would have been much less. This can be easily worked out by substituting the price after excise, ₹ 16,500 (at point E_2') in the equation of demand. The loss of sales, in that case, would have been 1350 sets (101,850 – 100,500). If it is a unit subsidy instead of a unit tax, $\Delta CS = +111{,}903{,}750$; $\Delta PS = +47{,}958{,}750$; $\Delta R = -162{,}225{,}000$; $\Delta W = -2{,}362{,}500$ (See Figure 2.48 (b))].

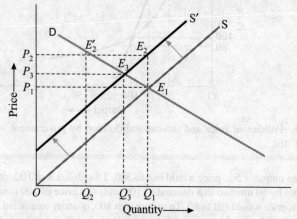

FIGURE 2.50 Effect of unit tax. Levy of excise shifts the supply curve upwards to left by the magnitude of the excise. $OQ_1 = 105{,}000$; $OP_1 = 15{,}000$, $OP_2 = 16{,}500$ and $OP_3 = 16{,}050$ (the new market price). While new market demand is $OQ_3 = 101{,}850$, the new equilibrium takes place at E_3, where market price is ₹ 16,050 per set. The new equilibrium takes place at the intersection of the demand curve $Q^D = 150{,}000 - 3P$ and the new supply curve $Q^S = 7P - 10{,}500$. The initial supply curve passes through the origin and its equation can be written as $P = (1/7) Q^S$. The new supply curve, parallel to the initial one, has an intercept on the vertical axis equal in magnitude to the money value of the excise duty. Following the form $y = mx + c$, it is, thus, $P = (1/7) Q^S + 1{,}500$, which reduces to $Q^S = 7P - 10{,}500$ on clearing the fraction. The number of the sets demanded at the new equilibrium is 101,850, as obtained by solving the equations of demand and the new equation of supply.]

48. Examine Figure 2.51 in which the short- and the long-run supply curves are given by

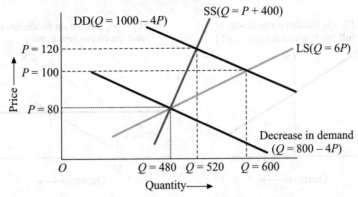

FIGURE 2.51 Effect of a decrease in demand on income and prices in short- and long-runs.

$$Q^S = P + 400 \text{ (short-run)}$$
$$\text{and, } Q^S = 6P \text{ (long-run)}$$

respectively while demand curve faced by the producers is:

$$Q^D = 1{,}000 - 4P$$

Now suppose a decrease in demand arises due to a sudden drift in consumers' tastes and preferences. The resulting demand curve is:

$$Q^D = 800 - 4P$$

Can we deduce from these observations that when demand decreases, receipts from sale as well as prices both decrease whether supply is elastic (flatter) or inelastic (steeper), but the price falls more sharply when supply is inelastic (steeper) than when it is elastic (flatter). Calculate the changes in income and prices to support your answer.

[**Ans. Yes** In short-run price falls from 120 to 80 per unit (33.33%) while it falls from 100 to 80 per unit (20%) in the long-run. Income in short-run falls from 62,400 to 38,400 (38.5%) while it falls from 60,000 to 38,400 (36%) in the long-run.]

49. Go through the following sketches carefully and examine the statement that the burden of excise tax varies directly with the price elasticity of supply and inversely with the price elasticity of demand on consumers while it varies in exactly opposite manner with the respective elasticities on the producers.

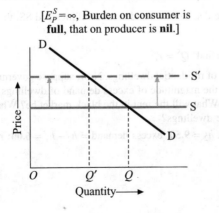

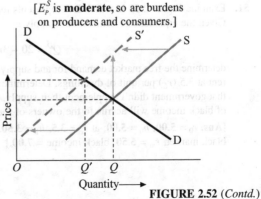

FIGURE 2.52 (*Contd.*)

FIGURE 2.52 (*Contd.*)

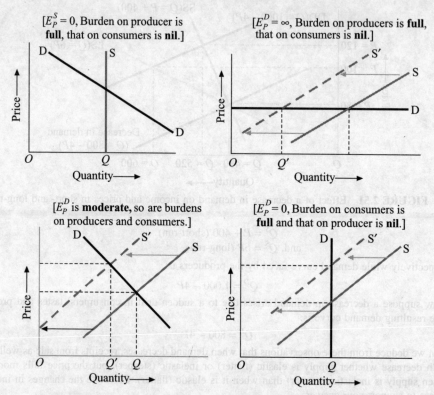

FIGURE 2.52 Levy of excise shifts the supply curve upwards to left.

50. Question 49 can also be split into two parts:
    (a) Show that the burden of unit tax on consumers varies directly with price elasticity of supply and inversely with price elasticity of demand.
    (b) Show that the burden of unit tax on producers varies inversely with the price elasticity of supply and directly with price elasticity of demand.

51. Examine Figure 2.53 in which DD represents the demand for residential dwellings and SS, their supply. Given the equations of demand and supply as

$$Q^D = 20 - 3r \quad \text{and} \quad Q^S = r,$$

determine the free market demand for and supply of residential dwellings. Now, suppose government fixes rent at 3.5 (r_C) per unit of dwellings. Determine the magnitude of excess demand of dwellings assuming that government didn't supplement their supply. What will the rent in the black market be? What amount of black income will accrue to the owners of the dwellings?

[**Ans.** $r_0 = 5.00$, $h_0 = 5.00$; at $r_c = 3.5$, $h_1 = 3.50$, $h_2 = 9.50$, excess demand $= h_2 - h_1 = 6.00$; rent in the black market, $r_m = 5.50$, black income $= 7.00$.]

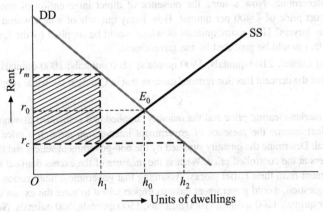

FIGURE 2.53 Rent control and emergence of black market.

52. How would your answer to Question 51 change if the supply equation of dwellings changes to $Q^S = 3r - 10$. Assuming that the supply curve is flatter in the long-run and steeper in the short-run, would you conclude that the rent control introduced by government would worsen the shortage of dwellings in the long-run?
    [**Ans.** $r_0 = 5.00$, $h_0 = 5.00$; $r_c = 3.5$, $h_2 = 9.50$, $h_1 = 0.50$; excess demand = 9.00, $r_m = 18.50$. Dwelling shortage changes to **9.00** units; **Yes**, becoming worse than before by **3.00** units.]

53. How is rent control executed? What are its possible implications?

54. What is a ceiling price? Why is it resorted to? Is it true to say that "a price control if not supported by appropriate policy of public distribution, would lead to the emergence of a black market as well as to a loss of social welfare?" Explain.
    [**Hint.** Refer to Figure 2.41]

55. What is a price floor? Why is it resorted to by the government? It is argued that 'it would be better and more efficient for the government to grant the difference of the minimum support price over the existing market price to the cultivators in cash rather than purchase the corn from them at the minimum support price to help them'. Do you agree with the argument? Explain with the help of a diagram.
    [**Hint.** Refer to Figure 2.40]

56. What are the essential components of the Public Distribution System (PDS)? How does it work?
    [**Hint.** Refer to Figures 2.40 and 2.41]

57. 'Income of the producers can be stabilized even when their outputs fluctuate widely provided that there is no regulatory intervention by government and that the demand curve faced by the producers is a rectangular hyperbola.' Discuss.
    [**Hint.** Refer to Figure 2.39]

58. 'Stabilizing quantity sold helps income stabilization but stabilizing price does not.' Explain giving reasons.
    [**Hint.** Refer to Figure 2.38]

59. 'Unplanned fluctuations in output lead to sharper fluctuations in price when the demand curve is inelastic (steeper) than when it is elastic (flatter).' Discuss.
    [**Hint.** Refer to Figure 2.36]

60. Quantity of wheat demanded in quintals in a local market is given by the equation
$$Q^D = 3,000 - 3P$$
    The equation of its supply is given as
$$Q^S = 7P$$

Determine the market-clearing price and the quantity demanded and sold at this price, assuming no government intervention. Now assume the presence of direct intervention of government through the minimum support price of ₹ 400 per quintal. How many quintals of wheat would be demanded by the non-government buyers? How many quintals of wheat would be supplied by the farmers? Determine the excess supply that would be procured by the government.

[**Ans.** ₹ 300 per quintal, 2100 quintals; 1800 quintals; 2800 quintals; 1000 quintals.]

Now suppose that the demand function remains same as that in Question 60, while supply function changes to

$$Q^S = 2P$$

61. Determine the market-clearing price and the quantity supplied and demanded assuming no intervention by government. Next assume the presence of government intervention through a price control at a price of ₹ 500 per quintal. Determine the quantity supplied by the non-government sellers and the quantity demanded by the consumers at the controlled price. What is the measure of the excess demand that would have to be met by government from their buffer stocks. Assuming that government intervention is limited only to the locality in the question, would government have to import wheat to meet the excess demand?

[**Ans.** ₹ 600 per quintal, 1200 quintals; 1000 quintals; 1500 quintals; 500 quintals. **No**, government would not have to import wheat because they have a buffer stock of 1000 quintals already procured by them.]

62. For demand and supply conditions of question 60, suppose govt. chose indirect intervention policy through the introduction of excise tax of ₹ 30 on each quintal of wheat produced. How would the market price and the equilibrium quantity change in consequence? In what proportion would the excise tax be shared between the farmer and the consumer? What revenue would it raise for the state?

[**Ans.** Equilibrium price and quantity before the introduction of unit excise tax are ₹ 300 per quintal of wheat and 2100 quintals of wheat. After the introduction of the tax, the respective values of price and quantity in equilibrium would be ₹ 321 per quintal and 2037 quintals. The burden of excise tax on the consumer is ₹ 21 per quintal and that on the farmer is ₹ 9 per quintal. The proportion of sharing the unit tax between the farmer and the consumer, therefore, is 9: 21 or 3: 7. Revenue generated for the state is ₹ 30 × 2037 = ₹ 61, 110.]

63. Demand and supply functions for a consumer product are as given below:

$$Q^D = 5000 - 6P, \text{ and}$$
$$Q^S = 4P$$

Determine the equilibrium price and quantity. Now suppose that the country is practicing free-trade policy with the rest of the world and that the world price of the consumer product is ₹ 300 per unit. How would the free-trade policy affect the social welfare and the domestic industry? Assume that the domestic industry is operating at a fixed cost of ₹ 400 per unit. Next, suppose that government decides to protect the domestic industry. How would the social welfare be affected when

(a) government resorts to complete elimination of the imports through import tariff?
(b) Partial elimination of imports through (i) tariff (ii) import quota, allowing the domestic industry to recover the costs only?

[**Ans.** Equilibrium price = ₹ 500 per unit, equilibrium quantity = 2000 units, free trade leads to a loss of producer's surplus of ₹ 320,000 and a gain in consumer's surplus of ₹ 520,000. Net gain in social welfare is 200,000 and the imports amount to 2000 units of the product. The domestic industry suffers a loss ₹ 100 per unit and may close down. (a) Domestic industry would regain its lost surpluses while consumer's would loose what they gained under free trade. The social welfare would fall by ₹ 200,000 (b) (i) Under partial elimination of imports through tariff as suggested, gain in producer's surplus is ₹ 140,000, loss in consumer's surplus is ₹ 290,000 and gain in government revenue from the levy of tariff is ₹ 100, 000 [100 × (2600 − 1600)]. Net effect on social welfare = +140,000 − 290,000 + 100,000 = −50,000 when compared to the situation of free trade. But when compared to the situation of full protection, which led to a loss of social welfare by ₹ 200,000; loss of social welfare can be seen to fall by ₹ 150,000 (Figure 2.45, Note that government receipts from tariff under full protection are nil because imports are nil). (b) (ii) If import quota be resorted to, instead of import tariff, government receipts from tariff would be zero and thus the net effect on social welfare now would be $-150,000$ ($140,000 - 290,000$) as compared to the situation of free trade.]

64. Supply and demand functions for a consumer product are as given below:
$$Q^D = 100,000 - 4P$$
and
$$Q^S = 6P$$
Determine the equilibrium price and quantity. Now suppose that government intervenes through a subsidy of ₹ 2000 per unit on the market price. How would it affect the consumer's and the producer's surpluses? What would it cost the government? How would your answer change, if instead of subsidy, government levies a unit tax at the same rate on the market price?
[**Hint.** Treat subsidy as a negative tax. Equilibrium price and quantity are ₹ 10000 and 60000 units respectively. Under subsidy, $\Delta CS = + ₹\ 74,880,000$; $\Delta PS = + 49,920,000$; cost of subsidy to government = ₹ 129,600,000; change in social welfare = **– ₹ 4,800,000** (deadweight loss). Under unit tax, $\Delta CS = - ₹\ 69,120,000$; $\Delta PS = -₹\ 46,080,000$; revenue to government, $\Delta R = 110,400,000$. Change in social welfare, $\Delta W = $ **–₹ 4,800,000**.]

65. Given the demand and the supply functions for labour hours as below:
$$L^S = 10W,$$
and
$$L^D = 600 - 10W$$
where, W is the wage rate per hour of labour and L^S and L^D are respectively the supply and demand of labour in millions of labour hours.

(a) Determine the free market wage rate and employment. Now suppose that the government fixes the minimum wage rate at ₹ 40 per labour hour (a wage floor). How would the employment of labour hours be effected?

(b) Suppose that instead of a minimum wage, government paid a subsidy of ₹ 10 per hour per employee to the employers. What would be the level of employment and the equilibrium wage rate now?

[**Ans.**

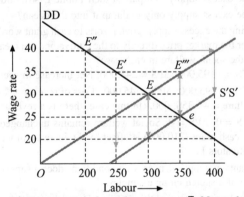

FIGURE 2.54 Equilibrium wage and employment are ₹ 30 per hour and 300 million hours respectively. At the minimum wage of ₹ 40, demand is 200 million working hours while supply is 400 million working hours. Hike in wage rate reduces employment by 100 (= 300 – 200) million working hours and creates an excess supply of 200 (= 400 – 200) million labour hours. When wage subsidy of ₹ 10 per hour is granted to the employers, employment increases to 350 million working hours as the supply curve shifts downwards. The new equilibrium wage is ₹ 25 per hour. To provide 350 million working hours, workers require a wage rate of ₹ 35 per hour. This shows that one labour hour costs the employers a wage of ₹ 25 per hour (net of subsidy). In other words, employers transfer the entire subsidy to the workers. [The reader can see the effect of wage subsidy. Equation of new supply curve is $L^S = 10W + 100$. A simultaneous solution of this and the demand curve is (350, 25).]

66. 'Import tariff and quotas do protect domestic industry for sure but affect the social welfare adversely.' Explain.
    [**Hint.** Refer to Figure 2.44.]
67. 'Price floor and price ceiling, if not supported by adequate measures by government, distorts market mechanism and adversely affects social welfare.' Discuss with explanatory diagrams.
    [**Hint.** Refer to Figures 2.40 and 2.41.]
68. 'Price ceiling, if matched by positive measures by government, helps not only in elimination of the black market but also in raising the social welfare.' Examine the authenticity of the statement giving reasons in support.
    [**Hint.** Refer to Figure 2.41.]
69. 'When demand decreases, sales decrease whatever the elasticity of supply but fall in price is sharper when supply is inelastic than when it is elastic.' Explain the statement with the help of the diagrams.
    [**Hint.** Refer to Figure 2.37.]
70. What are the implications of the rent controls? Show that rent control causes housing shortages that worsen in the long-run.
    [**Hint.** Refer to Figure 2.43.]
71. What is meant by income stabilization? How can government help stabilization of the cultivators income under wide fluctuations in corn production? Explain with the help of the diagrams.
    [**Hint.** Refer to Figure 2.47.]
72. 'Cropping pattern in India is governed by the last year's prices.' Examine the statement and support your comments with diagrams. Under what conditions can the agricultural production be stabilized? Explain with diagrams.
73. How would the consumers' and the producers' surpluses change after the introduction of the minimum support price in Question 60 when
    (a) govt. procures the excess supply as a part of their Public Distribution System (PDS)?
    (b) govt. procures the excess supply only to dump it into the ocean?
    (c) instead of procuring the excess supply, govt. resorts to cash grant worth the difference of the minimum support price over the market price directly to the cultivators as a measure of protection? What would be the effect on the social welfare in each case?
    [**Ans.** (a) $\Delta CS = -195,000$; $\Delta PS = 245,000$; Net increase in social welfare = 50,000.
    (b) $\Delta CS = -195,000$; $\Delta PS = 245,000$; Loss of revenue = ₹ 400, 000. Net decrease in social welfare = –₹ 350, 000. (In this case, there is a revenue loss of ₹ 400,000.)
    (c) $\Delta CS = 0$; $\Delta PS = 0$; Social welfare remains unchanged as the loss of welfare through the cash grant (210,000) is offset by the increase in welfare by an equal amount to the cultivators.]
74. Explain the determinants of supply. Under what conditions does a supply curve depict a dual behaviour? Explain with the help of a sketch citing examples.
75. Does a supply curve always have a positive slope? Draw the supply curve of labour hours of skilled workers in relation to their hourly wages. How would you justify its dual behaviour?
76. The situation in the previous question is not without a parallel. Supply curve of lendings of the private money lenders also portrays an identical trend in relation to the rate of interest applicable to such secured or unsecured loans. Explain the phenomenon with a neat sketch and justify the dual behaviour of the curve.
77. Demand and supply functions for a product are given as $Q^D = 3,000 - 3P$ and $Q^S = 7P$. Determine equilibrium price and quantity. Now suppose unit excise is levied on the product at the rate of ₹ 30 in the 1st year, ₹ 35 in the 2nd year, ₹ 40 in the 3rd year, ₹ 45 in the 4th year and ₹ 50 in the 5th year. Calculate the corresponding magnitudes of the deadweight loss suffered by the society for each of the five years. Is there any relation between the magnitudes of the unit tax levied by government and the magnitudes of

the deadweight loss suffered by the society? Graph the relationship with magnitudes of the unit tax on the horizontal axis and those of the deadweight loss on the vertical axis. What inference do you draw?

[Ans.

Year	Unit excise	Market price after unit excise	Deadweight loss
1	30	321.00	945.00
2	35	324.50	1286.25
3	40	328.00	1680.00
4	45	331.50	2126.25
5	50	335.00	2525.00

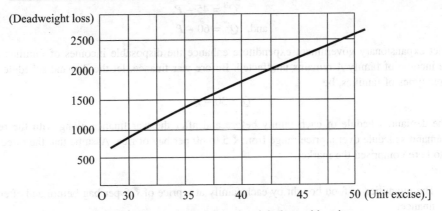

FIGURE 2.55 Variation of dead weight loss with unit tax.

78. Would your observations in (Question 77) change if the State chose to grant subsidies of the same measures in each of the five years instead of levying unit excise? Calculate magnitudes of the deadweight loss suffered at each level of subsidy in each of the five years and graph the relationship between the two.

CASE STUDY: THE FAD THEORY OF FAMINES

Decline in availability of staple food leads to famines responsible for massive casualities due to starvation and epidemics. Nobel laureate Prof. Amartya Sen, in his study on poverty and famines*, calls the phenomenon as the FAD [Food Availability Decline] theory of famines. His study covers famines of Bengal (1943), Ethiopia (1973) and Bangladesh (1974). According to Prof. Sen, Bengal Famine was caused by the war time (World War II) boom in public expenditure which led to general expansion of the purchasing power. This, in turn, resulted in a substantial rise in price of rice, the common staple food of the people of Bengal. War time finance gave a sizable boost to the disposable income of a segment of people of Bengal. The other segment comprising low income majorities, however, had no share in it. The benefitiaries, driven by the fear of the conjectural non-availability of essential goods, indulged in panic-buying and storing of essential commodities giving rise to a sudden spurt in demand and hence in price. This accounts for the demand side of the factors that led to a rise in prices of essential commodities. To make the matters worse,

---

* Sen, Amartya, 'Poverty and Famines': An Essay of Entitlement and Deprivation, Oxford University Press, 1981

the supply side too didn't lag behind. Supply shocks resulting from the prohibition of inter-province flow of the essential goods and from suppression of stocks by traders and farmers in anticipation of a further rise in price aggravated the price situation further. Thus, the food availability decline in Bengal in 1943 was not a consequence of crop failure nor of any lapses in distribution and transportation, but of the relative fall of the real income of the low income people who were not as lucky as the middle and the high income people in availing of a share in the disposable income enhanced by expansionary war finance. They were no longer in a position to buy the basic minimum quantity of rice needed for their survival. According to Prof. Sen, the supply of rice in Bengal in 1943 was 13% higher than what it was in the non-famine year 1941.

To illustrate, let us take three typical families—Family A, family B and family C respectively from the low-income, middle-income and the high-income segments of the people. Further, let their respective demand schedules, after war finance, be given as

$$Q^A = 30 - P,$$
$$Q^B = 45 - P,$$
$$\text{and,} \quad Q^C = 60 - P$$

Further, let expansionary government expenditure enhance the disposable incomes of families B and C while the income of family A remains unaffected. Before war finance, let the demand schedule for each of the three types of families, be

$$Q = 30 - P$$

Sketch the demand schedule of each family before and after the war finance along with the respective market demand schedule over a price range from ₹ 5 to 60 per bag of rice. Assume that the three families referred to here comprised the market.
Determine:

(i) The quantities of food bought by each family at a price of ₹ 5 per bag before and after the war finance.

(ii) The total market demand, before and after the war finance, at a price of ₹ 5 per bag of rice; assuming these three families only comprised the market.

(iii) How would your answers to (i) and (ii) above change when the price rises to ₹ 30 per bag of rice?

(iv) How would your answers to (i) and (ii) above change when the price rises to ₹ 45 per bag of rice?

(v) At what price would families A and B reach their starvation points?

(vi) Had the public distribution system existed in Bengal in 1943, what measures would you recommend it to undertake against the crisis?

[Ans. (i) Before : 25 bags each.
After : 25 bags, 40 bags and 55 bags, respectively.
(ii) Before : 75 bags.
After : 120 bags.
(iii) Answer to (i) : Before   : 0 bags each.
After : 0 bags, 15 bags and 30 bags, respectively.
Answer to (ii) : Before   : 0 bags
After : 45 bags.
(iv) Answer to (i) : Before   : 0 bags each.
After : 0 bags, 0 bags and 15 bags.
Answer to (ii) : Before   : 0 bags
After : 15 bags.

(v) Family A reaches its starvation point at a price of ₹ 30 per bag of rice, while family B, reaches it at a price of ₹ 45 per bag of it.
(vi) Under PDS, the government of Bengal should import rice from other states and should undertake distribution of it through the fair price shops at a price below ₹ 30 per bag depending on its procurement price. If the procurement price be ₹ 10.00 per bag, the distribution price can be above ₹ 10, but below ₹ 30.]

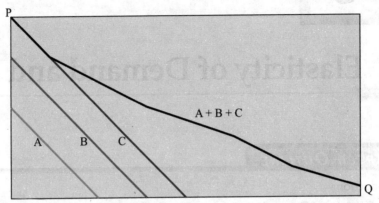

FIGURE 2.56 Demand curves of Families A, B and C are labeled by letters A, B and C respectively. The market demand curve is a horizontal summation of these three and is labeled as (A + B + C).

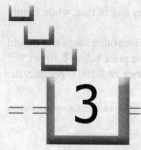

3

Elasticity of Demand and Supply

CHAPTER OUTLINE

Introduction
- Elasticity of Demand
- Elasticity of Supply
- Partial Price Elasticities
- Key Terms and Concepts
- Exercises

INTRODUCTION

Elasticity of demand or supply refers to its flexibility to a change in one of its determinants while all other determinants remain unchanged. For instance, price-elasticity of demand refers to responsiveness of demand to a change in market price, while all other determinants of demand except price remain unchanged. Similarly, income-elasticity of demand is responsiveness of demand to a change in income while all other determinants of demand except income remain unchanged.

The concepts of elasticity of demand and supply are very important in the study of market behaviour. Policy matters related to pricing and positioning of products, analysis of their profitability, decisions pertaining to procurement and stocking of raw materials, employment of man-power, scheduling of production, strategies of advertising the product, selection of the appropriate distribution channels and decisions regarding the stock levels of the finished products—all depend on respective elasticities of demand and supply.

Let us study them in requisite detail in this chapter.

3.1 ELASTICITY OF DEMAND

Elasticity of demand is defined as its *responsiveness to a change in one of its determinants while the other determinants remain unchanged*. We define some of the elasticities below before discussing them in detail.

3.1.1 Price Elasticity

It is defined *as the responsiveness of demand to a change in price, while all the other things except the product price remain unchanged*. It's measured as a ratio of the proportionate change in demand to the proportionate change in price.

Thus, *price elasticity* of demand, denoted by E_P^D, may be expressed as:

$$E_P^D = \frac{\text{Proportionate change in demand}}{\text{Proportionate change in price}}$$

$$= \frac{(Q_2 - Q_1)/Q_1}{(P_2 - P_1)/P_1} \tag{3.1}$$

$$= \frac{(Q_2 - Q_1)}{(P_2 - P_1)} \times \frac{P_1}{Q_1}$$

$$= \frac{\Delta Q}{\Delta P} \times \frac{P}{Q} \tag{3.2}$$

where
- $Q_2 \equiv$ quantity demanded at price P_2
- $Q_1 \equiv$ quantity demanded at price P_1
- $\Delta Q \equiv$ change in quantity demanded due to a change ΔP in price
- $Q \equiv$ initial level of demand at initial price P.

3.1.2 Income Elasticity

Income elasticity of demand is defined as its *responsiveness to a change in income while all other things except income remain unchanged*. Income elasticity of demand is measured as a ratio of the proportionate change in quantity demanded to the proportionate change in income while all other things remain unchanged. Thus, income elasticity of demand, denoted by E_Y^D, is given as:

$$E_Y^D = \frac{\text{Proportionate change in demand}}{\text{Proportionate change in income}}$$

$$= \frac{(Q_2 - Q_1)/Q_1}{(Y_2 - Y_1)/Y_1}$$

$$= \frac{(Q_2 - Q_1)}{(Y_2 - Y_1)} \times \frac{Y_1}{Q_1}$$

$$= \frac{\Delta Q}{\Delta Y} \times \frac{Y}{Q} \tag{3.3}$$

where

$Q_2 \equiv$ quantity demanded at income Y_2
$Q_1 \equiv$ quantity demanded at income Y_1
$\Delta Q \equiv$ change in demand due to change ΔY in income
$Q \equiv$ initial demand at initial level of income, Y.

3.1.3 Cross-price Elasticity

It is defined as *responsiveness of demand for good A to a change in price of good B, while all other things except the price of good B remain unchanged*. Here, goods A and B are related goods (substitutes/complements). It is measured as a ratio of the proportionate change in demand for good A to the proportionate change in price of good B. Thus, *cross-price elasticity*, denoted as $E^D_{P(CROSS)}$ is given as

$$E^D_{P(CROSS)} = \frac{\text{Proportionate change in demand for good } A}{\text{Proportionate change in price of good } B}$$

$$= \frac{(Q^A_2 - Q^A_1)/Q^A_1}{(P^B_2 - P^B_1)/P^B_1}$$

$$= \frac{(Q^A_2 - Q^A_1)}{(P^B_2 - P^B_1)} \times \frac{P^B_1}{Q^A_1}$$

$$= \frac{\Delta Q^A}{\Delta P^B} \times \frac{P^B}{Q^A} \qquad (3.4)$$

where

$Q^A_2 \equiv$ quantity demanded of good A at price P^B_2 of B
$Q^A_1 \equiv$ quantity demanded of good A at price P^B_1 of B
$\Delta Q^A \equiv$ change in demand of good A due to a change in price ΔP^B of good B
$Q^A \equiv$ quantity demanded of good A at a price P^B of B.

Before proceeding any further, let us construct some numerical illustrations to demonstrate calculation of the elasticities defined above.

ILLUSTRATION 3.1:

(a) Calculate price elasticity of demand when a rise in price from ₹ 10 per unit to ₹ 12 per unit of a product lowers its demand from 1,000 to 800 units in a local store.
(b) When income of a consumer increases from ₹ 10,000 to ₹ 12,000, his demand for a product rises from 20 to 30 units of it. Calculate income elasticity of demand.
(c) When price of tea in a local cafe rises from ₹ 4 a cup to ₹ 5 a cup, demand for coffee rises from 30 cups a day to 40 cups a day despite no change in coffee prices. Calculate cross-price elasticity of demand.
(d) A 20% rise in price of ink leads to 30% fall in the demand of ink-pens. Calculate the cross-price elasticity of demand.

Solution:

(a) $P_1 = 10$, $Q_1 = 1000$ units
$P_2 = 12$, $Q_2 = 800$ units

∴
$$\Delta P = 12 - 10$$
$$= 2$$
$$\Delta Q = 800 - 1000$$
$$= -200$$

Thus,
$$E_P^D = \frac{\Delta Q}{\Delta P} \times \frac{P_1}{Q_1}$$

$$= \frac{-200}{+2} \times \frac{10}{1000}$$

$$= -1.00$$

(The negative sign signifies that the good is a normal one.)

(b) $Y_1 = 10,000$, $Y_2 = 12,000$
$Q_1 = 20$ units, $Q_2 = 30$ units

$$\Delta Q = 30 - 20$$
$$= 10$$
$$\Delta Y = 12,000 - 10,000$$
$$= 2000$$

∴
$$E_Y^D = \frac{\Delta Q}{\Delta Y} \times \frac{Y}{Q}$$

$$= \frac{10}{2000} \times \frac{10,000}{20}$$

$$= +2.5$$

(The positive sign of the income elasticity signifies that the good is a normal one.)

(c) $P_1^{tea} = 4$ per cup, $Q_1^{coffee} = 30$ cups
$P_2^{tea} = 5$ per cup, $Q_2^{coffee} = 40$ cups

$$\Delta Q^{coffee} = 40 - 30$$
$$= +10$$
$$\Delta P^{tea} = 5 - 4$$
$$= +1$$

$$E_P^D \text{ (CROSS)} = \frac{+10}{+1} \times \frac{4}{30}$$

$$= +4/3$$
$$= +1.333$$

(The positive sign of the cross-price elasticity signifies that the two goods are substitutes.)

(d) $\quad \Delta P^{\text{ink}}/P^{\text{ink}} = +20\%$
$$= 0.20$$
$$\Delta Q^{\text{pen}}/Q^{\text{pen}} = -30\%$$
$$= -0.30$$
$$E_P^D \text{ (CROSS)} = \frac{-0.30}{+0.20}$$
$$= -1.5$$

(The negative sign of the cross-price elasticity signifies that the two goods are complements.)

Having gone through the process of calculation of the elasticity, let us turn to the types, degrees and determinants of the price elasticity of demand.

3.1.4 Types of Price Elasticity of Demand

Price elasticity is generally referred to as:

1. Arc price elasticity, and
2. Point price elasticity.

1. Arc price elasticity: The arc price elasticity is slightly different from the price elasticity defined above. We have seen above that the price elasticity is given as

$$E_P^D = \frac{Q_2 - Q_1}{P_2 - P_1} \times \frac{P_1}{Q_1}$$

Here, changes in demand and prices are taken as the proportionate changes with respect to the original levels of demand (Q_1) and price (P_1). If the two points are separated by a larger distance on the demand curve, it is customary to express the changes in demand and price as proportionate changes of the average values rather than the original values (Figure 3.1). Thus,

$$E_P^D = \frac{Q_2 - Q_1}{P_2 - P_1} \times \frac{(P_1 + P_2)/2}{(Q_1 + Q_2)/2}$$

$$= \frac{Q_2 - Q_1}{P_2 - P_1} \times \frac{(P_1 + P_2)}{(Q_1 + Q_2)} \quad\quad (3.5)$$

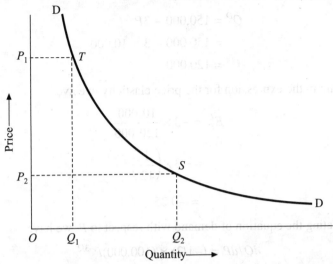

FIGURE 3.1 Arc price elasticity: when the two points on the demand curve are separated by a large distance, the changes in demand and price are expressed as a percentage of the average values of demand and price rather than of their original values.

2. *Point price elasticity:* Point price elasticity refers to the price elasticity at a point on the demand curve. In other words, it accounts for the price elasticity of demand in the close proximity of the point, that is, proportionate change in demand in response to an infinitesimally small change in price at the point. The point price elasticity, thus, has its relevance to situations in which either the equation of the demand curve is given or the demand curve itself is given. To understand, let us refer to the following illustration.

ILLUSTRATION 3.2:

(a) Quantity demanded, Q^D, of a product is given as a function of its price as below:

$$Q^D = 150{,}000 - 3P$$

Calculate price elasticity of demand at a price, $P = 10{,}000$.

(b) Quantity demanded, Q^D, of a product is given as

$$Q^D = 100{,}000/\sqrt{P}$$

Calculate price elasticity of demand at a price, $P = 10{,}000$.

(c) Given the demand curve and given a point on it, obtain an expression for the elasticity of demand.

Solution:

(a) $E_P^D = dQ/dP \times P/Q$ (For a point price elasticity, changes in Q and P have to be infinitesimally small.)

Differentiating the equation of demand with respect to price, we have

$$dQ/dP = -3$$

Quantity demanded, when $P = 10,000$

$$Q^D = 150,000 - 3P$$
$$= 150,000 - 3 \times 10,000$$
$$= 120,000$$

Substituting in the expression for the price elasticity, we ave

$$E_P^D = -3 \times \frac{10,000}{120,000}$$
$$= -3 \times \left(\frac{1}{12}\right)$$
$$= -0.25$$

(b) Differentiating the equation of demand with respect to P, we have

$$dQ/dP = (-1/2) \times (100,000)P^{-3/2}$$

Value of the derivative at $P = 10,000$

$$dQ/dP = (-1/2) \times (100,000)(10,000)^{-3/2}$$
$$= -1/20$$
$$= -0.05$$

$$\therefore E_P^D = \left(\frac{dQ}{dP}\right)_{(P=10,000)} \times \left(\frac{P}{Q}\right)_{(P=10,000)}$$
$$= -0.05 \times \frac{10,000}{1000}$$
$$= -0.50$$

(c) *Point price elasticity at a given point on a given demand curve*: In Figure 3.2, AB is the linear demand curve on which, point $T(Q, P)$ is given. We have to determine price elasticity of demand at this point. Take a point $S(Q', P')$ close to $T(Q, P)$ so that $PP' = TR = \Delta P$ and $QQ' = RS = \Delta Q$. In Figure 3.3, DD is a non-linear demand curve on which point $T(Q, P)$ is given. Draw AB tangential to DD at T. Take point $S(Q', P')$ close to point $T(Q, P)$ on AB as shown. As soon as AB, tangential to DD at point T is drawn, we can forget the non-linear demand curve DD for all practical purposes.

Geometrical treatment, from this point onwards, would refer to both the figures.

$$E_P^D = (\Delta Q/\Delta P) \times (P/Q)$$
$$= (QQ'/PP') \times (P/Q)$$
$$= (RS/TR) \times (OP/OQ)$$
$$= (QB/QT) \times (OP/OQ) \qquad \text{(since } RS/TR = QB/QT, \text{ as } \Delta TRS \sim \Delta TQB)$$

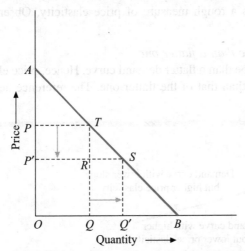

FIGURE 3.2 AB is the demand curve. T and S are two points on it. Price elasticity at point $T(Q, P)$ is required. Point $S(Q', P')$ is taken in the proximity of point T, so that $PP' = TR = \Delta P$; $OQ' = RS = \Delta Q$.

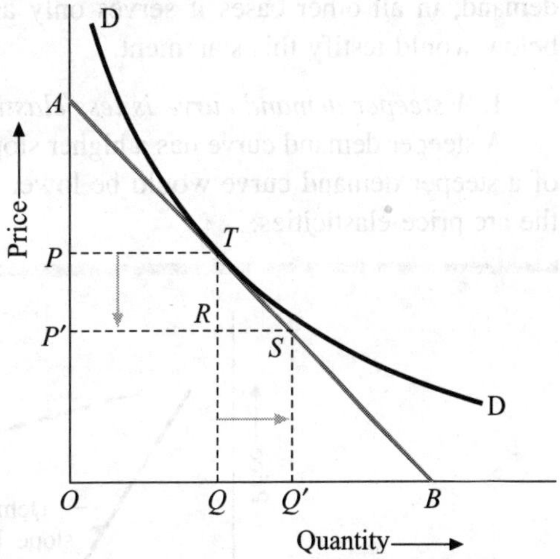

FIGURE 3.3 DD is a non-linear demand curve. T is a point on it, at which price elasticity is required. A tangent, AB, is drawn to DD at point T. Point $S(Q', P')$ is taken in the proximity of T so that $PP' = TR = \Delta P$; $QQ' = RS = \Delta Q$.

$$= (QB/OP) \times (OP/OQ) \quad \text{(since } QT = OP\text{)}$$
$$= QB/OQ$$
$$= BQ/QO$$
$$= BT/TA \quad \text{(since } BQ/QO = BT/TA, \text{ as } \Delta BQT - \Delta BOA\text{)}$$
$$= \frac{\text{Length of the lower segment}}{\text{Length of the upper segment}}$$

Thus, price elasticity of demand at a point on the demand curve is given as

$$E_P^D = \frac{\text{Length of the lower segment}}{\text{Length of the upper segment}} \qquad (3.6)$$

3.1.5 Relationship between Price Elasticity of Demand and the Slope of the Demand Curve

We have seen that the price elasticity of demand,

$$E_P^D = (dQ/dP) \times (P/Q)$$
$$= 1/(dp/dQ) \times (P/Q)$$
$$= 1/m \times P/Q \qquad (3.7)$$

where, m = slope of the demand curve.

Thus, price elasticity of demand is inversely related to the slope of the demand curve and directly to the (P/Q) ratio. Except to the extreme cases of $m = 0$ and $m = \infty$ where slope m of the demand curve is an over-riding factor and acts as a perfect measure of price elasticity of demand, in all other cases it serves only as a rough measure of price elasticity. Observations below would testify this statement.

1. *A steeper demand curve is less elastic than a flatter one*

A steeper demand curve has a higher slope than a flatter demand curve. Hence, price elasticity of a steeper demand curve would be lower than that of the flatter one. The reference here is to the arc price elasticities.

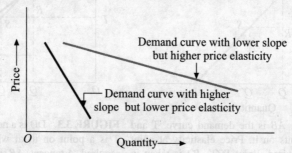

FIGURE 3.4 A steeper demand curve is less elastic than a flatter one.

Following the argument, a horizontal demand curve, with slope $m = 0$, is infinitely elastic while a vertical demand curve, with slope $m = \infty$, has price elasticity as low as zero. The former is known as perfectly elastic while the latter, as perfectly inelastic.

2. *Two linear demand curves originating from the same point on the vertical axis have same price elasticity of demand at a given price despite their different slopes (Figure 3.5).* From Figure 3.5, linear demand curves, AB and AC, originating from point A on the vertical axis and meeting x-axis in points B and C have same price elasticity at price OP. Corresponding points on AB and AC are T and S respectively.

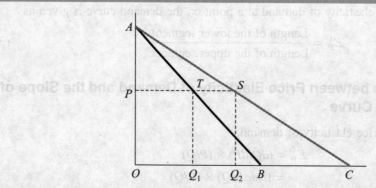

FIGURE 3.5 The two demand curves, AB and AC, originating from same point A on the vertical axis and meeting the horizontal axis in different points B and C, have the same price elasticity at price OP. Price elasticity at point T on AB is the same as that on S on CD.

$$E_P^D \text{ at point } T \text{ on } AB = \frac{\text{Lower segment}}{\text{Upper segment}}$$

$$= BT/TA$$

$$= OP/PA \qquad \text{(since } \Delta APT \sim \Delta AOB)$$

$$E_P^D \text{ at point } S \text{ on } AC = \frac{\text{Lower segment}}{\text{Upper segment}}$$

$$= CS/SA$$

$$= OP/PA \qquad \text{(since } \Delta APS \sim \Delta AOC)$$

$\therefore E_P^D$ at $T = E_P^D$ at S. Hence, the statement.

3. *For two parallel linear demand curves, the price elasticities of demand at a given price are not the same despite same slopes (Figure 3.6)*

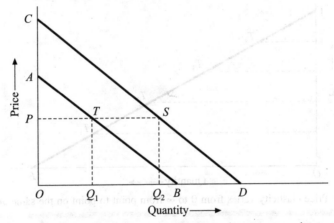

FIGURE 3.6 The price elasticities of two linear parallel demand curves at a given price are not the same despite same slopes.

Consider linear demand curves, AB and CD, parallel to each other. At a given price, take points T and S on AB and CD respectively. The price elasticities at these points are BT/TA and DS/SC which by geometry can be shown to be OP/PA and OP/PC. From the Figure, $PA \neq PC$, the elasticities at the points T and S are different.

$$E_P^D \text{ at } T = \frac{\text{Lower segment}}{\text{Upper segment}}$$

$$= BT/TA$$

$$= OP/PA \qquad (3.8)$$

$$\text{(since } \Delta APT \sim \Delta AOB, BT/TA = OP/PA)$$

$$E_P^D \text{ at } S = \frac{\text{Lower segment}}{\text{Upper segment}}$$

$$= DS/SC$$

$$= OP/PC \qquad (3.9)$$

(since $\triangle CPS \sim \triangle COD$, $DS/SC = OP/PC$)

From Eqs. (3.8) and (3.9), we have

$$= OP/PA \neq OP/PC \qquad \text{(since } PA \neq PC\text{)}$$

∴ Price elasticities are not the same at points T and S, despite same slopes of AB and CD.

4. *Price elasticity on a linear demand curve varies from point to point between 0 and ∞ (Figure 3.7).*

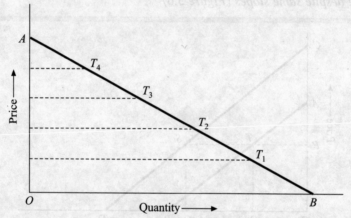

FIGURE 3.7 Price elasticity varies from 0 to ∞ from point to point on the same demand curve.

Take points T_1, T_2, T_3 and T_4 on linear demand curve AB so that $BT_1 = T_1 T_2 = T_2 T_3 = T_3 T_4 = T_4 A = d$, a fixed length.

At point B, price elasticity $= 0/BA = 0$

At point T_1, price elasticity $= BT_1/T_1A = d/4d = 1/4$

At point T_2, price elasticity $= BT_2/T_2A = 2d/3d = 2/3$

At point T_3, price elasticity $= BT_3/T_3A = 3d/2d = 3/2$

At point T_4, price elasticity $= BT_4/T_4A = 4d/d = 4/1$

At point T_5, price elasticity $= BA/0 = 5d/0 = \infty$

Price elasticity of demand thus varies from 0 to ∞ on a linear demand curve as we move from the lowest point on it to the highest one despite same slope of the demand curve at every point on it.

5. *For two intersecting demand curves, their price elasticities are different at the point of their intersection (Figure 3.8).*

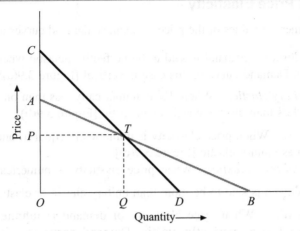

FIGURE 3.8 For intersecting demand curves, their price elasticities are different at the point of their intersection.

Suppose *AB* and *CD* are the two linear demand curves intersecting each other at point *T* (Figure 3.8).

Price elasticity of *AB* at *T* = *BT*/*TA* = *OP*/*PA*   (since $\triangle APT \sim \triangle AOB$)

Price elasticity of *CD* at *T* = *DT*/*TC* = *OP*/*PC*   (since $\triangle CPT \sim \triangle COD$)

But from Figure 3.8, it is evident that *OP*/*PA* ≠ *OP*/*PC*   (since *PA* ≠ *PC*)

6. *When demand curve is a rectangular hyperbola, price elasticity of demand is unitary at every point on it (Figure 2.39, Chapter 2).*

We have seen that a rectangular hyperbola can be described by the equation

$$xy = \alpha$$

For a demand curve with price *P* on *y*-axis and quantity *Q* on *x*-axis, the equation of the demand curve (rectangular hyperbola) can be expressed as

$$PQ = \alpha$$

Differentiating it with respect to *P* implicity, we have

$$P(dQ/dP) + Q \cdot 1 = 0$$

$$\Rightarrow \quad (dQ/dP) = -(Q/P)$$

$$\Rightarrow \quad E_P^D = (dQ/dP) \times (P/Q)$$

$$= -(Q/P) \times (P/Q)$$

$$= -1$$

The expression being independent of *P*/*Q*, price elasticity of demand is unitary at every point on the demand curve in question.

3.1.6 Degree of Price Elasticity

Depending on the numerical values of the price elasticities, demand curves are often classified as:

(a) *Perfectly inelastic:* Demand is said to be perfectly inelastic when E_P^D is numerically equal to zero. Demand curve in this case is vertical [Figure 3.9(a)].

(b) *Less than unitary elastic:* When E_P^D is numerically less than one $\left(\left|E_P^D\right|<1\right)$, demand is said to be less than unitary elastic or inelastic [Figure 3.9(b)].

(c) *Unitary elastic:* When price elasticity is numerically equal to one $\left(\left|E_P^D\right|=1\right)$, demand is referred to as unitary elastic [Figure 3.9(c)].

(d) *More than unitary elastic:* When price elasticity is numerically greater than one $\left(\left|E_P^D\right|>1\right)$, demand is said to be more than unitary elastic or elastic [Figure 3.9(d)].

(e) *Perfectly elastic:* When price elasticity of demand is infinitely high $\left(\left|E_P^D\right|=\infty\right)$, demand is said to be perfectly elastic. Demand curve in this case is horizontal [Figure 3.9(e)].

Figure 3.9 shows different degrees of price elasticity of demand.

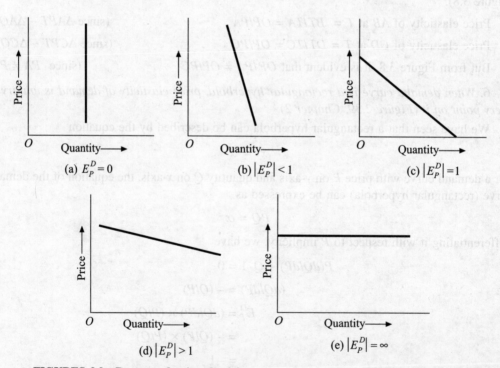

FIGURES 3.9 Degrees of price elasticity: (a) perfectly inelastic demand, (b) less than unitary elastic demand, (c) unitary elastic demand, (d) more than unitary elastic demand and (e) perfectly or infinitely elastic demand.

3.1.7 Measurement of Price Elasticity of Demand

Theoretically, there are three methods of measuring price elasticity of demand. Two of them, we have already discussed in this section. The reference here is to the first two summarized below. The third one, the Marshall's total outlay method, has not so far been mentioned.

1. *Flux's proportionality method:* The method, already mentioned in the definition of the price elasticity of demand as

$$E_P^D = \frac{\text{Proportionate change in demand}}{\text{Proportionate change in price}}$$

$$= \frac{\Delta Q}{\Delta P} \times \frac{P}{Q}$$

is known as the Flux's proportionality method of measuring the price elasticity of demand.

2. *Graphical or Geometrical method*: This method is based on the slope of the demand curve. A steeper demand curve has a lower price elasticity and flatter one, a higher price elasticity. The method is also used to measure price elasticity at a point on the demand curve, given as the ratio of the length of the lower segment to that of the upper segment.

3. *Marshall's total outlay method**: This method is based on changes in total expenditures with changes in product price (Table 3.1).

TABLE 3.1 Demonstration of Marshall's total outlay method of measuring price elasticity of demand

	Individual A		Individual B		Individual C	
Price	Q	TE	Q	TE	Q	TE
5	20	100	20	100	20	100
4	22	88	25	100	30	120
2	30	60	50	100	75	150
	$\left|E_P^D\right|<1$		$\left|E_P^D\right|=1$		$\left|E_P^D\right|>1$	

---

*When total expenditure on a product varies directly with price, the price elasticity of demand is less than unitary $\left(\left|E_P^D\right|<1\right)$; when it varies inversely with price, the price elasticity of demand is more than unitary $\left(\left|E_P^D\right|>1\right)$ and when the total expenditure remains unaffected by price changes, the price elasticity is unitary $\left(\left|E_P^D\right|=1\right)$. These observations, demonstrated in Table 3.1, can also be proved by calculus. Let the total expenditure (total outlay) be given as

$$TE = P \cdot Q$$

Differentiating TE with respect to P, we have

$$d(TE)/dP = Q \cdot 1 + P \cdot dQ/dP$$
$$= Q[1 + (P/Q) \cdot (dQ/dP)]$$
$$= Q[1 - \{-(dQ/dP) \cdot (P/Q)\}]$$
$$= Q\left[1 - \left|E_P^D\right|\right] \quad \text{(Note that } E_P^D \text{ is negative for a normal good.)}$$

When TE varies directly with P, it is an increasing function of P. Hence, $d(TE)/dP > 0$ *(Contd.)*

Q represents quantity in units and TE, the total expenditure. Individual A reduces his expenditure from 100 to 60 as the price of the product falls. According to this method, the price elasticity must be numerically less than one. For individual B, total expenditure remains unchanged as the product price falls. For him, price elasticity is unitary. In case of individual C, total expenditure increases as price falls. Price elasticity for him is more than unitary. Instead of providing an absolute measure of price elasticity the method helps its classification as unitary, less than unitary or more than unitary.

3.1.8 Factors Affecting Price Elasticity of Demand

Price elasticity of demand depends on the following factors:

1. *Nature of commodity:*   Elasticity of demand for any commodity depends upon the category of commodity to which it belongs. For instance, if the commodity belongs to necessities, such as, salt, food, etc. its price elasticity is very low but if it belongs to luxuries, its price elasticity is high. Likewise price elasticity is close to zero for prestige goods, such as, jewels, rare coins, rare paintings, etc.

2. *Availability of substitutes:*   Commodities with no substitutes have inelastic demands while those having close substitutes have highly elastic demands. For instances, a rise in price of tea reflects in a rise in demand of coffee even when coffee prices do not fall. Cross demand of coffee therefore is highly elastic.

3. *Multiplicity of use:*   Demand for goods that have more than one use is generally more elastic. For instance, commodities such as milk, coal and electricity that have multiple uses have highly elastic demands. On the contrary, single use goods have comparatively less elastic demands.

4. *Nature of use:*   Some commodities are jointly demanded. For example, a car is demanded jointly with petrol and an ink-pen, jointly with ink. The car is useless without petrol and so is the ink-pen without the ink. If the demand for cars is less elastic, so is the demand for the petrol. The same is the case with the demand of ink pens with that of the ink. The elasticity of demand of one commodity depends upon that of the related commodity.

5. *Deferred consumption:*   Commodities whose consumption can be deferred have elastic demands. For instance, when price of the consumer durables such as refrigerators, TVs, etc. is high or expected to fall, their demand is postponed.

6. *Habits:*   Some people get habituated or addicted to consumption of commodities like coffee, tea, or cigarettes of a particular brand. Their demands for these goods are highly inelastic.

(*Footnote contd.*)

$$\Rightarrow \quad Q\left[1 - \left|E_P^D\right|\right] > 0 \Rightarrow \left|E_P^D\right| > 1$$

When TE varies inversely with P, it is a decreasing function of P. Hence, $d(\text{TE})/dP < 0$

$$\Rightarrow \quad Q\left[1 - \left|E_P^D\right|\right] < 0 \Rightarrow \left|E_P^D\right| > 1$$

And, when TE remains passive to price changes, $d(\text{TE})/dP = 0$

$$\Rightarrow \quad Q\left[1 - \left|E_P^D\right|\right] = 0 \Rightarrow \left|E_P^D\right| = 1$$

That proves Marshall's Theorem.

7. *Income group of the consumer:* Demands of individuals belonging to a higher income group are generally less elastic. Whether price rises or falls, it does not matter for the rich who take a liking for a product.

8. *Proportion of income spent*: When proportion of consumer's income spent on a product is small, its demand is generally less elastic.

9. *Price level:* When the price level is high, demand for commodities is elastic; and when it is low, demand is less elastic.

10. *Time factor:* The shorter the time period of demand, the lesser the price elasticity and the longer the time period, the higher the price elasticity. If a consumer has to buy a product at short notice, he/she cannot wait for price to fall nor can he/she think of a way out or of a substitute. If installation of a particular brand of electric metre is made a precondition of electric supply all of a sudden, consumers have to buy the device whatever the price. If given time and choice, they may find cheaper substitutes or other producers may come up with cheaper substitutes. Producers of the brand in question feel compelled to keep the time factor in mind while setting price of such products.

3.2 ELASTICITY OF SUPPLY

Elasticity of supply is defined as responsiveness of supply to a change in one of its determinants while all other determinants remain unchanged. It is, thus, responsiveness of supply to a change in price while all other determinants of supply remain unchanged. Like price elasticity of demand, price elasticity of supply, is measured as a ratio of the proportionate change in supply to a proportionate change in price.

$$E_P^S = \frac{\text{Proportionate change in quantity supplied}}{\text{Proportionate change in price}}$$

$$= \frac{(Q_2 - Q_1)/Q_1}{(P_2 - P_1)/P_1}$$

$$= \frac{\Delta Q/Q}{\Delta P/P}$$

$$= (\Delta Q/\Delta P)(P/Q) \tag{3.10}$$

where

$Q_1 \equiv$ quantity supplied at price P_1

$Q_2 \equiv$ quantity supplied at price P_2

$\Delta Q \equiv$ change in quantity supplied from the initial supply of Q

$\Delta P \equiv$ change in price from the initial price of P.

For infinitesimally small changes in supply and price, the price elasticity of supply can also be expressed in terms of derivatives of Q with respec to P as

$$E_P^S = (dQ/dP) \times (P/Q)$$

As in case of the elasticity of demand, the elasticity of supply too can be defined as arc price elasticity and point price elasticity. Arc price elasticity can be expressed as

$$E_P^S = \frac{(Q_2 - Q_1)/[(Q_1 + Q_2)/2]}{(P_2 - P_1)/[(P_1 + P_2)/2]}$$

$$= \frac{(Q_2 - Q_1)/(Q_1 + Q_2)}{(P_2 - P_1)/(P_1 + P_2)} \qquad (3.11)$$

Here changes in quantity and price are expressed as proportions of the average values of the price and quantity rather than of their initial values.

The expression for the point price elasticity at a point on the supply curve, can be obtained geometrically as shown in Figure 3.10.

In Figure 3.10 (a), the supply curve is a straight line passing through the origin. For point price elasticity at point $T(Q, P)$, take a point S (Q', P') close to it so that quantity supplied increases by $\Delta Q (= Q' - Q)$ in response to a rise in price by $\Delta P (= P' - P)$.

$$\begin{aligned} E_P^S &= \Delta Q/\Delta P \times P/Q \\ &= TR/RS \times OP/OQ & (\Delta Q = QQ' = TR, \Delta P = PP' = RS) \\ &= OQ/QT \times OP/OQ & (TR/RS = OQ/QT, \text{ as } \Delta TRS \sim \Delta OQT) \\ &= 1.0 & (\text{since, } QT = OP) \end{aligned}$$

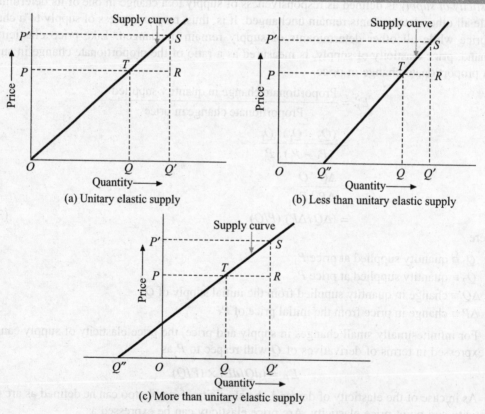

FIGURE 3.10 Point price elasticity of linear supply curves.

Thus, the price elasticity of supply at a given point on the linear supply curve through origin is unitary.

In Figure 3.10(b), likewise

$$E_P^S = \Delta Q/\Delta P \times OP/OQ$$
$$= OQ'/PP' \times OP/OQ \quad \text{(since } \Delta Q = QQ', \Delta P = PP')$$
$$= TR/RS \times OP/OQ \quad \text{(since } QQ' = TR, PP' = RS)$$
$$= Q''Q/OP \times OP/OQ$$
$$\quad \text{(since } TR/RS = Q''Q/OP \text{ as } \Delta TRS \sim \Delta Q''Q'T)$$
$$= Q''Q/OQ$$
$$< 1.00 \quad \text{(since } Q''Q < OQ)$$

Thus, the price elasticity of supply at a point on it is less than unitary if the linear supply curve intersects the quantity axis (x-axis).

In Figure 3.10(c), the linear supply curve intersects the price-axis (y-axis). Proceeding likewise, the point price elasticity at point $T(Q, P)$, can be worked out as

$$E_P^S = Q''Q/OQ$$
$$> 1.00 \quad \text{(since } Q''Q > OQ)$$

Thus, price elasticity of supply for a linear supply curve at a point on it is more than unitary if the supply curve intersects the price axis (y-axis).

Alternatively, the supply equations for the curves in Figures 3.9(a), (b) and (c) can be identified, respectively, as

$$P = mQ \quad [3.12(a)]$$
$$P = mQ - C \quad [3.12(b)]$$
$$P = mQ + C \quad [3.12(c)]$$

Differentiating 3.12(a) with respect to P, we have

$$1 = m(dQ/dP)$$
$$\Rightarrow (dQ/dP) = (1/m)$$
$$\therefore E_P^S = (1/m).(P/Q), \quad [\text{as } E_P^S = (dQ/dP)\cdot(P/Q)]$$
$$= (1/m).(mQ/Q), \quad (\text{as } P = mQ)$$
$$= (1/m).(m)$$
$$= 1$$

Differentiating 3.12(b) with respect to P, we have

$$1 = m(dQ/dP)$$
$$\Rightarrow (dQ/dP) = (1/m)$$
$$\therefore E_P^S = (dQ/dP)\cdot(P/Q) \quad [E_P^S = (dQ/dP)\cdot(P/Q)]$$
$$= (1/m)\cdot[(mQ - C)/Q] \quad (\text{as } P = mQ - C)$$
$$= (1/m)\cdot(m - C/Q)$$
$$= (1/m)\cdot m - (1/m)(C/Q)$$

$$= 1 - (C/mQ)$$
$$< 1$$

Similarly, differentiating 3.12(c) with respect to P, we have

$$1 = m(dQ/dP)$$
$$\Rightarrow \qquad dQ/dP = 1/m$$
$$\therefore \qquad E_P^S = (dQ/dP) \cdot (P/Q)$$
$$= (1/m) \cdot [(mQ + C)/Q] \qquad \text{(as } P = mQ + C\text{)}$$
$$= (1/m) \cdot (mQ/Q) + [(1/m) \cdot (C/Q)]$$
$$= 1 + (C/mQ)$$
$$> 1$$

3.2.1 Degrees of Price Elasticity of Supply

Degrees of price elasticity of supply (Figure 3.11) follow the same pattern as the degrees of price elasticity of demand. As has already been explained, a horizontal supply curve is infinitely elastic, a vertical one is perfectly inelastic, one passing through origin is unitary elastic, one having an intercept on the vertical axis is more than unitary elastic and the one having an intercept on the horizontal axis is less than unitary elastic. Some observations about the price elasticity of supply need to be made here:

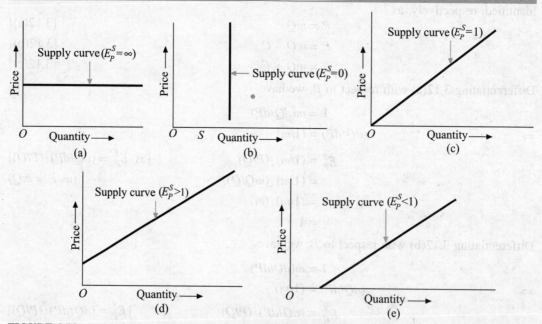

FIGURE 3.11 (a) perfectly elastic supply, (b) perfectly inelastic supply, (c) unitary elastic supply, (d) more than unitary elastic supply, (e) less than unitary elastic supply.

1. *Price elasticity of supply, like that of demand, is inversely related to the slope of the supply curve in general*

$$E_P^S = (dQ/dP) \cdot (P/Q)$$
$$= [1/(dP/dQ)] \, (P/Q)$$
$$= (1/m) \, (P/Q) \qquad (3.13)$$
$$= \alpha \cdot (1/m) \qquad \text{(where } \alpha = P/Q\text{)}$$

The supply curve with a higher slope is less elastic than one with a lower slope given the same value of (P/Q) for the two. In other words, for the intersecting supply curves, the price elasticity of supply is lower for the steeper curve and higher for the flatter one at the point of intersection. For the horizontal and the vertical supply curves, the slope of the supply curve is an overriding factor. The (P/Q) ratio for these extreme situations becomes immaterial due to the extreme values of m, which are 0 and ∞ respectively.

2. *For the linear parallel supply curves, slope has nothing to do with the price elasticity of supply*

The fact is self-evident. For linear parallel supply curves, slope is same for all of them. Elasticity of supply, in such cases depends on the intercepts made by them on the price axis. As seen earlier in this section, price elasticity of supply is unitary for a supply curve passing through origin, more than one for a supply curve making positive intercept on price axis and less than one for a supply curve making a negative intercept on the price axis. As is the case with the slope of demand curve as a measure of the price elasticity of demand, slope of the supply curve too is a rough measure of price elasticity of supply.

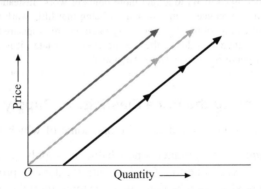

FIGURE 3.12 In the figure above, all the three supply curves have identical slopes but the one (marked with two arrows) passing through the origin is unitary elastic, the one (marked with one arrow) having an intercept on the vertical axis is more than unitary elastic and the one, marked with three arrows, having an intercept on the horizontal axis, is less than unitary elastic. Refer to the equations 3.12(a), 3.12(c) and 3.12(b) in that order and the respective expressions of the price elasticities of supply as obtained therein.

3. *Price elasticity of supply for a normal good is always positive while price elasticity of demand for it is always negative. The opposite is the case with the two in respect of the goods for which the supply and the demand curves slope downwards and upwards respectively.* We have discussed the upward slope of the demand curve already. The supply curve slopes downwards in certain cases. One such case is demonstrated below.

Supply curve for labour hours in response to the rising rate of hourly wage, or, the supply curve for loanable funds in response to the rising rate of interest assumes a negative slope as shown in Figure 3.13.

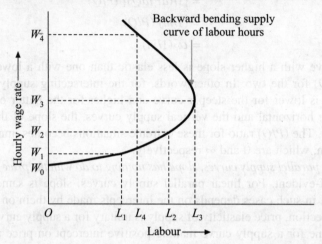

FIGURE 3.13 When wage rate is low, say W_0, supply of labour hours is zero. Workers find work unrewarding. Employers raise the wage rate to W_1 to lure them to work with the result that OL_1 hours of work are supplied. But employers in need of more hours of work from them, raise the wage rate further to W_2 with the consequence that OL_2 hours of work are provided. The supply is maximum, OL_3 hours of work, at the wage rate of W_3. Now suppose the wage rate is further hiked to W_4 to attract more hours of work. Instead of supplying more hours of work, the workers rather choose to reduce them. The reason being that little work fetches more than sufficient income to the workers due to high rate of hourly wage. They begin to prefer leisure to labour. Up to a wage rate of W_3, supply of labour hours is increased due to the income effect, but later, it is decreased due to the leisure effect. As a result, the supply curve bends backwards beyond W_3.

3.2.2 Factors Influencing the Price Elasticity of Supply

Elasticity of supply depends upon a number of factors, some of which are as given below:

1. *Nature of the product:* If a product is perishable, its supply is inelastic. It has to be sold whatever the price within a certain period. On the contrary, durable products have higher price elasticity of supply. Such products can be conveniently stored until the market offers a fair price for them. For some of the agricultural products that are perishable, their supply is inelastic. For others also, supply is inelastic due to inelastic supply of land.

2. *Nature of production costs:* If the costs decline with level of output, supply of such goods is highly elastic. On the contrary, if the costs rise with the output, supply is inelastic in nature.

3. *Nature of production technique:* If the technique of production is complex, the supply of products is inelastic. On the contrary, if the technique is simple and cheap, the supply is highly elastic.

4. *Nature of production period:* If the period of production is long, supply lags behind the demand and is usually inelastic in nature. For instance, supply of wheat is inelastic until the harvest time.

5. *Future expectations:* If price is expected to go up in future, current supply becomes inelastic. Sellers hold back the stocks with a view to come out with them at the time when they expect the price to go up.

6. *Degree of shiftability of resource:* If resources possessed by the producers can be shifted from current use to other uses, supply of other products can be increased when price of these products rises. Multi-product firms keep shifting their resources from production of one good to that of another on the basis of the price offered by the market. Thus, supply of some of the products of a multi-product firm is usually highly elastic.

3.3 PARTIAL PRICE ELASTICITIES

In our analysis so far, demand has been treated as a function of only one variable—be it price, consumers' income, or prices of related goods. While considering variations in demand in response to changes in one of them, we implicitly or explicitly assumed that the other determinants of demand remain unchanged. In real world, other determinants *do* change along with the one in question. A fall in price of the product may not take place in isolation. It might lead to a fall in price of a substitute or might even be a consequence of a fall in price of the said substitute. Likewise, a rise in price often leads to a rise in income of the consumers. We know that the salaries and wages of the working class get automatically adjusted upward through the system of additional dearness allowance which is linked to the price indices. That is what is meant by the 100% neutralization of inflation (price rise). In respect of some category of workers, neutralization of inflation may be partial only. Whatever the case, consumers' income rises every time price rises. It is a different matter whether it rises in full measure or in part. So long as it rises with rising prices, *ceteris paribus* clause can no longer be enforced. In fact, it is an unrealistic assumption. Its authenticity lies in the cause of analysis of the true nature of the relationship between two variables. For instance, the effect of a rise in price on demand may be offset by an appropriate rise in income. One might be led to believe that demand remains unaffected by the said changes in price and income. We know that this is not true. Study of price–demand relationship reveals that demand falls in response to a rise in price and that of income–demand relationship reveals that demand rises in response to a rise in income. The analysis of the two relationships, each in isolation from the other, helps understanding why demand remains unaffected when income and price both rise. The purpose of assumptions, thus, in any analysis, are never the over-simplification of the complex phenomena but splitting the complex phenomena in simple constituents to facilitate study of each in isolation from the others so that the complex phenomena remains no longer complex whenever its analysis is called for.

Treating demand of a product, A, as a function of its own price P_A, consumers' income, Y, and prices of the substitutes and/or complements, P_B, we can express the demand function as

$$Q_A^D = a - bP_A + cY - dP_B \qquad (3.14)$$

Equation (3.14) shows that Q^D varies inversely with P_A, directly with Y and inversely with P_B. Had we not analyzed the relationships individually, it would not have been possible for us to use the negative or the positive signs in the equation as we have done above. The use of the negative sign before P_B indicates that the products A and B are complements.

For the demand function in Eq. (3.14), three determinants influence demand simultaneously. Hence, we have three elasticities to deal with here. They are:

1. Price elasticity with respect to own price, E_{PA}^D
2. Income elasticity, E_Y^D
3. Cross-price elasticity with respect to the price of the complement B, E_{PA}^D

They are known as the partial elasticities and are given as:

$$E_{PA}^D = (\partial Q_A/\partial P_A)(P_A/Q_A) \tag{3.15}$$

$$E_{PB}^D = (\partial Q_A/\partial P_B)(P_B/Q_A) \tag{3.16}$$

$$E_Y^D = (\partial Q_A/\partial Y)(Y/Q_A) \tag{3.17}$$

The first component in each expression is the partial derivative. If the demand function is of the following type,

$$Q_A^D = aY/bP_B P_A \tag{3.18}$$

Or logarithmically of the type,

$$\log Q_A^D = \log a + \log Y - \log P_B - \log b - \log P_A \tag{3.19}$$

Differentiating Eq. (3.19) partially with respect to P_A, P_B and Y, we have

$$\partial Q_A/\partial P_A = Q_A \cdot (-1/P_A) \tag{3.20}$$

$$\partial Q_A/\partial Y = Q_A \cdot (1/Y) \tag{3.21}$$

$$\partial Q_A/\partial P_B = Q_A \cdot (-1/P_B) \tag{3.22}$$

Substituting these values in Eqs. (3.15), (3.16) and (3.17), we have

$$E_{PA}^D = (\partial Q_A/\partial P_A)(P_A/Q_A) = -1.00$$

$$E_{PB}^D = (\partial Q_A/\partial P_B)(P_B/Q_A) = -1.00$$

$$E_Y^D = (\partial Q_A/\partial Y)(Y/Q_A) = +1.00$$

Partial elasticities are not always unitary as above. Their values depend on the nature of the demand function. The reader is advised to verify the fact for the demand function

$$Q_A^D = a \cdot (P_A)^{-b} (P_B)^{+c} (Y)^{+d} \tag{3.23}$$

KEY TERMS AND CONCEPTS

Arc price elasticity of demand It is the ratio of proportionate change in demand with respect to the average demand to a proportionate change in price with respect to the average price.

Arc price elasticity of supply It is price elasticity of supply over the specified arc/segment of the supply curve. It is measured as a ratio of the proportionate change in quantity supplied with respect to the average supply along the arc/segment to the proportionate change in price with respect to the average price along the arc/segment of the supply curve.

Backward bending supply curve Supply curve of labour hours bends backwards when wage rate is raised beyond a certain level.

Cross-price elasticity of demand Responsiveness of demand of one product to a change in the price of a related good, when other things remain unchanged.

Degree of shiftability of resources.

Degrees of price elasticity of demand On the basis of its numerical value, price elasticity of demand is classified as:

1. Perfectly elastic, when price elasticity is ∞ (horizontal demand curve).
2. More than unitary elastic demand, when price elasticity > 1.
3. Unitary elastic demand, when price elasticity = 1.
4. Less than unitary elastic demand, when price elasticity < 1.
5. Perfectly inelastic demand, when price elasticity = 0 (vertical demand curve).

Elasticity of demand Responsiveness of demand to a change in one of its determinants while other determinants remain unchanged.

Measurement of the elasticity of demand It is measured as a ratio of the proportionate change in quantity demanded to a proportionate change in one of its determinants while other determinants remain unchanged.

Elasticity of supply It is the responsiveness of quantity supplied to a change in one of its determinants while other determinants remain unchanged.

Factors influencing the price elasticity of demand

1. Nature of commodity.
2. Availability of the substitutes.
3. Multiplicity of use.
4. Nature of use.
5. Deferred consumption.
6. Habits.
7. Income group of the consumer.
8. Proportion of income spent on the product.
9. Price level.
10. Time factor.

Important observations about the price elasticity of demand

1. Point price elasticity varies from point to point on a demand curve while arc price elasticity is the same over the entire arc or segment of the demand curve.
2. A steeper demand curve is less elastic than a flatter demand curve.
3. Two linear demand curves originating from the same point on the vertical axis (price-axis) and meeting the horizontal axis (quantity-axis) in two different points, have same price elasticity at a given price, despite different slopes.
4. Two linear parallel demand curves have different price elasticities at a given price despite same slope.
5. For intersecting demand curves, price elasticities are different at the point of intersection.

Measurement of cross-price elasticity of demand It is measured as a ratio of the proportionate change in quantity demanded of one product to a proportionate change in price of a related good, when other things remain unchanged.

Measurement of income elasticity of demand It is measured as a ratio of the proportionate change in quantity demanded to a proportionate change in income when other things remain unchanged.

Measurement of price elasticity of demand It is measured as a ratio of the proportionate change in quantity demanded to a proportionate change in price when other things remain unchanged.

Methods of measuring the price elasticity of demand

1. Flux's proportionality method:

$$\text{Price elasticity} = \frac{\text{Proportionate change in demand}}{\text{Proportionate change in price}}$$

2. Graphical method:
3. Marshall's total outlay method:
   Price elasticity is less than unitary when total expenditure on the product falls with price.
   Price elasticity is unitary when total expenditure remains unchanged in response to falling prices.
   Price elasticity is more than unitary when total expenditure increases with falling prices.

Point price elasticity of demand It is price elasticity of demand at a given point on the demand curve. It is given as the ratio of the length of the lower segment to that of the upper segment of the demand curve.

Point price elasticity of supply Price elasticity of supply at a given point on the supply curve.

Price elasticity of supply It is responsiveness of quantity supplied to a change in the price offered for the product by the market, while other things remain unchanged.

Factors influencing the price elasticity of supply

1. Nature of product.
2. Nature of production costs.
3. Nature of production techniques.
4. Nature of production period.
5. Future expectations.

Measurement of price elasticity of supply It is measured as a ratio of proportionate change in quantity supplied to a proportionate change in price offered by the market for the product, other things remaining unchanged.

Observations about the price elasticity of supply

1. Price elasticity of supply is 1 for a linear supply curve passing through the origin.
2. Price elasticity of supply is less than 1 for the linear supply curve intersecting the horizontal axis.
3. Price elasticity of supply is more than 1 for a linear supply curve intersecting the vertical axis.
4. Linear parallel supply curves have different price elasticities despite same slope.

EXERCISES

A. Short Answer Questions

Define the following (1 through 4):
1. Price elasticity of demand
2. Cross-price elasticity of demand
3. Price elasticity of supply
4. Income elasticity of demand

5. What is the significance of the sign of the cross-price elasticity?
6. What is the significance of the sign of the income elasticity?
7. What is the significance of the sign of the price elasticity of demand?
8. Explain the flux's method of measuring the price elasticity of supply.
9. What is the significance of the sign of the price elasticity of supply?
10. Name three factors that influence the price elasticity of demand.
11. Name three factors that influence the price elasticity of supply.

B. Long Answer Questions

12. Find elasticity of demand in each case at the indicated point:
    (a) $Q^D = 100{,}000/P$; $P = 100$.
    (b) $Q^D = 150{,}000/\sqrt{P}$; $P = 10{,}000$.
    (c) $Q^D = 10 + 3Y$; $Y = 15{,}000$. ($Y \equiv$ income)
    (d) $Q^D_{COFFEE} = 2 + 3P_{TEA}$; $P_{TEA} = 4$.
    (e) $Q^D_{INK\text{-}PENS} = 100 - 3P_{INK}$; $P_{INK} = 20$.
    [**Ans.** (a) -1, (b) -0.50, (c) $+0.9998$, (d) $+0.857$, (e) -1.50.]
13. Explain the total outlay method of determining the price elasticity of demand.
14. Show that the price elasticity of demand at a point on the demand curve is equal to the ratio of the length of the lower segment to that of the upper segment of the demand curve.
15. Show that the price elasticity of demand is unitary at every point on the demand curve:

$$Q = 1000/P$$

   [**Hint.** $E^D_P = (dQ/dP)(P/Q)$
   $= (-1000/P^2)\{P/(1000/P)\}$
   $= (-1000/P^2)\{P^2/1000\}$
   $= -1.00$]

16. Show that the price elasticity of demand varies inversely as the slope of the demand curve. What condition would you like to impose for the validity of this observation?

   [**Hint.** $E^D_P = (dQ/dP)(P/Q)$
   $= (1/dP/dQ)(P/Q)$
   $= (1/m)(P/Q)$

   where, $m \equiv$ the slope of the demand curve. $P/Q =$ constant]

17. What is the significance of the observation in Question 16? Explain with the help of a neat sketch.
18. Show that the price elasticity of demand varies from point to point on the same demand curve, from a lowest of zero to a highest of infinity.
19. For two linear parallel demand curves, show that the price elasticity of demand is not the same at a given price.
20. For two linear demand curves, originating from the same point on the vertical axis but touching the horizontal axis at the different points, show that the price elasticity of demand is same at a given price despite different slopes.

21. Given two linear demand curves, parallel to each other, mark off a point on each at which the price elasticity of demand is the same for each of them. Justify your choice of points geometrically or otherwise.
   [**Hint.** Let AB and $A'B'$ be two linear demand curves, parallel to each other. Draw a ray OR through the origin, intersecting the demand curve AB at point T and $A'B'$ at point S.
   Now make use of the similarity of triangles,
   $$\triangle OTB \sim \triangle OSB' \text{ and } \triangle OTA \sim \triangle OSA'$$
   to show that $BT/TA = B'S/SA'$

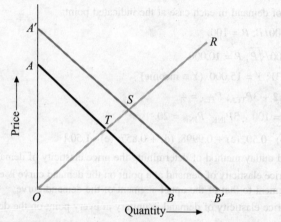

FIGURE 3.14 The required points are T on AB and S on $A'B'$

Alternatively, deduce that the price elasticity is same at points T and S on the grounds that:
   (a) The slopes of the two curves are the same at these points, and
   (b) The ratio of P/Q is also the same at each of these two points because each one lies on the ray, OR.]
22. Given two linear intersecting demand curves, show that the price elasticity of demand is not the same for the two at the point of intersection.
23. With the help of neat sketches, demonstrate different degrees of price elasticity.
24. On what factors does the price elasticity of demand depend?
25. What is meant by the market demand curve? Obtain the market demand curve from the data given below:

Price	10	8	6	4	3
Quantity A :	20	30	50	100	120
demanded B :	15	25	60	150	270
by C :	10	20	80	190	410

Calculate price elasticity of demand for each market segment when price falls from 10 to 6? Also calculate price elasticity of market demand for same change in price.
   [**Ans.** −3.75, −7.50, −17.50, −8.06]
26. The following data relate the demand schedule to the respective price elasticities of demand. Some of the entries are, however, missing. Find them and complete the table:

Elasticity of Demand and Supply

Price	100	80	75	70	60
Quantity demanded :	50	–	120	–	200
E_P^D :	–	–5.0	–	–3.75	–

[**Ans.** Q: 50, 100, 120, 150, 200. E_P^D: —, –5.0, –3.33, –3.75, –2.33]

27. Given the price elasticity of demand as –3, by what per cent would the consumption drop when the price of the product rises by 10%?
 [**Ans.** 30%]

28. Price of a product falls by 10%. In consequence, the total expenditure of the consumer rises by 20%. What can you say about the price elasticity of demand?
 [**Ans.** Total expenditure, E = Price · Quantity = PQ.

 The per cent increase in $E = \Delta E/E = \Delta(PQ)/PQ$

 $\Delta E/E = [P\Delta Q + Q\Delta P]/PQ$, (by product rule, $\Delta PQ = P\Delta Q + Q\Delta P$)

 $= P\Delta Q/PQ + Q\Delta P/PQ$

 $= \Delta Q/Q + \Delta P/P$

 As $\Delta E/E = 20\%$; $\Delta P/P = -10\%$, we have

 $\Delta Q/Q = 20\% + 10\% = 30\%$

 ∴ $E_P^D = (\Delta Q/Q)/(\Delta P/P)$

 $= 30/(-10) = -3$]

29. A doctor increases his consultation fee from ₹ 100 to ₹ 150. This leads to fewer patients per day but higher daily income for him. It rises from ₹ 10,000 to ₹ 12,000. What can you say about the price elasticity of demand from these observations?
 [**Ans.** –0.40. Following Marshall's total outlay method, elasticity of demand, in this case, is less than one in numerical terms. This is so because total expenditure of the patients increases with increasing price (fee). Since actual changes in price and quantity demanded are given, we can calculate actual value of E_P^D here.

 $P_1 = 100$, $Q_1 = 10,000/100 = 100$ patients

 $P_2 = 150$, $Q_2 = 12,000/150 = 80$ patients

 Thus, $E_P^D = \Delta Q/\Delta P \times P/Q$

 $= -20/50 \times 100/100$

 $= -0.40$

 Note that the expression, $\Delta E/E = [\Delta Q/Q] + [\Delta P/P]$ as derived in Question no. 28 is better suited for estimation of E_P^D at a point when changes in price and quantity are expressed as a percentage of original price and quantity. For actual changes in price and quantity if we employ Flux's proportionality method, the result would not tally with that obtained using the expression obtained in Question no. 28. Reader can verify that

 $\Delta E/E = [(12000 - 10000)/10000] = 0.20$

 $\Delta P/P = [(150 - 100)/100] = 0.50$

If we employ the expression of (Q. 28) for calculation of $\Delta Q/Q$, we get

$$\Delta Q/Q = (\Delta E/E) - (\Delta P/P)$$
$$= 0.20 - 0.50$$
$$= -0.30 \text{ or } 30\% \text{ fall in demand.}$$

and,
$$E_P^D = \Delta Q/Q \div \Delta P/P$$
$$= -0.30/0.50$$
$$= -0.60$$

Note that $\Delta Q/Q$ as calculated from actual data in this question is (–20%) and not (–30%). This explains the discrepancy between the values of price elasticities. The expression obtained in Question no. 28 is thus not applicable when actual values and changes therein are given.

When actual values are given, the correct methodology for estimation of $\Delta Q/Q$ is as given below:

$$\Delta E/E = [E_2 - E_1]/E_1$$
$$= [P_2 Q_2 - P_1 Q_1]/P_1 Q_1$$
$$= [P_2 Q_2 - P_2 Q_1 + P_2 Q_1 - P_1 Q_1]/P_1 Q_1$$

(adding and subtracting $P_2 Q_1$ in the numerator)

$$= [P_2(Q_2 - Q_1) + (P_2 - P_1)Q_1]/P_1 Q_1$$
$$= [P_2 \Delta Q + \Delta P \cdot Q_1]/P_1 Q_1$$
$$= P_2/P_1 [\Delta Q/Q_1] + \Delta P/P_1$$

$\Rightarrow \quad 0.20 = 150/100 \, (\Delta Q/Q) + (50/100)$

$\Rightarrow \quad \Delta Q/Q = -0.20$, not -0.30 as obtained from the expression in (Question no. 28).]

30. Price of a product increases by 10%. As a result, total expenditure on the product decreases by 50 %. What can you say about the price elasticity of demand for this product?
    [**Ans.** –6.00]

31. Arrange the following in ascending order of magnitude of the price elasticity of demand.
    (a) Salt, (b) Soap, (c) Penicillin, (d) Ice-cream, (e) Diamonds
    [**Ans.** Salt, Soap, Penicillin, Diamonds, Ice-cream]

32. Calculate price elasticity of supply if a rise in market price from ₹ 100 per unit to ₹ 110 per unit leads to an increase in quantity supplied from 10,000 to 18,000 units.
    [**Ans.** 8]

33. Quantity supplied is related to the price as

$$Q = 3P$$

Calculate price elasticity of supply at $P = 1000$.
[**Ans.** 1]

34. Show that a linear supply curve passing through origin is unitary elastic at every point on it.
35. Show that a linear supply curve having an intercept on the vertical axis is more than unitary elastic at every point on it.
36. Show that a linear supply curve having an intercept on the horizontal axis is less than unitary elastic at every point on it.

37. Two linear supply curves intersect each other at a point. Which one of the two would have a higher price elasticity at the point of intersection? Explain with help of a sketch.

38. Arrange the following supply schedules:
    (a) $Q = 3P + 20$
    (b) $Q = 3P$
    (c) $Q = 3P - 20$

    in ascending order of magnitude of the elasticity of supply. Give reasons in support of your answer.
    [**Ans.** Schedule 3, Schedule 2, Schedule 1]

39. Consider the following individual and market supply schedules:

Price (₹ /unit)	Firm A (units)	Firm B (units)	Firm C (units)	Industry (units)
100	20	—	30	50
120	40	20	40	10
130	30	40	80	150
140	50	30	120	200

    Plot the supply schedules of the firms and the industry. Calculate the price elasticity of supply for firm C when the price of the product goes up from ₹ 120 to ₹ 140.
    [**Ans.** 12]

40. Suppose a consumer spends whole of his income on two goods—X and Y. Let his income be $\overline{M}$ and the prices of X and Y, P_X and P_Y respectively. Show that both the goods can't be inferior.
    [**Ans.** Since the consumer spends whole of his income on these two goods

    $$\overline{M} = xP_X + yP_Y \qquad (1)$$

    Differentiating Eq. (1) with respect to $\overline{M}$, we have

    $$1 = P_X \cdot dx/d\overline{M} + P_Y \cdot dy/d\overline{M} \qquad (2)$$

    $\Rightarrow$
    $$1 = [x \cdot P_X/\overline{M} \cdot [\{dx/d\overline{M}\} \cdot \{\overline{M}/x\}] + [yP_Y/\overline{M}] \cdot [\{dy/dM\} \cdot \{\overline{M}/y\}] \qquad (3)$$

    (multiplying and dividing the first-term of the right-hand side of equation (2) by $x/\overline{M}$, and the second, by $y/\overline{M}$)

    $\Rightarrow$
    $$K_X \cdot \eta_X + K_Y \cdot \eta_Y = 1 \qquad (4)$$

    Where

    $K_X \equiv xP_X/\overline{M} \equiv$ proportion of income spent on good X

    $K_Y \equiv yP_Y/\overline{M} \equiv$ proportion of income spent on good Y

    $\eta_X \equiv$ income elasticity of demand for good X

    $\eta_Y \equiv$ income elasticity of demand for good Y

    K_X and K_Y are both positive fractions. Each represents proportion of income spent on the respective goods.
    If both of η_X and η_Y are negative, the left-hand side of Eq. (4) would be a negative number which is not possible as the right-hand side is +1. However, one of the two can be negative subject to the condition that the expression on the left-hand side is +1. Likewise, both the elasticities can be positive subject to the condition that the left-hand side is equal to +1. Thus, either both of the income elasticities are positive or just one of them is positive, but both can't be negative. Hence both the goods can't be inferior goods.]

41. A consumer spends 30% of his income on X and the rest on Y. Find the income elasticity of demand for good X, given that the income elasticity of demand for good Y is

   (a) 0.50
   (b) 1.00
   (c) 1.50
   (d) 0.00
   (e) 4.00

   [**Ans.** (a) +2.17, (b) 1.00, (c) −0.17, (d) +3.33, (e) −6.00]
   [**Hint.** Use equation (4) of question (40). For instance, in part (a), $\eta_Y = 0.50$, $K_Y = 0.70$, $K_X = 0.30$. Hence,

   $$0.30\,(\eta_X) + 0.70\,(0.50) = 1$$
   $$\Rightarrow \quad \eta_X = (1 - 0.70 \times 0.50)/0.30$$
   $$= (0.65)/0.30$$
   $$= +2.17]$$

42. An individual spends whole of his income on two goods X and Y. Suppose an increase in price of X induces an increase in demand for commodity Y. Can you infer anything about the price elasticity of demand for good X?

   [**Ans.** Greater than 1. Use Marshall's total outlay method. A rise in price of commodity X raises demand of commodity Y. This means that expenditure incurred on commodity Y increases. Therefore, expenditure on X must decrease. This happens in response to a rise in price of X. Since a rise in price of X reduces expenditure on X, the price elasticity of X must be greater than 1 according to Marshall's total outlay method.]

43. Suppose a consumer spends her entire income on purchase of two commodities X and Y. Suppose further that the consumer's price elasticity of demand for commodity X is less than 1. Using calculus, prove that X and Y are complements.

   [**Ans.** We know that the consumer's budget line in this case would be

   $$xP_X + yP_Y = \bar{M} \tag{1}$$

   where, $\bar{M}$ is consumer's fixed income which she spends on goods X and Y at respective prices of P_X and P_Y. Differentiating Eq. (1) with respect to P_X, we have

   $$x \cdot 1 + P_X \cdot \frac{dx}{dp_X} + Y \cdot \frac{dP_Y}{dP_X} + P_Y \cdot \frac{dy}{dP_X} = 0$$

   $\Rightarrow \quad [1 + (dx/dP_X)(P_X/x)] + y \cdot 0 + [P_Y/x][dy/dP_X] = 0$

   (dividing on both the sides by x and substituting $dP_Y/dP_X = 0$)

   $\Rightarrow \quad [1 + E^X_{PX}] + [P_Y/x][dy/dP_X] = 0$

   $\Rightarrow \quad [1 + E^X_{PX}] + [P_Y/x][\{dy/dP_X\}\{P_X/y\}]\{y/P_X\} = 0$

   (multiplying and dividing the second term by P_X/y)

   $\Rightarrow \quad [1 + E^X_{PX}] + [P_Y/x][E^Y_{PX}]\{y/P_X\} = 0$

   $\Rightarrow \quad (y \cdot P_Y/x \cdot P_X)\,E^Y_{PX} = -[1 + E^X_{PX}]$

   $\Rightarrow \quad E^Y_{PX} = -(x \cdot P_X/y \cdot P_Y)[1 + E^X_{PX}]$

   $\quad\quad\quad = -\alpha\beta$; where, $(x \cdot P_X/y \cdot P_Y) = \alpha\,(\alpha > 0), [1 + E^X_{PX}] = \beta\,(\beta > 0)$

   $\Rightarrow \quad E^Y_{PX} < 0$

[*Note:* $\alpha > 0$ because $(x \cdot P_X / y \cdot P_Y) > 0$ and $\beta > 0$ because $[1+ E_{PX}^X] > 0$ whenever $|E_{PX}^X| < 1$. Given that $|E_{PX}^D| < 1$, we have $E_{PX}^Y < 0$ {take $E_{PX}^X = \pm 1/2$ or $\pm 3/4$ to understand}]

$\Rightarrow$ The cross-price elasticity of demand for good Y with respect to the price of good $X(E_{PX}^Y)$ is negative.
$\Rightarrow$ X and Y are complements (cross-price elasticity is negative for the complements).

44. Demand for a product A, is a function of its own price P_A, price of the substitute P_B and income of the consumers Y. It is given as

$$Q_A^D = 1000 - 7P_A + 0.50Y + 1.25P_B$$

Determine partial elasticities at a point of time when $P_A = 120$, $P_B = 100$ and $Y = 5000$.
[**Ans.** $E_{PA}^A = -0.302$, $E_{PB}^A = +0.045$, $E_Y^A = +0.898$]

C. Essay Type Questions

45. Explain the factors that influence the price elasticity of demand.
46. Explain the factors that influence the price elasticity of supply.
47. "Slope of the demand curve is a rough measure of the price elasticity of demand." Examine the statement.
48. Go through (Question no. 50) of Chapter 2 and examine the statement for its validity. Split the statement into its constituents (four parts) and establish each separately.

4

Approaches to Demand Analysis and Consumer Behaviour

CHAPTER OUTLINE

Introduction
- Theory of Demand—Cardinal Utility Approach
- Theory of Demand—Ordinal Utility or Indifference Curve Approach
- Expansion Path
- Price Effect and Its Components—The Income and the Substitution Effects
- Applications of Indifference Curves
- The Composite Commodity Theorem
- Critique of Indifference Curve Approach
- The Revealed Preference Approach
- Key Terms and Concepts
- Exercises
- Case Study: The Food Stamp Programme and Social Welfare

INTRODUCTION

In Chapter 2, we discussed how market demand and supply curves lead to market equilibrium. We also saw there how these curves are obtained through horizontal summation of the individual demand and supply curves. In our analysis, we resorted to the laws of demand and supply to draw the individual demand and supply curves. Little did we think then of the equilibrium of an individual consumer or an individual producer, who, by all means, are responsible for individual demand and individual supply curves.

In this chapter, we will take up the equilibrium of an individual consumer and in the next, we will take up that of an individual producer.

For the equilibrium of individual consumer, we first need to discuss various approaches to demand analysis. Traditionally, there are three of them:
(a) Marshallian Cardinal Utility Approach
(b) Hicks–Allen Indifference Curves Theory or Ordinal Utility Approach, and
(c) Samuelson's Revealed Preference Approach

Let us take them up in their requisite detail below:

4.1 THEORY OF DEMAND—CARDINAL UTILITY APPROACH

The concept of utility owes its origin to Jeremy Bentham and his fellow utilitarians of eighteenth century. It, however, acquired its precise meaning in nineteenth century through the collective efforts of W.S. Jevons, L. Walrus, Carl Menger and Alfred Marshall. The emerging concept, called **marginal analysis**, finally formed the basis of the theory of consumer behaviour.

Leaving alone the definitions of utility, as given by these economists, let us focus on their essence. Utility of a product refers to its capability of satisfying human needs. Its most important feature is its subjectivity. That is, a product possessing utility for one consumer may not possess any for another. For instance, a book on biology is said to possess utility for a student of biology, but not for a student of economics. This is so because the former has a need for it, while the latter hasn't. Also, the former is willing to pay for it, while the latter isn't. This explains subjectivity of utility. It is, however, not to be confused with 'usefulness'. Despite having no utility for an economics student, the book, if gifted to him/her, may come of some use to him/her. For instance, he may use it as a décoration piece on his/her bookshelf to impress visitors or may sell it off to a student of biology or to a scrap-vendor. As for him/her, it is a book on economics that possesses utility. Thus, if a product has the capability to satisfy a human need, it is said to possess utility for the individual in question, else, it does not. What more, a product may possess utility for one consumer, but disutility for another. One man's mutton may be another's poison!

Another feature common to the definitions of utility was its measurability. Bentham invented a unit for its meaurement. He called it '**util**' though he failed to provide a precise definition to it. Alfred Marshall, on the other hand, felt contented with the notion of its numerical measurement through monetary units.

4.1.1 Assumptions of Cardinal Utility Approach

Assumptions underlying this approach to demand analysis are as stated below:

1. *Rationality of consumer:* The consumer is a rational person, aiming at maximization of total utility. The maximization is subject to the constraint imposed by his income, which is fixed. A rational consumer attempts to attain as high a level of total utility as is possible for him with the given level of income.

2. *Utility is cardinal:* Utility of a commodity is numerically measurable. The most convenient measure of utility is the quantity of money which a consumer is prepared to pay for a unit of the commodity.

3. *Constant marginal utility of money:* This assumption was regarded essential for a monetary measure of utility. No measuring rod can serve as a standard measure if it is elastic or flexible itself in its length. If the marginal utility of money (the utility of an additional unit of

money) changes with a change in the level of consumer's income, money as a measuring rod of utility of a commodity would become an elastic ruler, measuring different utilities of the same unit at different levels of a consumer's income. A ten-rupee note would have much higher utility for a poor consumer than for a rich consumer. Money as a flexible measuring rod would become inappropriate for measurement of utility of a product*.

4. *Diminishing marginal utility of commodity:* The utilities gained from the consumption of successive units of a commodity have a diminishing trend. In other words, marginal utility of a commodity diminishes each time a consumer has an additional unit of the commodity for his consumption.

5. *Additivity of utility:* The total utility of a basket of goods is the sum-total of the utilities of the individual commodities in the basket.

If there are n commodities in the basket with quantities $x_1, x_2, \ldots, x_n$; the total utility is given as

$$U = f(x_1, x_2, \ldots, x_n) = U_1(x_1) + U_2(x_2) + \cdots + U_n(x_n)$$

The additivity assumption was, however, dropped in the later versions of the cardinal utility theory.

4.1.2 Consumer's Equilibrium

In a single commodity model, a consumer buys quantity x of the commodity X or retains his money income M, which is given. The consumer will attain his equilibrium when the marginal utility of $X(MU_X)$ is equated to the market price of the commodity (P_X). That is,

$$MU_X = P_X** \tag{4.1}$$

---

* Also see, A. Koutsoyiannis, *Modern Microeconomics,* 2nd ed., The Macmillan Press Ltd., p.14.

**To derive the condition, let us express consumer's problem through a mathematical model:

Consumer's objective: Maximization of total utility, $U = f(x)$

Consumer's limitation: Budget constraint, $[x.P_X] \leq M$

Consumer's problem is one of constrained maximization. It can be solved by maximizing the excess of the utility derived over the utility foregone in terms of money income sacrificed. Let the excess be Φ, so that,

$$\Phi = U - x \cdot P_X$$

Given the price of $X(P_X)$, differentiating Φ with respect to x to get

$$d\Phi/dx = dU/dx - P_X$$

Setting $d\Phi/dx$ at zero for maximization, we have

$$dU/dx = P_X$$
$$\Rightarrow MU_X = P_X$$

This gives the necessary condition of maximization. To find the sufficient condition, differentiate Φ with respect to x for the second time so that

$$d^2\Phi/dx^2 < 0$$
$$\Rightarrow d^2U/dx^2 < 0$$
$$\Rightarrow d(dU/dx) < 0$$
$$\Rightarrow d(MU_X)/dx < 0$$
$$\Rightarrow \text{Slope of } MU_X < 0$$

Note that the assumption of diminishing MU also requires $d(MU_X)/dx < 0$. The assumption is thus well founded mathematically.

If $MU_X > P_X$, the consumer can increase his satisfaction by having more of X, else, if $MU_X < P_X$, the consumer can increase his satisfaction by cutting the consumption and holding his income unspent. In a multiple commodity model, the condition of the consumer's equilibrium may be expressed as

$$MU_X/P_X = MU_Y/P_Y = \cdots = MU_n/P_n \qquad (4.2)$$

In other words, the consumer will be in equilibrium when the ratios of the marginal utilities of the individual commodities to their market prices are same.

It is possible to derive demand curve of a commodity from Eq. (4.1), as shown in Figure 4.1.

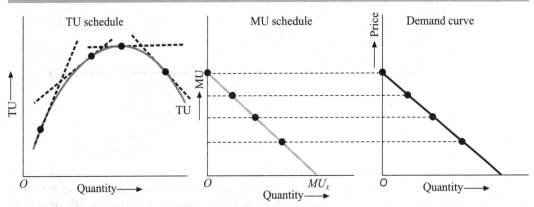

FIGURE 4.1 Derivation of demand curve from the marginal utility schedule: In the first panel, tangents are drawn to the TU schedule to show how slope of MU_X diminishes with increasing x. MU_x schedule in panel second demonstrates the fact. Numerical equality of MU_X to P_X gives the demand curve in third panel.

The diminishing MU_X schedule gives the demand schedule through point-to-point correspondence between MU_X and P_X as shown in the figure by means of the horizontal projections.

Let us now demonstrate how a consumer in a one-commodity world reaches equilibrium. Think of a consumer who has to decide the optimal number of bananas to consume with a given budget. Suppose the price of a banana is fixed at ₹ 2 and our consumer is hungry having nothing else available. Suppose further that the consumer buys bananas piece-by-piece and marginal utilities of successive pieces are ₹ 8 for the first, ₹ 7 for the second, ₹ 6 for the third and so on; diminishing by one rupee each time an additional piece is bought (Table 4.1). Proceeding this way, marginal utility of the 7th banana works out at ₹ 2. It is quite obvious that so long as the consumer is hungry and so long as the marginal utility of a banana is higher than its price, the consumer would continue buying them if his budget permits. The optimal number of bananas that must be bought is thus *seven* (Figure 4.2). He may go at most for the 8th if still hungry but that would not be in line with the *rationality assumption*.

TABLE 4.1 Marginal Utility (MU) schedule for consumption of bananas

No. of bananas consumed:	1	2	3	4	5	6	7	8	9	10	11	12
Marginal utility (₹):	8	7	6	5	4	3	2	1	0	−1	−2	−3
Price (₹):	2	2	2	2	2	2	2	2	2	2	2	2

The equilibrium level of consumption of bananas is thus *seven* as the marginal utility of the seventh banana equals its price, ₹ 2. For each of the subsequent pieces, marginal utility is less than its price.

The illustration explains Marshall's cardinal utility approach which is based on the subjectivity and numerical measurability of utility. A consumer attempts maximization of the excess of utility derived over the sacrifice of purchasing power made.

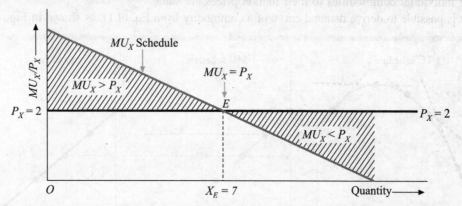

FIGURE 4.2 Equilibrium level of consumption of bananas: Equilibrium of the consumer takes place at E, the point where $MU_X = P_X$. The MU curve slopes downward from left to right demonstrating the law of diminishing marginal utility. Price of the product being fixed, the horizontal price line cuts the MU curve E, the point of equilibrium.

4.1.3 Critique of the Cardinal Utility Approach

The cardinal utility approach suffers from the following drawbacks:

1. The second assumption of the cardinal utility is unrealistic. Utility is an abstract attribute like honesty, intelligence, etc. Numerical measurement of such attributes is not possible in absolute terms.
2. The assumption of constant marginal utility of money is also unrealistic. Every additional unit of money spent on a commodity has a higher utility than that possessed by the preceding unit of it spent. In other words, marginal utility of money increases with increasing expenditure. Similarly, use of money as a numerical measure of utility is inappropriate. Marginal utility of money is different at different levels of income. How can then money be used as a measuring rod for utility when its own value is unstable?
3. The law of diminishing marginal utility of a commodity has been established from introspection with little empirical support. We know that marginal utility of commodity diminishes only for certain goods in certain circumstances. For instance, in the illustration in Figure 4.2, if a consumer has one banana in breakfast each morning, the marginal utility of each of the 12 bananas may be same everyday. It diminishes only when all of them are consumed at a point of time one after another. Moreover, marginal utility of a commodity such as money or diamond never diminishes. The same is the case with a lot of other durable and semi-durable goods.

4.2 THEORY OF DEMAND–ORDINAL UTILITY OR INDIFFERENCE CURVE APPROACH

The indifference curve approach to analysis of demand was initiated by the English economist *F. Y. Edgeworth* (1881). It was extended by the Italian economist *Vilfredo Pareto* (1906) and Soviet economist *Eugen Slutsky* (1915). Logical perfection to it was however given by two English economists *R. G. D. Allen* and *J. R. Hicks (1934)**. *J. R. Hicks* further developed it in his books 'Value and capital' (1939)** and 'Revision in Demand Theory' (1956).

Before coming to the indifference curve approach to demand, let us outline its main assumptions first.

4.2.1 Assumptions of Indifference Curve Approach to Demand

1. *Rationality of the consumer:* Consumer is assumed to be a rational person, always aiming at maximization of his utility given his income and prices of goods. He is further assumed to possess all the relevant information to serve his objectives.

2. *Utility is ordinal:* Axiomatically, consumer is capable of ranking different baskets of goods in order of his preferences. In other words, the consumer need not know the absolute numerical measures of utilities possessed by two baskets of, say, apples and oranges but for sure he knows which one of them he would prefer over the other.

3. *Diminishing marginal rate of substitution*[†]*:* Consumers' preferences are ranked in terms of indifference curves, assumed convex to the origin. In other words, the rate at which a consumer foregoes quantities of one good (say, Y) for the sake of an additional unit of the other (say, X) depicts a diminishing trend as more and more of the latter (X) are had. This implies that *the slope of the indifference curve increases from left to right as we go down the curve.* Marginal rate of substitution of X for Y (written as $MRS_{X,Y}$), representing the numerical value of the slope of the indifference curve, therefore, diminishes with successive additional doles of good X had in place of Y.

---

* J.R. Hicks and R.G.D. Allen, *A Reconsideration of the Theory of Value,* Economica (1934)
** J.R. Hicks,*Value and Capital*, Oxford University Press,1939. J.R. Hicks got a Nobel prize for this work.
[†] The assumption of diminishing marginal rate of commodity substitution was made by the proponents of the indifference curve approach basically to avoid the mention of diminishing marginal utilities and monetary measurement thereof. The objective was to steer clear of the concept of cardinal utilities and their monetary measurements. The reasons for this were mainly two – *first*, monetary measure of abstract things like utility/ marginal utility poses several problems apart from the problem of their subjectivity. *Second*, marginal utility of money itself being nonconstant – increasing with increasing expenditure and decreasing with increasing income – the problem of monetary measurement of utilities and marginal utilities poses further complications. How could a measuring rod as elastic and as flexible as money be used as a standard measure of another parameter? That was why exponents of the cardinal utility had explicitly assumed that marginal utility of money is constant. This we know attracted a lot of criticism from several corners. Despite their efforts, the exponents of the ordinal utility approach could succeed only in avoiding the explicit mention of the diminishing marginal utility. Its concept and its measurement however remained intact implicitly in the assumption of diminishing marginal rate of commodity substitution, as evidenced below.

We know that the slope of a curve, at any point on it, is equal to the slope of the tangent to the curve at that point. The utility function, as seen earlier, is

$$U = f(x, y)$$

(contd.)

4. *Total utility of the consumer depends on the quantities of commodities consumed:* If $x_1, x_2, ..., x_n$ represent quantities of goods $X_1, X_2, ..., X_n$, the total utility U is given by

$$U = f(x_1, x_2, ..., x_n)$$
$$= u_1(x_1) + u_2(x_2) + \cdots + u_n(x_n)$$

5. *Consistency and Transitivity of choice:* Consumer is assumed to be consistent in his choices, that is, if he chooses Bundle A over Bundle B in one period, he will not choose Bundle B over Bundle A in another period, when both the bundles are available to him. Symbolically,

If $\qquad\qquad A > B$, then $B \not> A$

In like manner, his choices are also characterized by transitivity, that is if Bundle A is preferred over Bundle B and Bundle B over C, then Bundle A is preferred over Bundle C. Symbolically,

If $\qquad\qquad A > B$ and if $B > C$, then $A > C$

4.2.2 Indifference Curves (ICs)

Suppose the consumer is in a two-commodity world. He consumes quantities x and y of goods X and Y respectively. Prices of the two goods are given as P_X and P_Y. Total utility derived by the consumer from these quantities is U, given as

$$U = f(x, y) \qquad (4.3)$$

Here, U is a function of x and y. It shows that utility, U, depends on the quantities of the two goods consumed. To derive a fixed level of utility, $\bar{U}$, a consumer may have more of X with less of Y or more of Y with less of X. Level of utility derived from each being the same, our consumer will be indifferent in between the two. In other words, it would not matter whether he has more of X with less of Y or more of Y with less of X so long as he has the same level

---

(*Footnote contd.*)
where, $U = \bar{U}$, constant for an indifference curve and x and y are the quantities of commodities X and Y. The expression for the slope of the IC can be had from the expression of the total defferential,

$$dU = (\partial U/\partial x)\cdot dx + (\partial U/\partial y)\cdot dy$$
$$= MU_X \cdot dx + MU_Y \cdot dy$$

Since $U = \bar{U}$ for an indifference curve, $dU = d\bar{U} = 0$. Substituting this in the expression above, we have

$$dy/dx = -(MU_X/MU_Y)$$

The left-hand side represents the slope of the indifference curve. Its numerical value, defined as the $\mathbf{MRS}_{X,Y}$ is given as

$$\mathbf{MRS}_{X,Y} = |dy/dx| = |-(MU_X/MU_Y)| = |(MU_X/MU_Y)|$$

Clearly, diminishing $\mathbf{MRS}_{X,Y}$ implies diminishing MU_X for the preferred commodity X and/or increasing MU_Y for the sacrificed commodity, Y. Hence the concept of the diminishing marginal utilities is implicit in the assumption of diminishing marginal rate of commodity substitution.

of utility from each of the two. To demonstrate, let the two commodities be oranges (X) and apples (Y). Then, so long as the utility derived by the consumer from 10 oranges with 50 apples is the same as that derived from 50 oranges with 10 apples or from 20 oranges with 30 apples, the consumer in question will be, indifferent in between these combinations. For him, one bundle is as good as another. Plotting the combinations (10, 50), (20, 30) and (50, 10) of the two fruits with oranges on the x-axis and apples on y-axis and joining the points by means of a smooth curve, we get a curve called the *indifference curve*. The nomenclature is deliberate. One can use *fixed utility curve* as an alternative but use of *indifference curve* is to emphasize consumer's indifference in between the bundles each of which offers the same utility to the consumer. Here, the curve is *convex to the origin* (Figure 4.3). Consumer's preferences that lead to an indifference curve such as this are called *convex preferences*.

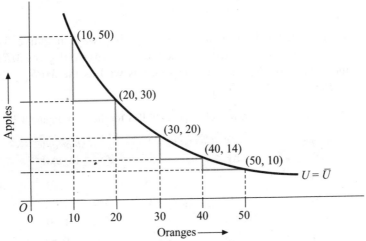

FIGURE 4.3 Indifference curve (IC): It is the locus of all possible combinations of two goods each of which offers same level of satisfaction (utility, $\bar{U}$) to the consumer to the extent that the consumer turns indifferent in between any two of them. Each of the combinations (10, 50), (20, 30), (30, 20), (40, 14) and (50, 10) in the figure stands for the same level of utility, $\bar{U}$ with the result that the consumer turns indifferent in between any two of them. The combinations here lead to an indifference curve convex to the origin. Consumer's preferences such as these are known as convex preferences. Note how the rate of sacrifice of apples changes each time 10 additional oranges are had by the consumer. The rate, called the Marginal Rate of Substitution of X for Y, written as $MRS_{X,Y}$, depicts a diminishing trend from left to right along the curve. $MRS_{X,Y}$ can therefore be defined as the rate at which commodity Y is sacrificed by the consumer per additional unit of commodity X had.

An *indifference curve* (IC) can thus be defined as *the locus of various combinations of quantities of two goods each of which offers the same level of satisfaction (utility $\bar{U}$) to the consumer to the extent that the consumer turns indifferent in between any two of them*. Utility derived by the consumer being fixed, the utility function of Eq. (4.3) transforms to

$$\bar{U} = f(x, y) \tag{4.4}$$

where, $\bar{U}$ is fixed level of utility derived from bundles (x, y).

The slope of the curve portrayed in Figure 4.3 is negative. It increases as we go down the curve from left to right. Its numerical value $|\Delta y/\Delta x|$, called the Marginal Rate of substitution of X for Y would therefore diminish from left to right along the curve. Written as $MRS_{X,Y}$, it is given is

$$MRS_{X,Y} = \left| \frac{\text{Quantity of } Y \text{ foregone } (\Delta y)}{\text{Quantity of } X \text{ gained } (\Delta x)} \right|$$

$$= \left| \frac{\Delta y}{\Delta x} \right|$$

$$= -\left(\frac{\Delta y}{\Delta x} \right)$$

$$= |\text{Slope of IC}| \quad (4.5)$$

Note that the ratio of a change in Y to a change in X is always negative for a downward sloping curve. Its numerical value, $|\Delta y/\Delta x|$, also defined as $[-(\Delta y/\Delta x)]$ gives $MRS_{X,Y}$. Table 4.2 demonstrates the mechanism of determining the slope as well as the $MRS_{X,Y}$. Shortly, we are going to show that $MRS_{X,Y} = |MU_X/MU_Y|$

TABLE 4.2 Determination of slope and MRS for the IC in Figure 4.3

Oranges (X)	Apples (Y)	Changes		Slope of IC ($\Delta y/\Delta x$)	$MRS_{X,Y}$ $|\Delta y/\Delta x|$
		Δy	Δx		
10	50	–	–	–	–
20	30	–20	+10	–2.00	2.00
30	20	–10	+10	–1.00	1.00
40	14	–06	+10	–0.60	0.60
50	10	–04	+10	–0.40	0.40

In Table 4.2, as quantity of X increases, that of Y decreases. Thus, changes in y are negative, while those in x, positive. The ratio $\Delta y/\Delta x$ is negative. It increases from (–2.00) to (–0.40) from left to right along the Indifference Curve (IC). The numerical value (modulus) of the slope, defined as **MRS**$_{X,Y}$, decreases from 2.00 to 0.40 as we go down the curve. The fact is known as the *law of diminishing marginal rate of substitution of X for Y*.

Consumer preferences such as these that lead to an indifference curve convex to the origin or to the diminishing marginal rate of commodity substitution are known as convex preferences, as stated earlier. Such preferences lead to negative slope of the indifference curve and are called the *monotonic preferences*. To provide an illustrative definition, if (x_1, y_1) is a bundle (combination) of two goods and if (x_2, y_2) is a bundle of two goods with at least as much of both the goods and more of one, then consumer's preference to (x_2, y_2) over (x_1, y_1), written as $(x_2, y_2) > (x_1, y_1)$, is known as the monotonic preference. How could such preferences lead to a negative slope? To understand, see Figure 4.4. Such preferences imply 'more is better' which is abbreviated as **MIB**. As the saying goes, excess of everything is bad, the assumption of MIB holds only to a certain point in consumption. If goods are consumed beyond this point, called the point of satiation, *'more is no longer better'*.

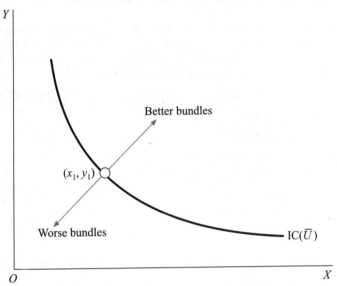

FIGURE 4.4 Monotonic preferences: Bundle (x_1, y_1) lies on the indifference curve, $\bar{U}$. Bundles with at least as much of both the goods and more of one, if preferred by a consumer, would imply his **monotonic preferences**. Starting from bundle (x_1, y_1) and moving anywhere up and to the right is moving to the preferred zone while moving down and to the left is moving to the non-preferred zone. All the better bundles in the preferred zone imply at least as much of two goods as offered by a bundle on the IC and more of one. The IC, therefore, serves as the lower boundary of the preferred zone. This is possible only when the IC is negatively sloped, as in the figure.

Preference to bundle (3, 3) over bundles (0, 0), (0, 1), (0, 2), (0, 3), (1, 0), (1, 1), (1, 2), (1, 3), (2, 0), (2, 1), (2, 2), (2, 3), (3, 0), (3, 1) and (3, 2) is a monotonic preference. It implies at least as much of both the goods as each of the rejected bundles offer and more of one of the two goods. Assuming linear preferences the indifference curve that serves as the lowest boundary of the preferred zone has bundles (1, 0) and (0, 1); the lowest-but-one boundary of the preferred zone has bundles (2, 0), (1, 1) and (0, 2); the lowest-but-two boundary of the preferred zone has bundles (3, 0), (2, 1), (1, 2) and (0, 3); the lowest-but-three boundary of the preferred zone has bundles (3, 1), (2, 2), (1, 3) while the lowest-but-four boundary of the preferred zone has bundles (3, 2) and (2, 3). The highest boundary for the data given contains bundle (3, 3). Each of them represents a distinct IC. Ranking of the ICs in order of preference is shown in Table 4.3. Each of the six ICs has a negative slope. Bundle (3, 3) is an *isolated bundle*. It would fall on the highest IC provided such IC exists. Existence or non-existence of an IC for an isolated bundle depends on whether the nature of the consumer's preferences is known or not. In our case the nature of the consumer preferences being given as linear, as in Figure 4.5, the bundle (3, 3) would fall on a linear IC. Had the consumer preferences been convex, it would have fallen on a convex IC as in Figure 4.3. Ranking the bundles as in Table 4.3, we can draw ICs at least for the bundles ranked 1 to 6 (Figure 4.5). Given that the preferences are linear, as in this case, it is possible to ascertain an IC for each one of the bundle-sets listed against each rank. Figure 4.5 depicts ICs for bundle-sets ranked 1 to 6 in Table 4.3.

TABLE 4.3 Given the consumer preferences as linear, all the bundles except that in bold faced figures are ranked in order of utility levels $U_6 > U_5 > U_4 > U_3 > U_2 > U_1$ (Figure 4.5). Bundles ranked from 1 to 6 can all be portrayed through linear ICs under the assumption of linear preferences. ICs, one above the other, representing distinct levels of utilities, comprise an **Indifference Map**.

Ranks	Bundles	Indifference Curves (ICs)
1	(3, 3)	U_6
2	(2, 3), (3, 2)	U_5
3	(1, 3), (2, 2), (3, 1)	U_4
4	(1, 2), (2, 1), (0, 3), (3, 0)	U_3
5	(0, 2), (1, 1), (2, 0)	U_2
6	(0, 1), (1, 0)	U_1
7	**(0, 0)**	

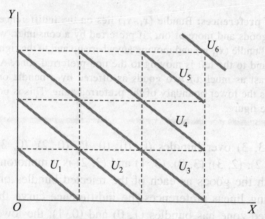

FIGURE 4.5 Given consumer's preferences as linear, bundles representing identical utility levels are portrayed on one IC. There are six ICs as shown. The lowest one having zero quantities of both the goods is not portrayed because it offers no utility to the consumer. In order of preference, $U_6 > U_5 > U_4 > U_3 > U_2 > U_1$. The lowest boundary of the preferred zone is defined by U_1 and the highest by U_6. Each of the six has a negative slope, confirming the fact that the preferences represented by it are monotonic preferences. When consumer's preferences are linear the locus of $f(x, y) = \bar{U}$ is a straight line with a downward slope. It can be given by $ax + by = c$, where a, b and c are all constants. ICs are linear when the two goods in question are **perfect or net substitutes** of each other. As discussed later in this section, perfect substitutes are rare in real world. What we often come across are **close or gross substitutes** like pepsi and coke, tea and coffee, etc. Note that $MRS_{X, Y}$ is constant for a linear IC.

Besides monotonic, convex and linear preferences, consumers are known to have quasi-linear preferences as in Figure 4.6, discrete preferences as in Figure 4.7, Cobb Douglas preferences as in Figure 4.8 and homothetic preferences as in Figures 4.43 to 4.45.

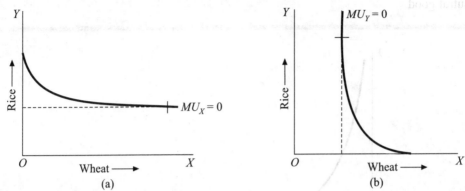

FIGURE 4.6 Quasi-linear preferences: When ICs are partly linear and partly non-linear, they are called *quasi-linear*. As in panel (a), consumer has a marked preference for good Y over good X. After a certain level of consumption, good X behaves like a neutral good offering no utility to the consumer who turns reluctant to give away good Y for good X. An example from the real world is provided by the marked preference to rice over wheat depicted by certain communities in India. The case in panel (b) is, in a way, opposite of the case in panel (a). Here, good Y turns neutral to the consumer after a certain level of its consumption. Utility offered by it becomes zero with the result that the consumer refuses to exchange his preferred commodity X for it. The example cited above may be reverted to explain the phenomenon. Certain communities in India depict a marked preference for wheat over rice. Algebraic expression for the IC in the left panel may take the form $U = y + \log x$ or $U = y + \sqrt{x}$ while that for the IC in the right panel may take the form $U = x + \log y$ or $U = x + \sqrt{y}$.

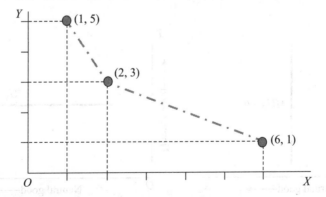

FIGURE 4.7 Discrete preferences: When goods are consumed or bought in whole number or non-fractional units, consumer's preferences are called **discrete or integer preferences**. For instance, cars and scooters can never be bought or used in fractional quantities. One can have one car with 5 scooters or 2 cars with 3 scooters or 6 cars with 1 scooter but no one can have 1.45 cars with 3.68 scooters or 1.93 pencils with 3.23 pencil cutters. Note that $MRS_{X, Y}$ is ill-defined in this case.

In the same way, commodities can be classified as neutral goods as in Figure 4.9 and bad goods (economic bads) as in Figures 4.10 to 4.12. Utility contributed by a unit of the neutral good is zero and that by a unit of an economic bad is negative. Cigarettes and alcohol are both economic bads as both are injurious to health. For a student of economics, a book on biology is a neutral good.

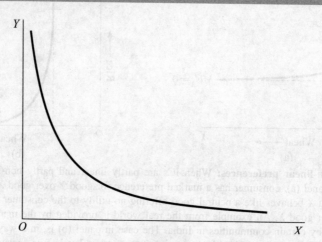

FIGURE 4.8 Cobb Douglas preferences: Such preferences refer to bundles generated by a utility function resembling the Cobb Douglas production function, $\bar{Q} = f(L, K) = AL^\alpha K^\beta$. Following the pattern, the utility function describing such preferences is $\bar{U} = f(x, y) = Ax^\alpha y^\beta$. For instance, a utility function $\bar{U} = 100\, x^{1/3} y^{2/3}$ represents Cobb Douglas preferences. It leads to an IC distinctly convex to the origin. The preferences portrayed are monotonic and $MRS_{X,Y}$ diminishes from left to right.

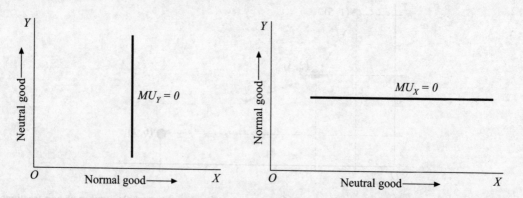

FIGURE 4.9 One of the two goods is a neutral good: When Y is a neutral good ($MU_Y = 0$), the IC is a straight line parallel to the y-axis (left panel) and when X is a neutral good ($MU_X = 0$), it is a straight line parallel to the x-axis (right panel). Note that $MRS_{X,Y}$ is infinite in the left panel and zeo in the right panel.

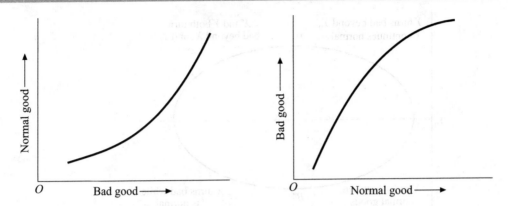

FIGURE 4.10 One of the two goods is a bad good: When good X is a bad good (such as cigarettes, liquor, etc.), $MU_X < 0$ (negative). The IC in this case (left panel) develops a positive slope (depicting non-monotonic preferences) with convexity to the axis (x-axis) measuring the bad good. Alternatively when Y is a bad good, $MU_Y < 0$ (negative). The IC (right panel) again assumes a positive slope (depicting non-monotonic preferences) with its convexity to the axis (y-axis) measuring the bad good.

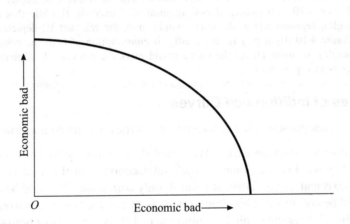

FIGURE 4.11 When both goods are bad goods: When each of the two goods is an economic bad (one is, say, liquor and the other, cigarettes) so that $MU_X < 0$ and $MU_Y < 0$ (both causing disutility), the IC is concave to the origin depicting *non-convex or concave preferences*. The consumer has to give up some quantity of one bad good if he desires to have more of the other. Note that $MRS_{X,Y}$ increases from left to right in this case.

Changes in shapes of ICs caused by variations in consumer preferences or the nature of one or both of the two goods consumed are quite interesting. Before proceeding to the analysis of consumer's equilibrium, it would be in order to discuss some of these shapes and to study some interesting properties of the indifference curves.

According to the saying *excess of everything is bad*, even normal goods turn bad if consumed beyond a certain limit. The situation is potrayed in Figure 4.12.

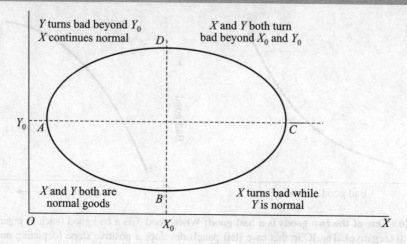

FIGURE 4.12 *Excess of everything is bad* is demonstrated here through the changing slope of the IC. Consumption of goods X and Y beyond quantities X_0 and Y_0 proves bad for the consumer. In case consumption is restricted to X_0 of X and Y_0 of Y, segment AB of the curve would mark the relevant IC depicting convex preferences (bottom-left quadrangle); if consumption of X exceeds X_0 while that of Y restricted to Y_0 (bottom-right quadrangle), segment BC of the curve would mark the relevant IC depicting non-monotonic preferences as in Figure 4.10 (left panel), if consumption of Y exceeds Y_0 while that of X restricted to X_0 (top-left quadrangle), segment AD of the curve would mark the relevant IC depicting non-monotonic preferences as in Figure 4.10 (right panel), and finally, if consumption of both the goods exceeds X_0 and Y_0 (top-right quadrangle), segment DC of the curve would mark the relevant IC depicting non-convex or concave preferences as in Figure 4.11.

4.2.3 Features of Indifference Curves

The indifference curves possess a few interesting properties. Let us demonstrate them below:

1. *The ICs never intersect an axis:* We establish the property by contradiction. Suppose, to the contrary, they do. Let the points of their intersection with the axes be points A and B respectively on x-axis and y-axis. Then, at point A, only commodity X would be consumed while at B, only Y would be consumed. This shows that only one of the two goods would be consumed at these points. This violates the implicit assumption that IC is the locus of non-zero quantities of the two goods that yield a fixed level of utility for the consumer (Figure 4.13). Our assumption is therefore false. This establishes the property.

2. *A higher IC represents a higher utility:* Figure 4.14 establishes the property. Monotonicity of preferences implying more is better (MIB) comes handy in this regard. Combinations on U_2 represent more of at least one of the two goods than those on U_1. That establishes the property.

3. *ICs do not intersect each other:* The property can be established by contradiction. Let there be two ICs offering distinct utilities U_1 and U_2. Suppose, if possible, that the two intersect each other at point $E(x_0, y_0)$. The point (x_0, y_0) is a combination of two goods which represents a definite utility, say U_0. Since the point lies on both the ICs, $U_1 = U_2 = U_0$. But $U_1 \neq U_2$ as given. Our assumption, therefore, leads us to a contradiction. Hence, it is false and the two distinct ICs

never intersect each other. An alternative method of establishing the property is demostrated in Figure 4.15.

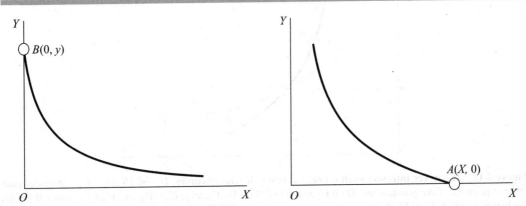

FIGURE 4.13 **ICs never intersect the axes:** In the left panel, IC is assumed to intersect y-axis at point $B(0, y)$ and in the right panel, it is assumed to intersect x-axis at point $A(x, 0)$. At each of these points, only one good is consumed. This leads to a violation of the implicit assumption that ICs trace out positive quantities of the two goods that offer a certain level of utility to the consumer. Our assumption thus leads us to a contradiction and is therefore false.

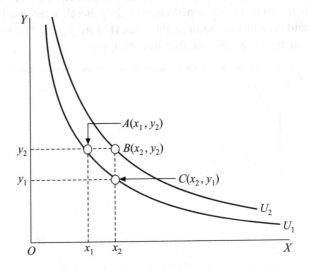

FIGURE 4.14 **A higher IC represents higher utility:** A higher IC stands for a higher utility and a lower IC, for a lower utility. U_1 is a lower IC while U_2, a higher one. Take points A, B and C as shown so that points A and C fall on U_1 and B on U_2. Points A and B are in a horizontal line while points C and B, on a vertical line. Utility derived at point $B(x_2, y_2)$ is higher than what it is at point $A(x_1, y_2)$ or at $C(x_2, y_1)$. The conclusion follows from assumption 4 of the IC approach or from the MIB-assumption implied by the monotonicity of preferences. Thus, U_B (meaning utility at point B) > U_A or U_C. Note that $U_A = U_C$ because points A and C both lie on same IC, U_1. At point B, a consumer may have more of at least one of the two goods than what he may at points A or $C(x_2 > x_1$ and $y_2 > y_1)$.

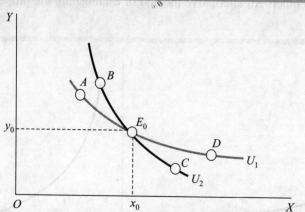

Figure 4.15 ICs never intersect each other: Let two indifference curves, U_1 and U_2 ($U_1 \neq U_2$), intersect each other at point E_0. Take points A and D on U_1 and C and B on U_2. Clearly, $U_A = U_D$ and $U_B = U_C$. Since B lies on the higher IC (U_2), $U_B > U_A$. Likewise, point D lies on higher IC (U_1), $U_D > U_C$ or $U_A > U_B$ (since, $U_D = U_A$ and $U_B = U_C$). The conclusions $U_B > U_A$ and $U_A > U_B$ contradict each other. Hence our assumption that the two distinct ICs intersect each other leads us to a contradiction and hence is false. ICs, therefore, do not intersect each other.

4. *No two ICs are parallel to each other:* The fact that ICs do not intersect each other does not necessarily imply that they are parallel to each other. In fact ICs may be best described as parts of the elliptical curves (oval-shaped curves). In general, inter-spacing between any two is maximum in the middle and minimum at the ends (Figure 4.16). The ICs, therefore, neither intersect each other nor they are even parallel to each other.

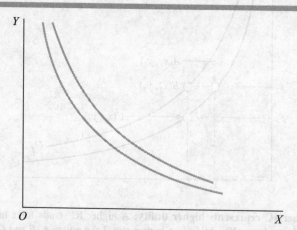

FIGURE 4.16 No two ICs are parallel to each other: Inter-spacing between the ICs is not the same in the middle as that at the ends.

5. *ICs are convex to the origin:* The assumption of diminishing marginal rate of commodity substitution (Assumption 3) was intended to ensure convexity of IC to the origin. The assumption implies that the numerical value of the slope of an IC diminishes from left to right along the IC. In other words, the actual value of the slope (with the negative sign) increases along the curve

from left to right. This, in the language of differential calculus, implies that the slope of the curve (dy/dx) is an increasing function of x. That is,

$$d(dy/dx)/dx > 0$$

or
$$d^2y/dx^2 > 0 \qquad (4.6)$$

That is, an IC convex to the origin implies that $d^2y/dx^2 > 0$. In other words, Eq. (4.6) provides the necessary condition for IC to be convex to the origin. Is the condition a sufficient one as well? The answer is in affirmative*.

Proceeding likewise, the reader can show that $d^2y/dx^2 = 0$ is the necessary and sufficient condition for linearity of IC and that $d^2y/dx^2 < 0$ is the necessary and sufficient condition for concavity of IC to the origin.

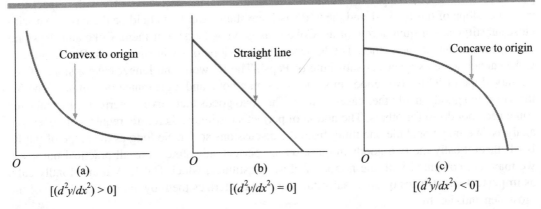

FIGURE 4.17 ICs are convex to the origin: In (a) second-order derivative of y with respect to x is positive, in (b), it is zero and in (c) it is negative. In other words, MRS diminishes in (a), increases in (c) and is unchanged in (b) from left to right along the respective curves. Curves in (b) and (c), therefore, cannot represent indifference curves according to the IC theory.

---

*We can establish the fact in either of the following two ways:

(1) Whenever $d^2y/dx^2 > 0$, we must show that the IC has to be convex to the origin.

$$d^2y/dx^2 > 0$$
$\Rightarrow \quad d(dy/dx)/dx > 0$
$\Rightarrow \quad (dy/dx)$ is an increasing function of x
$\Rightarrow \quad$ Slope of IC increases with increasing x
$\Rightarrow \quad MRS_{X,Y}$ decreases with increasing x
$\Rightarrow \quad$ IC is convex to origin.

Thus, expression 4.6 provides the necessary and sufficient condition for the convexity of IC.

(2) When $d^2y/dx^2 \not> 0$ or when $d^2y/dx^2 \leq 0$ we must show that the IC is non-convex to the origin.

Let $\quad d^2y/dx^2 = 0$
$\Rightarrow \quad d(dy/dx)/dx = 0$
$\Rightarrow \quad (dy/dx) = $ constant
$\Rightarrow \quad$ IC is linear (non-convex)

(contd.)

4.2.4 Conditional Properties of the Indifference Curves

Under special circumstances, ICs possess exceptional shapes. Let us consider the following:

1. *For perfect substitutes, if any, ICs are linear:* If the two goods were perfect substitutes of each other, the indifference curves would be linear with constant marginal rate of commodity substitution as shown in Figure 4.17(b). There is a big *if* here that deserves a little discussion. Is it possible for any two goods to be perfect substitutes of each other? If yes, do they deserve to be treated as two different goods? Pepsi in can and Pepsi in bottle can serve as perfect substitutes of each other provided both have same price, same quantity and offer same level of satisfaction. But then, are the two different products to be plotted on two different axes? Two cigarettes of the same brand are perfect substitutes of each other but they are not treated as two different products. If two goods are perfect substitutes of each other, the derivative of y with respect to x = -1, i.e. slope of the IC is -1 and the MRS is 1(constant). But that could be the case even with close substitutes. For quite a few of us, Coke is as good as Pepsi. For them, Coke and Pepsi are perfect substitutes of each other. The IC would have a slope of -1 in such cases. But for others, Coke cannot serve as a perfect substitute of Pepsi. The IC would no longer have a slope of -1. Unitary slope of IC for two goods in some cases may not stand a guarantee of unitary slope for the same two goods in all other cases as well. Thus two goods that serve as perfect substitutes for some need not do so for others. The notion of perfect substitutes, therefore, requires an extensive analysis. We may conclude one thing from the discussions so far. So long as the slope of the IC is -1, theoretically the two goods in question are perfect substitutes. For all practical purposes, we may feel contented with the notion of close substitutes, which Hal R. Varian* fondly calls as **imperfect substitutes** or gross substitutes and characterizes them by the positive slope of the cross demand, i.e. by

$$dPx/dy > 0 \qquad (4.7)$$

For our purpose, a simple distinction between the perfect and the close substitutes would serve the purpose. A red pencil is a perfect substitute of a blue pencil for someone who does not care about the colour. A pen and a pencil are by no means perfect substitutes.

2. *For perfect complements, ICs are L-shaped:* Two goods are said to be *perfect complements* provided one is completely useless without the other. For example, ink and ink-pens are perfect complements. In like manner, petrol and petrol-car are also perfect complements. But for a car that is designed to run on petrol as well as on the cooking gas, car and petrol are simply *gross*

Footnote (Contd).

Now let $d^2y/dx^2 < 0$
$\Rightarrow$ $d(dy/dx)/dx < 0$
$\Rightarrow$ (dy/dx) is a decreasing function of x
$\Rightarrow$ Slope of IC decreases with increasing x
$\Rightarrow$ MRS$_{X,Y}$ increases with increasing x
$\Rightarrow$ IC is concave (non-convex) to origin.

The arguments show that a positive non-zero value of the second-order derivative of y with respect to x serves as the necessary and sufficient condition for convexity of IC.

* Hal R. Varian, *Intermediate Microeconomics*, 5th ed., W. W. Norton & Company, New York, p. 112.

complements. Left foot shoe and the right foot shoe are perfect complements if they are of the same colour, same size and same make. In terms of cross demand, two goods are said to be perfect complements provided slope of the cross-demand is negative, i.e.,

$$dPx/dy < 0 \qquad (4.8)$$

Comparing Eqs. (4.7) and (4.8), the reader may have an idea about complements and substitutes. To avoid advanced treatment at this stage, it would better to treat these two definitions to relate to the **gross substitutes** and **gross complements**. Figure 4.18 demonstrates the nature of the IC for the perfect complements.

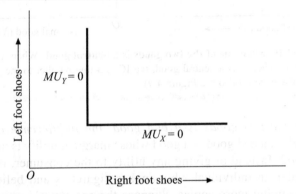

FIGURE 4.18 IC for perfect complements: IC for perfect complements is made up of two linear segments—one horizontal and the other vertical. Along the horizontal segment, marginal utility of the right foot shoes is zero and so is that of the left foot shoes along the vertical segment.

The utility function for perfect complements takes the form:

$$U = f(x, y)$$
$$= \text{minimum of } \{ax, by\} \qquad (4.9)$$

That is, if $ax < by$, $U = \{ax, ax\}$; and if $ax > by$, $U = \{by, by\}$. In the former case, the utility is equivalent to that derived from ax pairs of the perfect complements while in the latter case, utility is equivalent to that derived from by pairs of the perfect complements. For example, suppose you have 4 pairs of shoes—4 left foot shoes matched with 4 right foot shoes. Utility derived from them is the utility derived from these 4 pairs. Now suppose you add 4 right foot shoes so that you have 4 left foot shoes with 8 right foot shoes. The utility derived now is min{8, 4}, which is utility derived from 4 right foot shoes and 4 left foot shoes or utility derived from 4 pairs of shoes only. Likewise, if 4 left foot shoes are added, $U = \min \{4, 8\}$, which is utility derived from 4 right foot shoes and 4 left foot shoes or utility derived from just 4 pairs of shoes. The additional left foot shoes or the additional right foot shoes have zero marginal utilities.

3. *When one of the two goods is a neutral good, the IC is a straight line parallel to the axis on which the neutral good is measured (Figure 4.19).*

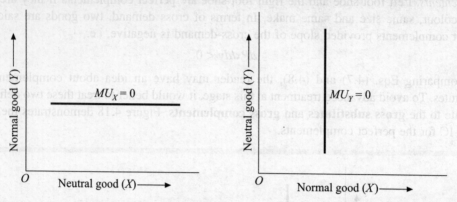

FIGURE 4.19 **Shape of IC when one of the two goods is a neutral good:** When X is a neutral good, the IC is parallel to the x-axis and when Y is a neutral good, the IC is a line parallel to the y-axis. A neutral good is one whose Marginal Utility is zero (also see Figure 4.9).

4. *When one of the two goods is a bad good, the indifference curve has a positive slope:* As stated earlier, a bad good is a good whose marginal utility is negative. For instance, cigarette is a bad good. Instead of giving any utility to the consumer, it causes injury to his health. Let us consider an individual who smokes cigarettes and believes that he can get away with it by consuming more apples. Suppose the consumer's estimate of the marginal utility of a cigarette is (−5) and that of the an apple is (+10). Different combinations of these two goods that give him a definite level of utility are as given in Table 4.4. Representing cigarettes on the x-axis and apples on the y-axis, we get an upward sloping indifference curve as shown in Figure 4.20.

TABLE 4.4 Data for the shape of IC when one of the two goods is bad

Number of cigarettes smoked :	2	4	8	10	12	16	20
Number of apples consumed :	3	4	6	7	8	10	12
Total utility :	20	20	20	20	20	20	20

5. *When both the goods are bad goods, the IC is a downward sloping one with its concavity to the origin:* When both the goods are bad goods, such as cigarettes and alcohol, the consumer derives disutility from the consumption of either or both. Different combinations of the bad goods that cause a fixed level of disutility lead to an indifference curve that slopes downwards with its concavity to the origin. Figure 4.21 portrays such an indifference curve. Reader can try some combinations of such goods. If the quantity consumed of one of the two is increased, that of the other is to be decreased so as to maintain a fixed level of disutility. Consumer preferences of this type are referred to as the *concave preferences*, as shown earlier in this section.

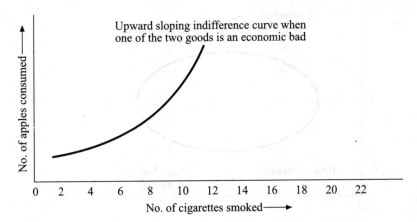

FIGURE 4.20 **Shape of the IC when one of the two goods is a bad good:** When one of the two goods is an economic bad, the consumer has to increase the quantity of the normal good so as to neutralize the disutility caused by increasing quantities of the economic bad. It is through such adjustments that the consumer retains a fixed utility, say, 20 units (Table 4.4) [also see Figure 4.10].

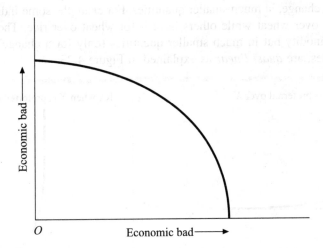

FIGURE 4.21 **Shape of the IC when both goods are bad goods:** When both goods are bad goods, the indifference curve has its concavity to the origin. Such preferences are termed **concave preferences** (also see Figure 4.11).

6. *When each of the two goods turns bad after a certain level of consumption, shape of the IC changes:* As the saying goes, excess of everything is bad. Many goods turn bad if consumed beyond a certain limit. Indifference curves for such goods are portrayed in Figure 4.22.

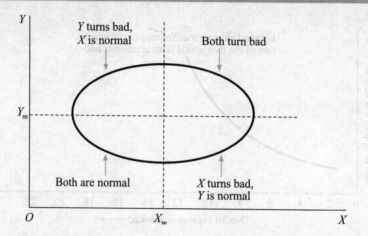

FIGURE 4.22 Changes in the shape of the IC with changing nature of the two goods: If consumed up to (X_m, Y_m), both goods behave as normal goods; beyond X_m of X and Y_m of Y, both turn bad (also see Figure 4.12).

7. *When consumer has a marked preference for one of the two goods, ICs are quasi-linear:* There are people who strongly prefer one good over the other. They can, however, have the other good but only for a change, in much smaller quantities. For example, some Indians have a marked preference for rice over wheat while others have it for wheat over rice. They do consume the non-preferred commodity but in much smaller quantities (only for a change). The indifference curves, in such cases, are *quasi-linear* as explained in Figure 4.23.

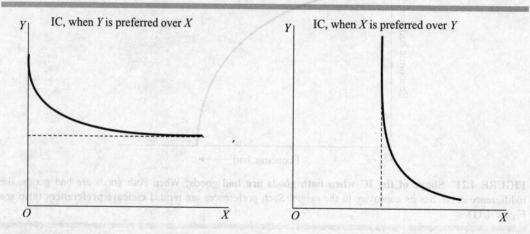

FIGURE 4.23 ICs are quasi-linear when one of the two goods is preferred over the other: When consumer has a strong preference for Y over X (left panel) or for X over Y (right panel), the IC is quasi-linear. In either case, the consumer does not want to have less than a certain minimum of the preferred commodity (also see Figure 4.6).

After knowing the indifference curves, their nature and their properties clearly, we are all set to discuss consumer's equilibrium with the help of indifference curves.

4.2.5 Consumer's Equilibrium

Consumer's equilibrium in a two-commodity world requires familiarity with indifference curves and budget line. The concept of indifference curves already introduced, we need to introduce the concept of budget line in its requisite detail. Just as an IC is the locus of points representing different combinations of quantities of two goods that offer a fixed level of satisfaction (utility) to the consumer, a budget line is the locus of points representing different combinations of quantities of two goods that cost the consumer a fixed amount of money (budget) at the given prices. The set of points on the budget line is known as the **budget set**. Figure 4.24 shows the shape of the budget line. It slopes downwards with a slope numerically equal to the price ratio, P_X/P_Y.

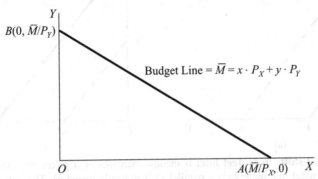

FIGURE 4.24 Consumer's budget line: The budget line AB ($\bar{M} = x \cdot P_X + y \cdot P_Y$) is a join of A ($\bar{M}/P_X$, 0) and B (0, $\bar{M}/P_Y$). Its slope is $-(P_X/P_Y)$.

Price of Y remaining the same, a fall in price of commodity X decreases the price ratio causing an outward pivotal shift in the budget line while a rise in it, increases the price ratio causing an inward pivotal shift in the budget line (Figure 4.25).

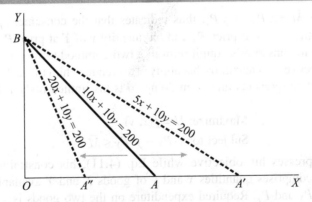

FIGURE 4.25 Pivotal shifts in budget line: Price of Y remaining the same, a fall in price of X pivots the budget line BA upwards to BA' and a rise in it pivots it downwards to BA''. If $\bar{M} = 200$, $P_X = 10$ and $P_Y = 10$, the budget line BA is $200 = 10x + 10y$. If P_X falls to 5, it pivots to BA' ($200 = 5x + 10y$) and if it rises to 20, it pivots to BA'' ($200 = 20x + 10y$).

When income of the consumer increases while product prices remain unchanged, or when prices of both the goods fall in the same proportion while consumer's income remains unchanged, the budget line undergoes a parallel shift upwards [Figure 4.26(a)]. The opposite is the effect on the budget line of a decrease in income while product prices remain unchanged or of a simultaneous increase in product prices by a fixed proportion when consumer's income remains unchanged [Figure 4.26(b)].

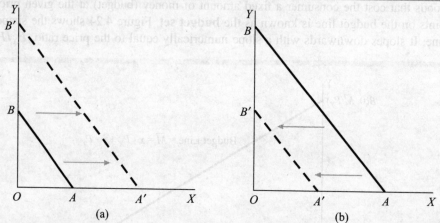

FIGURE 4.26 Parallel shifts in budget line: If income increases or if prices of both the goods fall in the same proportion, the budget line undergoes a parallel shift upwards (panel a). The opposite is the effect of a decrease in income or a simultaneous increase in prices of the two goods by the same proportion (panel b). For example, if consumer's income doubles from 200 to 400 when prices of both the goods remain unchanged at 20 and 10 respectively or when prices of both the goods fall to half as much each, i.e. to 10 and 5 respectively when income of the consumer remains unchanged at 200, the budget line shifts upwards to right, parallel to itself, as shown in panel (a). The opposite is the effect when income of the consumer falls to half as much, to 100, with unchanged prices of the two goods or when prices of the two goods increase to twice as much each, i.e. to 40 and 20 respectively while income remains unchanged at 200 (panel b).

The budget line, $\bar{M} = x \cdot P_X + y \cdot P_Y$, thus indicates that the consumer spends whole of his income, $\bar{M}$, on quantity x of X at price P_X and on quantity y of Y at price P_Y.

Let us now turn to consumer's equilibrium in a two-commodity world.

Consumer's objective is to maximize his utility. This requires him to reach the highest possible indifference curve. What prevents him from doing so is his limited budget. Mathematically, he intends to

$$\text{Maximize: } U = f(x, y) \qquad (4.10)$$
$$\text{Subject to: } x \cdot P_X + y \cdot P_Y \leq \bar{M} \qquad (4.11)$$

Equation (4.10) expresses his objective while Eq. (4.11), his constraint. Here, the utility maximizing bundle comprises quantities x and y of goods X and Y available to the consumer at respective prices P_X and P_Y. Required expenditure on the two goods is $x \cdot P_X + y \cdot P_Y$, which the consumer has to finance from his budget, $\bar{M}$. Constraint (4.11) requires expenditure on two goods to be less than or equal to $\bar{M}$. Assumed to be a utility maximizer, a consumer has to make the most of the available budget. Hence, the constraint $x \cdot P_X + y \cdot P_Y \leq \bar{M}$ is converted to $x \cdot P_X + y \cdot P_Y = \bar{M}$. The mathematical expression of the consumer's problem now transforms to

Approaches to Demand Analysis and Consumer Behaviour

$$\text{Maximize: } U = f(x, y) \quad (4.12)$$

$$\text{Subject to: } x \cdot P_X + y \cdot P_Y = \overline{M} \quad (4.13)$$

It is to be noted that the problem is no longer one of simple maximization. Had it been so, use of simple calculus would have taken care of it. The problem instead relates to constrained maximization, which we need to convert into simple maximization. Employing the technique of Lagrange's multiplier*, we merge the constraint and the objective function to develop a composite function for the purpose and apply calculus thereafter. The condition of consumer's equilibrium that works out is

$$MU_X/MU_Y = P_X/P_Y \quad (4.14)$$

---

*We explain here the Lagrange's Method of constrained maximization. It requires familiarity with partial differentiation. Re-writing Eq. (4.13) as

$$xP_X + yP_Y - \overline{M} = 0$$

and developing a composite function, Φ, with the help of the Lagrange's multiplier, λ, a constant, we have:

$$\Phi = U - \lambda(xP_X + yP_Y - \overline{M})$$

Differentiating Φ partially with respect to x, y and λ, we have

$$\partial\Phi/\partial x = \partial U/\partial x - \lambda P_X = 0 \quad (1)$$

$$\partial\Phi/\partial y = \partial U/\partial y - \lambda P_Y = 0 \quad (2)$$

$$\partial\Phi/\partial \lambda = -(xP_X + yP_Y - \overline{M}) = 0 \quad (3)$$

From Eqs. (1) to (3), we have

$$\partial U/\partial x = \lambda P_X$$

$$\partial U/\partial y = \lambda P_Y$$

and

$$xP_X + yP_Y = \overline{M}$$

Implying, in that order,

$$MU_X = \lambda P_X$$

$$MU_Y = \lambda P_Y$$

$$\Rightarrow \quad MU_X/MU_Y = P_X/P_Y \quad (4)$$

Equation (4) gives the required condition of equilibrium of the consumer. Here,

$$\partial U/\partial x = MU_X \quad \text{and} \quad \partial U/\partial y = MU_Y$$

The mathematical requirement for maximization of a function of two variables comprises the following three conditions:
1. The first-order partial derivatives are zero, i.e.

$$\partial\Phi/\partial x = 0 \quad \text{and} \quad \partial\Phi/\partial y = 0$$

2. The second-order partial derivatives are negative at the point where the first-order partial derivatives are zero, i.e.

$$\partial^2\Phi/\partial x^2 < 0 \quad \text{and} \quad \partial^2\Phi/\partial y^2 < 0$$

3. The product of the second order partial derivatives is greater than the square of the cross partial derivatives, i.e.

$$(\partial^2\Phi/\partial x^2)(\partial^2\Phi/\partial y^2) > (\partial^2\Phi/\partial x\,\partial y)^2$$

The right-hand side of Eq. (4.14) gives the price ratio* of the two goods while its left-hand side gives $MRS_{X,Y}$**.

For diagrammatic representation of the consumer's equilibrium, we require to superimpose the budget line (Figure 4.24) and the indifference map (Figure 4.27) into same commodity space (Figure 4.28). The latter, the indifference map, consists of a number of indifference curves, one above the other, representing distinct levels of utilities available to the consumer.

The highest attainable IC for the consumer is U''. Consumer's budget line BA touches U'' at e (Figure 4.28). At this point, the slope of the budget line $(-P_X/P_Y)$ is equal to the slope of U'' $(-MU_X/MU_Y)$ and the equilibrium basket of the consumer is (x_e, y_e).

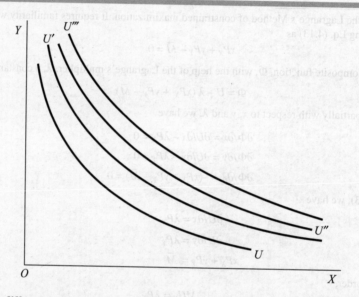

FIGURE 4.27 Indifference map. Consumer's indifference map comprises indifference curves U, U', U'' and U''', where, $U''' > U'' > U' > U$. The one closest to the origin (U) represents the lowest level of utility available and the one farthest away from the origin represents the highest level of it.

---

*Differentiating Eq. (4.13) with respect to x, we have

$$(dy/dx) = -(P_X/P_Y) \qquad (5)$$

Equation (5) gives the slope of the budget line. Its numerical value gives the price ratio of the two goods.
**Substituting $U = \bar{U}$ in the expression of total differential

$$dU = (\partial U/\partial x) \cdot dx + (\partial U/\partial y) \cdot dy \qquad (6)$$

With
$$dU = d\bar{U}$$
$$= 0 \qquad (\bar{U} \text{ is constant})$$

Equation (6) read with this, gives

$$(dy/dx) = -(MU_X/MU_Y) \qquad (7)$$

Equation (7) gives the slope of the indifference curve. Its modulus gives the $MRS_{X,Y}$.

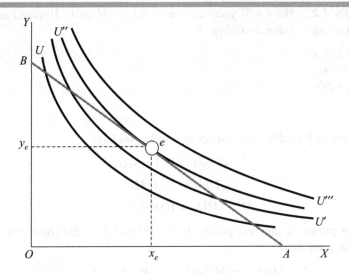

FIGURE 4.28 Consumer's quilibrium: Consumer's budget line AB ($\bar{M} = x \cdot P_X + y \cdot P_Y$) touches the indifference curve U'' at e. At this point, slope of the indifference curve is equal to the slope of the budget line. In other words, $MRS_{X,Y} = P_X/P_Y$. Equilibrium basket of the consumer is (x_e, y_e).

ILLUSTRATION 4.1: Given the utility function

$$U = 1000\, x^{1/3}\, y^{2/3}$$

and the consumer's budget

$$3000 = 100x + 50y$$

determine the equilibrium basket for the consumer.

Solution: Differentiating the utility function partially with respect to x and y, we have

$$\partial U/\partial x = (1000/3) \cdot (y/x)^{2/3} = MU_X$$
$$\partial U/\partial y = (2000/3) \cdot (x/y)^{1/3} = MU_Y$$
$$\therefore \qquad MU_X/MU_Y = (y/2x)$$

Given the prices of the two goods, $P_X = 100$ and $P_Y = 50$ (From the equation of the budget line), we have

$$(y/2x) = (100/50)$$
$$\Rightarrow \qquad y = 4x$$

Substituting in the equation of the budget line, we have

$$x = 10, \text{ and } y = 40$$

This gives the equilibrium basket for the consumer.

ILLUSTRATION 4.2: How will your answer to the problem in Illustration 4.1 change if the utility functions were given as follows?

(a) $U = 100x + 50y$
(b) $U = 50x + 100y$
(c) $U = 200x + 50y$

Solution:

(a) Differentiating partially with respect to x and y, we have

$$\partial U/\partial x = 100 = MU_X$$
$$\partial U/\partial y = 50 = MU_Y$$
$$\therefore \quad MU_X/MU_Y = 100/50 = 2$$

Given the prices of the two goods, $P_X = 100$ and $P_Y = 50$ (from the equation of the budget line), we have

$$MRS_{X,Y} = MU_X/MU_Y = P_X/P_Y = 2$$

That is, $MRS_{X,Y} = P_X/P_Y$ for all baskets represented by the utility function or by the budget line. In other words, the budget line and the indifference curve coincide each other, as shown in Figure 4.29. This implies existence of **infinitely many solutions**, that is, one basket on the budget line or indifference curve is as good as another. Note that a linear indifference curve indicates that the two goods are perfect substitutes.

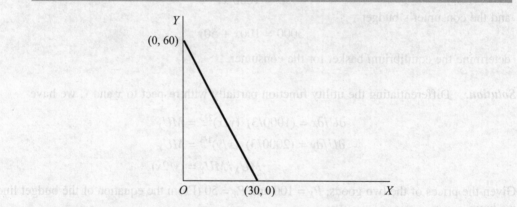

FIGURE 4.29 Infinitely many solutions: Utility function ($U = 100x + 50y$) coincides with the budget line ($3000 = 100x + 50y$), yielding infinitely many solutions.

(b) Differentiating partially with respect to x and y, we have

$$\partial U/\partial x = 50 = MU_X$$
$$\partial U/\partial y = 100 = MU_Y$$
$$\therefore \quad MU_X/MU_Y = 50/100 = 1/2$$

Given the prices of the two goods,
$$P_X = 100 \text{ and } P_Y = 50$$
we have
$$P_X/P_Y = 100/50 = 2$$
Clearly,
$$MU_X/MU_Y < P_X/P_Y$$
IC is therefore flatter than the budget line.
Goods being substitutes, (0, 60) would optimize consumer's utility (Figure 4.30).

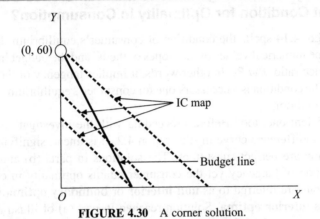

FIGURE 4.30 A corner solution.

(c) Differentiating partially with respect to x and y, we have
$$\partial U/\partial x = 200 = MU_X$$
$$\partial U/\partial y = 50 = MU_Y$$
$$\therefore \quad MU_X/MU_Y = 200/5 = 4$$

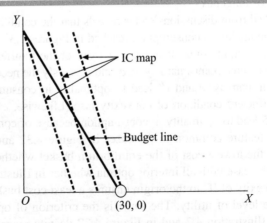

FIGURE 4.31 A corner solution.

Given the prices of the two goods, $P_X = 100$ and $P_Y = 50$, we have

$$P_X/P_Y = 100/50 = 2$$

Clearly,

$$MU_X/MU_Y > P_X/P_Y$$

This time, IC is steeper than the budget line.

Again, the utility function being linear, the goods are substitutes. (30, 0) would optimize consumer's utility (Figure 4.31).

4.2.6 Is Tangency of the Budget Line to the Indifference Curve a Sufficient Condition for Optimality in Consumption?

We have seen that Eq. 4.14 spells the condition of consumer's equilibrium. In simple words, it implies equality of the numerical values of the slopes of the IC and the budget line, that is, equality of $MRS_{X, Y}$ to the price ratio, P_X/P_Y. In other words, it implies tangency of the budget line to the indifference curve. The condition is a necessary one for consumer's equilibrium and is often referred to as the first order condition.

But, is it a sufficient one, too? Before proceeding with the investigation, let us first cast a look at the shape of indifference curve in Illustration 4.2. It is linear, signifying the fact that the two goods in question are perfect substitutes. The solutions in parts (b) and (c) fail to satisfy the necessary condition of tangency yet the consumer attains optimality in consumption at the corners. Such solutions are referred to as **non-interior** or **boundary optima** while that reached in Illustration 4.1, as **interior optima**. Solution reached in part (a) of illustration 4.2, implying infinitely many solutions, may be referred to as both – **a non-interior optima** as well as an **interior optima**. Interior optima of Illustration 4.1 is a unique one, satisfying the necessary condition of tangency. Boundary optima, such as those in parts (b) and (c) of Illustration 4.2 and that in Figure 4.32 do not satisfy the necessary condition of tangency, yet, optimality in consumption is reached in each of these cases.

Cases of interior optima such as those in Figures 4.33 and 4.35 involve non-unique tangents. Not all points of tangency in Figure 4.34 imply optimality in consumption despite satisfying the necessary condition of tangency.

Conclusion reached from discussions so far reveals that the condition of tangency is **necessary, but not sufficient**. Optimality in consumption reached in Figures 4.32 to 4.35 reveals the sufficient condition of consumer's equilibrium. It is the convexity of the indifference curve to the origin. In Figure 4.34, each of the three points, namely, e, e' and e'' satisfy the necessary condition of tangency, but only two of them, namely, e and e'' lead to optimality in consumption. This is so because e and e'' satisfy the sufficient condition of convexity also. Likewise, cases of kinky preferences in Figures 4.33 and 4.35 lead to optimality in consumption because of convexity of IC to the origin.

The singlemost feature common to the cases in Figure 4.32 and those in parts (b) and (c) of Illustration 4.2 is the lowest cost of the equilibrium basket whether IC is convex to origin or linear. The same is the case with all interior optima whether in Illustration 4.1 or in Figures 4.33 and 4.35. Thus, convexity of IC to the origin ensures a least cost basket to the consumer without a compromise in the level of utility. The same is the criterion of optimality in consumption in parts (b) and (c) of Illustration 4.2 and in Figure 4.32 despite respective absence and presence of convexity.

The criterion of **utility maximizing least cost basket (UMLCB)** is thus the over-riding criterion of optimality in consumption. It embraces the criterion of convexity of IC to the origin as well. Barring the extreme cases of boundary optima, convexity of IC to the origin serves as a sufficient condition for optimality in consumption but Utility Maximizing Least Cost Basket (UMLCB) criterion as the sufficient condition of consumer's equilibrium has a wider and universal applicability.

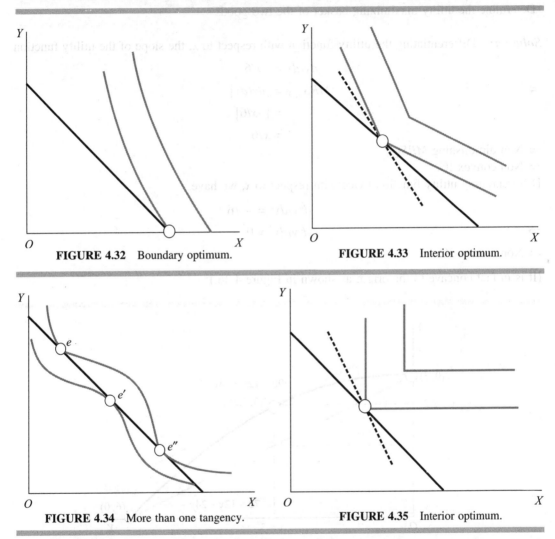

FIGURE 4.32 Boundary optimum.

FIGURE 4.33 Interior optimum.

FIGURE 4.34 More than one tangency.

FIGURE 4.35 Interior optimum.

As assumed by the exponents of the indifference curve approach to the theory of demand and as established in property 5 of indifference curves, the necessary and sufficient condition for the convexity of IC to the origin is the diminishing $MRS_{X,Y}$ along the IC from left to right or the positive non-zero value of second-order derivative of y with respect to x; i.e.

$$d^2y/dx^2 > 0 \qquad (4.15)$$

Let us have an illustration to drive the concept home.

ILLUSTRATION 4.3: Given the utility function as

$$12y = 36 - x^2$$

and the budget line as

$$M = 12x + 24y$$

Determine the utility maximizing basket of the two goods.

Solution: Differentiating the utility function with respect to x, the slope of the utility function

$$dy/dx = -x/6$$

$\Rightarrow \quad MRS_{X,Y} = |dy/dx|$

$$= |-x/6|$$

$$= x/6$$

$\Rightarrow$ Non-diminishing $MRS_{X,Y}$
$\Rightarrow$ Non-convex IC.

Differentiating utility function twice with respect to x, we have

$$d^2y/dx^2 = -1/6$$

$\Rightarrow \quad d^2y/dx^2 \not> 0$

$\Rightarrow$ Non-convex IC.

(It is in fact concave to the origin as shown in Figure 4.36.)

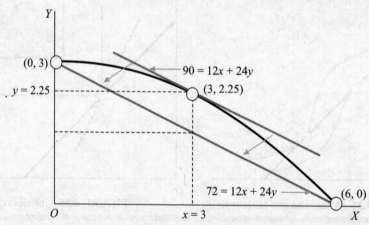

FIGURE 4.36 Tangency of budget line to the IC is not a sufficient condition of optimality in consumption. According to this, optimal basket is (3, 2.25) which would cost the consumer a sum of ₹ 90 (12 × 3 + 24 × 2.25 = 90). The consumer can obtain the same utility at (0, 3) costing him a sum of ₹ 72 (12 × 0 + 24 × 3 = 72) or at (6, 0) costing him an equally lower sum of ₹ 72 (12 × 6 + 24 × 0 = 72). Why should the consumer spend 90 at (3, 2.25) when he/she can get same utility at (0, 3) or at (6, 0) at an expense of ₹ 72.00? The condition of tangency proves insufficient here in optimization of utility.

Differentiating budget line with respect to x, the slope of the budget line
$$dy/dx = -1/2$$
The necessary condition of equilibrium requires tangency of the budget line to the indifference curve. Accordingly, equilibrium is described by

Slope of the budget line = Slope of the IC
$$\Rightarrow -1/2 = -x/6$$
$$\Rightarrow x = 3$$

The corresponding value of y can be obtained by substituting for x in the utility function. It is $y = 2.25$.

Combination (3, 2.25), shown by hollow circle in Figure 4.36, marks optimality in consumption as described by the necessary condition of tangency. Consumer's cost of the basket is 90 (12 × 3 + 24 × 2.25). The same level of utility is available to the consumer at the corners (6, 0) and (0, 3) at a cost of 72 (12 × 6 + 24 × 0 or 12 × 0 + 24 × 3), which is lower than 90. **The condition of tangency is, therefore, not sufficient for consumer's equilibrium.**

The condition sufficient for the purpose is the condition of convexity of IC to the origin. This does not exist here. Yet, the consumer can avail optimality in consumption at (0,3) or (6,0) through the existence of **UMLCB**. We have already seen that IC, in this case, is **non-convex** ($d^2y/dx^2 \not> 0$). Nevertheless, **UMLCB** exists and at two points (6, 0) and (0, 3). The consumer may attain optimality in consumption at either point on the non-convex IC.

The illustration demonstrates that the necessary condition of tangency of the budget line to the IC is not a sufficient one for optimality in consumption. For this, the criterion of utility maximizing least cost basket (UMLCB) serves as an over-riding criterion. It ensures optimality in consumption (consumer's equilibrium) irrespective of presence or absence of convexity of IC to the origin. Maximization of utility for a given budget or minimization of budget for a given level of utility are both incorporated in it under utility maximization at least cost. Each of points e or e'' in Figure 4.34 maximizes utility for a given budget (least cost) while e' does not. Baskets (0, 3) and (6, 0) in Figure 4.36 maximize utility at least cost while (3, 2.25) does not. Note that points e and e'' in Figure 4.34 satisfy the necessary condition of tangency as well as the sufficient condition of UMLCB but point e' in Figure 4.34 and point (3, 2.25) in Figure 4.36 satisfy the necessary condition but not the criterion of UMLCB. Note also that equilibrium is a state of balance from which no consumer has an incentive to deviate.

Accordingly, all the optima discussed above, be they interior optima or exterior optima, constitute different states of equilibria.

4.3 EXPANSION PATH

Equilibrium position once reached remains stable until there is a change in consumer's budget, his/her preferences or product prices. Given the preferences, a change in budget with product prices remaining unchanged or a change in prices upwards or downwards in the same proportion with the budget remaining unchanged, the equilibrium position also changes. The locus traced out by the equilibrium point here is called the **Income Consumption Curve (ICC)**. On the other hand, given the preferences and budget, a change in price of one of the two goods while that of the other remaining unchanged, the locus traced by the equilibrium point is called the **Price Consumption Curve (PCC)**. Each of the two in general is known as the **expansion path**.

4.3.1 Income Consumption Curve (ICC)

Prices of the two goods remaining the same, a change in budget, if positive (increase), the budget line would shift upwards parallel to itself; and the same, if negative (decrease), the budget line would shift downwards parallel to itself. Equilibrium position would shift accordingly, that is, it would shift upwards in response to a positive change in budget and downwards in response to a negative change in it. *When equilibrium position changes due to changes in budget alone, the locus traced out by the equilibrium point (the expansion path), whether upwards or downwards, is called the* **income consumption curve** (ICC) (Figure 4.37). For normal goods, ICC slopes upwards, as shown (Figure 4.37). Consumer's income (budget) remaining the same, exactly identical effect is realized on the pattern of consumption when prices of the two goods fall in the same proportion. This is so because consumer's budget line shifts upwards, parallel to itself, when income alone increases or when prices alone fall by the same proportion for the two goods (Figure 4.26a).

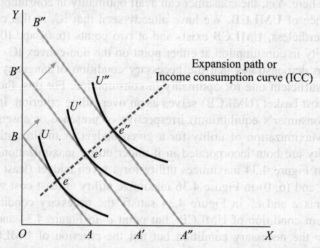

FIGURE 4.37 Income consumption curve: It is the locus traced out by the equilibrium points in response to changes in consumer's budget, prices of the two goods remaining the same. In the figure, consumer's budget line shifts upwards, parallel to itself, from position AB to $A'B'$ and then to $A''B''$ as consumer's income increases. Both goods being **normal**, equilibrium position shifts from e to e' and then to e''. Consumption of both the goods increases each time in consequence. The locus of points e, e' and e'' is called the expansion path or income consumption curve (ICC). Points on ICC signify changing pattern of consumption of the two goods as consumer's income changes.

A decrease in income alone or a proportionate increase in product prices alone would cause a downward parallel shift in the budget line (Figure 4.26b). Equilibrium points would shift downwards but the locus traced by them would appear identical to that in Figure 4.37 with the only difference that point e will be in position e'' and e'' in position e.

The expansion path is different when one of the two goods is an inferior one (Figure 4.38) or it is a basic necessity (Figure 4.39).

In Figure 4.38, equilibrium takes place at point E where budget line AB touches indifference curve, U. The consumer buys X and Y units of the two goods. When consumer's income rises to $A'B'$, his equilibrium shifts to point E' on a higher indifference curve, U'. The consumer buys X' and Y' of the two goods ($X' < X$, $Y' > Y$). An increase in consumer's income leads to a decrease in consumption of X and an increase in consumption of Y. Commodity X is thus an inferior good while commodity Y is a normal good. Given the price of good X, if its consumption decreases in response to an increase in consumer's income, good X is an **inferior good** and the expansion path (income consumption curve) bends backwards as shown in Figure 4.38.

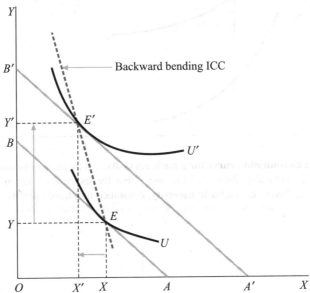

FIGURE 4.38 **Income consumption curve for an inferior good:** An increase in consumer's income shifts the budget line outward from AB to $A'B'$, given no change in the prices of the two goods. If consumption of good X falls from OX to OX', X is certainly an **inferior good**. In the figure, equilibrium shifts from point E to point E' which lies to the left of point E. The ICC bends leftwards as shown. As a result, consumption of X falls while that of Y increases. Clearly, X is an **inferior good** while Y a normal one.

Likewise, given the prices of the two goods, if an increase in consumer's income leaves consumer's demand for a commodity unaffected, the commodity in question is a **basic necessity** and the expansion path (income consumption curve) is vertical (Figure 4.39). Basic necessities are goods that have to be consumed in fixed quantities whatever the income of the consumer. Food, salt and clothing are all basic necessities for most of us. We have to have them in requisite quantities irrespective of our income levels. A vertical income consumption curve indicates that a fixed quantity of the product in question is demanded irrespective of whether income of the consumer rises or falls.

The ICCs discussed above relate only to normal goods, inferior goods and basic necessities.

There is a big possibility that each one of the above may behave as a normal good up to a certain level of its consumption. Thereafter, some of them may behave like a basic necessity (Figure 4.40) and some like an inferior good (Figure 4.41). The left panel of each figure portrays such behaviour of good X while the right panel, that of good Y.

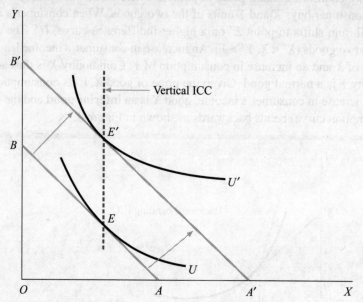

FIGURE 4.39 Income consumption curve for a basic necessity: An increase in income shifts the equilibrium from point E to point E', vertically above it. This shows that the increase of income leaves demand for X unaffected. Commodity X, therefore, is a **basic necessity**, consumed in a fixed quantity.

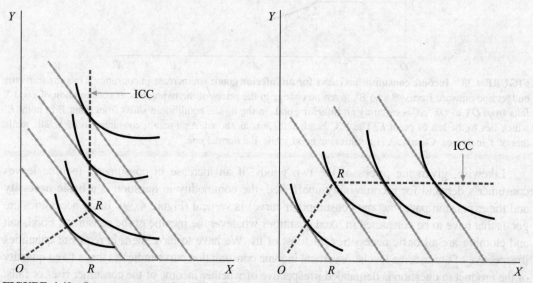

FIGURE 4.40 Income consumption curve for a commodity that behaves like a basic necessity after a certain level of consumption: Segment OR of the ICC has a positive slope in both the panels, indicating the fact that both the commodities behave as normal commodities along OR. Beyond point R in the left panel, X behaves as a basic necessity and in the right panel, Y behaves as a basic necessity.

Approaches to Demand Analysis and Consumer Behaviour   169

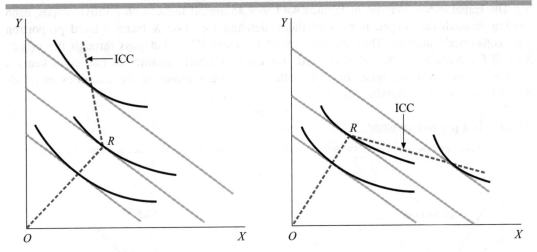

FIGURE 4.41 Income consumption curve for a commodity that behaves as an inferior good after a certain level of its consumption: The ICC has a positive slope along OR. That is both the goods behave as normal goods along this segment of ICC. Beyond point R, X behaves as an inferior good in the left panel and Y behaves as an inferior good in the right panel. This is evident from the sharp turn of the ICC towards y-axis in the left panel and towards x-axis in the right panel.

4.3.2 Engel Curves

An Engel curve, named after Ernest Engel, the propounder of the *Law of Family Expenditure*, shows quantities of a good (say X) which a consumer will consume at various levels of income, given consumer's tastes, preferences and the prices of the goods in question. Representing income on the vertical axis and quantities of good X consumed on the horizontal axis, Engel curves may be derived from the corresponding ICCs, as shown in Figures 4.42 to 4.50.

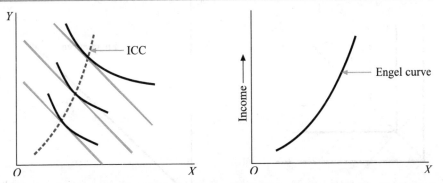

FIGURE 4.42 Derivation of an Engel Curve: For an ICC with a positive slope, the Engel curve, showing variation of the quantity of good X consumed with rising levels of income, also has a positive slope as shown in the right panel. Note that it is income that is measured on the y-axis in the right panel. The axes in the left panel represent quantities of goods X and Y while in the right panel, they represent quantity of X on the x-axis and money income on the y-axis.

The Engel curves derived in Figures 4.43 to 4.45 are all linear with positive slopes, each passing through the origin. For all of them, demand for good X bears a fixed proportion with consumer's income. They all correspond to linear ICCs that pass through the origin. Such ICCs contain bundles of two goods for each of which quantity of one good bears a fixed proportion with the quantity of the other. If x and y represent the quantities of goods X and Y, y/x is a fixed number, that is,

$$y = mx \qquad (4.16)$$

where m is a positive constant.

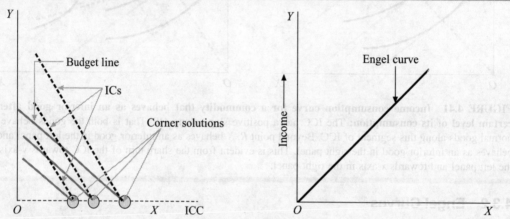

FIGURE 4.43 Derivation of Engel Curve for a good when consumer preferences are linear: When the two goods are perfect substitutes, the ICs are linear as shown in the left panel. The Engel curve for good X is a positively sloped straight line passing through origin. Its equation can be given as, $M = x\,P_X$, where x is quantity of X, M is income and P_X, the price of X, also representing the slope of the Engel curve.

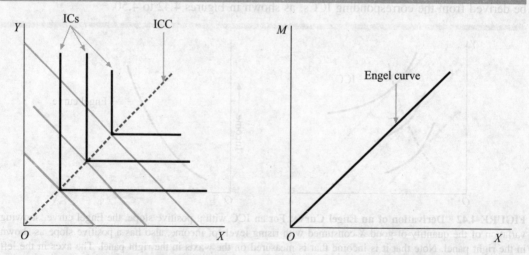

FIGURE 4.44 Derivation of Engel Curve for a good that is a perfect complement of the other good: For perfect complements, ICs are L-shaped, represented by the function $U = \min(x, y)$. Equation of the Engel Curve can be given as, $M = x \cdot (P_X + P_Y)$, with a slope of $(P_X + P_Y)$.

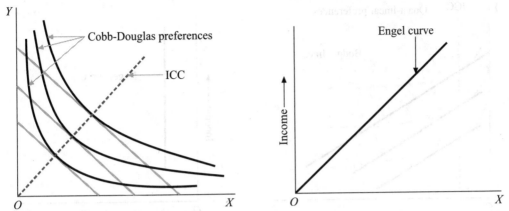

FIGURE 4.45 **Derivation of Engel Curve for a good when consumer preferences are Cobb-Douglas preferences:** When the indifference curves resemble the shape of the curve $U = x^a y^{1-a}$ (Cobb-Douglas function), the ICC is linear with positive slope. The equation of the Engel Curve can be given as, $M = x \cdot P_X/a$ [refer to Illustration 4.1 for proof], with a slope of P_X/a.

Consumer preferences that lead to such ICCs are called ***homothetic preferences***. In simple words, if ICCs are characterized by the Eq. (4.34), consumer preferences are homothetic preferences. Such preferences refer to

1. The linear indifference curves for perfect substitutes
2. The L-shaped indifference curves for perfect complements
3. The Cobb-Douglas indifference curves, also known as Cobb-Douglas preferences.

In case of the perfect substitutes, the demand function for good X is $x = M/P_X$ and the equation of the Engel curve is $M = x \cdot P_X$. Clearly the slope of the Engel curve is P_X, which is fixed because price of X is fixed.

In case of the perfect complements, the demand function for good X is $x = M/(P_X + P_Y)$ and the equation of the Engel curve is $M = x \cdot (P_X + P_Y)$. Clearly the slope of the Engel curve is $(P_X + P_Y)$ which is fixed because prices of the two goods are fixed. In case of the Cobb-Douglas preferences, the demand function for good X is $x = a \cdot M/P_X$ and the equation of the Engel curve is $M = x \cdot P_X/a$. The slope of the Engel curve is P_X/a, which is fixed.

Engel curves, in general, need not be straight lines passing through origin and having a positive slope. When income of the consumers increases, demand for a good may, and in fact it generally does, increase more proportionately or less proportionately than the increase in income. The three cases discussed above are exceptionally simple ones. Figure 4.39, discussed above, is an example in which demand for good X does not increase in the same proportion in which consumer's income does. Another example of this type of demand–income relationship is provided by the *quasi-linear preferences*. Such preferences give a vertical ICC, as shown in the left panel in Figure 4.46. The Engel curve for quasi-linear preferences is also a vertical line, as shown in the right panel.

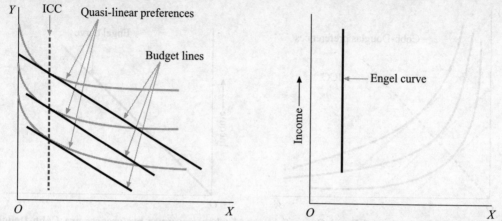

FIGURE 4.46 Derivation of Engel Curve for a good when consumer preferences are quasi-linear: ICC for quasi-linear preferences is a vertical line as shown in the left panel. The Engel curve, as derived in the right panel, is also a vertical line. The extra income with the consumer is not spent on good X. Instead, whole of the increase of income is spent on good Y. For example, suppose an individual has an income M, a part of which he spends on, say, pens and the rest, he retains in the form of cash for buying a variety of goods such as pencils, erasers, notebooks, etc. In a two-commodity world, income retained by a consumer in cash to buy a variety of goods other than good X is termed the **composite commodity** Y and, as such, is represented on the vertical axis.

Quasi-linear preferences refer to the indifference curves that are partly linear and partly non-linear. Examples of the utility functions describing them are:

1. $U = \sqrt{x} + y$ \hfill (4.17)
2. $U = \log x + y$ \hfill (4.18)

When commodity X is a basic necessity, such as salt, the Engel curve that results (Figure 4.47) is again vertical. Such commodities are consumed in fixed quantities by the households.

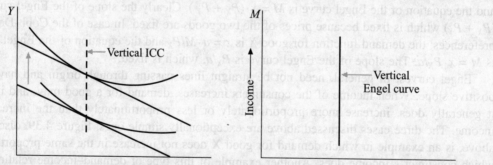

FIGURE 4.47 Derivation of Engel curve for a basic necessity: For basic necessities such as salt, ICC and hence the Engel curve is vertical.

For inferior goods, the ICC bends backwards as seen from Figure 4.38. Engel curve derived for inferior goods also has a negative slope as shown below in Figure 4.48.

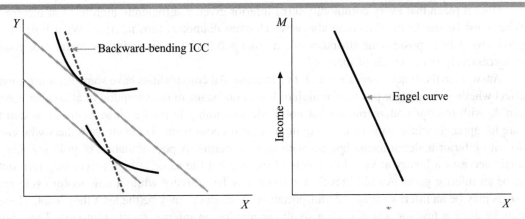

FIGURE 4.48 Derivation of Engel curve for an inferior good: For X, an inferior good, ICC bends towards y-axis as shown in the left panel. The Engel curve derived also bends towards the income axis as shown in the right panel.

4.3.3 Can Engel Curve for a Commodity be Partly Upward Rising, Partly Vertical and Partly Backward Bending?

Figure 4.49 shows Engel curve for a commodity that assumes different roles in different income groups. In the lowest income group, it behaves like a normal good; in the middle income group, like a basic necessity and in the high income group, it behaves as an inferior good. Alternatively, when consumer's income is below Y_1, consumption of X would rise as income rises from 0 to Y_1, when consumer's income is above Y_1 but below Y_2, consumption of X remains fixed at OX_1 as income rises from Y_1 to Y_2 and when consumer's income is above Y_2, consumption of X begins to fall each time income rises above Y_2. In the last lap, the commodity behaves like an inferior good.

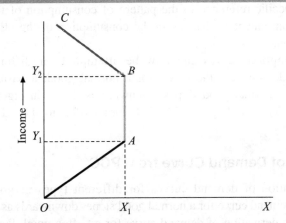

FIGURE 4.49 Derivation of Engel curve for a good that behaves as a normal good, a basic necessity and as an inferior good in different income groups: Engel curve for commodity X in different income groups does not possess a uniform slope. X behaves as a normal good when income is below Y_1, it behaves as a basic commodity when income is above Y_1 but below Y_2 and it behaves as an inferior good when income is above Y_2.

Does it mean that every commodity turns inferior given a sufficiently high level of income? What must be the level of income above which even diamonds turn inferior? What type of a good must X be to possess the attributes of a normal good, a basic necessity and an inferior good at successively rising levels of income?

Answers to these questions are not all that straight. All commodities have some demonstration effect whether negative or positive or high or low at one stage of consumption or at another. One can do with inferior undergarments but not while swimming in public view. Many of us don't care for apparels while some of us are quite particular about them. There are yet others who can do with inferior undergarments but not with inferior outfits. A poor imitation of gold jewellery might serve as a luxury at very low levels of income but the same at high levels may turn out to be an inferior good. An old bicycle for some may be a luxury while a new motor cycle for others may be an inferior means of transportation. A small car may be the least they want. There may be quite a few for whom even a small car may be an inferior family transport. There are others for whom nothing short of a Rolls Royce will do. Even the most precious diamonds may fall short of their standard for some provided something superior to diamonds exists ! There is no limit to human desire to demonstrate exclusive status before others who are less fortunate. In crux, every commodity turns inferior given sufficiently high level of income.

4.3.4 Price Consumption Curves (PCCs)

Expansion path is slightly different when price of only one good falls or rises, income of the consumer remaining the same. Expansion path in this case signifies changing pattern of consumption of the two goods in response to a change (rise or fall) in price of only one good and is called the **price consumption curve (PCC)** (Figure 4.50).

The locus, the equilibrium point traces out in response to the changes in price of one of the two commodities while nominal income of the consumer and the price of the other good remain unchanged, is defined as the Price Consumption Curve (PCC). Also known as the Price Offer Curve, it has specific reference to the pattern of consumption of the commodity whose price rises or falls. Consequential changes in the consumption of the other commodity are of secondary consideration.

The price consumption curves can now be attempted for different types of goods. Figures 4.51 to 4.53 demonstrate the PCCs for a normal good, a basic necessity and for a Giffen good. PCC for a normal good slopes downward as shown in Figure 4.51 while that for basic necessity is a vertical line (Figure 4.52). PCC for a Giffen good bends backwards as shown in Figure 4.53.

4.3.5 Derivation of Demand Curve from PCC

Let us attempt derivation of demand curves for different types of goods from their price consumption curves. Demand curve for a normal good slopes downwards as shown in Figure 4.54.

Let us next turn to derivation of demand curve for a Giffen good. Figure 4.55 explains the mechanism. The figure portrays direct variation of quantity demanded with price, other things remaining the same.

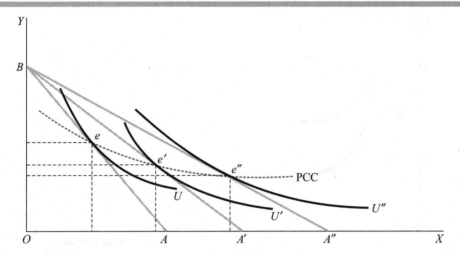

FIGURE 4.50 Derivation of price consumption curve: A fall in price of X, other things remaining the same, causes an outward pivotal shift in the budget line (Figure 4.25). In consequence, the consumer buys more of the good in question provided it is a normal good, same of it provided it is a basic necessity and less of it provided it is a Giffen good. A basic necessity refers to a good, such as salt, which is consumed in a fixed quantity irrespective of the magnitudes of a rise or fall in its price or in consumer's income. A Giffen good refers to a good consumed in lesser quantity when its price falls and in larger quantity when its price rises. The changing pattern of consumption of the two goods in response to a fall or a rise in price of one good is the **price consumption curve**. In Figure, an outward pivotal shift is caused in the budget line by a fall in price of X. Initially, it shifts from BA to BA' and then to BA''. Accordingly, equilibrium shifts from e to e' and then to e''. Joining them by means of a smooth curve, we get the PCC traced out by the equilibrium point.

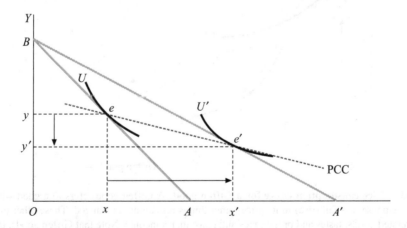

FIGURE 4.51 Price consumption curve for a normal good: Consumer is in equilibrium at e on budget line BA, enjoying utility U. He consumes Ox of X and Oy of Y. Other things remaining same, price of X falls with the result that the budget line BA pivots to BA'. Consumer's equilibrium shifts to e' on BA' where utility enjoyed by him is U'. He consumes Ox' of X and Oy' of Y. As a result, consumption of X increases by xx' while that of Y falls by yy'. The curve joining e and e' gives the PCC. It slopes downward.

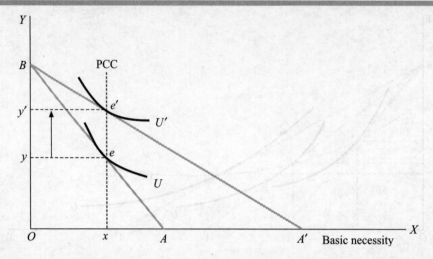

FIGURE 4.52 Price consumption curve for a basic necessity: When X is a basic necessity, the PCC is a vertical line. The consumer does not increase consumption of X, instead, whatever income is released from the consumption of the cheaper necessity X, it is diverted to the consumption of Y.

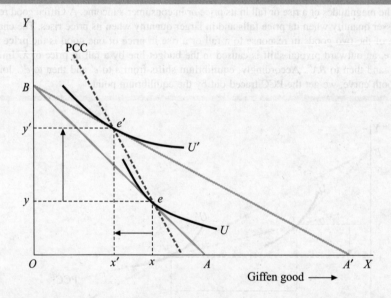

FIGURE 4.53 Price consumption curve for a Giffen good: A Giffen good refers to a good whose demand falls (rises) in response to a fall (rise) in its price, other things remaining unchanged. These other things include prices of the related goods, tastes and preferences and consumer's income. Note that Giffen goods, by definition, are different from inferior goods. Inferior goods are goods whose demand falls (rises) when consumer's income rises (falls), other things remaining unchanged. The other things here include price of the product, prices of the related goods and consumer's tastes and preferences. As in the figure, a fall in price of product X pivots the consumer's budget line from BA to BA'. X being a Giffen good, its demand falls from Ox to Ox'. The PCC, therefore, bends backwards as shown.

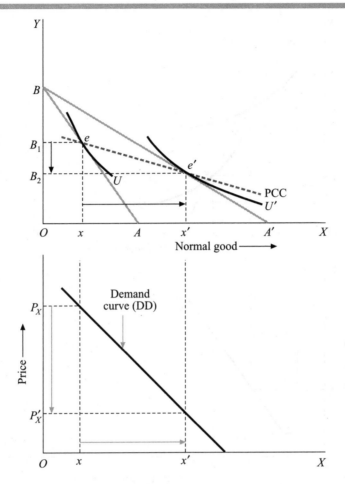

FIGURE 4.54 Derivation of demand curve for a normal good from its PCC: The upper panel shows the price consumption curve for a normal good, X (same as that in Figure 4.51). On y-axis, we measure quantity of commodity Y, whose price is assumed constant. The vertical axis can thus be used to measure consumer's income, real as well as nominal. OB can thus represent a measure of consumer's nominal income, $OB \times P_Y$, given that P_Y is fixed. At point e, consumer buys Ox of X and possesses nominal income OB_1. This implies that he has exchanged income BB_1 for quantity Ox of X at a price P_X (say). Price P_X can thus be expressed as, $P_X = BB_1/Ox$. Now suppose price of X falls to P'_X. The consumer buys Ox' of X spending an income of BB_2 and retaining that of OB_2 at e'. Price, P'_X is thus equal to BB_2/Ox'. Draw projections from e and e' vertically downwards to mark-off quantities Ox and Ox' on the quantity axes in the upper and the lower panels. Note that the lower panel is drawn with its y-axis aligned to the y-axis of the upper panel. This is done for the convenience of marking off the quantities Ox and Ox' in the lower panel. Marking off the corresponding prices P_X and P'_X on the price axis in the lower panel and joining points (Ox, P_X) and (Ox', P'_X) by means of a smooth curve, we obtain the desired demand curve DD as shown. As drawn, it is linear but it may be non-linear too depending on the nature of demand for the product in question. In either case, it slopes downwards from left to right for a normal good.

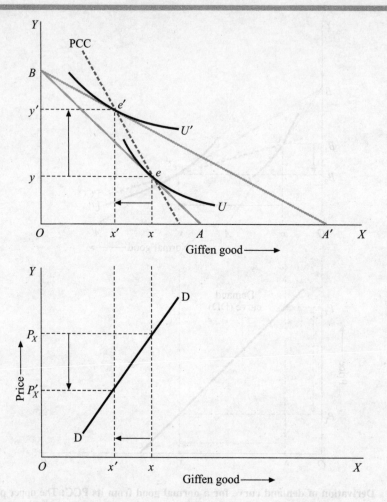

FIGURE 4.55 Derivation of demand curve for a Giffen good from its PCC: Price consumption curve for X, a Giffen good, is as shown in the upper panel. It is more or less same as that in Figure 4.53. Derivation of its demand curve follows the same procedure as for a normal good (Figure 4.54). Projections from points e and e' mark off quantities Ox and Ox' of X demanded at prices P_X and P'_X. Joining points (Ox, P_X) and (Ox', P'_X), we get the desired demand curve DD that slopes upwards from left to right for the Giffen good. DD as drawn is linear. It may be non-linear too depending on the nature of demand for the product in question.

Demand curve for necessities is vertical as quantity demanded remains unchanged whatever the price. We derive it from its PCC (Figure 4.52) following the same procedure as for normal or Giffen goods. Figure 4.56 demonstrates it.

Derivation of demand curve for commodity X, a normal good, is worked out in Figure 4.57 when commodity Y is a basic necessity with its price fixed. Price consumption curve (PCC) in this case is a horizontal line as shown in the upper panel while demand curve for X is a rectangular hyperbola.

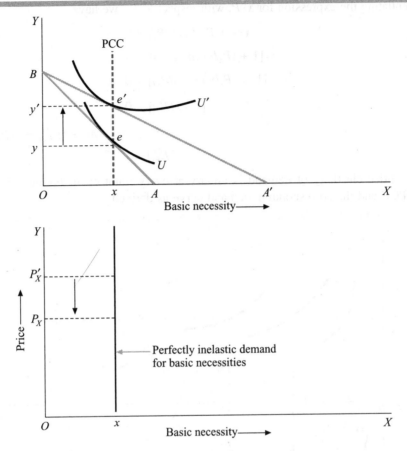

FIGURE 4.56 Derivation of demand curve for a basic necessity from its PCC: The figure portrays derivation of demand curve for a basic necessity from its price consumption curve. Note that the price consumption curve is vertical and so is the demand curve for X when X is a basic necessity. As shown, it is perfectly inelastic. Quantity bought remains same whatever the price of commodity X.

Commodity Y being a basic necessity with its price assumed constant, expenditure on Y is fixed as only a fixed quantity of it is demanded. That is, $y \cdot P_y$ remains constant irrespective of the magnitude of increase or decrease in consumer's real income in response to a fall or a rise in price of X. The PCC for X is thus a horizontal line as whole of the increase (decrease) in consumer's real income caused by a fall (rise) in price of X is spent (adjusted) on consumption of X alone. Consumption of Y remains unaffected and so does expenditure $(y \cdot P_y)$ incurred on it in the process. In a nutshell, nominal income spent on $Y(y \cdot P_y)$ and nominal income spent on X $(x \cdot P_x)$ both remain fixed by virtue of the fixed budget at the disposal of the consumer. Note that $x \cdot P_x$ is the difference of budget $\bar{M}$ over $y \cdot P_y$, that is,

$$x \cdot P_x = \bar{M} - y \cdot P_y$$
$$= K, \text{ a constant.}$$

Differentiating the expression for $x \cdot P_x$ with respect to P_x, we have

$$x \cdot 1 + P_x \cdot [dx/dP_x] = 0$$
$$\Rightarrow \quad x \cdot [1 + (P_x/x)(dx/dP_x)] = 0$$
$$\Rightarrow \quad [1 - (-P_x/x)(dx/dP_x)] = 0$$
$$\Rightarrow \quad [1 - |E^D_{Px}|] = 0$$

where $|E^D_{Px}| = (-P_x/x)(dx/dP_x)$

$$\Rightarrow \quad |E^D_{Px}| = 1$$

That is, price elasticity of demand is unitary at every point on it. Figure 4.57 shows the horizontal PCC and the corresponding demand curve as derived.

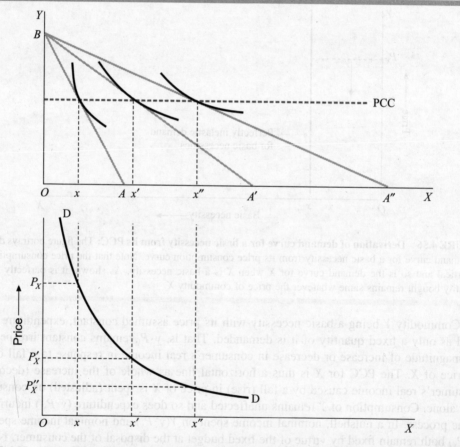

FIGURE 4.57 Derivation of demand curve for a normal good when the other good is a basic necessity with fixed price: When Y is a basic necessity and X, a normal good, every fall in price of X leads to an equivalent rise in demand of X. Y, a basic necessity is bought and consumed in fixed quantity, y. PCC for X is a horizontal line and the demand curve for commodity X that results from it is a rectangular hyperbola having unitary price elasticity at every point on it.

4.3.6 Special Cases of Substitutes, Complements and Discrete Goods

When goods X and Y are perfect substitutes, IC is linear with a downward slope. The demand curve for X (lower panel, Figure 4.58) as derived from the PCC (Figure 4.58, upper panel) has a non-uniform slope.

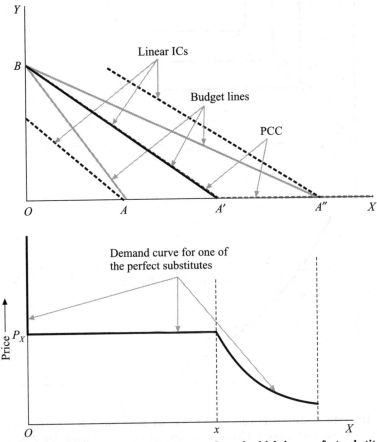

FIGURE 4.58 Derivation of demand curve for a normal good which is a perfect substitute of the other good: In the upper panel, budget line BA pivots outwards first to BA' and then to BA'' in response to a fall in price from P_X to P_X' and finally to P_X''. The indifference curves for perfect substitutes being linear, infinitely many solutions emerge as the budget line BA' coincides with the second lowest of them. Thereafter, with further pivotal of the budget line, corner solutions result all of which fall on the x-axis. For infinitely many solutions, the PCC is a downwardly sloping line coinciding with the budget line BA' and for the corner solutions on the x-axis, the PCC is a horizontal line coinciding with the x-axis. The demand curve for X is perfectly inelastic for prices higher than P_X, perfectly elastic at a price equal to P_X and it is moderately elastic for prices below P_X as shown in the lower panel.

As regards for perfect complements, PCC is an upwardly sloping curve as shown in Figure 4.59 (upper panel) and the demand curve derived from it has a normal shape as shown in the same figure in its lower panel.

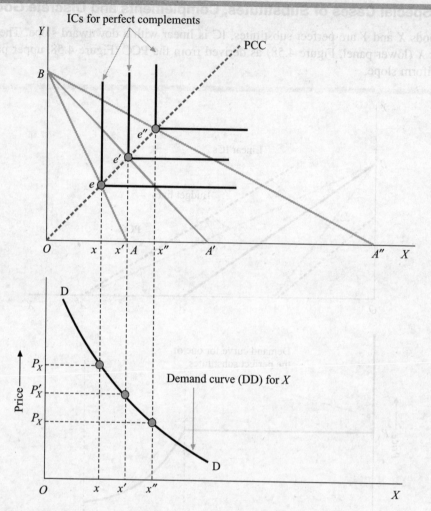

FIGURE 4.59 Derivation of demand curve for a normal good which is a perfect complement of the other good: Price consumption curve for good X, a complement of the fixed-priced-good Y, is a straight line passing through the origin as shown in the upper panel. PCC is the locus of the equilibrium points e, e' and e''. Quantities demanded—x, x' and x''—at prices P_X, P_X' and P_X'' respectively are marked off in the lower panel as shown. Joining the points we have the demand curve, DD in the lower panel.

For perfect complements, ICs are L-shaped. Derivation of PCC and from it that of the demand curve for good X (price of Y assumed fixed) is demonstrated in Figure 4.59. In its upper panel, PCC obtained slopes upwards and in its lower panel, demand curve derived from the PCC, slopes downwards.

The last one among the special cases is the case of discrete goods. We have already discussed the nature of ICs for such goods. Here we will explore the possibilities of deriving the price consumption curve and from it, those of deriving the demand curve for good X (Figure 4.60).

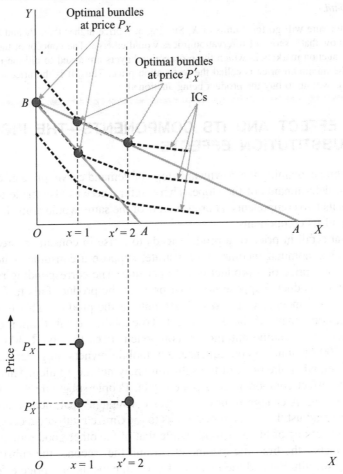

FIGURE 4.60 Derivation of demand curve for a discrete good: In the upper panel, at a price P_X (budget line BA), there are only two discrete bundles—one with $x = 0$ units of X and the other with $x = 1$ unit of X that can be bought despite a large part of the IC coinciding with BA. This is so due to discreteness of consumer preferences. At a lower price P'_X (on the budget line BA'), there are again two bundles—one with $x = 1$ unit of X and the other with $x' = 2$ units of X that can be bought despite a large part of the IC coinciding with BA'. Again, this is so due to discreteness of consumer preferences. Units of X at prices P_X and P'_X are indicated by solid circles. A close look at the upper panel reveals that there is no price consumption curve. The reason is that X is to be bought in whole units. Even the demand curve is discontinuous due to this reason. It has two distinct segments each perfectly inelastic. At price P_X, the consumer is indifferent between consuming and not consuming. If he feels that P_X is high enough, he will buy only zero units of X and if he feels that the price is not high enough, he will buy $x = 1$ unit. Please refer to the broken horizontal segment at price P_X (lower panel). This price P_X is called the **reservation price** which can be defined as the price at which the consumer is indifferent between consuming and not consuming the product. In case price falls below P_X but keeps higher than P'_X, the consumer will not increase the consumption of the good beyond one unit of X. If it is at the level of P'_X, the consumer will again turn indifferent between consuming 1 unit or 2 units. If he feels price P'_X is not low enough, he will continue to consume 1 unit. But if he feels P'_X is low enough, he may go for 2 units. In the figure, when price is P_X, the consumer may buy 0 unit of X or 1 unit of X. But when price is P'_X, he may buy 1 unit of X or 2 units of X. He will be as undecided at P'_X as at P_X. P'_X will thus serve as **another reservation price**. If price falls below

(Contd.)

FIGURE 4.60 (*Contd.*)

P_X', the consumer for sure will go for 2 units of X. Starting at a price higher than P_X and taking several prices below it, one can show that a series of reservation prices would emerge. The concept of the reservation price is borrowed from the auction markets in which the prospective buyers are asked to bid the price above a certain minimum price. The minimum price is called the reservation price. Thus, it is the price at which the seller or the owner himself is willing to buy the product being auctioned.

4.4 PRICE EFFECT AND ITS COMPONENTS—THE INCOME AND THE SUBSTITUTION EFFECTS

In Section 2.3, while explaining the downward slope of demand curve, price effect was mentioned as one of the two determinants of the slope. There, reference was also made to substitution and income effects as its two components. A brief review of the same would come handy in explaining the price effect and its components.

We know that a fall in price of a product leads to a rise in consumer's real income despite no change in his/her nominal income. To illustrate, suppose a consumer's nominal income is ₹ 100 and the current price of a product is ₹ 20 per unit. The corresponding real income works out at 5 units of the product. Suppose now that price of the product falls to ₹ 10 per unit. As a result, consumer's real income would rise to 10 units of the product. This is what is known as the income effect component of the price effect. To explain the substitution effect component, suppose that price of a genuine automobile component rises to, say, ₹ 300 per unit from an initial level of ₹ 200 per unit. In consequence, automobile-owners, in general, choose a cheaper substitute for it even when the price of the substitute may not have fallen. This is what is known as the substitution effect component of a price effect. People substitute a costlier product by a cheaper one in general. A change in price changes consumers' real income and simultaneously influences them to readjust their preferences so as to maximize total satisfaction. Thus, the effect of a change in price of one of the two goods while that of the other good remains fixed manifests itself into two effects—the first, the income effect and the second, the substitution effect. We will segregate the substitution and the income effect components of a price effect in this section with the help of the ICs. The objective is to understand the consumers' behaviour better. The common approaches in this regard are the following two:

1. Compensatory Variation Hypothesis of Hicks
2. Constant Real Income Hypothesis of Slutsky

Let us take up the two in this very order.

1. The Compensatory Variation Hypothesis of Hicks

Figure 4.61 explains Hicksian Compensatory Variation Hypothesis of splitting the price effect into its components for a normal good.

Now, according to our sign convention introduced in Figure 4.62, the *price effect* is *positive* for normal goods, *zero* for *basic necessities* and *negative* for *Giffen goods*. The *substitution effect*, on the other hand, is *positive* in all the three cases and the *income effect* is *positive* for *normal goods*, *negative* for *basic necessities* and *negative* for *Giffen goods*.

Following the method of Figure 4.61, we can split the price effect into its components for basic necessities and Giffen goods too as shown in Figures 4.62 and 4.63.

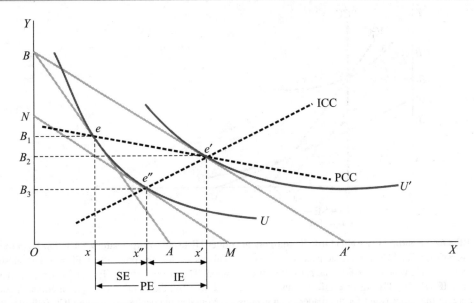

FIGURE 4.61 Segregation of the price effect under Hicksian Compensatory Variation Hypothesis: Let the consumer be in equilibrium at the point e where he enjoys utility U on budget line BA. Here, he consumes Ox of X, a normal good, at a cost of BB_1 real income. Now, price of Y remaining unchanged, let price of X fall from P_X to P'_X. In consequence, his budget line pivots from BA to BA' and he moves from e to e'. At this point, he attains a higher utility (U') consuming Ox' of X at a cost of BB_2 real income. Additional quantity of X consumed due to a fall in its price is xx' ($Ox' - Ox$). This is known as the **price effect** (PE). To split it into its components of substitution and income effects, draw NM parallel to BA' in such a way that it just touches the initial IC (U) at e''. This amounts to a withdrawal of real income BN from the consumer so that he is stripped off the increase in real income caused by the fall in price of X under the Compensatory Variation Hypothesis of Prof. Hicks. Withdrawal of BN under the hypothesis is such that allows him, though by pushing him down the IC, to retain just that level of satisfaction which he enjoyed before the fall in price of X. This allows him to have more of the cheaper good in lieu of some quantity of good Y whose price is unchanged. In other words, MN allows the consumer to move down on U to e'' to choose Ox'' of X with B_1B_3 less of good Y. The consumer substitutes xx'' of X for B_1B_3 of Y. This is known as the **substitution effect** (SE) component of the price effect (xx'). Clearly, xx'' is its measure. Now, let the withdrawn income (BN) be returned to the consumer. This would take him back to e' allowing him an additional $x''x'$ of X purely by virtue of the restoration of the withdrawn income. Hence, $x''x'$ is a measure of the **income effect** (IE) component of the price effect. Treating the price effect, substitution effect and income effect all positive*, we observe that $xx' = xx'' + x''x'$. Here, xx' = price effect (PE), xx'' = substitution effect (SE) and $x''x'$ = Income effect (IE). Thus, PE = SE + IE.

---

*The sign of price effect is taken as positive here because consumption of X increases in response to a fall in its price. The opposite would the case be when X is a Giffen good. A fall in its price is followed by a decrease in the quantity demanded of a Giffen good. The price effect for a Giffen good is, therefore, negative according to this convention. As quantities demanded increase by virtue of substitution and income effects here, each of them too is taken as positive. The rule of thumb is to take the sign of change in demand of X as positive whenever the demand of X increases and take it negative whenever it decreases irrespective of whether the price falls or rises or whether the commodity in question is a normal good, a basic necessity or a Giffen good.

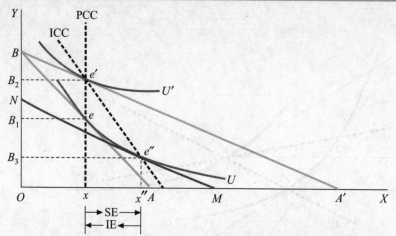

FIGURE 4.62 Splitting price effect into its components under Hicksian Compensatory Variation Hypothesis for basic necessities: The PCC for a basic necessity is vertical. This means that the price effect, PE = 0. The substitution effect, SE = $+xx''$, which is positive as per our sign convention. The income effect, IE = $-x''x$, which is negative. PE = SE + IE. The negative income effect is just strong enough to offset the positive substitution effect. A complete description of the figure is left for the reader as an exercise*. (Note that the backward bending ICC indicates that the income effect component of the price effect is negative. **This shows that the basic necessities are inferior goods**.)

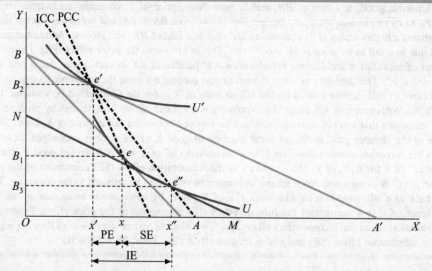

FIGURE 4.63 Splitting price effect into its components under Hicksian Compensatory Variation Hypothesis for Giffen goods: The PCC for Giffen goods is negatively sloped. The price effect, PE = $-xx'$. The substitution effect, SE = $+xx''$. The income effect, IE = $-x''x'$. Note that the negative income effect is so strong that it not only offsets the positive substitution effect, but also renders the price effect negative. Thus, $-xx' = xx'' + (-x''x')$ or PE = SE + IE. A complete description of the figure is left for the reader as an exercise*. (Note that the backward bending ICC indicates that the income effect component of the price effect is negative. **The commodity is not only a Giffen good but also an inferior one**.)

*Follow the pattern of Figure 4.61.

2. Constant Real Income Hypothesis of Slutsky

Slutsky's approach was a little different from that of Prof. Hicks. Unlike Hicksian Compensatory Variation Hypothesis of restoring the original level of utility to the consumer, it provided for restoration of the original basket to the consumer while withdrawing his/her income to isolate the substitution effect component. That way, withdrawal of real income was a little less than that under Hicksian Compensatory Variation Hypothesis as the budget line *NM* was required to pass through the initial equilibrium point *e* rather than of passing tangentially to the initial indifference curve *U* at point e''. A comparative analysis of the two versions is provided for a normal good, basic necessity and a Giffen good in Figures 4.64 to 4.66.

Slutsky's approach is considered more realistic because it seeks to segregate the income and the substitution effects by withdrawing all the additional real income accruing to the consumer in consequence to a fall in the price of *X*. As against this, Hicksian Hypothesis seeks to withdraw a little more of the real income than what is necessary to undo the increase in real income. The purpose of the latter is to put the consumer back on the initial IC so that he/she may retain the initial level of utility purely through a movement from one point on it to another.

Slutsky's substitution effect did not relate to the same IC while Hicksian substitution effect did. That way Hicksian version is more logical while Slutsky's, more realistic.

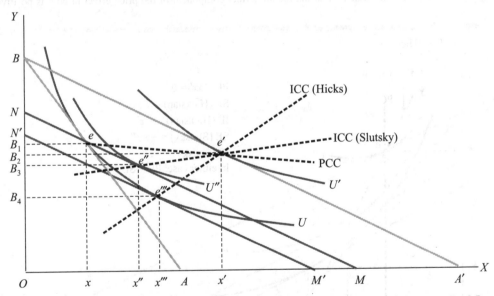

FIGURE 4.64 Segregation of the price effect into its components by Slutsky's Constant Real Income Hypothesis: The consumer enjoys utility *U* at point *e* on the budget line *BA*. He enjoys *Ox* of *X* and *ON'* of *Y*. A fall in price of *X* pivots his budget line to *BA'* on which he attains his equilibrium at point *e'* enjoying utility *U'* through consumption of *Ox'* of *X* and OB_1 of *Y*. The price effect is *xx'*, which is positive. To split it into its components of SE and IE, budget line *NM*, parallel to *BA'*, is drawn through point *e* so that the consumer may retain his original level of real income after withdrawal of *BN* real income under the Constant Real Income Hypothesis of Slutsky. *Thus, according to Slutsky's Constant Real Income Hypothesis,*

(Contd.)

FIGURE 4.64 (*Contd.*)

real income BN, not BN' of Hicksian Compensatory Hypothesis, should be withdrawn from the consumer so that NM drawn parallel to BA' may pass through e, the initial point of equilibrium. This is essential for the consumer. He must buy the original basket under Constant Real Income Hypothesis. His real income, after withdrawal of BN, is given by ON. But with this real income, the consumer may attain a utility of U'', which is higher than the utility enjoyed by him earlier at e ($U'' > U$). Hence, the consumer will attempt utility maximization by moving onto U'' from the present level of the utility, U. Slutsky calls this movement from e to e'' as the substitution effect. Its measure in terms of commodity X is equal to xx'' which is positive according to our sign convention. Now if the income withdrawn from him is reverted back to him, the consumer will promptly go back to e' to enjoy U' on BA'. The movement from e'' to e' is income effect component of the price effect. In terms of X, its measure is $x''x'$, which too is positive. Thus, the price effect, $PE = xx'$, substitution effect, $SE = xx''$ and the income effect, $IE = x''x'$. Clearly, $xx' = xx'' + x''x'$; or, $PE = SE + IE$, which is what is known as the Slutsky's Theorem. The reader can easily compare this version with its Hicksian counter part by drawing $N'M'$, parallel to BA' and touching the original indifference curve, U at the point e'''. Under the Compensatory Variation Hypothesis of Prof. Hicks, one has to withdraw more income than what one has to withdraw under Constant Real Income Hypothesis of Slutsky. Note further that the substitution effect under the Constant Real Income Hypothesis leaves the consumer with higher level of utility than that under the Compensatory Variation Hypothesis ($U'' > U$). In terms of their measures in quantity of X, Hicksian Substitution Effect is larger than the substitution effect due to Slutsky ($xx''' > xx''$). Likewise, the measure of the income effect is lower under Hicksian Compensatory Variation Hypothesis than that under the Constant Real Income Hypothesis of Slutsky. (Note that the upward sloping ICCs under both the versions indicate that the income effect component of the price effect in both is positive.)

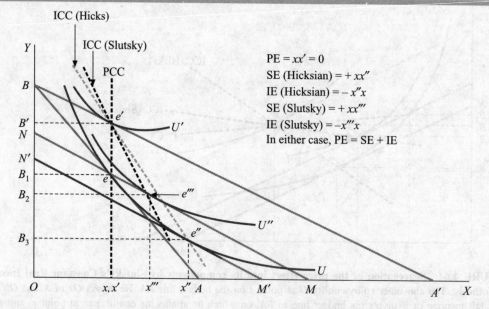

FIGURE 4.65 Comparison of the two versions of splitting price effect for a basic necessity: ICCs for the basic necessities must bend backwards to indicate the negativity of the income effects under each of the two hypotheses (Hicksian and Slutsky's). $PE = xx' = 0$, SE (Hicksian) $= xx''$, IE (Hicksian) $= -x''x$, SE (Slutsky) $= xx'''$, IE (Slutsky) $= -x'''x$. In either case, $PE = SE + IE$.

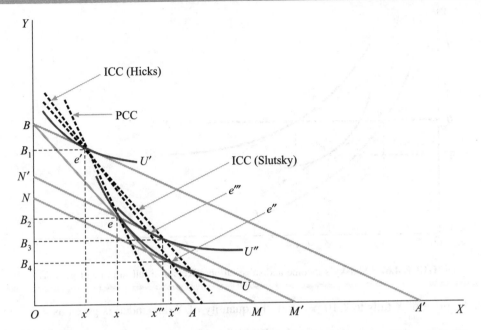

FIGURE 4.66 Comparison of the two versions of splitting the price effect for a Giffen good: PE = $-xx'$, SE (Hicksian) = $+xx''$ and IE (Hicksian) = $-x''x'$. Hicksian Theorem, PE = SE + IE, holds as $-xx' = +xx'' - x''x'$. Likewise, SE (Slutsky's) = $+xx'''$, and IE (Slutsky's) = $-x'''x'$. Slutskian Theorem, PE = SE + IE, holds as $-xx' = +xx''' - x'''x'$.

Some illustrations of Slutsky's theorem

ILLUSTRATION 4.4: A consumer spends whole of his income, ₹ 1000, on two goods, X and Y. The price of good Y is fixed at ₹ 50 per unit while that of X varies. The current price of X is ₹ 20 per unit and it falls to ₹ 10 per unit after a week. The quantity demanded of X is given as a function of its own price and the consumer's income as

$$x = M/5P_x$$

Determine the substitution and income effects under Constant Real Income Hypothesis of Slutsky.

Solution: Refer to Figure 4.67. When the price of X is ₹ 20 per unit, the quantity demanded of it is given by the demand function. It is

$$x = 1000/(5 \times 20)$$
$$= 10 \text{ units of } X \ (= Ox)$$

Income spent on X
$= x \cdot P_X$
$= 10 \times 20$
$= 200 \ (= BB')$

Income left to be spent on Y
$= 1000 - 200$
$= 800 \ (= OB')$

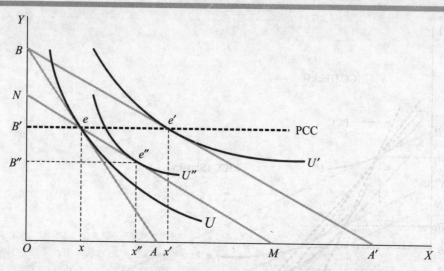

FIGURE 4.67 Slutsky's income and substitution effects of a fall in price of good X.

When the price of X falls to ₹ 10 per unit, the quantity of X demanded is given as

$$x' = 1000/(5 \times 10)$$
$$= 20 \, (= Ox')$$

The price effect,
$$xx' = Ox' - Ox$$
$$= 20 - 10$$
$$= 10$$

Money spent on X after the fall in price, $= x' \cdot P_X$
$$= 20 \times 10$$
$$= 200$$

The amount, the consumer spends on X before and after the fall in its price is the same (coincidence). PCC is thus a horizontal line. Points e and e' are the equilibrium points. Now suppose income BN is withdrawn from the consumer so that he returns to point e on the new budget line NM, i.e. to the original basket comprising quantity Ox of X and OB' of Y. As the price of Y remains unchanged, the consumer spends the same amount on Y as before (i.e. $OB' = 800$) but his expenditure on X has gone down to $B'N$ due to a fall in its price.

$$B'N = 10 \times 10$$
$$= 100$$

Thus, the income ON left with the consumer after withdrawal of income BN, may be given as

$$ON = OB' + B'N$$
$$= 800 + 100$$
$$= 900$$

Income withdrawn, thus, is 1000 − 900 = 100. To find the measure of the substitution effect, let us calculate Ox''. This is given by the demand function when income 900 is substituted for M and price, ₹ 10 for P_X.

$$x'' = 900/(5 \times 10)$$
$$= 18 \ (= Ox'').$$

The substitution effect (SE), therefore, is

$$SE = Ox'' - Ox$$
$$= 18 - 10$$
$$= 8$$

PE, as calculated above, is 10. Therefore, the income effect

$$IE = PE - SE$$
$$= 10 - 8$$
$$= 2.$$

4.4.1 Splitting the Price Effect into Substitution and Income Effects When the Price of X Rises

So far we have discussed how to split price effect of a fall in price of good X (price of Y remaining the same) into its components of substitution and income effects. In this section, let us have a feel of splitting price effect into its componenets of substitution and income effects when price of a good rises instead of falling. A rise in price of X, other things remaining same, causes a pivotal of the budget line inwards from BA to BA', shifting equilibrium from e to e' (Figure 4.68). The rise in price reduces consumer's real income. Under Compensatory Variation Hypothesis of Hicks, NM is drawn parallel to BA', touching original IC (U) at e''. Movement from e to e' marks price effect while that from e' to e'' marks income effect. Movement from e to e'' is substitution effect.

Resorting to our sign convention, we observe that Hicksian Theorem, $PE = SE + IE$, holds. For its comparison with the Slutsky's version, $N'M'$ is drawn parallel to BA' passing through e as required by Slutsky's Constant Real Income Hypothesis. As evident from Figure 4.68, Slutsky's Theorem also holds just as Hicksian Theorem does.

Reader can try splitting price effect into its components for basic necessities and Giffen goods for a rise in price of X.

4.5 APPLICATIONS OF INDIFFERENCE CURVES

Apart from their role in explaining the complexity of the consumers' behaviour, indifference curves play a very important role in the study of many complicated economic phenomena. For example, study of consumers' surplus, cost of living, investors' portfolio management, time preference theory of interest, efficiency of exchange, allocative efficiency of resources, gains from foreign trade, social welfare maximization and time preference theory of consumption and saving over the life cycle are some of the important theoretical premises where indifference curves come handy in the study and analysis. Even more important is the role played by the indifference curves in policy formulations in respect of rationing, fixation of wages, evaluation of alternative tax policies, alternative grants of

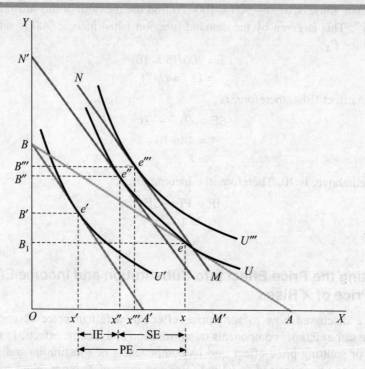

FIGURE 4.68 Splitting price effect into its components when price of one good rises instead of falling: Under our sign convention, PE is negative $(-xx')$, so is SE $(-xx'')$ and IE $(-x''x')$. Hicksian theorem, PE = SE + IE, can be checked to hold as $(-xx') = (-xx'') + (-x''x')$. On the same lines, Slutsky's theorem with PE $(-xx')$, SE $(-xx''')$ and IE $(-x'''x')$ can also be checked to hold.

---

assistance to people and evaluation of effectiveness of taxing wage income from the view point of its impact on labour productivity. For the sake of convenience, we divide these applications into two broad categories:

1. Applications in economic theory
2. Applications in policy formulations.

Let us take them in that order.

1. Applications of indifference curves in economic theory

(a) *In the study of consumer surplus*

In Chapter 2 the concept of consumer surplus was employed frequently while evaluating the effects of direct and indirect interventions of State in the free-play of price mechanism. Our purpose there was to analyse the effects of government policies on social welfare. Here we use the concept to determine consumer surplus of an individual consumer when his demand for a product is known or when his preferences through indifference curves are given.

Given the individual's demand, the consumer surplus is given by the area between the demand curve and the normal price (Figure 4.69).

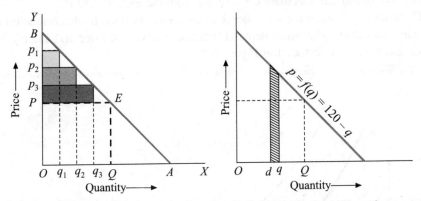

FIGURE 4.69 Consumer Surplus (CS) through a simple demand schedule: Given the consumer demand curve AB, the surplus possessed by a consumer is given by the area of $\triangle BEP$. It measures the excess of income which a consumer is willing to forego for a product over that being sacrificed currently.

As is clear from the figure (left panel), the consumer is willing to pay a price p_1 for quantity q_1, p_2 for quantity q_2 and p_3 for a quantity q_3. The amounts he is willing to spend are respectively $p_1 \cdot q_1$, $p_2 \cdot q_2$ and $p_3 \cdot q_3$. What he actually spends for these quantities are respectively $P \cdot q_1$, $P \cdot q_2$ and $P \cdot q_3$. The excess incomes he is willing to forego are thus respectively $(p_1 - P) \cdot q_1$, $(p_2 - P) \cdot q_2$ and $(p_3 - P) \cdot q_3$. The total excess income the consumer is willing to forego is shown by the shaded region, that is, $(p_1 - P) \cdot q_1 + (p_2 - P) \cdot q_2 + (p_3 - P) \cdot q_3$. The measure of CS, thus, is

$$CS = (p_1 \cdot q_1 + p_2 \cdot q_2 + p_3 \cdot q_3) - P(q_1 + q_2 + q_3)$$
$$= (\Sigma p \cdot q) - P(\Sigma q)$$

The CS so measured is a little less than the area under the demand curve that lies above price OP. That is, it is less than the area of $\triangle BEP$ by the areas of the triangular regions above the shaded rectangles. This is so due to discrete changes taken in quantity demanded. Were these changes infinitesimally small so that quantity demanded may be changed without significant changes in price, the areas of these triangular regions can be reduced to zero and the measure of CS may be raised to the area of $\triangle BEP$ (right panel). The CS can then be measured as

$$CS = \int_{q=0}^{q=Q} (p - P) \cdot dq \qquad \text{(See Chapter 1 also)}$$

Given the consumer's demand as $p = f(q)$, $CS = \int_{q=0}^{q=Q} [f(q) - P] \cdot dq$

$$= F(Q) - PQ.$$

Here, $F(Q)$ is the value of the definite integral of $f(q)$ with $0 \le q \le Q$.

To elaborate suppose the demand function is $p = 120 - q$ and the consumer is currently consuming 60 units of the product at a price of ₹ 60 each, the measure of CS works out as

$$CS = \int_{q=0}^{q=60} [120 - q - 60] \cdot dq$$

$$= 120q - (1/2)\,q^2 - 60q \Big|_0^{60}$$

$$= 7200 - 1/2 \times 3600 - 60 \times 60 = 1800.$$

To verify, the reader can calculate CS directly from the area of $\triangle BEP$.

Alfred Marshall is credited for the concept of consumer surplus. Its determination in respect of an individual consumer with given demand function or levels of price and quantity of current consumption has been demonstrated in Figure 4.70.

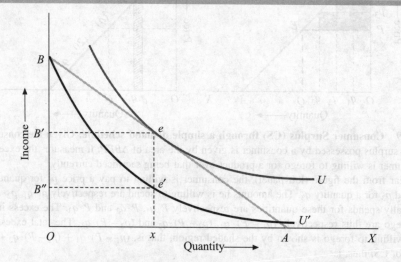

FIGURE 4.70 Consumer Surplus through indifference curves under Marshallian assumption of constant MU of money: Consumer's budget line BA touches the indifference curve U at e where he consumes quantity x of X, spending income BB'. Draw U' vertically parallel to U through point B, the point of maximum income the consumer has allocated for the commodity X. U' cuts the vertical line through the point of initial equilibrium at point e'. This implies that the consumer is willing to sacrifice an income BB'' instead of BB' for the product rather than remain without it. Income of $B'B''$ ($= BB'' - BB'$) which the consumer is willing to forego for the product over and above what he is currently spending on it, is the Marshallian measure of the consumer surplus. The reason for drawing the U' through the point of highest income is to ensure that the basket at the point of highest income lies on his indifference curve.

Income represented on the y-axis may be nominal or real. One way to conveniently resolve the dilemma is to treat commodity Y as a **composite commodity** whose price is fixed at ₹ 1 per unit. In such a case the quantity of Y represented on the y-axis would be equal to the number of rupees of nominal income the consumer has. While consuming commodity X, the consumer may be regarded to be converting a part of the units of the composite commodity into the units of good X. For instance, suppose his nominal income is ₹ 100 which is represented as 100 units of the composite commodity on y-axis. At point e', he is having quantity Ox of X and OB'' of Y. This would imply that he has converted BB'' units of the composite commodity into the Ox quantity of X and is still having OB'' units of the composite commodity which thus can be defined as the quantity of a commodity equal in magnitude to the number of rupees of the nominal income the consumer possesses.

The determination of CS through the indifference curves under Marshallian assumption of constant marginal utility of money is demonstrated in Figure 4.70 and under Hicksian relaxation of this assumption, in Figure 4.71.

Just as Marshallian cardinal utility theory of demand is based on his assumption of constant marginal utility of money, his estimate of consumer surplus too is based on it. Accordingly, the estimate of consumer surplus works out at $B'B''$. The technique is also explained in

Figure 4.71. Suppose the consumer is in equilibrium at point e on his budget line AB, enjoying utility U through consumption of quantity Ox of X. Income sacrificed by him for this quantity is BB'. To determine the CS under the assumption of constant marginal utility of money, let the indifference curve U pass through B, the point of highest income allocated by him for the commodity. Let this indifference curve be U''. Note that the curve is kept vertically parallel to the original curve U. This is essential due to the assumption of constant marginal utility of money. The income now sacrificed by the consumer for the quantity Ox of X is BB''. Excess income thus sacrificed by the consumer is $B'B''$ ($BB'' - BB'$). This gives Marshallian measure of consumer surplus (Figure 4.71).

While commenting on his assumptions of the cardinal utility approach to demand, it was pointed out that the assumption of constant marginal utility of money is highly unrealistic. Relaxing the assumption on this ground, the measure of the consumer surplus would work out smaller than its Marshallian Counterpart. Figure 4.71 demonstrates the point. The indifference curve U when allowed to pass through B, the point of highest income allocated by the consumer for commodity X, would assume the shape of U'' instead of U' as it would be no longer vertically parallel to U due to the relaxation of the assumption of constant marginal utility of money. U'' tends to approach U with increasing consumption of X. The reason for this is the increasing marginal utility of money with increasing expenditure on X. As more and more of X is bought by the consumer, his/her tendency to forego less and less of income for it increases due to increasing MU of money. As a result, U'' is flatter than U'. Instead of sacrificing BB'', the consumer sacrifices only BB''' for quantity Ox and the CS works out at $B'B'''$ ($BB''' - BB'$, Figure 4.71). Evidently, $B'B''' < B'B''$.

Recall that Hicks in his ordinal utility approach to demand analysis had relaxed the assumption of constant marginal utility of money and still maintained the inverse relationship between price and demand. The measure of consumer surplus ($B'B'''$) so obtained is at times referred to as the Hicksian measure of it therefore.

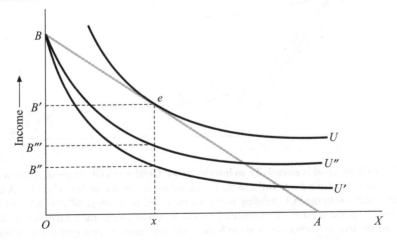

FIGURE 4.71 Consumer surplus without the assumption of constant MU of money: Relaxing the assumption, the IC through B would not be vertically parallel to U. Instead, it would be flatter like U''. The CS would be $B'B'''$ instead of $B'B''$.

(b) *Every Giffen good is an inferior good but its converse need not be true*

As in Figure 4.38, the income consumption curve for an inferior good bends towards y-axis. An increase in income, other things remaining unchanged, results in a decrease in demand for the inferior good, say X. Here, the other things referred to include price of X along with prices of the related goods, tastes, preferences and fashions. As against this, when good X is a Giffen good, it is the price consumption curve that bends towards y-axis as shown in Figure 4.53. This implies that a fall in price of good X results in a decrease in its demand, other things remaining unchanged. The other things referred to here include consumer's income, prices of the related goods, tastes, preferences and fashions. *In sum, when demand of good X falls in response to a rise in income (other things remaining unchanged), X is an inferior good but when demand of good X falls in response to a fall in price of X (other things remaining unchanged), it is a Giffen good.* This sums up the distinction between the two types of goods as far as their definitions are concerned.

A little in-depth analysis, however, reveals a complication. Let us cast a glance at Figures 4.72 and 4.73. Figure 4.72 reveals the fact that a Giffen good is an inferior good and an inferior good is a Giffen good. Figure 4.73, on the contrary, reveals that X, an inferior good, is not a Giffen good. This explains that the line dividing the two types of goods is a blurred one. As regards Giffen goods, they are essentially inferior; but as regards inferior goods, they need not be Giffen goods always.

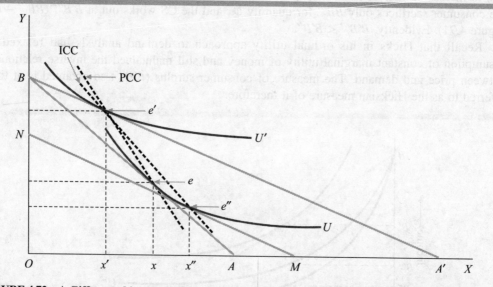

FIGURE 4.72 **A Giffen good is essentially an inferior good:** Good X is a Giffen good. A fall in its price pivots the consumer's budget line from BA to BA' and the consumer moves from e on U to e' on U'. A fall in its price, thus, lowers its demand with the PCC bending towards y-axis. NM is drawn parallel to BA' touching the initial indifference curve, U at the point e''. This amounts to withdrawal of an income by the magnitude BN from the consumer. When the income withdrawn is given back to the consumer, he promptly moves from e'' on U to e' on U. In other words, an increase in income of the consumer results in a decrease in demand of commodity X and the ICC bends towards the y-axis. Thus, a backward bending PCC leads to a backward bending ICC. Hence, a Giffen good is essentially an inferior good. Price effect and income effect are both negative for a Giffen good.

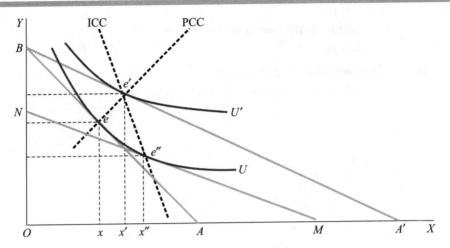

FIGURE 4.73 An inferior good need not be a Giffen good: Commodity X, in this case is an inferior good but not a Giffen good. The income consumption curve bends towards y-axis indicating that less of X is demanded at higher incomes, other things remaining unchanged. The Price consumption curve, on the other hand, has a positive slope indicating that more of X is demanded at lower prices other things remaining unchanged. Commodity X for sure is an inferior good but not a Giffen good. In terms of PE, SE and IE, we observe that IE is negative while PE, positive.

(c) *Indifference curve analysis of the cost of living*

Indifference curve analysis can be used to investigate whether a consumer is better off or worse off after a period of time, over which, product prices and consumers' income both change. The basic assumption the analysis requires is that the consumer must spend whole of his income on the two goods under consideration in all time periods, that is, he must choose a point on his budget line in all time-periods.

Let us examine the following:

(i) *A consumer is better off in the current period than in the base period if his income index is higher than the Laspeyres price index (Figure 4.74).*

Expressed symbolically, the theorem implies that the consumer is better off if,

$$(Y_T/Y_0) \times 100 > L \tag{4.19}$$

where, $Y_T \equiv$ consumer's current income;

$Y_0 \equiv$ consumer's income in the base period;

$L \equiv$ Laspeyres price index.

Recall from Statistics that Laspeyres price index is defined as the cost of the base year's basket at current prices, that is,

$$L = [(\Sigma q_0\, p_T)/(\Sigma q_0\, p_0)] \times 100 \tag{4.20}$$

where, $q_0 \equiv$ quantity consumed in the base period,

$p_0 \equiv$ price in the base period

$p_T \equiv$ price in the current period, T

Let us also note that

$Y_T =$ income in current period, T

$$= \Sigma q_T p_T \quad (4.21)$$
Y_0 = income in the base period
$$= \Sigma q_0 p_0 \quad (4.22)$$

Figure 4.74 demonstrates the statement.

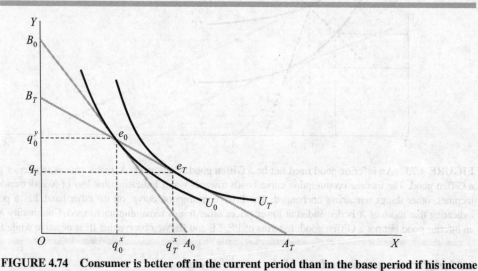

FIGURE 4.74 Consumer is better off in the current period than in the base period if his income index is higher than the Laspeyres price index: $B_0 A_0$ represents the initial budget line defined by $Y_0 = \Sigma q_0 p_0 = q^x_0 \cdot p^x_0 + q^y_0 \cdot p^y_0$. The consumer is in equilibrium at point e_0, consuming basket (q^x_0, q^y_0) at the base period's prices p^x_0 and p^y_0 respectively. Now suppose prices of the two goods change to p^x_T and p^y_T in the current period. As a result, the budget line changes to $B_T A_T$, defined by $Y_T = \Sigma q_T \cdot p_T = q^x_T \cdot p^x_T + q^y_T \cdot p^y_T$. Laspeyres price index implies cost of the base year's basket at current year's prices $(\Sigma q_0 p_T)$ expressed as a ratio of the cost of base years basket at base year's prices $(\Sigma q_0 p_0)$. For this, base year's basket must be available to the consumer at current prices. This can happen in two ways:

1. *When e_0 falls on $B_0 A_0$ as well as on $B_T A_T$ (as in the figure):* Draw $B_T A_T$ through initial equilibrium (e_0). This would signify that the initial basket is still available to the consumer at e_0 in the current period, that is, on $B_T A_T$. Base year's basket costs $\Sigma q_0 p_0$ in base year's prices and $\Sigma q_0 p_T$ in current year's prices. In other words, $\Sigma q_0 p_T = \Sigma q_0 p_0 = Y_0$. The consumer may however choose the basket at e_T (q^x_T, q^y_T), particularly when it falls on a higher indifference curve U_T, as in the figure, indicating that the consumer is better off in the current period at e_T than in the base period at e_0. Thus, consumer is better off at e_T even when $\Sigma q_0 p_T = \Sigma q_T p_T$. [If the consumer chooses e_0 on $B_T A_T$, he spends $\Sigma q_0 p_T$ ($= q^x_0 \cdot p^x_T + q^y_0 \cdot p^y_T$) $= \Sigma q_T p_T (= q^x_T \cdot p^x_T + q^y_T \cdot p^y_T)$ yet remains on lower indifference curve (U_0).]

2. *When e_0 falls on $B_0 A_0$ but lies below $B_T A_T$ (not shown in the figure):* Draw $B_T A_T$ through a point above e_0 on $B_0 A_0$. This also ensures the base year's basket to the consumer in the current year's prices because e_0 now lies below $B_T A_T$, implying, $\Sigma q_0 p_T < \Sigma q_T p_T$. Again the consumer would be better off at e_T. Hence, $\Sigma q_0 p_T \leq \Sigma q_T p_T$. If $\Sigma q_0 p_T = \Sigma q_T p_T$, the consumer is better off at e_T. Ans if $\Sigma q_0 p_T < \Sigma q_T p_T$, still the consumer is better off at e_T. In particular, having $\Sigma q_0 p_T < \Sigma q_T p_T$ and dividing on both sides by $\Sigma q_0 p_0$, we have

$$\Sigma q_0 p_T / \Sigma q_0 p_0 < \Sigma q_T p_T / \Sigma q_0 p_0$$
$\Rightarrow \quad (\Sigma q_0 p_T / \Sigma q_0 p_0) \times 100 < (\Sigma q_T p_T / \Sigma q_0 p_0) \times 100$ (multiplying both the sides by 100)
$\Rightarrow \quad L < (Y_T/Y_0) \times 100$ or $(Y_T/Y_0) \times 100 > L$ (Rearranging the terms)

Thus, if current period's income index is greater than the Laspeyres price index, the consumer is better off in the current period.

(ii) *A consumer is worse off in the current period than in the base period if his income index is lower than the Paasche price index* (Figure 4.75).

Expressed symbolically, the theorem implies that the consumer is wrose off if,

$$(Y_T/Y_0) \times 100 < P \tag{4.23}$$

where, P is Paasche price index defined as

$$P = (\Sigma q_T p_T / \Sigma q_T p_0) \times 100 \tag{4.24}$$

All the symbols here have the same meaning as in the previous theorem.

Figure 4.75 demonstrates the proof of the theorem.

(d) *ICs and Fisher's time preference theory of interest*

The time preference theory of interest is associated with the name of Irving Fisher who defined interest as an "index of the community's preference for a dollar of present over a dollar of future income". Time preference, is thus preference of having a certain amount today rather than at a point of time in future. Interest is the price of enjoying future income at present. It is determined by the rates of "marginal rate of time preference" and "marginal return over cost." Marginal rate of time preference, also known as the rate of willingness, refers to willingness to borrow. If the rate of willingness is higher than the rate of interest, the individual would borrow, and if it is lower than the rate of interest, the individual will lend. The rate of return over cost is the discount rate at which the net present values of the alternative investment opportunities get equalized. If the rate of return over cost is higher for an investment opportunity than the market rate of interest, the individual would prefer to invest rather than lend at the market rate of interest. In the opposite case, when the rate of return over cost is lower than the market rate of interest, the individual would prefer to lend for the interest rather than go for low return investment.

For determination of the rate of interest, therefore, we require:

(i) *The willingness curves:* Which are none other than the indifference curves representing various combinations of the present and the future incomes each of which offers the same level of utility to an individual. It is to be noted that some individuals prefer future income to present income while others prefer present income to the future income. For instance, it is observed that people from business community in general prefer future income to present income. The latter for most of them is quite high while the former for them is uncertain. They lack income assuring schemes such as old age pensions. For them the only way to provide for future is to save now and invest for future income streams, particularly for their old age. They are thus the potential sources of loans. Unlike them, there is the salaried class who prefer present income to future income. Individuals in this category feel secure about old age. Certainty of retirement benefits such as old-age pensions, provident fund, gratuity and the like assure them a secure future. Even their monthly salaries rise steadily as they proceed towards their retirement. The main problem of the people in this category is the low pay scales accruing to them at the entry stage. It is at this time that most of them want to enjoy the luxuries of the consumer-durables. Therefore, they invariably tend to borrow to buy consumer durables such as cars, flats, TVs, etc. They are, thus, the potential consumers of the loans.

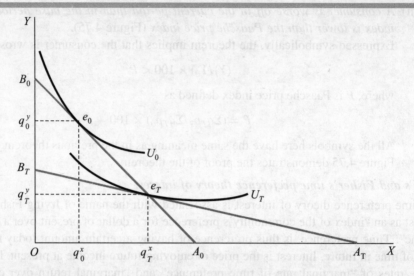

FIGURE 4.75 Consumer is worse off in the current period than in the base period if his income index is lower than the Paasche's price index: Let B_0A_0 represents the initial budget line defined by $Y_0 = \Sigma q_0 p_0 = q^x{}_0 \cdot p^x{}_0 + q^y{}_0 \cdot p^y{}_0$. The consumer is in equilibrium at e_0, consuming basket $(q^x{}_0, q^y{}_0)$ in the base period's prices $p^x{}_0$ and $p^y{}_0$ respectively. Now suppose that the prices of the two goods change to $p^x{}_T$ and $p^y{}_T$ in the current period. As a result, the budget line changes to $B_T A_T$, defined as $Y_T = \Sigma q_T p_T = q^x{}_T \cdot p^x{}_T + q^y{}_T \cdot p^y{}_T$. Paasches price index implies the ratio of cost of the current year's basket at current prices to that of the current year's basket at base year's prices. For this, let $B_T A_T$ intersect $B_0 A_0$ at e_T, which lies below e_0. This signifies that the initial basket (q_0) lies above $B_T A_T$ and is therefore no longer available to the consumer in the current period. The consumer therefore chooses the basket (q_T) at e_T, which lies on a lower indifference curve (U_T). This indicates that the consumer is worse off in the current period than in the base period. To show that income index is less than Paasch's price index, let us define basket e_T in base period's prices as $\Sigma q_T p_0 = q^x{}_T \cdot p^x{}_0 + q^y{}_T \cdot p^y{}_0$. Let us discuss the following possibilities:

1. *When* $\Sigma q_T p_0 = \Sigma q_0 p_0 = \Sigma q_T p_T$: Here, $\Sigma q_T p_0 = \Sigma q_0 p_0$ because e_T and e_0 both fall on same budget line $(B_0 A_0)$ and $\Sigma q_0 p_0 = \Sigma q_T p_T$ because e_T falls on both the budget lines. The consumer chooses q_T at e_T in preference to q_0 at e_0 despite identical costs because q_0 is no longer available to him at current prices. He is on a lower indifference curve (U_T) and hence, worse off at e_T despite $\Sigma q_0 p_0 = \Sigma q_T p_0$.

2. *When* $\Sigma q_0 p_0 > \Sigma q_T p_0$: From the figure, e_0 lies above $B_T A_T$. Hence e_0, though on a higher indifference curve, is not available to the consumer at the current prices. He has to do at a lower indifference curve (U_T), being worse off than before.

In particular, having $\Sigma q_0 p_0 > \Sigma q_T p_0$, dividing on both sides by $\Sigma q_T p_T$, inverting and multiplying each side by 100, we have

$\Sigma q_0 p_0 / \Sigma q_T p_T > \Sigma q_T p_0 / \Sigma q_T p_T$ (dividing by $\Sigma q_T p_T$)

$\Rightarrow \quad \Sigma q_T p_T / \Sigma q_0 p_0 < \Sigma q_T p_T / \Sigma q_T p_0$ (Inverting the ratio)

$\Rightarrow \quad [\Sigma q_T p_T / \Sigma q_0 p_0] \times 100 < [\Sigma q_T p_T / \Sigma q_T p_0] \times 100$ (Multiplying both sides by 100)

$\Rightarrow \quad [Y_T / Y_0] \times 100 < P$ (Multiplying both sides by 100)

That is, the consumer is worse off if the current period's income index is less than the Paasche price index.

The willingness curves for people who prefer future income to present income and those who prefer present income to future income are shown in Figures 4.76(a) and (b). Both depict quasi-linear preferences. For those who are neutral to present and future incomes, the willingness curves resemble the shape of the IC as in Figure 4.76(c).
All the three depict convex preferences.

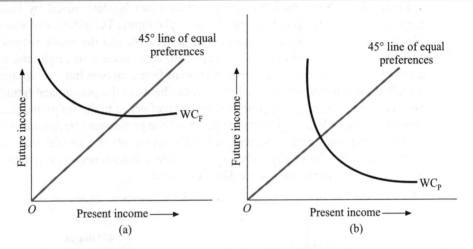

FIGURE 4.76(a) The willingness curve (WC$_F$) for those who prefer future income to present income. (WC$_F$) is said to mark negative time preferences.

FIGURE 4.76(b) The willingness curve (WC$_P$) for those who prefer present income to future income is said to mark positive preferences.

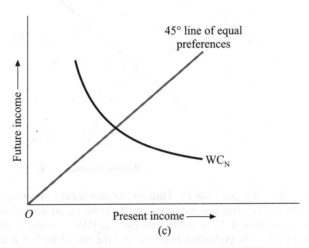

FIGURE 4.76(c) Willingness curve for neutral time preferences (WC$_N$) between the present and future incomes is symmetric about the 45° line representing equality of preferences between present and future incomes, that is, if more of one is preferred, more of the other also has to be chosen along the 45° line.

(ii) *The transformation curves:* The rate of return over cost or the net capital productivity is represented by the transformation curves that depict the rate at which one type of income is transformed into the other. A transformation curve, like a production possibility curve, represents various combinations of the present and the future incomes that are possible to realize with given endowment. As expected transformation curves are concave to the origin.

Figure 4.77 shows how the rate of interest can be determined by Fisher's time preference with the help of these two tools. In the figure, TC is the transformation curve which represents various combinations of the present and the future incomes that are possible with given endowment. As expected, it is concave to origin and its slope is given by the marginal rate of transformation of future income into present income. The ray OR depicts the points of equal preferences between the present and future incomes. WC_F represents the negative time preference (preference to the future incomes over the present incomes), WC_P represents the positive time preference (preference to the present incomes over the future incomes) and WC_N represents the neutral time preferences (shown separately for clarity). The rate of interest is determined at the point of tangency between the transformation and willingness curves.

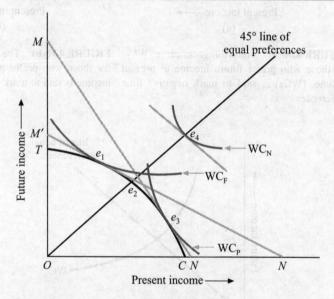

FIGURE 4.77 ICs and Fisher's Time preference theory of interest: If the willingness curve is WC_P, it touches the transformation curve at the point e_3. At this point, willingness is positive and so is the rate of interest. If the willingness curve is WC_N, it would touch the transformation curve at the point e_2. The time preference is neutral and the rate of interest is zero. If the willingness curve is WC_F, it would touch the transformation curve at the point e_1. At this point, time preference is negative. The rate of interest would be negative. Neutral time preference is indicated by the slope ($=-1$) of the WC_N (shown separately at e_4 to avoid congestion) at the point e_2, positive time preference is indicated by the slope (absolute value greater than 1) of WC_P at the point e_3 and the negative time preference is indicated by the slope of WC_F (numerically less than 1) at the point e_1.

(e) *ICs and gains from foreign trade*

ICs prove effective tools for analysis of gains from trade and specialization. To demonstrate, let us take a closed economy, producing and consuming at a point *e* on the production possibility curve TC (Figure 4.78). At this point, the economy produces and consumes Ox of X and Oy of Y. The community indifference curve attained by it is U. Point e is the point of tangency between the production possibility curve TC and the community indifference curve U. The domestic price ratio for the two goods is P_X/P_Y. It represents the slope of the price line PP. Now suppose the economy opens up to the rest of the world. Let the international price ratio for the two goods be P'_X/P'_Y, represented by the slope of the international price line eP'. Since eP' is steeper than PP, either $P'_X > P_X$ or $P'_Y < P_Y$ or both. This implies that either price of X has risen or that of Y, fallen or both taken place simultaneously.

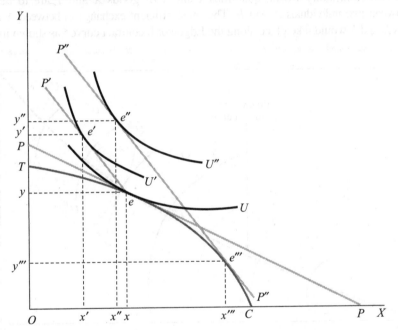

FIGURE 4.78 ICs and Gains from foreign trade: Before opening up to the rest of the world, the country produces and consumes at *e* where the domestic price line PP touches its PPC (TC) and the community indifference curve (U). It produces and consumes Ox of X and Oy of Y. Now suppose it enters foreign trade. International price line, eP', being steeper than the domestic price line, PP, product X fetches a higher price in the international market while product Y is cheaper there. The country would export xx' to the rest of the world and import yy' from it in consequence. By doing this, it attains a higher indifference curve, U'. Movement from U to U' marks the **gains from exchange**. Drawing a line $P''P''$ parallel to eP' and touching the PPC at e''', we get the point of optimal production which the country would undertake to maximize its total gains from trade. At this point, it will produce much more of X ($Ox''' > Ox$) with much less of Y ($Oy''' < Oy$). In the process it would exchange the excess of X ($x''x'''$) with $y''y'''$ of Y and thus attain a much higher level of utility, U''. Movement from U to U'' marks the **total gain from trade**. This comprises of two movements—the *first,* movement from U to U' which marks the **gains from exchange**, and the *second,* movement from U' to U'' which marks **gains from specialization**.

As a result, the country would consume at e' on $U'(U' > U)$. At this point, it would consume $Ox'(Ox' < Ox)$ of X and $Oy'(Oy' > Oy)$ of Y, exporting xx' of X and importing yy' of Y. In the process, it will attain a higher indifference curve $U'(U' > U)$. This gain in utility, called the *gain from exchange*, results from exchange of excess of high priced X produced domestically with low priced Y produced abroad. This would encourage the country to specialize in production of X. As a result, it would produce at the point e''' on its PPC, where the international price line $P''P''$, parallel to eP' (why?), touches it. As regards its consumption, the country will consume at e'' on U'' ($U'' > U'$). Movement from U' to U'' marks the gains accruing to the country from specialization. *The total gain from trade* is thus made up of *gains from exchange* and *gains from specialization*.

(f) Efficiency in distribution of commodities

Assuming a two-commodity world, quantities x and y of goods X and Y are to be distributed, suppose, between two individuals A and B. The most efficient exchange in-between A and B of the commodities X and Y would take place along the Edgeworth contract curve* as shown in Figure 4.79.

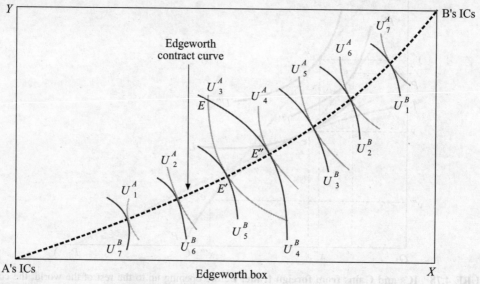

FIGURE 4.79 Efficiency in distribution of commodities: A's ICs (from bottom left to right, in grey) depicting different levels of his utilities, touch the respective ICs of B (from top right left, in black). The locus of the points of tangency (broken curve in black), called the **Edgeworth contract curve**, depicts points of efficient exchange of the commodities between consumers A and B. The points of tangency represent the points at which the slopes of the ICs of the two consumers are the same. In other words, the marginal rates of substitution of one commodity for the other for the two consumers are equal on the Edgeworth contract curve, i.e.

$$MRS^A_{X,Y} = MRS^B_{X,Y}$$

Exchange at any other point except those on the contract curve can be shown to be inefficient. For instance, consider the point E at which the ICs U^A_3 and U^B_4 meet each other. Evidently, exchange of the two commodities between the two consumers at E is inefficient because it is possible to increase the utility of at least one of the two consumers without adversely affecting that of the other, that is, at point E' or E''.

---

* Named after Edgeworth, who first used this construction.

(g) *Efficiency in allocation of the productive resources*

Allocation of labour and capital on production of goods X and Y (Figure 4.80) is efficient if made along the contract curve exactly in the same manner in which exchange of X and Y in part (f) above is made in-between consumers A and B.

In place of ICs, we take isoquants of the two goods. Efficient allocations of labour and capital between production of goods X and Y are possible along the contract curve. Allocations made elsewhere in the box can be shown inefficient on the same lines as in part (f).

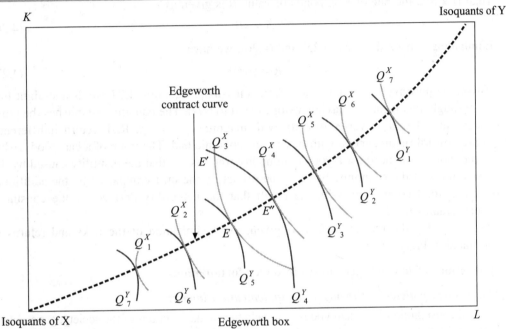

FIGURE 4.80 Efficiency in allocation of productive resources: Isoquants of goods X and Y (in grey and black respectively) touch each other along the contract curve. Thus, labour and capital get efficiently allocated between the alternative productions of commodities X and Y along the contract curve. An isoquant is the producers' indifference curve which shows their indifference in-between different combinations of labour and capital that lead to production of the same quantity of a commodity. The contract curve is the locus of the points at each of which the slopes of the isoquants are the same, i.e.

$$MRTS^X_{L,K} = MRTS^Y_{L,K}$$

Like MRS, MRTS (Marginal Rate of Technical Substitution of one factor of production for the other) for a commodity represents the numerical value of the slope of the isoquant for that commodity.

(h) *Optimality in investor's portfolio management*

Here we employ indifference curves to explain Tobin's portfolio optimization theory. According to Tobin, instead of holding their assets either in cash or in bonds, individuals tend to hold it in some combination of the two. In fact, they prefer to hold that combination of the two which helps them to optimize the risk and return associated with their bond-holdings.

Optimization of risks means their minimization and optimization of returns means their maximization. Simultaneous realization of the two is not easy as higher returns are usually associated with higher risks*. Minimization of risks may lead to minimization of returns as well. *No pains no gains* truly describes the situation. The technique of portfolio optimization draws its parallel in the technique of consumers' equilibrium.

Let R denote the total returns from bonds of value B. If r is the rate of return,

$$R = rB \qquad (4.25)$$

Total risk S at the rate of s on bonds of value B is given as

$$S = sB \qquad (4.26)$$

Eliminating B from the Eqs. (4.25) and (4.26), we have

$$R = (r/s)S \qquad (4.27)$$

If risks be portrayed on x-axis and returns on y-axis, Equation 4.27 yields a straight line passing through the origin and having a slope equal to (r/s). The equation establishes the point that magnitude of returns varies directly with magnitude of risks. Risk–return indifference curves are upward rising curves, with risk as an economic bad. The more of a bad good (risks) is had, the more is the need for a good commodity (returns) so that the disutility caused by the successive units of the economic bad may be off set by the utility imparted by the additional units of the good commodity with the result that the net utility derived by the consumer (investor) remains fixed.

Assuming that the rate of interest is given, the optimization of the risks and returns is demonstrated in Figure 4.81.

2. Applications of indifference curves in policy formulations

(a) *Government policies of subsidy and supplementary income*

To increase consumption of certain goods or to help the weaker sections of the society, government resorts to schemes such as grant of cash or subsidization of certain essential commodities. In the former case, cash is transferred to the vulnerable sections to enable them to buy the desired products at the prevailing market prices. It is a type of transfer payment intended to supplement the income of the weaker sections. In the latter case, government makes goods available to the people at the prices below the market levels. The price difference is borne by the government. Both the schemes aim at increasing social welfare, the cost of which is borne in each case by the government. To evaluate the costs and benefits, let us refer to Figure 4.82.

(b) *Direct tax versus indirect tax*

A direct tax is a non-shiftable tax. Income tax is an example. Its incidence and impact both fall on the same person. It is levied on income of an individual and is paid by the individual on whose income it is levied. An indirect tax, on the other hand, is a shiftable tax. Its incidence and impact need not fall on the same person. Sales tax is an example. It is levied on the sale of a product. It is shared between the buyer and the seller in a ratio depending upon the relative price elasticities of demand and supply of the product.

---

*See also the risk and uncertainty bearing theory of profit, Chapters 15 and 22.

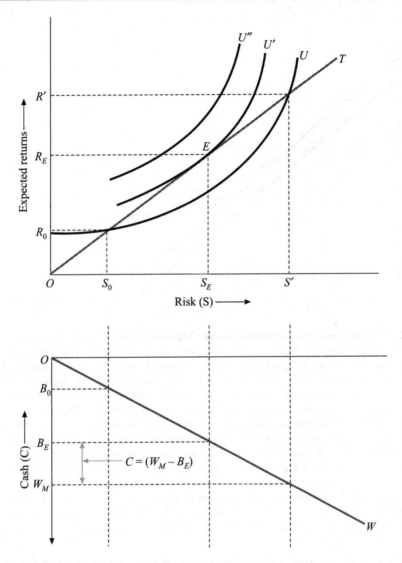

FIGURE 4.81 Optimality in investor's portfolio management: The upper panel shows the ray OT, representing optimum combinations of risk and return, and the risk–return indifference curves, U, U' and U'', showing various combinations of the risks and returns that yield same level of satisfaction to the portfolio holder. The point of tangency between OT and the indifference curves is the point of optimality of risk–return mix. Here, it is the indifference curve U' that touches the ray OT at point E. This gives the optimal combination of the risk and the return. The lower panel measures risks on the horizontal axis and bond-holding of the investor on the vertical (downward) axis. The ray OW shows different combinations of risks and bond-holdings, indicating higher risks are associated with higher bond-holdings. The investor would hold OB_E worth of wealth in bonds and the rest $OW_M - OB_E$ or C, in cash.

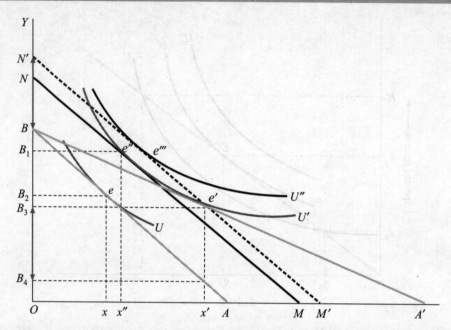

FIGURE 4.82 Subsidy versus supplementary income: The grant of subsidy pivots the consumer's budget line from BA to BA'. The consumer buys more of $X(Ox')$ in consequence at point e', sacrificing an income of BB_3. To buy this quantity of X before the grant of subsidy the consumer had to forego an income of BB_4. The cost of subsidy is, therefore, equal to B_3B_4. Due to the subsidy, the consumer is able to attain a higher indifference curve, U'. Now suppose government wants to know the amount of the supplementary income that would have to be given to retain the consumer at the same indifference curve at which he has reached due to the grant of subsidy. For this purpose, a straight line NM, parallel to BA, is drawn touching U' at e''. The amount of the supplementary income, thus is equal to NB. Note that the consumer is equally well off in each case but it costs government less ($NB < B_3B_4$) when assistance is given in the form of cash (supplementary income). Alternatively, had government decided to spend a fixed amount B_3B_4, whether through subsidy or through supplementary income the consumer would have been better off with the supplementary income BN' equal in value to subsidy B_3B_4. That way the consumer would have attained a higher utility U'' at e'''. Quite often, the choice between the two depends on factors other than the costs and the benefits. If the economy is experiencing inflation, the grant of subsidy is a better option but if it is under depression, the supplementary income is more suitable.

A direct tax reduces the consumer's disposable income while an indirect tax increases the market price of the commodity on which it is levied. A direct tax causes a downward parallel shift the consumer's budget line while an indirect tax causes an inward pivotal shift in it. Both affect the consumption of a product. Effect of an indirect tax is direct on the consumption of the product on which it is levied. The levy affects the consumption of the product directly through an increase in its market price. The effect of a direct tax on the consumption of products is indirect as their market prices remain unaffected while the purchasing power of the consumer gets eroded by its levy. Figure 4.83 compares the effects of the two on the consumer's utility.

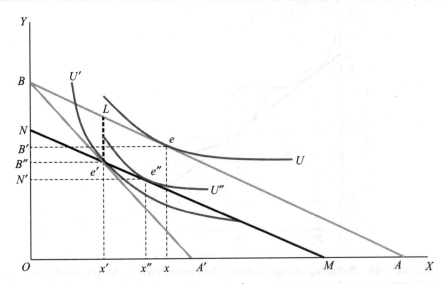

FIGURE 4.83 Direct tax versus indirect tax: Suppose the consumer is enjoying utility U at point e on his budget line BA. He consumes quantity Ox of X sacrificing income BB'. Now suppose an indirect tax is levied on X. This raises its price leading to a downward pivotal shift in the budget line from BA to BA'. The consumer attains his equilibrium at e' on BA' enjoying utility U' ($U' < U$). His consumption of X drops from Ox to Ox', while sacrifice of income increases from BB' to BB''. At e', indirect tax paid by the consumer is Le'. Now suppose government wishes to see the effect of an equal direct tax on consumers' welfare. For this, budget line NM is drawn parallel to BA and passing through e'. Note that BN is the magnitude of direct tax which is equal to Le' (Why?), the indirect tax. In other words, revenue to government is the same whether direct tax is levied or indirect tax is levied. However, the direct tax takes the consumer to a higher utility U'' at e''. Thus direct tax is preferable to the indirect tax from the viewpoint of the consumer.

As regards government, it realizes same revenue in either case. Even otherwise, a direct tax is preferable to the indirect tax because it possesses the attribute of certainty of revenue. The indirect tax does not possess this attribute. Governments often prefer direct tax of lower magnitude to an indirect tax of higher magnitude because of this. After all, a bird in hand is better than two in the bush!

(c) *Rationing policy*

We take up two types of rationing problems here:

(i) *When community is sharply divided in respect of their preferences between two basic necessities:* Suppose there are two goods—rice and wheat—one of which is preferred by one segment of the community while the other by the other segment. Both are basic necessities. Suppose further that government is regulating the supply of the two through fair price shops. Given the consumers' income and the prices of the two goods as fixed by government, the alternative possibilities of rationing the two commodities are shown in Figure 4.84.

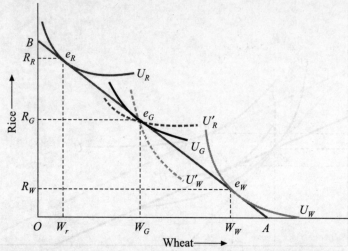

FIGURE 4.84 Rationing of commodities when community is sharply divided in respect of its preferences: Let each consumer have the same budget and hence the same budget line, BA. Also, let the commodities be wheat and rice and their prices P_W and P_R as fixed by government. The indifference curves U_W and U_R are both quasi-linear, indicating existence of consumers with marked preferences for wheat and rice. As opposed to them, indifference curve UG indicates neutrality of preference signalling existence of consumers who are not particular for either commodity. The equilibrium baskets for the three segments of the consumers are marked at e_R, e_G and e_W respectively. If government decides to distribute the two goods at e_G, the segment, which prefers rice gets less of it with more of wheat and that, which prefers wheat gets less of it with more of rice. They would have no use for the excess commodity delivered and would fall on lower indifference curves each. Those who prefer rice fall from U_R to U'_R ($U'_R < U_R$) and those who prefer wheat fall from U_W to U'_W ($U'_W < U_W$). Those who have the balanced preferences (U_G) are the only happy people.

Social welfare can be significantly raised if the government adopts a little flexibility in distribution by granting each segment its desired basket. The flexibility costs nothing to the government yet benefits the segments preferring rice and wheat by lifting them to higher indifference curves U_R and U_W, respectively. *Thus, when community is sharply divided in respect of its preferences between two necessities, flexibility in their distribution by the government to suit the consumer preferences cost government nothing, but raises social welfare to its optimum.*

(ii) *Rationing under different constraints imposed on the consumers*: Rationing often involves three types of constraints:

1. Budget Constraint,
$$x \cdot P_X + y \cdot P_Y \leq \bar{M} \tag{4.28}$$

where, x and y are the quantities of the two goods X and Y; P_X and P_Y are the prices per unit of X and Y respectively and $\bar{M}$ is the money income at the disposal of the consumer.

2. Ration Point Constraint,
$$x \cdot T_X + y \cdot T_Y \leq \bar{T} \tag{4.29}$$

where, x and y represent the quantities of goods X and Y; T_X and T_Y represent prices in terms of ration-points per unit of commodities X and Y respectively while $\bar{T}$ represents the total ration-points allocated to a consumer. Point rationing is often introduced during the periods of wage-price controls. Ration points are allotted to the consumers and prices per unit of rationed commodities in terms of ration points, apart from their money prices, are fixed.

3. Time Constraint,

$$x \cdot t_X + y \cdot t_Y \leq \bar{t} \tag{4.30}$$

where, x and y represent the quantities of goods X and Y; t_X and t_Y represent expenditures of time per unit of consumption of commodities X and Y respectively while $\bar{t}$ represents the total time at the disposal of the consumer. Time serves as an economic good.

The consumer has to make a choice of a bundle that maximizes his satisfaction under the stipulated limits of money income, ration-points and/or time costs.

Symbolically, when all the three constraints are operative in simultaneity, the bundle must satisfy the following conditions:

$$\text{Maximize:} \quad U = f(x, y) \tag{4.31}$$

$$\text{subject to:} \quad (1)\ x \cdot P_X + y \cdot P_Y \leq \bar{M} \tag{4.28}$$

$$(2)\ x \cdot T_X + y \cdot T_Y \leq \bar{T} \tag{4.29}$$

$$(3)\ x \cdot t_X + y \cdot t_Y \leq \bar{t} \tag{4.30}$$

The condition (4.31) requires that the bundle must lie on the highest possible indifference curve. The constraints (4.28), (4.29) and (4.30) require that the bundle costs him at most $\bar{M}$ of income, $\bar{T}$ of the ration-points and $\bar{t}$ of total time.

Clearly, the feasible baskets would comprise positive quantities of the two goods confined to the region bound by all the three constraints. One that maximizes the utility would fall on the periphery of the region at one of its vertices. Here, we demonstrate situations in which only budget and ration-point constraints are operative. The reader can try other situations discarding any one of the three constraints or taking all the three constraints at a time. The technique remains the same.

In our case, three different possibilities emerge:

1. Budget at the disposal of the consumer is relatively scarce.
2. Ration-points at the disposal of the consumer are relatively scarce.
3. When budget is relatively scarce in respect of commodity X while ration-points are scarce in respect of commodity Y or vice-versa.

Figures 4.85, 4.86 and 4.87 respectively demonstrate the process of attainment of bliss in each case.

In the foregone discussions, if the ration-point constraint be replaced by the time constraint, the technique of determining consumer's bliss-point remains unchanged in every respect. The problem arises when a trade-off between money and time gets involved. The trade-off is a reality. Workers trade-off their time for money-income and vice-versa depending on their preferences and changes therein that take place from time to time. When more income is needed, leisure-time is sacrificed by them and when more leisure-time is needed, it is income that is foregone by them.

In the applications that follow, we are going to discuss how workers determine the appropriate supply of their hours of work in response to the existing structure of hourly wage rate. For the purpose, we need to introduce the concepts of leisure–income trade-off as also that of leisure–income indifference curves in the next application.

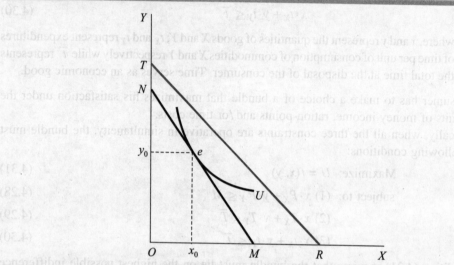

FIGURE 4.85 Rationing under relative scarcity of budget: When budget (MN) is relatively scarce, the budget constraint is the binding one. It is closer to the origin while the ration-point constraint is farther away from it. The consumer attains his optimal basket at $e(x_0, y_0)$. Clearly, the ration-point constraint turns redundant.

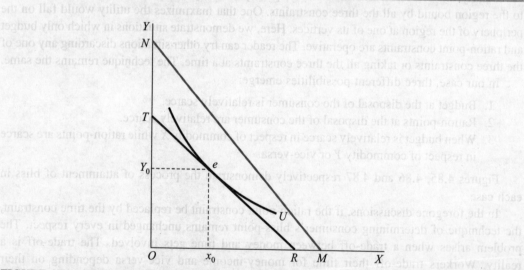

FIGURE 4.86 Rationing under relative scarcity of ration points: When ration-points (RT) are relatively scarce, the ration-point constraint is the binding one. It is closer to the origin while the budget constraint is farther away from it. The consumer attains his optimal basket at $e(x_0, y_0)$. Clearly, the budget constraint turns redundant.

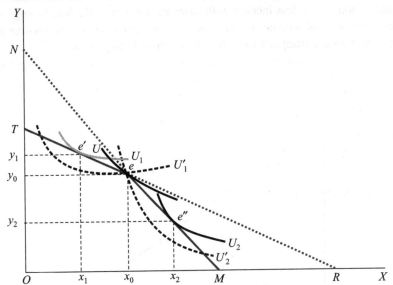

FIGURE 4.87 **Rationing when budget is relatively scarce in respect of commodity X and ration points are relatively scarce in respect of commodity Y:** When budget is relatively scarce in respect of X and ration-points are relatively scarce in respect of Y, the budget line (MN) is steeper than the ration-point line (RT). The two intersect each other at e (x_0, y_0). If both constraints are binding, the consumer attains optimality at $e(x_0, y_0)$. But, if the budget constraint alone is binding, the consumer may raise his utility level to U_2 [at $e''(x_2, y_2)$], which is higher than U'_2. Note that U'_2 stands for same utility level as U (why?). That is possible by giving away some of the ration points for money if the same be permissible. Likewise, if the ration-point constraint is binding, the consumer may raise his utility level to U_1 [at e' (x_1, y_1)], which is higher than U'_1. Note that U'_1 stands for same utility level as U (why?). That is possible by giving away some of the money income for ration points if the same is permissible. [Note that $U'_1 < U_1$ and $U'_2 < U_2$, while U'_1 and U'_2 both pass through e and represent the same utility level as U]. If the trade-off between money and the ration points be non-permissible, which is what is a reality, the bliss point shall remain the point e (x_0, y_0). In this case, utilities U_1 and U_2 shall remain unattainable to the consumer.

(d) Choice between leisure and income

As an individual, a worker has at most 24 hours at his disposal to divide between leisure and work. The number of hours he devotes to work or the number of hours he keeps for leisure depends on several factors.

The *first* one is the prevailing hourly wage. In general, if the hourly wage is high, supply of labour hours is high and if it is low, the supply of labour hours is low. On the other hand, if the wage rate is too high or too low, the supply of labour hours is low in either case. A too low wage proves a disincentive to work and so does a too high wage. Workers find work unrewarding when wage rate is too low and too rewarding when the wage rate is too high. In the latter case, little work fetches them sufficient income for their needs. As a result, they begin to prefer leisure to labour.

The *second* one is wage income. Desire for higher income compels workers to supply more hours of work or to acquire rare skills which command higher wage rates. People acquire special skills so that little work may fetch them higher incomes and they may have the desired number of leisure hours each day.

At a given rate of hourly wage, the leisure-income trade-off would mean association of less leisure with more income and less income with more leisure. *Given the hourly wage rate, different combinations of leisure and income trace a straight line called the leisure-income trade-off line.* The line slopes downward from left to right, as shown in Figure 4.88.

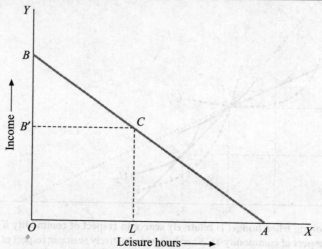

FIGURE 4.88 Leisure-income trade-off line: Leisure-income trade-off line, *BA*, slopes downwards from left to right. The *x*-axis represents leisure hours while the *y*-axis, the money income. At point *O*, leisure hours enjoyed by the worker are zero. In other words, he is devoting all the 24 hours to work at this point. As a result he is entitled to the maximum income, *OB*. The income w is thus associated with *AO* hours (24 hours) of work or zero hours of leisure. At point *A*, time devoted to leisure is *OA* hours (all the 24 hours) and that devoted to work is zero. Money income associated to this point is therefore zero. At *C*, leisure hours enjoyed by the worker are *OL* and the money income associated is *OB'*. The income is thus associated with *AL*, hours of work. Hourly wage rate, therefore, would work out as $w = OB'/AL$. Clearly, it represents the slope of the segment *CA*. In the same way, income *OB* being associated with *AO* hours (24 hours) of work, the hourly wage rate or the slope of the line can also be given as, $w = OB/AO$. The two expressions of w are identical. Thus, $w = OB'/AL = OB/AO$. Each one gives the slope of the leisure-income trade-off line, *AB* as *C*, *A* and *B* are collinear. *Given the wage rate per hour, the locus of the different combinations of leisure and income would trace a straight line.*

Likewise, *The locus of various combinations of leisure and income that offer the worker a fixed level of satisfaction is called the leisure–income indifference curve* (Figure 4.89). The worker is indifferent in-between any two because he derives same utility at each. If he has fewer hours of leisure, he would have more wage income or if he has more hours of leisure, he would have lesser income earned. Much depends on the worker's preferences between leisure and income. Like all other indifference curves for normal goods, a leisure–income indifference curve is convex to the origin. In other words, worker's preferences for leisure and income are *convex*.

A worker's choice of a combination of leisure hours and money income follows the same technique as does a consumer's choice of a basket of two goods. In equilibrium, the worker enjoys *OL* hours of leisure with *OB'* of money income (Figure 4.90). This income accrues to him from *AL* hours of work. The wage rate per hour of work is, thus, given by

$$w = OB'/AL \tag{4.31}$$

We are now all set to discuss some important applications of leisure-income curves.

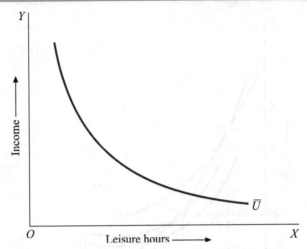

FIGURE 4.89 **The leisure-income indifference curve:** The leisure–income indifference curve traces different combinations of leisure hours enjoyed and incomes earned that offer the same utility to a worker. Worker's preferences for leisure and income that lead to an indifference curve convex to the origin are known as the **convex preferences**. The leisure–income indifference curves thus possess all the properties of the indifference curves discussed earliar.

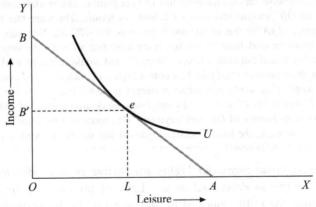

FIGURE 4.90 Equilibrium of the worker is the point of tangency, e, of BA to U.

(i) *Overtime wage rate has to be higher than the normal wage rate:* To induce workers to extend their work-hours beyond the normal hours, the hourly wage rate to be offered should be higher than the normal wage rate.

In other words, the overtime wage rate should be higher than the normal wage rate to induce workers to supply additional hours of work.

With the help of leisure–income trade-off lines and the leisure–income indifference curves, we are in a position to explain the logic behind the higher overtime wage rates (Figure 4.91).

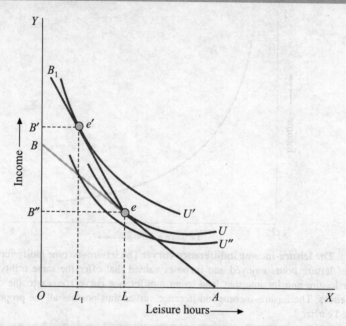

FIGURE 4.91 Overtime wage versus normal wage: The leisure–income indifference curve (U) is tangential to the leisure–income trade-off line (BA) at point e. The worker supplies AL hours of work at this point for OB'' income and enjoys OL hours of leisure. The wage rate for the routine work is equal to the slope of eA (or that of BA) and is given as $w = OB''/AL$. Now suppose employer requires LL_1 hours of overtime work from the worker. If the wage rate offered is the same as that for the routine work, the worker would fall onto a lower utility, U'' and would refuse to work overtime. In order to motivate him, the employer must take him onto a higher IC such as U' by offering him a higher rate of overtime wage. This would necessitate a steeper trade-off line eB_1 beyond point e. The worker would attain higher utility U' at e' on it by supplying the desired number of additional hours of work. This would yield an income of OB' and leave only OL_1 hours of leisure for him. With the possibility of higher overtime wage, the leisure–income trade-off line develops a kink at e.

(ii) *Taxing wage-income turns out highly productive in underdeveloped countries but counter-productive in developed ones:* Levy of tax on wage-income reduces wage rate and hence the utility enjoyed by the workers. In the underdeveloped countries, workers find it unbearable. To compensate the loss of income to taxation, the workers choose to forego more leisure and supply more hours of work. The affect on working habits of the people in developed countries is opposite. Fall in wage rate in consequence to taxation of wage income is matched by them by a reduction in supply of labour hours. Workers in advanced countries are economically better-off in comparison to their counterparts in underdeveloped countries. As a result, they find work unattractive at lower wage rate and reduce their supply of labour hours in consequence. Figures 4.92 and 4.93 demonstrate the effect of taxation of wage income on the working habits of the people in the underdeveloped and developed countries.

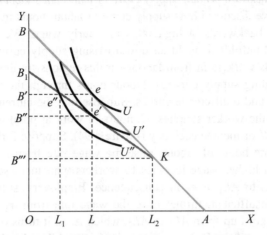

FIGURE 4.92 Effect of taxing wage income on work in poor countries: A worker in an underdeveloped country increases supply of labour-hours in response to taxation of wage incomes beyond OB''' at $t\%$ of the wage rate (income of OB''' being exempted from the levy). As a result, the leisure–income trade-off line AB bends downwards to AKB_1 at K. The worker pays a tax of $B'B''$ with wage income falling from OB' to OB'' for AL hours of work at e'. He slips down from U to U'. The worker, if poor or one from a poor country, is most likely to move to e'' enjoying even lesser utility (U'') than that he did in the post-tax position at e'. Note that he supplies more hours to retain his pre-tax level of income, OB'. Thus, taxation of hourly wage in underdeveloped countries or in respect of poor workers proves highly productive.

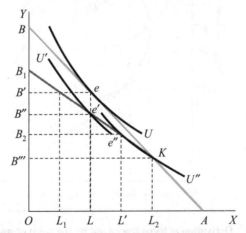

FIGURE 4.93 Effect of taxing wage income on work in rich countries: A worker in an advanced nation, on the contrary, decreases the supply of labour-hours in response to taxation of wage income beyond OB''' at $t\%$ of the wage rate (income of OB''' being exempted from the levy). As a result, the leisure–income trade-off line AB bends downwards to AKB_1 at K. The worker pays a tax of $B'B''$ with wage income falling from OB' to OB'' for AL hours of work. He slips down from U to U'. The worker, if affluent, or one in an affluent country, may choose either to remain at e', or to move to e'', a position where he is better-off on U'' than on U', by supplying fewer hours, AL', ($AL' < AL$). This would reduce his output and hence the total product of the firm. Thus, taxation of hourly wage in affluent countries proves counter-productive.

(iii) *Derivation of backward-bending supply curve of individual's labour hours:* In Section 2.7 (Figure 2.14) we discussed how supply curve of labour hours in respect of an individual worker bends backwards at high rates of hourly wage. We also observed that the backward bend unfolds to yield an upward rising supply curve in the long-run when free entry hauls workers in from labour-surplus regions. In this section, we derive the backward bending supply curve of labour hours through the tools of leisure–income trade-off lines and indifference curves. Suppose that the current wage rate per labour-hour is w and the worker supplies AL hours of work at point e, enjoying OL hours of leisure and OB' of income each day (Figure 4.94). Suppose further that the employers, in need of more hours of labour, raise the wage rate from w to w_1 as an incentive. This results in higher wage-incomes to workers who increase the supply of labour-hours from AL to AL_1 at e_1 in consequence. Employers, still finding the supply of labour-hours insufficient, further raise the wage rate from w_1 to w_2. In consequence, labour supply goes up from AL_1 to AL_2, which is, as it turns out, the maximum at the disposal of the workers. If the wage rate be further hiked by the employers from this

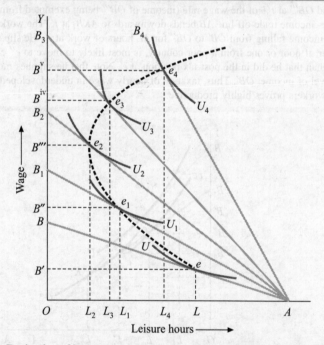

FIGURE 4.94 Derivation of locus traced out by the point of worker's equilibrium: The worker is supplying AL hours at e when the wage rate is $w(BA)$. Finding supply insufficient, employers increase the wage rate to $w_1(B_1A)$, and in consequence, supply increases to AL_1 hours. Employers continue to increase wages to lure more and more hours of work until at w_2, supply of labour hours reaches a maximum of AL_2. Thereafter, any further hike in wage rate is matched by a decrease in supply of labour hours first to AL_3 and finally to AL_4. The broken curve shows how the locus of the equilibrium looks. In the figure, x-axis measures leisure-hours and y-axis income.

level to w_3 level or even to a higher level, the effect on supply of labour hours is opposite. The workers, instead of increasing the supply, decrease it each time wage is hiked by the employers with a view to lure more hours of work. This unexpected behaviour of workers is due to leisure effect. Workers begin to value leisure activities at higher levels of income accruing to them due to higher wage-rates. Little work now fetches them a high income. Initially, they had increased the supply of labour hours to raise income to the desired level. Now that the desired level of income is attained with fewer hours of work they begin to prefer leisure to labour. Figures 4.94 and 4.95 demonstrate the behaviour of the workers. The reference here is to the supply of labour-hours of skilled workers. In case of unskilled or non-specific labour, the question of backward bend in the supply curve seldom arises as the same is highly wage elastic. Figures 4.94 and 4.95 demonstrate derivation of the backward bending supply curve of labour hours of skilled worker.

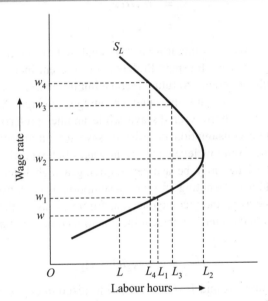

FIGURE 4.95 Derivation of the backward bending supply curve of labour hours: At wage w, hours OL (equal to AL in Figure 4.94) of work are supplied initially. Now wage rate is raised to w_1 due to which supply goes to OL_1 (= AL_1 of Figure 4.94). The trend goes on until wage rate is w_2 at which the supply of labour hours is maximum at OL_2 (= AL_2 of Figure 4.94). Any hike in wage rate is matched by a cut in the supply of labour hours first to OL_3 (= AL_3 of Figure 4.94) and then to OL_4 (= AL_4 of Figure 4.94). In this figure, x-axis represents labour-hours and y-axis, the hourly wage-rate, w. The supply curve of labour hours of an individual bends backwards as shown.

(e) Consumption and saving over the life cycle

In the time preference theory of interest (Figure 4.77), we employed willingness curves to represent a wealth-holder's preferences for present and future incomes. A willingness curve was defined as a locus of different combinations of present and future incomes that offer same level of utility to the wealth-holder. One combination of the two incomes is as good as another so much so that the wealth-holder turns indifferent in between them. The willingness curve, therefore, was none other than a wealth-holder's indifference curve between the present and the future incomes. An indifference curve such as willingness curve may be described algebraically by

$$U = \alpha xy + \beta \tag{4.32}$$

where,

$x \equiv$ current income

$y \equiv$ future income

α, β are constants.

The slope of the utility function in Eq. (4.32) may be given as

$$dy/dx = -[(\partial U/\partial x)/(\partial U/\partial y)]$$
$$= -\alpha y/\alpha x$$
$$= -y/x \tag{4.33}$$

We can extend our notion of willingness curve to analyse how a rational individual plans his consumption and savings over his lifespan. Preference to present income implies preference to current consumption while preference to future income implies preference to future consumption. The former leads to dissavings while the latter encourages savings. An individual preferring current consumption tends to borrow or dissave while another preferring future consumption tends to curtail his current consumption in order to save for future consumption. The former may be a worker suffering from low levels of current wages but expecting high levels of assured future incomes while the latter may be a trader enjoying a high level of current income but fearing tough days in old age. Denoting current consumption as c_1, consumption one year from now as c_2, current income as y_1 and income one year from now as y_2, the expression for current consumption of an individual preferring present income to income accruing to him one year from now may be given as:

$$c_1 = y_1 + [y_2/(1 + r)] \tag{4.34}$$

where, r is the rate of interest and $[y_2/(1 + r)]$ is the discounted value of income one year from now.

That is, the individual prefers to consume not only his current income y_1 but also the discounted value of his income y_2 accruing to him one year from now. One can also look upon $[y_2/(1 + r)]$ as the amount borrowed now at $100r$ per cent per annum, which may be paid off one year from now by the then income of y_2.

For an individual who prefers future consumption c_2 to current consumption of y_1, the expression may be given as:

$$c_2 = [y_1 (1+ r)] + y_2 \tag{4.35}$$

where, $[y_1 (1 + r)]$ is the amount the individual would get one year from now by investing his current income y_1 at $100r$ per cent compounded annually.

But if $c_1 < y_1$, $s_1 = y_1 - c_1$, and supposing that he consumes whole of the income during the year only, the future consumption would be

$$c_2 = s_1 (1 + r) + y_2$$
$$= (y_1 - c_1)(1 + r) + y_2$$
$$\Rightarrow \quad c_2 + (1 + r) c_1 = y_1 (1 + r) + y_2 \qquad (4.36)$$

Expression (4.36) represents a straight line when c_1 is represented on x-axis and c_2 on y-axis. The expression assumes that current consumption is less than the current income and whole of the future income along with the current savings as also the interest on these savings are to be consumed in future.

If $c_1 > y_1$, the individual would borrow in the current period and repay his borrowings along with interest in future from the future income y_2. In such a case,

$$c_2 = y_2 - (c_1 - y_1)(1 + r)$$
$$\Rightarrow \quad c_2 + c_1 (1 + r) = y_2 + y_1 (1 + r) \qquad (4.37)$$

Expressions (4.36) and (4.37) are both identical, each yielding a straight line when plotted with c_1 on x-axis and c_2 on y-axis. If $c_1 = 0$,

$$c_2 = y_2 + y_1 (1 + r), \text{ which is the same as Eq. (4.35)}.$$

And if $\quad c_2 = 0$,

$$c_1 = y_1 + [y_2/(1 + r)], \text{ which is the same as Eq. (4.34)}.$$

Thus, Eq. (4.36) or (4.37) would represent the consumer's budget line with a slope of

$$dc_2/dc_1 = -[1 + r] \qquad (4.38)$$

Replacing c_1 for x and c_2 for y in Eq. (4.32), we have

$$U = \alpha\, c_1 c_2 + \beta$$
$$\Rightarrow \quad dc_2/dc_1 = -c_2/c_1 \qquad (4.39)$$

For optimality of the combination (c_1, c_2), the budget line should be tangential to the indifference curve (Figure 4.96). This requires that the slope of the indifference curve must be equal to that of the budget line. That is,

$$dc_2/dc_1 = -c_2/c_1$$
$$= -[1 + r]$$
$$\Rightarrow \quad c_2/c_1 = [1 + r] \qquad (4.40)$$

The analysis above is based on the assumption that 'future' refers to a period of one year from now. It can be extended to any period n years from now by replacing the term $[1 + r]$ by $[1 + r]^n$.

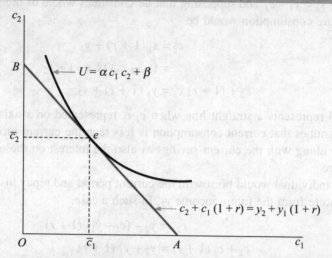

FIGURE 4.96 Consumption and savings over life-time: Consumption and saving over life-time, viewed as current consumption and future consumption, assuming that the life-span comprises only these two periods. The model can be extended to any number of periods. The optimal levels of the current and the future consumption are $[\bar{c}_1, \bar{c}_2]$.

4.6 THE COMPOSITE COMMODITY THEOREM

All the applications of the indifference curves discussed above are limited to a two-commodity world. The world we live in is a multi-commodity world in which we produce and consume a number of commodities. What is the utility of the indifference curve analysis if it cannot be applied to the real world problems to obtain their solutions? Is there a way to make this tool applicable to a multi-commodity world?

The concept of composite commodity provides an answer to the question. Through it we can extend the applicability of indifference curves to a multi-commodity world. What we need to do is to define commodity Y as a composite commodity representing a basket of a number of goods other than commodity X. Here, X may be a major item of consumption, such as food, on which we spend a sizeable part of our budget on regular basis. Commodity Y would then represent a heterogeneous basket of all other goods except X. The question that arises now is to decide how to measure good Y on the vertical axis? Adding up of the quantities of shirts, bicycles, TVs, tables, chairs, etc. together to determine the quantity of Y makes no sense! The only other alternative left to account for the quantity of the composite commodity is to add up the monetary values of all the goods included in it. To illustrate, let the money value of all the goods contained in the heterogeneous basket of composite commodity add up to ₹ 20,000. Good Y can then be quantified as 20,000 units of composite commodity, each priced at rupee one. Thus, *a composite commodity can be defined as the money value of all the goods consumed other than good X*. When none of X is consumed, the quantity of Y consumed would be equal to the numerical value of the budget, $\bar{B}$ When Y is not consumed at all, the quantity of good X woud be $\bar{B}/P_x$ where P_X is the price of good X. As per definition of the composite commodity, price of its each unit would be $P_Y = 1$. The slope of the budget line $(-P_X/P_Y)$ would be simply $(-P_X)$.

The numerical value of total expenditure on all the commodities other than commodity X is thus interpreted as the quantity of the *composite commodity*. The results of the indifference curve analysis with this notion of the composite commodity would yield the optimal basket of commodity X and the optimal expenditure on all goods other than commodity X. Hicks in his *Value and Capital* has worked this out in the form of the *Composite Commodity Theorem*.

To illustrate, suppose a consumer spends a sum of ₹ 10,000 on food and non-food items (composite commodity). The price of food is, say, ₹ 50 per unit. Hence, he would buy a maximum of 200 units of food or a maximum of 10,000 units of the non-food items each or any linear combination of the two. The budget line is the join of points (200,0) and (0,10,000) with a slope of $(-P_X)$, which is equal to (-50) as in this case. Note that the price of the composite commodity Y would be rupee one per unit. The equilibrium of the consumer can be shown as in Figure 4.97 (not to scale).

The analysis reduces to the same format as that employed earlier in the chapter while discussing the price consumption curves or deriving the demand curve for good X.

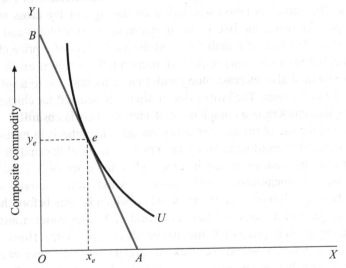

FIGURE 4.97 Consumer's equilibrium in a multi-product world, the composite commodity theorem: In a multiple-commodity world, a consumer's equilibrium can be looked upon as one in which commodities are classified as food and non-food items (composite commodity). Of the budget $\overline{B}$, the consumer can spend at most $\overline{B}/P_X$ on food and at most $\overline{B}/P_Y$ with $P_Y = 1$ on non-food items (composite commodity). Note that the slope of the budget line AB is very high (equal to P_x). At point e, the budget line is tangent to the indifference curve $\overline{U} = f(x, y)$. If $\overline{B}$ is ₹ 10,000 and $P_x = 50$, the budget line would have a slope of (-50) connecting points A (200, 0) and B (0, 10000). If $x_e = 120$ units of food, costing ₹ 6000 at $P_x = 50$, y_e is 4000 units of non-food items bought at $P_Y = ₹ 1.00$ per unit. A fall or a rise in price of X would pivot the budget line outwards or inwards and an increase or a decrease in income would shift the budget line parallel to itself outwards or inwards as the case be. Accordingly, price consumption and income consumption curves can be visualized and demand curves can be derived following the usual procedure.

4.7 CRITIQUE OF INDIFFERENCE CURVE APPROACH

The indifference curve approach to demand analysis is treated by economists as a major advancement in the study of consumers' behaviour. The reasons cited for this are the following:

1. Less stringent assumptions

The indifference curve analysis is based on assumptions less stringent than those of the cardinal utility analysis. This approach is superior to the cardinal utility analysis in that it does not depend on the unrealistic assumptions of cardinality of utility and constancy of the marginal utility of money.

2. Its utility in measurement of consumers' surplus

Indifference curve analysis provides a framework for the measurement of consumers' surplus which is very important in welfare economics and in government policy formulations. Estimate of consumers' surplus helps government in formulation of appropriate tax policies with a view to maximize social welfare.

3. Its utility in classification of goods as substitutes and complements

Indifference curve analysis lays down a better criterion for classification of goods as substitutes and complements. The earlier criterion was based on the sign of the cross price elasticity of demand. If the sign is positive, the two goods in question are substitutes and if it is negative, they are complements. The rule of thumb followed the total effect of a price change and led to absurd conclusions. For instance, suppose price of mutton falls to half as much. In consequence, demand for chicken would also increase along with that of mutton due to a substantial increase in real income of the consumers. The cross price elasticity of demand for chicken would then be negative, implying that chicken is a complement of mutton! This is absurd!

Hicks* suggested the use of the compensatory variation hypothesis in measurement of cross price elasticity of demand. According to him, cross price elasticity of demand should be measured after compensating for the change in real income. When the price of X falls, the real income of the consumer rises. Compensatory variation requires withdrawal of enough income from the consumer so that he may fall back onto the same IC on which he was before the fall in price of X. Now, if a fall in price of X leads to a fall in demand of Y, after compensating for the rise in real income caused by a fall in price of X, the two goods are substitutes. However, the Hicksian criterion, although theoretically sound, yet lacks in practicability because one needs to know the consumer preferences before knowing which way the demand of good Y would move after compensating for the rise in real income caused by a fall in price of X. Hence, the usual approach of the sign of cross price elasticity continues to be more feasible and practicable.

Despite the important advantages of the indifference curve analysis, the approach suffers from a few serious drawbacks. Some of which are outlined below:

1. Assumption of convexity of consumer preferences

ICs are axiomatically assumed to be convex to the origin. The theory has failed to establish this convexity.

---

*J. Hicks, *Value and Capital* (Oxford University Press, 1946) 2nd ed., pp. 42–52.

2. Little validity of ordering of consumer preferences

Consumer's ability and rationality of ordering his preferences is highly questionable. Even consumer preferences change quite fast. Hence, even if ordering them be possible, their validity is short-lived.

3. Retention of some of the weaknesses of the cardinalist approach

The indifference curve theory has retained most of the weaknesses of the cardinalist school. For instance, it has retained the strong assumption of rationality of the consumer as also the concept of marginal utility. The latter is implicit in the definition of the marginal rate of commodity substitution (See Section 4.2, p. 137).

4. It overlooks important influences on consumer's behaviour

The theory has ignored important influences of advertising, habits, impulsiveness and speculative nature on consumer behaviour. Such influences have a great significance in price–output decisions of the firms.

Despite these drawbacks, the indifference curve theory continues to be a major advancement in the study of consumer behaviour.

4.8 THE REVEALED PREFERENCE APPROACH

Paul A. Samuelson introduced the term *revealed preference* in 1938 through his article *Consumption Theory in Terms of Revealed Preference*. Later, in 1947, it appeared again in his book, 'Fundamentals of Economic Analysis'.

Samuelson's revealed preference hypothesis is treated as yet another major breakthrough in the 'theory of demand'. It establishes the law of demand directly from its axioms making no use of indifference curves and their restrictive assumptions.

The hallmark of the theory of revealed preference is that it is behaviourist rather than introspective as in Hicks–Allen approach of indifference curves. By choosing a basket of goods in a given budgetary situation, a consumer under the revealed preference theory is said to have revealed his preference for that basket over the rest implying that they are all either inferior or costlier (Figure 4.98).

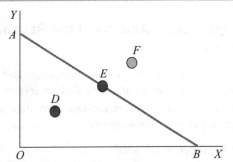

FIGURE 4.98 Baskets revealed inferior, preferred or unaffordable: AB is the budget line. Baskets D and E are affordable but basket F is not because it lies above the budget line of the consumer. Suppose the consumer chooses basket E on the budget line. This implies that he reveals his preference for this basket. All other baskets are either costlier (such as F) or inferior (such as all the baskets other than E on AB as also those such as D below it). In the figure, the choice of basket D would violate the assumption of rationality on the grounds that it does not maximize the consumer's utility. Axiomatically, the basket *revealed preferred* must maximize the consumer's utility.

Derivation of demand through the revealed preference theory is based on the following assumptions:

1. *Rationality:* Consumer is assumed to be a rational person who prefers baskets that include more quantities of the commodities.
2. *Consistency:* Consumer is consistent in his behaviour. If he chooses a bundle A in a situation in which bundle B is also available to him, he will not choose bundle B in any other situation in which bundle A is also available to him.

Symbolically,

$$\text{If } A > B, \text{ then } B \not> A.$$

3. *Transitivity:* In any particular situation,

$$\text{if } A > B \text{ and } B > C \Rightarrow A > C.$$

4. *Revealed preference axiom:* The consumer, by choosing a basket of goods in a given budgetary situation, reveals his preference for that particular basket. The chosen basket maximizes (axiomatically) his utility and the rest of the baskets on the budget line are revealed inferior.

4.8.1 Derivation of Demand under the Revealed Preference Theory

Suppose AB (Figure 4.99) is the budget line of a consumer. Suppose further that the consumer chooses a basket L on AB, revealing thereby his preference for the basket over all the rest. Now suppose price of X falls. Given the price of Y, his budget line AB pivots outwards to AB' (Figure 4.99). This shows an increase in consumer's real income. Under the constant real income hypothesis, an income equivalent to length AM on y-axis needs to be withdrawn from the consumer so that he may, if he likes, choose the same level of consumption as before (point L). Figure 4.99 explains the process of derivation of the law of demand given that X is a normal good.

The law of demand established in Figure 4.99 is known as *Samuelson's fundamental theorem of consumption*. The theorem states that *"Any good (simple or composite) that is known always to increase (decrease) in demand when money income alone rises (falls) must definitely shrink (expand) in demand when its price alone rises (falls)"*.

4.8.2 The Weak and the Strong Axioms of the Revealed Preference Theory

We made a mention of the ordering principles (consistency and transitivity) of consumer preferences while listing the assumptions of the revealed preference theory. Now we combine the ordering principles with the revealed-preference-axiom to state and establish the Weak and the Strong Axioms of the revealed preference theory:

Weak Axiom of Revealed Preference (WARP)

If bundle (x_1, y_1) is directly revealed preferred to bundle (x_2, y_2), the two bundles being different from each other, it cannot happen that bundle (x_2, y_2) would be directly revealed preferred to bundle (x_1, y_1).

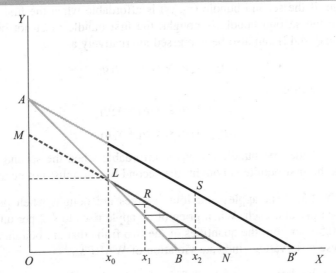

FIGURE 4.99 Derivation of demand curve from revealed preference theory: The consumer has revealed his preference for basket L on his budget line AB. This implies all other baskets are either inferior or costlier for the consumer. A fall in price of X increases his real income. As a result, his budget line pivots outwards to AB'. If X is a normal good, its income elasticity of demand is positive. From Samuelson's Fundamental Theorem of Consumption, X would expand in demand when price alone falls. That is, a fall in price of X must be associated with a rise in its demand. To see, suppose income AM is temporarily withdrawn from the consumer to strip him off the rise of real income caused by a fall in price of X. In consequence, budget line AB' shifts downwards through a vertical distance AM. The shifted line is MN, which passes through point L. The consumer may, if he likes, retain the same basket at L but in all likelihood, he would prefer a basket in the triangular region LBN (shaded), excluding baskets rejected already by him on the segment LB. He would not choose a basket on LB because of his consistency as he has already rejected all the baskets on LB below point L. Again, he would not choose a basket on LA as he has already rejected them all. The question of choosing a basket on LM does not arise because he has already rejected much better bundles on LA lying above LM. Thus, partly by virtue of consistency and partly by virtue of rationality, the consumer would choose baskets only in the triangular region LBN. Among the baskets in the triangular region LBN, he must choose a basket on segment LN below point L by virtue of his rationality. Choosing a basket, such as that at R, on segment LN or above LB is in line with both, his rationality and consistency. It is in line with rationality because a basket such as R enables him to have more of at least one of the two goods than any other basket below segment LN in the triangular region and it is in line with his consistency because he can't prefer a basket already rejected by him. In case, the withdrawn income is not restored to the consumer, the substitution effect is zero if he chooses basket L. If X is a normal good, i.e. it has a positive income elasticity and if the withdrawn income is retrieved back to the consumer, he would choose a basket on AB' somewhere to the right of the point L. Thus, the consumer would consume more of X in response to a fall in its price provided it is a normal good.

In other words, if a bundle (x_1, y_1) is bought at prices (p_1, q_1) and a different bundle (x_2, y_2) is bought at (p_2, q_2), then if

$$x_1 p_1 + y_1 q_1 \geq x_2 p_1 + y_2 q_1 \tag{4.41}$$

it must *not* be the case that

$$x_2 p_2 + y_2 q_2 \geq x_1 p_2 + y_1 q_2$$

Instead,

$$x_2 p_2 + y_2 q_2 < x_1 p_2 + y_1 q_2 \tag{4.42}$$

In simple language, if the second bundle (x_2, y_2) is affordable when the first bundle (x_1, y_1) is bought, then when the second bundle is bought, the first bundle must not be affordable. The conditions (4.41) and (4.42) can also be expressed alternatively as:

If
$$x_2 p_2 + y_2 q_2 \geq x_1 p_2 + y_1 q_2 \quad (4.43)$$

then, it *must not* be the case that

$$x_1 p_1 + y_1 q_1 \geq x_2 p_1 + y_2 q_1$$

Instead,
$$x_1 p_1 + y_1 q_1 < x_2 p_1 + y_2 q_1 \quad (4.44)$$

In simple language, if the first bundle (x_1, y_1) is affordable when the second bundle (x_2, y_2) is bought, then when the first bundle is bought, the second bundle must not be affordable.

ILLUSTRATION 4.5: Six apples and four oranges are bought when prices of the two fruits are rupee one per unit each. When price of an apple rises to ₹ 2 per unit and that of an orange falls to ₹ 0.50 per unit, the quantities of the two fruits that are bought are 8 apples and 3 oranges. Do these observations indicate violation of WARP?

Solution: Relating the data given to the definition of WARP, we have:

$$x_1 = 6, \; y_1 = 4; \; p_1 = 1, \; q_1 = 1$$
$$x_2 = 8, \; y_2 = 3; \; p_2 = 2, \; q_2 = 0.50$$

(Please see Figure 4.100)

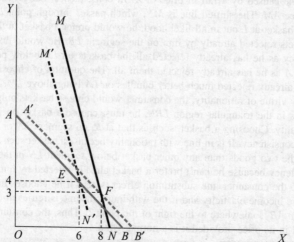

FIGURE 4.100 (Illustration 4.5): Six apples (measured on x-axis) and 4 oranges (measured on y-axis) are bought (point E, budget line AB) at a price of rupee one per unit of each. Clearly, consumer's budget is ₹ 10. When price of apples goes up to ₹ 2 per unit and that of oranges, to ₹ 0.50 per unit, he buys 8 apples and 3 oranges. His budget is now ₹ 17.50 (budget line MN). He is at point F, buying 8 apples and 3 oranges. When he buys bundle $E(6, 4)$, bundle $F(8, 3)$ is not affordable to him (at the existing prices of rupee one each) and when he buys bundle $F(8, 3)$ at new prices, bundle $E(6, 4)$ is affordable to him at new prices. The first bundle $E(6, 4)$ is affordable when the second bundle $F(8, 3)$ is bought; hence, when the first bundle $E(6, 4)$ is bought, the second bundle $F(8, 3)$ must not be affordable. This being true, **WARP is not violated**.

According to condition (4.43),
$$x_2p_2 + y_2q_2 = 8 \times 2 + 3 \times 0.50$$
$$= 17.50$$
$$x_1p_2 + y_1q_2 = 6 \times 2 + 4 \times 0.50$$
$$= 14.00$$

Clearly,
$$17.50 > 14.0$$
$$\Rightarrow \quad x_2p_2 + y_2q_2 \geq x_1p_2 + y_1q_2$$

If $\quad x_2p_2 + y_2q_2 \geq x_1p_2 + y_1q_2$

then it *must not* be the case that
$$x_1p_1 + y_1q_1 \geq x_2p_1 + y_2q_1 \quad \text{[From condition (4.44)]}$$

Instead, $\quad x_1p_1 + y_1q_1 < x_2p_1 + y_2q_1$
$$x_1p_1 + y_1q_1 = 6 \times 1 + 4 \times 1 = 10$$
$$x_2p_1 + y_2q_1 = 8 \times 1 + 3 \times 1 = 11$$

Clearly,
$$10 < 11$$
$$\Rightarrow \quad x_1p_1 + y_1q_1 < x_2p_1 + y_2q_1$$
$$\Rightarrow \quad x_1p_1 + y_1q_1 \not\geq x_2p_1 + y_2q_1$$

WARP, therefore, is not violated and the buying behaviour of the consumer is consistent.

ILLUSTRATION 4.6: In the previous illustration, let
$$x_1 = 2, y_1 = 4; p_1 = 2, q_1 = 4$$
$$x_2 = 4, y_2 = 2; p_2 = 4, q_2 = 2$$

Investigate whether WARP is violated or not.

Solution: From condition (4.43),
$$x_2p_2 + y_2q_2 = 4 \times 4 + 2 \times 2$$
$$= 20$$
$$x_1p_2 + y_1q_2 = 2 \times 4 + 4 \times 2$$
$$= 16$$

Therefore,
$$x_2p_2 + y_2q_2 \geq x_1p_2 + y_1q_2$$

Hence, condition (4.43) is satisfied.

To see that condition (4.44), i.e. $(x_1p_1 + y_1q_1 < x_2p_1 + y_2q_1)$ is also satisfied, we have

$$x_1p_1 + y_1q_1 = 2 \times 2 + 4 \times 4$$
$$= 20$$
$$x_2p_1 + y_2q_1 = 4 \times 2 + 2 \times 4$$
$$= 16$$

But,
$$20 \not< 16$$
$$x_1p_1 + y_1q_1 \not< x_2p_1 + y_2q_1$$

Hence, condition (4.44) is not satisfied. WARP is, therefore, violated and the buying behaviour of the consumer is inconsistent.

Calculations show that WARP is violated because Eq. (4.44) is not satisfied. The same result can be reached if we plot the data provided as in earlier illustration. Figure 4.101 demonstrates the point.

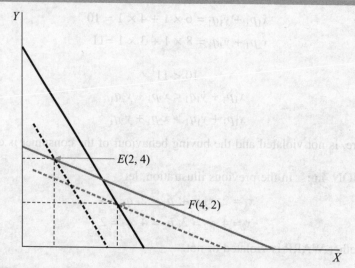

FIGURE 4.101 (Illustration 4.6): 'If bundle $E(2, 4)$ is affordable when bundle $F(4, 2)$ is bought, then when $E(2, 4)$ is bought, $F(4, 2)$ must not be affordable'. This is the condition for WARP to hold. But we observe that $E(2, 4)$ is affordable at prices $(4, 2)$ when $F(4, 2)$ bundle is bought, but when $E(2, 4)$ is bought at prices $(2, 4)$, $F(4, 2)$ bundle must not be affordable but it is! Budget lines in grey represent prices $(2, 4)$ while those in black represent prices $(4, 2)$. **WARP is violated and hence buying behaviour of the consumer is inconsistent.**

Checking WARP in Case of Several Choices of Bundles

When the bundles are more than two, the methods discussed above often turn out inconvenient. Let us, therefore, develop a compact method convenient enough for checking WARP in all cases.

Consider the observations given in Table 4.5.

TABLE 4.5 Choice of bundles at different price-sets

Observations	Prices		Bundles	
	p	q	x	y
1.	2	4	3	6
2.	4	2	6	3
3.	2	2	6	6

Expenditures incurred on each of the three bundles at each of the three price-sets can be calculated and listed in the form of a table (Table 4.6). Entry in row 1, column 1 of the table is 30 (2 × 3 + 4 × 6). It represents expenditure to be incurred on first bundle (3, 6) at the first price-set (2, 4). Likewise, entry in row 3 and column 2 is 18 (2 × 6 + 2 × 3). It represents expenditure to be incurred on second bundle (6, 3) at third price-set (2, 2). Entry in row 2 and column 1 is 24 (3 × 4 + 6 × 2). It represents expenditure to be incurred on first bundle (3, 6) at second price-set (4, 2). The rest of the entries are calculated similarly. Column 1 of the table shows expenditures to be incurred on bundle 1 at the three price-sets, column 2 shows expenditures to be incurred on second bundle at the three price-sets and column 3 shows expenditures to be incurred on the third bundle at the three price-sets. Likewise, row 1 shows expenditures to be incurred on the three bundles at the first price-set, row 2 shows that to be incurred on the three bundles at second price-set and row 3 shows expenditures to be incurred on the three bundles at the third price-set. Table 4.6 thus shows expenditures to be incurred on different bundles at each of the three price-sets.

TABLE 4.6 Expenditures on bundles at different price-sets

Prices \ Bundles	1	2	3
1	30	24*	36
2	24*	30	36
3	18*	18*	24

Entries along the diagonal from top-left to bottom-right in Table 4.6 indicate actual expenditures incurred on the three bundles at the respective price-sets. Other entries in each row indicate how much he would have spent had he chosen a different bundle. Starred entries indicate that the corresponding bundle is affordable in comparison to those actually bought (entries in the diagonal from top-left to the bottom-right). For instance, entry in row 3, column 1, which is 18, represents the cost of bundle 1 at the price-set 3, which the consumer had to incur, had he chosen bundle 1 instead of bundle 3 actually bought by him at this price-set. The actual cost of bundle 3 bought by the consumer is 24, which is more than that he had to incur had he chosen bundle 1 at this price-set instead of bundle 3. Thus, at the price-set 3, bundle 3 is revealed preferred to bundle 1. This implies that the latter is revealed inferior despite its affordability at the existing price-set. Likewise, bundle 3 is revealed preferred even to bundle 2 at the price-set 3. Bundle 2 is actually bought at the price-set 2 and is revealed preferred to bundle 1 at this price-set. The bundles corresponding to the starred entries are revealed inferior to the corresponding bundles in the diagonal from top-left to bottom-right of the table actually bought and hence revealed preferred.

The next step is to investigate whether the consumer is consistent in making his choices or not. The investigation involves a pair of entries along the diagonal from top-left to bottom-right, in respect of each of which, we require investigating whether a starred entry exists immediately to the left (right) of one and to the right (left) of the other. If they do, WARP is violated; else, it is not. It is only these starred entries that enter the test of consistency. Entries without a star to the left or those without a star to the right of the diagonal entries do not require a test of consistency on the grounds that they are all unaffordable.

If the choices are consistent, WARP is satisfied; else, it is violated. In the present context, let us take the first two entries in the diagonal, namely, 30 (row 1, col. 1) and 30 (row 2, col. 2). The first one (row 1, column 1) has a starred entry (24*) immediately to its right (row 1, col. 2) while the second one (row 2, col. 2) also has a starred entry (24*) immediately to its left (row 2, col. 1). WARP is therefore violated implying inconsistent consumer choices. The mechanism of the test is simple. Bundle 2(row 2, col. 2) was purchased when bundle 1 (row 2, col. 1) was affordable (24* < 30); then when bundle 1 (row 1, col. 1) is purchased, bundle 2 (row 1, col. 2) must not be affordable if WARP is to be satisfied. In other words, 24* (row 1, col. 2) should not be less than 30 (row 1, col. 1) for WARP to be satisfied! But as the facts stand, 24* (row 1, col. 2) is less than 30 (row 1, col. 1). WARP, therefore, is violated, making current choices of the consumer inconsistent.

To clarify the point further, let us take the last two entries in the diagonal, namely, 30 (row 2, col. 2) and 24 (row 3, col. 3). The choices are obviously consistent as there does not exist a starred entry to the right of 30 (row 2, col. 2) while a starred entry to the left of 24 (row 3, col. 3) does. Looking at it from the viewpoint of 'vice versa', a starred entry to the left of 24 (row 3, col. 3) exists but a starred entry to the right of 30 (row 2, col. 2) does not. That shows that bundle 3 (row 3, col. 3) is bought when bundle 2 (row 3, col. 2) is affordable but when bundle 2 (row 2, col. 2) is bought, bundle 3 (row 2, col. 3) is not affordable. To satisfy WARP, when bundle 2 (row 2, col. 2) is purchased, bundle 3 (row 2, col. 3) must not be affordable. This is true as bundle 3 (row 2, col. 3) costs more (36) than bundle 2 (row 2, col. 2) which costs only 30. WARP is thus satisfied in this case.

The reader is advised to test the first and third entries along the diagonal for consistency. Proceeding likewise, it can easily be shown that consumer's choices are again consistent as WARP is not violated. Bundle 3 (row 3, col. 3) is bought when bundle 1(row 3, col. 1) is affordable and when bundle 1 (row 1, col. 1) is bought, bundle 3 (row 1, col. 3) is not affordable as required for satisfaction of WARP.

As a rule of thumb, we can conclude that if entry (i, j) in Table 4.6 contains a star and if entry (j, i) in the table also contains a star, then the diagonal entries (i, i) and (j, j) indicating actual purchases of the consumer signify violation of WARP and hence inconsistency in the buying behaviour of the consumer.

Problems in Illustrations 4.5 and 4.6 are easier to solve this way. Presenting in the format of Table 4.6, we have

TABLE 4.7 (Illustration 4.5) When bundle 2 (row 2, col. 2) is bought, bundle 1 (row 2, col. 1) is affordable and when bundle 1(row 1, col. 1) is bought, bundle 2 (row 1, col. 2) is not affordable as required by WARP. Choices are therefore consistent

Price sets \ Bundles	1(6, 4)	2(8, 3)
1(1, 1)	10	11
2(2, 0.50)	14*	17.50

TABLE 4.8 (Illustration 4.6) When bundle 2 (row 2, col. 2) is bought, bundle 1 (row 2, col. 1) is affordable and when bundle 1 (row 1, col. 1) is bought, bundle 2 (row 1, col. 2) **is affordable**. This violates WARP. Choices are therefore inconsistent

Price sets \ Bundles	1(6, 4)	2(8, 3)
1(4, 2)	18	16*
2(2, 4)	16*	20

Through the criteria laid down, the reader can verify that WARP is not violated in the situation of Illustration 4.5 while it is violated in the latter case.

Strong Axiom of Revealed Preference (SARP)

If (x_1, y_1) is revealed preferred to (x_2, y_2) [either directly or indirectly], the two bundles being different from each other, it can't happen that (x_2, y_2) would be revealed preferred to (x_1, y_1) directly or indirectly.

WARP implies that if bundle A is revealed preferred directly to another bundle B, then we should never observe B being directly revealed preferred to A. This is what consistency in choices implies.

Revealed preference is said to be indirect if a bundle is revealed preferred to another through transitivity. That is, if bundle A is revealed preferred to bundle C and bundle C is revealed preferred to a third bundle B, then, bundle A is said to be revealed preferred to bundle B indirectly. SARP implies that if a bundle A is revealed preferred to another bundle B directly or indirectly, then we should never observe bundle B revealed preferred to bundle A directly or indirectly. The main point of difference between WARP and SARP is that the revealed preference is direct in WARP while it can be direct as well as indirect in SARP.

Checking SARP

Consider Table 4.9 of costs in respect of four bundles at four price-sets. The table follows the pattern of Table 4.6, which expressed costs of each of the three bundles at each of the three price-sets.

On the basis of reasoning similar to that for checking WARP, we observe that bundle 1 (first row) is revealed preferred to bundle 2 (first row) and bundle 2 (second row) is revealed preferred to bundle 3 (second row).

Bundle 1 ⇐ Bundle 2 ⇐ Bundle 3

By virtue of transitivity, bundle 1 is revealed preferred indirectly to bundle 3.

Bundle 1 ⇐ Bundle 3 (A)

Star in parenthesis in the first row, third column indicates that bundle 1 is revealed preferred to bundle 3 inirectly.

TABLE 4.9 Indirect preferences and SARP

Prices \ Bundles	1	2	3	4
1	20 (*)	10*	22 (*)	25
2	21	20	15*	30
3	30	32	25	24*
4	20*	40	45	35

Likewise, bundle 3 (third row) is revealed preferred to bundle 4 (third row) and bundle 4 (fourth row) is revealed preferred to bundle 1 (fourth row).

Bundle 3 ⇐ Bundle 4 ⇐ Bundle 1

Hence, bundle 3 is revealed preferred to bundle 1 indirectly. This can be represented as below:

Bundle 1 ⇒ Bundle 3 (B)

From (A) and (B), it is clear that SARP *is violated*. From A, bundle 1 is revealed preferred to bundle 3 indirectly (bundle 1 is revealed preferred to bundle 2, which, in turn, is revealed preferred to bundle 3) and from B, bundle 3 is revealed preferred to bundle 1 indirectly (bundle 3 is revealed preferred to bundle 4, which, in turn, is revealed preferred to bundle 1). For non-violation of SARP, bundle 3 must not be preferred to bundle 1 if bundle 1 has already been preferred to bundle 3. Consumer's preferences, here, are inconsistent therefore.

To drive the concept home, let us take another illustration (Table 4.10).

TABLE 4.10 Indirect preferences and SARP

Bundles \ Prices	1	2	3
1	24	14*	26 (*)
2	25	24	19*
3	16	19	14

Bundle 1 is revealed preferred to bundle 2, which, in turn, is revealed preferred to bundle 3, as shown in Table 4.10 by means of the arrows. Bundle 1 is thus indirectly preferred to bundle 3 but bundle 3 is **not preferred** to bundle 1 directly or indirectly. SARP therefore is **not violated** and the consumer **is consistent** in his preferences.

Critique of Revealed Preference Theory

As stated earlier, Samuelson's revealed preference theory is a major advancement to the theory of demand. It helps to derive demand curve without a reference to the concepts of utility and convexity of the indifference curves. It also lays down the basis of construction of the cost of living indices and their use in the study of consumer's welfare.

The theory, however, is not free from criticism. Economists often subject it to criticism on the following grounds:

1. According to Prof. Armstrong, the revealed preference theory ignores the possibility of indifference in the consumer's behaviour. It is likely that a consumer may face bundles equally desirable and may find it difficult to choose between them or to reveal his preference for one over the other.
2. The theory takes into account price as the singlemost determinant of consumer's behaviour. In real world, a consumer's behaviour is influenced by a number of socioeconomic considerations, other than that of the price.
3. Samuelson's derivation of demand is conditional as it requires positive income elasticity as a necessary condition for the negative price elasticity.
4. The theory is silent about Giffen Paradox in which income elasticity is negative.
5. Samuelson's basic axiom that choice reveals preference has been widely questioned. A consumer may choose a bundle today and another tomorrow. For example, an individual may purchase more potatoes with less onions today due to their relative prices and money income in his possession at the time of purchase. The next day, he may reverse the order of choice due to the size of income in possession despite identical relative prices.

In the words of Prof. Tapas Majumdar*, *"This axiom is invalid for situations where the individual choosers are known to be capable of employing strategies of game theory type."* Moreover, Samuelson's theory leaves little or no room for demand forecasting so crucial for planning and scheduling production.

---

* Tapas Majumdar, *The Measurement of Utility,* Macmillan & Co. Ltd., London, 1966, p. 139.

KEY TERMS AND CONCEPTS

Approaches to demand analysis There are three approaches to the analysis of demand:
1. Marshallian cardinal utility approach
2. Hicks-Allen's indifference curve approach
3. Samuelson's revealed preference approach.

Assumptions of the cardinal utility analysis It is based on the following assumptions:
1. Consumer is a rational person
2. Utility is cardinal
3. Marginal utility of money is constant
4. Marginal utility of the commodity diminishes with the level of consumption
5. Additivity of utility.

Assumptions of the revealed preference theory
1. Rationality of the consumer.
2. Consistency of choice.
3. Transitivity of choice.
4. Revealed preference axiom.

Cardinal utility Refers to the concept of numerical measurement of utility in terms of monetary units.

Cardinal utility approach So long as the marginal utility of a product exceeds its price, demand for the additional units of a product continues. As soon as the marginal utility equals the price, demand reaches its saturation.

Critique of cardinal utility approach Marshall's cardinal utility approach is subjected to criticism on several counts:
1. The assumption of the cardinal utility is unrealistic.
2. The assumption of constant marginal utility of money is also unrealistic.
3. The law of diminishing marginal utility of commodity is based more on introspection than on empirical studies.

Cobb–Douglas preferences Utility function described by a homogeneous function such as the Cobb-Douglas function $U = Ax^{\alpha} \cdot y^{\beta}$, where α, β are constants, represent such preferences.

Compensatory variation hypothesis A hypothesis employed by Hicks to split the total effect of a fall (rise) in price of a good into its components of substitution and income effects. Hicksian hypothesis requires adjustment of the rise (fall) in income caused by a fall (rise) in price of a good in such a way that the consumer retains his original level of utility in consequence. Hicks, for the purpose, drew a budget line representing income net of that withdrawn touching the original indifference curve. The new budget line was drawn parallel to the budget line resulting in consequence of the change in price (budget line NM in Figure 4.61).

Composite commodity It is a bundle of goods, heterogeneous in character, when quantified in terms of units of money. For example, 2 pens each priced at ₹ 20 and 3 notebooks each priced at ₹ 10 would constitute 70 units of a composite commodity (money value of pens, ₹ 40 + money value of notebooks, ₹ 30 = 70 units of composite commodity each priced at rupee one). Goods represented by a composite commodity being heterogeneous in nature cannot be accounted by a single unit except units of money.

Constant real income hypothesis A hypothesis employed by Slutsky to split the total effect of a fall (rise) in price of a good into its components of substitution and income effects. Slutsky's hypothesis requires adjustment of the rise (fall) in income caused by a fall (rise) in price of a good in such a way that the consumer retains his original equilibrium basket (his real income) in consequence. Slutsky, for the purpose, drew a budget line representing income net of that withdrawn through the original point of equilibrium. The new budget line was drawn parallel to the budget line resulting in consequence of the change in price(budget line *NM* in Figure 4.64).

Consumer surplus   It represents excess of expenditure a consumer is willing to incur, over and above that being actually incurred by him on a product, so that he may not have to do without it during its scarcity.

Convex preferences   Consumer preferences that lead to an indifference curve convex to the origin. Utility functions such as $U = Ax^\alpha y^\beta$ describe convex preferences.

Demerits of revealed preference theory

1. According to Prof. Armstrong, the revealed preference theory ignores the possibility of indifference in the consumer's behaviour. It is likely that a consumer may face bundles equally desirable and may find it difficult to choose between them.
2. The theory takes into account price as the sole factor influencing the consumer's behaviour. In real world, a consumer is influenced by a number of socioeconomic considerations.
3. Samuelson's derivation of the demand law is conditional as it requires positive income elasticity as a necessary condition for the negative price elasticity.
4. The theory is silent about Giffen Paradox in which income elasticity is negative.
5. Samuelson's basic axiom that choice reveals preference has been widely questioned. A consumer may choose a bundle today and another tomorrow. For example, an individual may purchase more potatoes with less onions today due to their relative prices and money income in his possession at the time of purchase. The next day, he may reverse the order of choice due to the size of income in possession despite same relative prices.

Discrete preferences   When goods are demanded in whole (non-fractional) units, the indifference curve is a broken or a discontinuous curve. Consumer preferences of this type are referred to as discrete preferences.

Engel curve   An Engel curve, named after Ernest Engel, the propounder of the *Law of Family Expenditure*, shows variation of quantities of a good (say *X*) consumed with variation in consumer's income, given his tastes, preferences, fashions, product prices and prices of the related goods. Representing income on the vertical axis and the quantities of good *X* on the horizontal axis, Engel curves as derived from the ICCs are shown in Figures 4.40 to 4.45.

Gross and net substitutes   Gross substitutes refer to the close substitutes like coke and pepsi. Net substitutes are perfect substitutes such as ball point pens of same brand, colour and price.

Homothetic preferences   The type of consumer preferences that lead to the linear income consumption curve passing through the origin are referred to as the homothetic preferences. Consumer preference in respect of perfect substitutes, perfect complements and Cobb–Douglas utility functions are homothetic preferences.

Income consumption curve   Locus traced by consumer's equilibrium point in response to parallel shifts in the budget line.

Indifference curves   An indifference curve is the locus of different combinations of two goods that yield the same utility (level of satisfaction) each to the consumer. As a result, the consumer turns indifferent in-between any two of them.

   Conditional properties of indifference curves   Under given conditions, ICs show the following properties:

1. For perfect substitutes, ICs are negatively sloped straight lines.
2. For perfect complements, ICs are *L*-shaped.
3. An IC is a horizontal line when *X* is a neutral good and a vertical line, if *Y* is a neutral good.

4. If one of the two goods is an economic bad, IC would have a positive slope.
5. When both the goods are the economic bads, ICs slope downward with concavity to the origin.
6. When each of the two goods turns bad after a certain level of consumption, ICs may have a peculiar oval shape.
7. When consumers have a marked preference for one of the two goods, ICs are quasilinear.
8. ICs are discontinuous for discrete goods.

Demerits of indifference curves Despite being a major advancement in the analysis of demand, indifference curves suffer from several drawbacks:

1. *Assumption of convexity of consumer preferences:* ICs are axiomatically assumed to be convex to the origin. The theory is said to have failed to establish this convexity.
2. *Little validity of ordering of consumer preferences:* Consumer's ability and rationality of ordering his preferences is highly questionable. Even consumer preferences change quite fast. Hence, even if ordering them be possible, their validity is short-lived.
3. *Retention of some of the weaknesses of the cardinalist approach:* The indifference curve theory has retained most of the weaknesses of the cardinalist school. For instance, it has retained the strong assumption of rationality of the consumer as also the concept of marginal utility. The latter is implicit in the definition of the marginal rate of commodity substitution.
4. *It overlooks important influences on consumer's behaviour.*

Merits of indifference curves Indifference curves are considered as a major advancement in the demand theory. They possess the following merits:

1. Based on less stringent assumptions.
2. Serve as an instrument of measurement of the consumers' surplus.
3. Help classification of substitutes and complements.

Properties of indifference curves Indifference curves possess the following properties:

1. The ICs never cut each other
2. A higher IC represents a higher utility
3. ICs do not intersect each other
4. No two ICs are parallel to each other
5. ICs are convex to the origin. The necessary and the sufficient condition for convexity of the IC to the origin, is that the second order derivative of y with respect to x must be positive.

Indifference curve approach A consumer attempts to reach the highest possible indifference curve with given budget limitation. He attains his equilibrium at the point where indifference curve is tangential to the budget line. In other words, the condition of equilibrium is the equality of the slopes of the two.

Assumptions of the indifference curve approach The indifference curve approach is based on the following assumptions:

1. Rationality of the consumer
2. Utility is ordinal
3. Diminishing marginal rate of commodity substitution
4. Total utility derived from consumption depends on quantity of commodity consumed
5. Consistency and transitivity of choice.

Leisure income indifference curves Locus of various combinations of leisure hours and income levels that offer the same level of utility to the worker.

Leisure income trade-off line Different combinations of leisure hours and associated income levels that correspond to a given rate of hourly wage. Such combinations trace a straight line depicting the rate at which leisure hours are exchanged by the workers for wage-income.

Marginal rate of commodity substitution The rate at which a consumer foregoes quantities of one good (say, Y) for the sake of some additional quantities of another good (say, X) depicts a diminishing trend as more and more of the latter (X) are had. This implies that the **slope** of the indifference curve **increases** from left to right as we go down the curve. Marginal Rate of Substitution of X for Y (written as $MRS_{X,Y}$), generally representing the numerical value of the slope of the indifference curve, thus, diminishes with successive additional doles of good X in place of Y.

Merits of revealed preference theory Samuelson's revealed preference theory is a major advancement to the theory of demand. It provides direct way to derive the demand curve, that is, without the use of the concepts of utility and convexity of indifference curves. It also provides the basis of construction of index numbers of the cost of living and their use in consumer welfare.

Monotonic preferences If (x_1, y_1) be a bundle of two goods and if (x_2, y_2) is a bundle of two goods with at least as much of both the goods and more of one, consumer's preference to (x_2, y_2) over (x_1, y_1) written as $(x_2, y_2) > (x_1, y_1)$, is called the monotonic preference.

Price consumption curve Locus traced by consumer's equilibrium point in response to pivotal movements in the budget line, caused by changes in price of one of the two goods while that of the other remaining unchanged.

Quasi-linear preferences Consumer preferences that lead to an indifference curve partly linear and partly non-linear. Utility function such as $U = \sqrt{x} + y$ or $U = x + \sqrt{y}$ or $U = \log x + y$ or $U = x + \log y$ describe quasi-linear preferences.

Reservation price Price at which a consumer is indifferent between consuming and not consuming a good. If price falls below this price the consumer will increase consumption by one unit of the product. The price has relevance to the demand of the discrete goods (Figure 4.51).

Samuelson's fundamental theorem of consumption "Any good (simple or composite) that is known always to increase (decrease) in demand when money income alone rises (falls) must definitely shrink (expand) in demand when its price alone rises (falls)."

Strong axiom of revealed preference theory (SARP) If a bundle A is revealed preferred to a different bundle B directly or indirectly, then it would never happen that bundle B is revealed preferred directly or indirectly to bundle A.

Utility Utility of a product refers to its property of satisfying human needs or desires. It is subjective in nature and should not be confused with 'usefulness' of the product.

Weak axiom of revealed preference theory (WARP) If a bundle A is revealed preferred to a different bundle B directly, then it would never happen that bundle B is revealed directly preferred to bundle A.

EXERCISES

A. Short Answer Questions

1. State the law of diminishing marginal utility. Is it essential for the law of demand?
2. State the significance of the assumption of constant marginal utility of money in cardinal utility theory of demand.
3. State the assumption of the diminishing marginal rate of commodity substitution.
4. State the main drawbacks of the Marshallian cardinal utility approach to the theory of demand.
5. The following schedule gives the number of bananas consumed and the total utility derived at each level of consumption by a consumer. Given that the price of bananas as fixed at ₹ 2 per banana, determine the optimal level of consumption.

Number of bananas :	1	2	3	4	5	6	7	8
TU :	5	9.5	13.5	17	20	22.5	24.5	26

[**Ans.** Seven bananas.]

6. Outline the main assumptions of the cardinal utility approach to the theory of demand.
7. Point out the main assumptions of the indifference curve analysis of the theory of demand.
8. Provide an explanation to the law of the diminishing marginal rate of commodity substitution.
9. What are indifference curves? Explain with the help of a rough sketch.
10. Explain why ICs can't intersect each other.
11. Show that a higher IC offers a higher level of satisfaction to the consumer.
12. Sketch the likely shape of the indifference curves in each of the following cases:
    (a) When both the goods are bad goods.
    (b) When one of the two is a bad good.
    (c) When one of the two is a neutral good.
    (d) When both of them are perfect substitutes.
    (e) When both of them are perfect complements.
    (f) When both goods turn bad after a given level of consumption.
13. How does a consumer attain his equilibrium under the cardinal utility theory of demand?
14. Given the market price,

$$P = 10,$$

and the utility function,

$$U = 20 + 4\sqrt{[(x-10)]}$$

Obtain the necessary and sufficient conditions of the consumer's equilibrium.

[**Ans.** The necessary condition is $MU = P$ while the sufficient condition is $\partial (MU)/\partial x < 0$. In simple language, marginal utility of the commodity must be equal to the price of the product as a necessary condition of equilibrium and law of diminishing marginal utility must operate as the sufficient condition. Accordingly, the necessary condition is $\sqrt{(x-10)} = 0.2$ and the sufficient condition is $x > 10$. Refer back to the conditions of the equilibrium under cardinal utility theory.]

15. In Question 14, determine the quantity demanded in equilibrium and the corresponding level of the total utility derived by the consumer?

[**Ans.** $x = 10.04$, $U = 20.8$.]

16. What is meant by the rationality of the consumer and the cardinality of the utility?
17. Why is the assumption of constant marginal utility of money essential in the cardinal utility approach to the theory of demand?
18. If the successive units of a commodity be consumed at intervals rather than in a continuity, what do you think would happen to the law of diminishing marginal utility of the commodity?
19. For whom do you think is the marginal utility of money higher–a rich person or a poor person?
20. What would happen to the marginal utility of money if the consumption expenditure is on the rise continuously?
21. The total utility at different levels of consumption is as given below:

Units consumed:	1	5	10
Total utility:	20	60	85

If the price is fixed at ₹ 10 per unit, determine the equilibrium level of demand.
[**Ans.** 5.]

22. *The ordering principle of the consumer preferences has little validity*–Examine.
23. Give an example of a utility function that well describes the requirements of the perfect complements.
24. *An apple is good for health while a cigarette, injurious to it*. What kind of an IC would you expect for a consumer who consumes both in quantities that stabilize the net of the total utility.
25. *Excess of everything is bad*. Substantiate the statement from cardinal utility theory of demand.
26. Give an example of a utility function that describes the quasi-linear preferences. Sketch the corresponding indifference curve.
27. Define the price consumption and the income consumption curves. What is the distinguishing feature between them?
28. State the weak and the strong axioms of the revealed preference theory with specific reference to their distinguishing feature.
29. A consumer spends whole of his income on two goods X and Y. When his income is ₹ 100, the price of good X is ₹ 5 per unit of it and that of Y is ₹ 10 per unit of it. What can you infer about $MRS_{X,Y}$ at the optimum?
    [**Ans.** In equilibrium, $MRS_{X,Y} = |-P_X/P_Y| = |-5/10| = 0.50.$]
30. Suppose that prices of all the goods double between 1994 and 2004 while incomes of the consumers triple over the period. Would the Laspeyre's price index for the year 2004 with 1994 as the base be less than 2, greater than 2 or just equal to 2? Would the consumer be better off in the current year than in the base year?
    [**Ans.** Laspeyre's price index is defined as $L = \Sigma q_0 p_t / \Sigma q_0 p_0$. Since, $P_t = 2P_0$, $L = (\Sigma q_0 p_t / \Sigma q_0 p_0) = (2\Sigma q_0 p_0 / \Sigma q_0 p_0) = 2.00$. Now income index is $Y = (\Sigma q_t p_t / \Sigma q_0 p_0) = 3.00$. Thus, $Y > L$, the consumer is better off in 2004 than in 1994. It is not difficult to see that quantity demanded, q_t has gone up 1.5 times the base year's quantity (doubling of prices has had an adverse effect on quantity demanded). Consumer can thus afford 1.5 times of what he did in 1994, but according to the assumption of Laspeyre's price index, he consumes the base year's quantity in the current year. Laspeyre's price index would therefore be exactly 2.00. However, the consumer is better off in current year than in the base year by virtue of $Y > L$. He has the potential to consume more. It is a different matter that he does not.]
31. Show that the substitution effect for the perfect complements is zero.
32. A consumer consumes two goods X and Y. If commodity X is rationed and the constraint is binding, what is the effective consumption set? Explain with the help of the indifference curves.
33. Distinguish between the net and the gross substitutes.
34. A consumer is indifferent between bundles A and B and also between B and C but he is known to strictly prefer A to C. Which property of the indifference curves is violated by such behaviour of the consumer?
    [**Ans.** Transitivity.]
35. Show that if the indifference curves were concave to the origin, the consumer would never consume both the goods together.
    [**Ans.** A corner solution.]
36. A consumer consumes two goods in a fixed proportion. What would the likely shape of the indifference curve be?
37. Marginal rate of commodity substitution is equal to their price ratios. What does this statement imply? Explain with the help of a sketch.
38. Each of the two goods X and Y turns bad after 10th unit of its consumption. Sketch the likely shape of the IC if 20 units of each may at most be consumed by an individual?

39. For which of the following goods is a price increase likely to lead to a substantial income effect?
 (a) Salt (b) housing (c) theatre ticket and (d) food.
 [**Hint.** Use PE = SE + IE.]

40. Suppose MU of good X is 20 while its price is ₹ 4 per unit and MU of Y is 50 while its price is ₹ 5 per unit. The individual to whom this information applies is spending ₹ 20 on each good. Is he maximizing his satisfaction? On the basis of this information can you choose an optimal combination for him? why or why not?
 [**Ans.** The condition of equilibrium is $(MU_X/MU_Y) = (P_X/P_Y)$, but 20/50 ≠ 4/5. Hence, the consumer is not maximizing his satisfaction. Since MU_X and MU_Y are both constant, the IC is linear as for perfect substitutes. Moreover, IC being flatter than the budget line [(20/50) < (4/5)], a corner solution (0,8) would be the optimal solution.]

41. 'In a two-commodity world, the income consumption curve approaches the x-axis as consumer's income rises. Then, commodity X represented on the x-axis is an inferior good.' Comment.

42. Depict pollution on x-axis and electricity on y-axis. What would the family indifference curve look like if
 (a) pollution is a bad commodity and electricity is a good commodity.
 (b) pollution is a neutral commodity and electricity is a good commodity.

43. If Coke and Pepsi are perfect substitutes for a consumer, the slope of the indifference curve is –1. What should the price ratio be if the optimal bundle consists of positive amounts of both Coke and Pepsi?
 [**Ans.** 1, For positive quantities of the two goods, IC and the budget line must coincide, else, it will be a corner solution with one of the two goods bought being zero in quantity.]

44. Show that Marshall's analysis can't account for Giffen goods.

45. An individual's marginal utilities for good X and Y are as given below:

$$MU_X = 40 - 5x, \quad MU_Y = 20 - 3y.$$

Determine $MRS_{X,Y}$ when the consumption basket is $x = 3$, $y = 5$. If $P_X/P_Y = 5$, Is the basket an optimal one?
 [**Ans.** $MRS_{X,Y} = 5/1$, yes.]

46. Draw the income consumption curves
 (a) when both the goods are perfect complements.
 (b) when one of the two is an inferior good.

47. A consumer is found spending whole of his income on good Y. His income is ₹ 100, price of X is ₹ 2 per unit and that of Y is ₹ 4 per unit. What can you say about the $MRS_{X,Y}$ at the optimum?
 [**Ans.** Spending whole of the income on Y implies a corner solution with 0 of X. In such a case, the IC must have a lower slope than that of the budget line (Figure 4.30). $MRS_{X,Y}$ would then be less than the numerical value of the slope of budget line, i.e. less than 1/2.]

48. The slope of the compensated demand curve is unambiguously negative or zero. Do you agree? Explain your answer with the help of a sketch.
 [**Ans. Figure 4.102.** Substitution effect of a price change can't be less than zero, according to our sign convention. It is zero for perfect complements for which the compensated demand curve would be vertical with a slope of ∞. For other categories of goods, the substitution effect is non-zero or positive (as per our sign convention). As a result, the compensated demand curve would either be vertical (slope = ∞) or negatively sloped as shown. It will therefore be always less elastic than the normal demand curve.]

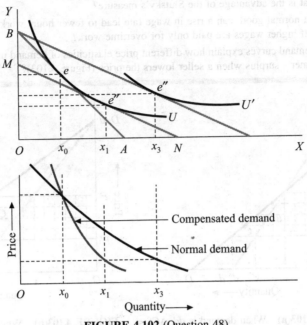

FIGURE 4.102 (Question 48)

49. Is it true to say that the compensated demand curve is less elastic than the usual demand curve? Explain with the help of a sketch.

   [**Hint.** Question no. 48.]

50. If the price consumption curve is parallel to the x-axis (representing commodity X), what must be the price elasticity of demand for X?

   [**Ans.** (Refer to Figure 4.57) Since PCC is a horizontal line, it follows that xP_X is constant. It is so because yP_Y is constant ($xP_X = M - yP_Y$). Differentiating $xP_X = K$, where, K = constant with respect to P_X, we get

$$x + P_X (dx/dP_X) = 0$$
$\Rightarrow \qquad x[1 + (P_X/x)(dx/dP_X)] = 0$
$\Rightarrow \qquad [1 + E^D{}_{PX}] = 0/X = 0$
$\Rightarrow \qquad E^D{}_{PX} = -1$

Thus, price elasticity is unitary at every point on the demand curve derived from a horizontal PCC. Note that a demand curve for which price elasticity is unitary at every point on it is a rectangular hyperbola (the equation of which is $xy = K$).]

B. Long Answer Questions

51. An individual consumes two goods X and Y. His utility function is given as $U = y + \log x$, where x and y are the quantities of X and Y.
   Draw an indifference map depicting his preferences. Show that the Engel curve for X is a vertical line. Can X be a Giffen good?

   [**Ans.** As Engel curve is a vertical line (Figure 4.46), commodity X cannot be an inferior good. If X is a Giffen good, it has to be an inferior good also (refer to the application that every Giffen good is an inferior good but the converse need not be true). Since, it is not an inferior good, it can't be a Giffen good either.]

52. Show graphically the substitution and the real income effects of a price change as per Hicks and Slutsky's versions. What is the advantage of the Slutsky's measure?

53. If leisure is a normal good, can a rise in wage rate lead to fewer hours worked? How would the result be modified if higher wages are paid only for overtime work?

54. Using two demand curves explain how different price elasticities of demand influence changes in the size of the consumer's surplus when a seller lowers the price (Figure 4.103)?

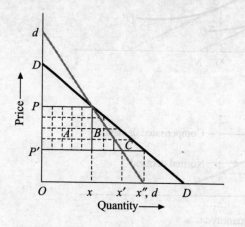
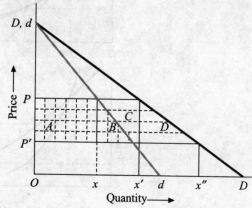

FIGURE 4.103(a) When demand is dd, $\Delta CS = A + B$. When demand is DD, $\Delta CS = A + B + C$. Size of ΔCS is higher by 'C' when demand is DD than when it is dd. Demand DD is more elastic than demand dd. Hence, the size of ΔCS is higher for more elastic demand.

FIGURE 4.103(b) When demand as dd, $\Delta CS = A + B$. When demand is DD, $\Delta CS = A + B + C + D$. Size of ΔCS is higher by '$C + D$' when demand is DD than when it is dd. Demand DD is more elastic than dd. Hence, the size of ΔCS is higher for more elastic demand.

55. A farmer has a single crop, potatoes, for the support of his family. He consumes some and sells the remainder to obtain income to spend on other goods. Assuming a given price of potatoes and given prices of all other goods, illustrate the equilibrium position of the farmer using indifference curves anlysis.

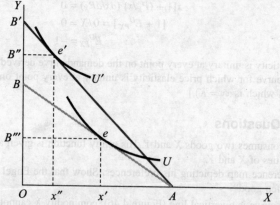

FIGURE 4.104 Suppose the farmer has a stock OA potatoes (x-axis). Price of the other goods (composite commodity, represented on y-axis) is fixed at 1. At the existing price of potatoes, say P_X, the farmer can buy

(Contd.)

FIGURE 4.104 (*Contd.*)

OB quantity of other goods if he sells the entire stock of potatoes (leaving nothing for self consumption). Suppose, he retains Ox' for self consumption and sells $x'A$ at the existing price to buy OB''' quantity of the other goods. He is thus in equilibrium at e, enjoying utility, U. Now suppose price of potatoes goes up to, say P'_X. Clearly, the farmer would like to sell more of potatoes, say $x''A$, retaining only Ox'' for self consumption. Sale of larger quantity of potatoes at higher price fetches him more of other goods at point e where he enjoys OB'' of other goods and Ox'' of potatoes. His utility rises to U'. Here, it is not difficult to see that $P_X = OB/OA$ and $P'_X = OB'/OA$. The reader must note the difference in the treatment of the farmer's equilibrium. In deviation from the usual treatment of the consumer's equilibrium, the situation has been dealt with on the lines of the worker's equilibrium who exchanges leisure hours for wage-income.

56. A consumer has strictly convex preferences. When price of petrol is ₹ 30 per litre the consumer buys 16 litres of it. A per unit tax of ₹ 2 is levied and in consequence, his petrol consumption drops to 14 litres. The consumer is given a lump-sum rebate of ₹ 28 to compensate for the tax. Explain through the indifference curves that the consumer is worse-off in the latter case (Figure 4.105).

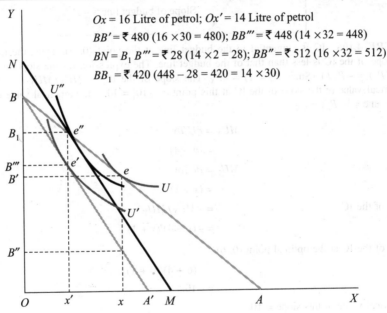

FIGURE 4.105 The consumer is buying 16 litres (Ox) of petrol at e at the price of ₹ 30 per litre, spending ₹ 480 (on BA). Now suppose a unit tax of ₹ 2 per litre is levied on petrol consumption. This shifts the budget line of the consumer to BA'. In consequence, the consumer reduces petrol consumption to 14 litres, spending ₹ 448 on BA' at the point e'. Here, he enjoys utility U' ($U' < U$). The consumer is compensated for the tax paid by him on 14 litres of petrol in the form of a rebate of ₹ 28 (14 × 2 = 28). This shifts his budget line BA', parallel to itself, to NM (NM representing a budget of ₹ 476 = 448 + 28, the sum of the rebate and the amount spent on petrol after the levy). He is at the point e'', enjoying less utility U'' ($U'' < U$). The consumer is thus worse off even after the grant of the rebate.

57. Suppose the utility function of a consumer over apples (x) and oranges (y) is given as

$$U = [x + 1][y + 4].$$

The consumer maximizes his utility subject to his budget constraint $x \cdot P_X + y \cdot P_Y \leq \bar{M}$, where, $P_Y = 1$. Demonstrate that a sufficient condition for his optimal consumption to be $[0, 6]$ is $P_X > 10$. Draw a diagram as well.

[**Ans.** Since the equilibrium basket is $(0, 6)$, it is a corner solution, as shown in the Figure 4.106.]

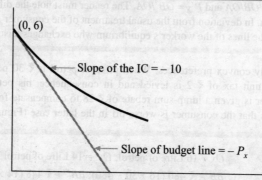

FIGURE 4.106 IC is tangential to the budget line at the point $(0, 6)$. Thus, the numerical value of the slope of the IC is less than that of the budget line. The expression for the slope of the budget line is $(-P_X/P_Y) = -P_X/1$ (Since $P_Y = 1$) $= -P_X$. The slope of the IC $= -MU_X/MU_Y = -10$ [at $(0, 6)$]. The numerical value of the slope of the IC at this point $= |-10| = 10$. The numerical value of the slope of the budget line $= |-P_X| = P_X$.

$$MU_X = \partial U/\partial x$$
$$= (y + 4)$$
$$MU_Y = \partial U/\partial y$$
$$= (x + 1)$$

Slope of the IC
$$= -MU_X/MU_Y$$
$$= -(y + 4)/(x + 1)$$

Slope of the IC at the optimal point $(0, 6)$
$$= -(6 + 4)/(0 + 1)$$
$$= -10.$$

Numerical value of this slope $= 10$.

Slope of the budget line is
$$= (-P_X/P_Y)$$
$$= -P_X/1 \text{ (Since } P_Y = 1)$$
$$= -P_X$$

Its numerical value
$$= |-P_X|$$
$$= P_X$$

Since numerical value of the slope of the IC at $(0, 6)$ < numerical value of the slope of the budget line,
$$10 < P_X$$
Or
$$P_X > 10.]$$

58. 'In the cardinal utility theory, the assumption of diminishing marginal utility has been established introspectively but read with the assumption of utility maximizing rationality of the consumer, it is established automatically.' Examine the statement.

    [**Hint.** Show that $MU_X = P_X$ and that $\partial(MU)/\partial x < 0$.]

59. 'The assumption of diminishing marginal rate of commodity substitution automatically establishes the convexity of the indifference curves.' Discuss.

    [**Hint.** Diminishing MRS implies increasing dy/dx. This requires $d^2y/dx^2 > 0$, which in turn implies convexity of the IC to the origin. Refer to the proof of this property of the ICs.]

60. A worker has strictly convex preferences for leisure and a consumption good. Let his endowment time be T hours which he can devote to work and/or leisure. His only source of income is work. What is the shape of his labour supply curve:

    (a) Leisure is a normal good.

    (b) Leisure is an inferior good.

    [**Hint.** If leisure is a normal good, a hike in wage rate (a rise in price of leisure) leads to fewer hours of leisure or more hours of work. In consequence, the supply curve of labour hours would have a positive slope. If leisure is an inferior good, a hike in wage rate (a rise in price of leisure) would lead to a rise in demand for leisure (a fall in supply of labour hours). The supply curve of the labour hours would bend backwards. See Figure 4.107.]

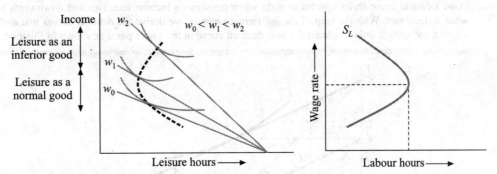

FIGURE 4.107 Derivation of supply curve of labour hours when leisure is a normal good.

61. Suppose a consumer's demand for a good is given as

    $$x = 10 + [\bar{M}/10P_X],$$

    where,

    x = quantity of good X,

    $\bar{M}$ = income,

    P_X = Price of X.

    Given his income as ₹ 120 per day and the price of good X as ₹ 4 per unit, measure the substitution and the income effects of a fall in price from ₹ 4 per unit to

    (a) ₹ 3 per unit,

    (b) ₹ 2 per unit.

    [**Ans.** (a) PE = 1.0, SE = 0.57, IE = 0.43

    (b) PE = 3.0, SE = 1.7, IE = 1.3.]

62. A consumer's buying behaviour of goods X and Y in two price situations is observed as

Observations	Prices		Bundles	
	P_X	P_Y	X	Y
1	6	3	6	6
2	5	5	10	0

Which consumption bundle has he revealed preferred to the other ? Does his buying behaviour reveal violation of the Weak Axiom of Revealed Preference?

[**Ans.** None. The consumer buys whatever is affordable. At first price set, second bundle is unaffordable and at the second price set, the first one is unaffordable.

		Bundles	
		1	2
Price set	1	54	60
	2	60	50

No violation of WARP.]

63. Depict and explain the shift of demand curve for a commodity due to a change in consumer's income with the help of indifference curves.

[**Ans.** Demand curve shifts upward to right when consumer's income increases and downwards to left when it decreases. With the help of the indifference curves, we derive the demand curves first and then we shift the budget lines to obtain the new demand curve in the lower panel as shown in Figure 4.108.]

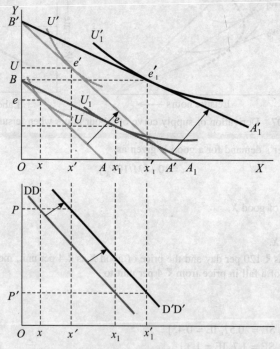

FIGURE 4.108 In the upper panel, BA is the initial budget line on which the consumer is in equilibrium at the point e enjoying utility U and consuming quantity x of good X. A fall in price of X, from P to P',

(Contd.)

FIGURE 4.108 (*Contd.*)

leads to a pivotal shift in it to BA_1. The consumer moves to e_1 on BA_1 where he enjoys utility U_1, consuming quantity x_1 of good X. Drawing projections downwards from e and e_1, we mark off points (x, P) and (x_1, P') in the lower panel as shown. Joining these points, we obtain the demand curve DD. Now, suppose consumer's income increases. In consequence, his budget lines will undergo parallel shifts (BA to $B'A'$ and BA_1 to $B'A'_1$) leading to shifts in equilibrium points from e and e_1 to e' and e'_1 respectively. Quantities demanded will increase from x and x_1 to x' and x'_1 respectively (x and x' are demanded at price P while x_1 and x'_1 at P'). Dropping projections from e' and e'_1, we mark off points (x', P) and (x'_1, P') in the lower panel as shown. Joining them we get the demand curve D'D'.

64. Assume that a consumer's income consumption curve for good X is vertical. Show that the demand curve for good X must be downward sloping.

    [**Ans.** When ICC is vertical, as shown in Figure 4.109, the income effect on consumption of commodity X is zero, i.e. IE = 0.

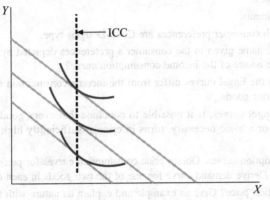

FIGURE 4.109 A vertical ICC for X. We know that **price effect** is equal to the sum of the **substitution** and the **income effects**. When income effect is zero for good X, price effect = substitution effect. According to our sign convention, substitution effect can never be negative (or it can never be positive according to the opposite convention used by many scholars). What this implies, is that a fall in price leads to a rise in quantity demanded of good X by virtue of the substitution effect. (This we define as the positive substitution effect while some economists define this as a negative substitution effect.) But since the substitution effect is equal to the price effect due to zero income effect, even the price effect is positive implying that more of X would be demanded in response to a fall in price of the good. This implies inverse relationship between price and quantity of X demanded and hence downward sloping demand curve.]

65. The utility function for a consumer is as expressed below:

$$U = 1000 \, x^{1/3} \, y^{2/3}$$

The budget at his disposal is ₹ 10,000. Obtain the consumer's demand equations for the two goods and hence determine the equilibrium basket when prices of the two goods are $P_X = 50$, $P_Y = 20$ per unit of each. Also draw a sketch and mark off the equilibrium basket on it.

[**Ans.** Equations of demand for goods X and Y are respectively $x = 10{,}000/3P_X$ and $y = 20{,}000/3P_Y$. The equilibrium basket is (200/3, 1000/3).]

66. Suppose the utility function for the consumer in Question 65 takes one of the following forms:
    (a) $U = 50x + 20y$
    (b) $U = 20x + 50y$
    (c) $U = 80x + 40y$

    Other things remaining the same (as in Question 65) comment on the possibility of determination of the equilibrium basket in each case. Draw sketches and comment on the nature of the solutions.

    [Ans. (a) The IC will coincide with the budget line leading to infinitely many solutions.

    (b) Equilibrium solution does not exist. Goods being perfect substitutes, a corner solution at (0, 500) would result.

    (c) No equilibrium solution is possible. However, a corner solution at (0, 500) results.]

67. Show that the condition of tangency between the IC and the budget line is a must for the equilibrium of the utility maximizing consumer.

68. Define an income consumption curve. Sketch the income consumption curve when the two goods involved are:
    (a) Perfect substitutes.
    (b) Perfect complements.
    (c) Those for which consumer preferences are Cobb-Douglas type.

    What is the specific name given to the consumer's preferences depicted by the above three cases from the viewpoint of the nature of the income consumption curve?

69. In what respects do the Engel curves differ from the income consumption curves. Derive Engel curves for normal and inferior goods.

70. With the help of Engel curves, is it possible to conclude that every good, irrespective of whether it is normal, inferior or a basic necessity, turns inferior at sufficiently high levels of income? Explain with diagrams.

71. Define price consumption curves. Obtain price consumption curves for perfect substitutes, complements and discrete goods. Derive demand curve for one of the two goods in each case.

72. What is the reservation price? Give an example and explain its nature with the help of a diagram.

73. Define price consumption curves and use them to derive the demand curves for
    (a) A Giffen good
    (b) A Normal good.

74. Define homothetic preferences. Explain the common characteristics of such preferences with the help of necessary diagrams.

75. Explain the compensatory variation hypothesis. How does it help classification of goods into substitutes and complements ?

76. Explain the technique of splitting the price effect into its components of substitution and income effects for a
    (i) Giffen good
    (ii) Normal good
    (iii) Basic necessity.

77. Explain the constant real income hypothesis. Use it to split the price effect into its components of substitution and income effects for a normal good and a Giffen good.

78. Compare Hicksian compensatory variation hypothesis with Slutsky's constant real income hypothesis from the viewpoint of segregating the substitution and the income effects. Which one, according to you, is more realistic and which more logical?

79. A consumer spends whole of his income on two goods X and Y. The equation of demand for good X is as given below:

$$x = \bar{M}/10P_X,$$

where x is the quantity of good X demanded at price P_X while M is consumer's income. Given that $\bar{M} = 1000$, $P_X = 20$, measure the price effect, the substitution effect and the income effect when the price of X falls to 10.

[**Ans.** PE = 5.0, SE = 4.5, IE = 0.5.]

80. In the previous question, if the demand equation for good X is

$$x = 10 + [\bar{M}/10P_X],$$

Income of the consumer, $\bar{M} = 1200$ and the price of X, $P_X = 30$, determine the measures of the price effect, the substitution effect and the income effect when the price of good X falls to 20

[**Ans:** PE = 2.00, SE = 1.3, IE = 0.7.]

81. Define consumer's surplus. Explain how is it determined in Marshallian economics. For the sake of demonstration, take the linear demand given by the equation:

$$Q = 2.0 - 0.05P,$$

where Q is quantity demanded at price P.

Assume the market price to be ₹ 20 per unit of the output. In what single aspect does the Marshallian concept of the consumer's surplus differ from the Hicksian concept? Point out some uses of consumer's surplus.

82. Employ indifference curves to bring out the difference between Marshallian and Hicksian concepts of consumer's surplus.

83. 'Every Giffen good is an inferior good but the converse need not be true.' Explain with the help of the indifference curves. With the help of indifference curves, show that an individual is better off in the current period as compared to the base period provided the income index is higher than the Laspeyre's price index.

84. With the help of indifference curves, show that an individual is worse off in the current period as compared to the base period provided the current period's income index is smaller than the Paasche's price index.

85. Explain Fisher's time preference theory of interest with the help of indifference curves.

86. With the help of indifference curves, show that gains from international trade comprise gains from exchange and gains from specialization.

87. Suppose there are two individuals in an economy who produce and consume two goods X and Y. With the use of the indifference curves show how these two goods can be efficiently shared between them.

88. Suppose an economy produces two goods by employing two factors of production, namely labour and capital. Use indifference curves for efficient allocation of these two factors between production of the two goods.

89. With the help of indifference curves, show how an investor optimizes his portfolio.

90. Compare the effects of the direct and indirect taxes on the welfare of the consumers with the help of the indifference curves.

91. With the help of indifference curves, compare the efficacy of the alternative schemes of subsidy and the supplementary income (also known as cash subsidy or cash grant) in an economy passing through the phase of (a) depression (b) prosperity.

92. Compare the alternative policies of direct and indirect taxes from the viewpoint of their effectiveness in generating revenue for government.

93. 'When a society is divided sharply between marked preferences for two goods, it is possible to increase social welfare if government adopts a little flexibility in rationing of these commodities.' Explain with the help of indifference curves. How would your answer change if a third segment of society emerges with preferences as balanced as the existing policy of distribution?

94. What is meant by point rationing? How do consumers attain maximization of utility when
    (a) the budget possessed by them is scarce.
    (b) the ration points at their disposal are scarce.
    (c) the budget is scarce in respect of commodity X.
    (d) the ration points are scarce in respect of commodity Y.

95. Define leisure–income trade-off and leisure–income indifference. Employ these concepts to show how a worker can optimally divide his day between work and leisure.

96. With the help of the leisure–income trade-off lines and the leisure income indifference curves, show why the overtime wages must be higher than the normal wages?

97. Employ leisure income trade-off lines to show that taxing wage income proves highly productive in under developed countries but highly counter productive in advanced countries.

98. With the help of leisure–income curves, show that a hike in wage rate leads to a cut in hours worked only when leisure is a normal good.

99. How can the current and the future levels of consumption be optimally determined with the help of indifference curves? Explain. How would you substantiate the life cycle hypothesis of income on the basis of your observations?

100. Define a composite commodity. Show how Hicksian composite commodity theorem helps extension of indifference curve theory to a multi-commodity world.

101. Outline the assumptions of the revealed preference theory of demand. Distinguish between the Weak Axiom of Revealed Preference (WARP) and the Strong Axiom of Revealed Preference (SARP) theory.

102. State and establish Samuelson's Fundamental Theorem of Consumption. How far can the theorem be used in demand forecasting in the real world situations?

103. Compare the cardinalist and the ordinalist approaches to the theory of demand. Which approach do you find better and why?

104. Compare the indifference curve theory of demand with that of the revealed preference.

105. What are monotonic preferences? Use a numerical illustration to explain.

CASE STUDY: THE FOOD STAMP PROGRAMME AND SOCIAL WELFARE

The U.S. Federal government, under its **Food Stamp Act of 1964,** introduced Food Stamp Programme as a measure of relief to the weaker sections of society. Under it, the government allotted food stamps to the weaker sections at subsidized prices. The full monthly allotment was food coupons worth $153. The amount of subsidy granted depended on the level of income of the allottees—the poorer the allottee, the higher the subsidy granted. "A family of four with a monthly income of $300, paid $83 for the full monthly allotment of the food stamps. If a family of four had a monthly income of $100, the cost of the full monthly allotment would have been $25 only*". This formed the crux of the pre-1979 Food Stamp Programme in U.S., which served as an ad valorem subsidy on food with the rate of subsidization depending on the household income. Considering a family of four with monthly income of $100, the rate of subsidization

---

* Hal R. Varian, *Intermediate Economics*. W.W. Norton & Company. New York., London., 5th ed., pp. 29–31. The original source: *Food Stamps and Nutrition*, American Enterprise Institute, 1975.

of food worked out at 84% (monthly allotment of $153 subsidized to $25, amounts to a subsidy of $128 which expressed in per cent terms works out at 84% approximately).

Representing food on horizontal axis and other goods as composite commodity on y-axis, the mechanism of drawing the budget lines of the consumer with and without the food stamps may be represented as in Figure 4.110(a).

In post-1979 period, Food Stamp Programme was modified by the U.S. government. Food coupons worth $200 were allotted free of cost to the eligible households. As in Figure 4.110(a), mechanism of the budget lines of the consumer, with and without the food stamps, is depicted as shown in Figure 4.110(b). Consider households A and B, each with 4 members and monthly income of $100. With the help of the indifference curves, demonstrate the equilibrium positions in each of the following cases and comment on the relative state of the consumer's welfare:

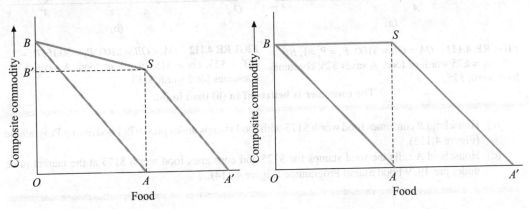

FIGURE 4.110(a) Pre-1979 Food Stamp Programme: With Food units on x-axis and money income or composite commodity ($P_Y = 1$) on y-axis, BA represents consumer's budget line with a slope of -1. Note that $OA = 153$ units of food each priced at $1 ($P_X = 1$) and OB represents income of $153 needed to buy 153 units of food without food stamps. Under the food stamp scheme, a consumer if allowed a subsidy of 84%, would be able to get full monthly allotment of 153 units just for $25 ($BB'$). Slope of BS being -0.16 ($P_X = 0.16$), the consumer enjoys OB' ($128) of income with 153 units of food. If he wishes to have more of food, he can do so along SA'. His budget line with food stamp scheme is BSA', with a kink at S.

FIGURE 4.110(b) Post-1979 Food Stamp Programme: With food units on x-axis and money income/composite commodity ($P_Y = 1$) on y-axis, BA is consumer's budget line with a slope of -1. Note that $OA = 200$ units of food each priced at $1 ($P_X = 1$) and OB represents money income $200 (200 units of composite commodity) needed to buy 200 units of food without food stamps. In the post-1979 scheme, 100% subsidy is allowed. The consumer is able to buy full monthly allotment of 200 units of food at no cost. Thus, in the post-1979 scheme, consumer's budget line is BSA', with a kink at S. If the consumer wishes to have additional units of food, he will be on segment SA'. As regards the first 200 units, he has them and still has an income of $200 for other commodities.

(a) Household A consumes food worth $75 without food stamps under pre-1979 Food Stamp Programme (Figure 4.111).
(b) Household A consumes food worth $153 with food stamps under pre-1979 Food Stamp Programme (Figure 4.112).

[Ans.

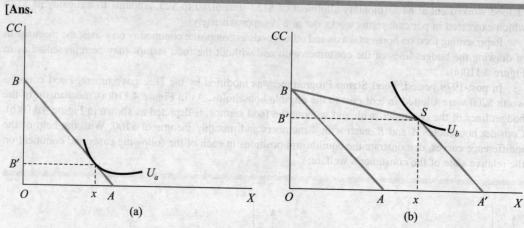

FIGURE 4.111 $OA = OB = \$100$, $P_x = P_y = 1$, $BB' = \$75$, $Ox = \$75$ worth of food. A saves $25, consumes food worth $75.

FIGURE 4.112 $OA = OB = \$100$, $P_x = \$0.16$, $P_y = 1$, $BB' = \$25$, $Ox = \$153$ worth of food. A saves $75, consumes food worth $153.

The consumer is better-off in (b) than in (a).

(c) Household B consumes food worth $175 with food stamps under pre-1979 Food Stamp Programme (Figure 4.113).

(d) Household A sells the food stamps for $125 and consumes food worth $175 at the market price under pre-1979 Food Stamp Programme (Figure 4.114).

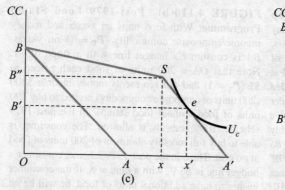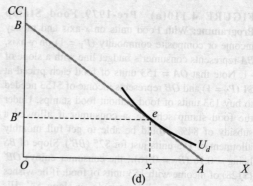

FIGURE 4.113 $OA = OB = 100$, $Ox = \$153$ worth of food, $Ox' = \$175$, $BB' = BB'' + B''B' = \$(25 + 22) = \$47$. Slope of SA' being 1, $B'B'' = xx' = 175 - 153 = 22$. $OB' = \$53$. Consumer saves $53.

FIGURE 4.114 $OA = OB = 200$, $BB' = \$175$, $OB' = 25$, $Ox = \$175$ worth of food. Consumer saves $25, has food worth $175.

The consumer in (c) is better-off than that in (d).

(e) Household B consumes food worth $80 without food stamps under post-1979 Food Stamp Programme (Figure 4.115).

(f) Household B consumes food worth $250 with food stamps under post-1979 Food Stamp Programme (Figure 4.116).

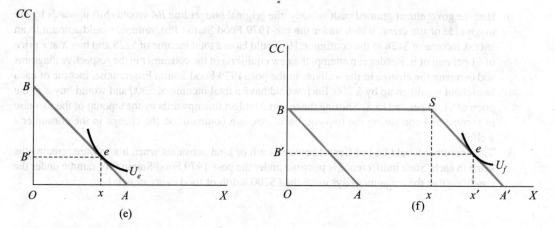

FIGURE 4.115 $OA = OB = 100$, $Ox = \$80 = BB'$. $OB' = \$20$. Consumer saves $\$20$, consumers food worth of $\$80$.

FIGURE 4.116 $OA = OB = 100$, $Ox = \$200$, $BB' = \$50 = OB' = xx'$. $Ox' = 250$. Consumer saves $\$50$, consumes food worth $\$250$.

The consumer in (f) is better-off than that in (e).

(g) Household B sells the food stamps for $\$175$ and consumes food worth $\$250$ at the market price under post-1979 Food Stamp Programme (Figure 4.117).

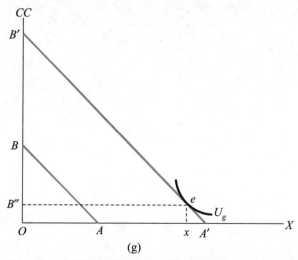

FIGURE 4.117 $OA = OB = \$100$, $BB' = \$175 = AA'$, $OB'' = \$25$, $Ox =$ food worth $\$250$. Consumer saves $\$25$. *Clearly he is worse off in (g) than in (f)*.

(h) Had the U.S. government decided to grant food subsidy in cash, how would your answers in (a), (b), (c), (e), and (f) change? Will the consumers be better off under the cash subsidy? Give reasons in support of your answers.

(i) Is it possible for a household to be indifferent between the cash and kind subsidies in any of the above cases?

(j) Had the government granted cash subsidy, the original budget line BA would shift upwards by the magnitude of the grant, which under the pre-1979 Food Stamp Programme, would amount to an excess income of $128 to the consumer. He would have a total income of $228 and buy X at a price of $1 per unit of it. Reader can attempt the new equilibria of the consumer in the respective diagrams and compare the change in the welfare. In the post-1979 Food Stamp Programme, income of each household would go up by $ 200. Each would have a total income of $300 and would buy X at the price of $1.00 per unit of X. Shifting the original budget line upwards by the amount of the increase in income and comparing the two equilibria, one can comment on the change in the consumer's welfare.

(k) The consumer would be indifferent between cash or kind subsidies when his welfare remains the same in each. Such indifference is possible under the post-1979 Food Stamp Programme under the condition that the consumer buys more than $200 worth of food every month.]

5

Production and Producer's Equilibrium

CHAPTER OUTLINE

Introduction
- Factors of Production
- Production Function
- Short-run Production
- Long-run Production
- Isocost and Isoquant Curves
- Producer's Equilibrium
- Returns to Variable Proportions and Returns to Scale
- Features of Cobb–Douglas Production Function and Elasticity of Factor Substitution
- Economic and Non-economic Regions of Production
- Influence of Technical Progress on Position and Shape of an Isoquant
- *Key Terms and Concepts*
- *Exercises*

INTRODUCTION

We have seen that we need to produce a good or a service to raise our incomes to desired levels. Some of us are industrialists, producing tangible goods in their factories, while others are the salaried individuals, providing intangible services. Be it a tangible good or an intangible service, both are products. Both possess utility and hence both are capable of satisfying human needs. A product is nothing but a bundle of utility, capable of satisfying human needs. Nature has bestowed many gifts on mankind, some of which already possess the desired level of utility while others lack it. Even those things that already possess utility, require more utility to be added so that their utility level may rise to the level desired by consumers. Even to other things that lack utility, producers create and add it, to satisfy human needs. It is this addition or creation of utility that is known as *production*.

Production may, thus, be defined as creation or addition of utility to the basic materials. Utility is said to be created in sand when sand is converted into bricks. Sand, by itself, has no utility. Building a house with these bricks, adds more utility to the utility of bricks. This is known as addition of utility. *The process of creation or addition of utility is called the production process.* It is essentially a directed or an intended activity which involves space (land or building), manpower (workers or labour), materials (basic inputs), tools or machines (real capital) and an organizer (the entrepreneur) to organize the activity. For instance, a producer of readymade garments needs a building where his designers and tailors work on cloth with the help of scissors and sewing machines to convert cloth into garments. *Thus, the production-process can be defined also as a directed activity of adding value to the basic inputs.*

5.1 FACTORS OF PRODUCTION

The things essential for the production can, thus, be identified as:

1. Land and building
2. Labour
3. Capital – real (such as, plant equipment, machinery) and financial (such as money)
4. Entrepreneur (the organizer who procures all the above and combines them in a desired manner so as to convert the basic materials into the finished products).

All these are known as the four factors of production.
Let us attempt to know a little more about each one:

1. *Land and building:* Land-building is a fixed factor of production. This is so because it is not possible to increase its supply at short notice whenever more of it is needed to increase production. Generally, the factor is owned by the producer but can also be had on monthly rentals from its owners. From the viewpoint of the firm (the factory producing goods or services), whether it is owned by the owner of the firm or rented from someone else for the purpose, it is simply a factor of production to be compensated by the firm every month at the market rate of rent in the same way in which man-power and other factors of production are. If the owner of the firm owns land-building, rent is paid to him by the firm every month and is known as the *imputed rent*. It should be borne in mind that the firm is a separate entity and its 'owner', in technical terms, is no more than a creditor who provides for productive factors such as land-building, capital and entrepreneurial skills to the firm. He, therefore, is to be compensated by the firm for all these just as other factors are.

2. *Capital:* Capital refers to productive assets that participate in production directly. Examples are tools, equipment, machinery and plant. In fact, there are two types of capital—real capital and financial capital. Real capital refers to tangible productive assets participating directly in production while financial capital refers to cash, shares debentures and such other instruments that do not take part in production process directly but help procurement and use of

factors of production. Capital, in economics, refers to real capital. Compensation made to this factor by the firm is interest. Capital, like land-building, is treated fixed in short run but unlike land-building, it is variable in the long-run.

3. *Labour:* Labour refers to man-power or human resource participating in production. It includes workers of all categories—skilled or unskilled, menial or manual, specific or non-specific, experienced or inexperienced. It is compensated by the firm on the basis of its market price. From the viewpoint of the firm's liability, labour is divided into two categories—permanent labour and temporary labour. Compensation made to the permanent labour is known as *salary* while that made to the temporary labour, as wages. Apart from salary, permanent labour is entitled to some compensation in kind, such as, rent-free accommodation, medical reimbursements, free transport and retirement benefits. Even the entrepreneur is a part of the man-power entitled to compensation for his/her organizational skills in one way or the other. Temporary or ad hoc labour, as the name suggests, is hired only for specific purposes or durations and is compensated accordingly at a predetermined wage.

Labour, except certain categories of it, is treated variable both in short-run and long-run.

4. *Entrepreneur:* Commonly known as producer or owner of the firm, an entrepreneur is a factor of production generally befitting no single or precise description. He is a risk-taker who ventures all his eggs to the same basket with a conviction that he would not let any harm come to it. He is confident of success of his venture. He thinks he knows what he is doing and that no amount of distraction can ever deviate him from the path he has set for his activities. What more, he is even a perfectionist, according to some thinkers.

Entrepreneurial skills are also treated fixed in short- and long-run.

5.2 PRODUCTION FUNCTION

Under identical conditions, 10 workers move more bricks than 2 workers. A larger firm produces more quantity of a product than a smaller one. Using the term *output* for the quantity of a product produced and *input* for the amount of factors of production employed for the purpose, we can say that output varies directly with input, in these cases. A situation may arise later when increasing an input, other things remaining the same, may lead to a fall in the output. *A mathematical relationship between units of output and units of an input is known as the production function.* In the example above, let the number of bricks moved be Q and the number of workers, L. Assuming that one worker moves 500 bricks per day on an average, the number of bricks moved per day, can be mathematically expressed as:

$$Q = 500L \tag{5.1}$$

Equation (5.1) expresses output Q in terms of input L and shows how Q varies directly with L. If L is 1, Q is 500; if L is 2, Q is 1000 and if L is 10, Q is 5000. A mathematical relationship such as this [Eq. (5.1)], provides an example of the production function. In general, it can be expressed as

$$Q = f(L) = \alpha L \tag{5.2}$$

where, α is a symbolic representation of 500.

Equation (5.2) represents a production function of a firm employing a single variable factor of production, namely labour. The production function of a firm employing all the four factors of production, in like manner, can be represented as:

$$Q = f(B, L, K, E) \qquad (5.3)$$

where
$B \equiv$ units of factor land-building
$L \equiv$ units of factor labour
$K \equiv$ units of factor capital
$E \equiv$ units of factor entrepreneur.

Likewise, the production function for a firm employing two factors of production, namely L and K, can be represented as:

$$Q = f(L, K) \qquad (5.4)$$

A typical production function involving two variable factors of production is the Cobb-Douglas production function used commonly to describe production situations in general. It is given as

$$Q = AL^\alpha K^\beta \qquad (5.5)$$

where
$A \equiv$ a constant, called efficiency parameter
$L \equiv$ quantity of labour
$K \equiv$ quantity of capital
$\alpha, \beta \equiv$ positive constants

the ratio $\alpha/\beta \equiv$ factor intensity.

For the purpose of numerical illustration, let $A = 100$, $\alpha = 1/3$ and $\beta = 2/3$. Further, let $L = 1000$ units of labour and $K = 216$ units of capital. The quantity of output is then given as:

$$Q = 100 \times (1000)^{1/3} \times (216)^{2/3}$$
$$= 100 \times (10) \times (36)$$
$$= 36,000 \text{ units of output}$$

Factor intensity, $\alpha/\beta = (1/3) \div (2/3) = 1/2$. The higher the ratio, the more labour intensive is the technique of production. Similarly, the lower the ratio, the more capital intensive the technique is. Also, the higher the value of the efficiency parameter, the higher the efficiency of production. For instance, if $A = 200$ in this illustration, $Q = 72,000$ units of output despite same quantities of labour and capital employed. You will learn more about production functions later in the chapter. Production functions for firms employing only three factors of production can be expressed in the same manner.

Production, from the viewpoint of the variability of factors of production, is classified into following four categories:

1. *Very short-run production:* This refers to a production situation in which time period is too short to increase any factor of production to increase output if so desired.

2. *Short-run production:* This refers to a production situation in which time period is too short to increase more than one factor of production to increase output if so desired. Usually, it is labour that can be increased in case of short-run production.

3. *Long-run production:* This refers to a production situation in which time period is too short to increase more than two factors of production to increase output if so desired. Usually, it is labour and capital which are possible to be increased in this case.

4. *Very long-run production:* This refers to a production situation in which time period is long enough to increase all the factors of production with a view to increase output. Increasing factors other than labour and capital generally requires a period long enough to be termed *very long-run*. Production with all the factors variable is termed *very long-run production*.

Very short-run production is too static to require any analysis. Similarly, very long-run production is too dynamic to require any analysis. In the latter case, everything changes including technology and above all, tastes and preferences of consumers. This might render the product too obsolete to be demanded. On the basis of these arguments, it is only short-run and long-run productions that deserve analysis.

5.3 SHORT-RUN PRODUCTION

As stated above, short-run production refers to that production situation in which all the factors except labour are fixed. Higher levels of outputs can only be realized through an increase in labour input only. Let us construct a numerical illustration to show various aspects of short-run production.

TABLE 5.1 Short-run production (Returns to a variable factor)

Capital ($K = \bar{K}$)	4	4	4	4	4	4	4	4	4
Labour, L (units)	1	2	3	4	5	6	7	8	9
Output, Q (units)	8	20	36	48	55	60	60	56	50
Marginal Product (MP)	8	12	16	12	7	5	0	−4	−6
Average Product (AP)	8	10	12	12	11	10	8.6	7	5.56

Stage I Stage II Stage III

Factors other than labour are all fixed. Units of capital available are 4. When units of labour are increased as shown in Table 5.1, the total output increases initially at a slow pace. It picks up thereafter and reaches its maximum of 60 units at 6 units of labour. If additional units of labour be employed, particularly the 7th unit, total product remains unchanged at 60 units, indicating that the 7th unit of labour has contributed nothing to the total product. If 8th unit of labour be employed, the total product declines from 60 to 56 units indicating that the 8th unit of labour has contributed negative units to the total product. This implies that the 8th unit of labour has caused a damage to the total product of the earlier 7 units. Let us define average and marginal products before proceeding any further.

Average Product* of labour, AP, is defined as output per unit of labour and may be given as:

$$AP = Q/L$$

---

*The terms Average Product, Marginal Product and Total Product are loosely used here to represent Average Physical Product (APP), Marginal Physical Product (MPP) and Total Physical Product (TPP). The term *physical* is used to stress that they are in terms of commodity units and not in terms of their money values. The reader can use the terms either way.

AP increases from 8 units per worker to a maximum of 12 units per worker. Thereafter, it declines steadily to 5.56 units per worker.

Marginal Product is defined as an addition to the total product per additional unit of labour employed. It can also be given as the ratio of the change in total output to a change in the number of units of labour employed. Thus,

$$MP = \frac{\text{Change in total product}}{\text{Change in labour units employed}}$$

$$= \frac{\Delta(TP)}{\Delta L}$$

$$= (\Delta Q / \Delta L)$$

$$= (dQ/dL)$$

Marginal product of labour (MP_L) is 8 at $L = 1$. It increases to a maximum of 16 per worker at $L = 3$. Thereafter, it declines to -6 per worker at $L = 9$.

Diagrammatically, TP, AP and MP in this illustration are portrayed as in Figure 5.1.

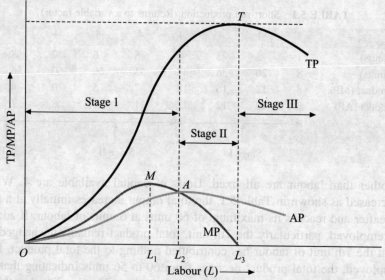

FIGURE 5.1 TP, MP and AP in short-run production: MP rises faster than AP initially. It reaches its maximum at M and begins to decline thereafter. AP reaches its maximum at the end of stage I at A and it too begins to decline steadily thereafter. Stage II terminates at the point where TP is maximum (at T) or at the point where MP = 0 (at L_3). The III stage begins right after this point. The point of intersection between AP and MP marks the end of stage I, while MP = 0 marks the end of the stage II. Note that MP reaches its maximum at M while AP is still on rise, reaching its maximum at A and falling steadily thereafter but at a pace slower than that of MP. The point at which TP is maximum (point T), MP = 0.

Nature of TP, AP and MP curves leads to three stages of production as described in Figure 5.1. In stage I, the average product steadily rises as successive units of labour input are employed. *The stage is characterized as the stage of increasing returns to the variable factor labour.* This implies that the average product of the variable factor labour has an increasing tendency in stage I. The marginal product also rises in this stage but before the end of the stage, it begins to decline to meet the average product curve at its maximum. *The point of intersection of MP and AP marks the end of first stage and also that of the increasing returns to the variable factor labour.* Average product thereafter falls steadily while the marginal product falls much faster. It reduces to zero at the point where the total product is maximum. *Stage II is characterized as the stage of the diminishing returns to the variable factor labour.* In this stage, MP falls keeping below AP through nonzero values. *This stage is also characterized as the stage in which total product increases but at a diminishing rate.* The stage reaches its end at the point where MP = 0 or TP is maximum.

In the third stage, total product of labour (TP_L) develops a declining trend as marginal product of labour (MP_L) turns negative. *This stage is characterized as the stage of negative returns to the variable factor labour.* Every additional unit of labour, if employed, leads to a decrease in total output.

Returns to variable factor labour imply outputs realized in return to increasing doles of labour input. As factors other than labour are all fixed, the proportion of labour to the fixed factors varies with additional units of labour employed. Returns to the variable factor labour, are, thus, also known as *returns to variable proportions*. At the initial level of employment of labour, such returns have a tendency to increase. Later, they develop a tendency to diminish and finally to turn even negative as doles of labour are further increased. Increasing, diminishing and negative returns to variable proportions taken together comprise *the law of diminishing returns*.

In the language of G. J. Stigler*,"*As equal increments of one input are added; the inputs of other productive services being held constant, beyond a certain point the resulting increments of product will decrease, i.e. the marginal products will diminish.*"

According to F. Benham**,"*As the proportion of one factor in a combination of factors is increased, after a point, first the marginal and then the average product of that factor will diminish.*"

According to P. A. Samuelson[†],"*An increase in some inputs relative to other fixed inputs will, in a given state of technology, cause output to increase; but after a point the extra output resulting from the same additions of extra inputs will become less and less.*"

K. E. Boulding[††] is of the view that the expression *diminishing returns* is a loose one because it can be variously interpreted. He, therefore, avoids the use of the expression and names it "*the Law of Eventually Diminishing Marginal Physical Productivity*" and defines it thus: "*As we increase the quantity of any one input which is combined with a fixed quantity of the other inputs, the marginal physical productivity of the variable input must eventually decline.*"

Whatever the terminology, the law of diminishing returns to variable proportions can be stated as *the law of initial increasing returns to a variable input followed by steadily decreasing returns to its successively increasing units employed with fixed quantities of collaborating factors of production*. The law, anyhow, remains *a combination of the stages of increasing, diminishing and negative returns to a variable input, given that other inputs remain unchanged.*

---

* G.J. Stigler, *Theory of Price*, The Macmillan Co., 1953, p. 111
** F. Benham, *Economics*, 2nd ed., 1960, p. 110
[†] P.A. Samuelson, *Economics*, 8th ed., p. 25
[††] K.E. Boulding, *Economic Analysis*, p. 589

The reasons for increasing, diminishing and negative returns to variable proportions are explained in the following paragraphs.

The main reason for the increasing returns to variable proportions is the indivisibility of certain fixed factors of production. Such factors cannot be had in smaller quantities to suit a smaller size of the variable factor. As the size of the variable inputs increases, the proportion of its combination with the fixed factors tends to approach optimality in factor combination. This leads to fuller utilization of the fixed factor. That provides an explanation for increasing returns to variable proportions in the initial stages of production. To illustrate, suppose a machine requires 10 workers to operate it at its full capacity. If only two workers be employed, they won't be able to exploit its full capacity with the result that the total as well as the average products will both be small. As the number of workers is increased, the machine approaches its fuller utilization and the marginal product of the variable factor rises. In consequence, the average product of the variable factor sustains its rising trend until it reaches its maximum at an employment of 10 workers.

The reason for the decreasing returns to variable proportions is partly the over-crowding of the fixed factors by the units of the variable factor and, partly the non-homogeneity of the additional units of the variable factor. The additional units of the variable factor fail to match the earlier units in their productivity due to lack of their experience with and adjustment to the fixed factors. As a result, marginal and average products both decline with the rising level of employment.

Finally the *reason for the negative returns to variable proportions is partly the over-crowding of the fixed factor by the units of the variable factor and, partly the depreciation of the fixed factors that leads to their frequent break-downs.* As a result, the marginal product of the variable factor becomes negative and the total and the average products both register a steep fall.

Which stage of production do producers prefer?

From the analysis above, it is clear that no producer would like to produce in the third stage of production. Each additional unit of the variable factor employed has a negative marginal product with the result that the total product falls rapidly.

Likewise, no producer would like to remain even in the first stage of production which is characterized for rising average product. So long as average product is rising, producers feel tempted to employ additional units of labour until they eventually enter the second stage of production. In this stage too, they continue employment of the variable factor until they reach that level at which the marginal product of the factor is zero. This is so due to their twin objectives of competitiveness and market share. The objective of competitiveness requires minimization of cost per unit of output so that price per unit set may be at its lowest. To minimize the cost per unit, fixed costs need to be spread on a largest quantity. To achieve this, producers continue employment of the variable factor as long as the marginal product of the factor is anything greater than zero. In the same way, large market share cannot be possible unless product price is low and no demand is refused. Producers, therefore, need to produce as large a quantity as possible.

5.4 LONG-RUN PRODUCTION

We have seen that short-run is long enough for the producers but only for increasing the labour input alone. As against this, long-run refers to that time period which is long enough for the producers to increase capital input also. Production in long-run, thus, takes place under two variable factors—labour and capital. The two are collaborated by producers in a fixed ratio called *scale*. For instance, if 6 units of labour input are collaborated with 2 units of capital, *the scale is 6:2 (or 3:1)*. Now suppose more is desired to be produced. This would require more of labour and capital. The two would have to be increased but in such a way that their ratio (scale) remains unchanged at 3:1. The inputs for the purpose can thus be 9: 3 or 12: 4 or 15: 5 or such other combinations of the two for each of which, the ratio of the two is 3:1. Quantities of output realized in consequence to the increasing units of the two inputs in a given ratio or scale are referred to as *returns to scale*.

Let us construct a numerical illustration. For the purpose, let the scale be 5: 2. Units of output realized in consequence to increasing doles of inputs in this scale are, say, as shown in Table 5.2.

TABLE 5.2 Long-run production (Returns to scale)

Labour (L) :	5	10	15	20	25	30	35	40	45
Capital (K) :	2	4	6	8	10	12	14	16	18
Total Output :	10	15	25	40	55	70	80	85	88

|←——— IRS ———→|←— CRS —→|←——— DRS ———→|

where, IRS ≡ Increasing returns to scale, CRS ≡ Constant returns to scale and DRS ≡ decreasing returns to scale.

As the factor inputs are increased from combination (5, 2) to combination (20, 8), the output increases from 10 units to 40 units; first by 5 units, then by 10 units and finally by 15 units. This implies that the total product increases at an increasing rate in response to increasing employment of inputs in the scale of 5: 2. The phenomenon is termed *increasing returns to scale* (IRS).

As the factor inputs are increased further from combination (15, 6) to (30, 12), total product increases from 25 units to 70 units at the fixed rate of 15 units each time the factor inputs are increased in the scale of 5: 2. The phenomenon is termed *constant returns to scale* (CRS).

Likewise, as the factor inputs are increased even further from the combination (25, 10) to (45, 18), total product increases from 55 units to 88 units, first by 15 units, then by 10 units, thereafter by 5 units, and finally, by 3 units. This implies that the total product increases at a decreasing rate in response to increasing employment of inputs in the scale of 5:2. This phenomenon is termed as *decreasing returns to scale* (DRS).

The *law of returns to scale can be stated as a combination of IRS, CRS and DRS. Accordingly, when employment of units of the variable factors of production is increased in a given scale, the total product increases initially at an increasing rate* (IRS), *then at a constant rate* (CRS) *and finally at a decreasing rate*(DRS).

IRS, CRS and DRS taken together are referred to as *diminishing returns to scale*. The reason for this is the long-run tendency of production that stabilizes in the stage of decreasing returns to scale. The preceding stages of increasing and constant returns to scale finally appear as the passing phases in production.

Returns to scale can also be analyzed mathematically if production function were known. We will do that in Section 5.7 while distinguishing returns to variable proportions from returns to scale.

IRS, CRS and DRS can also be explained with the help of isoquants. Section 5.7 will take care even of this technique.

5.4.1 Causes of Increasing, Constant and Decreasing Returns to Scale

Increasing returns to scale take place due to **indivisibilities of fixed factors**. Such fixed factors can't be had in smaller sizes to suit the smaller size of output initially produced with smaller quantities of variable inputs. As the size of variable inputs increases, the fixed factors get closer and closer to their fuller utilization. This brings in increasing returns from the additional units of the variable factors. Apart from the indivisibility of land-building, plant-equipment and machinery, known as **technical indivisibility**, there exists an indivisibility of managerial skill, known as **managerial indivisibility**, as well. Trained and skilled management produces better results with progressing plant size than with a plant size being underutilized. Same is the case with trained and experienced workers. They also produce better results with progressing size than with a plant size being underutilized.

Decreasing returns to scale take place due to **wear and tear of fixed factors (depreciation), overgrowth of plant size and exhaustibility of natural resources**. All of them lead to diseconomies in production. Depreciation affects productivity adversely, not only of the fixed factors but also of the collaborating factors such as labour. Oversized plants reduce efficiency of management. This leads to diminishing returns to management. Exhaustibility of natural resources too causes diseconomies in production.

Constant returns to scale result from **built-in reserve capacity in the plant and non-homogeneity of variable factors of production**. Plants are often planned by producers with some reserve capacity as a precautionary measure. Provision for production in shifts or that of accommodating more of the variable factors if needed in the building are usual practices. This imparts some flexibility of size to the fixed factors to accommodate additional units of the collaborating variable factors. Productivity of the variable factors, labour in particular, is usually much lower than that of the labour already in operation. This is the effect of learning of the existing units. Such non-homogeneity of the variable factors stabilizes returns to scale.

5.5 ISOCOST AND ISOQUANT CURVES

Isocost and the isoquant curves play the same role in producers' equilibrium as that played by the budget line and the indifference curves in consumer's equilibrium. In fact, isocost curve is a producer's budget line while an isoquant, his indifference curve. The reader having familiarity with the budget-line and the indifference curve will sort of feel like having a revision of the two while going through them.

5.5.1 Isocost Curves

For the sake of convenience, suppose that the producer is employing two variable factors, namely labour (L) and capital (K). Suppose further that the price of one unit of labour is w and that of one unit of capital is r. A producer employing L units of labour and K units of capital would thus have to spend ($w \cdot L + r \cdot K$) by way of the factor cost. This represents producer's total cost (C) and is expressed as

$$C = w \cdot L + r \cdot K \tag{5.6}$$

Isocost curve is the locus traced out by various combinations of L and K, each of which costs the producer the same amount of money $\overline{C}$. In Eq. (5.6), if we substitute $(C = \overline{C})$, we get the equation of the isocost curve.

$$\overline{C} = w \cdot L + r \cdot K \tag{5.7}$$

Differentiating Eq. (5.7) with respect to L, we have

$$dK/dL = -w/r \tag{5.8}$$

This gives the slope of the producer's budget line (isocost curve, Figure 5.2).

Price of capital remaining unchanged, a fall in price of labour leads to an outward pivotal shift in the isocost line and a rise in it, to an inward pivotal shift in it. The reader can try the shifts following the pattern of Figure 4.25 (Chapter 4).

Fall and rise in prices of both by the same proportion cause parallel outward and inward shifts in it respectively. The pattern is the same as that of Figure 4.26 (Chapter 4).

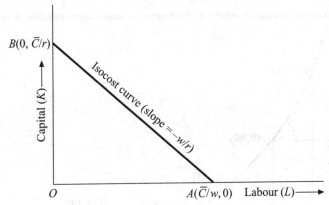

FIGURE 5.2 Isocost curve BA slopes downward from left to right. Its slope is OB/OA which is equal to $\overline{C}/r \div \overline{C}/w = w/r$ in magnitude (without sign). Points on BA represent combinations of L and K that cost the same amount of money, $\overline{C}$ to the producer.

5.5.2 Isoquant Curves

Locus traced out by different combinations of labour (L) and capital (K), each of which leads to production of the same quantity of output, is known as the isoquant (same quantity) curve. Output produced by different combinations of L and K is, say, $\overline{Q}$, then

$$\overline{Q} = f(L, K) \tag{5.9}$$

Equation (5.9), which can be obtained by substituting $Q = \overline{Q}$ in Eq. (5.4), is known as the equation of the isoquant curve. Just as we demonstrated the $MRS_{X,Y}$ in respect of indifference curves through hypothetical data (Table 4.2), we demonstrate the Marginal Rate of Technical Substitution of factor L for K ($MRTS_{L,K}$) for isoquants in Table 5.3.

TABLE 5.3 Marginal rate of technical substitution

Combination	L	K	Slope of the IQ = $\Delta K/\Delta L$	$MRTS_{L,K} = |\Delta K/\Delta L|$
1.	20	80	—	
2.	40	60	$-20/20 = -1.00$	1.00
3.	60	45	$-15/20 = -0.75$	0.75
4.	80	32	$-13/20 = -0.65$	0.65
5.	100	22	$-10/20 = -0.50$	0.50
6.	120	14	$-8/20 = -0.40$	0.40
7.	140	8	$-6/20 = -0.30$	0.30

As is obvious from Table 5.3, the slope of the isoquant curve ($\Delta K/\Delta L$) increases from -1.00 to -0.30 while the $MRTS_{L,K}$ ($|\Delta K/\Delta L|$) diminishes from 1.00 to 0.30 as we move from combination 1 to 7. Each of these combinations is assumed to yield same level of output so that the producer is indifferent in between any two. Figure 5.3 demonstrates the isoquant curve, which like an indifference curves, is convex to the origin.

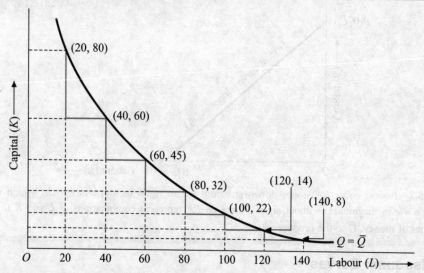

FIGURE 5.3 Isoquant $Q = \bar{Q}$, like an IC, is convex to origin. Movement down the curve to right implies decreasing sacrifice of capital units each time a fixed number (20) of labour units is put in additionally. The decreasing sacrifice of units of capital per additional unit of labour put in, is numerically given by $|\Delta K/\Delta L|$ and is known as the Marginal Rate of Technical Substitution of L for $K (MRTS_{L,K})$.

5.5.3 Properties of Isoquants

Isoquants, abbreviated as IQs, possess the same properties as those of the indifference curves. For the convenience of the reader, we just state them here.

1. IQs never intersect the two axes.
2. A higher IQ implies a higher level of output.

3. IQs never intersect each other.
4. IQs are never parallel to each other. Interspacing between them is least at the ends and maximum in the middle.
5. IQs are convex to the origin. **Convex isoquants** possess continuous substitutability of K and L over a stretch. Beyond this stretch, K and L are not substitutable for each other.
6. If L and K are perfect substitutes of each other, the IQ, called **linear isoquant**, is linear. A linear isoquant implies that either factor can be used in production.
   If an isoquant has several linear segments separated by kinks, the isoquant is called **kinked isoquant** or **activity analysis isoquant** or **linear programming isoquant**. Such isoquants are used in linear programming.
7. If L and K are perfect complements of each other, the IQ is L-shaped. Such isoquant is known as **input-output isoquant** or **Leontief isoquant**, after Leontief, the inventor of input–output analysis. There is only one combination of L and K available for production. It is the corner point of L-shaped isoquant.
8. If marginal product of one of the two factors is zero, IQ is parallel to the axis on which the factor with zero marginal product is represented.
9. If one of the two factors has negative marginal product, the IQ slopes upwards from left to right.
10. If both the factors have negative marginal products, the IQ is concave to the origin.
11. If the producer has a preference for a factor of production, the IQ is quasi-linear.
12. If the factors to be employed in whole number units only, the IQ is discontinuous.

The reader is advised to draw the figures on the lines of those drawn for ICs with changed labeling of the two axes.

5.6 PRODUCER'S EQUILIBRIUM

Just as we classified our study of consumer's equilibrium in two parts—one in which we assumed our consumer in a one-commodity world and the other in which we assumed him in a two-commodity world, we take up the study of producer's equilibrium too on the same lines in two parts. In the first part, we study how a producer employs an optimal quantity of a single variable factor of production and in the second part, we study how he does the same in case of two variable factors of production.

5.6.1 One Variable Factor Case

Suppose our producer employs only one variable factor of production. Let it be labour. Quantity, Q, of the product would then depend on the quantity, L, of labour alone. Q can thus be expressed as a function of L as

$$Q = f(L) \tag{5.10}$$

Suppose further that price of labour is w per unit. Let the total cost of producing Q units of the product be C. Then,

$$C = w \cdot L \tag{5.11}$$

Producer's equilibrium, here, may imply either of the following two:

1. **Maximization of output with given cost, that is,**

   Maximize: $Q = f(L)$ (Objective function)

   Subject to: $\overline{C} = w \cdot L$ (Constraint)

2. **Minimization of cost with given target of production, that is,**

   Minimize: $C = w \cdot L$ (Objective function)

   Subject to: $\overline{Q} = f(L)$ (Constraint).

Equilibrium of the producer is governed by the same condition, whichever the case. To obtain the condition, let us, for simplicity, assume that factor market is competitive, that is, price of labour is determined through its demand and supply at the point of their intersection. That is,

$$w = \text{constant}$$

Keeping in view the objective and the constraint, the condition of equilibrium may be spelled out as

$$MP_L = w^* \qquad (5.12)$$

when both are measured in same units, say, money.

According to the law of diminishing marginal productivity of a factor, the marginal physical product of an input diminishes with increasing number of units of the input employed in the long-run. Assuming the input price as fixed, producers' equilibrium can be determined in the same way as the consumers' equilibrium. Consider the data in Table 5.4 for a firm employing only one variable factor, labour.

From Table 5.4 marginal product of labour decreases with increasing doles of labour input. The MP_L curve, thus, has a negative slope.

Measuring the marginal product on the vertical axis and the labour input on the horizontal axis, we can determine the producers' equilibrium as in Figure 5.4, assuming that the price of each unit of labour is ₹ 10.

---

*Formulating the mathematical model for the firm employing only one variable factor, labour, we have:

$$\text{Maximize: } Q = f(L)$$

$$\text{Subject to: } \overline{C} = \overline{w} \cdot L$$

Developing a function,

$$\Phi = Q - \overline{C}$$
$$= Q - \overline{w} \cdot L$$

where, Φ can be considered to represent the excess of the value of the output over the total costs. This reduces the problem of constrained maximization into one of simple maximization. Differentiating Φ with respect to L, we have

$$d\Phi/dL = dQ/dL - \overline{w}$$
$$= 0. \qquad \text{(necessary condition for maximization)}.$$

$\Rightarrow \qquad dQ/dL - w = 0$

$\Rightarrow \qquad MP_L - w = 0$

$\Rightarrow \qquad MP_L = w$

Here, $dQ/dL = MP_L$ (marginal product of labour) and $d\Phi/dL = 0$ for maximization. It can also be verified that $d^2\Phi/dL^2 < 0$, because MP_L curve has a negative slope due to law of diminishing marginal productivity of labour in the long-run.

TABLE 5.4 MP_L schedule for a firm employing only one variable input labour

Input units (L) :	0	1	2	3	4	5	6	7	8
Total product :	0	20	38	54	68	70	80	88	94
Marginal product :	0	20	18	16	14	12	10	8	6
Cost/unit of L :	10	10	10	10	10	10	10	10	10

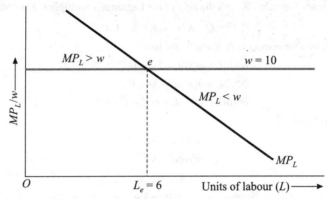

FIGURE 5.4 Equilibrium of a producer employing one variable input, labour. MP_L decreases with increasing employment of labour while cost of each unit of labour is fixed. Equilibrium takes place at the point where $MP_L = w$, the wage rate or the cost per unit of labour.

5.6.2 Two Variable Factors Case

Suppose our producer employs two variable factors, namely labour and capital. He produces quantity Q of a product employing quantity L of labour and K of capital. The production function then takes the general form,

$$Q = f(L, K) \tag{5.13}$$

Given the prices of labour and capital as w and r respectively, the cost function may be expressed as

$$C = w \cdot L + r \cdot K \tag{5.14}$$

As seen in the case of one variable factor, producers' equilibrium refers to either of the following two:

1. Determination of cost-minimizing employment of L and K to produce a predetermined quantity, $\bar{Q}$ of the product:
   The problem can be mathematically expressed as

   Minimize: $C = w \cdot L + r \cdot K$ (Objective function)

   Subject to: $\bar{Q} = f(L, K)$ (Constraint)

2. Determination of the output-maximizing employment of L and K when the producer is on a fixed budget, $\bar{C}$:
   The problem can be mathematically expressed as

   Maximize: $Q = f(L, K)$ (Objective function)

   Subject to: $\bar{C} = w \cdot L + r \cdot K$ (Constraint)

In either case, the condition of equilibrium is the same

$$[MP_L/MP_K] = [w/r]* \qquad (5.15)$$

Here, MP_L and MP_K are marginal products of labour and capital and w and r are the fixed prices of the two.

---

* Re-writing constraint, $\bar{C} = w \cdot L + r \cdot K$

as, $w \cdot L + r \cdot K - \bar{C} = 0$

and developing a composite function, Φ, with the help of the Lagrange's multiplier, λ, a constant, we have:

$$\Phi = Q - \lambda(w \cdot L + r \cdot K - \bar{C}) \qquad (1)$$

Differentiating Φ partially with respect to L, K and λ, we have

$$\partial\Phi/\partial L = \partial Q/\partial L - \lambda w = 0; \qquad (2)$$
$$\partial\Phi/\partial K = \partial Q/\partial K - \lambda r = 0; \qquad (3)$$
$$\partial\Phi/\partial\lambda = -(w \cdot L + r \cdot K - \bar{C}) = 0 \qquad (4)$$

From Eqs. (2) to (4), we have

$$\partial Q/\partial L = \lambda w, \qquad (5)$$
$$\partial Q/\partial K = \lambda r \qquad (6)$$

and $\qquad w \cdot L + r \cdot K = \bar{C} \qquad (7)$

$\Rightarrow \qquad MP_L = \lambda w \qquad$ [from 5]

and, $\qquad MP_K = \lambda r \qquad$ [from 6]

$\Rightarrow \qquad MP_L/MP_K = w/r \qquad (8)$

Equation (8) gives the required condition of equilibrium of the producer. Here,

$$\partial Q/\partial L = MP_L$$
$$\partial Q/\partial K = MP_K$$

The mathematical requirement for maximization of a function of two variables comprises the following three conditions:

1. The first-order partial derivatives are zero, i.e. $\partial\Phi/\partial L = 0$ and $\partial\Phi/\partial K = 0$
2. The second-order partial derivatives are negative at the point where first-order partial derivatives are zero, i.e.

$$\partial^2\Phi/\partial L^2 < 0 \text{ and } \partial^2\Phi/\partial K^2 < 0$$

3. The product of the second-order partial derivatives is greater than the square of the cross partial derivatives, i.e.

$$(\partial^2\Phi/\partial L^2)(\partial^2\Phi/\partial K^2) > (\partial^2\Phi/\partial L \, \partial K)^2$$

The right-hand side of Eq. (8) gives the numerical value of the slope of the isocost curve.
The left-hand side is the slope of the IQ. To show this, let us consider the total differential for the function $Q = f(L, K)$] as

$$dQ = (\partial Q/\partial L) \cdot dL + (\partial Q/\partial K) \cdot dk \qquad (9)$$

Substituting $dQ = d\bar{Q} = 0$ (since $\bar{Q} = Q$ on an isoquant), we have from (9)

$$0 = (MP_L)dL + (MP_K)dk \qquad (10)$$

From (10), we have

$$-dK/dL = MP_L/MP_K$$

Or, $\qquad MRTS_{L,K} = MP_L/MP_K$

Thus, $\qquad -dK/dL = MRTS_{L,K} = MP_L/MP_K =$ slope of the isocost line $= w/r \qquad (11)$

The left-hand side of Eq. (5.15) is $MRTS_{L,K}$, representing numerical value of the slope of the isoquant and its right-hand side is the numerical value of the slope of the isocost line. In totality, the condition can be stated as

$$MRTS_{L,K} = -dK/dL = [MP_L/MP_K] = [w/r] = \text{Slope of isocost line}. \qquad (5.16)$$

To demonstrate producer's equilibrium diagrammatically, let us superimpose the isocost line (Figure 5.2) on the isoquant map (Figure 5.5) as in Figure 5.6. The highest isoquant touched by the isocost gives producer's equilibrium at the point of tangency. (If the isocost does not touch any isoquant, the reader can draw an additional one in between any two of them for the purpose.)

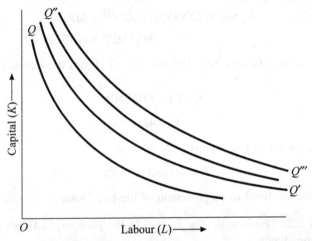

FIGURE 5.5 Producer's isoquant map comprises isoquants Q, Q', Q'' and Q'''. Thus, $Q''' > Q'' > Q' > Q$. The one closest to the origin (Q) represents the lowest level of output and the one farthest away from the origin represents the highest level of it.

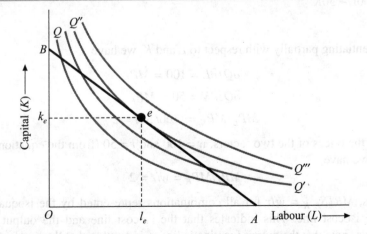

FIGURE 5.6 Producer's isocost line AB ($\overline{C} = w \cdot L + r \cdot K$) touches the isoquant Q'' at e. At this point, slope of the isoquant is equal to the slope of the isocost line. In other words, $MRTS_{L,K} = w/r$. Equilibrium level of employment of labour and capital is (l_e, k_e).

ILLUSTRATION 5.1: Given the output function

$$Q = 1000 \, L^{1/3} K^{2/3}$$

and the consumer's budget

$$3000 = 100L + 50K$$

determine the equilibrium level of employment for the producer.

Solution: Differentiating the output function partially with respect to L and K, we have

$$\partial Q/\partial L = (1000/3) \cdot (K/L)^{2/3} = MP_L$$
$$\partial Q/\partial K = (2000/3) \cdot (L/K)^{1/3} = MP_K$$

$\therefore \qquad MP_L/MP_K = (K/2L).$

Given the prices of the two factors, $w = 100$ and $r = 50$ (From the equation of the isocost line given), we have

$$(K/2L) = (100/50)$$

$\Rightarrow \qquad K = 4L$

Substituting in the equation of the isocost line, we have

$$L = 10 \text{ and } K = 40$$

This gives the equilibrium level of employment of the two factors.

ILLUSTRATION 5.2: How will your answer to the problem in Illustration 5.1 change if the isoquant functions were:

(a) $Q = 100L + 50K$
(b) $Q = 50L + 100K$
(c) $Q = 200L + 50K$.

Solution:

(a) Differentiating partially with respect to L and K, we have

$$\partial Q/\partial L = 100 = MP_L$$
$$\partial Q/\partial K = 50 = MP_K$$

$\therefore \qquad MP_L/MP_K = (100/50) = 2$

Given the prices of the two factors, $w = 100$ and $r = 50$ (from the equation of the isocost line), we have

$$MP_L/MP_K = w/r = 2$$

That is, $MRTS_{L,K} = w/r$ for all combinations represented by the isoquant function or by the isocost line. This indicates that the isocost line and the output function both coincide (note that the output function is linear, indicating that the two factors are perfect substitutes). There exist infinitely many solutions, that is, any factor combination on the isocost line is as good as any other on it (Figure 5.7).

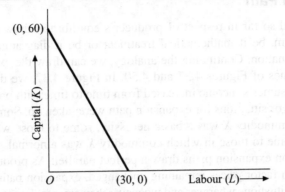

FIGURE 5.7 **Infinitely many solutions:** Output function ($Q = 100L + 50K$) coincides with the isocost line ($3000 = 100L + 50K$), yielding infinitely many solutions.

(b) Differentiating partially with respect to L and K, we have

$$\partial Q/\partial L = 50 = MP_L$$
$$\partial Q/\partial K = 100 = MP_K$$
$$\therefore MP_L/MP_K = (50/100) = 1/2$$

Given the prices of the two factors, $w = 100$ and $r = 50$ (From the equation of the isocost line), we have,

$$w/r = (100/50) = 2$$

Clearly, $1/2 \neq 2$ ($MRTS_{L,K} \neq w/r$)

(IQ is flatter than the isocost line)
Goods being the substitutes, (0, 60) would optimize producer's output (Figure 5.8).

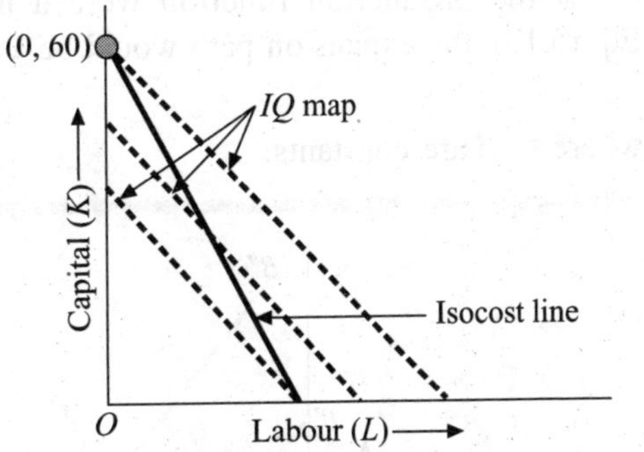

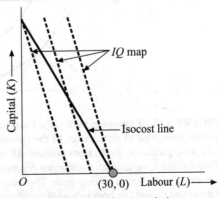

FIGURE 5.8 Corner solution.

(c) Differentiating partially with respect to L and K, we've

$$\partial Q/\partial L = 200 = MP_L$$
$$\partial P/\partial K = 50 = MP_K$$
$$\therefore MP_L/MP_K = (200/50) = 4$$

Given the prices of the two factors, $w = 100$ and $r = 50$ (From the equation of the isocost line), we have

$$w/r = (100/50) = 2$$

Clearly, $4 \neq 2$ ($MRTS_{L,K} \neq w/r$)

(This time, IQ is steeper than the isocost line.)
Again, output function being linear, the goods are substitutes. (30, 0) would optimize producer's output (Figure 5.9).

FIGURE 5.9 Corner solution.

5.6.3 Expansion Path

Discussions conducted so far in respect of producer's equilibrium draw a perfect parallel with consumer's equilibrium, be it mathematical treatment or be it diagrammatic representation or be it conceptual explanation. Continuing the analogy, we can draw the expansion path of a firm following the techniques of Figures 4.37 and 4.50. In Figure 4.37, we dealt with consumption expansion path as consumer's income increased from time to time with product prices remaining unchanged. A number of situations for expansion path were taken up. Some related to expansion paths (ICCs) when commodity X was a basic necessity, some to those when commodity X was an inferior one and some to those in which commodity X was a normal good turned later to an inferior one. Production expansion paths draw a perfect parallel. As producer's budget increases from time to time with factor prices remaining unchanged, expansion paths in production can be drawn under different situations wherever and whenever they emerge. For instance, some labour can be a basic necessity and some inferior. Expansion paths can be drawn for all of them on the same lines. In the same way, when price of one of the two factors rises or falls from time to time while that of the other remains unchanged, expansion paths in production follow the trend of Figure 4.50. For ready reference and for demonstrating the amendments in the figures, we show the situations of Figures 4.37 and 4.50 in Figures 5.10 and 5.11(a).

If the production function were a homogeneous production function, such as one in Eq. (5.17), the expansion path would be a straight line passing through origin.

$$Q = AL^\alpha K^\beta \tag{5.17}$$

where α, β are constants.

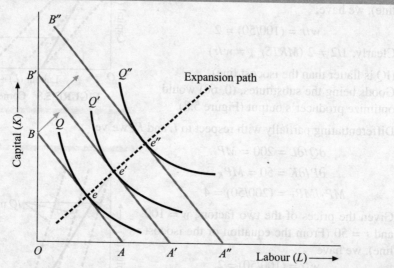

FIGURE 5.10 Expansion path is the locus traced by the equilibrium points in response to changes in producer's budget from time to time, prices of the factors remaining the same. In the figure, producer's budget line shifts upwards, parallel to itself, from position AB to $A'B'$ and then to $A''B''$ each time producer's income increases. Both factors being normal, equilibrium position shifts from e to e' and then to e''. Employment of both the factors increases each time in consequence. The locus of points e, e' and e'' is called expansion path in production. As labour and capital can both be varied simultaneously, the expansion path represents a **long-run expansion path**.

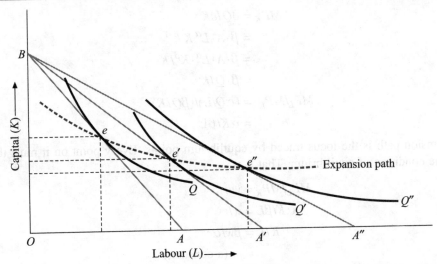

FIGURE 5.11(a) Long-run expansion path when price of one factor changes: A fall in price of L, other things remaining the same, causes an outward pivotal shift in the isocost line. In consequence, producer employs more of the factor in question provided it is a normal one. The changing pattern of employment of the two factors in response to a fall or a rise in price of one is also known as expansion path in production. In the figure, an outward pivotal shift is caused in the isocost line by a fall in price of L. Initially, it shifts from BA to BA' and then to BA''. Accordingly, equilibrium shifts from e to e' and then to e''. Joining these points by means of a smooth curve, we get the required curve **(a long-run expansion path)**.

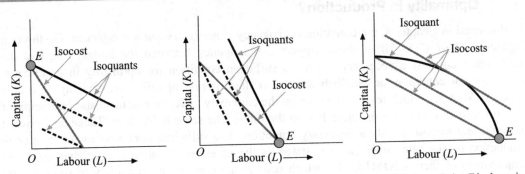

FIGURE 5.11(b) Condition of tangency is necessary but not sufficient for equilibrium: Point E is the point of optimality in production in each case. Condition of tangency is not defined in case of linear isoquants and is insufficient in case of concave isoquants.

To show, let us calculate MP_L and MP_K for this function through partial differentiation.

$$MP_L = \partial Q/\partial L$$
$$= \alpha \cdot A \cdot L^{\alpha-1} \cdot K^{\beta}$$
$$= \alpha \cdot A \cdot L^{\alpha} \cdot K^{\beta}/L$$
$$= \alpha Q/L$$

Likewise,

$$MP_K = \partial Q/\partial K$$
$$= \beta \cdot A \cdot L^\alpha K^{\beta-1}$$
$$= \beta \cdot A \cdot L^\alpha \cdot K^\beta / K$$
$$= \beta \cdot Q/K$$
$$MP_L/MP_K = (\alpha Q/L)/(\beta Q/K)$$
$$= \alpha K/\beta L$$

Expansion path is the locus traced by equilibrium points. Every point on it must therefore satisfy the condition of equilibrium. That is,

$$MP_L/MP_K = w/r$$
$$\Rightarrow \quad \alpha K/\beta L = w/r$$
$$\Rightarrow \quad K/L = \beta w/\alpha r$$
$$= m \text{ (a constant)}$$

(Since w, r, α, and β are all constants)

$$\Rightarrow \quad K = m \cdot L \quad (5.18)$$

Equation (5.18) represents a straight line passing through the origin. That establishes the fact that expansion path passes through the origin and is linear when production function is homogeneous.

5.6.4 Is Tangency of Isocost to Isoquant a Sufficient Condition for Optimality in Production?

As discussed in Chapter 4, the condition of tangency is *necessary but not sufficient*. Go through Figures 4.32 to 4.35. All of them support that tangency between the budget line and the indifference curve is a necessary but not a sufficient condition for optimality in production. The sufficient condition, as established there, is the criterion of utility maximizing least cost basket (**UMLCB**), which rests at the core on the convexity of IC on one hand and optimality of the corner solution in case of linear ICs on the other. The same holds here. Tangency between isoquant and isocost is only a necessary condition. The sufficient condition for optimality in production on the same lines can be stated as the criterion of output maximizing least cost employment of factors (**OMLCEF**), which rests at the core on the convexity of isoquants on one hand and optimality of the corner solution in case of linear IQs on the other. The reader is advised to recall Illustrations 4.2 and 4.3 with Q, L, K and C in place of U, x, y and M. Here, we feel contented with diagrams showing optimality in production when isoquants are linear and concave [Figure 5.11(b)].

5.7 RETURNS TO VARIABLE PROPORTIONS AND RETURNS TO SCALE

Returns to variable proportions, also known as returns to a variable factor, are short-run phenomena. Returns to scale, on the other hand, refer to long-run production situations. Returns to variable proportions refer to that production situation in which all the factors of production are constant except one, namely labour. As against this, returns to scale refer to that production situation in which two factors of production are variable. Returns to variable proportions end up in negative returns while returns to scale end up in decreasing returns to scale.

We can distinguish between the two graphically through isoquants and mathematically through the production function. Let us first demonstrate the use of production function for the purpose. The function we take is the Cobb–Douglas Production Function (Eq. 5.17).

Mathematical Presentation of Returns to Scale and Returns to Variable Proportions

Recall Cobb–Douglas Production Function (Eq. 5.17)

$$Q = AL^\alpha K^\beta \qquad (5.17)$$

where, Q represents units of output produced; α, β are constants, A is efficiency parameter, and L and K are units of labour and capital.

(i) *Returns to variable proportions or returns to a variable factor:* In this case, all the factors are fixed except labour. Substituting $K = \bar{K}$ (fixed) in the equation, we have

$$Q = AL^\alpha \bar{K}^\beta = A'L^\alpha \qquad (5.19)$$

where,

$$A' \equiv A \times \bar{K}^\beta = a \text{ constant (since } A, \bar{K}, \beta \text{ are all constants)}$$

Now let the variable input labour be doubled so that current employment $L' = 2L$. Let output realized in consequence be Q'. Then,

$$\begin{aligned}
Q' &= A'(L')^\alpha & \text{[from Eq. (5.19)]} \\
&= A' \times (2L)^\alpha \\
&= A' \times 2^\alpha L^\alpha \\
&= 2^\alpha \times (A'L^\alpha) \\
&= 2^\alpha \times Q & \text{[from Eq. (5.19)]}
\end{aligned}$$

If $\alpha > 1$, say 2, then

$$Q' = 2^2 \times Q = 4Q$$

Doubling the variable factor labour thus leads to 4 times the original output. This implies more than proportionate increase in output or *increasing returns to a variable factor, labour.*

If $\alpha = 1$,

$$\begin{aligned}
Q' &= 2^1 Q \\
&= 2Q
\end{aligned}$$

Doubling the variable input labour thus leads to proportionate increase in output. *This implies constant returns to the variable input, labour.*

If $\alpha < 1$, say 1/2,

$$\begin{aligned}
Q' &= 2^{1/2} \times Q \\
&= \sqrt{2} \times Q \\
&= 1.414Q
\end{aligned}$$

Doubling the variable input labour thus leads to less than proportionate increase in output. *This implies decreasing returns to a variable factor, labour.*

(ii) *Returns to scale:* In long-run production, L and K both are variable. Let them both be doubled so that

$$L' = 2L$$

and $$K' = 2K$$

Substituting in equation

$$Q' = A(L')^\alpha (K')^\beta$$

we have

$$Q' = A(2L)^\alpha (2K)^\beta$$
$$= 2^{(\alpha+\beta)} \times AL^\alpha K^\beta$$
$$= 2^{(\alpha+\beta)} Q \qquad \text{[from Eq. (5.17)]}$$

If $\alpha + \beta > 1$, say 2,

$$Q' = 2^2 Q$$
$$= 4Q$$

Doubling the factor inputs thus leads to 4 times the original output implying more than proportionate increase in it. This gives *increasing returns to scale.*

If $\alpha + \beta = 1$,

$$Q' = 2^1 Q$$
$$= 2Q$$

Doubling the factor inputs in this case doubles the output implying an increase in it by the same proportion. This gives *constant returns to scale.*

Finally, If $\alpha + \beta < 1$, say 1/2,

$$Q' = 2^{1/2} Q$$
$$= \sqrt{2} Q$$
$$= 1.414 Q$$

Here, doubling the factor inputs leads to less than proportionate increase in output. This implies *decreasing returns to scale.*

Mathematical presentation of returns is thus a simple exercise.

Graphical Presentation of Returns to Scale and Return to Variable Proportions

(i) *Return to scale:* The returns to scale may be presented graphically by the distances on a *product line* or an *isocline* intercepted by successsive isoquants, that is, isoquants that show levels of output in multiples of some base quantity, e.g. $Q, 2Q, 3Q$, etc.

A *product curve* shows movement of a point from one isoquant to another in consequence to changes in quantities of input (s). It passes through origin when both the factors vary simultaneously in a given proportion. We get a linear product curve, called *product line*, when production function is homogeneous. If the product line subtends equal angles with the axes, it is called an *isocline*. If only one factor varies, the product line resulting is parallel to the axis measuring the variable factor. In Figure 5.12, product curves are product lines due to homogeneity of production functions and in Figure 5.13, they are non-linear due to non-homogeneity of the production function. Figure 5.14 shows the *increasing returns to scale*, Figure 5.15, the *constant returns to scale* and Figure 5.16 shows the *decreasing returns to scale*.

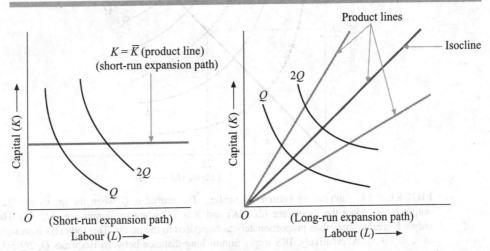

FIGURE 5.12 Short-run and long-run expansion paths. In the left panel, one factor (K) is held constant while the other varies in short-run. The product line (a short-run expansion path) is a horizontal line at a distance of $\bar{K}$ from the origin. In the right panel, both the factors are variable. The product lines (long-run expansion paths) pass through the origin. If the factors are combined in equal measures (such as, one unit of L combined one unit of K or 5 units of L combined with 5 units of K), the product line is equally inclined to the two axes and is called an isocline. Both the panels represent homogeneous production functions. You will earn about them in the next section.

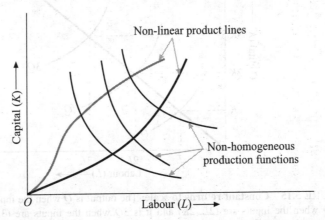

FIGURE 5.13 Expansion paths when production functions are non-homogeneous. Product lines are non-linear when production functions are non-homogeneous.

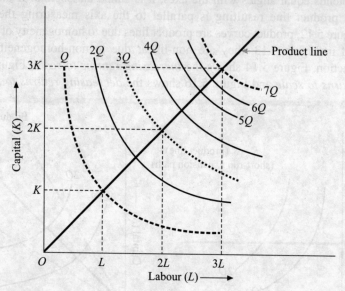

FIGURE 5.14 Increasing returns to scale: The output is Q when the inputs are (L, K). The output is $3Q$ when the inputs are $(2L, 2K)$ and it is $7Q$ when the inputs are $(3L, 3K)$. Hence, the output increases more than proportionately as compared to the inputs. This indicates increasing returns to scale (IRS). Alternatively, IRS imply diminishing distance between isoquants Q, $2Q$ $3Q$, ..., etc. along the product line.

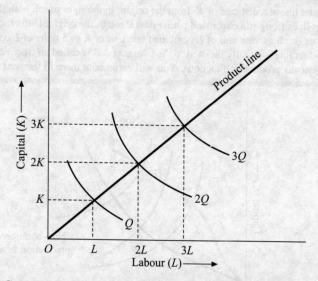

FIGURE 5.15 Constant returns to scale: The output is Q when the inputs are (L, K). The output is $2Q$ when the inputs are $(2L, 2K)$ and it is $3Q$ when the inputs are $(3L, 3K)$. Hence, the output increases in the same proportion in which inputs do. This indicates constant returns to scale (CRS). Alternatively, CRS imply constant distance between the isoquants Q, $2Q$, etc. along the product line.

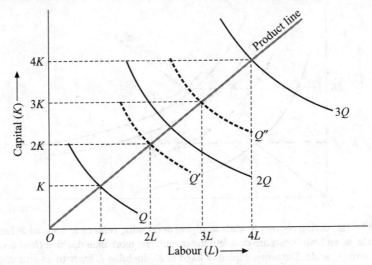

FIGURE 5.16 Decreasing returns to scale: The distance between the successive isoquants $Q, 2Q, 3Q, \ldots$, etc. along the product line has an increasing trend. This shows that the output increases less proportionately than the increase in inputs. In other words, when the inputs are doubled, the output realized (Q') is less than doubled; when the inputs are tripled, the output realized (Q'') is less than tripled; and so on. This indicates decreasing returns to scale.

(ii) *Returns to variable proportions:* Returns to a variable factor, say labour, may be shown graphically by interspacing between successive isoquants in the product line drawn at a distance $K = \bar{K}$ from the x-axis. Isoquants drawn correspond to outputs that are multiples of some base level of output, Q. Collaborating factor of production, capital, being fixed, varying outputs are realized only through varying units of labour input.

A horizontal line drawn at a distance $\bar{K}$ from the origin, serves as the product-line while demonstrating returns to a variable factor labour (returns to variable proportions). Figures 5.17 to 5.19 demonstrate returns to a variable proportions when returns to scale being realized are respectively increasing, constant and decreasing.

In sum, whatever the returns to scale, returns to a variable factor are, in all likelihood, diminishing returns. Mathematically speaking, in case of increasing returns to scale (IRS), if $\alpha + \beta = 2$, return to variable factor labour may be increasing when $1 < \alpha < 2$, constant when $\alpha = 1$ and may be decreasing when $\alpha < 1$. Much depends on the strength of IRS, that is on the value of $(\alpha + \beta)$. For IRS, $(\alpha + \beta) > 1$, which implies that $(\alpha + \beta)$ may have any value greater than 1. If it is 1.1, returns to scale would have an increasing trend, no doubt, but the strength of IRS would be weak. Value of α for increasing returns to variable proportions may then be anywhere between 1 and 1.1. But its most probable value should be less than 1 implying decreasing returns to variable proportions. When strength of IRS is high, that is, value of $(\alpha + \beta)$ is high, the likelihood of α having a high value is also high and so is that of increasing returns to variable proportions. Thus, when returns to scale are strong enough to offset the diminishing marginal productivity of the single variable factor labour, returns to variable proportions have an increasing trend. The case, however, is rare.

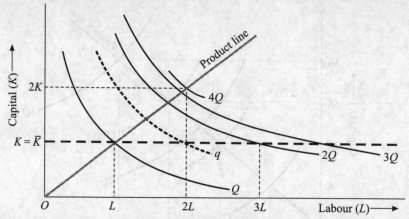

FIGURE 5.17 **Increasing returns to scale implying decreasing returns to a variable factor:** Under increasing returns to scale, when both inputs are doubled, the output gets more than doubled (four times, say). This implies increasing returns to scale. But when capital is fixed at K, doubling L leads to an output q, which is much less than doubled ($q < 2Q$). Likewise, when labour is further increased to $3L$, the output is $2Q$, which is much less than tripled. Thus, when returns to scale realized have an increasing trend, returns to a variable factor labour (returns to variable proportions) have a diminishing trend.

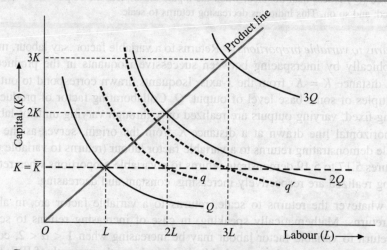

FIGURE 5.18 **Constant returns to scale implying decreasing returns to a variable factor:** Under constant returns to scale, when both inputs are doubled, the output also gets doubled and when both are tripled, the output also get tripled. But when capital is fixed at $K = \bar{K}$ doubling L leads to an output q, which is much less than doubled and increasing it three times leads it to q', again less than even $2Q$. Thus, when returns to scale realized have a constant trend, returns to a variable factor labour (returns to variable proportions) have a diminishing trend.

Under constant returns to scale (CRS), $\alpha + \beta = 1$ and α has a very high probability of being less than 1 implying decreasing returns to variable proportions. Under decreasing returns to scale (DRS), $\alpha + \beta < 1$ and α has every chance of being less than 1 implying decreasing returns to variable proportions.

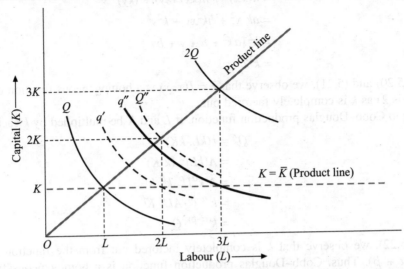

FIGURE 5.19 Decreasing returns to scale implying decreasing returns to a variable factor: Under decreasing returns to scale, when both the inputs are doubled, the output realized is Q'', which is much less than doubled and when both of them are further increased to three times as much, the output realized is $2Q$, which is less than $3Q$. With capital fixed at $\bar{K}$ when L is increased to $2L$, the output realized is q', which is much less than $2Q$ and when L is increased to $3L$, the output realized is q'', which is much less than $3Q$. Thus, returns to a variable factor labour have a diminishing trend given that returns to scale are following a decreasing trend.

5.8 FEATURES OF COBB–DOUGLAS PRODUCTION FUNCTION AND ELASTICITY OF FACTOR SUBSTITUTION

In Section 5.2, while discussing the production functions, we made a brief mention of Cobb–Douglas production function [Eq. (5.5)]. For ready reference, we restate it below.

$$Q = AL^\alpha K^\beta \tag{5.5}$$

Here, Q is the output, L and K are the quantities of labour and capital, A is a constant called the efficiency parameter and α and β are positive constants.

Cobb–Douglas production function is a homogeneous production function of degree $(\alpha + \beta)$. Before proceeding any further let us first see what a homogeneous function is.

A homogeneous function is a function in which if the independent variables be multiplied by a constant, k, then it must be possible to factor k out of the function completely. The power n of k is called the degree of homogeneity of the function.

To demonstrate, let Z be a function of x and y such that

$$Z = f(x, y) = ax^2 + h x y + by^2 \tag{5.20}$$

Multiplying the independent variables x and y by k each in (5.20), we have, the new function, Z'

$$Z' = f(kx, ky)$$

$$\begin{aligned}
&= a(kx)^2 + h(kx)(ky) + (ky)^2 \\
&= ak^2x^2 + hk^2xy + k^2y^2 \\
&= k^2[ax^2 + hxy + by^2] \\
&= k^2 Z
\end{aligned} \qquad (5.21)$$

From Eqs. (5.20) and (5.21), we observe that $Z = f(x, y)$ is a homogeneous function of degree 2 (power of k is 2) as k is completely factored out.

Coming to Cobb–Douglas production function, if L and K be multiplied by k each, we have

$$\begin{aligned}
Q' &= f(kL, kK) \\
&= A(kL)^\alpha (kK)^\beta \\
&= A \, k^\alpha L^\alpha \cdot k^\beta K^\beta \\
&= k^{(\alpha+\beta)} \cdot AL^\alpha K^\beta \\
&= k^{(\alpha+\beta)} \cdot Q
\end{aligned} \qquad (5.22)$$

From Eq. (5.22), we observe that k is completely factored out from the function and has a power of $(\alpha + \beta)$. Thus, Cobb–Douglas production function is a homogeneous function of degree $(\alpha + \beta)$.

Now we can turn to features of the Cobb–Douglas production function.

5.8.1 Features of Cobb–Douglas Production Function

1. The marginal product of labour (MP_L) is equal to α times its average product (AP_L):

$$\begin{aligned}
MP_L &= \partial Q / \partial L \\
&= \alpha \cdot AL^{\alpha-1} K^\beta \quad \text{(differentiating partially w. r. t. } L\text{)} \\
&= \alpha \cdot AL^\alpha K^\beta / L \\
&= \alpha \cdot Q / L \\
&= \alpha \cdot AP_L
\end{aligned} \qquad (5.23)$$

2. Differentiating Eq. (5.5) partially with respect to K, similarly, it can be shown that

$$\begin{aligned}
MP_K &= \beta \cdot Q / K \\
&= \beta \cdot AP_K
\end{aligned} \qquad (5.24)$$

3. The marginal rate of technical substitution of L for K, written as $MRTS_{L,K}$, can be expressed from Eq. (5.16) as

$$\begin{aligned}
MRTS_{L,K} &= -dK/dL \\
&= MP_L / MP_K \\
&= (\alpha \cdot Q/L)/(\beta \cdot Q/K) \quad \text{[from Eqs. (5.23) and (5.24)]} \\
&= (\alpha \cdot K)/(\beta \cdot L)
\end{aligned} \qquad (5.25)$$

4. Elasticity of factor substitution for Cobb–Douglas prodution unction, σ, is 1. It is given as

$$\sigma = \frac{\text{Percentage change in } (K/L)}{\text{Percentage change in MRTS}}$$

$$= \frac{d(K/L)/(K/L)}{d(\text{MRTS})/(\text{MRTS})}$$

$$= \frac{d(K/L)/(K/L)}{d(\alpha \cdot K/\beta \cdot L)/(\alpha \cdot K/\beta \cdot L)} \quad \text{[from Eq. (5.25)]}$$

$$= \frac{d(K/L) \cdot (\alpha \cdot K/\beta \cdot L)}{(\alpha/\beta) \cdot d(K/L) \cdot (K/L)}$$

(α, β sorted out as constants)

$$= \frac{(\alpha/\beta) \cdot d(K/L) \cdot (K/L)}{(\alpha/\beta) \cdot d(K/L) \cdot (K/L)}$$

(α, β sorted out as constants)

$= 1$.

5. Factor intensity for a Cobb–Douglas production function is defined as the ratio of α/β. The higher the ratio the more labour intensive the technique of production and lower the ratio the more capital intensive it is.

6. The coefficient A in this production function gives the efficiency of the factors of production in the organization. The two firms with same L, K, α, β would produce different outputs due to different values of A. Alternatively, two firms producing same output with different factor quantities do so due to the difference in their efficiency parameter, A. For instance, let

$$1000 = 100 \, L^\alpha K^\beta \text{ for one firm, and}$$

$$1000 = 200 \, L^\alpha K^\beta \text{ for the other firm}$$

Then, it is the second firm that is more efficient because it requires less of $L^\alpha K^\beta$ to produce same output.

7. The value of $\alpha + \beta$ for a Cobb–Douglas production function gives the nature of returns whether they are increasing, constant or decreasing.

If $\alpha + \beta < 1$, we have decreasing returns to scale.

If $\alpha + \beta = 1$, we have constant returns to scale.

If $\alpha + \beta > 1$, we have increasing returns to scale.

But, $\alpha + \beta$ for a Cobb–Douglas production function is its degree of homogeneity. Hence, a Cobb–Douglas production function of degree one depicts constant returns to scale, that of degree greater than one depicts increasing returns to scale and that of degree less than one, depicts decreasing returns to scale [for demonstration, see Section 5.7 (ii), p. 280].

5.9 ECONOMIC AND NON-ECONOMIC REGIONS OF PRODUCTION

Production is viable on that part of the isoquant on which $MRTS_{L,K}$ diminishes from left to right. The segment of the isoquant we are referring to is the segment convex to the origin (Figure 5.20). It lies between points A and B. At these points, tangents drawn are either horizontal (as at A) or vertical (as at B). A point A, $MP_L = 0$ and at point B, $MP_K = 0$.

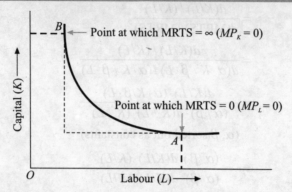

FIGURE 5.20 Economically viable segment of an isoquant: It is the segment between A and B that is economically viable for production.

If we draw an isoquant map economically viable for production, each one of them would have points such as those between A and B. At the lower ends they are indicated by points A, A_1, A_2, A_3, A_4, etc. and at the upper ends they are indicated by points B, B_1, B_2, B_3, B_4, etc. Joining all the points at the lower ends and all the points at the upper ends to the origin by means of smooth curves, we get *the lower and the upper ridge lines* which bound the region *economically viable* for production. Regions below the lower ridge line and those above the upper ridge line are all economically non-viable and are thus called *non-economic regions* (Figure 5.21).

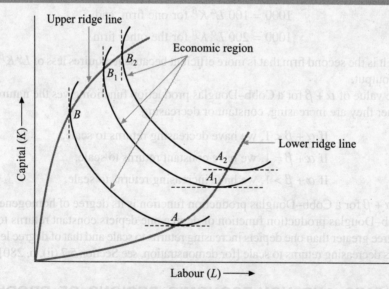

FIGURE 5.21 Ridge lines: The upper ridge line is the locus of points B, B_1, B_2, while the lower one is that of points A, A_1, A_2. The region between the two is the economic region and that below the lower one and above the upper one is the non-economic region from the viewpoint of production. The reader can verify that production on segments of isoquants above the upper ridge line and below the lower ridge line involves higher costs due to requirement of more of capital or more of labour or more of both to produce the same volume of output.

5.10 INFLUENCE OF TECHNICAL PROGRESS ON POSITION AND SHAPE OF AN ISOQUANT

Advancements in production-technology influence the position of the total product curve and the isoquant. Such changes bring about an increase in efficiency of the collaborating factors with the result that more is possible to produce with same inputs. In consequence, total product curve shifts upwards and isoquant, downwards as shown in Figure 5.22.

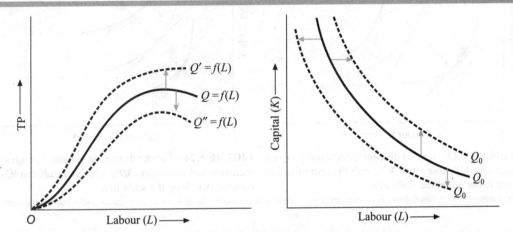

FIGURE 5.22 Technical progress and the shifts TPs and IQs: Technical progress increases productive efficiency of the organization. This leads to higher production. Total product curve shifts upwards and isoquant shifts downwards. A downward shift in IQ shows same output with lesser inputs while an upward shift in it shows same output with more of inputs. A technological progress boosts production while a technological deterioration affects it adversely.

Apart from shifts in TP and IQ curves, technological progress may also change their shapes. For instance, if technical progress is **capital deepening**, change in the shape of the isoquants is as shown in Figure 5.23, if it is **labour deepening**, the change in it is as shown in Figure 5.24 and if technical progress is **neutral**, the shape of the isoquant remains unchanged as shown in Figure 5.25.

Capital deepening technical progress is one which shifts IQs downwards along the scale line in such a way that the IQs turn flatter as they slide down. In other words, slope of an isoquant increases (or, $MRTS_{L,K}$ decreases) each time it slides down along the scale line. This happens due to the fact that capital deepening technical progress increases MP_K more than MP_L.

Labour deepening technical progress is one which shifts IQs downwards along the scale line in such a way that the IQs turn steeper as they slide down. In other words, slope of an isoquant decreases (or, $MRTS_{L,K}$ increases) each time it slides down along the scale line. This happens due to the fact that labour deepening technical progress increases MP_L more than MP_K.

Finally, **neutral technical progress** is one which shifts IQs downwards along the scale line in such a way that the IQs retain the same slope as they slide down. In other words, slope of an isoquant remains unaffected (or, $MRTS_{L,K}$ remains unaffected) each time it slides down along the scale line. This happens due to the fact that neutral technical progress increases MP_L and MP_K both by the same proportion.

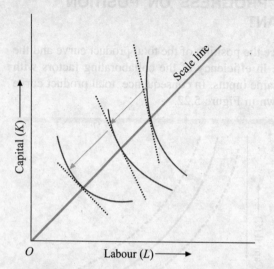
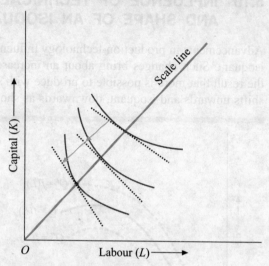

FIGURE 5.23 Capital deepening technical progress increases MP_K more than MP_L with the result that IQs turn flatter along the scale line.

FIGURE 5.24 Labour deepening technical progress increases MP_L more than MP_K with the result that IQs turn steeper along the scale line.

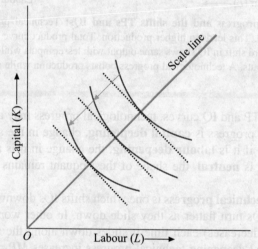

FIGURE 5.25 Neutral technical progress increases MP_L and MP_K each by same proportion with the result that IQs retain same slope along the scale line.

KEY TERMS AND CONCEPTS

Capital deepening technical progress is one which shifts IQs downwards along the scale line in such a way that the IQs turn flatter as they slide down. In other words, slope of an isoquant increases (or, $MRTS_{L,K}$ decreases) each time it slides down along the scale line. This happens due to the fact that capital deepening technical progress increases MP_K more than MP_L.

Economic region It is the region of the viability of production. It lies in between the upper and the lower ridge lines.

Elasticity of factor substitution The elasticity of factor substitution for Cobb–Douglas producion function, denoted as σ, is given as

$$\sigma = \frac{\text{Percentage change in } (K/L)}{\text{Percentage change in MRTS}}$$

$$= \frac{d(K/L)/(K/L)}{d(\text{MRTS})/\text{MRTS}}$$

Entrepreneur It refers to anyone who ventures all sorts of risks by procuring and/or staking factors of production to the process of production.

Financial capital It refers to paper titles such as shares, bonds, debentures and such other documents that entitle the holder to procure real assets.

Homogeneity of a function A homogeneous function is a function in which if the independent variables be multiplied by a constant, k, then it must be possible to factor k out of the function completely. The power n of k is called the degree of homogeneity of the function.

Isocline The product line inclined equally to the two axes. A product line is the locus of the combinations of labour and capital that a producer can choose to increase or decrease the output.

Isocost curve Different combinations of L and K that cost a producer same amount of money. The equation of the curve is, $\overline{C} = w \cdot L + r \cdot K$; $\overline{C} = $ constant.

Isoquant Different combinations of L and K that help the producer to produce same quantity of output. The equation of the isoquant is, $\overline{Q} = f(L, K)$, where, $\overline{Q} = $ constant.

Labour deepening technical progress is one which shifts IQs downwards along the scale line in such a way that the IQs turn steeper as they slide down. In other words, slope of an isoquant decreases (or, $MRTS_{L,K}$ increases) each time it slides down along the scale line. This happens due to the fact that labour deepening technical progress increases MP_L more than MP_K.

Law of returns to scale When units of all the variable factors of production are increased keeping the proportion (scale) of their combination unchanged, the patterns of output realized in response are known as the returns to scale. The law of returns to scale states that the output realized increases at an increasing rate in the beginning, at a constant rate thereafter and at a decreasing rate finally when the units of all the variable factors are increased successively in the same proportion.

    Causes of increasing returns to scale The main cause of increasing returns to scale is indivisibility of fixed factors of production.

    Causes of the constant returns to scale The main causes of constant returns to scale comprise learning of existing factors and the non-homogeneity of additional ones.

    Causes of the decreasing returns to scale Depreciation of some fixed factors of production and diminishing returns accruing to the management due to oversized plant are the main causes of the decreasing returns to scale.

Law of variable proportions or returns to a variable factor The law refers to a pattern in which output in return to increasing doles of an input while all other factors of production are fixed is realized. When units of one variable factor of production are increased successively, output produced increases at an increasing rate (increasing returns) initially, decreasing rate (decreasing returns) thereafter and at negative rate (negative returns) finally. Increasing, decreasing and negative returns in production in response to employment of successively increasing units of one variable factor of production while all other factors are held constant, taken together, are called the diminishing returns to variable proportions or diminishing returns to a variable factor.

Causes of decreasing returns to variable proportions The main causes for decreasing returns to variable proportions are over-crowding of fixed factors by the variable factor and the non-homogeneity of the units of the variable factor of production.

Causes of increasing returns to variable proportions Indivisibility of fixed factors of production is the main cause of increasing returns to variable proportions.

Causes of negative returns to variable proportions The main causes of negative returns to variable proportions are the over-crowding and the depreciation of the fixed factors of production.

Lower ridge line It is the locus of the points on the isoquants, at each of which, $MP_L = 0$.

Neutral technical progression is one which shifts IQs downwards along the scale line in such a way that the IQs retain the same slope as they slide down. In other words, slope of an isoquant remains unaffected (or, $MRTS_{L,K}$ remains unaffected) each time it slides down along the scale line. This happens due to the fact that neutral technical progress increases MP_L and MP_K each by the same proportion.

Producers' equilibrium It refers to that level of employment of factor—inputs which either maximizes the total output with given budget or minimizes total costs for given output target. In either case the point of equilibrium is the point at which the marginal product of a variable factor bears a fixed ratio with its price. Thus,

$$\frac{MP_L}{P_L} = \frac{MP_K}{P_K} = \ldots = \text{constant}.$$

If the firm is employing only one variable factor, say labour, the condition of the equilibrium is MP_L/P_L = constant.

Production It refers to creation or addition of utility to basic inputs or materials.

Factors of production They refer to the elements such as land, labour, capital and entrepreneur which participate in the production process.

Long-run production It refers to that production situation in which at least two factors of production are possible to be increased with a view to increase the output.

Production function It refers to a mathematical relationship that expresses the physical units of output in terms of the physical units of the factors of production.

Production process It is the process of creation or addition of utility to basic inputs or materials. It essentially involves combination of the factors of production for the purpose.

Short-run production It refers to a production situation in which not more than one factor of production is possible to be increased with a view to increase the output.

Stage of production producers prefer Producers prefer the second stage of production in which average product of the variable factor steadily declines with its increasing number of units employed. Producers reject the third stage due to negative marginal product of the variable factor. They overshoot the first stage due to ever-rising value of the average product of the variable factor. In the second stage, producers prefer the point of maximum total output (MP = 0) so that they may maximize their market share and may at the same time enhance their competitiveness.

Real capital It refers to capital such as plant, equipment, machinery, etc. that take part in production directly.

Upper ridge line It is the locus of the points on the isoquants, at each of which, $MP_K = 0$.

EXERCISES

A. Short Answer Questions

Define the following (1 through 12):
1. Production
2. Production process
3. Real capital
4. Financial capital
5. Entrepreneur
6. Increasing returns to variable proportions
7. Decreasing returns to variable proportions
8. Negative returns to variable proportions
9. Marginal physical product
10. Increasing returns to scale
11. Constant return to scale
12. Diminishing returns to scale
13. Why is very short-run production of little significance in the study of production?
14. Why is very long-run production of little significance in the study of production?
15. How short is the 'short-run' in the short-run production?
16. How long is the 'long-run' in the study of long-run production?
17. What is meant by returns in production?
18. What is meant by variable proportions?
19. What is meant by scale in production?
20. What is meant by returns to scale?
21. What is meant by producers' equilibrium?
22. What is the condition for the producers' equilibrium when a single variable factor is in use?
23. What is the condition for the producers' equilibrium when more than one factor of production is variable?
24. What is a production function?
25. Name two factors of production?
26. What is total physical product?
27. What is meant by average physical product?
28. What can you say about each of the following when the total product curve is rising?
    (a) Average product   (b) Marginal product $[AP_L > 0; MP_L > 0]$
29. What can you say about the following when the total product curve is at its peak?
    (a) Average product   (b) Marginal product $[AP_L > 0; MP_L = 0]$
30. What can you say about the following when the total product curve is falling?
    (a) Average product   (b) Marginal product $[AP_L > 0; MP_L < 0]$
31. How does the shape of the average product curve differ from that of the marginal product curve?
32. How is the total physical product derived from the marginal physical product schedule?

[**Hint.** Refer to Section 5.3 or to $\int_0^L MP_L \cdot dL$]

33. Through a rough sketch show that the marginal product curve falls even when the average product curve is still on the rise?

34. Name the factors responsible for any three of the following:
    (a) Increasing returns to variable proportions.
    (b) Negative returns to variable proportions.
    (c) Decreasing returns to variable proportions.
    (d) Increasing returns to scale.
    (e) Constant returns to scale.
    (f) Decreasing returns to scale.

    [**Ans.** (a) Indivisibility of fixed factors. (b) Depreciation and over-crowding of fixed factors. (c) Overcrowding of fixed factors and non-homogeneity of variable factors. (d) Indivisibility of fixed factors. (e) Non-homogeneity of variable factors. (f) Depreciation and over-crowding of fixed factors.]

35. If two factors of production have same price, what is the slope of the isocost curve?

    [**Ans.** -1. Numerical value of the slope of the isocost is given as w/r.]

36. Under what conditions would $Q = AL^\alpha K^\beta$ lead to (a) increasing (b) constant and (c) decreasing returns to scale? Explain.

37. Under what conditions would the function in question 36 lead to increasing, decreasing and constant returns to a variable factor labour?

38. Figure 5.26 shows two isoquants, each representing the same output but one lying above the other. Is it possible? Explain.

    [**Ans.** Yes, the one that is lower is more efficient.]

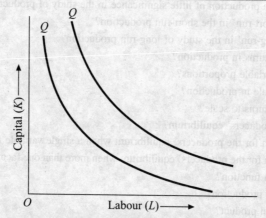

FIGURE 5.26 Two isoquants representing the same output.

39. There are two firms, each producing same quantity. The production functions of the two are given as:

    $$\text{First}: \quad 500 = A L^\alpha K^\beta$$
    $$\text{Second}: \quad 500 = B L^\alpha K^\beta$$

    Under what condition would the first firm be
    (a) more efficient than the second?
    (b) less efficient than the second?
    (c) as efficient as the second?

    Give reasons in support of your answer.

    [**Ans:** (a) $A > B$ (b) $A < B$ (c) $A = B$.]

40. What conditions would you impose for economic feasibility of production? Explain.

B. Long Answer Questions

41. Distinguish between the short-run and the long-run production.
42. Distinguish between returns to variable proportions and the returns to scale.
43. Which of the three stages of production do the producers like to operate and why?
44. Explain the phenomenon of diminishing returns to variable proportions. What are the factors responsible for it?
45. Explain the phenomenon of diminishing returns to scale. What are the factors responsible for it?
46. What is meant by the producers' equilibrium? Plot the data given below and determine the point of the producers' equilibrium.

L (units) :	1	2	3	4	5	6	7	8	9	10
MP_L (units) :	80	70	60	50	40	30	20	10	0	−10
P_L (₹/unit) :	40	40	40	40	40	40	40	40	40	40

Where, MP_L is the marginal product of labour, P_L is the price per unit of labour.

[**Ans.** Equilibrium level of employment = 5 units of labour.]

47. For the data in (Q. 46), determine the total and the average products at each level of employment of labour units, assuming that the marginal product of labour is zero when number of units of labour employed are zero.
48. The average product of labour at the employment levels of 0, 1, 2, 3, 4, 5, 6, 7, 8, 9 and 10 units is respectively 0, 8, 9, 10, 11, 12, 12, 11, 10, 8.89 and 7.8, in units of output. Determine the total and the marginal products. Plot them along with the average product and mark off the three stages of production distinctly. What are the distinctive features of the three stages of production in this case?
49. The marginal product of a variable input at different levels of its employment is as given below:

Units of input :	0	2	3	4	5	6	7	8	9	10	11	12
MP :	0	3	9	11	13	15	16	10	2	0	−2	−4

Determine total and average products of the input and graph them. Distinctly mark-off different stages of production on your graph and outline their distinctive features.

[**Hint.** The corresponding total products are 0, 6, 15, 26, 39, 54, 70, 80, 82, 82, 80 and 76 while the average products are 0, 3, 5, 6.5, 7.8, 9, 10, 10, 9.1, 8.2, 7.27 and 6.33. MP of 2 units of input is given to be 3. This means that

$$\frac{\text{Change in TP}}{\text{Change in inputs}} = 3$$

Change in TP = 3 × change in inputs
$$= 3 \times [2 - 0]$$
$$= 6$$

∴ Total product = original product + change in TP
$$= 0 + 6$$
$$= 6.]$$

50. If the marginal product of a factor is falling, does it mean that its average product is also falling? Explain using diagrams.

[**Hint.** Refer to Figure 5.1 or 5.27.

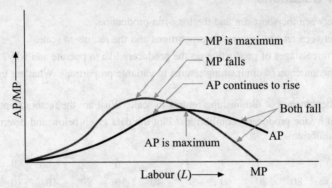

FIGURE 5.27 (Question 50): MP and AP from Figure 5.1 are drawn here for ready reference. Now answer the question.]

51. Examine each of the following functions for homogeneity and determine the degree of homogeneity for those which are homogeneous

   (a) $Z = ax + by + c$.
   (b) $Z = ax^2 + by^2 + 2hxy$.
   (c) $Z = axy$.
   (d) $Z = \sqrt{[ax^2 + 2hxy + by^2]}$.
   (e) $Z = 5 x^{1/3} y^{2/3}$.

   [**Ans.** (a) Not homogeneous. (b) Homogeneous of degree 2. (c) Homogeneous of degree 2. (d) Homogeneous of degree one. (e) Homogeneous of degree one.]

52. For a production function $Q = A L^\alpha K^\beta$, where α, β are both positive, show that if the marginal product of labour is falling, the marginal product of capital can't be falling when increasing returns accrue in production.

   [**Ans.** $\quad MP_L = (\partial Q/\partial L) = \alpha A L^{\alpha-1} K^\beta$

   Falling MP_L implies that
   $$\partial(MP_L)/\partial L < 0$$
   $\Rightarrow \qquad \alpha(\alpha-1) AL^{\alpha-2} K^\beta < 0$
   $\Rightarrow \qquad \alpha < 1$

   (Since all other terms on the left are non-negative)

   For increasing returns,
   $$\alpha + \beta > 1$$
   $\Rightarrow \qquad -\alpha < (\beta - 1)$

   The statement can be split into two parts

   (a) $-\alpha < (\beta - 1) < 0$, when, $\beta < 1$; and
   (b) $-\alpha < 0 < (\beta - 1)$, when, $\beta > 1$

   Now,
   $$\partial(MP_K)/\partial K = \beta(\beta - 1) AL^\alpha K^{\beta-2}$$

   If $(\beta - 1) < 0$, $\partial(MP_K)/\partial K < 0 \Rightarrow MP_K$ is falling.

   If $(\beta - 1) > 0$, $\partial(MP_K)/\partial K > 0 \Rightarrow MP_K$ is rising.

Thus for increasing returns in production ($\alpha + \beta > 1$), if MP_L is falling ($\alpha < 1$); it does not matter whether MP_K is falling or rising so long as $\beta > 1 - \alpha$, $0 < \alpha < 1$. In fact, MP_K can be falling when $\beta < 1$ or rising when $\beta > 1$. To understand, let $\alpha = 0.8$ and $\beta = 0.7$. Each is less than 1 yet ($\alpha + \beta$) = 1.5, which is greater than 1. This implies increasing returns with MP_L and MP_K both falling. Next, let $\alpha = 0.6$ and $\beta = 1.2$ so that ($\alpha + \beta$) = 1.8. This implies increasing returns to scale with MP_L falling and MP_K rising.]

53. In Question 52, can the same be said when constant or diminishing returns accrue in production? Substantiate your answer.

    [**Ans.** For constant returns in production,

    $$\alpha + \beta = 1$$

    $\Rightarrow \quad\quad\quad\quad\quad\quad\quad \beta = 1 - \alpha \quad\quad\quad\quad\quad$ (Since MP_L is falling, $0 < \alpha < 1$)

    Then, $0 < \beta < 1$ or $\beta - 1 < 0$

    $\Rightarrow \partial(MP_K)/\partial K < 0$, as $\partial(MP_K)/\partial K = \beta(\beta - 1) AL^\alpha K^{\beta-2}$

    $\Rightarrow MP_K$ is also falling.

    Thus, for constant returns in production, if MP_L is falling, MP_K is also falling.
    For decreasing returns in production,

    $$\alpha + \beta < 1$$

    $\Rightarrow \quad\quad\quad\quad\quad\quad\quad \beta - 1 < -\alpha$

    $\Rightarrow \quad\quad\quad\quad\quad \beta - 1 < 0$, for all α such that $0 < \alpha < 1$

    $\Rightarrow \quad\quad\quad\quad\quad\quad MP_K$ is also falling.

    Thus, for decreasing returns in production, if MP_L is falling, MP_K too is falling.]

54. With the help of a neat sketch, define the ridge lines and the economic and the non-economic regions of production.
55. Define the elasticity of factor substitution. Show that it is constant for a Cobb–Douglas production function irrespective of its degree of homogeneity.
56. What are the three stages of production? Which one of these do the producers prefer and why?
57. What are the causes of increasing, decreasing and constant returns to scale?
58. State and explain the law of variable proportions.

C. Essay Type Questions

59. Distinguish between the returns to scale and the returns to variable proportions.
60. What are the isoquants? Explain their essential features.
61. Given the production and the cost functions as

    $$Q = 500 \, L^{1/4} \, K^{3/4}$$
    $$C = w \cdot L + r \cdot K$$

    Derive the demand curves for labour and capital with a view to maximizing the output when the cost is limited to ₹ 10,000. Would your answer change if the objective shifts to cost minimization with a desired level of output? Give reasons in support of your answer. Determine the equilibrium levels of employment of the factors in each case, given $w = 100$ and $r = 75$. Also draw sketches to show the main point of difference.

    [**Ans.** Demand curves for labour and capital are $L = 2500/w$; $K = 7500/r$
    No. Equilibrium level of employment of labour and capital is $L = 25$, $K = 100$ when $w = 100$ and $r = 75$
    The main point of difference, apart from the objectives of the firm, rests in the diagrammatic representation of the two. For the first one, maximization of output under given budget is diagrammatically reached

through tangency of the budget line to the *highest isoquant* while for the second one, minimization of cost under given target of output is diagrammatically reached through tangency of isoquant to the *lowest isocost*. In the former case, we draw an *isoquant-map* while in the latter, we draw an *isocost-map*. In the former case, we look for highest isoquant touching the given budget line while in the latter case, we look for lowest isocost line touching the given isoquant.]

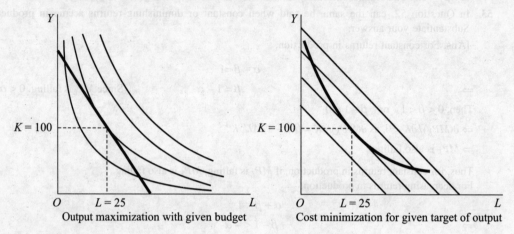

Output maximization with given budget   Cost minimization for given target of output

62. Explain with sketches the situations in which the condition of tangency of the isocost to the isoquant proves insufficient for equilibrium in production. How is optimal employment of factors determined in each of these situations?

63. Examine the role of technical progress on production. Distinguish between capital deepening technical progress and labour deepening technical progress. How is neutral technical progress different from the above two?

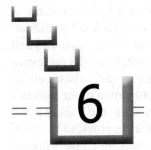

6

Cost and Revenue

Chapter Outline

Introduction
- Classification of Costs
- Cost Functions and Traditional Theory of Costs
- Modern Theory of Costs
- Economies and Diseconomies of Scale
- Revenue Curves
- Linear Break-even Analysis
- Non-linear Break-even Analysis
- Key Terms and Concepts
- Exercises

INTRODUCTION

None of the factors of production referred to in the previous chapter can be had for free. In fact, each of them commands a price. The one in shorter supply commands a higher price and the one in abundance commands a lower price. Higher or lower–there is a price attached to every factor. Hiring labour costs—its wage, hiring land-building costs—its rent and borrowing financial capital costs—its interest. What's more, even an entrepreneur is not for free. The least he/she needs to be compensated with is his/her opportunity cost. Quite often, it is much more that is needed to compensate the entrepreneur for his/her entrepreneurial skills. Expenses incurred by a firm on various factors of production are known as its *factor costs*. Total expenditures incurred by the firm on production form its *total cost*.

Cost, thus, can be defined as a compensation, cash or kind, made by a firm to a factor of production for its contribution to the production process. For instance, cost incurred on labour, commonly known as *compensation of employees*, includes cash payments such as salaries and wages, kind payments such as rent-free accommodation, free medical care, free gifts on festive occasions and social security contributions. The last one refers to firm's monthly contributions towards workers' provident fund. Such contributions are always a fixed proportion of the worker's basic salary. The fund grows in time to a sizeable amount and is passed on to the worker at the time of leaving service. Rent-free accommodation refers to residential quarters provided by a firm to its workers free of charge. In case a firm does not possess enough quarters for all the workers, it compensates those without quarters by paying them house-rent at specified rates every month so that they may avail accommodation for themselves elsewhere. Payment of house rent to the workers by way of house rent allowance (HRA) is quite common. Free medical care refers to free medical treatment of the workers and their family-members in the firm's dispensary. If a firm does not have a dispensary or hospital of its own for providing such services, it reimburses medical expenses incurred by the workers on their treatment in hospitals prescribed by the firm. Many firms have a practice of distributing free gifts to workers on festive occasions. Diwali gifts to workers in India is an example.

All these provisions cost the firm money. Taken together, they are known as the *compensation of employees*.

Price of land-building is the rent which represents compensation for its use in production.

Price for the use of financial capital is *interest* but price for the use of real capital is expenditure incurred on its maintenance. Plant, equipment and machinery—all suffer wear and tear, called *depreciation*, when used. Firms often provide for it under the head of *depreciation allowance*, set aside usually in anticipation of the damage.

Price of an entrepreneur is his *opportunity cost*. It may be defined as the cost of opportunity foregone for the sake of current opportunity. To understand, suppose an individual gives up working as a manager in a firm which pays him ₹ 100,000 per month, so that he may start his own venture as an entrepreneur. The opportunity cost of enterpreneurship for him is the opportunity of earning ₹ 100,000 per month as a manager. In other words, opportunity cost can also be defined as *income from the next best alternative use* possible, even though it may not have been resorted to ever before.

The entrepreneur, in our illustration, would expect at least ₹ 100,000 per month from his current venture for the contribution of his entrepreneurial skills. In case he contributes some other factors also, such as, land-building and financial capital, he would be entitled to rent and interest as well.

Receipts in terms of money from the sale of output are termed *revenue*. It is the money value of output sold. It is from this revenue that all the factors are compensated for their contribution ultimately. Total receipts from sale of entire output is termed *total revenue*.

6.1 CLASSIFICATION OF COSTS

Depending on the nature, costs are classified into a number of categories. Let us examine the following categories which are highly relevant to our analysis of costs:

Explicit and implicit costs: Explicit costs are *costs of external factors of production none of which is owned by the producer*. Costs of inputs such as raw materials purchased and labour employed/hired are two examples of explicit costs. Electricity consumed in production is yet another example. As against this, *costs of factors owned and provided by the producer himself are the implicit costs*. Examples of implicit costs are the costs of self-provided land-building, financial capital and the entrepreneurial skills. Rent, interest and opportunity cost are thus examples of the implicit costs.

From the viewpoint of an accountant, total cost of production comprises explicit costs alone but from the viewpoint of an economist, it comprises explicit and implicit costs both. The accountant's concept treats implicit costs as a part of the firm's profit while the economist's concept treats it as a part of the total cost.

Money costs and real costs: Money costs, also known as *private costs*, refer to total expenses incurred by producers in monetary terms on production. Such costs include costs of only those factors of production in respect of which monetization is possible. For instance, determination of monetary value of services of labour is possible through market forces but determination of the same in respect of services of an entrepreneur is not possible due to lack of monetization of anxiety, stress and fatigue that an entrepreneur suffers round the clock to ensure smoothness of production. No money value can serve as an adequate measure of such contribution, leave alone the measure of the opportunity cost. There are no price tags possible for anxiety suffered and leisure sacrificed. Such qualitative aspects are highly difficult, if not impossible, to monetize. Sufferings of society from noise and air pollution, likewise, are no less difficult to monetize. Production invariably inflicts such sufferings whether borne by an entrepreneur or by the society. In absence of monetization, it is difficult to compensate the concerned for their services or sufferings. They are thus non-money costs or external costs, which don't enter cost-sheets. *Real costs* comprise the *money costs* and the *external costs both*.

Sunk costs and future costs: An expenditure already incurred is called a *sunk cost* provided it is not possible to recover or withdraw it. For example, costs incurred on digging the foundation for a building are irrecoverable while those incurred on purchase of a machine or a house are recoverable through resale of the asset. Sunk costs are said to be *irrelevant* for decision making. Once incurred, sunk costs become *unavoidable costs*.

On the other hand, *future costs* are costs to be incurred in future. For example, additional costs associated with setting up of an additional plant in days to come are future costs. By all means, such costs are avoidable and hence highly relevant from the viewpoint of decision making.

Private cost and social cost: Private cost, also known as the money cost, refers to the cost of production actually incurred by a firm in terms of money. All money costs are the private costs. As against this, *social cost* refers to cost of producing a commodity to the society as a whole. It includes private cost as well as the cost of sufferings of the society (external costs) on account of water, noise and air pollution. As seen earlier, the latter component of the social cost is a non-monetized one. The social cost may be higher or lower than the private cost depending on whether the external costs are positive or negative. The concept of social cost is of high significance in social cost and benefit analysis.

Fixed and variable costs: Fixed costs refer to costs of fixed factors of production. Land, building, plant, equipment and machinery are a few examples of fixed factors of production. Fixed costs remain fixed whether output produced is high or low or zero. Cost of all the fixed factors taken together is termed *total fixed cost* (TFC). Figure 6.1 demonstrates the behaviour of the TFC curve in relation to the level of output.

As against this, the *variable cost* varies with the level of output. Variable cost refers to the cost of variable factors of production. Examples of variable cost include costs of raw-materials, labour, power, fuel and depreciation. Such costs increase with an increase in output. Variable cost of all the units of an output taken together is termed *total variable cost* (TVC). The total variable cost as a function of the output is portrayed in Figure 6.2.

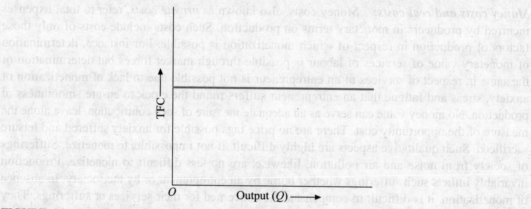

FIGURE 6.1 Relationship of total fixed cost with the level of the output: The curve is a horizontal line, indicating that TFC is constant at all levels of output.

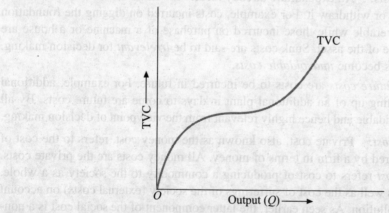

FIGURE 6.2 Total variable cost as a function of output: TVC increases rapidly at the initial levels. It becomes stable over a certain level of output. Thereafter, it regains its initial momentum and shoots up quite fast as shown.

6.2 COST FUNCTIONS AND TRADITIONAL THEORY OF COSTS

The total cost of producing an output, Q, comprises two components—total fixed cost and total variable cost. The first component is independent of the level of the output while the second component varies with it. To demonstrate, suppose a firm's total fixed cost is ₹ 50,000. The variable cost per unit of commodity produced is ₹ 15. Expression for the total cost of producing Q units of the product, thus, is given as:

$$TC = TFC + TVC$$
$$= 50,000 + 15Q \qquad (6.1)$$

Equation (6.1) if plotted for different levels of output, gives a linear total cost curve (Figure 6.3).

Total cost function, as discussed above, is one of the simplest kind. Before we discuss the more realistic cost functions, let us first define the average and marginal costs and their equations for the linear cost function of the type depicted by Eq. (6.1). For the sake of general treatment, we take its general form given by Eq. (6.2).

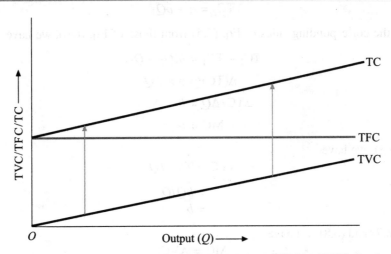

FIGURE 6.3 Derivation of linear TC through vertical summation of TFC and TVC: Total cost as a function of output, Q, is portrayed as a straight line. Its intercept on the vertical axis is equivalent to TFC which in our illustration is 50,000. TFC, when plotted, yields a horizontal line. TVC = 15Q is also a straight line. It slopes upwards but passes through the origin.

$$TC = a + bQ \qquad (6.2)$$

where, TC is the total cost, a is TFC, and b is variable cost per unit of output.

Average total cost (ATC) or simply *the average cost* (AC) may be defined as the *total cost per unit of output*.

Thus,

$$ATC \text{ or } AC = TC/Q$$
$$= (TFC + TVC)/Q$$

$$= (TFC/Q) + (TVC/Q)$$
$$= AFC + AVC \qquad (6.3)$$

where, AFC is the average fixed cost and is defined *as the total fixed cost per unit of the output* while AVC is the average variable cost and is defined as *the total variable cost per unit of the output.* Alternatively, from Eq. (6.2),

$$AC = (a + bQ)/Q$$
$$= (a/Q) + (bQ/Q)$$
$$= (a/Q) + b \qquad (6.4)$$

Likewise, marginal cost (MC) can be defined *as a change in total cost* (TC) *per unit change in the total output* (Q). To obtain an expression for the marginal cost*, let the initial level of output be Q_1. Let it now be increased to Q_2. Further, let the corresponding total costs be TC_1 and TC_2 so that

$$TC_1 = a + bQ_1 \qquad (6.5)$$
and,
$$TC_2 = a + bQ_2 \qquad (6.6)$$

Subtracting the corresponding sides of Eq. (6.5) from those of Eq. (6.6), we have

$$TC_2 - TC_1 = b(Q_2 - Q_1)$$
$$\Rightarrow \quad \Delta(TC) = b \times \Delta Q$$
$$\Rightarrow \quad \Delta TC/\Delta Q = b$$
$$\Rightarrow \quad MC = b \qquad (6.7)$$

From Eq. (6.3), we have
$$AVC = TVC/Q$$
$$= bQ/Q$$
$$= b \qquad (6.8)$$

From Eqs. (6.7) and (6.8), we have
$$MC = AVC$$

That is, the marginal cost is the same as the average variable cost. From Eq. (6.4), $AFC = a/Q$, which implies that AFC is infinitely large when $Q = 0$ and $AFC = 0$ when Q is infinitely large.

A more realistic total cost curve is a non-linear one. It can be obtained through vertical summation of TFC and the TVC of Figures 6.1 and 6.2. Figure 6.5 explains the mechanism.

ATC, as a sum of AFC and AVC can be derived and shown as in Figure 6.4 (not to scale) along with MC. The total fixed cost curve (Figure 6.1) is a horizontal one, that is, $TFC = a$, where a is total fixed cost. The TVC curve, however, has a peculiar nature (Figure 6.2). It resembles the lateral inversion of the alphabet 'S'. A non-linear TVC of this type may result from a cubic expression in Q. For instance,

---

*The expression for the marginal cost can alternatively be obtained by differential calculus. Differentiating Eq. (6.2) with respect to Q, we have $d(TC)/dQ = b$, as a is constant.

$$TVC = bQ - cQ^2 + dQ^3 \quad (6.9)$$

where, b, c and d are constants and Q is output in units. Total cost curve, thus, can be expressed as

$$TC = a + bQ - cQ^2 + dQ^3 \quad (6.10)$$

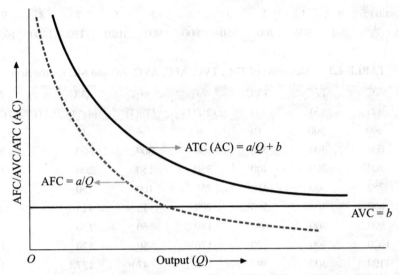

FIGURE 6.4 AFC, AVC, MC and AC curves associated with a linear total cost function: In the figure, AVC = MC = b. Thus, MC and AVC curves both coincide with each other and both are horizontal. Average fixed cost curve is a rectangular hyperbola. AC is derived as a vertical summation of AFC and AVC (not to scale).

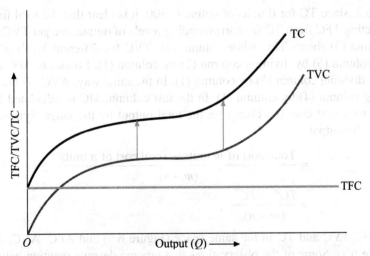

FIGURE 6.5 Derivation of the total cost curve through vertical summation of TFC and non-linear TVC: The TVC curve passes through the origin and is non-linear. The TFC curve is a horizontal line as usual. The TC curve is derived as a vertical displacement of TVC upwards by a distance equal to TFC in magnitude.

Before proceeding any further with this cost function, let us first derive the total cost curve with the help of Figures 6.1 and 6.2. Figure 6.5 explains the process.

Let us now construct a numerical illustration to analyze the behaviour TC, TFC, TVC, AFC, AVC, AC and MC. Suppose a firm has the total cost schedule of Table 6.1.

TABLE 6.1 Total cost schedule of a firm

Q (units):	0	1	2	3	4	5	6	7	8	9	10
Total cost (₹):	300	600	700	750	800	900	1020	1190	1400	1650	2300

TABLE 6.2 Calculation of TFC, TVC, AFC, AVC, AC and MC for the firm

Q	TC	TFC	TVC	AC	AFC	AVC	MC
(1)	(2)	(3)	(4)	(2)/(1)	(3)/(1)	(4)/(1)	$[TC^m - TC^n]/(m-n)$
0	300	300	0	∞	∞	0	–
1	600	300	300	600	300	300	300
2	700	300	400	350	150	200	100
3	750	300	450	250	100	150	50
4	800	300	500	200	75	125	50
5	900	300	600	180	60	120	100
6	1020	300	720	170	50	120	120
7	1190	300	890	170	42.9	127.1	170
8	1400	300	1100	175	37.5	137.5	210
9	1650	300	1350	183.3	33.3	150	250
10	2300	300	2000	230	30	200	650

In Table 6.2, since TC for 0 units of output is 300, it is clear that the total fixed cost (TFC) is 300. Subtracting TFC from TC for corresponding levels of output, we get TVCs for each level of these. Column (3) shows TFC while column (4), TVC for different levels of output. AC is calculated in column (5) by dividing column (2) by column (1). Likewise, AFC is calculated in column (6) by dividing column (3) by column (1). In the same way, AVC is obtained in column (7) by dividing column (4) by column (1). In the last column, MC is calculated by dividing the change in the total cost due to a change in the total output by the latter. Symbolically, MC of the mth unit of the output

$$= \frac{\text{Total cost of } m \text{ units} - \text{Total cost of } n \text{ units}}{(m-n)}$$

$$= \frac{TC^m - TC^n}{(m-n)}$$

Let us plot TFC, TVC and TC in the same space (Figure 6.6) and AFC, AVC, AC and MC in another (Figure 6.7). Some of the observations that emerge deserve mention below:

(a) Among MC, AVC and AC, it is the MC that falls at the fastest and the AC the slowest. When it comes to rise, MC again is the fastest and the AC the slowest.

(b) It is the MC that reaches its minimum first. The next to do so is AVC and the last, the AC.
(c) After attaining its minimum, MC begins to rise while AVC and AC still continue to fall. AVC begins its upward journey as soon as it is intersected by the fast-rising MC at its lowest point. AC continues to fall even when MC and AVC are both on their upward journeys already. AC joins the other two only after getting intersected by the fast-rising MC.

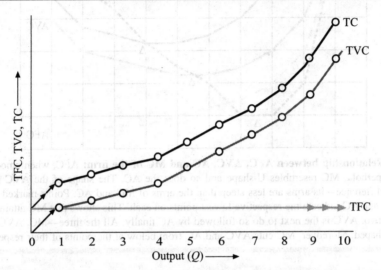

FIGURE 6.6 TFC, TVC and TC of the firm derived from the data of Table 6.1. The TFC (marked with three arrows), TVC (marked with one arrow) and TC (marked with two arrows) represent data of Table 6.2 by joining the points through linear segments. The points, if joined by means of a smooth curve, would resemble the curves in Figure 6.5.

Plotting the AFC, AVC, AC and MC in the same space likewise, we obtain U-shaped curves as shown in Figure 6.7.

Mathematical treatment: Let us now return to the 3rd degree equation of the TC function, i.e. Eq. (6.10).

$$AC = TC/Q$$
$$= [a + bQ - cQ^2 + dQ^3]/Q$$
$$= a/Q + bQ/Q - cQ^2/Q + dQ^3/Q$$
$$= a/Q + b - cQ + dQ^2$$
$$= AFC + AVC$$

where,
$$AFC = a/Q,$$
$$AVC = b - cQ + dQ^2$$

The equation of the MC curve can be obtained by differentiating the TC function with respect to Q.

$$MC = d(TC)/dQ = b - 2cQ + 3dQ^2$$

AFC, when plotted, gives a rectangular hyperbola while AVC and MC give a parabola each. All the curves are sketched (not to scale) in Figure 6.8.

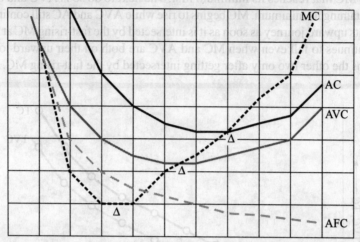

FIGURE 6.7 Relationship between AFC, AVC, AC and MC of the firm: AFC, when smoothened, gives a rectangular hyperbola. MC resembles U-shape and so does the AC. The shape of the AVC is also similar but there is one difference—its arms are less steep than the arms of MC and AC. Points marked by hollow 'Δ' under MC, AVC and AC indicate the respective lowest points on each. This shows that MC attains its minimum before the other two. AVC is the next to do so followed by AC finally. All the three—MC, AVC and AC—are more or less U-shaped. Moreover, MC cuts AVC and AC from below at the points of their respective minima.

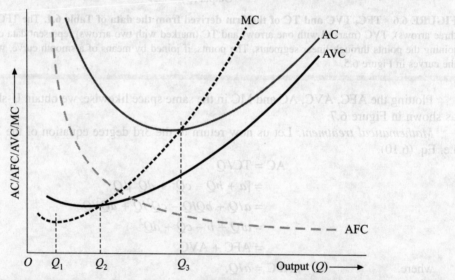

FIGURE 6.8 Relationship between AFC, AVC, AC and MC for a cubic total cost function: All the curves except AFC are U-shaped. This indicates that each of them falls for some initial range of output, reaches its minimum at a certain level of output and begins to rise once at its lowest. Of the three (MC, AVC and AC), MC attains its minimum before the other two while AVC attains it next and AC, the last. MC is minimum at Q_1, AVC at Q_2 and AC at Q_3. MC cuts AVC and AC at their respective minima. The initial fall in cost shows increasing returns and later rise in it shows decreasing returns in production. The level of output at which AC is minimum is the optimal level and the corresponding plant size, the optimal plant size.

6.2.1 Relationships among AC, AVC and MC in the Short-run

In the traditional theory of cost, AC, AVC and MC curves are all U-shaped in short-run. That is, each one exhibits an initial fall over a certain range of output, hits its lowest and shoots up thereafter. Such behaviour of the curves is indicative of diminishing returns to variable proportions (Chapter 5) that set in production in short-run. Initial increasing returns cause a steep fall in these curves. The decreasing returns that follow thereafter slow down the fall and the curves hit their respective lowest points before shooting up again due to negative returns following finally. Figure 6.9 demonstrates the behaviour of the three curves. Let us compare AC and MC first.

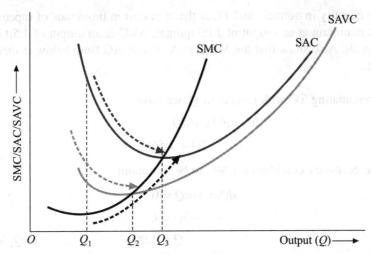

FIGURE 6.9 Behaviour of AC, AVC and MC in short-run: When AC falls, so does the MC but at a faster pace, keeping itself below the AC curve. MC reaches its minimum before AC does and it begins to rise thereafter. MC rises beyond the output OQ_1 while AC continues to fall till it reaches its minimum at the output OQ_3 where it is cut from below by the rising MC. Thus, AC is falling even when MC has begun to rise. Beyond the lowest point on the AC, both the curves rise but MC rises at a faster pace, keeping itself above the AC curve. Behaviour of the AVC is rather modest. It falls until output level rises to OQ_2 where it is cut from below by MC. Thereafter, it begins its upward journey as shown.

AC and MC are both alike in nature in short-run but for the following three basic differences*

1. When AC falls, so does MC but at a faster rate.
   MC < AC so long as AC falls.

---

*Relationship between AC and MC can be understood also through calculus. For the purpose, let us express the total cost as the product of AC and the output produced.

TC = cQ, where, c = AC (a function of output, Q) and Q = output.
Since MC = $d(TC)/dQ$, differentiating TC with respect to Q, we have

$$MC = d(TC)/dQ = c + Q \cdot (dc/dQ)$$
$$= AC + Q \cdot (\text{slope of AC})$$

(Contd.)

2. MC attains its minimum earlier than AC. While AC continues to fall, MC starts rising steeply from its lowest point. As soon as AC touches its lowest point, MC meets it from below. Thus, MC = AC, where AC is the least.
3. When AC begins its upward journey from its lowest point, MC is already on it and rising at a much faster pace. Thus, MC > AC so long as AC rises.

The relative behaviour of AVC and MC can be described by taking AVC in place of AC throughout the three points above. An illustration is in order to drive the concepts home.

ILLUSTRATION 6.1: Consider the total cost function

$$TC = 2 + 3Q - 1.5Q^2 + 0.5Q^3$$

where, Q is the quantity in quintals and TC is the total cost in thousands of rupees. Show that MC reaches its minimum at an output of 1.00 quintal, AVC at an output of 1.50 quintals and AC at 2.00 quintals. Also show that the MC cuts AVC and AC from below at their respective minimum points.

Solution: Differentiating TC with respect to Q, we have

$$MC = d(TC)/dQ$$
$$= 3 - 3Q + 1.5Q^2$$

According to the necessary condition for MC to be minimum

$$d(MC)/dQ = 0$$
$$\Rightarrow -3 + 3Q = 0$$
$$\Rightarrow Q = 1.00 \qquad (OQ_1 \text{ in Figure 6.9})$$

According to the sufficient condition,

$$d^2(MC)/dQ^2 > 0$$

at the point where MC is minimum.

Differentiating the expression for the MC twice successively, we have

$$d^2(MC)/dQ^2 = +3$$

This being greater than zero, MC is least at $Q = 1.00$ quintals of output. Minimum of MC = ₹ 1.5 thousand per quintal.

From the total cost function given, we have

$$TVC = 3Q - 1.5Q^2 + 0.5Q^3$$

(*Footnote contd.*)

When AC falls, its slope is negative, when AC is minimum, its slope is 0 and when AC rises, its slope is positive. With this notion, we can interpret the expression for MC as:

1. MC > AC, when slope of AC is positive (AC is rising),
2. MC = AC, when slope of AC = 0 (AC is minimum), and
3. MC < AC, when slope of AC is negative (AC is falling).

$$AVC = 3 - 1.5Q + 0.5Q^2$$

According to the necessary condition for AVC to be minimum,

$$d(AVC)/dQ = 0$$

$\Rightarrow \qquad -1.5 + Q = 0$

$\Rightarrow \qquad Q = 1.50 \qquad (OQ_2 \text{ in Figure 6.9})$

According to the sufficient conditions,

$$d^2(AVC)/dQ^2 = +1.0$$

This being greater than zero, AVC is least at $Q = 1.50$ quintals of output. Minimum of AVC = ₹ 1.875 thousand per quintal. Value of MC at $Q = 1.5$ is also 1.875 thousand. This shows that MC = AVC at $Q = 1.50$, the level of output at which AVC is the minimum.

Now, $\qquad AC = TC/Q$

$\qquad\qquad = 2/Q + 3 - 1.5Q + 0.5Q^2$

According to the necessary condition for AC to be minimum,

$$d(AC)/dQ = 0$$

Differentiating the expression for AC with respect to Q, we have

$$d(AC)/dQ = -2/Q^2 - 1.50 + 1.00Q$$

$\Rightarrow \qquad -2/Q^2 - 1.50 + Q = 0$

$\Rightarrow \qquad Q^3 - 1.50Q^2 - 2 = 0$

$\Rightarrow \qquad 2Q^3 - 3Q^2 - 4 = 0$

$\Rightarrow \qquad (Q - 2)(2Q^2 + Q + 2) = 0$

$\Rightarrow \qquad Q = 2.00 \qquad (OQ_3 \text{ in Figure 6.9})$

According to the sufficient condition,

$$d^2(AC)/dQ^2 = 4/Q^3$$

This being positive at $Q = 2$, AC is minimum at $Q = 2$ quintals of output. Minimum of AC is ₹ 3.00 thousand per quintal. MC at this level is also ₹ 3.00 thousand per quintal. This shows that MC cuts AC where AC is the minimum. To sum, MC, AVC and AC attain their respective minima at $Q = 1$, $Q = 1.5$ and $Q = 2$. MC cuts AVC and AC where they are least. Since MC begins to rise much earlier than the AVC and AC, it cuts them from below.

The U-shape of the short-run average and the marginal cost curves reflects the law of variable proportions. In the short-run, all the factors of production are not variable. In fact, it is labour that is generally considered variable in the short-run. The rest of the productive factors, as explained earlier, are fixed. As the successive units of the variable factor are employed in the short-run, the average and the marginal costs decline with every additional unit employed.

The marginal cost declines faster than the average cost. When it reaches its minimum, the average cost is still in the process of falling. Ultimately, MC begins to rise due to the diseconomies arising from the overcrowding of the fixed factors by the variable factor, labour. Soon MC meets AC at the point where AC is minimum. This point is referred to as the *optimal point* and the corresponding plant size is known as the *optimal plant size*. If output is expanded beyond this point, both AC and MC shoot up, MC again taking the lead. In illustration 6.1, the optimal plant size is $Q = 2$ which corresponds to the point of equality between MC and AC. From the illustration, MC = AC = 3 at $Q = 2$, the point of optimality of the plant.

ILLUSTRATION 6.2: [Derivation of the short-run MC and AVC from AP_L and MP_L] A firm employs only one factor of production, namely labour. The factor is available in abundance at a stable price. To produce Q units of output, the firm employs L units of labour at a price $\bar{w}$. Obtain expressions for AVC and MC in terms of average and marginal products of labour. Can AVC and MC curves be derived from average and marginal product curves of labour? Explain.

Solution: The information given befits the situation of short-run production. AP_L and MP_L curves follow the inverted U-shape as shown in Figure 5.1 (Chapter 5). Total cost of producing Q units of output with L units of labour has no TFC component. Thus,

$$TC = TVC$$
$$= \bar{w} \cdot L$$

$\therefore$
$$AVC = TVC/Q$$
$$= \bar{w} \cdot L/Q$$
$$= \bar{w}/(Q/L)$$
$$= \bar{w}/AP_L$$

This shows that AVC varies inversely as AP_L. It is infinitely large when $AP_L = 0$.
Hence,

(i) when AP_L increases with L, AVC must decrease,
(ii) when AP_L is maximum, AVC must be minimum, and
(iii) when AP_L decreases with L, AVC must increase.

Figure 6.10 demonstrates the point.
Similarly, as MC = MVC, we have

$$MC = d(TVC)/dQ$$
$$= d(\bar{w} \cdot L)/dQ$$
$$= \bar{w} \cdot (dL/dQ)$$
$$= \bar{w}/(dQ/dL)$$
$$= \bar{w}/MP_L$$

This shows that MC varies inversely as MP_L. It is infinitely large when $MP_L = 0$
Hence,

(i) when MP_L increases with L, MC must decrease,
(ii) when MP_L is maximum, MC must be minimum, and
(iii) when MP_L decreases with L, MC must increase.

Figure 6.10 demonstrates the point.

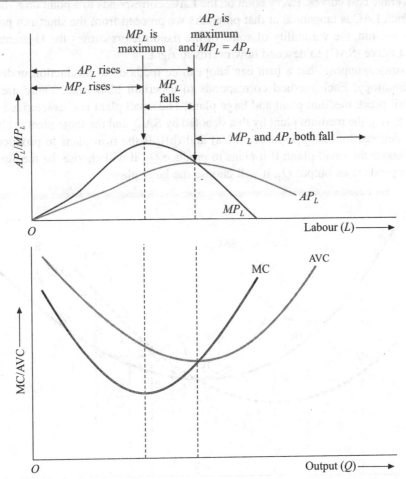

FIGURE 6.10 Derivation of MC and AVC from MP_L and AP_L schedules: Note the inverse relationships of AVC to AP_L and MC to MP_L. AVC is infinite when AP_L is zero and MC is infinite when MP_L is zero. Likewise, MC is minimum when MP_L is maximum and AVC is minimum when AP_L is maximum. AVC and MC are same when AP_L and MP_L are same.

6.2.2 Long-run Cost Curves in the Traditional Theory

The theory of costs discussed so far is the traditional theory of short-run costs. According to this theory, each of the average and the marginal cost curves in the short-run is U-shaped. As stated earlier, all the factors except labour are fixed in supply in the short-run, while all but labour and capital are fixed in the long-run, but none of them is fixed in the very long-run.

The long-run cost curves, also known as the *planning curves**, are derived from the short-run cost curves. The long-run average cost curve (LAC) is an enveloping curve to the

---

*Koutsoyiannis, A., *Modern Microeconomics*, 2nd ed., The Macmillan Press Ltd. London and Basingstoke, 1979, p. 113.

short-run average cost curves. Every point on the LAC, corresponds to a point on a short-run cost curve to which LAC is tangential at that point. As we proceed from the short-run production to that of the long-run, the variability of some of the fixed factors causes the U-shaped short-run average cost curve (SAC) to descend downwards to right.

To illustrate, suppose that a firm can adopt three methods of production under the given state of technology. Each method corresponds to a certain plant size. There are thus three plants—small plant, medium plant and large plant. The small plant is characterized by the cost denoted by SAC_1, the medium plant by that denoted by SAC_2 and the large plant is characterized by the cost denoted by SAC_3 [Figures 6.11(a) and (b)]. If the firm plans to produce an output Q_1, it will choose the small plant; if it plans to produce Q_2, it will choose the medium plant and if it plans to produce an output Q_3, it will choose the large plant.

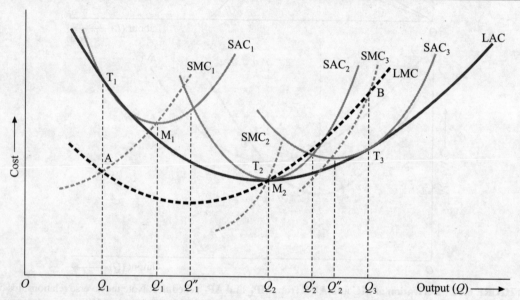

FIGURE 6.11(a) Derivation of long-run cost curves (LAC and LMC) from short-run cost curves (SACs and SMCs): When demand is Q_1'' or less, the firm resorts to the small sized plant (SAC_1) to satisfy it. SAC_1 is short-run average cost curve implying high initial costs due to non-variability of other factors except the variable factor labour. If demand exceeds Q_1'', the firm increases plantsize to SAC_2 and continues with it until demand exceeds Q_2'. When demand exceeds Q_1'', the firm saves by adopting plant SAC_2 and so does it by adopting plant size SAC_3 when demand exceeds Q_2'. The plant size SAC_3 serves the purpose of the firm but only up to Q_3, level of demand. Beyond this level even this plant proves expensive. The firm needs to vary one or more of its fixed factors again if it intends to reduce costs. This initiates decreasing returns in production. According to the traditional theory, the LAC curve is the one that envelops the SAC curves. Note that SAC_1 touches LAC at T_1 (at the output of Q_1), SAC_2 touches it at M_2 (at the output of Q_2) and SAC_3 touches it at T_3 (at the output of Q_3). The LAC curve thus does not necessarily contain the minimum points of SACs and is always flatter than them. The LMC, on the other hand, is derived by joining points of intersection of corresponding SMCs with perpendiculars drawn from the points T_1, T_2 and T_3 to the quantity axis. It is thus a join of points A, T_2 and B as shown. The shape of the curves owes its origin to increasing and decreasing returns to scale resulting from respective economies and diseconomies.

Suppose the firm is producing Q_1 with the small plant (SAC_1) when demand for its product increases beyond Q_1. As is clear from Figure 6.11(a) it can expand its output up to Q_1'' with the same plant (SAC_1) but to expand it beyond this level, say to Q_2', it will have to resort to the medium plant (SAC_2) and to expand it even beyond Q_2', it will have to resort to the large plant (SAC_3). Output Q_1 corresponds to point T_1 on SAC_1, Q_2 to point T_2 (M_2) on SAC_2 and output Q_3 to point T_3 on SAC_3. Joining points T_1, T_2 and T_3 by means of a smooth curve, the curve so obtained envelopes all the three SACs and is known as the *long-run average cost curve* (LAC).

To derive the corresponding LMC, draw perpendiculars from points T_1, T_2 and T_3 on the quantity axis so that they cut SMC_1, SMC_2 and SMC_3 at points A, M_2 and B respectively. Joining these points, we get the LMC.

We need to make a few observations about the LMC here:

1. When the output planned is less than Q_1, $SMC_1 < LMC$.
2. When the output planned is equal to Q_1, $SMC_1 = LMC$.
3. When the output planned is more than Q_1 but less than Q_1'', $SMC_1 > LMC$.
4. When the output planned is larger than Q_1'' but smaller than Q_2, $SMC_2 < LMC$.
5. When the output planned is equal to Q_2, $SMC_2 = LMC$.
6. When the output planned is larger than Q_2 but less than Q_2', $SMC_2 > LMC$.
7. When the output planned is more than Q_2' but less than Q_2'', $SMC_3 < LMC$.
8. When the output planned is equal to Q_3, $SMC_3 = LMC$.

The long-run AC and MC curves under constant returns to scale are overlapping and horizontal, containing the minimum points of the respective SACs [Figure 6.11(b)].

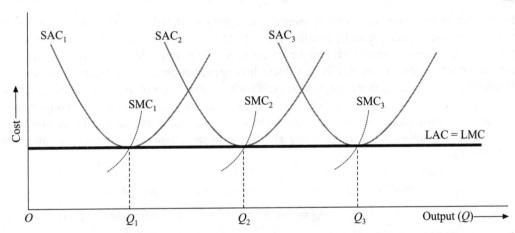

FIGURE 6.11(b) Derivation of LAC and LMC under constant returns: LAC and LMC curves under constant returns to scale are overlapping and horizontal containing the minimum points of the respective SACs.

It is necessary to point out one difference between the short-run and long-run curves. While arms of the short-run average and the marginal cost curves stand steeply upwards like those of the alphabet–U, those of the corresponding long-run cost curves droop sideways as shown in Figure 6.12.

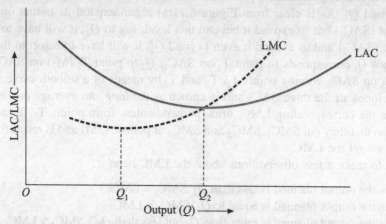

FIGURE 6.12 Long-run average and marginal cost curves have flatter, arms. Their respective minima occur at OQ_2 and OQ_1.

6.2.3 Derivation of the Long-run Total Cost Curve for a Firm from its Expansion Path

Equilibrium of a firm in the long-run employing two variable factors is described by the condition

$$\frac{MP_L}{MP_K} = \frac{w}{r} \qquad \text{[from Eq. (5.15)]}$$

The left-hand side represents slope of isoquant and the right-hand side, that of isocost. Given the factor prices, the isocost shifts parallel to itself outwards as the producer's budget expands. More of both factors are employed and the producer is able to jump onto a higher isoquant each time his isocost shifts outwards. Given a linear homogeneous production function, the shifting equilibrium points trace a linear expansion path such as one given by $K = mL$ [Figure 5.10] in respect of Cobb–Douglas production function. Thus, a higher output is associated with higher costs.

The total cost curve can be derived from the expansion path of a firm as shown in Figure 6.13. The upper panel in the figure shows the linear expansion path and the lower, the total cost curve.

Long-run total cost curve can also be derived mathematically. The process is demonstrated below. Let quantity produced, Q, be given by a homogeneous production function,

$$Q = f(L, K) = AL^\alpha K^\beta \qquad \text{where } \alpha \text{ and } \beta \text{ are constants.}$$

Let us assume that each of α and β is less than 1 so that each of MP_L and MP_K diminishes with increasing employment of labour and capital. Further, let the firm's budget be given as $\overline{C}$ and let the quantities of labour and capital the firm can afford with this budget be L and K. Then

$$\overline{C} = wL + rK$$

where, w and r are unit prices of inputs L and K.

Also, let the objective of the firm be maximization of output, given the budget. For converting the problem of constrained maximization into one of simple maximization, let us use Lagrangian λ to develop a composite function Φ, so that

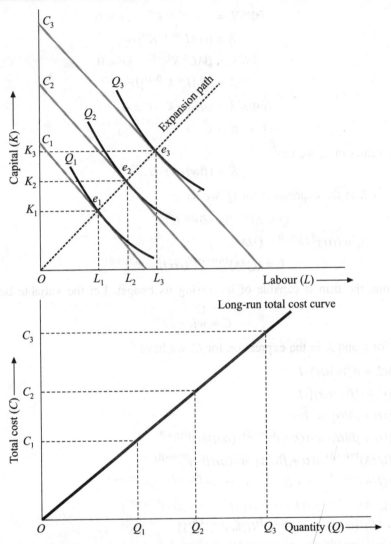

FIGURE 6.13 Expansion path of a firm and its long-run total cost curve: In the upper panel, the firm is at equilibrium initially at e_1. It employs input combination (L_1, K_1) at a cost of C_1 and produces quantity Q_1 of output. With an increase in its budget from C_1 to C_2, the firm moves to e_2, employing (L_2, K_2) and producing Q_2. If the budget increases further to C_3, the firm would move to e_3, employing combination (L_3, K_3) and producing quantity Q_3 of output. The locus of equilibrium points e_1, e_2 and e_3 represents the firm's expansion path. The lower panel shows quantities Q_1, Q_2 and Q_3 produced at respective costs C_1, C_2 and C_3. Joining points (Q_1, C_1), (Q_2, C_2), and (Q_3, C_3) long-run total cost curve is obtained as shown.

$$\Phi = AL^\alpha K^\beta - \lambda [wL + rK - \overline{C}]$$

The objective of the firm can now be fulfilled by maximizing Φ. Differentiating Φ partially with respect to L, K and λ, we have

$$\partial\Phi/\partial L = \alpha AL^{(\alpha-1)} K^\beta - \lambda w = 0$$

$\Rightarrow$
$$\lambda = [\alpha AL^{(\alpha-1)} K^\beta]/w$$

$$\partial\Phi/\partial K = \beta AL^\alpha K^{(\beta-1)} - \lambda r = 0$$

$\Rightarrow$
$$\lambda = [\beta AL^\alpha K^{(\beta-1)}]/r$$

$$\partial\Phi/\partial\lambda = wL + rK - \overline{C} = 0$$

$\Rightarrow$
$$wL + rK = \overline{C}$$

Equating the values of λ, we have

$$K = (\beta w/\alpha r)\cdot L$$

Substituting for K in the expression for Q, we have

$$Q = AL^\alpha (\beta w/\alpha r)^\beta L^\beta$$

$\Rightarrow \quad (\beta w/\alpha r)^\beta L^{(\alpha+\beta)} = Q/A$

$\Rightarrow \quad L = (Q/A)^{1/(\alpha+\beta)} \cdot (\alpha r/\beta w)^{\beta/(\alpha+\beta)}$

In the long-run, the firm is capable of increasing its budget. Let the variable budget for the long-run be

$$C = wL + rK$$

Substituting for L and K in the expression for C, we have

$C = wL + r(\beta w/\alpha r)\cdot L$

$\quad = [w + r(\beta w/\alpha r)]\cdot L$

$\quad = [(\alpha+\beta)/\alpha]\cdot w\cdot L$

$\quad = [(\alpha+\beta)/\alpha]\cdot w\cdot (Q/A)^{1/(\alpha+\beta)}\cdot (\alpha r/\beta w)^{\beta/(\alpha+\beta)}$

$\quad = (Q/A)^{1/(\alpha+\beta)}\cdot [(\alpha+\beta)/\alpha]\cdot w\cdot (\alpha r/\beta w)^{\beta/(\alpha+\beta)}$

$\quad = (Q/A)^{1/(\alpha+\beta)}\cdot (\alpha+\beta)\cdot (w/\alpha)\cdot \{(\alpha r)^{\beta/(\alpha+\beta)}/(\beta w)^{\beta/(\alpha+\beta)}\}$

$\quad = (Q/A)^{1/(\alpha+\beta)}\cdot [(\alpha)(w/\alpha)\cdot \{(\alpha r)^{\beta/(\alpha+\beta)}/(\beta w)^{\beta/(\alpha+\beta)}\}$

$\qquad + (\beta)\cdot (w/\alpha)\cdot \{(\alpha r)^{\beta/(\alpha+\beta)}/(\beta w)^{\beta/(\alpha+\beta)}\}]$

$\quad = (Q/A)^{1/(\alpha+\beta)}\cdot [w\cdot \{(\alpha r)^{\beta/(\alpha+\beta)}/(\beta w)^{\beta/(\alpha+\beta)}\}$

$\qquad + (\beta)\cdot (w/\alpha)\cdot \{(\alpha r)^{\beta/(\alpha+\beta)}/(\beta w)^{\beta/(\alpha+\beta)}\}]$

$\quad = (Q/A)^{1/(\alpha+\beta)}\cdot [w^{\alpha/(\alpha+\beta)}]\cdot [r^{\beta/(\alpha+\beta)}]\cdot [(\alpha/\beta)^{\beta/(\alpha+\beta)} + (\alpha/\beta)^{-\alpha/(\alpha+\beta)}]$.

From the cost function above, it is clear that

(i) C increases as Q does

(ii) C increases as w does

(iii) C increases as r does

If the firm is experiencing constant returns to scale, $(\alpha + \beta) = 1$, the cost function then reduces to

$$C = (Q/A) \cdot [w^\alpha] \cdot [r^\alpha] \cdot [(\alpha/\beta)^\beta + (\alpha/\beta)^{-\alpha}]$$

The reader can try the dual of the problem for deriving the cost function. Results in both the cases for the long-run total cost function are the same. The dual of this problem would require minimization of cost, given the level of output to be produced. The composite function associated would be

$$\Phi = wL + rK - \lambda [AL^\alpha K^\beta - \bar{Q}]$$

6.3 MODERN THEORY OF COSTS

(a) Short-run Costs

The traditional view of U-shaped short-run cost curves has been widely questioned on several grounds. In 1939, George Stigler suggested short-run average variable cost curve to have a flat stretch at the bottom over a range of output (Figure 6.14). The reason, a number of modern firms these days build such plants that facilitate a wide range of output at a fixed level of average variable cost in short-run. The range of output referred to here is known as the *reserve capacity* of the firm. The short-run average variable cost, thus, is U-shaped with a flat stretch at its bottom as shown in Figure 6.14. In Modern Theory, it is referred to as a *saucer-shaped short-run average variable cost curve* (Saucer-shaped SAVC).

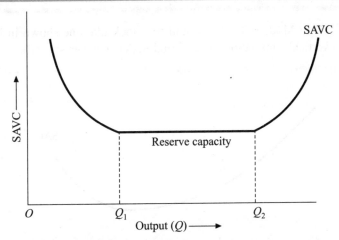

FIGURE 6.14 The Modern Theory of short-run AVC: According to this theory, average variable cost curve in the short-run is saucer-shaped. The flat stretch at the bottom begins at an output OQ_1 and continues until OQ_2. The firm can thus produce output Q_1Q_2 at the same AVC, which is also the lowest.

The average fixed cost (AFC) curve, in the Modern Theory, remains same as that in the Traditional Theory. Under reserve capacity, however, the shape of the AFC curve will look like one shown in Figure 6.15.

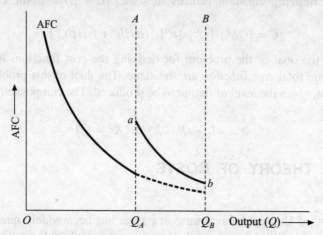

FIGURE 6.15 AFC in Modern Theory: The largest capacity of machinery sets an absolute upper limit to expansion of output (boundary B). The smallest capacity of machinery sets a lower limit to expansion of output (boundary A). Boundary A, however, is not the absolute boundary of the lower limit of output because the firm can expand output beyond Q_A by having more hours of labour through overtime wages. This however raises average fixed cost beyond Q_A. The AFC for expanded output is shown by segment 'ab', which is higher above the AFC curve of the traditional theory (without reserve capacity). Note that the fixed costs include maintenance costs of land–building, depreciation of machinery, salaries of permanent staff comprising of the direct labour (associated directly with production) and indirect labour (administrative and office staff). In absence of the reserve capacity in machinery, the AFC would be an unbroken rectangular hyperbola, as in Traditional Theory of costs.

The short-run AC in Modern Theory would thus look like one shown in Figure 6.16. It is obtained through a vertical summation of AFC and SAVC (saucer-shaped).

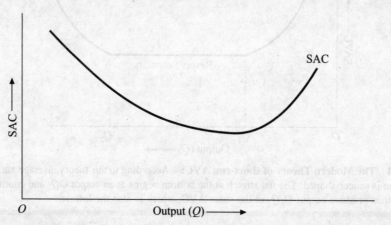

FIGURE 6.16 SAC in Modern Throry: The short-run AC (SAC), as obtained through vertical summation of average fixed cost and short-run average variable cost in the modern theory of costs has a shape as shown in the figure. The steep fall until the lower limit (Q_1, Figure 6.14) of the reserve capacity is retarded by the flat stretch, $Q_1 Q_2$, of the SAVC. Thereafter, a steep rise is revived as shown.

The short-run marginal cost curve (SMC) in Modern Theory is as shown in Figure 6.17. It follows its usual shape before and after the flat stretch of SAVC but coincides with it over its flat stretch as shown.

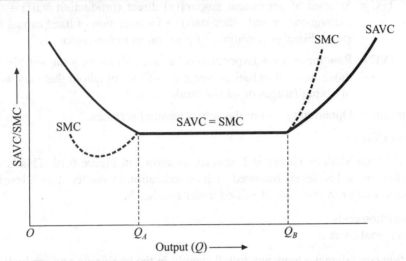

FIGURE 6.17 SMC and SAVC in the Modern Theory: Over the flat stretch of the reserve capacity, SMC = SAVC. To the left of it and to its right, the marginal cost curve demonstrates its normal behaviour expected of it in conformation to the fall and rise of SAVC.

All the short-run cost curves in the Modern Theory of costs can now be portrayed together as shown in Figure 6.18.

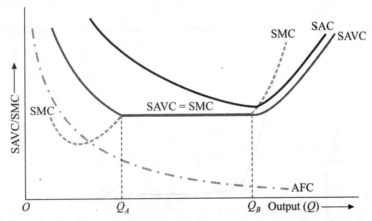

FIGURE 6.18 Short-run cost curves in the Modern Theory of costs: As portrayed in the figure, AFC and SAC both turn flatter over the stretch of the reserve capacity but before and after the reserve capacity, the two maintain their normal behaviour. The curves, as expected, conform to the behaviour of the saucer-shaped SAVC.

The short-run total cost can, thus, be expressed as

$$TC = TFC + TVC + \text{Normal profits}$$

where

TFC = Salaries of permanent labour [(a) direct (production staff) + (b) indirect (administrative and office-staff)] + Depreciation of fixed capital (machinery, etc.) + Fixed expenditures of plant on its maintenance

TVC = Raw materials + Expenditures incurred on running the machinery (such as those incurred on fuel, power, etc.) + Costs of labour that vary with the level of output (wages of ad hoc workers, etc.)

Normal profits = Opportunity cost of the entrepreneurial services.

(b) Long-run Costs

Long-run AC in the Modern Theory is L-shaped, as shown in Figure 6.19. This is so due to a steep fall in the cost at low levels followed by its stabilization thereafter at high levels of output in the long-run. Long-run costs are classified under two heads:

1. Production costs
2. Managerial costs

Production costs depict a tendency to fall steeply in the beginning and gradually thereafter as the scale of production increases. This is due to technical economies which are substantial in the beginning, but insignificant thereafter as a certain level of output is reached or as all the technical economies get exhausted. The firm is said to have reached a certain *minimum optimal scale* for the given technology. If a new technology is introduced at a higher level of output, it must be cheaper to operate; or, if the existing technology is continued, some economies must still be achievable at higher output levels. For instance, bulk purchases of inputs, such as raw materials, may lead to substantial savings for the firm due to quantity discounts accruing to it.

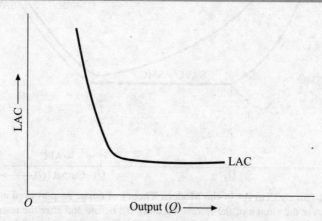

FIGURE 6.19 LAC in Modern Theory: The L-shaped long-run average cost curve implied by the modern theory of costs.

As regards *managerial costs*, they may rise at very large scales of production but the rise in them is more than offset by the falling production costs. Managerial costs vary from one size of plant to another as there are specific levels and managerial techniques to suit specific plant sizes. When the plant size is small, managerial costs diminish with expansion of output but when plant size is large, managerial costs may register a slow rise with each expansion of output. As mentioned earlier, such rise in managerial costs is more than offset by the substantially falling production costs. Hence, the chance of the long-run average cost to rise is completely ruled out.

To derive the LAC implied by the modern theory of costs, we start with the SACs of three plant sizes. According to R. W. Clower and J. F. Due, a plant is said to be used 'normally' when it operates at a level between two-thirds and three-quarters of its capacity*. Assuming that each of the three plants is operating at its two-thirds capacity, called the *load factor*, LAC can be derived by joining points corresponding to this capacity of each plant as shown in Figure 6.20.

As soon as the *minimum optimal scale of plant* is reached at $\overline{Q}$ LAC turns stable at its lowest (horizontal segment). The minimum optimal scale of plant may be defined as a certain level of output at which all possible economies stand exhausted, that is, no further reduction in costs is possible. In our case, this happens during production in its third plant size at an output level of $\overline{Q}$.

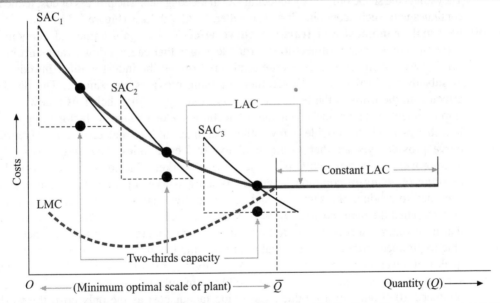

FIGURE 6.20 Derivation of LAC from SACs in modern theory: Derivation of long-run average cost curve (LAC) from respective short-run average cost curves (SACs) as implied by the modern theory of costs. On each of the three SACs, a point corresponding to utilization of two-thirds of its capacity is marked-off as shown. A smooth join of the three gives the desired LAC. Corresponding LMC keeps below LAC as shown. It joins LAC at the latter's lowest point (at an output level of $\overline{Q}$) where all the possible economies stand exhausted. Thereafter, LMC overlaps LA. The level of output $\overline{Q}$ at which all possible economies stand exhausted is called the **minimum optimal scale of plant**.

---

*R.W. Clower and J.F. Due, *Microeconomics* (Irwin–Dorsey, 1972), p. 232.

As regards the derivation of LMC curve, many writers including Bain* believe that it would be below the LAC curve so long as the latter falls and would coincide with it as soon as it turns stable at its lowest. Figure 6.20 shows the position of LMC.

6.4 ECONOMIES AND DISECONOMIES OF SCALE

6.4.1 Internal and External Economies

(i) **Internal economies:** When a firm increases its plant size or when it increases the number of its plants, the economies that accrue to the firm are referred to as *internal economies of scale*. Economies arising from an increase in the size of a single plant are known as *intra-plant economies of scale* while those arising from an increase in the number of the plants, irrespective of whether the firm continues to produce the same product in the new plants or different products therein are known as *inter-plant economies of scale*.

Both types of economies, intra-plant and inter-plant, are internal economies of scale. They determine the shape of the long-run average cost curve (LAC) of the firm, which at times is also called its *scale curve*. All internal economies are subject to internal decisions. They affect the shape of LAC by reducing AC in the long-run. The process of cost reduction continues until such economies last. Thereafter, LAC stabilizes (Figure 6.20).

(ii) **External economies and learning curve effect:** As against internal economies, *external economies* are subject to external decisions that cause a downward shift in the firm's LAC. Such economies accrue to all the firms in the industry alike. Introduction of subsidy on fertilizers by Government of India provides an example. The decision affected all the firms in the fertilizer industry alike by shifting their LACs downwards. Improvement of technique or change of technology or change in factor prices in an industry as a whole provide a few other examples of external economies. *Learning curve* provides yet another example of external economies. *Learning curve* refers to improvement in productive efficiency of the workers due to repetitive work. It is *learning by doing* in common language. When a worker operates the same machine everyday to produce the same product in a repetitive manner, he becomes a part of a system called the *man-machine system*. He gets so well versed in operating the machine that it becomes a second nature to him. His efficiency increases. In consequence, he is able to produce more of a better quality at the same labour-cost or same of an identical quality at lower labour-cost to the firm. Generally, the latter is the case. To demonstrate, suppose a worker is paid a wage of ₹ 6000 per month. In the first month of work, he produced 1000 units of a product. Assuming labour cost as the only cost, the worker produced output at an average cost of ₹ 6 per unit in the first month.

Richer in experience with the machine, the worker produced 1200 units of the same product next month at an average cost of ₹ 5. This leads to a reduction in AC by as much as $16^2/3 \%$.

If learning continues at the same rate, the production cost per unit would fall each month to $83^1/3 \%$ of what it was the previous month. Here, $83^1/3 \%$ or 0.833 is called the *learning rate* of the worker. If the unit cost in the initial stage is a and the learning rate of the worker is $r \%$ per month, the cost per unit in the nth month is given as

---

* J.S. Bain, *Barriers to New Competition* (Harvard University Press, Cambridge, Mass., 1956), p. 63.

$$C_n = ar^{n-1} \qquad (6.11)*$$

To demonstrate, let the initial cost a be ₹ 100 and learning rate r be 0.8, the cost per unit in the 4th month ($n = 4$) would work out as

$$\begin{aligned} C_4 &= (100)(0.8)^{4-1} \\ &= (100)(0.8)^3 \\ &= (100)(0.512) \\ &= ₹ 51.20 \end{aligned}$$

A little effort with a calculator gives the LAC schedule (Table 6.3) for the worker for the first 6 months.

TABLE 6.3 LAC schedule for a worker with learning rate of 0.80

Month of work (n) :	$n = 1$	$n = 2$	$n = 3$	$n = 4$	$n = 5$	$n = 6$
LAC per unit per month :	100	80	64	51.2	40.96	32.77

Falling LAC in consequence to learning by doing at a stable learning rate of 0.8 per month is plotted in Figure 6.21 for the worker.

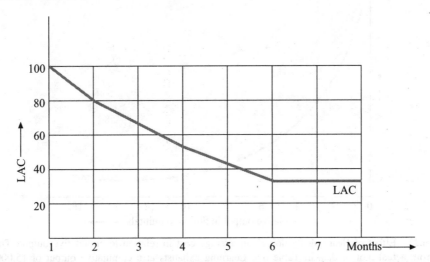

FIGURE 6.21 Learning curve for a worker: Effect of learning on AC—When the worker is in the process of **learning by doing** at a stable learning rate of 0.80 per month, LAC falls each month to 80% of its value the previous month. Learning being cumulative, a stage is reached when it gets exhausted. As soon as this happens, LAC is stabilized at its lowest.

---

*The reader with a little familiarity with geometric progression would easily recognize that the expression in Eq. (6.11) is none other than the expression for the nth term of the progression with first term a and the common ratio r. For slower or low quality workers, effect of learning on cost may be slower, following an arithmetic progression [$C_n = a + (n-1)d$] instead of a geometric progression.

This is the effect of 'learning by doing' on the efficiency of a worker. Note that the effect of learning of a worker on his efficiency is portrayed through reduction in AC per period of learning process of the worker. The concept is highly useful in performance appraisal of an employee. Learning rates differ from worker to worker and so must their emoluments and perks. A number of corporations conduct biannual/annual appraisals to ascertain the performance graph of each worker. This helps in promotions and granting of financial incentives to workers.

Effect of learning or the learning curve effect is viewed in yet another sense as well. As cumulative output of a firm increases, average cost (AC) declines with increasing volume of cumulative output. The relationship is portrayed in Figure 6.22. Hypothetical data in Table 6.4 form the basis of the relationship in the figure.

According to Petersen and Lewis*, the relationship can be expressed through the equation,

$$LAC = BQ^\alpha \qquad (6.12)$$

where, B and α are constants and Q, cumulative output.

The relationship [Equation (6.12)] can be estimated through regression techniques** using the data given in Table 6.4. The estimated equation can be used to forecast average cost when cumulated output desired by the firm is known.

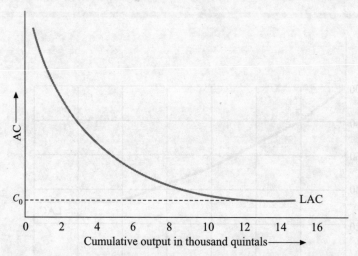

FIGURE 6.22 Effect of 'learning by doing' on average cost in relation to cumulative output. The curve is obtained from actual plot of data in Table 6.4. Learning exhausts at a cumulative output of 15,000 quintals. Average cost stabilizes at its lowest of ₹ 2.62 per quintal.

TABLE 6.4 Average cost schedule

Cumulative output :	1000	1500	2500	4000	6000	9000	15000
AC :	10.00	8.00	6.4	5.12	4.10	3.28	2.62

*H. Craig Petersen and W. Cris Lewis, *Managerial Economics,* 3rd ed., p. 556.
**See Appendix A at the end of this book.

Robert S. Pindyck and Daniel L. Rubinfeld* have expressed the learning curve effect in terms of labour inputs (L) per unit of output as a function of cumulative units of output (N) produced. It is given as

$$L = A + BN^{-\beta} \tag{6.13}$$

where, L is the quantity of labour input used per unit of output, N is the cumulative units of output and A, B, β are all constants such that A, $B > 0$ and β lies between 0 and 1.

When $N = 1$, $L = A + B$. This implies that labour input required per unit of output for the first unit produced is $(A + B)$.

When $\beta = 0$, $L = A + B$ which is the same as that for the first unit produced. This shows that $\beta = 0$ implies no learning.

When $\beta > 0$ and $N \to \infty$, $L \to A$. Thus A represents the minimum quantity of the labour input required per unit of output when all learning has exhausted.

When $\beta = \frac{1}{2}$, $L = A + B(N)^{-\frac{1}{2}}$.

When $\beta = 0.31$, every doubling of the cumulative output (N) results in a fall in the labour input requirement by about 19%, as shown below:

When cumulative output $= N$, $\beta = 0.31$,

$$L - A = B(N)^{-0.31}$$

When cumulative output $= 2N$, $\beta = 0.31$ and labour input per unit of output $= L'$,

$$\begin{aligned} L' - A &= B(2N)^{-0.31} \\ &= 2^{-0.31} (BN^{-0.31}) \\ &= 0.81666 (L - A) \quad [\because (BN^{-0.31}) = L - A] \\ &= 81\% \text{ of } (L - A) \quad \text{(approximately)} \end{aligned}$$

(let $2^{-0.31} = x$, then $\log x = -0.31 \log 2 = \overline{1}.90669$. Thus, $x = $ antilog $\overline{1}.90669 = 0.80666$.)

That shows 19% fall in the labour input requirement per unit of output.

The authors* have calculated labour input required for different levels of cumulative output assuming $A = 0$ and $\beta = 0.32$ for illustration.

The nature of the learning curve in all the methods is the same while the purposes served are different. The first, Eq. (6.11), worked out by the author, relates the effect of the learning process of a worker over time on the average cost of the product; the second, Eq. (6.12), worked out by Petersen and Lewis relates AC to cumulated output and the third, Eq. (6.13), worked out by Rubinfeld and Pindyck, relates labour input requirement to the cumulated output.

Distinction between internal and external economies of scale

As mentioned earlier, internal economies are subject to internal decisions that affect the shape of LAC. So long as such economies exist or are available, average cost falls but as soon as they are exhausted, average cost stabilizes at its lowest unless some diseconomies cause an increase in it.

---

*Robert S. Pindyck and Daniel L. Rubinfeld, *Microeconomics*, 3rd ed., pp. 220–223.

External economies, on the other hand, are subject to external decisions that cause a downward shift in LAC. Even learning curve behaves as an external economy in so far as its effect on LAC is concerned.

The distinction between the two is demonstrated in Figure 6.23.

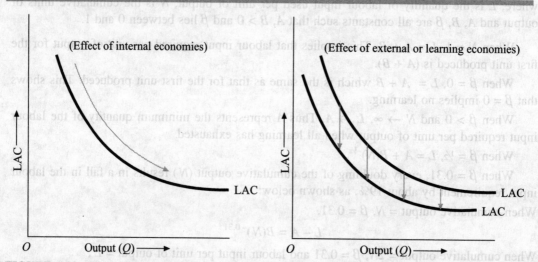

FIGURE 6.23 Distinction between internal and external economies: In the left panel, LAC falls due to availability of internal economies while in the right panel, LAC shifts downwards due to availability of external economies. Economies caused by learning also cause a similar shift in LAC. The only difference is that learning economies do not cause an exactly parallel shift in LAC. This is so because process of learning is cumulative and continuous at least up to the level of optimality of the current size of the plant. Reduction in cost is higher at the start of learning. It assumes a diminishing trend thereafter. As a result, LAC and LAC' get closer to each other at a higher level of output.

Generally, learning causes a non-parallel shift in LAC. To understand, let the learning rate be 0.80 while average costs at various levels of output are, in rupees, given as 10, 9, 8, 6 and 5 per period. Costs reduced in consequence to learning at each level are respectively 8, 7.2, 6.4, 4.8, and 4.0, registering a reductions of 2, 1.8, 1.6, 1.2 and 1.00 at the respective levels. That establishes the statement made in Figure 6.23 about non-uniformity of shift in LAC caused by learning.

Expression for the average cost per unit of output in Eq. (6.11) has been obtained on the assumption that the learning process of a worker is related to time period spent by the worker in production. It gives average cost per unit of output per lot produced in a particular time period. Learning curves of this type are highly suitable for performance appraisal of workers. Fixing of wages, determination of time of wage hike, promotion or of confirmation in a job, apart from determining the quantum of productivity-linked bonus may all acquire a rational basis when learning curve is the criteria.

Expression for average cost per unit of output in Eq. (6.12) above correlates effect of learning on AC to the cumulated output and is highly suitable for forecasting average cost at desired levels of cumulated outputs.

Cost–output elasticity and economies of scale

Internal economies lower the average cost of production continuously until their exhaustion while external economies and the learning curve effect shift the average cost curve downward as shown in Figure 6.23. A measure of the two therefore appears necessary.

Economies and diseconomies of scale are often measured in terms of the cost–output elasticity, E_C, defined as a ratio of proportionate change in total cost of production to a proportionate change in output.

$$E_C = \frac{\text{Proportionate change in total cost}}{\text{Proportionate change in output}}$$

$$= \frac{\Delta C / C}{\Delta Q / Q}$$

$$= (\Delta C / \Delta Q) \div (C / Q)$$

$$= MC / AC \qquad (6.14)$$

Clearly, $E_C = 1$, when $MC = AC$; $E_C < 1$, when $MC < AC$; and $E_C > 1$, when $MC > AC$

$E_C < 1 \Rightarrow$ existence of economies of scale

$E_C > 1 \Rightarrow$ existence of diseconomies of scale

$E_C = 1 \Rightarrow$ existence of neither

The expression $[1 - E_C]$ is called the **Scale Economies Index** (SEI) given as

$$SEI = 1 - E_C$$

$$= 1 - MC / AC$$

$$= (AC - MC) / AC \qquad (6.15)$$

When $MC = AC$, $SEI = 0$ implying absence of economies and diseconomies.

When $MC < AC$, $SEI > 0$ implying presence of the economies of scale.

Finally, when $MC > AC$, $SEI < 0$ implying existence of diseconomies.

6.4.2 Classification of Economies of Scale

Economies of scale, whether intra-plant or inter-plant, are classified into following two categories:

1. Pecuniary economies
2. Real economies

1. Pecuniary economies: Pecuniary economies result when productive inputs are availed by producers at much lower costs through their bulk purchasing. As the plant size expands, inputs needed are bought in bulk qualifying producers to quantity discounts. Economies such as these are strictly monetary and accrue to firms due to bulk purchases of inputs at lower costs. Large sized firms have the advantage of availing cheaper financial capital, cheaper labour and cheaper transport for their large sized consignments.

2. Real economies: Real economies are those associated with reduction in the physical quantity of inputs such as raw materials, labour and capital per unit of output. Such economies may be classified as production economies, selling and marketing economies, managerial economies and transport and storage economies—all accruing to the firms due to better technology and supervision.

Different classifications of the economies of scale are schematically presented in Table 6.5.

TABLE 6.5 Classification of economies of scale

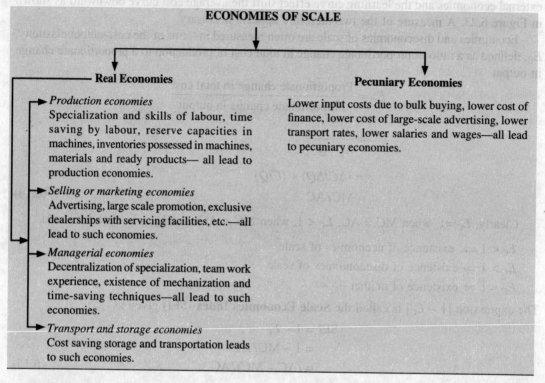

6.4.3 Economies of Scope

In addition to economies of scale, there exist a few other economies as well that lead to cost saving. For example, production of related goods often results in cost reduction when carried out in same plant under same supervision of management. Related goods such as cars and trucks, air conditioners and refrigerators, audio and video cassettes, etc. can share common production techniques, common raw materials, common plants and equipment and above all, common managerial supervision. Joint production may thus lead to substantial cost saving in such cases. Cost savings so caused are referred to as **economies of scope**.

To demonstrate, suppose a firm manufactures Q_1 cars at a cost of $C(Q_1)$ and Q_2 pick-up vans at a cost of $C(Q_2)$ in separate plants. Total cost incurred thus is $C(Q_1) + C(Q_2)$. Production of the two in a single plant costs $C(Q_1, Q_2)$. Cost saving so caused is $[C(Q_1) + C(Q_2) - C(Q_1, Q_2)]$. This expressed as a ratio of $C(Q_1, Q_2)$ gives the **degree of scope economies**, SC.

$$SC = \frac{[C(Q_1) + C(Q_2) - C(Q_1, Q_2)]}{C(Q_1, Q_2)} \quad (6.16)$$

SC can be negative, zero or positive. When negative, it implies diseconomies of scope, when positive, it implies economies of scope and when zero, it implies absence of both. Joint production is advantageous when SC > 0.

Advantages of joint production can also be studied with the help of production possibility curves (Figure 6.24). The curves trace out possible combinations of Q_1 and Q_2 that can be produced with given inputs employed fully and efficiently. The production possibility curve for cars and pick-up vans if concave to origin, such as N_1, joint production is advantageous; if linear, such as N_2, joint production is neither advantageous nor disadvantageous and if convex to origin, such as N_3, joint production is disadvantageous.

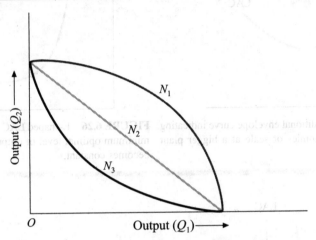

FIGURE 6.24 PPCs and economies of scope: Joint production is advantageous when PPC is concave to origin as in case of N_1, disadvantageous when PPC is convex to origin as in case of N_3 and neither when PPC is linear as in case of N_2.

6.4.4 Diseconomies of Scale

We have seen how internal economies of scale lead to a falling LAC with increasing output. We have also seen how external economies cause a downward shift of LAC.

There is, however, a great deal of disagreement among economists on following issues:

1. Are there diseconomies in existence at very large scales of output? (leading to traditional envelope curve of Figure 6.25).
2. Is there a minimum optimum scale of output in existence at which all possible economies get reaped so that LAC may remain constant at its lowest beyond that? (leading to L-shaped LAC of Figure 6.26).
3. Are there economies of scale, however small, in existence at all levels of output? (leading to inverse J-curve of Figure 6.27).

Empirical evidence supports that there exist *no diseconomies* of scale at high levels of output. That rejects the traditional enveloping LAC of Figure 6.25. But then no empirical support exists to establish conclusively that costs remain constant beyond a certain minimum optimal scale (Figure 6.26) or fall continuously with expanding plant (Figure 6.27). Thus, while the enveloping LAC is rejected, the L-shaped LAC and the inverse J-shaped LAC are not conclusively established by empirical studies either.

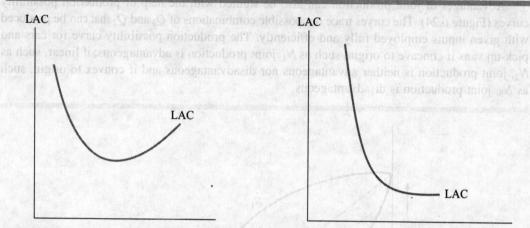

FIGURE 6.25 Traditional envelope curve indicating existence of diseconomies of scale at a bigger plant size.

FIGURE 6.26 L-shaped LAC indicating existence of minimum optimal level of output beyond which LAC becomes constant.

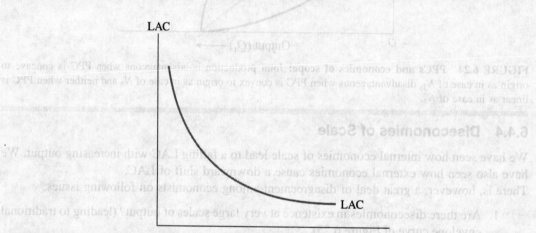

FIGURE 6.27 Inverse J-curve indicating existence of some economies of scale at all levels of output.

6.5 REVENUE CURVES

The term **revenue** or **total revenue** in economics refers to total receipts from sale of the output. For instance, total revenue from sale of 1000 units produced by a firm is the simple multiplication of this quantity with its market price per unit. If the latter is ₹ 20 per unit, the total revenue realized from sale would be ₹ 20,000.

In the numerical illustration above, we have assumed that the market price of each unit is fixed and it remains so for all the units offered by a producer for sale. The situation refers to a competitive market in which price once fixed remains so throughout the market period due to the presence of competition among the sellers each of whom is a price-taker. By the expression **price taker** we mean a seller who sells his product at a price fixed by market forces of demand and supply. Refer to illustration 1.1 (Chapter 1). The market price determined by the market forces is ₹ 15,000 per TV-set. Competitive sellers being price takers sell their product at this price. A simple multiplication shows that the total revenue from the sale of 105,000 TV-sets is ₹ 15.75 crores.

If the market price fixed by the market forces be $\bar{P}$ and the quantity sold Q, the total revenue, TR, can be expressed as

$$\text{TR} = \bar{P} \times Q \tag{6.17}$$

The expressions for the average and the marginal revenues, in this case, can be obtained as below.

The **Average Revenue** (AR) is defined as revenue per unit of product sold and is given as

$$\begin{aligned} \text{AR} &= \text{TR}/Q \\ &= \bar{P} \times Q/Q \\ &= \bar{P} \end{aligned} \tag{6.18}$$

Likewise, the **Marginal Revenue** (MR) is defined as a change in the total revenue caused by an additional unit sold. If the total revenue from the sale of Q_0 units is TR_0 and that from the sale of Q_1 units, TR_1, the marginal revenue,

$$\begin{aligned} \text{MR} &= \frac{\text{Change in total revenue}}{\text{Change in quantity sold}} \\ &= \frac{\text{TR}_1 - \text{TR}_0}{(Q_1 - Q_0)} \\ &= \frac{\Delta(\text{TR})}{\Delta Q} \\ &= \frac{d(\text{TR})}{dQ} \end{aligned} \tag{6.19}$$

The last expression refers to the change in total revenue, $d(\text{TR})$ caused by an infinitesimally small change, dQ, in quantity sold. Since price is fixed at $\bar{P}$,

$$\text{TR}_0 = \bar{P} \times Q_0$$

and

$$\text{TR}_1 = \bar{P} \times Q_1$$

∴

$$\begin{aligned} \text{MR} &= (\text{TR}_1 - \text{TR}_0)/(Q_1 - Q_0) \\ &= (\bar{P} \times Q_1 - \bar{P} \times Q_0)/(Q_1 - Q_0) \\ &= \bar{P}(Q_1 - Q_0)/(Q_1 - Q_0) \\ &= \bar{P} \end{aligned} \tag{6.20}$$

Thus, *in a competitive market*, $AR = MR = \bar{P}$, as shown in Figure 6.28.

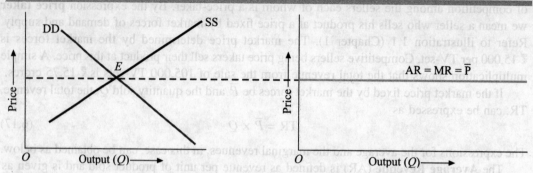

FIGURE 6.28 AR and MR in a competitive market: The market price is $\bar{P}$, as determined by the market forces of demand and supply in the left panel. The competitive firm, being a price taker, has to adopt this price. As a result, AR = MR = $\bar{P}$ as shown in the right panel. The firm is prepared to sell unlimited output at this price. AR and MR curves are both horizontal and coincidental.

A numerical illustration would drive the concept home. Consider the schedule of sales in Table 6.6.

TABLE 6.6 Relationship between AR and MR of a competitive seller

Output :	1	2	10	15	20	30	50	60	80	100
TR :	10	20	100	150	200	300	500	600	800	1000
AR :	10	10	10	10	10	10	10	10	10	10
MR :	10	10	10	10	10	10	10	10	10	10

AR = MR = 10 at all levels of sales. AR and MR are calculated through Eqs. (6.18) and (6.20).

When a single producer operates in the market, he dictates the price and is known as **price maker**. MR and AR for a price maker are different*. He usually starts with a high price and goes on lowering it whenever he feels his sales are stuck up. In other words, he faces a downward sloping demand curve:

$$P = a - bQ \tag{6.21}$$

where, a and b are fixed numbers, P is price and Q, quantity demanded. Price is no longer fixed in this case. The seller/producer exercises control over it by regulating the supply and is known as a monopoly producer/seller.

Total revenue,

$$TR = \text{Price} \times \text{Quantity sold}$$
$$= P \times Q$$

---

*For a price maker, $P \neq \bar{P}$. MR $= d(TR)/dQ = d(PQ)/dQ = P \cdot 1 + Q\, dP/dQ = P\left[1 + \dfrac{Q}{P} \cdot \dfrac{dP}{dQ}\right]$
$= P\left[1 + \dfrac{1}{(P/Q)dQ/dP}\right] = P\left[1 - \dfrac{1}{-(P/Q)(dQ/dP)}\right] = P\left[1 - \dfrac{1}{|e|}\right] = AR\left[1 - \dfrac{1}{|e|}\right]$. Here, $|e|$ is numerical value of elasticity which is negative and AR = TR/Q = PQ/Q = P. Thus, MR for a price maker is a function of AR and price elasticity of demand.

$$= (a - bQ) \times Q$$
$$= aQ - bQ^2 \qquad (6.22)$$

AR, from definition, is given by

$$AR = TR/Q$$
$$= PQ/Q$$
$$= P$$
$$= a - bQ \qquad (6.23)$$

MR, from Eq. (6.22), is obtained as

$$MR = d(TR)/dQ$$
$$= d(aQ - bQ^2)/dQ$$
$$= a - 2bQ \qquad (6.24)$$

(on differentiation)

Comparison of Eqs. (6.23) and (6.24) leads to the following observations:

1. The slope of the MR curve is $(-2b)$ while that of the AR curve is $(-b)$. In other words, MR is twice as steep as the AR curve.
2. The value of the output at which AR = 0, is (a/b) while that of it at which MR = 0, is $(a/2b)$. In other words, MR bisects all the horizontal intercepts between the vertical axis and the AR curve.

A numerical illustration would help understanding the concepts. Consider Table 6.7.

TABLE 6.7 Relationship between AR and MR of a single seller

Output:	1	2	3	4	5	6	7	8	9	10	11	12	13	14	15	16	17	18	19	20	21
TR:	20	38	54	68	80	90	98	104	108	110	110	108	104	98	90	80	68	54	38	20	0
AR:	20	19	18	17	16	15	14	13	12	11	10	9	8	7	6	5	4	3	2	1	0
MR:	20	18	16	14	12	10	8	6	4	2	0	-2	-4	-6	-8	-10	-12	-14	-16	-18	-20

Using,

$$AR = TR/Q,$$

and

$$MR = \Delta(TR)/\Delta Q,$$

we calculate AR and MR for the data in the table and observe that MR falls twice as fast as AR. AR = 0, when $Q = 21$ (Figure 6.30) and MR = 0 when $Q = 11$. It can be seen that 1/2 of $(21 - 1)$ is equal to $(11 - 1)$. Note that AR and MR do not initiate from the vertical axis in this illustration. Instead, they initiate from the vertical line through $Q = 1$. In Eqs. (6.23) and (6.24), AR and MR initiated from the vertical axis. Figures 6.29 and 6.30 demonstrate the point.

6.6 LINEAR BREAK-EVEN ANALYSIS

Break-even in context to TR and TC refers to equality of the two. That is,

$$TR = TC$$

Linear break-even also means the same with one difference. TR and TC are both essentially linear for linear break-even. TR under competitive conditions is essentially linear as price of the product is fixed. That is,

$$\text{TR} = \bar{P} \times Q \qquad (6.25)$$

As regards TC, it is also linear whenever TVC is. That is,

$$\text{TC} = a + bQ \qquad (6.26)$$

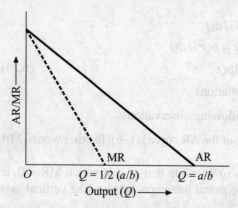

FIGURE 6.29 Relationship between AR and MR where, $\text{AR} = a - bQ$, $\text{MR} = a - 2bQ$. When plotted, both curves originate from the vertical axis. MR is twice as steep as AR and bisects all horizontal intercepts between AR and the vertical line through $Q = 0$ (the vertical axis).

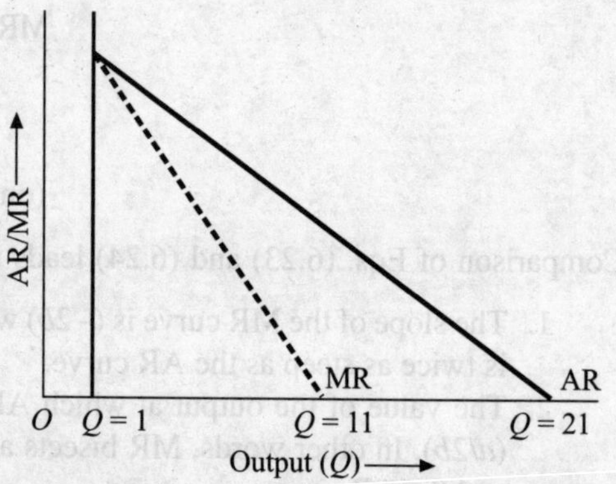

FIGURE 6.30 Relationship between AR and MR, the latter being twice as steep as the former. MR bisects the horizontal intercepts between AR and the vertical line through $Q = 1$.

For break-even,

$$\text{TR} = \text{TC}$$
$$\Rightarrow \qquad \bar{P}Q = a + bQ$$
$$\Rightarrow \qquad (\bar{P} - b) \times Q = a$$
$$\Rightarrow \qquad Q = a/(\bar{P} - b) \qquad (6.27)$$
$$\Rightarrow \qquad = \frac{\text{TFC}}{(\text{Competitive price} - \text{Variable cost}) \text{ per unit}}$$

where, $\bar{P}$ is competitive price per unit of output, b is variable cost per unit of output and a is the total fixed cost (TFC).

In case the firm also desires a fixed profit $\bar{\pi}$, then

$$\text{TR} = \text{TC} + \bar{\pi}$$
$$\Rightarrow \qquad \bar{P}Q = a + bQ + \bar{\pi}$$

$\Rightarrow \quad (\bar{P} - b)Q = a + \bar{\pi}$

$\Rightarrow \quad Q = (a + \bar{\pi})/(\bar{P} - b)$ (6.28)

$$= \frac{(TFC + \text{desired profit})}{(\text{Competitive price} - \text{Variable cost}) \text{ per unit}}$$

Figure 6.31 demonstrates determination of the break-even output with and without the profit desired by the firm.

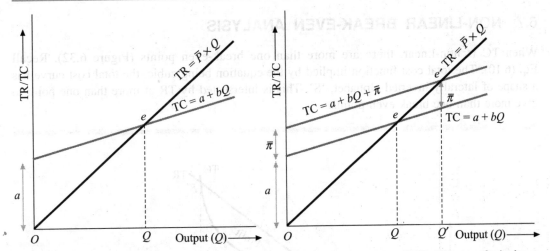

FIGURE 6.31 Linear break-even with and without profit: Break-even output (OQ) without profits is shown in the left panel and break-even output (OQ') with profits is shown in the right panel. TR passes through the origin while TC and TC + $\bar{\pi}$ make an intercept on the vertical axis.

ILLUSTRATION 6.3: A firm has incurred a fixed cost of 200,000. The variable cost per unit of output is 20 and the competitive price, 30.

(i) Determine the break-even output.
(ii) How would your answer to (i) change if the firm desires a profit of 50,000?

Solution:

(i) From Eq. (6.27), break-even output,

$$Q = a/(\bar{P} - b)$$

$$Q = \frac{200{,}000}{(30 - 20)}$$

(Substituting $a = 200{,}000$, $\bar{P} = 30$ and $b = 20$ in the expression)

$= 20{,}000$ units.

(ii) From Eq. (6.28), break-even output with a fixed profit is given as

$$Q = (a + \bar{\pi})/(\bar{P} - b)$$
$$= \frac{(200,000 + 50,000)}{(30 - 20)}$$

(Substituting $a = 200,000$, $\bar{P} = 30$ and $b = 20$ and $\bar{\pi} = 50,000$ in the expression)

$$= (250,000)/(10)$$
$$= 25,000 \text{ units.}$$

6.7 NON-LINEAR BREAK-EVEN ANALYSIS

When TC is non-linear, there are more than one break-even points (Figure 6.32). Recall Eq. (6.10). The total cost function implied by the equation being cubic, the total cost curve has a shape of laterally inverted alphabet, 'S'. This is intersected by TR at more than one point to give more than one break-even points.

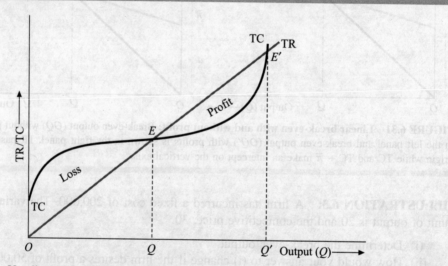

FIGURE 6.32 Non-linear break-even analysis: When the cost curve is non-linear, there exist more than one break-even points ($E, E', \ldots$). Break-even outputs can be obtained by setting TR equal to TC.

Setting TR equal to TC, we obtain a cubic expression having three roots.

$$\bar{P}Q = a + bQ - cQ^2 + dQ^3$$
$$\Rightarrow \quad dQ^3 - cQ^2 + (b - \bar{P})Q + a = 0$$

Given a, b, c and d, the equation can be solved to give three values of Q provided the coefficient, $d \neq 0$. In case $d = 0$, the equation reduces to a second-degree equation having only two roots.

When TR and TC are both non-linear, again more than one break-even point would result. Setting TC = TR, we have

$$a + bQ - cQ^2 + dQ^3 = PQ$$
$$= (\alpha - \beta Q) \cdot Q$$
$$= \alpha Q - \beta Q^2$$
$$\Rightarrow dQ^3 + (\beta - c)Q^2 + (b - \alpha)Q + a = 0$$

Given a, b, c, α, β and d, the equation can be solved to give three values of Q provided the coefficient, $d \neq 0$. In case, $d = 0$, the equation reduces to a second-degree equation having only two roots.

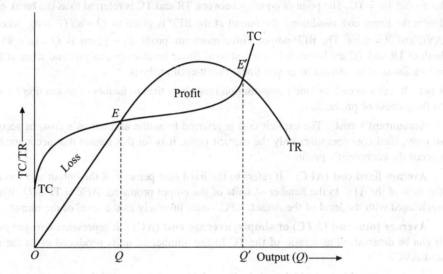

FIGURE 6.33 Non-linear break-even with TR and TC both non-linear: When both the curves are non-linear, the break-even points obtained by setting TR = TC are still more than one. TR is a second degree curve under non-competitive conditions of downward sloping demand, $P = \alpha - \beta Q$. TR, thus, is given as TR = $\alpha Q - \beta Q^2$.

Break-even analysis, whether linear or non-linear, is a very effective tool of determining the least volume of output that helps producers to break-even with the production costs. An output less than this if targetted in production would land the firm in loss. This is so due to heavy fixed costs usually involved. Producers are therefore keen on ascertaining the least size of output particularly at the initial levels so that they may escape the likely loss. The problem usually relates to average cost which has to be reduced to such levels that may allow producers to set a viable price. At higher levels with established product market, the firms can afford to charge a mark-up also to allow desired levels of profit.

The biggest drawback of the tool is that break-even outputs often prove non-viable due to fractional or decimal values. A break-even output of say 10.46 jet planes turns non-viable for obvious reasons. The exact quantity cannot be produced because it is not in whole numbers and rounding it off up or down defeats the very purpose of the analysis.

KEY TERMS AND CONCEPTS

Average revenue (AR) It is the revenue realized per unit of the output sold. It can be determined as a ratio of the total revenue (TR) realized to the quantity sold. Thus, AR = TR/Q = PQ/Q = P, where, P is price expressed as a function of quantity sold, given that the firm is a price maker (monopoly). The AR curve must slope downwards like a demand curve in this case. For competitive market, the firms are price takers. They adopt the price determined by the market forces of demand and supply. The price, thus, is fixed, $P = \overline{P}$. Hence, AR = TR/Q = $\overline{P}Q/Q = \overline{P}$ and the AR curve is horizontal.

Break-even analysis At the initial stages of production, TR < TC. This leads to losses to the firm. The firm, therefore, attempts to flyover these losses by deciding the minimum output to be produced as a single lot so that TR = TC. The point of equality between TR and TC is referred to as the break-even point (BEP). Under the linear cost conditions, the output at the BEP is given as $Q = a/(\overline{P} - b)$, where, a = TFC, b = AVC and $\overline{P}$ = price. The BEP output with a minimum profit, $\overline{\pi}$, is given as $Q = (a + \overline{\pi})/(\overline{P} - b)$. When both of TR and TC are linear, it is referred to as linear break-even analysis and when at least one of them is non-linear, it is referred to as non-linear break-even analysis.

Cost It refers to cash or kind compensation made by a firm to factors of production for their contribution to the process of production.

Accountant's cost The explicit cost is referred to as the accountant's cost. In accountant's concept of costs, total cost comprises only the explicit costs. It is for this reason that accountant's profits always exceed the economist's profits.

Average fixed cost (AFC) It refers to the fixed cost per unit of the output and can be determined as the ratio of the TFC to the number of units of the output produced. AFC = TFC/Q. While TFC remains unchanged with the level of the output, AFC varies inversely as the level of the output.

Average total cost (ATC) or simply, average cost (AC) It represents cost per unit of the output. It can be determined as a ratio of the TC to the number of units produced or as the sum of the AFC and AVC.

Average variable cost (AVC) It is the variable cost per unit of the output and can be determined as a ratio of the TVC to the number of units of output produced. AVC = TVC/Q.

Economist's cost The sum of the explicit and implicit costs is referred to as the economist's cost. In the economist's concept of costs, total cost comprises both—the explicit cost and the implicit cost. It is for this reason that the economist's estimate of profit is always less than that of an accountant.

Explicit cost It is the cost incurred by a producer on external factors of production. External factors of production refer to those factors that are procured by the producer from outside or those none of which is owned by him. Examples are labour, raw-materials, power-fuel, etc.

Future costs Future costs, also known as the avoidable or escapable costs, refer to costs based on business expectations. For instance, policy decisions involving expansion programmes of business involve future costs.

Implicit cost It refers to the cost of the factors of production provided by the entrepreneur himself to his firm. He is entitled to receive the incomes accruing to them. For example, the entrepreneur is entitled to the rent accruing to land-building if provided by himself to his firm. Here, rent is an implicit cost. In the other case, if it is hired from some one else, it is an explicit cost.

Marginal cost (MC) It refers to the change in TC per unit change in output. It can also be defined as the change in the total cost caused by production of an additional unit of it.

Money costs Money costs, also known as the private costs, refer to the production costs measured or incurred in terms of money. Only those costs enter into the money costs that are possible to be estimated in monetary terms. Loss of health caused to the society by the factory pollution is difficult to estimate in terms of money and hence is not a part of the money costs. Money costs comprise the explicit and the implicit costs.

Opportunity cost It refers to the cost of the opportunity foregone for the sake of current opportunity. For instance, the opportunity cost of an entrepreneur is the income he might have earned from employment as a manager in some other firm which he has sacrificed for managing his own. Alternatively, it represents likely income from the next best alternative use of his skills even though it may never have been resorted to by the entrepreneur.

Real costs Real costs refer to true costs of production. Such costs comprise *money costs* and *external costs*. The external costs refer to non-monetary costs such as those of entrepreneurial services that involve anxiety, patience, waiting, sacrifice of leisure and social life and the like. None of these is subject to measurement by any measuring rod whatsoever. Another example of the external costs is the cost of sufferings inflicted by air and noise pollution upon the society. Such costs never form a part of the private costs not only because of the lack of monetization but more so because of the lack of social responsibility on the part of the producers. Real cost is, thus, the sum of the money cost (or the private cost) and the external cost.

Social costs Also known as real cost of production, the social cost is the sum total of the private cost and the external cost. Social costs are used in social cost and benefit analysis of a project or productive unit. If the social cost is more than the private cost, the external cost is positive or social benefit is negative. This is known as negative externality. In the opposite case, when the social cost is less than the private cost, the social benefit is positive. This is known as positive externality.

Sunk costs The sunk costs, also known as unavoidable costs, refer to the expenditures that have already been incurred and cannot be recovered. All the costs incurred in the past actually are the sunk-costs.

Total cost (TC) It is the sum of the TFC and the TVC.

Total fixed cost (TFC) It refers to the cost incurred on the fixed factors of production. It remains unchanged even when output is increased or decreased. It has to be incurred irrespective of the level of output being produced.

Total variable costs (TVC) It depends on the level of output being produced. It increases with an increase in the level of output and decreases with a decrease in it and is incurred on the variable factors of production, such as, labour, raw materials, fuel and power, etc.

Cost-output elasticity Economies and diseconomies of scale are often measured in terms of cost-output elasticity, E_C. It can be defined as the ratio of proportionate change in total cost of production to proportionate change in output.

$$E_C = \frac{\text{Proportionate change in total cost}}{\text{Proportionate change in output}}$$

$$= \frac{\Delta C / C}{\Delta Q / Q}$$

$$= (\Delta C / \Delta Q) \cdot (C/Q)$$

$$= MC/AC.$$

Clearly, $E_C = 1$, when MC = AC, $E_C < 1$, when MC < AC and $E_C > 1$, when MC > AC.

$E_C < 1 \Rightarrow$ existence of economies of scale.

$E_C > 1 \Rightarrow$ existence of diseconomies of scale.

$E_C = 1 \Rightarrow$ existence of neither.

Depreciation Also known as consumption of capital, depreciation refers to wear and tear of productive assets in the process of production.

Economies of scales When average cost of production falls with increase in plant size, the phenomenon is referred to as economies of scale. Economies of scale are said to be *external* if the phenomenon is a consequence of some external changes such as changes in government policies and they are said to *internal* if the phenomenon is a consequence of some internal changes. When the phenomenon is limited to a single plant, it is known as *intra-plant economies of scale* and when it extends to all the plants of the firm, it is referred to as *inter-plant economies of scale*. Intra-plant and inter-plant economies are components of internal economies.

Envelope curve It refers to the U-shaped LAC curve of the traditional theory of costs which envelopes firm's short-run average cost curves characterizing its various plant sizes. It signifies the presence of diseconomies at higher scale of production.

Inverse J-curve It refers to the LAC characterizing the belief that some economies of scale always exist in production and cause the LAC to maintain its declining trend at all scales of production. The belief defies the requirement of attaining the minimum optimal plant size and holds that the costs continue to decline with the scale though the decline may be small at sufficiently large scales. *Empirical evidence in support of L-shaped and inverse J-shaped LAC curves is, however, inconclusive although it conclusively rejects the existence of the envelop curve and the diseconomies of scale at higher scale of production.*

L-shaped curve It is the LAC curve as implied by the modern theory of costs. The curve characterizes a continuously falling average cost until it stabilizes at its minimum at the firm's *minimum optimal plant size* where it is believed to stay ever after as per this theory.

Learning curve Also known as 'learning by doing', it refers to improvement in the efficiency of the workers in consequence to their repetitive participation in production as an integral part of man-machine system. The rate at which production cost per unit changes is called the *learning rate* and its effect on production costs, the *learning curve effect*. Historical decline in cost per unit of output when portrayed with cumulative output leads to a curve called the *learning curve* that falls from left to right continuously until all the learning possibilities get exhausted.

Marginal revenue (MR) It is defined as a change in TR per unit increase in quantity sold. Thus, MR = $\Delta(TR)/\Delta Q$ or $d(TR)/dQ$. For a price maker (monopoly), MR slopes downwards and is twice as steep as the AR curve. For a competitive firm, MR = $d(TR)/dQ = d(\bar{P} \times Q)/dQ = \bar{P}$, price being fixed. Thus, for a competitive market, AR = MR = $\bar{P}$. Both the curves are horizontal and coincidental.

Modern theory of long-run costs According to the modern theory of costs, LAC curve is L–shaped due to economies of large-scale production accruing to the firm.

Modern theory of short-run costs In the modern theory of costs, the SAVC and the SMC retain their traditional U-shape but with a flat stretch at the bottom representing the existence of reserve capacity in the firm. SAC, however, does not possess the flat stretch. SAVC curve possesses a saucer-like shape.

Reserve capacity It refers to the range of output over which, short-run average variable cost (SAVC) is constant. According to the Modern Theory, producers build the plants with a view to accommodate sudden spurt in demand without having to bear higher costs.

Scale curve It is another name given to LAC curve which falls with expansion of the plant size.

Scale economy index $(1 - E_C)$ is defined as scale economy index.

Scope economies Such economies refer to cost saving caused by joint production of related products that make use of common resources, plant, equipment or machinery. Separate production of such products leads to diseconomies due to suboptimal use of common equipment and managerial supervision. For instance, production of cars and pickup vans uses identical lathe machines, painting and assembling units, skilled workers, managerial supervision, etc. and can be accomplished at much lower cost if carried out in a common plant rather than in separate plants.

Degree of scope economies It is measured as a ratio of cost saved to the joint cost of production. It can be expressed as

$$SC = \frac{[C(Q_1) + C(Q_2) - C(Q_1, Q_2)]}{C(Q_1, Q_2)}.$$

Total revenue (TR or R) It represents money value of output sold. In other words, it represents sales proceed which is equal to the product of price and quantity sold, i.e. R (or TR) $= P \times Q$.

Traditional theory of short-run costs According to this theory, AC, AVC and MC are all U-shaped. The reasons for this are the initial increasing returns to the variable proportions followed by decreasing returns thereafter and negative returns finally. Due to such returns, when AC falls, so does MC so that MC < AC; when AC is the least, MC = AC and when AC rises, so does MC so that MC > AC. Of the three, it is the MC that reaches its minimum first, followed by AVC next and by AC, finally. MC cuts AVC and AC at their respective minima in its upward movement.

Traditional theory of the long-run costs According to this theory, the long-run average and the marginal cost curves retain the U-shape but with drooping arms, i.e. their arms fall flatter. The long-run average cost curve (LAC) is derived from the short-run average cost curves (SACs) as an enveloping curve to them. Likewise, the long-run marginal cost curve (LMC) is derived from the short-run marginal cost curves (SMCs).

EXERCISES

A. Short Answer Questions

Define the following: (1 through 16)
1. Depreciation
2. Opportunity cost
3. Explicit cost
4. Implicit cost
5. Private cost
6. Social cost
7. Real cost
8. Money cost
9. Sunk cost
10. Future cost
11. Total fixed cost
12. Total variable cost
13. Average variable cost
14. Average fixed cost
15. Average total cost

16. Marginal cost
17. Briefly introduce the traditional theory of short-run cost curves.
18. Briefly introduce the traditional theory of the long-run average cost curve.
19. What is the modern theory of the short-run average variable cost curve?
20. What is the modern theory of the long-run average cost curve?
21. Explain saucer-shaped SAVC curve.
22. Explain L-shaped average cost curve.
23. Explain Average Revenue (AR) and Marginal Revenue (MR).
24. Show that AR=MR= $\bar{P}$ for a competitive firm.
25. Draw a rough sketch of AR for a monopoly firm.
26. Draw a rough sketch of MR for a monopoly firm.
27. What is the linear break-even analysis?
28. Which of AC, AVC and MC reaches its minimum first and which last?
29. At what point are the AC and the MC same? Explain with the help of a rough sketch.
30. At what point are the AVC and the MC same? Show with the help of a rough sketch.
31. Can AC be falling when MC is rising? Draw a rough sketch to explain.
32. Can AC be falling when AVC is rising? Draw a rough sketch to explain.
33. Can AC and AVC be falling when MC is rising? Show with the help of a rough sketch.
34. Classify the following into fixed cost and variable cost:
    (a) Rent for the factory building.
    (b) Salaries to the permanent staff.
    (c) Interest on capital.
    (d) Wages paid to the casual workers.
    (e) Cost of the raw materials.
    (f) Depreciation.
    (g) Minimum electricity bill.
    (h) Electricity charges beyond the minimum.
35. What is the reserve capacity? Explain with the help of a diagram.
36. What is a learning curve? Explain the learning curve effect with the help of an example.
37. Account for the shape of the average fixed cost curve as implied by the modern theory of costs.
38. What is an inverse J-curve? Explain with the help of a diagram.
39. Account for the shape of the L-shaped LAC.
40. Distinguish between the interplant and the intraplant economies of scale.
41. Distinguish between the internal and the external economies of scale.
42. What are the real economies? What are the components of the real economies?
43. Define pecuniary economies. How do they arise?
44. Define the diseconomies of scale. What is their effect on LAC and what do empirical observations say about the existence of such economies?
45. What is meant by minimum optimal scale of plant? How does it effect LAC?
46. Define scale economy index? How can it be used to detect presence or absence of scale economies?
47. Define economies of scope. How can they be measured?
48. What is cost-output elasticity? How is it related to scale economy index?
49. What is the main difference between linear and non-linear break-even analysis?

B. Long Answer Questions

50. How can TVC be obtained from the marginal cost curve?

   [**Ans.** Area under the MC curve gives TVC. This can be easily seen from the following:

   We know that $d(TC)/dQ = MC$.

   $\Rightarrow \qquad d(TC) = (MC)dQ$

   $\Rightarrow \qquad \int d(TC) = \int (MC)dQ$

   $\Rightarrow \qquad TC = \int (MC) \cdot dQ$

   TVC can be found by subtracting TFC from TC or simply by evaluating the definite integral

   $$\int_0^Q MC \cdot dQ$$

   The reader can verify the result by taking any total cost function. Here, we demonstrate the result by taking a general function:

   $$TC = a + bQ + cQ^2$$

   Since, $\qquad MC = d(TC)/dQ$

   $\qquad \qquad \quad = b + 2cQ$

   $\int (b + 2cQ)dQ = bQ + 2c(Q^2/2) + a \qquad$ (a is the constant of integration)

   $\qquad \qquad \qquad = a + bQ + cQ^2$

   $\qquad \qquad \qquad = TFC + TVC$

   $\therefore \quad$ Area under the MC curve $= \int_0^Q MC \cdot dQ = \int_0^Q (b + 2cQ) \cdot dQ = bQ + cQ^2 \big|_0^Q$

   $\qquad \qquad \qquad \qquad \qquad \quad = bQ + cQ^2 - 0 = bQ + cQ^2$

   $\therefore \qquad \qquad \qquad \qquad$ TVC = Area under the MC curve

   The reader with a little familiarity with differentiation and integration would have no difficulty in understanding the result.]

Distinguish between (51 through 58):

51. Explicit and implicit cost
52. Private and social cost
53. Money cost and real cost
54. Sunk cost and future cost
55. Total fixed cost and total variable cost
56. AC and MC
57. AVC and MC
58. AVC and AC
59. With the help of a neat sketch, show that under increasing returns to variable proportions of the three, it is the MC that reaches its minima first, the AVC next and the AC finally.
60. Given, $TC = 2 + 3Q - 1.5Q^2 + 0.5Q^3$. Show that the MC attains its minimum at $Q = 1.0$, the AVC at $Q = 1.50$, and the AC at $Q = 2.00$. Determine the minimum values of the three and show that MC = AVC at the point where AVC is minimum and that MC = AC at the point where AC is minimum.

61. Given, TC = $a + bQ + cQ^2$. Show that MC = AC = $b + 2\sqrt{(ac)}$ at $Q = \sqrt{(a/c)}$ where AC is minimum.

    [**Ans.** Since
    $$TC = a + bQ + cQ^2,$$
    $$MC = d(TC)/dQ$$
    $$= b + 2cQ$$
    and,
    $$AC = TC/Q$$
    $$= a/Q + b + cQ$$

    For minimization of AC, $d(AC)/dQ = 0$ and $d^2(AC)/dQ^2 > 0$

    Differentiating AC with respect to Q, we have $-a/Q^2 + c = 0$, as the necessary condition for minimization.

    $\Rightarrow \qquad cQ^2 - a = 0$

    $\Rightarrow \qquad Q = \sqrt{(a/c)}$

    Differentiating AC twice with respect to Q, we have

    $$d^2(AC)/dQ^2 = 2a/Q^3 = \frac{2c\sqrt{c}}{\sqrt{a}} \qquad \text{[at } Q = \sqrt{(a/c)}\text{]}$$

    which is certainly positive as $a > 0$, $Q > 0$

    The value of MC at $Q = \sqrt{(a/c)}$ can be seen to be $b + 2c\sqrt{(a/c)}$ or $b + 2\sqrt{(ac)}$. Likewise value of AC at this point can also be seen to be $b + 2\sqrt{(ac)}$.]

62. Given, TC = $300 + 2Q + 3Q^2$. Show that AC is minimum at $Q = 10$ units and that AC = 62 = MC at this point.

63. Given, MC = $2 + 6Q$. Find an expression for TC, if TC = 300 at $Q = 0$. Find the area under the MC curve (Figure 6.34) and show that it is equal to TVC.

    [**Ans.**

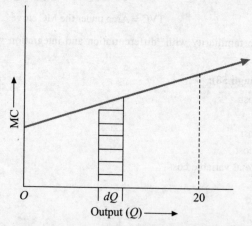

FIGURE 6.34 (Question 63) In the figure, MC curve is shown with the arrowhead. It is a linearly upward rising curve with a positive slope ($2c$). Taking a thin stripe of width dQ and height MC (the width dQ is infinitesimally small so that the stripe is a rectangle of length MC).

The area of the thin stripe, dA, called the area element, is

$$dA = MC \cdot dQ$$

But, $\qquad d(TC) = MC \cdot dQ \qquad$ (By definition)

$\therefore \qquad dA = d(TC)$

$\qquad\qquad = MC \cdot dQ$

$\therefore \qquad TC = \int MC \cdot dQ$

$\qquad\qquad = \int (2 + 6Q) dQ$

$\qquad\qquad = 2Q + 3Q^2 + K \qquad$ (where, K = constant of integration.)

When, $\qquad Q = 0, TC = 300$

Thus, $\qquad TC = 300 + 2Q + 3Q^2 \qquad$ (where, $TVC = 2Q + 3Q^2$)

Area under the MC curve between $Q = 0$ and Q, when $MC = 2 + 6Q$, is

$$A = \int_0^Q (2 + 6Q) dQ$$

$$= 2Q + 3Q^2 \Big|_0^Q$$

$$= 2Q + 3Q^2 - 0$$

MC curve being a straight line, the area under it between the vertical lines $Q = 0$ and $Q = 20$ (say) is equal to the area of the trapezium with parallel sides of lengths 2 ($MC = 2$ at $Q = 0$) and 122 ($MC = 122$ at $Q = 20$) and the distance of separation between them $20(20 - 0)$, which can be seen to be

$$= 1/2\ (20)\ (2 + 122)$$

$$= 1240.$$

The same can be obtained by substituting $Q = 20$ in the expression for the TVC.

Thus, $\qquad TVC = 2Q + 3Q^2$ at $Q = 20$

$\qquad\qquad = 2 \times 20 + 3 \times (20)(20)$

$\qquad\qquad = 1240.]$

64. A firm's total cost schedule is as given in the following table:

Output :	0	1	5	10	12	15	20
TC :	300	305	385	602	756	1005	1540

Obtain TFC, AFC, TVC, AVC, ATC (AC) and MC schedules. Sketch the schedules.

65. A firm's TFC is 500 and its MC schedule is as given below:

Output :	0	2	4	6	8	10	12	14	16	18	20	22	24
MC :	–	340	300	200	150	120	120	130	150	175	215	300	340

Work out TC, TVC, AC, AVC and AFC schedules. Sketch them on the same graph.

66. Given the total revenue schedule for the sales of a firm as below:

Units sold :	1	2	5	10	20	25	40	50	100
TR :	20	40	100	200	400	500	800	1000	2000

Work out the AR and MR schedules and sketch them on the same graph. Why are the schedules identical'

67. Given the TR schedule for sales of a firm as below:

Units sold :	1	2	3	4	5	6	7	8	9	10	11	12
TR :	20	38	54	68	80	90	98	104	108	110	110	108

Work out the AR and MR schedules and sketch them on the same graph. What can you say about their shapes? Why the schedules differ from those obtained in Q. 66?

68. Given the equation of demand:

$$Q^d = 1000 - 4P,$$

where the symbols have their usual meaning. Obtain expressions for total revenue, average revenue and marginal revenue. Draw their rough sketches and find the levels of output at which:

(a) AR = 0,

(b) MR = 0, and

(c) TR is maximum.

Estimate slopes of AR and MR. Can we conclude that

(i) MR is twice as steep as AR?

(ii) MR bisects all horizontal intercept between the vertical axis and the AR when $P = 0$? $P = 125$?

Calculate the price elasticity of demand at $Q = 500$. Find AR and MR at this point and show that

$$MR = AR [1 - (1/E_P^D)].$$

[**Ans.** $TR = 250Q - 0.25Q^2$; $MR = 250 - 0.5Q$; $AR = 250 - 0.25Q$

(a) AR = 0 at $Q = 1,000$;

(b) MR = 0 at $Q = 500$;

(c) TR is maximum at $Q = 500$. Slope of AR = -0.25; slope of MR = -0.50

(i) Yes

(ii) When $P = 0$ (horizontal axis), the horizontal intercept between the vertical axis and the AR curve is 1000 units (Figure 6.35). MR meets it at its midpoint which is 500 units away from the origin. When $P = 125$, MR = 125 at $Q = 250$ and AR = 125 at $Q = 500$. The horizontal intercept between the vertical axis and the AR curve is 500 units. MR bisects it at $Q = 250$ (Figure 6.35)

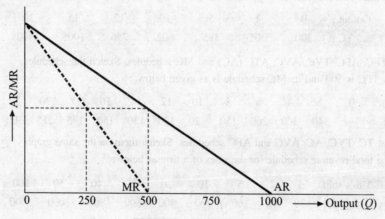

FIGURE 6.35 (Question 68).

$$E_P^D = (dQ/dP)(P/Q).$$

Differentiating the equation of demand w.r.t. P, we have

$$dQ/dP = -4, P/Q \text{ at } Q = 500 \text{ is } 125/500 = 0.25.$$
$$\therefore \quad E_P^D = -4 \times 0.25 = -1.0$$

MR, at $Q = 500$, is 0 and AR, at $Q = 500$, is 125.
We observe that $0 = 125 [1 - 1/1]$.

69. In general, let the quantity demanded, Q, be given as

$$Q = a - bP$$

Obtain expressions for TR, AR and MR. Find the slopes of AR and MR. Verify that MR is twice as steep as AR. Show that MR bisects all the horizontal intercepts between the vertical axis and the AR curve. Also show that

$$MR = AR[1 - (1/e)],$$

where, e is the price elasticity of demand.

[Ans. Rewriting the equation of demand, making P as its subject, we have

$$P = a/b - (1/b)Q$$
$$TR = PQ$$
$$= [a/b - (1/b)Q]Q$$
$$= (a/b)Q - (1/b)Q^2$$
$$AR = TR/Q$$
$$= (a/b) - (1/b)Q \qquad (1)$$
$$MR = d(TR)/dQ$$
$$= (a/b) - 2(1/b)Q \qquad (2)$$

From (1) and (2), the slopes of the AR and the MR curves are $(-1/b)$ and $(-2/b)$, respectively. Therefore, MR is twice as steep as AR curve.
Next, take any horizontal intercept between the vertical axis and the AR curve at $P = t$. Then,

$$AR = MR = t \text{ at } P = t.$$

Substituting in Eqs. (1) and (2) respectively, we have

$$t = (a/b) - (1/b)Q \Rightarrow Q = a - bt \qquad (3)$$
$$t = (a/b) - 2(1/b)Q \Rightarrow Q = 1/2(a - bt) \qquad (4)$$

Comparing Eqs. (3) and (4), we have the fact that the MR bisects all the horizontal intercepts between the price axis and the AR curve. Now,

$$TR = PQ$$
$$\therefore \quad MR = d(TR)/dQ$$
$$= P + Q(dP/dQ) \qquad \text{(differentiating by the product rule)}$$
$$= P[1 + (Q/P)(dP/dQ)]$$
$$= P[1 - 1/\{-(dQ/dP)(P/Q)\}]$$
$$= AR[1 - 1/|e|], \qquad \text{where, } |e| = \{-(dQ/dP)(P/Q)\}.]$$

70. Explain the concept of the linear break-even analysis. What is its significance in production decisions in short-run? Obtain expressions for the break-even outputs with or without profit.

71. A firm is operating in short-run. Its fixed cost is 250,000 while average variable cost is 37.50 and price, 50.00. Determine the lot size the firm should produce to avoid loss. What must the lot-size be if the firm wants to earn a minimum profit of 50,000?

[**Ans.** 20,000; 24,000.]

72. Consider a point where a straight line from the origin is tangent to the total cost curve. Which of the following will be true?

(a) Average cost is minimum,
(b) Average cost equals the marginal cost,
(c) Average cost equals average fixed cost plus average variable cost,
(d) All the above.

[**Ans.** (d). Refer to the Illustration 6.1. Figure 6.36 demonstrates the working.

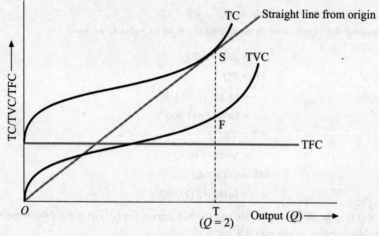

FIGURE 6.36 (Question 72).

(a) In the figure, straight line OS from origin touches the TC curve at point S. Perpendicular from S meets the x-axis at T. Average cost at S may be defined as

$$AC = \frac{\text{Total Cost (ST)}}{\text{Output(OT)}}$$

$$= \frac{ST}{OT}$$

$$= \text{Slope of OS}$$

Every point other than point S on TC lies above the tangent OS. Therefore, average cost (AC) for every point other than the point S on TC is higher than that at S. Thus, AC (Slope of OS at S) is minimum at S. In other words, AC is minimum at the point of tangency of the ray from origin to the TC curve.

(b) MC at $S = d(TC)/dQ$ at S.

$\quad\quad\quad = $ Slope of TC at S.

= Slope of OS at S.

= AC.

(c) AC at S = $\dfrac{ST}{OT} = \dfrac{SF + FT}{OT} = \dfrac{SF}{OT} + \dfrac{FT}{OT}$ = AFC + AVC (SF = TFC, FT = TVC and OT = output)

(d) From (a), (b) and (c), slope of the tangent to TC from the origin = AC = AVC + AFC = MC. But AC being minimum at S or at a point where MC = AC, **all the four alternative choices are correct**.

Alternative Explanation: As an alternative demonstration, refer to illustration 6.1.

$$TC = 2 + 3Q - 1.5 Q^2 + 0.5Q^3$$
$$MC = 3 - 3Q + 1.5Q^2$$
$$TFC = 2$$
$$TVC = 3Q - 1.5Q^2 + 0.5Q^3$$
$$AFC = 2/Q$$
$$AVC = TVC/Q$$
$$= 3 - 1.5Q + 0.5Q^2$$

We have seen that AC is minimum at $Q = 2$. At this point,

$$\text{Value of AC} = 2/2 + 3 - 1.5 \times 2 + 0.5\,(2)^2 = 1 + 3 - 3 + 2$$
$$= 3.$$
$$\text{Value of MC} = 3 - 3(2) + 1.5\,(2)^2 = 3 - 6 + 6$$
$$= 3 = \text{Value of the slope of TC at } Q = 2.$$

MC is the slope of the TC and it is equal to 3 at the output level where AC is minimum or where MC = AC. Tangent, OS, drawn to TC from the origin meets TC at point S. At this point, value of MC must be equal to the value of the slope of this tangent. Therefore, point S is the point of tangency between TC and the straight line from origin. At this point, as seen above, MC = AC and AC is minimum.

At $Q = 2$, AFC = 2/2 = 1

At $Q = 2$, AVC = $3 - 1.5(2) + 0.5\,(2)^2 = 2$

Clearly, AC = MC = AFC + AVC at the point where the straight line from the origin touches the total cost curve.]

73. Obtain the short-run average variable cost curve as implied by the modern theory of costs.
74. Derive the L-shaped long-run average variable cost curve from the short-run variable cost curve. Also obtain the corresponding LMC curve.
75. Obtain the LAC and the LMC from the respective short-run cost curves, as implied in the traditional theory of costs.
76. Given that the learning rate is 80 % and the current cost per unit of output is ₹ 10,000 for the first lot. Calculate the unit costs for the first six lots and plot the 80 % learning curve. Also explain the basic difference between the scale economies and the learning curve effect.

   [**Ans.** Unit costs per lot for the first six lots are respectively 10,000; 8000; 6400; 5120; 4096; and 3277.]
77. What is the learning curve effect? Draw a 90 % learning curve assuming that initial AC = 1000 per lot.
78. Compare the LACs as implied by the traditional and the modern theories of cost. How do the implications of the inverse J-curve differ from those of these curves? Explain with brief reference to the implications of the empirical studies.

79. What is the effect of externalities on the short-run average and marginal cost curves? Explain with the help of sketches how social cost curves with negative/positive externalities can be obtained.

[**Hint.** Externalities would lead to shifts in the average and the marginal cost curves. Treat these cost curves as private cost curves and draw the corresponding social cost curves for negative and positive externalities.]

80. Suppose that the market price is fixed at ₹ 100 per unit while the variable cost per unit is ₹ 40. Determine the break-even output when (a) the total fixed cost is ₹ 60,000, (b) the total fixed cost is ₹ 60,000 and the desired profit is ₹ 30,000. Determine the break-even turnover in each case.

[**Ans.** (a) 1000 units (b) 1500; ₹ 100,000 and ₹ 150,000 respectively.]

81. Given the equation of demand, $P = 100 - 2Q$, where the symbols have their usual meaning. Find the equations of the total revenue and the marginal revenue. Show that MR curve is twice as steep as the AR curve. Find the output at which

(a) MR = 0, (b) AR = 0.

Show that MR meets the horizontal axis at the mid-point of the intercept between the vertical axis and the AR curve. Take a line parallel to the horizontal axis and at a distance of 50 from the x-axis. Would MR bisect the intercept made on this line too between the vertical axis and the AR curve? What conclusion can you draw from it? Find the price elasticity of demand at the point where MR = 0. What is the price elasticity of demand at the point where $Q = 12.50$? Find the values of MR and AR at $Q = 12.50$. Do the answers satisfy the equation MR = AR $(1 - 1/e)$?

[**Ans.** TR = $P \times Q = (100 - 2Q) \times Q = 100 Q - 2Q^2$. MR = $d(TR)/dQ = 100 - 4Q$. Slope of MR = -4; Slope of AR = -2 {Since, AR = $100 - 2Q$}

$\therefore$ MR is twice as steep as AR curve (Figure 6.37).

(a) Now, Since MR = 0;

$$100 - 4Q = 0 \Rightarrow Q = 25$$

(b) Since AR = 0;

$$100 - 2Q = 0 \Rightarrow Q = 50.$$

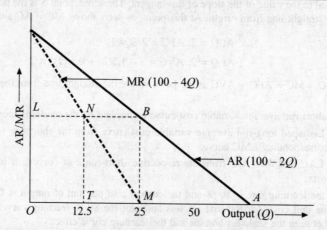

FIGURE 6.37 (Question 81) OA = 50, OM = 25; therefore, OM = 1/2 (OA). The horizontal intercept between the vertical axis and the AR curve on the x-axis is OA = 50; MR bisects it at M. The horizontal intercept between the vertical axis and the AR at a vertical distance of 50 from the x-axis is LB = 25. MR cuts it at N, and LN = 12.50. $\therefore$ LN = 1/2 LB. Thus, all horizontal intercepts between the vertical axis and the AR curve are bisected by the MR curve.

Thus, MR bisects the horizontal intercept between the origin and the point where AR = 0. A line parallel to the horizontal axis and at a distance of 50 would cut MR and AR both at the points where MR = 50 = AR.

$\therefore$ $\quad\quad\quad\quad\quad\quad\quad\quad\quad 100 - 4Q = 50$

$\Rightarrow$ $\quad\quad\quad\quad\quad\quad\quad\quad\quad Q = 12.50$ (OT);

and, $\quad\quad\quad\quad\quad\quad\quad\quad\quad 100 - 2Q = 50$

$\Rightarrow$ $\quad\quad\quad\quad\quad\quad\quad\quad\quad Q = 25$ (OM).

The price elasticity of demand where MR = 0, can be calculated by putting this value in

$$MR = AR\,(1 - 1/|e|).$$

Thus,
$$e = 1.$$

When, $Q = 12.50$, MR $= 100 - 4\,(12.50) = 50$, and AR $(P) = 100 - 2\,(12.50) = 75$

Thus, price elasticity of demand at $P = 75$ and $Q = 12.50$ is

$$|e| = |\{dQ/dP\}\,\{P/Q\}|$$
$$= |\{-1/2\}\,\{75/12.50\}|$$
$$= 3$$

Substituting MR = 50, AR = 75 and $|e| = 3$ in MR = AR $(1 - 1/|e|)$, we see that the equation is satisfied; i.e. $50 = 75\,(1 - 1/3) = 50.]$

C. Essay Type Questions

82. 'Cost curves implied by the modern theory of costs are more realistic than those implied by the traditional theories of costs.' Examine critically.
83. 'Production costs are not just what producers take into account.' Discuss.
84. 'Economies of scale never exhaust.' Examine the statement.
85. 'Linear and non-linear analyses have their own places in the real world production situations.' Discuss.
86. For a firm employing one variable factor, labour, obtain expressions for average variable and marginal costs from the expressions of the average and marginal products of the factor. Also derive the AVC and MC curves from the respective average and marginal product curves of the factor.
87. From the expression of the expansion path of a firm employing two variable factors of production, obtain an expression for the total cost. How can the total cost curve be obtained from the expansion path of the firm geometrically? Explain.
88. What are economies of scope? Define degree of scope economies and explain how production possibility curves can be used to show existence or absence of economies of scope.
89. Define cost-output elasticity and scale economy index. Show how can each be used to explain existence or absence of scale economies in production. To demonstrate your answers, take (i) AC = 20 and MC = 10, (ii) AC = MC = 15, and (iii) AC = 20 and MC = 30.

Project Work

Prepare a project on '*Bhopal Gas Tragedy of Eighties – The Social Costs of Production*'.

7

Market Forms

CHAPTER OUTLINE

Introduction
- Assumptions of Perfect Competition
- Fluctuations in Market Price and Their Effect on the Price of a Competitive Firm
- Monopoly and Its Features
- Forms and Features of Imperfect Market
- Economic Efficiency of a Market
- Key Terms and Concepts
- Exercises

INTRODUCTION

Market refers to any place or location where a product, be it a tangible commodity or an intangible service, is exchanged for money between seller(s) and buyer(s). It is a place of exchange, be it a household, a roadside, a pavement, or even a street corner that may fit into this description. The essential feature is the presence of the buyer(s) and seller(s) with an intent of exchange. Markets known for sale and purchase of particular commodities or services are generally named or known after them. Capital market, money market, stock market, car market, spare parts market, fruit market, vegetable market, etc. are a few examples. Such markets have specific locations so that buyers and sellers may get therefore a fair deal for themselves. There are markets where prices are fixed and uniform throughout and markets where such certainties don't exist. The former is called a **perfect market** while the latter, an **imperfect** one. In other words, a market where price distortions are least is a perfect or a competitive market while one, where the price distortions are common, is an imperfect market. One of the causes responsible for market imperfections is the existence of a single seller or a single buyer dictating the price. Market with a single seller is called a **monopoly** while that with a single buyer, a **monopsony**. Market with exactly two sellers is called a **duopoly**, while that with exactly two buyers, a **duopsony**. A variant of duopoly is **oligopoly** in which the number of sellers is more than two but limited to a few. Likewise, a variant of duopsony is **oligopsony** in which the number of buyers is more than two but limited to a few. A market with a large number of monopoly sellers dealing with close substitutes such as different brands of toothpastes or those of cigarettes constitute a **monopolistic market** or a **monopolistic competition**.

The word *competitive* emphasizes that we are not dealing with *monopoly* and the word *imperfect* emphasizes that we are not dealing with *perfect competition**. The markets can thus be classified as in Table 7.1.

TABLE 7.1 Classification of markets

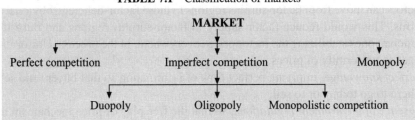

7.1 ASSUMPTIONS OF PERFECT COMPETITION

The most important feature of a competitive market is its uniformity of price. As seen in Chapter 2, price in a competitive market is determined through interaction of market forces of demand and supply. All the firms in the market adopt this price and are therefore known as **price takers**. The mechanism is demonstrated in Figure 7.1.

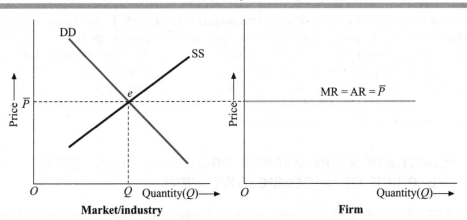

FIGURE 7.1 A competitive firm as a price taker: Demand and supply determine the market price (left panel) which every firm in the market adopts for its product (right panel). A price-taker competitive firm, thus, has a perfectly elastic demand curve for which $AR = MR = \bar{P}$.

---

*R.G. Lipsey, *An introduction to Positive Economics*, 7th ed., p. 257.

The reasons why the competitive firms feel compelled to adopt the market price would become apparent to the reader from the following features of a competitive or a perfect market.

1. *Large number of buyers and sellers*, so that no single seller or buyer may dictate the price.
2. *Homogeneity of product*, so that price may not be distorted on the grounds of visible differences among the units of the same product.
3. *Free entry and free exit*, so that the firms may move in or out of the industry in the event of deficient or excess supply. This is essential for price stability.
4. *Perfect mobility of factors of production*, so that production costs may remain unchanged. This is essential for uniformity of costs. Differences in factor prices lead to differences in production costs and hence in output prices. If factors of production are perfectly mobile, factors can move from factor-surplus regions to those factor-deficient, obviously for better terms. This would reduce factor supply in factor-surplus regions and raise it in factor-deficient ones stabilizing the factor prices everywhere, in the process. Uniformity of costs leads to uniformity of prices.
5. *Perfect knowledge*, implying perfect flow of information so that buyers and sellers know where to go to buy or to sell.
6. *Absence of government regulations*, so that the free play of price mechanism may not be obstructed by govt. regulations of tariff, subsidy, rationing, price ceilings and price floors. Most of these regulations are highly distortionary.
7. *Absence of transportation costs*, so that price may not get distorted by them in distant markets.
8. *Profit-maximization*, so that no firm chases objectives such as one of *beggar-thy-neighbour*. At times, a large firm resorts to price cuts despite losses suffered, only to oust its rivals so that it may have the entire market to itself later. A perfect firm is assumed to have no other objective than that of profit maximization.

It is not very difficult to see that a perfect competition is a myth. In real world, it is difficult to realize it. Presence of government regulations, presence of heavy transportation costs, absence of perfect knowledge and perfect mobility of factors and prevalence of the *beggar-thy-neighbour* policies—all make existence of perfect competition impossible. It is, however, possible to realize the first three requisites, namely, the large number of buyers and sellers, the homogeneity of product and the free entry and free exit in the real world. A market form possessing these three attributes is known as the **Pure Competition**.

7.2 FLUCTUATIONS IN MARKET PRICE AND THEIR EFFECT ON THE PRICE OF A COMPETITIVE FIRM

Market price refers to the price prevailing at a point of time in the market. As against this, normal price refers to a price that stretches itself over a period of time. It can be the market price that remains stable over a period of time or even an average of the fluctuating market prices over that period of time. Fluctuations in market price over a period of time are common observations. They take place due to market imperfections and get transmitted in equal measure to all the competing firms.

As mentioned in Section 7.1, a perfect competition is a myth. Even in pure competition, market price fluctuates over time due to following reasons:

(a) Shifts in demand.
(b) Shifts in supply.
(c) Government regulations.

We have discussed the three in their requisite detail in Chapter 2 but only in respect of the market/industry as a whole. We did not discuss their effects on the constituent firms there. Let us do it now.

(a) Shifts in demand

Shifts in demand are caused by shift factors, namely change in income of the consumers, change in prices of the related goods and change in tastes, preferences and fashions. A favourable change, shifts the demand curve upwards to right while an unfavourable one shifts it downwards to left (Figure 7.2). An increase or a decrease in population also leads to an upward or a downward shift in demand.

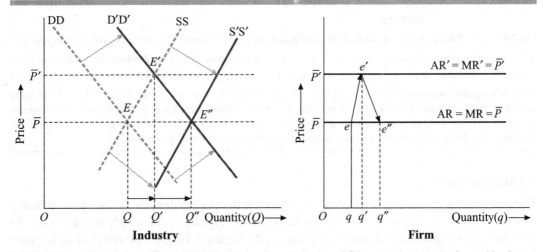

FIGURE 7.2 Effect of an upward shift in demand on the price of firms: An increase in demand leads to a rise in the market price, other things remaining unchanged. As a result, demand shifts from DD to D'D', industry equilibrium from $E(Q, \bar{P})$ to $E'(Q', \bar{P}')$ and that of a firm, from $e(q, \bar{P})$ to $e'(q', \bar{P}')$. To restore the old price, supply needs to be increased through a parallel shift in it from SS to S'S'. This shifts the industry equilibrium from $E'(Q', \bar{P}')$ to $E''(Q'', \bar{P})$ and that of a firm, from $e'(q', \bar{P}')$ to $e''(q'', \bar{P})$ as shown. As an example from the real world, when market demand for food grains rises from DD to D'D', the market price rises from $\bar{P}$ to $\bar{P}'$. To restore original price at $\bar{P}$, producers or government must increase supply. In case producers fail, government may do so through its public distribution system (PDS). Under PDS, many states resort to procuring foodgrains directly from the cultivators at the harvest time or to importing them and then distributing them through fair price shops during their scarcity. This shifts market supply curve from SS to S'S'. Alternatively, government may also influence price to some extent by introducing subsidy on the sale of scarce goods. In the former case, each fair price shop must get $(q'' - q')$ extra grains to supply and in the latter, amount of subsidy must be appropriately determined to ensure desired effect on price [Figure 2.42(d), Chapter 2].

Exactly opposite is the case when demand decreases. Figure 7.3 demonstrates the point.

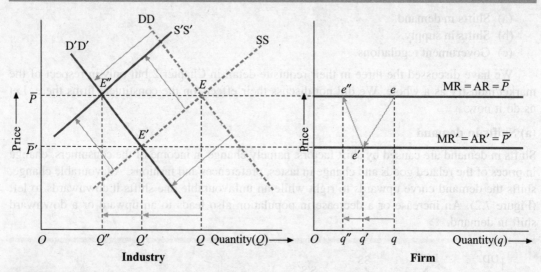

FIGURE 7.3 **Effect of a downward shift in demand on price of firms:** Downward to left shift in demand; shifts industry equilibrium from $E(Q, \bar{P})$ to $E'(Q', \bar{P}')$. In consequence, firm's equilibrium shifts from $e(q, \bar{P})$ to $e'(q', \bar{P}')$. To restore price at $\bar{P}$, an upward to left shift in supply from SS to S'S' is called for. This shifts industry's equilibrium from $E'(Q', \bar{P}')$ to $E''(Q'', \bar{P})$ and that of the firm, from $e'(q', \bar{P}')$ to $e''(q'', \bar{P})$. In order to restore price, industry must hold back quantity $Q''Q$ and a firm, quantity $q''q$. Alternatively, government must buy quantity $Q''Q$ directly from the producers. As a measure to prevent the resurgence of the problem, contractionary fiscal and monetary policies to squeeze producers credit may be introduced.

(b) Shift in supply

The effect of an increase or a decrease in supply on the price-output decisions of the industry and the firm can be explained on similar lines. Increase/decrease in supply is caused by the shift factors as explained in Section 2.7 (Chapter 2). Figure 7.4 shows the effect of an increase in supply on the price-output decisions of industry and firm while Figure 7.5 shows that of a decrease in it on them.

In Figure 7.4, industry may resort to aggressive marketing to increase demand in order to retain the original level of price. This may require influencing consumers' tastes, preferences, etc. or penetrating new market segments or even going deeper into the same market segment.

When supply decreases, the supply curve shifts upwards to left and the market price rises in consequence. To restore it back to its original level, demand needs to be decreased from DD to D'D' (Figure 7.5).

We have seen how market forces influence the price-output decisions of a competitive firm. In all the above cases, the free play of the market forces remains undisturbed so long as government does not intervene. Let us now examine how government intervention influences free play of market forces and hence price-output decisions of the industry and firms.

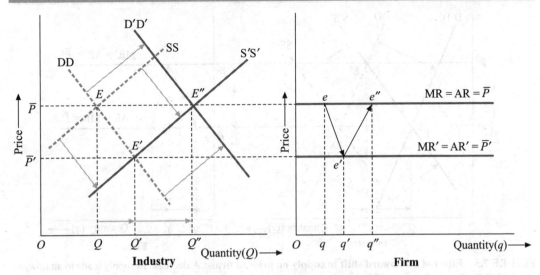

FIGURE 7.4 Effect of a downward shift in supply on the price of firms: Increase in industry supply lowers price from $\bar{P}$ to $\bar{P}'$. To restore it, demand needs to be increased, as shown, from DD to D'D'. Increase in supply shifts the industry's equilibrium from $E(Q, \bar{P})$ to $E'(Q', \bar{P}')$ and that of the firm, from $e(q, \bar{P})$ to $e'(q', \bar{P}')$. While an increase in demand from DD to D'D' shifts industry's equilibrium from $E'(Q', \bar{P}')$ to $E''(Q'', \bar{P})$ and that of the firm, from $e'(q', \bar{P}')$ to $e''(q'', \bar{P})$. As discussed in Section 2.2 (Chapter 2), an increase in demand can be brought about by suitably influencing the shift factors, such as, income of the consumers, prices of the related goods, or consumers' tastes, preferences and fashions. But, income of the consumers cannot be increased at will nor can the prices of the related goods. What can firms do on their own is to resort to aggressive marketing strategies to penetrate deeper into the market segments or to explore new market segments for the purpose. It is, however, possible that increase in supply may automatically result in an increase in consumers income in the long-run unless it is caused purely by certain technological breakthroughs. In case increase in supply is caused through additional employment of factors, income of the consumers is likely to go up in consequence. Also, government if keen on price stabilization may resort to an expansionary fiscal policy and monetary authority if striving for price stability may resort to expansionary monetary policies.

(c) Government regulations

(i) *Direct intervention:* In respect of protected industries, government often resorts to *price floors* with a view to ensure a certain minimum support price to the producers. A price floor is a price fixed by the government above the market price and is maintained at that level through deliberate action. In the process, government has to resort to purchasing the excess supply itself (Figure 7.6).

During harvests, the Indian government procures food grains at the floor-price to retain people's interest in cultivation as a source of livelihood. In India, a little over 68% of the labour force derives its livelihood from agriculture. To prevent the flight of the rural labour to the already over-populated urban areas suffering from problem of massive unemployment of the educated, it becomes imperative for the state to retain the rural workforce to the rural occupations only. Apart from this, a sound agricultural sector is needed by the State not only for self-sufficiency in production of food but also for rapid economic development of the nation.

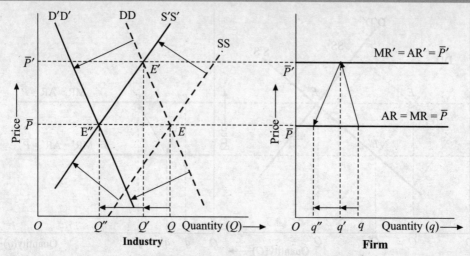

FIGURE 7.5 Effect of an upward shift in supply on price of firms: A decrease in supply leads to an upward-to-left shift in the supply curve. This increases price. In consequence, market demand drops from Q to Q'. The firm, being a price-taker, adopts the higher price and suffers a fall in its quantity from q to q'. To restore price at the original level, market demand needs to be decreased to D'D'. As a short-run measure, government must resort to contractionary fiscal policy and monetary institutions to contractionary monetary policy.

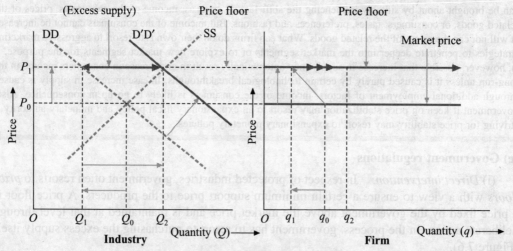

FIGURE 7.6 Effect of a price floor on a firm's price output decisions: During harvests, market price of foodgrains is P_0 which is lower than the minimum support price P_1. At P_0, quantity of foodgrains sold by the cultivators is Q_0. The procurement department of government now enters the market offering the cultivators the assured price P_1 ($P_1 > P_0$). At this price, supply of foodgrains is Q_2 while demand by private buyers is only Q_1. The resulting excess supply, $(Q_2 - Q_1)$, is bought by the procurement department at P_1. This distorts the market price. An individual seller (farmer), selling q_0 at P_0 now sells q_1 to the private buyers at P_1 and the rest of his share of the excess supply, $(q_2 - q_1)$, he sells to the procurement department of government. Here price P_1 is the floor-price, below which, market price is not allowed by government to fall.

In addition to the above, a welfare state also needs to protect the interest of common consumers against the exploitative trade practices of the intermediaries resorted to by them often during the off-season when supply of foodgrains is lean. The state has to ensure supply of essential commodities to people at fair prices during such periods. This is done by government by pegging the price of essential commodities below the market level and undertaking to supply the deficits itself. The price so fixed by government is called the *price-ceiling*. The stocks raised by the procurement department during the harvests at the price floor come handy in this regard. Procurement of foodgrains at prices remunerative enough (*through price-floors*) for the cultivators on the one hand and their distribution at prices reasonable enough (*through price-ceiling*) to the common people on the other, constitute the essential ingredients of the public distribution system (PDS) in India. Figure 7.7 demonstrates working of the price-ceiling as practised by the welfare states.

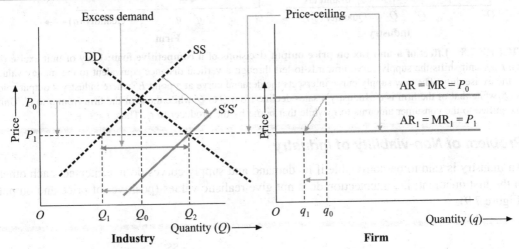

FIGURE 7.7 Effect of price ceiling on price output decisions of firms: The private sellers supply Q_0 at a price P_0 while an individual seller supplies only q_0 at this price. Now suppose the public distribution department enters the market to provide the essential commodity at P_1 ($P_1 < P_0$). This results in excess demand of ($Q_2 - Q_1$). The private sellers supply only Q_1 at P_1 while one of them may supply only q_1. The rest of the supply to meet the excess demand comes from government.

(ii) *Indirect intervention:* Price-floor and price-ceiling discussed above are examples of *direct intervention* by government in the free play of price mechanism. In addition, government resorts to some indirect methods as well to influence the market price. Such methods, called *indirect intervention*, include levy of sales-tax and excise-duty. Sales-tax is a unit tax levied at a certain percentage of the product-price on each unit sold [see Figure 2.42(b), (c), Chapter 2]. Excise-duty, on the other hand, is a unit tax levied as a fixed amount, usually a percentage of production cost, on each unit produced [Figure 2.42(a), Chapter 2]. Levy of these taxes results in an upward-to-left shift in the supply curve (see also exercises 45, 47, 60, 61, 62 and 64 of Chapter 2). Here we will briefly introduce the effect of these unit taxes on price-output decisions mainly of the firm (Figure 7.8).

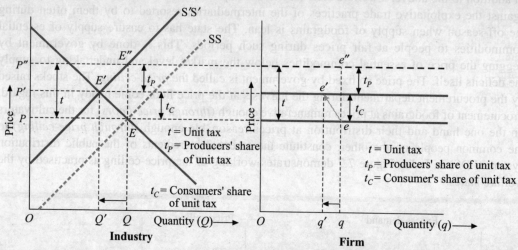

FIGURE 7.8 Effect of a unit tax on price output decisions of a competitive firm: Levy of unit excise of Rs. t per unit shifts the supply curve upwards-to-left through a vertical distance equivalent to the money value of the excise duty. The new supply curve intersects the demand curve at a point E' where industry's output sold is Q' while that of the firm is q'. Industry's sales decline from Q to Q' while those of the firm from q to q'. Unit tax shifted to the consumer amounts to t_C while that borne by the producer to t_P. Thus, $t = t_C + t_P$.

Problem of Non-viability of Industry

An industry is said to be non-viable if its demand and supply curves do not intersect each other in the first quadrant; i.e. intersection does not give realistic values (positive) of price and output (Figure 7.9).

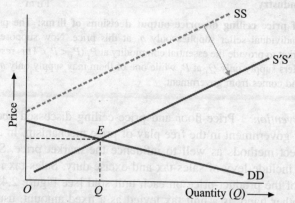

FIGURE 7.9 Problem of non-viability of a competitive industry: When demand (DD) does not intersect supply (SS) in the positive quadrant, the industry is said to be non-viable. Given the demand (DD), supply (SS) needs to be shifted downwards-to-right to make it viable. Suppose industry desires to produce and sell at least OQ quantity. It has to shift the supply SS to S'S'. This can be accomplished either through a price-cut for same quantity or through an increase in quantity supplied at the same price. Both the situations are impossible unless the production costs are slashed significantly.

Features of a Competitive Firm

A firm under perfect competition is, thus, a price-taker. It has to adopt the price fixed by the market forces of demand and supply. Its AR and MR are both horizontal and overlapping, each equal to the market price, $\overline{P}$ irrespective of the quantity transacted; that is, AR = MR = $\overline{P}$ for a competitive firm for all levels of its output.

In the long-run, a competitive firm earns normal profits by producing an output at the lowest average cost. The output of a firm corresponding to the lowest average cost is called its *optimal output* and the corresponding plant size is known as its *optimal plant size or optimal capacity*. A competitive firm always operates at its optimal capacity in the long-run.

Consumers' welfare is the highest under a competitive firm as they enjoy the highest level of consumption at lowest price.

In the light of these features, we will work out how a competitive firm takes decisions in respect of its output and price in the next chapter.

7.3 MONOPOLY AND ITS FEATURES

Monopoly is a market structure with a single seller. There exist barriers to entry of new firms in this market. The factors that lead to evolution and perpetuation of monopoly are as given below:

1. *Control over strategic raw materials:* Some firms/producers possess exclusive ownership of crucial raw materials or exclusive knowledge of production techniques. They, therefore, monopolize production of output requiring such exclusive factors. For example, countries with petroleum deposits monopolize production and supply of crude petroleum.

2. *Patent rights for a product or for a production process:* If a firm or producer develops a product or a production process of his own and gets it patented, the firm or the producer comes to possess the sole right to produce the output or to use the process in question. For example, firms producing certain brands of soft drinks, photocopiers, cigarettes, or automobiles enjoy monopoly power in production of these goods. Period for which patent rights are granted in respect of a product or process is called its *patent life*. No Goods or technologies can be imitated during their patent life by other producers.

3. *Government licensing:* If a firm or a producer is licensed to produce a product in respect of which none else has production rights, the firm or the producer comes to acquire monopoly power by virtue of the license.

4. *The size of the market:* If the market size is small so that a single producer can comfortably meet the entire demand under economical conditions, he gains monopoly power. For example, production of services such as transport, electricity and communication exhibit substantial economies of scale and require a single platform.

5. *Entry-limiting pricing policy:* A firm or a producer pursuing a limit pricing policy often prevents entry of new firms. A pricing policy such as this may be combined with aggressive advertising and product differentiation so as to make new entry unattractive. The entry-limiting price is the lowest that a monopoly can set on the upper half of the AR curve without inducing entry.

Features of Monopoly

1. As a single seller facing a large number of buyers, a monopolist is a price maker

With AR and MR distinct, each sloping downwards from left to right, a monopoly firm sets profit-maximizing price along the upper half* of its AR curve and profit maximizing output along the falling part of its AC curve. This it does at the output level where its marginal cost curve cuts its MR curve from below (the necessary and the sufficient condition for profit maximization)**.

In Section 6.5 (Chapter 6), we discussed AR and MR curves in some detail. Let us list some of the results we had arrived at:

(1) AR and MR both slope downwards
(2) MR is twice as steep as AR when AR is linear.
(3) MR bisects all the horizontal intercepts between the vertical axis and the AR-curve
(4) MR as a function of AR is given as $MR = AR(1 - 1/|e|)$.

2. A monopoly tends to restrict entry

As explained in Figure 7.10, a monopoly resorts to entry limiting price to restrict potential entrants. If needed, it also resorts to aggressive advertising to ensure brand loyalty. It does all in the line of perpetuation of its monopoly power.

3. A monopoly resorts to price discrimination

Price-discrimination is a practice of charging different prices for identical or same product from different consumers at same time in the same market or from same consumer at different times in the same market or from same consumer at same time in different markets. The first one is called the **personal discrimination**, the second, the **inter-temporal discrimination** and the third,

---

* This can be easily shown with the help of the expression for MR in terms of AR and 'e' as demonstrated below:
Since $MR \geq 0$ for a monopoly,

$AR(1 - 1/|e|) \geq 0$
$\Rightarrow \quad (1 - 1/|e|) \geq 0 \quad$ (as AR is always ≥ 0)
$\Rightarrow \quad 1 \geq 1/|e|$
$\Rightarrow \quad |e| \geq 1 \quad$ (Upper half of the AR curve)

** Profit (π) for a firm is given as
$$\pi = TR - TC$$
Differentiating π with respect to output Q, we have
$$d\pi/dQ = d(TR)/dQ - d(TC)/dQ$$
$$= MR - MC$$
As per the necessary condition of profit-maximization, the first-order derivative of π with respect to Q must be zero.
$$\therefore \quad MR = MC$$
For sufficient condition of profit-maximization,
$$d^2\pi/dQ^2 < 0$$
Differentiating once again, we have
$$d^2\pi/dQ^2 = d(MR - MC)/dQ = d(MR)/dQ - d(MC)/dQ$$
$$= \text{Slope of MR} - \text{Slope of MC}$$
For this to be negative, Slope of MR < Slope of MC; Or, MC must cut MR from below.

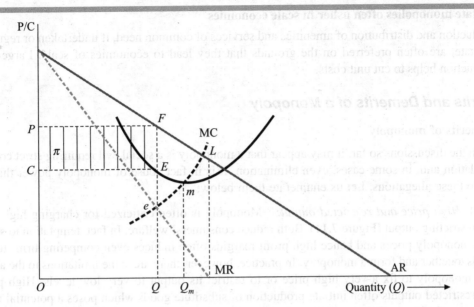

FIGURE 7.10 Entry limiting pricing policy of a monopoly: For a monopoly, AR and MR both slope downwards from left to right as shown. Profit maximization requires MC to cut MR from below. This happens at e. Corresponding output is OQ and price, QF or OP. Average cost is OE or OC. Profit earned is the area of the shaded rectangle, CEFP. Note that price set by the monopoly corresponds to the upper half of AR curve and the falling part of the AC. Optimal plant size is OQ_m which corresponds to point m of minimum average cost. A monopoly always prefers to operate a suboptimal plant, retaining what at times is referred to as its excess capacity, QQ_m. Point L on AR is the mid-point of AR. It corresponds to MR = 0. A monopoly can't set a price below point L on AR. If it does, its MR would be negative. Price corresponding to point L is the lowest price a monopoly can set. This price is termed as the entry limiting price which a monopoly sets only to bar potential entrants. New entrants would have to set a price lower than this but the same would lead to heavy losses to them due to negative MR.

the **geographical discrimination**. Monopolies, whether private, state-owned or state-regulated, invariably resort to price discrimination. Private monopolies do it for maximization of profits while state-regulated monopolies do it for recovery of costs or for regulating consumption among different uses or different individuals. Domestic and commercial uses of power are subject to different rates of tariff in India and so are different slabs in domestic consumption of power. Indian Railways charge different fares for AC and non-AC journeys. Non-AC journey is treated as basic necessity of common people and is duly subsidized while AC journey is treated as a luxury and hence duly subjected to higher fares. Another example of State discrimination is **peak-load pricing**. It implies different rates for peak hours and off-peak hours of demand.

We will study price discrimination in its requisite detail in Section 9.6 of Chapter 9.

4. Monopoly power reduces social welfare

A monopoly, if private, restricts supply and charges a higher price (Figure 7.11). This adversely affects social welfare which is much lower than what it is under competitive conditions. You will learn more about the loss of social welfare under monopoly in Section 9.4 of Chapter 9.

5. State monopolies often usher in scale economies

Production and distribution of amenities and services of common need, if undertaken or regulated by state, are often preferred on the grounds that they lead to economies of scale. Large-scale production helps to cut unit costs.

Merits and Demerits of a Monopoly

Demerits of monopoly

From the discussions so far, it may appear that a monopoly is a social evil requiring strict control, regulation and, in some cases, even elimination. It is in fact abuse of monopoly power that has led to these allegations. Let us enumerate them below:

1. *High price and restricted output:* Monopoly is often criticized for charging high price and restricting output (Figure 7.11). Both reduce consumers' welfare. In fact, temptation to secure high monopoly prices and hence high profit margins often induces even competing firms to join hands together and form a monopoly. In practice, however, there are some limitations to the ability of a monopoly to fix a very high price or to restrict its output to very low levels. High prices and restricted outputs often initiate production of substitute goods which poses a potential threat to monopoly power. The possibility of government intervention poses yet another threat to it.

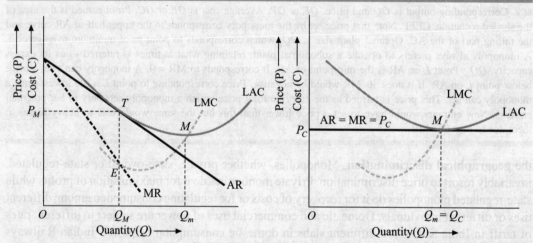

FIGURE 7.11 Monopoly charges a higher price and supplies lower quantity than a competitive firm in the long-run: Output Q_m corresponds to the lowest point, M, on the LAC in each panel. It is thus the optimal output for a monopoly (left panel) as well as for a competitive firm (right panel). The monopoly in its bid to maximize its profit produces Q_M at E where its LMC cuts its MR from below. Price set by price-maker monopoly is P_M. Thus it produces a sub-optimal output along the falling part of its LAC. As against this, a competitive firm maximizes its profit at M where its LMC cuts its MR from below. Corresponding output is Q_C and price, P_C. Evidently, $Q_m = Q_C$, implying that the competitive firm produces at its optimal level. Monopoly output Q_M is less than the competitive output Q_C while monopoly price P_M is higher than the competitive price P_C. This shows that consumers are better off with a competitive firm than with a monopoly.

2. *Biased Allocation of Economic Resources:* The profit intent of the monopoly firms leads them to produce luxury goods that yield high profit margins. Production of such goods is generally high-tech to which smaller competitive firms lack access. In absence of competitors, the monopoly succeeds in sustaining monopoly power which enables it to fix a high price for its product by restricting its supply. It also succeeds in restricting factor employment thereby factor prices above their competitive rates. In other words, a monopoly leads to a general distortion of distribution and allocation of resources.

3. *Discouraging the Technological Progress:* Generally all monopolies shy away from spending on research and development. Most of them rather try their best to abandon development of new technology so that they may avoid heavy investment on it. If a monopoly opts for advanced technology, it does so only with a view to bar entry to new firms. Here, the objective is to sustain monopoly power.

4. *Unfair Trade Practices:* A monopoly resorts to all sorts of unfair practices to oust its rivals. It may indulge in a cut-throat-competition with them including pricing below the production cost if it helps in throwing the rivals out or forcing them to merge with it. For instantce, the trust companies frequently resort to fixing ridiculously low prices with a view to force rivals either to quit or to merge with the trust companies. As soon as the purpose is served, the trust companies revert back to high price and make good the loss suffered by them in the process. A case of unfair trade practices can be cited from the past. It relates to a system of secret rebates in freight charges an American trust company availed from the railway companies by threatening them not to patronize them if such rebates were not granted. The railway companies yielded under compulsion and the trust company gained an edge over its rivals who soon ran out of steam paying higher freight charges. The trust company enjoyed the fruits of fixing lower prices due to its lower costs of transportation. A number of countries, including India, now have an anti-trust legislation to deal with such unfair trade practices. The MRTP Act of 1969 in India is such a legislation enacted to permit only those mergers, acquisitions and trade practices that increase efficiency and prevent those that enhance the monopoly power of the trust companies.

5. *Exploitation of Corrupt System:* There are many instances from the US to support that monopolies bribe corrupt legislators to prevent passing of legislation against their unfair trade practices and many more to support that they brive even judges to interpret the anti trust laws favourably. Monopolies, even elsewhere, are not far behind in exploiting the corrupt politicians and judges in availing special favours to strengthen their monopoly power. Influencing political parties by making substancial contributions to their election-funds is a common practice in most of the democracies. The obliged political parties reciprocate the favours as soon as they resume power. They come out with such economic policies that benefit the monopolies at least during the tenure of their regime.

Anti-trust-legislation, however strict, proves to little consequence at times due to such manipulative potential of the monopoly firms.

Merits of monopoly

Before we get carried away with some of the negative features of the monopoly, let us look at its positive features also. A monopoly possesses the following merits:

1. *Potential to stand depression:* Due to its extensive financial resources, a monopoly firm can survive the shocks of falling prices and consequential losses, which, to small-sized competitive firms, prove fatal during the period of depression. Small competitive firms close down due to

losses while a monopoly firm not only fares through them but even succeeds in maintaining the price level too.

2. *Potential for research and development:* Due to its large financial resources, a monopoly can introduce any type of invention or improved technology which it deems crucial for its commercial success. On the contrary, small competitive firms turn commercially non-viable due to their inability to afford the technological innovations.

3. *Potential to face foreign competition:* A large monopoly is capable to compete with foreign firms mainly because of its scale economies resulting from its large-scale operations. It is for this reason that many European countries encourage formation of cartels and syndicates. Small competitive firms suffer from diseconomies and hence, fail to face foreign competition.

4. *As a remedy to unhealthy competition:* Many industries consist of a large number of inefficient firms indulging in unhealthy competition. Combining these firms into one, often leads to eliminate inefficiency, reduce costs and widen the markets through intelligent advertising.

5. *As a source of essential public utilities:* Industries producing essential goods and services need to operate on large-scale so that enough is produced to suffice the needs of the people at fair and uniform prices. Such industries require huge capital investment and hence are often state managed. Examples are public transport, power generation, water supply, communication and the like. They are all state monopolies. All operate on large-scale so that they may avail the benefits of scale economies and may provide basic amenities at fair and uniform price.

7.4 FORMS AND FEATURES OF IMPERFECT MARKET

Literally speaking, it should refer to a market form that is not perfect. Having had an idea of what a perfect market is, can we now define an imperfect market? Alright, let us try. An imperfect market must then be one that has features exactly opposite of a perfect market. If we list the features that way, we must get the features of an imperfect market. But, that is not true. An imperfect market, too, has a large number of buyers and in some forms of it, a large number of sellers as well (the monopolistic and the oligopolistic forms, for instance). The product, in an imperfect market, is neither non-homogeneous nor homogeneous. Instead, it consists of close substitutes standardized or non-standardized. In some forms of the imperfect market, even entry and exit are not barred! The conclusion is that the imperfect market is not the opposite of a perfect market in its literal sense. Instead, some of its features resemble the features of the perfect market itself. Then why do we call it an imperfect market? The basic reason is that the firms in the imperfect market have downward sloping AR and MR curves just as monopolies do. That is, like monopoly firms, firms in an imperfect market are price-makers rather than price-takers. But, we can't classify it even as a monopoly because there exist more than one seller in it. Thus, an imperfect market is neither opposite of a perfect market nor similar to a monopoly. It is simply a real world market structure that has some features of a perfect market and some of a monopoly.

It is often seen in three forms:

1. Duopoly

When there are exactly *two sellers* dealing in intrinsically identical but externally differentiated products, the market form is called **duopoly**. The external differentiation refers to the difference of looks caused by packaging, brand name or by external design. Intrinsically, products are the same or very close substitutes. Two brands of mineral water or unbranded mineral water sold by two sellers provides an example of a duopoly. Until very recently, the automobile industry in India was a duopoly. There were only two car-brands—the Ambassador and the Fiat. The vehicles possessed external as well as internal differences but served as close substitutes. The external differences related to the design and looks of the vehicles while the internal differences were those relating to fuel economy, engine-power, etc. Yet, the two formed close substitutes so long as their utility was concerned. However, both behaved like rivals. If one lowered the price, the other followed but if one raised the price the other did not. The degree of interdependence was very high. Duopoly often starts with price wars and ends up in a price-collusion. Action and reaction in respect of price and quantity supplied are common features. Price wars in between, however, do not lead to uncertainty or indeterminacy of equilibrium which is eventually reached despite action–reaction chain perpetuating the cut-throat competition between the two.

You will study the process of attainment of equilibrium in a later chapter (Chapter 11) through the models of Cournot, Edgeworth, Chamberlin, Sweezy and Baumol.

2. Oligopoly

When number of sellers is more than two but limited to a few, the market structure is referred to as an Oligopoly. Literally it means a few sellers. Some economists fix the number anywhere between 3 and 6 but there is no hard and fast rule in this regard. The market structure is characterized by high degree of interdependence, price wars or cartels with price leaderships, aggressive marketing methods and a fair degree of monopoly power. Oligopoly is classified as open or closed depending on existence or non-existence of entry of new firms. It is also classified as a pure oligopoly or a differentiated one depending on the nature of products whether they are homogeneous or differentiated. Petroleum industry is an example of pure oligopoly while automobile industry, that of a differentiated one.

There is yet another classification of oligopoly. This is of collisive oligopoly and collusive oligopoly. It is a collisive oligopoly if price wars persist and a collusive oligopoly if cartels get formed.

3. Monopolistic competition

Monopolistic competition is a market structure with large number of buyers and sellers dealing with externally differentiated close substitutes. Each seller acts like a monopoly to his loyalist buyers. Product differentiation being generally external–caused by packaging, external looks, or simply by brand positioning. Products are close substitutes of each other internally. Firms in monopolistic competition incur huge advertising or selling costs in order to position their products vis-à-vis other competing firms. The basic purpose of such advertising is to lure the consumers away from the competing brands by making them believe that the brand used by them is superior to other brands. That is why such advertising is sometimes referred to as *persuasive advertising*. Through it, the advertiser attempts to retain its market share. Another feature of the monopolistically competitive market is the existence of free entry and free exit which ensure only normal profits to the firms in the long-run. The abnormal profits of the short-run are driven to zero due to free entry. Likewise, short-run loss is also driven to zero due to free exit of firms. Price is greater than LMC but equal to LAC in the long-run. Examples of the monopolistic competition are provided by toothpaste and cigarette manufacturers. There is a high degree of brand loyalty among consumers. It is this loyalty that is exploited by a monopolistically competitive firm like a monopoly.

7.5 ECONOMIC EFFICIENCY OF A MARKET

To some economists, a market structure is economically efficient if it attempts **maximization of aggregate consumer and producer surpluses**. The reference here is to those who believe in positive economics. To them, all regulatory policies of government reduce economic efficiency of a free market by *obstructing* free-play of price-mechanism and hence by *reducing* aggregate consumer and producer surpluses. If we go by this criteria, regulatory measures of government restricting production and consumption of country-made liquor would affect economic efficiency of the market adversely by reducing aggregate consumer and producer surpluses. That way, restrictions on production and consumption of polluting chemicals would also have identical effects on economic efficiency of the market. There are a number of measures of government discussed in Chapter 2 that reduce aggregate consumer and producer surpluses and hence affect economic efficiency of the market adversely. Why then such measures are introduced? The answer to the question is not very difficult to seek. Welfare States introduce such regulatory measures for maximization of social welfare. Should not then the criterion of economic efficiency of a market be **maximization of aggregate social welfare** rather than **maximization of consumer and producer surpluses**? Even the latter aims at maximization of social welfare though of only certain segments of the society. *A more appropriate measure of economic efficiency of a market therefore is maximization of aggregate social welfare rather than of aggregate consumer and producer surpluses.* In respect of goods production and consumption of which cause no harm to any segment of the society or tend to maximize aggregate social welfare, a welfare state must leave free-play of market mechanism alone and it most often also does. State intervention takes place only when increase in aggregate consumer and producer surpluses fail to offset the decrease in social welfare caused by distortionary allocations or by their harmful effects such as pollution. Note that the concept of **maximization of aggregate social welfare** implies maximization of the excess of increase over decrease in social welfare. That way, production and consumption of even harmful products or their regulation by government would boost market efficiency if their positive effects offset their negative effects so that the net effect on aggregate social welfare is positive or at least zero.

In Chapter 2, we saw how government intervention in free play of price mechanism, if half-hearted, leads to loss of social welfare. It would be in order to review instances of price ceiling (Figure 2.41), price floor (Figure 2.40), specific unit excise (Figure 2.42a), subsidy (Figure 2.42d) and those of import tariff (Figures 2.44 to 2.46) that demonstrate how these policies of direct or indirect government intervention in the free play of market mechanism result in loss of social welfare *unless* appropriate remedial measures also accompany them. For instance, policy of price control (price-ceiling) may lead to emergence of a black market (Figure 2.41) causing deadweight loss *unless* government provides a back-up to its policy by supplying the excess demand so caused from its own sources. Price ceiling in India is supported by government through its system of public distribution channellized through fair price shops. In like manner, the price floors are supported by Indian government through its procurement system. Government of India does it on purpose of protecting the weaker sections of society against exploitative trade practices of intermediaries who purchase corn from the cultivators at the harvest-time at lower prices and sell it later when its price is high during its scarcity [see Chapter 2 for functioning of Public Distribution System (PDS)].

Policies of intervention, such as these, as executed by the State, are external to the market. When introduced, they cost the society significantly in terms of social welfare *unless* government executes them whole-heartedly. Cost of half-hearted policies, the loss of social welfare, is an **externality** that reduces efficiency of a competitive market. For the sake of efficient operation of the competitive market, the State must leave the market alone *unless* it is prepared to execute its policy strictly and whole heartedly.

Another factor that affects economic efficiency of a market adversely is **existence of asymmetric information** caused by **imperfect knowledge** and **failure of price-signalling**. The factor leads to market failure. Asymmetric information refers unequal knowledge about the product or its price among the buyers and sellers. Price-signalling refers to providing of signals by the price-leaders to buyers and sellers to finalize their buying and selling decisions.

For detailed treatment of social welfare maximization and efficiencies of exchange and resource allocation, see Chapter 16; for that of market failure due to asymmetric information, see Chapter 17 and that due to externality and public goods, see Chapter 18 of this text.

Discussion on efficiency of market has been included here because no discussion on markets is ever complete if it doesn't incorporate this aspects.

KEY TERMS AND CONCEPTS

Antitrust laws   Refer to rules and regulations that prohibit or restrain competition or tend to do so. MRTP Act in India is an Indian version of the antitrust legislation.

Competitive firm   A firm which is not a monopoly.

Direct intervention   It refers to direct government action to regulate price in the market through the instruments of price ceiling and price floor. It necessitates government involvement in sale and purchase of the product in the market.

Duopoly   A form of imperfect market in which there are just two sellers.

Features of duopoly   The market form has the following features:

1. Two sellers and a large number of buyers.
2. The products are close substitutes with external differentiation or they are identical ones.
3. Both are price makers operating like rivals with action—reaction games until they settle down in eventual equilibrium.
4. Entry is unattractive due to price wars and cut throat competitions.

Duopsony   A market form with exactly two buyers.

Excess demand   It refers to the excess of the quantity demanded over that supplied when price set is lower than the market clearing price.

Excess supply   It refers to the excess of quantity supplied over that demanded when price set is higher than the market-clearing price (market price).

Factors responsible for the monopoly power   The monopoly power evolves and perpetuates due to the following attributes:

1. Control possessed over strategic raw materials and exclusive knowledge of production techniques.
2. Patent rights owned for a product or production process.
3. Government licensing under trade barriers.
4. Size of the market.
5. Existence of entry limiting pricing.

Features of perfect competition The basic feature of the perfect competition is the uniformity of the market price throughout the market. To ensure this, a perfect market is assumed to possess the following features:

1. Large number of the buyers and the sellers.
2. Homogeneity of the product.
3. Free entry and exit.
4. Absence of transportation costs.
5. Absence of barriers.
6. Perfect knowledge.
7. Perfect mobility.
8. Profit maximization.

Indirect intervention It refers to government policy to give a desired tilt in market price through indirect methods such as levy of excise duty. Levy of such unit taxes leads to an upward-to-left shift in supply curve by the amount of tax levied per unit of the product. This results in sharing of the levy between consumers and producers in proportions depending on the relative price elasticities of demand and supply.

Market A place where goods and services are exchanged for money.

Imperfect market A form of market which is neither perfect nor a monopoly. In other words, it is a real world market structure in which some features of a perfect market and some of a monopoly are simultaneously present. Price is neither fixed nor uniform despite the presence of more than one seller.

Perfect market A form of market structure in which product price is uniform throughout the market. Every firm or seller in it is a price taker.

Monopolistic competition A form of imperfect market with many sellers each of whom acts like a price maker or a monopoly.

Feature of monopolistic competition It is a form of imperfect market possessing the following attributes:

1. Existence of large number of buyers and sellers.
2. Existence of externally differentiated, but internally identical products.
3. Existence of sellers each of whom acts as a price maker
4. Existence of free entry and exit.
5. Existence of high selling cost.

Monopoly A market form in which there is only one seller who is a price maker.

Demerits of monopoly A monopoly possesses a number of demerits, known as abuses of monopoly. Some of them are listed below:

1. Monopoly firms restrict supplies and charge a higher price.
2. They cause biased allocation of economic resources.
3. They discourage technology development.
4. They indulge in unfair trade practices.
5. They exploit the corrupt system for their advantage.

Features of monopoly A monopoly is characterized by the following features:

1. A single seller and a large number of buyers.
2. The single seller is a price maker with downward sloping AR and MR. The single seller fixes its price on the upper-half of the AR curve and produces along the falling part of AC curve. This helps monopoly to ensure an excess capacity for itself.
3. There exist barriers to entry of new firms.

4. Price discrimination is a common practice employed either to maximize profits (the case with private monopolies) or to recover the production costs or to regulate consumption (the case with government monopolies).

Merits of monopoly Despite exploitative nature of monopoly, it is true that a private monopoly if decent or a government monopoly in general can prove highly advantageous for the economy. Some of the merits of such monopolies are listed below:

1. Only a monopoly has the potential to stand depression.
2. Only a monopoly has the resources and the potential for research and development.
3. Due to its huge resources and scale economies, only a monopoly can face foreign competition.
4. Only a monopoly can check unhealthy competition that is so common among small competitive firms. This can be done through merging the inefficient competitive units together.
5. It is of common knowledge that monopoly alone is a potential source of public utilities. The best example is that of the State Electricity Boards in India that have not only survived the competition from the multinational giants but have also maintained supply of electricity at much lower rates despite common evils of pilferage, misuse and political interference.

Monopsony A market form with only one buyer.

Oligopoly A form of imperfect market in which there are a few (more than two) sellers.

Features of oligopoly The market form is an extension of duopoly and has the following features:

1. Few sellers (3 to 6) and a large number of buyers.
2. Products are either homogeneous or close substitutes with external differentiation.
3. All the firms are price makers with downward sloping AR curves.
4. Entry is unattractive due to price wars and cut throat competitions. Prices tend to be rigid or sticky once equilibrium is reached. Oligopoly often ends up in price leadership cartels.
5. A high degree of interdependence.

Oligopsony A market form with a few (more than two) buyers.

Price ceiling A price fixed by government with a view to protect the interests of the common consumers against higher prices prevailing in the market during its scarcity. As a back-up to the price-ceiling policy, government undertakes to supply the product at this price through fair price shops.

Procurement of foodgrains at the price floor and their distribution at the ceiling price form two essential components of the *Public Distribution System* (PDS) In India.

Price discrimination A practice of charging different prices for identical or same products by a monopoly from different individuals, at different times or in different regions. Private monopolies resort to it to maximize profits while government monopolies, to recover costs or to regulate consumption.

Price floor A price fixed by state with a view to ensure a certain minimum to producers to retain their interest in production. It is always over and above the prevailing market price. The *Minimum Support Price* guaranteed by government of India to the cultivators provides its example. As a back-up to the price-floor, government undertakes to purchase the product at this price through its procurement departments.

Price-maker A firm which fixes price of its own product.

Price-taker A firm which adopts the price fixed by market forces of demand and supply.

Pure competition A form of perfect market which has only first three features of it, namely large number of buyers and sellers, homogeneous product and free entry and exit. It is the realistic form of the perfect market.

Features of pure competition It is a form of perfect competition in which only first three features of it exist, namely

1. Large number of buyers and sellers,
2. Homogeneity of product and
3. Free entry and free exit.

EXERCISES

A. Short Answer Questions

Define the following: (1 through 20)

1. Market
2. Competitive firm
3. Monopoly
4. Perfect competition
5. Pure competition
6. Imperfect market
7. Monopsony
8. Duopoly
9. Oligopoly
10. Duopsony
11. Oligopsony
12. Monopolistic competition
13. Price floor
14. Price ceiling
15. Excess supply
16. Excess demand
17. Price taker
18. Price-maker
19. Patent rights
20. Patent life
21. Mention the features of pure competition.
22. What is meant by product differentiation?
23. How are the AR, MR and the price elasticity of demand interrelated?
24. A monopoly has estimated a price of 12 per unit for its profit maximization. It has so far sold 100 units. What should be the MR of the 101st unit if the price elasticity of demand is known to be 3 numerically?
    [Ans. 8.]
25. What is a non-viable industry? Draw a rough sketch to show why it is not viable?
26. How do the following affect the equilibrium price and quantity?
    (a) Rise in price of the substitute good.
    (b) Increase in the price of an input.
    (c) Introduction of a cost-saving technology.
    (d) Levy of excise on a commodity.
    (e) An increase in the excise rate.
    (f) A favourable change in the tastes of consumers.
27. When will each of the following imply a rise/fall in price without a change in quantity demanded/supplied?
    (a) An increase in demand.
    (b) A decrease in demand.
    (c) An increase in supply.
    (d) A decrease in supply.

[**Ans.** (a) When the supply curve is perfectly inelastic.
(b) When the supply curve is perfectly inelastic.
(c) When the demand curve is perfectly inelastic.
(d) When the demand curve is perfectly inelastic.]

28. When will each of the following imply an increase in quantity demanded/supplied without a change in price?
    (a) An increase in supply.
    (b) An increase in demand.
    [**Ans.** (a) When demand is perfectly elastic.
    (b) When supply is perfectly elastic.]
29. Suppose demand for a product increases. This raises the price of the product. What should the government do to restore the original price?
30. How will each of the following influence the market price of the product in question?
    (a) Increase in income of the consumers.
    (b) A fall in production of wheat due to failure of rains.
    (c) Import of wheat.
    (d) Export of onions.
    (e) Discovery of huge petroleum deposits under the land surface in India.
    (f) Entry of a foreign player in the domestic market with cheaper telephone instruments assuming that India does not levy any tariff on the product.
    (g) Entry of a foreign player in the domestic market with cheaper telephone instruments assuming that India levies enough tariff to protect domestic industry.
    [**Ans.** (a) Price would rise due to an upward to right shift in the demand curve.
    (b) Price would go up due to an upward to left shift in the supply curve.
    (c) Price would come down due to a downward to right shift in the supply curve.
    (d) Price would go up due to an upward to left shift in the supply curve.
    (e) Price would come down due to a downward to right shift in the supply curve.
    (f) Price would come down due to a downward to right shift in the supply curve.
    (g) No effect on price, because tariff levied would raise the price of foreign telephones to the domestic level or above.]
31. Mention the three forms of an imperfectly competitive market.
32. Define Break Even Price.
33. Show that the break–even price is always equal to the marginal cost for a competitive firm.
34. What features are common to the pure competition and the perfect competition? What features of the monopolistic competition resemble with those of the perfect competition?
35. What features of the monopolistic competition resemble those of the monopoly?
36. In what respects does a monopoly differ from a competitive firm?
37. What are selling costs? What is persuasive advertising? What is their main objective?
38. Give two examples of monopolistically competitive industry.
39. What are the conditions of long-run equilibrium of monopolistically competitive industry?
    [**Ans.** LMC must cut MR from below.]
40. Why is the demand curve of the monopolistically competitive firm more elastic than that of a monopoly?
    [**Ans.** This is so because the products are close substitutes and the action of one firm to lower the price is followed by the other firms. As a result, the demand curve of the monopolistically competitive firms becomes flatter.]
41. Explain how merger of smaller firms into a larger one proves more efficient?
    [**Hint.** It is so due to the economies of scale that accrue to a larger firm.]

B. Long Answer Questions

42. Outline features of perfect competition that make it a myth.
43. Distinguish between perfect competition and pure competition. Which of the two is unrealistic?
44. Compare perfect competition with monopolistic competition in respect of their features.
45. Distinguish between duopoly and oligopoly in respect of their features.
46. The demand curve faced by a monopoly is given as:

$$P = 100 - 2Q$$

Find equations of total and marginal revenues. Show that MR curve is twice as steep as AR curve. Find the level of output at which
   (a) MR = 0,
   (b) AR = 0.

Show that MR meets the horizontal axis at the mid-point of the intercept between the vertical axis and AR curve. Further, take a line parallel to the horizontal axis at a distance of 50 from it. Would MR bisect the intercept made on this line too by the vertical axis and AR curve? What conclusion can you draw from it? Find the price elasticity of demand at the point where MR = 0. Also, calculate the price elasticity of demand as well as MR and AR at $Q = 12.50$? Do the answers satisfy the equation MR = AR $(1 - 1/e)$?

[Ans.
$$TR = P \times Q = (100 - 2Q) \times Q = 100Q - 2Q^2$$
$$MR = d(TR)/dQ = 100 - 4Q$$

Its slope = -4; Slope of AR = slope of the demand curve = -2
∴ MR is twice as steep as AR.
Now, Since   AR = 0; $100 - 2Q = 0 \Rightarrow Q = 50$.
and   MR = 0 $\Rightarrow 100 - 4Q = 0 \Rightarrow Q = 25$.

Thus, MR bisects the horizontal intercept between the origin and the point where AR = 0 (Refer to Figure 7.12). A line parallel to the horizontal axis and at a distance of 50 would cut MR and AR both at the points where MR = 50 and AR = 50
∴ $100 - 4Q = 50 \Rightarrow Q = 12.50$; and, $100 - 2Q = 50 \Rightarrow Q = 25$.

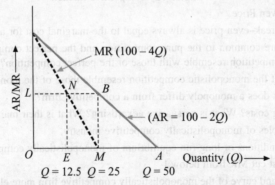

FIGURE 7.12 (Question 46) $OA = 50$, $OM = 25$; ∴ $OM = 1/2(OA)$. The horizontal intercept between the vertical axis and AR curve on the x-axis is $OA = 50$; MR bisects it at M. The horizontal intercept between the vertical axis and AR at a vertical distance of 50 is $LB = 25$. MR cuts it at N, and $LN = 12.50$. ∴ $LN = 1/2 LB$. Thus, all horizontal intercepts between the vertical axis and the AR curve are bisected by the MR.

The price elasticity of demand where MR = 0, can be calculated by putting this value in MR = AR $(1 - 1/e)$. Thus, $e = 1$.

When, $Q = 12.50$, MR = $100 - 4 (12.50) = 50$, and AR = $100 - 2 (12.50) = 75 = P$
Thus, price elasticity of demand at $P = 75$ and $Q = 12.50$ is

$$e = |\{dQ/dP\} \{P/Q\}|$$
$$= |\{-1/2\} \{75/12.50\}|$$
$$= 3$$

Substituting MR = 50, AR = 75 and $e = 3$ in MR = AR $(1 - 1/e)$, we see that the equation is satisfied; i.e. $50 = 75 (1 - 1/3) = 50$.]

47. What is meant by anti-trust legislation? Why has this legislation been enacted by so many countries? In what form does it exist in India?

C. Essay Type Questions

48. Show that the burden of unit excise on consumers is related inversely with the price elasticity of demand and directly with the price elasticity of supply while that on producers is related directly with the price elasticity of demand and inversely with the price elasticity of supply.

    [**Hint.** Refer to Q. 49 and 50 (Chapter 2).]

49. 'All monopolies—whether private or state-owned or regulated—are bad.' Examine the statement in the light of merits and demerits of a monopoly.

50. Explain the functioning of the public distribution system (PDS). It is said to be unfair because of its interference with free play of price mechanism. Discuss.

51. 'A monopoly stands not only for unfair trade practices, but also for inducing corruption.' Do you agree? Give reasons in support of your answer.

52. Explain the factors responsible for evolution and perpetuation of monopoly power. Would you recommend takeover of private monopolies by government? Why? Why not? Explain.

8

Price-output Decisions of a Firm under Perfect Competition

CHAPTER OUTLINE

Introduction
- Price-output Decisions of a Competitive Firm in the Short-run
- Price-output Decisions of a Competitive Firm in the Long-run
- Dynamic Changes and Industry Equilibrium
- Important Observations about Competitive Market
- Key Terms and Concepts
- Exercises

INTRODUCTION

We have seen in Chapter 7 that the basic goal of every firm, whether competitive or monopoly, is maximization of profit. We have also seen that profit (π) represents excess of total revenue (TR) over total cost (TC), i.e.

$$\pi = \text{TR} - \text{TC} \tag{8.1}$$

For an economist, profit is *abnormal* or *supernormal* when $\pi > 0$ and *normal* when $\pi = 0$. A firm is said to be earning normal profits when its TR is equal to its TC. The latter, TC, refers to the sum of explicit and implicit costs. This is the economist's version (Chapter 6). Profit, to an economist, means excess of TR over the sum of the explicit and implicit costs. To an accountant, TC refers only to the explicit costs. Thus, to an accountant, profit means excess of TR over the explicit costs only. The distinction between the accountant's and the economist's versions of profit can thus be understood from the relationship derived on next page:

Economist's profit = TR − (explicit cost + implicit cost)

= TR − explicit cost − implicit cost

= Accountant's profit − implicit cost.

Economist's and accountant's profits are also known as *economic* and *accounting profits* respectively.

Evidently, accountant's concept of profit overestimates it by as much as is the magnitude of the implicit costs. Alternatively, economist's concept of profit underestimates it by the same magnitude in relation to the accountant's concept. Of the two, economist's concept is more logical as it treats entrepreneur as a provider of factors for which he or she deserves compensation just as other factors do. Firm being an independent entity, it has to compensate all the factors for their contributions to production. For an economist, it is thus firm's profit, rather economic profit, that matters. Even the accounting concept treats a firm as a separate entity but when it comes to preparing the balance sheet. It is only the explicit costs that appear on the cost-side. The difference of receipts over costs gives what the accounting concept calls *gross profit*. The firm and the entrepreneur both appear as one entity at this stage. It is only the *profit and loss account* that treats the implicit costs as costs. Deducting them from the gross profit, it terms the residue obtained as *net profit*. Gross and net profits are thus alien concepts in economics. Nevertheless, net profit of accounting concept can be treated as the economic profit, as evident from this discussion.

The following identities sum up the discussion:

> Economic profit = TR − TC
> = TR − explicit cost − implicit cost
> = Accounting profit − implicit cost
> = Gross profit − implicit cost
> = Net profit
> Implicit cost = Rent on land and building + interest on capital + wages of management + depreciation charges + insurance charges

As stated earlier, we are concerned with the economist's concept of profit. Before returning to Eq. (8.1) for maximization of profit, let us recall that total revenue is the product of output and price, irrespective of whether the price is constant as in case of a competitive firm or variable as in case of a monopoly.

Now, differentiating π with respect to Q, we have

$$d\pi/dQ = d(TR)/dQ - d(TC)/dQ$$
$$= MR - MC \qquad (8.2)$$

As per the necessary condition of maximization, the first order derivative of π with respect to Q must vanish, i.e.

$$d\pi/dQ = 0 \qquad (8.3)$$

From Eqs. (8.2) and (8.3), we have

$$MR - MC = 0$$

$\Rightarrow$
$$MR = MC \qquad (8.4)$$

Equation (8.4) spells the necessary condition for profit maximization. The condition, however, is not a sufficient one. From calculus we know that first-order derivative must vanish for all stationary points. That way, condition (8.4) is a necessary condition even for the minimization of π. For maximization, the sufficient condition is the negativity of the second-order derivative of π with respect to Q at the point where the first-order derivative vanishes.

Differentiating Eq. (8.2) with respect to Q, we have

$$d^2\pi/dQ^2 = d(MR)/dQ - d(MC)/dQ$$
$$= \text{Slope of MR} - \text{Slope of MC}$$

This should be negative for maximization at the point where the first-order derivative vanishes. Thus,

$$\text{Slope of MR} - \text{Slope of MC} < 0$$

Or, $\qquad\qquad\qquad$ Slope of MR < Slope of MC $\qquad\qquad\qquad$ (8.5)

Equation (8.5) spells the sufficient condition for profit maximization. In simple terms *the necessary and sufficient conditions for maximization of profit imply that MC must cut MR from below*. The conditions are equally applicable to each and every profit maximizing firm irrespective of whether it is a competitive firm or a monopoly or an imperfect firm. Figures 8.1 and 8.2 demonstrate their applicability to a competitive firm and to a monopoly respectively.

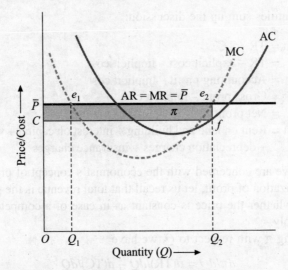

FIGURE 8.1 Competitive firm—a possibility for its equilibrium: For a price-taker competitive firm, $AR = MR = \bar{P}$ is a horizontal line, cut by the MC curve at e_1 from above and at e_2 from below. Point e_2 is the point of profit maximization (equilibrium), satisfying both the conditions. Shaded rectangle represents abnormal profit accruing to the competitive firm.

In both the figures, MC = MR at points e_1 and e_2, but slope of MR is less than that of MC only at e_2 in each. Hence, point e_2 is the point of equilibrium in each as MC cuts MR from below at this point.

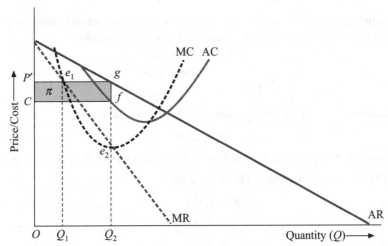

FIGURE 8.2 Monopoly—a possibility for its equilibrium: For a price maker monopoly, AR and MR both slope downward with MR keeping below AR. MC cuts MR at e_1 from above and at e_2 from below. Point e_2 is the point of profit maximization (equilibrium), satisfying both the conditions. Shaded rectangle represents abnormal profit accruing to the monopoly firm.

Profit per unit of output can be obtained by dividing on both the sides of Eq. (8.1) by Q. Thus,

$$\pi/Q = TR/Q - TC/Q$$

∴ Average profit = AR − AC (8.6)

From the discussions above, it is clear that *profit maximizing output is determined at the point where MC cuts MR from below and the profit-maximizing price is determined at the point at which the vertical line through the profit-maximizing output cuts the AR curve. Profit per unit of output is the excess of AR over AC at the profit-maximizing output.*

Profit per unit for a competitive firm (Figure 8.1) is '$e_2 f$' and that for a monopoly (Figure 8.2) is 'gf'. Let us construct a numerical illustration.

ILLUSTRATION 8.1: Given the market demand as

$$Q = 5000 - 10P,$$

the market supply as

$$Q = 10P,$$

and the total cost of a firm in the market, as

$$TC = 5000 + 750q - 30q^2 + (1/3)q^3;$$

where q is equilibrium level of output of a firm.
determine
(a) The market price.
(b) The AR and MR curves of the firm.
(c) The profit-maximizing price and output of the firm.
(d) Profit earned by the firm.
(e) Draw a rough sketch and mark off the equilibrium price and output and the profit earned by the firm.

Solution:

(a) Market price is determined at the point where market demand and market supply intersect. Thus, at the point where quantity demanded = quantity supplied,

$$5000 - 10P = 10P$$

$$\Rightarrow \qquad 20P = 5000$$

$$\Rightarrow \qquad P = 250$$

Substituting in the equation of demand or supply, we have

$$q = 2500.$$

(b) Since the firm is one of the firms selling at the price fixed by the market, it is a competitive firm. Price $P = \bar{P}$. Therefore, TR $= \bar{P} \times q$ and

$$\text{AR} = \text{TR}/q$$
$$= \bar{P} \times q/q$$
$$= \bar{P}$$
$$\text{MR} = d(\text{TR})/dq$$
$$= d(\bar{P} \times q)/dq$$
$$= \bar{P} \qquad \text{(from calculus)}$$

Thus, $\quad$ AR = MR
$$= \bar{P}$$
$$= 250 \qquad \text{[from part (a)]}$$

Thus, AR and MR curves are both same, a horizontal line at a distance of 250 from the quantity axis (Figure 8.3).

(c) Differentiating the total cost function with respect to q, we have

$$\text{MC} = d(\text{TC})/dq$$
$$= d[5000 + 750q - 30q^2 + (1/3)q^3]/dq$$
$$= 750 - 60q + q^2$$

As per the necessary condition, MC = MR, i.e.

$$750 - 60q + q^2 = 250$$
$$\Rightarrow \qquad q^2 - 60q + 500 = 0$$
$$\Rightarrow \qquad (q - 50)(q - 10) = 0$$
$$\Rightarrow \qquad \text{either } q = 50 \text{ or } q = 10$$

To ensure which of the two levels of the output maximizes the profit, let us apply the sufficient condition (slope of MR < Slope of MC). We know that the slope of MR = 0 because MR is a horizontal line.

$$\text{Slope of MC} = d(\text{MC})/dq$$
$$= d(750 - 60q + q^2)/dq$$
$$= 2q - 60$$

When $q = 10$,
$$\text{slope of MC} = 20 - 60$$
$$= -40\ (<0)$$

But slope of MR must be less than slope of MC. The sufficient condition, therefore, is not satisfied at $q = 10$. Hence, it is not the equilibrium output.
When $q = 50$,
$$\text{Slope of MC} = 100 - 60$$
$$= 40\ (>0)$$

Since $0 < 40$, the slope of MR < slope of MC and the sufficient condition is satisfied at $q = 50$. Hence, it is the equilibrium output. Price at this output is 250.

(d) Profit = TR − TC
$$= Pq - 5000 - 750q + 30q^2 - (1/3)q^3$$
$$= 250 \times 50 - 5000 - 750 \times 50 + 30 \times 50^2 - (1/3) \times 50^3$$
$$= 12500 - 5000 - 37500 + 75000 - 125000/3$$
$$= 10000/3$$
$$= 3333.33$$

Alternatively, for parts (c) and (d),

Since, $\quad\text{TR} = \overline{P} \times q$
$$= 250q$$

we have, $\quad \pi = \text{TR} - \text{TC}$
$$= 250q - [5000 + 750q - 30q^2 + (1/3)q^3]$$
$$= -5000 - 500q + 30q^2 - (1/3)q^3$$

Differentiating π with respect to q, we have
$$d\pi/dq = -500 + 60q - q^2$$

For profit maximization, $d\pi/dq = 0$

$\therefore \qquad -500 + 60q - q^2 = 0$

$\Rightarrow \qquad q^2 - 60q + 500 = 0$

$\Rightarrow \qquad (q - 50)(q - 10) = 0$

$\Rightarrow \qquad q = 50,\ q = 10$

Finding the second-order derivative of π with respect to q, we have
$$d^2\pi/dq^2 = 60 - 2q$$

At $q = 10$, $\qquad d^2\pi/dq^2 = 60 - 2 \times 10 = 40 > 0$

Thus, profit is not maximized at $q = 10$. Instead it is minimum at this output.

At $q = 50$, $\qquad d^2\pi/dq^2 = 60 - 2 \times 50 = -40 < 0$

Profit is, thus, maximized at $q = 50$.
The volume of profit at this level of output,

$$\pi = -5000 - 500 \times 50 + 30 \times (50)^2 - (1/3)(50)^3$$
$$= -71666.67 + 75000$$
$$= 3333.33$$

(e)

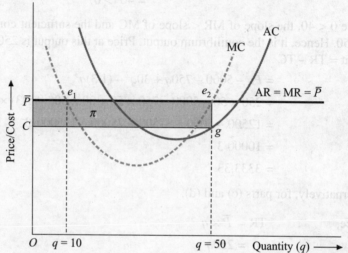

FIGURE 8.3 Illustration 8.1 MC = MR at $q = 10$ (point e_1) and $q = 50$ (point e_2). The point of equilibrium is the point corresponding to $q = 50$ where MC cuts MR from below. The profit maximizing output is, thus, 50 units and price, ₹ 250 per unit. The value of AC is $TC/q = 183.3333$ at the profit maximizing level. Profit per unit is ₹ 66.6666 and the total profit is ₹ 66.6666 × 50 = ₹ 3333.33.

8.1 PRICE-OUTPUT DECISIONS OF A COMPETITIVE FIRM IN THE SHORT-RUN

The short-run equilibrium is characterized by two things. *First*, the U-shaped average and marginal cost curves, and *second*, insignificant entry and exit of the firms. The latter ensures persistence of abnormal profits/losses in the short-run. The former, on the other hand, denoted as SAC (short-run average cost), SAVC (short-run average variable cost) and SMC (short-run marginal cost) with their typical U-shapes caused by the inability of the firm to increase some of its fixed factors, contribute further to sustenance of abnormal profits or losses. Under the circumstances, the equilibrium of a competitive firm in short-run involves either abnormal profits or losses or even normal profits as shown in Figures 8.4 to 8.6.

A common case of short-run equilibrium of a competitive firm is one in which the firm suffers loss and feels contented only with recovery of the total variable cost. The level of output at which this happens, refers to the lowest point on SAVC, as shown in Figure 8.6. Thus, in short-run a loss-making competitive firm *does not stop* its operations just when the horizontal demand curve faced by it (AR curve) slides below its SAC but it continues until it slides to the lowest point on its SAVC. The point is called **shutdown point** and the corresponding price and output, its **shutdown price** and **shutdown output**. Note that the firm's AR curve slides down when market price falls (Figure 8.6).

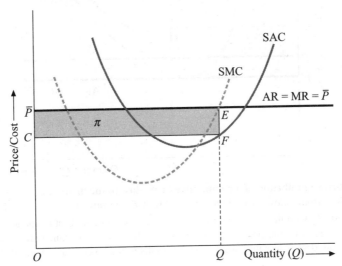

FIGURE 8.4 Short-run equilibrium of a competitive firm—abnormal profit: SMC cuts MR from below at E, which is the point of equilibrium. The firm's equilibrium output, therefore, is OQ. Equilibrium price and cost are determined at the points E and F respectively where AR and SAC are cut by the vertical line through E. Profit per unit is $AR - SAC = EF$ or $\bar{P}C$. The total profit is the area of the shaded rectangle, $CFE\bar{P} = OQ \times C\bar{P}$. As it is the excess of TR over TC (explicit + implicit), it is the **abnormal** or **supernormal profit**.

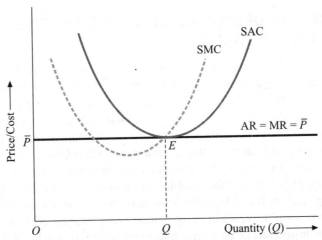

FIGURE 8.5 Short-run equilibrium of a competitive firm—normal profit: The second possibility of equilibrium of a competitive firm in short-run arises when SMC = SAC at E, the point of equilibrium. Here, SMC = SAC = AR = MR = $\bar{P}$. The possibility is rare but not impossible. The firm earns only normal profits.

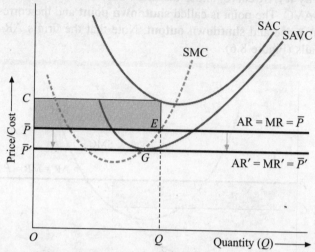

FIGURE 8.6 Short-run equilibrium of a competitive firm—loss to the firm: Equilibrium takes place at point E where SMC cuts MR from below. SAC lying above AR at E, the firm suffers loss in the short-run. If market price falls below $\bar{P}$, say to $\bar{P}'$ with the result that MR$'$ = AR$'$ = $\bar{P}'$ touches SAVC at G, the lowest point on SAVC, the equilibrium is reached at G, the point at which SMC = MR$'$. Point G is called **shutdown point**. The firm thus continues to operate despite loss until the market price falls to the level of this point. If it falls down further, the firm shuts down.

Figure 8.6 shows short-run loss accruing to a competitive firm. Nevertheless, the firm continues to operate until price falls to the level of the shutdown point, G. The firm feels contented only with the recovery of the total variable cost in the short-run. A further fall in price leads the firm to its closure.

8.2 PRICE-OUTPUT DECISIONS OF A COMPETITIVE FIRM IN THE LONG-RUN

The long-run equilibrium of a competitive firm is characterized by flatter AC and MC curves on one hand and free entry and exit of the firms on the other. In the long-run, therefore, a competitive firm makes only normal profits. The flatter cost curves result from variability of some of the factors that were fixed in short-run. Free entry and exit wipe out abnormal profit or loss accruing to a firm in the short-run due to insignificant entry or exit. Movement from short-run to long-run is automatic. Abnormal profits attract entry of new firms while losses force exit on vulnerable firms. Entry of new firms depresses price through a boost in supply while exit elevates it through a fall in supply. When market price falls, established firms may reduce their plant size before the vulnerable firms seek exit or the vulnerable firms may exit before the established firms reduce their plant-size. In the same way, when market price rises, established firms may expand their plant-size before new firms enter or new firms may enter before the established firms expand their plant-size. There are thus four alternative possibilities to long-run equilibrium in a competitive market. We discuss the adjustment process of attainment of long-run equilibrium characterized for normal profits below in the four cases:

1. New firms enter the market under short-run abnormal profits before an established firm expands its plant-size.

Suppose a competitive firm is currently making abnormal profits and contemplating an expansion of its plant. However, much before it succeeds in its endeavour, new firms, lured by abnormal profits, succeed in seeking entry. As a result, market supply increases and price falls until abnormal profits are completely driven to zero (Figure 8.7).

The firm in question has to sell lesser quantity, q' at a lower price $\bar{P}'$ instead of producing and selling q at $\bar{P}$ in the pre-entry period. The entry of new firms has eliminated its abnormal profit of π and reduced its market share from (q/Q) to (q'/Q').

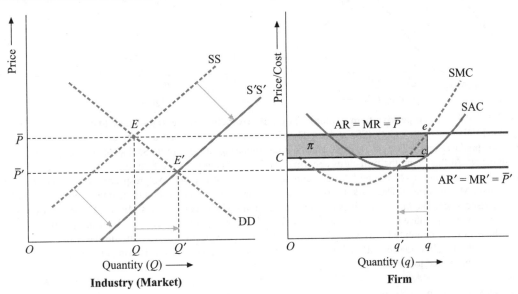

FIGURE 8.7 Abnormal profit of a competitive firm is driven to zero in the long-run by entry of new firms: In the left panel, Demand (DD) intersects Supply (SS) at E. Market Price is $\bar{P}$ and demand, Q. Entry of new firms shifts the supply curve to S'S', price to $\bar{P}'$ and quantity demanded to Q'. Assuming that the firm itself is not increasing its plant size, its cost curves remain unchanged while price falls to P' (right panel). Its market share declines due to presence of new firms. Its abnormal profit is driven to zero, that is, firm earns only the normal profit. Entry of new firms, thus, eliminates abnormal profit.

2. Established firms expand their plant-size before new firms enter the market under abnormal profits.

Suppose the firm itself decides to increase its plant size before the entry of new firms. In such a case, the short-run average cost curve of the firm descends downwards due to the scale economies that accrue to it. The firm produces more at a lower cost. The market supply increases and the market price comes down in consequence. The firm sells all that is produced at a lower market price. Its abnormal profit also disappears (Figure 8.8).

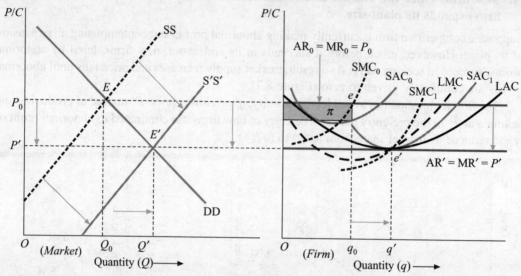

FIGURE 8.8 **A competitive firm expands its plant size before the entry of new firms:** In the left panel, Demand (DD) intersects supply (SS) at point E giving equilibrium price and quantity as P_0 and Q_0. The firm in question produces and sells q_0 at P_0 (right panel). It determines q_0 at e where its SMC_0 cuts its MR_0 ($= AR_0 = P_0$) from below. At this point, the firm earns abnormal profit, π. This induces the firm to expand its plant to produce more. In consequence, its SMC and SAC descend downwards to SMC_1 and SAC_1 respectively. The corresponding LAC and LMC are drawn. The market supply increases due to expansion of the firm and the market price falls to P' in consequence. The firm determines its output at the point where its LMC cuts MR' ($= AR' = P'$) from below at e'. The output produced by the firm at this point is q' which is sold at price P'. Abnormal profits disappear and the firm feels contented only with the normal profits. The question is why should the firm expand when it knows that its abnormal profits will disappear? The answer is to increase its competitiveness by lowering the price and hence to increase its market share.

3. Vulnerable firms exit under short-run losses before established firms are able to contract their plant size.

The case is exactly opposite of case (1). The smaller or the vulnerable firms fail to bear the loss and decide to quit. Exit of such firms reduces the market supply. In consequence, the market price rises. The remaining firms gain market share and their losses are made good without their contracting the plant size. They now begin to earn normal profits (Figure 8.9).

4. The loss making firms reduce their plant size before their exit.

Clearly, this is opposite of the case discussed in (2) above. Assume that a competitive firm is making loss in the short-run. It decides to reduce its plant size if possible. If it succeeds, its contribution to the market supply would decline and in consequence, the market price would rise. The firm being a price taker, would sell the current output at the higher market price. It would adjust its output in such a way that its loss gets eliminated. The firm would be in stable equilibrium with normal profits, as shown in Figure 8.10.

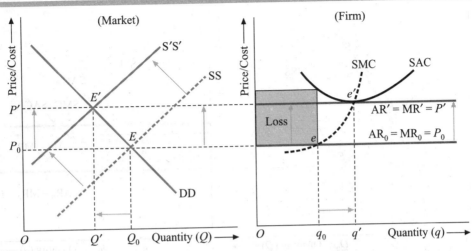

FIGURE 8.9 Vulnerable competitive firms quit before the established firms are able to contract their plant size: Exit of vulnerable firms due to losses, decreases market supply from SS to S′S′. This raises the market price from P_0 to P' and lowers the market supply from Q_0 to Q'. The competitive firm in question, is initially at e, producing and selling q_0 at price P_0 (= AR_0 = MR_0). It is suffering a loss, shown by the shaded rectangle. As soon as the exit of some firms takes place, price rises to P' (= AR' = MR'). The loss disappears at e' where the firm's SMC cuts its MR′ from below. Here SMC = SAC = AR′ = MR′. Note that the firm in question sells $q'(q' > q_0)$ at a higher price, P'. This is due to a substantial fall in market supply and a consequential rise in price. The firm in question, grabs the opportunity to supply more partly to operate at its optimal capacity and partly to get rid of losses. The firm earns normal profits in the long-run.

The long-run equilibrium of a competitive firm involves normal profits only. Figure 8.11 shows the ultimate equilibrium of the competitive firms whether it results in consequence of free entry/exit of firms or of their own action of expansion/contraction of the plant size. At this stage, the reader may concern with what the long-run equilibrium looks like rather than how is it reached.

8.3 DYNAMIC CHANGES AND INDUSTRY EQUILIBRIUM

In Section 7.2, we examined the effects of shifts in demand and supply on the price-output decisions of a competitive industry as also of a firm operating in it. In the same section, we also examined the effects of government intervention in the free play of the market mechanism (price mechanism) on the price-output decisions of the industry and the firm. Shifts in demand and supply and the direct and indirect interventions of government in the market mechanism are all known as dynamic changes. In the direct government intervention, we studied how price ceiling and price floor influence price output decisions of the industry and the firm operating in it. In the indirect government intervention, we studied how a levy of a unit tax or a grant of subsidy cause shifts in the supply curve of the industry and effect its price-output decisions along with those of each firm operating in it. Much earlier in Chapter 2 on price mechanism, we had taken up these dynamic factors to see their effects on the price mechanism and social welfare; and later in Chapter 3 on elasticity of demand and supply, we had studied the same for demand and supply curves of varying price elasticities.

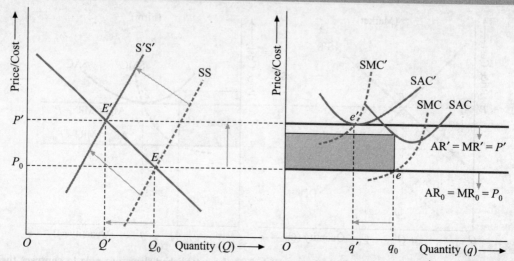

FIGURE 8.10 The loss making competitive firms contract their plant size before any of them exits: If a loss-making competitive firm cuts its plant size before any of its loss making competitors quit, market supply decreases from SS to S'S' with the result that market price increases from P_0 to P_1. Reduction in the plant size raises the SAC of the firm in question from SAC to SAC' and its SMC, from SMC to SMC'. The firm sells q' at P' instead of q_0 at P_0. The firm that incurred loss at $e(q_0, P_0)$, earns normal profit at $e'(q', P')$. Contraction of plant size by the loss making firm helps it in getting rid of its short-run loss despite higher costs. The notion of the long-run cost curves in this case is misleading. Such curves appear similar to the long-run curves of case (2) but the equilibrium does not, due to reduction in the plant size. One can treat the situation as opposite of that of case (2) but for the difference that output had increased of case (2) while it has decreased here.

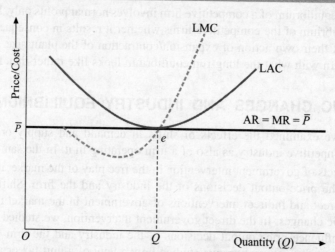

FIGURE 8.11 Long-run equilibrium of a competitive firm: In the long-run LAC is tangential to AR at 'e'. A competitive firm makes normal profits with flatter cost curves. At the point, LAC = LMC = AR = MR = $\bar{P}$. Output OQ corresponding to the lowest point on the firm's LAC is called its **optimal output or optimal capacity.**

What we omitted there, were the situations of demand-supply shifts under conditions of constant increasing and decreasing costs of production and situations that affected the AC and MC curves of a firm. Let us discuss them now.

1. Shifts in market demand under constant, increasing and decreasing cost conditions

(a) *Constant cost industry*

An industry is said to be a constant cost industry if prices of productive factors remain constant as industry output expands. Supply can therefore match every increase in demand at the same cost. Every time demand curve shifts upwards to right, supply curve shifts downwards to right by the same magnitude with the result that product price remains constant. Such adjustments of supply to demand lead to a horizontal industry supply curve called *long-run supply curve* (LRS).

The mechanism can be explained as follows. Other things remaining unchanged, an upward-to-right shift in demand pushes the price up, which in turn, increases profit margin, given the constant costs. Resulting abnormal profits to the constituent firms attract new firms. This increases supply by the same magnitude by which demand has increased. Identical increase in supply is a result of the constant costs and product price is restored at the original level.

In the figure (Figure 8.12, left panel), industry supply increases from S to S' retrieving the price back to the initial level, P. Shift in supply is equivalent to that in demand due to constant costs. While industry output expands by QQ', output of a firm in the industry increases by qq' initially, but returns back to the initial level, q as soon as price falls back to P (Figure 8.12, right panel). Additional demand is, thus, satisfied by the new firms. In case demand increases further, so would the output at the same price, following the same mechanism. Industry supply curve is horizontal in the long-run, as shown in the left panel (Figure 8.12).

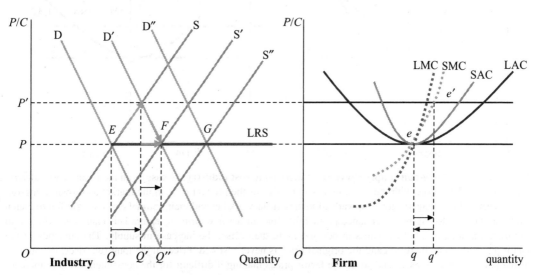

FIGURE 8.12 Long-run supply curve of a constant cost industry: In a constant cost industry, supply can be shifted by the same magnitude by which demand does. Every time demand curve shifts upwards to right, supply curve shifts downwards to right by the same magnitude. Initially, the product price increases from P to

P', but as soon as supply catches up with demand, it falls down to the original level (left panel). In case demand increases further, so does supply. It catches up with demand neck-to-neck due to constant costs. In the long-run, supply curve of industry turns horizontal, as shown.

Effect on price-output decisions of a firm in the industry is shown in the right panel. The firm being a price taker, it follows the price prevailing in the industry. When product price rises to P', given the costs, abnormal profits follow, which attract new entrants. As a result, industry supply increases and product price falls. The process continues until the abnormal profits are driven to zero and original price is restored. Each firm ends up supplying quantity q at the initial price P in the long-run. Additional output demanded is supplied by the new entrants.

(b) *Increasing cost industry*

An industry is said to be an increasing cost industry if prices of productive factors increase as industry output expands. In other words, production costs rise with an increase in output and so do the product prices and hence the abnormal profits. New firms enter, but the shifts in supply fail to match the shifts in demand.

The long-run supply curve of the industry slopes upwards as shown in Figure 8.13. While more is produced and supplied by the industry at higher prices (left panel), a firm's output remains unchanged (right panel)

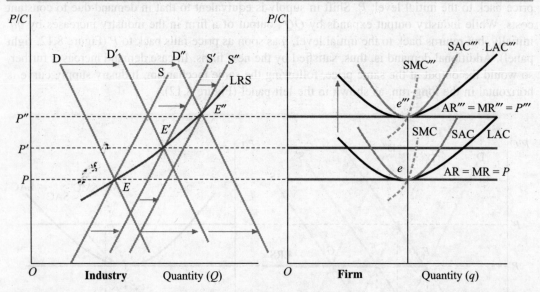

FIGURE 8.13 Long-run supply curve of an increasing cost industry: In case of an increasing cost industry, supply fails to keep pace with the shifts in demand. Price of the product rises in the market as shown. Long-run supply curve of the industry slopes upwards. Existing firms work beyond their optimal capacity, but fail to match shifts in demand. Rising prices enhance profitability and attract new firms to enter. This causes an increase in supply in the long-run, but the shifts in demand more than offset the increase in supply. The tendency of the factor prices to go up increases and the original price is never restored. Price, in the long-run, rises, the number of the new entrants increases and so do the factor prices making it difficult for the constituent firms to increase their market share, as shown.

(c) Decreasing cost industry

An industry is a decreasing cost industry if the factor prices decline as the industry output expands. Due to declining costs of production, industry supply increases by more than the increase in demand. The long-run supply curve of the industry slopes downwards as shown in Figure 8.14. Product price falls in long-run due to downward shifts in the cost curves of the firms. Such a supply curve characterizes presence of the external economies. Declining costs increase the firm's profitability and attract new firms. This may not allow a higher market share to any firm.

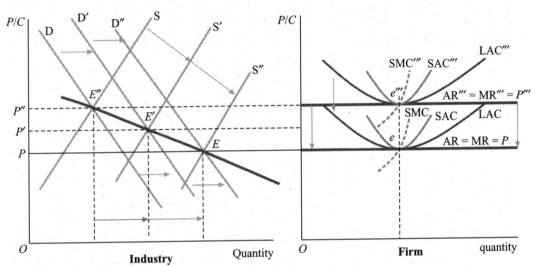

FIGURE 8.14 Long-run supply curve of a decreasing cost industry: In a decreasing cost industry, shifts in supply supersede the shifts in demand. Successively higher shifts in supply more than offset the shifts in demand with the result that product price falls and goes on falling. A fall in price alone must force exit on the vulnerable firms but if accompanied by a steeper fall in production costs, it rather attracts new firms. See how cost curves shifts downwards in the right panel. In all likelihood, existing firms operate at their existing (optimal) capacity with same market share. New firms enter and share the market with the established firms. Long-run supply curve of the industry slopes downwards as shown (Left panel).

(2) Effect of changes in the fixed and variable costs

(a) A change in TFC

A change in total fixed cost is followed by a change in average fixed cost and hence by a change in average total cost. If total fixed cost increases, so do the average fixed and average total costs. This results in an upward shift in the average cost curves. Average variable cost curves and marginal cost curves, however, remain unaffected by the changes. To illustrate, let us take the linear total cost function:

$$TC = a + bQ$$

where, a = TFC, b = average variable cost, TC = total cost and Q = output. For this function,

$$AFC = TFC/Q$$
$$= a/Q$$

$$AC = TC/Q$$
$$= (a + bQ)/Q$$
$$= a/Q + b$$
$$= AFC + b$$
$$AVC = TVC/Q$$
$$= b \cdot Q/Q = b$$
$$MC = d(TC)/dQ$$
$$= d(a + bQ)/dQ = b$$

Now suppose that TFC increases by 'h'. The total cost function now changes to

$$TC' = (a + h) + bQ$$
$$= TFC' + TVC$$

And,
$$AFC' = (a + h)/Q$$
$$= a/Q + h/Q$$
$$= AFC + h/Q.$$
$$\Rightarrow AFC' > AFC.$$
$$AVC' = TVC/Q$$
$$= bQ/Q$$
$$= b$$
$$= AVC$$
$$MC' = d(TC')/dQ$$
$$= d(a + h + bQ)/dQ$$
$$= b$$
$$= MC$$
$$AC' = TC'/Q$$
$$= (a + h)/Q + bQ/Q$$
$$= AFC + h/Q + b$$
$$= AFC + b + h/Q$$
$$= AC + h/Q$$
$$\Rightarrow AC' > AC.$$

Comparing the statements, we observe that an increase in TFC increases AFC and AC but leaves AVC and MC unaffected. The curves in their most general form, are presented as in Figure 8.15(a).

In respect of an industry, a change (say, an increase) in total fixed cost would affect only the supply curve which would shift upward to left by the magnitude of increase in the average cost. The effects on the firm's price and on the industry, are as shown in Figures 8.15(a) and (b) respectively. An increase in total fixed cost thus forces a competitive firm into loss.

Imposition of a lump-sum tax or of a profit tax has the same effect on the price output decisions of the industry and the firm as that of an increase in the TFC.

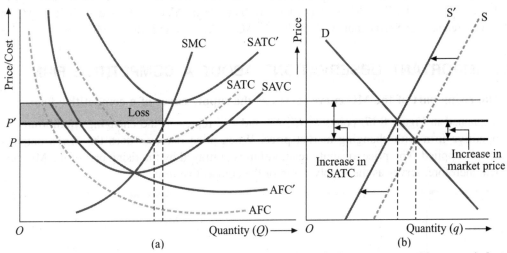

FIGURE 8.15 Effect of an increase in TFC on average and marginal cost curves and hence on industry demand and supply curves: (a) An increase in total fixed cost results in an increase in average fixed cost and average total cost. Respective curves shift upwards as shown while average variable cost and marginal cost remain un-affected and so do their curves. (b) An increase in SATC shifts the industry supply curve upwards to left by an equal vertical distance. The market price and hence the firm's price rises only to P'. Hence, an increase in total fixed cost forces a competitive firm into loss.

(b) *A change in the variable cost*

An increase in variable cost leads to an upward shift in AVC, AC and MC curves of a firm. As regards the industry, the market supply curve shifts upward to left as in Figure 8.15(b).

How do upward shifts in AC and MC, caused by a change in the variable cost, affect price output decisions of a firm? Figure 8.16 answers the question.

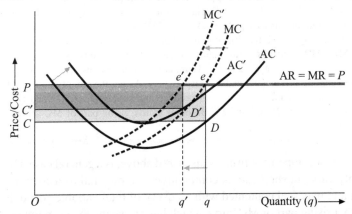

FIGURE 8.16 Effect of an increase in the variable cost on the cost curves: An increase in the variable cost leads to an upward shift in AC and MC. In consequence, firm's sale declines from q to q' and its profits decline from the rectangle $eDCP$ to the rectangle $e'D'C'P$.

Effect of an increase in TVC on the cost curves can also be understood mathematically. Let TVC be 'bQ' and TVC' = '$(b + h)Q$'. Clearly increase in AVC is 'h' and so is it in AC and MC. The reader can verify that AVC' = $b + h$, AC' = AC + h and MC' = MC + h.

8.4 IMPORTANT OBSERVATIONS ABOUT A COMPETITIVE FIRM

1. The rising part of the MC curve serves as the supply curve of a competitive firm.

As explained in Figure 8.17, points E, E', E'' and E''' represent the changing equilibrium of a competitive firm with changing market price. When price rises, so does the firm's output or quantity supplied. The price–quantity relationship is portrayed by the rising part of the MC-curve which, therefore, serves as the supply curve of the competitive firm.

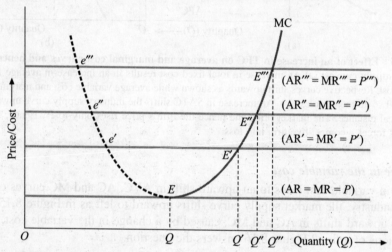

FIGURE 8.17 Rising part of MC as the supply curve of a competitive firm: The marginal cost curve, MC, cuts MR curve (AR = MR = P) from below at E. The equilibrium output is Q which the competitive firm would supply at price P. Now suppose market price rises to P' (AR' = MR' = P'). MC cuts MR' from below at E' where equilibrium output is Q' which the firm supplies at price P' (note that e', e'' and e''' cannot be equilibrium points as MC cuts MR', MR'' and MR''' from above at each of these points). In the same way, MC cuts MR'' and MR''' from below respectively at E'' and E'''. Here, equilibrium outputs are Q'' and Q''' respectively which the competitive firm supplies at prices P'' and P''' respectively. As per the condition of profit maximization, MC must cut MR from below. Evidently, the firm will produce and supply Q, Q', Q'' and Q''' at prices P, P', P'' and P''' respectively at points E, E', E'' and E'''. In other words, rising part of MC serves as the supply curve of a competitive firm.

The supply curve of a competitive firm, as discussed above, is a general case. One of its variations refers to its supply curve in short run. A competitive firm may fail to recover its total production cost in short-run and may feel contented with recovery of total variable cost only. In this case, its supply curve is that rising part of MC curve which lies above the lowest point on the SAVC curve (Figure 8.18).

As another variation of general case, we can refer to the long-run supply curve of a competitive firm. In long-run, a competitive firm operates at the lowest point on its LAC which is highly stable unless external economies or diseconomies crop up to shift it downwards or upwards respectively. Assuming existence of neither, we can treat the firm's LAC as highly stable. The firm produces quantity Q at 'e' (Figure 8.19), the lowest point on its LAC. If the market price rises, abnormal profits crop up which last only for a short span of time. Entry of firms soon restores the original price and quantity at point 'e'. If market price falls, losses crop up which force exit on vulnerable firms or initiate a contraction in firm's output. In either case the firm in question would supply at least quantity Q. Hence, Q or more would be supplied at a price of P or higher. The rising part of MC lying above point 'e' (shown in dark) would serve as the supply curve of the firm. Soon higher supply would restore price to P and supply to Q. In the event of a fall in market price, the firm would prefer to supply Q as this would ensure minimization of loss. Soon, vulnerable firms would quit and the market price would go up to the level of P. The firm in question would regain its normal profits. Hence, long-run supply curve of a competitive firm is that part of the rising MC which lies above the lowest point on its LAC (Figure 8.19).

Under constant cost conditions, LMC and LAC are both constant. They are both horizontal and coincidental. For equilibrium, LMC = LAC = AR = MR = P for a competitive firm with the result that long-run supply curve of a competitive firm under constant cost conditions is horizontal (Figure 8.20).

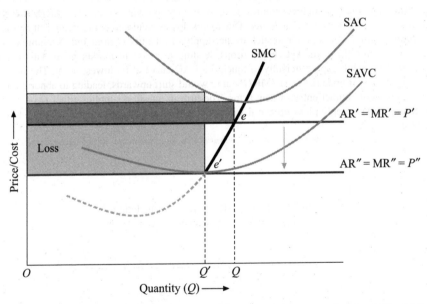

FIGURE 8.18 Short-run supply curve of a competitive firm is that part of rising MC which lies above the lowest point on SAVC: Short-run supply curve of the competitive firm is the solid part of the rising MC. The lowest point on this part is the lowest point on the SAVC. In other words, the competitive firms continue to produce, despite a fall in price from P' to P'', so long as they recover their total variable costs. As in figure, the firm would continue till its AR/MR curves touch the SAVC curve at its lowest point, e'. If price falls below this point, the firm would quit. Hence, only that part of the rising MC serves as the supply curve of the firm which lies above the SAVC. Note how loss changes with a fall in market price.

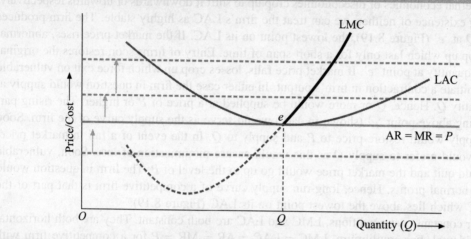

FIGURE 8.19 Rising part of MC curve, that lies above LAC, serves as the long-run supply curve of a competitive firm: Solid part of the rising LMC serves as the long-run supply curve of the competitive firm. LMC = LAC = AR = MR at the equilibrium point, e. Recall that a competitive firm always operates at the lowest point of its LAC. Quantity produced at this point is known as its optimal capacity.

If price falls, AR/MR/P curve would shift downwards but LAC would not unless some external economies accrue to the firm. In absence of such economies, LAC would remain where it is while AR/MR/P curve would slide down creating a gap between LAC and price. Due to this, losses would crop up forcing exit on the vulnerable firms. The firm in question would prefer to stick to the supply of quantity Q in its bid to minimize losses. With the exit of the vulnerable firms, market supply drops, leading to a rise in market price. This continues until the horizontal price line shifts up sufficiently to touch the LAC curve at its lowest point. The firm in question regains its normal profits. If price rises, AR/MR/P curve would shift upwards, leading to abnormal profits to the existing firms. This would attract entry of new firms. The firm in question supplies either Q or more at a price P or higher. Soon, market supply picks up and market price is restored at the earlier level of P. Even abnormal profits disappear.

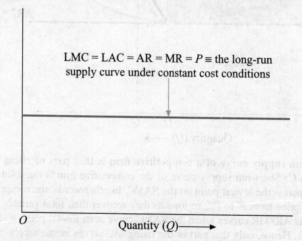

FIGURE 8.20 The long-run supply curve under constant cost conditions.

2. A competitive firm always operates at its optimal capacity in the long-run.

Refer to Figure 8.11. At the equilibrium, LAC = LMC = AR = MR = $\bar{P}$. The firm makes only the normal profit (zero economic profit). It produces at the lowest cost and sells its output at a price equal to the lowest average cost. If we compare a competitive firm with a monopoly (refer to Figure 7.11, Chapter 7) we would observe that a monopoly always produces along the falling part of the LAC (not on the lowest point of the LAC) and charges a price higher than its MC and MR both. This requires curtailment of quantity produced and sold. In the process, a part of the consumer's surplus as also a part of the producer's surplus are lost. The loss of social welfare so caused by monopoly is known as the *Dead Weight Loss**. At the moment, it would be enough to know that a competitive firm produces and sells more than what a monopoly does and charges a price less than what a monopoly does.

3. The lowest point on the average variable cost curve serves as the shutdown point of the firm.

A firm in competitive market, if unable to recover its total cost in short-run, does not quit unless it fails to recover its total variable cost as well. The observation is explained in Figure 8.18. Point e' in the figure is the firm's shutdown point. Here, we discuss various price ranges relevant to a competitive firm's operations in short-run (Figure 8.21).

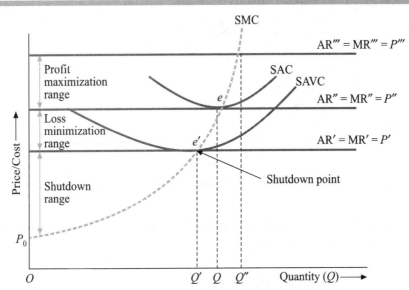

FIGURE 8.21 Shutdown point of a competitive firm in short-run: Point e' is the point of firm's shutdown as SAVC is lowest at this point. In case price falls below this point, a competitive firm operating in short-run would have to closedown. The closedown may take place anywhere between prices P_0 and P' (P_0 is lowest MC). A firm must shutdown at point e' only but sometimes it chooses to continue even below e' until price falls to the lowest point on MC, P_0. It does so to demonstrate its competence or to keep up its prestige for the sake of a **going concern** in its valuation. That is, a firm may stretch below its shutdown point for the sake of higher valuation at the time of its liquidation. The price range between P' and P'' is known as **loss minimization range** and the price range between P'' and P''', as **profit maximization range**.

---

* See Chapters 1 and 2.

4. Consumers' and producers' surpluses for competitive industry and firm.

As discussed earlier in Chapters 1 and 2, producers' surplus (PS) for a competitive industry may be defined as the excess of total revenue (TR) of the industry over its total cost (TC) of production.

It represents the area above the industry supply curve that lies below the horizontal line through the point of equilibrium. In Figure 8.22, shaded area marked a represents the producers' surplus.

As against this, the consumers' surplus (CS) may be defined as the area under the industry demand curve that lies above the horizontal line through the point of equilibrium. In Figure 8.22, consumers' surplus is represented by the shaded area marked b. In Chapter 2, we have discussed the concepts in much greater detail while analyzing effects of government intervention in free play of price mechanism.

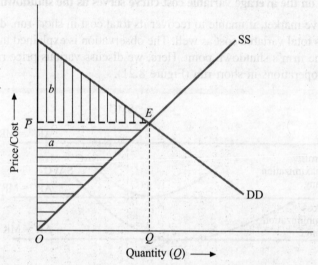

FIGURE 8.22 Producers' and Consumers' Surpluses: $a \equiv$ Producers' surplus; $b \equiv$ Consumers' surplus.

We can define producer's surplus in respect of a competitive firm as the excess of its total revenue (TR) over its total variable cost (TVC).

Thus, the producer's surplus (PS) of a competitive firm may be given as

$$PS = TR - TVC$$
$$= TR - TVC - TFC + TFC \quad \text{(adding and subtracting TFC)}$$
$$= TR - (TFC + TVC) + TFC$$
$$= (TR - TC) + TFC$$
$$= \pi + TFC, \text{ where, } \pi \equiv \text{firm's profit.}$$

Thus, a firm's surplus differs from its profit by an amount of TFC. The firm's surplus can also be represented as excess of price (P) over marginal cost (MC) of producing Q units of output (Figure 8.23).

Shaded region between the horizontal price line (AR = MR = P) and the MC curve gives a firm's surplus.

We know that

$$TR = \bar{P} \times Q$$

and that the area under the MC curve (See Q. 50 and 63, Chapter 6) = TVC. The expression for producer's surplus (PS) for a competitive firm is thus given as

$$PS = \bar{P} \times Q - TVC$$
$$= TR - \text{area under the MC curve}$$
$$= \text{the shaded area as in Figure 8.23}$$

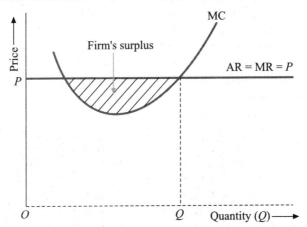

FIGURE 8.23 Producer's surplus in respect of a competitive firm is represented by the shaded area = area of the rectangle $OQEP$ – Area below the MC curve = TR – TVC.

From the discussions above and from Figure 8.11, optimality of its plant-size and its policy of product pricing at the level of MC make a competitive firm economically more efficient than any other firm in any market form.

Features of a competitive market make it too good to exist. No doubt, it is a myth. It is in fact an ideal market structure consumers and producers both dream for. Market imperfection is a reality. We will discuss them in Chapters 10*[1] and 11*[2]. Before that, we will take up monopoly, another extreme structure of a market in Chapter 9*[3]. Just as pure competition as a form of perfect competion is realistic, natural monopoly as a form of monopoly is also realistic. The most common forms are the three forms of an imperfect market, namely, *monopolistic competition, duopoly* and *oligopoly*. Chapter 10*[4] is devoted to monopolistic competition, while Chapter 11*[5] to duopoly and oligopoly.

---

*[1] Chapter 2 of *Microeconomics, Theory and Applications*, Part II by Chauhan, S.P.S., PHI
*[2] Chapter 3 of *Microeconomics, Theory and Applications*, Part II by Chauhan, S.P.S, PHI
*[3] Chapter 1 of *Microeconomics, Theory and Applications*, Part II by Chauhan, S.P.S., PHI
*[4] Chapter 2 of *Microeconomics, Theory and Applications*, Part II by Chauhan, S.P.S., PHI
*[5] Chapter 3 of *Microeconomics, Theory and Applications*, Part II by Chauhan, S.P.S., PHI

KEY TERMS AND CONCEPTS

Consumers' surplus (CS) It may be defined as the excess of consumers' disposable income over their current consumption expenditure, which, in the event of scarcity, they are willing to forego to retain their current level of consumption.

Deadweight loss It refers to the total loss of social welfare. A part of it is the social loss of consumers' surplus and the rest is the social loss of producers' surplus. Thus, **deadweight loss = the social loss of CS + the social loss of PS.**

Excess capacity When a firm operates along the falling part of its AC, it is said to be sub-optimal. The output it is producing is called sub-optimal output. Excess of the optimal output over the sub-optimal output is called the excess capacity of a firm. The concept has its relevance to long-run as the short-run is usually marked as a transitory period of the adjustment process. It is only the monopoly firm that possesses the excess capacity. The competitive firms always operate at their optimal capacity in the long-run.

Optimal capacity It refers to the optimal or the most economic level of output of a firm which must correspond to the lowest average cost or the lowest point on the average cost curve. It is only a competitive firm that operates at the optimal capacity in the long-run (Figure 8.11).

Price and MC for a competitive firm The price or the average revenue is always equal to the marginal cost at the equilibrium of a competitive firm, i.e. $P = MC$.

Producers' surplus (PS) It can be defined, in the like manner, as the excess of total revenue over total variable cost. The total revenue is the product of the price and quantity and the total variable cost is the area under the MC curve between $Q = 0$ and $Q = Q_C$ or Q_M depending on whether the firm is a competitive one or a monopoly. Here, Q_C is the equilibrium level of output of a competitive firm while Q_M is that of a monopoly.

Profit, π In common parlance, excess of total revenue over total cost (explicit + implicit) is called profit. Thus, profit $\pi = TR - TC$, where TC = explicit cost + implicit cost. When $\pi > 0$, it is known as **abnormal** or **supernormal profit,** when $\pi = 0$, it is called **normal profit** and when $\pi < 0$, it is known as **loss.** Some authors refer to it as **abnormal loss,** only to maintain symmetry of the negative deviation from $\pi = 0$. According to many, there is nothing like abnormal loss because there does not exist anything such as **normal loss**. Normal profit exists and refers to a situation in which all costs, explicit or implicit, including the opportunity cost of the entrepreneur, are equal to the total revenue at the market rate. Thus, use of the term **abnormal loss** in place of **loss** is inappropriate.

Economists' and accountants' concepts of profit According to economists' concept, profit is excess of total revenue over total costs that include implicit and explicit costs both. Thus, $\pi = TR -$ Explicit cost implicit cost. On the contrary, the accountants' concept treats profit as the excess of total revenue over explicit costs only. Thus, $\pi = TR -$ explicit costs. The total cost, according to the accounting concept, comprises only the explicit costs.

Shutdown point It is defined as the level of output at which average variable cost is minimum. It is the lowest level to which market price can fall without forcing the firms to closedown production (Figure 8.21).

Sufficient condition of profit maximization The sufficient condition of profit maximization is that MC must cut MR from below. This implies that the slope of the MR curve must be less than that of the MC curve. This results from setting the second-order derivative of π with respect to Q negative at the output where the first-order derivative is zero.

Supply curve of a competitive firm The rising part of the MC curve serves as the supply curve of a competitive firm (refer to Figures 8.17 to 8.19).

EXERCISES

A. Short Answer Questions

Define the following: (1 through 11)

1. Profit
2. Abnormal profit
3. Normal profit
4. Loss
5. Shut-down point
6. Optimal capacity of a firm
7. Sub-optimal output
8. Consumers' surplus
9. Producers' surplus
10. Excess capacity of a firm
11. Deadweight loss
12. What is the economists' concept of profit?
13. What is the accountants' concept of profit?
14. What is the necessary condition of profit maximization?
15. What is the sufficient condition of profit maximization?
16. Explain the concept of consumers' surplus with the help of an example.
17. Is it correct to say that $P = MC$ for a competitive firm whether it in short-run or long-run?
18. At which point on the LAC does a competitive firm produce in the long-run?
19. Given that $MR > 0$, how would the TR change with Q? [**Ans.** Increase]
20. How would the TR change with the output when $MR < 0$? [**Ans.** Decrease]
21. How would the TR change with the output when $MR = 0$? [**Ans.** Maximum]
22. Sketch the shape of the TR for a competitive firm.
23. How are AR and MR related for a competitive firm?

B. Long Answer Questions

24. Show that the supply curve for a competitive firm is the rising part of the MC curve.
25. Would the number of firms increase/decrease/remain unchanged when the firms in a competitive market are making
    (a) abnormal profits?
    (b) losses?
    (c) normal profits?

    [**Ans.** (a) Increase, (b) decrease, (c) unchanged.]
26. In long-run equilibrium of a competitive firm, show with the help of a sketch that $LAC = LMC = AR = MR$.
27. Show that the abnormal profits accruing to a competitive firm in the short-run disappear in the long-run due to free entry of new firms.
28. Show that losses accruing to a competitive firm in the short-run disappear in the long-run due to free exit of vulnerable firms.
29. LAC is minimum at an output of 20 units for a competitive firm. The minimum value of the average cost at this output is 30. The industry demand schedule is as given below:

Price:	15	20	25	30	35	40
Demand:	2000	1800	1500	1000	700	500

(a) Determined the market price and quantity sold.

(b) Assuming that each firm has the same market share, how many firms were there in the market?

(c) Suppose the industry adopts a cost-saving technology which shifts the LAC downwards so that the minimum average cost falls from 30 to 20 and the equilibrium output of a firm, from 20 to 15. How many firms will now operate in the industry?

[**Ans.** A competitive firm is a price taker. In the long-run equilibrium, AR = MR = LAC = LMC. The LAC must touch the AR = MR curve. Therefore, equilibrium price is equal to the minimum average cost which is 30. The market demand at this price is 1000 units. The output of the firm in equilibrium is 20 units. Therefore, the number of the firms in the market is 1000/20 = 50 (see Figure 8.24).

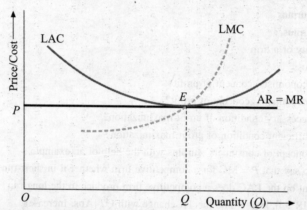

FIGURE 8.24 (Question 29) Equilibrium price is equal to the minimum value of the average cost. It is $OP = 30$. The market demand at this price is 1,000 units while firm's output is $OQ = 20$. Therefore, the number of firms is 1000/20 = 50.

Now the minimum average cost falls to 20. Therefore, the new price = 20. The market demand at this price is 1,800 units while the firm's output is 15 units. Therefore, the number of firms operating in the market is 1,800/15 = 120. Had the profit maximizing output of the competitive firm gone up to 30, the number of firms would have been 1,800/30 = 60.]

30. How would an increase in total fixed cost affect the price output decisions of (a) a competitive firm? (b) a competitive industry? Explain with the help of diagrams.

31. Suppose a lump-sum tax is levied annually on all the firms in an industry. How would it affect the price output decisions of the industry and the firm?

32. Suppose the variable cost of all the firms in an industry gets increased due to a levy of an indirect tax. What effect would it have on their price-output decisions? Use diagrams wherever necessary.

33. Show that a competitive firm always operates at its optimal capacity in the long-run.

34. Show that the rising part of the MC curve serves as the supply curve of a competitive firm.

35. What is shutdown point? Explain with the help of a diagram.

36. Show that the industry supply curve of a constant cost industry is a horizontal line showing that more is supplied by the industry at the same price. Why is it that a firm operating in the industry may fail to have a share in the increase of market demand?

37. Show that the industry supply curve of an increasing cost industry is an upward sloping line showing that more is supplied by the industry at a higher price. Why is it that a firm operating in the industry may fail to have a share in the increase of market demand?

38. Show that the industry supply curve of decreasing cost industry is a downward sloping line showing that more is supplied by the industry at a lower prices. Why is it that a firm operating in the industry may fail to have a share in the increase of market demand?

39. The market demand function of a competitive industry is represented by
$$Q = 10.5 - P,$$
where Q is aggregate quantity supplied by all the firms at a price P.
All the firms in the industry have identical cost function:
$$C = q - q^2 + 0.5q^3,$$
where C is the cost of a firm and q is the quantity produced by each
Calculate:
(a) the output produced by each firm in the long-run
(b) the long-run equilibrium price
(c) the equilibrium number of firms.

[**Ans.** (a) In the long-run, price charged by the competitive firm = minimum value of the average cost, LAC, given by
$$LAC = C/q$$
$$= 1 - q + 0.5q^2$$
It is minimum when
$$d(LAC)/dq = 0$$
and
$$d^2(LAC)/dq^2 > 0.$$
Differentiating LAC with respect to q, we have
$$d(LAC)/dq = -1 + q$$
$$= 0$$
$\Rightarrow$ $\qquad q = 1$
At this point, $\qquad d^2(LAC)/dq^2 = 1\ (> 0).$

Thus, LAC is minimum at $q = 1$. The value of the minimum LAC is 0.5 which is equal to the market price (A competitive firm is a price taker). Substituting in the equation of the market demand,
$$Q = 10.5 - P$$
$$= 10.5 - 0.5$$
$$= 10$$
which gives the industry demand. It is also equal to the industry supply at its equilibrium. Supply made by a firm is $q = 1$.
The number of firms in the industry is, therefore, $10/1 = 10$ firms.]

40. A competitive firm finds that at equilibrium level of output, its AR = 20, MC = 20 and AC = 60 while AVC = 16. Will the firm produce or shutdown? Explain with the help of a diagram. If price falls, up to what level can it bear the decline in the price? Can you be absolutely sure of your answer? Give reasons.
[**Ans.** It will produce because $P(= 20) >$ AVC $(= 16)$ and it will continue to produce at least to a fall in price up to 16. It will continue to produce even when price falls below 16 but how much below it is not certain because the minimum point on the AVC (V_0) is not known as is clear from Figure 8.25.

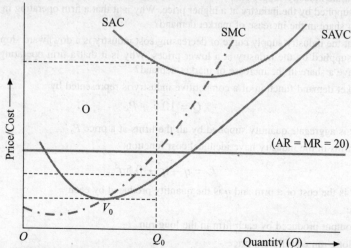

FIGURE 8.25 (**Question 40**) The shutdown point of the firm is V_0 (The point where SAVC is minimum) which certainly must be below the point where SAVC = 16. (Why)? The firm will continue to produce until the price falls to the level of V_0.]

41. In Illustration 8.1, suppose the data pertaining to demand and supply remain unchanged ($Q^D = 5,000 - 10P$; $Q^S = 10P$) but the cost function changes to

    (a) $TC = 10,000 + 750q - 30q^2 + (1/3)q^3$
    (b) $TC = 5,000 + 1000q - 30q^2 + (1/3)q^3$

    How would your answers to the questions therein change and why?

    [**Ans.** (a) market price = 250; market demand = 2,500; firm's AR = MR = 250; firm's profit maximizing output = 50 and price = 250; resulting profits (loss) = –1,666.67

    (b) market price = 250; market demand = 2,500; firm's AR = MR = 250; firm's profit maximizing output = 42.25 and price = 250; resulting profits (loss) = –8275.25]

C. Essay Type Questions

42. With the help of sketches, show that the loss or abnormal profit accruing to a competitive firm in the short-run is driven to zero by the free exit and free entry of the firms.
43. Explain how the price output decisions of the industry and firms operating in it be affected
    (a) when a lump-sum tax is levied by government
    (b) when a unit tax is levied by government.
44. Under what circumstances can the supply curve of a competitive firm be
    (a) the segment of rising MC that lies above the minimum of the AC?
    (b) the segment of rising MC that lies above the minimum of the AVC?
    (c) a horizontal line coinciding with AR and MR?

    Explain with the help of neat sketches.

Price-output Decisions of a Monopoly

CHAPTER OUTLINE

Introduction
- Price-output Decisions of Monopoly in Short-run
- Price-output Decisions of Monopoly in Long-run
- Monopoly Power and its Sources
- Social Cost of Monopoly Power
- Supply Curve of a Monopoly
- Price Discrimination
- Price-output Decisions of a Monopoly under Dynamic Changes
- Multiplant Monopoly
- Monopoly versus Competitive Firm
- Monopsony and Monopsony Power
- Key Terms and Concepts
- Exercises

INTRODUCTION

In Chapter 7, we discussed monopoly as a market form, its general traits, merits, demerits and factors responsible for its evolution and perpetuation. In this chapter, we take up how a monopoly firm makes its price-output decisions in short-run and long-run.

As discussed in Chapters 7 and 8, every firm, whether competitive or monopoly, aims at profit maximization as its main objective. We have also seen that the necessary and sufficient condition for fulfilment of this objective is that the firm's MC curve must cut its MR curve from below. As has been the case with a competitive firm, price-output decisions of a monopoly too require its average and marginal cost curves along with those of its average and marginal revenues. The only point of difference is the nature of the firm's AR and MR curves. For a competitive (price taker) firm, the AR and MR curves are both horizontal and coincidental [Eqs. (6.18) and (6.20)] while for a monopoly (price maker) firm, the two are distinct and downward sloping. They start from the same point but MR goes steeper than AR at all levels of output [Eqs. (6.23) and (6.24)]. As regards the average and marginal cost curves, they continue to be same as those in case of a competitive firm. Short-run and long-run equilibria are differentiated from each other on the basis of difference in the nature of the short-run and long-run average and marginal cost curves.

9.1 PRICE-OUTPUT DECISIONS OF MONOPOLY IN SHORT-RUN

A monopoly is thus a price maker with distinct and down-wardly sloping AR and MR curves. The short-run equilibrium of the firm is characterized by its short-run marginal cost curve (SMC) cutting its MR curve from below.

There emerge three possibilities for the equilibrium of a monopoly in short-run. In the first case, the monopoly makes abnormal profit (Figure 9.1); in the second, it makes normal profit (Figure 9.2) and in the third case, it suffers loss (Figure 9.3).

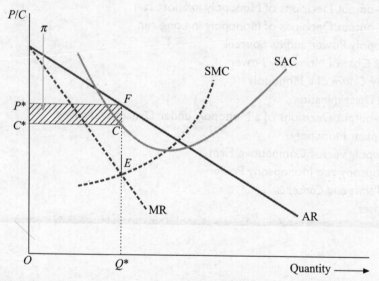

FIGURE 9.1 Short-run abnormal profit of monopoly: The short-run equilibrium of the monopoly takes place at point E, where SMC cuts MR from below, thereby, satisfying both the conditions of profit maximization. A vertical line through E cuts AR at F and SAC at C. The corresponding output is OQ^*, price is Q^*F or OP^* and average cost (AC) is Q^*C or OC^*. The profit per unit is C^*P^* and the total profit, π, given by the area of the shaded rectangle is $C^*P^* \times OQ^*$.

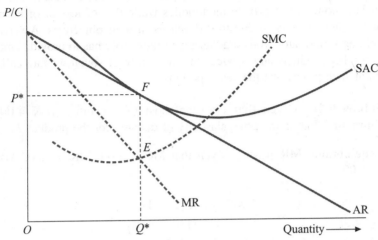

FIGURE 9.2 Short-run normal profit of a monopoly: Equilibrium takes place at point E. The profit-maximizing output is OQ^* and price, OP^*. In equilibrium, AR = AC = Q^*F. Profit per unit is 0. The firm makes only a normal profit.

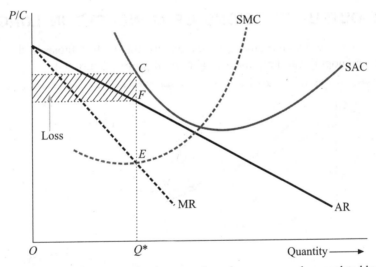

FIGURE 9.3 Short-run loss of a monopoly: A monopoly such as one owned or regulated by state may incur loss in short-run as shown by the shaded rectangle. The reason for the loss is the location of SAC which is higher than that of AR.

Being a price maker, a private monopoly enjoys every chance of avoiding loss. A government monopoly in a welfare-oriented economy, on the other hand, may run into loss due to price controls.

In each of the three cases, MC cuts MR from below and hence it is equal to MR at the equilibrium. As is obvious, the monopoly produces along the falling part of the short-run average cost curve (SAC) and sticks to the upper-half of its AR curve in each of three cases for its pricing decisions.

The short-run analysis of equilibrium of a monopoly firm reveals that the situation of abnormal profit (Figure 9.1) is common to private monopolies while that of loss or of normal profits, to government monopolies. This is so due to differences in their objectives. A private monopoly operates for profit as a motivator while a government monopoly has to provide amenities, public utilities and such other products and services that the cause of social welfare calls for. Also, it distributes them at such prices that the cause permits.

ILLUSTRATION 9.1: Given that marginal cost of a product is ₹ 4.00 and price, ₹ 8.00 in equilibrium. What is the price elasticity of demand for the product?

Solution: In equilibrium, MR = MC. Given that MC = 4.00, MR = 4.00. Also, given that $P = 8.00$, AR = 8.00.
We know that

$$MR = AR\,[1 - (1/|e|)]$$
$$\Rightarrow\quad 4 = 8\,[1 - (1/|e|)]$$
$$\Rightarrow\quad 1/|e| = 1 - (1/2)$$
$$\Rightarrow\quad |e| = 2$$
$$\Rightarrow\quad e = -2.$$

9.2 PRICE-OUTPUT DECISIONS OF MONOPOLY IN LONG-RUN

In the long-run, average and marginal cost curves are flatter than those in the short-run. The result is that no monopoly can help itself to abnormal profit (Figure 9.4).

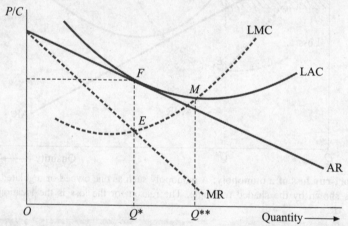

FIGURE 9.4 Long-run normal profit of a monopoly: Even in the long-run, a monopoly produces along the falling part of the average cost curve [LAC] and sticks to the upper-half of the AR curve for pricing. The optimal output is OQ^{**} [corresponding to the lowest point on the LAC] but a monopoly produces only OQ^* which is less than this. The difference of optimal output over the actual output of a monopoly is known as its **excess capacity**. It is Q^*Q^{**}. The monopoly earns only the normal profit. Note that the normal profit in this figure differs from the normal profit of Figure 9.2. Here, it is a consequence of long-run adjustments while in Figure 9.2, it is an eventuality of short-run.

9.3 MONOPOLY POWER AND ITS SOURCES

For a competitive firm, price is always equal to the marginal cost, whether it is operating in short-run or in long-run. As against this, price is always higher than the marginal cost for a monopoly. In fact, excess of price over MC expressed as a ratio of price is known as the **monopoly power** of a firm. This measure of the monopoly power was introduced by economist Abba Lerner in 1934 and is often known after the name of the economist as Lerner's Index of Monopoly Power*. Symbolically,

$$\text{Monopoly power of a firm} = \frac{P - MC}{P}$$

$$= \frac{AR - MR}{AR}$$

(Since $P = AR$ and $MC = MR$ at the equilibrium)

$$= \frac{AR - AR(1 - 1/|e|)}{AR}$$

[Since $MR = AR(1 - 1/|e|)$]

$$= \frac{AR[1 - 1 + 1/|e|]}{AR}$$

$$= \frac{1}{|e|} \qquad (9.1)$$

where, $|e|$ is the numerical measure of the price elasticity of demand.

Equation (9.1) shows that the monopoly power of a firm varies inversely as the numerical value of the price elasticity of demand. The horizontal AR curve being its demand curve, the monopoly power of a competitive firm is zero as the price elasticity of its demand is infinite. The same is infinitely large for a monopoly firm having perfectly inelastic AR curve ($e = 0$). When $e = 1$, monopoly power of a firm is also 1(100 %). *The steeper the demand curve faced by a firm, the higher the monopoly power of the firm.* In other words, the higher the price elasticity of demand of a firm, the lower the monopoly power it has. Price elasticity of demand is thus the main source of monopoly power. Its other sources comprise the number of buyers (market size) and the extent of interaction among them.

There are a number of problems associated with the measurement of monopoly power. Let us outline some of them below:

1. The firms must know the demand curves they are facing. This may not be as easy as it appears.
2. The firms must know their MCs. This being difficult, the firms use average variable cost in their calculations.
3. The dynamic aspects of pricing such as shifts in demand and the learning curve effects must not exist.

---

*Pindyck Robert S., and Daniel S. Rubinfeld, *Microeconomics*, 5th Ed., Pearson Education Inc. (2004), Delhi, pp. 333–334.

4. The firms must not resort to fixing price below its optimal level. To the contrary, they must resort to a pricing policy in which price is kept below the optimal level only with a view to avoid legal complications.

9.4 SOCIAL COST OF MONOPOLY POWER

The social responsibility of a firm, among other things, implies that the firm must provide quality product at a reasonable price to the consumers. From the discussions so far, it is evident that consumers cannot be as happy with a monopoly as with a competitive firm because the monopoly provides less at a higher price than what a competitive firm does. In other words, social welfare is lower under monopoly than that under a competitive firm.

Figure 9.5 demonstrates how a monopoly leads to loss of social welfare.

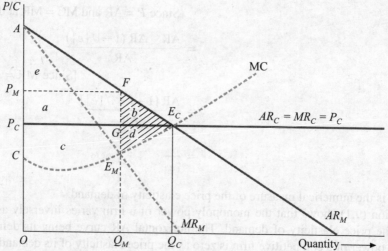

FIGURE 9.5 Social cost of monopoly: Let the firm be a competitive one initially, with its average and marginal revenue curves coincidental and horizontal ($AR_C = MR_C$). Its equilibrium takes place at E_C where it produces and sells quantity OQ_C at a price OP_C. Now suppose the firm transforms into a monopoly. Its AR_C and MR_C change respectively to AR_M and MR_M, both sloping downwards, MR_M being twice as steep as AR_M. As a monopoly, it fixes its equilibrium position at E_M where it produces quantity OQ_M to sell it at a price OP_M. Evidently, it supplies less [$OQ_M < OQ_C$] at a higher price [$OP_M > OP_C$] as a monopoly than as a competitive firm. The transformation leads to loss of social-welfare by a measure $FGE_M E_C$ [the shaded portion, ($b + d$)]. When the firm behaved as a competitive one, consumers enjoyed a surplus of $AP_C E_C$. Now they enjoy only $AP_M F$. They have thus lost a surplus worth the area of the trapezium $P_M P_C E_C F$ ($a + b$), of which, $P_M P_C GF$ ($= a$) is acquired by the firm in the form of gain in producer's surplus as a monopoly; and the rest, FGE_C ($= b$), accrues to none and hence is a loss of social welfare. In like manner, when the firm behaved as a competitive one, it enjoyed a surplus of $CE_M E_C P_C$ ($c + d$) as producer's surplus. Now it enjoys $CE_M FP_M$. Change in it involves a gain of $P_M P_C GF$ ($= a$) and a loss of $GE_M E_C$ ($= d$). The loss accrues to none and hence is a loss of social welfare. The total loss of social welfare is the sum of the two, i.e. $GE_M E_C$ ($= d$) + FGE_C ($= b$) = $FE_M E_C$ [$= (b + d)$]. The loss of social welfare, the **dead weight loss***, is a consequence of the firm's transformation into monopoly.

---

*An easier way of its analysis is computing change in social welfare as a sum of changes in consumer's and producer's surpluses, that is, $\Delta W = \Delta CS + \Delta PS = [e - (a + b + e)] + [(c + a) - (c + d)] = -(a + b) + (a - d) = -(b + d)$.

Loss of social welfare, $(b + d)$, called the deadweight loss, is a social cost of monopoly power. One part of it, b, represents loss of consumer's surplus and the other, d, that of producer's surplus. Consumer's surplus, as defined on several occasions in Chapter 2, represents excess of consumers' disposable income over their current consumption expenditure, which they are willing to forego to sustain their existing level of consumption in the event of scarcity. In the figure, it is represented by the area of triangle $AP_C E_C$ when the firm is a competitive one and by the area of triangle $AP_M F$ when it is a monopoly. Producer's surplus, likewise, is the excess of total revenue over the total variable cost. The total revenue is the product of price and quantity and total variable cost is represented by the area under the MC curve between $Q = 0$ and $Q = Q_C$ or Q_M depending on whether the firm is a competitive one or a monopoly. In the former case, the producer's surplus is $CP_C E_C$ $(c + d)$ and in the latter, it is $CP_M FGE_M$ $(c + a)$.

The social cost associated with monopoly makes it economically less efficient than a competitive firm. Causes responsible for the social cost include sub-optimal operations of monopoly and its policy of setting a price above its MC.

9.5 SUPPLY CURVE OF A MONOPOLY

A monopoly has no unique supply curve derived from its MC. Given the marginal cost curve, a monopoly may offer same quantity at different prices or different quantities at same price. Figure 9.6 demonstrates how a monopoly supplies same quantity at different prices and Figure 9.7 demonstrates how it supplies different quantities at same price.

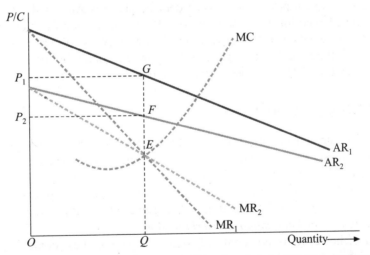

FIGURE 9.6 Monopoly supplies same quantity at different prices in different markets: The monopoly sells same quantity OQ at different prices in two markets. It charges OP_1 in market one with demand AR_1, and marginal revenue, MR_1 (at G) and OP_2 in market two with demand AR_2 and marginal revenue, MR_2 (at F). Note that its AR curves are non-parallel with different origins at the vertical axis and that corresponding MR curves intersect each other at point E.

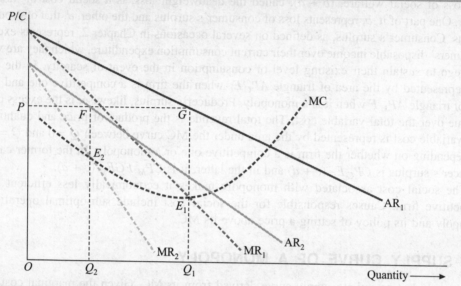

FIGURE 9.7 Monopoly supplies different quantities at same price in different markets: The monopoly sells different quantities, OQ_2 (when demand curve is AR_2) and OQ_1 (when demand curve is AR_1) at the same price (OP) in the two markets. Note that its AR curves are non-parallel with different origins at the vertical axis and that corresponding MR curves do not intersect each other.

In Figure 9.6, different prices, OP_1 (when demand curve is AR_1) and OP_2 (when demand curve is AR_2), are charged for the same quantity (OQ) by the monopoly in different markets.

In Figure 9.7, different quantities, OQ_1 (when demand curve is AR_1) and OQ_2 (when demand curve is AR_2), are offered at the same price (OP) by the monopoly in different markets.

From Figures 9.6 and 9.7, we observe that a monopoly firm has no unique supply curve.

9.6 PRICE DISCRIMINATION

A monopoly, if private, aims at profit maximization. They even resort to discriminatory pricing policies for the purpose. Price discrimination may be defined as a practice of charging different prices for same or identical products. The practice of charging different prices from different individuals is called *personal discrimination*, that of charging different prices at different places is called *geographical discrimination* and that of charging different prices at different points of time, is called the *time* or *intertemporal discrimination*.

The practice, however, is not confined to private monopolies alone. It extends also to professionals such as doctors, lawyers, chartered accountants who charge different fee for same or identical services from different persons, at different times or in different locations as also to certain state monopolies such as railways and electricity boards, which charge different rates for identical services on the basis of nature and quantum of their use. Private monopolies generally resort to geographical and time discrimination while government mon-opolies resort to use-based and slab-based discrimination. Price charged by private monopolies in domestic market is usually different from that charged by them in a foreign market, while price charged by state for electricity differs from domestic to commercial uses and from one level of consumption to another.

Thus, practice of price discrimination has gained ground even with the natural* or government regulated monopolies. Apart from use-based and slab-based discrimination government monopolies practice personal discrimination as well but with some justification. The best examples of the use-based and slab-based price are provided by the state electricity boards, which charge different rates for commercial and domestic use of power as also for its high or low levels (slabs) of power consumption. There are different rates for commercial and domestic use of power and so is the case with higher and lower slabs of power consumption in India. The same has been the case with State-run telephone services here. Lower rates have been applicable to lower call slabs. The ideology is simple. The state has to provide minimum basic services to the multitudes at affordable rates even if the rates charged fall short of average cost. The loss is offset by the higher rates charged on the lavish use of service. Indian Railways charge different fares for same journey from different individuals with some justification of higher rates through comforts and facilities offered.

The objectives of the private and the regulated monopolies are, however, different. While private monopolies do it for profit motive, the regulated monopolies do it for recovery of costs incurred or for regulation of consumption. The question that arises now is—'can such practices be carried out indefinitely?' To investigate, let us first see the conditions that are essential for the success of price discrimination:

(a) In respect of the geographical discrimination, the condition necessary for success of price discrimination is inequality of price elasticities of demand. To demonstrate, let us take the example of domestic and foreign markets with price elasticities of e_1 and e_2 respectively. Let the prices charged in these markets be respectively P_1 and P_2 and let the respective MRs in the two be denoted as MR_1 and MR_2. Then,

$$MR_1 = P_1\left[1 - \frac{1}{e_1}\right] \tag{9.2}$$

and
$$MR_2 = P_2\left[1 - \frac{1}{e_2}\right] \tag{9.3}$$

The condition of equilibrium requires equality of each of MR_1 and MR_2 to the firm's MC. That is,

$$MR_1 = MC = MR_2**$$
$$\Rightarrow \qquad MR_1 = MR_2$$

---

*A **natural monopoly** refers to a large-sized state monopoly with huge fixed costs and decliningly low AC and MC curves. Such monopolies often provide public utilities with a view to maximize social welfare. The important feature of such monopolies is their huge fixed costs which private monopolies often find difficult to shell out. Moreover, large scale operations help reduction in the marginal costs. This facilitates distribution of the utilities at low prices. Unlike a simple monopoly, a natural monopoly does not need to restrict entry of new firms therefore. Examples of natural monopolies are the state enterprises generating and distributing power and providing telephone services in India. Natural monopolies are either state operated or state regulated. A price equal to the marginal cost makes distribution Pareto-efficient but leads to a loss to the monopoly. A price equal to the average cost helps recovery of the total cost but renders distribution Pareto-inefficient as the quantity supplied falls. A profit-maximizing price is even worse from the viewpoint of Pareto efficiency [Figure 9.9]. A natural monopoly, therefore, resorts to discriminatory pricing policies which might be use-based and/or slab-based. The objective is twin-maximization of social welfare as well as recovery of costs.

**Monopoly profit
$$\pi = TR_1 + TR_2 - TC \qquad\qquad (Contd.)$$
$$= P_1Q_1 + P_2Q_2 - TC$$

$$\Rightarrow \qquad P_1\left[1-\frac{1}{|e_1|}\right] = P_2\left[1-\frac{1}{|e_2|}\right]$$

$$\Rightarrow \qquad \frac{P_1}{P_2} = \frac{\left[1-\dfrac{1}{|e_2|}\right]}{\left[1-\dfrac{1}{|e_1|}\right]} \qquad (9.4)$$

It can be verified that $P_1 > P_2$ when $|e_1| < |e_2|$.
For instance, if $|e_1| = 2$, and $|e_2| = 4$, then we have

$$\frac{P_1}{P_2} = \frac{\left[1-\dfrac{1}{4}\right]}{\left[1-\dfrac{1}{2}\right]}$$

$$= 1.50$$

$$\Rightarrow \qquad P_1/P_2 > 1$$
$$\Rightarrow \qquad P_1 > P_2 \qquad (9.5)$$

Thus, a higher price is set in a less elastic market and a lower one, in a more elastic market. If the price elasticities in the two markets were the same, the prices charged too would be the same, i.e. $P_1 = P_2$. This means price discrimination cannot be practiced if the two markets have identical price elasticities.

Apart from the condition of different price elasticities of demand in the two markets, segregation of the markets is also essential for the success of geographical price discrimination. If the markets are not segregated, consumers would trespass from the costlier to the cheaper market and the practice of price discrimination would collapse.

(b) In respect of personal discrimination, it is essential that the individuals must not belong to the same social group. This is particularly relevant to the case of price discrimination by professionals. A doctor charging different fees from individuals belonging to the same social groups cannot last long with such discriminatory policies. The patients would learn of it soon and he would lose at least those ones who he has over-charged.

(Footnote contd.)
Differentiating partially with respect to Q_1 and Q_2, we have

$$\partial\pi/\partial Q_1 = \partial(TR_1)/\partial Q_1 - \partial(TC)/\partial Q_1$$
$$= MR_1 - MC,$$

[since $Q = Q_1 + Q_2$, $\partial(TC)/\partial Q_1 = \{\partial(TC)/\partial Q\}\{\partial Q/\partial Q_1\} = MC \cdot 1 = MC$]

Likewise,
$$\partial\pi/\partial Q_2 = \partial(TR_2)/\partial Q_2 - \partial(TC)/\partial Q_2$$
$$= MR_2 - MC$$

For maximization of profits, first order partial derivatives must be equal to zero. Setting so, we have

$$MR_1 = MR_2 = MC$$

The reader can verify the second order and the cross-partial derivative conditions to hold good.

Discriminatory policies even of the regulated monopolies succeed only when consumers belong to different socio-economic groups so that the state has some rational justification for charging different prices for identical products. For example, charging a higher rail fare from rich passengers, only on the basis of their incomes, would be resented by the affected, but the same is not when it is done in the name of luxurious journey, such as airconditioned coaches.

9.6.1 The Objectives of Price Discrimination

For a private monopoly, the objective of price discrimination is maximization of its profit. This can be shown easily through Figure 9.8.

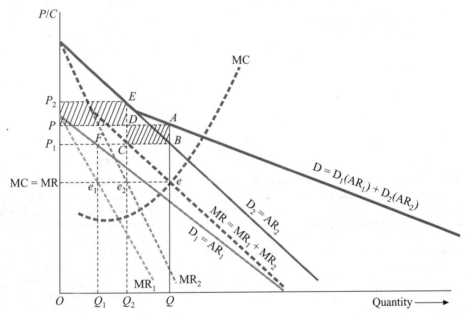

FIGURE 9.8 Discriminating monopoly earns higher revenue than a simple monopoly: A discriminating monopoly faces demand D_1 (AR_1) in the first market and D_2 (AR_2) in the second market. The respective MR curves are MR_1 and MR_2. The total market demand is $D(AR_1 + AR_2)$ and the aggregate marginal revenue curve is $MR = MR_1 + MR_2$. The market demand curve is obtained through the horizontal summation of AR_1 and AR_2 while the total MR curve, through that of the MR_1 and MR_2. Market equilibrium is determined at the point e, the point of intersection of MC and MR. The horizontal line through e meets MR_1 and MR_2 at e_1 and e_2 respectively. The discriminating monopoly sells Q_1 in market one at a price P_1 and Q_2 in market two at a price P_2 earning revenue OQ_1FP_1 from market one and OQ_2EP_2 from market two. Total revenue earned from the two markets through discriminatory policies is, thus, $OQ_1FP_1 + OQ_2EP_2$. If the monopoly behaves like a simple monopoly, it will sell output Q at a price P, earning a revenue of $OQAP$. It can be shown through geometry that $OQ_1FP_1 = Q_2QBC$ as $Q_2Q = Q - Q_2 = Q_1$. Area OQ_2DP is common to areas OQ_2EP_2 and $OQAP$. Revenue realized through discriminatory policy from the market two exceeds OQ_2DP by $PDEP_2$ (shaded) while that realized through discriminatory policy from market one (i.e. Q_2QBC) falls short of Q_2QAD by $CBAD$. Through discriminatory policy, the monopoly gets $PDEP_2$ more but $CBAD$ less than when behaving like a simple monopoly. From the figure, it is clear that $PDEP_2 > CBAD$. Thus, a monopoly earns higher revenue through price discrimination than without it. A higher revenue with same production costs would lead the monopoly to a higher profit.

A discriminating monopoly earns a higher profit than a simple monopoly as explained in Figure 9.8. A State monopoly, on the other hand, does not aim at profit. Instead, its objectives invariably focus on welfare maximization on the first count and recovery of production costs on the second. To serve these ends, a State monopoly uses an appropriate mix of marginal cost pricing, average cost pricing and/or profit-maximizing pricing, as explained in Figure 9.9.

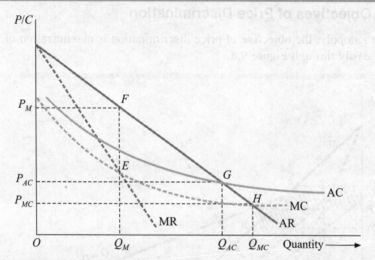

FIGURE 9.9 **Pricing policies of state monopolies:** State monopoly or a regulated monopoly may set profit maximizing price P_M and sell quantity Q_M or set a price P_{MC} = MC and sell quantity Q_{MC} or set a price P_{AC} = AC and sell quantity Q_{AC} or even evolve a mix of these policies in which P_{MC} is charged from low income people, P_{AC} from middle income people while P_M from high income people or may even introduce low pricing policy (P_{MC}) for low level of consumption and a high price policy (P_M) for high level of consumption. The latter relates to the consumption-slabs. Pricing of electric-power in India is an example of slab-pricing policy. Note that the MC and the AC curves for a **Natural Monopoly** are falling curves due to declining average and marginal costs. Also note that output Q_{MC} is Pareto-efficient but leads to negative profits while Q_{AC} is Pareto-inefficient but helps the cause of cost recovery but output Q_M generates profits but is even more Pareto-inefficient than Q_{AC} (See Section 16.2 for Pareto-efficiency).

9.6.2 Degrees of Price Discrimination

British economist A.C. Pigou* has classified price discrimination as third-, second- and first-degree price discrimination depending on the extent of consumer's surplus it helps to mop up. The three degrees of price discrimination are depicted in Figures 9.10, 9.11 and 9.12.

Suppose a monopoly has Q units to sell and the profit-maximizing price is P. In the third-degree price discrimination, the monopoly sets a price higher than the profit-maximizing price, P, to mop up a limited part of the consumer's surplus (shaded, Figure 9.10). In the second-degree price discrimination, the monopoly sets several prices above the profit maximizing level, to mop up a much larger part of the consumer's surplus (Figure 9.11). In Figure 9.12, the monopoly varies price along its demand curve for each unit it sells so as to mop up entire cosumer's surplus.

---

*Pigou, A.C., *The Economics of Welfare,* 4th Ed., Macmillan, 1950.

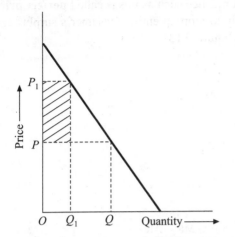
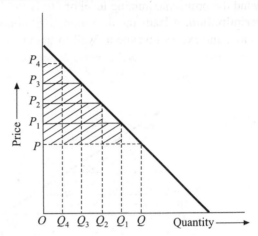

FIGURE 9.10 Third-degree price discrimination: Monopoly mops away a small part of the consumer's surplus by setting a price higher than the profit-maximizing level.

FIGURE 9.11 Second-degree price discrimination: Monopoly mops away a larger part of the consumer's surplus by setting prices higher than the profit-maximizing level several times.

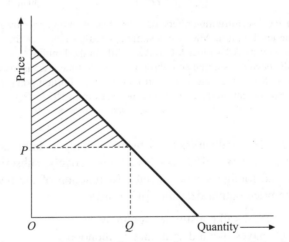

FIGURE 9.12 First-degree price discrimination: Monopoly mops away whole of the consumer's surplus by varying price continuously on the demand curve for each unit sold before the profit-maximizing level.

9.6.3 Effects of Price Discrimination

We have seen above how a discriminating monopoly increases its total revenue and hence total profits by reducing price of successive units of its output until its profit-maximizing price is reached. If a discriminating monopoly continues price-cutting even below its profit-maximizing level, the practice would lead to upward pivotal shifts in its MR each time price is cut until at last it coincides with its AR-curve. In the limiting case, MC = AR = MR at point e''' (Figure 9.13). Excess quantity sold beyond the profit-maximizing level of OQ is QQ''' and excess price-cut beyond the profit-maximizing level of OP is PP'''. A practice such as this is called **perfect price discrimination.** It leads the discriminating monopoly to mop up entire consumer's surplus and also to some excess revenue as well in the process (Figure 9.13).

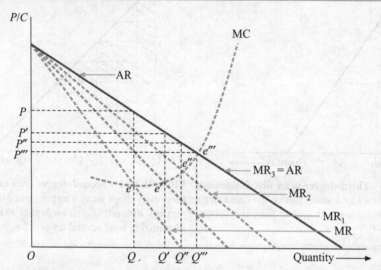

FIGURE 9.13 **Perfect price discrimination** refers to the practice of cutting price by a discriminating monopoly below its profit-maximizing level until its MR, which shifts upward-to-right each time an additional unit is sold at a lower price, coincides with its AR so that MC = AR = MR in the limiting case. The pivotal shifts in MR arise due to a rise in the MC beyond its initial equilibrium at e. Each time price is lowered by the firm below P, the equilibrium point and the MR-curve must both shift upwards (equilibrium point, from e to e''' and the MR curve, from MR to MR_3). The output produced and sold increases from OQ to OQ'''.

ILLUSTRATION 9.2: Demand curves faced by a monopoly in domestic and foreign markets are $Q_d = 32{,}000 - 0.4\, P_d$ and $Q_f = 18{,}000 - 0.1\, P_f$ respectively, subscripts d and f represent variables in domestic and foreign sectors. Total cost function of the firm is TC = $50{,}000 + 40{,}000\,Q$. Compare the price-output decisions of the firm

(i) when the firm behaves like a simple monopoly
(ii) when the firm behaves like a discriminating monopoly.

Calculate the profits earned by the firm in each case and show that a higher price is charged in the less elastic market and a lower one, in the more elastic market.

Solution:
(i) When the firm behaves like a simple monopoly

If the firm behaves like a simple monopoly, it would charge same price from both the markets. Given the demand functions of the two markets,

$$Q_d = 32{,}000 - 0.4\, P_d$$

and
$$Q_f = 18,000 - 0.1\, P_f$$

the market demand can be derived through horizontal summation of the two with $P_d = P_f = P$. Thus,

$$Q_D = Q_d + Q_f$$
$$= 32,000 - 0.4P + 18,000 - 0.1P$$
$$= 50,000 - 0.5P$$

Or
$$P = 100,000 - 2Q_D \qquad (9.6)$$

Total revenue,
$$TR = P \cdot Q_D$$
$$= [100,000 - 2Q_D] \cdot Q_D$$
$$= 100,000\, Q - 2Q^2 \qquad \text{(replacing } Q_D \text{ by } Q)$$

Given,
$$TC = 50,000 + 40,000Q \qquad (9.7)$$

The profit function can be expressed as

$$\pi = TR - TC$$
$$= 100,000Q - 2Q^2 - 50,000 - 40,000Q$$
$$= 60,000Q - 2Q^2 - 50,000 \qquad (9.8)$$

Differentiating the profit function with respect to Q, we have

$$d\pi/dQ = 60,000 - 4Q \qquad (9.9)$$

Setting $d\pi/dQ$ at zero for profit maximization, we have

$$60,000 - 4Q = 0$$

$\Rightarrow$
$$Q = 15,000$$
and
$$P = 70,000 \quad [\text{substituting } Q = 15,000 \text{ in Eq. (9.6)}]$$

Differentiating Eq. (9.9) with respect to Q once again, we have

$$d^2\pi/dQ^2 = -4$$

This satisfies the second order condition of maximization as $d^2\pi/dQ^2 < 0$ for all Q. Hence, monopoly profit is maximized at $Q = 15,000$ and $P = 70,000$.

Substituting these values in the profit function, we have

$$\pi = 60,000 \times 15,000 - 2 \times (15,000)^2 - 50,000$$
$$= 449,950,000$$

(ii) When the firm behaves like a discriminating monopoly

The profit function in this case is

$$\pi = TR_d + TR_f - TC$$

$$= P_d Q_d + P_f Q_f - TC$$
$$= [80{,}000 - 2.5Q_d]\, Q_d + [180{,}000 - 10Q_f]\, Q_f - 50{,}000 - 40{,}000Q \qquad (9.10)$$

Substituting, $Q = (Q_d + Q_f)$ in Eq. (9.10) and simplifying, we have

$$\pi = 40{,}000\, Q_d - 2.5\, (Q_d)^2 + 140{,}000\, Q_f - 10\, (Q_f)^2 - 50{,}000 \qquad (9.11)$$

The conditions of maximization of π, a function of two variables, Q_d and Q_f, require

(a) $\partial \pi/\partial Q_d = 0$ and $\partial \pi/\partial Q_f = 0$
(b) $\partial^2 \pi/\partial(Q_d)^2 < 0$ and $\partial^2 \pi/\partial(Q_f)^2 < 0$
(c) $[\partial^2 \pi/\partial(Q_d)^2]\,[\partial^2 \pi/\partial(Q_f)^2] > [\partial^2 \pi/\partial(Q_d)\,\partial(Q_f)]^2$

Differentiating Eq. (9.11) with respect to Q_d and Q_f partially, we have

$$\partial \pi/\partial Q_d = 40{,}000 - 5Q_d$$
$$= 0 \qquad \text{[as per condition (a)]}$$
$$\Rightarrow \quad Q_d = 8{,}000$$

and
$$\partial \pi/\partial Q_f = 140{,}000 - 20Q_f$$
$$= 0 \qquad \text{[as per condition (a)]}$$
$$\Rightarrow \quad Q_f = 7{,}000$$

Differentiating again partially with respect to Q_d and Q_f, we have

$$\partial^2 \pi/\partial(Q_d)^2 = -5$$

and
$$\partial^2 \pi/\partial(Q_f)^2 = -20$$

This satisfies condition (b). To meet condition (c), differentiate

$$\partial \pi/\partial Q_d = 40{,}000 - 5Q_d$$

partially with respect to Q_f or differentiate

$$\partial \pi/\partial Q_f = 140{,}000 - 20Q_f$$

partially with respect to Q_d so that

$$\partial^2 \pi/\partial(Q_d)\,\partial(Q_f) = 0$$
$$\Rightarrow \quad [\partial^2 \pi/\partial(Q_d)\,\partial(Q_f)]^2 = 0 \qquad (9.12)$$

Since $\partial^2 \pi/\partial(Q_d)^2 = -5$
and $\partial^2 \pi/\partial(Q_f)^2 = -20$

we have
$$[\partial^2 \pi/\partial(Q_d)^2]\,[\partial^2 \pi/\partial(Q_f)^2] = (-5)(-20) = +100 \qquad (9.13)$$

From Eqs. (9.12) and (9.13), we have

$$[\partial^2 \pi/\partial(Q_d)^2]\,[\partial^2 \pi/\partial(Q_f)^2] > [\partial^2 \pi/\partial(Q_d)\,\partial(Q_f)]^2$$

Hence, all the conditions of profit maximization are satisfied at

$$Q_d = 8{,}000 \text{ and } Q_f = 7{,}000$$

Corresponding prices from the respective demand functions are

$$P_d = 60{,}000 \text{ and } P_f = 110{,}000$$

The profit of the discriminating monopoly works out at

$$\pi = 649{,}950{,}000$$

[on substituting the values of P_f, P_d, Q_d, Q_f in Eq. (9.11)]

Comparing the results of (i) and (ii), we observe that the firm sells 1500 units of the output in each case but earns a higher profit (695,950,000 > 449,950,000) in the second case.

Price elasticity of demand in the domestic market

$$= (dQ_d/dP_d) \times (P_d/Q_d)$$
$$= (-0.4) \times (60{,}000/8{,}000)$$

[substituting for the derivative and for the variables from the data given]

$$= -3$$

Price elasticity of demand in the foreign market

$$= (dQ_f/dP_f) \times (P_f/Q_f)$$
$$= (-0.1) \times (110{,}000/7{,}000)$$
$$= -1.57143$$

As $|-3| > |-1.57143|$, domestic demand is more elastic than the foreign demand.

Price charged in the domestic market is 60,000 which is less than that charged in the foreign market (110,000).

This supports the observation that a *higher price is charged by a discriminating monopoly in the less elastic market and a lower price, in the more elastic market*.

9.6.4 Existence of Monopoly through Price Discrimination

In case demand functions in different sectors of a market are such that total demand obtained through their horizontal summation lies below the average cost curve, the monopoly firm cannot survive charging a uniform price like a simple monopoly. But its survival is quite possible if it resorts to discriminatory practices as shown in Figure 9.14.

9.6.5 Other Forms of Price Discrimination

There are two other forms of price discrimination:

1. Intertemporal Price Discrimination
2. Peak Load Pricing.

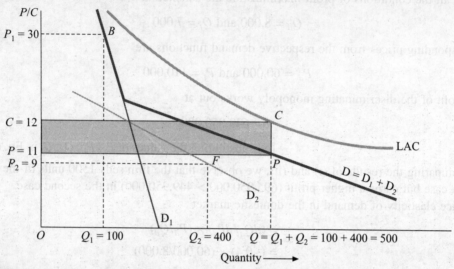

FIGURE 9.14 Existence of loss making monopoly through price discrimination: The monopoly faces a less elastic demand (D_1) in market 1 and a more elastic demand (D_2) in market 2. The total demand curve D is obtained through horizontal summation of D_1 and D_2. The long-run cost curve, LAC, lies above D at all levels of output. Let the total output be Q, which if sold at a uniform price P, would lead to a loss equal to area of the shaded rectangle. Resorting to price discrimination may help the firm not only in getting rid of the loss but also in making some profit. Charging a higher price P_1 in less elastic market (Market 1) and a lower price P_2 in more elastic market (Market 2) helps the firm in raising revenue equal in area to the sum of the areas of rectangles $OQ_1B\,P_1$ and $OQ_2F\,P_2$ so that it is larger than the area of the rectangle $OQPP$. A numerical illustration would help understanding the statement. Let $Q = 500$ units, $Q_1 = 100$ units, $Q_2 = 400$ units so that $Q = Q_1 + Q_2$. Let LAC = 40, 15 and 12 at $Q_1 = 100$, $Q_2 = 400$ and $Q = 500$ respectively. If the firm behaves like a simple monopoly and charges a uniform price of 11 (less than the average cost of 12) to sell the total output of 500 units, TR = 500 × 11 = 5,500 and TC = 500 × 12 = 6,000. The simple monopoly thus runs into a loss of 500. But if it charges a price of 30 in the first market to sell 100 units and a price of 9 in the second market to sell 400 units, TR= 30 × 100 + 9 × 400 = 6,600 which is higher than the total cost of producing 500 units. The loss-making monopoly, thus, would make a profit of 600 by resorting to price discrimination.

Let us introduce them briefly here.

1. Intertemporal Price Discrimination

Under this, consumers are segmented into groups with distinct price-elasticities of demand. A high price (P_1) is set for consumers with less elastic demand. After skimming all the cream from them, the discriminating monopoly turns to consumers with more elastic demand and sets a lower price for them. The process continues until no segment is left (Figure 9.15).

2. Peak Load Pricing

The practice of charging a high price during peak hours of demand is called *peak load pricing*. Charging a higher price during peak hours is efficient as MC is higher during peak hours. The practice is quite common to all monopolies whether they are private or State-operated. For instance, toll tax is higher on Delhi–Noida–Delhi toll bridge (DND-bridge) during peak hours than during off peak hours. Prices of woolens are higher during winters than during summers. Figure 9.16 explains the mechanism.

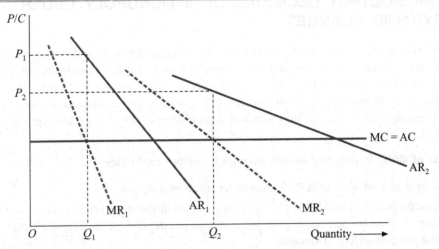

FIGURE 9.15 Intertemporal price discrimination: Consumers are divided into groups on the basis of their demand elasticities. Here, we discuss two groups—one with inelastic demand and the other with elastic demand. Initially, the firm fixes a high price in the less elastic market and skims all the cream from it. Later, the firm lowers the price for the consumers with more elastic demand. The consumers with less elastic demand are often the rich who cannot wait for price to fall. Others with elastic demand comprise masses who wait until price settles down. The objective of the firm is to maximize profits.

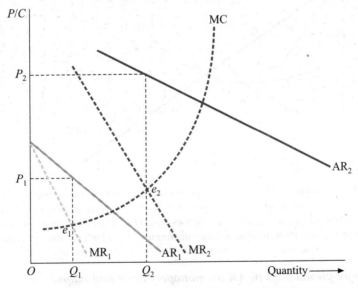

FIGURE 9.16 Peak load pricing: AR_2 and MR_2 represent the demand and the MR curves during the peak period while AR_1 and MR_1 represent those during the off peak period. MC curve cuts MR_2 at e_2, determining price as P_2 and it cuts MR_1 at e_1, determining price as P_1 [$P_2 > P_1$]. The firm sells quantity Q_2 at P_2 and Q_1 at P_1. A higher price during peak period is efficient as MC is higher.

9.7 PRICE-OUTPUT DECISIONS OF A MONOPOLY UNDER DYNAMIC CHANGES

Shifts in AR, MR and MC are consequences of changes known as dynamic changes. For instance, levy of unit tax shifts the MC curve upwards by the magnitude of the tax. A downward parallel shift in AR of a monopoly may be a consequence of entry of a stubborn rival. This is accompanied by a shift in the MR curve of the monopoly as well. Here, we discuss a few situations to show how some of such changes influence price-output decisions of a monopoly.

(a) Effect of shifts in demand on the monopoly output and price

(i) Effect of a pivotal shift in AR on monopoly price and output

An outward pivotal shift in AR may result in higher sale at the same price or same sale at higher price (Figure 9.17). In fact, changes in price and output depend on the extent of shift in AR as also on the price elasticity of demand.

Effect of an inward pivotal shift in AR is opposite. Quantity sold at the same price decreases or price of the same quantity falls. So do the profit margin and the supernormal profit.

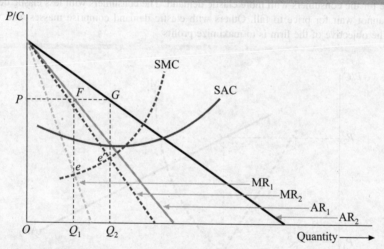

FIGURE 9.17 Effect of a pivotal shift in AR on price output decisions of a monopoly: Demand curve faced by the monopoly shifts from AR_1 to AR_2. In consequence, MR curve shifts from MR_1 to MR_2. Firm's equilibrium shifts from e to e' and output produced and sold increases from Q_1 to Q_2. Price charged remains unchanged at P even after the shift of demand. Profit margin and the supernormal profit both increase as evident from the figure.

(ii) Effect of a non-pivotal shift in AR on monopoly price and output

A non-pivotal shift may be parallel or non-parallel. It may lead to an increase in output and price both depending on the extent of shift and the price elasticity of demand faced by the monopoly firm (Figure 9.18).

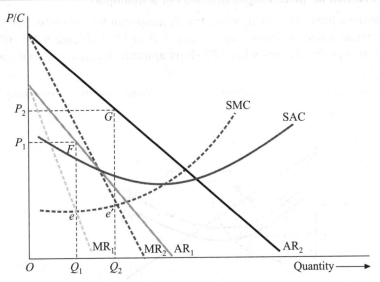

FIGURE 9.18 Effect of a non-pivotal shift in AR on price-output decisions of a monopoly: A non-pivotal shift in demand curve faced by a monopoly is accompanied by a non-pivotal shift in its MR curve. Price and output will both increase in consequence if the shift is upward and the same may be said for profit-margin and supernormal profit. Opposite is the result if the non-pivotal shift is downward.

If the price elasticity of demand also changes with the shift in demand, output may increase but the price may fall as shown in Figure 9.19.

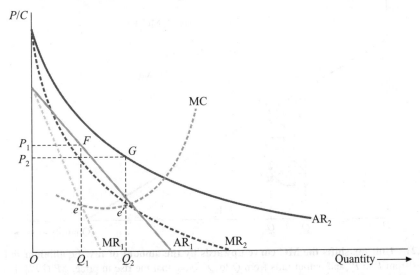

FIGURE 9.19 Effect of a pivotal shift accompanied by a change in price elasticity of demand: If a shift in demand is accompanied by a change in its linearity as well, the price charged by a monopoly falls while its output increases as shown in the figure.

(b) Effect of taxation on price-output decisions of a monopoly

Tax levied may be a lump-sum tax or a unit tax. A lump-sum tax causes an upward shift in AC (Figure 9.20), while a unit tax causes an upward shift in MC* (Figure 9.21). When AC shifts upwards, the firm's profit falls and when MC shifts upwards, its price rises but output and profit both fall.

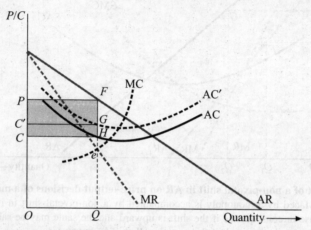

FIGURE 9.20 Levy of lump-sum tax shifts AC upwards to AC': This reduces the profit margin of the firm. MC curve remains unaffected and so are the firm's output and price. The only effect of the levy is a decline in firm's profits from rectangle $CHFP$ to rectangle $C'GFP$.

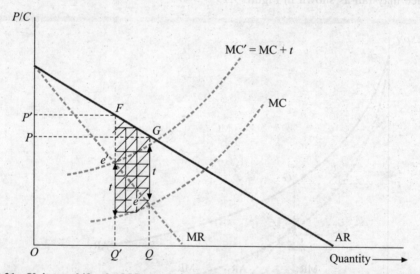

FIGURE 9.21 Unit tax shifts the MC curve upwards by the amount of tax: Equilibrium shifts from e to e', price rises from P to P' and output falls from Q to Q'. Note that the rise in price, ΔP (PP'), is less than the levy of the tax ($\Delta P < t$). Shaded region shows **deadweight loss**.

*See Section 8.3.

(i) *Effect of lump-sum tax*

Levy of a lump-sum tax shifts the average fixed cost curve upwards, leaving the MC curve, unaffected. As a result, equilibrium of a monopoly remains unchanged while its profit margin declines. Upward shift in AFC shifts the ATC upwards, which reduces the firm's profit margin and hence its total profit (Figure 9.20).

(ii) *Effect of a unit tax*

On the other hand, levy of a unit tax, t, shifts the MC curve upwards (see Section 8.3) to MC' (MC + t), as shown in Figure 9.21. From the figure, only a part of the tax is shifted onto the consumers, ΔP (PP') < t. So long as the AR and MR curves of the monopoly are linear, tax shifting onto the consumers would be only partial. Rest of it would be borne by the firm. We will examine three cases here.

(a) When both AR and MR are linear (Figures 9.22 and 9.23)

When demand (AR) is linear, so is corresponding MR [Eq. (9.16)]. Let MC be $\bar{c}$, a constant, leading to a horizontal MC curve as shown in Figure 9.22. Expressing AR curve as

$$P = \alpha - \beta Q \quad (9.14)$$

We have
$$TR = PQ$$
$$= (\alpha - \beta Q) \cdot Q$$
$$= \alpha Q - \beta Q^2 \quad (9.15)$$

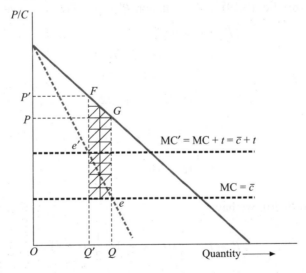

FIGURE 9.22 **Effect of a unit tax on price-output of a monopoly with linear AR and MR and fixed MC:** When MC is horizontal, shift in it caused by a unit tax leads to an increase in price by exactly half of the unit tax ($\Delta P = 1/2 \cdot t$). Equation (9.22) explains the result. The shaded region marks the **deadweight loss.**

Differentiating Eq. (9.15) with respect to Q, we have

$$MR = \alpha - 2\beta Q \qquad (9.16)$$

For equilibrium, MC = MR. Thus, when MC = $\overline{c}$

$$\alpha - 2\beta Q = \overline{c}$$

$$\Rightarrow \qquad Q = (\alpha - \overline{c})/2\beta \qquad (9.17)$$

Price at this output is

$$\begin{aligned} P &= \alpha - \beta Q \\ &= \alpha - \beta[(\alpha - \overline{c})/2\beta] \\ &= \alpha - (\alpha - \overline{c})/2 \\ &= \alpha + \overline{c}/2 - \alpha/2 \\ &= \frac{1}{2}(\alpha + \overline{c}) \end{aligned} \qquad (9.18)$$

Levy of unit tax t shifts MC to MC′, where, MC′ = MC + t = $\overline{c}$ + t. The new equilibrium requires

$$MC' = MR$$

$$\Rightarrow \qquad \overline{c} + t = \alpha - 2\beta Q'$$

$$\Rightarrow \qquad Q' = (\alpha - \overline{c} - t)/2\beta \qquad (9.19)$$

where, Q' = output at the new equilibrium

Substituting for Q' from Eq. (9.19) in the equation $P' = \alpha - \beta Q'$, we have

$$\begin{aligned} P' &= \alpha - \beta Q' \\ &= \alpha - \beta[(\alpha - \overline{c} - t)/2\beta] \\ &= \alpha - [(\alpha - \overline{c} - t)/2] \\ &= (2\alpha - \alpha + \overline{c} + t)/2 \\ &= \frac{1}{2}(\alpha + \overline{c} + t) \end{aligned} \qquad (9.20)$$

$$= \frac{1}{2}(\alpha + MC') \qquad (9.21)$$

(Since, $\overline{c} + t$ = MC′)

From Eqs. (9.18) and (9.20), we have

$$\begin{aligned} P' - P &= \frac{1}{2}(\alpha + \overline{c} + t) - \frac{1}{2}(\alpha + \overline{c}) \\ &= \frac{1}{2} \cdot t \end{aligned}$$

Thus,

$$\Delta P = \frac{1}{2} \cdot t, \text{ where, } \Delta P = P' - P \qquad (9.22)$$

Next, let MC $= \bar{c} + mQ$, where m, a constant, represents the slope of MC, as in Figure 9.23. Rewriting Eq. (9.17), we have

$$\alpha - 2\beta Q = \bar{c} + mQ$$

$$\Rightarrow \quad Q = (\alpha - \bar{c})/(m + 2\beta) \tag{9.23}$$

Substituting in $P = \alpha - \beta Q$, we have

$$P = \alpha - \beta(\alpha - \bar{c})/(m + 2\beta)$$
$$= (\alpha m + \alpha\beta + \beta\bar{c})/(m + 2\beta) \tag{9.24}$$

When tax is levied, Eq. (9.19) may be rewritten as

$$Q' = (\alpha - \bar{c} - t)/(m + 2\beta) \tag{9.25}$$

Substituting in $P' = \alpha - \beta Q'$, we have

$$P' = \alpha - \beta(\alpha - \bar{c} - t)/(m + 2\beta)$$
$$= (\alpha m + \alpha\beta + \beta\bar{c} + \beta t)/(m + 2\beta) \tag{9.26}$$

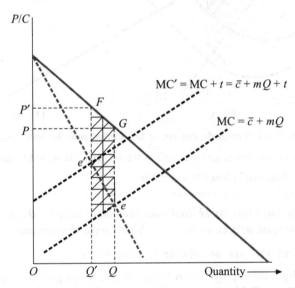

FIGURE 9.23 Effect of a unit tax on price-output of a monopoly with linear AR and MR and upward rising linear MC: When MC is linear and upward sloping, shift in it caused by a unit tax leads to an increase in price by less than half the tax ($\Delta P < 1/2 \cdot t$). Equation (9.29) explains the result. The shaded region marks **the deadweight loss.**

Subtracting Eq. (9.24) from Eq. (9.26), we have

$$P' - P = \beta t/(m + 2\beta) \tag{9.27}$$

[Expression (9.27) reduces to (9.22) as soon as we substitute $m = 0$ in it.]

From Eq. (9.27), we have

$$\Delta P = \beta t/(m + 2\beta) \tag{9.28}$$

Since $(m + 2\beta) > 2\beta$, $\beta t/(m + 2\beta) < \beta t/2\beta$ or $< \frac{1}{2} \cdot t$

Hence
$$\Delta P < \frac{1}{2} \cdot t \tag{9.29}$$

If MC is a second degree function, the tax shifted onto the consumer may be still less (Figure 9.24).

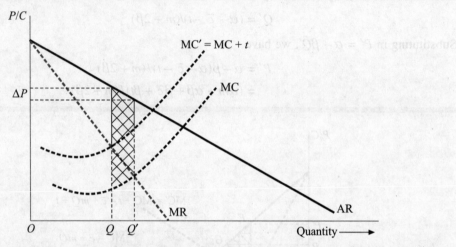

FIGURE 9.24 **When MC is a second degree curve tax shifted may be less than that when it is linear:** When MC curve is parabolic, as shown, less than half of the tax levied is shifted to the consumers $\left(\Delta P < \frac{1}{2} \cdot t\right)$. The shaded region shows **deadweight loss** due to taxation.

Thus, when MC is constant, tax shifted onto the consumers is 50% and when MC is linear sloping upward or a second degree curve, tax shifted onto the consumers is less than 50%.

(b) When both AR and MR are non-linear (Figure 9.25)

When demand faced by a monopoly is non-linear, such as that given by demand function,

$$P = k/(Q + a) \tag{9.30}$$

(where, k and a are constants)

Expression for TR may be given as

$$\text{TR} = PQ$$
$$= kQ/(Q + a) \tag{9.31}$$

Differentiating Eq. (9.31) with respect to Q, we have

$$\text{MR} = ak/(Q + a)^2 \tag{9.32}$$

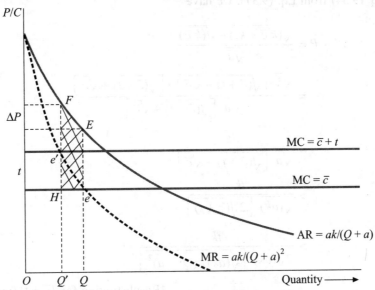

FIGURE 9.25 Both AR $[P = k/(Q + a)]$ and MR $= ak/(Q + a)^2$ are non-linear. MC is taken to be constant, MC $= \bar{c}$. When tax t is levied per unit of output, price-rise is higher than half the value of the tax. $\Delta P > \frac{1}{2} \times t$ Eq. (9.39). Note that demand in this case though non-linear, it is not a constant elasticity demand. The shaded region shows **deadweight loss** caused by unit tax.

If MC $= \bar{c}$, equilibrium output is given by

$$\bar{c} = ak/(Q + a)^2$$

$$\Rightarrow \qquad Q = \sqrt{(ak/\bar{c})} - a \qquad (9.33)$$

Substituting for Q in Eq. (9.30), we have

$$P = k/[(\sqrt{ak/\bar{c}}) - a + a]$$
$$= \sqrt{\{\bar{c}k/a\}} \qquad (9.34)$$

When unit tax t is levied, MC $= \bar{c} + t$. Post-tax equilibrium may be given as

$$\bar{c} + t = ak/(Q' + a)^2 \qquad (9.35)$$

(where Q' is new equilibrium quantity)

Whence,

$$Q' = \sqrt{\{(ak)/(\bar{c} + t)\}} - a \qquad (9.36)$$

Substituting for Q' in $P' = k/(Q' + a)$, we have

$$P' = k/\sqrt{\{(ak)/(\bar{c} + t)\}}$$
$$= \sqrt{k(\bar{c} + t)}/(\sqrt{a}) \qquad (9.37)$$

Subtracting Eq. (9.34) from Eq. (9.37), we have

$$P' - P = \frac{\sqrt{(k\overline{c} + kt)} - \sqrt{(k\overline{c})}}{\sqrt{a}}$$

$$= \frac{\sqrt{k} \cdot \left[\sqrt{(\overline{c}+t)} - \sqrt{\overline{c}}\right] \times \left[\sqrt{(\overline{c}+t)} + \sqrt{\overline{c}}\right]}{\sqrt{a} \cdot \left[\sqrt{(\overline{c}+t)} + \sqrt{\overline{c}}\right]}$$

$$= \frac{t\sqrt{k}}{\sqrt{a} \cdot \left[\sqrt{(\overline{c}+t)} + \sqrt{\overline{c}}\right]} \tag{9.38}$$

$$> \frac{tk}{\sqrt{(ak)} \cdot \left[2\sqrt{(\overline{c}+t)}\right]}$$

$$> \frac{tk}{2\sqrt{(ak)} \cdot \left[\sqrt{(ak)/(Q'+a)^2}\right]}$$

[Resubstituting for $(\overline{c} + t)$ from Eq. (9.35)]

$$> \frac{1}{2} \times \left[1 + \frac{Q'}{a}\right] \times t$$

$$\Rightarrow \quad \Delta P > \frac{1}{2} \times t \tag{9.39}$$

(c) When demand faced by a monopoly is a constant elasticity demand (Figure 9.26)

It can be seen that demand faced by a monopoly in part (b) is not a constant elasticity demand despite its non-linearity. As shown below, its price elasticity varies inversely with price

$$E_P^D = [dQ/dP] \times [P/Q]$$
$$= [(-k/P^2) \times \{P^2/(k - aP)\}]$$
$$= [k/(aP - k)] \tag{9.40}$$

For a demand function such as

$$Q = k/P^2 \tag{9.41}$$

price elasticity of demand is constant at every point on it.

$$E_P^D = [dQ/dP] \times [P/Q]$$
$$= [-2k/P^3] \times [P/(k/P^2)]$$
$$= [-2k/P^3] \times [P^3/k]$$
$$= -2 \text{ (constant)}$$

Rewriting Eq. (9.41) with P as its subject, we have

$$P = \sqrt{k}/\sqrt{Q} \tag{9.42}$$

Then
$$TR = PQ$$

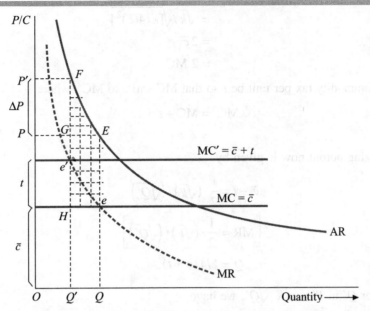

FIGURE 9.26 Constant elasticity demand (AR) faced by a monopoly leads to a non-linear MR: If MC = $\bar{c}$ (constant), equilibrium takes place at e where quantity Q is sold at price P. Levy of unit tax t shifts MC to MC′= $\bar{c} + t$ and the equilibrium to e' where quantity Q' is sold at price P'. Rise in price, $\Delta P(P'- P)$ is higher than the unit tax. In fact, $\Delta P = 2t$ [Eq. (9.50)]. The shaded region represents the loss of social welfare (deadweight loss) caused by unit tax.

$$= \left[\sqrt{k}/\sqrt{Q}\right] \cdot Q$$
$$= \sqrt{(kQ)}$$

And
$$\text{MR} = d(\text{TR})/dQ$$
$$= \frac{1}{2} \cdot (\sqrt{k})/(\sqrt{Q}) \qquad (9.43)$$

Now for simplicity, Let MC be constant so that
$$\text{MC} = \bar{c} \qquad (9.44)$$

Then profit-maximizing output and price are given by the condition
$$\text{MC} = \text{MR}$$
$$\Rightarrow \qquad \bar{c} = \frac{1}{2} \cdot (\sqrt{k})/(\sqrt{Q})$$
$$\Rightarrow \qquad Q = k/4(\bar{c})^2 \qquad (9.45)$$

Substituting this value of Q in Eq. (9.42), we have
$$P = \sqrt{k}/\sqrt{Q}$$

$$= \sqrt{k}/\sqrt{[k/4(\overline{c})^2]}$$
$$= 2\overline{c} \qquad (9.46)$$
$$= 2 \text{ MC}$$

Now let the commodity tax per unit be t so that MC shifts to MC', where

$$\text{MC}' = \text{MC} + t$$
$$= \overline{c} + t \qquad (9.47)$$

Profit-maximizing output now is given by

$$\overline{c} + t = \frac{1}{2} \cdot (\sqrt{k})/(\sqrt{Q'})$$
$$\left[\text{MR} = \frac{1}{2} \cdot (\sqrt{k})/(\sqrt{Q'}) \right]$$
$$\Rightarrow \qquad Q' = k/4(\overline{c} + t)^2 \qquad (9.48)$$

Substituting for Q' in $P' = \sqrt{K}/\sqrt{Q'}$, we have

$$P' = \sqrt{k}/\sqrt{[k/4(\overline{c}+t)^2]}$$
$$= 2 \cdot (\overline{c} + t) \qquad (9.49)$$

Subtracting Eq. (9.46) from Eq. (9.49), we have

$$P' - P = 2t$$

That is
$$\Delta P = 2t \qquad (9.50)$$

From Eq. (9.50), it is clear that increase in price is twice the value of the tax levied.

We have seen how a commodity tax influences monopoly price of a commodity. In our analysis, we made an implicit assumption that the unit tax levied remains fixed, at least during our analysis.

What if it varies from time to time? To see, let us consider the relation,

$$\text{MR} = \text{AR}[1 - 1/|e|] \qquad (9.51)$$
$$= P[1 - 1/|e|] \qquad (9.52)$$
$$\text{(Since AR} = P\text{)}$$

Also, since MR = MC at equilibrium, we have from Eq. (9.52) that

$$\text{MC} = P[1 - 1/|e|]$$

Or
$$P = \text{MC}/[1 - 1/|e|] \qquad (9.53)*$$

---

*Price P expressed as a function of MC and price elasticity of demand is known as the **mark-up price** of a monopoly. Coefficient $[1/\{1- (1/|e|)\}]$, the coefficient of mark-up, is always greater than 1 for a monopoly as its price elasticity of demand is always greater than 1 in equilibrium.

Now suppose MC increases to MC', where MC' = MC + t. Here t is the magnitude of the unit tax. If MC is constant, $\bar{c}$, we have

$$P' = (\bar{c} + t)/[1 - 1/|e|] \tag{9.54}$$

Differentiating Eq. (9.54) with respect to t (t being variable), we have

$$dP'/dt = 1/[1 - 1/|e|] \tag{9.55}$$

Since $\Delta P = (dP/dt) \cdot \Delta t$, we have

$$\Delta P = \{1/(1 - 1/|e|)\} \cdot \Delta t \tag{9.56}$$

We have seen in Chapter 7 that a monopoly sticks to the upper-half of its demand curve so that its MR $\geq$ 0. We have also seen that the price elasticity of demand, e, for the upper-half of the AR curve is numerically greater than 1, i.e. $|e| > 1$. The expression $1/|e|$, thus, is less than 1 and hence,

$$0 < \{1 - 1/|e|\} < 1$$

Therefore,

$$\{1/(1 - 1/|e|)\} > 1$$

Now, let $\{1/(1 - 1/|e|)\}$ be α so that $\alpha > 1$. The expression in Eq. (9.56), therefore, reduces to

$$\Delta P = \alpha \cdot \Delta t, \text{ where, } \alpha > 1 \tag{9.57}$$

Thus,

$$\Delta P > \Delta t$$

This implies that the increase in the product price is higher than the increase in the unit tax.

9.8 MULTIPLANT MONOPOLY

A multiplant monopoly, as the name suggests, has several plants operating generally in different locations. Product is homogeneous but production costs may be different in different plants. As it appears, the monopoly must choose one with the lowest production cost or prefer to operate a single plant to benefit from its economies of scale. The reasons for operating from different plants in different locations are the following three:

1. *Transportation costs:* When markets are widely scattered, distribution of products from a single plant involves huge transportation costs. This distorts price. Apart from this, if productive resources too are widely scattered, multiplant operations prove cost effective by eliminating transportation costs of resources.
2. *Deterrence to local entry:* Widely scattered potential markets often attract entry of local firms. A multiplant monopoly can check such entry more effectively.
3. *Supply lags:* A local plant can monitor demand and supply of a market more effectively than a plant located far away.

There are a few subjective reasons also that encourage multiplant operations of a monopoly. To some monopolies, diversification of production lends a sense of security; to others, smaller plants and markets are easier to handle; and, to a few others, multiplant operations help in allocative efficiency of the family members of the owner. To understand the price-output decisions of a multiplant monopoly, suppose, for simplicity, that a monopoly has two plants producing quantities Q_1 and Q_2 respectively at costs C_1 and C_2 where

$$C_1 = f(Q_1) \tag{9.58}$$

and

$$C_2 = g(Q_2) \tag{9.59}$$

Given the market demand as,

$$P = h(Q)$$
$$= h(Q_1 + Q_2) \tag{9.60}$$

The profit function of the multiplant monopoly can be expressed as

$$\pi = TR - TC$$
$$= R - C$$
$$= R - C_1 - C_2 \tag{9.61}$$

Clearly, π is a function of two variables, Q_1 and Q_2. Differentiating π partially with respect to Q_1 and Q_2, we have

$$\partial \pi / \partial Q_1 = \partial R / \partial Q_1 - \partial C_1 / \partial Q_1$$
$$= MR_1 - MC_1$$
$$= 0 \quad \text{(For maximization of profit)}$$

$\Rightarrow$

$$MR_1 = MC_1 \tag{9.62}$$

and

$$\partial \pi / \partial Q_2 = \partial R / \partial Q_2 - \partial C_2 / \partial Q_2$$
$$= MR_2 - MC_2$$
$$= 0 \quad \text{(For maximization of profit)}$$

$\Rightarrow$

$$MR_2 = MC_2 \tag{9.63}$$

But

$$MR_1 = \partial R / \partial Q_1$$
$$= (\partial R / \partial Q) \times (\partial Q / \partial Q_1)$$
$$= MR \times 1$$

$(\partial Q / \partial Q_1 = \partial (Q_1 + Q_2) / \partial Q_1 = 1$ as $\partial Q_2 / \partial Q_1 = 0)$

$$= MR \tag{9.64}$$

Likewise

$$MR_2 = MR \tag{9.65}$$

From Eqs. (9.62), (9.63), (9.64) and (9.65), we have

$$MR_1 = MR_2 = MR = MC_1 = MC_2 \tag{9.66}$$

Equation (9.66) provides the necessary condition of equilibrium of a multiplant monopoly. Sufficient conditions to ensure maximization of profit are:

1. $\partial^2\pi/\partial Q_1^2 < 0$ and $\partial^2\pi/\partial Q_2^2 < 0$
2. $(\partial^2\pi/\partial Q_1^2)(\partial^2\pi/\partial Q_2^2) > (\partial^2\pi/\partial Q_1\partial Q_2)^2$

Figures 9.27, 9.28 and 9.29 demonstrate equilibrium of the multiplant monopoly.

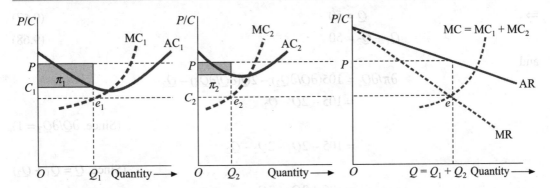

FIGURE 9.27 Plant with lower cost: The plant has a higher market share (Q_1) and a higher individual profit, π_1. Price and equilibrium are determined by the central agency.

FIGURE 9.28 Plant with higher cost: The plant has a lower market share (Q_2) and a lower individual profit, π_2. Price and equilibrium are both determined by the central agency.

FIGURE 9.29 Output of multiplant monopoly: It is determined by the intersection of MC and MR at e. Total output = Q, where $Q = Q_1 + Q_2$. Market price is the monopoly price P, which maximizes profit of multiplant monopoly.

An illustration would explain the working of multiplant monopoly.

ILLUSTRATION 9.3: A multiplant monopoly facing the market demand

$$Q = 105 - P$$

operates through two plants with production costs

$$C_1 = 5Q_1, \text{ and}$$
$$C_2 = 0.5Q_2^2$$

Determine:
1. Profit-maximizing output and price of the monopoly as also the amount of profit accruing to it.
2. Allocation of output among plants and individual profits accruing to them.

Solution: Profit,

$$\pi = TR - TC$$
$$= PQ - C_1 - C_2$$
$$= [105 - Q]Q - 5Q_1 - 0.5Q_2^2$$
$$= 105Q - Q^2 - 5Q_1 - 0.5Q_2^2$$

Differentiating π partially w.r.t Q_1 and Q_2, we have

$$\partial \pi / \partial Q_1 = 105(\partial Q / \partial Q_1) - 2Q(\partial Q / \partial Q_1) - 5$$
$$= 105 - 2Q - 5$$

(Since, $\partial Q / \partial Q_1 = 1$)

$$= 100 - 2Q$$
$$= 0$$

(For maximization of π)

$\Rightarrow \qquad Q = 50$ \hfill (9.67)

$\Rightarrow \qquad Q_1 + Q_2 = 50$ \hfill (9.68)

and

$$\partial \pi / \partial Q_2 = 105(\partial Q / \partial Q_2) - 2Q(\partial Q / \partial Q_2) - Q_2$$
$$= 105 - 2Q - Q_2$$

(Since, $\partial Q / \partial Q_2 = 1$)

$$= 105 - 2Q_1 - 2Q_2 - Q_2$$

(Since, $Q = Q_1 + Q_2$)

$$= 105 - 2Q_1 - 3Q_2$$
$$= 0$$

(For maximization of π)

$\Rightarrow \qquad 2Q_1 + 3Q_2 = 105$ \hfill (9.69)

Solution of simultaneous Eqs. (9.68) and (9.69) yields

$$Q_2 = 5$$
$$Q_1 = 45$$

Substituting for Q in the equation of demand, we have

$$P = 105 - Q$$
$$= 105 - 50$$
$$= 55$$

Substituting values of Q, Q_1 and Q_2 in the profit function, we have

$$\pi = 105Q - Q^2 - 5Q_1 - 0.5Q_2^2$$
$$= 105 \times 50 - (50)^2 - 5 \times 45 - 0.5 \times (5)^2$$
$$= 5250 - 2500 - 225 - 12.5$$
$$= 2512.50$$

Profit accruing to the first plant,

$$\pi_1 = PQ_1 - 5Q_1$$
$$= 55 \times 45 - 5 \times 45$$
$$= 2250$$

Profit accruing to the second plant

$$\pi_2 = PQ_2 - 0.5Q^2$$
$$= 55 \times 5 - 0.5 \times 25$$
$$= 262.50$$

To ensure maximization, we must have

$$\partial^2 \pi / \partial Q_1^2 < 0$$
$$\partial^2 \pi / \partial Q_2^2 < 0$$
$$(\partial^2 \pi / \partial Q_1^2)(\partial^2 \pi / \partial Q_2^2) > (\partial^2 \pi / \partial Q_1 \partial Q_2)^2$$

Successive differentiation of the profit function gives

$$\partial^2 \pi / \partial Q_1^2 = -2 \text{ (i.e. } \partial^2 \pi / \partial Q_1^2 < 0)$$
$$\partial^2 \pi / \partial Q_2^2 = -3 \text{ (i.e. } \partial^2 \pi / \partial Q_2^2 < 0)$$
$$(\partial^2 \pi / \partial Q_1^2)(\partial^2 \pi / \partial Q_2^2) = (-2) \times (-3) = 6;$$
$$(\partial^2 \pi / \partial Q_1 \partial Q_2) = -2 \text{ so that, } (\partial^2 \pi / \partial Q_1 \partial Q_2)^2 = 4$$

and hence

$$(\partial^2 \pi / \partial Q_1^2)(\partial^2 \pi / \partial Q_2^2) > (\partial^2 \pi / \partial Q_1 \partial Q_2)^2$$
(as 6 > 4)

9.9 MONOPOLY VERSUS COMPETITIVE FIRM

By this time, it must be clear to the reader that a monopoly is poles apart from a competitive firm in many ways. For ready reference, we enumerate some important differences below:

1. A competitive firm is a price-taker while a monopoly is a price-maker.
2. The AR and MR curves for a competitive firm are the same. When plotted, each gives a horizontal line coinciding with the other. In case of a monopoly, the two curves are distinct, each sloping downwards, MR being twice as steep as AR.
3. In the long-run, a competitive firm operates at its optimal capacity, i.e. it produces at the lowest average cost. As against this, a monopoly produces along the falling part of the average cost curve, retaining an excess capacity all along.
4. For a competitive firm, price is always equal to the marginal cost. For a monopoly, it is always higher than the marginal cost and is always determined along the upper-half of the AR curve. The ratio of excess of price over MC to the price is called the monopoly power of a firm.

$$\text{Monopoly Power of a firm} = (P - MC)/P = 1/|e| \qquad \text{[from Eq. (9.1)]}$$

That is, monopoly power of a firm is inversely related to the price elasticity of demand. For a competitive firm, price elasticity of demand being infinity, its monopoly power is zero. Even otherwise, the fact is a pre-established one as P = MC for a competitive firm.

In case of a monopoly, it is always non-zero, approaching infinity when $e = 0$ (for vertical AR).
5. Social welfare is higher under a competitive firm and lower under a monopoly. A monopoly sells less at a higher price than a competitive firm.
6. The rising part of the MC curve serves as the supply curve (Figures 8.17, 8.18 and 8.19) for a competitive firm while no supply curve exists for a monopoly. It can, in fact, supply different quantities at same price (Figure 9.7) or same quantity at different prices (Figure 9.6).
7. All monopolies, whether private or state-owned, resort to discriminatory pricing policies. Such practices cannot be possible for a competitive firm for which MR is always equal to AR.

A monopoly, therefore, is economically less efficient than a competitive firm. Its sub-optimal operations (excess capacity) and its policy of pricing above its MC are sufficient to substantiate the statement.

9.10 MONOPSONY AND MONOPSONY POWER

We have so far discussed how a single seller dictates price-output decisions. In Chapter 7, we discussed how a monopsony, a single buyer, does the same thing. When a single buyer buys a product, he is said to be receiving value. The total value (TV) received from Q units can be represented as

$$TV = vQ \qquad (9.70)$$

(where, v is the value per unit of a product and Q is the quantity of the product bought)
In exchange of the value received, the buyer incurs expenditure. Total expenditure (TE) incurred by him on Q units at price p can thus be represented as

$$TE = pQ \qquad (9.71)$$

(where, p is the price or expenditure incurred per unit of the product and Q is the quantity bought)
The net benefit (NB) of the buyer can be expressed as

$$NB = TV - TE \qquad (9.72)$$
$$= vQ - pQ$$

The buyer, being single and hence in a dictating position, has to determine the net benefit maximizing quantity that he should buy. The necessary and the sufficient conditions for the purpose are

$$d(NB)/dQ = 0 \text{ and } d^2(NB)/dQ^2 < 0$$

Differentiating Eq. (9.70) with respect to Q, we have

$$d(NB)/dQ = d(TV)/dQ - d(TE)/dQ$$
$$= MV - ME$$
$$= 0 \qquad \text{(as per the necessary condition)}$$

For the net benefit maximizing quantity the necessary condition thus is

$$MV = ME \tag{9.73}$$

Differentiating Eq. (9.70) once again with respect to Q, we have, for maximization,

$$d(MV - ME)/dQ < 0$$
$$\Rightarrow \qquad d(MV)/dQ < d(ME)/dQ$$
$$\Rightarrow \qquad \text{The slope of the MV curve} < \text{The slope of the ME curve} \tag{9.74}$$

According to the law of diminishing marginal utility, the MV curve must slope downwards and according to the increasing marginal utility of money, the ME curve must slope upwards.
For determining the net benefit maximizing quantity, the ME curve must therefore cut the MV curve from below as shown in Figure 9.30.

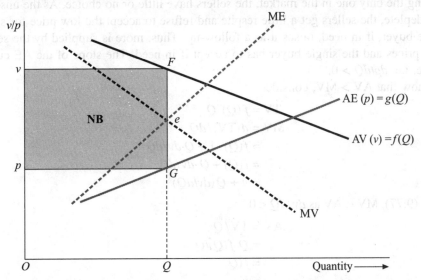

FIGURE 9.30 As per the conditions of net benefit maximization, ME cuts MV from below, as shown, at point e. The monopsony buys OQ spending Op per unit. The value received by the monopsony is Ov per unit and the net benefit maximized by it is the region **vGFp** (shaded).

Note that both v and p are functions of Q, i.e. $v = f(Q)$ and $p = g(Q)$. The former, $v = f(Q)$, is a decreasing function of Q so that $dv/dQ < 0$; and the latter, $p = g(Q)$, is an increasing function of Q, so that $dp/dQ > 0$. The net benefit is the difference of the average value v(AV) received over average expenditure p(AE) incurred per unit. The facts that we still need to establish are: (a) AE < ME, and (b) AV > MV.

To show that AE < ME, consider

$$TE = g(Q) \cdot Q$$

So that
$$ME = d(TE)/dQ$$
$$= g(Q) \cdot 1 + Q \cdot dp/dQ$$

$$= g(Q) \cdot 1 + Q \cdot dp/dQ$$
$$= p + Q \cdot \frac{dp}{dQ} \qquad (9.75)$$

And
$$AE = TE/Q$$
$$= [g(Q) \cdot Q]/Q$$
$$= g(Q)$$
$$= p \qquad (9.76)$$

From Eqs. (9.75) and (9.76), since $dp/dQ > 0$, we have
$$ME > AE$$

Note that $dp/dQ > 0$ because AE [$p = g(Q)$] is a supply curve, which slopes upwards as usual. The single buyer starts with a low price and increases it when sellers reject it. Quite often a low price is accepted by firms with large unsold stocks or by firms hard pressed for cash. The buyer being the only one in the market, the sellers have little or no choice. As the unsold stocks begin to deplete, the sellers get a little respite and refuse to accept the low price for subsequent units. The buyer, if in need, raises it as a follow-up. Thus, more is supplied by the sellers only at higher prices and the single buyer has to accept if in need. The slope of the AE curve, thus, is positive, i.e. $dp/dQ > 0$.

To show that AV > MV, consider
$$TV = f(Q) \cdot Q$$

Then
$$MV = d(TV)/dQ$$
$$= f(Q) \cdot 1 + Q \cdot dv/dQ$$
$$= f(Q) + Q \cdot dv/dQ$$
$$= v + Q(dv/dQ) \qquad (9.77)$$

From Eq. (9.77), MV < AV as $dv/dQ < 0$
and
$$AV = TV/Q$$
$$= Q \cdot f(Q)/Q$$
$$= f(Q)$$
$$= v$$

Note that AV is the demand curve of the single buyer for whom value of every additional unit has a diminishing trend by virtue of the law of diminishing marginal utility. Hence, MV < AV.

9.10.1 Monopsony Power and its Sources

We have seen that a monopoly charges a price higher than its MC and that monopoly power of a firm is given as $(P - MC)/P$. We have also seen that monopoly power is inversely related to price elasticity of demand.

On the same lines, we can define monopsony power as well. We have just shown that a monopsony pays a price (p) which is less than the MV of the product. The monopsony power can thus be defined as a ratio of the difference of the MV of a unit of product over its price to its price. Thus,

$$\text{Monopsony power} = (MV - p)/p$$
$$= (ME - p)/p$$

(Since MV = ME at the point of equilibrium)

$$= (p \cdot 1 + Q \cdot dp/dQ - p)/p$$

[From Eq. (9.75), ME $= p \cdot 1 + Q \cdot dp/dQ$]

$$= (Q/p) \times (dp/dQ)$$
$$= 1/[(p/Q) \times (dQ/dp)]$$
$$= 1/E_P^S \text{ or simply } 1/e_s \quad (9.78)$$

Thus, if the supply curve is perfectly elastic, that is, if the AE curve is horizontal as in the case of a competitive buyer, the monopsony power of the buyer is zero as ME = AE = p. In like manner, if elasticity of supply is zero (as for a perfectly inelastic supply), the monopsony power of the buyer would be ∞ (infinity).

Thus, among others, the main source of the monopsony power is the price elasticity of supply. The other sources that may contribute to the monopsony power are the number of buyers and the extent of interaction among them.

9.10.2 Social Costs of Monopsony Power

Just as the monopoly power has its social cost in the form of deadweight loss, so has the monopsony power too.

Deadweight loss caused by it is shown in Figure 9.31.

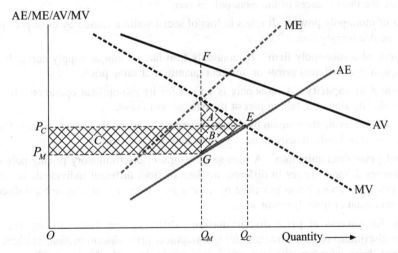

FIGURE 9.31 Let the competitive price and the quantity be P_C and Q_C: Now, suppose the buyer turns monopsonistic paying a price P_M for quantity Q_M [$P_M < P_C$ and $Q_M < Q_C$]. The change (loss) in the producer's surplus $= -(C + B)$ and that (gain) in the consumer's (buyer's) surplus $= +(C - A)$. The buyer gains C due to a fall in price but loses A due to loss of quantity ($Q_C - Q_M$). Thus, net loss of social welfare = Change in producer's surplus + Change in consumer's surplus $= -(C + B) + (C - A) = -(B + A)$, which being negative is a loss of social welfare (**a deadweight loss**).

The social cost of the monopsony power is thus a loss of social welfare (deadweight loss). Monopsony too, like a monopoly, causes loss of social welfare.

KEY TERMS AND CONCEPTS

Monopoly A single seller, producing along the falling part of AC and sticking to the upper-half of its demand curve for pricing. It has no unique supply curve and often resorts to discriminatory pricing policies to raise surpluses. It invariably sustains excess capacity due to its sub-optimal size of operations causing substantial loss of social welfare.

Natural monopoly A monopoly, having huge fixed costs and decliningly low AC and MC, operated or regulated by State and known for large-scale production and distribution of basic amenities or essential services, is called a natural monopoly. It may resort to marginal cost pricing if maximizing social welfare or to average cost pricing if recovering its production costs or even to profit-maximizing pricing if maximizing its profits. Nowadays, a natural monopoly mixes the three in suitable proportions to maximize social welfare without sacrificing its objective of cost-recovery.

Monopoly power Defined as a ratio of difference of price over marginal cost to the price and expressed as an index, it expresses strength of the monopoly character of a firm. It is inversely related to the price elasticity of demand.

$$\text{Monopoly power} = (P - MC)/P$$
$$= 1/|e|$$

For a competitive firm, the monopoly power is 0 and for a monopoly firm facing a unitary elastic demand, it is 1.00 or 100%. If the price elasticity of demand is 0, the monopoly power is infinite.

Sources of monopoly power Price elasticity of demand, number of firms and the extent of interaction among them are the three sources of the monopoly power.

Social cost of monopoly power It refers to loss of social welfare caused by monopoly practices. The loss is called the deadweight loss.

Supply curve of a monopoly firm A monopoly firm has no unique supply curve. It can resort to supply same quantity at different prices or different quantities at same price.

Monopoly and its capacity A monopoly is known for its sub-optimal operations. It retains excess capacity by producing along the falling part of its average cost curve.

Monopoly and its favourite zone on its demand curve A monopoly always sticks to the elastic zone of its demand. In other words, it sells along the upper half of its AR curve.

Monopoly and price discrimination A monopoly resorts to discriminatory pricing policies whenever possible. It charges different prices in different markets or from different individuals at different times. Accordingly, price discrimination as practiced by a monopoly is known as geographical discrimination or personal discrimination or time discrimination.

Conditions for success of price discrimination Different conditions are required for different types of price discrimination. For instance, for geographical price discrimination, markets are required to be segregated. Each must have its own price elasticity of demand. The monopoly can practice price discrimination until its marginal revenues in the segregated markets get equalized each to its marginal cost. Discrimination beyond this point proves non-profitable. In the same way, success of personal discrimination depends on differences in socio-economic status of the buyers and that of time discrimination, on the intensity of demand.

Objectives of price discrimination Different monopolies have different objectives to fulfil through price discrimination. For instance, private monopolies do it for maximization of profits or for raising surpluses while regulated monopolies do it for maximization of social welfare and recovery of the production costs. Intertemporal price discrimination aims at surpluses and peak-load pricing at efficiency and surpluses both. Slab and use based discriminations aim at distributional efficiency. In some cases, discrimination helps the cause of survival of some monopolies who face demand curves lying below their LACs.

Degrees of price discrimination Degrees of price discrimination refer to the extent to which a discriminating monopoly succeeds in mopping away the consumer's surplus. In third-degree price discrimination, it succeeds in mopping only a small part of the consumer's surplus by setting a price above the profit-maximizing level once. In second-degree price discrimination, it succeeds in mopping a larger part of the consumer's surplus by setting more than one price above the profit-maximizing level. In the first-degree price discrimination, it targets whole of the consumer's surplus even if it requires unit-to-unit price-setting above the profit-maximizing level.

Perfect price discrimination Under it, a monopoly reduces price for each successive unit even below the profit-maximizing level so that its MR undergoes pivotal shifts until it coincides with its AR.

Effects of perfect price discrimination Price discrimination if carried out beyond the profit-maximizing output or below the profit maximizing price, it leads to pivotal shifts in MR of the firm until it finally coincides with its AR. The effect of price discrimination comprises pivotal shifts in MR leading to maximization of total revenue.

Intertemporal price discrimination It refers to segmenting of the consumers according to their demand elasticities and setting price for each separately. The segment with less elastic demand is charged a higher price in the beginning and that with more elastic demand is charged a lower price later.

Peak load pricing It refers to a practice of charging a higher price for a product or service during peak periods of its demand rather than of charging a single price throughout. It helps raising surpluses and increasing distributional efficiency by setting a higher price when MC is high and a lower price when MC is low.

Mark-up pricing It refers to setting a price equal to MC marked up by the factor $1/\{1 - 1/|e|\}$. Thus, $P = MC/\{1 - 1/|e|\}$.

Price-output decisions of monopoly under dynamic changes Dynamic changes refer to distortionary factors comprising those causing shifts in demand and cost curves.

1. A pivotal shift in demand results in an increase in output without a change in price or an increase in price without a change in output.
2. A non-pivotal shift results in increase in both the price and the output.
3. A non-pivotal shift in demand results in an increase in output but a decrease in price provided price elasticity of demand also increases with the shift.
4. A lump-sum tax does not affect price and output of the monopoly. Instead, it decreases the firm's profits.
5. A unit tax affects price and output of the monopoly in a number of ways depending upon the nature of the demand and the marginal cost curves:
   (a) when demand curve is **linear** and MC curve **horizontal**, increase in product price is exactly half as much as the magnitude of the tax $[\Delta P = 1/2 \cdot t$, where t is tax].
   (b) when demand curve is **linear** and MC curve **rising**, increase in price is less than half the value of the tax $[\Delta P < 1/2 \cdot t$, where t is tax].
   (c) when demand curve is **non-linear** and MC curve **horizontal**, increase in price is more than the magnitude of the tax $[\Delta P > t]$.
   (d) when demand curve has **constant price elasticity** and **MC curve** is horizontal, increase in price is more than the magnitude of the tax $[\Delta P > t]$.

Monopsony It refers to a single buyer dictating price. A monopsony starts with a low price but has to pay increasing prices with increasing purchases.

Equilibrium of monopsony The necessary and the sufficient condition for the equilibrium is that the ME curve must cut the MV curve from below.

Monopsony power It is defined as the ratio of excess of ME over price to the price.

$$\text{Monopsony power} = (ME - p)/p$$
$$= 1/e_s$$

It is inversely related to the price elasticity of supply.

Social cost of monopsony Loss of social welfare is the cost of monopsony power.

Sources of monopsony power Elasticity of supply, number of buyers and the extent of interaction among them are the main sources of monopsony power.

EXERCISES

A. Short Answer Questions

Define the following: (1 through 8)
1. Monopoly power
2. Monopsony power
3. Price discrimination
4. Perfect price discrimination
5. Intertemporal price discrimination
6. Peak load pricing
7. Mark-up pricing
8. Natural monopoly
9. What are the sources of monopoly power?
10. What are the sources of monopsony power?
11. Explain geographical price discrimination and personal price discrimination.
12. What are the conditions for the success of price discrimination?
13. Enumerate three objectives of price discrimination.
14. What is meant by degrees of price discrimination?
15. State three features of monopoly.
16. State three important differences between a monopoly firm and a competitive firm.
17. State the most important effect of price discrimination.
18. With a neat sketch, show that a monopoly always sticks to the upper-half of the demand curve.
19. With the help of a neat sketch, show that a monopoly always operates at sub-optimal capacity.
20. In what respects is a natural monopoly different from a simple monopoly?
21. Given that the price elasticity of demand is -3. What is the monopoly power of a firm facing this demand curve?
    [Ans. 33.33%.]
22. Given that the price elasticity of supply is 2. What is the monopsony power of a buyer with this supply?
    [Ans. 50%.]
23. Given that the price elasticity of demand as -3 in the domestic market and -1.5 in the foreign market. Is it correct to say that the price charged by the monopoly in the domestic market would be half of that charged by it in the foreign market? Give reasons in support of your answer.
    [Ans. yes.]
24. Given MC = 4, price elasticity of demand = -3. Is it true to say that the price charged by the firm would be 6? Give reasons in support.
    [Ans. yes.]

25. For a firm whose monopoly power is 80%, is it true to say that the price elasticity of demand for the firm is -1.25 and the price of the product is five times its MC? Give reasons in support.
   [**Ans.** yes.]
26. Given the price elasticity of supply as 4. Determine the monopsony power of the buyer and show that the price paid for a unit of the product is 80% of the ME.
   [**Ans.** 25%.]
27. Given that the magnitude of tax on a commodity produced by a monopoly with constant costs is ₹ 10. By how much would the price rise when
   (a) demand curve faced by the firm is linear,
   (b) demand curve faced by a firm is non-linear,
   (c) demand curve faced by a firm is constant elasticity demand curve?
   [**Ans.** 5, more than 10, 20.]

B. Long Answer Questions

28. Show with the help of neat sketches that a monopoly has no unique supply curve.
29. With the help of a neat sketch, show that the output produced by a monopoly is always sub-optimal.
30. What is monopoly power? Show that the monopoly power varies inversely as the price elasticity of demand. What is the cost of the monopoly power? Explain with the help of a diagram.
31. What is monopsony power and what are its sources? Show that the monopsony power varies inversely as the price elasticity of supply. What is the cost of the monopsony power? Explain with the help of a diagram.
32. With the help of a neat sketch and a numerical illustration show that an otherwise loss-making monopoly may not only survive but may also convert its losses into profits through discriminatory pricing policy.
33. With the help of a neat sketch, demonstrate the effect of price discrimination.
34. Explain the mechanism of intertemporal price discrimination with the help of a sketch. What is the objective of this type of price discrimination?
35. Explain the mechanism of peak load pricing with the help of a neat sketch. Why is it referred to as an efficient way of distribution of essential services?
36. What is a natural monopoly? Explain its pricing policies that lead to (a) maximization of social welfare (b) recovery of production costs.
37. Explain the mechanism of price discrimination. What conditions are essential for its success? What are the main objectives of such practices?
38. How would price and output of a monopoly change when demand faced by it undergoes a pivotal shift outwards? How would your answer change if the shift in demand is non-pivotal?
39. How would a non-pivotal shift in monopoly demand affect its price-output decisions when the said shift is also accompanied by an increase in the price elasticity of demand with an increase in the level of monopoly output?
40. How does levy of a lump-sum tax affect the price-output decisions of a monopoly? Explain with the help of a diagram.
41. Given the linear monopoly demand and constant costs, how would price-output decisions of a monopoly be influenced by the levy of a specific unit tax? Draw a diagram and show with the help of calculus that the increase in price would be equal to half the value of the unit tax.
42. Given the linear monopoly demand and rising costs, how would price-output decisions of a monopoly be influenced by the levy of a specific unit tax? Draw a diagram and show with the help of calculus that the increase in price would be less than half the value of the unit tax.

43. A monopoly faces a non-linear demand. How would its price be affected by the levy of a specific unit tax when its MC curve is horizontal? Draw a diagram and show with the help of calculus that the increase in price would be higher than the magnitude of the tax.

44. A monopoly faces a constant elasticity demand. How would its price be affected by the levy of a specific unit tax when its MC curve is horizontal? Draw a diagram and show with the help of calculus that price would increase by twice the magnitude of the unit tax.

45. How would the price of a monopoly firm change in general in response to an increase in the unit tax already in practice? Draw a diagram and show with the help of calculus that the increase in price would be higher than the increase in value of the unit tax.

46. How does a monopsony determine its net benefit-maximizing quantity and price? Draw a diagram and mark-off the net benefit derived by the monopsony.

47. A monopoly faces a linear demand curve

$$P = 100 - 0.01Q$$

The firm's total cost function is

$$C = 30,000 + 50Q$$

(a) Determine:
   (i) profit-maximizing price and output
   (ii) magnitude of profit earned
   (iii) monopoly power
   (iv) rise in price in response to the levy of a unit tax of 10 and loss of social welfare caused by it

Draw a diagram and mark-off profits earned.

(b) Now suppose the firm was a competitive one before acquiring the monopoly power. Calculate the deadweight loss caused by this transition.

[**Ans.** (a) (i) $P = 75$; $Q = 2,500$; (ii) $\pi = 32,500$ (Figure 9.32); (iii) monopoly power = 33.33%; (iv) $\Delta P = 5$, deadweight loss = 13,750, Area of Trapezium $eGHF$. (b) 31,250 (see complete solution below).

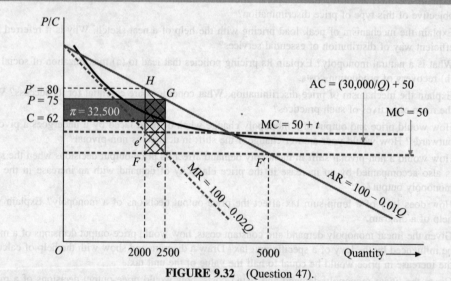

FIGURE 9.32 (Question 47).

(a) (i)
$$\text{profit}, \pi = TR - TC$$
$$= PQ - 30{,}000 - 50Q$$
$$= [100 - 0.01Q]Q - 30{,}000 - 50Q$$

Differentiating with respect to Q, we have
$$d\pi/dQ = 100 - 0.02Q - 50$$
$$= 50 - 0.02Q$$
$$\Rightarrow Q = 2{,}500 \text{ and } P = 75$$

[For maximization of profit, $d\pi/dQ = 0$]

(ii)
$$\pi = [100 - 0.01 \times 2{,}500] \times 2{,}500 - 30{,}000 - 50 \times 2{,}500$$
$$= 32{,}500$$

(iii) Elasticity of demand $= (dQ/dP) \times (P/Q)$
$$= (-100) \times (75/2500)$$
$$= -3$$

Monopoly power $= 1/|e|$
$$= 1/3$$
$$= 33.33\%$$

(iv) Note that output after the levy of tax (Figure 9.22) is given by
$$MC + t = MR$$
$$\Rightarrow 50 + 10 = 100 - 0.02Q$$
$$\Rightarrow Q = 2000$$
$$\Delta P = 1/2 \times t$$
$$= 1/2 \times 10$$
$$= 5$$
$$P' = 75 + 5$$
$$= 80$$

Deadweight loss due to tax = Area of the shaded region in Figure 9.22
$$= \frac{1}{2} \times (80 + 75) \times (2500 - 2000) - (2500 - 2000) \times 50$$
$$= 13{,}750$$

(b) As a competitive firm, it determined price through $P = MC$
$$\Rightarrow 100 - 0.01Q = 50$$
$$\Rightarrow Q = 5{,}000$$
And $P = 100 - 0.01 \times 5000$
$$= 50$$

Deadweight loss caused by the transition of the firm competitive to monopoly
$$= \text{Area of } \Delta GeF'$$
$$= 1/2 \times eF' \times eG$$
$$= 1/2 \times (5000 - 2500) \times (75 - 50)$$
$$= 31{,}250.$$

48. The demand curve faced by a monopoly is given as
$$Q = 2{,}560{,}000/P^2$$
Where, Q is the quantity demanded and P, the price. The total cost function is given as
$$C = 8{,}000 + 40Q$$

(a) Show that demand faced by the monopoly is a constant elasticity demand.
(b) Determine the profit maximizing price and output.
(c) Determine the magnitude of profit.
(d) Suppose a unit tax of ₹ 10 per unit is imposed. Show that the price increases by ₹ 20 per unit.
(e) Determine the new level of sales and the change in profit.
(f) Determine the loss of social welfare due to the levy of the unit tax.

[**Ans.** (a) Differentiating equation of demand with respect to P, we have

$$dQ/dP = -2 \times 2{,}560{,}000/P^3$$
$$E_P^D = (dQ/dP) \times (P/Q)$$
$$= (-5{,}120{,}000/P^3) \times [P/(2{,}560{,}000/P^2)]$$
$$= -(5{,}120{,}000/2{,}560{,}000) \times (P^3/P^3)$$
$$= -2.$$

The expression for E_P^D is free from P and Q. Hence the price elasticity of demand is constant for all levels of output and prices.

Demand curve, therefore, is a constant elasticity demand curve.

(b) Rewriting the equation of demand, we have

$$P = 1600/\sqrt{Q}$$
$$TR = \left(1600/\sqrt{Q}\right) \times Q$$
$$= 1600\sqrt{Q}$$
$$MR = d(TR)/dQ$$
$$= 1600 \times 1/2 \times (1/\sqrt{Q})$$
$$= 800/\sqrt{Q}$$

Differentiating the total cost function with respect to Q, we have

$$MC = 40$$

For maximization of profit, $MC = MR$

$$800/\sqrt{Q} = 40$$
$$\Rightarrow \qquad Q = \mathbf{400}$$

Substituting for Q, $\quad P = 1600\sqrt{(400)}$
$$= \mathbf{80}$$

(c) Profit, $\quad \pi = TR - TC$
$$= 1600\sqrt{Q} - 8{,}000 - 40Q$$
$$= 1600\sqrt{(400)} - 8{,}000 - 40 \times 400$$
$$= 32{,}000 - 8{,}000 - 16{,}000$$
$$= \mathbf{8{,}000}$$

(d) Since $t = 10$, the MC curve would shift upwards by 10 units so that at equilibrium,

$$MC + t = MR'$$
$$= 800/\sqrt{Q'}, \quad \text{(where } Q' = \text{quantity demanded after tax)}$$
$\Rightarrow \quad 40 + 10 = 800/\sqrt{Q'}, \quad (MC = 40)$
$\Rightarrow \quad Q' = 256 \text{ (New level of sales)}$

At this output, price P' is given as

$$P' = 1600/\sqrt{Q'}$$
$$= 1600/\sqrt{256}$$
$$= 100 \text{ (New level of price)}$$
$$\Delta P = P' - P$$
$$= 100 - 80$$
$$= 20$$

Thus, when unit tax is 10, increase in price is 20. The same result would have been obtained directly from Eq. (9.50).

(e) Total revenue after tax

$$TR' = P' \times Q'$$
$$= 100 \times 256$$
$$= 25,600$$
$$TC' = 8,000 + 40Q'$$
$$= 8,000 + 40 \times 256$$
$$= 18,240$$

After tax profit $= TR' - TC'$
$$= 25,600 - 18,240$$
$$= \mathbf{7,360}$$

(f) Sales have decreased from 400 units to 256 units and profit has gone down from 8,000 to 7,360. The shaded region in Figure 9.26 represents the loss of social welfare (deadweight loss) caused by tax. Its value can be found by the area under the demand curve from Q' to Q less the area of the rectangle $Q'QeH$. Thus,

$$\text{Deadweight loss due to tax} = \int_{Q'}^{Q} \left(1600/\sqrt{Q}\right) dQ - [400 - 256] \times 40$$
$$= \int_{256}^{400} \left(1600/\sqrt{Q}\right) dQ - 5,760$$
$$= 3200\sqrt{Q}\Big|_{256}^{400} - 5,760$$
$$= 12,800 - 5,760$$
$$= \mathbf{7040}.]$$

49. A monopoly faces a non-linear demand curve given by

$$P = 10,000/(Q + 40)$$

Its total cost function is given as

$$C = 2,100 + 40Q$$

Determine:

(a) Profit-maximizing price
(b) Profit-maximizing output
(c) Profit
(d) Rise in price when a commodity tax of ₹ 10 per unit is levied
(e) Price, profit and output after the levy of the unit tax
(f) Loss of social welfare due to the levy of the tax

[**Ans.** Refer to Figure 9.25

$$TR = PQ$$
$$= [10,000/(Q + 40)] \times Q$$
$$= [10,000\, Q/(Q + 40)]$$
$$\Rightarrow \quad MR = [(Q + 40) \times 10,000 - 10,000Q]/(Q + 40)^2$$
$$= 400,000/(Q + 40)^2$$
$$TC = 2100 + 40Q$$
$$\Rightarrow \quad MC = 40$$

For maximization of profit

$$MC = MR$$
$$\Rightarrow \quad 40 = 400,000/(Q + 40)^2$$
$$\Rightarrow \quad Q = 60$$

Substituting $\quad P = \mathbf{100}$

$$\text{Profit} = TR - TC$$
$$= 100 \times 60 - 2100 - 40 \times 60$$
$$= 6,000 - 4,500$$
$$= \mathbf{1,500}$$

Tax shifts the MC curve upwards by 10 units. Profit-maximizing output after tax is thus given by

$$MC + t = MR'$$
$$40 + 10 = 400,000/(Q' + 40)^2$$
$$Q' = \sqrt{8,000} - 40$$
$$= 89.4 \text{ (Approx.)} - 40$$
$$= \mathbf{49.4}$$

Substituting $\quad P' = 10,000/(Q' + 40)$
$$= \mathbf{111.86}$$

Rise in price $\quad \Delta P = P' - P$
$$= 111.86 - 100$$
$$= \mathbf{11.86}$$

Hence, Price rises by more than the unit tax.

Profit after the levy
$$= TR' - TC'$$
$$= 111.86 \times 49.4 - 2,100 - 40 \times 49.4$$
$$= 5,525.88 - 4,076$$
$$= \mathbf{1,449.88}$$

Clearly, profit has decreased.

Loss of social welfare = shaded area (Figure 9.25)

$$= \int_{49.4}^{60} [10{,}000/(Q+40)]\, dQ - (60 - 49.4) \times (40)$$
$$= 10{,}000\,(\log_e 100 - \log_e 89.4) - 424$$
$$= 10{,}000 \times 0.1121 - 424$$
$$= 1{,}121 - 424$$
$$= \mathbf{697}.]$$

50. Outline the main differences between a competitive firm and a monopoly in respect of their characteristic features.

C. Essay Type Questions

51. With help of diagrams explain how a monopoly reaches its price-output decisions in short and long periods. Examine critically the main points of departure of the natural monopoly from a simple monopoly in respect of these decisions.
52. Explain the practice of price discrimination in its various manifestations. Examine the conditions necessary for its success and comment on its objectives and effects. How can discriminatory pricing policies help a natural monopoly in respect of efficiency and existence?

10

Price-output Decisions of Monopolistically Competitive Firms

CHAPTER OUTLINE

Introduction
- Price-output Decisions of Monopolistically Competitive Firm in Short-run and Long-run
- Monopolistic Competition and Economic Efficiency
- Chamberlin's Large Group Models of Monopolistic Competition
- Comparison with Pure Competition
- Key Terms and Concepts
- Exercises

INTRODUCTION

We made a brief reference to monopolistic competition as a market form in Chapter 7. There, we observed that monopolistic competition is a market structure with large number of firms selling close substitutes, differentiated externally through packaging, appearances, brand names, etc. and internally through superficial attributes such as colour, odour, flavour and the like. Product differentiation of this type is created deliberately by producers either to gain an edge over their rivals or to acquire some monopoly power. The objective is a higher market share or a higher profit margin. Each firm behaves like a monopoly to its customers who take a liking for its product or turn brand loyal. Tobacco and toothpaste industries provide examples of monopolistic markets.

The market form resembles competitive market on two counts—*first*, it has a large number of buyers and sellers just as a competitive market has; and *second*, it possesses the feature of free entry and exit just as a competitive market does. The former, however, differs from the latter in respect of selling costs, homogeneity of product and uniformity of price. In a monopolistic market, product is non-homogeneous (differentiated) while in a competitive market, it is homogeneous.

A monopolistic market is characterized for selling costs while a competitive market, for uniformity of price.

In the same way, the market form resembles a monopoly too on certain counts. Like a monopoly, each firm in this market faces distinct and downward sloping AR and MR curves. They also produce along the falling part of AC and possess the usual monopoly power, causing loss of social welfare just like a monopoly. It is a different matter though that the loss of social welfare under a monopoly is of somewhat higher measure than what it is under a firm in this market form. As regards its differences from a monopoly, a firm in this market cannot resort to price discrimination nor can it restrict entry to new firms the way a monopoly can. Many monopolies are state regulated while firms in this market are autonomous.

A monopolistic market thus dangles between the extremes of a perfect market and a monopoly. It resembles each in some respects and differs from each in some others. Nevertheless, it is a real world market structure with its own traits, deserving a separate study just as each of the other two forms does.

Let us therefore turn to short- and long-run equilibria of a firm operating in a monopolistic market.

10.1 PRICE-OUTPUT DECISIONS OF MONOPOLISTICALLY COMPETITIVE FIRM IN SHORT-RUN AND LONG-RUN

As mentioned earlier, a firm in the monopolistic market faces downward sloping AR and MR curves. This is due to the monopoly power acquired by a monopolistically competitive firm partly through product differentiation and partly due to brand loyalty of its customers. The slope of the demand curve faced by a monopolistically competitive firm, however, is not as steep as that of the demand curve faced by a monopoly. The reason is the presence of a large number of firms selling close substitutes, due to which, the monopoly power of a firm in this market is relatively weak. Equilibrium of a firm can, however, be worked out on the same lines as in case of a monopoly. The short-run abnormal profits disappear with the entry of new firms in the long-run (Figure 10.1).

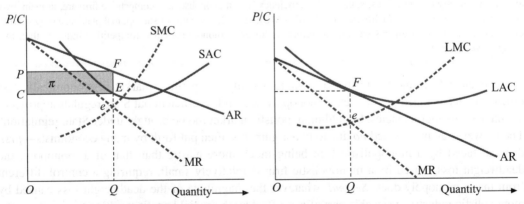

FIGURE 10.1 A monopolistic firm under short and long-run equilibria: A monopolistically competitive firm may earn abnormal profits in the short-run (left panel). With entry of new firms, abnormal profits disappear in the long-run (right panel). Market share of the firm declines with the entry of new firms and so does the market price. Entry shifts AR curve downwards. The right panel shows the long-run equilibrium. LAC is tangential to the AR curve in the long-run.

10.2 MONOPOLISTIC COMPETITION AND ECONOMIC EFFICIENCY

We have seen that a perfectly competitive firm has zero monopoly power ($1/e = 0$, as $e = \infty$ for a competitive firm) and hence it is economically the most efficient market structure. That way, a monopoly is the least efficient and a monopolistically competitive firm, moderately efficient because of its moderate monopoly power.

Comparison of the long-run equilibrium of a monopolistically competitive firm to that of a competitive firm reveals that the former is economically less efficient than the latter. Figure 10.2 serves the purpose.

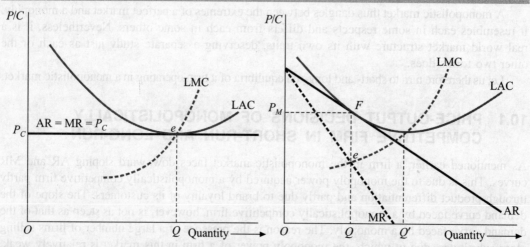

FIGURE 10.2 Competitive firm versus monopolistic firm in the long-run: A competitive firm sells more at a lower price than a monopolistically competitive firm. Price charged by a competitive firm is equal to its MC (P_C = MC) while that charged by a monopolistically competitive firm is higher than its MC (P_M > MC). The former operates at its optimal capacity while the latter sticks to the falling part of its AC, retaining thereby an excess capacity of QQ'. Thus, sources of inefficiency of a monopolistically competitive firm are, in main, two: (1) practice of charging a price higher than its MC (P > MC); and, (2) existence of sub-optimal plant size ($OQ < OQ'$) or excess capacity. Consumer's welfare, therefore, is lower in monopolistically competitive industry than in a competitive industry.

It is clear from the figure that a monopolistically competitive market is economically less efficient than a competitive market. A monopoly is even less efficient but State regulation provides a remedy to its inefficiencies. Should monopolistic market too be brought under State regulation? The answer is an unexpected *no* due to two arguments often put forth by many economists—*first*, demand faced by a monopolistic firm being much more elastic than that of a monopoly, the deadweight loss caused by a monopolistic firm is relatively small, requiring a control different from that a monopoly does. *Second*, whatever the magnitude of the deadweight loss caused by monopolistic industry, a sizeable part of it is offset by the social benefit resulting from the variety in products, which a wide range of consumers value and prefer (See Chamberlin's measure of excess capacity of a monopolistic firm, Figure 10.9).

10.3 CHAMBERLIN'S LARGE GROUP MODELS OF MONOPOLISTIC COMPETITION

Monopolistic industry may start with few firms but in due course of time the number of firms grows large. Group equilibrium in such cases turns highly complex, requiring several assumptions to restrict multiplicity of influences from interfering in the core analysis of market equilibrium. Chamberlin studied the market structure in its three variations called the Chamberlin's large group models. His models are based on following assumptions:

1. There are a large number of sellers in the group facing a large number of buyers.
2. The products of the sellers are differentiated, yet they are close substitutes of one another.
3. There is free entry and exit of firms in the group.
4. The goal of the firm is profit maximization, both in the short-run and in the long-run.
5. The factor prices and the technology are given.
6. The firm is assumed to behave as if it knew its demand and cost curves with certainty.
7. The long-run is made up of a number of identical short-run periods, which are assumed to be independent of one another in the sense that decisions of one period do not influence future periods nor are they influenced by the past periods.
8. Finally, Chamberlin made a *heroic assumption* that demand and cost curves both, for all the products, are uniform throughout the group. This requires consumer's preferences to be evenly distributed among sellers and a product differentiation of such negligibility that does not give rise to significant differences in costs.* Chamberlin made these assumptions to show the equilibrium of a firm as also that of the group it belonged to, on the same diagram. The heroic assumptions of Chamberlin lead to models which restrict inclusion in the group of similar products with different costs of production. He himself admitted that the assumptions are unrealistic and at a later stage he also relaxed them.

The two heroic assumptions of Chamberlin, namely, identical costs of production and evenly distributed consumer preferences among the products facilitated equilibrium of a firm as also that of the group on the same diagram through identical demand and cost curves.

Under these assumptions, Chamberlin developed his large group models. In the *first* model, existing firms are assumed to be in short-run equilibrium, realizing abnormal profits. The abnormal profits attract entry of new firms. Price adjustments so necessitated cause a downward shift in each firm's AR curve until it is tangential to its AC. In the *second* model, it is assumed that the number of firms in the industry is optimal, with no room for entry or exit of new firms and that the long-run equilibrium is reached through price adjustments of the existing firms. The *third* model is a combination of the first two—the equilibrium being reached through the price adjustments of the existing firms and also of the new firms entering the industry.

10.3.1 Model I: Equilibrium with New Firms Entering the Industry

This model is based on the assumption that each firm is in short-run equilibrium realizing abnormal profits and that the short-run abnormal profits attract entry of new firms, leading to a downward

---

*Chamberlin, *Theory of Monopolistic Competition*, pp. 82–83.

parallel shift in AR curve. Chamberlin employed traditional cost curves and avoided the use of MC and MR curves as far as possible, though the same was implicit all along in his treatment. The situation is shown in Figure 10.3.

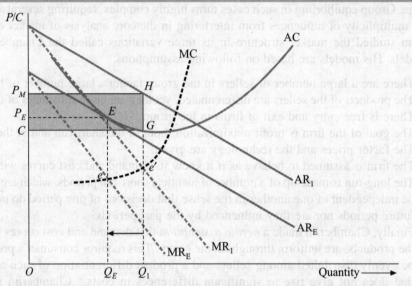

FIGURE 10.3 Equilibrium with new firms entering the industry: Each firm in the market is in equilibrium at point e', producing Q_1, selling it at P_M and earning abnormal profit of $CGHP_M$. Abnormal profits of the existing firms attract entry of new firms. This shifts the demand curve of each firm down to AR_E so that it touches the AC at E in equilibrium, where abnormal profit of each firm is driven to zero and market share to Q_E. The number of firms at this point is optimal and the industry equilibrium, stable.

The abnormal profits earned by the existing firms attract entry of new firms, leading to downward shifts in AR until it turns tangential to AC in equilibrium. Point E in Figure 10.3 is the point where this happens. Each of the firms earns normal profits here. Market share of each declines and the number of firms stabilizes. Equilibrium at E is stable with the result that entry/exit of a firm stops. Note that the group equilibrium here has been possible due to the heroic assumptions of identical cost and demand conditions.

10.3.2 Model II: Equilibrium with Price Competition

This model is based on the assumption that the number of firms in the group is optimal so that neither entry nor exit of a firm is called for. The ruling price in short-run is higher than the equilibrium price with the result that abnormal profit accrues to each firm in short-run. Each firm believes that it can increase its market share by lowering its price and that no other firm in the group will follow its course.

The analysis in this model resorts to a market share curve, DD. It is *the locus of points at which a firm in the group actually ends up selling its product each time it lowers its price*. The firm in question resorts to a price cut along its demand curve with a view to boost its market share, assuming that none of the fellow firms will follow its suit. However, each of the fellow firms thinks on identical lines independently at the same time and resorts to an identical price cut. As a result, each firm, instead of realizing the desired expansion of market share itself, ends up sharing it with the rest of the firms. Each one sells much less than what it anticipated at the time of introducing the price cut. Each one continues to believe that it is on its own demand curve shifted downwards in consequence to the price-cuts introduced by its fellow firms simultaneously and in complete disregard of its past experience to the contrary, it prepares itself for a repeat performance assuming once again that its fellow firms will not follow it in its price-cut. The process of successive price cuts continues and so does the shifting of the demand curve until abnormal profits of short-run disappear completely in the long-run (Figure 10.4).

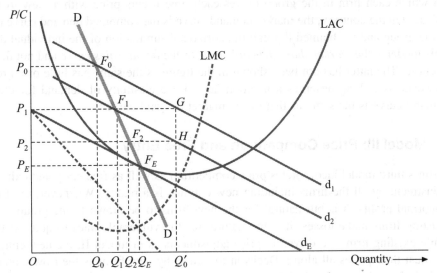

FIGURE 10.4 Equilibrium of existing firms with price competition: Market share demand curve DD, locus of points F_0, F_1, F_2 and F_E, represents price-output combinations of a monopolistic firm reducing its price with a view to boost its market share up to Q_0'. To understand, let the demand faced by the firm be d_1 and let the quantity sold by the firm at P_0 be Q_0 (point F_0). Note that P_0 is a non-equilibrium price. Further, suppose the firm decides to lower its price along its demand d_1 so that it may sell quantity Q_0' at G at a price P_1. The firm in question assumes that other firms in the group would continue to charge P_0 as before. Each of the other firms thinks on the same lines simultaneously and does the same independently. As a result, the firm in question as also all the other firms in the group, end up selling only Q_1 at F_1 instead of Q_0' at G. This shows that simultaneous and independent decision of each firm to lower its price to P_1 with a view to boost its market share to Q_0' results in a downward parallel shift in its demand from d_1 to d_2. All meet the same fate—an increase in the market share by $Q_0 Q_1$ each! The firms do not stop here but continue to behave in an identical manner independently until each one ends up at point F_E, earning normal profit only in the process. Note that F_E corresponds to the profit-maximizing output (Q_E) of each and that average cost curve LAC is tangential to demand d_E at F_E. Any further cut in price is unlikely as the resulting price would fall below the average cost, causing loss to each firm in the group. It would be interesting to note that each time a firm lowers its price, it does so thinking that it would move along its demand curve and would sell Q_0' but as the reality would have it, each ends up falling onto the same downwardly shifted demand curve or moving along the market share curve DD ultimately. DD is therefore known as the *actual sales curve* also. What is really surprising is the Chamberlin's assumption that each firm continues to lower its price believing that other firms in the group would not follow the suit despite its past experiences to the contrary! How could a firm be so myopic as not to be able to see beyond the tip of its nose?

Curves d_1, d_2 and d_E are the shifting demand curves of a firm in the group, d_1 being the initial position. Quantity Q_0' of the first mover would have been sold at a price P_1 had the rest of the firms in the group not moved simultaneously and shared its expected expansion $(Q_0' - Q_0)$ of demand. But they all did and the firm in question had to feel contented with sale of Q_1 instead of Q_0'. The same has been the experience of all the firms in the group. Simultaneous market sharing shifts the demand curve of each from d_1 to d_2.

The shift in question can be treated as a consequence of less than expected sales realized by each firm at a given price due to simultaneous moves of all the firms in the group.

One thing needs a clarification here. The market demand curve and the market share demand curve should not be confused for each other. The market share demand curve is the actual demand curve on which each firm in the group moves each time it cuts price with a view to boost its market share. On the contrary, the market demand curve is the combined demand curve of all the firms in the group and is obtained through the horizontal summation of the individual demands. DD in this model is the *market share demand curve* or the *actual sales curve* and not the market demand curve. The latter has not been shown in the figure as the same has little or no relevance here. However, one thing deserves a mention here. Price elasticity of demand for the market share demand curve is the same as that of the market demand curve*.

10.3.3 Model III: Price Competition and Free Entry

Chamberlin's third model incorporates price competition as well as free entry and exit together. Price adjustment by all the firms including new entrants is a reality. Whenever, existing firms make abnormal profits, it is but natural for the new firms to be drawn to the group. Likewise, when existing firms make losses, it is but natural for the vulnerable ones to quit. At the same time, while existing firms are driven to price adjustments as in model II, the new entrants also have to adjust their prices all along. Decision to join in by new firms is their own, that is, it is completely independent of the decisions of the existing firms. Moreover, every firm at the time of entry is confident of having a foothold for itself unless there is a writing on the wall that the group itself is sinking. In sum, entry and exit are regular features in a large group of firms and so is the process of price adjustments among them if their products are close substitutes. Figure 10.5 portrays the model.

---

*The fact can be easily proved by taking q as the share of a firm in the market demand Q. Thus, $q = kQ$, where k is a fixed proportion between 0 and 1. The price elasticity of market share demand curve can thus be determined as

$$\begin{aligned} E_{MSD} &= (dq/dP)(P/q) \\ &= [d(kQ)/dP][P/(kQ)] \\ &= (k/k)[dQ/dP][P/Q] \\ &= [dQ/dP][P/Q] \\ &= E_{MD} \end{aligned}$$

where, E_{MD} is the price elasticity of market demand while E_{MSD}, that of the market share demand of a firm.

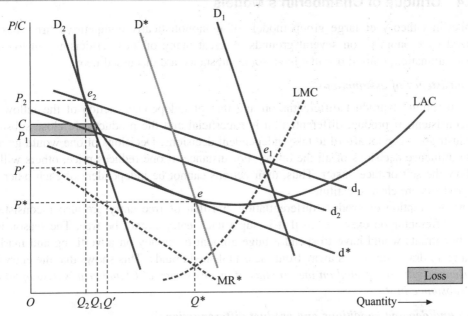

FIGURE 10.5 **Equilibrium of monopolistically competitive firms under price competition and free entry:** Suppose one of the existing firms in the group is enjoying abnormal profits at e_1 on its demand curve, d_1. The market share demand curve is D_1 at this point. Abnormal profits attract new firms whose entry shifts the market share curve D_1 downward-to-left (market share of each firm decreases due to entry of new firms). Such shifting of market share curve continues until it touches the LAC curve at point e_2. One may think that long-run equilibrium is reached as profits of all the players get driven to zero at e_2. This, however, is not true. The firm in question thinks that it can increase its profit as also its market share by reducing its price along its demand curve, d_1, assuming that none of the fellow firms would follow its suit. But each of the fellow firms independently thinks the same way and reduces its price simultaneously with the firm in question along d_1. As a result, none of firms realizes the expected increase in its profit or market share. Instead, each one finds itself on demand curve d_2, which is d_1 shifted vertically downwards. The result is a marginal increase in market share (Q_2Q_1) accompanied by a loss equal to the shaded rectangle to each firm. All the firms, along with the new entrants, meet the same fate. Each firm finds itself at the intersection of the market share curve D_2 and the shifted individual demand curve d_2, which falls below LAC causing it a loss to each equal to the shaded rectangle. Any further reduction in price by any of the firms in the group leads to a downward shift in the individual demand curve and forces them all to slide down along the market share demand curve, D_2. Losses to the vulnerable firms force them to quit. As a result, the market share curve, D_2 shifts upwards until it reaches position, D^* which corresponds to a position in which individual demand curve, d^* is tangential to the LAC curve at point e^*. Note that point e^* is the profit-maximizing point at which each firm sells Q^* at a price P^* and earns normal profits. Thus, e^* is the long-run equilibrium point.

Existence of price competition among the firms initiates a market share curve while simultaneous existence of entry and exit of new firms causes downward-to-left shifts in the market share curve, D_1, until it touches LAC. The common incentives of profit and market share attempted by each firm in the group through simultaneous price-cuts lead to downward-to-left shift in its demand curve, d_1. This may lead each to ultimate loss forcing an exit on the vulnerable firms. The end result is that the market share curve finally passes through the point of tangency between the LAC and the individual firm's demand curve, d^*.

10.3.4 Critique of Chamberlin's Models

Chamberlin's theory of large group models of monopolistically competitive firms has been criticized by economists on several grounds. A great many of these criticisms fail to stand a closer examination. Only those that have some substance are discussed here.

1. *Inconsistency of assumptions*

The assumption of product differentiation and that of independent action of the fellow firms are inconsistent. If product differentiation is superficial and the products are close substitutes, the industrialists cannot afford to take independent decisions. Decisions of one would go a long way to influence decisions of all the others. For instance, if one reduces price, others will have to follow the suit or face ouster. Thus, their actions cannot be independent of each other when their products are close substitutes.

The assumption of product differentiation and that of free entry are also inconsistent. If product differentiation exists, even if it is superficial, entry cannot be free. The reason is that the new entrants would have to spend a huge amount of money on advertising and marketing campaign to draw consumers away from the established brands. This shows that the entry is not free. *Hence, criticism leveled on the grounds of inconsistency of Chamberlin's assumptions has some substance in it.*

2. *Cost and demand conditions and product differentiation*

If product differentiation exists, even if it is superficial, the prices and the costs cannot be identical. If that is the case, Chamberlin's heroic assumption of identical demand and cost conditions is unrealistic and hence non-maintainable. The concept of industry and hence that of the group equilibrium stands exploded under these situations.

Hence, criticism on the basis of unrealistic assumption of identical cost and demand conditions too has substance in it.

3. *The concept of the largeness of the number of sellers is not clear*

The theory assumes a large number of sellers but it fails to specify what number of firms is large enough to qualify the myopic disregard of the competitors' actions or to distinguish the monopolistic competition from the other forms of imperfect competition such as oligopoly. *Criticism leveled on this ground also has substance in it.*

4. *The concept of price and the cross-price elasticity is vague*

The theory assumes that the products must have a high price elasticity and a high positive cross price elasticity of demand but it fails to specify how high these elasticities should be so as to ensure grouping of the products in the same industry group or classifying the products as close substitutes for the purpose? *Criticism based on this ground is also not invalid.*

5. *The theory is indeterminate*

P.W.S. Andrews* argues that demand curve will slope downwards only when products are directly sold to the consumers. What if they are sold as inputs to other manufacturers who are themselves profit maximisers? They will never offer a high price for a product supplied by others at a lower

---
* Andrews, P.W.S., *On Competition in Economic Theory*, Macmillan, 1964.

price. Thus the part of demand curve arising from the other manufacturers, traders, retailers and wholesalers cannot give rise to downward sloping demand curve. *As evident, criticism is not baseless.*

10.4 COMPARISON WITH PURE COMPETITION

For long-run equilibrium of a monopolistically competitive firm, LAC is tangential to AR at equilibrium. Price, $P = LAC$ but it is higher than MC and MR both, each of which are same at the equilibrium point.

As against this, for a firm in pure competition, the condition of equilibrium is $P = LAC = LMC = MR$.

As a result, a monopolistic firm supplies less at a higher price than what a firm in pure or perfect competition does. Profits in the long-run in both the cases would, however, be normal.

The monopolistic firms produce less than the optimal output, i.e. the average production cost for a monopolistically competitive firm is higher than its lowest while for a competitive firm it is always at its lowest.

Another point of deviation from a competitive industry as also of occasional criticism of a monopolistic market is its feature of 'too many, too small firms' each with *excess capacity* measured as the difference between the ideal output Q_F and the equilibrium or actual output Q_E as shown in Figure 10.6. Chamberlin, however, does not agree with this view. To him, criticism of the monopolistic competition and excess capacity is valid only when demand curve faced by a monopolistic firm is a horizontal one as in case of a firm in competitive market. In a monopolistic market with a

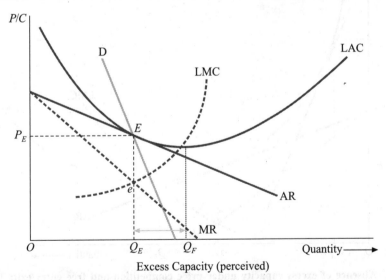

FIGURE 10.6 Perceived excess capacity as social cost of variety: Excess capacity of the monopolistically competitive firm as per the notion of excess capacity, is the excess of the optimal output (Q_F) over equilibrium output Q_E, that is, $Q_E Q_F$. To Chamberlin, this is the social cost of variety in products which the consumers desire and are also willing to pay for. With active price competition and free entry, there exists **no excess capacity** in a monopolistic market, according to Chamberlin.

downwardly sloping demand faced by a firm, Chamberlin argues, the socially optimal or ideal ouput cannot be Q_F when firms indulge in active price competition and enjoy free entry and exit. This is so because of product differentiation in existence in a monopolistic market reflecting consumer's desire for variety in products and their willingness to pay for it as well. Socially optimal output under these circumstances, to Chamberlin, is Q_E instead of Q_F. The excess of Q_F over Q_E (Figure 10.6), Chamberlin argues, is the **social cost of variety, not the excess capacity**.

The notion of *excess capacity* as portrayed in Figure 10.6, according to Chamberlin, is a misleading one. There exists, to Chamberlin, **no excess capacity** in a monopolistically competitive market under active price competition and free entry and exit. Under active price competition, a price-cut by a firm to boost its market share and profits is independently and simultaneously matched by the rest of the firms with the result that the demand curve faced by each firm slides downwards each time a price-cut is introduced. The position of the new demand curve falls farther and farther below the LAC, in each shift, leading the firms to higher and higher margins of loss (Figure 10.5). Entry and exit being free, the vulnerable firms unable to stand the burden of loss eventually exit with the result that the market share curve, D_2 shifts upwards to right until it occupies position D* in which it passes through the point of tangency *e* of LAC to the individual demand curve d* (Figure 10.5). Output at this point, Q_E, is socially optimal as explained earlier. The perceived excess capacity, $Q_E Q_F$ (Figure 10.6), is the **social cost of variety**. Monopolistic firms, Chamberlin argues, **cannot possess excess capacity** so long as active price competition and free entry and exit dominate the market (Figure 10.7).

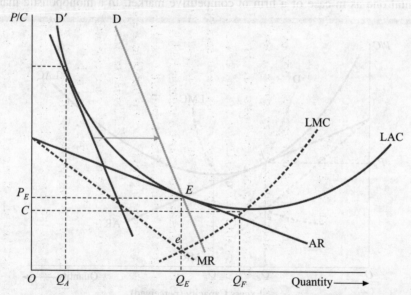

FIGURE 10.7 Absence of excess capacity under price competition and free entry-exit: There exists no excess capacity, according to Chamberlin, in a monopolistically competitive market with active price competition and free entry and exit. Socially optimal output = equilibrium output, Q_E. Least cost output, Q_F is never produced due to consumer's desire for product differentiation or variety. The difference, **$Q_E Q_F$, is thus the social cost of variety** instead of **excess capacity**.

The sources of excess capacity in a monopolistically competitive market, to Chamberlin, are *non-price competition and free entry and exit* (Figure 10.8). Due to non-price competition, demand curve faced by a firm does no longer slide downwards as it did in case of active price competition. As a result, each firm ignores its individual demand curve (dd) and focuses on its market share curve, D for its price-output decisions. Under non-price competition, dd remaining undisturbed and hence lying above the LAC, abnormal profits accrue to the existing firms.

This attracts entry of new firms which shifts the market share curve D downwards to left each time a new firm enters. The process of such shifts in D continues until it touches the LAC curve at e. The actual output, therefore, falls from Q_E to Q_A due to non-price competition and free entry and exit. The difference $Q_A Q_E$ thus represents **excess capacity** of a monopolistically competitive firm (Figure 10.8).

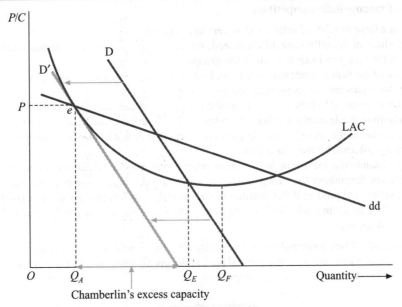

FIGURE 10.8 Non-price competition and free entry-exit as sources of Chamberlin's excess capacity: Non-price competition and free entry, according to Chamberlin, are the sources of excess capacity in monopolistically competitive market. Chamberlin argues that output is restricted by the monopolistic firms due to non-price competition. In this case, firms ignore their demand curve (dd) and stick to their market share curve (D) instead. Long-run equilibrium is reached only after free entry has shifted D to a position D' of tangency with the LAC curve.

Monopolistic competition is less efficient than a pure or perfect competition because price in it is higher and output lower than the corresponding price and output in the latter. As mentioned earlier, $P > MC$ for monopolistic firms, a sizeable monopoly power accrues to these firms that renders them less efficient than their competitive counterparts. If the monopolistic firms were coerced to produce a level of output at which $P = MC$, the firms would close-down in the long-run. The socially ideal output cannot be reached without destroying the entire private enterprise system.

KEY TERMS AND CONCEPTS

Excess capacity It is defined as the excess of the optimal level of output ($P = MC$) over the equilibrium level of output. All the firms whether monopoly or monopolistic possess the excess capacity due to the downwardly-sloping demand curve faced by them. It arises due to unexhausted economies of scale caused by restricted outputs.

Heroic assumptions of Chamberlin The assumption that both demand and cost curves are uniform throughout the group of the monopolistically competitive market.

Market share curve It is the actual demand curve faced by the monopolistically competitive firms. It represents the share of each firm in the total market demand.

Monopolistic competition It refers to a market structure with large number of buyers and sellers with free entry and exit, exchanging differentiated products that are close substitutes of each other.

Features of monopolistic competition

1. There is a large number of sellers and buyers in the group.
2. The products of the sellers are differentiated, yet they are close substitutes of one another.
3. There is free entry and exit of firms in the group.
4. The goal of the firm is profit maximization, both in the short-run and in the long-run.
5. The factor prices and the technology are given.
6. The firm is assumed to behave as if it knew its demand and cost curves with certainty.
7. The long-run is made up of a number of identical short-run periods, which are assumed to be independent of one another in the sense that the decisions of one period do not influence those of the future periods and are not affected by the past actions.
8. Finally, Chamberlin makes the heroic assumption that both demand and cost curves for all products are uniform throughout the group. This requires consumer's preferences to be evenly distributed among sellers and product differentiation of such negligibility which does not give rise to differences in costs.* Chamberlin made these assumptions to show the equilibrium of the firm and the group on the same diagram.

Price competition When monopolistically competitive firms resort to price reduction with a view to increase their market share and the consequential profits, the phenomenon is referred to as price-competition. Opposite of it is known as the non-price competition.

EXERCISES

A. Short Answer Questions

1. Distinguish between price competition and non-price competition.
2. Distinguish between market demand curve and market share demand curve.
3. What is meant by excess capacity?
4. How does excess capacity differ from the reserve capacity?
5. How does a monopoly firm differ from monopolistic firm?
6. What condition would you like to impose on the cross price elasticity of demand for (a) substitutes, (b) close substitutes?

---

* Chamberlin, *Theory of Monopolistic Competition*, pp. 82–83.

7. How can product differentiation be compatible with the attribute of close substitutes in monopolistic market?
8. Enumerate three important features of monopolistic market.
9. What is the single-most difference between monopolistic and pure competition?
10. How does a monopolistic firm reach its price-output decisions in short-run?
11. How does a monopolistic firm reach its price-output decisions in long-run?
12. Why is the market share curve steeper than the demand curve faced by an individual monopolistic firm?
13. Which of the two curves—market demand curve and the market share curve—would be (a) steeper; (b) farther away from the origin? Give reasons in support.
14. What are the heroic assumptions of Chamberlin regarding the group equilibrium of the monopolistically competitive firms? Why do you think they are named so?
15. To what factors does Chamberlin attribute the cause of the excess capacity? Why?
16. When does the demand curve faced by a monopolistically competitive firm shift downwards? Why?

B. Long Answer Questions

17. Distinguish between perfect competition and monopolistic competition.
18. Compare the long-run and short-run equilibrium of monopolistically competitive firm.
19. Show with the help of a diagram how a typical firm in monopolistically competitive market would reach its equilibrium with new firms entering the market.
20. Outline the assumptions resorted to by Chamberlin in his large group model. Is there any conflict between the assumptions?
21. How does a firm in monopolistic competition reach its equilibrium price-output decisions when firms in the group indulge in price competition?
22. How does a firm in monopolistic competition reach its equilibrium price-output decisions when firms in the group indulge in price competition and there is no barrier to entry and exit of the firms?
23. Price elasticity of the market share curve in the monopolistic competition is the same as that of the market demand curve. Does that mean that the two curves must be parallel? Give reasons in support of your answer.
24. With the help of a diagram demonstrate what do you mean by the notion of the excess capacity? Why does a monopoly possess it while a competitive firm does not?
25. How does Chamberlin justify that a monopolistically competitive firm does not possess any excess capacity? Give reasons in support of your answer.
26. Show that the main cause of the existence of the excess capacity in a monopolistically competitive market is the non-price competition.

C. Essay Type Questions

27. Is it true to say that short-run abnormal profits accruing to the monopolistic firms disappear in the long-run and that the share of the firms also declines in the long-run? Give reasons in support of your answer. Use diagrams.
28. Critically discuss Chamberlin's large group model of monopolistic competition when free entry of firms and price competition among the firms both exist.
29. Critically examine Chamberlin's theory of monopolistic competition.

Price-output Decisions under Oligopoly

CHAPTER OUTLINE

Introduction
- Simultaneous Quantity Setting: The Cournot Model with Costless Production
- Reaction Curve Approach to Cournot's Model—with and wihtout the Assumptions of Costless Production and Identical Costs
- Simultaneous Price Setting with Homogeneous and Heterogeneous Products—Bertrand's Model
- Quantity Leadership—Stackelberg Model
- Chamberlin's Oligopoly Model (Small Group Model)
- The Kinked Demand Model of Sweezy
- Cartels
- Price Leadership Models
- Critique of Price Leadership Models
- Contestable Market Theory
- Competition versus Collusion (The Prisoners' Dilemma)
- Prisoners' Dilemma
- Key Terms and Concepts
- Exercises

INTRODUCTION

In Chapter 10, we discussed one form of an imperfect market—the monopolistic competition. Let us take up its other form, **oligopoly**, in this chapter. The oligopoly, meaning a few sellers, is that form of an imperfect market which is characterized by standardized or differentiated products and a high degree of interdependence. When the number of sellers is just two, the market form is called a **duopoly** and when it is more than two but limited to a few, it is called an **oligopoly**. Literature on the subject refers to them by the general name of oligopoly.

Price quantity decisions of an oligopolistic firm may be independent or dependent. When such decisions are taken independently by a firm, the firm in question is called **price leader** if it initiates price setting and **quantity leader** if it initiates quantity setting. Rest of the firms follow the leader. If they follow the leader in setting the price, they are called **price followers** and if in setting the quantity, they are called **quantity followers**. The leader firm in each case takes its decision on its own, that is, without an idea of what other firms have in mind. The choices made by the other firms may be dependent on the leader firm's choice or independent of it, but if made simultaneously, they constitute a **simultaneous game** and if made after the leader's decision, they constitute a **sequential game**. The price-quantity decisions in which the leader firm finalizes its decisions in anticipation of those of the other firms or the other firms do the same in anticipation of the leader firm's decision or even on the basis of the leader firm's signals are all said to be **interdependent**. As yet another possibility, when firms, instead of competing with each other, decide to consult each other in a friendly manner before making their moves, they are said to be **colluding**. They constitute a **collusive oligopoly** indulging in a **cooperative game**. As against this, when the oligopolistic firms are on the war path, whether in respect of price or of quantity, the market form is termed as a **collisive oligopoly** indulging in a **non-cooperative game**.

Traditionally, there are two forms of an oligopoly –

(a) Non-collusive oligopoly, and
(b) Collusive oligopoly.

The first form is marked for price-quantity wars while the second, for cartels and price leaderships.

Reconciling, we classify the study of oligopoly as below:

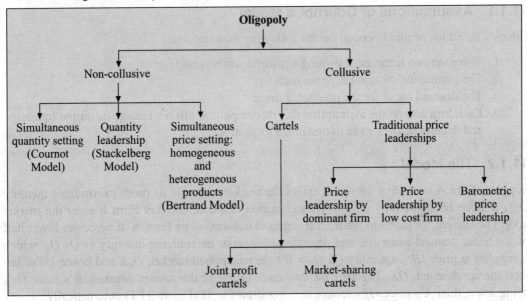

In Section 11.1, we take up the Cournot's original version of simultaneous quantity setting with costless production; in Section 11.2, we take up reaction curve approach to Cournot's simultaneous quantity setting with and without costless production through Stackelberg's isoprofit curves and in Section 11.3, we discuss Bertrand's simultaneous price setting for homogeneous and heterogeneous products through isoprofit curves. Section 11.4 provides an extension of Cournot's model to incorporate simultaneous quantity setting along with sophisticated quantity leadership through Stackelberg's sophisticated behaviourism; Section 11.5, with Chamberlin's small group oligopoly model and Section 11.6 deals with Sweezy's kinked demand models to conclude the treatment of non-collusive oligopoly.

Section 11.7 takes up collusive form of oligopoly with the discussion of cartels, Section 11.8 concludes it with that of price leadership models and Section 11.9 casts a critical look at price leadership models. Section 11.10 introduces Contestable market theory in brief; Section 11.11 provides an insight into competition versus collusion and Section 11.12 winds up the chapter with the discussion of Prisoners' Dilemma.

11.1 SIMULTANEOUS QUANTITY SETTING: THE COURNOT MODEL WITH COSTLESS PRODUCTION

This is an earliest duopoly model. It was developed by French economist Augustin Cournot in 1838.

The model may be presented in many ways. Let us begin with its original version, as illustrated by Cournot himself through an example of two sellers of mineral water, each owning a spring. The original version, though quite limited in its applicability due to its assumptions of identical products with zero production costs, can be extended to suit situations in which demands need not be identical nor costs identically zero. What is needed is relaxation of some of the assumptions of Cournot's original version, as would be evidenced in Section 11.2.

11.1.1 Assumptions of Cournot's Model

Cournot based his original version on the following assumptions:

1. There are two firms, each owning a mineral water spring.
2. The production costs are zero for each.
3. The demand curve for the product is linear.
4. Each firm acts on the assumption that its competitor will not change its output (quantity) and decides its own so as to maximize its profits.

11.1.2 The Model

Suppose, Firm A is the first mover. It enters the market and sells its profit maximizing quantity OQ_A at price OP_A. Quantity OQ_A = 1/2 the market demand, OX. Let Firm B enter the market now. The late entrant caters to the market segment unsupplied by Firm A. It perceives lower half of the linear demand as its AR and determines its profit maximizing quantity as $Q_A Q_B$, which it supplies at price OP_B. Quantity $Q_A Q_B$ = 1/2 the unsupplied market, $Q_A X$ and hence 1/4 of the total market demand, OX. Together the two cater to 3/4 of the market demand. B's price OP_B being lower than A's price OP_A, consumers get drawn to B (Figure 11.1) automatically.

Realizing this and assuming that B will not change its quantity, A reacts by readjusting its own to 1/2 the market uncatered by B. Thus A's supply in its second phase is 1/2 of (1 – 1/4), that is, 3/8 of the market demand. As regards reaction of B to this move of A, B would readjust its quantity to 1/2 the market left unsupplied by A. Assuming that A will not change its supply of 3/8 of the market demand, B would supply 1/2 of (1 – 3/8), that is, 5/16 of the total market demand in its second phase. The price charged by A will come down and that charged by B will go up each time a readjustment of quantity is made by either. The action-reaction chain continues indefinitely until a point is eventually reached at which each of the two supplies the same quantity, that is, 1/3 of market demand at the same price. This can be proved mathematically as follows.

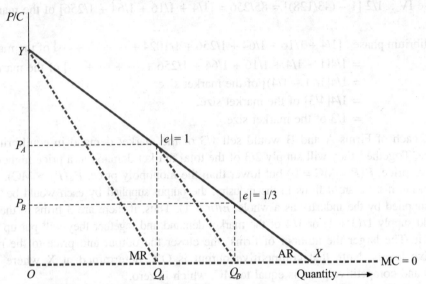

FIGURE 11.1 Simultaneous quantity setting under costless production—Cournot's duopoly model: Let YX represent the linear demand for mineral water and YQ_A, the corresponding MR curve. Production being costless, MC coincides with the horizontal axis (MC = 0). Profit-maximizing quantity and price for the first mover A are OQ_A and OP_A respectively, determined at the point where MC cuts MR. A vertical line through this point meets the linear demand YX at its midpoint where $|e| = 1$. Note that $OQ_A = 1/2$ of OX, Q_A being the midpoint of OX and X being the point where linear demand meets the quantity axis. Firm A thus supplies half the market demand at price OP_A. Now suppose Firm B enters the market. It caters to the unsupplied market (lower- half of the linear demand). Profit-maximizing quantity and price for Firm B are Q_AQ_B and OP_B respectively determined at Q_B, the point where MC cuts B's MR. Note that quantity sold by Firm B is half the unsupplied demand, so that $Q_AQ_B = 1/2 \ Q_A X = 1/4 \ OX$. Thus, Firm A, in its initial phase, supplies 1/2 of the market demand at price OP_A while Firm B, 1/4 of the market demand at price OP_B ($OP_B < OP_A$).

Quantities supplied by Firm A in its successive phases can be expressed as below:

Phase I   : 1/2 of the market size.
Phase II : 1/2 [1 – (1/4)] = 3/8 = [1/2 – (1/8)] of the market size.
Phase III : 1/2 [1 – (5/16)] = 11/32 = [1/2 – 1/8 –1/32] of the market size.
Phase IV : 1/2 [1 – (21/64)] = 43/128 = [1/2 – 1/8 –1/32 –1/128] of the market size.

...   .

Equilibrium phase: $[1/2 - 1/8\{1 + 1/4 + 1/16 + 1/64 + \cdots + \cdots + \cdots\}]$ of the market size.
$= [1/2 - 1/8\{1/(1 - 1/4)\}]^*$ of the market size.
$= [1/2 - 1/8\{4/3\}]$ of the market size.
$= [1/2 - 1/6]$ of the market size.
$= 1/3$ of the market size.

Quantities supplied by Firm B in its successive phases can be expressed as below:

Phase I   : $1/2 (1/2) = 1/4$ of the market size.
Phase II   : $1/2 [1 - (3/8)] = 5/16 = [1/4 + 1/16]$ of the market size.
Phase III : $1/2 [1 - (11/32)] = 21/64 = [1/4 + 1/16 + 1/64]$ of the market size.
Phase IV   : $1/2 [1 - (43/128)] = 85/256 = [1/4 + 1/16 + 1/64 + 1/256]$ of the market size.

...   .

Equilibrium phase : $[1/4 + 1/16 + 1/64 + 1/256 + 1/1024 + \cdots + \cdots + \cdots]$ of the market size.
$= 1/4[1 + 1/4 + 1/16 + 1/64 + 1/256 + \cdots + \cdots + \cdots]$ of the market size.
$= 1/4[1/(1 - 1/4)]$ of the market size.
$= 1/4[4/3]$ of the market size.
$= 1/3$ of the market size.

Thus, each of Firms A and B would sell 1/3 of the market demand in equilibrium at the same price. Together, they will supply 2/3 of the total market demand at a price higher than the competitive price, $P(P = MC = 0)$ but lower than the monopoly price, $P_A(P_A > MC)$.

In general, if there are n firms in the industry, the output supplied by each would be $1/(n + 1)$ and that supplied by the industry as a whole, $n/(n + 1)$. Thus, if there are 3 firms in the industry, each would supply $1/(3 + 1)$ or 1/4 of the market demand and together they will put up $3/(3 + 1)$ or 3/4 of it. The larger the number of firms' the closer the output and price to the respective competitive levels. Note that competitive output is OX, determined at X where $MC = P$ ($MC = 0$) and competitive price is equal to MC, which is zero.

Cournot's model, therefore, leads to a stable equilibrium. The model, however, is not free from criticism.

Comments

The model suffers from the following drawbacks:
1. The model does not say how long it will take to reach the equilibrium.
2. The assumption of costless production is unrealistic.
3. Though the model can be generalized to any number of firms, it is a closed model as entry of new firms is not provided for. The number of firms remains unchanged throughout the adjustment period.
4. The firms seem never to learn from their past experiences as each continues to assume repeatitively that the other would not change its quantity in its next phase even when there exists evidence to the contrary.

The model is thus subjected to criticism on the grounds of its unrealistic assumptions.

---

* Sum to infinity of a G.P. $(a + ar + ar^2 + ar^3 + \ldots + \ldots)$ with $|r| < 1$ is $a/(1 - r)$.

11.2 REACTION CURVE APPROACH TO COURNOT'S MODEL—WITH AND WITHOUT THE ASSUMPTIONS OF COSTLESS PRODUCTION AND IDENTICAL COSTS

The reaction curve approach* provides a more powerful treatment of oligopolistic markets. This is so because it no longer requires the highly unrealistic assumptions of identical demand and cost conditions. To begin, let us introduce the concept of isoprofit curves needed in derivation of the reaction curves geometrically.

An isoprofit curve for Firm A is the locus of points defined by different combinations of outputs of A and its rival B, which yield to A the same level of profit (Figure 11.2).

Similarly, *an isoprofit curve for Firm B is the locus of points defined by different combinations of outputs of B and its rival A, which yield to B the same level of profit (Figure 11.3).*

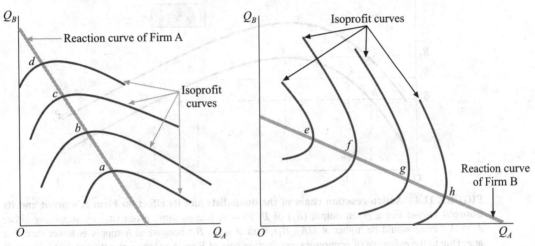

FIGURE 11.2 Isoprofit map and the reaction curve of Firm A.

FIGURE 11.3 Isoprofit map and the reaction curve of Firm B.

From the definitions given above it is clear that isoprofit curves are indifference curves with the following properties:

1. Isoprofit curves of a duopolist are concave to the axis on which its output is measured. That is, isoprofit curves of duopolist A are concave to the x-axis, while those of duopolist B are concave to the y-axis when output of A is measured on x-axis and that of B, on y-axis. The shape of the isoprofit curve of A shows that it can react to any level of B's output by adjusting its own so as to maintain a given level of profit, π_A, for itself. The same can be said about the shape of the isoprofit curve of B, which enables it to react to any level of A's output by adjusting its own so as to maintain a given level of profit, π_B, for itself.

---

*The concept of reaction curves approach is based on the concept of isoprofit curves based on Stackelberg's indifference curve analysis.

2. The farther away the location of the isoprofit curve of a duopolist from the corresponding axis, the higher the quantity supplied by its rival and the lower that supplied by the duopolist in question and the lower the magnitude of profit accruing to it (Figure 11.4). This is so because larger supply made by the rival lowers the market price and hence the profit margin of the duopolist in question already supplying less.
3. The peak of a higher isoprofit curve of duopolist A (implying lower levels of profit to A) lies to the left of the peak of its lower isoprofit curve. Likewise, the peak of B's isoprofit curve farther away from the y-axis lies lower below the peak of its isoprofit curve lying closer to the y-axis.

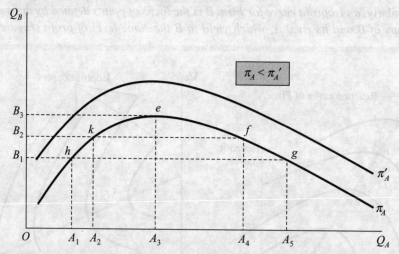

FIGURE 11.4 Action-reaction chain of the duopolists and its effect on Firm A's profit and its isoprofit curve: For a given output (B_1) of B, Firm A retains same profit (π_A) by supplying either A_1 or A_5. Price would be higher at $h(A_1, B_1)$, than at $g(A_5, B_1)$ because at h supply is lower than that at g. Due to the existence of economies, production cost of Firm A is lower at g than at h. A can retain therefore same profit (π_A) by supplying either A_1 or A_5, given B's supply as B_1. If B increases its supply from B_1 to B_2, Firm A must decrease it from A_5 to A_4, if at g, so that the total supply may remain same and the fall in price caused by B's increase in supply may be offset by the rise in it caused by a suitable decrease in supply of A to make the same profit (π_A); or, if at h, Firm A must increase it from A_1 to A_2 so that its production cost falls by the same proportion by which price has fallen in response to B's increase in supply. These adjustments of Firm A form a part of its reaction to the moves of Firm B so that Firm A may maintain the same level of profit (π_A) whether at h or k or f or g. If Firm B increases its supply even beyond B_2, say to B_3, Firm A has to increase its own from A_2 to A_3 if at k or decrease it from A_4 to A_3 if at f on the same grounds. In case B increases supply above B_3, A's isoprofit curve will shift upwards to (π_A'), indicating a decline in A's profits ($\pi_A' < \pi_A$).

The locus of the peaks (a, b, c, and d) on the isoprofit curves of Firm A (Figure 11.2) and that of the points (e, f, g and h) farthest from the vertical axis on isoprofit curves of Firm B (Figure 11.3) give the reaction curves of the two duopolists A and B in that order.

Having explained the process of derivation of reaction curves of the two duopolists from their isoprofit curves, the equilibrium of the market is determined as in Figure 11.5 at the point of their intersection.

The reaction curves for the two can also be obtained with the help of calculus. The process is demonstrated below:

Suppose the duopolists face the market demand curve,

$$P = a - bQ \tag{11.1}$$

where, a and b are positive constants; Q is the quantity demanded at price P; Q_1 of which is supplied by first duopolist and Q_2 by the second so that $Q = Q_1 + Q_2$
Differentiating $Q = Q_1 + Q_2$ with respect to Q_1 and Q_2 in that order, we have

$$dQ/dQ_1 = 1$$

and

$$dQ/dQ_2 = 1$$

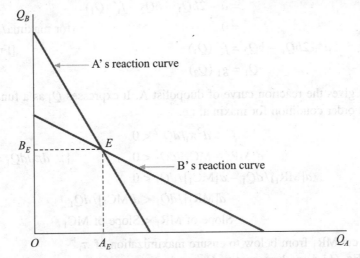

FIGURE 11.5 Reaction curve approach to duopoly equilibrium: Equilibrium of a duopoly takes place at the intersection of reaction curves of the firms. Equilibrium quantities of the two firms are A_E and B_E respectively.

(Assuming zero conjectural variations, i.e. $dQ_2/dQ_1 = dQ_1/dQ_2 = 0$ as each duopolist treats the rivals output as fixed.)

Let π_1 and π_2 be the profit functions of the duopolists 1 and 2 respectively. Then

$$\pi_1 = TR_1 - TC_1 \tag{11.2}$$
$$= P \times Q_1 - f_1(Q_1) \qquad [TC_1 = f_1(Q_1)]$$
$$= [a - bQ] \times Q_1 - f_1(Q_1)$$
$$= [a - b(Q_1 + Q_2)] \times Q_1 - f_1(Q_1)$$
$$= aQ_1 - bQ_1^2 - bQ_1 Q_2 - f_1(Q_1) \tag{11.3}$$

and

$$\pi_2 = TR_2 - TC_2 \tag{11.4}$$
$$= P \times Q_2 - f_2(Q_2) \qquad [TC_2 = f_2(Q_2)]$$
$$= [a - bQ] \times Q_2 - f_2(Q_2)$$

$$= [a - b(Q_1 + Q_2)] \times Q_2 - f_2(Q_2)$$
$$= aQ_2 - bQ_2^2 - bQ_1 Q_2 - f_2(Q_2) \qquad (11.5)$$

Differentiating Eq. (11.2) with respect to Q_1, we have

$$d\pi_1/dQ_1 = d(TR_1)/dQ_1 - d(TC_1)/dQ_1$$
$$= MR_1 - MC_1$$
$$= 0 \qquad \text{(for maxima/minima)} \quad (11.6)$$

Differentiating Eq. (11.3) with respect to Q_1, we have

$$d\pi_1/dQ_1 = a - 2bQ_1 - bQ_2 - d[f_1(Q_1)]/dQ_1$$
$$= a - 2bQ_1 - bQ_2 - f_1'(Q_1)$$
$$= 0 \qquad \text{(for maxima/minima)} \quad (11.7)$$

$\Rightarrow \qquad a - 2bQ_1 - bQ_2 = f_1'(Q_1) \qquad \text{[From Eq. (11.7)]}$

$\Rightarrow \qquad Q_1 = g_1(Q_2) \qquad (11.8)$

Equation (11.8) gives the reaction curve of duopolist A. It expresses Q_1 as a function of Q_2.
The second order condition for maxima, i.e.

$$d^2\pi_1/dQ_1^2 < 0$$

$\Rightarrow \qquad d[MR_1 - MC_1]/dQ_1 < 0 \qquad [\because d\pi_1/dQ_1 = MR_1 - MC_1]$

$\Rightarrow \qquad d[MR_1]/dQ_1 - d[MC_1]/dQ_1 < 0$

$\Rightarrow \qquad d[MR_1]/dQ_1 < d[MC_1]/dQ_1$

$\Rightarrow \qquad$ Slope of MR_1 < Slope of MC_1

$\Rightarrow$ MC_1 should cut MR_1 from below to ensure maximization of π_1

Differentiating Eq. (11.4) with respect to Q_2, we have

$$d\pi_2/dQ_2 = d(TR_2)/dQ_2 - d(TC_2)/dQ_2$$
$$= MR_2 - MC_2$$
$$= 0 \qquad \text{(for maxima/minima)} \quad (11.9)$$

Differentiating Eq. (11.5) with respect to Q_2, we have

$$d\pi_2/dQ_2 = a - 2bQ_2 - bQ_1 - d[f_2(Q_2)]/dQ_2$$
$$= a - 2bQ_2 - bQ_1 - f_2'(Q_2)$$
$$= 0 \qquad \text{(for maxima/minima)} \quad (11.10)$$

$\Rightarrow \qquad a - 2bQ_2 - bQ_1 = f_2'(Q_2) \qquad \text{[From Eq. (11.10)]}$

$\Rightarrow \qquad Q_2 = g_2(Q_1) \qquad (11.11)$

Equation (11.11) gives the reaction curve of duopolist B. It expresses Q_2 as a function of Q_1.
The second order condition for maxima, i.e.

$$d^2\pi_2/dQ_2^2 < 0$$

$\Rightarrow \qquad d[MR_2 - MC_2]/dQ_2 < 0 \qquad [\because d\pi_2/dQ_2 = MR_2 - MC_2]$

$$\Rightarrow \quad d[MR_2]/dQ_2 - d[MC_2]/dQ_2 < 0$$

$$\Rightarrow \quad d[MR_2]/dQ_2 < d[MC_2]/dQ_2$$

$$\Rightarrow \quad \text{Slope of } MR_2 < \text{Slope of } MC_2$$

$\Rightarrow MC_2$ should cut MR_2 from below to ensure maximization of π_2

The isoprofit curve of duopolist 1 for a given level of profit, $\bar{\pi}_1$ is given by Eq. (11.3). It can be expressed as

$$aQ_1 - bQ_1^2 - bQ_1Q_2 - f_1(Q_1) = \bar{\pi}_1 \qquad (11.12)$$

Likewise, isoprofit curve of duopolist 2 for a given level of profit, $\bar{\pi}_2$ is given by Eq. (11.5). It can be expressed as

$$aQ_2 - bQ_2^2 - bQ_1Q_2 - f_2(Q_2) = \bar{\pi}_2 \qquad (11.13)$$

Let us have a numerical illustration now.

ILLUSTRATION 11.1: The market demand faced by duopolists is given by

$$P = 100 - 0.4Q,$$

and their respective cost functions are

$$C_1 = 5Q_1, \text{ and } C_2 = 0.1Q_2^2$$

where, Q_1 and Q_2 are the quantities produced and supplied by duopolists 1 and 2 respectively so that $Q = Q_1 + Q_2$

Calculate:

(a) Reaction curves of the two.
(b) Quantities Q_1 and Q_2 produced and supplied by the two in equilibrium.
(c) Profits accruing to each in equilibrium.
(d) Market price and quantity transacted.
(e) Isoprofit curves of the two.
(f) How would your answers change under Cournot's assumptions?

Solution: The profit functions of the two can be expressed as:

$$\pi_1 = TR_1 - TC_1$$
$$= PQ_1 - 5Q_1$$
$$= [100 - 0.4Q] Q_1 - 5Q_1$$
$$= [100 - 0.4(Q_1 + Q_2)] Q_1 - 5Q_1$$
$$= 100Q_1 - 0.4Q_1^2 - 0.4Q_2Q_1 - 5Q_1$$
$$= 95Q_1 - 0.4Q_1^2 - 0.4Q_2Q_1 \qquad (11.14)$$

$$\pi_2 = TR_2 - TC_2$$
$$= PQ_2 - 0.1Q_2^2$$
$$= [100 - 0.4Q] Q_2 - 0.1Q_2^2$$
$$= [100 - 0.4(Q_1 + Q_2)] Q_2 - 0.1Q_2^2$$
$$= 100Q_2 - 0.4Q_2^2 - 0.4Q_1Q_2 - 0.1Q_2^2$$
$$= 100Q_2 - 0.5Q_2^2 - 0.4Q_1Q_2 \qquad (11.15)$$

Differentiating Eq. (11.14) with respect to Q_1, we have

$$d\pi_1/dQ_1 = 95 - 0.8Q_1 - 0.4Q_2$$

(Assuming zero conjectural variation, i.e. $dQ_2/dQ_1 = 0$)

$= 0$ (the necessary condition for maximization)

$\Rightarrow \quad Q_1 = (950/8) - 1/2 Q_2$ (11.16)

Equation (11.16) gives the reaction curve of duopolist 1.

Differentiating once again, we have

$$d^2\pi_1/dQ_1^2 = -0.8$$

which being negative, second order condition is also satisfied.

Differentiating Eq. (11.15) with respect to Q_2, we have

$$d\pi_2/dQ_2 = 100 - Q_2 - 0.4Q_1$$

(Assuming zero conjectural variation, i.e. $dQ_1/dQ_2 = 0$)

$= 0$ (the necessary condition for maximization)

$\Rightarrow \quad Q_2 = 100 - 0.4Q_1$ (11.17)

Equation (11.17) gives the reaction curve of duopolist 2.

Differentiating once again, we have

$$d^2\pi_1/dQ_1^2 = -1.0$$

which being negative, second order condition is satisfied.

Plotting Eqs. (11.16) and (11.17) on the same plane (Figure 11.6), the two intersect each other at E, which gives the equilibrium.

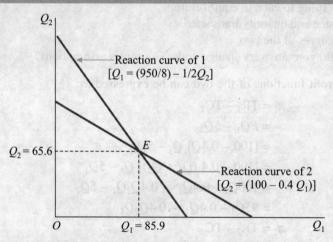

FIGURE 11.6 Equilibrium of the duopolistic market.

Solution of the simultaneous Eqs. (11.16) and (11.17) gives

$$Q_1 = 85.9$$
$$Q_2 = 65.6$$

and $\qquad Q = Q_1 + Q_2$
$\qquad\qquad = 85.9 + 65.6$
$\qquad\qquad =$ **151.5**

Market price $\qquad P = 100 - 0.4Q$
$\qquad\qquad = 100 - 0.4 \times 151.5$
$\qquad\qquad =$ **39.4**

Profits accruing to the two at the equilibrium are

$$\pi_1 = 95Q_1 - 0.4Q_1^2 - 0.4Q_2Q_1$$
$$= \textbf{2954.98 or 2955}$$
$$\pi_2 = 100Q_2 - 0.5Q_2^2 - 0.4Q_1Q_2$$
$$= \textbf{2154.3 or 2154}$$

Isoprofit curves for the two can be stated as

$$\bar{\pi}_1 = 95Q_1 - 0.4Q_1^2 - 0.4Q_2Q_1$$
and $\qquad \bar{\pi}_2 = 100Q_2 - 0.5Q_2^2 - 0.4Q_2Q_1$

Each of which represents locus of various combinations of Q_1 and Q_2 yielding the same level of profit, $\bar{\pi}_1$ in case of duopolist 1 and $\bar{\pi}_2$ in case of duopolist 2. Identifying $\bar{\pi}_1$ and $\bar{\pi}_2$ one can draw isoprofit maps for the two as in Figures 11.2 and 11.3. Isoprofit curves corresponding to the equilibrium can be obtained by substituting for $\bar{\pi}_1$ and $\bar{\pi}_2$ as calculated above.

The model reduces to Cournot's model as soon as we assume zero production costs. The profit functions change to

$$\pi_1 = 100Q_1 - 0.4Q_1^2 - 0.4Q_2Q_1$$
and $\qquad \pi_2 = 100\,Q_2 - 0.4Q_2^2 - 0.4Q_1Q_2$

Maximizing the profits, we get the reaction curves as

$$Q_1 = 125 - 0.5Q_2$$
and $\qquad Q_2 = 125 - 0.5Q_1$

Simultaneous solution of the equations leads to

$$Q_1 = 250/3$$
$$= \textbf{83.33}$$
and $\qquad Q_2 = \textbf{83.33}$ (Figure 11.7)
$$P = 100 - 0.4Q$$
$$= 100 - 0.4[(250/3) + (250/3)]$$
$$= 100 - 0.4[500/3]$$
$$= \textbf{100/3}$$

Market demand can be found by substituting $P = 0$ in the demand curve.

$$0.4Q = 100$$
$$\textbf{\textit{Q} = 250}$$

It is clear that each of the two sellers would supply 1/3 of the market demand at a price $P = 100/3$ which is what the original model of Cournot has predicted under zero production costs.

The illustration provides an insight into Cournot's model of duopoly under costless production and its reaction-curve-version with and without non-zero and non-identical costs of production. The assumption of costless production leads to equal market sharing ($Q_1 = 83.33$ and $Q_2 = 83.33$) and that of non-costless and non-identical production, to unequal market sharing ($Q_1 = 85.9$ and $Q_2 = 65.6$). The assumption of costless production leads to larger market size ($Q = 250$) and lower equilibrium price ($P = 33.33$) but that of non-zero production costs, to smaller market size ($Q = 151.5$) and higher equilibrium price ($P = 39.4$). Figure 11.7 shows Cournot's version of the reaction curve approach to duopoly.

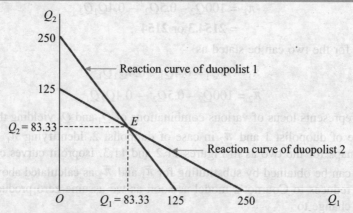

FIGURE 11.7 **Duopoly equilibrium in Cournot' version:** Reaction curves under Cournot's costless production.

11.3 SIMULTANEOUS PRICE SETTING WITH HOMOGENEOUS AND HETEROGENEOUS PRODUCTS—BERTRAND'S MODEL

Developed in 1883, Bertrand's model*, resembles Cournot's in its basic framework. The major point of difference is its simultaneous price setting as against simultaneous quantity setting of Cournot's. Each firm in it assumes that its rival firm will not change its price, while the firm in question sets its own; unlike Cournot's model in which each firm assumes that its rival firm will not change its quantity, while the firm in question sets its own. As another point of difference, price set in this model is equal to the marginal cost whereas it is always greater than the marginal cost in Cournot's model. As for its resemblance with the reaction curve approach to Cournot's model, isoprofit curves are incorporated even in this model and so is the maximization of individual profits instead of industry or joint profits. Figure 11.8 explains the process.

The model is presented with the analytical tools of the reaction curves derived from the isoprofit maps. An isoprofit curve of a firm, say A, represents same level of profits which will accrue to firm A from various levels of prices charged by it and its rival firm. The isoprofit curve of firm A is convex to the axis that measures the prices charged by it (P_A). Such shape of this curve indicates that the firm must lower the price charged by it to a certain level to meet the price cutting by its rival firm in order to maintain its profits at a certain level, say π_A. If the rival firm

---
* Bertrand, J., *Theorie Mathematique de la Rchesse Sociale, Journal des Savants*, Paris, 1883, pp.499–508.

continues to cut price, firm A will not be able to maintain its level of profit at π_A any longer and would have to climb down to a lower isoprofit curve π'_A. In the same way, isoprofit curves for B too can be explained. While isoprofit curves of A are convex to x-axis, measuring A's prices, isoprofit curves of B are convex to y-axis measuring B's prices. Note that the behaviour of the isoprofit curves in Bertrand's model is exactly opposite of the behaviour of the isoprofit curves in Stackelberg's analysis of the Cournot's model. In the latter, isoprofit curves of A are concave to x-axis, measuring quantities supplied by A; and, isoprofit curves of B are concave to y-axis, measuring quantities supplied by B. The equilibrium of the duopolistic market can be attained with the help of the reaction curves of the two sellers as derived in Figure 11.8 from the isoprofit curves. Note that the firms resort to marginal cost pricing and attempt equilibrium through maximization of individual profits rather than of joint profits.

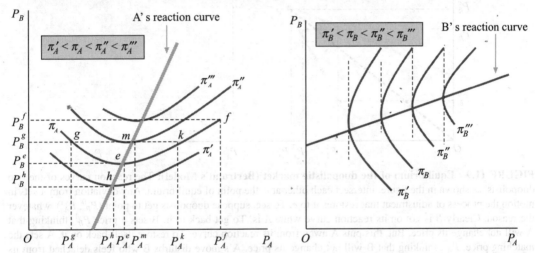

FIGURE 11.8 Derivation of the reaction curves of duopolists through their isoprofit curves (Bertrand's Model): Prices set by A are measured on x-axis and those set by B, on y-axis. In the left panel, an isoprofit curve represents combinations of different price levels of the two that yield same level of profit to A. The lowest isoprofit curve represents lowest level of profit to A and the highest, the highest level of it to it. π_A represents combinations such as $g(P_A^g, P_B^g)$, $e(P_A^e, P_B^e)$, $k(P_A^k, P_B^g)$ and $f(P_A^f, P_B^f)$ each of which entitles A to same profit π_A. When price set by B is P_B^g at g, that set by A has to be either P_A^g at g or P_A^k at k so that it may retain profit π_A whether at g or at k. At g, price set by A is lower than that set by it at k. This implies higher sales for A at g than at k with same profit to A at each point. If A sets a price P_A^m at $m(P_A^m < P_A^k)$, when price set by B is P_B^g, A jumps on to a higher isoprofit curve, π''_A. The reason for this is that A sells more at m than at k due to a lower price set by it at m. If B reduces its price to P_B^e at e, its sales would go up and sales of A would go down unless the latter also cuts its price from P_A^k to P_A^e ($P_A^e < P_A^k$). If B resorts to further price cutting, say to P_B^h, A would have to cut its price to P_A^h at h and fall onto a lower isoprofit curve, π'_A. The locus of the points of the lowest prices set by B on each of A's isoprofit curves (points h, e, m, etc.) gives A's reaction curve, which is an upward-sloping straight line, as shown.

In the right panel, isoprofit curves of B are drawn likewise. Each isoprofit curve is an indifference curve representing various combinations of the prices set by the two sellers that yield the same level of profit to B. The isoprofit curve to the rightmost indicates highest profit to B and that to the leftmost, indicates the lowest profit to it. The locus of the points of the lowest prices set by A on each of B's isoprofit curves gives B's reaction curve, again an upward rising straight line though flatter than A's reaction curve.

Figure 11.9 explains the mechanism of attainment of equilibrium through reaction curves drawn in the same space. The point of intersection of the two reaction curves gives the equilibrium of the duopoly.

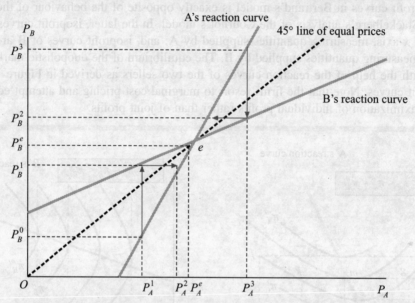

FIGURE 11.9 **Equilibrium of the duopolistic market (Bertrand's Model):** The reaction curves of the two duopolists, as shown in the figure, intersect each other at e, the point of equilibrium. Any deviation from it sets in motion the process of adjustment that restores it to e. To see, suppose duopolists get to point (P_B^0, P_A^1), whatever the reason. Clearly B is not on its reaction curve while A is. To get back to it, B sets a price P_B^1, thinking that A will not change its price. But, this puts A away from its reaction curve. To restore itself back on it, A sets the matching price, P_A^2, thinking that B will not change its price. A's move disturbs B who feels detached from its reaction curve again. The action-reaction chain continues until the two land at e with no incentive to depart from since the two regain their reaction curves simultaneously. Likewise, the reader can imagine the two at (P_A^3, P_B^3) and see how the two end up again in point e.

Comments

Note that Bertrand's model does not lead to maximization of the industry (joint) profits. As has been seen, the profit-maximizing isoprofit curves of the two firms are those that lie farthest away from the axes. This is so because each, while changing its price, assumes that its rival will not change its price. But as it turns out, the rival does. Firms never seem to learn from their past experiences. Industry profits can be increased when firms recognize their past mistakes and abandon the Bertrand pattern of behaviour.

Like Cournot's model, Bertrand's model too is a closed one. Both the models assume naïve behaviour of rivals, both fail to deal with entry and to incorporate selling costs, both fail to define the length of the adjustment process, both deal with firms producing homogeneous products, both assume simultaneity of the decisions—one in respect of choosing quantity while the other in respect of choosing price, both assume that market demand is accurately known, and above all, both are based on individual demand curves located under the convenient assumption of constant reaction curves. What more, both models subscribe to an interesting feature that the limit of duopoly is pure competition. Neither model refutes the other. Each is consistent with the other though each is based on different set of assumptions.

The main point of difference, apart from that of simultaneity of quantity setting in Cournot's model and price setting in Bertrand's model, is that costless production in Cournot's model ($MC_1 = MC_2 = 0$) does not imply zero prices to be charged by the firms while in Bertrand's model, it does. In Cournot's model, each firm chooses its profit-maximizing quantity by setting its MR equal to its MC, with emerging price, P, being higher than the MC ($P > MC$) at equilibrium. In Bertrand's model, simultaneous price setting by firms implies zero price and hence zero economic profit to each under costless production. Under the assumption of homogeneous product, no firm can survive by setting a price higher than the price set by its rival. Consumers reject a firm charging a higher price for a product available at a lower price elsewhere. As a consequence, the low price firm captures the market unless the high price firm also lowers its price. If a firm sets a price higher than that set by its rival, its rival does not follow the suit but if a firm sets a price lower than that set by its rival, the rival has to follow the suit. In such price competition, both the firms have to charge the price, which is equal to the marginal cost ($P = MC$). Under costless production, MC being zero, the price set by each firm is zero.

Under the assumption of homogeneity of product in the two models, firms have to set same price. This is true particularly when the firms have to choose price (Bertrand's model) instead of quantity (Cournot's model). Let us construct a numerical example to demonstrate the point.

ILLUSTRATION 11.2: A product with market demand given by

$$P = 120 - Q,$$

where Q is total quantity demanded at price P and being manufactured by two firms in the market with identical costs. Determine outputs of the two firms under

(a) Cournot pattern of simultaneous quantity setting?
(b) Bertrand's pattern of simultaneous price setting?

Assume production to be

(i) costless with $MC_1 = MC_2 = 0$,
(ii) non-costless with $MC_1 = MC_2 = 20$.

Solution: Let the equilibrium outputs of the two be Q_1 and Q_2 so that $Q = Q_1 + Q_2$

(a) When the firms follow Cournot's pattern of simultaneous quantity setting, the equilibrium condition for each firm is equality of its MR to its MC.

For the first firm,
$$MR_1 = d(TR_1)/dQ_1$$
$$= d[(120 - Q)Q_1]/dQ_1$$
$$= 120 - 2Q_1 - Q_2 \qquad \text{(Since } Q = Q_1 + Q_2\text{)}$$

For the second firm,

$$MR_2 = d(TR_2)/dQ_2$$
$$= d[(120 - Q)Q_2]/dQ_2$$
$$= 120 - 2Q_2 - Q_1 \quad \text{(Since } Q = Q_1 + Q_2\text{)}$$

(i) When production is costless, that is,

$$MC_1 = MC_2 = 0$$

The reaction curves for the two firms are obtained by setting $MR_1 = MC_1$ and $MR_2 = MC_2$. This yields:

$$Q_1 = 60 - 1/2Q_2, \text{ and}$$
$$Q_2 = 60 - 1/2Q_1$$

Solution of simultaneous equations yields

$$Q_1 = Q_2 = 40$$

Hence

$$Q = Q_1 + Q_2$$
$$= 80$$

Price set by each firm

$$P = 120 - Q$$
$$= 120 - 80$$
$$= 40.$$

(ii) When production is non-costless and

$$MC_1 = MC_2 = 20$$

the reaction curves for the two firms are obtained by setting $MR_1 = MC_1$ and $MR_2 = MC_2$. This yields:

$$Q_1 = 50 - 1/2Q_2, \text{ and}$$
$$Q_2 = 50 - 1/2Q_1$$

Solution of simultaneous equations yields

$$Q_1 = Q_2 = 100/3$$

Hence

$$Q = Q_1 + Q_2$$
$$= 200/3$$

Price set by each firm

$$P = 120 - Q$$
$$= 120 - 200/3$$
$$= 160/3$$

(b) When the firms follow Bertrand's pattern of simultaneous price setting, the equilibrium condition for each is equality of its price to its marginal cost.

(i) Under costless production

$$MC_1 = MC_2 = 0$$

Price set by the first firm

$$P_1 = MC_1$$
$$= 0$$

and that set by the second firm

$$P_2 = MC_2$$
$$= 0$$

The two firms sell **120 units** together and **60 units** individually.

(ii) When production is non-costless and

$$MC_1 = MC_2 = 20$$

Price set by the first firm

$$P_1 = MC_1$$
$$= 20$$

and that set by the second firm

$$P_2 = MC_2$$
$$= 20$$

The two firms sell **100 units** together and **50 units** individually.

Bertrand's model assumed that the products are homogeneous. In an oligopolistic market, some degree of product differentiation always exists. It may be in the external features or in features related to qualitative aspects such as product durability or product appeal arising from its design that products of one firm are perceived different from those of the other. In such cases, firms compete by choosing prices rather than quantities. To see how product differentiation influences price-competition, let us take up an example.

ILLUSTRATION 11.3: Demand functions of firms in a duopolistic market are given as

$$Q_1 = 150 - 2P_1 + P_2 \quad \text{[demand faced by the first firm]}$$
$$Q_2 = 150 - 2P_2 + P_1 \quad \text{[demand faced by the second firm]}$$

Suppose each firm has a fixed cost of 1000 and a variable cost of zero. Q_1 and Q_2 are quantities the two firms sell respectively at prices P_1 and P_2.
Obtain reaction curves for the two and determine their equilibrium price-outputs.

Solution: It is clear from the demand functions of the two firms that the quantity sold by each varies inversely as its own price but directly as the competitor's price. To derive the reaction curves of the two firms, let us derive their profit functions and impose conditions of profit maximization on each.

Profit function for the first firm

$$\pi_1 = TR_1 - TC_1$$
$$= P_1 Q_1 - C_1 \quad\quad [TC_1 \equiv C_1 = TFC + TVC = 1000 + 0 \times Q_1 = 1000]$$
$$= P_1[150 - 2P_1 + P_2] - 1000$$
$$= 150 P_1 - 2P_1^2 + P_1 P_2 - 1000$$

Differentiating π_1 with respect to P_1, we have

$$d\pi_1/dP_1 = 150 - 4P_1 + P_2$$
$$= 0 \quad\quad \text{(for maximization of profit)}$$
$$\Rightarrow \quad\quad P_1 = (75/2) + (1/4)P_2 \quad\quad (11.18)$$

Profit function for the second firm

$$\pi_2 = TR_2 - TC_2$$
$$= P_2 Q_2 - C_2 \quad\quad [TC_2 \equiv C_2 = TFC + TVC = 1000 + 0 \times Q_2 = 1000]$$
$$= P_2[150 - 2P_2 + P_1] - 1000$$
$$= 150 P_2 - 2P_2^2 + P_1 P_2 - 1000$$

Differentiating π_2 with respect to P_2, we have

$$d\pi_2/dP_2 = 150 - 4P_2 + P_1$$
$$= 0 \quad\quad \text{(for maximization of profit)}$$
$$\Rightarrow \quad\quad P_2 = (75/2) + (1/4)P_1 \quad\quad (11.19)$$

Equations (11.18) and (11.19) give the reaction curves of the two firms. Solving them simultaneously for P_1 and P_2, we have

$$P_1 = 50$$

and

$$P_2 = 50$$

The quantities sold by the two can now be determined by substituting these values in the respective demand functions. Thus,

$$Q_1 = 100$$

and

$$Q_2 = 100$$

Substituting P_1 and P_2 in the respective profit functions, we have

$$\pi_1 = 4000$$

and

$$\pi_2 = 4000$$

Plotting the reaction curves, we can show the solution as in Figure 11.10.

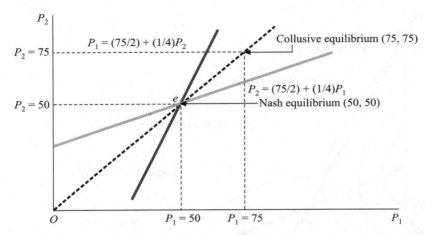

FIGURE 11.10 Nash equilibrium* in prices: The point of intersection of the two reaction curves marks Nash equilibrium. Each firm is charging a price of 50, selling 100 units and making a profit of 4000. Each firm is doing its best given the strategy of its rival. If the two firms are able to collude, they will charge the monopoly price to maximize joint profits. Under collusion, each firm can be seen to charge a price of 75, sell 75 units and to earn a profit of 4625. The solution (75, 75) is the collusive solution**.

11.4 QUANTITY LEADERSHIP—STACKELBERG MODEL

This model, treated as an extension of Cournot's model, was developed by the German economist Heinrich von Stackelberg. In the model, Stackelberg assumed that *one* duopolist is sufficiently sophisticated to recognize that his rival acts on Cournot's assumption. The recognition enables the sophisticated duopolist to determine the rival's reaction curve and to incorporate it in his own profit function before maximizing his profits like a monopolist.

The working of the model is demonstrated in Figure 11.11.

If one firm is a sophisticated leader while the other a follower, the equilibrium that emerges is a stable one as the follower acts as a naïve firm.

---

* Nash equilibrium refers to the equilibrium at which each firm does the best it can, given the strategy (price) of its rival. Concept of such equilibrium was first introduced by the mathematician John Nash in 1951. Ever since it is referred to as Nash equilibrium after the name of the mathematician.
** Under collusion, the firms will behave like a monopoly charging a common price, i.e. $P_1 = P_2 = P$, and will maximize the total profits, π.

$$\pi = \pi_1 + \pi_2$$
$$= 150P - 2P^2 + P^2 - 1000 + 150P - 2P^2 + P^2 - 1000$$
$$= 300P - 2P^2 - 2000$$

Differentiating the joint profit function with respect to P, we have

$$d\pi/dP = 300 - 4P$$
$$= 0 \qquad \text{(for maximization of profit)}$$

$\Rightarrow P = 75$. Substituting in the demand functions, $Q_1 = Q_2 = 75$ and in the profit functions, $\pi_1 = \pi_2 = 4625$.

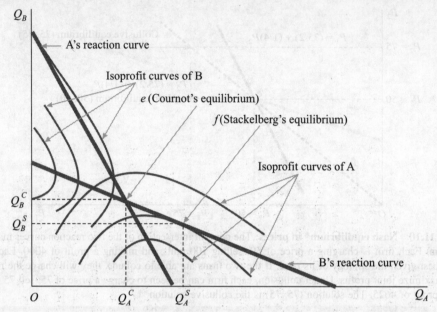

FIGURE 11.11 Stackelberg's duopoly model of quantity leadership: The reaction curves of the two firms may be derived from their isoprofits curves following the procedure of Figures 11.2 and 11.3. Point of intersection of the reaction curves, point $e(Q_A^C, Q_B^C)$, as in Figure 11.6 or 11.7, gives Cournot's equilibrium. Now, let Firm A be a sophisticated quantity leader and Firm B, a follower. As assumed by Stackelberg, the sophisticated leader knows the reaction curve of its rival who is acting on Cournot's assumptions. Accordingly, Firm A incorporates quantity supplied by Firm B into its profit function before maximizing it like a monopoly. Firm A thus determines its profit-maximizing quantity at point $f(Q_A^S, Q_B^S)$ where reaction curve of Firm B touches one of the isoprofit curves of Firm A. The follower reacts to this quantity leadership of Firm A by supplying Q_B^S as expected by Firm A. Opposite is the case when Firm B acts as a sophisticated leader. The reader can compare the situation of Stackelberg's quantity leadership equilibrium (point f) with that of Cournot's (point e).

If both the firms behave as sophisticated quantity leaders, each will attempt maximization of its own profit like a monopoly. The market situation will turn unstable leading to what is called **Stackelberg's disequilibrium**. This will initiate either a price war between the two continuing until one of them surrenders and turns a follower or a situation arises in which the two enter into a collusion.

Stackelberg's quantity leadership model has interesting implications, one of which is that the follower ultimately realizes that its naïve behaviour fails to pay-off. In consequence, a high degree of interdependence between the two emerges.

This model, however, does not apply to a market structure in which firms behave on Bertrand's assumptions. A sophisticated price leader can do nothing to maximize its own profits or to persuade the other to stop price cutting.

Mathematical treatment of Stackelberg's model

Suppose the firms face a linear demand curve

$$P = a - bQ$$

where, Q is the quantity demanded at price P. Suppose further that C_1 and C_2 are costs of producing quantities Q_1 and Q_2 respectively by the two firms. Also suppose that Firm 1 is the quantity leader and Firm 2, the follower. Quantities Q_1 and Q_2 have to be such that $Q = Q_1 + Q_2$ in equilibrium.

The profit function of Firm 1 can be given as

$$\pi_1 = PQ_1 - C_1$$
$$= [a - bQ]\, Q_1 - C_1$$
$$= [a - b(Q_1 + Q_2)]\, Q_1 - C_1$$
$$= aQ_1 - bQ_1^2 - bQ_1 Q_2 - C_1$$

Differentiating with respect to Q_1, we have

$$d\pi_1/dQ_1 = a - 2bQ_1 - bQ_2 - MC_1 \qquad (\because dQ_2/dQ_1 = 0)$$
$$= 0 \qquad \text{(for maximization)}$$
$$\Rightarrow \qquad Q_1 = [a - bQ_2 - MC_1]/2b \qquad (11.20)$$

The profit function of Firm 2, likewise, can be expressed as

$$\pi_2 = PQ_2 - C_2$$
$$= [a - bQ]\, Q_2 - C_2$$
$$= [a - b(Q_1 + Q_2)]\, Q_2 - C_2$$
$$= aQ_2 - bQ_2^2 - bQ_1 Q_2 - C_2$$

Differentiating with respect to Q_2, we have

$$d\pi_2/dQ_2 = a - 2bQ_2 - bQ_1 - MC_2 \qquad (\because dQ_1/dQ_2 = 0)$$
$$= 0 \qquad \text{(for maximization)}$$
$$\Rightarrow \qquad Q_2 = [a - bQ_1 - MC_2]/2b \qquad (11.21)$$

Equations (11.20) and (11.21) give the reaction curves of Firm 1 and Firm 2 respectively. Derivation of the reaction curves has so far followed the same steps as in reaction curve approach to Cournot's duopole.

Now that Firm 1 is a sophisticated quantity leader, it would incorporate quantity of Firm 2 [Eq. (11.21)] in its profit function before maximizing it.

Profit function of Firm 1 is now given as

$$\pi_1 = aQ_1 - bQ_1^2 - bQ_1\,[\{a - bQ_1 - MC_2\}/2b] - C_1$$
$$= aQ_1 - bQ_1^2 - (aQ_1/2) + (bQ_1^2/2) - 1/2\, MC_2 - C_1$$

Differentiating with respect to Q_1, we have

$$d\pi_1/dQ_1 = a - 2bQ_1 - a/2 + bQ_1 - MC_1 \qquad (\because d(MC_2)/dQ_1 = 0)$$
$$= 0 \qquad \text{(for maximization)}$$
$$\Rightarrow \qquad \mathbf{Q_1 = [(1/2)\cdot a - MC_1]/b} \qquad (11.22)$$

The second firm, being a quantity follower, determines its quantity by substituting this value of Q_1 in its reaction curve given by Eq. (11.21). Thus,

$$Q_2 = [a - b\{(1/2)a - MC_1\}/b - MC_2]/2b$$
$$= [(1/2)a + MC_1 - MC_2]/2b \qquad (11.23)$$

In case production costs are zero, that is,

$$MC_1 = MC_2 = 0$$

Then
$$Q_1 = a/2b \qquad (11.24)$$
and
$$Q_2 = a/4b \qquad (11.25)$$

Proceeding likewise, we can work out expressions for outputs of the two firms when Firm 2 acts as a sophisticated quantity leader and Firm 1, as a follower.

To show that Stackelberg's model is an extension of Cournot's, we can work out Cournot's equilibrium from that of Stackelberg. The only thing we need to do for the purpose is to set $Q_1 = Q_2$ and $MC_1 = MC_2 = 0$ in either of the reaction curves (11.20) or (11.21). For instance, from Eq. (11.20), we have

$$Q_1 = a/3b \qquad (11.26)$$
$$Q_2 = a/3b \qquad (11.27)$$

Note that market size is $Q = (a/b)$ which can be determined by substituting $P = 0$ in the market demand function, $P = a - bQ$. From Eqs. (11.26) and (11.27), we observe that each of the duopolists acting on Cournot's assumptions supplies 1/3 of the market size and from Eqs. (11.24) and (11.25), we observe that the sophisticated quantity leader supplies 1/2 of the market size while the follower, 1/4 of it.

Let us have a numerical illustration now.

ILLUSTRATION 11.4: For the demand and cost functions of illustration 11.1, determine the equilibrium quantities and price under:

(i) Cournot's assumptions of naïve behaviour of the duopolists
(ii) Quantity leadership of the first duopolist
(iii) Quantity leadership of the second duopolist
(iv) Stackelberg's sophisticated pattern of behaviour adopted by both

Solution:

(i) Illustration 11.1 answers part (i).
(ii) *When first duopolist is the sophisticated leader:* It will incorporate the second's reaction curve in its profit function before maximizing it like a monopolist.
Its profit function [Eq. (11.14)], after substituting for Q_2 in it from Eq. (11.17), appears as

$$\pi_1 = 95Q_1 - 0.4Q_1^2 - 0.4[100 - 0.4Q_1] \cdot Q_1$$
$$= 55Q_1 - 0.24Q_1^2 \qquad (11.28)$$

Differentiating with respect to Q_1, we have

$$d\pi_1/dQ_1 = 55 - 0.48Q_1$$
$$= 0 \quad \text{(for maximization)}$$
$$\Rightarrow \quad Q_1 = 55/0.48$$
$$= \mathbf{114.6} \quad \text{(correct to first place of decimal)}$$

Profit earned by the leader

$$\pi_1 = 55Q_1 - 0.24Q_1^2$$
$$= 55 \times 114.6 - 0.24(114.6)^2$$
$$= \mathbf{3151 \text{ (Approx.)}}$$

(Note that $Q_1 = 85.9$ under Cournot's model)
Substituting $Q_1 = 114.6$ in the follower's reaction curve [Eq. (11.17)], we have

$$Q_2 = 100 - 0.4Q_1$$
$$= 100 - 0.4(55/0.48)$$
$$= 100 - 45.8$$
$$= \mathbf{54.2}$$

(Note that $Q_2 = 65.6$ under Cournot's model)
Profit earned by the follower (Equation 11.15)

$$\pi_2 = 100Q_2 - 0.4Q_2^2 - 0.4Q_1Q_2 - 0.1Q_2^2$$
$$= 100 \times 54.2 - 0.5(54.2)^2 - 0.4(114.6)(54.2)$$
$$= 5420 - 1468.82 - 2484.53$$
$$= \mathbf{1468 \text{ (Approx.)}}$$

The total quantity supplied

$$Q = (Q_1 + Q_2)$$
$$= 114.6 + 54.2$$
$$= \mathbf{168.8} \quad \text{(as against 151.5 under Cournot's model)}$$

Market price

$$P = 100 - 0.4Q$$
$$= 100 - 0.4 \times 168.8$$
$$= 100 - 67.5$$
$$= \mathbf{32.5} \quad \text{(as against 39.4 in Cournot's model)}$$

(iii) *When the second firm is a sophisticated leader:* In this case, it is the second firm that will incorporate the reaction curve of the first in its profit function before maximizing it like a monopolist. Substituting for Q_1 from Eq. (11.16) in Eq. (11.15), we have

$$\pi_2 = 100\,Q_2 - 0.5Q_2^2 - 0.4\,(950/8 - 1/2Q_2)\cdot Q_2$$
$$= 52.5Q_2 - 0.3Q_2^2$$

Differentiating with respect to Q_2, we have

$$d\pi_2/dQ_2 = 52.5 - 0.6Q_2$$
$$= 0 \qquad \text{(for maximization)}$$
$$\Rightarrow \qquad Q_2 = 52.5/0.6$$
$$= \mathbf{87.5}$$

Profit earned by the leader,

$$\pi_2 = 52.5Q_2 - 0.3Q_2^2$$
$$= 52.5 \times 87.5 - 0.3\,(87.5)^2$$
$$= 4593.75 - 0.3 \times 7656.25$$
$$= 4593.75 - 2296.88$$
$$= \mathbf{2297\ (Approx.)}$$

Substituting $Q_2 = 87.5$ in the reaction curve of the follower (the first firm), we have

$$Q_1 = 950/8 - 1/2Q_2$$
$$= 118.75 - 1/2 \times 87.5$$
$$= 118.75 - 43.75$$
$$= \mathbf{75}$$

Profit of the follower (Equation 11.14),

$$\pi_1 = 95Q_1 - 0.4Q_1^2 - 0.4Q_2Q_1$$
$$= 95 \times 75 - 0.4\,(75)^2 - 0.4\,(87.5)\,(75)$$
$$= 7125 - 0.4 \times 5625 - 0.4 \times 6562.5$$
$$= 7125 - 2250 - 2625$$
$$= \mathbf{2250}$$

Total output

$$Q = (Q_1 + Q_2)$$
$$= 75 + 87.5$$
$$= \mathbf{162.5}$$

Market price

$$P = 100 - 0.4 \times 162.5$$
$$= \mathbf{35}$$

(iv) *When both firms adopt the sophisticated behaviour: A state of Stackelberg's disequilibrium:* Each firm in this case would compare its profit earned by it as a leader with that earned by it as a follower before taking its decision.
Profits of the first firm:

$$\text{As a leader} = \mathbf{3151}$$

$$\text{As a follower} = \mathbf{2250}$$

Clearly, the first firm will prefer to act as a leader.
Profits of the second firm:

$$\text{As a leader} = \mathbf{2297}$$

$$\text{As a follower} = \mathbf{1468}$$

Clearly, the second firm too will prefer to act as a leader.

In fact, each firm benefits from its sophisticated behaviour so much so that each would prefer to lead. As they proceed with their plans, they soon realize that their expectations cannot be fulfilled simultaneously. Price wars become inevitable unless they decide to collude for mutual gains.

11.5 CHAMBERLIN'S OLIGOPOLY MODEL (SMALL GROUP MODEL)

Chamberlin's oligopoly model accepts interdependence of firms and suggests that a stable equilibrium can be reached through a monopoly price provided firms in the market acknowledge their interdependence and attempt maximization of joint profits rather than of catering to individual profits independently. If the firms do not recognize their interdependence, he admits, the industry will reach an equilibrium either on Cournot's pattern of behaviour (acting independently to maximize own profit on the assumption that the rival firm will keep its output constant) or on Bertrand's pattern of behaviour (acting independently to maximize own profit on the assumption that the rival firm will keep its price unchanged). But can a business firm be as naïve as Cournot and Bertrand assumed or can it be so myopic as not to see beyond the tip of its nose? For instance, when a rival firm is observed in past changing its earlier decisions of output or price, how can one continue to assume that it would not in future? Business firms, after all, are in business for profits and the same if maximized through collusion or even without it through joint profit maximization, why should the firms not accept their interdependence?

Rejecting the assumption of independent action of own profit-maximization by a firm, Chamberlin argues that each firm would recognize its dependence on the rest for its price-output decisions and a monopoly solution comprising monopoly price and monopoly output would emerge as a stable industry equilibrium. Chamberlin assumes that a monopoly solution (joint profit-maximization) is possible even without collusion as the firms are intelligent enough to recognize their interdependence or to learn from their past mistakes and to adopt a position that is best for all concerned.

His model can be understood best in the duopoly framework with zero production costs. Figure 11.12 explains the working of his model.

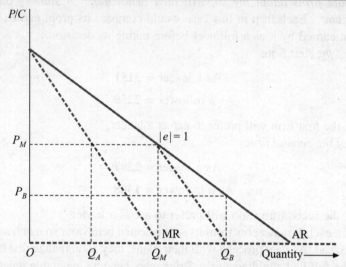

FIGURE 11.12 Chamberlin's oligopoly model: In the figure, AR is the demand curve faced by the duopolists. Corresponding MR intersects the MC curve (coinciding with the horizontal axis due to zero production costs) at Q_M, which gives the profit-maximizing output (OQ_M) supplied by duopolist A at price P_M. Now suppose duopolist B enters the market. It determines its profit-maximizing output $(Q_M Q_B)$ at Q_B where MC equals B's MR and meets 1/2 the demand of the unsupplied market at a price P_B. Duopolist A recognizing the fact that the price charged by B is lower than its own price P_M and that it would have to lose its customers to B soon, cuts its supply to 1/2 of OQ_M, that is, to OQ_A to make way for B to join it to supply the other half $(Q_A Q_M)$ at the joint profit-maximizing price P_M. B realizes an increase in its profit as it charges price P_M $(P_M > P_A)$ for same quantity $(Q_A Q_M = Q_M Q_B)$. It thus feels happy at A's move. On the other hand, A experiences a decrease in its profit to half as much but feels happy that it now has to supply only half as much. Had it not taken the initiative, it would have lost all its customers to B or would have to lower its price to P_B. This would have caused losses to it any way. The two, therefore, would supply half the market demand together at the profit-maximizing price P_M as if the two formed a monopoly.

Chamberlin's model, known as a small group model, suffers from the defect that it is a closed one like Cournot's. There is no room for entry in it as in case of Cournot's model. Moreover, there is ample empirical support that oligopolistic firms always start with price-wars though ending up in collusions sooner or later. Chamberlin's argument that firms are intelligent enough to recognize their interdependence may be valid but not at the initial stages of competition.

11.6 THE KINKED DEMAND MODEL OF SWEEZY

The kinked demand curve was employed by Hall and Hitch* in the article *Price theory and Business Behaviour* in 1939 not as a tool to determine price and output in oligopolistic market, but as an explanation of why price once determined on the basis of average cost principle, will remain *sticky*. It was Paul Sweezy** who, in his article *Demand under Conditions of Oligopoly* published in the same year, introduced the kinked demand curve as a tool to determine equilibrium in oligopolistic market. His model may be presented as in Figure 11.13.

---

* Hall, R.L. and C.I. Hitch, *Price Theory and Business Behaviour*, Oxford Economic Papers, 1939, pp. 12–45.
** Sweezy, Paul, *Demand under Conditions of Oligopoly*, Journal of Political Economy, 1939, pp. 568–737.

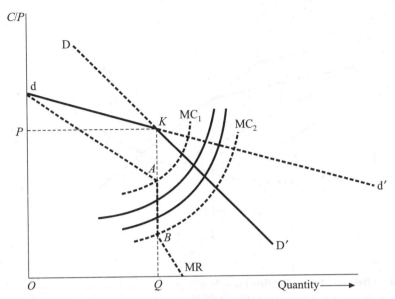

FIGURE 11.13 Sweezy's kinked demand model of sticky price: Demand curves dd′ and DD′ intersect at point K. DD′ is the market share curve while dd′, the demand curve of a typical firm. If the firm increases its price above P, other firms do not follow suit with the result that segment KD of the market share curve (DD′) becomes redundant. But if the firm lowers its price below P, other firms in the market follow suit and segment Kd' of the firm's demand curve dd′ becomes redundant. All the firms move along KD'. Thus, d KD', with a kink at K, serves as the demand curve of the oligopolistic firms. MR curve, due to the kink in demand d KD' at K, is discontinuous at K. Equilibrium of a typical firm in the market is given at the point of the kink. This is so because MC lies below MR to the left of K and above MR to its right. At the point of the kink, MC_1 cuts MR at point A and MC_2 cuts MR at point B. In between A and B, MC may cut AB anywhere without disturbing the equilibrium at K. MC is abnormally high at A and abnormally low at B. Such MCs are rare. Whether the MC is in position MC_1 or in position MC_2, equilibrium price and output remain unchanged. The price, thus, remains sticky at P despite changes in production costs.

11.6.1 Equilibrium of Oligopolistic Firms under Indirect Taxation

Levy of an indirect tax, such as the sales tax, affects production cost and hence price of all the firms in an oligopolistic market despite the fact that new MC (after fax) passes through the discontinuity of the MR curve. The point of kink shifts upwards to left due to tax shifting by firms onto consumers. Equilibrium price rises and equilibrium quantity falls (Figure 11.14). Every firm in the market increases price as production cost for all of them are equally affected by the levy. Demand curve of a typical firm undergoes an upward parallel shift from dk to $d'k'$ (Figure 11.14). Let us discuss another situation involving a pivotal shift in demand. It shifts the kink leftwards or rightwards horizontally (not upwards, as in Figure 11.14). Such a shift in demand affects the volume of output and not the level of price so long as MC passes through the range of the discontinuity of the new MR (Figure 11.15). In this case the shift in kink takes place along the price line. Cost curves remain unchanged in absence of tax.

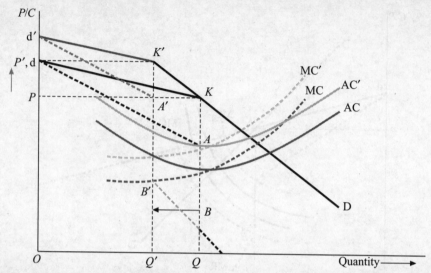

FIGURE 11.14 Effect of a Levy of indirect tax on oligopolistic equilibrium: Levy of tax shifts average cost curve from AC to AC′ and marginal cost curve, from MC to MC′. Increase in cost is reflected in an increase in price from P to P'. This results from the shift of demand from dKD to $d'K'D$. The kink shifts upwards to left from K to K'. Equilibrium price rises from P to P' but quantity falls from Q to Q'. Note that the cost curves pass through the discontinuity of the new MR curve.

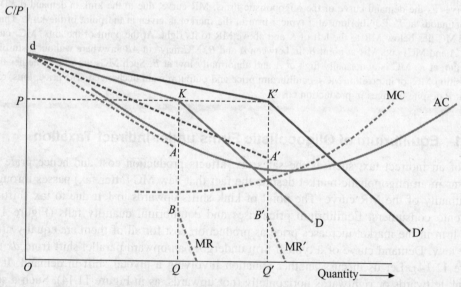

FIGURE 11.15 Effect of a Pivotal shift in demand on price-output decisions of an oligopolistic market: When demand shifts from dKD to $dK'D'$ in such a way that point of kink lies in the same horizontal line, output increases from Q to Q' while price remains unchanged so long as MC continues to pass through the range of the discontinuity of the MR curve.

11.6.2 Critique of Sweezy's Model

Sweezy's model, appearing very realistic at the first sight, reveals a few drawbacks at a closer look. The following ones deserve a special mention here:

1. The model does not define the level of price that maximizes profits.
2. The model also fails to indicate the level of price at which the kink occurs.
3. The model also fails to explain the price-output decisions of the firms.

The kinked demand curve model can explain only the stickiness of price, once reached, in a situation of changing costs and rivalry. And that is almost all about the utility of the model.

11.7 CARTELS

We have seen from Sections 11.1 to 11.6 how non-collusive oligopolistic firms reach their equilibria and how they cater to their individual goals of profit maximization instead of maximization of joint or industry profits. We have also seen that a monopoly solution maximizing joint industry profit is possible if the firms recognize or acknowledge their interdepence and aim at common interest. We have also had some idea of why recognition of inter-dependence fails to take precedence over individualism in an oligopolistic market. In Chapter 12, we will see how such failure leads to oligopolistic games. In the remaining part of Chapter 11, we will discuss the mechanism and consequences of the recognition of interdependence among oligopolistic firms. In this section, we discuss the mechanism and consequences of formation of a cartel, an important form of collusive oligopoly.

11.7.1 Cartels Maximizing Joint Profits

A cartel is a group of firms in direct secret agreement to reduce uncertainty arising from individualistic pursuits. In this particular case, the aim of the cartel is to maximize joint industry profits. The situation resembles one of a multiplant monopoly maximising its profits. For the sake of simplicity, assume that all the products in the oligopoly market are homogeneous. Such an oligopoly is called a **pure oligopoly**.

The firms appoint a central agency with sole authority not only to decide the total quantity to be produced and price to be charged to maximize industry profits, but also to decide allocation of the output among the firms of the cartel. The authority of the central agency is total in the sense that the agency enjoys access to the cost figures of the individual firms. All along, we assume for the sake of convenience that the agency estimates the market demand curve and the corresponding MR curve. Market MC curve is derived from the horizontal summation of the MC curves of individual firms. We further assume that there are only two firms in the cartel. Working of the cartel is explained in Figures 11.16, 11.17 and 11.18.

Central agency estimates demand and cost curves to determine quantity and price for the market as also for the constituent firms. Having access to costs of individual firms, the central agency determines MC of the industry through horizontal summation of MC_1 and MC_2, the marginal costs of the constituent firms. As is clear from Figure 11.18, the profit-maximizing output is determined at the point e where MC cuts MR from below. The output is Q and corresponding price, P. To allocate 'Q' among constituent firms, a horizontal line through e is drawn to cut MC_1

at e_1 and MC_2 at e_2. The points e_1 and e_2 determine quantities Q_1 and Q_2 that the two firms should produce and sell so that $Q = Q_1 + Q_2$. The constituent firms sell their allocations at monopoly price, P. The firm with lower cost (Figure 11.16) gets a higher market share (Q_1) and earns a higher profit than the firm with higher cost (Figure 11.17).

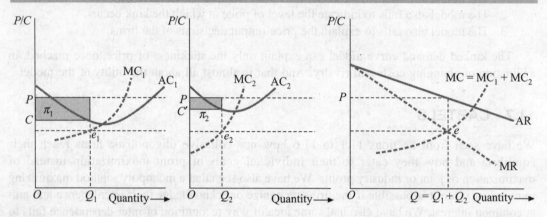

FIGURE 11.16 Firm with lower cost: The firm has a higher market share (Q_1) and a higher profit, π_1. Price and equilibrium are determined by the central agency.

FIGURE 11.17 Firm with higher cost: The firm has a lower market share (Q_2) and a lower profit, π_2. Price and equilibrium are determined by the central agency.

FIGURE 11.18 Joint output of the industry: It is determined by the intersection of MC and MR at e. Total output = Q, where $Q = Q_1 + Q_2$. Market price is the monopoly price P, which maximizes joint profits of the industry.

11.7.2 Mathematical Presentation of Joint Profit-maximizing Cartel

Joint profit maximization by a cartel follows the same methodology as that followed by a profit maximizing multiplant monopoly. The model, thus, can be presented as

Maximize: $\pi = \pi_1 + \pi_2$

Subject to: $C_1 = f_1(Q_1)$, $C_2 = f_2(Q_2)$ and demand, $P = f(Q)$

where

$Q = Q_1 + Q_2$
$\pi_1 = TR_1 - TC_1$
$\pi_2 = TR_2 - TC_2$
$\pi =$ Joint profit

Now,
$$\pi = \pi_1 + \pi_2$$
$$= TR_1 - TC_1 + TR_2 - TC_2$$
$$= TR_1 + TR_2 - TC_1 - TC_2 \quad \ldots \quad \ldots \quad (11.29)$$

Differentiating Eq. (11.29) partially with respect to Q_1 and Q_2, we have

$$\partial \pi / \partial Q_1 = \partial(TR_1)/\partial Q_1 - \partial(TC_1)/\partial Q_1$$

$$= MR_1 - MC_1$$
$$= 0 \quad \text{(for maximization of profit)}$$
$$\Rightarrow \quad MR_1 = MC_1 \quad \ldots \quad \ldots \quad \ldots \quad (11.30)$$
and
$$\partial\pi/\partial Q_2 = \partial(TR_2)/\partial Q_2 - \partial(TC_2)/\partial Q_2$$
$$= MR_2 - MC_2$$
$$= 0 \quad \text{(for maximization of profit)}$$
$$\Rightarrow \quad MR_2 = MC_2 \quad \ldots \quad \ldots \quad \ldots \quad (11.31)$$

From Eqs. (11.30) and (11.31), we have
$$MR_1 = MR_2 = MC_1 = MC_2 \quad \ldots \quad \ldots \quad \ldots \quad (11.32)$$

Rewriting Eq. 11.29 with $TR_1 + TR_2 = TR$ and differentiating it partially w.r.t. Q_1, we have

$$\partial\pi/\partial Q_1 = \partial(TR)/\partial Q_1 - \partial(TC_1)/\partial Q_1$$
$$= [\partial(TR)/\partial Q](\partial Q/\partial Q_1) - \partial(TC_1)/\partial Q_1$$
$$= MR - MC_1 \quad [\text{Since, } (\partial Q/\partial Q_1) = 1, \text{ as } Q = Q_1 + Q_2]$$

Proceeding likewise,
$$\partial\pi/\partial Q_2 = MR - MC_2$$

Incorporating these expressions in Eq. 11.32, we have
$$MR_2 = MR = MR_1 = MC_1 = MC_2 \quad (11.33)$$

Equation 11.33 spells the condition of joint industry profit maximization. The supplementary conditions are
$$\partial^2\pi/\partial Q_1^2 < 0$$
$$\partial^2\pi/\partial Q_2^2 < 0$$
and,
$$[\partial^2\pi/\partial Q_1^2][\partial^2\pi/\partial Q_2^2] > [\partial^2\pi/\partial Q_1\partial Q_2]^2$$

Before we evaluate joint profit maximization, let us have a numerical illustration.

ILLUSTRATION 11.5: Assume that the market demand is
$$P = 100 - 0.4Q, \text{ where, } Q = Q_1 + Q_2$$
and the two colluding firms have costs given by
$$C_1 = 5Q_1, \; C_2 = 0.1Q_2^2$$
How would the central agency allocate outputs to the two so as to maximize the joint profits?

Solution: The profit function
$$\pi = TR - TC_1 - TC_2$$
$$= PQ - 5Q_1 - 0.1Q_2^2$$
$$= (100 - 0.4Q)Q - 5Q_1 - 0.1Q_2^2$$
$$= 100Q - 0.4Q^2 - 5Q_1 - 0.1Q_2^2$$

Differentiating partially with respect to Q_1 and Q_2, we have

$$\partial\pi/\partial Q_1 = 100(\partial Q/\partial Q_1) - 0.8Q(\partial Q/\partial Q_1) - 5$$
$$= 100 - 0.8Q - 5 \quad \text{(Since, } \partial Q/\partial Q_1 = 1\text{)}$$
$$= 0 \quad \text{(for maximization of profit)}$$
$$\Rightarrow \quad 0.8\,Q = 95$$
$$\Rightarrow \quad Q = 950/8$$
$$= \mathbf{118.75}$$

and
$$\partial\pi/\partial Q_2 = 100(\partial Q/\partial Q_2) - 0.8Q(\partial Q/\partial Q_2) - 0.2Q_2$$
$$= 100 - 0.8Q - 0.2Q_2 \quad \text{(Since, } \partial Q/\partial Q_2 = 1\text{)}$$
$$= 0 \quad \text{(for maximization of profit)}$$
$$\Rightarrow \quad 0.2Q_2 = 100 - 0.8Q$$
$$= 100 - 0.8 \times (950/8)$$
$$= 5$$
$$\Rightarrow \quad Q_2 = 5/0.2$$
$$= \mathbf{25}$$
$$P = 100 - 0.4Q$$
$$= 100 - 0.4 \times 950/8$$
$$= \mathbf{52.5}$$

Profit
$$\pi = 100Q - 0.4Q^2 - 5Q_1 - 0.1Q_2^2$$
$$= 100 \times (95/0.8) - 0.4\,(95/0.8)^2 - 5\,(93.75) - 0.1\,(25)^2$$
$$= 11875 - 5640.625 - 468.75 - 62.5$$
$$= \mathbf{5703.125}$$

Note that
$$Q_1 = Q - Q_2$$
$$= 118.75 - 25$$
$$= \mathbf{93.75}$$

Thus, price fixed by the central agency is 52.5 and quantities allocated to the two oligopolists are 93.75 units and 25 units respectively.

Compare the data discussed in Illustrations 11.1, 11.4 and 11.5. There were two firms in each case facing same market demand and having similar cost conditions. In Illustrations 11.1 and 11.4, the firms were non-colluding firms while in Illustration 11.5, they are colluding in the form of a cartel to maximize joint profits. In Illustration 11.1, while setting their respective quantities, each firm believed in Cournot's assumption that the rival firm will not change its quantity. In Illustration 11.4, the firms behaved according to Stackelberg's assumptions that at least one of the firms is a sophisticated quantity leader. Price-output decisions in the three situations are accordingly different.

Critique of joint Profit Maximization

Despite the ease of theoretical working of joint profit maximization, It poses a number of problems in practice.

Let us make a list of them below:

1. *Estimation of market demand from individual demands is not perfect:* Individual firms find their demands highly elastic due to existence of perfect substitutes, while industry demand estimated by the central agency is usually much less elastic due to errors in its estimation. This leads to errors in derivation of MR curve.
2. *Erratic Estimation of MC:* As mentioned earlier, MC is obtained through horizontal summation of the individual MCs. Quite often, constituent firms don't reveal true costs with the result that MC estimated by the central agency is not realistic.
3. *Slow Process of Cartel Negotiations:* The process of allocation of outputs to the firms is not all that mechanical. Individual firms indulge in bargains of the market shares. By the time such bargains and negotiations reach their final shape, lot of water has flown under the bridge. The market they supply to are totally different from what they were expected by the central agency.
4. *Unsuitability of the High Cost Firms in the Cartel:* Existence of a high cost firm in the cartel with its MC much above the joint MC estimated by the central agency makes output allocation for this firm very irrational. The firm, thus, must close down and the process of cartelization must restart with firms having similar cost conditions. This may defeat the purpose of joint profit maximization.
5. *Fear of State Intervention:* If the central agency sets a price that generates high profits for the members there is a fear of government intervention defeating the purpose of cartelization.
6. *Members Wish to have a Good Public Image:* If members in the cartel wish to have a high public image, they may like to lower the price set by the central agency. This defeats the purpose of joint profit maximization.
7. *Entry of New Firms:* If the existing firms are having supernormal profits, the possibility of new entrants can't be ruled out. This once again comes in the way of joint profit maximization.
8. *Members Forego Individuality:* Members don't have freedom of product design and selling activities.

11.7.3 Market Sharing Cartels

This form of collusion is more common than joint profit maximizing cartels. The firms agree to share the market but retain a considerable degree of freedom in respect of styling, brand positioning and such other product-related decisions. Market sharing takes the following two forms:

(i) *Cartels with non-price competition agreements:*

The member firms in this cartel, called a 'loose' one, reach a consensus on price at which each one is allowed to sell any quantity. The price reached is a result of bargaining between low-cost and high-cost firms with low-cost firms pressing for a lower price while high-cost firms, for a higher one. The firms agree not to lower the price below the cartel price. They are, however, free to vary the style of their products or their selling strategies. In other words, the firms compete on a non-price basis enjoying their freedom of brand positioning and selling strategies so as to maximize their market shares.

Figure 11.19 demonstrates the working of the cartel. As is clear from the figure, such cartels are highly unstable as any firm may choose to break away from the cartel by opting to charge a price lower than the agreed one. This is particularly true in respect of a low-cost firm. Such cartels are thus highly unstable. It is due to absence of a formal agreement binding the members.

(ii) *Cartels with quota agreements:*

Another form of market-sharing cartel is one in which firms work out their quotas and agree to stick to them. In other words, they fix the quantities each member is to sell at the price agreed upon. Quotas are generally determined on the basis of production costs of the member firms. For instance, a firm with lower costs will have a higher quota and one with higher costs will have a lower quota. Under identical costs, quotas will be identical for all the forms in the industry. In case there are only two firms in the cartel, each firm will sell half the market demand (Figure 11.20). In case the costs are not identical, quotas will differ in accordance with the production costs as mentioned above or with the bargaining powers of the member firms. The bargaining power of a firm, however, depends on its past sales and/or its productive capacity.

Another form of market sharing is geographical allocation of market segments. Each firm is assigned a region and is instructed to restrict its sales to it.

As is evident from the discussions, cartels are closed models of market sharing. They are all fairly unstable due to lack of formalization of their formation. In the event of free entry and exit, their instability increases even further and return of price wars becomes highly probable.

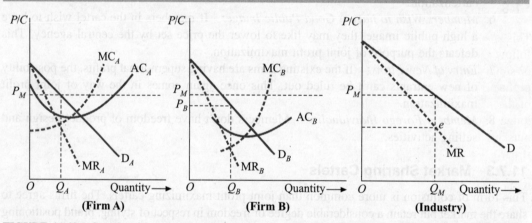

FIGURE 11.19 Cartels with non-price competition: A and B are the two firms in the cartel. Firm B is a low-cost firm while Firm A, a high cost one. The firms agree on the monopoly price, P_M. As per the agreement, none is to charge a price below this level. However, Firm B, a low-cost firm, has sufficient incentive to break away from the cartel by openly opting for a lower price with a view to increase its market share and to drive the high cost firm out of business. As soon as Firm B decides to break away, it sets a price (P_B) below P_M and the cartel breaks down. Even when the firms have identical cost structures, the cartels have an inherent tendency to collapse. Any firm may choose to charge a price slightly lower than the monopoly price and break away from the cartel unless there is a formal agreement binding it to the rest. Formal agreements require legal sanctity which is not possible as law does not permit formation of such collusions in most of the countries. The agreement defying firm, being a low-cost one, can drive the other firms out of business by drawing all their customers to itself by setting a lower price.

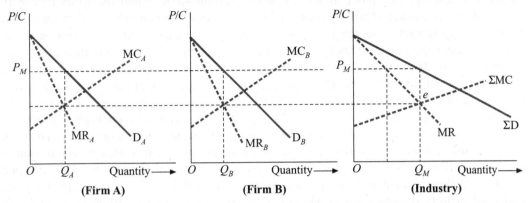

FIGURE 11.20 Cartels with equal quota agreements: In this type of market sharing, the firms have equal quotas due to identical costs. In case of two firms, each charges the monopoly price and sells half the market demand. In case of unequal costs, quotas too are unequal. In this case, quotas depend on bargaining powers of the firms, which in turn, depend on past sales incurred by them and/or their respective production capacities. Even this form of cartel is unstable. In the absence of a binding agreement, any firm may choose to breakaway from the cartel and to attempt maximization of its market share throwing other firms out by setting prices lower than the agreed monopoly price.

11.8 PRICE LEADERSHIP MODELS

This is another form of collusive oligopoly. One firm sets price, which the other firms accept and follow. The firm that sets price is called **price leader** and the rest that accept, **price followers** or simply **followers**. Needless to say that the followers accept the price even if it is below their profit-maximizing level. The main reason for such compliance by the followers is dominance of the price leader or its decision. Usually, the leader is a firm with lowest production cost or longest standing in the market or one equipped with best research facilities for the purpose. In a nutshell, it is a firm capable of carrying on its price decision independently and indefinitely even if it costs it a sizeable part of its profits.

Price leadership is a widespread phenomenon in business world. It may be practiced with or without an explicit agreement among the firms. Agreements are generally implicit or informal.

There are several forms of price leadership. The most common ones are the following:

(a) Price leadership by a low-cost firm.
(b) Price leadership by a dominant firm.
(c) Barometric price leadership.

Let us take them in that order.

11.8.1 Price Leadership by a Low-cost Firm

To understand the mechanism of price leadership by a low-cost firm, suppose there are two firms in the industry. Suppose, further that their products are identical but the production costs, different. Firm A is the low-cost firm and Firm B, the high cost one.

We can discuss the model in its two manifestations–*first*, when the firms decide in favour of equal market share (Figure 11.21) and *second*, when they decide against it (Figure 11.22). In each case, the low-cost firm, Firm A, sets its profit maximizing price as P_A and corresponding quantity as Q_A, while the high cost firm, Firm B, sets them as P_B and Q_B, respectively. If the firms do not collude, the chances of a price war are very high. The high cost firm will loose its market if it doesn't lower its price to the level of the low-cost firm's price or below it. If the high cost firm (B) adopts the low-cost firm's (A's) price, the act signals acceptance of the low-cost firm's (A's) price leadership by the high cost firm, B, but if B cuts its price below the price set by A, it signals beginning of a price war. To retain its market share, A would cut its price below the reduced price of B, which B would counter by a further price-cut. The action-reaction chain will continue until better sense prevails upon the two and they recognize their interdependence. Thus, B has either to accept A's price leadership or to face a price war in which A is in an advantageous position due to its lower costs of production. It is not that B has just these two alternatives only. There exists a third one as well before it. For instance, B can adopt A's price, but reduce its own quantity. In consequence, A will have to vary its quantity and will forego its profit maximizing position. As regards B, the option proves suicidal. The best course before B, thus, is to accept the price leadership of A, the low-cost firm.

The two firms must therefore collude. They can do so by allowing the low-cost firm's price and sharing the market either equally (Figure 11.21) or unequally (Figure 11.22).

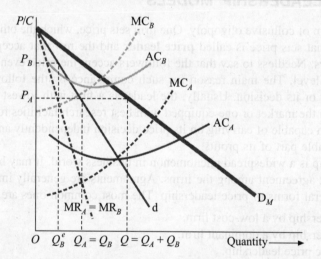

FIGURE 11.21 Low-cost price leader, firms with equal market share: Firm B faces demand d. Its MC cuts its MR to give equilibrium price P_B and equilibrium quantity Q_B^e. The market demand is D_M. Firm A, being the low-cost firm, sets a price P_A at which market demand is Q ($Q_A + Q_B$). The firms agree to share the market demand equally and sell Q_A and Q_B ($Q_A = Q_B = 1/2Q$). Note that Firm B has adopted the lower price P_A and has sold $Q_B = Q_A = 1/2Q$, which is higher than Q_B^e.

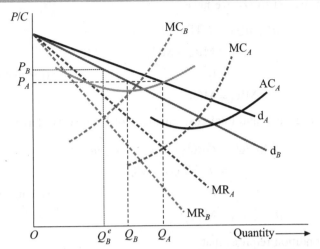

FIGURE 11.22 Low-cost price leader, firms with unequal market share: Firms A and B face demand curve d_A and d_B respectively. Their respective MRs are cut by their respective MCs to set prices P_A and P_B and quantities Q_A and Q_B^e. Firm A, being the low-cost firm, sets price P_A which Firm B adopts despite the fact that P_A is lower than its profit-maximizing price P_B. Firm B sells Q_B which is higher than its equilibrium quantity Q_B^e. The firms enjoy unequal market shares, Q_A and Q_B.

11.8.2 Mathematical Treatment of Price Leadership by Low-cost Firm

1. When firms have equal market shares

The market demand may be defined by the function

$$P = a - bQ$$
$$= a - b(Q_A + Q_B), \quad Q = Q_A + Q_B$$

where, Q_A and Q_B are outputs of Firms A and B respectively.

Their costs may be defined by the cost functions

$$C_A = f_A(Q_A)$$
$$C_B = f_B(Q_B)$$

Given that $AC_A < AC_B$, Firm A is the price leader.

Under the assumption of equal market shares, the firms will produce equal quantities, that is,

$$Q_A = Q_B$$

With this, the demand function in terms of the leader's quantity transforms to

$$P = a - 2bQ_A$$

The low-cost leader will set a price that maximizes its own profit,

$$\pi_A = TR_A - C_A$$
$$= PQ_A - C_A$$
$$= (a - 2bQ_A)Q_A - C_A$$

Differentiating with respect to Q_A, we have

$$d\pi_A/dQ_A = d(TR_A - C_A)/dQ_A$$
$$= MR_A - MC_A$$
$$= 0 \qquad \text{(for maximization of profit)}$$
$$\Rightarrow \quad MR_A = MC_A$$

Substituting the total revenue and total cost functions of Firm A, we have

$$d\pi_A/dQ_A = d(aQ_A - 2bQ_A^2 - C_A)/dQ_A$$
$$= a - 4bQ_A - MC_A$$
$$= 0 \qquad \text{(for maximization of profit)}$$
$$\Rightarrow \quad a - 4bQ_A = MC_A$$

The second order condition requires that

$$d^2 TR_A/dQ_A^2 < d^2 C_A/dQ_A^2$$

The leader firm thus produces Q_A and sells it at P_A while the follower firm adopts the leader's price and sells same quantity as the leader does. If the follower firm were to maximize its profits, it would produce Q_B^e and sell it at P_B.

However, $Q_B^e < Q_B$ and $P_B > P_A$. Adopting the leader's price might force the follower to suffer a loss of revenue. If it goes beyond the loss of revenue, that is, if it causes losses, the follower might decide to break away and produce much less and sell it at P_A only, forcing the leader thereby to a non-profit maximizing position.

ILLUSTRATION 11.6: Given the market demand

$$P = 180 - 4Q, \text{ where, } Q = Q_1 + Q_2$$

and the cost functions of the two firms

$$C_1 = 4Q_1$$
$$C_2 = 10Q_2$$

where

$$C_1 < C_2$$

Determine the price that the low-cost firm will set and the quantities the two firms will sell when they have resolved to share the market equally.

Solution: Since $C_1 < C_2$, the first firm is the price leader. To find the price it sets, let us derive its profit function

$$\pi_1 = PQ_1 - C_1$$
$$= (180 - 4Q) Q_1 - 4Q_1 \qquad \text{(since } C_1 = 4Q_1\text{)}$$
$$= [180 - 4(Q_1 + Q_2)] Q_1 - 4Q_1$$

$$= [180 - 4(Q_1 + Q_1)]Q_1 - 4Q_1$$

(since $Q_2 = Q_1$ under equal market sharing)

$$= [180 - 8Q_1]Q_1 - 4Q_1$$
$$= 176Q_1 - 8Q_1^2 \qquad (11.34)$$

Differentiating Eq. (11.34) with respect to Q_1, we have

$$d\pi_1/dQ_1 = 176 - 16Q_1$$
$$= 0 \qquad \text{(for maximization of profit)}$$
$$\Rightarrow \qquad 16Q_1 = 176$$
$$\Rightarrow \qquad \boldsymbol{Q_1 = 11}$$

Due to equal market sharing, quantity sold by the second firm

$$\boldsymbol{Q_2 = Q_1 = 11}$$

and industry sales

$$Q = Q_1 + Q_2$$
$$= 11 + 11$$
$$= 22$$

Price set by the leader

$$P = 180 - 4 \times 22$$
$$= 92$$

Profit of the leader

$$\pi_1 = 176Q_1 - 8Q_1^2$$
$$= 176 \times 11 - 8(11)^2$$
$$= 1936 - 968$$
$$= \boldsymbol{968}$$

Profit made by the follower

$$\pi_2 = [180 - 4Q]Q_2 - 10Q_2$$
$$= [180 - 4 \times 22] \times 11 - 10 \times 11$$
$$= 1012 - 110$$
$$= \boldsymbol{902}$$

Had the second firm not entered into collusion with the first, it would have maximized its profits by producing 170/16 or 10.6 units and charging a higher price,

$$P = 180 - 8(170/16)$$
$$= 95$$

The solution follows from maximization of the second firm's profit function

$$\pi_2 = [180 - 4Q]Q_2 - 10Q_2$$
$$= [180 - 8Q_2]Q_2 - 10Q_2$$
$$= 170Q_2 - 8Q_2^2$$
$$d\pi_2/dQ_2 = 0 \qquad \text{(for maximization of profit)}$$
$$\Rightarrow \qquad Q_2 = 170/16$$
$$= 10.6$$

2. When firms have unequal market shares

Let the firms decide to share the market unequally so that

$$Q_1/Q = k_1$$

and $$Q_2/Q = k_2 \qquad (k_2 = 1 - k_1)$$

where $$Q = Q_1 + Q_2$$

The reaction curves of the two firms can be expressed as

$$Q_1 = k_1 Q$$
$$= k_1 (Q_1 + Q_2)$$
$$= k_1 Q_2/(1 - k_1) \qquad \text{[for the first firm]}$$
$$Q_2 = k_2 Q$$
$$= k_2(Q_1 + Q_2)$$
$$= k_2 Q_1/(1 - k_2) \qquad \text{[for the second firm]}$$

Suppose Firm 1 is the price leader. It knows its demand and cost curves. To see how the firms reach their price-output decisions, let us have an illustration.

ILLUSTRATION 11.7: In an oligopolistic industry having two firms, the low-cost firm's estimates of its demand and cost functions are as given below:

$$P_1 = 210 - 5Q_1 - Q_2$$

and $$C_1 = 5Q_1^2$$

The firms agree to share the market demand in the ratio 2:1. The follower firm adjusts its output after the leader firm has decided its. Determine the equilibrium price-outputs of the two firms and comment on the results.

Solution: The reaction curve of the follower firm can be expressed as

$$Q_2 = k_2 Q_1/(1 - k_2)$$
$$= (1/3) Q_1/(1 - 1/3)$$
$$= 1/2 Q_1$$

The profit function of the first firm can now be expressed as

$$\pi_1 = TR_1 - TC_1$$
$$= P_1 Q_1 - 5Q_1^2$$
$$= [210 - 5Q_1 - Q_2]Q_1 - 5Q_1^2$$
$$= [210 - 5Q_1 - 1/2 Q_1]Q_1 - 5Q_1^2 \quad \text{(Since, } Q_2 = 1/2 Q_1)$$
$$= 210 Q_1 - 10.5 Q_1^2$$

Differentiating with respect to Q_1, we have

$$d\pi_1/dQ_1 = 210 - 21 Q_1$$
$$= 0 \quad \text{(for maximization)}$$

$\Rightarrow \qquad \mathbf{Q_1 = 10}$

and
$$Q_2 = 1/2 Q_1$$
$$= 1/2 \times 10$$
$$= \mathbf{5}$$

Price set by the first firm

$$P_1 = 210 - 5 \times 10 - 5$$
$$= \mathbf{155}$$

Profit earned by the first firm

$$\pi_1 = 210 Q_1 - 10.5 Q_1^2$$
$$= 210 \times 10 - 10.5 (10)^2$$
$$= 2100 - 1050$$
$$= \mathbf{1050}$$

The follower firm produces 5 units and sells them at a price of 155, set by the leader. For the latter, it is the profit-maximizing price, which it sets keeping in view the market share allotted to the former. The leader thus maximizes its own profit leaving the follower to abide with the market share allotted and market price set. The follower's position of profit or loss would depend on its costs.

11.8.3 Price Leadership by a Dominant Firm

The dominant firm model assumes existence of a large firm with a huge market share and a number of smaller firms with a small market share each.

The dominant firm knows the market demand, DD (Figure 11.23) and the collective supply of the smaller firms. It derives its demand curve and hence its MR curve, as explained in the figure. There is no agreement on market sharing. The smaller firms can drive the dominant firm to a non-profit-maximizing position by producing less than their collective supply.

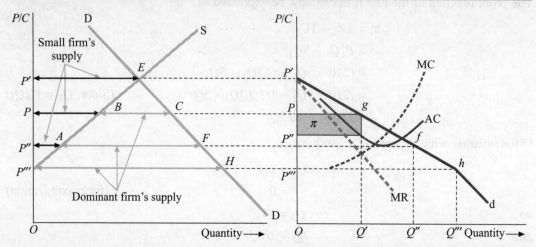

FIGURE 11.23 Price leadership by a dominant firm: DD is the market demand curve and P''' S, the supply curve of small firms, as estimated by the dominant firm. Intersection of the two gives market price P' and other firms' supply, $P'E$. At the point of intersection, supply of the dominant firm is evidently zero. Now suppose the dominant firm decides to supply entire market demand. What it needs to do is to cut price to P''' so that supply of the other firms may fall to zero. Market demand at P''' is $P'''H$ (left panel). If the firm meets this demand, it will end up at h (right panel) supplying quantity $P'''h$ or OQ'''. Joining points P' and h, the firm gets its demand curve, $P'h$. Treating it as its AR curve, the dominant firm obtains its MR curve, as shown in the right panel and determines its profit-maximizing quantity, OQ' (= BC) and price (P). The supply of the other firms at this price-level is PB. Once the dominant firm derives its demand curve $P'h$, which it does through its estimates of market demand DD and other firm's supply $P'''S$, it finalizes its profit-maximizing price P and quantity OQ' (= BC) leaving rest of the market demand (PB) for other firms to supply. The most important weapon the dominant firm possesses is its capacity to fix its profit-maximizing price P below the market price P'. Other firms have to accept the dominant firm's price even though it is below their market-clearing price. Note that the dominant firm could set its profit-maximizing price below the market price only because it was a low-cost firm. Note further that a price set by the dominant firm below its profit-maximizing level, would force it to a non-profit-maximizing position. To this, even other firms can force it by deciding to supply a quantity less than PB. The dominant firm would then have to supply more than its profit-maximizing quantity BC (or OQ') and would be forced to a non-profit-maximizing position, say, one at price P''. At P'', it supplies AF (= $P''f$, in the right panel), and is pushed not only to forego its profit maximization but also to run into loss (Point f on $P'h$, corresponding to price P'' which falls below AC). A price cut by the dominant firm below P''', leads it to move along the market demand curve DD itself (segment HD in the left panel and hd in the right panel).

11.8.4 Mathematical Treatment of Price Leadership of the Dominant Firm

Let the market demand, DD, be given as

$$Q^D = a - bP$$

while supply of small firms as

$$Q^S = cP \qquad \text{(where, } a, b \text{ and } c \text{ are all constants.)}$$

The equation of demand for the dominant firm, thus, can be expressed as

$$q = Q^D - Q^S$$
$$= a - bP - cP$$
$$= a - (b + c)P$$
$$\Rightarrow \quad P = (a - q)/(b + c) \tag{11.35}$$

Given the total cost function of the dominant firm as

$$C = t.q, \quad \text{where, } t \text{ is average cost.}$$

The profit function of the dominant firm can be expressed as

$$\pi = TR - TC$$
$$= P \cdot q - t \cdot q$$
$$= (P - t) \cdot q$$
$$= [\{(a - q)/(b + c)\} - t]q$$
$$= [(a - q) - t(b + c)] \, q/(b + c)$$

Differentiating with respect to q, we have

$$d\pi/dq = (a - 2q)/(b + c) - t$$
$$= 0 \qquad \text{(for maximization of profit)}$$
$$\Rightarrow \quad q = [a - t \cdot (b + c)]/2 \tag{11.36}$$

Price set by the dominant firm, on substituting for 'q' in Eq. (11.35), is

$$P = [a - a/2 + t(b + c)/2]/(b + c)$$
$$= [a + t(b + c)]/2\,(b + c)$$
$$= [a/\{2(b + c)\} + (1/2)t] \tag{11.37}$$

Total market demand on substituting this value of P in the given demand function is

$$Q^D = a - bP$$
$$= a - b[a/\{2(b + c)\} + (1/2)t]$$
$$= a - ab/\{2(b + c)\} - (1/2)bt$$
$$= \{ab + 2ac\}/\{2(b + c)\} - (1/2)bt \tag{11.38}$$

Supply of other firms, likewise, is

$$Q^S = cP$$
$$= ca/\{2(b + c)\} + ct/2 \tag{11.39}$$

Given relevant demand, supply and cost functions, equilibrium of industry under dominant price leadership can be determined.

ILLUSTRATION 11.8: Given the market demand as

$$Q^D = 100 - 0.6P$$

the other firms' supply as

$$Q^S = 0.4P$$

and the dominant firm's cost function as

$$C = 4q$$

Determine the equilibrium price and quantity of the dominant firm and the quantity supplied by the other firms.

Solution: Identifying the constants involved in Eqs. (11.35) to (11.38), we have

$$a = 100, \ b = 0.6, \ c = 0.4, \ t = 4$$

From Eq. (11.36), we have

$$q = [a - t \cdot (b + c)]/2$$
$$= [100 - 4 \cdot (0.6 + 0.4)]/2$$
$$= \mathbf{48}$$

From Eq. (11.37), we have

$$P = [a/\{2(b + c)\} + 1/2 t]$$
$$= [100/\{2(0.6 + 0.4)\} + 1/2 \cdot 4]$$
$$= \mathbf{52}$$

and from Eq. (11.38)

$$Q^D = \{ab + 2ac\}/\{2(b + c)\} - (1/2)bt$$
$$= \{100 \times 0.6 + 2 \times 100 \times 0.4\}/\{2(0.6 + 0.4)\} - (1/2) \times 0.6 \times 4$$
$$= (60 + 80)/2 - 1.2$$
$$= 70 - 1.2$$
$$= \mathbf{68.8}$$

and finally, from Eq. (11.39)

$$Q^S = cP$$
$$= [ca/2(b + c)] + [ct/2]$$
$$= [0.4 \times 100/2(0.6 + 0.4)] + 0.4 \times 4/2$$
$$= 20 + 0.8$$
$$= \mathbf{20.8}$$

The reader is advised to try the solution directly rather than employing the formulae derived in Eqs. (11.36), (11.37), (11.38) and (11.39) above.

11.8.5 Barometric Price Leadership

In barometric price leadership, a firm best equipped with techniques of market research or one with a proven record of success in setting prices for its products is taken as a price leader. In short, the firm accepted as a leader must serve as a barometer in reflecting changes in economic and business environment. It is not necessary for the leader to belong to the same industry. For instance, a steel industry may be treated as a barometric price leader for the motor car industry.

Barometric price leadership may be favoured on several grounds:

1. In most of the price leadership models discussed so far, the problem of rivalry among the large firms poses a threat to market stability. In a case like this, barometric price leadership is the only recourse and a fairly stable one too.
2. Followers can avoid calculations and recalculations under an environment of rapid changes. Barometric price leadership is highly convenient to them on this count.
3. Barometric price leader having a rich experience of market research proves a reasonably good forecaster of changes in cost and demand conditions in the industry. Following it is the only reasonable recourse for the firms.

11.9 CRITIQUE OF PRICE LEADERSHIP MODELS

Stability of oligopolistic market depends on price leader's power to enforce changes in price, whether positive (increase) or negative (decrease). This essentially requires the price leader to be a low-cost firm as well as a large-sized one. A high-cost firm cannot afford to set a low price. Likewise, a small firm with low costs cannot survive advertising and product-design wars often initiated by dominant firms. If a dominant firm loses its cost advantage, it loses its power to set a lower price. It also loses its power to set a higher price particularly when other firms are low-cost firms. Unless the leader is both, a low-cost firm and a large firm, its demand curve will have a kink leading to asymmetry in its power to set price. Its power to lower the price will be higher than its power to raise it.

Many times, the initiative to change price does not come from a low-cost firm or a large firm. Instead, it comes from a desperate firm requiring quick cash. Such firms reduce price significantly for fast cash when in financial crisis.

The traditional price leader is assumed to base its price on the marginalistic rule, MC = MR, so as to maximize its profits. This, however, is myopic as the profits earned, though lucrative, attract entry of new firms and the leader may in long-run lose its power and position both.

The traditional theory assumes absence of entry of new firms. Even if a stubborn firm forces its entry, the theory assumes that the new entrant will follow the leader. Such an assumption is based on the belief that the new entrant is a small beginner with high costs. This may not always be the case. At times, a new entrant may be a firm already established in some other industry but entering the one in question due to its capability to expand or to diversify. Also if the new firm has some absolute cost advantage over the other firms, the price leadership of any of the existing firms would face a potential threat.

11.10 CONTESTABLE MARKET THEORY

A contestable market is defined as one into which new firms may enter and produce under the same cost conditions as firms already operating and also as one from which firms can exit with no loss of capital*.

On the basis of this definition, a contestable market is expected to possess the following features:

1. The central feature of a contestable market is the extreme situation of smooth entry and exit. This cannot be possible unless exit and entry are both costless. In other words, either there are no fixed costs or there is no depreciation of assets so that an exiting firm does not have to incur loss while disposing of its productive assets at the time of exit. In the same way, entry too must not involve costs irrecoverable.

2. Abnormal profits do not persist in a contestable market. If the firms already operating in the industry earn supernormal profits, new firms get attracted. Entry being costless, the new entrants set the same price as that charged by the existing firms or even a price slightly lower than this. Entry of new firms continues as long as abnormal profits do. Excess supply caused by the new firms lowers the market price, evaporating the abnormal profits and making entry unattractive. If it persists, losses accrue to all the operating firms necessitating exit of the vulnerable ones. With exit of some firms, supply falls and market price rises. This continues until normal profits get restored and exit stops. In other words, the contestable market theory ensures zero economic profits and a price equal to MC to the operating firms (Figure 11.24).

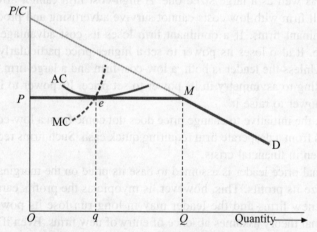

FIGURE 11.24 Equilibrium of a firm in a contestable market: Firms in a contestable market charge a price, $P = MC$, earning zero economic profit each. The Damocles' sword in the form of costless entry would continue to hang over their heads to prevent the firms from colluding or from gaining monopoly power. Each firm would behave as if it faced demand curve PM D. The portion MD of this demand curve would seldom be adopted by a firm due to the possibility of loss. In fact, each firm would treat the horizontal portion PM as its demand, as if it were in a competitive market. Each will sell quantity q at price P.

---

*Browning and Browning, *Microeconomic Theory and Applications*, Kalyani Publishers, New Delhi, 2nd Ed., p. 429.

3. Possibility of monopoly power of any firm in the industry is ruled out. The instant a firm assumes monopoly position, entry of new firms takes place and the monopoly power of the firm comes to an end.
4. Possibility of a collusion among the firms to charge a price higher than MC is also ruled out. The reason, once again, is the same—costless entry of new firms, which renders collusion completely ineffective. Figure 11.24 demonstrates equilibrium of a firm in the contestable market.

According to the contestable market theory, all the contestable firms would behave as if in a competitive market no matter what their number, large or small, is.

A very strong criticism of contestable market theory was put forth by William J. Shepherd* who disputed the assumption of the *costless entry and exit* of firms.

The most important thing about the contestable market theory is that the possibility of entry can have a powerful effect on the monopoly behaviour of a firm.

11.11 COMPETITION VERSUS COLLUSION (THE PRISONERS' DILEMMA)

In Section 11.3 (Figure 11.9), we examined how price competition with product differentiation leads to Nash equilibrium (also called non-cooperative equilibrium at times) in which each firm does its best to optimize its interest (profit in our case) given what its opponent has done. We have seen that resulting profit to each firm was ₹ 4000 from Nash equilibrium. It was higher than that accruing to a firm had it operated under perfectly competitive conditions but lower than that accruing to it (₹ 4625), had it chosen to collude. Collusion being illegal in many countries, firms prefer to cooperate with each other with a view to maximize their profits. In cooperative situations, a firm can set the profit-maximizing price (₹ 75) as if in collusion [Section 11.3, Figure 11.10] and expect the rivals to follow the suit. This does not require any formal or informal agreement. The only risk it involves is non-compliance by the rivals, who might, and more likely even would, set a price lower than the collusive level of ₹ 75 per unit once they come to know of it. The reason is obvious. A price below the collusive level, would help a firm to boost its market share as well as profit.

Referring back to collusive and Nash equilibria of Section 11.3, Figure 11.10, let us review the pay-offs under each. In Nash equilibrium, each firm charged a price of 50 and earned a profit 4000. In collusive equilibrium, each firm charged a price of 75 and earned a profit of 4625. Now assume one firm decides to charge collusive level of price (₹ 75 per unit) while the other continues to charge ₹ 50 as if in Nash equilibrium. The profit accruing to the former,

$$\pi_1 = P_1 Q_1 - C_1$$
$$= P_1 [150 - 2P_1 + P_2] - C_1$$
$$= 75 [150 - 2 \times 75 + 50] - 1000$$

---

*Shephard, William J., *Contestability versus Competition*, American Economic Review, 74, September 1984, pp. 572–87.

$$= 3750 - 1000$$
$$= 2750$$

and that accruing to the latter

$$\pi_2 = P_2 Q_2 - C_2$$
$$= P_2 [150 - 2P_2 + P_1] - 1000$$
$$= 50 \times [150 - 2 \times 50 + 75] - 1000$$
$$= 50 \times 125 - 1000$$
$$= 6250 - 1000$$
$$= 5250$$

Thus, if one sets a price at collusive level while the other at the Nash equilibrium level, profit earned by the low-price firm is 5250 and that by the high-price firm, 2750. Treating price setting as the strategies of the firms and the profits accruing to them in consequence as the resulting pay-offs, we can summarize the results in the form of a table (Table 11.1) called the pay-off matrix.

TABLE 11.1 Pay-off matrix for oligopolistic game: *Nash equilibrium* requires both firms to charge a price of 50. If Firm 1 chooses the strategy of charging a price of 50, its rival, Firm 2, will also choose the same and if Firm 2 chooses to charge the price of 50, Firm 1 too will choose to charge the same.

		Firm 2	
		Charge 50	Charge 75
Firm 1	Charge 50	[4000, 4000]	[5250, 2750]
	Charge 75	[2750, 5250]	[4625, 4625]

From the pay-off matrix, it is clear that both the firms will gain by cooperating with each other in charging the collusive price of ₹ 75 per unit. In this case, the two sell 150 (75 + 75) units collectively and earn a total profit of 9250 (4625 + 4625). If one firm decides to charge the collusive price (₹ 75 per unit) while the other continues with the Nash equilibrium price (₹ 50 per unit), the latter earns a higher profit (₹ 5250) than the former, who earns only ₹ 2750. In this case, the firm setting a higher price sells only 50 units while the other setting a lower price sells 125 units. The low-price firm gains in market share as well as in profits. The total sales amount to 175 (50 + 125) and total profits to ₹ 8,000 (5250 + 2750). In case both continue with the Nash equilibrium, total sales amount to ₹ 200 units (100 + 100) and profits to 8,000 (4000 + 4000).

Evidently, none of the two has an incentive to charge the collusive price. Each one fears that its deviation from Nash equilibrium would jeopardize its own interests of market share and profit and bestow the benefits on its opponent.

Charging collusive price requires a formal agreement to bind the firms to stick to the collusive price. As mentioned earlier on several occasions, an agreement such as this cannot be enforced through a court of law in the event of its breach. The best course left for the firms thus is to continue with Nash equilibrium.

11.12 PRISONERS' DILEMMA

Prisoners' dilemma provides a classic example of oligopolistic dilemma faced by a firm while introducing a price higher than that charged by its rival.

Let us go through the famous dilemma faced by two prisoners accused of collaborating in a crime. The two are kept in separate cells so that they may not communicate with each other. Each is asked to confess. If the two do, each gets five years' imprisonment but if neither does, each gets two years' imprisonment and if one of the two does while the other one does not, the one who does, gets one year's imprisonment while the other who does not gets ten years' imprisonment. The dilemma the prisoners face is to decide whether to confess or not.

Table 11.2 shows alternative options (strategies) before the two and the number of years of imprisonment (Pay-off) associated. The first entry in each bracket represents the number of years of imprisonment to Prisoner A and the second, the number of years of imprisonment to Prisoner B.

TABLE 11.2 Prisoner's dilemma—A situation parallel to oligopolistic game of Table 11.1: Each of the prisoners will confess according to the conditions of *Nash equilibrium*, unless there exists a way of knowing what the other has done. If the two are able to communicate, both will collude and decide against confessing.

		Prisoner B	
		Confess	Do not confess
Prisoner A	Confess	[5 years, 5 years]	[1 year, 10 years]
	Do not confess	[10 years, 1 year]	[2 years, 2 years]

The one who confesses first, gets the advantage of a mild punishment despite being equally involved in the crime. Each prisoner fears that the other would take the lead in confessing the crime and getting away with a milder punishment. In all likelihood, each would make a dash to confess so that he does not miss the advantage. In the next chapter (Table 12.11), a solution such as this is also reached through minimax and dominant strategies.

According to the condition of *Nash equilibrium*, one must do the best one can given what one's opponent has done. If Prisoner A chooses to confess, Prisoner B would do the best for him by choosing to confess and if Prisoner B is the first one to do that, Prisoner A would do the best for him by choosing to confess. That way top-left cell in Table 11.2 would mark *Nash equilibrium* but it does not because neither has a way of knowing what the other one has done or is doing.

It is not very difficult to see that the best strategy for each of the two prisoners would be not to confess, as each would get a milder punishment of 2 years' imprisonment. It is due to lack of communication between the two that they fail to make a resolve.

Oligopolistic firms find themselves in similar dilemma as that evidenced from Table 11.1. Each has to decide whether to compete and capture a larger share of the market at the rival's cost or to cooperate and coexist with the rival.

11.12.1 Implications of the Prisoners' Dilemma

There exists, however, a significant difference between the prisoners' dilemma and the dilemma faced by the oligopolistic firms. While prisoners get only one chance to choose a strategy, an oligopolist gets a number of chances, one after another, to learn from its past mistakes and to revise its earlier decision. It is, therefore, quite likely that the firms may cooperate among themselves for coexistence and mutual benefit.

On the contrary, even the other possibility is not ruled out. Many firms prefer to compete aggressively with a view to increase their market share rather than collude for moderate profits. In such cases, price wars result. This lends an element of uncertainty to the market structure. That should not, however, be allowed to imply that the oligopolistic firms do not have a desire for stability. Had it been so, price rigidity, considered to be a characteristic feature of oligopolistic market, would not have existed despite changes in costs and demands (Section 11.6) nor would cartels have had a chance to emerge nor would various types of price leaderships to evolve.

It is this desire for stability that the firms in oligopolistic market resort to *price signaling*, a practice of announcing a price hike (through media, for instance) much before executing it, so that the other firms may prepare to follow the suit. Such price signaling is a form of price leadership (Section 11.8).

KEY TERMS AND CONCEPTS

Assumptions of Bertrand's model   The model assumes that each firm expects its rival firm to keep its price constant (as against that of Cournot in which each firm expects its rival firm to keep its quantity constant), irrespective of its own decisions of pricing. Each firm faces the same demand curve and attempts maximization of its own profits.

Assumption of Cournot's duopoly model   Cournot established existence of a stable duopoly equilibrium with each firm selling $1/(n + 1)$th part of the market demand. In his original model, Cournot assumed two firms, each reaching its eventual equilibrium by supplying 1/3rd of the market demand under the following assumptions:

1. There are two firms each owning a mineral water spring.
2. The production costs are zero.
3. The demand curve for the product is linear.
4. Each firm acts on the assumption that its competitor will not change its output and decides its own so as to maximize profits.

Criticism of Cournot's model   The model suffers from the following drawbacks:

1. The model does not say how long will it take to reach the equilibrium.
2. The assumption of costless production is unrealistic.
3. Though the model can be generalized to any number of firms, it is a closed model as entry or exit of the firms are not taken into consideration. The number of firms remains unchanged throughout the adjustment period.
4. The firms never learn from their past experiences and continue to assume each that its rival would not change its quantity despite its experiences to the contrary.

Assumptions of the Chamberlin's model   Rejecting the assumption of independent action of duopoly firms, Chamberlin argues that they cannot be as naïve as Cournot and Bertrand assumed them to be. Chamberlin's argument sounds quite pragmatic as no business firm can afford to be so myopic as not to see beyond the tip of its nose. When rivals are caught in the act of changing their price-output policies in the past, how can one assume that they would not repeat the same in future? Business firms are in business with the sole objective of profit-maximization. If a collusion helps maximization of joint profits, why should they not go for it? It is business or profits that make them rivals rather than a personal vendetta. Chamberlin assumes that a monopoly solution or joint profit maximization can be achieved even without a collusion. His assumption is based on the fact that business firms are intelligent enough to recognize their interdependence, to learn from their past mistakes and to adopt a strategy in their best interest, which is vested in maximization of joint profits by charging a monopoly price.

Assumptions of the Stackelberg's model of sophisticated price leadership Stackelberg assumed that one duopolist is sufficiently sophisticated to recognize that its rival acts on Cournot's assumption. This recognition enables the sophisticated duopolist to determine the rival's reaction curve and to incorporate it in its own profit function before maximizing it like a monopoly.

Barometric price leadership In this type of a market structure, it is agreed formally or informally that all the firms in the industry will follow the price or price-changes of a firm better equipped with knowledge of prevailing market trends and hence is better poised to make forecasts than any other firm in the industry. In short, the firm chosen as the leader is considered as a barometer reflecting changes in economic environment. It is not necessary that the leader firm should belong to the industry itself. For instance, a steel industry may be chosen as a barometric price leader for the motor car industry.

Reasons for barometric price leadership Barometric price leadership may be favoured on several grounds:

1. Rivalry among large firms does not lend stability to earlier forms of price leadership. In a case like this, barometric price leadership is the only recourse and a fairly stable one too.
2. Followers can avoid calculations and recalculations under an environment of rapid changes. Barometric price leadership is highly convenient to them on this count.
3. Barometric price leader having rich experience of market research proves a reasonably good forecaster of changes in cost and demand conditions in the industry. Following it is the only reasonable recourse for the firms.

Cartels A cartel is a group of firms in direct secret agreement to reduce uncertainty arising from individualistic pursuits. The aim of the cartel is to maximize the joint industry profits or determine the market shares of the members in it.

Colluding The term refers to connivance of oligopolistic firms in setting price and quantity to maximize collective gains.

Collusive equilibrium When oligopolistic firms cooperate with each other to maximize their collective gains like a monopoly, the price-output decisions so reached are referred to as collusive equilibrium.

Collusive or cooperative game When colluding or cooperating firms in an oligopolistic market fall in line with one another in respect of their price-output decisions with a view to optimize their collective interests, the phenomenon is called a collusive or co-operative game.

Interdependence When firms in an oligopolistic market take their price-quantity decisions in recognition of the likely or anticipated decisions of the opponents, the phenomenon is referred to as interdependence. In an oligopoly market, price-quantity decisions of a firm depend on guessed or anticipated decisions of rivals giving rise to interdependence.

Isoprofit curves An isoprofit curve for firm A is the locus of points defined by different levels of output of A and its rival B, which yield to A the same level of profit.

Features of the isoprofit curves The isoprofit curves are indifference curves with following features:

1. Isoprofit curves of a duopolist are concave to the axis on which the firm's output is measured.
2. The farther the isoprofit curve from the axis, the lower the profit of the firm in question.

3. For Firm A whose output is measured on the *x*-axis, the highest points of the successively higher isoprofit curves lie to the left of the highest points of the successively lower isoprofit curves. For Firm B whose output is measured on *y*-axis, the rightmost points of the successively farther isoprofit curves from the axis, lie to the right of the rightmost points of the successively closer isoprofit curves to the axis.

Kinked demand model of Sweezy The model incorporates the firm's demand curve and its market share curve to derive a demand curve with a kink at the point of intersection of the two. The kinked demand is derived on the assumption that the firms follow their competitors in price cutting but not in price hiking. Through the model, Sweezy established that price is determined at the point of the kink and it remains sticky there even when production costs vary.

Critique of Sweezy's model Sweezy's model appears to be very realistic at the outset. A little in-depth analysis, however, reveals that the model suffers from the following drawbacks:

1. The model does not define the level at which price will be set in order to maximize profits.
2. The model also fails to explain the level at which the kink will occur.
3. The model also fails to explain the price output decisions of the firms.

The kinked demand curve model can explain stickiness of price in a situation of changing costs and rivalry. And that is almost all about the utility of the model.

Nash equilibrium Nash equilibrium refers to an equilibrium in which each firm does the best it can to optimize its interest given what its rival has done. No firm has any incentive to change its strategy once it attains Nash equilibrium. The concept of this equilibrium was first introduced by the mathematician John Nash in 1951. Ever since it is known as Nash equilibrium after the name of the mathematician.

Non-collusive or collisive oligopoly The term refers to the warring firms in an oligopoly market. The firms indulge in price wars which relate to price-cutting by other firms in retaliation to price-cutting initiated by one of them.

Price follower An oligopolistic firm that adopts the price set by the price leader.

Price leader An oligopolistic firm that takes the lead in setting product price.

Price leadership This is another form of collusive oliogopoly in which one firm sets the price while others follow it. The price setting firm is known as the price leader. The follower firms prefer to abide with the price set by the leader, even if it amounts to a departure from their profit-maximizing behaviour. The main reason for such compliance is to avoid uncertainty of their competitors' reactions. Price leadership is widespread in the business world. It may be practiced either through an explicit agreement among the firms or even informally. There are several forms of price leadership. The most common ones are the following:

1. Price leadership by a low-cost firm.
2. Price leadership by a dominant firm.
3. Barometric price leadership.

Price signalling In cooperative oligopoly, one of the firms sends signals for a price change well in advance. This is known as price signalling. The cooperating firms follow the signal to maximize collective gains.

Prisoner's dilemma Prisoners' dilemma provides a classic example of oligopolistic dilemma faced by a firm while introducing a price higher than that charged by its rival.

The famous dilemma is faced by two prisoners accused of collaborating in a crime. The two are kept in separate cells so that they may not communicate with each other. Each is asked to confess. If the two confess, each gets five years' imprisonment but if neither does, each gets two years' imprisonment and if one of the two confesses while the other one does not, the one who confesses gets one year' imprisonment while the other who does not gets ten years' imprisonment. The dilemma the prisoners face is to decide whether to confess or not?

Quantity follower An oligopolistic firm that sets its supply on the basis of supply of the quantity leader.

Quantity leader An oligopolistic firm that takes the lead in setting its supply.

Reaction curves A reaction curve of a firm represents its profit-maximizing output as a function of its opponent's output which is given.

Sequential game Action–reaction chain in an oligopoly is known as a sequential game. A firm's action of a change in its price or quantity is retaliated by its rivals through adjustments in price-quantities of theirs. The chain comprises sequential games.

Simultaneous game When firms in oligopoly take price-quantity decisions independently and simultaneously, the game is referred to as the simultaneous game.

Sophisticated price leadership When a duopolist firm incorporates the reaction curve of its rival into its profit function before maximizing it, the output and price so determined by the firm, impart the firm the status of a sophisticated price leadership.

EXERCISES

A. Very Short Answer Questions

Define the following (1 through 21):
1. Price leader
2. Price follower
3. Quantity leader
4. Quantity follower
5. Sequential game
6. Simultaneous game
7. Interdependence
8. Collusive game
9. Non-collusive game
10. Isoprofit curve
11. Nash equilibrium
12. Sophisticated price leader
13. Price rigidity
14. Cartel
15. Contestable market
16. Barometric price leader
17. Reaction curve
18. Kinked demand curve
19. Dominant price leader
20. Prisoners' dilemma
21. Costless entry and exit
22. Outline the main assumptions of Cournot's duopoly model.
23. Outline the main properties of the isoprofit curves.
24. Outline the main drawbacks of Sweezy's kinked demand curve model.
25. Outline the main types of cartel.

26. On what grounds are the price leadership models criticized?
27. Under what circumstances does a barometric price leadership evolve?
28. What can pose a potential threat to the dominant price leadership?
29. How does the prisoner dilemma differ from the oligopolistic dilemma?
30. In what respects does the Bertrand's model differ from that of Cournot?

B. Short Answer Questions

Distinguish between (31 through 39):

31. A price leader and a quantity leader
32. A sequential game and a simultaneous game
33. A collusive game and a non-collusive game
34. A Nash equilibrium and a collusive equilibrium
35. A price leader and a sophisticated price leader
36. Stackelberg's model and those of Cournot and Bertrand
37. Chamberlin's model and other models of duopoly
38. A low-cost price leader and a dominant price leader
39. Joint profit maximizing cartels and market sharing cartels
40. With the help of neat sketches, show how a kinked demand curve can be derived. What is the significance of the kink?
41. What would happen to the price rigidity if the marginal cost curve of a firm failed to pass through the gap of the discontinuity in its marginal revenue curve?
42. What would happen to the price rigidity if the demand curve undergoes a
    (i) pivotal shift,
    (ii) a parallel shift
    given that the marginal cost curve of the firm continues to pass through the discontinuity in its marginal revenue curves?
43. What can lead to the break-down of an otherwise undefeatable low-cost price leadership? Explain.
44. Demonstrate the prisoners' dilemma with the help of an hypothetical example.
45. With the help of kinked demand curves, explain the effect of an indirect tax on the equilibrium price and quantity of the oligopolistic firms.

C. Long Answer Questions

46. Show through simple arithmetics that an equilibrium position is eventually reached in Cournot's duopoly model and that each seller supplies 1/3 of the total market demand in equilibrium.
47. How can the Stackelberg's model of duopoly be treated as an extension of the Cournot's model?
48. Show that the conclusions of Cournot's model (Q. 46) can also be reached through the reaction curves of the duopolists.
49. Consider a Cournot's duopoly model with aggregate demand given by

$$P = a - bQ, \text{ where, } Q = q_1 + q_2$$

Production being costless, show that each duopolist's output in equilibrium is 1/3 of the competitive output. Illustrate with the help of a diagram.

[**Ans.** Market demand can be obtained by setting price P = MC in the equation of demand. MC being zero under costless production, quantity demanded (Figure 11.25) may be given by

$$Q = a/b$$

The total revenue to first firm
$$TR_1 = P \times q_1$$
Production cost being zero under costless production, the profit function for the first firm
$$\pi_1 = TR_1 - TC_1$$
$$= P \times q_1 - 0$$
$$= [a - b \cdot Q] \cdot q_1$$
$$= a \cdot q_1 - b \cdot (q_1 + q_2) \cdot q_1$$
$$= a \cdot q_1 - b \cdot q_1^2 - b q_2 q_1$$

Differentiating with respect to q_1 partially, we have
$$\partial \pi_1 / \partial q_1$$
$$= a - 2b \cdot q_1 - b q_2$$
$$= 0 \qquad \text{(for maximization of profit)}$$
$\Rightarrow \qquad q_1 = (a - b q_2)/2b \qquad (11.40)$

Likewise
$$q_2 = (a - b q_1)/2b \qquad (11.41)$$

Equations (11.40) and (11.41) give the reaction curves of the two firms.
Solving them simultaneously, we have
$$q_1 = q_2 = 1/3 \cdot (a/b) = 1/3 \text{ of the total market demand.}$$

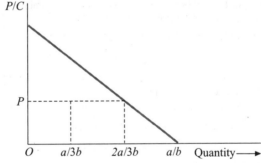

FIGURE 11.25 Cournot's stable equilibrium: Each firm supplies 1/3 of market demand at a price $P = a/3$.]

50. In a constant cost industry with zero costs, the demand function is given as
$$P = 16 - Q$$
Estimate price and output assuming the firm to be a (a) monopoly, (b) Cournot's duopoly firm and (c) competitive firm.

[**Ans.** Profit function for monopoly
$$\pi = TR - TC$$
$$= PQ - 0$$
$$= [16 - Q]Q$$
$$= 16Q - Q^2$$

Differentiating with respect to Q, we have

$$d\pi/dQ = 16 - 2Q$$
$$= 0 \quad \text{(for profit maximization)}$$

$\Rightarrow Q = 8$, corresponding price, $P = 16 - 8 = 8$, and monopoly profit $= 8 \times 8 = 64$.

In case the firm is a Cournot's duopoly firm, the profit function for the first firm is given as

$$\pi_1 = PQ_1 - 0$$
$$= 16Q_1 - (Q_1 + Q_2)Q_1$$
$$= 16Q_1 - Q_1^2 - Q_1Q_2$$
$$\partial\pi_1/\partial Q_1 = 16 - 2Q_1 - Q_2$$
$$= 0 \quad \text{(for maximization of profit)}$$

$\Rightarrow \qquad\qquad Q_1 = 8 - 1/2 Q_2$

Likewise $\qquad\qquad Q_2 = 8 - 1/2 Q_1$

Solution of the simultaneous equations leads to $Q_1 = Q_2 = \mathbf{16/3}$

Price
For a perfect market
$$P = 16 - \left(\frac{16}{3} + \frac{16}{3}\right) = \frac{16}{3} \qquad (\because \ Q = Q_1 + Q_2)$$

$$P = MC$$

But $\qquad\qquad MC = 0$

Substituting this in $\qquad Q = 16 - P$, we have

$$Q = \mathbf{16}.]$$

51. How is the Cournot–Nash equilibrium determined? Why is it stable? Why don't the duopolists set an output at joint profit-maximizing level by tacit collusion?

52. The market demand faced by an industry is given as

$$Q = 150 - P$$

The marginal cost = 0. Calculate the equilibrium values of price and output under monopoly, Cournot's duopoly and perfect competition.

[**Ans.** $P = 75$, $Q = 75$; $P = 50$, $Q = 100$ ($Q_1 = Q_2 = 150/3 = 50$); $P = 0$, $Q = 150$.]

53. The demand function faced by duopolists A and B is given as

$$P = 10 - 0.1Q$$

The marginal costs for the two are

$$MC_A = 2 \text{ and } MC_B = 3 \text{ respectively.}$$

Find the reaction functions of each and the quantities each would produce in equilibrium. How would your answer change if the two behaved strictly in accordance with Cournot's assumptions?

[**Ans.** A's reaction curve, $Q_A = 40 - 0.5Q_B$; B's reaction curve, $Q_B = 35 - 0.5Q_A$; $Q_A = 30$, $Q_B = 20$.

In case they behave strictly on Cournot's pattern, $MC_A = MC_B = 0$

A's reaction curve, $Q_A = 50 - 0.5Q_B$; B's reaction curve, $Q_B = 50 - 0.5Q_A$; $Q_A = 100/3$, $Q_B = 100/3$.]

54. Using the kinked demand curve model, explain how a reduction in the marginal cost might not lead to any change in price or output.

55. Explain how the kinked demand curve hypothesis supports the view that prices in an oligopolistic market tend to be stable.

56. Can a kinked demand curve arise in a duopoly market with homogeneous product? If so, what would be its shape? What would be the equilibrium price and quantity?

57. The largest firm in the industry produces 30% of the total output. The industry demand curve is unit elastic and the elasticity of supply of other firms is 3.0. What is the elasticity of demand for the largest firm? Will it be larger or smaller for other firms?

[**Ans.** Quantity largest firm produces, $q = 0.30$ of D, where, $D =$ industry output. Thus,

$$q/D = 0.30$$

Then, $\quad S/D = 1 - 0.30 = 0.70$, where, $S =$ supply of the other firms.

Now, $\quad q = D - S$ (see the dominant price leadership model)

Differentiating with respect to P, we have

$$dq/dP = dD/dP - dS/dP$$

$\Rightarrow \quad [(dq/dP)(P/q)](q/P) = [(dD/dP)(P/D)](D/P) - [(dS/dP)(P/S)](S/P)$

$\Rightarrow \quad e \cdot (q/P) = E_D \cdot (D/P) - E_S \cdot (S/P)$

$\Rightarrow \quad e = E_D \cdot (D/q) - E_S (S/q)$

$\quad\quad = -1/0.30 - 3 [(S/D)/(q/D)]$, given $E_D = -1$, $E_S = 3$

$\quad\quad = -10/3 - 3 [(0.70)/(0.30)]$

$\quad\quad = -10/3 - 3 (7/3)$

$\quad\quad = -3.33 - 7$

$\quad\quad = -\mathbf{10.33}$.]

58. Suppose the market demand curve for a commodity is

$$P = 70 - Q$$

Suppose further that there are two firms each with constant MC of 10. Assuming they behave as Cournot's duopolists, what will be the price and the industry output? Compare them with those of pure monopoly and perfect competition.

[**Ans.** Price $P = 30$, $Q = 40$; Price $P = 40$, $Q = 30$; Price $P = 10$, $Q = 60$.]

59. What are the essential features of the kinked demand curve model of oligopoly? Explain and contrast with the competitive model of the industry.

60. State and explain the concept of a Cournot's equilibrium. Bring out precisely its difference from a profit-maximizing behaviour.

61. (a) Distinguish between the nature of the kink in the demand curve when an oligopolist is selling in
   (i) Sellers' market (ii) Buyers' market.
   (b) Show that the demand curve of the dominant price leader has a kink at a price low enough for the smaller firms to continue.

[**Ans.** (a) (i) Nature of the kinked demand curve for the sellers' market (Figure 11.26):

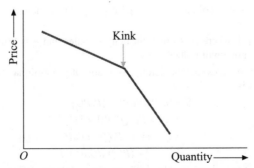

FIGURE 11.26 Competitors follow only a decrease in price (not an increase) in sellers' market.

(ii) Nature of the kinked demand curve for the buyers' market (Figure 11.27):

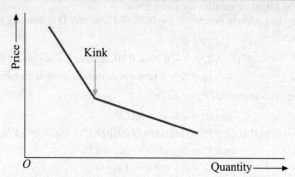

FIGURE 11.27 Competitors follow only an increase in price (not a decrease) in buyers' market.

(b) Refer to dominant price leadership model.]

62. Two firms producing outputs Q_1 and Q_2 at zero cost each, face demand curve

$$P = 1200 - Q, \text{ where, } Q = Q_1 + Q_2$$

The second firm is caught in the act of discharging pollutants. Environmental Regulations imposed on it in consequence, have increased its marginal cost to 600 while that of the first firm remains unchanged.

(a) Determine the monopoly price and output.
(b) Reaction curves of the two firms under new cost conditions.
(c) The respective prices, outputs and the profits of the two firms under the changed cost structure.

[**Ans.** (a) Monopoly price $P = 600$, output $= 600$
(b) Reaction curve of the first, $Q_1 = 600 - 1/2Q_2$
Reaction curve of the second, $Q_2 = 300 - 1/2Q_1$
(c) Price $P = 600$, $Q_1 = 600$, $Q_2 = 0$
Profit of the first $= 360,000$
Profit of the second $= 0$.]

63. Explain the process of simultaneous price setting in Bertrand's model and show that it does not lead to a maximization of industry profits.
64. Show that abnormal profits to a firm cannot arise in a contestable market.
65. Can a firm acquire monopoly power in a contestable market? Explain your answer.
66. Can firms in a contestable collude and charge a price higher than the marginal cost? Give reasons in support of your answer.
67. Show that $S = 1 - |e|$, where S is price elasticity of sales and e is price elasticity of demand. Hence, deduce that a fall in price will reduce sales.

[**Ans.** Price elasticity of sales may be defined as a ratio of proportionate change in sales to proportionate change in price, that is,

$$S = [d(PQ)/dP] \times [P/PQ]$$
$$= [Q + P(dQ/dP)] \times [1/Q]$$
$$= Q \times [1 + (P/Q)(dQ/dP)] \times [1/Q]$$
$$= [1 - \{-(P/Q)(dQ/dP)\}]$$
$$= [1 - |e|] \qquad (QED)$$

Thus, $S > 0$ whenever, $|e| < 1$

⇒ $[d(PQ)/dP] \times [P/PQ] > 0$, whenever, $|e| < 1$
⇒ $[d(PQ)/dP] > 0$, whenever, $|e| < 1$ [Since, $(P/PQ) > 0$ always.]
⇒ Sales function is an increasing function of P, whenever, $|e| < 1$
⇒ Sales increase with an increase in price and decrease with a decrease in it, whenever, $|e| < 1$

It can also be deduced, likewise, that sales increase with a decrease in price and decrease with an increase in it provided $|e| > 1$.

D. Essay Type Questions

68. Let the market for a product be represented by a duopoly in which the firms produce outputs q_1 and q_2. Let the demand function be given as

$$P = 100 - 2Q, \text{ where, } Q = q_1 + q_2$$

The marginal cost faced by each firm is 4. Determine:

(a) The reaction functions of the two duopolists.
(b) The price and the output of each duopolist assuming that they do not collude.
(c) Price and output of each assuming that they stick to Cournot's assumptions.
(d) Price and output of each assuming that they stick to Chamberlin's assumptions.
(e) Price and output of each assuming that one of them is a sophisticated price leader.
(f) Price and output of each when both demonstrate the sophisticated behaviour.

[**Ans.**(a) Reaction function for the first firm: $q_1 = 24 - 1/2 q_2$
Reaction function for the second firm: $q_2 = 24 - 1/2 q_1$

(b) Price-output decisions of the firms under non-collusive equilibrium:
Equilibrium takes place at the point of intersection of the reaction curves given in (a). Thus,

$$q_1 = 16, q_2 = 16, P = 36, Q = 16 + 16 = 32$$

(c) Cournot's assumptions include costless production, under which reaction curves of the firms would change to

$$q_1 = 25 - 1/2 q_2 \text{ and } q_2 = 25 - 1/2 q_1$$

A solution of simultaneous equations yields

$$q_1 = q_2 = 50/3, P = 100/3$$

(d) Under Chamberlin's assumptions, the equilibrium is monopoly equilibrium with

$$Q = 24(q_1 = q_2 = 1/2 \times 24 = 12) \text{ and Price } P = 52$$

(e) The leader's price $P = 28$, quantity = 24, profit = **576**
The follower's price $P = 28$, quantity = 12, profit = **288**

(f) When both demonstrate the sophisticated behaviour, each would calculate its price, output and profits first as a leader and then as a follower.
When first firm is a leader, $q_1 = $ **24**, $P = $ **28**, $\pi_1 = $ **576**
If the first firm is a follower, $q_1 = $ **12**, $P = $ **28**, $\pi_1 = $ **288**

Evidently the first firm would prefer to act as a leader. Exactly similar would be the case with the second firm. The resulting situation leads to a disequilibrium called the Stackelberg's disequilibrium as both cannot be leaders at the same time.]

69. (a) Obtain equilibrium outputs of Cournot's duopolists through the reaction curves approach when the firms face non-identical and non-zero costs.

(b) For outputs Q_1 and Q_2 of two firms, given the market demand function as

$$P = 200 - 0.5Q, \text{ where, } Q = Q_1 + Q_2$$

and cost functions as

$$C_1 = 10Q_1$$
$$C_2 = 1/2Q_2^2$$

Determine:
(i) the reaction functions of the two firms
(ii) their equilibrium outputs Q_1 and Q_2
(iii) market price P
(iv) respective profits earned by the two.

[**Ans.** (i) Reaction curve for the first firm: $Q_1 = 190 - 1/2Q_2$
Reaction curve for the second firm: $Q_2 = 100 - 1/4Q_1$
(ii) $Q_1 = 160$, $Q_2 = 60$
(iii) $P = 90$
(iv) $\pi_1 = 12,400$; $\pi_2 = 3,600$.]

70. For the data given in Q. 69 (b), work out Stackelberg's equilibrium under each of the following situations:
    (a) when the first duopolist is a sophisticated leader
    (b) when the second duopolist is a sophisticated leader
    (c) when both are sophisticated leaders.

    Also determine the profits earned by each of them in each case. Comment on the stability of equilibrium in each case.

    [**Ans.** (i) When the first firm is a sophisticated price leader,

    $Q_1 = 187$, $P = 80$, Profit $\pi_1 = 13,046.67$; $Q_2 = 53$, $P = 80$, $\pi_2 = 2844.46$

    (ii) When the second firm is a sophisticated price leader

    $Q_2 = 70$, $P = 87.50$, $\pi_2 = 3675$; $Q_1 = 155$, $P = 87.50$, $\pi_1 = 12,012.50$

    (iii) From the above, it is clear that each firm would like to be a sophisticated price leader due to higher profits associated. The same being impossible simultaneously, Stackelberg's disequilibrium would be the consequence.]

71. (a) Explain Bertrand's model of duopoly equilibrium under heterogeneous outputs.
    (b) Given the demand functions faced by the two duopolists as

    $$Q_1 = 300 - 2P_1 + P_2, \text{ and}$$
    $$Q_2 = 300 - 2P_2 + P_1$$

    The total fixed cost incurred by each is 10,000 while variable costs are zero in each case. Work out:
    (i) Nash equilibrium and the corresponding profits earned by the two
    (ii) Collusive equilibrium and the corresponding profits earned by each.

    [**Ans.** (i) Nash equilibrium: $P_1 = 100 = P_2$, $Q_1 = 200 = Q_2$, $\pi_1 = 10,000 = \pi_2$
    (ii) Collusive equilibrium: $P_1 = 150 = P_2$, $Q_1 = 150 = Q_2$, $\pi_1 = 12,500 = \pi_2$.]

72. Demand for a product is given by the demand function:

    $$Q = 4,000 - P$$

    where, Q is the quantity sold in the market at a price P. Suppose there are two producers with cost functions:

    $$C_1 = 10Q_1 + 1/2Q_1^2$$
    $$C_2 = 10Q_2 + 1/2Q_2^2$$

    sharing the market demand between them.

(a) Unable to collude, the two firms act as short-run perfect competitors. What are the equilibrium values of their outputs, the price P and respective profits?

(b) Suppose the two firms somehow recognize the oligopolistic nature of market and behave on Cournot's pattern. Determine the equilibrium values of their outputs, price P and their respective profits.

(c) Suppose the second duopolist conjectures the first to behave on Cournot's pattern, and decides to behave on Stackelberg's pattern himself, what are the equilibrium values of their outputs, price P and the respective profits?

(d) Now suppose that the two firms decide to collude, what are the equilibrium values of their outputs, the price P and respective profits?

[**Ans.** (a) Each firm would equate its MC to its price P. $Q_1 = 1330 = Q_2$, $P = 1340$

$$\pi_1 = 8,84,450 = \pi_2$$

(b) $Q_1 = 997.5 = Q_2$, $P = 2005$, $\pi_1 = 14,92,509.38 = \pi_2$

(c) Second firm is a sophisticated leader. $Q_2 = 1140$, $Q_1 = 950$, $P = 1910$

$$\pi_2 = 15,16,200; \quad \pi_1 = 13,53,750$$

(d) If the two collude, they will behave like a monopoly with TR = $4000Q - Q^2$ and $\Sigma MC = 1/2Q + 10$. Note that MC of each firm is $MC_i = 10 + Q_i$, $i = 1, 2$. A horizontal summation of the MC curve gives the monopoly MC as MC = $10 + 1/2Q$. The reader can verify by identification of MC as say 10, 20, 30 and calculating the corresponding values of Q_1, Q_2. At a particular value of MC, find $Q_1 + Q_2$, plot or fit the equation of the curve. The process is similar to that of determining the market demand through the horizontal summation of the individual demand curves. Now, MR = MC for monopoly equilibrium. $Q = 1596$, $P = 2404$, $Q_1 = Q_2 = 798$. Joint profit = $31,84,020$ (shared equally). Note that the total cost function can be arrived at either through horizontal summation of the individual cost function or through integration of the joint MC curve. Also note that the profits made by both are higher under collusion than under competition.]

73. Assume that the market demand is

$$P = 200 - 0.5Q, \text{ where, } Q = Q_1 + Q_2$$

and the two colluding firms have costs given by

$$C_1 = 10Q_1, \quad C_2 = 1/2 Q_2^2$$

How would the central agency allocate the outputs to the two so as to maximize the joint profits? What would the respective profits be?

[**Ans.**

$$\pi = \pi_1 + \pi_2$$
$$= TR - TC_1 - TC_2$$
$$= (200 - 0.5Q)Q - 10Q_1 - 1/2 Q_2^2$$
$$= 200Q - 0.5Q^2 - 10Q_1 - 1/2 Q_2^2$$

$d\pi/dQ_1 = 200(dQ/dQ_1) - 0.5(2Q)(dQ/dQ_1) - 10$
$= 200 - Q - 10$, since $dQ/dQ_1 = 1$ when $Q = Q_1 + Q_2$
$= 190 - Q$
$= 0$ \hfill (for maximization of profit)

$\Rightarrow \qquad Q = 190$

$d\pi/dQ_2 = 200(dQ/dQ_2) - 0.5(2Q)(dQ/dQ_2) - Q_2$
$= 200 - Q - Q_2$, since $dQ/dQ_2 = 1$ when $Q = Q_1 + Q_2$
$= 0$ \hfill (for maximization of profit)

		$Q_2 = 200 - Q$
$\Rightarrow$		$= 200 - 190$
		$= \mathbf{10}$
Thus		$Q_1 = Q - Q_2$
		$= 190 - 10$
		$= \mathbf{180}$
Price		$P = 200 - 0.5Q$
		$= 200 - 0.5 \times 190$
		$= \mathbf{105}$
Profit		$\pi_1 = 105 \times 180 - 10 \times 180$
		$= \mathbf{17,100}$
Profit		$\pi_2 = 105 \times 10 - 1/2 \times (10)^2$
		$= \mathbf{1,000}.]$

74. (a) Given the market demand

$$P = 205 - 5Q, \text{ where, } Q = Q_1 + Q_2$$

and, the cost functions of the two firms

$$C_1 = 5Q_1$$
$$C_2 = 10Q_2 \qquad (C_1 < C_2)$$

Determine the price that the low-cost firm will set and the quantities that the two firms will sell when they have resolved to share the market equally.

[**Ans.** $Q_1 = Q_2 = 10$, $P = 105$, $\pi_1 = 1000$, $\pi_2 = 950$.]

(b) In an oligopolistic industry with two firms, the low-cost firm estimates its demand and cost functions as

$$P_1 = 220 - 5.5\ Q_1 - Q_2, \text{ and}$$
$$C_1 = 5Q_1^2$$

The firms agree to share the market demand in the ratio 2:1 with the follower firm, reacting by adjusting its output in response to that of the first according to his reaction curve. Determine the equilibrium price outputs and profits of the two firms and comment on the results.

[**Ans.** $Q_1 = 10$, $Q_2 = 5$, $P = 160$, $\pi_1 = 1100$, Profit of the second firm is indeterminate due to lack of its cost data.]

75. The market demand and the cost functions of the duopolists are

$$P = 200 - 0.5Q \qquad \text{where, } Q = Q_1 + Q_2$$
$$C_1 = 10Q_1$$

and $\qquad C_2 = 1/2 Q_2^2$

(Q_1 and Q_2 are the quantities supplied by the two duopolists)

Determine the equilibrium quantities and the market price under:

(a) Cournot's assumptions of naïve behaviour of the duopolists
(b) Quantity leadership of the first duopolist
(c) Quantity leadership of the second duopolist
(d) Stackelberg's sophisticated pattern of behaviour adopted by both

[**Ans.** (a) $Q_1 = 160$, $Q_2 = 60$, $P = 90$, $\pi_1 = 12{,}800$, $\pi_2 = 3600$
(b) $Q_1 = 560/3$, $Q_2 = 160/3$, $P = 80$, $\pi_1 = 13{,}066.67$, $\pi_2 = 2844.44$
(c) $Q_1 = 155$, $Q_2 = 70$, $P = 87.50$, $\pi_1 = 12{,}012.50$, $\pi_2 = 3675$
(d) When first firm is a leader, $Q_1 = 560/3$, $P = 80$, $\pi_1 = 13{,}066.67$
When first firm is a follower, $Q_1 = 155$, $P = 87.50$, $\pi_1 = 12012.50$
When second firm is a leader, $Q_2 = 70$, $P = 87.50$, $\pi_2 = 3675$
When second firm is a follower, $Q_2 = 160/3$, $P = 80$, $\pi_2 = 2844.44$
Clearly each firm earns a higher profit as a leader than as a follower.
Each would like to lead rather than to follow. It is a state of disequilibrium.]

76. Given the market demand function

$$Q^D = 1000 - 6P$$

the other firms' supply function as

$$Q^S = 4P - 40$$

and the dominant firms' cost function as

$$C = 60q$$

Determine the equilibrium price and quantity of the dominant firm and the quantity supplied by the other firms. Estimate the profits of the dominant firm. Now suppose the dominant firm intends to drive the other firms out of business. What price would you advise the dominant firm to set for the purpose? What profits would the dominant firm earns in this case?

[**Ans.** Equilibrium price and quantity of the dominant firm: $P = 82$, $q = 220$
Quantity supplied by the other firms = 288
Profit earned by the dominant firm = 4840
To drive the other firms out of business, price should be such that equates Q^S to 0.
Such a price is given by $4P - 40 = 0$, or $P = 10$. At this price, the dominant firm would be called for to supply 940 units incurring a loss of 47,000. In this case the dominant firm should not be advised to attempt to drive other firms out of business.]

77. Given the demand functions faced by the two duopolists as

$$Q_1 = 300 - 2P_1 + P_2, \text{ and}$$
$$Q_2 = 300 - 2P_2 + P_1$$

The total fixed cost incurred by each is 10,000 while variable costs are zero in each case. Work out:

(a) Nash equilibrium and the corresponding profits earned by the two.
(b) Collusive equilibrium and the corresponding profits earned by each.
(c) The profits earned by each if the first firm sets the price at the collusive level while the second does not.
(d) The profits earned by each if the second firm sets the price at the collusive level while the first does not.
(e) The pay-off matrix and
    (i) the best strategy for both
    (ii) the likely strategy the two would follow.

[**Ans.** (a) $P_1 = P_2 = 100$, $Q_1 = Q_2 = 200$, $\pi_1 = 10{,}000 = \pi_2$
(b) $P_1 = P_2 = 150$, $Q_1 = Q_2 = 150$, $\pi_1 = 12{,}500 = \pi_2$
(c) When the first firm sets the collusive price while the second does not, the profit of the first firm is 5,000 and that of the second is 15,000

(d) When the second firm sets the collusive price while the first does not, the profit of the first firm is 15,000 and that of the second is 5,000

(e) The pay-off matrix: (i) Both should raise price. (ii) none would raise price.

		Firm 2	
		Sets $P = 100$	Sets $P = 150$
Firm 1	Sets $P = 100$	{10,000; 10,000}	{15,000; 5,000}
	Sets $P = 150$	{5,000; 15,000}	{12,500; 12,500}

The first entry in each cell represents the pay-off of Firm 1 while the second, that of Firm 2. Top-left cell would give Nash equilibrium if Firm 2 chooses Column 1 whenever Firm 1 chooses Row 1 and Firm 1 chooses Row 1 whenever Firm 2 chooses Column 1. Here, suppose Firm 1 sets price of 100. In consequence, Firm 2 will also settle for the same price, instead of the other one of 150. Thus, Firm 2 does for a higher pay-off of 10,000 that accrues to it at a price of 100 than that of 5,000 that would accrue to it at a price of 150. Thus, Firm 2 chooses Column 1 whenever Firm 1 chooses Row 1. Next, investigate what Firm 1 would do when Firm 2 chooses Column 1. If the answer is Row 1, the top-left cell [Row 1; Column 1], gives the Nash Equilibrium, otherwise not. Test each cell in this manner for Nash equilibrium. A pay-off matrix may contain more than one Nash equilibrium. In this case, there exist only one, that is, in the top-left cell.]

78. Write a comprehensive note on oligopolistic games, bringing out clearly the similarities and dissimilarities of the dilemma faced by the oligopolists with that faced by the prisoners in the famous prisoners' dilemma.

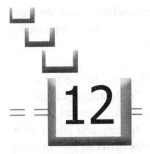

Game Theory

CHAPTER OUTLINE

Introduction
- Pay-off Matrix, Strategies and Equilibria Revisited
- Non-zero-sum Games under Pure Strategies [Nash Equilibrium in Pure Strategies]
- Non-zero-sum Games under Mixed Strategies [Nash Equilibrium in Mixed Strategies]
- Non-zero-sum Games under Maximin/Minimax Criteria
- Non-zero-sum Games [Assorted Applications]
- Non-zero-sum Mixed Strategy Games of Incomplete/Imperfect Information
- Zero-sum Games
- Key Terms and Concepts
- Exercises

INTRODUCTION

In Section 11.11, we observed how oligopolistic firms react to their rivals' actions and with what consequences. In fact, the activity can be interpreted as a high-stake game in which players' objective is to boost their short-run and/or long-run gains by outguessing their rivals. The gains referred to here are total gains comprising market shares and economic profits. Many important insights into oligopolistic markets have been achieved through **game theory**, initiated in 1950s by mathematician John Von Neumann and economist Oskar Morgenstern.

The technique was designed to evaluate situations where individuals and organizations had conflicting objectives including strategies of dating and mating, parlour games, legal and political negotiations and negotiations of wages between unions and firms.

In this chapter, we will discuss some fundamental concepts of nomenclature and structure of the game theory. Although its political and courtship applications are far more interesting, discussions in this chapter will confine to its use in the economic setting.

Let us first introduce the terminology of the game theory.

A **strategy** refers to a course of action devised to achieve desired goals. In the theory of games, players devise several alternative strategies to serve their ends. For instance, candidates use film stars during their election campaigns to draw people as one strategy while local celebrities for the purpose as another. When a player adopts a single strategy and sticks to it, he/she is said to be resorting to a **pure strategy** but when he/she shuffles between two or more strategies with a view to keep his/her opponents guessing, he/she is said to be resorting to a **mixed strategy**. For instance, use of either film stars or of local celebrities in all the campaigns provides an example of the **pure strategy** while that of film stars in some constituencies and local celebrities in others at random, that of a **mixed strategy**. The situation of a mixed strategy is probabilistic in nature (that is, each of the alternative strategies has a probability of being adopted or not adopted) while that of a pure strategy is deterministic, as the strategy once adopted is continued for ever.

Outcomes of the alternative strategies of a player against those of his/her rival in terms of returns are known as **pay-offs**. For example, in Table 12.1, Contestant A's pay-offs from 'use of filmstars' are (0) and (+3) and from 'use local celebrities', (–2) and (–1) respectively, against Contestant B's strategies of 'use of filmstars' and 'use of local celebrities'.

TABLE 12.1 Pay-off matrix—Zero-sum game: Figures in the cells show pay-offs (gain of votes) to Politician A from the corresponding strategies of his own against those of his rival. Pay-offs with negative signs show A's loss and those without a sign or with a positive sign show A's gain. For instance, figure 0 in the top-left cell indicates that A's pay-off (gain of votes) is zero when both contestants adopt the strategy 'use of film stars' in their campaigns. Figure 3 in the top-right cell indicates that A's pay-off (gain of votes) is positive (he gains 3 lac votes) from his strategy of 'use of film stars' in his campaigns as against B's strategy of 'use of local celebrities'. Figure (– 2) in the bottom–left cell and figure –1 in the bottom-right cell indicate that A's pay-off from his strategy of 'use of local celebrities' is negative, i.e., he loses 2 lac and 1 lac votes to politician B against the latter's strategies of 'use of film stars' and 'use of local celebrities', respectively. Gain of one is the loss of the other. For example gain of 3 lac votes by A is the loss of 3 lac votes to B so that (+3) + (–3) = 0. This is true for each entry in the cells. That is why single figures are used in the cells in a zero-sum game. The game has a dominant strategy equilibriumin in the top-left cell, the confluence of the dominant strategies of the two contestants.

		Candidate B	
		Use of film stars	Use of local celebrities
Candidate A	Use of film stars	0	+3
	Use of local celebrities	– 2	–1

From the viewpoint of total gain or loss, games are classified as zero-sum and non-zero-sum. A **zero-sum game** refers to a game in which gain of one is loss of the other so that the sum of the gain (treated as positive) and the loss (treated as negative) is zero. For example, votes gained by a contestant due to his/her use of film stars in his/her election campaign are votes lost by his/her opponent (s), as the total votes in the constituency or total votes polled in it are fixed. If the contestant in question polls 3 lac more votes due to this strategy, his/her opponent(s) loses (lose) an equal number so that the sum of votes gained by the contestant and those lost by his/her opponent(s) is zero. Table 12.1 shows the tabular presentation of the pay-offs. As pointed out, there are two contestants in the game–Contestant A and Contestant B. Each one of them has two strategies—'use of film stars' or 'uses of local celebrities'. If both uses film stars in their campaigns, neither gains or loses any votes. If Contestant A uses film stars while Contestant B uses local celebrities, the former gains 3 lac votes while the latter loses the same number. If Contestant A uses local celebrities while contestant B uses film stars, the former loses 2 lac votes while the latter gains the same number. If both uses local celebrities, Contestant A loses 1 lac votes while Contestant B gains them. The sum of votes gained by one and those lost by the other in consequence to their respective strategies of campaigning is equal to zero in each case.

A **non-zero-sum-game**, as the name suggests, refers to a game in which the sum of one player's gain and another's loss is non-zero, that is, gain of one need not imply loss of the other. An oligopolistic game such as one discussed in Table 12.2 is a non-zero-sum game. In the table, there are two players—Firm 1 and Firm 2. Each one has two strategies—'no price change' and 'price increase'. If both attempt the strategy of price increase simultaneously, both realize same increase in pay-offs (from 10 to 60) each. If one sticks to 'no price change' while the other switches to 'price increase', the one who sticks to 'no price change' realizes an increase of 90 (from 10 to 100) in pay-off while the other who turns to 'price increase', suffers a loss of 6 (from 10 to 4) in it. The sum of the changes in the pay-offs of the two firms is non-zero. The reason for this is that the total profit to be earned by the two is not fixed like the total votes in the constituency in the example of a zero-sum-game.

TABLE 12.2 **Pay-off matrix—Non-zero sum game:** The table shows the strategies of the two firms of retaining the current price or increasing it along with the corresponding profits accruing to them in consequence. First entry in each cell is the profit accruing to the first firm and the second, that accruing to the second firm. If neither firm increases price, profits accruing to them are ₹ 10 million each and if both firms resort to 'price increase', profits accruing to them are ₹ 60 million each. If the first firm increases price while the second firm does not, profit earned by the first firm is ₹ 4 million while that earned by the second firm is ₹ 100 million and if the first firm sticks to 'no price change', while the second firm goes for 'price increase', profit earned by the first firm is ₹ 100 million while that earned by the second firm is ₹ 4 million only. From the definition, it can be verified that 'no price change' is the dominant strategy for each firm and the *top-left cell* at the confluence of the dominant strategies of the two provides a *dominant strategy equilibrium* of the game. The top-left cell also provides a Nash equilibrium as well. If Firm 1 adopts 'no price change', Firm 2 does its best by choosing the same and if Firm 2 adopts 'no price change', Firm 1 does its best by choosing the same. Apart from these two in the top-left cell, the game also has a *collusive* or *cooperative equilibrium* in the *bottom-right cell*. If the two firms collude for a simultaneous increase in price, each can boost its profit to ₹ 60.00 million (bottom-right cell).

		Firm 2	
		No price change	Price increase
Firm 1	No price change	{10, 10}	{100, 4}
	Price increase	{4, 100}	{60, 60}

When there are only two competitors or players in a game, it is called a **two-person or two-player game.** On the contrary, if the game involves more than two, say n, the game is termed as an *n-person or n-player game.*

A **cooperative game** is one in which the players are assumed to be rational enough to realize that their mutual interest rests in cooperation with each other on all courses of action that benefit at least one of them without affecting any of the rest adversely. On the contrary, a **non-cooperative game** is one in which the players do not cooperate with each other either due to lack of communication or due to placing self-interest above the interest of the others or even due to *beggar-my-neighbour policy* adopted by them. The best example of the cooperative game is the **collusive equilibrium** (Section 11.3, Figure 11.10) and that of the non-cooperative game is the simultaneous confession by the prisoners in **prisoners' dilemma** (Section 11.12, Table 11.2).

A strategy is a **dominant strategy** for a player provided its outcome is most favourable among all the alternative strategies, no matter what his/her opponent (s) does (do). In the same way, a strategy is a **dominated strategy** for its player if its outcome is most unfavourable among all the alternative strategies, no matter what his/her opponent (s) does (do). In Table 12.2, the dominant strategy for Firm 1 is 'no price change' because the firm earns higher profits under it [10 when Firm 2 adopts 'no price increase' and 100 when Firm 2 adopts 'price increase'] than under the strategy of 'price increase' [4 when Firm 2 adopts 'no price change' and 60 when Firm 2 adopts 'price increase']. Likewise, the 'dominant strategy' for Firm 2 is also 'no price change', the reader can verify.

Also, it can be verified that 'price increase' is the dominated strategy for both.

When each player has a dominant strategy, the confluence of the dominant strategies is called **dominant strategy equilibrium**. In Table 12.2, dominant strategy for each firm is 'no price change'. The confluence of the dominant strategies of the two, the top-left cell implying a pay-off of 10 each, provides an example of the dominant strategy equilibrium. Each player adopts his/her dominant strategy regardless of what his opponent does.

As against the dominant strategy equilibrium, the **Nash equilibrium**, named after the American mathematician John Nash, refers to the equilibrium in which **each player does the best he can given what his opponent has done or is doing**. In Table 12.2, the top-left cell provides a Nash equilibrium. If Firm 1 chooses 'no price change', Firm 2 does the best it can by choosing 'no price change' because its pay-off (10) from 'no price change' is higher than its pay-off (4) from 'price increase' and if Firm 2 chooses 'no price change', Firm 1 does the best it can by choosing 'no price change' because its pay-off (10) from 'no price change' is higher than its pay-off (4) from 'price increase'. Again, the top-left cell in the pay-off matrix provides a Nash equilibrium as well. **Note that the dominant strategy equilibrium is essentially a Nash equilibrium but its converse need not be true**. The game in Table 12.3 possesses two Nash equilibria—one in top-left cell and the other in bottom-right cell, but no dominant strategy equilibrium at all.

TABLE 12.3 Absence of a dominant strategy equilibrium but presence of two Nash equilibria in top-left and bottom-right cells.

		Firm 2	
		No price change	Price increase
Firm 1	No price change	{10, 10}	{12, 4}
	Price increase	{4, 12}	{20, 20}

The player who takes the lead in choosing the strategy is known as an **active player** while the other who makes his choice after knowing the rival's choice is known as a **passive player**. We will discuss more about it in Section 12.2.

12.1 PAY-OFF MATRIX, STRATEGIES AND EQUILIBRIA REVISITED

At the heart of the game theory is the concept of **pay-off matrix**. As explained earlier, a strategy is a course of action and the pay-off is its outcome or result. In Table 12.2, as seen earlier, strategies available to the firms are 'no price change' and 'price increase'. The pay-offs accruing to the players from their respective strategies against those of their rivals when arranged systematically in the form of a table constitute a **pay-off matrix**, such as ones shown in Tables 12.1, 12.2 or 12.3.

In Table 12.2, there are four possible combinations of the strategies—*first*, both the firms go for price-change, *second*, neither goes for price change, *third*, Firm 1 increases its price while Firm 2 does not, and *fourth*, Firm 2 increases its price while Firm 1 does not. The outcomes of each of the four combinations in terms of monetary gains constitute a pay-off matrix such as that in Table 12.2. The first number in each cell is the pay-off accruing to the first firm and the second number, that accruing to the second firm in consequence to their respective strategies. From Table 12.2, it is clear that the first firm is better off if it sticks to the strategy of 'no price change' no matter what the second firm does as the profits of the first firm are higher from 'no price change' (10 > 4 and 100 > 60) than from 'price increase', irrespective of whether its opponent sticks to 'no price change' or decides to increase it. Thus, 'no price change' is the *dominant strategy* for Firm 1. It can be shown on similar lines that it is so even for second firm, that is, 'no price change' irrespective of whether the first firm sticks to 'no price change' or decides in favour of 'price increase'. 'No price change' is thus, a dominant strategy for each. The cell at the confluence of the dominant strategies of the two, the top-left cell, gives the dominant strategy equilibrium. Each will continue with 'no price change' and earn a profit of ₹ 10 million. Such equilibria, however, are not so common. They exist only when dominant strategies do.

If the two firms reach an understanding and decide to go for 'price increase' simultaneously, both can boost their profits to ₹ 60 million each (bottom-right cell). Equilibrium such as this, known as the **collusive** or **cooperative equilibrium**, is possible only when better sense prevails upon the firms inducing them to cooperate with each other in pursuing the mutual interest. As is clear from the pay-off matrix, the tendency of each firm would be to break away from the other and to switch over to a lower price secretly to boost its own profit assuming that its rival would continue with 'price increase'. The betraying firm may dash to a profit of ₹ 100 million if it returns back to 'no price change' position but the advantage ceases to exist as soon as its betrayal is exposed to the other firm.

The pay-off matrix for a zero-sum game looks a little different. In the example of two politicians, A and B, contesting an election from the same constituency. Each resorts to two popular strategies of election campaign—the use of film stars and/or the use of local celebrities—to attract voters to attend their election speeches. The outcomes of the strategies in terms of votes gained by each are shown in Table 12.1, showing gains of votes by A. A positive entry indicates gain, a negative entry indicates loss and a zero entry indicates neither. Use of film stars is the dominant strategy for both as each stands to gain maximum whatever strategy the other chooses. Since the dominant strategies for both are known, their confluence gives a **dominant strategy equilibrium**. Needless to say, the equilibrium is a stable one. Use of local celebrities is a dominated strategy for each because it offers them a lower pay-off than the other strategy.

Games can, thus, be classified under the heads of 'non-zero-sum games' and 'zero-sum games'. Each of them can further be subdivided into pure strategy and mixed strategy games.

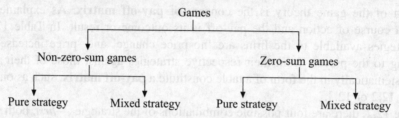

12.2 NON-ZERO-SUM GAMES UNDER PURE STRATEGIES [NASH EQUILIBRIUM IN PURE STRATEGIES]

Pay-off matrix in Table 12.2 provides an example of a non-zero-sum game under pure strategies. It leads to a dominant strategy equilibrium. As stated earlier, a dominant strategy equilibrium sounds good when it happens but such equilibria are rare in the real world.

Now, consider the pay-off matrix in Table 12.3. It is a non-zero-sum game with no dominant strategy for any firm. A dominant strategy equilibrium is, therefore, ruled out. The game, however, possesses two Nash equilibria. Known after the name of the American mathematician, John Nash, who developed it in 1951, a Nash equilibrium deserves a more extensive exposition than a mere mention as in the introductory part of the chapter. It may be defined *as a pair of expectations about each player's choice such that, when the other player's choice is revealed, neither player wants to change his behaviour*. In alternative terminology, Nash equilibrium refers to *a set of strategies such that none of the players in the game can improve his pay-off, given the strategy of his opponent*. According to the alternative definition, if Firm 1 chooses 'no price change', the best that Firm 2 can do is to choose 'no price change' because its pay-offs under 'no price change' is higher than that under 'price increase' [10 > 4]. Now if Firm 2 chooses 'no price change', the best that Firm 1 can do is to choose 'no price change' because its pay-off under 'no price change' is higher than that under 'price increase'[10 > 4]. The top-left cell of the pay-off matrix in Table 12.3 thus, provides a Nash equilibrium. It can be seen that the game in Table 12.3 possesses yet another Nash equilibrium in bottom-right cell despite the fact that no dominant strategies exist.

According to the earlier definition, suppose Firm 1 expects Firm 2 to choose 'no price change' and chooses 'no price change' itself. Later, when choice of Firm 2 is revealed as 'no price change', Firm 1 would not be able to improve its pay-off by switching over to 'price increase' and hence, would continue with its strategy of 'no price change'. Likewise, suppose Firm 2 expects Firm 1 to choose 'no price change' and decides in favour of 'no price change' itself. Later, when choice of Firm 1 is revealed as 'no price change', Firm 2 would not be able to improve its pay-off by switching over to 'price increase' and hence, would continue with its strategy of 'no price change'. In consequence, the top-left cell in the pay-off matrix provides a Nash equilibrium. In a nutshell, given the choice of the strategy of one player, the second player chooses the strategy that maximizes his (second player's) pay-off.

12.2.1 Nash Equilibrium has Two Limitations

1. There can be more than one Nash equilibria in a game

As evidenced from pay-off matrix in Table 12.3, the game possesses two Nash equilibria—one in top-left cell as discussed earlier and the other in bottom-right cell as detailed here. If Firm 1 adopts 'price increase', Firm 2 would do its best by adopting 'price increase' as its pay-off from the same is higher than its pay-off from 'no price change' (20 > 12) and if Firm 2 adopts 'price increase', Firm 1 would do its best by adopting 'price increase' as its pay-off from the same is higher than its pay-off from 'no price change' (20 > 12). Existence of multiple Nash equilibria does not pose as much of a serious problem as does the non-existence of any.

2. There can be no Nash equilibrium in a game

Consider the pay-off matrix in Table 12.4. If Firm 1 adopts 'no price change', Firm 2 will do its best by adopting the same as its pay-off from it is higher than that from 'price increase' (10 > 8) but if Firm 2 adopts 'no price change', Firm 1 *will not* adopt the same as its pay-off from it is lower than that from 'price increase' (10 < 12). Top-left cell, therefore, *does not* provide a Nash equilibrium. The same can be said about each of the other three cells in the pay-off matrix. For instance, if Firm 1 adopts 'price increase', Firm 2 will do its best by adopting the same as its pay-off from it is higher than that from 'no price change' (12 > 10) but if Firm 2 adopts 'price increase', Firm 1 *will not* adopt the same as its pay-off from it will be lower than that from 'no price change' (8 < 12). No Nash equilibrium is, therefore, possible for the game in Table 12.4 in pure strategies.

TABLE 12.4 Existence of no Nash equilibrium in pure strategies

		Firm 2	
		No price change	Price increase
Firm 1	No price change	{10, 10}	{12, 8}
	Price increase	{12, 10}	{8, 12}

Mixed strategies, however, provide at least one Nash equilibrium for the game in Table 12.4. The process is demonstrated in Section 12.3.

12.3 NON-ZERO-SUM GAMES UNDER MIXED STRATEGIES [NASH EQUILIBRIUM IN MIXED STRATEGIES]

12.3.1 The Need for Mixed Strategies

Strategies that we have discussed so far are *pure strategies*, in which, a player chooses a strategy and sticks to it. As stated earlier, pure strategies fail to yield a position of equilibrium at times. Oligopolistic firms may compete with each other for maximization of their market shares and profits but by no means would they like to sustain an aura of uncertainty over their business activities. In fact they strive for a balance or equilibrium, sooner or later, so that they may operate with some certainty of the desired and deserved goals. All the competition that exists among them is only to ensure them their due, which is, to make the most of their potential and capabilities. The firms in the market thus strive for the goals of stability and growth they believe they deserve well at least in the long-run. They may, therefore, resort to shuffling of their strategies if their desire for a stable equilibrium calls for, i.e. they may resort to mixed strategies to attain a stable equilibrium.

12.3.2 Mixed Strategies and Nash Equilibrium

A mixed strategy is one in which a player randomizes his choice of a strategy by assigning probabilities to each choice and then choosing a strategy on the basis of these probabilities, which can be assigned to each strategy on the basis of the frequency of its use by the players in the past. For instance, suppose Firm 1 has been observed resorting to 'no price change' strategy on 60% of the times, the probability of adopting this strategy by the firm is 0.60 and that of the alternative strategy of 'price increase' would then be 0.40. Similarly, for Firm 2, probabilities may be assigned to each of its alternative strategies.

We have seen that the pay-off matrix in Table 12.4 possesses neither a dominant strategy equilibrium nor a Nash equilibrium under pure strategies. We intend to show here that it possesses at least one Nash equilibrium under mixed strategies. For that, let us first see how probabilities for different cells may be calculated.

Let the two firms resort to the strategy of 'no price change' with probabilities p and q, respectively. The probability of the strategy of 'price increase' for Firm 1 would then be $(1 - p)$ and that for Firm 2, $(1 - q)$. Accordingly, probabilities can be assigned to each cell in the pay-off matrix assuming that firms (players) choose strategies independently and simultaneously (Table 12.5).

TABLE 12.5 Probability of both the firms adopting the strategy of 'no price change' is pq, that of both adopting the strategy of 'price increase' is $(1 - p)(1 - q)$, that of the first firm adopting 'no price change' and the second firm adopting 'price increase' is $p(1 - q)$ and finally, that for the first firm adopting 'price increase' and the second firm adopting 'no price change' is $(1 - p)q$.

		Firm 2	
		No price change	Price increase
Firm 1	No price change	pq	$p(1-q)$
	Price increase	$(1-p)q$	$(1-p)(1-q)$

The expected pay-offs of the firms from each strategy-mix can also be computed for Table 12.4 and shown as in Table 12.6.

TABLE 12.6 Expected pay-offs of the two firms under different strategy-mixes for the game in Table 12.4

		Firm 2	
		No price change	Price increase
Firm 1	No price change	$[10pq, 10pq]$	$12p\{(1-q), 8p(1-q)\}$
	Price increase	$\{12(1-p)q, 10(1-p)q\}$	$\{8(1-p)(1-q), 12(1-p)(1-q)\}$

Expected pay-offs of the two firms for the game in Table 12.4 are:

$$E_1 = 10pq + 12(1-p)q + 12p(1-q) + 8(1-p)(1-q) \text{ (for Firm 1)} \tag{12.1}$$

and, $E_2 = 10pq + 10(1-p)q + 8p(1-q) + 12(1-p)(1-q)$ (for Firm 2) (12.2)

In matrix notation, Eqs. (12.1) and (12.2) can be expressed as:

$$E_1 = f(p, q) = (p \ 1-p) \cdot (A_1) \cdot \begin{bmatrix} q \\ 1-q \end{bmatrix}$$

(Where, $A_1 \equiv$ pay-off matrix of Firm 1 under different strategies of its own against those of its opponent)

$$= (p \ 1-p) \begin{bmatrix} 10 & 12 \\ 12 & 8 \end{bmatrix} \begin{bmatrix} q \\ 1-q \end{bmatrix} \tag{12.3}$$

and,

$$E_2 = g(p, q) = (p \ 1-p) \cdot (A_2) \cdot \begin{bmatrix} q \\ 1-q \end{bmatrix}$$

(Where, $A_2 \equiv$ pay-off matrix of Firm 2 under different strategies of its own against those of its opponent)

$$= (p \ 1-p) \begin{bmatrix} 10 & 8 \\ 10 & 12 \end{bmatrix} \begin{bmatrix} q \\ 1-q \end{bmatrix} \tag{12.4}$$

Table 12.7 shows expected pay-offs of the two firms under selected values of p and q.

TABLE 12.7 Expected pay-offs of Firms 1 and 2 resorting to the strategies of 'no price change' with probabilities p and q and 'price increase' with probabilities $(1-p)$ and $(1-q)$, respectively as given by Eqs. (12.1) and (12.2) for different values of p and q are shown in the table. The highest and the lowest pay-offs that Firm 1 can avail of are 11 and 8, respectively while those Firm 2 can avail of are 12.00 and 9.33. Each firm strives for maximization of its expected pay-off. In the table, *no unique* values of p and q exist that may ensure both the firms of their respective maximum pay-offs, 11 and 12, simultaneously. Firm 2's maximum pay-off of 12 corresponds to $p = 0$ and $q = 0$ at which Firm 1's expected pay-off is 8, not 11. Likewise, probability set that ensures an expected pay-off of 11 to Firm 1 fails to ensure that of 12.00 to Firm 2.

p	0	1/4	1/3	1/2	**1/2**	3/4	1	**2/3**	1/2	2/3	1/3	2/3	1	**2/3**
q	0	1/4	1/3	1/2	**1**	3/4	1	**2/3**	2/3	2/3	2/3	1/3	2/3	**1**
E_1	8.00	9.63	10.00	10.50	**11.00**	10.63	10.00	**10.67**	10.67	10.67	**10.67**	10.67	10.67	**10.67**
E_2	12.00	10.75	10.44	10.00	**10.00**	9.75	10.00	**9.78**	10.00	9.69	**10.22**	9.56	9.33	**10.00**

A Nash equilibrium would result when probability of one firm resorting to a strategy is known to the other firm and the latter shuffles its strategies accordingly to serve its interest best. For instance, if probability with which Firm 1 resorts to 'no price change' be given as 2/3 ($p = 2/3$) Firm 2 will resort to 'no price change' with probability q so that its expected pay-off from 'no price change' may be the same as that from 'price increase', that is,

$$10 \times 2/3 \times q + 10 \times (1-2/3)q = 8 \times 2/3 \times (1-q) + 12 \times (1-2/3)(1-q)$$

$\Rightarrow \qquad (58/3)q = 28/3$

$\Rightarrow \qquad q = 14/29$

Firm 2's expected pay-off from 'no price change' is 4.83 and so is it from 'price increase'. Firm 2's total expected pay-off is thus, 9.66.

Nash equilibrium demonstrated here is based on the assumption that Firm 1's strategy-mix ($p = 2/3$, $1 - p = 1/3$) is known to Firm 2 either from Firm 1's past behaviour or from Firm 2's subjective assessment of Firm 1's probabilities of shuffling its strategies. If it is based on Firm 1's past behaviour, the game may be a **non-simultaneous** one. On the other hand, if it is based on subjective assessment of probabilities, it may be a **simultaneous game**.

Next, given Firm 2's probability of resorting to 'no price change' as $2/3$ ($q = 2/3$), Firm 1 will resort to 'no price change' with probability p so that its expected pay-off from 'no price change' may be the same as that from 'price increase', that is,

$$10 \times 2/3 \times p + 12 \times p \times (1 - 2/3) = 12 \times (1 - p) \times 2/3 + 8 \times (1 - p)(1 - 2/3)$$
$$\Rightarrow (64/3)p = 32/3$$
$$\Rightarrow p = 1/2$$

Firm 1's expected pay-off from 'no price change' is 5.33 and so is it from 'price increase'. Firm 1's total expected pay-off is thus, 10.66.

Again, Nash equilibrium demonstrated here is based on the assumption that Firm 2's strategy-mix ($q = 2/3$) is known to Firm 1 either from Firm 2's past behaviour or from Firm 1's subjective assessment of Firm 2's probabilities of shuffling its strategies. As above, the game may be a non-simultaneous one, if based on Firm 2's past behaviour or a simultaneous one if based on the subjective assessment of Firm 2's probabilities by Firm 1.

When the game is independent and simultaneous, Firm 1 can attempt maximization of its pay-off by differentiating its pay-off function with respect to p. Differentiating Eq. (12.1) with respect to p, we have

$$\partial E_1/\partial p = 10q - 12q + 12(1 - q) - 8(1 - q)$$
$$= 4 - 6q \qquad (12.5)$$

The second order condition of maxima, however, is not satisfied as $\partial^2 E_1/\partial p^2 = 0$. Nevertheless, we can follow its modified version to determine the simultaneous equilibrium.

The methodology can best be explained through the following steps:

Step 1: Find values of q over which pay-off maximizing firm's expected pay-off (E_1) increases, decreases or remains constant. Here, E_1 is an increasing function of p over **$0 < q < 2/3$**, as the required condition,

$$\partial E_1 / \partial p > 0$$
$$\Rightarrow 4 - 6q > 0 \qquad \text{[From Eq. (12.5)]}$$
$$\Rightarrow q < 2/3$$

Likewise, E_1 is a decreasing function of p over **$2/3 < q < 1$**, as the required condition,

$$\partial E_1 / \partial p < 0$$
$$\Rightarrow 4 - 6q < 0 \qquad \text{[From Eq. (12.5)]}$$
$$\Rightarrow q > 2/3$$

And, E_1 is constant when $q = 2/3$, as the required condition,

$$\partial E_1/\partial p = 0$$

$$\Rightarrow \qquad 4 - 6q = 0 \qquad \text{[From Eq. 12.5]}$$
$$\Rightarrow \qquad \mathbf{q = 2/3}$$

Step 2: Now plot p as a function of q as in panel (a) (Figure 12.1). When $q < 2/3$, E_1 increases with p. This implies that the best response of Firm 1 $(p, 1 - p)$ to the strategy mix $(q, 1 - q)$ of Firm 2 is to resort to 'no price change' with $p = 1$ (dotted line at $p = 1$). When $q > 2/3$, E_1 decreases with p. This implies that the best response of Firm 1 $(p, 1 - p)$ to the strategy-mix $(q, 1 - q)$ of Firm 2 is to resort to 'price increase' with $p = 0$ (dotted line at $p = 0$). When $q = 2/3$, Firm 1 will be indifferent between the two strategies as shown by the dotted line at $q = 2/3$.

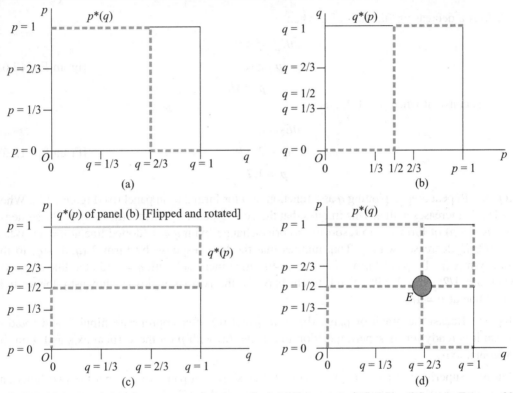

FIGURE 12.1 Panel (a) shows p as a function of $q[p^*(q)]$ as per calculations of Step 1. For $q < 2/3$, Firm 1's best response $(p, 1 - p)$ to Firm 2's strategy mix $(q, 1 - q)$ is to resort to 'no price change' $(p = 1)$; for $q > 2/3$, Firm 1's best response $(p, 1 - p)$ to Firm 2's $(q, 1 - q)$ is to resort to 'price increase' $(p = 0)$ and for $q = 2/3$, Firm 1 is indifferent between its strategies. In panel (b), q is portrayed as a function of p as per calculations in Step 3. When $p > 1/2$, Firm 2's best response $(q, 1 - q)$ to Firm 1's strategy-mix $(p, 1 - p)$ is 'no price change' with $q = 1$, when $p < 1/2$, Firm 2's best response $(q, 1 - q)$ to Firm 1's $(p, 1 - p)$ is to resort to 'price increase' with $q = 0$ and when $p = 1/2$, Firm 2 is indifferent between the strategies. Panel (c) presents the graph of panel (b) after its transformation through flipping and rotating it so that it is ready for its superimposition into panel (a). Panel (d) shows graphs of panels (a) and (c) superimposed into the same space to give the position of equilibrium through the intersection of the two. In equilibrium, the strategy mix of Firm 1 is (1/2, 1/2) and that of Firm 2 is (2/3, 1/3). This constitutes Nash equilibrium.

Step 3: Repeat Step 1 with the pay-off function of Firm 2 (Eq. 12.2), maximizing E_2 with respect to q this time. Differentiating Eq. 12.2 with respect to q, we have:

$$\partial E_2/\partial q = 10p + 10(1-p) - 8p - 12(1-p)$$
$$= 4p - 2 \qquad (12.6)$$

Clearly, E_2 is an increasing function of q when

$$\partial E_2/\partial q > 0$$
$$\Rightarrow \qquad 4p - 2 > 0 \qquad \text{[From Eq. 12.6]}$$
$$\Rightarrow \qquad \mathbf{p > 1/2}$$

and, E_2 is a decreasing function of q when

$$\partial E_2/\partial q < 0$$
$$\Rightarrow \qquad 4p - 2 < 0 \qquad \text{[From Eq. 12.6]}$$
$$\Rightarrow \qquad \mathbf{p < 1/2}$$

and, it is constant when $p = 1/2$, since

$$\partial E_2/\partial q = 0$$
$$\Rightarrow \qquad 4p - 2 = 0 \qquad \text{[From Eq. 12.6]}$$
$$\Rightarrow \qquad \mathbf{p = 1/2}$$

Step 4: Repeat Step 2, plotting q as a function of p for Firm 2 as in panel (b) (Figure 12.1). When $p > 1/2$, E_2 increases with q. This implies that the best response by Firm 2 ($q, 1-q$) to the strategy-mix ($p, 1-p$) of Firm 1 is to resort to 'no price change' with $q = 1$ (dotted line at $q = 1$). When $p < 1/2$, E_2 decreases with q. This implies that the best response by Firm 2 ($q, 1-q$) to the strategy-mix ($p, 1-p$) of Firm 1 is to resort to 'price increase' with $q = 0$ (dotted line at $q = 0$). When $p = 1/2$, Firm 2 will be indifferent between the two strategies as shown by the vertical dotted line at $p = 1/2$.

Step 5: Recast the graph of panel (b) as in panel (c) after appropriate flipping and rotating so that it is ready for its superimposition into panel (a) with p on the vertical axis and q on the horizontal axis.

Step 6: Superimpose panel (c) into panel (a) as shown in panel (d) so that the two functions [$p^*(q)$ and $q^*(p)$] may intersect each other at point E ($P = 1/2, Q = 2/3$).

Step 7: Calculate the value of the game by substituting for p and q in either of the Eq. (12.1) or (12.2).

This gives $E_1 = \mathbf{10.67}$ and $E_2 = \mathbf{10.00}$

The same results follow if we grant the assumption that a player turns indifferent between its strategies if its expected pay-off from each is the same no matter how the other player shuffles his/her strategies. In Step 2 above, Firm 1 turns indifferent between its strategies when its rival employs 'no price change' with a probability of 2/3 and 'price increase' with a probability of 1/3. Likewise, in Step 4, Firm 2 turns indifferent between its strategies when Firm 1 shuffles its strategies with a probability of 1/2 each.

In the game of Table 12.4, Firm 1's indifference between 'no price change' and 'price increase' at Firm 2's strategy-mix of $(q, 1 - q)$ implies that Firm 1's pay-off from its 'no price change' is equal to its pay-off from its 'price increase'.

Firm 1's pay-off from 'no price change' $= 10q + 12(1 - q)$
$$= 12 - 2q$$
Firm 1's pay-off from 'price increase' $= 12q + 8(1 - q)$
$$= 4q + 8$$

Equating the two, we have,
$$12 - 2q = 4q + 8$$
$$\Rightarrow \quad 6q = 4$$
$$\Rightarrow \quad \mathbf{q = 2/3;\ 1 - q = 1/3}.$$

Likewise, Firm 2's indifference between 'no price change' and 'price increase' at Firm 1's strategy-mix of $(p, 1 - p)$ implies that Firm 2's pay-off from its 'no price change' is equal to its pay-off from its 'price increase'.

Firm 2's pay-off from 'no price change' $= 10p + 10(1 - p)$
$$= 10$$
Firm 2's pay-off from 'price increase' $= 8p + 12(1 - p)$
$$= 12 - 4p$$

Equating the two, we have,
$$12 - 4p = 10$$
$$\Rightarrow \quad 4p = 2$$
$$\Rightarrow \quad \mathbf{p = 1/2;\ 1 - p = 1/2}.$$

Evidently, the results obtained are exactly the same as those obtained from differentiation of the expected pay-off functions [Step 1 through Step 7]. The reader can follow either of the two but the latter is strongly recommended due to its simplicity and economy of time.

This shows that a mixed strategy yields at least one Nash equilibrium where pure strategies fail. Note also the fact that *all dominant strategy equilibria are Nash equilibria but not all Nash equilibria are dominant strategy equilibria.* 'No price change' is the dominant strategy for both the players (Table 12.2). The top-left cell of the pay-off matrix provides the dominant strategy equilibrium. The same cell can be shown to constitute a Nash equilibrium as well under pure strategies. However, in Table 12.3, the top-left and bottom-right cells each yields a Nash equilibrium but not a dominant strategy equilibrium.

12.4 NON-ZERO-SUM GAMES UNDER MAXIMIN/MINIMAX CRITERIA

12.4.1 Maximin Criteria

In highly competitive oligopolistic situations, von Neumann and Morgenstern suggested, a decision-maker may adopt a **risk-averse strategy**. The strategy, also known as a **loss-avoidance**

strategy, requires a player to choose the best from the worst possible pay-offs offered by the strategies available, no matter what other decision makers do. Accordingly, each player in the game determines the minimum possible pay-off offered by each of his/her strategies against each of his/her rival's strategies. He/she then chooses the best among these worst pay-offs and adopts the strategy corresponding to it. The decision criterion is known as the maximin criterion or also as **maximin strategy,** signifying choice of the maximum pay-off from among the minimum possible ones offered by the available strategies. In other words, it amounts to maximization of the minimum pay-offs offered by the alternative strategies open to a player against those of his/her rival(s).

Thus, each player determines the least pay-off each strategy offers and then decides to play the strategy corresponding to the maximum of these minimum pay-offs, called the **maximin**.

Consider the game in Table 12.8. The game already has two Nash Equilibria in top-right and bottom-left cells. The maximin strategy equilibrium takes place in the top-left cell, which is different from either of the two Nash equilibria in top-right and bottom-left cells. To see what risk aversion actually means, refer to Table 12.9. The minimum gains to Firm 1 are (−10) from 'don't invest' and (−100) from 'invest'. Of the two, Firm 1 must choose one that yields higher pay-off under the maximin-criterion. In the same way, the minimum gains to Firm 2 are 5 from 'don't invest' and 10 from 'invest'. Of the two, Firm 2 would choose one that yields higher pay-off under the maximin-criterion.

TABLE 12.8 Product choice problem equilibrium in maximin criterion: In applying the maximin criterion, each firm first determines its minimum pay-off that could result from each strategy available to it. As shown in the table, for Firm 1, it is 6 from the strategy of 'no new product' and 4 from the strategy of 'new product' and for Firm 2 too, incidentally, it is 6 from the strategy of 'no new product' and 4 from the strategy of 'new product'. In the next step, each firm is to choose the maximum of these minimum pay-offs assured. The result is that neither firm decides in favour of introducing the 'new product' because the minimum assured by 'no new product' (6) is higher than the minimum (4) assured by the strategy of 'new product'. This places each firm in top-left cell. The maximin criterion thus, leads to an equilibrium which is different from either of the two Nash equilibria– the *first* in top-right cell and the *second* in bottom-left cell. The reason rests on loss avoidance of the maximin criterion instead of profit maximization of Nash equilibrium. The latter, in the top-right cell, implies that Firm 1 should not introduce the new product if Firm 2 already has it introduced; and that in the bottom left cell, implies that Firm 2 should not introduce the new product if Firm 1 already has it introduced. The risk-averse strategy implies that none should introduce a new product unless speculating.

		Firm 2		
		No new product	New product	Row minimum
Firm 1	No new product	{8, 8}	{6, 12}	6
	New product	{12, 6}	{4, 4}	4
	Column minimum	6	4	

TABLE 12.9 Nash equilibrium versus maximin strategy equilibrium: It is clear from Table 12.9 that Firm 2 has a dominant strategy (invest) while Firm 1 has none. Dominant strategy equilibrium is, thus, not possible. However, a Nash equilibrium (bottom- right cell) exists. Both the firms maximize pay-offs by adopting the strategy 'invest'. If Firm 2 chooses 'invest', the best Firm 1 can do is to 'invest' and if Firm 1 chooses 'invest', the best Firm 2 can do is to choose the same. If Firm 2 with a dominant strategy of 'invest' is irrational and Firm 1 is a first mover, the safe course for Firm 1 is to turn risk-averse and avoid 'invest' no matter what its opponent does. This can be shown conveniently through maximin strategy. The minimum pay-off assured to Firm 1 is (–10) from 'don't invest' and (–100) from 'invest'. Under the maximin criterion, Firm 1 must choose the higher of the two, that is, (–10) which corresponds to 'don't invest'. In the same way, minimum pay-offs to Firm 2 from the two strategies are 5 and 10. Of these, 10 being higher must be chosen by Firm 2. The maximin equilibrium is the top-right cell. However, if Firm 2, a docile firm, is a first mover, Firm 1 would do better by comparing its expected pay-off from each of its strategies before finalizing its choice. This requires knowing the probabilities with which Firm 2 shuffles its strategies. Suppose Firm 2 adopts 'don't invest' on 20 % of the times. The expected pay-off to Firm 1 is [0.20 × 5 + 0.80 × (–10)], which is (–7) from 'don't invest' and [0.20 × (–100) + 0.80 × (20)] or (–4) from 'invest'. Since (–4) > (–7), Firm 1 would do better by investing than by not investing in this case. In case the probability of not investing by Firm 2 is 50%, the expected pay-offs to Firm 1 from the two strategies are (–2.50) from 'don't invest' and (–40) from 'invest'. Since (–2.50) > (–40), Firm 1 must resort to 'don't invest' in this case. Similarly, when Firm 1 is docile, Firm 2 can go for a risk-averse strategy. When both are rational, the two would stick to Nash equilibrium in bottom-right cell.

		Firm 2		
		Don't invest	Invest	Firm 1 minimum
Firm 1	Don't invest	{5, 5}	{–10, 10}	–10
	Invest	{–100, 6}	{20, 12}	–100
	Firm 2 minimum	5	10	

12.4.2 Minimax Criterion

Instead of maximizing profits, a player in losses may have to minimize them under loss avoidance strategy. This can be possible through a minimax criterion. The criterion, like a maximin criterion, is a risk-averse criterion requiring determination of a course of action that relates to the minimum of the maximum losses likely from the available strategies. Many non-cooperative games can be resolved through minimax criterion but their outcomes may not always be desirable for the participants and also for the society. Take for example, the problem of prisoner's dilemma (Table 11.2) reproduced here in Table 12.10. The minimax equilibrium takes place in the bottom right cell.

12.5 NON-ZERO-SUM GAMES [ASSORTED APPLICATIONS]

In this section, we will take up a few specific applications of non-zero-sum games. These applications would include, among others, the special cases of Repeated and Sequential Games as well.

12.5.1 APPLICATION 12.1: Problem of the Couple [The Battle of Sexes]

A young couple prefers to spend the weekend out together but has different tastes in entertainment. Husband loves going to club but not without wife while wife, going to theatre but not without husband. The pay-off matrix is shown in Table 12.11. The game has two Nash equilibria in pure strategies, one in which the two go together to the club and the other in which they go together to the theatre. The husband has a preference for the first, while the wife, for the second. Neither of the two would want to change, given the choice of the other.

TABLE 12.10 Prisoner's dilemma: Two suspects convicted of collaborating in a crime are kept in separate cells so that they may not communicate in-between. The outcome of 'do not confess' for both amounts to 2 years in jail each, that of 'confess' for both amounts to 5 years in jail each and that of one confessing while the other not, amounts to 10 years in jail for the one who doesn't and 1 year in jail for the other who does. Under minimax criterion, each of the two prisoners determines the maximum number of years in jail each strategy may lead to, and thereafter, each adopts the strategy that relates to the minimum of these maximum punishments. As a result, each one confesses and each one gets 5 years in jail, yielding a **minimax equilibrium** in bottom-right cell. The same is the result if we work out a **dominant strategy equilibrium**. For each suspect, 'confess' is the dominant strategy and the bottom-right cell rests at the confluence of the dominant strategies of the two. Note that Nash equilibrium is not workable here as none of the two suspects has a way of knowing what the other one has done or is doing. Note further that the solution reached through common sense in Table 11.2 (Chapter 11) is none other than the one reached here through minimax and dominant strategies.

		Suspect 2		
		Do not confess	Confess	Row maximum
Suspect 1	Do not confess	{2, 2}	{10, 1}	10
	Confess	{1, 10}	{5, 5}	5
	Column maximum	10	5	

TABLE 12.11 Problem of the couple: Nash equilibria exist in top-left and bottom-right cells

		Wife	
		Club	Theatre
Husband	Club	{10, 5}	{0, 0}
	Theatre	{0, 0}	{5, 10}

Apart from the Nash equilibria in pure strategies, there exists an equilibrium in mixed strategies as well. To see, let wife's probability of going to 'club' be q so that of her going to 'theatre' is $(1-q)$. For the husband to turn indifferent between 'club' and 'theatre', his expected pay-off from going to 'club' must be the same as that from going to 'theatre'. That is,

$$10q + 0 \cdot (1-q) = 0 \cdot q + 5 \cdot (1-q)$$
$$\Rightarrow \qquad 15q = 5$$
$$\Rightarrow \qquad q = 1/3, \text{ and}$$
$$1 - q = 2/3.$$

Likewise, if the husband plays 'club' with the probability p, the wife will turn indifferent between 'club' and 'theatre' when her expected pay-off from playing 'club' is the same as that from playing 'theatre', i.e.,

$$5p + 0 \cdot (1-p) = 0 \cdot p + 10 \cdot (1-p)$$
$$\Rightarrow \qquad 15p = 10$$
$$\Rightarrow \qquad p = 2/3, \text{ and}$$
$$1 - p = 1/3.$$

Husband's total expected pay-off

$$= 10pq + 0(1-p)q + 0 \cdot p(1-q) + 5(1-p)(1-q)$$
$$= (10)(2/3)(1/3) + (0)\,1/3\,(1/3) + (0)(2/3)(2/3) + (5)(1/3)(2/3)$$
$$= 20/9 + 0 + 0 + 10/9$$
$$= 30/9.$$
$$= \mathbf{10/3}$$

Wife's total expected pay-off

$$= 5pq + 0 \cdot (1-p)q + 0 \cdot p(1-q) + 10(1-p)(1-q)$$
$$= (5)(2/3)(1/3) + (0)(1/3)(1/3) + (0)(2/3)(2/3) + (10)(1/3)(2/3)$$
$$= 10/9 + 20/9$$
$$= 30/9$$
$$= \mathbf{10/3}$$

Thus, apart from the two Nash equilibria in pure strategies, there exists one in mixed strategies as well. The husband must play 'club' with a probability of 2/3 and the wife must play it with a probability of 1/3. It can be seen that none of the two could be better-off in mixed strategies by any deviation from these probabilities.

12.5.2 APPLICATION 12.2: Matching Coins [Matching Pennies]

There are two players, A and B. Each one flips its coin at the same time and reveals its outcome to the other. If the outcomes match, that is, if both are heads or both are tails, Player A wins ₹ 100 from Player B and if the outcomes don't match, that is, if A's toss reveals a head, while B's toss reveals a tail or vice versa, Player B wins ₹ 100 from Player A. Identifying strategies as tossing of heads and tails, the pay-off matrix can be presented as in Table 12.12. As is evident from the table, none of the two strategies is a dominant strategy for either player. Hence, dominant strategy equilibrium is ruled out. A closer look at the table also reveals that a Nash equilibrium too is out of question in pure strategies. None of the two players knows the outcome of the other's toss before tossing its own. Mixed strategy, however, yields a Nash equilibrium.

Proceeding on the same lines as in the previous application, if Player B plays 'heads' with a probability of q, Player B would be indifferent between the strategies of 'heads' and 'tails' if the expected payoffs are same from each. That is,

$$100q + (-100)(1-q) = (-100)q + 100(1-q)$$
$$\Rightarrow \qquad 400q = 200$$
$$\Rightarrow \qquad q = 1/2, \text{ and}$$
$$1 - q = 1/2$$

Likewise, when Player A plays 'heads' with a probability of p, Player B would be indifferent between the strategies of 'heads' and 'tails' if the expected payoffs are same from each. That is,
$$(-100)p + 100(1-p) = 100p + (-100)(1-p)$$
$$\Rightarrow \qquad 400p = 200$$
$$\Rightarrow \qquad p = 1/2, \text{ and}$$
$$\Rightarrow \qquad (1-p) = 1/2.$$

Total expected pay-off of the player A,
$$E_A = 100pq + (-100)p(1-q) + (-100)(1-p)q + 100(1-p)(1-q)$$
$$= (100)(1/2)(1/2) + (-100)(1/2)(1/2) + (-100)(1/2)(1/2) + (100)(1/2)(1/2)$$
$$= 0$$

Total expected pay-off of the player B,
$$E_B = (-100)pq + 100p(1-q) + 100(1-p)q + (-100)(1-p)(1-q)$$
$$= (-100)(1/2)(1/2) + 100(1/2)(1/2) + (100)(1/2)(1/2) + (-100)(1/2)(1/2)$$
$$= 0$$

The expected pay-offs for both are the same. Mixed strategy of heads and tails with probabilities of 1/2 each yields a Nash equilibrium. None of the players can improve its pay-off by deviating from the probability of 1/2 for playing 'heads' and 1/2 for playing 'tails'. To check, suppose the Player A 'heads' with a probability of p and 'tails' with a probability of $1-p$, while the Player B continues to play the two strategies with the probability of 1/2 each.

TABLE 12.12 Game of Matching the Coins

		Player B	
		Heads	Tails
Player A	Heads	{100, –100}	{–100, 100}
	Tails	{–100, 100}	{100, –100}

The expected pay-off of Player A
$$= (100)p(1/2) + (-100)p(1/2) + (-100)(1-p)(1/2) + (100)(1-p)(1/2)$$
$$= 50p - 50p + 50p - 50p - 50 + 50$$
$$= 0$$

The expected pay-off of Player B
$$= (-100)p(1/2) + (100)p(1/2) + 100(1-p)(1/2) + (-100)(1-p)(1/2)$$
$$= -50p + 50p - 50p + 50p + 50 - 50$$
$$= 0$$

The expected pay-offs of the two players are the same when Player A attempts to improve its pay-off by a change in his probability of playing 'heads' or 'tails', given the probability of its opponent as 1/2 for each strategy. The same can be said of the other player if it attempts to improve its pay-off by a change in its probabilities given the probability of the Player A as 1/2 for each strategy. The reader can verify the statements by assigning numerical values to p such as 3/4, 1/4, 2/3, etc.

12.5.3 APPLICATION 12.3: Repeated Games

We have seen how firms find themselves in prisoners' dilemma while making price-output decisions in an oligopolistic market. Is it possible to have a wayout of this dilemma? Before we investigate the possibility of an answer to this question, let us first recall from Section 11.9 that the 'prisoners' dilemma' is a one time game for the suspects who have no way of knowing each other's moves. That is, they don't get a second chance of improvising their moves. As against this, such games in an oligopolistic market are *repetitive* in nature. The firms face them week after week, month after month or year after year. Moreover, moves of one firm form no secret to the other at the time it decides to improvise. Consider the game in Table 12.13 as an illustration.

Due to *repetitive nature* of the game, it is possible for the competitors in an oligopolistic market to develop an understanding to cooperate with each other for common objectives. Consider the pay-off matrix in Table 12.13. The two firms in the game face a dilemma whether to continue with the low price strategy or adopt a high price strategy. The problem is posed by the high price strategy which, if played by one but not by the other, may cause substantial loss to the firm that plays it and substantial gains to the other that does not play it. But, if both the firms cooperate and play 'high price', both stand to gain much higher profits (50, 50) than the equilibrium profits (10, 10).

TABLE 12.13 Pricing Problem: If one firm adopts 'high price' while the other does not, the one who does, suffers loss while the other who doesn't, reaps a rich harvest. However, if both adopt 'high price' simultaneously, both stand to realize substantial gains. Also, the first one to switch to 'high price' stands to lose substantially as its rival firm doesn't follow its suit for obvious reasons. In absence of a perfect collusion, therefore, both continue to play 'low price' strategy, which yields for each a reasonable payoff through dominant strategy equilibrium that is also a Nash equilibrium. The dilemma faced by the firms draws a parallel with the prisoner's dilemma but for the difference of *repetitive nature* of the oligopolistic games. If one of the firms starts with a high price and if the other does not follow the suit or returns back to the 'low price' after initially cooperating with the first mover, the first mover also returns to the low price and the two end up in top-left cell, which, as mentioned above, is already labeled as both a Nash equilibrium and a dominant strategy equilibrium in pure strategies.

		Firm 2	
		Low price	High price
Firm 1	Low price	{10, 10}	{100, −50}
	High price	{−50, 100}	{50, 50}

According to a study conducted by Robert Axelrod*, what works out best for the oligopolistic markets in such situations is a '**tit-for-tat**' strategy. A player would start off with 'high price'

---

* Robert Axelrod, *The Evolution of Cooperation* (New York; Basic Books, 1984).

strategy and would continue with it so long as its competitor cooperates and charges a high price but if it does not (i.e., continues with the 'low price' strategy or turns back to it after initial cooperation), it would itself turn to the 'low price' strategy ultimately.

If the game continues for *infinitely long period* or *for ever,* a 'tit-for-tat' strategy leads to a cooperative game in which firms settle for a 'high price' for ever. They sense that others will adopt the 'tit-for-tat' strategy or will learn from their repeated experiences to behave rationally and opt for a 'high price' ultimately. A firm deciding to charge a low price in any period may make high profits in that period but it also knows from its past experiences that its rivals in the market suffering substantial losses currently due to its adoption of 'low price' strategy will follow its suit in the subsequent periods with the result that its abnormal profits of today will disappear tomorrow. Moreover, its non-cooperation with the price-hiking firms will signal its selfishness to them, who, in consequence, will also decide to return back to 'low price' eliminating thereby, the non-cooperating firm's advantage with immediate effect. This serves as a deterrent to a firm planning to betray the resolve of the firms in the market to play 'high price'. In an infinitely long period, therefore, better sense is bound to prevail upon all the firms with the consequence that none of them will ever dare to betray the resolve and a *cooperative game* is bound to be an ultimate consequence.

But if the game continues over a *limited* or *finite period,* a firm may decide to go for the 'low price' strategy in the ultimate period thinking it would be too late by then for the others to harm its interest through the 'tit-for-tat' strategy. But then, even other firms may think on the same lines, i.e., switch to the 'low price' strategy in the ultimate period. Under the suspicion, the firm in question may decide to undercut price in the *penultimate* period. Again, what if the other firms also think of the same? Its likelihood, by no means, can be deemed insignificant. Outguessing each other for own gain may continue until all the firms decide to under-cut price right in the first period, ending eventually in the top-left cell (Nash equilibrium) of Table 12.13. The game thus, turns out to be a *non-cooperative one* due to limited time period.

As most of the competitors do not expect to live for ever, the 'tit-for-tat' strategy seems to have little value and the competitors appear stuck up in the prisoners' dilemma. But then the realization that no one is to live for ever itself is of little consequence as all the competitors know that each one of them would be succeeded by its descendent sooner or later and the game would have to go for ever. Hence, what seems to be the most likely outcome is a cooperative game.

The only situations that threaten the cooperative game relate to shifting demand and cost conditions as also the number of the participating firms, which turns large. Uncertainties about demand and cost conditions make it difficult to reach any implicit understanding among the firms to cooperate while explicit understandings are of little consequence due to anti-trust legislation. Moreover, cost differences, if existent, lead to price differences threatening thereby, the survival of the cooperative game.

12.5.4 APPLICATION 12.4: Sequential Games—Benefit of First Mover

In most of the games discussed so far, players make their moves almost simultaneously. When one player makes its moves only after the other has, the game is called a sequential game. **Stackelberg's duopoly model** discussed in Section 11.4 provides an example. One of the two firms sets its quantity only after the other one has.

Consider the pay-off matrix in Table 12.14. Each of the two firms has to decide whether to introduce a new product or to continue with the old one. As is obvious, the first one to introduce the new product has all the advantages of a pioneer in the field. It can set a market skimming price for its product and enjoy monopoly power at least until the rival firm is in a position to introduce a substitute. By then, even consumers get used to the pioneer's product, showing reluctance to switch over to its substitutes introduced later. Word processing and spread-sheet softwares provide good examples. Users acquire proficiency in the use of the first mover's product and resist its substitute unless it offers sufficient incentive. Table 12.14 shows advantages of being the first mover. Assume that the firms use maximin criterion to finalize their decision. If the firms announce their decision to introduce the new product independently and simultaneously, neither will succeed in its endeavour given the pay-offs and the decision criterion. The maximin for Firm 1 is –10 and so is it for Firm 2. Each corresponds to 'no new product'.

TABLE 12.14 Sequential game: Benefit of being the first mover in the market

		Firm 2	
		No new product	Introduce new product
Firm 1	No new product	{5, 5}	{–10, 20}
	Introduce new product	{20, –10}	{–12, –12}

Now suppose it is a sequential game. Firm 1 introduces the new product as a first mover. The strategy for Firm 2 will now be to stay out to retain a higher pay-off (–10) through 'no new product' than that (–12) through 'introduce new product'. Consequently, Firm 1 will earn a pay-off of 20 as the only supplier. Firm 1 has, thus, benefitted significantly from its being the first mover in the market.

12.5.5 APPLICATION 12.5: Sequential Games—Product Choice

For another application of sequential games, refer to the pay-off matrix in Table 12.15. The game involves two fast food firms each with varieties F_1 and F_2. If both the firms market the same variety, be it F_1 or F_2, the pay-offs to the two are smaller but identical (each earns a pay-off of 2), but if they market different varieties, Firm 1 marketing variety F_1 while Firm 2 marketing F_2 or Firm 1 marketing F_2 while Firm 2 marketing F_1, the pay-offs to the two are higher but unequal (one that markets F_1, gets a pay-off of 3 while the one that markets F_2, gets a pay-off of 6). This makes it a sequential game.

TABLE 12.15 Product choice problem: From the pay-offs, it is clear that both the firms realize smaller pay-offs when both decide to introduce the same food. On the contrary, both gain higher pay-offs when one introduces one food while the other, the other one. If Firm 1 takes lead in introducing the foods, it would gain more by introducing F_2 instead of F_1. Firm 2 will have to follow with Food F_1. Instead, if Firm 2 takes the lead, it will introduce F_2 instead of F_1 and Firm 1 will have to come up with F_1 instead of F_2. Much would depend on the sequence in which moves are executed by the two.

		Firm 2	
		F_1	F_2
Firm 1	F_1	{2, 2}	{3, 6}
	F_2	{6, 3}	{2, 2}

Each expecting a higher pay-off from F_2, tries its best to market it first. Suppose Firm 1 succeeds in taking the lead. As a result, the best Firm 2 can do is to come out with F_1 (pay-off from F_1 being 3 while that from F_2, 2). Next, suppose Firm 2 succeeds in taking the lead. The best Firm 1 can do is to come out with F_1 (pay-off from F_1 being 3 while that from F_2, 2). The beneficiary in either case is the first mover.

At times, a sequential game is more convenient to analyze through a decision tree. Its decision tree presentation is called the **extensive form of a game**. For the game of Table 12.15, the extensive form is shown in Figure 12.2:

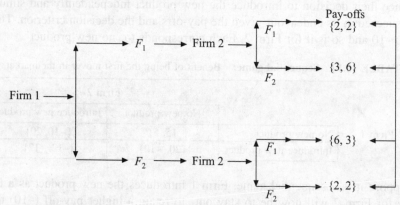

FIGURE 12.2 **Game of Table 12.15 in its extensive form:** Pay-offs to the firms from each sequence are shown in the last column. If Firm 1 introduces F_1, the possible responses of Firm 2 would comprise introducing F_1 with a pay-offs of 2 and F_2 with a pay-off of 6. Evidently, Firm 2 will prefer introducing F_2. The respective pay-off to Firm 1 would be 2 when Firm 2 introduces F_1 and 3 when it introduces F_2. Similarly, if Firm 1 introduces F_2, the responses of Firm 2 would comprise introducing F_1 with a pay-off of 3 and F_2 with a pay-off of 2. As obvious, Firm 2 will prefer introducing F_1 in this case. The respective pay-off to Firm 1 would be 6 when Firm 2 introduces F_1 and 2 when it introduces F_2. To work out the solution, move leftwards from right in the direction of the arrows. When Firm 1 is the first mover, it will prefer introducing F_2 while Firm 2 will follow it up by introducing F_1 for ensuring the best it can (a pay-off of 3). On the contrary if Firm 2 is the first mover, the best sequence for the two would comprise introduction of F_2 by Firm 2, and that of F_1 by Firm 1 as a follower. It is the first mover that gains more from the game.

As explained in the figure, if Firm 1 is the first mover, it should introduce food F_2 leaving food F_1 as the best choice for Firm 2. On the contrary, if Firm 2 is the first mover, it should introduce food F_2 leaving food F_1 for Firm 1.

The reader can verify that the game (Table 12.15) has no dominant strategy equilibrium. It, however, has two Nash equilibria (top-right and bottom-left cells) in pure strategies and one Nash equilibrium (Firm 1 introducing F_1 with probability $p = 1/5$ and F_2 with probability 4/5 while Firm 2 introducing F_1 with probability 1/5 and F_2 with probability 4/5) in mixed strategies with a total expected pay-off of 5.6 to each. But these solutions have no relevance unless the game is a simultaneous one.

12.5.6 APPLICATION 12.6: Limit Pricing and Short- and Long-run Profits

We have seen that abnormal profits of short-run attract new firms. If it happens, supply would increase and price would fall making a dent in the abnormal profits of the existing firm(s). If an existing firm enjoys monopoly power in the market, that is, if it is the only producer, it would leave no stone unturned to restrict new firms. In Figure 7.10, we observed how a monopoly restricts entry of new firms through what is called *limit pricing*. Under it, the entry barring monopoly can afford to set a price as low as that at L (Figure 7.10) without suffering any loss. The new entrants, on the contrary, have to set a much higher price even to break-even. This is so due to their smaller scale of operation. Suffering already from low levels of recognition, the new entrants fail to sell their output unless they set a price below the average cost. This is sufficient to show them exit and leave the market entirely to the existing monopoly.

The practice can be extended to monopolistic/oligopolistic firms that wish to sustain short-run abnormal profits in the long-run as well. They can do so through the entry limiting pricing model of Bain*. According to it, a price below the profit maximizing level of P_m would stabilize long-run profits of the entry barring monopolistic/oligopolistic firms (Curve II, Figure 12.4). On the contrary, if entry of the new firms is not restricted profits of the existing firms assume a declining trend in the long-run (Curve I, Figure 12.4).

Economic profits from a profit maximizing price, P_m, to a firm (Figure 12.3) in each period are depicted by profit stream of Curve I (Figure 12.4). Note that the economic profit is substantial in short-run, but it goes on declining steadily in the long-run as the new firms drawn by the abnormal profits of the short-run join in. The new entrant will have to produce at least Q_n to break-even at P_m. Outputs below this level will force it to loss and quit in consequence. Sensing entry, the existing firm lowers its price below P_m, the profit maximizing level, to make the matters worse for the new entrants. In case the new firm is stubborn enough to quit, the existing firm can conveniently lower its price even further to the level of P_L, a price corresponding to zero marginal revenue, necessitating for the new entrant to produce at least Q'_n to break-even. Production of such outputs for the new entrants at a cost as low as that of the existing firm is generally a difficult proposition. No doubt, entry-limiting price would reduce the existing firm's profit in short-run as shown, but it would stabilize it in the long-run in a growing market. If the market is a growing one, the long-run profit of the existing firm will grow due to size of the sale at the entry-limiting price. This would ensure the firm a fairly stable profit stream as shown by Curve II (Figure 12.4).

In deviation to Bain's model of entry limiting pricing, **Stigler's Model of Open Oligopoly** observes that the firms generally aim at maximization of the sum of the present values$^\phi$ of the profit stream.

To see what Stigler's Model implies, let us consider the following two profit streams. The first one depicts profits that decline with time when entry of the new firms is not restricted and the second, on the other hand, depicts a profit stream that remains stable with time when entry of the new firms is restricted:

---

*Bain, J.S., "A Note on Pricing in Monopoly and Oligopoly," *American Economic Review*, pp. 448–464, March 1949.
$^\phi$ For present value and its calculation, please see Chapter 15 of this book.

Stream I: 160, 80 and 40 at the end of periods 1, 2 and 3, respectively, when entry is not restricted
Stream II: 100, 100 and 100 at the end of periods 1, 2 and 3, respectively, when entry is restricted

According to Bain's entry limiting pricing, the existing firm must restrict entry of new firms for a stable profit stream depicted by Curve II in Figure 12.4, but according to Stigler's Open Oligopoly Model, it must aim at maximization of the present value of the profit stream whether it is possible by restricting the entry of new firms or by not doing so.

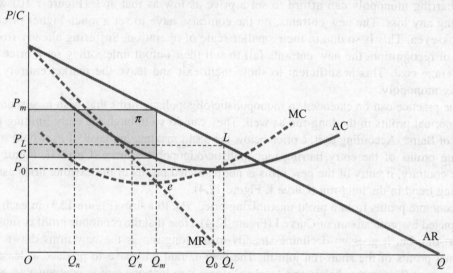

FIGURE 12.3 Entry limiting pricing: AR-curve of the monopoly represents the market demand for the product. The firm determines its equilibrium at e where its MC cuts its MR from below. Equilibrium output and price so determined by the firm are Q_m and P_m, respectively. Abnormal profit accruing to the firm is shown by the shaded rectangle. The size of the profit attracts entry of new firms. This may pose a potential threat to the future profit-stream of the monopoly (chances of a threat to its current profits are low due to higher production costs of the new entrants at their entry levels). As a safeguard, the monopoly can expand its output beyond Q_m, at least to the level of Q_0, the level of optimality in production. This it can without suffering a loss. If required, the firm can expand it further to Q_L, the level at which its MR = 0. Even at this level, price (P_L) is higher than AC, ensuring the firm of some profits. On the contrary, the new entrants, due to diseconomies of scale would have to produce lower output at higher cost, forced, therefore, to set a price higher than that of the existing monopoly. Losses suffered will force an exit on the new entrants. The large firm may return to profit maximizing price as soon as the threat of new entry clears off. If not, it may continue to lower the price further till its AR cuts its AC, just to make sure that none of the new entrants remain in competition. A price, such as P_L is called the entry-limiting price and the practice is referred to as **limit-pricing**.

When the rate of discount is high, say 20% per period, the sum of the present values of the first stream is 212.03 and that of the second, 210.64. Clearly, Stigler's Model would prescribe stream I for the existing firm, that is, not restricting entry of new firms.

When the rate of discount is low, say 10% per period, the sum of the present values of the first stream is 241.61 and that of the second, 248.68. Clearly, Stigler's Model would prescribe stream II for the existing firm, that is, restricting entry of the new firms.

Stigler's Open Oligopoly Model, thus provides a better insight into the problem posed by the new entry. Unlike Bain's model of entry restriction, it explains when entry restriction is called for and when it is not.

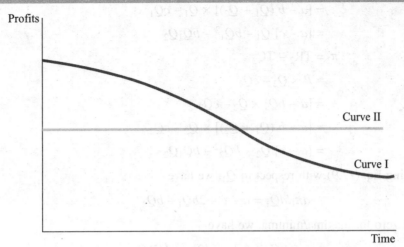

FIGURE 12.4 Curve I represents declining profit stream of a monopoly when entry of new firms is free. Curve II represents stable profit to the monopoly when entry of new firms is restricted.

12.5.7 APPLICATION 12.7: Cournot–Nash Equilibrium [Simultaneous Quantity Setting]

As discussed in Chapter 11, Cournot's model (1838) provides a classic example of game theory. It appears, Cournot sensed a duopoly equilibrium on the lines of Nash equilibrium more than a century ago. Let us revisit Cournot's duopoly model through reaction curves as in Section 11.2.

Suppose the duopolists face market demand given by

$$P = a - bQ \tag{12.7}$$

where, a and b are positive constants and Q is quantity demanded at price P.

Q_1 is supplied by first duopolist and Q_2 by second, so that $Q = Q_1 + Q_2$. The highest price, P is 'a', corresponding to $Q = 0$ and highest demand is 'a/b', corresponding to $P = 0$. From the viewpoint of practical considerations, $Q < a/b$ so that $P > 0$.

Differentiating $Q = Q_1 + Q_2$ with respect to Q_1 and Q_2, we have

$$dQ/dQ_1 = 1 + dQ_2/dQ_1, \text{ and } dQ/dQ_2 = 1 + dQ_1/dQ_2$$

Assuming zero conjectural variations, i.e., $dQ_2/dQ_1 = dQ_1/dQ_2 = 0$, as each duopolist treats the rivals output as fixed, we have $dQ/dQ_1 = dQ/dQ_2 = 1$.

Products of the two being homogeneous with identical costs, $TC_1 = cQ_1$ and $TC_2 = cQ_2$, where, c is average cost per unit. Let π_1 and π_2 be the profit functions of the Duopolists 1 and 2, respectively. Then,

$$\pi_1 = TR_1 - TC_1 \tag{12.8}$$
$$= P \times Q_1 - cQ_1$$
$$= [a - bQ] \times Q_1 - cQ_1$$

$$= [a - b(Q_1 + Q_2)] \times Q_1 - cQ_1$$
$$= [a - c]Q_1 - bQ_1^2 - bQ_1Q_2 \tag{12.9}$$

and,
$$\pi_2 = TR_2 - TC_2$$
$$= P \times Q_2 - cQ_2$$
$$= [a - bQ] \times Q_2 - cQ_2$$
$$= [a - b(Q_1 + Q_2)] \times Q_2 - cQ_2$$
$$= [a - c]Q_2 - bQ_2^2 - bQ_1Q_2 \tag{12.10}$$

Differentiating Eq. (12.9) with respect to Q_1, we have
$$d\pi_1/dQ_1 = a - c - 2bQ_1 - bQ_2$$

Setting it at zero for maxima/minima, we have
$$\Rightarrow \qquad \boldsymbol{Q_1 = (a - c)/2b - (1/2)Q_2} \tag{12.11}$$

Equation (12.11) gives the reaction curve of Duopolist 1 (Figure 12.5).

The second order condition, $d^2\pi_1/dQ_1^2 = -2b$ (negative). This ensures maximization of π_1. Differentiating Eq. (12.10) with respect to Q_2, we have
$$d\pi_2/dQ_2 = a - c - 2bQ_2 - bQ_1$$

Setting it at zero for maxima/minima, we have
$$\Rightarrow \qquad \boldsymbol{Q_2 = (a - c)/2b - (1/2)Q_1} \tag{12.12}$$

Equation (12.12) gives the reaction curve of Duopolist 2 (Figure 12.5).

The second order condition, $d^2\pi_2/dQ_2^2 = -2b$ (negative). This ensures maximization of π_2.

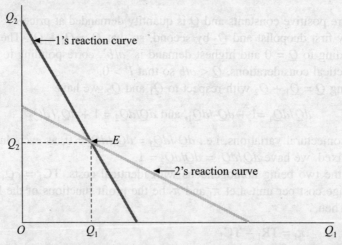

FIGURE 12.5 Equilibrium outputs, (Q_1, Q_2) are given at the intersection of the reaction curves.

Solving Eqs. (12.11) and (12.12) for Q_1 and Q_2, we get the Cournot–Nash equilibrium outputs of the two as

$$Q_1 = Q_2 = (a - c)/3b$$

and market price,
$$P = a - bQ$$
$$= a - 2b(a - c)/3b$$
$$= (2c + a)/3$$

Substituting for P, Q_1 and Q_2 in the profit functions of the two, we have

$$\pi_1 = \pi_2 = (a - c)^2/9b$$

Treating the players as joint profit maximizers, joint profit,

$$\pi = PQ - cQ$$
$$= (a - bQ)Q - cQ$$
$$= (a - c)Q - bQ^2$$

Differentiating with respect to Q and setting the derivative equal to zero for maximization, we have

$$Q = (a - c)/2b = Q_m, \text{ monopoly output,}$$
$$P = (a + c)/2 = P_m, \text{ monopoly price,}$$

and
$$\pi = (a - c)^2/4b = \pi_m, \text{ monopoly profit.}$$

Output produced and profit earned by each are $Q_m/2$ and $[(a - c)^2/8b]$*, respectively. Note that the expressions for Q_1, Q_2, π_1, π_2, Q_m, P_m, and π_m would be different when $TC_1 \neq TC_2$.

If one of the firms decides to sell $Q_m/2$ at P_m thinking that the other firm will follow its suit and do the same, but the other firm, to the contrary, adopts Cournot's pattern of behaviour, charging $(2c + a)/3$ instead of $(c + a)/2$, the one that charges the monopoly price loses its market while the other, following Cournot's pattern of behaviour, captures whole of it because of its lower price $[(2c + a)/3 < (c + a)/2]$. The result is that the former makes zero economic profit, while the latter gets away with entire profit $(\pi_1 + \pi_2)$, which the two were expected to earn together following Cournot's pattern of behaviour. Now let us express the game in its normal form in Table 12.16.

TABLE 12.16 Cournot–Nash equilibrium: Top-left cell provides Cournot–Nash Equilibrium. Top-right and bottom-left cells provide neither Cournot's equilibrium nor Nash's. The last cell, at the bottom right provides monopoly equilibrium which maximizes joint profits of the two firms. This is neither Nash equilibrium nor Cournot equilibrium. Note how monopoly output $Q_m/2$, set by only one, leads to zero profit to it.

		Firm 2	
		$Q_2 = (a - c)/3b$	$Q_m/2 = (a - c)/4b$
Firm 1	$Q_1 = (a - c)/3b$	$[(a - c)^2/9b; (a - c)^2/9b]$	$[2\{(a - c)^2/9b, 0\}]$
	$Q_m/2 = (a - c)/4b$	$[0, 2\{(a - c)^2/9b\}]$	$[(a - c)^2/8b; (a - c)^2/8b]$

*Monopoly profit, $\pi_m = PQ_m - cQ_m$. For its maximization, $d\pi_m/dQ_m = 0 \Rightarrow Q_m = (a - c)/2b; P = (a + c)/2$ and $\pi_m = (a - c)^2/4b$.

ILLUSTRATION 12.1: Let the market demand faced by the duopolists be

$$P = 100 - 0.5 Q, Q = Q_1 + Q_2$$

and their respective cost functions,

$$C_1 = 5Q_1, \text{ and } C_2 = 5Q_2$$

Work out Cournot–Nash Equilibrium.

Solution: Following the method of Illustration 11.1, Chapter 11, the reaction curves of the two duopolists are:

$$Q_1 = (95) - 1/2\ Q_2, \text{ and}$$
$$Q_2 = (95) - 1/2\ Q_1$$

Plotting the equations on the same plane (Figure 12.5), the two intersect each other at E, which gives the equilibrium. From the reaction curves, we have

$$Q_1 = 190/3$$
$$Q_2 = 190/3$$

And,
$$Q = Q_1 + Q_2$$
$$= 380/3$$

Market price,
$$P = 100 - 0.5Q$$
$$= 100 - 0.5 \times 380/3$$
$$= 110/3$$

Profits accruing to the two at the equilibrium are

$$\pi_1 = 95\ Q_1 - 0.5Q_1^2 - 0.5\ Q_2 Q_1$$
$$= \mathbf{18050/9}, \text{ and}$$
$$\pi_2 = 95Q_2 - 0.5Q_2^2 - 0.5Q_1 Q_2$$
$$= \mathbf{18050/9}$$

respectively.

Market demand at zero price (costless production) is 200 units* and at non-zero costs, as in this case, it is 190**.

It is clear that each duopolist supplies 1/3 of the market demand at the equilibrium.

In the normal form of the game, strategies of the two firms are to choose between $Q_i (i = 1, 2)$ and $(Q_m/2)$ while pay-offs refer to the profits accruing to the firms under each strategy. Monopoly output, $Q_m = (a - c)/2b = 95$, monopoly price $P_m = (a + c)/2 = 105/2$ and monopoly profit = $(a - c)^2/4b = 9025/2$. Of the two firms, each has to choose between strategies $Q_i = 190/3$ and $Q_m/2 = 95/2$ for pay-offs $\pi_i = 18050/9$ and $\pi_m/2 = 9025/4$. According to Cournot–Nash equilibrium, the obvious choice is the former. In its tabular form, the game is shown in Table 12.17.

---

* It can be found by substituting $P = 0$ in the demand curve.

** It can be found by substituting $P = MC(MC = 5)$ in the demand function.

TABLE 12.17 Cournot–Nash equilibrium (Simultaneous quantity setting): The two duopolists have two strategies —$(Q_i, Q_m/2)$. Q_i ($i = 1, 2$) = 190/3 and $Q_m/2$ = 95/2. Pay-offs from each strategy-mix as given in the table are calculated under Cournot and monopoly patterns of behaviour of the two. The two firms operate independently and simultaneously under their own beliefs and calculations. The strategy choice goes in favour of quantity strategy (Q_1, Q_2), the top-left cell, which forms both—a Cournot equilibrium as well as a Nash equilibrium. If Firm 1 chooses Q_1, Firm 2 does its best by choosing Q_2 and if Firm 2 chooses Q_2, Firm 1 does its best by choosing Q_1. The game offers high payoffs in bottom-right cell to each player if the two choose to collude. The cell may be treated as providing **Chamberlin's equilibrium** which is a consequence of Chamberlin's argument that business firms cannot be so irrational as not to see beyond the tip of their noses. Sooner or later business sense would prevail upon them and the two would collude to maximize joint profits through a monopoly equilibrium. Chamberlin's argument is not without substance as no personal vendetta is strong enough to take precedence over the business objective of profit maximization.

		Firm 2	
		$Q_2 = (190/3)$	$Q_m/2 = (95/2)$
Firm 1	$Q_1 = (190/3)$	{18050/9, 18050/9}	{36100/9, 0}
	$Q_m/2 = (95/2)$	{0, 36100/9}	{9025/4, 9025/4}

In the event when $TC_1 \ne TC_2$, the expressions for $Q_1, Q_2, \pi_1, \pi_2, Q_m, P_m$, and π_m would be different from what we observed above*. For a numerical illustration, refer to illustrations 11.1 and 11.5. From the former, simultaneous solution of the reaction curves yields $Q_1 = 85.9$ and $Q_2 = 65.6$. Price, P is 39.4 and profits to the two are $\pi_1 = 2955$ and $\pi_2 = 2154$. From the latter, $Q_1 = 93.75$, $Q_2 = 25$, $P = 52.5$, and joint profit of the two, π_m, is 5703. Share of the first firm in

---

* To see, let $TC_1 = c_1 Q_1$ and $TC_2 = c_2 Q_2^2$. Expressions for π_1 and π_2 can be written as

$$\pi_1 = PQ_1 - c_1 Q_1 = (a - bQ)Q_1 - c_1 Q_1, \text{ and } \pi_2 = PQ_2 - c_2 Q_2^2 = (a - bQ)Q_2 - c_2 Q_2^2$$

differentiating π_1 with respect to Q_1 and π_2 with respect to Q_2, we obtain the reaction curves of the two as

$$Q_1 = (a - c_1)/2b - 1/2 Q_2, \text{ and } Q_2 = [a - bQ_1]/2(b + c_2)$$

A simultaneous solution yields,

$$Q_1 = [2(b + c_2)(a - c_1) - ab]/[b(3b + 4c_2)], \text{ and } Q_2 = (a + c_1)/(3b + 4c_2)$$

Now,
$$Q = Q_1 + Q_2$$
$$= [2(b + c_2)(a - c_1) - ab]/[b(3b + 4c_2)] + (a + c_1)/(3b + 4c_2)$$
$$= [(2(b + c_2)(a - c_1) + bc_1]/b(3b + 4c_2)$$

Substituting,
$$P = a - b[(2(b + c_2)(a - c_1) + bc_1]/b(3b + 4c_2)$$
$$= [(a + c_1)(b + 2c_2)/(3b + 4c_2)]$$

Substituting in profit functions,

$$\pi_1 = \frac{[(a + c_1)(b + 2c_2) - c_1(3b + 4c_2)]}{(3b + 4c_2)} \times \frac{[2(b + c_2)(a - c_1) - ab]}{b(3b + 4c_2)}$$

$$= \frac{[(a + c_1)(b + 2c_2) - c_1(3b + 4c_2)][2(b + c_2)(a - c_1) - ab]}{b(3b + 4c_2)^2}$$

$$\pi_2 = \frac{[(a + c_1)^2 (b + c_2)]}{(3b + 4c_2)^2}$$

If the firms opt for joint profit maximization, we differentiate the joint profit function,

$$\pi = \pi_1 + \pi_2$$
$$= PQ_1 + PQ_2 - c_1 Q_1 - c_2 Q_2$$
$$= (a - bQ) \times Q - c_1 Q_1 - c_2 Q_2^2$$

(contd.)

the monopoly profit is given as $\pi_{m1} = 4453$ that of the second, as $\pi_{m2} = 1250$. The game in its normal form with unequal costs can be shown as in Table 12.17(a).

TABLE 12.17(a) **Cournot–Nash equilibrium** takes place in top-left cell. Due to cost differences, shares of the two firms in joint profit maximization are shown in bottom-right cell. The bottom-left and top-right cells show that the firm in Cournot's pattern captures the market while the one in joint profit maximization earns zero economic profit.

		Firm 2	
		In Cournot's Pattern	In joint Profit Maximization
Firm 1	In Cournot's Pattern	{2955, 2154}	{4085, 0}
	In joint Profit Maximization	{0, 3269}	{4453, 1250}

12.5.8 APPLICATION 12.8: Bertrand–Nash Equilibrium [Simultaneous Price Setting for Homogeneous Products]

Bertrand's model*, developed in 1883, differs from Cournot's in that it assumes that firms actually choose prices rather than quantities as in Cournot's model. Strategy spaces are, thus, different in the two models.

The main point of difference, apart from that of simultaneity of quantity setting in Cournot's model and price setting in Bertrand's model, is that costless production ($MC_1 = MC_2 = 0$) in Cournot's model does not imply zero prices to be charged by the firms while in Bertrand's model, it does. In Cournot's model, each firm chooses its profit maximizing quantity by setting its MR

Footnote (contd.)
with respect to Q_1 and Q_2 and set the value of each derivative at zero to get monopoly outputs.

$$d\pi/dQ_1 = a - 2b\,Q - c_1 \quad \text{[since } dQ/dQ_1 = 1 \text{ and } dQ_2/dQ_1 = 0 \text{ because } Q = Q_1 + Q_2]$$
$$= 0 \quad \text{[For maximization]}$$
$$Q = (a - c_1)/2b$$
$$= Q_m, \text{ where } Q_m = \text{monopoly output.}$$

and,
$$d\pi/dQ_2 = a - 2bQ - 2c_2 Q_2 \quad \text{[since } dQ/dQ_2 = 1 \text{ and } dQ_1/dQ_2 = 0 \text{ because } Q = Q_1 + Q_2]$$
$$= 0 \quad \text{[For maximization]}$$
$\Rightarrow$ $\quad Q_2 = c_1/2c_2 \quad$ [Substituting for Q as $(a-c_1)/2b$]
Now, $\quad Q_1 = Q - Q_2$
$$= [(a - c_1)c_2 - bc_1]/2bc_2$$

Substituting in demand function, we have
$$P = a - bQ$$
$$= (a + c_1)/2$$

Substituting, monopoly profit,
$$\pi = \pi_1 + \pi_2$$
$$= PQ_1 - c_1 Q_1 + PQ_2 - c_2 Q_2^2$$
$$= [(a+c_1)/2] \times [\{(a-c_1)c_2 - bc_1\}/2bc_2] - c_1[\{(a-c_1)c_2 - bc_1\}/2bc_2] + [(a+c_1)/2] \times [c_1/2c_2] - c_2[c_1/2c_2]^2$$
$$= \pi_m, \text{ the monopoly profit.}$$

Note that share of the first firm in the monopoly profit is,
$$\pi_{m1} = PQ_1 - c_1 Q_1, \text{ where } Q_1 = [(a-c_1)c_2 - bc_1]/2bc_2$$
and that of the second firm is
$$\pi_{m2} = PQ_2 - c_2 Q_2^2, \text{ where } Q_2 = c_1/2c_2$$

* J. Bertrand, 'Theorie Mathematique de la Rchesse Sociale', *Journal des Savants* (Paris, 1883), pp. 499–508.

equal to its MC with the emerging price, P, being higher than $MC (P > MC)$ at the equilibrium. In Bertrand's model, simultaneous price setting by firms implies setting prices equal to the marginal costs ($P = MC$). Under homogeneity of product, no firm can survive by setting a price higher than the price set by its rival. Consumers reject a firm charging a higher price for the one charging a lower price. In consequence, the low-price firm captures the market unless the high price firm also lowers its price. If a firm sets a price higher than that set by its rival, its rival does not follow the suit, but if a firm sets a price lower than that set by its rival, the rival has to follow the suit. In a price competition such as this, each firm has to set a price equal to its marginal cost, which is same when their products are homogeneous.

To demonstrate Bertrand–Nash equilibrium for homogeneous products under costless and non-costless conditions, let us represent the cases of Illustration 11.2 (Chapter 11) in the normal forms of the oligopolistic games.

(i) **When production is costless with $MC_1 = MC_2 = 0$ [Table 12.18(a)]**

TABLE 12.18(a) From the calculations of Illustration 11.2 (Chapter 11), price set by each duopolist under costless conditions and Bertrand's pattern is zero. Total market demand is 120 units (Putting $P = 0$ in the demand function $P = 120 - Q$) of which each caters to half as much, that is, 60 units. Profit to each in consequence is zero (Top-left cell). If the firms collude to maximize joint profits, like a monopoly, the joint output is 60 units (corresponding to MR = MC = 0) price is $P_m = 60$. Each firm sells half as much of 60 at a price, $P_m = 60$, earning in the process a profit of 1800 each. However, if Firm 1 follows Bertrand's pattern while Firm 2, that of a monopoly (Chamberlin's) or if Firm 2 follows Bertrand's pattern while Firm 1, that of a monopoly (Chamberlin's), profit accruing to each in either case is zero. Profit of one that sets zero price is zero and so is it of the other if it opts to set a monopoly price. Cosumers reject the one charging a monopoly price, entitling it to a zero profit and buy from the other setting a zero price, entitling it to a zero profit due to zero price and zero cost. *The game can be said to have a Bertrand–Nash equilibrium in the top-left cell and a collusive equilibrium in the bottom-right cell.*

		Firm 2	
		$P_2 = 0$	$P_m = 60$
Firm 1	$P_1 = 0$	{0, 0}	{0, 0}
	$P_m = 60$	{0, 0}	{1800, 1800}

(ii) **When production is non-costless with $MC_1 = MC_2 = 20$ [Table 12.18(b)]**

TABLE 12.18(b) From the calculations of Illustration 11.2 (Chapter 11), price set by each duopolist under non-costless conditions and Bertrand's pattern is 20. Total market demand is 100 units (Putting $P = 20$ in the demand function $P = 120 - Q$) of which each caters to half as much, that is, 50 units. Revenue to each, in consequence, is 1000 (Top-left cell). If the firms collude to maximize joint profits, like a monopoly, the joint output is 50 units (corresponding to MR = MC = 20) and price is $P_m = 70$. Each firm sells half as much of 50 at a price, $P_m = 70$, raising in the process a revenue of 1750 each. However, if Firm 1 follows Bertrand's pattern while Firm 2, that of a monopoly (Chamberlin's) or if Firm 2 follows Bertrand's pattern while Firm 1, that of a monopoly (Chamberlin's), revenue accruing to the one following the Bertrand's pattern is 2000 because it caters to entire market demand of 100 units at a price of 20, while that accruing to the one behaving like a monopoly is zero because consumers reject its product due to higher price charged. Note the use of 'revenue' instead of 'profit' because AC is not known precisely. *The game can be said to have a Bertrand–Nash equilibrium in the top-left cell and a collusive equilibrium in the bottom-right cell.*

		Firm 2	
		$P_2 = 20$	$P_m = 70$
Firm 1	$P_1 = 20$	{1000, 1000}	{2000, 0}
	$P_m = 70$	{0, 2000}	{1750, 1750}

12.5.9 APPLICATION 12.9: Bertrand–Nash Equilibrium [Simultaneous Price Setting for Heterogeneous Products]

Although, Bertrand's model assumed homogeneity of product, some degree of heterogeneity always arises in an oligopolistic market. It may be in the external features or in features related to qualitative aspects, such as, product durability or product appeal arising from its design or positioning that the products of one firm are perceived different from those of the other. In such cases, firms compete by choosing prices rather than quantities.

To demonstrate Bertrand–Nash equilibrium for heterogeneous products, let us represent the case of Illustration 11.3 (Chapter 11) in the normal form of the oligopolistic games.

> **ILLUSTRATION 12.2:** Demand functions of firms in a duopolistic market are given as:
>
> $Q_1 = 150 - 2P_1 + P_2$ [demand faced by first firm]
> $Q_2 = 150 - 2P_2 + P_1$ [demand faced by second firm]
>
> Suppose each firm has a fixed cost of 1000 and a variable cost of zero. Q_1 and Q_2 are quantities the two firms sell respectively at prices P_1 and P_2.
> Obtain reaction curves for the two and determine their equilibrium price-outputs.

Solution: It is clear from the demand functions of the two firms that the quantity sold by each varies inversely as its own price, but directly as the competitor's price. To derive the reaction curves of the two firms, let us derive their profit functions, as in Illustration 11.3, and impose conditions of profit maximization on each.
The two can be expressed as,

$$\pi_1 = 150 P_1 - 2P_1^2 + P_1 P_2 - 1000, \text{ and}$$
$$\pi_2 = 150 P_2 - 2P_2^2 + P_1 P_2 - 1000$$

Differentiating π_1 with respect to P_1, π_2 with respect to P_2 and setting each at zero, we obtain the reaction curves as

$$P_1 = (75/2) + (1/4)P_2 \quad (12.13)$$
$$P_2 = (75/2) + (1/4)P_1 \quad (12.14)$$

Solving them simultaneously for P_1 and P_2, we have

$$P_1 = 50 \quad \text{and} \quad P_2 = 50$$

Substituting in demand functions, we get

$$Q_1 = 100 \quad \text{and} \quad Q_2 = 100$$

Making substitutions in the profit functions, we get

$$\pi_1 = 4000 \quad \text{and} \quad \pi_2 = 4000$$

Plotting the reaction curves, we can show the solution as in Figure 12.6. The normal form of the game and its equilibrium is shown in Table 12.18(c).

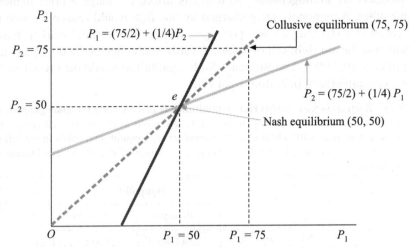

FIGURE 12.6 Bertrand–Nash equilibrium in prices: The point of intersection of the two reaction curves marks Nash equilibrium. Each firm is selling 100 units at a price of 50 each and each making a profit of 4000. Each is doing its best given the strategy of its rival. If the two firms are able to collude, they will charge the monopoly price to maximize joint profits. Under collusion, each firm can be seen to sell 75 units at a price of 75 and to earn a profit of 4625. The solution (75, 75) is the collusive solution*.

TABLE 12.18(c) Bertrand–Nash equilibrium (simultaneous price setting for heterogeneous products): The players are the two duopolists, Firm 1 and Firm 2. Their price strategies are P_i (i = 1, 2) and P_m, the joint profit maximizing price and the corresponding pay-offs are as depicted in the table. $P_1 = 50$ and $P_2 = 50$ form the dominant strategy for each leading to a dominant strategy equilibrium in top-left cell. The same, evidently, is the Bertrand–Nash equilibrium as well. If the duopolists collude and charge the monopoly price, $P_m = 75$, they both can be better off in bottom-right cell. Collusions such as this being illegal, collusive equilibrium is rare unless the two demonstrate the Chamberlin's pattern of behaviour. In absence of a formal agreement, the probability of one of the two to choose the Bertrand's price of 50 to sell 125 units for a higher pay-off of 5250 is very high. The other must better follow the suit or continue with the joint profit maximizing price of 75 to sell only 50 units and earn a lower profit of ₹ 2750 in the process. The ultimate is that the latter follows the suit of the former for a stable equilibrium in the top-left cell.

		Duopolist 2	
		$P_2 = 50$	$P_m = 75$
Duopolist 1	$P_1 = 50$	{4000, 4000}	{5250, 2750}
	$P_m = 75$	{2750, 5250}	{4625, 4625}

---

*Under collusion, the firms will behave like a monopoly charging a common price, i.e. $P_1 = P_2 = P$, and will maximize the total profits, π.

$$\pi = \pi_1 + \pi_2$$
$$= 150P_1 - 2P_1^2 + P_1P_2 - 1000 + 150P_2 - 2P_2^2 + P_1P_2 - 1000$$
$$= 150P - 2P^2 + P^2 - 1000 + 150P - 2P^2 + P^2 - 1000 \quad (\because P_1 = P_2 = P)$$
$$= 300P - 2P^2 - 2000$$

(contd.)

In case products are **homogeneous**, no firm can afford to charge a price higher than that charged by the other. A monopoly price charged by one firm would reduce its economic profit to zero. The competitor charging a lower price, gets away with the entire market share and joint profit. The entries in the top-right cell of Table 12.18(d) would then be (8000, 0) and those in the bottom-left cell of it, (0, 8000). The Bertrand–Nash equilibrium would then result in the top-left cell and collusive equilibrium, in bottom-right cell.

TABLE 12.18(d) Bertrand–Nash equilibrium (simultaneous price setting for homogeneous products): As explained above, a firm charging a monopoly price gets zero profit while the other charging a price under Bertrand's behaviour gets away with whole of it. Dominant strategy equilibrium exists in top-left cell and so does the Bertrand–Nash equilibrium. Under the cooperative conditions, the collusive equilibrium takes place in the bottom-right cell.

		Duopolist 2	
		$P_1 = 50$	$P_m = 75$
Duopolist 1	$P_1 = 50$	{4000, 4000}	{8000, 0}
	$P_m = 75$	{0, 8000}	{4625, 4625}

12.5.10 APPLICATION 12.10: Quantity Leadership [Stackelberg Model]

The model, treated as an extension of Cournot's model, as discussed in Section 11.4, was developed by the German economist Heinrich von Stackelberg. In the model, Stackelberg held that *one* duopolist is sufficiently sophisticated to assume that its rival acts on Cournot's pattern. The assumption enables the sophisticated duopolist to determine the rival's reaction curve and to incorporate it in its own profit function before maximizing it like a monopolist.

The working of the model has been detailed in Section 11.4 (Chapter 11).

If one firm is a sophisticated leader while the other, a follower, the resulting equilibrium is highly stable as the follower acts as a naïve firm.

If both the firms behave as sophisticated quantity leaders, each will attempt maximization of its own profit like a monopoly, incorporating the other's reaction curve in its profit function. The market situation, as a result, turns unstable leading to what is called **Stackelberg's disequilibrium**. This will initiate either a price war between the two, continuing until one firm surrenders and turns a follower, or, the two firms collude for a collusive equilibrium.

Stackelberg's quantity leadership model has interesting implications. One of them is the ultimate realization by the follower that its naïve behaviour fails to pay-off. As a result, the leader-follower pattern of behaviour is replaced by a high degree of interdependence between the two.

The model, however, does not apply to a market structure in which firms behave on Bertrand's assumption. A sophisticated quantity leader can do nothing to increase its profits

---

Footnote (contd.)

Differentiating the joint profit function with respect to P, we have

$d\pi/dP = 300 - 4P$

$= 0$ (for maximization of profit)

$\Rightarrow \quad P = 75$. Substituting in the demand functions, $Q_1 = Q_2 = 75$ and in the profit functions, $\pi_1 = \pi_2 = 4625$.

like a Cournot-type of firm by bluffing its naïve rival about its quantity or persuading it not to under-cut its price.

To demonstrate the game, let us recall the following results of Section 11.4, given that the linear demand, $P = a - bQ$, where, Q is the quantity demanded at price P of which Q_1 comes from first firm and Q_2, from the second so that $Q = Q_1 + Q_2$.

The reaction curves, as worked out in Section 11.4, are given as

$$Q_1 = [a - bQ_2 - MC_1]/2b \tag{12.15}$$

and
$$Q_2 = [a - bQ_1 - MC_2]/2b \tag{12.16}$$

Firm 1, being the sophisticated quantity leader, would incorporate quantity of Firm 2 [Eq. (12.16)] in its own profit function before maximizing it and calculates its profit maximizing quantity as

$$Q_1 = [(1/2)a - MC_1 + (1/2)MC_2]/b \tag{12.17}$$

Firm 2, the quantity follower, determines its quantity by substituting this value of Q_1 in its reaction curve given by Eq. 12.16. This has been worked out as

$$Q_2 = [(1/2)a + MC_1 - (3/2)MC_2]/2b \tag{12.18}$$

If the production is costless, $MC_1 = MC_2 = 0$ and the equilibrium outputs of the two as worked out in Section 11.4, can be given as

$$Q_1 = a/2b \tag{12.19}$$

and,
$$Q_2 = a/4b \tag{12.20}$$

Proceeding likewise, expressions have been worked out in Section 11.4 for the outputs of the two firms when Firm 2 acts as sophisticated quantity leader and Firm 1, as a follower.

It has also been shown that Stackelberg's model reduces to Cournot's as soon as $Q_1 = Q_2$ and $MC_1 = MC_2 = 0$ are set (here, in Eqs. 12.15 and 12.16). We observe that

$$Q_1 = a/3b \tag{12.21}$$

and
$$Q_2 = a/3b \tag{12.22}$$

Note that market size is $Q = (a/b)$ which can be determined by substituting $P = 0$ in the market demand function, $P = a - bQ$. From Eqs. (12.21) and (12.22), we observe that each of the duopolists acting on Cournot's pattern supplies 1/3rd of the market demand and from Eqs. (12.19) and (12.20), we observe that the sophisticated quantity leader supplies 1/2 of the market size while the follower, 1/4th of it.

Let us re-work Illustration 11.5 to understand Stackelberg's sophisticated quantity leadership model.

ILLUSTRATION 12.3: From the demand and cost functions of Illustration 11.1, determine the equilibrium quantities and prices under:

   (i) the quantity leadership of the first duopolist
   (ii) the quantity leadership of the second duopolist
   (iii) Stackelberg's sophisticated pattern of behaviour adopted by both

Solution:

The demand function in Illustration 11.1 was:

$$P = 100 - 0.4Q, \text{ where, } Q = Q_1 + Q_2$$

and the cost functions of the two firms were:

$$C_1 = 5Q_1, \; C_2 = 0.1Q_2^2$$

The reaction curves of the two firms simultaneously setting quantities were:

$$Q_1 = 950/8 - 1/2 Q_2 \text{ and,}$$
$$Q_2 = 100 - 0.4 \, Q_1$$

Equilibrium level of outputs were $Q_1 = 85.9$ and $Q_2 = 65.6$ while market price was 39.4. Profits to the two firms were $\pi_1 = 2955$ and $\pi_2 = 2154$

If the firms were to maximize joint profits, $Q_1 = 93.75$, $Q_2 = 25$, $P = 52.5$, $\pi_1 = 4453$ and $\pi_2 = 1250$. (See Illustration 11.5)

(i) *When first duopolist is the sophisticated quantity leader:* Duopolist 1 being the sophisticated quantity leader, he will incorporate Duopolist 2's quantity in his profit function before maximizing it like a monopolist. Thus,

$$\pi_1 = 95Q_1 - 0.4Q_1^2 - 0.4(100 - 0.4Q_1)Q_1$$
$$= 55Q_1 - 0.24Q_1^2$$

The profit maximizing quantity of the quantity leader,

$$Q_1 = \mathbf{114.6}$$

And, the corresponding quantity of the follower,

$$Q_2 = 100 - 0.4 \times 114.6$$
$$= \mathbf{54.2}$$

Price set is 32.5, by substituting for Q, which is 168.8, in the demand function. Profit earned by the leader at $Q_1 = 85.9$ and $P = 32.5$,

$$\pi_1 = 32.5 \times 114.6 - 5 \times 114.6$$
$$= \mathbf{3151} \text{ (approx.).}$$

And that earned by the follower,

$$\pi_2 = 32.5 \times 54.2 - 0.1 \times (54.2)^2$$
$$= \mathbf{1468} \text{ (approx.).}$$

(ii) *When second duopolist is the sophisticated quantity leader:* Duopolist 2 being the sophisticated quantity leader, he will incorporate duopolist 1's quantity in his profit function before maximizing it like a monopolist. Thus,

$$\pi_2 = (100 - 0.4Q)Q_2 - 0.1Q_2^2$$
$$= 52.5Q_2 - 0.3Q_2^2$$

The profit maximizing quantity of the quantity leader,

$$Q_2 = \mathbf{87.5}$$

And, the corresponding quantity of the follower,

$$Q_1 = 950/8 - 1/2(Q_2)$$
$$= 75$$

Price set is 35, by substituting for Q, which is 162.5, in the demand function.
Profit earned by the leader at $Q_2 = 87.5$ and $P = 35$,

$$\pi_2 = 35 \times 87.5 - 0.1\ (87.5)^2$$
$$= \mathbf{2297}\ \text{(approx.)}.$$

And that earned by the follower,

$$\pi_1 = 35 \times 75 - 5 \times 75$$
$$= \mathbf{2250}\ \text{(approx.)}.$$

(iii) *When both firms adopt the sophisticated behaviour: A state of Stackelberg's disequilibrium:* Each firm in this case would compare its profit earned by it as a leader with that earned by it as a follower before taking its decision.
Profits of the first firm,

As a leader = **3151**

As a follower = **2250**

Clearly, the first firm will prefer to act as a leader.
Profits of the second firm,

As a leader = **2297**

As a follower = **1468**

Clearly, the second firm too will prefer to act as a leader.
In fact, each firm benefits from its sophisticated leadership so much so that each would prefer to lead. As they proceed with their plans, they soon realize that their expectations cannot be fulfilled simultaneously. Price wars become inevitable and the game turns indeterminate unless they decide to collude for mutual gains.
To present the normal form of the game recall the situation of joint profit maximization by the two firms in Illustration 11.5 with the same demand and cost functions as in this illustration. There, the price fixed for the purpose was 52.5 and quantities sold were 93.75 units by the first firm and 25 units by the second. Profits accruing to the two were,

$$\pi_1 = P \times Q_1 - C_1$$
$$= 52.5 \times 93.75 - 5 \times 25$$
$$= \mathbf{4453}$$
$$\pi_2 = P \times Q_2 - C_2$$
$$= 52.5 \times 25 - 0.1 \times 25^2$$
$$= \mathbf{1250}$$

TABLE 12.19 When Firm 1 is the leader; Firm 2, the follower while one or both are joint profit maximizers: The strategies here are sophisticated quantity leadership by the first firm and followership by the second against pursuance of joint profit maximization. Price set under the former is 32.5, while that under the second, 52.5. When one of the two sets a higher price, that is 52.5, it incurs loss of sales and profits while the other, who sets a lower price, reaps a rich harvest by selling the entire demand of 168.8 units (Bottom-left or top-right cells). If both pursue joint profit maximization (Bottom-right cell), the first earns 4453 while the second, 1250 only. If the first firm acts as a sophisticated leader while the second, a follower; the profits to the leader and the follower are 3152 and 1468, respectively.

The dominant strategy for Firm 1 is sophisticated quantity leadership and for Firm 2, followership. The two strategies intersect in *top-left cell* yielding a dominant strategy equilibrium. The same provides Nash equilibrium as well.

		Firm 2	
		As Follower	As Joint Profit Maximizer
Firm 1	As Leader	[3151, 1468]	[4642, 0]
	As Joint Profit Maximizer	[0, 2637]	[4453, 1250]

TABLE 12.20 When Firm 2 is the leader; Firm 1, the follower while one or both are joint profit maximizers: The strategies here are sophisticated quantity leadership by the second firm and followership by the first against pursuance of joint profit maximization. Price set under the former is 35, while that under the second, 52.5. When one of the two sets a higher price, that is 52.5, it incurs loss of sales and profits while the other, who sets a lower price, reaps a rich harvest by selling the entire demand of 162.5 units (Bottom-left or top-right cells). If both pursue joint profit maximization (Bottom-right cell), the first earns 4453 while the second, 1250 only. If the second firm acts as a sophisticated leader while the first, a follower; the profits to the leader and the follower are 2297 and 2250, respectively.

The dominant strategy for Firm 2 is sophisticated quantity leadership and for Firm 1, followership. The two strategies intersect in *top-left cell* yielding a dominant strategy equilibrium. The same provides Nash equilibrium as well.

		Firm 2	
		As Leader	As Joint Profit Maximizer
Firm 1	As Follower	[2250, 2297]	[4875, 0]
	As Joint Profit Maximizer	[0, 3047]	[4453, 1250]

As is clear from Tables 12.19 and 12.20, joint profit maximization by the two is not an equilibrium position. Sophisticated behaviour, whether by Firm 1 or by Firm 2, yields a dominant strategy equilibrium and hence a Nash equilibrium as well.

If we compare the sophisticated behaviour with Cournot's reaction curve approach of simultaneous quantity setting (Illustration 11.1), the outcome of the analysis is the same as above. In other words, sophisticated behaviour again yields a dominant strategy equilibrium and hence a Nash equilibrium (Tables 12.21 and 12.22).

TABLE 12.21   When Firm 1 is the leader; Firm 2, the follower or one or both follows Cournot's pattern: The strategies here are sophisticated quantity leadership by the first firm and followership by the second against pursuance of simultaneous quantity setting under Cournot's pattern. Price set under the former is 32.5, while that under the second, 39.4. When one of the two sets a higher price, that is 39.4, it incurs loss of sales and profits while the other, who sets a lower price, reaps a rich harvest by selling the entire demand of 168.8 units (Bottom-left or top-right cells). If both pursue simultaneous quantity setting under Cournot's pattern (Bottom-right cell), the first earns 2955 while the second, 2154 only. If the first firm acts as a sophisticated leader while the second, a follower, the profits to the leader and the follower are 3152 and 1468, respectively.

The dominant strategy for Firm 1 is sophisticated quantity leadership and for Firm 2, followership. The two strategies intersect in *top-left cell* yielding a dominant strategy equilibrium. The same provides Nash equilibrium as well.

		Firm 2	
		As Follower	Under Cournot's Pattern
Firm 1	As Leader	[3151, 1468]	[4642, 0]
	Under Cournot's Pattern	[0, 2637]	[2955, 2154]

TABLE 12.22   When Firm 2 is the leader; Firm 1, the follower or one or both follows Cournot's pattern: The strategies here are sophisticated quantity leadership by the second firm and followership by the first against pursuance of simultaneous quantity setting under Cournot's pattern. Price set under the former is 35, while that under the second, 39.4. When one of the two sets a higher price, that is 39.4, it incurs loss of sales and profits while the other, who sets a lower price, reaps a rich harvest by selling the entire demand of 162.5 units (Bottom-left or top-right cells). If both pursue simultaneous quantity setting under Cournot's pattern (Bottom-right cell), the first earns 2955 while the second, 2154 only. If the second firm acts as a sophisticated leader while the first, a follower; the profits to the leader and the follower are 2297 and 2250, respectively.

The dominant strategy for Firm 2 is sophisticated quantity leadership and for Firm 1, followership. The two strategies intersect in *top-left cell* yielding a dominant strategy equilibrium. The same provides Nash equilibrium as well.

		Firm 2	
		As Leader	Under Cournot's Pattern
Firm 1	As Follower	[2250, 2297]	[4875, 0]
	Under Cournot's Pattern	[0, 3047]	[2955, 2154]

12.6   NON-ZERO-SUM MIXED STRATEGY GAMES OF INCOMPLETE/IMPERFECT INFORMATION

Mixed strategy games discussed so far are games of complete and perfect information. A game of **complete information** is one in which each player's pay-off function is common knowledge and a game of **perfect information** is one in which each information set is a singleton. Likewise, a game of **symmetric information** refers to a game in which no player has information different from what his rival has. Apart from being games of perfect, complete and symmetric information, they are the games of **certainty** as well because there existed no uncertainty about the pay-offs resulting from different strategies once a player makes a move. Cropping up of uncertainty at any stage in a game is referred to as **nature's move**. A game is said to be a **certain** game if nature does not make a move once a player does.

The games that we take up in this section are the games of incomplete, imperfect, asymmetric and uncertain information. Incompleteness of information means incompleteness of players' beliefs about the pay-off functions, while its imperfectness means existence of information sets that are **non-singleton**. The reason behind the incompleteness of players' beliefs about pay-off functions is their subjectivity requiring mechanical updating through **Bayesian Decision Rule** as in **Bayes Nash Equilibrium**. This lends some rationality, called **Bayesian Rationality** or **Bayesianism**, to the subjective beliefs or subjective estimates of probability attached to a pay-off.

To understand Bayes Nash Equilibrium and the terminologies introduced, consider Firms A and B. Let the strategies of Firm A be A_1 and A_2 and those of Firm B, B_1 and B_2. Further, let the pay-off sets (matrices) be given by Tables 12.23(a), (b) and (c) with B's estimates of pay-offs with respective probabilities 60%, 30% and 10%.

TABLE 12.23(a) Pay-offs to strategies A_1, A_2 of Firm A against strategies B_1, B_2 of Firm B are shown in the table. Evidently two Nash equilibria exist in pure strategies–*one*, in the *top-left cell* and the *other*, in the *bottom-right cell*. There exists no dominant strategy for either player. Firm B's subjective estimate of these pay-offs is 60%.

		Firm B	
		B_1	B_2
Firm A	A_1	[3, 3]	[–1, –1]
	A_2	[–1, –1]	[1, 1]

TABLE 12.23(b) Firm B's subjective estimate of these pay-offs is 30%. There is no dominant strategy for either player. The game, however, has a Nash equilibrium in pure strategies in the *bottom-right cell*.

		Firm B	
		B_1	B_2
Firm A	A_1	[6, 2]	[0, 3]
	A_2	[–1, –1]	[1, 4]

TABLE 12.23(c) Firm B's subjective estimate of these pay-offs is 10%. There is no dominant strategy for either player. The game has, however, two Nash equilibria–*one* in the *top-left cell* and the *other* in the *bottom-right cell*.

		Firm B	
		B_1	B_2
Firm A	A_1	[0, 0]	[–1, –1]
	A_2	[–1, –1]	[3, 3]

Now, suppose Firm A knows which of the pay-off sets (a), (b) and (c) actualizes, while Firm B does not. The latter, however, estimates the likelihood of pay-off set (a) to be the actual one as 60%, pay-off set (b) to be that as 30% and pay-off set (c) to be that as 10%. These estimates of the probabilities made by Firm B are of subjective nature. The game is thus one of *incomplete information* as the actual pay-off set is not of common knowledge as Firm B does not know it. It is of *asymmetric information* as Firm B does not know the actual pay-off set while its rival, Firm A, does. The game is also one of *certainty* as Nature does not make a move after the players made theirs. Also, the game is one of *imperfect information* as the pay-off set is not a singleton, at least to Firm B, which views it as any one of the three – (a), (b) and (c).

To analyse the game better, we employ **Harsanyi transformation** and remodel the game as in Figure 12.7. Nature makes the first move and chooses pay-off sets (a), (b) or (c) with probabilities of 60%, 30% and 10%. Note that these probabilities are the subjective estimates of the probabilities attached to each by Firm B. Firm A is able to observe Nature's move but Firm B is not, despite the fact that the probabilities with which Nature chooses pay-off sets (a), (b) and (c) are the same as those estimated by Firm B. Accordingly, Firm A makes a move and chooses Strategy A_1. Firm B, not sure whether Nature has chosen pay-off set (a) or (b) or (c), updates its estimates using **Bayesian Decision Rule***.

Firm A will choose A_1 when the pay-off set is either (a) or (b), but it will choose A_2 when pay-off set is (c). This is so because A_1 is unattractive for Firm A when pay-off set is (c). Firm B, before responding, will first update the probabilities of (a), (b) and (c) using Bayesian decision rule.

In the process, Firm B will rule out pay-off set (c) on the grounds of the lowest pay-off it offers to Firm A when Firm A chooses A_1, which it already has. Thus, Firm B would update the probabilities of pay-off sets (a), (b) and (c) under its belief that Firm A having chosen A_1 would never choose pay-off set (c). Using Bayesin decision rule, the updated probabilities of Firm B can be worked out as follows:

$$P[(a)/A_1] = \frac{P[(a)]\,P[A_1/(a)]}{P[(a)]\,P[A_1/(a)] + P[(b)]\,P[A_1/(b)] + P[(c)]\,P[A_1/(c)]}$$

$$= \frac{0.60 \times 1.00}{0.60 \times 1.00 + 0.30 \times 1.00 + 0.00 \times 1.00}$$

$$= 2/3\,(\approx \mathbf{0.67})$$

$$P[(b)/A_1] = \frac{P[(b)]\,P[A_1/(b)]}{P[(a)]\,P[A_1/(a)] + P[(b)]\,P[A_1/(b)] + P[(c)]\,P[A_1/(c)]}$$

$$= \frac{0.30 \times 1.00}{0.60 \times 1.00 + 0.30 \times 1.00 + 0.00 \times 1.00}$$

$$= 1/3\,(\approx \mathbf{0.33})$$

---

* Refer to Bayes Theorem, "If an event E can only occur in conjunction with one of the n mutually exclusive and exhaustive events $A_1, A_2, A_3, \ldots, A_n$ and if E actually occurs, the probability that it was preceded by a particular event A_i ($i = 1, 2, \ldots, n$) is given by

$$P(A_i/E) = \frac{P(A_i)P(E/A_i)}{\Sigma P(A_i)P(E/A_i)}$$

if $i = 1$, we have

$$P(A_1/E) = \frac{P(A_1)P(E/A_1)}{\Sigma P(A_1)P(E/A_1)}$$

$$P[(c)/A_1] = \frac{P[(c)] \, P[A_1/(c)]}{P[(a)] \, P[A_1/(a)] + P[(b)] \, P[A_1/(b)] + P[(c)] \, P[A_1/(c)]}$$

$$= \frac{0.00 \times 1.00}{0.60 \times 1.00 + 0.30 \times 1.00 + 0.00 \times 1.00}$$

$$= 0/9 \; (\approx 0.00)$$

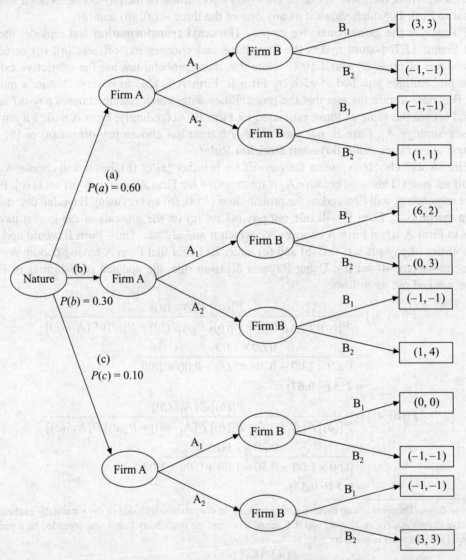

FIGURE 12.7 The three possibilities $P(a) = 0.60$, $P(b) = 0.30$, and $P(c) = 0.10$ of pay-offs as estimated subjectively by Firm B and viewed as Nature's moves through Harsanyi transformation of the game.

Given that the updated probability of pay-off set (a) is 0.67 and that of pay-off set (b) is 0.33, Firm B's best response to Firm A's choice of A_1 would be B_1 because its expected pay-off is higher than that from B_2. Firm B's expected pay-off from B_1 is 8/3 [2/3 × (3) + 1/3 × (2)] and from B_2 is 1/3 [2/3 × (–1) + 1/3 × (3)]. (Note that Firm B's best response to A_1 of Firm A, had the pay-off set actually been (b), would be B_2, not B_1, because its pay-off from B_2 is 3 which is higher than that from B_1 which is 2.) Thus, Firm B's best response to Firm A's choice of A_1 is B_1 in pay-off set (a).

But when Firm A chooses A_2, Firm B's best response is B_2. In this case, Firm B will rule out pay-off set (a) while updating its probabilities of the three pay-off sets on the grounds of lower pay-off to Firm A from it.

$$P[(a)/A_2] = \frac{P[(a)] P[A_2/(a)]}{P[(a)] P[A_2/(a)] + P[(b)] P[A_2/(b)] + P[(c)] P[A_2/(c)]}$$

$$= \frac{0.60 \times 0.00}{0.60 \times 0.00 + 0.30 \times 1.00 + 0.10 \times 1.00}$$

$$= \mathbf{0.00}$$

$$P[(b)/A_2] = \frac{P[(b)] P[A_2/(b)]}{P[(a)] P[A_2/(a)] + P[(b)] P[A_2/(b)] + P[(c)] P[A_2/(c)]}$$

$$= \frac{0.30 \times 1.00}{0.60 \times 0.00 + 0.30 \times 1.00 + 0.10 \times 1.00}$$

$$= \mathbf{3/4}$$

$$P[(c)/A_2] = \frac{P[(c)] P[A_2/(c)]}{P[(a)] P[A_2/(a)] + P[(b)] P[A_2/(b)] + P[(c)] P[A_2/(c)]}$$

$$= \frac{0.10 \times 1.00}{0.60 \times 0.00 + 0.30 \times 1.00 + 0.10 \times 1.00}$$

$$= \mathbf{1/4}$$

The reason for matching A_2 with B_2 by Firm B is its higher expected pay-off, 3.75 from B_2 than that from B_1, which is –1. **Bayesian equilibrium**, therefore, comprises [$A_1/(a)$, $A_1/(b)$, $A_2/(c)$; B_1/A_1, B_2/A_2].

In case of Firm A, its best responses are simple so long it uses non-random choices of its strategies. In case it randomizes its choices of strategies with probabilities 0.3, 0.4 and 0.3, the reader would just need to replace the probability of 1.00 [of $P(A_i/(a)$ or (b) or (c)] in calculations above by these probabilities in that order. But, that would be the case of mixed strategy Bayesian equilibrium.

12.7 ZERO-SUM GAMES

Zero-sum games, as defined earlier in the chapter, refer to games in which one player's gain is another's loss. When equilibrium position in these games is reached under pure strategies, the games are referred to as **zero-sum pure strategy games** and when this happens under mixed strategies, the games are referred to as the **zero-sum mixed strategy games**.

12.7.1 Zero-sum Pure Strategy Games—Minimax-Maximin Principles

To understand application of minimax and maximin principles to a zero-sum game, refer to Table 12.24. It represents payoffs to Firm A from its strategies A_1, A_2, A_3 and A_4 against the strategies B_1, B_2, B_3, B_4 and B_5 of Firm B, its rival. Negative entries in the table indicate Firm A's loss or Firm B's gain while positive ones indicate Firm A's gain or Firm B's loss. For instance, entry in first row (A_1) and first column (B_1), 2, implies Firm A's gain of 2 from its strategy A_1 against its rival's strategy B_1. The same for Firm B implies its loss from its strategy B_1 against its rival's strategy A_1. In general, entry at the intersection of row A_i and column B_j, written as (A_i, B_j), indicates Firm A's gain from its strategy A_i against its rival's strategy B_j. Likewise, (B_j, A_i) indicates Firm B's loss from its strategy B_j against its rival's strategy A_i. A row minimum indicates Firm A's least payoff from its corresponding strategy no matter which strategy Firm B adopts. Likewise, a column maximum indicates highest loss to Firm B from its corresponding strategy no matter which strategy Firm A adopts. Under the maximin principle, Firm A chooses the maximum value from amongst these row minima. In the table, the row minima are -1, -1, 5, and -3 corresponding to the strategies A_1, A_2, A_3 and A_4 respectively. The highest (maximum) of them is 5, corresponding to strategy A_3. This is **maximin**, implying maximum of the minimum values. Firm A will adopt strategy A_3 which ensures the highest of the lowest possible payoffs. Likewise, under the minimax principle, Firm B chooses the minimum value from amongst the column maxima. In the table, the column maxima are 15, 10, 5, 13 and 11 corresponding to the strategies B_1, B_2, B_3, B_4 and B_5 of Firm B, respectively. The lowest of them is 5. This is **minimax**, implying minimum of the maximum values. Firm B will adopt strategy B_3, which ensures the lowest of the highest possible losses to it. If Firm A's maximin is the same as Firm B's minimax, the corresponding entry is called the **saddle point** of the game. In our case here the saddle point is entry at (A_3, B_3), i.e., 5. The saddle point indicates the **value of the game**, that is, the gain or loss involved in the game. Value of the game is 5 here.

TABLE 12.24 Maximin-minimax equilibrium of a zero-sum game: Firm A's maximin is the same as Firm B's minimax. Strategy-mix (A_3, B_3) is thus the *saddle point* and the corresponding intersectional entry in the table, i.e., **5** is the *value of the game*.

		Firm B					
		B_1	B_2	B_3	B_4	B_5	Row minimum
	A_1	2	-1	3	5	6	-1
	A_2	-1	7	1	3	11	-1
Firm A	A_3	15	7	5	13	11	5 (Maximin)
	A_4	0	10	-3	1	0	-3
Column maximum		15	10	5 (Minimax)	13	11	Maximin = 5 = Minimax (Saddle Point)

12.7.2 Zero-sum Pure Strategy Games—Dominant Strategy Principle

Dominant strategy of a player is one that offers the player pay-offs higher than those offered by an alternative strategy no matter what strategies the opponent plays. A strategy offering lower pay-offs than the dominant strategy is accordingly called a **dominated strategy**. In the game of Table 12.25, strategy A_1 of Firm A dominates over its strategy A_3 in pay-offs no matter which strategy its rival, Firm B, adopts. Between the two, strategy A_1 of Firm A is a dominant strategy, while strategy A_3, a dominated strategy. In the same way, strategy B_2 of Firm B dominates over its strategy B_4 in sacrifices (losses) no matter which strategy Firm A plays. Sacrifices made by Firm B under strategy B_2 are of lower magnitude than those made under B_4. Accordingly, strategy B_2 is a dominant strategy for Firm B while strategy B_4, a dominated one.

In other words, a row in the table having every element more than or equal to the corresponding elements in another row represents the *dominant row* and the latter, the *dominated one*. In the same way, a column in the table having every element less than or equal to the corresponding elements in another column represents the *dominant column* and the latter, the *dominated one*. Clearly, the dominated row/column can be deleted from the pay-off matrix for obvious reasons.

TABLE 12.25 The table demonstrates the principle of dominance: Strategies A_1 and B_2 are the dominant strategies for Firms A and B, respectively over their respective strategies, A_3 and B_4, the dominated ones (shaded).

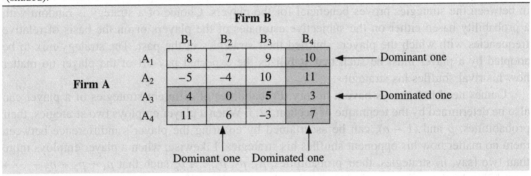

TABLE 12.26 **The reduced matrix:** A matrix obtained after deleting the dominated rows and columns is a *reduced matrix*. In the present case, it is not possible to reduce the matrix further in absence of the dominated rows and columns.

		Firm B		
		B_1	B_2	B_3
Firm A	A_1	8	7	9
	A_2	-5	-4	10
	A_4	11	6	-3

Deleting the dominated row and the dominated column from the matrix, the pay-off matrix that results is called the **reduced matrix**. It has rows A_1, A_2, and A_4 and columns B_1, B_2 and B_3 (Table 12.26). Investigating further for dominated rows and columns, we observe that no more such rows and columns exist. The principle of dominance can therefore be no longer applied now to reduce it further. We can however find the saddle-point through the minimax principle. The row minima for rows 1, 2 and 3 are 7, – 5 and – 3 respectively. Maximum of these minima is 7 (maximin). The column maxima for columns 1, 2 and 3 are 11, 7 and 10 respectively. The minimum of these maxima is 7(minimax). Thus, Maximin = Minimax = 7. Entry at (A_1, B_2), i.e., 7 is the saddle point as well as the value of the game (Table 12.27).

TABLE 12.27 Existence of saddle point under minimax-maximin principle: Saddle point = (A_1, B_2), i.e., 7 is the confluence of A_1 and B_2. It provides the solution of the game, the value of which is 7.

		Firm B			
		B_1	B_2	B_3	Row Minimum
	A_1	8	7	9	7
Firm A	A_2	−5	−4	10	−5
	A_3	11	6	−3	−3
Column Maximum		11	7	10	
			Minimax		

12.7.3 Zero-sum Mixed Strategy Games

Zero-sum games with no saddle point possess no solution in pure strategies. In such cases, shuffling in between the strategies proves beneficial for the players. Choice of a strategy is random with a probability based either on the subjective estimates of the players or on the basis of relative frequencies with which the players shuffled their strategies in the past. The strategy-mix to be adopted by a player must be such that stabilizes the expected pay-off of the player no matter how his rival shuffles his strategies.

Games need not always have a history. Probabilities of different strategies of a player can also be determined by the technique of Section 12.3. When a player employs two strategies, their probabilities, p and $(1 - p)$, can be ascertained by ensuring the player's indifference between them no matter how his opponent shuffles his strategies. Likewise, when a player employs more than two (say, n) strategies, their probabilities, $p_1, p_2, p_3, \ldots, p_n$ such that $p_1 + p_2 + p_3 + \cdots + p_n = 1$, can be determined again by ensuring the player's indifference between the strategies no matter how his opponents shuffles his strategies.

To demonstrate, suppose there are two players, namely, Firm A and Firm B. Suppose further that player A employs strategies A_1 and A_2 with probabilities p and $(1 - p)$, while player B employs strategies B_1 and B_2 with probabilities q and $(1 - q)$. Firm A turns indifferent between its strategies A_1 and A_2 when its expected pay-off from each is the same no matter how Firm B shuffles its strategies. Consider pay-off matrix of Table 12.28.

TABLE 12.28 Zero-sum mixed strategy game: The matrix shows pay-offs to Firm A or losses to Firm B. The strategies A_1, A_2, B_1 and B_2 are employed by the firms with probabilities p, $1 - p$, q and $1 - q$, respectively.

		Firm B	
		$B_1(q)$	$B_2(1 - q)$
Firm A	$A_1(p)$	a_{11}	a_{12}
	$A_2(1 - p)$	a_{21}	a_{22}

For the pay-off matrix of Table 12.28.

Firm A's expected pay-off from $A_1 = a_{11} \times q + a_{12} \times (1 - q)$

Firm A's expected pay-off from $A_2 = a_{21} \times q + a_{22} \times (1-q)$

Firm A will be indifferent between A_1 and A_2 when

$$a_{11} \times q + a_{12} \times (1-q) = a_{21} \times q + a_{22} \times (1-q)$$

$\Rightarrow \quad q[(a_{11} + a_{22}) - (a_{12} + a_{21})] = a_{22} - a_{12}$

$\Rightarrow \quad q = \dfrac{a_{22} - a_{12}}{(a_{11} + a_{22}) - (a_{12} + a_{21})}$ \hfill (12.23)

Likewise, Firm B turns indifferent between its strategies B_1 and B_2 when its expected pay-off from each is the same no matter how Firm A shuffles its strategies. For the pay-off matrix of Table 12.28,

Firm B's expected pay-off from $B_1 = a_{11} \times p + a_{21} \times (1-p)$

Firm B's expected pay-off from $B_2 = a_{12} \times p + a_{22} \times (1-p)$

Hence,

$$a_{11} \times p + a_{21} \times (1-p) = a_{12} \times p + a_{22} \times (1-p)$$

$\Rightarrow \quad p[(a_{11} + a_{22}) - (a_{12} + a_{21})] = a_{22} - a_{21}$

$\Rightarrow \quad p = \dfrac{a_{22} - a_{21}}{(a_{11} + a_{22}) - (a_{12} + a_{21})}$ \hfill (12.24)

Alternatively, expressing the total expected pay-offs of Firm A as

$$E(p, q) = a_{11} \times pq + a_{21} \times (1-p)q + a_{12} \times p(1-q) + a_{22} \times (1-p)(1-q)$$

and differentiating it partially with respect to p, we have

$$\partial E/\partial p = a_{11} \times q - a_{21} \times q + a_{12} \times (1-q) - a_{22} \times (1-q)$$
$$= [(a_{11} + a_{22}) - (a_{21} + a_{12})q - (a_{22} - a_{12})]$$

Setting it equal to zero for maximization, we have

$\Rightarrow \quad q = \dfrac{a_{22} - a_{12}}{(a_{11} + a_{22}) - (a_{21} + a_{12})}$ \hfill (12.25)

Now, differentiating it partially with respect to q, we have

$$\partial E/\partial q = a_{11} \times p + a_{21} \times (1-p) - a_{12} \times p - a_{22} \times (1-p)$$
$$= [(a_{11} + a_{22}) - (a_{21} + a_{12})]p - (a_{22} - a_{21})]$$

Setting it equal to zero for maximization, we have

$\Rightarrow \quad p = \dfrac{a_{22} - a_{21}}{(a_{11} + a_{22}) - (a_{21} + a_{12})}$ \hfill (12.26)

Note that expressions for p and q in Eqs. (12.23) and (12.24) are same as those in Eqs. (12.25) and (12.26). Substituting for p and q in the expression for $E(p, q)$, we have the value of the game. Note further that same values of p and q would be obtained if we process total expected profit of Firm B instead of Firm A.

ILLUSTRATION 12.4: Investigate the game below for the equilibrium solution and the value of the game.

		Firm B	
		B_1	B_2
Firm A	A_1	25	10
	A_2	5	15

Solution: Suppose Firm A resorts to its strategies A_1 and A_2 with probabilities p and $1 - p$ while Firm B resorts to its strategies B_1 and B_2 with probabilities q and $1 - q$. Firm A would turn indifferent between A_1 and A_2 when its expected pay-off from each is the same no matter how Firm B shuffles its strategies. That is,

$$25q + 10(1 - q) = 5q + 15(1 - q)$$
$$\Rightarrow \qquad 25q = 5$$
$$\Rightarrow \qquad \mathbf{q = 1/5,\ 1 - q = 4/5}$$

Likewise, Firm B would turn indifferent between B_1 and B_2 when its expected pay-off from each is the same. No matter how Firm A shuffles its strategies. That is,

$$25p + 5(1 - p) = 10p + 15(1 - p)$$
$$\Rightarrow \qquad 25p = 10$$
$$\Rightarrow \qquad \mathbf{p = 2/5,\ 1 - p = 3/5}.$$

Total expected pay-off of Firm A,

$$E(p, q) = 25pq + 10p(1 - q) + 5(1 - p)q + 15(1 - p)(1 - q) \qquad (12.27)$$

With $p = 2/5$ and $q = 1/5$,

$$E(2/5, 1/5) = 25(2/5)(1/5) + 10(2/5)(4/5) + 5(3/5)(1/5) + 15(3/5)(4/5)$$
$$= 325/25$$
$$= 13.$$

Firm A's expected gain is Firm B's expected loss in a zero-sum game. The value of the game is thus, **13**. The same results are obtained when Eq. (12.27) is differentiated partially with respect to p and q. That is,

$$\partial E/\partial p = 25q + 10(1 - q) - 5q - 15(1 - q)$$
$$= 25q - 5$$
$$= 0 \qquad \qquad \text{(For maximization)}$$

$$\Rightarrow \qquad q = 1/5, \text{ and}$$

$$\partial E/\partial q = 25p - 10p + 5(1-p) - 15(1-p)$$

$$= 25p - 10$$

$$= 0 \qquad \text{(For maximization)}$$

$$\Rightarrow \qquad p = 2/5$$

The reader can make use of formulae in Eqs. (12.23) and (12.24) for determining the values of p and q directly. Zero-sum mixed strategy games can also be solved graphically as well as by linear programming methods.

KEY TERMS AND CONCEPTS

Bayesianism or Bayesian rationality Estimates of probabilities of payoffs through Bayes Theorem to eliminate their subjectivity or to lend rationality to such estimates is called Bayesianism or Bayesian rationality.

Cooperative and Non-cooperative games A *cooperative game* is one in which the players cooperate with each other to pursue the common goals. As against this, a *non-cooperative game* is one in which they compete with each other. For example, if the two prisoners cooperate and decide not to confess, both get acquitted and the game is a cooperative one, but if they compete with each other to be the first to confess, each with the objective of milder punishment, the game is a non-cooperative one.

Dominant strategy equilibrium and Nash equilibrium The *dominant strategy equilibrium* takes place when each player has a dominant strategy. It occurs at the intersection of the dominant strategies of the two. It is highly stable as no player has an incentive to deviate from it. On the other hand, a *Nash equilibrium* refers to that equilibrium in which a player does the best he can given what his opponent has done. Every dominant strategy equilibrium leads to a Nash equilibrium, but every Nash equilibrium does not lead to a dominant strategy equilibrium.

Game of certainty: A game in which nature does not make a move once a player does is a game of certainty.

Game of complete information When each player's pay-off function is common knowledge, the game is one of complete information.

Game of perfect information When each information set is singleton, the game is one of perfect information.

Game of symmetric information When no player has information different from what its rival has, the game is one of symmetric information.

Game theory A theory that deals with decision-making process when two or more rational opponents match their strategies under conditions of competition or conflict, each striving to steal a march over its rival to serve its interest. It involves anticipation of the competitor's moves by each and formulation of its own that would counter them best and would help it to maximize its gain or minimize its loss.

Limit pricing Also known as *entry limiting pricing*, refers to that pricing policy of a monopoly/oligopoly firm in which it sets a price below the profit maximizing level so as to keep entry of new firms restricted / limited. Abnormal profits under profit maximizing price attract entry of new firms which affects the market share of the existing ones. A price set by the existing firms below the profit maximizing level falls below the average production cost of the new entrants. This forces them to exit due to losses.

Nature's move Cropping up of uncertainty at any stage is a game is known as nature's move.

Non-zero-sum game When gain to one does not imply loss to others, the game is referred to as the *non-zero-sum game*. In a non-zero-sum game both or all the players may gain or lose simultaneously as the total to be gained or lost is not fixed. For example, gains to the oligopolistic firms could be simultaneous in consequence to the moves initiated by them.

Pay-off matrix A tabular representation of outcomes of respective strategies of the players in terms of gains or losses to them is known as the *pay-off matrix*. For example, a tabular representation of profits earned by oligopolistic firms in response to their strategies of 'price increase' or 'no price increase' is a pay-off matrix (Table 12.4).

Repeated and non-repeated games A game like that of the prisoner's dilemma is a one-time game or a *non-repeated game*. It is played only once, that is, the players do not get a second go at it. As against this, most of the oligopolistic games that are played repeatedly time and again are called the *repeated games*. The players get back to play them repeatedly, and thus, get opportunities to improvise.

Saddle point The pay-off corresponding to the strategy-mix of the players, for which maximin of one is equal to the minimax of the other, is called the *saddle point* of the game. As the name suggests, it is this point that signifies the stability of the equilibrium of the game.

Sequential games In a *sequential game*, the pay-offs to the players depend on the sequence in which they play their strategies. For example, a player who takes the lead in moving to the market first by introducing a new product stands to gain while the other who follows stands to lose. To avoid loss, the follower must refrain from introduction of the new product.

Strategy A *strategy* is a course of action taken by one of the participants in a game.

Dominant and dominated strategies A strategy of a player which is superior in pay-offs to its other strategy/strategies, no matter what strategy its opponent plays, is called a *dominant strategy* while the other strategy/strategies disposed off as inferior to it is/are termed as *dominated strategy/strategies*. For instance, if the strategy of 'no price change' produces higher profits to a player than what the strategy of 'price increase' does, no matter what strategy its opponent plays, it is a dominant strategy while the strategy of 'price increase' is a dominated one.

Maximin and minimax principles A *maximin principle* refers to the maximum of the minimum possible gains resulting to a player from all the strategies at its disposal. The maximin strategy is employed only by the maximizing player. On the contrary, a *minimax principle* refers to the minimum of the maximum possible losses resulting from all the strategies available to it. The minimax principle is employed only by the loss minimizing player.

Pure strategies and mixed strategies When a player resorts to the same strategy each time it makes a move, it is said to be resorting to a *pure strategy*. For example, when an oligopolistic firm resorts to 'price increase' each time it makes a move, it is said to be resorting to pure strategy. On the contrary, when a firm uses a combination of strategies so that the opponents are kept guessing as to which strategy would the firm in question adopt on a particular occasion, the strategy is termed as a *mixed strategy*. For instance, if a firm resorts to the strategy of 'price increase' or 'no price increase' at random, the strategy would be a mixed strategy.

Two-person and *n*-person games When there are only two players, it is a two-person game and when there are more than two of them, it is an *n*-person game.

Zero-sum games When gain of one is the loss of the other in a game involving two players or gains of some are the losses of the others in a game involving many players, the game is called a *zero-sum game*. In a zero-sum game, the total gain is fixed so that the gain of one is the loss of the other, for example, number of votes gained by one contestant in an election represent those lost by other contestants, size of electorate being fixed.

EXERCISES

A. Short Answer Questions

Define the following (1 through 20):
1. Game theory
2. Zero-sum games
3. Non-zero sum games
4. Pure strategy
5. Mixed strategy
6. Dominant strategy
7. Cooperatives games
8. Non-cooperative games
9. Dominant strategy equilibrium
10. Nash equilibrium
11. Pay-off matrix
12. Minimax principle
13. Maximin principle
14. Saddle point
15. Repeated game
16. Non-repeated game
17. Sequential games
18. Limit pricing
19. Stigler's Open Oligopoly Model
20. Dominated strategy

B. Long Answer Questions

Distinguish between (21 through 27):
21. Zero-sum and non-zero sum games
22. Pure and mixed strategies
23. Dominant and dominated strategies
24. Cooperative and non-cooperative games
25. Dominant strategy equilibrium and Nash equilibrium
26. Maximin and minimax principles
27. Repeated and non-repeated games
28. Show that at least one Nash equilibrium exists under mixed strategies.
29. With the help of a neat sketch, explain the concept of limit pricing.
30. Explain the working of the Stigler's oligopoly model.
31. Show that the existence of the dominant strategy equilibrium implies existence of a Nash equilibrium, but existence of a Nash equilibrium does not imply the existence of a dominant strategy equilibrium.
32. Show that the zero-sum games without a saddle point can be solved with the help of mixed strategies.
33. How can the prisoner's dilemma model be used to explain a price war between duopolists? Explain.

34. Would a firm which plans to shut down in two years from now be more likely to favour limit pricing or an open oligopoly model? Explain.

C. Essay Type Questions

35. Two firms produce a homogeneous product for which variable costs are zero.
    The market demand for the product is given as:

    $$P = 1200 - 4Q,$$

    where, $Q = Q_1 + Q_2$,
    Q_1 = the output of the first duopolist
    Q_2 = the second duopolist

    Determine the Nash equilibrium output and price

    [**Ans.** Each will produce 100 units and sell them at a price of 400.]

36. Two firms can either reduce their prices or keep them at the present level. If firm A cuts the price, it will earn a profit of ₹ 20 million if firm B also cuts the price and that of ₹ 40 million if firm B does not change the price. If firm A makes no change in price, it will earn ₹ 0 million if firm B reduces price and ₹ 10 million if firm B makes no change in price. The outcomes for firm B are the same as those for the firm A (For outcomes of B, read the question again after substituting B for A and A for B).
    (a) Develop a pay-off matrix
    (b) Does the game possess a Nash equilibrium?
    (c) Does either firm have a dominant strategy? Explain.
    (d) Does a dominant strategy equilibrium exist? If yes, find it out.
    (e) Does an equilibrium in mixed strategies also exists? If yes, find it out.

    [**Ans.** (a)

		Firm B	
		Cuts the price	Does not cut the price
Firm A	Cuts the price	{20, 20}	{40, 0}
	Does not cut the price	{0, 40}	{10, 10}

    (b) Yes, when both cut price, (c) Yes, it is price cut for both, (d) dominant strategy equilibrium also exists, it is the same as the Nash equilibrium, (e) Yes, find it out yourself]

37. Two firms of the same product must independently decide whether to install a new machine. The pay-off matrix is shown here:

		Firm 2	
		New machine	No new machine
Firm 1	New machine	{10, 10}	{0, 20}
	No new machine	{20, 0}	{5, 5}

    (a) If they both use maximin decision criterion, what will be the outcome?
    (b) Does any firm possess any dominant strategy? Explain.
    (c) Does a dominant strategy equilibrium exist? if yes, determine it.
    (d) Does a Nash equilibrium also exist? If yes, determine it.
    (e) Does an equilibrium in mixed strategies exist? If yes, determine it.

    [**Ans.** (a) The bottom right cell; (b) Yes, no new machine for both; (c) Yes, bottom right cell; (d) Yes, the same as in (c); (e) No, none.

38. If the pay-off matrix in question 37 be replaced by the following pay-off matrix, how will your answers to questions (a) to (e) change?

Firm 2

	New machine	No new machine
Firm 1 New machine	{8, 8}	{6, 12}
No new machine	{12, 6}	{4, 4}

39. What is a tit-for-tat strategy? Why is it a rational strategy for infinitely repeated prisoner's dilemma?
40. Two competing firms are each contemplating to introduce a new product. Each will decide whether to produce product A or product B or product C. They have to make their choices at the same time. The resulting pay-offs are as shown as below:

Firm 2

		A	B	C
	A	{−20, −20}	{0, 20}	{20, 40}
Firm 1	B	{20, 0}	{−40, −40}	{−10, 30}
	C	{40, 20}	{30, −10}	{−60, −60}

Are there any Nash equilibria in pure strategies? If so, what are they? If both firms employ maximin strategies, what outcome will result? If firm 1 uses maximin strategy and firm 2 knows this, what will firm 2 do?

[**Ans.** (a) Yes, there are two of them, first: (C, A) and second: (A, C). If both firms choose according to maximin, Firm 1 will choose A and firm 2 will choose A, each with a pay-off of −20. (c) Firm 2 will choose C in order to maximize pay-off at (20, 40).]

41. Using the dominance criterion solve the game in the table below giving the pay-offs for player A:

Player B

		I	II	III	IV	V
	I	4	8	6	16	8
Player A	II	10	12	6	14	16
	III	12	14	18	16	14
	IV	8	4	16	8	6

[**Ans.** Optimal strategy for A = **III**, Optimal strategy for B = **I**; Value of the game = **12**.]

42. Using the dominance criterion, solve game in the table below giving the pay-offs for player A:

Player B

		I	II	III	IV
	I	70	70	50	10
Player A	II	60	40	30	0
	III	80	100	0	20
	IV	110	120	20	30

[**Ans.** Player A plays strategy I with probability of 0.20 and strategy IV with probability of 0.80 while player B plays strategy III with probability of 0.40 and strategy IV with a probability of 0.60. Expected gain to A = 13 and expected loss to B = 13.]

43. A monopoly firm faces the market demand:
$$P = 360 - 5.5Q$$
The cost function of the firm is given as:
$$TC = 328 + 200Q - 9Q^2 + (1/4)Q^3$$

Determine the profit maximizing output and price. Also estimate the abnormal profits accruing to the firm. Assuming that abnormal profits attract new firms, what must be the level of average cost of a new entrant so that it can just break-even? What is the level of its output at this point? Given that AC falls with expansion of output, what price must the existing monopoly set to limit entry of new firms or to force an exit on the one just entered?

What is the present value of the profit stream of the existing monopoly assuming existence of no competitors over

(a) coming three years
(b) infinitely many years

given that the rate of interest remains unchanged at
(i) 10%
(ii) 20%.

Now assume that entry of new firms continues and the existing monopoly is compelled to undercut the price (profit-maximizing price) by ₹ 10 per unit of output in each of the coming three years, What would be the present value of its profit streams assuming the same discount rates of (i) 10% and (ii) 20%? Would the monopoly be better off in the coming three years by undercutting price by ₹ 10 per unit each year successively? Explain.

[**Ans.** Profit is maximized at an output of 20 and profit-maximizing price is ₹ 250 per unit. This can be verified by maximizing the profit function

$$\pi = TR - TC$$
$$= 360Q - 5.5Q^2 - 328 - 200Q + 9Q^2 - (1/4)Q^3$$
$$= -328 + 160Q + 3.5Q^2 - (1/4)Q^3$$

Differentiating, we have
$$d\pi/dQ = 160 + 7Q - 3/4 Q^2$$

Setting the first order derivative at zero, the profit maximizing output, Q, is 20. Substituting it in the demand function, price, P is 250 and in the profit function, profit, π is 2272. For the new entrant to break-even, its AC must be at most at the level of price. Equating the expression of AC to 250, we observe that the new entrant must produce 4 units.

If the monopoly firm decides to bar the entry or force an exit on the firm just entered, it will have to undercut price below the profit maximizing level. Such price would be the entry limiting price and would be given by setting the firm's MR at zero. MR is $360 - 11Q$.

Equating it to zero, $Q = 360/11$ and entry limiting price, P_L, is 180. This will discourage new entrants or force exit on the just entered firm operating at AC = 250. The present value of the monopoly profit stream assuming no competitors

(a) (i) over the next 3 years when discounting rate is 10%

It is $(2272/1.1) + (2272/1.21) + (2272/1.331) = 5650.11$, and

(a) (ii) over the next 3 years when discounting rate is 20%

It is $(2272/1.2) + (2272/1.44) + (2272/1.728) = 4785.93$.

The present value of the monopoly profit stream assuming no competitors

(b) (i) over infinitely many years when discounting rate is 10%

It is $(2272/0.10) = 22,720$, and

(b) (ii) over infinitely many years when discounting rate is 20%
It is (2272/0.20) = 11,360

In the event the monopoly undercuts price by ₹ 10 per unit per year successively to restrict entry of new firms, price, output and profit in each of the three years may be given as below:

Year	Price	Output	Profit
1	240	240/11	2231.3
2	230	260/11	2103.0
3	220	280/11	1893.1

Present Value (PV) at 10% = 2231.3/1.1 + 2103/ 1.21 + 1893.1/ 1.331 = 5188.8
Present Value (PV) at 20% = 2231.3/1.2 + 2103/ 1.44 + 1893.1/ 1.728 = 4415.3

Clearly, entry limiting pricing generates lower profits than profit maximizing pricing at both the rates.]

44. Given the market demand as $P = 100 - Q$, the cost functions of the two firms as $C_1 = 4Q_1$ and $C_2 = 4Q_2$; determine the reaction curves and the Cournot's equilibrium. Present Cournot–Nash equilibrium in its normal form.

[**Ans.** Reaction curves: (1) $Q_1 = 48 - 1/2\ Q_2$, (2) $Q_2 = 48 - 1/2\ Q_1$; Cournot's equilibrium: $Q_1 = Q_2 = 32$, $P = 36$. Normal form of Cournot's equilibrium:

		Firm 2	
		In Cournot's Pattern	In Joint Profit Maximization
Firm 1	In Cournot's Pattern	{1024, 1024}	{2048, 0}
	In Joint Profit Maximization	{0, 2048}	{1152, 1152}

45. Given the market demand as $P = 100 - Q$, the cost functions of the two firms as $C_1 = 4Q_1$ and $C_2 = 1/2 Q_2^2$; determine the reaction curves and the Cournot's equilibrium. Present Cournot–Nash equilibrium in its normal form.

[**Ans.** Reaction curves: (1) $Q_1 = 48 - 1/2\ Q_2$, (2) $Q_2 = 32 - 1/2 Q_1$; Cournot's equilibrium: $Q_1 = 38.4$, $Q_2 = 19.2$, $P = 42.4$.
Normal form of Cournot's equilibrium:

		Firm 2	
		In Cournot's Pattern	In Joint Profit Maximization
Firm 1	In Cournot's Pattern	{1474.6, 629.8}	{2212, 0}
	In Joint Profit Maximization	{0, 783.6}	{2112, 200}

Note that a dominant strategy equilibrium also exists. It is Cournot's Pattern of behaviour for both.]

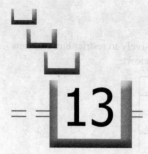

13

Sales Maximization

CHAPTER OUTLINE
Introduction
- Baumol's Static Models
- Baumol's Dynamic Model
- Key Terms and Concepts
- Exercises

INTRODUCTION

W.J. Baumol** presented two models to emphasizes his point that a modern firm pursues sales maximization as a more plausible goal than the traditional one of profit maximization. The deviation of a modern firm from its traditional goal arises due to separation of its ownership from its management. Among the reasons for pursuance of sales revenue maximization by a modern firm with a satisfactory level of profit, the following ones figure prominently:

1. Salaries and perks of the top management are correlated more closely with sales than profits.
2. Bankers and financial institutions treat sales-volume as a yardstick of a firm's performance while financing its business activities.
3. Labour unions' demand for better perks and working conditions can be tackled more satisfactorily when sales are growing than when they are declining.
4. Large sales with steadily high growth lend prestige to the management while large profits go into the pockets of the shareholders only.

---

* Baumol, W.J., *Business Behavior, Value and Growth,* Macmillan, New York, 1959. Revised ed. Harcourt, Bruce & World, Inc. 1967.

5. Growing sales lead a firm to scale economies and hence enhance its competitiveness. This helps the firm in meeting its social responsibility of providing quality goods at reasonable prices on one hand and boosting its market share on the other.
6. Large and steadily growing sales empower management to adopt a competitive tactics while low and declining sales obstruct it.

A modern firm, therefore, prefers growing sales with reasonable profits to spectacular profits.

Apart from this transformation in the behaviour of a firm, separation of its ownership from its management has led to several other transformations in its attitudes. A modern firm now desires stability with growth and believes that its decisions, unless of radical nature (calling forth major changes), would produce no changes in its rivals' behaviour. Expansion of its activities and size makes it more and more introvert due to the complexity of internal organization and decision-making process. The latter, for instance, involves passing through several stages before finalization by the top management and is therefore too lengthy to attract competitors' reactions before a considerable length of time. Moreover, large sized firms work to a blueprint comprising a variety of rules of thumb to simplify the complexities of product pricing, budgeting advertising expenditures, inventory control and the like. Product pricing follows a set practice of applying a mark-up to costs, advertising expenditures and inventory levels are usually a predetermined proportion of total revenue or sales. Such decisions do not need to take rivals' actions into account.

Despite these transformations of attitudes of the oligopolistic firms and their desire for a quiet life necessitating tacit collusion and orderly behaviour, the firms feel concerned about rivals' reactions to radical policy changes that influence their market shares. It is on this count that Baumol concedes existence of interdependence among firms as the main feature of the oligopolistic markets.

The two types of models, Baumol presented to establish his argument are:

  (i) Static model
  (ii) Dynamic model

Static model has four versions:

  (a) A single product model, without advertising
  (b) A single product model, with advertising
  (c) A multiproduct model, without advertising
  (d) A multiproduct model, with advertising

Dynamic model too may have as many versions, but here we discuss it only in the first version. Let us first study Baumol's static models.

13.1 BAUMOL'S STATIC MODELS

Let us first list the assumptions of these models:
  (a) The time horizon of the firm is a single period.
  (b) The firm attempts maximization of sales revenue with a profit constraint during this period.

(c) The profit constraint is exogenously determined keeping in view shareholders' expectations.
(d) It is assumed that the cost and revenue curves are conventional, that is, the cost curves are U-shaped and the demand curve is downward-sloping.

13.1.1 Model 1: Static Single Product Model without Advertising

Figure 13.1 demonstrates the working of this model. TR-curve shows behaviour of sales revenue with output and the inverted 'S' shaped TC-curve, that of total cost of production.

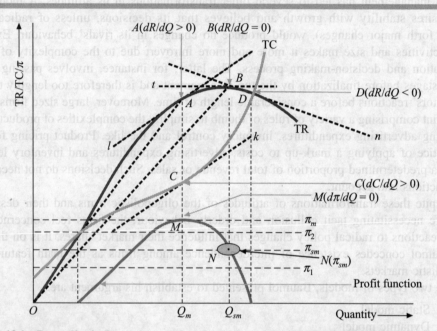

FIGURE 13.1 Baumol's single product model of sales maximization without advertising: Sales revenue is maximized at Q_{sm}, the level at which $dR/dQ = 0$ (point B on TR) but profit is maximized at Q_m, the level of output at which $d\pi/dQ = 0$ (point A on TR). Maximum profit is π_m, and profit at sales revenue maximizing level is π_{sm}. If the minimum acceptable profit to the shareholders is π_1 ($\pi_1 < \pi_{sm}$), the profit constraint proves in-operative as management is already ensuring them a higher level of it (π_{sm}) at the level of sales maximization. But if the minimum acceptable profit to the shareholders is π_2 ($\pi_2 > \pi_{sm}$), the management cannot ensure them this without giving up its objective of sales maximization. Thus, π_2 is an operative constraint because it lies above π_{sm}. If shareholders stick to profit maximization, sales cannot be maximized. Output in this case is Q_m and profit earned is π_m. The sales maximizing output is thus Q_{sm}, which allows a profit of π_{sm} to the shareholders.

Implications of Baumol's static single-product model

The following are the implications of Baumol's sales maximization model (without advertising):

1. A sales maximizer will never choose a level of output at which price elasticity is different from unity

For a sales maximizer, price elasticity of demand has to be unitary. Sales maximization implies maximization of total revenue, which requires as the first order condition and

$$dR/dQ = 0$$

$$d^2R/dQ^2 < 0$$

as the second order condition.
The first order condition, in simple language, means

$$MR = 0$$

$$\Rightarrow AR[1 - (1/|e|)] = 0$$

$$\Rightarrow |e| = 1$$

The second order condition ensures negative slope of the MR curve.

2. A sales maximizer sells a larger quantity at a lower price than what a profit maximizer does

A profit maximizer produces Q_m and sells it at a price higher than that charged by a sales maximizer. Figure 13.1 supports the statement. To show the same by calculus, we need to set the derivatives of profit and sales revenue functions with respect to Q each at zero so that

$$d\pi/dQ = 0$$

and

$$d(TR)/dQ = 0$$

The former implies equality of MR to MC (equality of slope of TR to the slope of TC, that is, $l \parallel k$). This corresponds to points A on TR and C on TC. The level of output is Q_m. Second order derivative of π must be negative implying slope of MR to be less than that of MC.

The latter implies zero slope of TR, which corresponds to point B on it. The level of output is Q_{sm} ($Q_{sm} > Q_m$).

TR is an increasing function of Q to the left of point B (at point A, for instance) and a decreasing function of it to its right (at point D, for instance). It is thus maximum at point B where $Q = Q_{sm}$.

This shows that sales-maximizing output (Q_{sm}) is higher than the profit-maximizing output (Q_m).

Next, we can show that profit-maximizing price (P_m) is higher than the sales-maximizing price (P_{sm}). We know that profit-maximizing price

$$P_m = \text{Average revenue at point } A$$

$$= TR/Q_m \text{ at point } A$$

$$= \text{Slope of ray } OA$$

and sales-maximizing price

$$P_{sm} = \text{Average revenue at point } B$$

$$= TR/Q_{sm} \text{ at point } B$$

$$= \text{Slope of ray } OB$$

A simple comparison reveals that

$$\text{Slope of ray } OA > \text{Slope of ray } OB.$$

$$\Rightarrow \qquad P_m > P_{sm}$$

$\Rightarrow$ Profit-maximizing price > Sales-maximizing price

3. The sales maximizer earns a lower profit than a profit maximizer

The conclusion is clear enough from Figure 13.1. Sales-maximizer's output (Q_{sm}) corresponds to point N on the profit function where profit earned is π_{sm} while profit-maximizer's output (Q_m) corresponds to point M on the profit function where profit earned is π_m.

4. Effect of an increase in total fixed costs

An increase in TFC shifts TC vertically upwards as in Figure 13.2. Baumol claims that the sales maximizers in the real world do in fact change their price-output decisions whenever overheads increase. This he claims has a better predictability than the traditional profit maximization hypothesis.

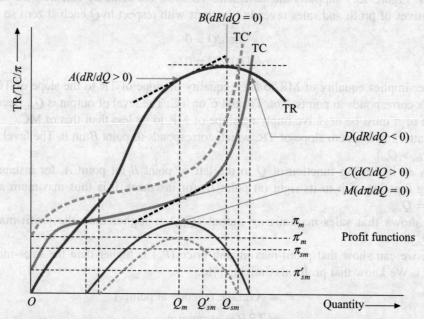

FIGURE 13.2   Effect of an increase in overheads on sales maximizer's price output decisions: An increase in TFC shifts TC vertically upwards. This results in a downward shift in the profit function. To ensure same profit (π_{sm}) to the shareholders, management would have to reduce output to Q'_{sm}. To do this, the management would have to pass the cost increase onto price with the result that TR would also undergo a vertically upward shift so that output Q'_{sm} falls exactly below the highest point on the new TR curve (TR', not shown in the figure to avoid congestion). In a nutshell, effect of an increase in TFC results in a shift in the sales maximizer's equilibrium, due to which, the sales maximizer sells less at a higher price, given π_{sm} as the acceptable level of profit to the shareholders. As regards its effect on profit maximizer, it is none in short-run because TFC does not concern him in the short-run. In case the sales maximizer succeeds in convincing the shareholders to accept π'_{sm} instead of π_{sm}, sales can still be maximized without charging the increased cost on price. Note that π_m falls to π'_m in consequence to the profit maximizer's inability to pass the cost increase onto price.

5. Effect of an imposition of a lump-sum tax

A lump-sum tax increases the TFC. Its effect on the equilibrium of a sales maximizer is exactly the same as the effect of an increase in TFC. The case, however, is different with the profit maximizer. The reader can verify that the profit maximizer would not change his equilibrium but bear the tax himself (Figure 13.2).

6. Effect of a specific tax

A specific tax is levied per unit of output. It would shift the profit function downwards but to the left as shown in Figure 13.3.

7. Effect of an increase in variable cost

The effect of an increase in variable cost is same as that of an imposition of a specific tax. Profit and the sales maximizers both will reduce their outputs and increase their prices, with the latter having to reduce his output by much more than the profit maximizer (Figure 13.3).

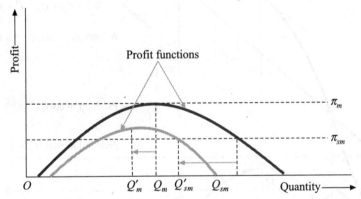

FIGURE 13.3 Effect of a specific tax on price output decisions of sales maximizer and profit maximizer: Given the profit constraint, the sales maximizer would reduce the output from Q_{sm} to Q'_{sm} and would increase the price to pass the specific unit tax onto the consumers. The profit maximizer too would reduce the output from Q_m to Q'_m and increase the price. However, the sales maximizer would have to reduce the output by much more than the profit maximizer.

8. Effect of a shift in demand

An outward shift in the AR (demand) curve would increase output and sales revenue both. However, increase in price would not be certain. In fact price would depend on the extent of shift in demand, as also, on the cost curves of the firm.

13.1.2 Model 2: Static Single Product Model with Advertising

Assumptions of the model include the following:

1. The goal of the firm is sales maximization subject to the profit constraint exogenously determined.

2. Sales revenue increases with advertising expenditure, that is, $dR/dA > 0$ where, A is the advertising expenditure. This implies that sales increase every time advertising expenditure is increased, that is, demand curve shifts upward to right every time advertising expenditure is increased.
3. Production costs are independent of advertising.
4. Product price is constant.

A sales maximizer would have to spend more on advertising than a profit maximizer. Figure 13.4 explains how this model works. The graphical presentation of Baumol's sales-maximizing model with advertising is inconsistent with his assumptions and inferences. In particular, assumptions (2), (3) and (4) do not fit into their slots.

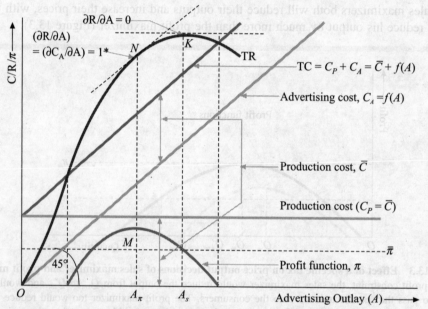

FIGURE 13.4 Baumol's Static Model with Advertising: Production cost (C_P) is independent of advertising outlay (A) and is shown by means of a horizontal line, $C_P = \bar{C}$. Advertising cost, C_A is given by a 45°-line* as $C_A = f(A) = A$, the advertising outlay (represented on x-axis). Total Cost curve (TC) is obtained through vertical summation of advertising cost (C_A) and production cost (C_P). Thus, TC $(C) = C_P + C_A = \bar{C} + f(A) = \bar{C} + A$. Now let the minimum profit desired by the shareholders be $\bar{\pi}$. If the sales maximizing advertising (A_s) corresponds to this level of profit, the shareholders will be as much happy as sales maximising management. Profit-maximizing advertising is given by A_π, which corresponds to M, the highest point on the profit function, π. At A_π, slope of TR curve is equal to that of the total cost curve, TC.

The model assumes that sales revenue increases with advertising outlay A (i.e. $\partial R/\partial A > 0$). Given the price as fixed, sales would increase only when volume of output increases. But production cost assumed independent of advertising, total output Q will remain constant and so will the sales revenue given the price. How can then sales revenue increase with advertising?

---

*$C_A = f(A)$ being inclined to the horizontal axis at 45°, slope of the curve = $\tan 45° = 1$

Alternatively, if sales increase with advertising, given the volume of output, product price must increase but the same is assumed constant. Assumptions (2), (3) and (4) are therefore, inconsistent.

In short, Baumol's graphical presentation (Figure 13.4) is inconsistent with Baumol's contentions and implications. Scholars like Sandmeyer*, Haveman and DeBartolo**, Kafoglis and Bushnell[†] among others have pointed out this deficiency of Baumol's model. They suggest that TR curve would shift upwards with increasing expenditure on advertising. As a result, equilibrium revenue and advertising expenditure will both be higher while output may be lower and price higher in the new equilibrium position. However, Baumol's mathematical model incorporates the possibilities of changes in price, output and advertising.

Let us present Baumol's mathematical version before presenting the graphical version as modified by M. Kafoglis and R. Brusnell[†] and C.J. Hawkins[††].

Mathematical Presentation of Baumol's Model 2

Baumol's sales maximization model with advertising can be stated as a constrained maximization problem as below:

Maximize: $R = f(Q, A)$

Subject to: $R - C - C_A = \bar{\pi}$, where, $C = g(Q)$ = production cost, $C_A = h(A)$.

Employing Lagrange's multiplier, it can be converted into a simple maximization problem, as stated below:

$$\text{Maximize: } \Phi = R - \lambda[R - C - C_A - \bar{\pi}], (\lambda < 0) \tag{13.1}$$

Differentiating partially with respect to Q, A, and λ, we have

$$\partial\Phi/\partial Q = \partial R/\partial Q - \lambda[\partial R/\partial Q - \partial C/\partial Q] = 0 \tag{13.2}$$

$$\partial\Phi/\partial A = \partial R/\partial A - \lambda[\partial R/\partial A - \partial C_A/\partial A] = 0 \tag{13.3}$$

$$\partial\Phi/\partial\lambda = [R - C - C_A - \bar{\pi}] = 0 \tag{13.4}$$

Equation (13.2) implies

$$\partial C/\partial Q = [1 - (1/\lambda)] \partial R/\partial Q$$

$\Rightarrow \qquad \partial C/\partial Q > \partial R/\partial Q, [\lambda \text{ being} < 0, 1 - (1/\lambda) > 1] \tag{13.5}$

$\Rightarrow \qquad \partial C/\partial Q \div \partial R/\partial Q = [1 - (1/\lambda)] > 1 \tag{13.6}$

Equation (13.3) implies

$$\partial C_A/\partial A = [1 - (1/\lambda)] \partial R/\partial A$$

$\Rightarrow \qquad \partial C_A/\partial A \div \partial R/\partial A = [1 - (1/\lambda)] > 1 \tag{13.7}$

$\Rightarrow \qquad \partial C_A/\partial A > \partial R/\partial A \tag{13.8}$

---

* Sandmeyer, R.L., *Baumol's Sales Maximization Model: Comment*, American Economic Review, 1964.

** Haveman, R. and G. DeBartolo, *The Revenue Maximization Oligopoly Model: Comment*, American Economic Review, 1968, pp.1355–8.

[†] Kafoglis, M. and R. Bushnell, *The Revenue Maximization Oligopoly Model: Comment*, American Economic Review, 1970.

[††] Hawkins, C.J., *The Revenue Maximization Oligopoly Model: Comment*, American Economic Review, 1970.

While, $\partial R/\partial A = \partial C_A/\partial A = 1$ at the profit-maximizing advertising expenditure, A_π (Figure 13.4).

For sales maximizing advertising, from equation 13.8, $\partial R/\partial A < \partial C_A/\partial A$ (In the figure, $\partial R/\partial A = 0$ and $\partial C_A/\partial A = 1$ at $A = A_s$, the sales-maximizing advertising expenditure). Advertising expenditure would thus be higher for a sales maximizer than for a profit maximizer ($A_s > A_\pi$). Given $\lambda < 0$, from Eqs. (13.6) and (13.7), the condition of equilibrium is

$$\partial C/\partial Q \div \partial R/\partial Q = [1 - (1/\lambda)] = \partial C_A/\partial A \div \partial R/\partial A; \ (\lambda < 0) \qquad (13.9)$$

Also, for a sales maximizer, MC > MR (as sales maximizing output is higher than profit maximizing output) while MR = $P[1 - (1/|e|)]$. Substituting for MR, MC > $P[1 - (1/|e|)]$ implying MC > P. Also, MR < P for all $|e| \geq 1$. Reconciling, MC > P > MR. A sales maximizer, therefore, charges a price less than MC but more than MR. Note that,

$$R = f(Q, A), \ C = g(Q) \text{ and advertising expenditure, } C_A = h(A).$$

Modified Graphical Presentation of Baumol's Model 2

Modified graphical version of Baumol's model (Figure 13.7) is derived through superimposing the cost curve (Figure 13.5) and the revenue curve (Figure 13.6).

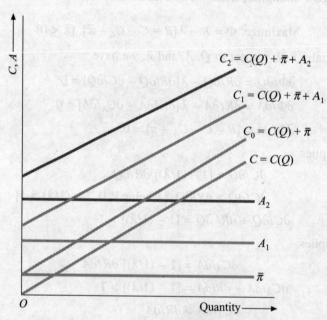

FIGURE 13.5 Total cost (C) is equal to the sum of production cost $C(Q)$, advertising expenditure A and minimum profit desired by shareholders. Production cost varies proportionally with output. Levels of advertising expenditures are independent of output. While the curve representing expenditure on advertising is a horizontal line such as A_1 or A_2, production cost curve is a positively sloped curve through the origin. Total cost curve is obtained through vertical summation of minimum profit constraint, advertising expenditure, and production cost. Thus, $TC_i = C(Q) + A_i + \bar{\pi}, i = 1, 2, \ldots$

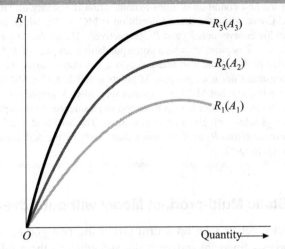

FIGURE 13.6 Sales revenue curve shifts upwards each time advertising outlay is increased. There is a distinct TR curve corresponding to a distinct level of advertising expenditure.

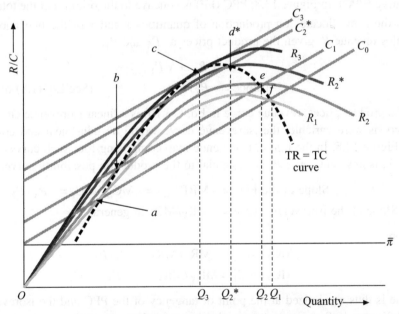

FIGURE 13.7 Baumol's model 2, modified graphical presentation: Superimposing TR and TC curves on the same plane, we get locus of points at each of which TR = TC for various levels of outputs. R_1, R_2 and R_3 are revenue curves corresponding to advertisinging expenditures A_1, A_2 and A_3. While curve R_3 touches the total cost curve C_3 at a single point (point c), curve R_1 intersects cost curve C_0 at points a and f and R_2 intersects cost curves C_1 at points b and e. Joining the points a, b, c, e and f by means of a smooth curve, we obtain the dotted curve which indicates equality of TR and TC at points a, b, c, e, and f. If more curves at various advertising outlays be drawn, each point on the dotted curve will mark equality between corresponding levels of revenue and cost curves. The dotted curve called *Haveman and DeBartolo Curve* is often referred to as '*TR = TC Curve*'. The firm attains its sales maximization (equilibrium) at the highest point (point d^*) on the

TR = TC Curve. Note that the first condition of sales maximization is equality of TR to TC, which is satisfied at every point on TR = TC Curve while the second condition is MC > MR, which is satisfied d^*, e and f. But points e and f correspond to lower revenues, R_2 and R_1, respectively. Hence the only point that maximizes sales with given profit constraint $\pi = \bar{\pi}$ is point d^* which corresponds to a revenue of R_2^*, total cost of C_2^*, output of Q_2^* and advertising outlay of A_2^*. Note also that points a and b don't satisfy the second condition of sales maximization with profit constraint nor does point c. At points a and b, MC < MR and at point c, MC = MR. Though revenue R_3 is the highest at c but MC is not greater than MR. A simple sales maximizer producing Q_3 at point c would have to reallocate resources from advertising to production until output increases to Q_2^* so that MC > MR for maximization of sales with given profit constraint. This will lead to a fall in price (from R_3/Q_3 to R_2^*/Q_2^*) but the loss of revenue (from R_3 to R_2) is more than offset by the additional revenue generated from increased production (from Q_3 to Q_2^*).

13.1.3 Model 3: Static Multi-product Model without Advertising

For the sake of simplicity, let us take up a firm producing two goods, X and Y. The firm has fixed amounts of resources—financial and/or real—and employs them fully and efficiently with available technology to produce quantities x and y of the two goods. The locus of different combinations of the two that are possible to be produced under the given conditions is a production possibility curve (PPC). In Figure 13.8, PPC (FF) is concave to the origin. Let the total resources be $\bar{C}$, which the firm allocates on production of quantities x and y of the two goods so as to maximize sales revenue R, given the product prices as P_X and P_Y.

$$R = x P_X + y P_Y \qquad (13.10)$$

(Slope $= -P_X/P_Y$) [See Eq. (1.8) of Chapter 1]

Given the product prices, revenue curve in Eq. (13.10) is a linear isorevenue curve. If prices of the two goods were variable, the isorevenue curve would be non-linear and convex to the origin as in Figure 13.8. In the figure, isorevenue map comprising four such curves is shown.

At point e, isorevenue curve R_3 is tangential to the production possibility curve, FF.

Slope of the PPC $= -\text{MRPT}_{X,Y} = -\text{MC}_X/\text{MC}_Y = -P_X/P_Y$

Slope of the isorevenue curve $= -\text{MR}_X/\text{MR}_Y$ in general.

At e, therefore,

$$-\text{MC}_X/\text{MC}_Y = -\text{MR}_X/\text{MR}_Y = -P_X/P_Y$$
$$\Rightarrow \quad \text{MC}_X/\text{MC}_Y = \text{MR}_X/\text{MR}_Y = P_X/P_Y$$

Sales revenue is thus maximized at the point of tangency of the PPC and the isorevenue curve. Graphically, Figure 13.8 portrays the mechanism of sales revenue maximization in a two-commodity world. Given the product prices, isorevenue curves are linear like PP in Figure 13.8.

13.1.4 Model 4: Static Multi-product Model with Advertising

In the last model, we saw how a static single product model without advertising was extended to its two-commodity version. It is possible to extend it even further to include more than two commodities through composite commodity theorem. Graphical presentation of such models is also possible in a two-dimensional space.

The condition of equilibrium of a static multiproduct model (Model 3) remains unaffected in presence of advertising so long as we assume that advertising expenditure is independent of quantities of the outputs. That is, the composite function, here, may be expressed as

$$\Phi = R - \lambda[R - C - C_A - \overline{\pi}], \quad (\lambda < 0) \tag{13.11}$$

where $C_A = h(A_i) = \Sigma A_i = A_1 + A_2 + \cdots + A_n, \quad C = g(Q_i)$
and $R = f(Q_i, A_i); \quad i = 1, 2, \ldots, n$

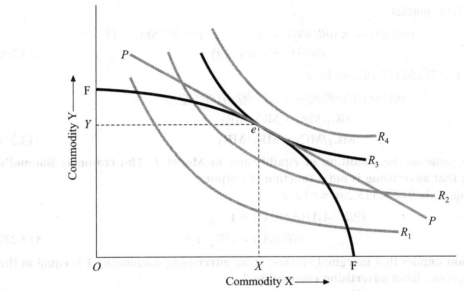

FIGURE 13.8 Baumol's multi-product model without advertising: The condition of sales revenue maximization requires tangency between PPC (FF) and the isorevenue curves (R_1, R_2, R_3 or R_4). It is satisfied at point e where the PPC touches R_3. Isorevenue curves for commodities X and Y are convex to the origin. At e, $MRPT_{X,Y}$ = numerical value of the slope of the isorevenue curve $(MR_X/MR_Y) = (MC_X/MC_Y) = (P_X/P_Y)$.

Treating Q_1 as the quantity of one commodity and Q_2, that of the composite commodity and differentiating Φ partially with respect to Q_1, Q_2, A_1, A_2 and λ; where A_1 and A_2 are expenditures incurred on advertising the two, we have

$$\partial \Phi / \partial Q_1 = \partial R / \partial Q_1 - \lambda[\partial R / \partial Q_1 - \partial C / \partial Q_1] = 0 \tag{13.12}$$
$$\partial \Phi / \partial Q_2 = \partial R / \partial Q_2 - \lambda[\partial R / \partial Q_2 - \partial C / \partial Q_2] = 0 \tag{13.13}$$
$$\partial \Phi / \partial A_1 = \partial R / \partial A_1 - \lambda[\partial R / \partial A_1 - \partial C_A / \partial A_1] = 0 \tag{13.14}$$
$$\partial \Phi / \partial A_2 = \partial R / \partial A_2 - \lambda[\partial R / \partial A_2 - \partial C_A / \partial A_2] = 0 \tag{13.15}$$

and $$\partial \Phi / \partial \lambda = [\dot{R} - C - C_A - \overline{\pi}] = 0 \tag{13.16}$$

Equation (13.12) implies
$$\partial C / \partial Q_1 = [1 - (1/\lambda)] \partial R / \partial Q_1$$
$\Rightarrow \quad \partial C / \partial Q_1 > \partial R / \partial Q_1, \qquad [\lambda \text{ being} < 0, 1 - (1/\lambda) > 1]$
$\Rightarrow \quad \partial C / \partial Q_1 \div \partial R / \partial Q_1 = [1 - (1/\lambda)] \tag{13.17}$

Equation (13.13) implies

$$\partial C/\partial Q_2 = [1 - (1/\lambda)] \partial R/\partial Q_2$$
$$\Rightarrow \partial C/\partial Q_2 > \partial R/\partial Q_2, [\lambda \text{ being} < 0, 1 - (1/\lambda) > 1]$$
$$\Rightarrow \partial C/\partial Q_2 \div \partial R/\partial Q_2 = [1 - (1/\lambda)] \qquad (13.18)$$

Equation (13.14) implies

$$(\partial R/\partial A_1) - \lambda (\partial R/\partial A_1) = -\lambda \qquad (\because \partial C_A/\partial A_1 = 1)$$
$$\Rightarrow \partial R/\partial A_1 = -\lambda/(1 - \lambda) \qquad (13.19)$$

Equation (13.15) implies

$$(\partial R/\partial A_2) - \lambda (\partial R/\partial A_2) = -\lambda \qquad (\because \partial C_A/\partial A_2 = 1)$$
$$\Rightarrow \partial R/\partial A_2 = -\lambda/(1 - \lambda) \qquad (13.20)$$

From Eqs. (13.17) and (13.18), we have

$$(\partial C/\partial Q_1)/(\partial R/\partial Q_1) = (\partial C/\partial Q_2)/(\partial R/\partial Q_2)$$
$$\Rightarrow \text{MC}_1/\text{MR}_1 = \text{MC}_2/\text{MR}_2$$
$$\Rightarrow \mathbf{MC_1/MC_2 = MR_1/MR_2} \qquad (13.21)$$

This is the same as the condition of equilibrium in Model 3. The reason is Baumol's assumption that advertising is not a function of outputs.

From Eqs. (13.19) and (13.20), we have

$$(\partial R/\partial A_1)/(\partial R/\partial A_2) = 1$$
$$\Rightarrow (\partial R/\partial A_1) = (\partial R/\partial A_2) \qquad (13.22)$$

The condition implies that marginal revenue from advertising commodity 1 is equal to the marginal revenue from advertising commodity 2.

From Eqs. (13.17) and (13.18), we have for a sales maximizer that $\text{MC}_i > \text{MR}_i$ while $\text{MR}_i = P_i[1 - (1/|e_i|)]$. Substituting for MR_i, $\text{MC}_i > P_i[1 - (1/|e_i|)]$ implying $\text{MC}_i > P_i$. Also, $\text{MR}_i < P_i$ for all $|e_i| \geq 1$. Reconciling, $\text{MC}_i > P_i > \text{MR}_i$ ($i = 1, 2$). A sales maximizer, therefore, charges a price less than MC but more than MR.

13.2 BAUMOL'S DYNAMIC MODEL

Static models of Section 13.1 suffer from two drawbacks: *first*, time horizon is short and *second*, profit constraint is exogenously determined. In Baumol's dynamic model, these drawbacks do not exist any more. Profit constraint is endogenously determined and the time horizon stands extended to the lifetime of the firm.

Assumptions of the model

The dynamic model is based on the following assumptions:

1. The firm attempts to maximize growth of its sales over its lifetime.
2. The profit being the main source of financing growth is an instrumental variable determined endogenously.
3. Demand and cost curves have the traditional shapes—demand curve sloping downwards and cost curves having traditional U-shape.

13.2.1 The Model

The model involves

(a) sales growth function, $g = f(\pi, R)$, where, π = profit and R = current sales; and
(b) iso-present-value function, $g = (1/\alpha)S - (\beta/\alpha)R$, where, α and β are constants of proportionality and S is the sum of the present values of the annual sales of the firm over its lifespan, that is, $S = \Sigma PV$, where,

$$\Sigma PV = \sum_{t=0}^{t=n} R[(1+g)^t/(1+r)^t], t = 0, 1, 2, 3, \ldots, n$$

'PV' stands for present values and R, for current sales.
Let us discuss them in their requisite detail.

(a) Sales Growth Function:

To obtain the function, let the annual rate of growth of sales be g per cent per annum of the current sales (R). Sales after 0,1, 2, 3, ..., n years of the firm's operation may then be expressed as R, $(1 + g)R$, $(1 + g)^2 R$, $(1 + g)^3 R$, ..., $(1 + g)^n R$ respectively. Further, let r be the market rate of interest, assumed fairly stable over the firm's lifespan. The sum, S, of the present values of the future annual sales, thus, can be expressed as

$$\begin{aligned} S &= \Sigma PV \\ &= R + R\left[\frac{(1+g)}{(1+r)} + \frac{(1+g)^2}{(1+r)^2} + \frac{(1+g)^3}{(1+r)^3} + \cdots + \frac{(1+g)^n}{(1+r)^n}\right] \\ &= \sum_{t=0}^{t=n} R\left[\frac{(1+g)^t}{(1+r)^t}\right], \quad t = 0, 1, 2, 3, \ldots, n \end{aligned} \quad (13.23)$$

The firm attempts to maximize, S, the sum of the present values of its yearly sales stream over its lifetime.

As is evident, S varies directly with R and g but inversely with the rate of interest, r. Given the rate of interest, r, S would vary directly with R and g only. To maximize S, the firm must have the largest possible values of R and g. As assumed, sales growth rate, g, being financed by the firm's internal profits, it can be expressed as a function of profit π and the current sales R. Thus,

$$g = f(\pi, R) \quad (13.24)$$

But profit π itself is a function of production cost C, growth rate g, interest rate r and current sales, R, so that

$$\pi = h(g, r, R, C) \quad (13.25)$$

In fact, growth function in Eq. (13.24) may be derived from the profit function in Eq. (13.25) under given conditions of r and C. Functions in these equations are identical when r and C are both fixed. They can be portrayed diagrammatically as in Figure 13.9.

When r and C are given, Eq. (13.24) follows from Eq. (13.25) and expresses sales growth g as a function of π and the current sales, R. Values of g and R increase simultaneously so long as π increases and reaches its maximum, but thereafter, g and π both decrease with increasing value of R.

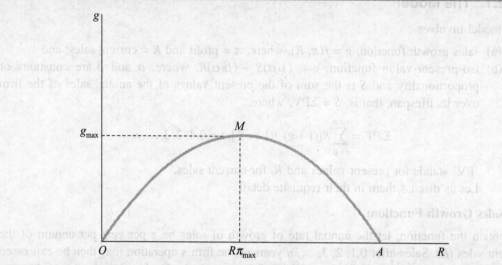

FIGURE 13.9 Sales growth function: The sales growth function (OMA), as portrayed in the figure, or as expressed in Eq. (13.24) or as derived from Eq. (13.25) under given cost and interest rate conditions, is at its peak at $R = R\pi_{max}$. At this level of sales, annual growth of sales, g, is also maximum (g_{max}). Along segment OM of the growth function, g increases as R and π increase but beyond OM, g decreases as R increases and π decreases. In other words, g and R both increase simultaneously up to point M but thereafter, it is only R that increases while the other two decline simultaneously.

(b) Iso-present-value function

From Eq. (13.23), the sum of present values of firm's annual sales over its lifetime is given as

$$S = \sum_{t=0}^{t=n} R\left[\frac{(1+g)^t}{(1+r)^t}\right], \quad (t = 0,1,2,3,\ldots n)$$

As mentioned earlier, S varies directly with R and g but inversely with r. When r is given, S varies only with R and g and can be expressed as below:

$$S = \alpha g + \beta R \tag{13.26}$$

Expressing g as a function of R and S from Eq. (13.26), we have

$$g = (1/\alpha)S - (\beta/\alpha)R \tag{13.27}$$

From Eq. (13.27), given S, it is clear that a firm has to choose a high R if it has chosen a low g; or a low R if it has chosen a high value of g. In other words, Eq. (13.26) or (13.27) describes an **iso-present-value curve**, which traces the locus of different combinations of g and R that stand for a given S. A look at either equation reveals that these curves are linear with slope $[-(\beta/\alpha)]$ and intercept $[(1/\alpha)S]$. Figure 13.10 demonstrates the iso-present value map.

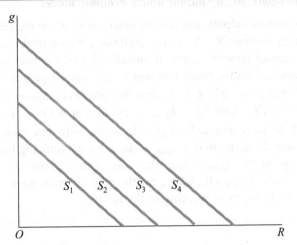

FIGURE 13.10 *Iso-present-value map*, showing iso-present-value curves S_1, S_2, S_3 and S_4 representing four levels of sums of the present values of annual sales. The highest one represents the highest value of S and the lowest one, the lowest value of it.

Determination of equilibrium values of g and R

The equilibrium choice of g and R relates to a point on the highest possible iso-present-value curve reachable with a given sales growth function. In other words, equilibrium values of g and R are determined at the point e where highest S-curve touches the sales growth function given by Eq. (13.24). The mechanism of determining the equilibrium point is demonstrated below in Figure 13.11.

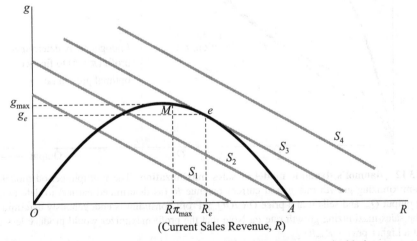

FIGURE 13.11 *Determination of equilibrium values of g an R:* Highest attainable iso-present-value curve under given sales growth function (*OMA*) is S_3. It touches the growth function at e which determines g_e and R_e that maximize the sum of the present values of the future stream of revenues.

Determination of sales-maximizing output under dynamic model

Sales- and profit-maximizing outputs may now be determined, given the sales maximizing growth rate g_e and current sales revenue R_e. We have determined the optimal combination of g_e and R_e that maximized the sum of present values of annual sales of the firm over its entire lifespan. The TR and TC curves, as also the profit function π, can now be plotted in the same space with endogenously determined profit $\pi = \bar{\pi}$ to finance the sales-maximizing growth rate, g_e.

From the point T on TR where TR = R_e, a perpendicular is drawn to the x-axis to meet the profit curve at N and the horizontal axis at Q_{sm}. Endogenously determined profit, $\pi = \bar{\pi}$ forms a horizontal line passing through point N. Q_{sm} is the sales-maximizing output.

Profit-maximizing output, $Q_{\pi m}$ is less than the sales-maximizing output, Q_{sm}. A sales maximizer sells Q_{sm} at a price OR_e/OQ_{sm} while a profit maximizer sells $Q_{\pi m}$ at a price $OR_{\pi m}/OQ_{\pi m}$. Figure 13.12 explains working of the model.

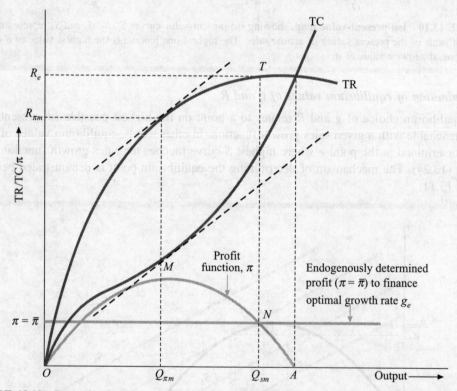

FIGURE 13.12 Baumol's dynamic model of sales maximization: The multiple-period model, makes use of the sales-maximizing growth rate g_e and current revenue R_e (as determined earlier) to determine the sales-maximizing output Q_{sm} and sells it at a price OR_e/OQ_{sm}. Profit constraint is endogenously determined at $\pi = \bar{\pi}$ to finance the sales-maximizing growth rate g_e. Note that the profit maximizer would produce less ($Q_{\pi m} < Q_{sm}$) and sell it at a higher price $OR_{\pi m}/OQ_{\pi m}$.

The multiperiod dynamic model of Baumol can be modified to allow for an exogenously determined minimum profit acceptable to the shareholders as also to allow for advertising and other multiproduct activities of the firms.

A multiperiod model is identical in its predictions to a single period model. Some of its predictions can be summarized here for ready reference:

1. Output will be higher and price lower for a sales maximizer than for a profit maximizer.
2. Lump-sum tax would cause an increase in price and a decrease in output. However, the tax would fail in its objective of distributive justice. The sales maximizer would shift the burden of the lump-sum tax to the consumers.
3. Levy of a specific tax will cause a larger decrease in output and a larger increase in price of a sales maximizer than of a profit maximizer.
4. An outward shift in demand would cause an increase in output and advertising both but its effect on price would be uncertain.
5. An increase in variable cost leads a sales maximizer to an increase in price and a decrease in output but its effect on a profit maximizer's price and output would be somewhat smaller.

KEY TERMS AND CONCEPTS

Endogenously-determined profit constraint It refers to the profit planned by the sales-maximizing firm to finance the optimum rate of growth of future sales over the lifetime of the firm. It has its relevance only to the dynamic model of sales maximization.

Exogenously-determined profit constraint It refers to minimum acceptable profit which is must for the shareholders to maintain their interest in the firm's operations. It is imposed on the sales-maximizing firm by the shareholders' interest.

Iso-present-value curves These curves represent possible combinations of current sales (R) and growth rate (g) of a firm's future sales over its lifetime, yielding the same present value of its future sales.

Models of sales maximization Baumol has presented two types of sales maximization models: static models and dynamic models.

Static model A Static model refers to a short period (single period) analysis. It has four versions:

(a) A single product model, without advertising
(b) A single product model, with advertising
(c) A multiproduct model, without advertising
(d) A multiproduct model, with advertising.

Assumptions of the static model The model is based on the following assumptions:

(a) The time horizon of the firm is a single period.
(b) During this period, the firm attempts to maximize sales revenue subject to a profit constraint.
(c) The profit constraint is exogenously determined by the shareholders' demands and expectations of a minimum profit, which is must for them.
(d) It is assumed that the cost and revenue curves are conventional, that is, the cost curves are U-shaped and the demand curve is downward-sloping.

Implications of the static model The static model leads to the following implications:

1. A sales maximizer will never choose a level of output at which price elasticity is different from unity.

2. A sales maximizer sells a larger quantity and charges a lower price than what of a profit maximizer does.
3. The sales maximizer earns a lower profit than a profit maximizer.
4. Effect of an increase in total fixed costs: An increase in TFC shifts the TC vertically upwards as in Figure 13.2. Baumol claims that sales maximizers in the real world do in fact change their price-output decisions whenever overheads increase. This he claims has a better predictability than the traditional profit maximization hypothesis.
5. Effect of an imposition of a lump-sum tax: A lump-sum tax increases the TFC. Its effect on the equilibrium of the sales maximizer is exactly the same as that of an increase in TFC. The case, however, is different with the profit maximizer. The reader can verify that the profit maximizer would not change his equilibrium but bear the tax himself (Figure 13.2).
6. Effect of a specific tax: A specific tax is levied per unit of output. It would shift the profit function downwards but to the left as shown in Figure 13.3.
7. Effect of an increase in variable cost: The effect of an increase in variable cost is same as that of an imposition of a specific tax. Profit maximizers and sales-maximizers will both reduce their outputs and increase their prices, with the sales maximizer having to reduce his output by much more than the profit maximizer (Figure 13.3).
8. Effect of a shift in demand: An outward shift in the AR (demand) curve would increase output and sales revenue both. However, increase in price would not be certain. In fact, price would depend on the extent of shift in demand, as also, on the cost curves of the firm.

Dynamic model Dynamic model refers to lifetime (multi-period) analysis of a firm. This, too may have as many variations as static models.

Assumptions of the dynamic model

1. The firm attempts to maximize the growth of its sales over its lifetime.
2. The profit being the main source of financing the growth of sales, it is an instrumental variable determined endogenously.
3. Demand and cost curves have the traditional shapes, demand curve sloping downwards and cost curves resembling their traditional U-shape.

Implications of the dynamic model Output and advertising expenditures will be higher and price lower for a sales maximizer than for a profit maximizer. Lump-sum tax would cause an increase in price and a reduction in output while a specific tax will lead the sales maximizer to a larger reduction in output and a larger increase in price as compared with a profit maximizer.

Sales maximization A practice of maximization of sales revenue, $R = PQ$, by a modern firm. Often, firms maximize sales with a certain minimum profit acceptable to the shareholders.

Arguments in favour of sales maximization

1. Salaries and perks of the top management are correlated more closely with sales than profits.
2. Bankers and financial institutions treat sales-volume as a yardstick of a firm's performance while financing its business activities.
3. Labour unions' demand for better perks and working conditions can be tackled more satisfactorily when sales are growing than when they are declining.
4. Large sales with steadily high growth lend prestige to the management while large profits go into the pockets of the shareholders only.
5. Growing sales lead a firm to scale economies and hence enhance its competitiveness. This helps the firm in meeting its social responsibility of providing quality goods at reasonable prices on the one hand and boosting its market share on the other.
6. Large and steadily growing sales empower management to adopt a competitive tactics while low and declining sales obstruct it.

EXERCISES

A. Short Answer Questions

1. What really is meant by sales maximization?
2. Give three reasons for maximization of sales rather than profits.
3. Mention three assumptions of the static models of sales maximization.
4. Mention three implications of Baumol's static model without advertising.
5. What is exogenously-determined profit constraint?
6. What is endogenously-determined profit constraint?
7. What are iso-present-value curves?
8. What is the main difference in the static and the dynamic models of sales maximization?
9. Mention three assumptions of Baumol's dynamic model.
10. Mention three implications of Baumol's dynamic model.
11. Name the factors on which the sum of the present values of the future annual sales of a firm depend.
12. What is the condition for determination of the optimal rate of growth of future annual sales of a firm over its lifetime?
13. "A sales maximizer will never choose an output at which price elasticity of demand is different from unity." Explain.
14. How does an outward shift in the AR curve affect the output and the sales of a sales maximizer? Explain.

B. Long Answer Questions

15. "A sales maximizer sells more at a lower price than what a profit maximizer does." Discuss.
16. Is it true to say that the profits earned by a sales maximizer are always lower than those earned by a profit maximizer? Give reasons for your answer.
17. Explain the effect of a lump-sum tax or on sales and profits of
    (a) the sales maximizer.
    (b) the profit-maximizer.
18. How does levy of a specific tax affect output and profits of
    (a) the sales maximizer?
    (b) the profit-maximizer?
19. How does an increase in the variable costs affect output and sales of
    (a) the sales maximizer?
    (b) the profit-maximizer?
20. Give three reasons in favour of sales revenue maximization as practiced by the management.
21. What are the main points of difference between the goals of sales maximization and profit maximization?
22. What is a non-operative profit constraint? How does it affect sales maximizer's equilibrium under given profit constraint?
    [**Ans.** Non-operative profit constraint refers to a profit constraint which lies below the profit constraint already in operation in sales maximization. A non-operative profit constraint does not affect the sales maximizer's equilibrium at *e* (Figure 13.13).]

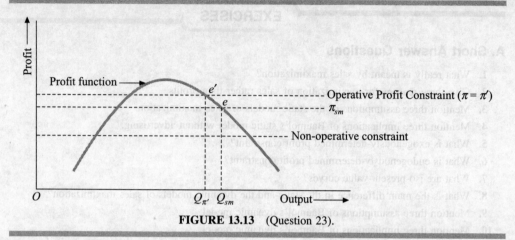

FIGURE 13.13 (Question 23).

23. What is meant by operative constraint? How does it affect the sales maximizer's equilibrium?

   [**Hint.** A profit constraint which lies above the profit constraint already in operation is an operative constraint. For instance, $\pi = \pi'$ in Figure 13.13 is said to be an operative constraint as it lies above π_{sm}, the profit constraint already in operation. When executed, it reduces sales ($Q_{\pi'} < Q_{sm}$) and sales revenue both (point e' in Figure 13.13.]

24. Given the demand function, $P = 100 - Q$, and the total cost function TC $= 500 + 7Q + Q^2$. Determine
   (a) Profit-maximizing quantity, price, sales and the volume of profit.
   (b) Sales-maximizing quantity, price, sales and the volume of profit.
   (c) Sales-maximizing quantity, price, sales and the volume of profit when profit constraint is $\pi = 50$.

   [**Ans.** (a) π = TR − TC
   $= PQ - (500 + 7Q + Q^2)$
   $= 100Q - Q^2 - 500 - 7Q - Q^2$

   Employing the first order condition of profit maximization, that is, $d\pi/dQ = 0$, we have
   $$100 - 2Q - 7 - 2Q = 0$$
   $\Rightarrow$ $\qquad Q = 23.25$
   and $\qquad P = 76.75$
   $\qquad$ TR $= 76.75 \times 23.25$
   $\qquad\qquad = 1784.44$
   $\qquad \pi = 1784.44 - [500 + 7 \times 23.25 + (23.25)^2]$
   $\qquad\qquad = 581.13$

   The second order condition, $d^2\pi/dQ^2 = -4$ for all values of Q. Hence,
   $$d^2\pi/dQ^2 < 0$$

   (b) TR $= 100Q - Q^2$
   For maximization of sales revenue, $d(\text{TR})/dQ = 0$
   $\Rightarrow \qquad 100 - 2Q = 0$
   $\Rightarrow \qquad Q = 50$

and
$$P = 50$$
$$TR = 2500$$
$$\pi = 2500 - 3{,}350$$
$$= -850$$

(c) Setting $\pi = 50$ and substituting it in the profit function, we have
$$50 = 100Q - Q^2 - 500 - 7Q - Q^2$$
$$\Rightarrow \quad 2Q^2 - 93Q + 550 = 0$$
$$\Rightarrow \quad Q = 39.55, 6.95$$

Thus, sales are maximized at $Q = 39.55$
Corresponding price, $P = 60.45$
$$TR = PQ = 2390.8.]$$

25. Show that $S = 1 - e$, where S = price elasticity of sales and e = price elasticity of demand. Hence deduce that a fall in price will reduce the sales when $|e| < 1$.

    [**Ans.** Price elasticity of sales is defined as the ratio of the proportionate change in sales to a proportionate change in price.
$$S = [d(PQ)/dP]\,[P/PQ]$$
$$= (1/Q)\,[Q + P(dQ/dP)]$$
$$= (1/Q)\,Q\,[1 - \{-(dQ/dP)(P/Q)\}],$$
$$= (1 - |e|), \quad |e| = |(dQ/dP)(P/Q)| = -(dQ/dP)(P/Q) \quad \text{(Proved)}$$

    When $\quad |e| < 1,\ S > 0$
    $\Rightarrow$ Price elasticity of sales is positive
    $\Rightarrow dR/dP > 0 \Rightarrow$ Sales vary with price. That is, when price falls, so do the sales.]

26. A firm with limited resource produces quantities x and y of two goods X and Y. The transformation curve that relates these quantities is as given below:
$$80y = 5999 - x^2 - 2x$$

    Find the sales-maximizing outputs of the two goods. Assume product prices as fixed at 60 and 40 respectively for X and Y. Also determine the sales revenue.

    [**Ans.** $x = 59,\ y = 30;\ R = 4740.]$

27. A firm with limited resource produces quantities x and y of two goods X and Y. The transformation curve that relates these quantities is as given below:
$$12y = 36 - x^2$$

    Find the sales-maximizing outputs of the two goods. Assume product prices as variable, implying a non-linear isorevenue curve:
$$R = 1500 x^{1/3}\, y^{2/3}$$

    Also determine the sales revenue.

    [**Ans.** $\text{MRPT}_{X,\,Y} = dy/dx = -x/6$ (On differentiating the equation of the PPC w.r.t x)
    Slope of the isorevenue curve
$$dy/dx = -(\partial R/\partial x) \div (\partial R/\partial y)$$
$$= -[(1500/3)\,(y/x)^{2/3}] \div [(3000/3)\,(x/y)^{1/3}]$$
$$= -y/2x$$

For sales revenue maximization,
Slope of the PPC = Slope of the isorevenue curve

$\Rightarrow \quad -x/6 = -y/2x$

$\Rightarrow \quad y = x^2/3$

Substituting in the equation of the PPC, we have

$$x^2 = 36/5$$
$$x = 2.6833$$

and
$$y = 2.4$$

Sales revenue $= 1500 x^{1/3} y^{2/3}$
$= 1500 (2.6833)^{1/3} (2.4)^{2/3}$
$= 1500 \times 2.491$
$= 3737.]$

C. Essay Type Questions

28. Explain Baumol's sales maximization model, under the conditions of no advertising or selling expenditures. Comment on some of its implications in economic theory.
29. Explain Baumol's sales maximization model, under the presence of advertising or selling expenditures. Comment on some of its implications in economic theory.
30. Explain Baumol's static multiproduct model of sales maximization under the conditions of no advertising or selling expenditures.
31. Explain Baumol's static multiproduct model of sales maximization under the presence of advertising or selling expenditures.
32. Explain Baumol's dynamic model of sales maximization. Critically examine some of its implications in economic theory.

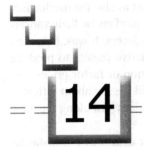

14

Determination of Factor Prices

CHAPTER OUTLINE

Introduction
✧ When Both Factor and Product Markets are Competitive
✧ When Factor Market is Competitive but Product Market is not
✧ When Product Market is Competitive but Factor Market is not
✧ When None of the Two Markets is Competitive
✧ Pricing of Factors when a Firm Employs More than One Variable Factor
✧ Market Supply and Market Demand of Factors
✧ Concluding Remarks and Marginal Productivity Theory of Distribution
✧ Rental Element in Factor Pricing
✧ Key Terms and Concepts
✧ Exercises

INTRODUCTION

To sell its product, a firm needs a market called the **product-market**. In Chapter 7, we have discussed its various forms. In Chapter 8, we have studied how price-output decisions are made by a firm in a competitive product market. In Chapters 9, 10 and 11, we have learnt how these decisions are reached by the firms in monopoly, monopolistic and inoligopolistic product markets.

We have also seen in Chapter 5 that a firm needs factors of production, which it procures from a market called the **factor-market**. The term refers to a market in which factors of production such as land, labour, capital, etc. are made available to the producers, or, to a market from where producers procure these factors of production. By now, there must be some realization in mind that a producer is sandwiched between two markets—the product market and the factor market.

Of the two, we have so far discussed various forms of a product market as also the mechanism of price-output decisions therein but little has been said about the factor markets or their various forms or their role and functioning in factor employment decisions of producers. It was, however, mentioned in Chapter 5 as to how a producer varies quantities of productive factors to produce the desired amount of a product in short and long periods. Also, a mention of factor prices was made in Chapter 6 while accounting for the production costs. But little did we say about different forms of a factor market or about its mechanism of determining factor prices. All along we have in fact been sparing the discussions for this chapter.

On the lines of a product market, even a factor market has a number of forms. For instance, it is said to be competitive when factor-owners are price takers or monopoly when they are price makers. In a competitive factor market, supply of productive factors is unlimited at fixed prices while in a monopoly factor market, it varies with factor prices. A factor market is said to be an imperfect one when some of its features are derived from a competitive factor market and the rest from a monopoly factor market. Availability and prices of productive factors go a long way to influence production costs and hence product prices. In the same way, the product price offered to the producers by a product market goes a long way to influence factor demand and factor prices. It is after all the revenue realized from the sale of the product that finances factor demand. That is the reason why theories of factor price determination are, at times, referred to as **theories of distribution**.

In this chapter, we, therefore, take up factor markets and theories of distribution. Since nature of demand and supply of factors of production depends on the structure of commodity and factor markets, we propose to study factor price determination in the following four combinations:

1. When both product and factor markets are competitive.
2. When factor market is competitive but product market is not.
3. When product market is competitive but factor market is not.
4. When none of the two is competitive.

Let us discuss them one-by-one in that order, but before that, let us enumerate factors on which demand and supply of factors of production depend.

Determinants of demand for factors of production

Demand for a factor of production depends on the following:

1. *Price of the factor:* The higher the price of a factor, the lower is its demand.
2. *Marginal physical product of the factor:* The higher the MPP of a factor, the higher is its demand.
3. *Price of the commodity produced by the factor*: The higher the price of the commodity produced by the factor, the higher is the demand for the factor.
4. *Amount of the collaborating factors available:* If the collaborating factors are not available, the main factor too would not be in demand. Its price would therefore fall.
5. *Prices of the collaborating factors:* If they are high, the demand for the main factor would be low.
6. *Technological progress:* If the technology improves, the demand for factors of production would go up. Upgraded technology increases marginal physical product of a factor and hence its demand.

Determinants of supply of factors of production

The following are the determinants of supply of a factor of production:

1. *Price of the factor:* The higher the price offered for a factor, the higher is its supply.
2. *Tastes of the labour factor:* Labour's tastes and preferences define the trade-off between leisure and work. If labour is leisure loving, it would not set out to work unless the reward is lucrative.
3. *Size of the population:* Higher the population size, the higher the supply of labour.
4. *Labour-force participation rate:* If it is high, the supply of labour too would be high. The labour-force participation rate refers to the proportion of labour-force offering for work. In many societies, women do not come out to work. Labour force participation rate is therefore low as men are the only bread-winners in such communities.
5. *Occupational, educational and geographical distribution of the labour force:* It is yet another determinant of labour supply, which depends on the proportion of labour engaged in primary, secondary or tertiary occupations or on the proportion of the educated or of rural or urban labour to the total labour force.

Bearing these facts in mind, let us return back to factor pricing under the assorted situations.

14.1 WHEN BOTH FACTOR AND PRODUCT MARKETS ARE COMPETITIVE

Supply of factor

A competitive factor-market implies existence of a large number of suppliers of factor services and an equally large size of factor-demand, so that, no single seller or buyer of factor-services may influence factor-price determined by the market forces. Individual factor suppliers provide factor-services in unlimited quantities at this price. This means that individual supply curve of a factor is perfectly elastic (horizontal), such as one shown in Figure 14.1.

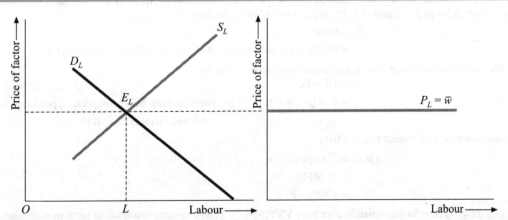

FIGURE 14.1 Demand and supply determine the factor price at E_L. Market demand for factor is OL and market price of a factor is P_L or $\bar{w}$. At this price, a supplier offers unlimited factor-services. The horizontal curve in the right panel is the supply curve of the individual factor.

For the sake of convenience, quantity of a factor is denoted by L and its price by P_L or w (if variable) or $\bar{w}$ (if fixed).

Demand for a factor

Producers demand productive factors for production of goods and services. It would, therefore, be subject to a number of influences as pointed out in the introduction of this chapter.

When product market is competitive, demand curve of factor L can be shown to be

$$P_L = \text{VMP}_L* \qquad (14.1)$$

where, P_L is price of one unit of L and VMP_L is the value of its marginal physical product (MPP_L). In a competitive product market where product price P is fixed at $\bar{P}$, we have

$$\text{VMP}_L = \text{MPP}_L \times \bar{P}$$

When factor market is competitive, factor price P_L is also fixed, say, at $\bar{w}$. Supply curve of factor L is

$$P_L = \bar{w} \qquad (14.2)$$

That is, factor owners supply unlimited quantity of L at $\bar{w}$.

From Eqs. (14.1) and (14.2), equilibrium level of employment of the factor L by a firm may then be given as

$$\text{VMP}_L = P_L** \qquad (14.3)$$

---

* Denoting TR as TRP_L of the factor L and differentiating it with respect to L, we have

$$d(\text{TRP}_L)/dL = d(PQ)/dL$$

$\Rightarrow \qquad \text{MRP}_L = d(\bar{P} \times Q)/dL$ [Product market being competitive, product price $P = \bar{P}$ (fixed)]

$\qquad \qquad \quad = \bar{P} \times (dQ/dL)$

$\qquad \qquad \quad = \bar{P} \times \text{MPP}_L \qquad$ [as $dQ/dL = \text{MPP}_L$]

$\qquad \qquad \quad = \text{VMP}_L$, that is, $\text{MRP}_L = \text{VMP}_L$ in a competitive product market.

Due to diminishing marginal productivity of a factor, MPP_L declines each time a unit of L is added. Hence MPP_L curve is a downward sloping curve showing inverse variation of MPP_L to the quantity of L and so is the VMP_L curve. Since price paid to a unit of L, P_L, is equal to its MRP_L, we have

$$P_L = \text{MRP}_L$$
$$\quad = \text{VMP}_L, \text{ the demand curve of } L \text{ in a competitive product market.}$$

** We know that a producer aims at maximization of profit, given by

$$\pi = \text{TR} - \text{TC}$$
$$\quad = \bar{P} \times Q - \bar{w} \times L \qquad \text{[Both markets being competitive, product price}$$
$$\qquad \qquad \qquad \qquad \qquad = \bar{P} \text{ and factor price} = \bar{w}]$$

Differentiating π with respect to L, we have

$$d\pi/dL = \bar{P}\,[dQ/dL] - \bar{w}$$
$$\qquad \quad = \bar{P}.\text{MPP}_L - \bar{w}$$
$$\qquad \quad = \text{VMP}_L - \bar{w}$$

Setting $d\pi/dL$ at zero for maximization, we have $\text{VMP}_L = \bar{w}$ [The necessary condition of profit maximization] For the sufficient condition to be satisfied, $d^2\pi/dL^2$ must be negative. Differentiating π with respect to L twice, we have

$$d^2\pi/dL^2 = d(\text{VMP}_L)/dL, \text{ which is negative because of negative slope of MPP}_L.$$

The price and quantity of the factor employed by a producer is determined at a point where its demand and supply curves intersect each other. Figures 14.2 and 14.3 demonstrate the mechanism. Note that we have proceeded in the analysis thus far on the assumption that the producer is employing only one variable factor of production. This may not be the case with the firms in general. In the long-run, for instance, every firm operates with two or more variable factors. The analysis of factor pricing when a firm employs more than one variable factor of production is spared for Section 14.5.

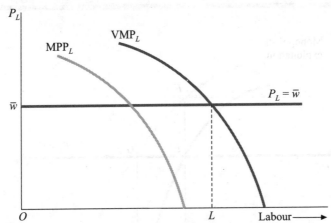

FIGURE 14.2 MPP_L, VMP_L and supply of a factor in a competitive factor market: The figure portrays the downward sloping portion of the Marginal Physical Product curve of the factor (MPP_L). As VMP_L curve represents the money value of Marginal Physical Product of L, $VMP_L = \bar{P} \times MPP_L$, where $\bar{P}$ is the price of the product, which is fixed in a competitive product market. $P_L = VMP_L$ is thus the demand curve of factor and $P_L = \bar{w}$ is its supply curve. Note that, MPP_L is the same as MP_L, the marginal product, the extra P is inserted only to stress physical units.

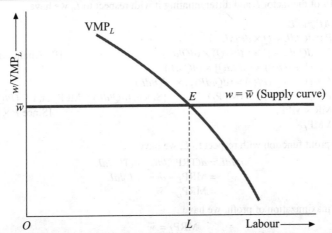

FIGURE 14.3 Equilibrium level of employment of a factor in competitive factor and product markets: In a competitive factor market, supply curve is horizontal while the demand curve in a competitive product market is the VMP_L curve, sloping downward as shown. The two curves intersect each other at E, the point of equilibrium. The equilibrium level of factor demand is OL and the equilibrium level of factor price is $\bar{w}$.

14.2 WHEN FACTOR MARKET IS COMPETITIVE BUT PRODUCT MARKET IS NOT

Factor market being competitive, supply curve of a factor continues to be horizontal, that is, $P_L = \bar{w}$, as in Section 14.1. When the product market is not competitive implying that the product price P is not equal to $\bar{P}$, the demand curve of factor is $P_L = \text{MRP}_L \neq \text{VMP}_L$*. Since equilibrium is determined by the forces of demand and supply, its condition in this case is

$$\bar{w} = \text{MRP}_L^{**} \tag{14.4}$$

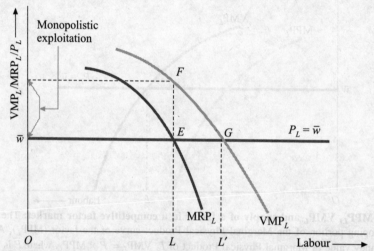

FIGURE 14.4 Supply curve of a factor in a competitive factor market is a horizontal line, $P_L = \bar{w}$ while its demand curve, due to non-competitive product market, is its MRP_L curve. The two intersect each other at E, the
(contd.)

---

* Denoting TR as TRP_L of the factor L and differentiating it with respect to L, we have

$$d(\text{TRP}_L)/dL = d(PQ)/dL$$

$$\Rightarrow \quad \text{MRP}_L = P \times dQ/dL + Q \times dP/dL$$

$$= P \times dQ/dL + Q \times (dP/dQ) \times (dQ/dL) \quad \text{[By Chain rule of differentiation]}$$

$$= P \times [1 + (Q/P) \times (dP/dQ)] \times (dQ/dL)$$

$$= P \times [1 - 1/\{-(P/Q) \times (dQ/dP)\}] \times (dQ/dL)$$

$$= P \times [1 - 1/\{|e|\}] \times (\text{MPP}_L) \quad \text{[Since, } (dQ/dL) = \text{MPP}_L \text{ and } \{-(P/Q) \times (dQ/dP)\} = |e|\text{]}$$

$$= \text{MR} \times \text{MPP}_L \quad \text{[Since } P \times [1 - 1/\{|e|\}] = \text{MR]}$$

$$\neq \text{VMP}_L$$

** Differentiating the profit function with respect to L, we have

$$d\pi/dL = d(\text{TRP}_L)/dL - d(\text{TC})/dL$$

$$= \text{MRP}_L - d(\bar{w} \times L)/dL$$

$$= \text{MRP}_L - \bar{w}$$

Setting $d\pi/dL$ at 0 for maximization of profit, we have

$$\text{MRP}_L = \bar{w}$$

Differentiating $d\pi/dL$ once again for second order condition, we have

$$d^2\pi/dL^2 = d(\text{MRP}_L)/dL = d(\text{MR} \cdot \text{MPP}_L)/dL = \text{MR} \cdot d(\text{MPP}_L)/dL + \text{MPP}_L \cdot d(\text{MR})/dL$$

$$< 0. \text{ [Since, MR} > 0, d(\text{MR})/dL < 0, \text{MPP}_L > 0 \text{ and } d(\text{MPP}_L)/dL < 0.$$

Figure caption (contd.)...
point of equilibrium. Equilibrium level of factor employment is OL and equilibrium price, $\bar{w}$. Had the product market been competitive, the factor price corresponding to OL level of employment would have been higher by EF, which, therefore serves as a measure of monopolistic exploitation of the factor. It arises due to monopoly power of the producer in the product market.

Equilibrium under a competitive product market would, however, have occurred at G, the point of intersection of VMP_L and the supply curve of the factor. Employment of factor would have been higher, that is, OL' while factor price would have remained unchanged at $\bar{w}$. It is due to monopoly power of the producers in the product market that he pays each factor EF less or employs LL' less of them, causing, thereby, *monopolistic exploitation* of the factors.

As evident from Figure 14.4, monopoly power of a firm in the product market makes MRP_L curve as the demand curve causing less employment of factors or paying less to each than when the firm was competitive in the product market. This results in **monopolistic exploitation** of factors.

14.3 WHEN PRODUCT MARKET IS COMPETITIVE BUT FACTOR MARKET IS NOT

In this situation, product price $P = \bar{P}$, but $w \neq \bar{w}$. The supply curve of the factor is, therefore, non-horizontal (Figure 14.5), while its demand curve is the VMP_L curve (As in Section 14.1), while the supply curve of the factor is a function of L, given as $w = f(L)$, where, L is the quantity of the factor supplied. The necessary and sufficient conditions for the firm's equilibrium can be spelled out as

$$VMP_L = ME_L, \qquad [14.5]*$$

and, $\qquad$ slope of VMP_L < slope of $ME_L \qquad [14.6]**$

where, ME_L is marginal expenditure given by $d(TE_L)/dL$ and TE_L, the total expenditure, given by wL.

Note that ME_L is steeper*** than AE_L, where AE_L is the average expenditure, given as (TE_L/L), which works out at $w = f(L)$, whose slope is (dw/dL).

---

* To prove, differentiate $\pi = \bar{P}.Q - w.L$ with respect to L.

$$d\pi/dL = \bar{P}.(dQ/dL) - w - L.(dw/dL)$$
$$= \bar{P}.(MPP_L) - [w + L.(dw/dL)]$$
$$= VMP_L - ME_L$$

where, ME_L is Marginal Expenditure on labour, given as $d(TE_L)/dL$. Since $TE_L = w.L$, we have,

$$ME_L = d(w.L)/dL$$
$$= w + L\,(dw/dL) \qquad \text{[Using product rule of differentiation]}$$

Setting $d\pi/dL$ at zero for the necessary condition, we have

$$VMP_L = ME_L$$

** To prove, differentiate the expression for $(d\pi/dL)$ with respect to L once again, we have

$$d^2\pi/dL^2 = d(VMP_L)/dL - d(ME_L)/dL$$

Since $d^2\pi/dL^2$ must be negative for sufficient condition, $d(VMP_L)/dL - d(ME_L)/dL < 0$ or slope of VMP_L < slope of ME_L.

***Slope of the ME curve $= d(ME_L)/dL$
$\qquad = d[w + L.dw/dL]/dL$
$\qquad = dw/dL + dw/dL + L.d^2w/dL^2$
$\qquad = 2.(dw/dL) + L.d^2w/dL^2$
$\qquad > dw/dL (\text{slope of } AE_L)$

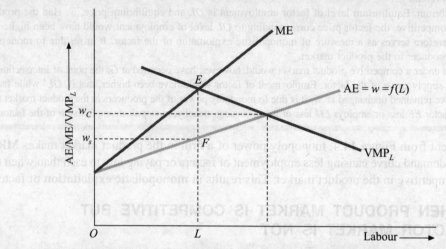

FIGURE 14.5 Equilibrium level of employment of a factor when factor owner is a monopoly and the producer, a competitive one: Equilibrium takes place at E, where $\text{ME} = \text{VMP}_L$. From E, draw a perpendicular onto x-axis, cutting the AE curve at F. Draw from F a perpendicular onto y-axis, to meet it at the point w_S on it. OL is the equilibrium level of employment and ow_S ($= FL$) is the equilibrium level of factor price. Note that ME is steeper than AE, where $\text{AE} = \text{TE}/L = wL/L = w = f(L)$, the supply function.

The employer is competitive in product market ($P = \bar{P}$) having VMP_L as its demand curve for factors. Since $w = f(L)$, the employer is monopsonistic (single buyer of factor) in the factor market. It starts with a low factor price and increases it only when its demand for factor is not met at that price. From the figure, it is clear that w_C is the factor price that corresponds to the point of intersection of factor supply $[w = f(L)]$ and factor demand $\text{VMP}_L \cdot (w_C - w_S)$ represents *monopsonistic exploitation* of factor.

Also, note that the total expenditure on labour, $\text{TE}_L = w \cdot L = f(L) \cdot L$, where, $w = f(L)$ is the supply curve of the factor. Average expenditure on labour, AE_L, is defined as TE_L/L or $w \cdot L/L = w$. Average expenditure on labour, AE_L, is also known as average wage (AW) and Marginal expenditure on it (ME_L), as marginal wage (MW) when factor in question is the labour factor.

Monopsony power of the producer (employer) in the factor market leads to a factor price lower than its competitive level, subjecting the factors thereby to an exploitation called *monopsonistic exploitation*. Its measure is the difference of competitive wage over the monopsonistic wage, i.e., $w_c - w_s$.

14.4 WHEN NONE OF THE TWO MARKETS IS COMPETITIVE

In this case, $w \neq \bar{w}$ and $P \neq \bar{P}$. The profit function can be spelled out as

$$\pi = P \cdot Q - w \cdot L \tag{14.7}$$

where, P is the product price, a function of quantity (Q) sold in the product market, and w is the factor price, a function of factor quantity (L) transacted in the factor market. Producer's equilibrium in the factor market can then be given by the following necessary and sufficient conditions:

$$\text{MRP}_L = \text{ME}_L \quad \text{(Necessary)} \qquad [14.8]*$$

and, $\quad$ slope of MRP_L < slope of ME (Sufficient) $\qquad$ [14.9]**

Thus, slope of MRP_L < the slope of the ME curve as a sufficient condition for profit maximization. The necessary and sufficient conditions taken together imply that MRP_L must cut ME curve from above. The producer's equilibrium in such a market is demonstrated in Figure 14.6. Equilibrium factor price is w_s and equilibrium quantity of factor employed is $O_L \cdot w_s$, w_m and w_c are, respectively monopsonistic, monopolistic and competitive factor prices. The total exploitation of labour, $(w_c - w_s)$, comprises monopolistic exploitation $(w_c - w_m)$ and monopsonistic exploitation $(w_m - w_s)$.

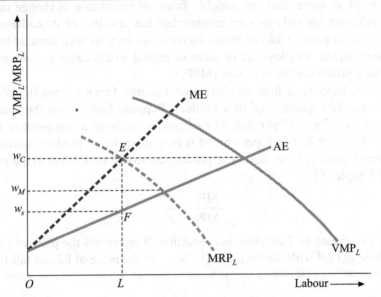

FIGURE 14.6 Equilibrium level of employment and price of a factor when none of the factor and product markets is competitive: Equilibrium in factor employment when none of the factor and product markets is competitive takes place at E, where, MRP_L of the factor intersects its ME-curve from above. A perpendicular
(contd.)

---

*Differentiating with respect to L, we have

$$d\pi/dL = P(dQ/dL) + Q \cdot (dP/dL - w - L \cdot (dw/dL)) \quad \text{[Using the product rule of differentiation]}$$
$$= [P + Q \cdot (dP/dQ)](dQ/dL) - w - L \cdot (dw/dL)$$
$$= P \cdot [1 + (Q/P) \cdot (dP/dQ)] \cdot (dQ/dL) - [w + L \cdot dw/dL]$$
$$= \text{AR} \cdot [1 - 1/|e|](\text{MPP}_L) - \text{ME}_L$$
$$= \text{MR} \cdot (\text{MPP}_L) - \text{ME}_L \quad \text{[Since, MR} = \text{AR} \cdot (1 - 1/|e|), \text{ and, ME}_L = w + L \cdot dw/dL]$$
$$= \text{MRP}_L - \text{ME}_L$$

Setting $d\pi/dL$ at 0 for the necessary condition, we have

$$\text{MRP}_L = \text{ME}_L$$

**For sufficient condition, differentiating the profit function twice with respect to L, we have

$$d^2\pi/dL^2 = d(\text{MRP}_L)/dL - d(\text{ME}_L)/dL$$
$$= \text{slope of MRP}_L - \text{slope of ME}_L$$

and imposing $d^2\pi/dL^2 < 0$, we have, slope of MRP_L < slope of ME_L

Figure caption (contd.)...
from E onto the x-axis meets the AE curve at F. FL or w_s measures the price a producer pays to a factor at the equilibrium while OL measures the equilibrium quantity of factor employed. Note that w_m is the monopolistic factor price and w_c the competitive one while w_s is the monopsonistic factor price. The total exploitation of labour, $(w_c - w_s)$ comprises monopolistic exploitation $(w_c - w_m)$, which would persist even when the employer does not have a monopsony power in the factor market and the rest, $(w_m - w_s)$ attributable to the monopsony power of the firm in the factor market.

14.5 PRICING OF FACTORS WHEN A FIRM EMPLOYS MORE THAN ONE VARIABLE FACTOR

When a firm employs more than one variable factor of production, a change in price of one factor would influence not only its own employment but also that of its collaborating factors. For instance, a fall in price of labour would increase not only its own demand but also that of the collaborating capital. Employment of more of capital would cause an outward shift in the marginal physical product curve of labour (MPP$_L$).

To elaborate, suppose a firm employs two variable factors, namely, labour (L') and capital (K') to produce quantity Q' of a product. Suppose further that the current prices of the two factors are w' and r' per unit of each respectively in a competitive factor market and the price of the product is P per unit of it in a competitive product market. The profit-maximizing employment of the factors of production would be subject to the condition [See Eq. (5.20) of Chapter 5]

$$\frac{\text{MP}_L}{\text{MP}_K} = \frac{w'}{r'} \qquad (14.10)$$

Point $e'(L', K')$ in Figure 14.7 satisfies this condition. It represents the point of tangency of the budget line (isocost) AB with the isoquant Q'. Now let the price of labour fall from w' to w''.

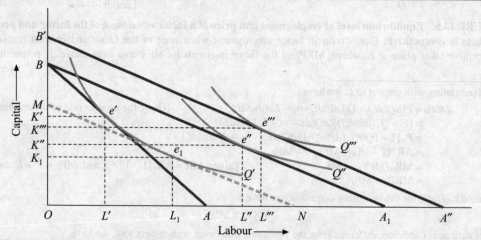

FIGURE 14.7 Effect of a fall in price of one factor on its employment and also on employment of its collaborating factor: The firm is in equilibrium at point e', producing Q' with the help of labour L' and capital K'.

(contd.)

Figure caption (contd.)...
The respective prices of the two factors along the budget line AB are w' and r'. Now, let the price of labour fall to w'' with the result that the budget line AB pivots outward to A_1B (price r of the capital remaining unchanged). In consequence, the producer moves onto a higher isoquant Q'' and attains a new equilibrium at e'', employing L'' of labour and K'' of capital to produce Q'' of the output. Note that a fall in price of labour leads not only to more of labour but also to more of capital being employed by the firm though increase in employment of capital is smaller than that of labour. The Price Effect of a fall in w is $L'L''$ of which $L'L_1$ is the Substitution Effect and L_1L'', the Output Effect. The latter draws an analogy with the Income Effect of a fall in price of a product. The firm thus has employed more of labour and capital in response to a fall in price of labour alone, capital prices remaining unchanged.

The discussion so far assumes that the firm has a fixed amount of money to spend on these two factors. In other words, the total expenditure is assumed constant. But a firm cannot maximize its profits as a constant expenditure firm, particularly, when price of one of the two factors has fallen. The profit-maximizing output before this change in the labour price was Q'. Let the same be now Q'''. The level of expenditure required for the purpose is $A'B'$ touching the isoquant Q''' at e''', as shown. That way, employment of labour and capital both has to increase even further to L''' and K'''. This is known as the Profit Maximizing Effect. The Substitution Effect decreases MPP_L of labour as more labour employed crowds fixed capital. The Output Effect combined with the Profit Maximizing Effect leads to sufficient increase in the employment of capital with the result that the MPP_L of the now-cheaper labour increases significantly to shift the MPP_L curve of the cheaper factor outward.

In consequence, producers would employ more of labour, which in turn, would disturb labour-capital ratio partly by virtue of the substitution effect and partly by virtue of the output effect. Substitution effect would come into play when a firm or producer substitutes cheaper labour for capital whose price remains unaffected while output effect (identical to the income effect of a fall in price of a product in consumer's equilibrium) arises when a firm or producer attempts to optimize output under changed levels of labour and capital employment. In fact, price effect of a fall in price of factor, comprises substitution and output effects just as price effect of a fall in price of a product comprises substitution and income effects. The output effect coupled with the profit-maximizing effect, however, may lead to employment of more of both the factors ultimately despite a fall in price of only one (Figure 14.7). The motive of profit-maximization would prompt the producer to shell out more to buy more of both the factors of production. The additional expenditure required for the purpose can be determined as explained in Figure 14.8.

Note that additional employment of capital following the output and the profit-maximizing effects of a fall in price of labour leads to a rise in MPP_L of labour. This causes outward shifts in the MPP_L curve each time price of factor labour falls (Figure 14.9). Demand for labour is thus derived by joining points of resulting labour employment (L) at each level of wage (w) in accordance with the corresponding VMP_L curve. Thus, joining (L', w'), (L'', w'') and (L''', w''') respectively on $VMP_{L'}$, $VMP_{L''}$ and $VMP_{L'''}$ (Figure 14.9) gives the labour demand curve, d_L.

For a firm employing more than one variable factor of production, the demand curve for a variable factor is not the simple VMP_L curve. Instead, it is the d_L-curve derived as above.

In the same way, demand for a factor by a firm employing more than one variable factor and having monopoly power in the product market is not the simple MRP_L curve. Instead, it is the d_L-curve derived as above.

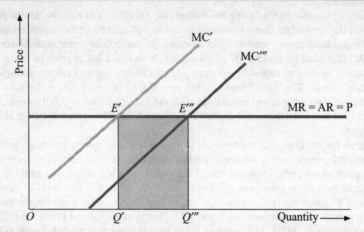

FIGURE 14.8 Q' is the profit-maximizing output as it corresponds to point E' where MC′ cuts MR from below. When price of labour falls, so does the marginal cost. MC′ shifts downward to MC‴. The new MC cuts MR from below at point E'''. Profit-maximizing output increases from Q' to Q''', requiring an additional expenditure to the tune of $Q'E'E'''Q'''$ (shaded area) to be incurred for the purpose.

Thus, VMP_L curve serves as the demand curve for labour when the firm employs only one variable factor and operates in a competitive product market, but if it employs more than one variable factor, the demand curve is d_L, which is derived as in Figure 14.9 from the VMP_L curves. In like manner, MRP_L curve serves as the demand curve for labour when the firm is a monopoly in the product market employing only one variable factor. In case it employs more than one variable factor, the demand curve, d_L, is derived from its MRP_L curves as in Figure 14.9. The only difference is that MRP_L curves replace VMP_L curves.

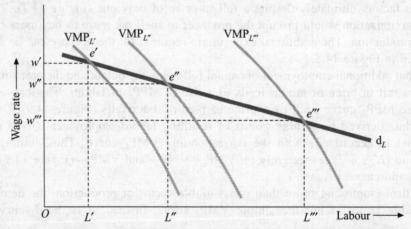

FIGURE 14.9 Every time wage rate falls, VMP_L of labour increases due to increasing MPP_L. Joining points E' (L', w'), E'' (L'', w'') and E''' (L''', w'''); demand curve d_L for the factor labour is obtained. Note that d_L is different from VMP_L.

14.6 MARKET SUPPLY AND MARKET DEMAND OF FACTORS

We have observed in Chapter 2 how supply curve of hours of skilled work from an individual bends backwards at sufficiently high rates of hourly wages (Figure 14.10). The reference here is to the negatively sloped segment of the supply curve of labour hours. At high wage-rates, an individual worker's preference for leisure increases with the result that supply of labour hours decreases. The backward bend so caused in the supply curve has a very simple explanation. Fewer hours of work fetch sufficiently higher levels of income for the worker who develops a tendency to curtail supply of labour hours at higher rates of hourly wages.

The market supply of labour hours, however, has no backward bend. It has a continuously rising trend (Figure 14.11) instead. The phenomenon has an explanation in *perfect mobility* feature of a competitive factor market. Higher wages in labour deficient regions attract labour from labour surplus (low wage) regions with the result that the backward bend in the supply curve straightens out. Also, a high wage rate serves as an incentive for labour to acquire skills through higher studies and special training programmes. Both these factors lead to a steadily rising market supply curve of labour hours (Figure 14.11).

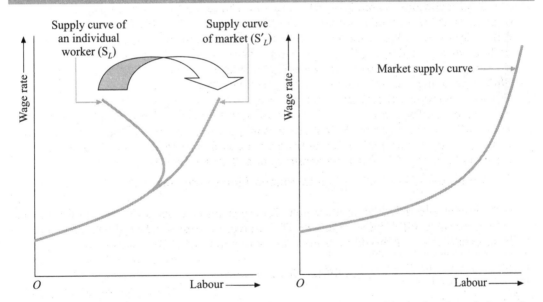

FIGURE 14.10 Backward bending supply curve of an individual's hours of skilled work gets straightened when workers from low-wage regions join in, lured by higher wages. S_L gets straightened to S'_L.

FIGURE 14.11 Positively-sloped **market supply** curve due to free entry and perfect mobility of skilled workers from low-wage regions. It is obtained through horizontal summation of the supply curves of the individual workers.

It is this market supply curve that has been employed in Figure 14.1 to derive the horizontal supply curve of individual workers in a competitive factor market.

Market demand is derived through a horizontal summation of the individual demands. As for the market demand for a factor, it is not just the simple horizontal summation of individual demands that serves the purpose. Instead, it is the horizontal summation of the individual demands adjusted for shifts caused by the shift factors. For instance, a fall in product price causes a downward parallel shift in factor demand portraying the relationship between quantity of factor demanded and its price (see determinants of factor demand in the introductory paragraphs of this chapter). To explain, suppose price of labour falls leading to an increase in labour employment by all the firms in the market. This increases total output and its supply, which in turn, lowers the product price and hence to a fall in value of the marginal product (VMP_L/MRP_L) of labour at all levels of its employment. In consequence, a firm's demand curve for labour shifts downwards to left. The new demand curve so obtained for the firm is its *adjusted demand curve*. Market demand for factors is obtained through horizontal summation of the adjusted demand curves of all the firms in the market. Figure 14.12(a) demonstrates the adjustment process which shifts labour demand from d_L to d_L', the latter being the adjusted demand curve for labour by a firm in the market.

Figure 14.12(b) gives the market demand, D_L', for labour, which is a result of a horizontal summation of individual demands, d_L', of all the firms in the market. A simple horizontal summation of all the unadjusted d_L curves would have given a market demand, D_L, requiring final adjustment as shown.

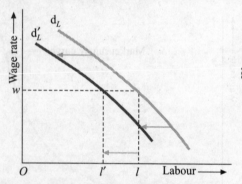

FIGURE 14.12(a) Individual firm's demand curve (d_L) shifts downwards due to a fall in product price, one of the shift factors. Product price falls when product supply increases due to higher employment of labour in consequence to a fall in wage rate. Thus, d_L shifts to d'_L, the adjusted demand curve.

FIGURE 14.12(b) D'_L is the market demand resulting from the horizontal summation of adjusted demands of individual firms. Horizontal summation of unadjusted demands leads to D_L.

One important use of the market demand for factors is the estimation of bargaining power of the labour unions through it. As shown in Figures 14.13 and 14.14, *the bargaining power of the trade unions is inversely related to the price elasticity of factor demand.*

In other words, union's bargaining power is maximum when price elasticity of factor demand is zero and it is minimum when price elasticity of factor demand is maximum. The relationship can be explained as below.

When price elasticity of factor demand is zero, the demand curve is vertical. Labour union can force as high a wage hike as it desires without fearing any retrenchment of fellow-workers (Figure 14.13). Likewise, when price elasticity of factor-demand is non-zero (elastic demand), no wage-hike can be forced by a labour union on the employer without suffering retrenchment of fellow workers in consequence (Figure 14.14). A wage-hike of $w_0 w_1$ may be matched by a retrenchment of $L_0 L_1$ workers.

In summary, union's bargaining power varies inversely as the price elasticity of factor demand.

14.7 CONCLUDING REMARKS AND MARGINAL PRODUCTIVITY THEORY OF DISTRIBUTION

In Sections 14.1 to 14.4, we have discussed pricing of factors by a producer when he employs only one variable factor. In Section 14.1, where factor and product markets are both competitive, the condition of equilibrium was $\overline{w} = \text{VMP}_L = \overline{P} \times \text{MPP}_L$, in Section 14.2, where factor market is competitive, while product market isn't, it was $\overline{w} = \text{MRP}_L = \text{MR} \times \text{MPP}_L$, in Section 14.3, where product market is competitive, while factor market isn't, it was $\text{ME} = \text{VMP}_L = \overline{P} \times \text{MPP}_L$ and in Section 14.4, where none of the two markets is competitive, the condition of equilibrium was $\text{ME} = \text{MRP}_L = \text{MR} \times \text{MPP}_L$. These conditions were obtained without using any specific theories of distribution. What we resorted to was simple calculus to fulfil the objective of profit-maximization, which every producer pursues.

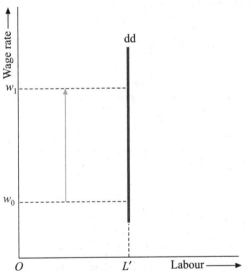
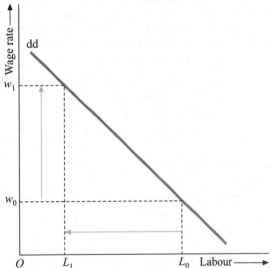

FIGURE 14.13 Suppose market demand is perfectly inelastic and the union presses for a wage hike from an initial w_0 to w_1. The employer cannot but concede as odds are against him. The union has all the bargaining power to achieve its desired ends.

FIGURE 14.14 Suppose market demand is elastic and the union presses for a wage hike from an initial w_0 to w_1. The employer can match union's threat of strike by a counter threat of retrenchment of $L_1 L_0$ workers. This reduces the bargaining power of the union.

Each of these conditions has one thing in common on its right hand side. It is MPP_L or marginal physical product of the factor. The right hand side of each condition expresses the value of marginal physical product of a factor that has to be paid to the factor under different conditions of the factor and product markets. All these results conform to the tenets of what is called the *marginal productivity theory of distribution*, which states that every factor of production is paid the value of its marginal physical product.

The case in Section 14.5, which relates to employment of more than one variable factor of production by the producers, provides no exception to the marginal productivity theory of distribution. In fact, it is an extension of the theory to many variable factors though in some of them it may not be all that simple. But, if we assume that it is, the profit maximizing combination of all the variable factors would be one in which the value of the marginal physical product of each factor employed is equal to its price. For example, suppose that there are two variable factors employed, namely, labour (L) and capital (K). Suppose, further that their prices are $\bar{w}$ and $\bar{r}$ (Factor and product markets both competitive), respectively. For profit maximizing combination of L and K,

$\bar{w}$ = value of the MPP_L of L = $(\bar{P}/MR) \times MPP_L$
$\bar{r}$ = value of the MPP_K of K = $(\bar{P}/MR) \times MPP_K$

Thus,
$$\frac{\bar{w}}{\bar{r}} = \frac{(\bar{P}/MR) \times MPP_L}{(\bar{P}/MR) \times MPP_K} = \frac{MPP_L}{MPP_K} \qquad [14.11]*$$

---

* For mathematical treatment, $\pi = TR - TE = PQ - (wL + rK)$; where, P is the price of the product, given as a function of quantity (Q) as $P = f(Q)$; w is the price of labour, given as a function of its quantity (L) as $w = g(L)$ and r is the price of capital, given as a function of its quantity (K) as $r = h(K)$.

Differentiating the profit function partially with respect to L and K, we have

$\partial \pi / \partial L = [P(\partial Q/\partial L) + Q(\partial P/\partial L)] - [w + L(\partial w/\partial L)]$
$\qquad = [P(\partial Q/\partial L) + Q(\partial P/\partial Q)(\partial Q/\partial L)] - [w + L(\partial w/\partial L)]$ (using chain rule of differentiation)
$\qquad = [P + Q(\partial P/\partial Q)](MPP_L) - ME_L$ (where, $(\partial Q/\partial L) = MPP_L$, $[w + L(\partial w/\partial L)] = ME_L$)
$\qquad = MR \times MPP_L - ME_L$
$\qquad = MRP_L - ME_L$ (MR $\times MPP_L = MRP_L$)
$\qquad = 0$ (Necessary condition for maximization of π)
$\Rightarrow \quad MRP_L = ME_L$ \hfill (1)

And,

$\partial \pi / \partial K = [P(\partial Q/\partial K) + Q(\partial P/\partial K)] - [r + K(\partial r/\partial K)]$
$\qquad = [P(\partial Q/\partial K) + Q(\partial P/\partial Q)(\partial Q/\partial K)] - [r + K(\partial r/\partial K)]$ (using chain rule of differentiation)
$\qquad = [P + Q(\partial P/\partial Q)](MPP_K) - ME_K$ (where, $(\partial Q/\partial K) = MPP_K$, $[r + K(\partial r/\partial K)] = ME_K$)
$\qquad = MR \times MPP_K - ME_K$
$\qquad = MRP_K - ME_K$ (MR $\times MPP_K = MRP_K$)
$\qquad = 0$ (Necessary condition for maximization of π)
$\Rightarrow \quad MRP_K = ME_K$ \hfill (2)

Dividing corresponding sides of (1) by those of (2), we have

$\qquad\qquad MRP_L/MRP_K = ME_L/ME_K$
$\Rightarrow \qquad (MR \times MPP_L)/(MR \times MPP_K) = ME_L/ME_K$
$\Rightarrow \qquad MPP_L/MPP_K = ME_L/ME_K$ \hfill (3)

The expression can also be written as

$$MPP_L/MPP_K = \bar{w}/\bar{r}$$

as soon as the firm loses its monopsony power. ME_L would then be equal to $\bar{w}$ and ME_K, to $\bar{r}$.

The expression in Eq. (14.11) summarizes the contention of the marginal productivity theory of distribution.

Assorted applications and implications of the theory

1. *Exploitation of labour*

According to Joan Robinson, a productive factor is said to be exploited by its employer if it is paid a price less than the value of its marginal product (VMP). The practice of paying less than the value of marginal product is common with the firms having monopoly power in the product market (leading to what is known as monopolistic exploitation of the factor) or monopsony power in the factor market (leading to what is known as monopsonistic exploitation of the factor). The two are demonstrated below for the factor, labour.

(a) *Monopolistic exploitation of labour*

When a firm enjoys monopoly power in the product market and employs one variable factor, its demand curve for labour (Section 14.2) is the MRP_L curve (instead of the VMP_L curve). This leads to monopolistic exploitation of labour as portrayed in Figures 14.15 and 14.16.

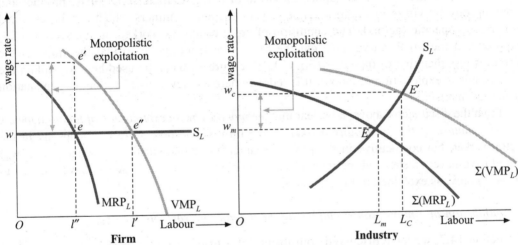

FIGURE 14.15 When the firm is competitive in product-market, equilibrium level of employment is l' at e'' but when it is monopolistic in product market, equilibrium level of employment is l'' at e. Monopolistic exploitation is ee'.

FIGURE 14.16 When the industry is competitive in the product-market, equilibrium level of employment is L_C at E' but when it is monopolistic in product market equilibrium level of employment is L_m at E. Monopolistic exploitation is $w_c - w_m$.

Note that the supply curve of labour, S_L, is horizontal for an individual firm in a competitive labour market while its demand curve is the VMP_L curve when the firm is competitive in the product market and the MRP_L curve when it is monopolistic in the product market (Figure 14.15). The monopolistic firm employs l'' labour at e. The corresponding wage a competitive firm would pay is ee' higher, giving ee' as a measure of monopolistic exploitation. Had the firm in question been a competitive one, it would have employed l' labour at e'', at the competitive wage, w.

In Figure 14.16, labour market supply, S_L, slopes upwards as all the firms in the industry face a competitive labour market. Had they been competitive in the product market as well, the equilibrium would have taken place at E' and the labour employed at w_c wage would have been L_C. The industry, however, enjoying monopoly power in product market, employs L_m labour at w_m wage. The magnitude of the monopolistic exploitation is $w_c - w_m$ [Note that ΣVMP_L and ΣMRP_L, the demand curves of the industry, are flatter than the VMP_L and MRP_L, the demand curves of an individual firm].

(b) Monopsonistic exploitation of labour

When a firm has monopsonistic power in the factor market and monopolistic power in the product market, it pays the factor a price not only less than its VMP_L but also less than its MRP_L. Refer to Figure 14.6 (Section 14.4). Equilibrium worked out there refers to one in which none of the labour and product markets is competitive, that is, the firm is a monopoly (single seller of product) in the product market and monopsony (single buyer of labour) in the factor market [A single uranium mining company in a small town provides an example of a firm with monopoly power in the product market and monopsony power in the factor market. It is a monopoly by virtue of being a single seller of its product and a monopsony by virtue of being a single buyer of uranium miners which can be assumed as perfectly specific factors]. The condition of equilibrium, as worked out in Section 14.4, requires that the MRP_L curve must cut the ME curve from above so that the slope of the former is less than that of the latter [Eq. (14.9)]. Figure 14.6 can be used here to explain the monopsonistic exploitation of labour. It is redrawn here as Figure 14.17 for better explanation of the mechanism.

From the discussions above, it is clear that the *monopsonistic exploitation of labour depends on the structure of the commodity market*. If the firm in question, were a monopsony in the factor-market, but competitive in the product market, the monopolistic component $(w_c - w_m)$ would have never existed and the monopsonistic exploitation $(w_c - w_s)$ would have reduced to $(w_c - w_f)$ only, as explained in Figure 14.18.

2. Equilibrium of a monopsonist employing more than one variable factor

In Section 14.7, we have discussed equilibrium of a firm facing a non-competitive product market and hiring two variable factors from a competitive factor market. The condition of equilibrium, as obtained therein, was given by Equation 14.11. Now suppose, the firm is the only buyer (monopsony) of these the two factors. The monopsony power in the factor market implies capability of a firm to dictate the factor prices. Such firms begin employment of factors at the lowest possible prices and raise them subsequently only when factors reject the prices offered and refuse to supply factor services. Those desperate for employment succumb to exploitative practices of the firm, but those not so desperate, refuse to oblige. On the contrary, if the firm is desperate to hire more factors, it comes out with higher factor prices to attract more factors.

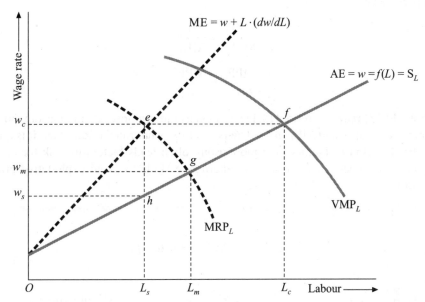

FIGURE 14.17 Due to monopoly power of the firm in the product market, its demand curve for labour is its MRP_L curve while the supply curve of labour faced by the firm in the labour market is its AE curve sloping upwards steadily. Had the labour market been competitive, the demand curve would have been the VMP_L curve, the competitive wage would have been w_c and employment, L_c at the equilibrium point, f. Had the firm been a simple monopoly in the product market, the monopolistic wage would have been w_m and employment, L_m (treating MRP_L as the firm's demand curve for labour and its AE curve as the supply curve of labour) at the equilibrium point, g. The difference of w_c over w_m, i.e. $(w_c - w_m)$ measures the *monopolistic exploitation of labour*. But since the firm has monopsony power in the labour market, it determines its profit-maximizing employment of labour at the point e where its MRP_L curve cuts its ME curve from above. A perpendicular from point e onto the labour axis determines its profit-maximizing employment L_s and profit-maximizing wage, w_s at h where perpendicular from e hits the AE curve. Thus, $(w_c - w_s)$ measures the monopsonistic exploitation of labour, of which, $(w_c - w_m)$ arises purely due to the monopoly power of the firm in the product market and $(w_m - w_s)$, purely due to its monopsony power in the factor market.

In Section 14.4, we have worked out the conditions of equilibrium of a firm employing a single variable factor and facing non-competitive product and factor markets. We have applied these conditions to a firm having monopoly power in the product market and monopsony power in the input market.

Let us extend our analysis to the firm employing more than one variable factor of production. Let the firm in question employ two variable factors of production, namely, labour (L) and capital (K). Expressing its profit function as

$$\pi = TR - TE$$
$$= PQ - (wL + rK) \qquad (14.12)$$

where, P is the price of the product, given as a function of quantity (Q) as $P = f(Q)$; w is the price of labour, given as a function of its quantity (L) as $w = g(L)$ and r is the price of capital, given as a function of its quantity (K) as $r = h(K)$.

Differentiating Eq. (14.12) partially with respect to L and K, as in the derivation of Eq. (14.11), we have

$$\frac{\text{MPP}_L}{\text{MPP}_K} = \frac{\text{ME}_L}{\text{ME}_K} \qquad (14.13)$$

Or,

$$\frac{\text{MPP}_L}{\text{ME}_L} = \frac{\text{MPP}_K}{\text{ME}_K} \qquad (14.14)$$

Equation (14.13) reduces to Eq. (14.11) as soon as the firm loses its monopsony power. ME_L would then be equal to $\overline{w}$ and ME_K, to $\overline{r}$. The possibility is not ruled out. In fact, it is quite likely to happen. Exploitation of factors by a monopsony often leads factors to look for alternatives. They may move to other places or acquire alternative skills to avoid exploitative practices of the monopsony.

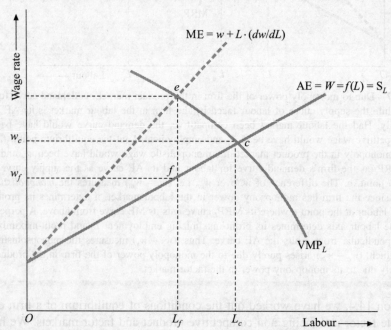

FIGURE 14.18 The size of the monopsonistic exploitation depends on the structure of the commodity market. If the commodity market is competitive, MRP_L curve becomes redundant and VMP_L curve takes its place. Competitive wage (w_c) is determined at the point c where VMP_L curve (demand curve for labour) cuts the AE curve (supply curve of labour). Equilibrium level of employment of labour at this point is L_c. Since the firm enjoys monopsony power in the labour market, the equilibrium condition requires that the VMP_L curve must cut the ME curve from above [see Eq. (14.6)]. This happens at point e, the point of equilibrium of the monopsonist. A perpendicular from e onto the labour axis gives the equilibrium level of employment as L_f and the wage as w_f. Thus, ($w_c - w_f$) measures the monopsonistic exploitation, which is much smaller than ($w_c - w_s$) of Figure 14.17. To conclude, the size of monopsonistic exploitation is much larger when the firm possesses monopoly power in the product market than when it does not.

3. Indeterminacy of the equilibrium of bilateral monopoly

When a single seller (Monopoly) faces a single buyer (Monopsony), the resulting market structure is called a bilateral monopoly. As seen earlier, a uranium mining company in a small town provides a good example of a bilateral monopoly. In factor market, it is a single buyer of uranium miners and in the product market, it is a single seller of its product. But, that doesn't set the ground for a bilateral monopoly unless the single buyer of labour faces a single seller of labour. As a single buyer of labour, the firm starts with the lowest initial wages which it raises only when workers reject them. Miners though highly specific (suited only to uranium mining), have to accept wages offered sooner or later or get unionized to protect their interests. Suppose, they go for the second option and come up with a strong union which restricts labour supply in the event the firm does not come up with a fair deal. Unionized miners thus assume the role of a single seller of labour (monopoly), while the uranium company, the only employer of labour serves as a single buyer (monopsony) of labour. This sets up a bilateral monopoly. Figure 14.19 explains its equilibrium, which is indeterminate.

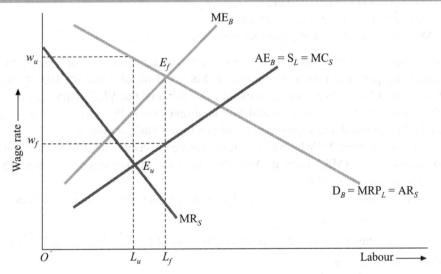

FIGURE 14.19 Indeterminacy of equilibrium of a bilateral monopoly: The monopsony firm determines its equilibrium at E_f, the point where its MRP_L curve cuts its ME_B curve from above. Thus, monopsony would like to employ L_f labour at a wage of w_f. Note that the wage offered by the firm is much less than its MRP_L. Labour union acting as a monopoly in the labour market, determines its equilibrium at E_u, the point of intersection of the union's MC curve [MC_S, the AE curve of labour buyer (AE_B)] with its MR curve (MR_S) from below. The trade union thus would like to supply L_u of labour at a wage of w_u. Note that AE_B, the supply curve of labour, is treated by the trade union as its MC curve (MC_S) while MRP_L curve of the firm is treated by it as its AR curve (AR_S). The monopsony firm wants to employ $L_f (L_f > L_u)$ of labour at a wage rate $w_f (w_f < w_u)$ while the trade union wants to supply $L_u (L_u < L_f)$ of labour at a wage rate $w_u (w_u > w_f)$. Equilibrium is thus indeterminate (E_u being different from E_f). How much of labour is employed and at what wage would depend on the relative bargaining powers of the two sides. Note that subscript 'S' is used for seller of labour while subscript B, for its buyer.

Note that average expenditure curve of labour-buyer (AE_B), the firm, is treated by the labour union as its marginal cost curve (MC_S) and the MRP_L curve of the firm is treated by the labour union (Single seller of labour) as its average revenue curve (AR_S). Labour union derives its marginal revenue curve (MR_S) from its AR_S curve.

Single buyer of labour (firm) and single seller of it (labour union) reach their own equilibria which do not relate to the same point in labour-wage space. No unique equilibrium is possible under the circumstances. That, however, does not mean that the firm would close down. Sooner or later the two sides would come to terms somewhere in between. Who gains what would depend on the relative bargaining powers of the two.

4. *Labour union versus competitive employer-firm: union's objectives and their attainment*

As is obvious, the basic objective of a trade union is to protect its members against exploitative practices of the employers. With passage of time, trade unions gain strength and go far beyond the traditional objective of protecting their members against exploitation. A trade union today may pursue any of the following objectives:

(a) Maximization of employment,
(b) Maximization of the total wage-bill, and
(c) Maximization of the total gains to the union as a whole.

To see how a trade union attempts these objectives, let us assume that the employer firm possesses neither monopoly power nor monopsony power. Market demand curve for labour under these assumptions would be the horizontal summation (ΣVMP_L) of the VMP_L curves of all the firms and market supply curve of labour would be the simple upwardly sloping curve as shown in Figure 14.20. The demand and supply curves intersect each other at point e.

The trade unions treat ΣVMP_L curve as their average revenue curve (AR_s) and derive their marginal revenue curve (MR_s) from it. Also, they treat the market supply of labour (S_L-curve) as their marginal cost curve (MC_s).

Let us see now how trade unions attempt each one of the above three objectives.

(a) *Maximization of employment*

Employment is maximized at e, the point of intersection of market demand and supply.

(b) *Maximization of the total wage-bill*

For maximization of the total wage-bill, the first order derivative of TR_s must be zero. In alternative language, $MR_s = 0$. This happens at point e' where OL' of labour is employed at wage rate w'. Note that wage-bill is maximized but level of employment falls from OL to OL' while wage rate rises from w to w'.

(c) *Maximization of total gains to the union*

As explained in Figure 14.20, total gains are maximized at the point where MC_s of labour cuts its MR_s from below. This happens at e''. Level of employment falls further to OL'' while wage rate rises further to w''.

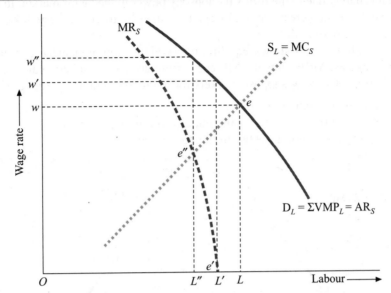

FIGURE 14.20 Alternative objectives of a trade union and their attainment when buyer firm is competitive: Employment is maximized at e, the point where market demand and supply intersect each other. OL of labour is employed at w wage. Maximization of total wage bill takes place at e' where $MR_S = 0$ (TR_S is maximum). Note that total wage is maximized at lower level of employment ($OL' < OL$) but at higher wage rate w' ($w' > w$). For maximization of total gains to the labour unions, their MC_s curve must cut their MR_s curve from below. This happens at point e'' where OL'' labour is employed at wage rate w'''. Note again that w'' is the highest wage rate and OL'' is the lowest level of employment.

5. How far are the labour unions beneficial to their members?

The extent to which labour unions benefit their members depends on two things:

(a) *The elasticity of demand for labour*

When demand for labour is highly inelastic, a labour union can prove highly effective in forcing a wage hike without sacrificing the cause of employment of its members (Figures 14.13 and 14.14). Let us now examine the same proposition in a slightly different way in Figure 14.21.

The left panel shows equilibrium of a competitive labour market. The steeper demand, D_L (inelastic), the flatter demand, d_L (elastic) and the upwardly sloping supply curve, S_L, intersect at e. The competitive wage is w_c and employment, OL. Now suppose, labour union goes for a wage hike to the level of w'. The union will have to sacrifice employment of LL' labour if the labour demand is inelastic (D_L) and of LL'' labour if it is elastic (d_L). This shows that the sacrifice of labour employment for a given wage hike varies directly with wage-elasticity of labour demand or the wage hike for a given sacrifice of labour employment varies inversely with it.

The right panel shows identical effects of union's moves in respect of a single firm in the labour market.

(b) *Monopsonistic power of the employer-firm*

If the employer-firm possesses monopsonistic power in the factor market and practices monopsonistic exploitation, labour union can reduce the size of the monopsonistic exploitation at least by that part of it which is purely due to the firm's monopsony power in the factor market. In addition, the union can also enforce an increase in total wage bill either by forcing a wage-hike or by raising the level of employment or both.

Figure 14.22 (left panel) shows equilibrium level of employment (L_s) of labour at the monopsonistic wage w_s. MRP_L cuts the ME curve from above at e, a perpendicular from which meets the AE curve at s. Now suppose workers form a union with an objective of

(i) Maximization of employment, or
(ii) Maximization of wage-rate for the initial level of employment, or
(iii) Attempting a situation in between the above two

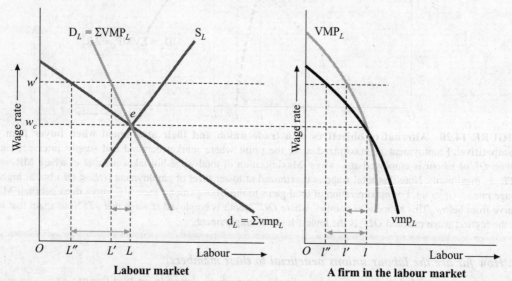

FIGURE 14.21 **Bargaining power of the trade unions and the elasticity of factor demand revisited:** Left panel shows the equilibrium of a competitive labour market. Demand and supply curves intersect each other at e. OL of labour is employed at competitive wage rate w_c. Labour employed by a firm in the labour market is shown in the right panel. Now suppose the labour union agitates and succeeds in getting a wage-hike. The new wage is, say, w'. If the market demand curve is relatively inelastic (D_L), loss of employment to the members of the union is only $L'L$; but if it is relatively elastic (d_L), loss of employment is $L''L$, which is higher ($L''L > L'L$). In respect of a firm, if the labour demand is relatively inelastic (VMP_L), the loss of employment to the members of the union is $l'l$, but if it is relatively elastic (vmp_L), the loss of employment is $l''l$, which is higher ($l''l > l'l$). This shows that the wage-hike enforced by the unions, benefits the members only when labour demand curve is inelastic than when it is elastic.

(i) *Maximization of employment:* If the union intends to maximize employment, it can set a wage w' at e', the point of intersection of demand (MRP_L) and supply (AE_L). The wage so set (w') will be equal to MRP_L and the level of employment to L' ($L' > L_s$) (Figure 14.22, left panel), where L_s is the level of employment when the firm has monopsony power in the factor market.

(ii) *Maximization of wage-rate for the initial level of employment:* This has been shown in the right panel of Figure 14.22. Union pushes the wage-rate up to w'' level for the existing level of employment, OL_s. Wage bill increases from $OL_s sw_s$ to $OL_s ew''$. The operative supply curve of labour is $w''e\,B'AE_L$, with a kink at the point B' and corresponding marginal expenditure curve is made up of two discontinuous segments $w''e\,B'$ and BME_L. Wage rate w'' is the highest attainable wage for the labour union. If it tries to push its luck further to have a wage rate higher than w'', it would have to do with an employment less than OL_s due to the discontinuity in the ME curve.

(iii) *Attempting a situation in between the above two:* Union can attempt a situation in between the two extremes of employment maximization and wage rate maximization for the initial level of employment. That way, union can attempt employment betwee OL_s and OL' and wage rate between W_s and W''.

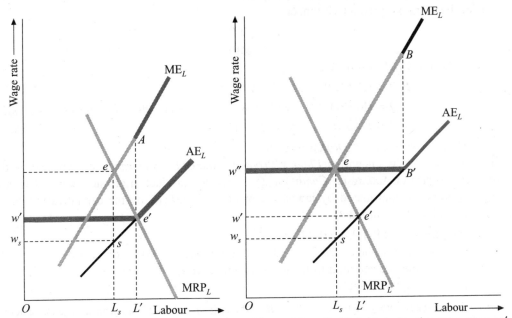

FIGURE 14.22 Monopsonistic buyer firm versus labour union: In the left panel, union sets a wage w' at e', the intersection of demand (MRP_L) and supply (AE_L). The operative supply curve of labour now is $w'e'\,AE_L$ with a kink at e' and the operative marginal expenditure curve is $w'e'AME_L$, with two discontinuous segments $w'e'$ and AME_L. Note that $(w' - w_s)$, the purely monopsonistic component of the total exploitation of labour under monopsony, is eliminated. This helps maximization of employment as well. Monopolistic exploitation though still continues. Labour union has thus succeeded in reducing total exploitation of labour to the size of the monopolistic exploitation. Wage rate and employment have both increased. Wage bill also increases from $(OL_s\,sw_s)$ to $(OL'e'w')$. In the right panel, labour union attempts maximization of the wage rate for the existing work force, OL_s. The maximum it can raise it is to the level of w''. If the union succeeds, wage bill would increases from $OL_s sw_s$ to $OL_s ew''$. The operative supply curve of labour would be $w''eB'AE_L$, with a kink at B' and corresponding marginal expenditure curve would be made up of two discontinuous segments $w''eB'$ and BME_L. Wage rate w'' is the highest attainable wage for the labour union. If the union tries to push its luck further to have a wage rate higher than w'', it would have to do with employment less than OL_s due to the discontinuity in ME_L curve. However, union can also attempt an intermediate situation between employment maximization and wage rate maximization. That way, union can attempt employment between OL_S and OL' and wage rate between w_S and w''.

6. Marginal Productivity Theory and Product Exhaustion Theorem

Marginal productivity theory requires that a factor must be paid the value of its marginal physical product. If every factor is paid this value, the total product of the firm must get exhausted to fufil the basic accounting identity, *product = income*. Let us investigate whether the theory stands this test. The objective is not to establish the theory, but to investigate whether the mathematical tools employed in this chapter to evolve a scientific method of factor pricing stand the test of theoretical expectation. The accounting identity requires that the value of the product must get exhausted by the factor payments. Mathematically speaking,

$$P.Q = w.L + r.K \qquad (14.15)$$

Here, output Q is sold at price P, and the firm employs two factors, namely labour (L) and Capital (K) at prices w and r per unit, respectively.

Under the marginal productivity theory,

$$w = P.\text{MPP}_L,$$

and,
$$r = P.\text{MPP}_K$$

Substituting in Eq. 14.15, we have

$$P.Q = (P.\text{MPP}_L).L + (P.\text{MPP}_K).K \qquad (14.16)$$
$$\Rightarrow \quad Q = (\text{MPP}_L).L + (\text{MPP}_K).K \qquad \text{(Cancelling } P \text{ from both the sides)}$$
$$\Rightarrow \quad Q = L.(\partial Q/\partial L) + K.(\partial Q/\partial K) \qquad (14.17)$$

where, $(\partial Q/\partial L) = \text{MPP}_L$ and $(\partial Q/\partial K) = \text{MPP}_K$.

Equation (14.17) is known as *Euler's Product Exhaustion Theorem**, known also as the *Adding-up Problem* or *Adding-up Condition*. Q is the total product in physical units of which, $L.(\partial Q/\partial L)$ units are contributed by labour factor and $K.(\partial Q/\partial K)$ by the capital factor. From Eq. (14.16), value of the product,

$$(PQ) = (P.\text{MPP}_L).L + (P.\text{MPP}_K).K$$
$$= \text{Total value of MPP}_L \text{ of labour} + \text{total value of MPP}_K \text{ of capital}$$
$$= \text{Income accruing to labour} + \text{Income accruing to capital}$$
$$= \text{Income (Total)}.$$

---

* Euler's Theorem states that $rQ = L(\partial f/\partial L) + K(\partial f/\partial K)$; where, $Q = f(L, K)$ is a homogeneous function of degree r in L and K, so that, $f(\lambda L, \lambda K) = \lambda^r f(L, K)$. When $r = 1$ (i.e., $Q = f(L, K)$ is a homogeneous function of degree 1 in L and K), $f(\lambda L, \lambda K) = \lambda f(L, K)$ and the theorem reduces to

$$Q = L(\partial f/\partial L) + K(\partial f/\partial K). \text{ Then, } Q = f(L, K) = Lf(1, K/L) = L\phi(K/L).$$

Then,
$$(\partial Q/\partial L) = \phi(K/L) + L\phi'(K/L)(-K/L^2)$$
$$= \phi(K/L) - \phi'(K/L)(K/L)$$
$$\Rightarrow \quad L(\partial Q/\partial L) = L\phi(K/L) - K\phi'(K/L).$$

Likewise, it can be shown that

$$K(\partial Q/\partial K) = K.L.\phi'(K/L)(1/L)$$
$$= K\phi'(K/L).$$

Adding, we have

$$L(\partial Q/\partial L) + K(\partial Q/\partial K) = L\phi(K/L) - K\phi'(K/L) + K\phi'(K/L)$$
$$= L\phi(K/L)$$
$$= Lf(1, K/L)$$
$$= f(L, K)$$
$$= Q.$$

Hence the theorem, $\quad Q = L(\partial Q/\partial L) + K(\partial Q/\partial K) = L.\text{MPP}_L + K.\text{MPP}_K$

Euler's theorem of product exhaustion is based on the assumption that the production function is a homogeneous one. Clark, Wicksteed and Walras, in their theorem of product exhaustion, showed that the assumption of homogeneity of the production function is not necessary.

Clark-Wicksteed-Walras 'product exhaustion' theorem* states that paying the factors the value of their marginal physical product leads to exhaustion of total value of the product in long-run competitive equilibrium, regardless of whether the production function is homogeneous or not.

Note that the theorem applies only in the long-run competitive equilibrium in which LAC is constant and the input elasticity of output is unitary.

14.8 RENTAL ELEMENT IN FACTOR PRICING

So far, we have discussed pricing of variable factors of production that possess a marginal product. Units of variable labour and capital possessing a marginal product are priced effectively through marginal productivity theory. Like labour, capital is assumed divisible here with its units possessing a marginal product each. One example of divisible capital is raw materials and another is financial capital. Their units possess a marginal product each. Raw materials can be priced effectively through the theory, but pricing of financial capital, an indirect factor, involves interest element too, which necessitates a separate theory of pricing. This is therefore taken up in Chapter 15. Nevertheless, the theory goes well in pricing of raw materials.

Not all factors are divisible into smaller units with a marginal product attached to each. For example, land and building are not only indivisible, but also fixed in their supply in long-run and short-run, respectively. The factor land is fixed in supply in long-run, while the factor building is fixed in its supply even in short-run. Both, as mentioned above, possess the attribute of indivisibility. The marginal productivity theory is of no use in pricing of such factors. A separate treatment is must for the purpose. Pricing of the factor building is based on the concept of **quasi-rent** and is being taken up in this very section. The same is the case with pricing of the factor land. It is based on the concept of **economic-rent** and is also being taken up in this section. In other words, this section is devoted to rental element in pricing of land and building.

---

*Under product exhaustion,

$$Q = (MPP_L).L + (MPP_K).K$$
$$\Rightarrow dQ = (MPP_L).dL + (MPP_K).dK$$
$$= (MPP_L)(\lambda L) + (MPP_K).(\lambda K)$$

[That is, if all factors are increased in the same proportion, λ, $(dL/L) = \lambda = (dK/K)$, $dL = \lambda L$ and $dK = \lambda K$]

$$= \lambda[(MPP_L).L + (MPP_K).K]$$
$$\Rightarrow dQ/\lambda = (MPP_L).L + (MPP_K).K$$
$$\Rightarrow QdQ/Q\lambda = (MPP_L).L + (MPP_K).K \quad \text{(multiplying and dividing on left by } Q\text{)}$$
$$\Rightarrow Q(dQ/Q)/\lambda = (MPP_L).L + (MPP_K).K$$
$$\Rightarrow Q.e = (MPP_L).L + (MPP_K).K$$

[Where, e is the input elasticity of the output $= (dQ/Q)/\lambda = (dQ/Q)/(dL/L) = (dQ/Q)/(dK/K)$]

$$\Rightarrow P.Q.e = (P.MPP_L).L + (P.MPP_K).K \quad \text{[Multiplying both the sides by } P\text{]}$$

The resulting equation proves the Clark-Wicksteed-Walras 'product exhaustion' theorem provided $e = 1$, which actually is the case when constant returns to scale accrue in production, i.e.,

$$\frac{dQ/Q}{dL/L} = \frac{\% \text{ change in } Q}{\% \text{ change in } L} = e = 1; \quad \text{and} \quad \frac{dQ/Q}{dK/K} = \frac{\% \text{ change in } Q}{\% \text{ change in } L} = e = 1$$

Rental element enters in pricing of some real capital, a direct factor, as well. But that, as in case of financial capital, also involves the interest element and is therefore spared for Chapter 15.

Let us now turn to pricing of land and building through the concepts of rent and quasi-rent.

(a) *Factors with supply fixed in the long-run*

Economic rent may be defined as a payment to a factor, made over and above its opportunity cost. The opportunity cost, also known as transfer earning of a factor, refers to its earning from its next best alternative use. Alternatively, it can be defined as the cost of opportunity foregone by a factor for the sake of its current use. Thus,

Economic Rent = Actual Earning of a Factor − Opportunity Cost of the Factor

If a factor has no alternative use, its opportunity cost is zero. In this case, economic rent of the factor would be equal to its actual earning.

Before proceeding any further, it would be appropriate to first explain the concepts of economic rent, actual earnings and opportunity cost through an illustration.

ILLUSTRATION 14.1: Given the equation of demand for a factor

$$Q_F^D = 100{,}000 - 3P_F$$

and that of its supply

$$Q_F^S = 2P_F$$

where, Q_F^D is the quantity of the factor demanded at a price P_F and Q_F^S is its quantity supplied at P_F.

Determine:

(a) The actual earning of the factor,
(b) The opportunity cost of the factor, and
(c) Economic rent of the factor

Solution:

(a) In equilibrium, $Q_F^D = Q_F^S$. Equilibrium price and quantity are $P_F = 20{,}000$ and $Q_F = 40{,}000$. Actual earning of the factor = $40{,}000 \times 20{,}000$ = **800,000,000**.

(b) Opportunity cost, the cost of the next best alternative use of the factor, is given by the area of the region below the supply curve in the equilibrium position. It is thus the area of $\triangle OAe$ (Figure 14.23), which is given by $1/2 \times OA \times Ae$. Substituting $OA = 40{,}000$ and $Ae = 20{,}000$, we have area of $\triangle OAe = 1/2 \times 40{,}000 \times 20{,}000 = 400{,}000{,}000$.

(c) Economic rent, an excess of actual earning of the factor over and above its opportunity cost, is thus 400,000,000 (that is, 800,000,000 − 400,000,000). Alternatively, it is the excess of the area of rectangle $OAeB$ over that of the $\triangle OAe$. From the figure, it is clearly the area of $\triangle OBe$, given by $1/2 \times OB \times Be$. Substituting, $OB = 20{,}000$ and $Be = 40{,}000$, we have, area of $\triangle OBe = 400{,}000{,}000$.

In fact, actual earning of the factor (Area of the rectangle $OAeB$) can be split into two parts—one, the opportunity cost (Area of triangle OAe) and the other, the economic rent (Area of

ΔOBe). Thus, economic rent refers to any payment made to a factor in excess of its opportunity cost. Economic rent, in this sense, is a surplus. Alfred Marshall called it the **producer's surplus** defined as the area above the supply curve but below the level of equilibrium price. In the same way, opportunity cost may be treated as producer's total variable cost (TVC) defined as the area below the supply curve (in case of industry) or below the MC curve (in case of a firm) that lies below the equilibrium level of quantity. Since, supply curve shows MC of offering an additional unit of a factor, the opportunity cost can be treated as TVC (Chapter 6).

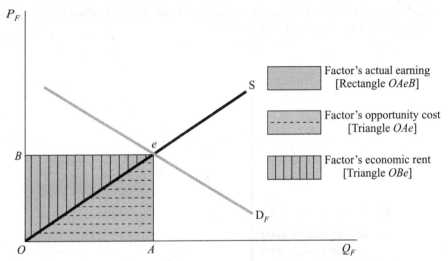

FIGURE 14.23 Demand and supply curves of the factor intersect at e. Equilibrium price is ₹ 20,000 per unit and equilibrium quantity of the factor employed is 40,000 units. Opportunity cost is the area of the triangle OAe while actual earning of the factor is the area of the rectangle $OAeB$. Economic rent is the area of the triangle OBe. Thus, opportunity cost = Area of triangle OAe = 1/2 $(OA) \cdot (Ae)$ = 1/2 (40,000) $\cdot$ (20,000) = 400,000,000. Actual earning = 40,000 × 20,000 = 800,000,000 and the economic rent = 1/2 × 40,000 × 20,000 = 400,000,000.

$$\text{Economic Rent} = \text{Actual Earnings} - \text{Opportunity Cost}$$
$$= \text{Total earning} - \text{TVC}$$
$$= \text{Producer's surplus.}$$

The only point of difference here is that the producer's surplus and the TVC in economic theory have appeared so far in context of production of commodities, with the quantity of the output on the horizontal axis.

The concept of economic rent, called the *Modern Theory of Rent,* is based on the concept of the opportunity cost or transfer earnings as introduced earlier.

Modern economists like Mrs. Joan Robinson have identified an element of rent in the incomes of all the factors of production. According to her, economic rent is the payment to a factor over and above what is necessary to keep the factor in current use. It is this concept that has been referred to above in the beginning of this section.

Productive factors in modern theory are classified into three categories for pricing them:

(i) Perfectly specific factors (with perfectly inelastic supply).
(ii) Perfectly non-specific factors (with perfectly elastic supply).
(iii) Factors neither perfectly specific nor perfectly non-specific.

Let us take them in that order.

(i) *Perfectly specific factors (with perfectly inelastic supply):* Perfectly specific factors have a high degree of specialization. They are suited only for a particular use with the result that their opportunity cost is zero. Due to a high degree of specialization, their supply curve is perfectly inelastic (vertical). Whole of their actual earning forms their economic rent therefore (Figure 14.24).

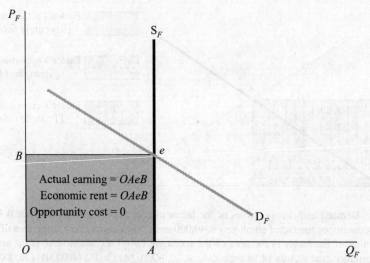

FIGURE 14.24 Supply curve of perfectly specific factors is perfectly inelastic (vertical). Factor price is determined at e, the point where demand and supply curves intersect each other. Quantity employed of the factor is OA and price accruing to it is OB. Area under the supply curve is zero and so is the opportunity cost of the factor. Economic rent is equal to the actual earning of the factor. Note that the economic rent is maximum when elasticity of supply of the factor is minimum (zero).

(ii) *Perfectly non-specific factors (with perfectly elastic supply):* Factors that have little or no specialization to their credit and are commonly available in unlimited supply at a given price refer to perfectly non-specific factors. The supply curve for such factors is perfectly elastic (horizontal). They can be put to any use with identical productivity with the result that their actual earning is equal to their opportunity cost. Such factors, therefore, command no rent (Figure 14.25).

(iii) *Neither perfectly specific nor perfectly non-specific factors:* When factors are neither perfectly specific nor perfectly non-specific, the supply curve is neither vertical nor horizontal as shown in Figure 14.26. The factors have an opportunity cost as also an economic rent. This is the most general case.

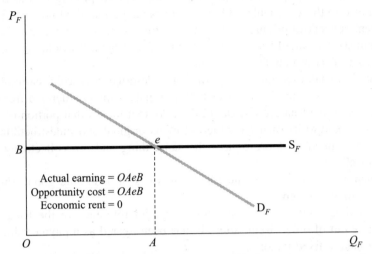

FIGURE 14.25 Demand for and supply of the perfectly non-specific factors intersect each other at e, where OA quantity of factors is employed at price OB. As the supply curve is perfectly elastic (horizontal), the area under the supply curve is equal to the area of the rectangle $OAeB$. Thus, actual earning of the perfectly non-specific factors is the same as their opportunity cost. Their economic rent is, therefore, zero. Note that economic rent is the minimum (zero) when elasticity of supply of the factors is infinite.

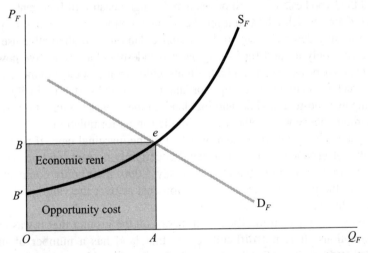

FIGURE 14.26 When factors are neither perfectly specific nor perfectly non-specific, the supply curve is neither perfectly elastic nor perfectly inelastic. It is moderately elastic as shown. Economic rent ($B'Be$) is neither as high as in Figure 14.24 nor is it as low as in Figure 14.25. Likewise, opportunity cost ($B'OAe$) is neither as low as in Figure 14.24 nor is it as high as in Figure 14.25. Just as the elasticity of supply is moderate, so are the economic rent and the opportunity cost.

An important inference that emerges from the analysis is that size of economic rent varies inversely as the price elasticity of supply while that of the opportunity cost, directly with it.

The concept of economic rent is applicable not only to pricing of the fixed factors of production but also to those variable such as labour having a marginal product. The question of applying the rent concept to pricing of the fixed factors perhaps cropped up when some of the classical economists like David Ricardo used it in pricing of land. It would, therefore, be in order to have a fair idea of Ricardian Theory of rent.

Ricardo and Marshall used the concept of rent to describe the surplus earnings derived from land and other free gifts of nature. To Marshall, rent means income derived from ownership of land and other free gifts of nature. To David Ricardo, rent means that portion of the produce of the land, which is paid to its owner for the use of its original and indestructible powers. Both these concepts of rent mean more or less the same thing and are collectively known as the **classical theory of rent**.

To a layman, rent is the price paid for the services of a durable good. This, however, is known as the **contractual rent**.

To understand rent in its true connotations, a brief reference to the Ricardian theory of rent would not be out of order. Rent, after all, has been treated as a payment for the use of the productivity of land, a fixed factor.

According to David Ricardo, rent is that portion of the produce of land, which is paid to the landlord for the use of its original and indestructible powers. It is known as **rent of productivity difference** or **of fertility difference**. To Ricardo, it is the generosity of nature that causes it. In his opinion, nature has been generous in gifting fertile soil to the mankind. To him, rent is price determined rather than price determining. That is, rent would be high when price of corn produced on it is high. Ricardo rejected the hypothesis that corn prices may be high because of high rent.

In Ricardian theory which admitted a number of assumptions, rent accrues only to land. Some of its assumptions really deserve attention. For instance, land has no alternative use except that for cultivation, it accrues only to land for its original and indestructible productive power, some lands are more fertile than others and command higher rents, cultivation is subject to the law of diminishing returns, market structure is competitive, superior land is cultivated first, and finally, land that returns just the cost of inputs is no-rent land or marginal land. Some of these assumptions found an explicit mention in Ricardian theory while others were implicit in its formulation.

Rent thus is an excess produce of land over that of the marginal land. If cost of production is 2,000 and if value of produce is also 2,000, land is certainly no-rent land or marginal land. But if the value of its produce is more than the cost, say 5,000, it certainly commands a rent equal to the difference of the produce over the production cost or over the value of the produce of the marginal land. In this case rent would be 3,000.

Modern economists rejected the Ricardian theory on the ground that it was based on highly unrealistic assumptions. It is not difficult to see that land has a number of uses other than cultivation and that the power of soil responsible for rent is neither original nor indestructible. In fact, it can be duplicated through chemical treatment of soil and it also gets dissipated with its prolonged use for cultivation. Likewise, perfect competition is a myth and rent is more often price determining rather than price determined. Land is not the only factor that earns rent. In fact, all the factors of production command rent, depending on their degree of specialization. According to Mrs. Joan Robinson, rent accrues to every factor of production. Ricardian theory of rent thus deserves nothing more than academic interest. In factor pricing, it is the concept of economic rent that has its utility in pricing of factors with fixed supply in the long-run.

(b) Factors with supply fixed in short-run

We have seen that supply of land is fixed whether in short-run or long-run. The most important thing about this factor is that its supply cannot be increased even in the long-run. As stated earlier, there exist a number of factors whose supply is fixed in short-run but not in long-run. For instance, most of the man-made assets such as buildings are fixed in supply in short-run but not in long-run. In the event of a rise in their demand in short-run, market prices of such factors shoot up and so does the total revenue realized by their owners. Just as a common producer feels contented with recovery of total variable cost (TVC) in short-run, suppliers of productive factors are contented with recovery of TVC in short-run. Excess of total revenue (TR) over TVC realized by factor owners in short-run is called **quasi-rent**. It is a residual payment that disappears in the long-run with an increase in the factor supply. Thus, quasi-rent disappears in the long-run while economic rent persists.

To understand this, let us analyze the short-run equilibrium of a competitive firm (Figure 14.27).

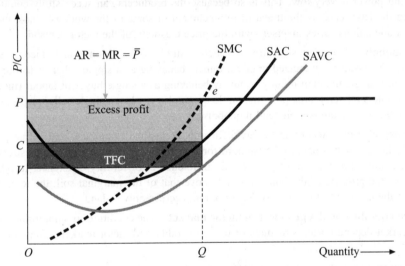

FIGURE 14.27 Equilibrium of a competitive firm in short-run takes place at e, the point where firm's SMC cuts its MR from below. In the present case, the firm is earning an Excess Profit, and at the same time, recovering its total fixed cost (TFC) as well. In short-run, firms are generally contented with the recovery of the total variable cost (TVC), which it pays to its variable factors. Anything earned above TVC, goes to the factors with fixed supply. This is so due to high opportunity cost of the fixed factors. Excess of total revenue (TR) over the TVC is thus the *Quasi-rent*. It is the sum of the excess profit and TFC, as is evident from the following:

$$\begin{aligned}
\text{Quasi-rent} &= \text{TR} - \text{TVC} \\
&= (\text{Excess profit} + \text{TFC} + \text{TVC}) - \text{TVC} \\
&= \text{Excess profit} + \text{TFC} \\
&= \text{The shaded area (light as well as dark)}
\end{aligned}$$

Rising demand of the fixed factor in short-run increases its opportunity cost as also the residual earning of the factor or its quasi-rent. Fluctuations in the market price of fixed factors influence the size of quasi-rent. An increase in it increases the size while a decrease, decreases it.

In sum, price paid to a factor fixed in supply in the long-run is called its **rent** while that paid to a factor fixed in supply in the short-run is called its **quasi-rent**. Rent persists in the long-run while quasi-rent disappears in the long-run with increasing factor supply.

KEY TERMS AND CONCEPTS

Average expenditure (AE)   It is the ratio of total expenditure incurred by a producer on all the units of a factor to the units of the factor employed.

$$AE = TE/L, \text{ where, TE is the total expenditure.}$$

Bargaining power of the trade unions   Trade unions often agitate for wage hike; sometimes they succeed in their motives, sometimes, they do not. Their success or failure depends on their bargaining power, which in turn, depends on the price elasticity of factor demand. When the factor demand is highly inelastic, the bargaining power of the trade unions is very high but when it is less inelastic or highly elastic, their bargaining power is very low. This is so because the producers can successfully counter the threat of agitation in the latter case by the threat of retrenchment of some of the workers. Thus, the bargaining power of the trade unions varies inversely with the price elasticity of the factor demand.

Bilateral monopoly   A market structure in which a single seller (Monopolist) faces a single buyer (monopsonist). For instance, unionized uranium miners behaving as a single seller of labour (monopoly) on one side and a single uranium mining company behaving as a single buyer of labour (monopsony) on the other constitute a bilateral monopoly. In simple terminology, when a single seller faces a single buyer, the resulting market structure is a bilateral monopoly.

Classical theory of rent   According to David Ricardo, a classical economist, rent is that portion of the produce of the land, which is paid to the landlord for the use of the original and the indestructible powers of the soil. It is known as the rent of productivity difference or of fertility difference. In other words, it is the excess of the produce of the land over and above that of the marginal soil, the lowest grade land returning only the costs of production. To Ricardo, rent accrues only to land.

Conditions of equilibrium of a producer in factor market   The conditions of equilibrium of a producer in a factor market depend on the structures of the commodity and factor markets. They are summarized as below:

1. $\overline{w} = VMP_L$, when the product and the factor markets are both competitive.
2. $\overline{w} = MRP_L$, when the factor market is competitive but product market is not.
3. $ME = VMP_L$, when the product market is competitive but the factor market is not.
4. $ME = MRP_L$, when none of the two is competitive.

Demand curve faced by a labour union   Employer firm's MRP_L/VMP_L curve serves as the demand curve for the labour union.

Demand curve of a firm for labour   It is the VMP_L curve when the employer firm is competitive in the product market; but if it is monopolistic, the demand curve of labour is its MRP_L curve.

Determinants of demand for a factor of production   Demand for a factor of production depends on the following factors:

1. Price of the factor.
2. Value of the marginal physical product of the factor.
3. Price of the product.
4. Amount of the collaborating factors available.

5. Price of the collaborating factors.
6. The state of technology progress.

Determinants of supply of a factor of production The supply of the factors of production depends on the following factors:

1. Price of factor.
2. Tastes of the factor-owners in respect of their preferences for leisure or labour.
3. Size of the population.
4. Labour force participation rate.
5. Occupational, geographical and educational distribution of the labour force.

Factor-market A market in which factors of production are exchanged for money.

Marginal expenditure (ME) It is the change in TE per unit change in the level of the employment of a factor.

$$ME = \Delta(TE)/\Delta L = d(TE)/dL$$

Marginal physical product of a factor It is the quantity of physical output produced by an additional unit of a factor.

Marginal revenue product of capital (MRP$_K$) It is the money value of the product of an additional unit of capital employed. It is given by the product of the MPP of capital and the product price (MR).

Marginal revenue product of labour (MRP$_L$) It is the money value of the product of an additional unit of labour employed. It is given by the product of the MPP of labour and the product price (MR).

Market demand curve for labour Market demand for labour is the horizontal summation of the individual VMP$_L$ curves of all the firms in the industry when the product market is competitive; but if it is monopolistic, the market demand is the horizontal summation of the individual MRP$_L$ curves of all the firms.

Market supply of labour It is an upward rising curve.

Modern theory of rent Modern economists like Mrs. Joan Robinson, rejecting the classical theory of rent, used the term *economic rent* for rent and defined it as the payment to a factor over and above what is required to keep the factor in its current employment. In alternative terminology, economic rent is defined as a payment made to a factor in excess of its opportunity cost or transfer earnings. Thus,

$$\text{Economic Rent} = \text{Actual Earning} - \text{Opportunity Cost}$$

Monopolistic exploitation of labour When a producer with monopoly power in the product market, pays labour a price less than the price accruing to labour employed by a producer in a competitive product market, the exploitation of labour is said to be monopolistic. In other words, when labour is paid less than its VMP$_L$ but equal to its MRP$_L$, the practice is referred to as the monopolistic exploitation of labour.

Monopsonistic exploitation of labour When a producer with monopsony power in the labour market and monopoly power in the product market pays a factor a price less than its VMP$_L$, the exploitation of labour goes beyond the monopolistic exploitation and is called the monopsonistic exploitation. The size of the monopsonistic exploitation depends on the structure of the commodity market. It is less when commodity market is competitive and more when it is monopolistic.

Objectives of labour unions Labour unions, in general, have three objectives:

1. Maximization of employment
2. Maximization of the total gains for union
3. Maximization of total wages.

Product exhaustion theorem The 'product exhaustion' theorem states that paying the factors the value of their marginal physical product leads to exhaustion of the total value of the product.

Product market A market in which products are exchanged for money.

Quasi-rent Excess of Total Revenue (TR) over the TVC is called the *quasi-rent*. For instance, most of the man-made assets such as buildings are fixed in their supply in short-run. Such factors command a very high price if their demand shoots up in short-run. Quasi-rent is a residual payment accruing to such factors in short-run over and above the TVC. It disappears in the long-run with increasing supply of the factor. Thus, *quasi-rent* disappears in the long-run while *economic rent* persists.

Relationship between MRP_K and VMP_K The VMP_K is the money value of the marginal physical product of capital when the product market is competitive while MRP_K is the money value of the marginal physical product of capital when the product market is a monopoly.

$$VMP_K = \bar{P} \cdot MPP_K = AR \cdot MPP_K$$
$$MRP_K = MR \cdot MPP_K$$

Clearly, both are same in a competitive product market, i.e. when $MR = AR = \bar{P}$, but they are not when the product market is a monopoly. In fact, $MRP_K < VMP_K$ in a monopoly product market as $MR < AR$ in it.

Relationship between MRP_L and VMP_L The VMP_L is the money value of the marginal physical product of labour when the product market is competitive while MRP_L is the money value of the marginal physical product of labour when the product market is a monopoly.

$$VMP_L = \bar{P} \cdot MPP_L = AR \cdot MPP_L$$
$$MRP_L = MR \cdot MPP$$

Clearly, both are same in a competitive product market, i.e. when $MR = AR = \bar{P}$, but they are not when the product market is a monopoly. In fact, $MRP_L < VMP_L$ in a monopoly product market as $MR < AR$ in it.

Supply curve of a labour union For a labour union, the AE_L curve of the employer firm serves as its supply curve. The union treats this curve as its MC-curve, which forms its supply curve.

Supply curve of labour for a firm It is a perfectly elastic (horizontal) curve when the employer firm is competitive in the factor market; but if it is monopsonistic, the supply curve is the AE_L curve of the employer firm.

Theory of distribution Also known as the theory of factor pricing, it states that each factor is paid a price equal to the value of its marginal physical product.

Value of the marginal physical product of capital (VMP_K) It is the money value of the product of an additional unit of capital employed. It is given by the product of the MPP of capital and the product price (AR).

Value of the marginal physical product of labour (VMP_L) It is the money value of the product of an additional unit of labour employed. It is given by the product of the MPP of labour and the product price (AR).

Wage and profit-maximizing effects of a fall in the wage rate Just as a fall in product price leads to a price effect, a fall in the wage rate leads to a *wage-effect,* which results in consequence of an increased employment of labour. Wage-effect is followed by the profit-maximizing effect provided the employer firm is not a constant cost firm (Figures 14.7 and 14.8). Wage-effect comprises substitution and output effects, analogous to substitution and the income effect-components of a price effect.

EXERCISES

A. Short Answer Questions

Define the following:

1. Product market
2. Factor market
3. Theory of distribution
4. VMP_L
5. MRP_L
6. VMP_K
7. MRP_K
8. Marginal expenditure
9. Average expenditure
10. Monopolistic exploitation of a factor
11. Monopsonistic exploitation of a factor
12. Economic rent
13. Quasi-rent
14. Marginal productivity theory
15. Product exhaustion theorem
16. What are the factors that would shift the demand curve of a factor?
17. What are the factors that would shift the supply curve of a factor?
18. On what factors does the bargaining power of the trade unions depend?
19. What is the difference between VMP and MPP?
20. When would the VMP_L be equal to the MRP_L?
21. When would the VMP_K be equal to the MRP_K?
22. What is the difference between TVP and TPP?
23. What is the difference between VMP and MRP?
24. What would happen to the TVP when MPP is positive? Negative?
25. What would happen to the TVP when VMP is positive? Negative?
26. How can TVP of a factor can be derived from its VMP curve?
27. How are the factor demand curve and the VMP curve related?
28. Name any three factors that determine the demand for a factor of production.
29. Name any three factors that determine the supply of factors of production.
30. What is the condition of equilibrium of a producer when the factor and the product-markets are both competitive?
31. What is the condition of equilibrium of a producer when the factor market is competitive, but the product market isn't?
32. What is the condition of equilibrium of a producer when the product market is competitive, but the factor market isn't?
33. What is the condition of equilibrium of a producer when none of the two markets is competitive?

B. Long Answer Questions

Distinguish between (34 through 39):

34. VMP and MRP of a factor.
35. Rent and economic rent.
36. Rent and quasi-rent.
37. Monopolistic exploitation and the monopsonistic exploitation.
38. Perfectly specific and perfectly non-specific factors.
39. Euler's product exhaustion theorem and Clark-Wicksteed-Walras 'product exhaustion' theorem.
40. Explain the factors that determine the demand of a factor of production.
41. Explain the factors that determine the supply of a factor of production.
42. Explain the monopolistic exploitation with the help of a diagram.
43. What is meant by the bargaining power of the trade union?
44. How are the market demand and market supply curves obtained from the individual demand and supply curves of a factor?
45. The marginal physical product of labour is as given in the table below:

Labour units :	1	2	3	4	5	6	7	8	9	10	11
MPP :	1	2	5	10	20	30	20	10	5	2	0

Determine TPP, APP, TVP and VMP_L for each level of employment when product market is competitive with price of the product fixed at ₹ 10 per unit. Here, APP is Average Physical Product. TPP is Total Physical Product, and TVP is Total Value of Physical Product and VMP_L is the Value of the Marginal Physical Product of labour.

46. What will the equilibrium level of employment of labour be if the labour market is also competitive in Question 45 with wage fixed at ₹ 100?
    [**Ans.** 8 Labour-units.]

47. Given that the labour and the product markets are both competitive with product-price as ₹ 10 per unit and wage as ₹ 50 per labour unit. The MPP schedule for certain employment of the labour units is given as:

Labour units :	5	6	7	8	9	10
MPP :	8	7	6	5	4	3

Obtain the demand and the supply schedules of labour faced by a firm in the labour market and sketch them. Determine the equilibrium level of employment of the labour units.
[**Ans.** 8 Labour-units.]

48. The demand curve of labour in the labour market is as given below:
$$w = 120 - 2L$$
and the supply curve as:
$$w = 3L$$
Determine the equilibrium level of employment and wage. Suppose labour participation rate increases. In consequence, the supply of labour increases to:
$$w = 3L - 20$$
How would the equilibrium level of employment and wage change now?
[**Ans.** 24, 72; 28, 64.]

49. The VMP_L curve for a firm is given as:
$$VMP_L = 100 - 3L$$

The supply of labour is given as
$$w = 2L$$
Determine the number of workers the firm would employ. What wage would the firm offer to the workers?
[**Ans.** 20; 40.]

50. "Supply curve of skilled labour by an individual worker bends backwards at high wage rates while the market supply curve steadily slopes upwards." Explain.

51. Show that the condition of equilibrium of a firm employing two variable factors, namely, labour and capital, is
$$(w/r) = (MPP_L/MPP_K)$$

52. Demand curves for labour in two markets are respectively $w = 100 - 3L$ and $w = 100 - 7L$. Sketch the curves. Suppose that the wage rate is ₹ 50 per worker in the first market and 40 per worker in the second market. Suppose further that the labour unions in both the markets decide to agitate to enforce a 40 % hike in wages. In which market do you think the union has the better chances of success and why?
[**Ans.** In the Second Market. The demand curve in the second market is less elastic.]

C. Essay Type Questions

53. What is a bilateral monopoly? Is it true to say that equilibrium is indeterminate in a bilateral monopoly?
54. Show that the size of monopsonistic exploitation depends on the structure of the commodity market.
55. Show that the size of the economic rent accruing to a factor of production depends on the price elasticity of its supply.
56. What are the various objectives the trade unions are formed to serve? Explain with the help of a figure how trade unions can attempt these objectives.
57. 'When demand for labour is highly inelastic, the labour union can prove highly beneficial to its members by raising the wage rate without sacrificing much of the employment of the labour.' Discuss with the help of sketches.
58. 'If the employer-firm possesses monopsonistic power in the factor-market, the labour union can reduce the size of the monopsonistic exploitation at least by that part of it, which is purely due to the firm's monopsony power in the factor market.' Discuss.
59. What is quasi-rent? In what respects does it differ from the economic rent? Can quasi-rent be negative? Give reasons in support of your answer.
60. Demand (Q^D) for and the supply (Q^S) of a factor of production are given respectively by the equations
$$3Q^D = 96 - 8P$$
and
$$Q^S = \sqrt{(16P - 80)};$$
where, P is the price of the factor. Sketch the curves and determine the following:
    (a) Actual Earnings of the factor in the equilibrium,
    (b) Transfer Earnings of the factor at the equilibrium level of employment, and
    (c) Economic Rent accruing to the factor.

[**Ans.** $Q^D = Q^S$ at the point of equilibrium. Therefore, equilibrium-level of employment and price are $Q = 8$ and $P = 9$. The actual earning of the factor is $9 \times 8 = 72$, as is clear from Figure 14.28.

$$\text{Area under the supply curve} = \int_0^8 \left[5 + \left(\frac{1}{16}\right)Q^2 \right] dQ$$
$$= 5Q + (1/48)Q^3 \Big|_0^8$$

$$= 40 + (32/3)$$
$$= 152/3$$
$$= \mathbf{50.67}$$
$$\therefore \quad \text{Transfer Earnings} = \mathbf{50.67}$$
$$\Rightarrow \quad \text{Economic rent} = \text{Actual Earnings} - \text{Transfer Earnings}$$
$$= 72 - 50.67$$
$$= \mathbf{21.33.}]$$

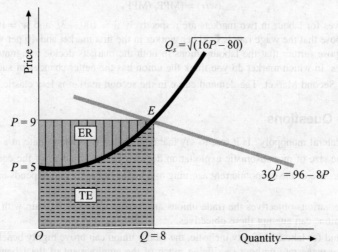

FIGURE 14.28 Demand and supply curves intersect each other at point E (8, 9). The area of the rectangle shaded (gray) shows actual earnings (AE) of the factor, the area shaded with broken lines shows transfer earnings (TE) and the area shaded with vertical lines shows the economic rent (ER).

61. Suppose that the total cost function for Q units of a factor fixed in supply in short-run is given as
$$TC = 2 + 3Q - 1.5Q^2 + 0.5Q^3$$
where, TC is measured in thousands of rupees and Q is in Quintals of the factor fixed in supply in the short-run. Suppose further that the market price of the factor currently is ₹ 3,000 per quintal of the factor. Due to sudden rise in demand of the factor, its price shoots up to ₹ 7,500 per quintal. Determine:

   (a) Quasi-rent when P = ₹ 3,000 per quintal
   (b) Quasi-rent when P = ₹ 7,500 per quintal

   [**Ans.** (a) TC = $2 + 3Q - 1.5Q^2 + 0.5Q^3$. Therefore,
   TFC = 2
   TVC = $3Q - 1.5Q^2 + 0.5Q^3$
   AVC = $3 - 1.5Q + 0.5Q^2$
   MC = $3 - 3Q + 1.5Q^2$
   AC = $2/Q + 3 - 1.5Q + 0.5Q^2$

Drawing rough sketches of AC, AVC and MC as in Figure 14.29, we have $\pi = 0$, TFC = 2.
Profit-maximizing output is given by the condition MC = MR. Thus, $3 - 3Q + 1.5Q^2 = 3$. This gives $Q = 2$. It can be verified that MC is minimum at $Q = 1$, AVC at $Q = 1.5$ and AC is minimum at $Q = 2$.

Also, minimum of AC is 3 and so is MC at E, where $Q = 2$. Normal profits ($\pi = 0$) accrue to the seller but TFC is recovered. Therefore, the quasi-rent is equal to TFC. Alternative method to find quasi-rent is to find TR – TVC at the point of equilibrium.

$$TR = 2 \times 3 = 6.$$

$$TVC = \int_0^2 MC\, dQ$$

$$= \int_0^3 MC\, dQ = 22.5 - \int_0^3 [3 - 3Q + 1.5Q^2]\, dQ$$

Quasi-rent = TR – TVC = 6 – 4 = 2 (₹ 2,000; as above).]

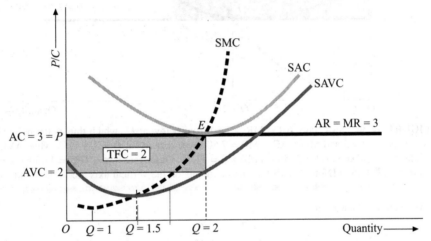

FIGURE 14.29 SMC cuts AR = MR = 3 from below at E, which thus is the point of equilibrium. At this point $Q = 2$ and AC = MC = AR = MR = 3. Note that AC is minimum at $Q = 2$. This implies normal profit or zero abnormal profit. AVC at $Q = 2$ is 2. The shaded area represents TFC, which is the difference of TC over TVC. The quasi-rent = π + TFC = 0 + TFC = TFC = 2. Thus, economic rent is ₹ 2,000. [Note that TFC of 2 represents 2,000 because TC is measured in thousands of rupees.]

(b) Profit-maximizing quantity (Figure 14.30) is given by the equality of MC to MR. Thus, $3 - 3Q + 1.5 Q^2 = 7.5$ (Since, MR = AR = P = 7, 500; which is 7.5 in terms of the units involved in the equation). Solving for Q, we have

$$1.5Q^2 - 3Q - 4.5 = 0$$
$\Rightarrow \quad 1.5(Q + 1)(Q - 3) = 0$
$\Rightarrow \quad Q = 3$

Profit, π = TR – TC
$= 7.5 \times 3 - [2 + 3 \times 3 - 1.5\,(3)^2 + 0.5(3)^3]$
$= 22.5 - [11]$
$= \mathbf{11.5}$

Quasi-rent

$= \pi + \text{TFC}$
$= 11.5 + 2$
$= \mathbf{13.5}$ (which in actual terms is ₹ 13,500)

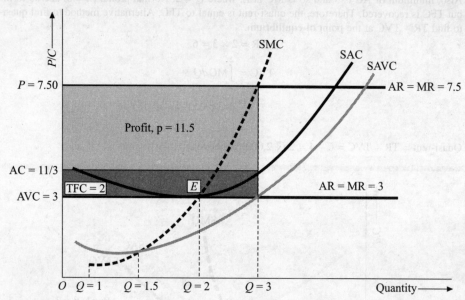

FIGURE 14.30 SMC cuts AR = MR = 7.50 from below at E', which thus is the point of equilibrium. At this point $Q = 3$ and MC = AR = MR = 7.50. Note that AC at $Q = 3$ is 11/3, while AVC = 3. TFC = 2 while $\pi = (P - AC) \times Q = (7.50 - 11/3) \times 3 = 11.50$. Quasi-rent = π + TFC = 11.50 + 2 = 13.50, which represents ₹ 13,500 [Note that all the measurements on the vertical axis are in thousands of rupees.]

Alternatively, Quasi-rent

$$= TR - TVC$$
$$= 7.5 \times 3 - \int_0^3 MC\, dQ = 22.5 - \int_0^3 [3 - 3Q + 1.5Q^2] dQ$$
$$= 22.5 - 9$$
$$= \mathbf{13.5} \text{ (which in actual terms is ₹ 13,500; as above).}]$$

62. Given the production function for a commodity,

$$Q = AL^\alpha K^\beta$$

Show that the Euler's product exhaustion theorem is satisfied irrespective of the product-price; as the total product gets exhausted by paying the factors the value of their marginal physical product but Clark-Wicksteed-Walras Theorem is not unless $\alpha = \beta = 1$.

63. Suppose that the producer in Question (62) is operating under the budget constraint,

$$\bar{C} \leq 12,000$$

and that $\alpha = 1/3$, $\beta = 2/3$, $w = 100$, $r = 80$, $P = 200$ and $A = 1200$. Determine the equilibrium-level of employment of L and K. Is the Euler's product exhaustion theorem satisfied at the point of equilibrium? How about the Clark-Wicksteed-Walras 'product exhaustion' theorem? Is it also satisfied at the point? Explain.

[**Ans.** Equilibrium level of employment is $L = 4$, $K = 10$. Euler's theorem is satisfied but the other one is not because input elasticity of output is not unitary.]

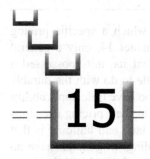

15

Investment Decisions and Capital Asset Pricing

CHAPTER OUTLINE

Introduction
✧ Types of Interest Rates
✧ Concept of Discounting Rates and Determination of Present Value (PV)
✧ Net Present Value Criterion for Capital Investment Decisions
✧ Investment Decisions of Consumers
✧ Intertemporal Production Decisions
✧ Decision Under Risk
✧ Key Terms and Concepts
✧ Exercises

INTRODUCTION

In Chapter 14, we discussed pricing of certain productive factors. We saw how factors having a marginal product (variable factors) as also those having no marginal product (fixed factors) can be priced. We also saw that variable factors such as labour possess the attribute of divisibility while fixed factors do not. Among the latter, not all are fixed for ever in their supply. Some of them, such as buildings/structures are fixed in supply only in short-run while others such as land are fixed in their supply even in long-run. We saw how the concept of economic rent is applied to pricing of factors fixed in supply in long-run and how the concept of quasi-rent is applied to pricing of factors fixed in supply in short-run. The reason for the need of a different set of theories for pricing the fixed factors, as discussed in Chapter 14 and also pointed out above, is that most of these factors are not only indivisible but are also durable in nature, subject to a repetitive use year after year over infinitely long periods.

Variable factors thus stand apart for their distinctive feature of divisibility which lends each of their units the attribute of marginal productivity. Next, consider raw material. It has divisibility due to which each of its units possesses a marginal product. Hence, it can be priced like any other variable factor.

In this Chapter, we take up yet another category of factors for which a specific pricing technique is called for. It comprises real and financial capital. In Chapter 14, only a general discussion on pricing of capital was conducted on the assumption that its units possessed a marginal product. This suited pricing of raw materials only, having little to do with the durable and indivisible capital assets and capital investments. Rental concepts too have little applicability to pricing of these factors due to involvement of the interest element in their pricing decisions exogenously. Another point of difference of capital investments from land and building is that the capital investments have a definite life span while land and building, in general, have an infinitely long life span. That provides another reason why capital is not clubbed with land and building but is treated as a separate factor of production.

To elaborate what investment decisions and capital pricing mean, suppose an equipment has a life span of one year. Before turning into scrap at the end, it yields a revenue of ₹ 1100. The scrap is disposed off for ₹ 220.00. Assuming that the rate of interest is fairly stable at 10% per annum compounded annually over the period and that the rate of inflation is zero, it is not difficult to find the maximum price of the equipment. Using the compound interest formula, $A = P(1 + r/100)^n$ with $A = ₹ 1320(1100 + 220)$, $n = 1$, and $r = 10\%$, we have, $P = A/(1 + r/100)^n = 1320/(1 + 10/100)^1 = ₹ 1200.00$. That is, the maximum price of the capital asset is ₹ 1200 and so is the maximum amount of investment to be made by the investor on the equipment. Suppose, the provider of the capital asset fixes its price at ₹ 1000, the investor would find the investment profitable because he gains ₹ 200 over the alternative of lending ₹ 1000 for 1 year at 10%. Lending would yield ₹ 1100 at the end of the year which is as good as ₹ 1000 in the beginning of the year, while investment in the equipment yields ₹ 1200. The investor, thus, gains ₹ 200 if he goes for capital investment. The producer of the capital asset has to bear in mind the viability of the capital investment by the investor while pricing the capital asset apart from his production costs of the capital asset. This was a simple illustration of investment and capital pricing decisions that will occupy our attention through out this chapter. Note also that the rate of interest in the formula, $P = A/(1 + r/100)^n$, is called the *rate of discount* and $1/(1 + r/100)^n$, the *discounting factor* (DF) for n years.

Before coming to such discussions, therefore, it is imperative to have a little grasp of interest rates, their main types and their determination so that we may know which one to use and where.

15.1 TYPES OF INTEREST RATES

Interest is the price that borrowers pay to the lenders for the use of funds. It is determined through interaction of demand and supply of loanable funds.

Demand for loanable funds comprises two components. *First,* demand for loanable funds by firms which need funds for investment in capital. *Second,* demand for loanable funds by the households who need funds for durables or for consumption levels higher than those their current incomes support. A segment of households tend to borrow in anticipation of substantial growth of incomes in future. Both components of demand for loanable funds vary inversely as the rate of interest, less being borrowed at higher rates and more at lower rates. The total demand (D_T) is a horizontal summation of the firms' demand (D_F) and the household demand (D_H) as shown in Figure 15.1.

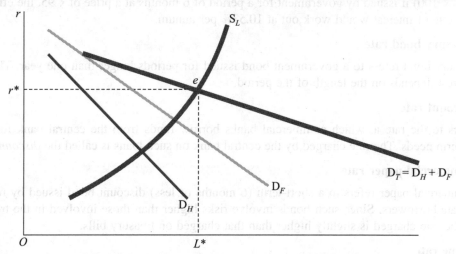

FIGURE 15.1 Determination of rate of interest: Representing the quantity of loanable funds on the horizontal axis and the rate of interest on the vertical axis, the total demand for loanable funds can be derived through horizontal summation of individual demands of the households (D_H) and the firm's (D_F), as shown. Equilibrium rate of interest is determined at e, the point where the demand and the supply curves intersect each other.

As against the behaviour of demand for loanable funds, their supply varies directly with the rate of interest. The most important source of loanable funds is the segment of the society enjoying a very high level of income currently but feeling somewhat insecure about it in future. The segment consists generally of people from business world who invest surpluses of their current incomes for high returns so that they may enjoy the current level of consumption even after their retirement from active work.

Equilibrium rate of interest r^* and equilibrium level of loans L^* are determined as shown in Figure 15.1. Fluctuations in the interest rate can be caused either by shift factors or by government regulations or by the monetary policies of the central bank.

Coming to the types of the interest rates, let us include the following ones for the purpose of our analysis in this chapter:

1. Treasury bill rate

A treasury bill refers to a short-term (a year or less) bond issued by government at a price less than the redemption value of the bond. For instance, a bond of face value of ₹ 100 (redemption

---

* To see the calculation, let the annual rate of interest be r.
Interest accrued,
$$I = 100 - 95 = 5.$$
Using simple interest formula,
$$I = P \times r \times t/100$$
Implying,
$$r = (100 \times I)/(P \times t)$$
$$= \frac{100 \times 5}{95 \times (1/2)}$$
$$= 10.53\%$$

value = ₹ 100) if issued by government for a period of 6 months at a price of ₹ 95, the effective annual rate of interest would work out at 10.53% per annum.

2. Treasury bond rate

A treasury bond refers to a government bond issued for periods longer than one year. The rate of interest depends on the length of the period.

3. Discount rate

It refers to the rate at which commercial banks borrow funds from the central bank for their short-term needs. The rate charged by the central bank on such loans is called the *discount rate*.

4. Commercial paper rate

A commercial paper refers to a short-term (6 months or less) discount bond issued by reputed corporate borrowers. Since such bonds involve risks higher than those involved in the treasury bills, the rate charged is slightly higher than that charged on treasury bills.

5. Prime rate

It refers to a rate used by commercial banks as a rate of reference in their lending activities. It is highly stable as it is fixed by the central bank as a part of its credit policy. In India, Prime Lending Rate (PLR) provides an example of this rate. Commercial banks base their rate of lending on PLR.

6. Corporate bond rate

It refers to the rate applicable to long-term corporate bonds issued by a corporation. The rate, varies considerably from corporation to corporation depending on its financial strength.

The rate of interest for our analysis of investment decisions in this chapter would be any common rate possessing the attributes of stability at least over a period of one year and popularity in day-to-day lendings or borrowings. It could be any rate of interest, even a hypothetical one. The objective is to demonstrate the working of investment decisions.

15.2 CONCEPT OF DISCOUNTING RATES AND DETERMINATION OF PRESENT VALUE (PV)

Income expected in future is generally viewed by its recipients in current prices. The phenomenon is referred to as **money illusion** and is common to the investors. An insurance policy for a sum of ten crores of rupees may sound quite lucrative when subscribed than when realized after a period of 20 years at its maturity. The subscriber rides the high horse of imagination dreaming of what he/she would be capable of doing with an amount like this—buy a decent luxury house with open surroundings, have a luxury imported car and still afford to have a fat bank balance waiting in the bank next block! Let him wait 20 years dreaming like that until he lays his hands on the assured sum of ten crores. All his/her illusions, dreams melt into thin air as soon as he/she steps into the market. The amount possessed is hardly sufficient for a two/three bedroom flat, leave alone the luxury house with open surroundings, the luxury imported car and the much relished fat bank-balance in the bank next block. All the disappointment he/she faces would have been avoided had he/she taken into his/her consideration the rate at which the value of money is eroding.

A rational subscriber must determine the present values (PVs) of the assured sum and the insurance premia to be paid year after year over the period of 20 years to qualify for this sum. Subtracting the present value of the investment stream from the present value of the assured sum gives the **net present value (NPV)** of the investment stream. If it is positive, investment is viable; else, it is not. In this section, we are going to discuss such issues but first let us cast a closer look at the rate of discount.

Rate of discount or discounting rate may be defined as the rate at which an income expected in future if discounted over the period would reduce into its value (present value) today. In other words, it can be defined as *the rate of compound interest at which the present value if lent now would amount to the income expected n years hence.* For instance, a sum of ₹ 1,000 if lent now for 3 years at 10% per annum, compounded annually, would amount to ₹ 1331 at the end of the period. In other words, an income of ₹ 1331 expected 3 years hence if discounted at 10% over the period of three years would yield ₹ 1,000 today. Here, the rate (10%) serves as the discounting rate as it reduces the sum expected (1331) after 3 years into its value today (1,000).

From the compound interest formula, we have

$$A = P\{1 + (r/100)\}^n \tag{15.1}$$

if $r = 10, n = 3$ and $P = 1,000$

$$A = 1,000 \times \{1 + (10/100)\}^3$$
$$= \mathbf{1,331}$$

Also, from the same formula [Eq. (15.1)]

$$P = A/\{1 + (r/100)\}^3 \tag{15.2}$$
$$= 1331/\{1 + (10/100)\}^3$$
$$= 1331/1.331$$
$$= \mathbf{1,000}$$

The present value of ₹ 1331 expected three years later is thus ₹ 1,000. The investment that fetches this amount 3 years later is also ₹ 1,000. The net present value of the investment, equal to the difference of the present value of the sum expected over the cost of investment, is zero (= 1000 − 1000).

In other words, an investment of ₹ 1,000 today in a bond maturing at ₹ 1,331 three years hence has a net present value of zero when discount rate is 10%. This leaves the investor indifferent to investing or not investing as he/she neither gains nor loses.

Now, suppose the same bond costs the investor ₹ 800 instead of ₹ 1,000. Other things remaining unchanged, NPV is ₹ 200 (1000 − 800) and the investment is certainly profitable.

Also, suppose rate of discount is 5% instead of 10%. Other things remaining unchanged, NPV is ₹ 149.77 (1,149.7678 − 1,000) and the investment is again profitable.

But if price of the bond is ₹ 1,200 instead of ₹ 1,000, other things remaining unchanged, NPV of the investment is negative 200(1000 − 1200) when the discount rate is 10% per annum and it is negative 124.85 (875.15 − 1000) when the rate of discount is 15%, other things remaining unchanged. In either case, investment is not advisable.

Criteria of non-negative NPV thus proves highly useful in taking investment decisions. Equation (15.2), giving P as directly related to A and inversely related to r, the discount rate, can now be re-stated using PV for P and DF for $[1/\{1+ (r/100)\}^n]$ is

$$PV = \frac{A}{\{1+(r/100)\}^n}$$

$$= A \times DF \tag{15.3}$$

where

$$DF = \frac{1}{\{1+r/100\}^n} \tag{15.4}$$

$$= \text{Discounting factor for a period of } n \text{ years.}$$

DF at the discounting rate of 10% is $[1/(1 + 0.10)^3]$ or $[0.7513148]$ for a period of 3 years, $[1/(1 + 0.10)^2]$ or $[0.826446281]$ for a period of 2 years and $[1/(1+ 0.10)^1]$ or 0.909090909 for a period of 1 year. This implies that present value (PV) of a future income of ₹ 1.00 is ₹ 0.7513148 if scheduled to be realized after 3 years; ₹ 0.826446281 if scheduled to be realized after 2 years; and ₹ 0.909090909 if scheduled to be realized after 1 year. Mathematical Tables provide values of DF for various periods at various rates of discount. One such table is provided here (Table 15.1) for ready reference of the reader.

TABLE 15.1 Discounting factor

Interest rate \ Period (yrs.)	1 Yr.	2 Yrs.	3 Yrs.	4 Yrs.	5 Yrs.	10 Yrs.	20 Yrs.	30 Yrs.
0.01	0.990	0.980	0.971	0.961	0.951	0.905	0.820	0.742
0.02	0.980	0.961	0.942	0.924	0.906	0.820	0.673	0.552
0.03	0.971	0.943	0.915	0.888	0.863	0.744	0.554	0.412
0.04	0.962	0.925	0.889	0.855	0.822	0.676	0.456	0.308
0.05	0.952	0.907	0.864	0.823	0.784	0.614	0.377	0.231
0.06	0.943	0.890	0.834	0.792	0.747	0.558	0.312	0.174
0.07	0.935	0.873	0.816	0.763	0.713	0.508	0.258	0.131
0.08	0.926	0.857	0.794	0.735	0.681	0.463	0.215	0.099
0.09	0.917	0.842	0.772	0.708	0.650	0.422	0.178	0.075
0.10	0.909	0.826	0.751	0.683	0.621	0.386	0.149	0.057
0.15	0.870	0.756	0.656	0.572	0.497	0.247	0.061	0.015
0.20	0.833	0.694	0.579	0.482	0.402	0.162	0.026	0.004

15.2.1 Sum of the Present Values of Future Income Streams

Before proceeding further, it is imperative to distinguish between stock and flow concepts. **Stock**, such as capital stock, refers to the quantity of some resource or material possessed at a point of time while **flow**, such as cash flow, refers to quantities that flow in or out over a period of time or at regular intervals to or from the stocks possessed. Water in a reservoir at a particular point of time is referred to as a stock while hourly inflow or outflow of it in terms of a rate such as litres per hour, as a flow. Amount of capital such as raw-materials possessed by a firm at the start of an accounting year is referred to as capital stock, which, if subtracted from that at the end of the accounting year, as a change in stock or a flow. A balance of ₹ 10,000 in a bank account at the beginning of a financial year constitutes stock concept but an addition of ₹ 1,000 over a year by way of interest or a deposit by the account holder as a flow concept.

Throughout the rest of the chapter, we will be frequently referring to terms like 'capital', 'investment' and incomes earned from them at regular intervals during the lifetime of the capital or tenure of the investment. The former would constitute stocks while the latter, cash flow.

Investments are made for future income streams or cash flows. For the purpose of analysis, let us classify them into the following categories:

1. When annual inflow of income is fixed and so is period of time and rate of interest

Suppose an individual is about to enter his retirement period. He wants a cash flow of ₹ 48,000 per annum every year-end during the next 10 years. Assuming that the rate of interest is 10% per annum and that it is expected to remain stable at least over the period in question. How much should he invest now to ensure the required cash flow?

Clearly, he must invest an amount equal in value to the sum of the discounted cash flows. The direct and a bit lengthier way of doing this is to calculate the present value of each cash flow at 10% over the periods of 1, 2, 3, 4, ..., 10 years and then add them up to arrive at the desired level of investment (PV). It can be given as

$$PV = \frac{48,000}{(1+0.10)} + \frac{48,000}{(1+0.10)^2} + \frac{48,000}{(1+0.10)^3} + \cdots + \frac{48,000}{(1+0.10)^{10}}$$

$$= \frac{48,000}{(1+0.10)} \left[1 + \left\{ \frac{1}{(1+0.10)} + \frac{1}{(1+0.10)^2} + \frac{1}{(1+0.10)^3} + \cdots + \frac{1}{(1+0.10)^9} \right\} \right]$$

$$= (AR)[1 + R + R^2 + R^3 + \cdots + R^9]; \text{ where, } A = 48,000, R = \left[\frac{1}{(1+0.10)} \right]$$

Employing the expression for the sum to first n terms of the Geometric Progression in the square brackets, we have

$$S_n = 1 + R + R^2 + R^3 + \cdots + R^{n-1}$$

$$= \left[\frac{(1-R^n)}{(1-R)} \right]^{*1}$$

[*1] For a Geometric Progression with first term 1 and common ratio R, the sum of the first n terms, is written as
$$S_n = 1 + R + R^2 + R^3 + \cdots + R^{n-1}$$
Multiplying on both the sides by R, we have
$$RS_n = [R + R^2 + R^3 + R^4 + \cdots + R^n]$$
Subtracting the expression RS_n from S_n, we have
$$(1-R)S_n = [1 - R^n]$$
or,
$$S_n = [1 - R^n]/(1-R)$$

with $R = 1/(1 + r)$, this reduces to

$$S_n = [(1 + r)/r] \times [1 - \{1/(1 + r)\}^n]^{*2}$$

Substituting in the expression for PV, we have

$$PV = \{A/(1 + r)\} \times \{(1 + r)/r\} \times [1 - \{1/(1 + r)\}^n]$$
$$= \{A/r\} \times [1 - \{1/(1 + r)\}^n]^{*3} \qquad (15.5)$$

Substituting, $A = 48{,}000$; $r = 0.10$ and $n = 10$; we have

$$PV = \{48{,}000/0.10\} \times [1 - \{1/(1 + 0.10)\}^{10}]$$
$$= (480{,}000) \times [1 - 1/2.5937]$$
$$= (480{,}000) \times 0.6145$$
$$= 294{,}960$$

The amount to be invested now must, thus, be ₹ 294,960 to ensure the desired cash flow.

Since, $(1 + r)^n \to \infty$ as $n \to \infty$; $\{1/(1 + r)^n\} \to 0$ and $\{1 - 1/(1 + r)^n\} \to 1]$. Thus, for a perpetual cash flow of 'A' per annum at the discount rate of 'r' per annum from Eq. 15.5 through its adjustment would require an investment now given by

$$PV = \frac{A}{r} \qquad (15.6)$$

Substituting for A and r in Eq. (15.6), we have

$$PV = \frac{48{,}000}{0.10}$$
$$= 480{,}000$$

This is certainly higher than 294,960 despite the same annual cash flow and the same rate of discount. The reason is the nature of cash flow which turns for ever.

2. When the annual inflow of income is fixed and so is the period of time but the rate of interest varies from year to year

Since the rate of interest is no longer fixed, the expression for PV would get transformed to

$$PV = \frac{A}{(1+r_1)} + \frac{A}{(1+r_1)(1+r_2)} + \frac{A}{(1+r_1)(1+r_2)(1+r_3)} + \cdots +$$
$$+ \cdots + \cdots + \frac{A}{(1+r_1)(1+r_2)(1+r_3)\ldots(1+r_n)} \qquad (15.7)$$

where, $r_1, r_2, r_3, \ldots, r_n$ are the interest-rates for years $1, 2, 3, \ldots, n$.

[*2] Substituting $R = 1/(1 + r)$, in $S_n = [1 - R^n]/(1 - R)$ and simplifying, we have

$$S_n = [(1 + r)/r]/[1 - \{1/(1 + r)\}^n]$$

[*3] Substituting the expression of S_n in the expression for PV, we have

$$PV = A\{1/(1 + r)\}\{(1 + r)/r\} \times [1 - \{1/(1 + r)\}^n]$$
$$= (A/r) \times [1 - \{1/(1 + r)\}^n]$$

(3) When period of time is fixed but annual inflow of income as also the rate of interest vary from year to year

The expression for the PV would, in this case, transform to

$$PV = \frac{A_1}{(1+r_1)} + \frac{A_2}{(1+r_1)(1+r_2)} + \frac{A_3}{(1+r_1)(1+r_2)(1+r_3)} + \cdots +$$

$$+ \cdots + \cdots + \frac{A_n}{(1+r_1)(1+r_2)(1+r_3)\cdots(1+r_n)} \tag{15.8}$$

where, $r_1, r_2, r_3, \ldots, r_n$ are the interest-rates and $A_1, A_2, A_3, \ldots, A_n$ are the annual cash flows for years 1, 2, 3, ..., n.

For annual cash flow(s) or annual income stream(s), the term in common use is annuity (annuities).

Now that we have learnt how to find the sum of present values of annuities expected in future, we can proceed to discuss investment decisions of individuals as also those of firms.

Before that, let us have a few applications of what we have learnt so far.

ILLUSTRATION 15.1: A bank officer has to decide whether to go for the Voluntary Retirement Scheme (VRS) offered by the bank or to continue to work as usual. He is 54 now (1st Jan., 2005) and the retirement age for the bank officers is 60 years. If he decides to continue to work with the bank he would be entitled to a salary of ₹ 3 lakhs in 2005, that 5% higher next year and so on till the day of his retirement. The mortality rate as per the estimates of an insurance company for a person of his age is 0.9% for 2005, 1.0% for 2006, 1.1% for 2007 and so on; increasing by 0.1% each year, till it is 1.4% for 2010, the year of his retirement (The day of his retirement is 31st of December, 2010). If the current rate of interest for discounting purposes is 10%, determine what single payment to the officer is must to help him decide in favour of VRS. Assume that all other benefits such as old-age-pension, gratuity, etc. would remain same either way the officer decides and that the income accruing to the officer in a year is treated as accredited to him in the beginning of that year.

Solution: If the officer decides to go for VRS in the beginning of 2005, he will have to forego his salary for the period of six years. To begin with he will have to forego ₹ 300,000 for the year 2005, which is to accrue to him with a probability of 0.991(1 – 0.009), given the mortality estimate of 0.9% or 0.009. His expected loss for 2005, thus, is ₹ 300,000 × 0.991 = ₹ 297,300. The present value of the expected loss of salary in the nth year, Y_n, may be given as

$$Y_n = \frac{Y_0 [1+g]^n \times [1-m_n]}{[1+r]^n} \tag{15.9}$$

where, g represents the growth rate of the annual salary (5% in the present case), $(1 - m_n)$ represents the probability of the officer's survival in the year n, given m_n as an estimate of the mortality rate in the year n and $1/(1 + r)^n$ is the discounting factor over a period of n years at a discount rate of $r\%$. For the year 2005, if we take $n = 0$, $Y_0 = Y_0 [1 + .05]^0 [1 - 0.009]/(1 + 0.10)^0 = 0.991 Y_0$. Likewise, for 2006, $n = 1$ and $Y_1 = Y_0 [1 + .05]^1 [1 - 0.010]/(1 + 0.10)^1$ and for the year 2007, $n = 2$, $Y_2 = Y_0 [1 + .05]^2 [1 - 0.011]/(1 + 0.10)^2$ and so on. For each of the coming 6 years, we calculate present values of the expected salaries and add them up to arrive at an amount which must be paid to the bank officer as an incentive to decide in favour of the VRS. The reader can verify that this amount is ₹ 15,88,944. Table 15.2 shows the relevant calculations in a systematic manner.

Column (3) shows how the officer's salary grows from year-to-year, Column (4) shows probabilities of the officer's survival, Column (5) shows the discounting factors for years $n = 0, 1, 2, 3, \ldots$, etc. and Column (6) shows how the present values of the expected annual cash flows are computed.

Note that the officer is to retire from service on 31st Dec, 2010. Therefore, there is no need to calculate the present value of the expected income for $n = 6$. The sum of the present values of the expected incomes is ₹ 15,88,937. This is must for the officer for opting VRS. The officer would have a temptation of gaining a lump-sum-income without the tension of work. He can invest the amount at 10% (the prevailing rate of interest) and ensure a perpetual annual income of ₹ 1,58,894* (approximately, ₹ 13,241 per month) apart from the usual service benefits such as old-age pension, gratuity, etc.

TABLE 15.2 Calculation of the PVs of the expected cash flows

Year	n	$Y_0(1+g)^n$	$(1-m_n)$	DF $[1/(1+r)^n]$	Discounted present value $Y_n = Y_0(1+g)^n(1-m_n)/(1+r)^n$
2005	0	$Y_0 = 300{,}000\,(1.05)^0$ = 300,000	0.991	1.00000	$Y_0 = 300{,}000 \times 0.991 \times 1$ = 297,300
2006	1	$Y_1 = 3{,}000{,}000\,(1.05)^1$ = 315, 000	0.990	0.90909	$Y_1 = 315{,}000 \times 0.990 \times 0.90909$ = 283,500
2007	2	$Y_2 = 300{,}000\,(1.05)^2$ = 330,750	0.989	0.82645	$Y_2 = 330{,}750 \times 0.989 \times 0.82645$ = 270,342
2008	3	$Y_3 = 300{,}000\,(1.05)^3$ = 347,288	0.988	0.75132	$Y_3 = 347{,}288 \times 0.988 \times 0.75132$ = 257,793
2009	4	$Y_4 = 300{,}000\,(1.05)^4$ = 364,652	0.987	0.68301	$Y_4 = 364{,}652 \times 0.987 \times 0.68301$ = 245,823
2010	5	$Y_5 = 300{,}000\,(1.05)^5$ = 382,885	0.986	0.62032	$Y_6 = 382{,}885 \times 0.986 \times 0.62032$ = 234,186
2011	6	—	—	—	—
				TOTAL:	₹ 15,88,944

In case he chooses to invest this amount only for the next 6 years, he would get a cash flow

$$A = r\,\text{PV} \div [1 - 1/(1+r)^n] \qquad \text{[Refer to Eq. (15.5)]}$$
$$= 0.10 \times 15{,}88{,}944 \div [1 - 1/(1.10)^6]$$
$$= ₹\,3{,}64{,}833.$$

Had he chosen to continue to work and had he survived at least up to his retirement, he would have received an average undiscounted cash flow of ₹ 3,40,096 per annum (The reader can verify

---

*From Eq. (15.6), perpetual annual cash flow at 10% would work out as much as $A = r \times \text{PV} = 0.10 \times 15{,}88{,}944 = 1{,}58{,}894$.

this by adding up the figures in column (3) and dividing the sum by 6). He would thus benefit by opting for VRS, which ensures him a larger amount, ₹ 3,64,833 per annum without a pain. In the event of death, the officer would not get the salary for the remainder period but by opting for VRS, the cash flows would continue to come to his nominees.

From the discussions on VRS so far, all appears pink and roses about the scheme. Realty, however, is different. A number of beneficiaries have come to regret their decision of opting for the scheme. It is not so because of any mismatch between the action and the deed on the part of the bankers, but it is so because of the failure of beneficiaries to make the most of the opportunity. A good many of them planned their investments well, but only a very few could execute the plans. The majority allowed their dear ones to influence their investment decisions. Once derailed, they stayed derailed from the track set and could not realize the benefits they had in mind at the time of opting for VRS. A number of other experiences from other sectors as well stand testimony to the observations. The VRS opting officers, despite their superior financial skills, failed to execute their investment plans under family pressures for conspicuous consumption. In consequence, they ended up moneyless, jobless and even friendless sooner than they thought. That has little to do with the scheme but quite a bit to caution those contemplating to go for it!

ILLUSTRATION 15.2: An investor purchases government bonds, each with a face value of ₹ 10,000 and a maturity period of 10 years. The bond offers an interest of 15% per annum on its face value, which is to be remitted to the holder of the bond at the end of each financial year. At the end of the maturity period, the holder has to surrender the bond and get the face value back. What is the investor's gain? Assume the market rate of interest to remain at 8% per annum throughout the tenure of the bond.

Solution: Interest accruing to the investor each year = 15% of ₹ 10,000
= ₹ 1,500.

This amount forms the annual cash flow for the investor over a period of 10 years. At the end of 10th year, he would also get the cash redemption of his initial investment. To investigate his gain, we need to calculate the present value of all the cash flows.

$$PV = \frac{1500}{(1+.08)^1} + \frac{1500}{(1+.08)^2} + \frac{1500}{(1+.08)^3} + \cdots + \frac{1500}{(1+.08)^{10}} + \frac{10{,}000}{(1+.08)^{10}}$$

$$= \frac{1500}{(1+.08)^1} \times \left[1 + \frac{1}{(1+.08)^1} + \frac{1}{(1+.08)^2} + \cdots + \frac{1}{(1+.08)^9}\right] + \frac{10{,}000}{(1+.08)^{10}}$$

$$= \frac{1500}{1.08} \left[\frac{1 - \frac{1}{(1.08)^{10}}}{1 - \frac{1}{1.08}}\right] + \frac{10{,}000}{(1.08)^{10}}$$

$$= \frac{1500}{0.08} \times \left[1 - \frac{1}{(1.08)^{10}}\right] + \frac{10{,}000}{(1.08)^{10}}$$

$$= 18{,}750 \times [1 - 0.463] + 4630$$

$$= 10{,}068.75 + 4630$$

$$= 14{,}699 \text{ (approximately).}$$

By investing ₹ 10,000 today, the investor is entitled to ₹ 14,699 today. The investment leads to a net gain of ₹ 4,699, which is the net present value of the investment.

15.2.2 Effective Yield

Effective yield or rate of return can be defined as percentage return on the market price (present value) of a bond or investment that an investor receives on it. Note that it has little to do with the face value of bond or with the initial amount of investment. In other words, effective yield is that rate of discount which equates the present value of the annuities to the market price of the bond or investment. Here, market price refers to the worth of the bond/investment in the eyes of the buyers and sellers. For instance, consider a perpetual bond of face value of ₹ 1000 and yielding an annuity of ₹ 100 perpetually. Its effective yield, from Eq. (15.6), is $r = A/PV = 100/800 = 12.5\%$ if the market price (PV) of the bond is ₹ 800, $100/1000 = 10\%$ if its market price (PV) is 1000 and it is $100/1250 = 8\%$ if its market price (PV) is 1250. Note that market price of the bond is its present value, not its face value. The sum of the present values of an annual income stream (annuities) may be more than the face value of the bond or equal to it or even less than it. The same is the case with the effective yield of an investment. It is the rate of return on its present value, not on the amount invested.

Determination of r is simple and direct from Eq. (15.6), but the same is quite complicated in respect of Eq. (15.10) as worked out for fixed duration investments below.

$$PV = [A/(1 + r) + A/(1 + r)^2 + A/(1 + r)^3 + \cdots + A/(1 + r)^n] + F/(1 + r)^n$$
$$= [A/r\{1 - 1/(1 + r)^n\}] + F/(1 + r)^n \qquad (15.10)$$

where n is the number of years of the tenure and F, the redemption value payable at the end of the tenure. One can try to compute r by hit and trial method from Eq. (15.10). A calculator may come handy in this regard.

As an alternative, r can be read directly from a graph between PV and r. Figure 15.2(a) portrays the relationship between PV and r for perpetuities. It is a rectangular hyperbola. Figure 15.2(b) portrays it for the fixed duration investments/bonds. It slopes downward, but its shape deviates from that of a rectangular hyperbola. The effective yield at a given PV in either case can be read directly from the graphs if drawn to the scale. Graph between PV and r for perpetuities is relatively a simple one [Figure 15.2(a)]. That, in respect of fixed tenure bonds [Eq. (15.10)], however, needs calculation of PV at different values of r for given A, n and F. PVs at $r = 5\%$, 8%, 10% and 20% when $A = $ ₹ 1500, $n = 10$ and $F = $ ₹ 10,000, are respectively ₹ 17,720; 14,699; 13,070 and 7905 as in case of Illustration 15.2. Plotting them against r, as shown separately in Figure 15.3, it gives a curve as in panel (b) of Figure 15.2. It slopes downwards, but its shape differs from that of a rectangular hyperbola. The effective yield at PV = 10,000 can be read from the graph, if plotted to the scale. It is exactly 15%.

As yet another alternative, r can also be determined through its interpolation from discounting tables.

Using discounting tables, it is 15% in respect of Eq. (15.10) for the data of Illustration 15.2. The simple conclusion that emerges from the analysis is that the effective yield is higher for a bond of fixed tenure than for a perpetual one, given the PV.

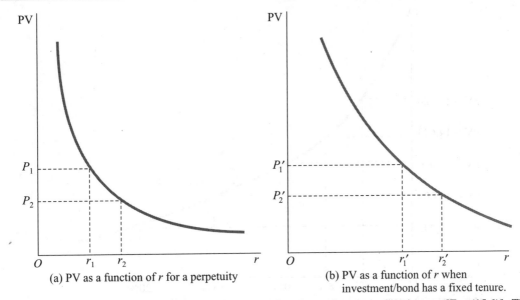

FIGURE 15.2 Panel (a) portrays PV of a perpetual bond as a function of r, the rate [Eq. (15.6)]. The curve is a rectangular hyperbola. The present value of the income stream of a perpetual bond is high when the rate is low and low when the rate is high. For instance, let the annuity of a perpetual bond be ₹ 100. When the rate of discount is 5%, its PV is 2,000 and when it is 20%, its PV is 500. If the perpetual bond has a price of ₹ 2,000, its effective yield would be 5% [$r = A/PV = 100/2000$], but if its price is ₹ 500, its effective yield would be 20% [$r = A/PV = 100/500$]. At each point on the rectangular hyperbola, $PV \times r = A$.

In the right panel, PV of a bond of fixed maturity is plotted against the rate of discount. Notice the difference between the shapes of the two curves. In each case, one can find PV of the bond, given the rate r of discount, or the rate r of discount, given the PV. However, for a bond of fixed maturity period, mathematical calculation of the rate of discount is not as direct and as simple as for a perpetuity, but its estimation from the graph certainly is.

One important conclusion that emerges from the two schedules is that effective yields are higher for the same PV under the fixed tenure of bond/investment than for the perpetual ones with identical present values.

Certainly, fixed tenure investment is better than a perpetual one because of a higher effective yield at a given PV.

The criteria for making a choice between perpetuity and a fixed tenure bond when bond price (PV) and the cost of its purchase are same for both is the fixed tenure bond because of its higher effective yield. In general, it is the Net Present Value (NPV), defined as

$$\text{NPV} = \text{PV} - \text{cost of investment} \qquad (15.11)$$

Investors go for that investment which offers highest NPV.

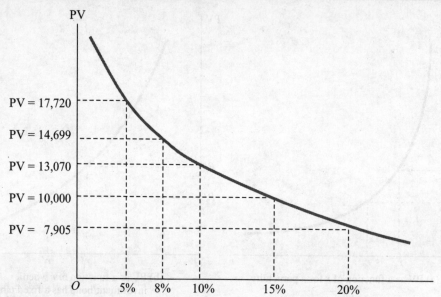

FIGURE 15.3 PVs of 17,720 at 5%; 14,699 at 8%; 13,070 at 10%; and 7,905 at 20% are plotted at the respective rates under the assumption of fixed tenure of the investment ($n = 10$ years), given A and F. The actual plot can be used for reading the rate directly from it for a given value of PV or for reading the PV directly for a given rate or for reading the r directly for a given PV. When PV is 10,000, the rate or the effective yield is 15%.

15.3 NET PRESENT VALUE CRITERION FOR CAPITAL INVESTMENT DECISIONS

Capital investment in any venture involves huge stakes. It generally involves a sizeable chunk of money committed to a venture. Implicit is the assumption that the investment would lead to long-term gains to investors. Evidently, no one would like to invest if it is known to lead to a loss. Capital investment decisions, therefore, are important decisions that require a considerable analysis of future prospects of business and hence of investment.

This, in turn, involves analysis of following five aspects:

1. Cost of capital

Normally, the price at which the capital asset is acquired is called the *cost of capital*. The higher the cost, the greater the need for weighing its pros and cons. First and foremost is the size of the cost. All else same, the lower the size of the cost, the lower the magnitude of the risk and the better it is for the investor.

2. Cost of investment

It is the opportunity cost of money that is committed to acquisition and use of productive assets for value addition. At times, investors use their idle cash for the purpose, but quite often, they resort to borrowing from financial institutions. In either case, there is an *opportunity cost* involved. If they employ their own funds, the opportunity cost is the return expected from their alternative uses. For instance, the investor may go for government bonds or may even choose to lend as an alternative source of income. And, if they resort to borrowing for it, they have to pay interest to the lenders. Interest from alternative use of their idle cash and/or interest on the borrowed funds, both constitute the cost of investment. If it is high, investment is less likely to come off.

3. Cash flows from investments

All else same, an investment with larger and longer cash flows in future is preferable to one with lower and shorter cash flows. Here the phrase 'all else same' refers to identical capital costs, identical opportunity costs, identical discount rates and identical business and economic environment. The last one refers to exogenous factors such as conditions of inflation, deflation and government policies, etc. that affect business prospects.

4. Discount rates

We have seen that the present value of a future cash flow varies inversely as the rate of discount. The higher the rate of discount, the lower the present value of the future cash flow. We have also seen that it is the interest rate that is often used to discount the future cash flows. There are at least 6 different types of interest rates as discussed in Section 15.1. Which of them is most appropriate for the purpose, we have had a brief discussion of it at the end of the section. Apart from them, one may even suggest two more—the real and the nominal rates of interest. While choice of interest rate for discounting purposes may depend on the nature of investment, choice from the real and the nominal rates of interest depends on the state of inflation, deflation or even the risk factors involved. At the outset, let us decide to count on the opportunity cost of an investment to serve as the discount rate unless otherwise specified.

5. Real and nominal discount rates

A nominal discount rate is the actual rate of discount without a correction for inflation, deflation or risks. On the contrary, the real discount rate refers to the rate of discount duly adjusted for all these. For example, when the inflation rate is 5%, the real discount rate would work out at 7% (12%, − 5%) when 12% is the stock market rate of discount.

Nominal rate of discount thus has to be adjusted for inflation. In the eventuality of risks, the rate of discount can be determined from the expression:

$$r_e - r_f = \beta(r_m - r_f) \tag{15.12}$$

Here, $r_e \equiv$ expected or real rate of discount,

$r_f \equiv$ risk free rate of discount,

$r_m \equiv$ stock market rate of discount, and

$\beta \equiv$ constant of proportionality, called **asset beta** and defined as a measure of the sensitivity of the asset's return to the market movements.

$(r_m - r_f) \equiv$ risk premium on the stock market rate of discount.

Thus, in the eventuality of risks, the real rate (r_e) of discount is given as

$$r_e = r_f + \beta(r_m - r_f) \tag{15.13}$$

Risk premium applies only to the *non-diversifiable risks* because they cannot be eliminated like the *diversifiable risks*. The latter can be averted by diversifying investment in more than one project.

Equation (15.12) is used to determine the discount rate in the Capital Asset Pricing Model (CAPM). (See Exercise 30 for illustration.)

Keeping all the five aspects of capital investment decision in view, the criterion for capital investment decisions, the Net Present Value (NPV), is the difference of the discounted present values of the future cash flows over the cost of the capital asset.

$$\text{NPV} = \text{PV} - \text{Cost of capital}$$

$$= \frac{A_1}{(1+r)^1} + \frac{A_2}{(1+r)^2} + \frac{A_3}{(1+r)^3} + \cdots + \frac{A_n}{(1+r)^n} + \frac{S}{(1+r)^n} - C \qquad (15.14)$$

Where, $A_1, A_2, A_3, \ldots, A_n$ are annuities, C is the cost of the capital, S is the scrap value of the capital asset after its life span of n years and r is the rate of discount. An illustration would do at this stage.

ILLUSTRATION 15.3: A firm has to invest ₹ 10 lakhs in a factory which is expected to yield a profit stream of ₹ 1.5 lakhs per year for the next 10 years. At the end of this period, the factory is to be disposed off to a scrap vendor for a sum of ₹ 1 lakh. Should the firm go for the investment when

(a) the rate of discount is the stock market rate of 10%,
(b) the rate of inflation is expected to be 5% per annum, and
(c) the risk free rate is 4% and the asset beta, 0.5?

Solution: Here, $C = 10$ lakhs

$$A_1 = A_2 = A_3 = \cdots = A_n = A = 1.50 \text{ lakhs}$$

$$S = 1.0 \text{ lakh}$$

(a) $r = 0.10$. Employing formula (15.14), we have

$$\text{NPV} = -C + A/(1+r)^1 + A/(1+r)^2 + A/(1+r)^3 + \cdots + A/(1+r)^n + S/(1+r)^n$$

$$= -10 + 1.50/(1.1)^1 + 1.50/(1.1)^2 + 1.50/(1.1)^3 + \cdots + 1.50/(1.1)^{10} + 1/(1.1)^{10}$$

$$= -10 + (1.50/0.10)\,[1 - 1/(1 + 0.10)^{10}] + 1/(1.1)^{10}$$

$$= -10 + 15\,[0.614] + 0.386$$

$$= -10 + 9.225 + 0.386$$

$$= -\,0.404$$

NPV being negative, it implies a loss of 0.404 lakh of rupees (₹ 40,400). The capital investment is, therefore, non-viable.

(b) $r = 0.10 - 0.05 = 0.05$. Employing the formula, we have

$$\text{NPV} = -10 + [1.50/(0.05)]\,[1 - 1/(1.05)^{10}] + 1/(1.05)^{10}$$

$$= -10 + 30\,[0.386] + 0.614$$

$$= -10 + 11.580 + 0.614$$

$$= +\,2.194$$

The NPV being positive, investment is viable.

(c) $\because r_f = 0.04, r_m = 0.10, \beta = 0.50$

$\therefore r = 0.04 + 0.5(0.10 - 0.04)$

$= 0.04 + 0.03$

$= 0.07$

$\text{NPV} = 10 + (1.50/0.07)[1 - 1/(1.07)^{10}] + 1/(1.07)^{10}$

$= -10 + 21.4286 [0.492] + 0.508$

$= +1.051$

NPV being positive, investment is again viable.

ILLUSTRATION 15.4: A firm has to decide which of the two alternative options of investment it should go for. The first one requires a sum of ₹ 8 lakh for a period of 3 years and is expected to pay back a sum of ₹ 2.22 lakh at the end of 1st year, ₹ 4.84 lakh at the end of 2nd year and ₹ 2.662 lakh at the end of 3rd year. The second one requires a sum of ₹ 10 lakh but assures a sum of ₹ 1.20 lakh per annum forever. Which of the two, he should go for if the rate of discount is 10% per annum? Assume no inflation, no deflation and no risks involved.

Solution: We need to calculate the NPV of each of the two income streams. NPV of the first one is given as

$\text{NPV}_1 = -8 + 2.2/(1.10)^1 + 4.84/(1.10)^2 + 2.662/(1.10)^3$

$= -8 + 2.000 + 4.000 + 2.000$

$= 0.$

The second one is a perpetual one. Its NPV is given by

$\text{NPV}_2 = -10 + (1.20/0.10)$ [$\because$ PV of a perpetuity is A/r, Eq. (15.6)]

$= +2.00.$

Clearly, the second option is a better one.

Note that NPV for the first investment is zero. **A rate of discount that leads to a zero NPV is called the Marginal Efficiency of Capital (MEC).** It is defined as that rate of discount which equates the sum of the PVs of all the annuities equal to the cost of the capital.

ILLUSTRATION 15.5: A firm has to decide whether to go for a capital investment that requires ₹ 10 lakh to be invested in the beginning of the first year, ₹ 5.0 lakh in the beginning of the second year and ₹ 2.0 lakh in the beginning of the third year. In the first 3 years, no return is expected. At the end of the 4th year, some sales are expected but a loss of ₹ 2.0 lakh is unavoidable. Thereafter, a steady profit stream of ₹ 2.0 lakh is expected at the end of each year till the end of the 20th year when the capital reduces to scrap and is disposed off for ₹ 1.0 lakh. Employ the NPV criterion to advise the firm. Assume a stable discount rate of 10% over the tenure of the investment.

Solution: In this case, capital investment is spread over a period of 3 years. The 4th year also has a negative cash flow. NPV at 10% per annum works out at

$$\text{NPV} = -10 - 5/(1.10)^1 - 2/(1.10)^2 - 2/(1.10)^4 + 2/(1.10)^5 + 2/(1.10)^6 + \cdots$$
$$+ 2/(1.10)^{20} + 1/(1.10)^{20}$$
$$= -10 - 4.545 - 1.653 - 1.366 + 2/(1.10)^5 [1 + (1/1.10) + \cdots + 1/(1.10)^{15}] + 1/(1.10)^{20}$$
$$= -17.564 + \{1/(1.10)^4\}(2/0.10)[1 - 1/(1.10)^{16}] + 1/(1.10)^{20} \qquad \text{[From Eq. (15.5)]}$$
$$= -17.564 + 20\{0.683\}[0.782] + 0.149$$
$$= -17.564 + 10.682 + 0.149$$
$$= -17.564 + 10.831$$
$$= \mathbf{-6.732}$$

Since the NPV is negative, investment is not advisable.

Note that first four cash flows are negative and that there is no return at the end of the 3rd year. Returns follow steadily with effect from the end of the 5th year and continue till the end of the 20th year. Even the scrap value of the worn out capital asset is realized at the end of the 20th year.

15.4 INVESTMENT DECISIONS OF CONSUMERS

Investment decisions of consumers are not much different from those of producers. In a way, they are quite similar to the capital investment decisions of producers. Both invest in durable goods. Producers acquire them for further production while consumers acquire them for consumption of services derived from them. For instance, a car is acquired by a firm as a capital asset and is used by it as such for further production. On the contrary, a consumer acquires it not for further production but for consumption of its services. A firm compares the cost of a durable asset with the present value of its future cash flows while a consumer compares its cost with the market value of the service the asset is expected to provide.

Suppose a household purchases a car at a price of C. Its life span is 5 years and the average annual value of the transport service and the running expenditure are rupees S and E respectively. The two become applicable from day one. At the end of its life-span, the car is disposed off as scrap for T. Assuming the discount rate to be r, the expression for the NPV of the investment in the car is given as

$$\text{NPV} = -C + (S-E) + \frac{[S-E]}{(1+r)^1} + \frac{[S-E]}{(1+r)^2} + \frac{[S-E]}{(1+r)^3} + \cdots + \frac{[S-E]}{(1+r)^5} + \frac{T}{(1+r)^5} \qquad (15.15)$$

Note that the first cash flow $(S - E)$ has not been discounted on the grounds that it accrues to the investor during first year and deemed to have been realized on the first day of it. The second cash flow is discounted for one year because it accrues during 2nd year and deemed to have been realized on the first day of it. If $S = ₹\,90,000$, $E = 40,000$ and $r = 8\%$, $C = 250,000$, $T = 25,000$

$$\text{NPV} = -250,000 + (90,000 - 40,000) + \frac{(90,000 - 40,000)}{(1.08)^1} + \cdots + \frac{(90,000 - 40,000)}{(1.08)^4} + \frac{25,000}{(1.08)^5}$$

$$= -250,000 + 50,000 + \frac{50,000}{0.08} \times [1 - 1/(1.08)^4] + \frac{25,000}{(1.08)^5} \qquad \text{(from Eq. 15.5)}$$

$$= -250,000 + 50,000 + 165,625 + 17,015 \qquad \text{(correct to nearest rupees)}$$
$$= -₹\ 17,360$$

NPV being negative, investment in car is not viable.

This was a simple illustration. In real world, services derived from a car, its running expenditures or discount rates may not all be constant. The NPV of the cash flows, in that case, would be given as

$$\text{NPV} = -C + (S_0 - E_0) + \frac{[S_1 - E_1]}{(1+r_1)} + \frac{[S_2 - E_2]}{(1+r_1)(1+r_2)} + \cdots + \frac{[S_5 - E_5]}{(1+r_1)(1+r_2)\ldots(1+r_5)}$$
$$+ \frac{T}{(1+r_1)(1+r_2)\ldots(1+r_5)} \qquad (15.16)$$

According to Rubinfeld and Pindyck*, *"consumers must often make trade-offs between up-front versus future payments."* What this implies is comparing costs of purchasing the durable with those of leasing it. If leasing proves cheaper than buying, why not lease? Obviously, the authors have a case. The only question that remains to answer is how to find out which option is *really* cheaper? In the words of Rubinfeld and Pindyck, "Which is better-buying or leasing? The answer depends on interest rate. If the interest rate is very low, buying the car is preferable because present value of the future lease payments is high. If the interest rate is high, leasing is preferred, because the present value of the future lease payments is low".

The authors appear to have given only little thought to the problem as the conclusion they have arrived at is only partially correct. It is not the discounted present values or the interest rates that have the sole say in the matter. Table 15.3 below stands testimony to the fact that

TABLE 15.3 Comparison of leasing and buying options

Options Rate of Discount	NPV of buying the car	NPV of leasing the car		
		When monthly lease is ₹ 3000	When monthly lease is ₹ 3500	When monthly lease is ₹ 4000
5%	$= -250,000 + 54000$ $+ 54000/0.05 \times$ $[1 - \{1/(1.05)^4\}]$ $+ 25000/(1.05)^5$ $= ₹\ 15,072$	$= 18000 + 18000/0.05$ $\times [1 - \{1/(1.05)^4\}]$ $= ₹\ 81,828$	$= 12000 + 12000/0.05$ $\times [1 - \{1/(1.05)^4\}]$ $= ₹\ 54,552$	$= 6000 + 6000/0.05$ $\times [1 - \{1/(1.05)^4\}]$ $= ₹\ 27,276$
10%	$= -250,000 + 54000$ $+ 54000/0.10$ $\times [1 - \{1/(1.10)^4\}]$ $+ 25000/(1.10)^5$ $= -₹\ 9297$	$= 18000 + 18000/0.10$ $\times [1 - \{1/(1.10)^4\}]$ $= ₹\ 75,060$	$= 12000 + 12000/0.10$ $\times [1 - \{1/(1.10)^4\}]$ $= ₹\ 50,040$	$= 6000 + 6000/0.10$ $\times [1 - \{1/(1.10)^4\}]$ $= ₹\ 25,020$
20%	$= -250,000 + 54000$ $+ 54000/0.20$ $\times [1 - \{1/(1.20)^4\}]$ $+ 25000/(1.20)^5$ $= -₹\ 46,173$	$= 18000 + 18000/0.20$ $\times [1 - \{1/(1.20)^4\}]$ $= ₹\ 64,593$	$= 12000 + 12000/0.20$ $\times [1 - \{1/(1.20)^4\}]$ $= ₹\ 43,062$	$= 6000 + 6000/0.20$ $\times [1 - \{1/(1.20)^4\}]$ $= ₹\ 21,519$

* Rubinfeld and Pindyck, *Microeconomics*, 5th ed., Pearson Education, p. 550.

interest rate alone or discounted present values alone cannot serve as a decisive factor as the author's claim. The table shows *that it is the monthly leasing rate that is equally important*. In other words, it is the NPV rather than the PV that serves as the sole criterion for making a choice between the two options. Therefore, one must go for the option with a higher NPV.

The table relates to the problem of buying or leasing a new car priced at ₹ 250,000. The individual, on an average, consumes transport services worth ₹ 7,500 per month and the operating cost of the car is ₹ 3,000 per month. The car, whether bought or leased, is used from day one of its purchase or lease. There are three leasing companies offering the vehicle to the consumer. Due to competition, monthly lease rates available to the consumer are ₹ 3,000 per month, ₹ 3,500 per month and ₹ 4,000 per month. All charges are assumed to be made annually in the beginning of each year. Assuming that the car turns into scrap at the end of 5 years and that it is disposed off to a scrap vendor for a consideration of ₹ 25,000 only.

We compare the buying and the leasing options at three discount rates—5%, 10%, and 20%. As per our assumption, the annual value of car services to the consumer is ₹ 90,000, annual running cost is ₹ 36,000 and annual lease rates are ₹ 36,000, ₹ 42,000 and ₹ 48,000. If the consumer buys the car, the annual benefit inflow would be ₹ 54,000 which would have to be discounted at the given discount rates. Alternatively, if the consumer goes for the leasing option, the net annual inflow of the service benefit under different leasing rates would be ₹ 18,000 (= 90,000 − 36,000 − 36,000), ₹ 12,000 (= 90,000 − 36,000 − 42,000) and ₹ 6,000 (= 900,000 − 36,000 − 48,000), respectively.

The NPVs of buying and leasing options at three different rates of discount are as shown in Table 15.3.

The following conclusions follow from a close look at the table:

1. As the discount rate increases, the NPVs decline for buying option as well as for the leasing options.
2. Leasing option is better than buying option at all rates of discount, low or high, and at all leasing rates.

This proves the point that Rubinfeld and Pindyck have given only little thought to the problem before making the statement.

Problems related to consumers' investments, as evident from this illustration, depend on evaluation by them of services of the durables. Quite often, a large number of durables are not acquired so much for the sake of their services as for "keeping up with the Joneses." For instance, new cars are often bought not because the old ones have turned troubleshooters but because new ones are essential to keep up with the Joneses. A consumer has to buy a new car mainly because his neighbour has bought one. It is a different matter that the car bought may remain parked at the residence for the best part of its lifespan as a status symbol. In most of the metropolitan cities in India, this proves an important cause of parking problems. How to evaluate transport services derived in such cases?

Most of the consumers resort to borrowing from financial institutions to purchase such durables. In such cases, a steady EMI (equated monthly installment) over the tenure of the loan contributes an additional running expenditure to be accommodated in E in Eq. (15.15). This affects the cash flows of the buying option adversely.

The case of purchasing a house is not much different from that of buying a car. To buy a house, a much larger investment is needed which is mostly borrowed from financial institutions on interest. EMIs of the loan may be treated as the monthly lease, clubbed with the running expenditures to constitute outflows of cash. The value of services of a house owned can be estimated by its monthly rental paid otherwise by the consumer for identical dwelling. Income tax rebates are usually granted to those who borrow for buying durables such as a house. This benefit can be added to the value of the services derived. The tenure of such loans extends to a much longer period, quite often spanning over the entire working life of an investor. Cost-benefit analysis in such cases through NPV criterion gains higher significance and so does the determination of appropriate discount rate. With these considerations, NPV of an investment in a house follows much the same process as that in any other durable.

15.5 INTERTEMPORAL PRODUCTION DECISIONS

Due to learning curve effect, current production serves as an investment for future production. Learning and experience acquired through current production prove highly cost-effective in future production. Learning economies reduce average cost in the long-run. The cost benefits so realized in the long-run serve as a return on the learning effort made in current production. It is in this sense that current production serves as an investment for future production. Productive investment in capital, therefore, goes far beyond the cash flows that follow. Cost saving is a reward that accrues on capital investment over and above the cash flows that result in consequence. Production decisions thus involve intertemporal considerations such as these apart from the capital investment decisions.

Production with a depletable resource, however, has an adverse effect on production cost in future. For instance, production of petroleum from crude oil depletes the non-replenishable deposits of the crude oil. This leaves lesser crude for future production. Production decisions must take such factors into account, while making huge capital investments in such productions.

The intertemporal decisions, therefore, relate to comparison of current and future costs and benefits of use of a depletable resource. To demonstrate, suppose that the cost of the crude oil is rupees C per unit, while its current price is P_t. Suppose, further that price will rise to P_{t+1} next year and that the discount rate is r which is fairly stable. Given that the crude reserves are limited, how should the crude extraction be regulated to maximize the total gains?

A little reasoning leads us to the following rules:

1. Do not use the crude now, if

$$(P_t - C) < \frac{(P_{t+1} - C)}{(1+r)} \qquad (15.17)$$

that is, if the current year's profit is less than the discounted present value of the next year's profits. This implies that excess of P over C rises faster than the market rate of interest.

2. Use the crude now, if

$$(P_t - C) > \frac{(P_{t+1} - C)}{(1+r)} \qquad (15.18)$$

that is, if the current year's profit is higher than the discounted present value of the next year's profits. This implies that excess of P over C rises slower than the market rate of interest.

3. It does not matter whether you use now or next year, if

$$(P_t - C) = \frac{(P_{t+1} - C)}{(1+r)} \qquad (15.19)$$

that is, if the current year's profit is the same as the discounted present value of the next year's profits. This implies that excess of P over C rises at the same rate as the market rate of interest.

15.5.1 Price Behaviour of using Depletable Resources in a Competitive Industry

Production with depletable resources leads to steadily rising opportunity costs and hence product prices. Rate of price rise is higher under market imperfections than under competitive conditions. Let us first have a feel of price rise of such products in a competitive market.

We know that each investor would attempt to maximize returns on investment, but presence of competitors, would not allow the price rise to go beyond the rate of interest, r, as evident from condition in Eq. (15.19). Thus, the excess of price over the marginal cost of extraction must grow at a rate equal to the market rate of interest. Price next year, P_{t+1}, would then be given as

$$P_{t+1} = C + (1+r)(P_t - C) \qquad (15.20)$$

The result in Eq. (15.20) is referred to as the **Hotelling rule*** of pricing depletable or exhaustible resources. Normally, for competitive markets, price is equal to the marginal cost ($P = MC$). In case of exhaustible resources, price has to be a little higher than the marginal cost so as to include the **user cost**, which is none other than the opportunity cost of the exhaustible resource. A seller of the exhaustible resource now evidently foregoes the opportunity of selling it in future.

Two observations arise:

1. Price of petroleum products, using exhaustible crude resource, has to be higher than the MC ($P > MC$) despite competitive nature of the product market. This is so due to the user cost which must be included in the price.
2. The excess of price over the marginal cost ($P - MC$) must rise at the rate equal to the market rate of interest (*Hotelling rule*).

Now suppose the initial price is P_0, and marginal cost is C. Then, $(P_0 - C)$ must grow at the market rate of interest, the rate of return on other assets, as depicted by Eq. (15.20). In case of the rule depicted by Eq. 15.17, supply of resource in future will increase lowering its future price if not sold now and if sold now in accordance to rule depicted by Eq. 15.18, its supply in future will decrease raising it future price. Hence the Hotelling rule. Diagrammatically, growth of $P_0 - C$ and its effect on the quantity demanded is demonstrated in Figure 15.4.

---

*The rule is known after Harold Hotelling who first demonstrated it in *The Economics of Exhaustible Resources*, Journal of Political Economy 39 (April 1931); p. 137–75.

15.5.2 Price Behaviour of using Depletable Resource by a Monopoly

We have seen how excess of price over marginal cost must grow in a competitive market at market rate of interest for exhaustible resources. In fact, it is the excess of MR over MC rather than that of price over MC that grows at the market rate of interest. Instead of MR, we have used price to suit our convenience knowing that the two are the same for the competitive firms.

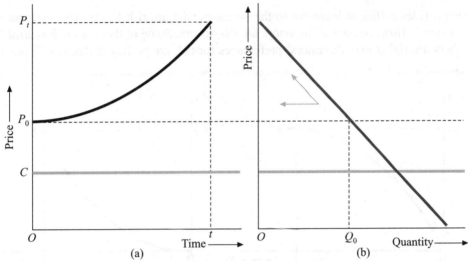

FIGURE 15.4 Variation of $(P_0 - C)$ with time (Left panel) and that of demand with price (Right panel) for using exhaustible resources. Right panel shows direction of price-quantity movements in future when exhaustible resource is used in production.

Now that the industry is no longer competitive, we may revert back to MR in place of price, P. As the monopolist is known to regulate total output, it will produce a quantity for which excess of MR over MC grows at the rate of interest.

$$(MR_{t+1} - C) = (1 + r)(MR_t - C) \qquad (15.21)$$

Note that Eq. (15.21) reduces to Eq. (15.20) as soon as we substitute P_{t+1} in place of MR_{t+1}.

In respect of a monopolist, the excess of price over the MC would rise at a rate higher than the market rate of interest, given that excess of MR over MC rises at the rate of interest. This is so because a monopolist, unlike a competitive firm, faces a demand curve that slopes downward. Given the price-quantity movements by panel(b) of Figure 15.4, the monopolist allows the excess of price over MC to grow at a rate higher than the rate of interest and hence exhausts the depletable resource at much slower a rate than that at which a competitive firm does. That way a monopolist can be considered to be a greater conservationist than a competitive firm.

15.6 DECISION UNDER RISK

So far, we focused on investment decisions that were based on information known with certainty. For instance, values of annuities and discount rates were known to us with certainty in all the cases.

Risk theory of returns, which we discussed in Section 4.5 under optimality in investor's portfolio management through risk-return indifference curves, is certainly a very effective tool in investment decisions. In Eq. 4.27, we established the proportionality of returns (R) and risk (S) as

$$R = (r/s)S$$

where r is the rate of return and s is the rate of risk associated.

The equation implies that the higher the risk involved, the higher the return to follow (*Figure. 4.81*).

This provides sufficient incentive to the investors who are risk lovers. They believe in 'no pains, no gains'. However, not all investors are risk-lovers. Some of them are *risk neutral*, while some others are *risk-averse*. Investors' preferences for risk are portrayed through Figure 15.5.

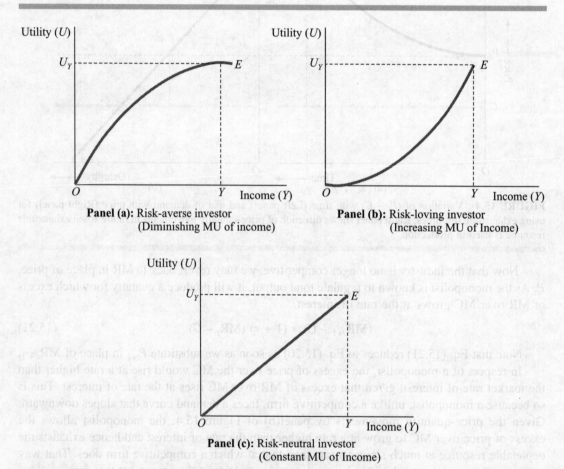

Panel (a): Risk-averse investor
(Diminishing MU of income)

Panel (b): Risk-loving investor
(Increasing MU of Income)

Panel (c): Risk-neutral investor
(Constant MU of Income)

FIGURE 15.5 As leveled, the panels show risk preferences of investors. In Panel (a), the investor is said to be risk-averse. The marginal utility of income for him has a diminishing trend.

In Panel (b), the investor is said to be risk-lover. The marginal utility of income for him has a rising trend.
In Panel (c), the investor is risk neutral as the marginal utility of income for him is constant.

It is necessary to distinguish here between *risk* and *uncertainty*. When there are several alternative options before a decision maker with no statistical probabilities attached, the situation is referred to as one of uncertainty, but when these options have statistical probabilities attached on the basis of past experience or otherwise, it is said to be one of risk. Probabilities attached may be on the basis of past experiences or past data or even purely subjective ones. *Investment decisions under risks* are more reliable than those *under uncertainty*, therefore because they have rational calculations behind. The Decision Theory, thus, involves

1. Decisions under Certainty,
2. Decisions under Risk, and
3. Decisions under Uncertainty.

A detailed study is being spared here for Chapter 22.

KEY TERMS AND CONCEPTS

Annuity It refers to the annual cash flows to the investor, accruing to him in return of investments made.

Capital asset pricing model (CAPM) In this model, price of a capital asset is determined employing the asset beta, risk premium, and risk-free rate of return (see Q. 30 for demonstration).

Commercial paper rate A commercial paper refers to a short-term (6 months or less) discount bond issued by reputed corporate borrowers. Since such bonds involve risks higher than those involved in the treasury bills, the rate charged is slightly higher than that charged on treasury bills.

Corporate bond rate It refers to the rate of interest paid by the corporations on their long-term loans. Corporations issue bonds for long periods at this rate, which varies considerably from corporation to corporation depending on its financial strength.

Discount rate It refers to the rate at which the commercial banks borrow funds from the central bank for their short-term needs. The rate charged by the central bank on such loans is called the *discount rate*.

Diversifiable and non-diversifiable risks Investments invariably involve an element of risk. Some of the risks can be averted by diversifying the investment into several projects rather than relying on a single project. Such risks are called the diversifiable risks. The other risks are the non-diversifiable ones that cannot be averted through diversification. They have to be incurred.

Hotelling rule of price variation for products using exhaustible resource The rule states that the excess of the marginal revenue over the marginal cost rises at the market rate of interest. That is,

$$(MR_{t+1} - C) = (1 + r)(MR_t - C)$$

In respect of a competitive product market, this rule can be modified as

$$(P_{t+1} - C) = (1 + r)(P_t - C)$$

Where, MR_{t+1} = marginal revenue in the year $t + 1$, C = marginal cost of production, r = rate of interest, MR_t = marginal revenue in the year t, P_t = product price in the year t, P_{t+1} = product price in the year $t + 1$.

Net present value It refers to the excess of the present values of the future income streams (annuities) over the cost of the capital. NPV = PV – C.

Perpetuity It refers to a bond with infinite maturity period. It is also known as the perpetual bond. Such bonds have no redemption except that they cause a perpetual income stream to the investor.

Prime rate It refers to that rate, which is used as a rate of reference by banks for short-term loans to their corporate borrowers. This rate is highly stable as it does not fluctuate frequently. In India, Prime Lending Rate (PLR) provides an example of this rate. While lending, banks base their rate of interest on this rate.

Present value It refers to the current value of a payment expected in future. To arrive at it, the expected payment is discounted at some appropriate rate of interest.

Rate of interest Interest is the price that borrowers pay to the lenders for the use of their funds. The rate of interest is determined through the interaction of demand and supply of the loanable funds.

Real and nominal discount rates Real discount rate refers to that rate of interest which has been adjusted for inflation while the nominal rate of discount refers to the actual rate of interest that includes the inflation rate as a part of it. In other words, nominal rate of discount is the unadjusted rate while the real rate of discount is the rate adjusted for inflation. For instance, let the inflation rate be 5% when the nominal rate of discount is 12%. The real rate of discount would then be 12 − 5 = 7%.

Risk premium It refers to the excess of the stock market rate of discount (r_m) over the risk-free rate (r_f) of discount. The risk premium accrues only to those investments that involve the non-diversifiable risks. The expected rate of discount (r_e) is a certain proportion (β) of the risk premium added to the risk-free rate of discount.

Thus, $$(r_e) = (r_f) + (\beta)[(r_m) - (r_f)]$$

Here β, called the asset beta, is the constant of proportionality which depends on the price movements of the asset in relation to the per cent movement in the market. If the per cent movement in the market is 1.0% and the expected movement in the price of asset is 5%; the asset β would be 5.0 as shown below:

$$\beta = \frac{r_e - r_f}{r_m - r_f} = \frac{5\%}{1\%} = 5.0$$

Treasury bill rate A treasury bill refers to a short-term (a year or less) bond issued by the government at a price less than the redemption value of the bond. For instance, a bond of face value of ₹ 100 (redemption value = ₹ 100) if issued by government for a period of 6 months at a price of ₹ 95, the effective annual rate of interest would work out to be 10.53% per annum.

Treasury bond rate A treasury bond refers to a government bond issued for periods longer than one year. The rate of interest depends on the length of the period.

User cost of production It is the opportunity cost of future production. A producer using exhaustible resources in production, sacrifices through its current use an opportunity of using it in future production. He, therefore, adds the user cost of production to the marginal production cost to arrive at the price of the product.

Risk-averse investor One for whom marginal utility of income diminishes with increasing income.

Risk-loving investor One for whom marginal utility of income increases with increasing income.

Risk-neutral investor One for whom marginal utility of income remains unaffected with increasing income.

EXERCISES

A. Very Short Answer Questions

Define the following:
1. Interest
2. Corporate bond rate
3. Treasury bond rate
4. Treasury bill rate
5. Commercial paper rate
6. Discount rate of interest
7. Prime lending rate
8. Present value
9. Net present value
10. Annuity
11. Perpetuity
12. User cost of production
13. Risk free rate of discount.
14. Stock market rate of return
15. Expected rate of discount
16. Asset beta
17. Risk premium
18. Effective yield
19. A risk-loving investor
20. A risk-averse investor
21. A risk-neutral investor

B. Long Answer Questions

Distinguish between (22 through 27):
22. Real and nominal rates of discount
23. Diversifiable and non-diversifiable risks
24. Risk-loving investor and risk-averse investor
25. Risk-averse investor and risk-neutral investor
26. Present value and net present value
27. Hiring and purchasing
28. Calculate the present value of a payment of ₹ 1000 expected 2 years hence. Assume that the market rate of interest is
    (a) 10% for both the years
    (b) 10% for the first year and 8% for the second year
    [**Ans.** (a) 826.45 (b) 841.75.]
29. Explain the loanable funds theory of determining the rate of interest.
30. An investment entitles an investor to a perpetual income stream of ₹ 1,000 per annum. It costs him ₹ 10,000. Another investment costs him ₹ 3500 now and entitles him to an income stream of

₹ 1100 after 1 year, ₹ 2420 after 2 years, and ₹ 1331 after 3 years. Which of the two would you advise him to go for? Assume that the rate of interest is 10% per annum for the period.

[**Ans.** Second, NPV of the 1st is zero and that of the second is +500.]

31. Given the market rate of interest as 10% per annum and the inflation rate as 4% per annum for next 3 years, determine the present value of a bond which is expected to yield ₹ 1100, 2420 and 1331 after 1, 2 and 3 years respectively.

    [**Ans.** ₹ 4309.06.]

32. Government bonds with face value of ₹ 1000 each are available for a price of ₹ 900. The bonds are redeemable after 6 months at the face value. Determine the treasury bill rate.

    [**Ans.** 22.22%.]

33. An individual, on the verge of his retirement, is expecting a sizeable amount of provident fund, gratuity, etc. at the retirement. For a perpetual income of ₹ 120,000 per annum, what minimum amount should he invest? Assume that the rate of interest is stable at 8% per annum.

    [**Ans.** ₹ 15 lakhs.]

34. A capital asset has a life span of 6 years. It requires an investment of ₹ 5 lakhs and yields a steady income of ₹ 1 lakh per annum over its life span. Its scrap value is ₹ 50,000 and the market rate of interest over the period is 10%. Would you advise in favour of this investment? Give reasons in support of your answer.

    [**Ans.** No, NPV = −₹ 36,275.]

35. How would your answer to Question 34 change if the rate of interest were 7.5% instead of 10%?

    [**Ans.** Investment is viable at 7.5%, NPV = +₹ 1733.33.]

36. In Question 34, interest rate is stable at 10% as given but general price-level is to go up at the rate of 4%. Would you decide in favour of the investment?

    [**Ans.** Yes, NPV = +₹ 26,916.67.]

37. A capital asset has a life span of 5 years left. It is expected to yield ₹ 10 lakhs per annum during this period. Thereafter, it is to be disposed off as scrap for ₹ 2 lakhs. The expected rate of return on the stock market is 12%, risk-free rate of return is 4% and asset beta is 0.6. What must be the minimum price at which you would advise the asset to be disposed off if so desired by the owner?

    [**Ans.** The expected rate of return,

    $$r_e = r_f + \beta(r_m - r_f)$$
    $$= 0.04 + 0.6(0.12 - 0.04)$$
    $$= 0.088$$
    $$= 8.8\%$$

    The present value of the asset,

    $$PV = \frac{A}{r}\left[1 - \{1/(1+r)^n\}\right] + \frac{S}{(1+r)^n}$$

    Substituting $A = 10$ lakhs, $S = 2$ lakhs, $n = 5$ years, $r = 8.8\%$, in the expression, we have

    $$PV = \frac{10}{0.088}\left[1 - \{1/(1.088)^5\}\right] + \frac{2}{(1.088)^5}$$
    $$= 113.6363636 \times [1 - 1/1.5245598] + 2/1.5245598$$
    $$= 39.09919976 + 1.311854$$
    $$= ₹ \; 40.41105376 \textbf{ lakhs.}$$

    The current price of the capital asset is ₹ 40,41,105.]

38. Show that the effective yield from perpetuity is lower than that from a bond of fixed maturity despite identical present values.

39. Show that the present value of a perpetuity is lower than that of a bond of fixed maturity despite identical effective yields.
40. Obtain an expression for the present value of an income stream when the annual inflow of income is fixed and so is the period of time and the rate of interest.
41. Obtain an expression for the present value of an income stream when the annual inflow of income is fixed and so is the period of time but the rate of interest varies from year to year.
42. Obtain an expression for the present value of an income stream when the period of time is fixed but the annual inflow of income as also the rate of interest vary from year to year.
43. Explain the Capital Asset Pricing Model (CAPM) and its ingredients.
44. Distinguish between diversifiable and non-diversifiable risks. How can the two be reconciled in investment decisions?
45. What is meant by risk premium and asset beta? What role do the two play in pricing of a capital asset?
46. Do we need a separate theory for investment decisions of the consumers? Explain with the help of an illustration.
47. What are intertemporal production decisions? In what respects such decisions differ from the other investment decisions? Explain.
48. 'Price in a competitive product market is always equal to the marginal cost of production.' Do you agree? Explain the role of the user cost of production.
49. As far as production with exhaustible resources is concerned, a monopolist is a greater conservationist than a competitive industry.' Do you agree? Give reasons in support of your answer.
50. What is the role of the risk premium in determining the NPV of an investment? Explain.
51. What are the determinants of NPV? How far is it true to say that NPV depends solely on the market rate of interest? Give reasons in support of your answer.

C. Essay Type Questions

52. Critically evaluate the role of the NPV criterion in investment decisions.
53. 'Investment is a risky business.' Critically examine the statement. How far does the saying 'No pains no gains' go with the statement?
54. 'Production with depletable resources certainly requires a different treatment'—Critically examine the statement with particular reference to product pricing. How does production with depletable resources by a competitive industry differ from that by a monopolist?
55. A firm has to decide whether to go for a capital investment that requires ₹ 20 lakhs to be invested in the beginning of the first year, ₹ 10.0 lakhs in the beginning of the second year and ₹ 5.0 lakhs in the beginning of the third year. In the first 3 years, no return is to follow. At the end of the 4th year, some sales are expected but a loss of ₹ 1.0 lakh is unavoidable. Thereafter, a steady profit stream of ₹ 4.0 lakhs is expected at the end of each year till the end of the 20th year, when the capital reduces to scrap and is sold off for ₹ 2.0 lakhs. Employ the NPV criterion to advise the firm. Assume a stable discount rate of 8% over the tenure of the investment.
    [**Ans.** Investment is not advisable, NPV = -7.8282]
56. A bank officer has to decide whether to go for the Voluntary Retirement Scheme (VRS) offered by the bank or to continue to work as usual. He is 54 now (1st Jan., 2005) and the retirement age for the bank officers is 60 years. If he decides to continue to work with the bank he would be entitled to a salary of ₹ 4 lakhs in 2005, that 5% higher next year and so on till the day of his retirement. The mortality rate as per the estimates of an insurance company for a person of his age is 0.9% for 2005, 1.0% for 2006, 1.1% for 2007 and so on; increasing by 0.1% each year, till it is 1.4% for 2010, the year of his retirement (The day of his retirement is 31st of December, 2010). If the current rate of interest for discounting purposes is 10%, determine what single payment to the officer is must to help him decide in favour of VRS?

Assume that all other benefits such as old-age-pension, gratuity, etc. would remain same either way the officer decides and that the income accruing to the officer in a year is treated as accredited to him in the beginning of that year.

[**Hint.** Follow the pattern of illustration 15.1, **Ans.** ₹ 21,18,591]

57. An individual has to decide whether to buy or lease a new car priced at ₹ 200,000. On an average the buyer consumes transport services worth ₹ 7,500 per month. The operating cost of the car is ₹ 3,000 per month and the buyer uses the car from day one of its purchase or lease. The lease rate of the car is ₹ 4,000 per month. All charges are assumed to be made annually in the beginning of the year over a period of 5 years. Assume that the car becomes scrap at the end of 5 years and, if bought, it is disposed off to a scrap vendor for a consideration of ₹ 25,000; else, it is returned to the leasing company. Would you advise him to buy the car? Assume a stable discount rate of 5%.

[**Ans.** Yes, NPVs of the two options are ₹ 65,072 (buying) and ₹ 27,276 (leasing).]

58. How would your answer to Question 57 change in each of the following situations:
    (a) Discount rate is 10% instead of 5%.
    (b) Monthly lease rate is ₹ 3000 instead of 4000.
    (c) Monthly lease rate is 3500 instead of 4000.

    [**Ans.** (a) No, NPVs of the two options are ₹ 40,705 (buying) and ₹ 25,056 (leasing).
    (b) No, NPVs of the two options are ₹ 65,072 (buying) and ₹ 81,827.11 (leasing).
    (c) No, NPVs of the two options are ₹ 65,072 (buying) and ₹ 54,551.41 (leasing).]

59. A firm has to decide which of the two alternative options of investment it should go for. The first option requires a sum of ₹ 6 lakhs for a period of 3 years. It is expected to pay back a sum of ₹ 2.20 lakhs at the end of the 1st year, ₹ 4.84 lakhs at the end of 2nd year and ₹ 2.662 lakhs at the end of the 3rd year. There is no other return in it except these. The second option requires a sum of ₹ 10 lakhs but assures a sum of ₹ 1.10 lakhs per annum forever. Which of the two, he should go for when the rate of discount is 10% per annum? Assume no inflation, no deflation and no risks involved.

    [**Ans.** The first one, the respective NPVs are ₹ 2 lakhs and ₹ 1.00 lakh.]

60. Make a comprehensive case on hire-purchase decisions with particular reference to cost and benefit analysis.

16

General Equilibrium and Economic Efficiency

CHAPTER OUTLINE
Introduction
✧ Path to General Equilibrium
✧ General Equilibrium Analysis: Efficiency of Exchange, Efficiency of Production and Efficiency of Product-mix
✧ Some Implications and Applications
✧ Market Failure and Its Sources
✧ Key Terms and Concepts
✧ Exercises

INTRODUCTION

So far, our study of equilibrium has confined itself to individuals or individual parts of the market. We have focussed on consumer's equilibrium (Chapter 4), producer's equilibrium (Chapter 5), product market equilibrium (Chapters 8, 9, 10 and 11) and factor market equilibrium (Chapter 14). Be it an individual consumer or an individual producer or be it an individual market-segment like product market, factor market, or be it a group of individual consumers or producers or of firms—we have studied them all in isolation to each other. In our study of factor markets, we discussed pricing of factors; in our study of product markets, we discussed pricing of products; in our study of firms, we discussed equilibrium of firms in respect of their price-output decisions under different market forms; in our study of equilibrium of a consumer, we studied utility maximization by a consumer under limited budget; and, in our study of equilibrium of a producer, we studied output maximization by a producer under given budget or cost minimization by him under given level of output to be produced. Little did we think in our analysis of a possible affect on a particular equilibrium of a change in equilibrium of a related market segment. For instance, while discussing equilibrium of a product market, we never bothered to analyse the affect of a change in factor market equilibrium nor did we ever think of the affect of a change in product market equilibrium on the equilibrium of the factor market. Our analysis of one equilibrium was in complete isolation to another. Throughout our study of individual units or of individual markets, our focus was on that particular unit or that particular market. In other words, we never bothered of interdependence of various market segments or of simultaneous equilibrium of entire market system despite our realization all along that the individual segments are related to each other and that changes in any of them go a long way to disturb the stability of the others. A shortfall in supply of labour increases wage rate in the factor market increasing thereby production cost and hence product price in the product market. Likewise, a change in product demand increases not only product price but also factor prices. Have not we completed a full circle? Yes, for sure we have and for sure we are face-to-face with a second cycle to get going. So much is the interdependence among the individual units or individual markets that a little disturbance in one spreads to the rest like a wild-fire.

Our study of individual units or individual markets, in isolation to each other, is known as the **partial equilibrium analysis** and our study of the interdependence among the individual units or of individual markets is known as the **general equilibrium analysis**. Partial equilibrium analysis is Marshallian* approach and is based on the *ceteris paribus* (all else same) assumption. Recall how frequently we have been resorting to the *ceteris paribus* clause in our analysis so far. In fact this clause concealed the interdependence of markets so that we may study the traits of individual units in their own environment first. In this chapter we introduce equilibrium in general or general equilibrium to explore possibilities of stability of the market system in an economy as also to investigate ways and means to reach it.

Let us first summarize important differences between partial and general equilibria (Table 16.1). As is obvious from the discussion, general equilibrium analysis refers to simultaneous equilibrium of all the economic units in the system with no restrictive assumptions. It was French economist Leon Walras** (1834–1910) who developed the general equilibrium model. In Walrasian model, the behaviour of each individual unit or market is presented by a set of equations. For instance a consumer buys goods and provides factor services. This leads to a set of equations depicting his behaviour. But there are so many consumers! In a Walrasian system, there are as many markets as there are commodities and factors of production. Each market has three types of functions—demand function, supply function and a market-clearing function. For the sake of simplicity, it would be better to explain the general equilibrium model by assuming two consumers (A and B, say), two commodities (X and Y, say) and two factors of production (L and K, say). The general equilibrium model then reduces to $2 \times 2 \times 2$[†] general equilibrium model for which it is not difficult to see that as many as 18 unknowns and 18 equations are involved. This makes the model solvable as the number of equations is just equal to the number of unknowns.

---

*Marshall, Alfred, *Principles of Economics*, Macmillan, 1920.

**Leon Walras, *Elements & Economie politique pure*, Lausanne, 1874. First translated in English by William Jaffe, Allan & Unwin, 1954.

[†]For a rigorous treatment of $2 \times 2 \times 2$ model, see H.G. Johnson, *Two-Sector Model of General Equilibrium*, Aldine Press, New york, 1971.

TABLE 16.1 Partial and general equilibrium analyses

Partial equilibrijm analysis	*General equilibrium analysis*
1. **Meaning:** Partial equilibrium refers to the equilibrium of only a part of the whole system. For instance, equilibrium of the product market to determine the price of the product, is partial equilibrium. It has nothing to do with the equilibrium of the factor market, nor with that of the producers. In the words of G.J. Stigler, "*A partial equilibrium is one which is based on only a restricted range of data; a standard example is price of a single product, the price of all other products being held fixed during the analysis.*" Determination of the product price through the interaction of product demand and product supply, while all other things remain constant (*ceteris paribus*) is an example of partial equilibrium.	1. **Meaning:** General equilibrium refers to the simultaneous equilibrium of all the markets operating in the system. For instance, simultaneous equilibrium of the factor market, the product market, the individual producer in respect of the employment of the factors, as also the individual consumer in respect of the quantities of the goods consumed is the general equilibrium. General equilibrium implies interdependence of all the segments of the economy. The concept of general equilibrium does not need assumptions like *ceteris paribus*.
2. **Methodology:** The methodology of partial equilibrium refers to determination of price and quantity in each market through the interaction of demand and supply curves drawn on the assumption of *ceteris paribus*.	2. **Methodology:** The father of general equilibrium analysis, Leon Walras, conceived economy as a system of simultaneous equations, describing the demands and supplies of all the commodities. The equations of the demand and supply of each product are expressed in terms of prices of all the products so that the effect of a change in any one of them on the rest may be studied directly.
3. **Applicability:** Partial equilibrium analysis forms the basis of microeconomic studies.	3. **Applicability:** The general equilibrium analysis serves as an important tool of resolving the macroeconomic controversies. It perceives the economy as a vast system of mutually interdependent markets. The nature of interdependence truly exposes the complexity of the system.
4. **Pioneers of partial equilibrium:** The most important exponent of the partial equilibrium analysis was Dr. Alfred Marshall whose work, magnum opus, *Principles of Economic* published in 1890 is considered as a leading work on Microeconomics.	4. **Pioneers of general equilibrium:** Leon Walras is considered as the father of the general equilibrium analysis. His work *Elements of Pure Economics* was published in French in 1874 and in English in 1954.

16.1 PATH TO GENERAL EQUILIBRIUM

Before coming to general equilibrium, let us have a glimpse of the nature and tendency of interdependence of individual markets. For the purpose, suppose two goods, X and Y, perfect substitutes of each other, are being produced by two perfectly competitive industries employing labour L and capital K from perfectly competitive markets. Suppose further that quantities of the two factors are fixed and that the production functions of the two goods are continuous with diminishing $MRTS_{L,K}$ and decreasing returns to scale. Also suppose that the industry producing X is labour intensive and that producing Y is capital intensive. The system is in initial equilibrium with consumers maximizing utility and producers maximizing profits.

Now suppose consumers' tastes and preferences tilt in favour of good X, leading to an upward to right shift in its demand from D_0 to D_1 and that for Y, the substitute, to a downward to left shift from d_0 to d_1. Figure 16.1 shows their effects on the respective quantities transacted and prices charged.

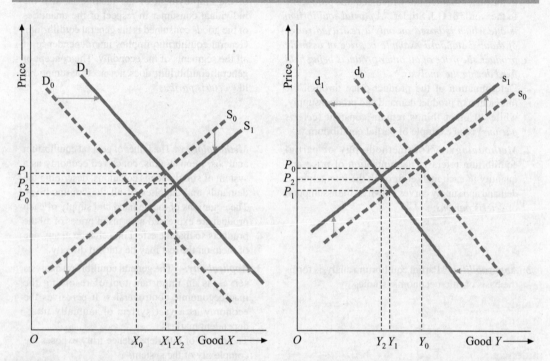

FIGURE 16.1 **Effect of an increase in demand for X on demand for its substitute Y and resource allocation:** In the left panel, demand for good X shifts upward to right from D_0 to D_1 due to a change in consumers' tastes and preferences. Quantity of X demanded increases from X_0 to X_1 and price rises from P_0 to P_1. Profits of industry X rise with the consequence that it tends to produce more of it by hiring more factors. Demand for factors increases and so does the production of X, leading to a downward to right shift in supply of X. This pushes price of X to P_2 and quantity to X_2. Since labour and capital are fixed and goods X and Y are perfect substitutes, factors from industry producing Y would move to industry producing X. As goods X and Y are substitutes and an increase in demand for X has led to a decrease in demand for good Y, price and demand for good Y would both fall. In consequence, demand for factors in industry producing Y would also fall. In a way, resources would shift from production of Y to production of X.

As an impact of a rise in demand of X, demand for Y falls and resources get shifted from production of good Y to production of good X. This is shown in Figure 16.2 through a production possibility curve.

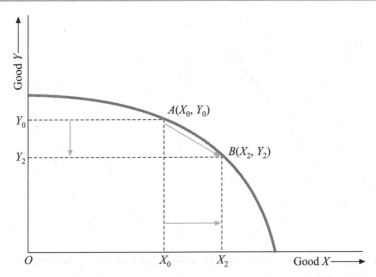

FIGURE 16.2 Resource re-allocation necessitated by an increase in demand of X and decrease in demand for Y: An increase in demand for X results in a decrease in demand of Y, as the two are perfect substitutes. When demand for X rises, so do the profits of the industry producing it. In like manner, when demand for Y falls so do the profits of the industry producing it. Increasing and decreasing profits call for a resource reallocation which takes place in favour of good X. Some resources are shifted from production of Y to production of X.

As assumed, commodity X is labour intensive and commodity Y, capital intensive. Demand for labour in industry X, therefore, increases more proportionately than the decrease in demand for it in industry Y. Labour released from industry Y falls short of labour demanded in industry X and the supply of commodity X fails to increase by as much as it should to offset the increase in demand for good X. As a result, rise in price of X is neutralized only partially (Figure 16.1), making X more profitable. On the other hand, a decrease in demand for Y leads to a decrease in demand for labour and capital both in industry Y but the decrease in capital-demand is much more than the decrease in labour-demand due to high capital intensity of commodity Y. Changes in demand for labour and capital in the two industries are portrayed in Figures 16.3 to 16.6.

In consequence to increased profitability of commodity X and decreased profitability of commodity Y, more of X and less of Y will be produced. This would necessitate reallocation of resources in favour of commodity X and against commodity Y. In Figure 16.2, movement from point A to point B along the PPC indicates resource reallocation.

Impact on demand of labour and capital in the industry producing commodity X is shown in Figures 16.3 and 16.4, while that on demand of labour and capital in the industry producing commodity Y is depicted in Figures 16.5 and 16.6.

Thus, a change in demand for good X initiates changes not only in demand and supply of substitute Y but also in demand and supply of labour and capital in the two industries. The effects trickle down to the firms operating in the two industries. The reader can draw projections to right of each figure to see how production and employment get influenced in respective firms in the consequence.

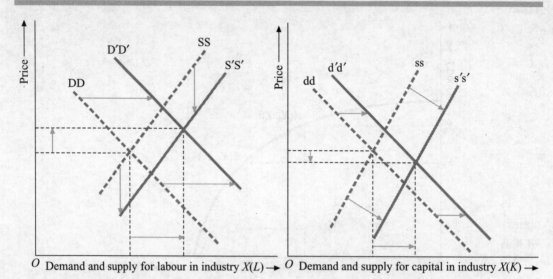

FIGURE 16.3 Increased demand for labour-intensive X leads to higher demand for labour but supply of labour being limited to the magnitude of labour released from industry Y. As a result, labour price rises.

FIGURE 16.4 Increased demand for labour-intensive X leads to a higher demand for capital also but the increase is much less than that for labour. Supply of it being higher due to release of capital from industry Y, its price falls.

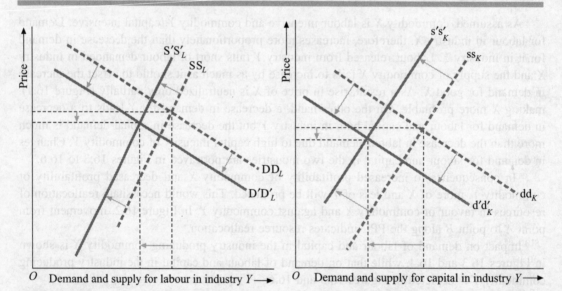

FIGURE 16.5 Demand and supply for labour fall in response to a fall in demand for good Y. As a result price and employment of labour fall in industry Y.

FIGURE 16.6 Demand and supply for capital fall in response to a fall in demand for good Y. As a result price and employment of capital fall in industry Y.

16.2 GENERAL EQUILIBRIUM ANALYSIS: EFFICIENCY OF EXCHANGE, EFFICIENCY OF PRODUCTION AND EFFICIENCY OF PRODUCT-MIX

General equilibrium in a $2 \times 2 \times 2$ model in competitive commodity and factor markets involves the following:

1. Efficient allocation of resources among firms (equilibrium of production).
2. Efficient distribution of commodities produced between the two consumers (equilibrium of consumption).
3. Efficient combination of products (simultaneous equilibrium of production and consumption).

The three constitute **marginal conditions of Pareto optimality or Pareto efficiency**. Pareto optimality or efficiency refers to a state of social well being in which it is not possible to make an individual better-off without making another worse-off.

Let us discuss these features of general equilibrium in requisite detail:

1. Equilibrium of production (efficiency of resource allocation)

This refers to efficiency of distribution of available factors among existing firms. Each firm desires a combination of labour and capital that lies on the highest isoquant available under the given budget or one that lies on the lowest isocost curve, given the output level to be produced. In either case, it requires efficiency of factor substitution by a firm for which,

$$\text{MRTS}_{L,K} = (\text{MP}_L/\text{MP}_K) = (w/r) \qquad (16.1)$$

where, w and r are the competitive prices of labour and capital; and, MP_L and MP_K are their marginal products respectively.

$\text{MRTS}_{L,K}$ stands for marginal rate of factor substitution, which is the ratio of MP_L and MP_K. For efficiency of factor substitution, this must be equal to the ratio of the corresponding factor prices, w/r (See Chapter 5).

Equilibrium of production requires efficiency of factor substitution by each firm. Under competitive conditions, ratio of factor prices (w/r) is given. Hence for each firm, its $\text{MRTS}_{L,K}$ must be equal to this ratio. Efficiency of factor substitution between firms producing goods X and Y would thus require

$$\text{MRTS}^X_{L,K} = \text{MRTS}^Y_{L,K} = (w/r) \qquad (16.2)$$

where, $\text{MRTS}^X_{L,K}$ stands for marginal rate of factor substitution of firm producing X and $\text{MRTS}^Y_{L,K}$ stands for that of the firm producing Y. Since $\text{MRTS}_{L,K}$ represents numerical value of the slope of an isoquant whereas (w/r) represents numerical value of the slope of an isocost, efficient allocation of factors L and K between production of goods X and Y would thus require isoquants of the two goods to satisfy condition in Eq. (16.2). Diagrammatically, this is shown in Figure 16.7.

The isoquants of the two firms are drawn with O as the reference point of the firm producing commodity X and O' as the reference point of the firm producing commodity Y. The respective isoquants are convex to the respective origins, O and O'.

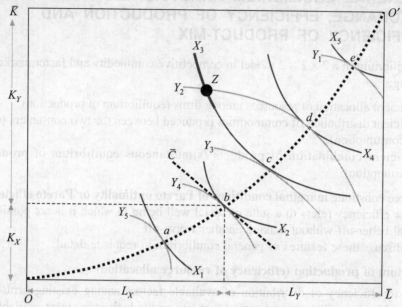

FIGURE 16.7 Edgeworth box of optimality of factor allocation: Given fixed quantities of labour ($\bar{L}$) and capital ($\bar{K}$), as measured on horizontal and vertical axes, isoquants of commodity X (X_i, $i = 1, 2, ..., 5$) are drawn with O as the origin, to which they all are convex and isoquants of commodity $Y(Y_i, i = 1, 2, ..., 5)$ are drawn with O' as the origin, to which they all are convex. The points at which the X and Y isoquants are tangential to each other, i.e. the points at which their slopes are equal, are marked as a, b, c, d, and e. At each of these, $(MRTS^X_{L,K}) = (MRTS^Y_{L,K})$. The locus, these points trace out, is known as **Edgeworth Contract Curve**. In the figure, curve OO', joining a, b, c, d, and e, is the Edgeworth Contract Curve. It defines possible allocations of labour and capital between production of X and Y. Points other than those on the contract curve lead to inefficiency of allocation as shown by extending isoquants X_3 and Y_2 to meet each other at point Z. Production of at least one of the two goods is less at Z than at either of the points c and d on the contract curve. At point $c(X_3, Y_3)$ more of Y is produced with same X than at $Z(X_3, Y_2)$ and at point $d(X_4, Y_2)$ more of X is produced with same Y than at Z. Thus, an allocation of inputs is efficient if it is made along the contract curve. Production of none of the two goods is possible to be increased along the contract curve without decreasing that of the other. That is what Pareto efficiency* requires. For equilibrium in input allocation, condition in Eq. (16.2) gives point b as the point of equilibrium on the contract curve. Note that the essential feature of the contract curve is equality of $MRTS^X_{L,K}$ and $MRTS^Y_{L,K}$ and that of equilibrium is equality of each to (w/r). In sum, there are infinite possibilities of efficient allocation of resources but only one of them leads to equilibrium.

From the discussion of Figure 16.7, it is clear that all the points on the contract curve lead to Pareto-efficient allocations of labour and capital for production of the two goods. This doesn't imply uniqueness of these allocations. However, one of these allocations that eventually satisfies the condition (Eq. 16.2) of maximizing joint profits under competitive equilibrium leads to uniqueness. Such an allocation emerges at b where X_2 of X is produced by X-industry employing L_X of $\bar{L}$ and K_X of $\bar{K}$ and Y_4 of Y is produced by Y-industry employing L_Y of $\bar{L}$ and K_Y of $\bar{K}$. Point b thus provides general equilibrium of production. The question that arises now is what if the consumers require a basket other than (X_2, Y_4)? The general equilibrium of production that

---

*Vilfredo Pareto, *Cours d' Economie politique*, Lausanne, 1897.

has been worked out right now will be of little consequence if quantities produced are no longer in demand.

Indications of change in consumer preferences reflect in product prices. As assumed in the beginning of the $2 \times 2 \times 2$ model, X and Y are substitutes. A rise in demand for X would raise its price which in turn would lower demand and price of Y. In consequence, production of X must increase and that of Y must decrease. As a result X-industry would climb up to a higher isoquant while Y-industry would climb down to a lower one. This would initiate a reallocation of resources leading to changes in input requirements and hence input prices w and r. The numerical value of the slope of the isocost will therefore change with changing $MRTS_{L,K}$ of the firms and so will the general equilibrium of production from point b to a higher point on the contract curve. To complete our discussion on equilibrium of production, we first need to obtain a production possibility curve from the contract curve and then we need to find out which basket the consumers actually require at a given set of prices.

Derivation of the production possibility curve from the edgeworth contract curve

In order to trace production possibility curve from the edgeworth contract curve, one needs to map into the commodity space, the quantities of goods X and Y corresponding to the points on the contract curve. Each point on the contract curve represents a point of tangency of X and Y isoquants. For instance, point a represents tangency of isoquants X_1 and Y_5, point b represents that of isoquants X_2 and Y_4, point c that of isoquants X_3 and Y_3 and so on. Each of the points a, b, c, d, and e on the contract curve OO' (Figure 16.7) represents a pair of isoquants touching each other. Quantities of X and Y represented by them are respectively (X_1, Y_5), (X_2, Y_4), (X_3, Y_3), (X_4, Y_2), and (X_5, Y_1). Plotting them with X on x-axis and Y on y-axis, and joining them by means of a smooth curve, we get the production possibility curve as shown in Figure 16.8.

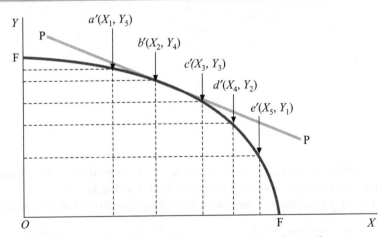

FIGURE 16.8 Derivation of production possibility curve from the edgeworth contract curve: Derivation of production possibility curve from the edgeworth contract curve involves plotting the combinations of X and Y corresponding to the points on the contract curve. Combinations corresponding to points a, b, c, d, and e on the contract curve OO' in Figure 16.7 are plotted with X on x-axis and Y on y-axis and are marked as a', b', c', d', and e' here. The locus of these points yields a curve concave to the origin. This is production possibility curve. Point b' at which $MRTS^X_{L,K} = MRTS^Y_{L,K} = (w/r)$ is the point of equilibrium in resource allocation between production of X and Y.

Determination of optimal product-mix

The slope of the production possibility curve, dy/dx, is negative. The rate at which one commodity is transformed into another is known as the marginal rate of product transformation or the marginal opportunity cost. Here, the rate at which commodity Y is converted into commodity X is called the marginal rate of product transformation of Y into X. Written as $\text{MRPT}_{X,Y}$, it is given as

$$\text{MRPT}_{X,Y} = \left|\frac{dy}{dx}\right|$$

$$= -\frac{f_x}{f_y} \quad \text{[Eq. (1.1), Ch-1]}$$

$$= -\frac{dy}{dx} \tag{16.3}$$

In our discussion of the problem of resource allocation (Chapter 1), we had taken the revenue function as

$$R = xP_x + yP_y$$

where, $\quad R \equiv$ revenue or sales proceeds,

x and $y \equiv$ the quantities of the two goods, X and Y, required to be produced for the optimality of resource allocation when their prices are P_x and P_y respectively.

It was shown that $\text{MRPT}_{X,Y}$ must be equal to the price ratio at the point of optimal resource allocation. To provide a proof to this statement we had employed Lagrange's method of constrained maximization. Implicit was the assumption of perfect competition. That was why P_x and P_y were treated as constant while differentiating the composite function Φ partially with respect to x and y. As price of a product is equal to its marginal cost in perfect competition, the condition for optimal resource allocation can be stated as

$$\text{MRPT}_{X,Y} = \left|\frac{dy}{dx}\right|$$

$$= -\frac{dy}{dx}$$

$$= \frac{P_x}{P_y} \tag{16.4}$$

$$= \frac{\text{MC}_x}{\text{MC}_y} \tag{16.5}$$

In sum, we had established and used condition in Eq. (16.4) for optimality of resource allocation, which, under the competitive condition, implies condition in Eq. (16.5).

In our analysis of general equilibrium, we can establish condition (16.5)* in slightly different way also.

---

* Total costs of production of x and y units of goods X and Y, employing labour L and capital K at prices w and r, respectively can be expressed as

$$\text{TC}_x = w \cdot L_x + r \cdot K_x \tag{1}$$

and
$$\text{TC}_y = w \cdot L_y + r \cdot K_y \tag{2}$$

where w and r are competitive prices of labour and capital, respectively. Differentiating Eqs. (1) and (2) with respect to X and Y, we have

$$d(\text{TC}_x)/dx = w \cdot (dL_x/dx) + r \cdot (dK_x/dx) \tag{3}$$

(contd.)

This strengthens the assertion that $f_x/f_y = MC_x/MC_y$. In sum, equilibrium of production requires production at point b (Figure 16.7), satisfying Eq. (16.3) and optimality of product-mix requires quantities X_2 and Y_4 to be produced at point b' (Figure 16.8), satisfying Eq. (16.5).

From the point of view of firms, general equilibrium of production is reached at point b' in the commodity space (Figure 16.8), which is a mapping of point b of the factor space (Figure 16.7).

2. Equilibrium of consumption (efficiency in distribution of goods)

In our discussions on equilibrium of production, we have seen that given a price set P_x and P_y for commodities X and Y, the two firms would produce quantities X_2 of X and Y_4 of Y at b' on the PPC in Figure 16.8. Continuing with $2 \times 2 \times 2$ model of general equilibrium, equilibrium of consumption refers to distribution of quantities X and Y between consumers A and B.

Edgeworth box once again proves handy in this analysis. We have seen in Chapter 4, that the condition of a consumer's equilibrium requires tangency of his indifference curve to his budget line. Symbolically, for consumer A,

$$MRS^A_{x,y} = [MU_x/MU_y] = [P_x/P_y] \qquad (16.6)$$

Likewise, for consumer B,

$$MRS^B_{x,y} = [MU_x/MU_y] = [P_x/P_y] \qquad (16.7)$$

Quantities of two goods being fixed as X_2 of X and Y_4 of Y, the efficiency of distribution between the two would require

$$MRS^A_{x,y} = [P_x/P_y] = MRS^B_{x,y} \qquad (16.8)$$

Resorting to the edgeworth box, let us draw A's indifference curves with O as the origin and those of B, with O' as the origin. The locus of points of tangency a, b, c, d, and e describes the contract curve, OO' (Figure 16.9).

Footnote contd.

$$d(TC_y)/dy = w \cdot (dL_y/dy) + r \cdot (dK_y/dy) \qquad (4)$$

In order to remain on the PPC, factors released from the decrease in commodity Y must be equal to the factors absorbed by the increase in the production of X, i.e.

$$dL_x = -dL_y \text{ and } dK_x = -dK_y$$

Substituting for dL_x and dK_x in Eq. (3), we have

$$MC_x = -[w \cdot (dL_y/dx) + r \cdot (dK_y/dx)] \qquad (5)$$

$$(\because d(TC_x)/dx = MC_x)$$

Likewise,

$$MC_y = w \cdot (dL_y/dy) + r \cdot (dK_y/dy) \qquad (6)$$

$$(\because d(TC_y)/dy = MC_y)$$

From Eqs. (5) and (6), we have

$$\begin{aligned}
\frac{MC_x}{MC_y} &= \frac{-[w \cdot (dL_y/dx) + r \cdot (dK_y/dx)]}{[w \cdot (dL_y/dy) + r \cdot (dK_y/dy)]/dy} \\
&= \frac{-[w \cdot (dL_y) + r \cdot (dK_y)]/dx}{[w \cdot (dL_y) + r \cdot (dK_y)]/dy} \\
&= \frac{-[w \cdot (dL_y) + r \cdot (dK_y)]}{[w \cdot (dL_y) + r \cdot (dK_y)]} \times \frac{dy}{dx} \\
&= (-)(dy/dx) \\
&= MRPT_{X,Y} \qquad \text{[From Eq. (16.3)]} \\
&= P_x/P_y
\end{aligned}$$

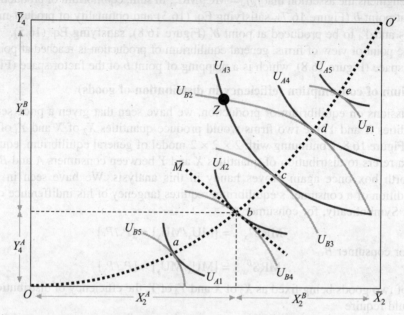

FIGURE 16.9 Edgeworth box of optimality of exchange of commodities: Indifference curves $U_{A1}, U_{A2}, ..., U_{A5}$ represent various utility levels available to consumer A while indifference curves $U_{B1}, U_{B2}, ..., U_{B5}$ represent those available to consumer B. A's utility curves are convex to O while those of B, convex to O'. Indifference curves of A are tangential to those of B at points $a, b, c, d,$ and e. The given quantities of the two goods that have to be shared between A and B are $\overline{X}_2$ and $\overline{Y}_4$ (Figure 16.7). Contract curve OO' is the join of points O, a, b, c, d, e and O'. As explained in Figure 16.7, it is not possible on the contract curve to increase utility of one consumer without decreasing that of another. Suppose welfare of consumer A is desired to be increased from that A is having at point b. This would require taking him to points $c, d,$ or e on the contract curve. A, in consequence, will attain higher utilities $U_{A3}, U_{A4},$ or U_{A5} but each time A attains a higher level of utility, B has to step down to lower levels of it. Thus, A's utility cannot be increased without making B worse-off. Hence, every point on the contract curve is Pareto efficient while every point elsewhere is Pareto–inefficient. As in Figure 16.7, compare point Z off the contract curve to another, c, on the contract curve. At point c, the two enjoy utilities U_{A3} and U_{B3} while at point Z, A continues with U_{A3} but B drops down to U_{B2}. Tangency of the respective indifference curves at points a, b, c, d and e implies equality of their slopes at these points $\mathrm{MRS}^A_{x, y} = \mathrm{MRS}^B_{x, y}$. This leads to existence of infinite number of Pareto-efficient possibilities of distribution of two goods between two consumers. Each of these corresponds to a particular set of prices of X and Y. For instance, corresponding to P_x and P_y, point b, satisfying $\mathrm{MRS}^A_{x, y} = \mathrm{MRS}^B_{x, y} = P_x/P_y$, is the Pareto-efficient distribution of two commodities. Point b, therefore, is an equilibrium point. If consumer's tastes and preferences shift in favour of commodity X, price of X rises and that of its substitute Y falls because its demand falls. In consequence, P_x/P_y would rise and the equilibrium position would shift away from point b on the contract curve.

Equilibrium of consumption, as explained in Figure 16.9, is reached at point b. Consumer A attains utility U_{A2} and consumer B, U_{B4} at this point.

3. Simultaneous equilibrium of production and consumption [efficiency in product-mix]

From the discussions so far, it appears that the condition,

$$\mathrm{MRS}^A_{x, y} = [P_x/P_y] = \mathrm{MRS}^B_{x, y} = \mathrm{MRPT}_{x, y} \qquad (16.9)$$

may be an over-riding factor in determining the equilibrium of production and consumption, provided the consumer is the sovereign king in the market (Figure 16.10). This is so because demand dictates price and hence production. Firms produce what market demands. From Figure 16.7, producers' equilibrium at point b though governed by condition in Eq. (16.3),

$$(MRTS^X_{L,K}) = (MRTS^Y_{L,K}) = (w/r)$$

it is subject to the condition in Eq. (16.4),

$$MRPT_{X,Y} = -\frac{dy}{dx} = \frac{P_x}{P_y}$$

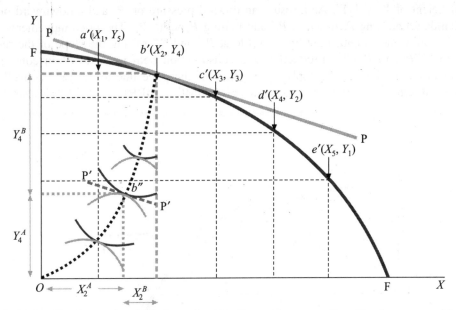

FIGURE 16.10 Simultaneous equilibrium of production and consumption: Simultaneous equilibrium of production and consumption implies general equilibrium in which two firms producing goods X and Y produce quantities X_2 of X and Y_4 of Y at b' while the two consumers A and B consume respectively the quantities $[X_2^A, Y_4^A]$ and $[X_2^B, Y_4^B]$ at b'' so that $X_2 = [X_2^A + X_2^B]$ and $Y_4 = [Y_4^A + Y_4^B]$. At b', price line PP is tangential to the PPC, that is, $MRPT_{X,Y} = [P_x/P_y]$ and at b'', price line P'P' drawn parallel to price line PP is tangential to the indifference curves of the two consumers, fulfilling the condition in Eq. (16.8). Taken together, the condition of general equilibrium or that of simultaneous equilibrium of production and consumption, as given in Eq. (16.9), is reached. This leads to attainment of the general equilibrium of an economy with two producers producing two goods, X and Y, employing two factors, L and K, and satisfying the demands of two consumers, A and B, at price set P_x and P_y.

Equilibrium of production [Eq. (16.2)], equilibrium of consumption [Eq. (16.8)] and simultaneous equilibrium of production and consumption [Eq. (16.9)] are all competitive equilibria. That makes general equilibrium of a 2 × 2 × 2 model a competitive equilibrium. From what we learnt about efficiency in Section 7.5, general equilibrium being a competitive one is efficient. It aims at maximization of aggregate producers' and consumers' surpluses or, more precisely, of social welfare.

16.3 SOME IMPLICATIONS AND APPLICATIONS

1. How efficient is the general equilibrium?

We have seen that a competitive market is highly efficient. General equilibrium being a competitive one must also be an efficient one. To establish the fact, let there be two firms in a competitive $2 \times 2 \times 2$ model of general equilibrium. Further, let production & consumption both take place initially at e (Figure 16.11) and let the competitive prices of goods X and Y be P_x and P_y. Now suppose that consumers decide to consume a different basket, say e', at the same price-set with an objective of a higher utility, U', if possible. Point e lies on the PPC, but point e' does not. Instead, it is much above the PPC though on the same price line PP (Figure 16.11). The basket (X', Y') demanded at e' for consumption is thus not available. It requires an excess of X by $X_1 X'$ and a deficient of Y by $Y_5 Y'$. As a result, an upward pressure on P_x and a downward pressure on P_y builds up pushing P_y down to P_y' and pulling P_x up to P_x'. The price movements follow the market adjustments until they finally settle at P_x'' and P_y'' raising the slope of the resulting price line $(P''P'')$ to P_x''/P_y''. Production and consumption both move to e'' in consequence. The general equilibrium at e'', implying tangency of the price line to the PPC as well as the consumers' indifference curve being competitive ($MC_x/MC_y = MRPT_{X,Y} = P_x''/P_y''$) is also efficient.

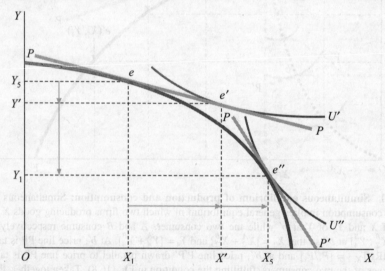

FIGURE 16.11 Efficiency of competitive equilibrium: Production and consumption are in general equilibrium at $e(X_1, Y_5)$. Is it possible to be better off at any other point, say e', with the same price set $(P_x \text{ and } P_y)$? Let us investigate. As is clear from the figure, Utility at e' is U' implying consumption of X' of X and Y' of Y. These quantities however don't correspond to the PPC as e' is above it. More of X by as much as $X_1 X'$ and less of Y by $Y_5 Y'$ needs to be produced and supplied. Demand for X being higher and that of Y being lower than their supplies, price of X comes under upward pressure and that of Y under downward pressure until the two settle at P_x'' and P_y'' respectively. As a result, the price line $P''P''$ turns steeper than PP and touches the PPC at e'' under the market adjustments. At e'', X_5 of X and Y_1 of Y are produced and consumed in ultimate equilibrium. Point e'', like point e, is the point of general equilibrium implying tangency of PPC, U'', and $P''P''$. Equilibrium at e'' is competitive and hence efficient like the equilibrium at e. However, e' is not the point of general equilibrium and hence the question of its efficiency doesn't arise.

2. Gains from free trade

Trade between two countries is favoured when both of them gain from it. Total gain accruing to a trading country comprises (1) gain from exchange, and (2) gain from specialization.

Gain from exchange refers to the advantage of buying a product at a price lower than the domestic price or selling another at a price higher than the domestic price. For instance, let the price of product X in India be ₹ 100 per unit. If India buys it from Australia at ₹ 80 per unit worth of Australian currency, India is said to be gaining from this exchange. It is a different matter that India would need Australian currency to give effect to this transaction. Now suppose Australia finds that it can have product Y from India at a price lower than the price prevailing in its own territory. India can sell product Y to Australia and raise Australian currency for buying product X. In the same way, Australia can raise enough Indian currency for buying product Y from India by selling product X to India. Equivalent foreign currencies can be had by the two from the international money market. Alternatively, they can work out a system of commodity exchange to avoid involving their currencies. If they do, India would exchange its Y for Australia's X and both the countries would gain from the exchange.

Gain from specialization, on the other hand, refers to the advantage of specializing in production of a product for which a country is more suited than other countries. Specialization enhances competitiveness of the specializing country through scale economies which cut production cost and reduce product price. For example, India, more suited to agricultural and labour intensive production, can enhance its competitiveness in the world market by specializing in production of the related products. Specialization has yet another benefit. Apart from reducing production cost it helps improving product quality as well. The specializing country gains market share by supplying better products at lower prices.

Trade transmits these advantages across the border to the trading partners. For instance, India, due to its richness of soil and suitable climatic conditions, is better poised for production of food; while UK, due to its capital endowments, is better suited for production of textiles. In other words, production of food is cheaper in India and production of textiles is cheaper in UK. Entering into trade helps India to consume cheaper textiles from UK and the latter to consume cheaper food from India. As a result, both the countries gain from trade.

To analyze the gains further, think of two countries, A and B. Country A has an advantage in production of X (food), while country B, has it in production of Y (clothing). Price of X in country A is P_x^A and that of it in country B is P_x^B. As assumed, $P_x^A < P_x^B$. Likewise, prices of Y in the two countries are P_y^A and P_y^B, and $P_y^A > P_y^B$ as assumed.

Suppose that the two countries are producing and consuming in isolation (no foreign trade), with Country A at points e_A [Figure 16.12(a)] producing and consuming (X_A, Y_A) and Country B at e_B [Figure 16.12(b)] producing and consuming (X_B, Y_B), respectively. Each is thus in general equilibrium on its own with respective utilities enjoyed given as U_A and U_B.

Now suppose the two enter in trade, with country A exporting its $X(P_x^A < P_x^B)$ to country B and importing Y from country B $(P_y^B < P_y^A)$ while country B exporting its $Y(P_y^B < P_y^A)$ to country A and importing X from country A $(P_x^A < P_x^B)$. That is, each is exporting what is cheaper in it and importing what is cheaper in the other. Figure 16.12(a) explains how country A climbs onto a higher indifference cure, U_A' by exchanging some of its X with some of country B's Y. Likewise, Figure 16.12(b) shows how country B climbs onto a higher indifference cure, U_B' by exchanging some of its Y with some of country A's X. The gains accruing to the two are the gains caused by the exchange of the products that are cheaper to produce in each in comparison to the other. Such gains are called *gains from exchange*.

To maximize the gains, each country then decides to specialize in production of that good which it can produce at lower costs than the other country. Due to specialization, country A [Figure 16.12(a)] moves from e_A to e_A''' in production (i.e., on its PPC) and from e_A to e_A'' in consumption, raising its utility level from U_A to U_A'' and country B [Figure 16.12(b)] moves from e_B to e_B''' in production (i.e., on its PPC) and from e_B to e_B'' in consumption, raising its utility level from U_B to U_B''. Country A specializes in production of X (cheaper in A but costlier in B) while country B specializes in production of Y(cheaper in B but costlier in A).

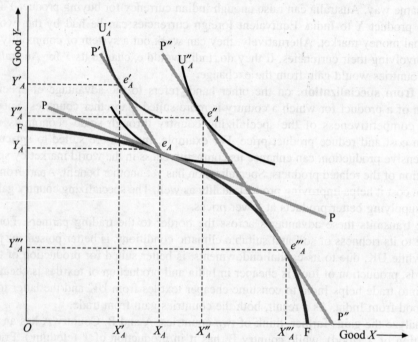

FIGURE 16.12(a) Gains from trade to country A: In the figure, country A is in general equilibrium at point $e_A(X_A, Y_A)$, that is, it is producing and consuming the basket (X_A, Y_A) and is enjoying utility U_A at the point. The commodity prices are P_x^A and P_y^A. Commodity X commanding a higher price in country B than what it does in the domestic territory of country A and commodity Y being cheaper in country B than in country A, the latter (country A) decides to trade with the former (country B). What prompts it to take this decision is quite logical, but let us analyze it in concrete terms. Since, $(P_y^B < P_y^A)$, the post-trade price line, $P'e_A$, in country A, becomes steeper than PP $[(P_x^A/P_y^B) > (P_x^A/P_y^A)]$. As a result, country A jumps onto a higher community indifference curve U_A' in the post trade period $(U_A' > U_A)$. This marks the gain from exchange accruing to country A in the post trade period. A rise in foreign demand for country A's product $X(P_x^A < P_x^B)$, country A decides to specialize in production of X. It moves to point e_A''' on its PPC for the purpose by shifting some of its resources from production of Y to production of X. This enables it to enjoy much more of the cheaper Y, which it imports from country B. In consequence, its community indifference curve shifts to a higher position at e_A'' where it now enjoys a higher utility U_A''. Movement from U_A' to U_A'' marks country A's gain from specialization. The total gain (TG) from trade is thus given as TG (movement from U_A to U_A'') = Gain from exchange (movement from U_A to U_A') + Gain from specialization (movement from U_A' to U_A''). Country A finally exports $(X_A''' - X_A'')$ to country B and imports $(Y_A''' - Y_A'')$ from it.

The total gains of the trading partners comprise the gains from exchange and gains from specialization. The mechanism of the shift in the general equilibrium of each country is demonstrated in Figures 16.12(a) and 16.12(b) for the two countries.

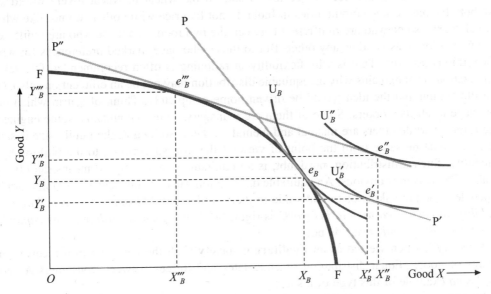

FIGURE 16.12(b) **Gains from trade to country B:** Country B is producing and consuming at point $e_B(X_B, Y_B)$ in its pre-trade period. $P_x^B > P_x^A$ and $P_y^B < P_y^A$, country B decides to enter in trade with country A. As soon as it does, its price line changes to $e_B P'$ which is flatter than PP $[(P_x^A/P_y^B) < (P_x^B/P_y^B)]$. As a result, country B jumps on a higher community indifference curve U_B'. This marks country B's **gain from exchange**.

A rise in foreign demand for country B's product $Y(P_y^B < P_y^A)$, country B decides to specialize in production of Y. It moves to point e_B''' on its PPC for the purpose by shifting some of its resources from production of X to production of Y. This enables it to enjoy much more of the cheaper X, which it imports from country A. In consequence, its community indifference curve shifts to a higher position at e_B'' where it now enjoys a higher utility U_B''. Movement from U_B' to U_B'' marks country B's **gain from specialization**. The total gain (TG) from trade is thus given as TG (movent from U_B to U_B'') = Gain from exchange (movent from U_B to U_B') + Gain from specialization (movement from U_B' to U_B''). Country B finally exports $(Y'''_B - Y''_B)$ to country A and imports $(X''_B - X'''_B)$ from it.

3. Equity versus efficiency

Is an efficient allocation of productive factors (L, K) between two goods (X, Y) equitable as well or is an efficient distribution of two goods (X, Y) between two consumers (A, B) equitable as well? In other words, we have to investigate whether efficiency implies equitability also.

Before finding an answer to these questions, let us first understand what actually the two imply. Suppose you have to distribute 10 chocolates and 20 toffees between two children, A and B. The concept of equity requires that chocolates and toffees must be distributed equally between A and B, that is, 5 chocolates and 10 toffees to each. Now suppose A prefers toffees and B prefers chocolates. That way, more toffees with fewer chocolates to A and more chocolates with fewer toffees to B would sure make both happier. An equitable distribution does not maximize the total welfare of the two. On the same lines, if the rationing department grants 20 kg of wheat and 20 kg of rice to each family of a particular size, the distribution may be an equitable one but not an efficient one also. May be one family has a marked preference for rice and the other for wheat. Granting all the rice to rice lovers and all the wheat to wheat lovers would sure make both happier. Some communities in India do not like rice while others do not like wheat. There also exist some who are indifferent between the two foods. To those who are indifferent, any combination is as good as any other. But to those who have marked preferences for wheat or rice, this is not true. That is why flexibility in rationing is often recommended for welfare maximization. That explains why an equitable distribution may not be an efficient one also. One more illustration and the idea would be driven home completely. Think of a firm which pays same wage to all its workers. Some of them are managers, some accountants, some engineers, some foremen while others are manual and menial workers. So long as the family size is same, wages too must be same from the point of view of the firm subscribing to the philosophy of equitability. Such a distribution, no doubt, is an equitable one, but by no means, an efficient one also. The reason is obvious. An equitable distribution, such as this, leaves no motivation for the people to acquire skills or to add value to their productivity! *'From each according to his capability, to each according to his work'* is right; but *'from each according to his capability, to each according to his need'* is not.

A society is often viewed as an **Egalitarian society** if all the members in it receive equal amounts of goods. Equal distribution of chocolates and toffees between consumers A and B provides an example of this type of a society.

A society is viewed as a **Utilitarian society** if it aims at maximization of the total utility of all its members. Granting all the chocolates to the chocolate lover and all the toffees to the toffee lover provides an example of a utilitarian society.

A society is viewed as **Market-oriented** if the distribution of goods is made on the basis of market mechanism (price mechanism). Payment of wages to workers in accordance with their market price provides an example of a market-oriented society.

A society is viewed as a **Rawlsian society** if it aims at maximization of the utility of the least-well-off individuals. For example, a society taxing the rich only to spend the tax proceeds on maximization of the utility of the poorest of the poor is a Rawlsian society. Thus, a state concentrating on welfare maximization of the poorest of the poor is a Rawlsian state.

A social welfare function may be devised through appropriate weighting of utilities intended for different communities in a society to fulfil the desired social objectives. For instance, a Rawlsian society would emphasize the utility of the poorest of the poor while an egalitarian society would assign equal weights to the utilities of all its members.

In our $2 \times 2 \times 2$ model, there are only two consumers, A and B. A social welfare function $\bar{w}$, involving utilities U_A and U_B, can be expressed, in general, as

$$\bar{w} = f(U_A, U_B) \tag{16.10}$$

It can be defined on the lines of an indifference curve as representing various combinations of utilities of the two consumers that stand for same level $\bar{w}$ of the social welfare. The shape of the social welfare function depends on the type of the function and the nature of the value judgements that determine weights attached to the individual utilities. A social welfare function with an explicit set of value judgements leads to social welfare contours, called **Bergson's* Welfare Contours**. Figure 16.13 portrays them.

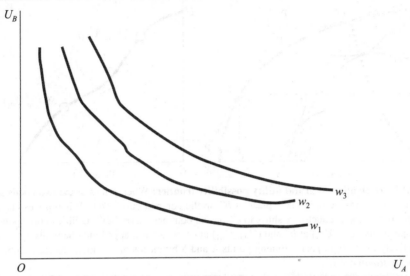

FIGURE 16.13 **Welfare function:** Bergson's welfare contours representing various combinations of U_A and U_B that yield same level of social welfare, $\bar{w}$. A higher contour represents higher social welfare and a lower one, a lower level of social welfare.

In order to determine the optimal level of social welfare, let us derive grand utility possibility frontier [Figure 16.14(b)]. It is the locus of utility combinations on the contract curve satisfying the condition in Eq. (16.8) for all price sets prevailing in a competitive market over a period of time. One such combination is shown at the point b'' in Figure 16.10, corresponding to the price set P_X and P_Y. For a price set different from P_X and P_Y, a different contract curve and hence a different combination (say, c'') is obtained [Figure 16.14(a)]. Utilities enjoyed by the two consumers at b'' and c'' are respectively, say, (U_{A2}, U_{B4}) and (U_{A6}, U_{B1}).

Each point on the grand utility possibility frontier represents allocations of the utilities that are not only Pareto-efficient, but also those that are in general equilibrium of perfect competition. They are Pareto-efficient because they correspond to the contract curve, the locus of the points, at each of which, the indifference curves of the two consumers are tangential to each other, that is,

$$\mathrm{MRS}^A_{X,\,Y} = \mathrm{MRS}^B_{X,\,Y}$$

They are in general equilibrium of perfect competition because each one of them satisfies the condition,

$$\mathrm{MRS}^A_{X,\,Y} = \mathrm{MRS}^B_{X,\,Y} = \mathrm{MRPT}_{X,\,Y} = P_x/P_y$$

A point above the grand utility possibility frontier is infeasible while one below it is Pareto-inefficient. The purpose of this discussion is to impress upon the reader that the grand utility possibility frontier can be treated as a budget line while determining the welfare-maximizing state with the help of the Bergson's welfare contours, as shown in Figure 16.15.

---

* A Bergson, *A Reformulation of Certain Aspects Welfare Economics Quarterly Journal of Economics*, 1937–38 pp. 310–34.

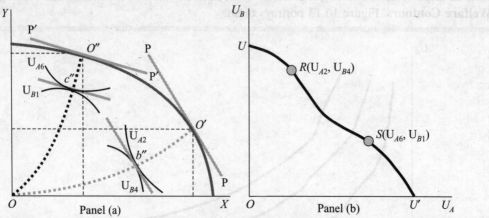

FIGURE 16.14 Derivation of grand utility possibility frontier: When prices of the two goods are P_x and P_y, the equilibrium of the product-mix takes place at b'' on the contract curve OO'. When prices change to P'_x and P'_y, the equilibrium of the product-mix shifts to c'' on the contract curve OO''. Utilities corresponding to these points are respectively (U_{A2}, U_{B4}) at b'' and (U_{A3}, U_{B1}) at c'', which if mapped into the utility space give points R and S, respectively in the right panel. Joining points R and S by means of a smooth curve, we obtain the *grand utility possibility frontier*, UU'.

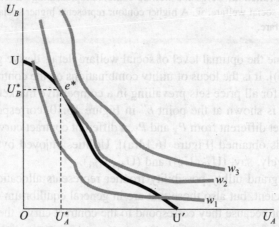

FIGURE 16.15 Attainment of point of bliss: In the figure, UU' is the grand utility possibility frontier and w_1, w_2 and w_3 are Bergson's social welfare contours. Welfare is maximized at the point where UU' is tangential to the highest possible welfare contour. In the figure, e^* is the point at which this happens. It is known as the *point of bliss*. Consumers enjoy utilities U^*_A and U^*_B at this point. Note that this allocation of utilities between the two consumers leads to Pareto-efficiency and general equilibrium under competitive conditions. Thus, the allocations are market oriented, but neither Egalitarian nor Rawlsian. In the presence of inequalities of income, a Rawlsian allocation would require maximization of the utility of the poorest of the poor. That way, allocation would have been made on any welfare contour available to the community but much above e^* if B is poorer than A and much below e^* if A is poorer than B. Similarly, an Egalitarian allocation would require equality of the utilities between the two, i.e. $U_A = U_B$ on the available welfare contour. There would be no need for the grand utility possibility frontier in either case. A utilitarian allocation would require several other considerations. For instance, one consideration is need-based allocation so that one who needs less gets less and one who needs more gets more. In the present case, welfare is maximized through market-oriented allocation. Efficiency is maximum, yet equity is out of question.

4. WALRAS' LAW: 'Value of the aggregate excess demand is identically zero'

Suppose, the initial quantities of the two goods (endowments) each consumers holds at prices P_x and P_y is M. That is, Consumer A holds (X_0^A, Y_0^A), while Consumer B, (X_0^B, Y_0^B) of the two goods at point M (Figure 16.16). Now suppose, Consumer A prefers to have (X_1^A, Y_1^A) at e_A, while Consumer B prefers to have (X_1^B, Y_1^B) at e_B at the going prices. Evidently, the choices of goods the two prefer to have do not exhaust the available supplies of X and Y. Moreover, the preferred baskets, known as the gross demands, are distinct. The excesses of the gross demands of the two goods over their endowments (quantities of the two goods held by the consumers) are known as their excess demands or net demands (Figure 16.16).

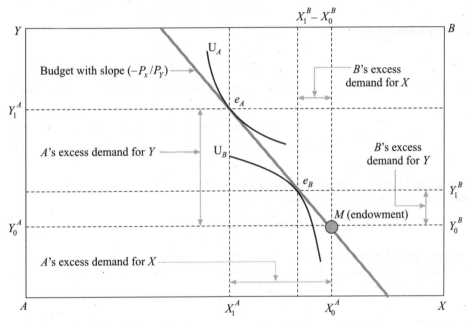

FIGURE 16.16   Walras' law–Value of aggregate excess demand is zero: In the figure, point M denotes the initial endowment of the two goods possessed by the two consumers at prices P_x and P_y. The two, however, prefer to consume at e_A (X_1^A, Y_1^A) and e_B (X_1^B, Y_1^B) respectively at the going prices. Gross demands of A and B for X and Y are

$$A\text{'s gross demand for } X = X_1^A$$
$$A\text{'s gross demand for } Y = Y_1^A$$
$$B\text{'s gross demand for } X = X_1^B$$
$$B\text{'s gross demand for } Y = Y_1^B$$

Initial demands of the two consumers for the two goods, in the like manner, are

$$A\text{'s initial demand for } X = X_0^A$$
$$A\text{'s initial demand for } Y = Y_0^A$$
$$B\text{'s initial demand for } X = X_0^B$$
$$B\text{'s initial demand for } Y = Y_0^B$$

(Contd.)

FIGURE 16.16 (*Contd.*)

Excess demands of A for goods X and Y are

$$E^A_X = X^A_1 - X^A_0 \quad \text{(Negative)}$$
$$E^A_Y = Y^A_1 - Y^A_0 \quad \text{(Positive)}$$

Likewise, excess demands of B for goods X and Y are

$$E^B_X = X^B_1 - X^B_0 \quad \text{(Positive)}$$
$$E^B_Y = Y^B_1 - Y^B_0 \quad \text{(Negative)}$$

Aggregate excess demand for
$$X = E^A_X + E^B_X$$
$$= X^A_1 - X^A_0 + X^B_1 - X^B_0$$
$$= (X^A_1 + X^B_1) - (X^A_0 + X^B_0) \tag{16.11}$$

Aggregate excess demand for
$$Y = E^A_Y + E^B_Y$$
$$= (Y^A_1 - Y^A_0) + (Y^B_1 - Y^B_0)$$
$$= (Y^A_1 + Y^B_1) - (Y^A_0 + Y^B_0) \tag{16.12}$$

Expressions (16.11) and (16.12) give the value of aggregate excess demands of the two goods. In value terms,

$$X^A_1 \cdot P_x + Y^A_1 \cdot P_y = X^A_0 \cdot P_x + Y^A_0 \cdot P_y$$

($\because$ Gross and endowment demands both lie on the same budget line).

$$\Rightarrow (X^A_1 - X^A_0) \cdot P_x + (Y^A_1 - Y^A_0) \cdot P_y = 0$$
$$\Rightarrow E^A_X \cdot P_x + E^A_Y \cdot P_y = 0 \tag{16.13}$$

$\Rightarrow$ **Value of aggregate excess demand of consumer A is zero.**
Proceeding exactly on the same lines, we have

$$(X^B_1 - X^B_0) \cdot P_x + (Y^B_1 - Y^B_0) \cdot P_y = 0$$
$$\Rightarrow E^B_X \cdot P_x + E^B_Y \cdot P_y = 0 \tag{16.14}$$

$\Rightarrow$ **Value of aggregate excess demand of consumer B is zero.**
$\Rightarrow$ *Value of aggregate excess demand of both the consumers for both the goods is zero.* This establishes **Walras' Law.**
From Eq. (16.13), it is clear that
either

$$E^A_X = E^A_Y = 0 \qquad (\because P_x \text{ and } P_y \text{ are non-zero})$$

implying that, $(X^A_1 - X^A_0) = (Y^A_1 - Y^A_0) = 0$
implying that, $X^A_1 = X^A_0$ and $Y^A_1 = Y^A_0$
implying that, $X^A_1 + Y^A_1 = X^A_0 + Y^A_0$

implying that, **A's gross demand = A's endowment** (16.15)

or
$$E^A_X \cdot P_x = -E^A_Y \cdot P_y \tag{16.16}$$

Likewise, from Eq. (16.14), it can be deduced that
either

B's gross demand = B's endowment (16.17)

or
$$E^B_X \cdot P_x = -E^B_Y \cdot P_y \tag{16.18}$$

Expressions (16.16) and (16.18) provide the components of **Walras' Law** while Eqs. (16.15) and (16.17) establish Pareto efficiency of Walrasian equilibrium (competitive equilibrium). However, Pareto efficiency of competitive equilibrium is established as first welfare theorem in the next implication.

The figure explains the proof of the Walras' Law which states that the value of the aggregate excess demand is identically zero.

5. Theorems of welfare economics

Let us now discuss two implications of the general equilibrium that lead to two theorems of welfare economics.

(a) *First theorem of welfare economics*

The theorem states that a **competitive or Walrasian equilibrium is Pareto efficient**. Let the competitive equilibrium be given at $e_1(X_1^A, X_1^B, Y_1^A, Y_1^B)$. We have to show that it is Pareto efficient as well. Although we have established the result indirectly in Figure 16.16, let us prove it here by contradiction.

Let the initial endowment of the consumers be as given by the point

$$M(X_0^A, X_0^B, Y_0^A, Y_0^B).$$

Now, suppose $e_1(X_1^A, X_1^B, Y_1^A, Y_1^B)$ is not Pareto efficient. Instead, let some other allocation, $e_2(X_2^A, X_2^B, Y_2^A, Y_2^B)$ such that $(X_2^A, Y_2^A) > (X_1^A, Y_1^A)$ and $(X_2^B, Y_2^B) > (X_1^B, Y_1^B)$ be Pareto efficient. Then

$$\left. \begin{array}{r} X_2^A + X_2^B = X_0^A + Y_0^B \\ Y_2^A + Y_2^B = Y_0^A + Y_0^B \end{array} \right\} \quad (16.19)$$

and

show that 2nd allocation is feasible.

And $\quad\quad\quad\quad (X_2^A, Y_2^A) > (X_1^A, Y_1^A)$

as also $\quad\quad\quad\quad (X_2^B, Y_2^B) > (X_1^B, Y_1^B)$

show that the 2nd allocation is preferable.
In that case, 2nd allocation must cost more. That is,

$$X_2^A \cdot P_x + Y_2^A \cdot P_y > X_0^A \cdot P_x + Y_0^A \cdot P_y$$

$$X_2^B \cdot P_x + Y_2^B \cdot P_y > X_0^B \cdot P_x + Y_0^B \cdot P_y$$

$\Rightarrow \quad (X_2^A + X_2^B) P_x + (Y_2^A + Y_2^B) P_y > (X_0^A + X_0^B) P_x + (Y_0^A + Y_0^B) P_y$

[Adding the corresponding sides]

$\Rightarrow \quad (X_0^A + X_0^B) P_x + (Y_0^A + Y_0^B) P_y > (X_0^A + X_0^B) P_x + (Y_0^A + Y_0^B) P_y$ [From Eq. (16.19)]

But, this cannot be true as no expression can be greater than itself.

Our assumption that 'the competitive (Walrasian) equilibrium at e_1 $(X_1^A, X_1^B, Y_1^A, Y_1^B)$ is not Pareto-efficient' is therefore false because it leads us to a contradiction. This proves the *First Theorem of Welfare Economics.*

(b) *Second theorem of welfare economics*

The theorem states that **a Pareto-efficient allocation is an equilibrium allocation**. A Pareto-efficient allocation implies tangency of the indifference curves to each other, implying identical slopes at the same point (Figure 16.17).

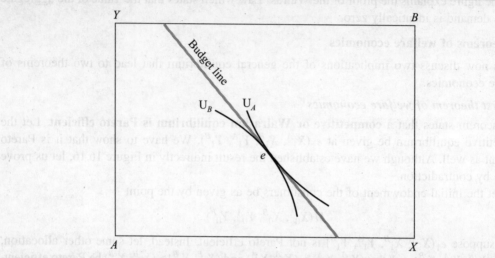

FIGURE 16.17 Pareto-efficient allocation as an equilibrium allocation: When consumers' preferences are convex, a Pareto-efficient allocation is an equilibrium allocation. This is so because of the condition of convexity of indifference curves for consumer's equilibrium.

But if the consumers' preferences are non-convex, as is the case in Figure 16.18, Pareto-efficiency of an allocation does not imply an equilibrium state of that allocation.

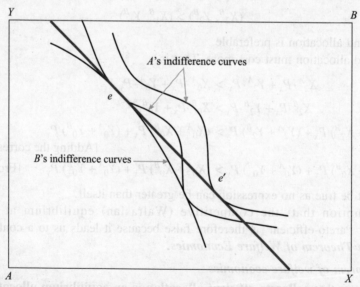

FIGURE 16.18 Pareto-efficient allocation as a non-equilibrium allocation: A Pareto-efficient allocation cannot be an equilibrium allocation when one of the two consumers has non-convex preferences. In the figure, allocation at e is Pareto-efficient but it cannot be achieved in a competitive market which requires convexity of the indifference curve to the origin. Note that A's indifference curve changes its convexity from left to right. In the middle, it is concave to origin.

The two theorems of welfare economics, as discussed above, have hardly had any reference to any explicit assumptions. Yet, some assumptions have existed all along implicitly. For instance, the first theorem of welfare economics, which states that a competitive equilibrium is Pareto-efficient, has two implicit assumptions:

First, each of the two consumers is concerned only about his or her own consumption, buying and consuming whatever he or she can at the competitive set of prices to maximize his or her satisfaction. Would this always lead to Pareto-efficiency? What if one cares about the other's consumption? If the answer is in affirmative, an externality is said to have occurred in consumption. For instance, suppose two students in a hostel share a room. One of them is a habitual smoker. His consumption of tobacco is sure to affect health of his room-mate by pushing him into passive smoking. This is an **externality in consumption**. The habitual smoker buys and consumes cigarettes to maximize his own utility but in the process, he affects the utility of the non-smoker adversely. The non-smoker might be tempted either to bribe the habitual smoker to smoke fewer cigarettes or to expose himself to air pollution. In either case, the passive smoker suffers a loss of welfare—be it bribing the habitual smoker to smoke less or be it spending money later on medical treatment. Welfare of the habitual smoker too suffers if he continues to smoke to his heart's content. In the presence of the consumption externalities, a competitive equilibrium hardly attains Pareto-efficiency. There always exist a number of ways to raise social welfare. If all the individuals in a society are allowed to buy and consume whatever their pockets and market prices permit them under competitive conditions, the state of social welfare would be far from being Pareto-efficient due to the presence of the **consumption externalities**.

Second, buyers and sellers behave competitively. If there are only two consumers in the edgeworth box, it is quite less likely that they take price as given. Individuals would recognize their market power and would be tempted to take advantage of it. Competitive equilibrium would change to monopsony equilibrium. The essential feature of 'large number of buyers and sellers' is must for the existence of competitive equilibrium and hence for Pareto-efficiency.

The second theorem of welfare economics states that every Pareto-efficient allocation is an equilibrium allocation under certain conditions. A Pareto-efficient allocation is one in which it is not possible to increase welfare of one without decreasing that of another. Suppose an economy is in a state of Pareto-efficiency and hence in a competitive equilibrium. This implies that social welfare cannot be increased any further. How then welfare states succeed in raising the level of social welfare through their monetary and fiscal policies? A tax reduces income and welfare of the rich but the tax-proceeds, when spent on the welfare of the poorer sections, lead to an increase in social welfare. Taxation is distortionary. If it leads to an increase in social welfare through equity and social justice on the one hand and on the other, it leads to an intervention in the free-play of market mechanism so crucial for a competitive equilibrium. A higher state of Pareto-efficiency can be achieved and the allocations may be far from being competitive.

6. The problem of fair allocation

A fair allocation is one that is equitable as well as Pareto-efficient. An equitable allocation is that allocation in which no individual prefers another's basket to his own. A Pareto-efficient allocation refers to that allocation which satisfies the condition implied by Eq. (16.9).

An equitable allocation does not mean equal distribution as one might think at the outset. It has been seen in the third implication above that an equal distribution may not be Pareto-efficient.

Distribution of 10 chocolates and 20 toffees between two consumers equally may not maximize the total utility of the two consumers when their preferences are sharply divided between toffees and chocolates, one preferring toffees while the other, chocolates. Recall from what you have learnt in indifference curve analysis about quasi-linear preferences. Granting, as desired, more toffees with fewer chocolates to one who prefers toffees and more chocolates with fewer toffees to one who prefers chocolates, would certainly raise social welfare, provided there is no room left for one consumer to envy another's basket.

A fair allocation, therefore, is one that is Pareto-efficient as well as equitable in this sense. An allocation such as one at point e in Figure 16.19 is a **fair allocation** while one, such as that at point S, is a **swapped allocation**. It lies on the budget line but is below the indifference curve of each consumer.

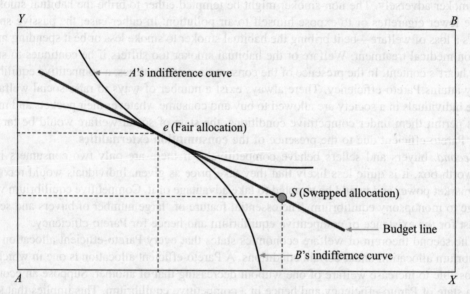

FIGURE 16.19 A fair allocation: Point e is the point of fair allocation in the edgeworth box. It is Pareto-efficient by virtue of satisfying the condition implied by Eq. (16.9). It is equitable also because it lies on the indifference curves of both the consumers with the result that no consumer envies another's basket. Point S represents swapped allocation which lies on the budget line but is below the indifference curves of the two consumers.

The purpose of these discussions is to highlight the implications of general equilibrium and Pareto-efficiency. General equilibrium, as discussed above, is based on several assumptions, which in real world, seldom exist. It is the complexity of the interrelationships among the economic entities, that calls for these assumptions. The purpose is to study crucial relationships under the microscope so that their true nature can be understood and analyzed. Once it is done, the assumptions can be relaxed and a truer general equilibrium can be attempted through an extension of the observations made. Economists have studied larger models that have wider implications to the real world problems.

The concept of general equilibrium and social welfare, as stated earlier, have different connotations in different economies. It is so because different economies have different sets of objectives—some believing in equal distribution while others subscribing to market orientation of distribution and yet others focussing on the welfare of the poorest of the poor. Market orientation of distribution has been gaining strength with the passage of time. It requires competitive conditions to hold and operate. As discussed above, such conditions are rare to hold and operate under distortionary pressures such as those resulting from direct and indirect interventions of governments of the nation states. Distortions such as these lead to market failure. We are going to introduce market failure and its causes in the next section.

16.4 MARKET FAILURE AND ITS SOURCES

Competitive markets fail to operate due to the following reasons:

1. Market power

When each of the sellers behaves like a monopoly with downward sloping and distinct ARs and MRs, quantity is determined by each by equating its MC to its MR; and price, by locating the point corresponding to this quantity on its AR curve. Such behaviour of monopolistic firms is possible either under product differentiation or under some informal agreement among the sellers. It cannot be sustained unless the regulatory authority is weak or the nature of the product itself grants market power to the sellers. Price charged is higher than the marginal cost as against that equal to MC charged by a competitive firm. Pareto-efficiency requires that

$$\text{MRPT}_{X,Y} = (P_x/P_y)$$

but

$$\text{MRPT}_{X,Y} = (MC_x/MC_y).$$

Hence, $\text{MRPT}_{X,Y}$ cannot be equal to (P_x/P_y) unless

$$(MC_x/MC_y) = (P_x/P_y)$$

which thus is possible only in a competitive market. Guilds of the sellers destroy competitive structure and empower the sellers with monopoly power.

Labour unions also play a similar role by distorting wages in favour of one product and against another so that

$$\text{MRTS}^X_{L,K} \neq \text{MRTS}^Y_{L,K}$$

Market power of the labour unions in an industry arises mainly because of limited supply of labour in that industry.

In sum, market power of the sellers destroys the competitive structure and poses as a potential source of **market failure**.

2. Lack of information

When the consumers lack information about a product, its quality, its price and its substitutes, they are at the mercy of the suppliers who take full advantage of their lack of information. As a result, many markets do not develop at all while many others develop beyond their due size.

'Perfect knowledge' is a requisite of the competitive market. In its absence, a competitive market ceases to exist and to operate.

3. Externalities

Presence of an externality, whether in consumption or in production, leads to distortionary factors, which influence consumption or production of a number of products. In our discussion on welfare theorems, we have already explained the role of consumption externalities. How a habitual smoker inflicts passive smoking on his room-mate and how it influences the room-mate's consumption, we have already seen. Production externalities, likewise, influence production by distorting production costs. Air, water, and noise pollution impose external costs and hence escalate actual costs of production. Alternatively, such externalities of production ultimately tend to escalate consumption costs when the society is made to bear these externalities in terms of expenditures incurred on medical care and health. Bhopal gas leakage tragedy of 1980s inflicted lot of sufferings on the society. People lost health due to it and wealth due to medical care it required. The industrial unit that caused it almost managed to get away as the judicial remedy they could manage proved nothing more than a drop in the ocean. The compensation they could get after years of court trials were peanuts as compared to the loss of life, health and wealth they had suffered. If the social cost is also made a part of the private cost of production, the production cost is much higher than usual and so is the product price, pushing demand for such products to very low levels. In the absence of such provisions, polluting industries reap the cost benefits.

4. Public goods

A **public good** refers to a product consumption of which cannot be restricted once the product is supplied. Many times, the very purpose of producing it is defeated due to this reason. For example, parks built for children often get reserved unofficially for other purposes with the result that children are invariably kept away from them. Consumption of a public good by one should not affect its consumption by another but it often does. Some members of the society extend their houses and reduce the open area meant for greenery and fresh air. Over utilization of a public good by some members to the extent that others are deprived of its use is known as the **tragedy of commons**. Proper regulation of the use of such goods either by the authorities or by a private agency may help the cause. Use or misuse of a public good which is free for all leads to failure of the market mechanism. Private poducers refrain from producing such goods due to their low profitability. Builders and developers prefer to cover the maximum plot area, leaving little or no open space. Covered area has a price while open area has not. Even if they allow open space, the occupants themselves would cover it up, defeating the very purpose for which it was meant. Production and use of public goods must be regulated by State if at all it is to serve its purpose.

We take up market failure due to asymmetric information in Chapter 17 and that, due to other factors in Chapter 18.

KEY TERMS AND CONCEPTS

Bliss point It is a point in the utility space at which the grand utility possibility frontier is tangential to the highest possible welfare contour.

Egalitarian society A society that believes in equal distribution of utility among all its members.

Equilibrium of consumption (efficiency of distribution of goods) This refers to efficiency of distribution of the available goods among the consumers. In other words, it refers to the efficiency in commodity substitution. The condition required for it is $MRS^A_{x,y} = [P_x/P_y] = MRS^B_{x,y}$.

Equilibrium of production (efficiency in distribution of factors) This refers to efficiency of distribution of available productive factors among the existing firms. In other words, it refers to the efficiency in factor substitution. It requires the condition $(MRTS^X_{L,K}) = (MRTS^Y_{L,K}) = (w/r)$.

Fair allocation A fair allocation is one that is equitable as well as Pareto-efficient. An equitable allocation is that allocation in which no individual prefers another's basket to his own.

Gains from trade General equilibrium before and after trade shows that trading countries gain from trade and community welfare increases for both. Gains accruing to the trading partners include gains from exchange and gains from specialization.

General equilibrium It refers to equilibrium of all the segments of the market in simultaneity. It involves a great deal of analysis of interdependence of different market segments. For example, equilibrium of all the economic entities including consumers, producers, factor markets, product markets, etc. taken together is general equilibrium.

Grand utility possibility frontier It is the locus of various combinations of the utilities enjoyed by consumers at the point of the general equilibrium, satisfying the condition

$$MRS^A_{x,y} = MRS^B_{x,y} = MRPT_{X,Y} = [P_x/P_y]$$

Market failure It refers to a state of market in which free play of price mechanism stands obstructed by market power, externalities, existence of public goods and lack of information. In this state, competitive conditions of exchange remain suspended.

Reasons of market failure There are four main reasons of market failure. They are

1. Market power
2. Externalities
3. Existence of public goods
4. Lack of information.

Market-oriented society A society that allows the market mechanism to guide distribution of utility among its members.

Partial equilibrium Equilibrium of just one segment of a market under the assumption that all other segments remain stable or unaffected. For example, equilibrium of product market under the assumption that other related market segments such as factor market, remain unaffected or unchanged. In other words, it refers to micro analysis under ceteris paribus assumption.

Rawlsian society A society that believes in maximization of the utility of the poorest of the poor.

Simultaneous equilibrium of production and consumption (efficiency of product-mix) As the term suggests it refers to general equilibrium. The conditions required are the conditions for the equilibrium of production and consumption along with the condition, $MRPT_{X,Y} = P_x/P_y$.

Social welfare function Welfare expressed as a function of the utilities enjoyed by consumers. In case there are two consumers enjoying utilities U_A and U_B, the general form of the welfare function is

$$w = f(U_A, U_B)$$

The function can be given the desired form through appropriate weighting of the individual utilities. A plot of the welfare function in the utility space is known as welfare contour.

Swapped allocation It is an allocation which is affordable (lies on the budget line of the consumer) but is below his indifference curve.

Theorems of welfare economics The first theorem of welfare economics states that competitive equilibrium, also known as general equilibrium or even as Walrasian equilibrium, is Pareto-efficient. The second theorem of welfare economics states that a Pareto-efficient allocation is an equilibrium allocation.

Tragedy of commons Overutilization of a public good by some members to the extent that others are deprived of its use is known as the tragedy of commons.

Utilitarian society A society that believes in maximization of the total utility of all its members.

Walras' law It states that the value of aggregate excess demand is identically zero.

EXERCISES

A. Very Short Answer Questions

Define the following:
1. Partial equilibrium
2. General equilibrium
3. Equilibrium in production
4. Equilibrium in consumption
5. Simultaneous equilibrium in consumption and production
6. Egalitarian distribution
7. Utilitarian distribution
8. Rawlsian distribution
9. Walras' law
10. Market-oriented distribution
11. Social welfare function
12. Grand utility possibility frontier
13. Bliss point
14. First theorem of welfare economics
15. Second theorem of welfare economics
16. Fair allocation
17. Market failure
18. Swapped allocations
19. Sources of market failure
20. Tragedy of commons

B. Short Answer Questions

Distinguish between:
21. Partial equilibrium and general equilibrium
22. Swapped allocation and fair allocation
23. An egalitarian allocation and Rawlsian allocation
24. Utilitarian and market oriented allocations

C. Long Answer Questions

25. Explain the mechanism of deriving the production possibility curve from the edgeworth contract curve.
26. What is the grand utility possibility frontier? How can it be obtained with the help of the edgeworth contract curve?
27. What are the social welfare contours? How can they be employed to determine the bliss point?
28. With the help of edgeworth box, show how equilibrium is reached in consumption.
29. With the help of edgeworth box, show how equilibrium is reached in production.
30. Two substitutes, X and Y, are being produced in an industry with given amounts of labour and capital. Production of X is labour intensive while that of Y is capital intensive. Due to some exogenous factors, demand tilts in favour of good X. What effect would it have on the equilibrium of the labour market?
31. Two substitutes, X and Y, are being produced in an industry with given amounts of labour and capital. Production of X is labour intensive while that of Y is capital intensive. Due to some exogenous factors, demand tilts in favour of good X. What effect would it have on the equilibrium of the capital market?
32. Country A has an advantage in production of X while country B has it in production of Y. The two enter in bilateral trade. Employing the concept of general equilibrium, show how a country A would benefit from bilateral trade.
33. Country A has an advantage in production of X while country B has it in production of Y. The two enter in bilateral trade. Employing the concept of general equilibrium, show how a country B would benefit from bilateral trade.
34. Is a competitive equilibrium Pareto-efficient too? Give arguments in support of your answer.
35. With the help of production possibility curve, show how efficient a competitive equilibrium is.
36. State and establish Walras' law.
37. Is every Pareto-efficient allocation a competitive allocation also? Give reasons in support of your answer.
38. Is it necessary for an efficient allocation to be an equitable one also? On what factors would the answer to this question depend? Give reasons in support of your answer.
39. What is an equitable allocation? Under what conditions would it be a fair allocation? Explain with the help of a diagram.
40. What is meant by externalities? How are they responsible for market failure?
41. What is meant by market power? How does it lead to market failure?
42. What are public goods? How does their existence lead to market failure?
43. What is the significance of perfect knowledge in a competitive market? Show how lack of information leads to market failure.
44. Show that all the allocations, other than those on the contract curve, are Pareto-inefficient.
45. How does market failure affect Pareto-efficiency? Give reasons in support.
46. Under what circumstances can market failure raise the social welfare?
47. What are the different concepts of equity? Which ones of them lead to Pareto-efficiency?
48. What is meant by tragedy of commons? What measures would you recommend to rectify the menace?

D. Essay Type Questions

49. Two substitutes, X and Y, are being produced in an industry with given amounts of labour and capital. Production of X is labour intensive while that of Y is capital intensive. Due to some exogenous factors, demand tilts in favour of good X. What effect would it have on the equilibrium of the labour and capital markets?
50. With the help of neat sketches show how simultaneous equilibrium of production and consumption is reached. What assumption is crucial for it?
51. Explain various requisites of Pareto-efficiency and show how they can be fulfilled in a $2 \times 2 \times 2$ model.
52. Write an essay on equity versus efficiency.

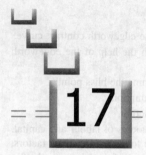

17

Markets with Asymmetric Information

CHAPTER OUTLINE

Introduction
- Mechanism of Market Failure due to Asymmetric Information
- Common Consequences of Asymmetric Information
- Remedies to Some Assorted Cases of Market Failure
- Efficiency Wage Theory
- Key Terms and Concepts
- Exercises

INTRODUCTION

In our analysis of competitive markets, we assumed that buyers and sellers possess perfect knowledge about the market, that is, the buyers possess perfect information about prices, product quality, availability and prices of the substitutes and such other details they need to know before making a purchase while the sellers possess perfect information about consumers' tastes, preferences, disposable incomes and all about the substitutes before offering a product for sale. Such assumptions were crucial for competitive markets. In reality, however, this is not so. Most often, buyers are seldom aware of the truth about prices, product quality, as also about prices and availability of substitutes at the time of making a purchase. In fact, they come to know of these things only after using the product for a while. The sellers invariably know more about these things than the buyers for obvious reasons. When some people know more than others about the product specifications, the phenomenon is termed as existence of **asymmetric information**. As an example, consider an individual who has purchased a brand new car for ₹ 500,000 a few months ago but wants to sell it now as he has to settle abroad. He is fully aware of its performance level. He knows how different or similar his car is in its performance today than when it was bought for the first time. Believing that his vehicle is almost as good as new and also has some additional accessories, he sets its price at ₹ 475,000! The vehicle has done hardly 400 km, yet, the maximum offer he gets from the market is ₹ 350,000! The market thus fails to get him its due price. His plight, perhaps, would not have been much different had he decided to sell it off the very next week of its purchase. The reason would have been and still is none other than the asymmetric information. The buyer is not sure of the quality and performance of the car even when one year warranty of free service against any manufacturing defect is transferable to him. The car is what Rubinfeld and Pindyck call it, a *'lemon'* for him. A number of suspicions surround the buyer. Why does the seller want to sell it the very next week? If he had no need for it, why did he buy it in the first place? Is there something seriously wrong with the car? Even when the buyer's engineers assure him of the genuineness of the car, he continues to be in two minds. Probably a substantial price cut may get him out of the dilemma.

Uncertainty of the quality and the size of investment are the two things responsible for the buyer's dilemma. He can't be sure of the quality unless he has run the car himself for some time. The seller, on the other hand, knows more about the car because he has used it himself for a while. Clearly, one party knows more about the product than the other. This is how asymmetric information leads to market failure. The term market-failure implies failure of market to give effect to the transaction even when buyer and seller both exist and so does the genuine product at the genuine price. The sources of market failure are mainly two – *first*, the existence of uncertainty in the minds of the buyers about product quality and *second*, the size of the investment at stake. Both of them originate from asymmetric information.

In Section 17.1, we examine how **quality uncertainties** lead to market failure with the result that high quality goods are driven out by the low-quality goods; in Section 17.2, we examine some common consequences of asymmetric information, in Section 17.3, we discuss remedies to some assorted cases of market failure and in Section 17.4, we take up efficiency wage theory of labour market. The basis again being market failure caused by asymmetric information.

17.1 MECHANISM OF MARKET FAILURE DUE TO ASYMMETRIC INFORMATION: LOW-QUALITY GOODS DRIVE HIGH QUALITY GOODS OUT OF THE MARKET

As mentioned, asymmetric information means that buyers of the product do not know about the product what sellers do or sellers do not know about it what buyers do. In either case, one of the requisites of a competitive industry (perfect knowledge) is flouted. As a result, either the product is under-valued or over-valued. Alternatively, either it fails to sell or it fetches a price different to its true price. The market mechanism thus fails to perform its main function.

Quality uncertainty among the consumers about a product refers to a dilemma a consumer faces about the product quality whether it is worth the price set for it or not. In other words, whether he must buy it or not at the price quoted for it! A rational consumer decides to play safe by going for a low-quality product. Of course, no use paying a higher price for a product that may turn out a low-quality one once it is bought and used. If all the consumers are equally risk-averse, demand schedule of high quality products shifts downwards-to-left as shown in the left panel of Figure 17.1. Quantity demanded now, OQ', and price offered OP', are below their true levels (OQ and OP) significantly. As against this, demand for low-quality goods shifts upwards-to-right, increasing both its quantity as well as price as portrayed in the right panel of Figure 17.1. Quantity transacted increases from Oq at Op to Oq' at Op' ($Oq' > Oq$ and $Op' > Op$).

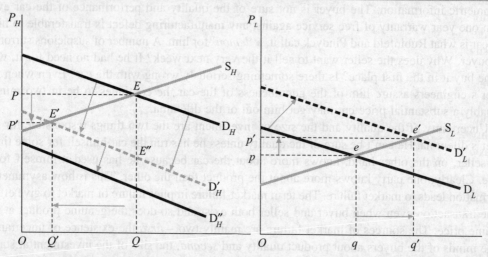

FIGURE 17.1 Quality uncertainty as a source of market failure: In the left panel, demand for high-quality goods D_H intersects their supply S_H at E, where, quantity OQ must be demanded at price OP. Due to asymmetric information, the same quantity is demanded at a much lower price at E'' as the quality uncertainty in the minds of the buyers forces them to treat a high-quality product as a low-quality one. This shifts their demand curve downwards to D'_H. Some of the sellers reject this price and refuse to sell. As a result, supply falls from OQ to OQ'. The new equilibrium takes place at E', the point where D'_H intersects S_H. Quantity of high-quality goods sold is OQ' at a price OP'. Due to quality uncertainty, demand curve may further slide down to D''_H, which does not intersect S_H at all. With this, market for high-quality goods fails. In the right panel, demand and supply of low-quality products intersect at point e, where quantity Oq of low-quality goods is transacted at price Op. Failure of the market for high-quality goods leads to an upward to right shift from D_L to D'_L in the demand curve of the low-quality goods. This raises sales of low-quality goods from Oq at price Op to Oq' at a higher price Op'. Quality uncertainty caused by asymmetric information thus leads to market failure in consequence to which low-quality goods drive-out the high-quality goods completely.

As evident, high quality goods get driven out of the market by the low-quality goods. This marks failure of the market. Sellers had all the information about the product quality which buyers lacked. The size of investment and the risk-averse nature of the buyers are two main sources of market failure caused by quality uncertainty. Other sources of market failure relate to supply side factors. Suppliers set a uniform price of certain service-products like insurance, unsecured loans, etc. only to learn in the process that their assessment of true cost of service was wrong in respect of the service buyers as will be evident in Section 17.2.

17.2 COMMON CONSEQUENCES OF ASYMMETRIC INFORMATION

Consequences of asymmetric information can be formalized as adverse selection, adverse pricing and adverse setting of interest rates. Let us have a brief introduction of each for clarity of concepts.

17.2.1 Adverse Selection

Quality uncertainties of consumers provide one example of asymmetric information. In the last section, we saw how it influenced consumers' behaviour, which resulted in *adverse selection* of goods. The term refers to adversity of making choice between high and low-quality goods by consumers. In consequence, they decide to play safe by offering the same price for high quality goods which they offer for the low-quality goods. The sellers of high quality goods either get driven out of the market or resort to distress sale as explained in Section 17.1. On the other hand, demand for the low-quality goods goes up at times increasing their prices in consequence. In sum, result, market mechanism fails in setting the true price of all the goods, be they high quality goods or low-quality goods. Adverse selection results from quality uncertainty caused by asymmetric information.

17.2.2 Adverse Pricing

Due to asymmetric information, sellers of certain services treat all the consumers of services alike and set a uniform price regardless of the fact that they are not and some of them might lead to much higher cost to the sellers to provide the service to them. This often results in loss to the service providers.

The best example is provided by medical-insurance service which is priced by insurance companies at a uniform rate regardless of the extent of risk involved in providing medical covers to the insuree. For instance, risk involved in insuring the old is higher than that involved in insuring the young. The old generally require more medical care than the young and the costs involved in the insurance cover to the old are higher than those involved in it to the young. Charging same premia from the old as from the young may lead to a break-even if the proportion of the latter among the insurees is high enough to offset losses caused by the most of the former. In absence of this, insurance companies refuse to provide such services to the people beyond a certain age.

As for the demand for insurance cover by the young is concerned, it is generally very low. The cover providers therefore to set a low premium for them to attract them to it which applies even to the middle or upper middle aged consumers as well. Given that the young being reluctant to avail of the services even at lower premia, their proportion among the insurees falls to low levels and the losses to the insurance companies rises to high levels.

This leaves little option before the insurance companies except to duck the claims by inserting stringent terms and conditions in the fine print or quit the business. This is unethical, but unavoidable. Some middle aged insurees too indulge in it to somehow avail of the cover. They manipulate information in connivance with insurance agents who strive for higher sales.

By this time, the reader must be able to understand how the stringent terms and conditions in the fine print have popularized insurance business among banks and financial institutions, private or public. What is needed is an analysis of the proportion of claims made on the insurance covers and the proportion of claims actually materialized. Considering the terms and conditions in the fine print, it is not difficult to see why the ratio of claims actualized to claims made is so low.

17.2.3 Adverse Setting of Interest Rates

Lending without collateral security is risky and therefore commands a higher return. The rate of interest such loans command comprise two components:

(i) Normal rate of interest or the opportunity cost of funds, and
(ii) Compensation for the risk bearing of the lender.

The first part accrues to the lender for allowing the borrower the use of funds for a period of time and the second part accrues for the risk undertaken if funds lent fail to return back. In absence of securities mortgaged, the outstanding amount is a loss to the lender. The riskier the lending, the higher the rate of interest it attracts.

Unsecured loans are therefore tempting to the lenders because of higher returns they offer. Much depends on the quality of the borrower. A high quality borrower is always punctual in repayment, but a low-quality borrower often defaults in repayment. Bankers and financial institutions extend such facilities through credit cards, personal loans and cash credit limits. Each one has its own rate of interest which is uniform to all who avail it. Some of them may turn out low-quality borrowers later, while others, high-quality ones. It is not easy to differentiate borrowers of one category from those of the other. In absence of track records of creditworthiness of borrowers, a uniform rate of interest makes lending sour to the lenders. A high-quality borrower keeps the outstanding balances low through regular repayments, while a low-quality borrower defaults. As a result, low-quality borrowers go for fresh credit cards to settle the liability on the old ones. They are, thus, compelled to hold several credit cards at a time from several banks. The practice continues until such borrowers reach a point of no respite. Bankers charge a very high rate of interest on such credit such as credit cards and personal loans.

The rate of interest on such loans is much higher than that on secured loans. The reason being the risk involved in absence of a collateral security as pointed out already. Bankers are tempted to give out such loans for higher returns believing that the returns rise in direct proportion to risks. They set a uniform rate for all the borrowers. It is clear that high quality borrowers would keep distance from such borrowings and the low-quality borrowers would multiply. The ultimate result is a low proportion of high-quality borrowers among the borrowers. But, then there is no way out to identify one type from the other. Bankers know much less about the creditworthiness of the borrowers than the borrowers themselves. The reason for high uniform rate of interest, thus, is none other than asymmetric information, leading as usual, to market failure.

There is no other remedy to it than the very source responsible for it. For instance, quality uncertainty about a used car can be eliminated by sending quality signals to the prospective buyers. Such signals must be indirect and must set all the quality uncertainties in the buyers' mind aside. Car dealers and brokers do the job successfully. Alternatively, quality signals may be given through media by the sellers. The practice is known as *market signalling*.

Many insurance companies have begun to charge a higher premium from older people and a lower premium from the younger people. Premium charged by them for insurance cover is no longer uniform. In fact, it reflects the extent of risk involved in the medical cover.

In the same way, bankers providing unsecured loans and credit cards may share computerized data pool to distinguish low-quality borrowers from high-quality borrowers. Such sharing of information is regarded as an intrusion in borrower's privacy, but from the viewpoint of the bankers and the credit card companies, it is necessary for the purpose. A recent regulation of the Reserve Bank of India, the central bank of the land, makes it mandatory for the bankers and the credit card companies to make available the details of their customers' transactions, exceeding a certain limit, to the regulatory bank. A recent system developed by credit information bureau maintains an information pool accessible only to the bankers, while granting advances to their customers. This has proved quite a help to distinguish low-quality borrowers from the high-quality ones.

A number of banks have started levying penal rates on defaulters and granting cash-back and such other incentives for timely repayments. The measures introduced have proved quite effective in checking the problem of market failure.

Let us examine some assorted cases of market failure and remedies best suited to them in Section 17.3.

17.3 REMEDIES TO SOME ASSORTED CASES OF MARKET FAILURE

In Section 17.1, we discussed how quality uncertainties caused by asymmetric information lead to market failure to the extent that the high-quality goods are driven-out by the low-quality goods. In this section, we take up specific remedies to some assorted incidences of market failure.

(a) Reputation and standardization

Quality uncertainty responsible for indecision on the part of buyers is tackled by some sellers through quality reputation which they build for their products. Some retail stores build up a reputation of replacing a product if reported defective by a customer while others provide free repairs followed by replacement if the customer is not satisfied. Large corporations run customer care departments to cater to customer's complaints. Some brands of television sets sold like hot cakes in India solely due to free after-sale service which included on-the-spot replacement of the defective piece by a brand new piece if the customer so desired. Some spare part stores in India have a nationwide reputation for genuineness of their components. The same is the case with a few car repair workshops in Delhi. All of them are known for quality so much so that a certificate or a cash-memo from them about the product puts all quality doubts to rest. Some courier service providers have built up a name for themselves through high quality service. People are willing to pay two to three times the market rate for their services.

Some restaurants and food suppliers have standardized their preparations to the effect that the same dish tastes the same whichever part of the year you have it from them.

Quality standardization by government agencies also helps to eliminate quality uncertainties. The quality marks such as 'ISI', 'AGMARK', etc. have stood the test of time in respect of product quality in India.

(b) Market signalling

It is a process by which sellers relay signals about quality of their products to the prospective buyers.

Manufacturers of high quality products use extensive guarantees and warrantees as quality signals to the prospective buyers. Manufacturers of low-quality products find such guarantees unaffordable. In fact, high quality products hardly require any repairs during the guarantee period, while their low-quality counterparts do. Such guarantees are quite likely to cost a fortune to the manufacturers of low-quality products. Guarantees and warrantees, as signals of high quality, help to eliminate quality uncertainties caused by asymmetric information. As a result, high quality goods retain their market.

In respect of high-tech consumer durables such as refrigerators, televisions, cars and the like, buyers know much less than the sellers about the dependability of the product. In absence of information, they treat all the brands as same in quality and settle for the cheapest ones. It is this phenomenon that drives high quality goods out of the market. Guarantees and warrantees and feature-wise pricing of the product-line prevent this from happening. Standard car manufacturing companies come up with a variety of the same product to help buyers to compare. For instance, petrol or diesel versions of the car, AC or non-AC versions, power windows or manual windows, power steering or non-power steering, etc. leave a wide range of choices that cater to every pocket and help comparison of high or low-quality products price-wise as well. To top it all, their salesmanship and advertising highlight quality and price both to help the buyer decide.

As yet another example, refer to the employee recruitment process. Employers conduct open tests, interviews and group discussions to select sincere and devoted workers. Not that their high grades are positively correlated with a candidate's sincerity and devotion to a job, but they signal quite a lot about a candidate's intelligence, capability to concentrate and control against distractions. Grades and degrees are quality signals which an employer looks for in a candidate apart from his/her general suitability to the organization. Even after recruitment tests, an employer prefers to retain a candidate for a year or half as a probationer. If the employee proves his worth during this period, he/she is recruited on permanent basis, else, relieved from the job. However, relieving too many workers, too, often imparts bad reputation to the employer who himself does not like experimenting with new staff every six-months or year. After all he has to produce goods at a settled price for which he needs high quality workers and wants them to settle down with work as soon as possible. Moreover, quality uncertainty caused by asymmetric information about the workers compels the employer to offer low initial wages to high and low-quality workers alike. This often discourages high-quality workers. To avoid this, employers advertise what they want and conduct tests to ensure they get what they want. Quality signals move across from one side to another—from employers to ascertain recruitment of high-quality workers and from workers to ensure job and wage deserved by them. Failure of factor market results from asymmetric information. A high quality worker may be fixed for low wages or a low-quality worker for high wages or both for low wages in absence of correct assessment of the workers' capabilities by the employers. Market signaling is a reliable tool to solve this problem.

Be it a factor market or a product market, it tends to fail in its main function of facilitating exchange of goods and services in absence of **market signaling**, which now can be defined as a system of sending signals by the sellers and buyers about the quality of products and services that are available.

3. Moral hazard

Moral hazard refers to a situation in which an individual's actions, if not supervised or monitored properly, may cause a serious loss to an organization whose interests are linked with the actions of the individual. Need for supervision arises due to immoral activities or habits. For instance, a worker with high morals is expected to deliver goods whether he/she is monitored or not, while another with low moral shirks work as soon as supervision is withdrawn. Careless and non-serious work leads to low productivity, breakdowns and wastages. In the same way, an individual may turn careless about the security of his house once he gets it insured. This is a moral hazard causing a loss to the insurance company. Quite often, people buy insurance cover by overstating the value of the insured property. This, they do on purpose, which is not pious. The insurance company falls prey and suffers loss due to this. It, therefore, becomes essential for the insurance company to assess and monitor the behaviour of the insuree. If a person turns careless about locking the doors and ensuring the functioning of the alarm system soon after buying an insurance-cover for his house, his intentions are clear. He would soon be seen making a claim for the stolen valuables from his house. The insurance company must monitor the behaviour of the insuree to avoid paying non-genuine claims. Insurees must realize that the cover is only a safeguard and that he/she has a moral duty to ensure safety norms expected of him/her.

To have an idea of insurance provider's loss, let the value of the insured items in the house be ₹ 10 lakh. If the owner locks the doors properly and installs an efficient burglar alarm, probability of theft is, say, 0.0005, but, if such safeguards are not taken, probability of theft is as high as, say, 0.01. Assuming no moral hazards (the owner exercises safety measures sincerely), the premium insurance company charges is ₹ 500(10,00,000 × 0.0005), which is a measure of expected loss to the insurance company. It charges this amount by way of premium from the insurees assuming no moral hazards. In the presence of moral hazards, the value of premium must be ₹ 10,000 (10,00,000 × 0.01). If the insurance company charges a uniform rate of ₹ 500, which is ₹ 9,500 short of what it should in the presence of moral hazards.

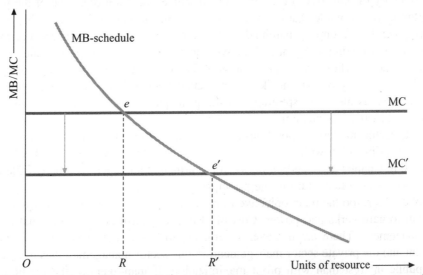

FIGURE 17.2 Effect of moral hazards: Marginal benefit declines each time a unit of resource is allocated to a particular use. The MB schedule, therefore, is a downward sloping curve, as shown. Marginal cost of each unit being given, the MC curve is a horizontal line, intersecting the MB curve at point e. Optimal quantity of resource to be allocated to this use is OR. Due to the presence of the moral hazard, the perceived marginal cost of the resource is MC′ (MC′ < MC) and the actual quantity of resource allocated to this use turns out to be OR'. Moral hazard therefore leads to over-allocation of resource to the present use by RR'.

As yet another illustration, we investigate how moral hazard influences allocative efficiency. Criterion for efficiency requires equality of marginal benefit of an additional unit of resource to its marginal cost. That is, MB = MC at the point of equilibrium.

Like the law of diminishing marginal utility, marginal benefit also diminishes with increasing number units of a resource allocated. Its schedule must therefore slope downwards like a marginal utility schedule. Given the marginal cost, the point of intersection of MB and MC schedules gives the point of efficient allocation of resource (Figure 17.2). However, due to presence of moral hazard, perceived marginal cost of a unit of resource (MC') is less than the actual marginal cost (MC).

It is not very difficult to see the role of asymmetric information in all these examples. The insurance company does not know whether an insuree continues or not to observe set precautions under which he/she seeks the insurance cover nor does a resource allocator know the real cost of resource per unit allocated to a certain use. Due to presence of moral hazards, the allocator allocates more resource (OR') at lower cost (MC') per unit, while the real cost (MC) per unit is higher (MC > MC') and the resource to be allocated at it (OR) is to be lower ($OR < OR'$). A work-shirker costs (MC) posing as a good worker to his employer, but deserves less (MC') in reality as a work-shirker. Low morality of the worker costs more to his employer. (For remedy, see Section 17.4). Such moral hazards can be checked through strict supervision, which has a cost and is quite cumbersome for the principal.

(d) Principal–Agent problem

Principal is the party whom a particular action affects, while **agent** is the party which acts. The owner of a firm, thus, is the principal and the manager, the agent. The **principal–agent problem** relates to diversity of objectives of the two. For instance, the main objective of the principal is maximization of profit, while that of the agent is maximization of sales (See Chapter 13). The principal is generally a group of shareholders whose main objective is to ensure a certain hassle-free return on their holdings. Agent's objective, therefore, turns to maximize sales with certain fixed return to the shareholders on their holdings. The objective, thus, deviates from principal's objective. Principal may or may not know the actual behaviour of the agent, while the agent knows his actions as also the aspirations of the principal. Thus, the cause of principal–agent problem is asymmetric information.

In private sector, modern corporations are controlled by management whose interests cluster around sales maximization with a fair return to the shareholders. Reasons for this have already been outlined in Chapter 13. The link between the principal and agent is a body called *board of directors* who ensure a fair return to the principal.

In public sector, too the main objective of management is growth and expansion. This helps management to gain perks and power. Cost of effective control is as high as that in case of a private management. There are however several departures in the behaviour of public sector management and the private sector management. Public sector management has to concern more with the public interest than with profit maximization. If man-agers of the public enterprises pursue objectives other than those specified by the public policy, their chances to continue in the high paying jobs get impaired.

The incentive system provides an answer to the otherwise cumbersome monitoring of agent's activities. Incentives may be monetary or non-monetary, but linked to the agents' performance.

Much depends on the aspirations of the agents, which may be pertaining to status, power, promotion or monetary benefits. The better the performance of the agents, the higher the incentive. Productivity-linked bonus and revenue sharing arrangements prove highly effective in motivating the management in achieving the principal's goals.

Organizations can't keep an eye on everything that the agents, do but they sure can set the agents' eyes on commensurate rewards which the agents can get if they help the organization to achieve its goals.

Revenue-sharing arrangement and productivity-linked bonus both prove highly effective in almost all the principal–agent problems.

17.4 EFFICIENCY WAGE THEORY

Efficiency wage theory prescribes for a high wage, called the **efficiency wage**, to serve as a check on work-shirking, a consequence of moral hazard. It is based on the principle that a better paid labour can afford to have better food and better health-care to work harder and better than his counterparts in the labour market. The wage is usually set higher than the wage-rate prevailing in the market, contrary to the observed practice of other firms to employ more hands on probation at the prevailing competitive wage and to throw out those ones at its end that are detected to be of low-quality. The other firms work on the traditional view of employing more workers at prevailing competitive wage to produce more at lower cost per unit (economies of scale) and realize higher sales and higher profits. Efficiency wage, in their view, being higher than the competitive wage, is not conducive to the objectives of a firm. Why then efficiency wage?

The answer to the question is provided by the Job–shirking Models. Low-quality workers, despite their habit of work shirking, get away with the same wage as that paid to a high-quality worker in most of the firms. This is partly due to lack of information about the productivity of a worker at the time of his recruitment and partly due to lack of supervision, of the worker's behaviour in the post recruitment period. We have already seen that monitoring the agent's behaviour not only involves costs of supervision, but is also cumbersome for the principals. In its absence, low-quality workers get their opportunity to shirk work. They have no fear of getting fired as alternative job opportunities at competitive wage are not difficult to pick. No doubt, asymmetric information is responsible for recruitment of low-quality workers, but easy availability of alternative options for fired workers at prevailing wage-rate helps them to sustain in employment. If a job-shirking worker gets the same wage that a non-shirking worker does, the result is market failure.

It is to check work shirking effectively that the efficiency wage theory prescribes introduction of efficiency wage. The theory seeks to attach a cost to the habit of shirking work. It is given by the difference of efficiency wage over the competitive wage. A job shirking worker can no longer afford to shirk work as the alternative openings available to him/her elsewhere would pay him/her a competitive wage which is much lower than the efficiency wage. If caught in the act of job shirking and fired from it in consequence, the job shirker would have to sacrifice the wage differential which, thus serves as the cost of work shirking to the worker. That is why many firms recruit workers at wages higher than the competitive wage.

Efficiency wage, thus, is that wage which serves as an incentive for the work-shirking worker not to shirk work. The question that arises now is how high the efficiency wage should be so that the worker does not shirk work? Let w_e be the efficiency wage. Also, let w^* be the competitive wage. The wage differential $(w_e - w^*)$ is, thus, the cost of work shirking.

Efficiency wage theory, however, is not without its side-effects. The most serious one of them is the unemployment caused as fewer workers are demanded at higher wages (Figure 17.3).

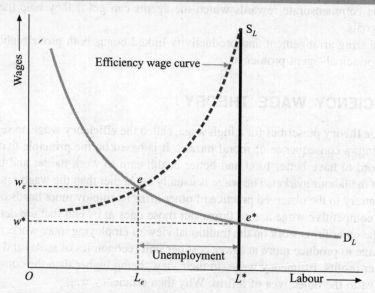

FIGURE 17.3 Effects of efficiency wage: Demand curve for labour, D_L, intersects the full employment supply, S_L, at e^*. Market clearing wage is w^* and employment, L^*. This signifies existence of full employment. Efficiency wage curve (dotted) is the supply curve of labour portraying relationship between efficiency wage w_e as a function of quantity of labour. Note that efficiency wage curve lies above the market-clearing wage, w^*. Efficiency wage, w_e is determined at e, the point of intersection of D_L and the efficiency wage curve. As $w_e > w^*$, unemployment to the tune of $(L^* - L_e)$ emerges. This explains why full employment, economies of large-scale production and profits otherwise possible under competitive conditions are foregone by a firm introducing efficiency wage to check work shirking.

The only catch in this model is that alternative job-options too might offer the efficiency wage to the workers, the likelihood of which is also quite high. If one firm is paying the efficiency wage to its workers as an incentive not to shirk work, there is no reason why the other firms would not follow the suit? If it happens, the model collapses. The best way to prevent work-shirking is introduction of revenue-sharing arrangement of wages or productivity-linked wages. Many firms in India do it. They offer a fixed low level of wage to every worker for coming to the place of work and for devoting the usual hours each day to the firm whether working or shirking. This wage could be as low as the opportunity cost of the worker. In a way, it could be that low which is must for a worker who comes to work but does nothing at all except whiling away the time. The only fear is that every worker might choose to do just that, but the plus point is that no one actually would, in the long-run. The reason is obvious—how long can a worker do with a very low wage just for the fun of shirking work, and that too, when all the alternative options offer the same deal? Sooner or later, the worker would get the better of himself and would devote seriously to work to earn maximum possible income by sharing revenue at a certain rate for his productivity!

Many corporations and large organizations these days do not want their workers to quit and join their rivals. There are several reasons for this:

1. A quitting worker carries the trade secrets of the organization to its competitors where he/she joins. No organization would want this to happen for obvious reasons.
2. No organization would like to experiment with new workers every now and then. A replacement usually requires some time to settle down with work. Until then, production in the organization suffers.
3. Frequent hire and fire of employees causes wastage of resources. Process of recruitment and training cost dearly to the organization.
4. Frequent hire and fire of employees also gives bad reputation in the job market. Even the faithful employees begin questioning their faithfulness.
5. Large organizations are usually preoccupied preventing their senior staff from being lured by smaller organizations who are always on the look-out for senior employees of the large organization to benefit from their experiences.

One may list many more reasons apart from these five. But, the fact remains. No organization can afford loosing its employees including of course even those shirking work, so long as it needs them or has to replace them. That is the reason why efficiency wage is introduced. A recent most trend of recruitment policy of such organizations deserves a mention here. Instead of their traditional policy of recruiting skilled staff from established management institutions, a large number of them have recently started catching them young and imparting them in-house training thereafter. The biggest advantage of this is that the employee has inadequate credentials to claim identical pay package or status elsewhere. He/she has no other recourse, but to remain faithful. Catching them at the undergraduate level and offering them packages otherwise offered to MBAs has been gaining ground in colleges of reputed universities in recent years. Some recruiters promise the youngsters to finance their MBA in a reputed institution abroad. Normally, candidates have to sign a bond with such organizations or have to mortgage their MBA degrees with them. In such cases employees cannot think of quitting ever after. Youngsters must clarify the terms and conditions before accepting such proposals. Unfortunately, the proposals are too lucrative to resist. Those who fall for them seldom worry about such considerations as signing a bond or mortgaging their degrees. An MBA from a reputed institution can quit if the job does not suit his tastes but youngsters signing a bond or mortgaging their degrees cannot. The author's objective is only to forewarn the youngsters.

KEY TERMS AND CONCEPTS

Adverse Selection It refers to a situation in which products of different qualities are sold at a single price due to asymmetric information.

Agent A person who acts on behalf of someone else.

Asymmetric Information When some people know more than others about the product specifications, the phenomenon is termed as asymmetric information. In simple words, asymmetric information means unequal information, i.e., some of us know more about something than others.

Cost of work-shirking It refers to the difference of efficiency wage over the competitive wage. In other words, it is the loss of wage that a worker would suffer by joining an alternative job elsewhere in the market.

Efficiency Wage It refers to the wage paid to a worker as an incentive for efficient work (not to shirk work). Efficiency wage is always higher than the market clearing or competitive wage.

Efficiency Wage Curve It portrays efficiency wages as a function of quantity of labour employed. In a way, it is the supply curve of labour when wages are efficiency wages. The curve always lies above the competitive wage.

Efficiency Wage Theory It refers to a concept that work-shirking can be prevented by offering wages higher than the competitive wages to the work-shirkers so that they avoid shirking work. If they don't, they would get fired and earn lower wages (competitive wages) form alternative jobs in the market.

Market Signaling It refers to a system of relaying signals about product quality for the benefit of the prospective buyers. The product may be a tangible one or an intangible one. For example, extensive guarantees and warrantees convey high quality of a tangible product while training, qualifications and length of experience convey information about the quality of a worker. Market signaling is resorted to by the sellers as a measure putting to rest all the quality uncertainties caused by asymmetric information in the minds of the prospective buyers.

Moral Hazard It refers to situations in which low morals of one party cause loss to another party when the former deviates from the agreed terms and conditions either on purpose or due to complacency. Carelessness and negligence creep in the behaviour of some individuals as soon as they realize that the cost is not theirs. As an example, take the case of a person who does not care to lock the doors properly just because he/she has bought insurance against theft.

Principal A person on whose behalf an action is taken by someone else.

Principal–Agent Problem When the principal and the agent do not have same goals and objectives, the problem is referred to as the principal–agent problem. For instance, the owner of a firm wants his management to maximize profits but the management pursues objectives other than that. One such objective is sales maximization. Incentives such as productivity linked bonus and/or revenue sharing by agents are often suggested to solve this problem.

Quality Uncertainty Buyers are often uncertain about the quality of used or high-tech products due to lack of information about them. As a result, they feel it convenient to treat high-quality goods as low-quality goods and offer lower prices for them. The result is that the high-quality goods get driven out of the market by the low-quality goods.

EXERCISES

A. Very Short Answer Questions

Define the following:
1. Asymmetric information
2. Adverse selection
3. Efficiency wage
4. Efficiency wage theory
5. Cost of work-shirking
6. Moral hazard
7. Market signaling
8. Quality uncertainty

9. Market failure
10. Principal–Agent problem
11. Efficiency wage curve

B. Short Answer Questions

12. Name two important factors responsible for market failure.
13. Suggest some of the measures to resolve the principal agent problem.
14. Suggest two ways to eliminate the problem of asymmetric information.

C. Long Answer Questions

15. 'Low-quality goods drive the high-quality goods out of the market.' Comment.
16. Enumerate the factors that lead to the problem of adverse selection. What are its implications?
17. Explain the concept of market signaling as a measure to solve the problem of quality uncertainty.
18. Explain the problem of moral hazard with reference to the insurance market.
19. Why does a principal–agent problem arise? How does it lead to market failure?
20. How can incentives such as bonus and profit sharing resolve the principal–agent problem? Explain with the help of an example.
21. How can the principal–agent model be employed to explain pursuance of objectives other than profit maximization by public enterprises?
22. How can reputation and standardization help to resolve the problem of quality uncertainty?
23. How can guarantees and warrantees help to resolve the problem of quality uncertainty?
24. How can asymmetric information lead to market failure? Explain with an example.
25. Critically examine the role of asymmetric information in the labour market.
26. Is there any link between adverse selection and moral hazard? Give reasons in support of your answer.
27. Discuss a few techniques of market signaling. Can they resolve the problem of asymmetric information?
28. Is it more profitable to employ workers at wages higher than the competitive wage? Give reasons in support.
29. What are the work-shirking models? How far does efficiency wage theory provide a solution to the problem of work shirking?
30. Why do firms employ fewer workers at higher wages when more of them are available at lower wages? Can this be treated as a cause of unemployment in industrialized countries? Explain.
31. How does moral hazard lead to inefficiency in resource allocation? Explain.
32. It is said that the premium should reflect the risks involved in medical insurance. Do you agree? Give reasons in support of your answer.

D. Essay Type Questions

33. Discuss the role of asymmetric information in market failure. What are the important manifestations of asymmetric information and how do they cause market failure? Suggest remedies in each case.
34. 'Efficiency wage theory may for sure serve as a safeguard against the problem of work shirking but at the same time it is highly undesireable from the viewpoint of growth and employment'. Discuss the statement substantiating your arguments appropriately. What alternatives to efficiency wage would you recommend to check work shirking?

18

Externalities and Public Goods

CHAPTER OUTLINE

Introduction
- Externalities and Market Failure
- Remedy to Market Failure Caused by Negative and Positive Externalities
- Public Goods
- Key Terms and Concepts
- Exercises

INTRODUCTION

In Chapter 16, we have outlined main sources of market failure. They are — market power, asymmetric information, externalities, and public goods. We have already discussed market power as a source of market failure in its requisite detail in earlier chapters. We have also discussed asymmetric information as a source of market failure in Chapter 17 in its requisite detail. Public good and externalities were, however, briefly introduced in Chapter 16, but not in their requisite detail there.

In this chapter, we take up externalities and public goods and study them to conclude the topic of market failure as outlined in Section 16.4.

We have had an elementary idea about what externalities and public goods are and how they can be treated as sources of market failure. In Section 18.1, we take up externalities in somewhat greater detail and discuss the mechanism through which they lead to market failure. In Section 18.2, we examine ways and means to rectify market failure caused by externalities. Finally in Section 18.3, we study public goods in somewhat greater detail along with the mechanism through which they cause market failure.

18.1 EXTERNALITIES AND MARKET FAILURE

Externalities refer to activities taking place outside a production or consumption system that extend their influence to the system to destabilize it. For instance, extensive construction of residential and commercial complexes affects agricultural production adversely by claiming the agricultural land. State authorities often acquire land from cultivators for construction of commercial and residential buildings on it. The activity for sure contributes much more to the national output and national employment than what agriculture does as more and more people get absorbed in construction activities and more and more people and organizations get adequate infrastructure for housing themselves and their economic activities. However, this causes a decline in food avaibility by leaving less land for cultivation apart from causing health hazards such as air and water pollution, adversely affecting productivity of manpower. Prices of dwellings and commercial complexes may come down due to increased supply, but prices of food may go up due to less food grains produced, while life expectancy and productive potential of general public comes down invariably in consequence. Without going into the question of justification of the State policy, one thing can be said for sure. The policy adversely affects agricultural production, life expectancy and productive potential of general public and hence is an externality. Actual cost of building construction would therefore work out much more than its private cost. The actual cost of construction must take into account additional expenditures incurred by general public on medical care and procurement of food.

The additional burden, on general public due to one additional unit of building constructed is known as Marginal External Cost (MEC). Thus, for every additional unit of building constructed, the actual cost of construction, called the Marginal Social Cost (MSC), is given as the sum of private cost (MC) and the Marginal External Cost (MEC). That is,

$$\text{MSC} = \text{MC} + \text{MEC} \qquad (18.1)$$

Assuming the market for buildings to be competitive and building prices to be given at $\bar{P}$ per unit, we can calculate the socially optimally output of buildings as shown in Figure 18.1.

When MSC > MC, externality is termed as negative externality. In other words, when social cost of production is higher than the actual or the private cost of production, the socially optimal output is *less* than the actual output and the **externality** is **negative**.

To elaborate further, increased industrial production increases national output; but at the same time, causes air, water and noise pollutions which disturb the ecological balance. Mankind has, in consequence, less of all the niceties such as vegetation, pure air, pure water and good food with more of all the economic bads. Industrial production thus leads to negative externalities, which destabilizes the ecological balance.

Thus, action of an economic decision-maker creates costs for others for which they are not compensated. There occurs an external diseconomy or negative externality for the society as a whole. In the above cases, society bears the costs of pollution caused by industrial production while industries don't. In the same way, the State policy of acquiring farm-land for construction of buildings imposes a cost on others or the society as a whole which the builders and developers don't bear.

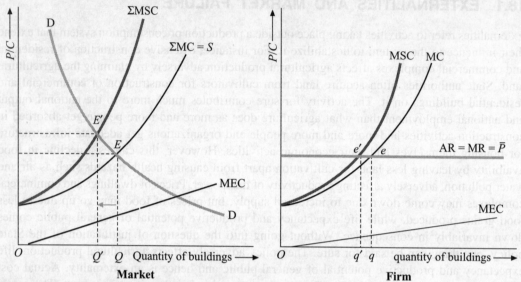

FIGURE 18.1 **Negative externality:** The left panel shows market demand (DD) for and market supply (ΣMC) of buildings. Market supply is a horizontal summation of the supplies of all the firms in the market. The socially optimal supply is given by the aggregate marginal social cost (ΣMSC), which is a vertical summation of MEC and ΣMC. Actual quantity supplied is OQ, while socially desirable supply is OQ' only. The right panel shows the firm's actual supply of buildings given by the MC curve whereas socially desirable supply of buildings given by the MSC, which is a vertical summation of MC and MEC. Actual quantity transacted by the firm is Oq, while socially desirable quantity is Oq'. What is clear from these discussions is that the industry is producing and supplying more than the socially desirable quantity and so is the firm. The reason is the diversion between the actual and social costs of production.

Thus, external diseconomies or negative externalities are caused by the divergence between private and social costs. The divergence is said to be negative because private cost (MC) is less than the social cost and the difference is borne by the society as a whole. It is also said to be negative because the society desires much less to be produced than what firms actually do.

When action of an economic decision-maker creates benefits for others for which the beneficiaries do not pay, there occurs an external economy or positive externality for the others and the society as a whole. For instance, suppose more flyovers, roads and highways are constructed by a welfare State. This certainly increases the social benefit for which the society does not pay as the welfare State levies no toll-tax or road-tax for the benefit created.

As another example of positive externalities, suppose an environmentalist uses unleaded petrol for running his car, paying $P = MC$. By using unleaded petrol, the environmentalist keeps the air cleaner without making anyone to compensate him for using the costlier fuel. The additional expenses incurred by him on better fuel are born by himself. This is the case of positive externality or external economy for society. The society would like many more car users to follow his example as marginal social benefit is higher than the private benefit of the car user (given by his demand curve, AR = MR = $\bar{P}$). In other words, Marginal Social Benefit (MSB) curve, as a vertical summation of the demand curve (AR = MR = $\bar{P}$) for better fuel and the Marginal External Benefit (MEB), would lie above the demand curve for better fuel as shown in Figure 18.2.

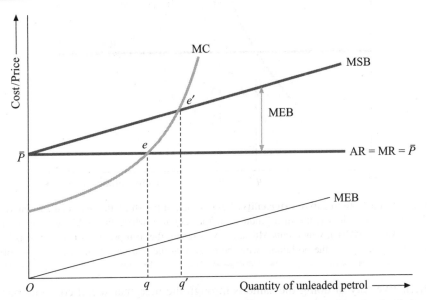

FIGURE 18.2 Positive externality: As shown, MEB rises with the quantity of unleaded petrol used. Private benefit of the fuel user is given by his demand curve, AR = MR = $\bar{P}$. As is clear, MSB is given by MSB = $\bar{P}$ + MEB. The environmentalist uses Oq quantity of unleaded fuel at e, where $\bar{P}$ = MC. Since MSB > $\bar{P}$, socially optimal quantity of unleaded fuel to be used is higher as at e'. Here, Oq' of it is what the society wants the users to use. To induce higher use of cleaner fuel, society must compensate the users by an equivalent of MEB.

Figure 18.2 shows that the use of the unleaded petrol is too less than what the society wants. In both the cases of the externalities, we observe that socially optimal or efficient outputs are different from those implied by the competitive equilibrium. This gives sufficient indication of market failure in respect of efficiency.

18.2 REMEDY TO MARKET FAILURE CAUSED BY NEGATIVE AND POSITIVE EXTERNALITIES

Remedy to market failure caused by externalities, in particular negative externalities, can be possible in a number of ways. For one, a unit tax, such as an output tax, affects production adversely by increasing the Marginal Cost (MC) by the amount of the tax (Figure 18.3). MC shifts upwards and profit-maximizing level of the output falls from Oq to Qq'. Thus, by suitably adjusting the amount of tax, output can be reduced to the levels socially optimal.

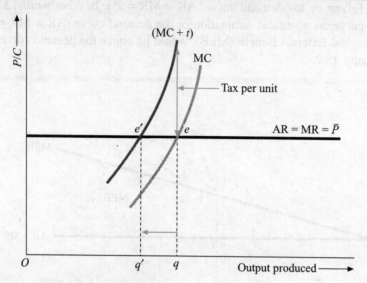

FIGURE 18.3 Remedy to negative externality: Levy of output tax shifts the marginal cost curve of the firm upward to left as shown. Initially, the firm produced output Oq at e, where firm's MC equals its MR. Levy of output tax shifts MC to MC + t, which cuts MR at e'. As a result, the firm produces Oq', which is less than Oq. This would reduce emission of the pollutants with the result that the marginal external cost is set off.

An alternative way of doing the same is through the marginal social cost and marginal cost of abatement (MCA). MCA measures additional cost to the firm of installing pollution control equipment. As the emission level of pollutants increases, so does the Marginal Social Cost (MSC). Likewise, as the extent of emission of pollutants increases, the Marginal Cost of Abatement (MCA) decreases as shown (Figure 18.4).

So far, we have studied problems of **externalities in production**. We have seen how such externalities lead to market failure and how they can be eliminated.

Let us now turn to **externalities in consumption**. Let us see how they lead to market failure and how the problem can be solved. Imagine a product whose consumption is limited only to the rich because of its high price. Let this price be the competitive price, $\bar{P}$. Let the quantity demanded at this price be Q (Figure 18.5). Price being high, many people find it unaffordable. The maximum they can shell out is say P' at which quantity demanded increases to Q'. But, a price as low as P' leaves no incentive for the producers to produce this quantity. This is an externality that leads to market failure by making consumption inefficient.

Before we proceed any further, let us recall that the product market here is competitive with supply curve characterized by MC = $\bar{P}$. Evidently, it is a horizontal line indicating that supply can be increased to any level at the fixed price, $\bar{P}$.

Socially optimal output Q' cannot be reached unless the price or MC falls to P'.

Now suppose, that State decides to increase social welfare through subsidy on this product. Under the circumstances, subsidy would cost government a sum of money equal to $(\bar{P} - P')(Q' - Q)$. Government would have to pay this amount to the producers, and in return, they reduce the market price by the amount of the subsidy, i.e. by $(\overline{P} - P')$ and have to sell quantity Q' at P'. This creates benefits for all the consumers alike irrespective of their financial status. Such benefits are called *external benefits* and the benefit accruing to the consumers per additional unit consumed is called the Marginal External Benefit (MEB). Note that MEB declines with the level of consumption just as the marginal utility does with it. Let us now analyze the effects of the subsidy on the welfare of consumers.

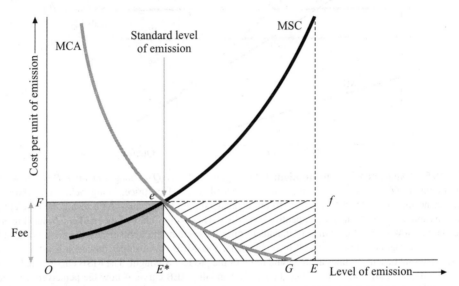

FIGURE 18.4 Choice between Abatement and Emission Fee: The MSC and the MCA intersect each other at point e. At this point, the level of emission is E^*, known as the standard level of emission. A firm emitting pollutants at level OE can thus be shown to benefit by paying an emission fee of E^*e up to its level of emission OE^* and by abating emission of pollution beyond this level. If the firm chose to pay the emission fee at the flat rate of E^*e per unit of emission without abatement, it pays a total fee given by the rectangle $OEfF$; if it chose to abate emission, it spends an amount given by the area under the MCA curve and if it chose to pay an emission fee of Ee^* per unit of emission for first OE^* units of emission and to abate emission thereafter, its total cost is an amount given by the sum of areas of the shaded rectangle (OE^*eF) and triangular region (E^*eG) below the MCA curve. Of the three, clearly the last option of paying emission fee up to OE^* level of emission and abating it beyond it is the cheapest option before the firm. Levy of emission fee or abating emission both cost the polluting firm dearly. This helps as a remedy for negative externality.

In Figure 18.5, DD is the market demand curve and SS, the supply curve. Introduction of subsidy shifts the supply curve down to S'S'. Initial equilibrium takes place at point e where quantity Q is bought at price $\overline{P}$. After introduction of subsidy, the new equilibrium takes place at point e''. The perceived demand curve is the Marginal Social Benefit Curve (MSB) which is calculated through the vertical summation of the private benefit given by the demand, DD and the marginal external benefit, MEB. That is, MSB = Private benefit represented by the demand curve DD + MEB = demand price + MEB.

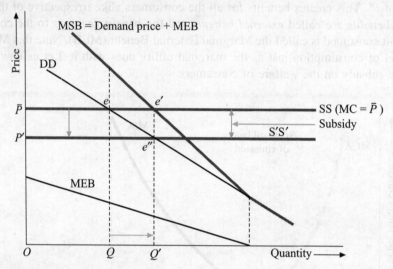

FIGURE 18.5 **Externality in consumption:** In the figure, quantity Q is bought at price $\bar{P}$ (point e). Socially desirable output is Q', which requires price to be reduced to P'. This price, being below the Marginal Cost (MC), leaves no incentives for the producers to produce and supply the product. As a result, the efficient level of consumption cannot be reached under competitive conditions. This marks failure of the market in achieving efficiency in consumption. Now suppose government intends to raise the welfare through subsidy. As soon as the subsidy is introduced, an external benefit arises to all the consumers. The MEB curve slopes downwards as an indication of the fact that external benefit declines as more and more of the product is bought. The MSB curve, which is obtained through the vertical summation of the demand curve DD and the MEB curve, is now the perceived demand curve. Producers getting a fixed amount per unit of the output from government by way of subsidy, treat S'S' as their supply curve instead of SS. The quantity bought now is Q' at a price P' at the point e''. This quantity would have been bought at P' in the pre-subsidy period, but the price in the pre-subsidy period was $\bar{P}$, not P'. The difference between the two, $(\bar{P} - P')$, represents the value of subsidy as also the excess of MSB over marginal private benefit marked by the demand curve DD. In mathematical terms, $e'e'' $ = subsidy = MSB − demand price = MEB. The benefit extended to the consumers is a *positive externality in consumption*. From the viewpoint of government, it is a re-allocation of welfare as the same had to be spent by government on providing amenities or public goods to people for their welfare. Government raises resources for such activities through indirect taxation.

In general, the remedy for market failure in production and consumption caused by negative and positive externalities is the condition of equality of Marginal Social Benefit (MSB) to the Marginal Social Cost (MSC). In a multi-product world, the ratio of MSB to MSC must be same for all the goods, i.e.

$$\frac{MSB_X}{MSC_X} = \frac{MSB_Y}{MSC_Y} = \ldots = \frac{MSB_Z}{MSC_Z}$$

18.3 PUBLIC GOODS

In Chapter 16, we have introduced a public good as a source of market failure.

A **public good** is a product, tangible or intangible, consumption of which cannot be restricted once it is supplied. This attribute of the good is known as the attribute of non-exclusion. Apart from this, it has yet another attribute called the attribute of **non-rival consumption**, that is, consumption of a public good by one does not affect its consumption by another. We had, in fact, referred only to its first attribute in Chapter 16 while mentioning it as a source of market failure.

To economists, a public good need not necessarily be a good provided by government. It may be any good that possesses the attributes of *non-exclusion* and *non-rival consumption*. As an illustration, let us take the example of a public park, use of which, cannot be reserved for some and denied to others. Every one has an equal access to it. This lends it the attribute of *non-exclusion*. A private lawn in a house does not possess this attribute. Only the owner of the house has an exclusive right to use it. Neighbours and others cannot claim an entry.

In like manner, use of a public park by one does not affect its utility to others. Even if many more join in, its utility remains unaffected. This lends it the attribute of non-rival consumption. A public park, therefore, is a public good.

National defence is another example of a public good. It possesses both the attributes of a public good. Any defence effort made cannot protect some and exclude others. Likewise, protection provided cannot be more for some and less for others.

The Free Rider Problem in Providing Certain Public Goods

An individual, who derives the benefits of a privately provided public good without bearing his share of the cost of providing it, is called a **free rider**. If the number of free riders increases, it becomes difficult, at times, impossible, for the private body to provide the public good for the benefit of the community. To illustrate, suppose the residents of a colony decide to sink a deep well of their own to solve the persistent water problem faced by the residents. The cost of the facility is ₹ 5 lakh and the number of families to benefit from it is 1,000. Share of each family in the cost works out at ₹ 500, but the benefit to each is estimated at ₹ 5,000. If it is left to the residents to volunteer to share the cost, the number of the volunteers would perhaps be very small. In fact, it may be small enough to raise the desired amount to provide the facility, which might thus have to be abandoned. Anticipating the free rider problem, if the resident welfare association decides to collect ₹ 2,500 from each of the 200 affluent families of the colony or if it makes it compulsory for each of the 1,000 families to contribute ₹ 500, they can succeed in having the facility. If the size of consumers is large and the facility is a public good, the number of free riders too would be large unless it is mandatory for all to contribute. It is only rational on the part of the free riders not to contribute because the facility is non-exclusive and non-rival.

There are a number of examples from the real world that provide evidence in support of the free rider problem. Shipra Estates Pvt. Ltd., a large construction company built a mini township in the suburb of Delhi and offered to provide 100% power back-up to all the residents at a nominal cost of ₹ 20,000 per flat as one-time payment with running costs to be shared equally on monthly basis by flatowners thereafter. The number of volunteers who accepted the proposal from the housing complex of over 1,000 families turned out to be as low as 20. As expected, the proposal had to be abandoned. The cost of generators and their sound proofing, etc. had been worked out at over ₹ 2 crores of rupees. In its next phase, the same company made the scheme a part of the package for the flat-buyers and it clicked. Needless to say that the scheme had the attributes of non-exclusion and non-rival consumption!

Efficiency in Provision of Public Goods

The criterion for efficient provision of goods, whether they are private goods* or public goods, is the same. It is the equality of Marginal Benefit (MB) derived from an additional unit to its Marginal Cost (MC), that is,

$$MB = MC$$

Note that we have deviated from the notations MSB and MSC deliberately to indicate that externalities, whether positive or negative, are not a part of the current discussion.

The main point of difference of a public good from a private good is related to the efficiency of its provision which requires adding up the marginal benefits of all its beneficiaries. This is not easy due to the attributes of non-exclusion and non-rival consumption of a public good. We have seen that a unit of a public good once provided cannot be confined to some beneficiaries and that the marginal utility is the same for all them.

Figure 18.6 explains the mechanism of efficient provision of public goods.

For the sake of simplicity, we assume two beneficiaries, one with demand D_1 and the other with demand D_2. The demands represent the marginal benefits derived by the respective consumers. The aggregate marginal benefit is calculated through vertical summation of D_1 and D_2. Marginal cost of production being given, the MC curve is horizontal.

Presence of free riders leads to externalities in consumption of a public good. Due to the presence of non-exclusion and non-rival consumption of a public good, free riders consume it without paying for it. This causes an externality in consumption, which leads to market failure. The presence of externalities in consumption makes it impossible to provide an efficient level of output of a public goods.

Patents

There is a great deal of hard work, research and investment behind an invention of a new product or production process. **Patent** is a legal tool that empowers the inventor to enjoy the monopoly power over its use. It helps to check the free rider problem. No one can use the invention without prior permission from the inventor at least over the **patent-life** of the invention. To illustrate, suppose a scientist invents a mosquito repellant. The know-how of the device helps its production and sale to the consumers. If the know-how is not patented, many free riding producers will use it to manufacture the device and make profits from its sale to the consumers. There is nothing wrong in the use of the knowledge to produce something so useful for mankind. What actually causes concern is that the research, investments and efforts made by the inventor go unrewarded. This goes a long way to discourage scientists and researchers from making similar efforts in future on such activities. Patent rights if vested with the inventor, no producer can use the know-how without the consent of the inventor. Inventor may charge a fee or royalty for granting the rights to the producer to use his invention for production of the mosquito repellant. So long as the producer sticks to the terms and conditions of the formal agreement with the inventor, he continues to enjoy the rights to use the invention. As long as the inventor enjoys the patent rights, the free rider problem that arises due to non-exclusive and non-rival consumption cannot crop up and the product too cannot be a public good. Market failure caused by externalities due to the presence of the free riders, thus, can be checked and the efficient provision of public goods becomes possible (Figure 18.6).

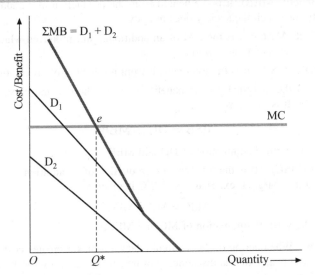

FIGURE 18.6 Efficient provision of a public good: Attributes of non-exclusion and non-rival consumption of public goods call for vertical summation of the marginal benefits, given by the demand curves of the two beneficiaries. Thus, $\Sigma MB = (D_1 + D_2)$. MC assumed fixed for all the units of the public good, efficient level of output of the public goods is determined at e, the point of intersection of MC and ΣMB. It is Q^*.

KEY TERMS AND CONCEPTS

Efficiency in Provision of Public Goods: Provision of public goods is efficient when total marginal benefit equals the marginal cost, that is,

$$\Sigma MB = MC$$

External Diseconomies When action of an economic decision maker creates costs for others for which he does not pay, there occurs an external diseconomy or negative externality for the others and the society as a whole.

External Economies When action of an economic decision-maker creates benefits for others for which he is not paid, there occurs an external economy or positive externality for the others and the society as a whole.

Externalities Externalities refer to activities taking place outside a production or consumption system that extend their influence to the system to destabilize it through market failure. When externalities take place in production, they are known as the externalities in production and when they take place in consumption, they are known as the externalities in consumption.

Free Rider Problem When number of free riders is large enough due to which production costs of the public good cannot be realized and provision of public goods becomes impossible.

Free Rider A consumer who consumes a public good without bearing its cost.

Marginal Cost of Abatement (MCA): MCA measures additional cost to the firm of installing pollution control equipment. The curve slopes downwards from left to right in indication that MCA declines with increasing level of the economic bad, such as emission of pollutants.

---

*Private goods refer to goods that do not possess the attributes of non-exclusion and non-rival consumption, not to the public goods provided by private bodies.

Marginal External Benefit (MEB): It is the benefit from the production of an additional unit of a good that goes to the society for which the society does not pay.

Marginal External Cost (MEC): It is the cost of an additional unit produced which is not borne by the producer but is borne by the society as a whole.

Marginal Social Benefit (MSB): It is the total benefit from production of an additional unit of output.

It is given as the sum of the marginal private benefit (given by the demand curve as the price) and the marginal external benefit. It is given as

$$MSB = DD + MEB$$

It is obtained through the vertical summation of DD and MEB.

Marginal Social Cost (MSC) It is the total cost of production of an additional unit of output, which is the sum of the MC and the marginal external cost. MSC is given as

$$MSC = MC + MEC$$

It is obtained through the vertical summation of MC and MEC.

Negative Externalities When action of an economic decision-maker creates costs for others for which he does not pay, there occurs an external diseconomy or negative externality for the others and the society as a whole.

Non-exclusive Goods Goods the consumption of which cannot be restricted once they are provided.

Non-rival Goods Goods the consumption of which by one person does leave less utility for the others.

Patents Legal rights of the inventor/innovator, which prevent the free riders from using the invention/innovation without his permission. Patents granted help to check the free rider problem and hence market failure caused by the externalities arising from the presence of free riders.

Positive Externalities When action of an economic decision-maker creates benefits for others for which he is not paid, there occurs an external economy or positive externality for the others and the society as a whole.

Public Goods Goods that possess the attributes of non-exclusion and non-rival consumption.

EXERCISES

A. Short Answer Questions

Define the following [1 through 16]:
1. Externality
2. Positive externalities
3. Negative externalities
4. Marginal social cost
5. Marginal social benefit
6. External economies
7. External diseconomies
8. Marginal cost of abatement
9. Public good
10. Free rider
11. Free rider problem
12. Patent

13. Utility of patent rights
14. Non-exclusive consumption
15. Non-rival consumption
16. Market failure
17. Give an example from the real world for externalities in production.
18. Give an example from the real world for externalities in consumption.
19. Give an example from real world for external economies.
20. Give an example from real world for external diseconomies.
21. Calculate marginal social cost for the 10th unit of a product if the total cost of production of first 9 units is 1800 and that of the first 10 units is 2000. Assume the marginal external cost of the 10th unit as 50. [**Ans. 250**]
22. Calculate marginal social benefit derived from 10th unit of a product if its demand price is ₹ 250. Assume the external benefit from first 10 units to be ₹ 1150 and that from the first 9 units is ₹ 1275. [**Ans.: 325**]
23. In questions 21 and 22, which externality is positive and which is negative?
24. Name the two attributes that are essential in a public good with examples.
25. How does the existence of free riders lead to externalities in consumption?
26. How do the consumption externalities lead to market failure?
27. Give an example non-exclusive consumption.
28. Give an example non-rival consumption.
29. Name two sources with remedies to the problem of market failure.
30. What is the condition of efficiency in provision of public goods? Would the condition remain unchanged in the presence of a free rider?

B. Long Answer Questions

Distinguish between [31 through 34]:
31. Negative and positive externalities
32. External economies and diseconomies
33. Marginal external benefit and marginal external cost
34. Marginal social benefit and marginal social cost
35. How does an externality in production lead to market failure? Suggest one remedy to it.
36. Can a public good be provided by private corporations?
37. What are public goods? How can an efficient provision of a public good be ensured? Explain.
38. How can commodity taxes serve as a remedy to the problem of market failure caused by externalities? Explain.
39. Explain how standard level of emission of pollutants be determined. How does it help to control pollution?

C. Essay Type Questions

40. How is an efficient level of output determined in the presence of negative externalities by an industry and by a firm? Explain with the help of a diagram.
41. How does the use of unleaded petrol by car owners lead to external benefits? Explain how would you determine the socially desirable quantity of unleaded petrol.
42. How can subsidy lead to a socially optimal level of consumption? Explain with the help of a diagram.
43. Write a short note on patent rights. How do they help to solve the free rider problem?

44. 'A public good cannot be provided efficiently by the private bodies but if the responsibility is assigned to government, it sure can be by the latter.' Discuss.
45. 'External costs, being bad, call for government intervention to reduce them; external benefits being good, call for no intervention by government.' Do you agree? Give reasons in support of your answer.
46. (a) The marginal cost of a facility is given as

$$MC = 100 + 3Q$$

Marginal revenue from the provision of the facility is ₹ 160. The facility, however, causes a positive externality to someone who is willing to pay ₹ 60 per unit of the facility. Determine

(i) the profit-maximizing output of the facility

(ii) economically-efficient output of the facility

[**Ans.** (i) Profit-maximizing output of the facility can be obtained by equating MC to MR. Thus,

$$100 + 3Q = 160$$
$$\Rightarrow Q = 20$$

which is the profit-maximizing output of the facility.

(ii) Marginal social benefit from the production of the facility is given as the sum of the marginal private benefit and the marginal external benefit

Thus, MSB = Marginal private benefit + Marginal external benefit
$$= 160 + 60$$
$$= 220.$$

For economically-efficient output of the facility, equate MSB to MC

$$MSB = MC$$
$$\Rightarrow 220 = 100 + 3Q$$
$$\Rightarrow Q = 40.]$$

(b) Marginal cost of a public good is fixed at MC = 92. Demand curves of Individuals A and B for the good are given as

$$Q = 60 - P_A \qquad \text{(For } A\text{)}$$
$$Q = 100 - (5/6) P_B \qquad \text{(For } B\text{)}$$

Determine the efficient level of provision of the public good.

[**Ans.** Due to non-exclusive nature of the public good, the marginal social benefit is calculated through the vertical summation of the demand curve. Thus,

MSB = Marginal private benefit of A + Marginal private benefit of B
$$= P_A + P_B$$
$$= (60 - Q) + (120 - 1.2 Q)$$
$$= 180 - 2.2Q$$

For efficient provision of the public good, MC = MSB

$$180 - 2.2Q = 92$$
$$\Rightarrow Q = 40.]$$

(c) At the point of competitive equilibrium, production of a good involves a marginal external cost of ₹ 80. Would an excise duty of ₹ 80 per unit achieve an efficient allocation of resource?

[**Ans.** Please refer to Figure 18.7 and also, Figures 9.1 and 9.3]

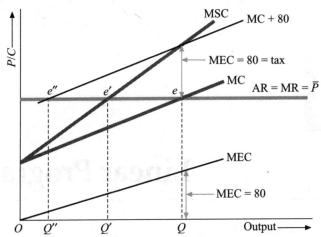

FIGURE 18.7 MC curve cuts the price line at e, leading to an output Q, which is not efficient due to the presence of MEC (presence of externalities). An efficient output requires MSC to be equated to the marginal private benefit, given by AR = MR = $\bar{P}$. The efficient output thus is Q'. A levy of excise per unit by the same amount as MEC, leads to a parallel-upward-to-left shift in the MC so that the new cost curve is MC + 80, which cuts the price line at e''. Here, output is Q'', which is less than Q'. Thus, an excise duty of the same amount as MEC does not lead to efficient allocation of resource.]

47. Discuss 'perfect competition is a myth and so is its efficiency.' Is it worth the time and effort to devote to them? Incorporate the real world and academic interests both.
48. Prepare a comprehensive case to tackle the social costs of production of health hazards. Refer to the Bhopal Gas Leakage Tragedy of 1984 as the basis of your project.

19

Linear Programming

CHAPTER OUTLINE

Introduction
- Constrained Maximization (Graphic Method)
- Constrained Maximization (Algebraic Method)
- Constrained Minimization (Graphic Method)
- Constrained Minimization (Algebraic Method)
- Assorted Applications
- The Dual Problem
- The Simplex Method
- Problem of Degeneracy in Linear Programming
- Special Cases
- Sensitivity Analysis
- Key Terms and Concepts
- Exercises

INTRODUCTION

In Chapter 4, we have observed how a consumer maximized his utility,

$$U = f(x, y) \qquad (19.1)$$

under the budget constraint,

$$x \cdot P_x + y \cdot P_y \leq M \qquad (19.2)$$

The consumer intended to choose utility maximizing quantities x and y of goods X and Y, given their prices as P_x and P_y and his budget, $\bar{M}$. In Chapter 5, we have also observed how a producer

maximized his output,
$$Q = f(L, K) \qquad (19.3)$$
subject to the cost constraint,
$$w \cdot L + r \cdot K \leq \overline{C} \qquad (19.4)$$

The producer intended to choose output maximizing factor quantities L and K of labour and capital, given their prices as w and r and given his budget, $\overline{C}$. The problem, be it of maximization of total utility under limited budget or be it one of maximization of total output under budgeted cost, was attempted as a constrained maximization, employing Lagrange's multiplier, λ, for transforming it into simple maximization. The utility function [Eq. (19.1)] and the output function [Eq. (19.3)] served as objective functions and were both non-linear while the budget limitations [Eqs. (19.2) and (19.4)], served as budget constraints and were both linear. Recall further, that the utility function was linear for perfect substitutes X and Y and so was the output function for perfect substitutes L and K.

Linear programming (LP) refers to a technique of a special set of constrained optimization problems where the objective function is linear and so are the constraints. It is a powerful decision-making tool employed in a variety of managerial applications. To demonstrate, let us take a few examples.

1. A firm manufactures two types of toys. Type A toy contributes a profit of ₹ 11 per unit while type B, that of ₹ 5 per unit. Both require three inputs—labour hours, machine hours and material-units. Requirements per unit and total availability of inputs are summarized in Table 19.1.

TABLE 19.1 Tabular Presentation of Production Problem

Toy type \ Inputs	Labour hours	Machine hours	Material-units	Contribution (₹ per unit)
A	3	1	2	11
B	1	1	5	5
Total requirements	300	140	550	

The objective is to find the product mix that maximizes total contribution, given the limitations of availability of inputs. Let the product mix comprise x units of type A and y units of type B. The total profit can now be expressed as:
$$\pi = 11x + 5y \qquad (19.5)$$
Limitations of the three inputs can, likewise, be expressed as:
$$3x + y \leq 300 \qquad (19.6)$$
$$x + y \leq 140 \qquad (19.7)$$
$$2x + 5y \leq 550 \qquad (19.8)$$
$$x, y \geq 0 \qquad (19.9)$$

The profit function in expression (19.5), called **objective function**, is to be maximized without violating any of the input constraints (19.6), (19.7) and (19.8), called

structural constraints and the quantity constraint (19.9) called **non-negativity constraint**.

Table 19.2 provides the mathematical formulation of the problem, called the model of **Linear Programming Problem (LPP-Model)**.

TABLE 19.2 LPP-Model of Profit Maximizing Product-mix Problem

Maximize $\pi = 11x + 5y$
Subject to: $3x + y \leq 300$
$x + y \leq 140$
$2x + 5y \leq 550$
$x, y \geq 0$

The optimal product mix satisfying the model, as attempted in Section 19.1, comprises $x = 80$ and $y = 60$. Reader can verify that the optimal product mix does not violate any of the three structural constraints or the non-negativity constraint and yields a profit of ₹ 1180. It exhausts labour and machine inputs fully but spares 90 units of material as un-utilized or idle. This is termed as existence of **idle capacity** in material-units.

2. As another illustration, suppose a dietician prescribes foods F_1 and F_2 to trainees of armed forces during winter. The costs per unit of F_1 and F_2 are estimated at ₹ 60 and ₹ 50, respectively. One unit of F_1 contains 4 units of carbohydrates and 15 units of fats while one unit of F_2 contains 5 units of carbohydrates and 9 units of fats. Every trainee needs a minimum of 320 units of carbohydrates and 720 units of fats daily. Additional units of fats and/or carbohydrates cause no adverse effects on the health of the trainees. Determine a cost minimizing food-mix that ensures the minimum amounts of nutrients to the trainees everyday.

Representing the information in tabular form on the pattern of Table 19.1, we get Table 19.3, as presented below.

TABLE 19.3 Tabular Presentation of the Diet Problem

Foods \ Ingredients	Fats	Carbohydrates	Cost (₹ per unit)
F_1	15	4	60
F_2	9	5	50
Minimum Requirement	720	320	

Formulating the LPP-model, we get Table 19.4.

TABLE 19.4 LPP-Model of the Cost Minimizing Diet Problem

Minimize: $C = 60x + 50y$	(19.10)
Subject to: $15x + 9y \geq 720$	(19.11)
$4x + 5y \geq 320$	(19.12)
$x, y \geq 0$	(19.13)

Expression (19.10) gives the objective (cost) function which needs to be minimized without violating the structural constraints (19.11) and (19.12) and the non-negativity constraint (19.13) Cost minimizing food mix, as worked out in Section 19.3, comprises $x = \mathbf{18.462}$ **units of** $\mathbf{F_1}$ and $y = \mathbf{49.230}$ **units of** $\mathbf{F_2}$. The minimum cost is ₹ 3569.22 while the trainees get the required minimum of the two ingredients.

Areas of application of LPP-models

Linear programming technique provides solutions to a variety of problems in decision making. Apart from determining profit maximizing product mix and cost minimizing food mix, the technique is of immense utility in transportation problem seeking to minimize the total cost of transporting consignments from different origins to various destinations, exhausting, in the process the capacities of the origins and the requirements of the destinations and in assignment problem seeking to maximize the total production by assigning different machines to different workmen, exhausting, their productive potentials under most economic conditions. Some assignment problems seek minimization of production costs or production periods by matching workmen to appropriate jobs or jobs to appropriate machines. Then, there are problems of determining the cost minimizing advertising-mix comprising audio, video or print media and cost minimizing feed-mix to cattle for desired production of beef, milk, etc. All these and many others may conveniently be solved with the technique to achieve the desired objectives.

Assumptions of LPP-models

The most important assumption of the LPP-models is the **linearity** of the functions involved whether they refer to the objective function or to the constraints. Profit function, cost function, revenue function, production function and the utility function must all be linear according to this assumption. The assumption requires constant coefficients of the variables throughout the model, apart from requiring them in the first degree. For instance, in a product-mix model, constant input costs ensure linearity of constraints and constant product prices ensure linearity of the objective function. Constant returns to scale ensure linearity of constraints while competitive market structure ensures linearity of objective function.

Assumption of linearity of functions in a LPP-model restricts it from admitting non-linear expressions for constraints and objective functions. Problems involving non-linear functions fall within the purview of non-linear programming.

19.1 CONSTRAINED MAXIMIZATION (GRAPHIC METHOD)

Refer to the problem in Table 19.1. Its graphical solution involves plotting the constraints to obtain the possible region of its solution called the **feasible region**. It is the polygon, OABCD (shaded) in Figure 19.1. The figure explains the mechanism of obtaining the optimal solution.

19.2 CONSTRAINED MAXIMIZATION (ALGEBRAIC METHOD)

Algebraic method involves drawing rough graphs of the inequalities and the profit function. There is no need to read off the coordinates of the vertices of the feasible polygon from its graph in this method. Instead, they are found through simultaneous solutions of the equations of the lines intersecting at each vertex. The biggest advantage of the method is that the constraints and the profit functions need not be plotted accurately. A rough sketch can serve the purpose. The other advantages include accuracy of the solution and economy of time. It yields a more accurate solution as the coordinates of the vertices are not read off from the graph, but calculated algebraically. It leads to economy of time as it no longer requies the to-the-scale plot of the functions and inequalities involved or, reading off the coordinates of optimal point accurately from the graph.

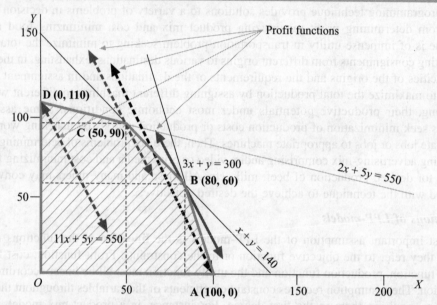

FIGURE 19.1 Equations involved in the three constraints are $3x + y = 300$, $2x + 5y = 550$ and $x + y = 140$. The straight lines represented by them are plotted and labeled accordingly in the figure. The regions bounded by the constraints (inequalities) are the regions below the lines corresponding, represented by the inequalities. The **feasible region** is the region common to all the inequalities in the first quadrant. It is limited to the positive quadrant due to the non-negativity constraints and is shown as the shaded polygon, **OABCD**. Coordinates of its vertices may be found through simultaneous solution of the equations of the lines intersecting each other. They are **O** (0, 0), **A** (100, 0), **B** (80, 60), **C** (50, 90) and **D** (0, 110). These coordinates may also be read off directly from the graph plotted to the scale. Identifying π as the suitable multiples of the LCM of 11 and 5, the coefficients of x and y in the profit function, $\pi = 11x + 5y$ may be plotted as a set of parallel lines passing through each vertex of the feasible region as shown. Profit maximizing product mix corresponds to the vertex lying on the profit line farthest away from the origin. Such a vertex is **B (80, 60)** and the corresponding profit is ₹ 1180 (= $11 \times 80 + 5 \times 60$).

The optimality of the solution is reached by substituting the coordinates of the vertices of the polygon in the objective function to identify the vertex that optimizes it. This gives the optimal product mix. The method is not much different from the graphical method.

To demonstrate, let us solve the problem of Table 19.2 by algebraic method.

A rough sketch of the equations involved in the constraints is shown in Figure 19.2. It gives the feasible region, OABCD. Vertex O is the intersection of $x = 0$ and $y = 0$; vertex

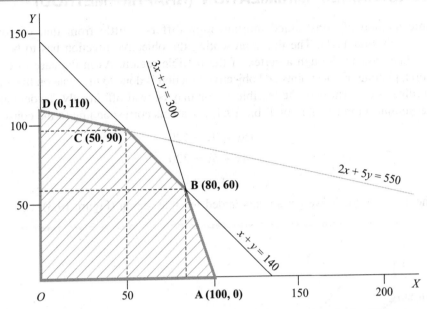

FIGURE 19.2 Rough sketch of the region bounded by the constraints gives the feasible region with vertices O, A, B, C and D. Coordinates of these vertices are found by solving the equations of lines intersecting at each. Substituting them in the profit function, we observe that profit is maximized at **B (80, 60)** and its value is ₹ **1180**.

A is the intersection of $y = 0$ and $3x + y = 300$; vertex B is the intersection of $x + y = 140$ and $3x + y = 300$; vertex C is the intersection of $x + y = 140$ and $2x + 5y = 550$; and, vertex D is the intersection of $x = 0$ and $x + y = 140$. From the simultaneous solution of the equations involved, coordinates of these vertices are (0, 0), (100, 0), (80, 60), (50, 90) and (0, 110), respectively. Substituting them in the profit function, we get the profit maximizing product mix (80, 60) as shown in Table 19.5.

TABLE 19.5 Computation of Profit Maximizing Product Mix

Vertex	x	y	Profit
O	0	0	$11 \times 0 + 5 \times 0 = 0$
A	100	0	$11 \times 100 + 5 \times 0 = 1100$
B	80	60	$11 \times 80 + 5 \times 60 = 1180$
C	50	90	$11 \times 50 + 5 \times 90 = 1000$
D	0	110	$11 \times 0 + 5 \times 110 = 550$

From the table, profit is maximized at B (80, 60). Its value is ₹ **1180**.

The two methods are not very different from each other. Graphic method requires actual and accurate plotting of the constraints and profit function while algebraic method requires algebraic calculations of coordinates of vertices of the feasible region. The optimal product mix is read-off from the graph while the same is computed from equations in the algebraic method.

19.3 CONSTRAINED MINIMIZATION (GRAPHIC METHOD)

The graphic method of constrained minimization differs a little from that of constrained maximization (Section 19.1). The line representing the objective function has to be closest to the origin while passing through a vertex of the feasible region. As in the case of constrained maximization, plotting of constraints and objective function is done to the scale on the graph paper so that coordinates of vertices of the feasible region may be read-off directly. To demonstrate, let us take the minimization problem of Table 19.4. Equations corresponding to the constraints are:

$$15x + 9y = 720$$
$$4x + 5y = 320$$
$$x, y = 0$$

Plotting them on the graph, we get an unbounded feasible region (Figure 19.3).

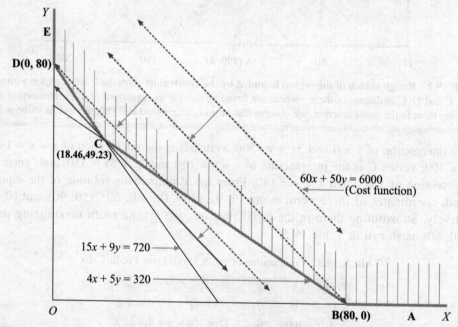

FIGURE 19.3 On plotting the constraints, the feasible region obtained is bounded below but unbounded above: The vertices that bound it below are B, C and D. Their coordinates are (80, 0), (18.46, 49.23) and (0, 80), respectively. Cost function is $60x + 50y = C$. Identifying C as 6000, a multiple of the LCM of 60 and 50, the cost function turns to $60x + 50y = 6000$. Plotting it, we get a cost line passing through point A (100, 0). Sliding it downwards so that it is closest to the origin while passing through a vertex of the feasible region bounded below, we observe that the cost is minimum at the vertex C (18.46, 49.23) which is the optimal food mix. The minimized cost is then ₹ 3569.1.

The cost minimizing product-mix is $x = 18.46$, $y = 49.23$* and the minimum cost, ₹ 3569.1.

---

* When the product–mix involves reading off fractional values of x and y, algebraic method comes handy.

19.4 CONSTRAINED MINIMIZATION (ALGEBRAIC METHOD)

Algebraic method of constrained minimization is much the same as that of constrained maximization. Rough sketches of the constraints are drawn and the coordinates of the intersectional points of any pair of them are determined by solving the corresponding equations, simultaneously. In the problem of Table 19.4, the two structural constraints intersect at C(18.46, 49.23). One of them, namely $4x + 5y = 320$, intersects with $y = 0$ at B (80, 0) and the other one, $15x + 9y = 720$, intersects with $x = 0$ at D (0, 80). Substituting the coordinates of the vertices in the objective function one by one (Table 19.6), we observe that it is minimized at C (18.46, 49.23). Optimal product mix thus, comprises $x =$ **18.46** and $y =$ **49.23** and the minimum cost is ₹ **3569.1** (Figure 19.4).

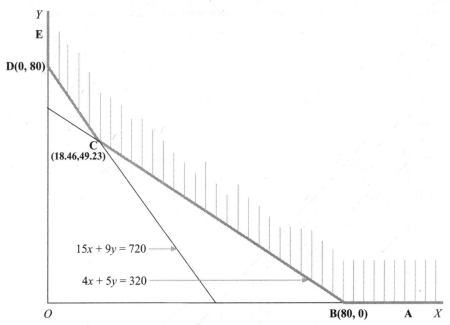

FIGURE 19.4 Algebraic method of constrained minimization problem gives the cost minimizing product mix at the point **C (18.46, 49.23)**. The corresponding value of the minimized cost is ₹ **3569.1**.

Table 19.6 shows calculation of the cost of each vertex.

TABLE 19.6 Computation of Cost Minimizing Product-Mix

Vertex	x	y	Cost
B	80	0	60 × 80 + 50 × 0 = 4800
C	18.46	49.23	60 × 18.46 + 50 × 49.23 = 3569.1
D	0	80	60 × 0 + 50 × 80 = 4000

19.5 ASSORTED APPLICATIONS

In this section, we take up a few applications of graphic and algebraic methods. The purpose is to provide a deeper insight into the utility of LPP technique in a day-to-day decision making.

ILLUSTRATION 19.1: A firm manufactures two types of leather belts. The first, Type A belt is a little superior in quality as compared to the other. It contributes ₹ 20 per piece. The other, Type B belt, is an economy brand contributing ₹ 15 per piece. Each Type A belt requires twice as much time to manufacture as each Type 'B' belt does. If the firm were to manufacture Type B belts only, it would have enough time for as many as 1000 of them per day. Each type of the belt requires 1 unit of leather per piece and the firm has enough of it for 800 pieces of either type per day. Each Type A belt requires a fancy buckle and the firm has at most 400 of them available per day. Each Type B belt requires an ordinary buckle and the firm has at most 700 of it available per day. Formulate the LPP-model and solve it graphically.

Solution:

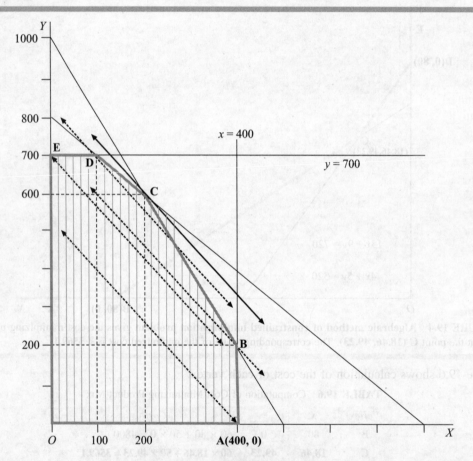

FIGURE 19.5 Constraints when plotted give OABCDE as the feasible region: Coordinates of the vertices can be read off from the graph as (0, 0), (400, 0), (400, 200), (200, 600), (100, 700), (0, 700), respectively. The profit function, $20x + 15y = \pi$, is plotted with $\pi = 6000$. The profit line corresponding to this function is the one that is closest to the origin. It is shifted upwards, parallel to itself, until it is farthest from the origin yet contains a vertex of the feasible region. Such a vertex is C (200, 600). Optimal product mix thus comprises **$x = 200$ and $y = 600$** and the profit earned is **₹ 13,000.**

Let the optimal product mix comprise x belts of Type A and y belts of Type B. The objective is to maximize profit,
$$\pi = 20x + 15y$$
subject to the constraints,
$$2x + y \leq 1000$$
$$x + y \leq 800$$
$$x \leq 400$$
$$y \leq 700$$
$$x, y \geq 0$$

Note that the *first structural constraint* has 2 as the coefficient of x and 1 as that of y. This is so, because each type A belt requires twice as much time to manufacture as each type B does. That way, if the firm has enough time for 1000 type B belts alone (put $x = 0$), it would have enough time for 500 type A belts alone (put $y = 0$). The *second structural constraint* indicates that the maximum number of two types of belts that can be manufactured with given quantity of leather, is 800. The *third* and the *fourth structural constraints* indicate that the number of Type A belts is limited to 400 and that of Type B belts, to 700 due to availability of buckles that is limited. Let us now plot the constraints and the objective function on the graph (Figure 19.5). Reader can try the algebraic method.

ILLUSTRATION 19.2: A manufacturer requires man-hours, machine-hours and cloth-material to produce two types of dresses. Profit per unit from dress 1 is ₹ 160 and that from dress 2 is ₹ 180. The manufacturer has enough man-hours for 60 pieces of dress 1 or 20 pieces of dress 2 or a linear combination of the two per day. Machine-hours, on the other hand, are sufficient enough for 36 pieces of dress 1 or 24 pieces of dress 2 or a linear combination, thereof, per day. Cloth-material available per day, likewise, is sufficient for 30 pieces of either type of dress or a linear combination thereof. Formulate a mathematical model of the problem and solve it graphically.

Solution: The profit function can be expressed, here, as:
$$\pi = 160x + 180y$$

The man-hours constraint is a straight line joining points (60, 0) and (0, 20). From the two-point-form of the equation of straight line, we have:
$$y - y' = \frac{(y'' - y')}{(x'' - x')}(x - x')$$

Treating (60, 0) as (x', y') and (0, 20) as (x'', y'') and substituting, we have:
$$y - 0 = \frac{(20 - 0)}{(0 - 60)} \times (x - 60)$$
$\Rightarrow \qquad 3y = -x + 60$
$\Rightarrow \qquad x + 3y = 60$

The region represented by the constraint must lie below the line. Thus,

$$x + 3y \leq 60.$$

Likewise, machine-hours and cloth-material constraints can be expressed, respectively, as

$$2x + 3y \leq 72, \text{ and}$$
$$x + y \leq 30$$

The mathematical model can now be presented as:

> **Maximize:** $\pi = 160x + 180y$
> **Subject to:** $x + 3y \leq 60$
> $2x + 3y \leq 72$
> $x + y \leq 30$
> $x, y \geq 0$

Plotting the constraints and the profit function on the graph, we have the feasible region and the optimal product mix as in Figure 19.6.

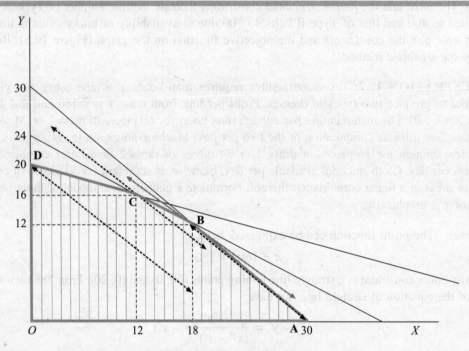

FIGURE 19.6 Feasible region is OABCD: Coordinates of the vertices are A (30, 0), B (18, 12), C (12, 16) and D (0, 20). The profit function passing through point B is farthest from the origin. The optimal **product mix** is $x = 18$ and $y = 12$ and corresponding profit, ₹ 5040.

The profit maximizing product mix under the given resource limitations comprises $x = 18$ and $y = 12$. The reader can try algebraic method as an exercise.

ILLUSTRATION 19.3: A local business firm is planning to advertise a special sale on radio and television. Its weekly advertising budget is ₹ 16,000. A radio commercial costs ₹ 800 per 30 second slot while a television commercial costs ₹ 4000 per 30 second slot. Radio slots can't be bought less than five in number while TV slots available are at the most four per week. Given that a TV slot is 6 times as effective as a radio slot in reaching consumers, how should the firm allocate its advertising budget to attract the largest number of them? How will the optimal solution be affected if availability of the television slots is no longer constrained?

Solution: Let x and y represent the number of radio and television slots, respectively, that should be contracted for maximization of consumer-exposure to the sale. The budget constraint can, therefore, be spelled as

$$800x + 4000y \leq 16000$$

As the number of radio slots has to be atleast 5 and that of television slots, at the most 4, we have to impose additional constraints

$$x \geq 5, \text{ and}$$
$$y \leq 4.$$

If we assume that a radio slot reaches 'n' consumers, the television slot would reach 6 times as many, i.e., $6n$ consumers. The total number of consumers reached, N, can then be expressed as:

$$N = nx + 6ny$$

Dividing both sides by n, we have

$$N/n = x + 6y$$
or,
$$m = x + 6y$$

where, $m = N/n$, which can be defined as the number of radio slots required to reach N consumers. Our purpose can be well served by maximizing 'm' subject to the constraints given.

LPP-model can now be expressed as:

> **Maximize:** $m = x + 6y$
> **Subject to:** $800x + 4000y \leq 16000$
> $x \geq 5$
> $y \leq 4$
> $x, y \geq 0$

When graphed, the model would look like one in Figure 19.7,
The firm should, therefore, go for 5 radio and 3 TV slots only.

If availability of television slots is no longer constrained (that is, when $y \leq 4$ is relaxed), the optimal solution would remain un-affected. In fact the constraint is redundant as evident from the figure.

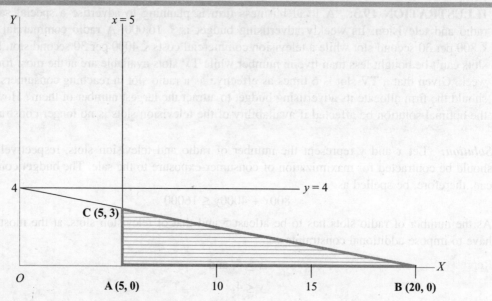

FIGURE 19.7 Employing algebraic method, coordinates of the vertices A, B and C of the feasible region (Δ ABC) are A (5, 0), B (20, 0) and C (5, 3). The vertex maximizing total exposure function ($m = x + 6y$) is C (5, 3) and the corresponding exposure is $m = 5 + 6 \times 3 = 23$.

ILLUSTRATION 19.4: With a view to provide an adequate product exposure to its consumers of high and middle incomes, a firm is planning an advertising campaign through visual and print media. Firm's advertising budget is ₹ 180,000. One spot on TV costs the firm ₹ 20,000 and one spot in print media costs it ₹ 12,000. The firm has decided not to buy more than 12 spots in print media as it has to contract atleast 6 spots on TV. One TV spot reaches 2000 families of high income consumers and 8000 families of middle income consumers while one spot in print media reaches 6000 families of high income consumers and 3000 families of middle income consumers. Assuming that every family reached purchases the firm's product and that a high-income family purchases twice as much as a middle income family, formulate the mathematical model to determine an optimal media mix for maximizing the firm's sales.

Solution: Let the optimal media mix comprise x TV spots and y print media spots. The objective is to maximize the number of buyers. The objective function, therefore, can be expressed as:

$$\text{Maximize: } N = (4000 + 8000)x + (12000 + 3000)y$$
$$= (12000)x + (15000)y$$

[Note that one high income family buys twice as much of it as a middle income family does. That way, as buyers, 2000 high income families exposed to one TV spot are equivalent to 4000 middle income families and 6000 high income families exposed to one print media spot are equivalent to 12,000 middle income families. Total number of families attracted through a TV exposure are, thus, 12000 (= 2 × 2000 + 8000). Likewise, total number of families attracted through a print media exposure are 15000 (= 2 × 6000 + 3000)].

The constraints can be expressed likewise as

$$20{,}000x + 12000y \le 180{,}000$$
$$y \le 12$$
$$x \ge 6$$
$$x, y \ge 0$$

The resulting mathematical model of LPP is

> **Maximize:** $N = (12000)x + (15000)y$
> **Subject to:** $20{,}000x + 12000y \le 180{,}000$
> $y \le 12$
> $x \ge 6$
> $x, y \ge 0$

Representing it graphically, the model would look like that in Figure 19.8.

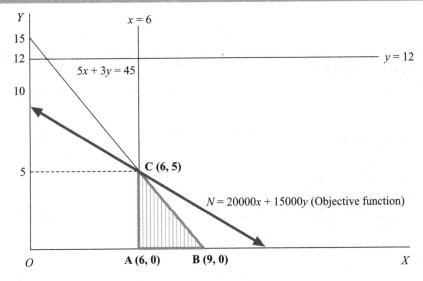

FIGURE 19.8 The feasible region bound by the constraints is ABC: Vertices A, B and C have coordinates (6, 0), (9, 0) and (6, 5). Following the algebraic method, the vertex that maximizes total exposure ($N = 12000x + 15000y$) is C (6, 5) and the maximum exposure is, thus, $N = 12000 \times 6 + 15000 \times 5 = \mathbf{147{,}000}$.

ILLUSTRATION 19.5: A firm employs man-hours M_1; machine hours M_2 and raw materials R_1 and R_2 to manufacture products A and B. The maximum of M_1 and M_2 available are 120 and 270 hours respectively but the minimum of R_1 and R_2 to be bought on the economic grounds are respectively 312 and 168 units. Man and machine hours required and raw-material units needed per unit of products A and B are as given in the following table. Production of none of the two products should exceed 25 units. Formulate the mathematical model and find the optimal product mix.

	Requirements per unit of the product				
	Machine Hours		Raw Materials		
Products	M_1	M_2	R_1	R_2	Profit per unit
A	3	3	13	4	500
B	3	9	8	7	125
Availability	120	270	312	168	

Solution: Let x and y be the quantities of the two products. The LPP-model can be expressed as:

Maximize: $\pi = 500x + 125y$

Subject to: $3x + 3y \leq 120$, or, $x + y \leq 40$

$3x + 9y \leq 270$, or, $x + 3y \leq 90$

$13x + 8y \geq 312$

$4x + 7y \geq 168$

$x \leq 25$

$y \leq 25$

$x, y \geq 0$

Optimal product mix, as worked out in Figure 19.9, comprises $x = 25$ and $y = 15$ and the corresponding profit, ₹ **14,375**.

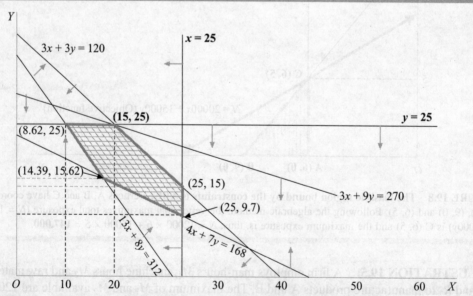

FIGURE 19.9 The feasible region (shaded) has vertices (8.62, 25), (14.39, 15.62), (25, 9.7), (25,15) and (15, 25). At these points, profit function ($\pi = 500x + 125y$) has values 7435, 9247, 13712, **14375** and 10625. Clearly, it is maximized at **(25, 15)** and its maximum value is **14375**.

19.6 THE DUAL PROBLEM

So far, our discussions have clustered around problems involving two variables. What if a problem involves three or more variables? Graphic solutions of such problems are not possible due to the difficulty of plotting constraints and objective functions in three or more dimensional space. To solve such problems, a much easier technique, called **simplex method,** is employed. Before proceeding with this method, let us introduce the concept of the **dual problem first**.

Suppose a firm produces quantities x, y and z of goods, X, Y and Z, employing man-hours (M) and raw material (R). Let input requirements per unit of X, Y and Z, total availability of inputs M and R and contributions per unit of the three products be given as in Table 19.7.

TABLE 19.7 Tabular presentation of the three variable problem

Product	Inputs		Profit/Unit
	M	R	
X	2	1	100
Y	6	5	400
Z	3	5	250
Availability	100	80	

Formulating the model, we have

$$\text{Maximize: } \pi = 100x + 400y + 250z \tag{19.14}$$
$$\text{Subject to: (1) } 2x + 6y + 3z \leq 100 \tag{19.15}$$
$$(2)\ x + 5y + 5z \leq 80 \tag{19.16}$$
$$(3)\ x, y, z \geq 0 \tag{19.17}$$

Clearly, graphical solution to this problem is difficult to visualize. Nevertheless, we can solve the problem graphically if we can transform it into its dual that involves two variables. The essential condition for this is that the number of structural constraints involved in the multivariable problem must be two, so that we may have two variables in its dual. This facilitates plotting constraints and profit function in a two-dimensional space.

To transform the problem into its dual, let us assume that the producer in question decides to lease his running firm to a friend for some time. As per terms, the lessor and the lessee have to reach an agreement on rentals of the productive inputs that must be charged per unit from the lessee so that the total rental cost of the lessee is as low as possible on the one hand and the total rental income of the lessor is at least as high as his current profits on the other. To demonstrate, let the rent per unit of inputs M and R be fixed at ₹ P and ₹ Q, respectively. The total rent on 100 units of M and 80 units of R is, thus, $100P + 80Q$. This must be kept minimum possible to protect the lessee's interest. As a result, the objective must be to minimize the total rental cost of the lessee, that is,

$$\text{Minimize: } C = 100P + 80Q$$

Now coming to the lessor's interest, P and Q fixed must be such that the lessor continues to earn at least ₹ 100 per unit of X, ₹ 400 per unit of Y and ₹ 250 per unit of Z produced from the inputs leased. From Table 19.7, for producing 1 unit of X, 2 units M and 1 unit of R are required. Hence, total rentals from 2 units of $M(2P)$ and 1 unit of $R(Q)$, that is, $2P + Q$, must be greater than or equal to ₹ 100, the magnitude of profit from 1 unit of X. That is,

$$2P + Q \geq 100$$

Likewise, for producing 1 unit of Y, 6 units M and 5 units of R are required. Hence, total rentals from 6 units of $M(6P)$ and 5 units of $R(5Q)$, that is, $6P + 5Q$, must be greater than or equal to ₹ 400, the magnitude of profit from 1 unit of Y. That is,

$$6P + 5Q \geq 400$$

Finally, for producing 1 unit of Z, 3 units of M and 5 units of R are required. Hence, total rentals from 3 units of $M(3P)$ and 5 units of $R(5Q)$, that is, $3P + 5Q$, must be greater than or equal to ₹ 250, the magnitude of profit from 1 unit of Z. That is,

$$3P + 5Q \geq 250$$

As rentals cannot be negative,

$$P, Q \geq 0$$

The model that results from the arrangements can be summarized as:

Minimize: $C = 100P + 80Q$	(19.18)
Subject to: $2P + Q \geq 100$	(19.19)
$6P + 5Q \geq 400$	(19.20)
$3P + 5Q \geq 250$	(19.21)
$P, Q \geq 0$	(19.22)

The former model [Expressions (19.14) through (19.17)] is called the **primal** while the latter [Expressions (19.18) through (19.22)], its **dual**.

A comparison of the primal with its dual leads to the following observations:

1. The maximization problem of primal transforms into one of the minimization in its dual.
2. The number of unknowns in the primal is three (x, y, z), which reduces to two (P, Q) in its dual.
3. The number of constraints in the primal is two, which is the same as the number of variables in its dual and the number of constraints in the dual is the same as the number of variables in the primal.
4. The stocks of inputs [100 and 80] that appear in the constraints of the primal, now appear as the coefficients of variables in the objective function of the dual and the coefficients of the variables in the objective function of the primal now appear as the stocks in the constraints of the dual.
5. The coefficients of the variables x, y, z in constraints (19.15) and (19.16) of the primal appear in that order as the coefficients of variables P and Q, respectively in the three constraints of the dual.
6. The '$\leq$' constraints of the primal change to '$\geq$' constraints of the dual.

These observations can help the reader to convert a maximization problem (primal) straight away into one of the minimization (dual) and vice-versa. The original problem, whether maximization problem or a minimization problem, is referred to as a **primal problem** while that obtained from its transformation, whether a maximization or a minimization problem, is referred to as its **dual problem**.

The solution of the *primal* in this case is *not possible* through graphic method but that of its *dual*, evidently is. It has been worked out in Figure 19.10. The rent of 1 unit of input M so determined is ₹ 25 and that of 1 unit of R, is ₹ 50. The corresponding total rental cost for the lessee is ₹ 6500.

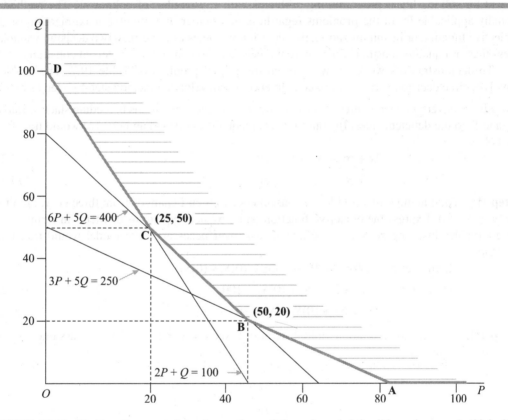

FIGURE 19.10 Plotting the constraints, the vertices of the unbounded feasible region are A (83.3, 0), B (50, 20), **C (25, 50)** and D (0, 100). Substituting their coordinates in the cost function (C = 100P + 80Q), we observe that the respective costs are 8330; 6600; **6500**; and 8000. Cost is, thus, minimized at **C (25, 50)**. It is **6500**. *The optimal product mix, therefore, is P = 25 and Q = 50.*

Inputs have, thus, been put to an alternative use by the owner (lessor) of the firm without adversely affecting his profits. The opportunity costs of the inputs here are ₹ 25 and ₹ 50 per unit of inputs M and R, respectively. They are better known as the **shadow prices** of the inputs.

While undertaking production himself, the lessor was entitled to profits of ₹ 100 per unit on X, ₹ 400 per unit on Y and ₹ 250 per unit on Z. Leasing the inputs required for producing one unit of each amounts to rental incomes of ₹ 100 ($2P + Q = 2 \times 25 + 50$), ₹ 400 ($6P + 5Q = 6 \times$

25 + 5 × 50) and ₹ 325 (3P + 5Q = 3 × 25 + 5 × 50) to the lessor. A simple comparison shows that the lessor is earning an excess profit of ₹ 75 (325 – 250) from leasing the input units (3 units of M and 5 units of R) required for producing one unit of Z. Leasing, therefore, appears a better option than self production. Doesn't it? To see, let us wait until we solve primal problem by **simplex method**.

19.7 THE SIMPLEX METHOD

Developed by George B. Dantzig in 1957, the simplex method is an iterative mathematical process meant for solving linear programming problems with any number of unknowns. The method is equally applicable to all the problems regardless of whether they involve maximization of the objective function or its minimization, two decision variables or more than two decision variables, 'less than or equal to constraints' or 'more than or equal to constraints' or mixed constraints.

To demonstrate its working, we take up the primal problem of Table 19.7. The problem involves three decision variables. For convenience, we develop the method step-by-step as below:

Step I: Convert the inequalities in the constraints into linear equations by adding slack variables S_1 and S_2 to the deficient sides. In consequence, inequalities (19.15) and (19.16) would transform as below

$$2x + 6y + 3z + S_1 = 100 \tag{19.23}$$

$$x + 5y + 5z + S_2 = 80 \tag{19.24}$$

Step II: Total number of variables in consequence to Step I changes from three (x, y, z) to five (x, y, z, S_1, S_2). Express the objective function and the linear equations of Step I in terms of the five variables inserting zero as a coefficient, wherever necessary. The model would transform as below

$$\text{Maximize: } \pi = 100x + 400y + 250z + (0)S_1 + (0)S_2 \tag{19.25}$$

$$\text{Subject to: } 2x + 6y + 3z + S_1 + (0)S_2 = 100 \tag{19.26}$$

$$x + 5y + 5z + (0)S_1 + S_2 = 80 \tag{19.27}$$

Step III: As an initial solution (initial iteration), set $x = y = z = 0$. That is, assume that the firm is kept idle. Then,

$$\pi = 0$$
$$S_1 = 100$$
$$S_2 = 80$$

Evidently when the firm is kept idle, profit earned is zero and the outputs are $S_1 = 100$ and $S_2 = 80$. Their contribution to the firm's profits is zero. Representing the initial iteration in the tabular form, the table we get would look like Table 19.8.

The second iteration is shown in Tableau 2 (Table 19.9). Entries in the 6th row, labeled Z_j, represent unit profits 80, 400, 400, 0, 80 contributed by the decision variables $(x, y, z, S_1$ and $S_2)$ at the rates 0 and 400 corresponding to the programme variables S_1 and y. The last row labeled $C_j - Z_j$ lists the opportunity cost of not including the decision variables in the current programme. Some of the entries in the opportunity cost row being greater than or equal to zero, another revision is called for. The column corresponding to the entry with the highest positive opportunity cost (20) in the

$C_j - Z_j$ row gives the *key column* and the entries in the last column labelled 'ratio' column give the ratios of quantities in the 'Qty' column to the corresponding entries in the key column. The least non-negative value of these ratios is 5 and hence the *key row* is the S_1 row corresponding to 5 this time. The intersectional element, 0.8, is the *key element* in the second iteration.

TABLE 19.8 **Initial iteration:** C_j represents contribution to profit made by one unit of the jth product. In the top row, entries 100, 400, 250, 0, 0 represent contributions made by one unit of the decision variables x, y, z, S_1 and S_2, respectively. In the extreme left column, entries under C_j represent contributions (0, 0) made by programme variables S_1 and S_2. Variables in the Product Mix (PM) row are decision variables (x, y, z, S_1 and S_2) and those in the product-mix column are programme variables S_1 and S_2. Entries in the quantity (Qty) column represent quantities of programme variables (S_1 and S_2). Entries in 4th and 5th rows represent coefficients of decision variables (x, y, z, S_1 and S_2) in Eqs. (19.26) and (19.27). Entries in 6th row, labeled Z_j, represents unit profits (0, 0, 0, 0, 0) contributed by the decision variables (x, y, z, S_1 and S_2) at the rates (0, 0) in C_j column for the programme variables, S_1 and S_2. The last row, labeled $C_j - Z_j$, lists the opportunity cost of not including the corresponding decision variables x, y, z, S_1 or S_2 in the current programme. As some of the entries in this row are greater than or equal to zero, the initial solution (initial iteration) is non-optimal, needing a revision. The process of revision, therefore, is initiated by locating the column corresponding to the highest positive opportunity cost in the $C_j - Z_j$ row. It is 400, which belongs to the '*y*-column'. This gives the **key column**. Entries in this column corresponding to the programme variables (S_1 and S_2) are 6 and 5, which are used to divide the corresponding entries in the 'Qty' column to obtain entries 16.67 and 16 in the 'ratio' column. The smallest non-negative entry, 16, in the 'ratio' column gives the **key row**. It is the row labelled S_2. Programme variable S_2 is, therefore, to be replaced along with its contribution, 0, by the decision variable y along with its contribution, 400. As the next step, key row is replaced by one obtained by dividing the existing key row by 5, the **key element**, also called the **pivotal element**. It is located at the intersection of the key row and the key column. The revised key row now has entries 400, y, 16, 0.20, 1, 1, 0, and 0.2. To complete the revision, all other rows also need replacement. Entries in the other rows are replaced by the difference of the existing entries over those obtained by dividing by the key number the product of the corresponding entries in the key row and the key column. There is only one other row, labeled as the S_1-row, in this problem. Each new entry in this row is obtained by the formula (19.28):

$$\text{Revised Entry} = \text{Existing Entry} - \frac{\left\{\begin{array}{c}\text{Corresponding number}\\ \text{in the key row}\end{array}\right\} \times \left\{\begin{array}{c}\text{Corresponding number}\\ \text{in the key column}\end{array}\right\}}{\text{Key Number}} \quad (19.28)$$

To demonstrate, 100 would be replaced by 4 [= 100 − (80 × 6)/5]; 2 by 0.8 [= 2 − (1 × 6)/5]; 6 by 0 [= 6 − (6 × 5)/5]; 3 by −3 [= 3 − (5 × 6)/5]; 1 by 1 [= 1 − (0 × 6)/5] and 0 by −1.2 [= 0 − (1 × 6)/5]. Thus, the numbers in the revised row are 4, 0.8, 0, −3, 1, and −1.2. They appear as shown in the 4th row of the revised table (Table 19.9).

			Initial iteration—Tableau: 1					
C_j →			100	400	250	0	0	
	PM →		x	y	z	S_1	S_2	
		Qty ↓						Ratio
0	S_1	100	2	6	3	1	0	16.67
0	S_2	80	1	5	5	0	1	16.00 ← Key row
		Z_j	0	0	0	0	0	
		$C_j - Z_j$	100	400 ↑ Key column	250	0	0	

TABLE 19.9 Second iteration: The revised rows (4th and 5th rows) of Table 19.8 appear respectively as 0, S_1, 4, 0.8, 0, −3, 1 and −1.2 and 400, y, 16, 0.2, 1, 1, 0 and 0.2. The Z_j row works out as 80, 400, 400, 0 and 80 and the $C_j − Z_j$ as 20, 0, −150, 0, and −80. The largest positive opportunity cost is 20. This gives the key column as indicated. Key row is the 4th row with least non-negative ratio, 5. The ratios are calculated as 4/0.8 (=5) and 16/0.2 (= 80). Key number is the intersectional number 0.8. As the opportunity cost row ($C_j − Z_j$) contains at least one non-negative non-zero value, the solution is not optimal and further iterations are needed. The table after revision of the rows is presented in Table 19.10 for the purpose.

C_j →			100	400	250	0	0	
	PM →		x	y	z	S_1	S_2	
		Qty						Ratio
0	S_1	4	0.8	0	−3	1	−1.2	5.0 ← Key row
400	y	16	0.2	1	1	0	0.2	80.00
		Z_j	80	400	400	0	80	
		$C_j − Z_j$	20	0	−150	0	−80	
			↑ Key column					

Third iteration (Table 19.10) provides the solution of the problem. The product mix that maximizes the profit comprises $x = 5$, $y = 15$, $z = 0$. Corresponding profit is ₹ **6500**.

As evident from the table (Table 19.10), solution of the dual (Expressions 19.18 through 19.22) can also be read off from the solution of its primal. Inverting the signs of the entries in columns labeled S_1 and S_2 in the opportunity cost row, we get 25 and 50 which provide values of P and Q involved in the dual. That is, $P = 25$ and $Q = 50$. The solution is exactly the same as that obtained by the graphical method of the dual in Figure 19.10. The lessor must therefore, charge a rent of ₹ 25 per unit of M and ₹ 50 per unit of R so that the rental cost of the lessee may be least possible and the rental revenue for the lessor may be at least as much as the lessor himself earned through self production. The corresponding rental cost for the lessee works out at ₹ 6500 (= 100 × 25 + 80 × 50) and the profit earned by the lessor through self production also works out as ₹ 6500 (= 100 × 5 + 400 × 15 + 250 × 0).

Now let us try to answer the question posed at the end of Section 19.6. The answer was reserved until the solution of the primal. Which is better for the owner–leasing or self-production? Leasing appeared a better option in Section 19.6 because a unit of Z appeared to contribute ₹ 325 through leasing instead of ₹ 250 through self-production, all else remaining the same. Now that the solution of the primal is before us, can we say that again? Evidently not. The solution reveals that the profit maximizing producer must not produce Z at all! At the same time, it also reveals that the maximized profit is no better than the rental revenue realized from leasing. What we can infer from this is that leasing is as good as self-production. It is neither better nor worse. Even otherwise we should bear in mind that the dual is formulated on the theoretical premise that the rental income from leasing must be at least as much as the maximized profits of the owner from self-production but the same must be subject to the condition that the rental cost of the lessee is minimum possible. This ensures that owner's maximized profits cannot exceed his rental receipts from leasing.

TABLE 19.10 **Third iteration:** Following the procedure, the revised solution works out as $x = 5$ and $y = 15$. Z_j and $C_j - Z_j$ are calculated following the same procedure to see if the $C_j - Z_j$ row contains any positive non-zero opportunity costs. Since, all the values of the opportunity cost row are either zero or negative, we have reached an optimal solution. Since Z does not appear in the PM column, it does not form a part of the solution. Maximized profit can be seen to be $\pi = 100 \times 5 + 400 \times 15 =$ **6500**. Observe the entries in $C_j - Z_j$ row under S_1 and S_2. They are -25 and -50. Inverting signs, we get 25 and 50 serving as a solution of the dual. Thus, $P = 25$ and $Q = 50$ comprise the solution of the dual. Refer to the graphic solution of the dual of this problem (Figure 19.10).

Third iteration—Tableau: 3

$C_j \rightarrow$			100	400	250	0	0	
	PM $\rightarrow$		x	y	z	S_1	S_2	
		Qty						Ratio
100	x	5	1	0	-3.75	1.25	-1.5	
400	y	15	0	1	1.75	-0.25	0.5	
		Z_j	100	400	325	25	50	
		$C_j - Z_j$	0	0	-75	-25	-50	

Thus, solution of a primal provides solution of its dual and solution of dual provides that of its primal. To demonstrate the latter point, let us work out solution of the dual as well through the simplex method.

Before that, one point needs clarification. Expressions 'primal' and 'dual' are interchangeable. That is, it is not necessary to use the term 'primal' for the maximization case and 'dual' for the minimization case. The one that is initially formulated is the primal problem and the other derived from it is the dual problem. Alternatively, if one is labelled as the primal problem the other should be labelled as its dual. Also, while variables $S_1, S_2, \ldots S_n$, called **slack variables**, are added on the deficient side of the inequalities with '$\leq$' signs in the structural constraints, the same are subtracted from the surplus sides of the inequalities with '$\geq$' signs and are called **surplus variables**.

To solve the dual [Eqs. (19.18) through (19.22)], we need to transform its 'greater than or equal to' inequalities into equations. This requires subtracting surplus variables from the surplus sides. Rewriting the constraints with surplus variables, we have

$$2P + Q - S_1 = 100$$
$$6P + 5Q - S_2 = 400$$
$$3P + 5Q - S_3 = 250$$

In the initial iteration, as soon as we set decision variables at zero, each of S_1, S_2 and S_3 assumes a negative value. To prevent this, artificial variables A_1, A_2 and A_3 are added, respectively to the three constraints on the left side of each, as shown below:

$$2P + Q - S_1 + A_1 = 100$$

$$6P + 5Q - S_2 + A_2 = 400$$
$$3P + 5Q - S_3 + A_3 = 250$$

A_1, A_2 and A_3 have to enter the objective function just as S_1, S_2 and S_3 have. However, unlike S_1, S_2 and S_3 which enter with zero coefficients, A_1, A_2 and A_3 appear in it with a high unit cost, M, each. The purpose is to involve high costs in the initial iteration to necessitate its revision subsequently. There is yet another reason for this. A high value of M ensures absence of A_1, A_2 and A_3 in the final solution. Recasting the dual model with S_1, S_2, S_3, A_1, A_2 and A_3 we have

Minimize: $C = 100P + 80Q + 0 \cdot S_1 + 0 \cdot S_2 + 0 \cdot S_3 + M \cdot A_1 + M \cdot A_2 + M \cdot A_3$
Subject to: $2P + Q - S_1 + 0 \cdot S_2 + 0 \cdot S_3 + A_1 + 0 \cdot A_2 + 0 \cdot A_3 = 100$
$6P + 5Q + 0 \cdot S_1 - S_2 + 0 \cdot S_3 + 0 \cdot A_1 + A_2 + 0 \cdot A_3 = 400$
$3P + 5Q + 0 \cdot S_1 + 0 \cdot S_2 - S_3 + 0 \cdot A_1 + 0 \cdot A_2 + A_3 = 250$
$P, Q \geq 0$

To work out the solution of the dual by simplex method, let us start with initial iteration with $P = Q = 0 = S_1 = S_2 = S_3$ (Table 19.11).

TABLE 19.11 Initial iteration: Entries in the Z_j row have been calculated at the rate of the contribution M made by each unit of A_1, A_2 and A_3. The entries are $(2 + 6 + 3)M$, $(1 + 5 + 5)M$, ..., $(0 + 0 + 1)M$, that is, $11M, 11M, -M, -M, -M, M, M$ and M. Accordingly, entries in $C_j - Z_j$ row are worked out as shown. Unlike the case with a maximization problem, entries in $C_j - Z_j$ row of a minimization problem have all to be positive or zero for optimality of the solution. In the present problem, $100 - 11M$ and $80 - 11M$ are both negative by virtue of our assumption of large M. Initial solution, therefore, is non-optimal needing further revision. Again, unlike the case with a maximization problem, key column of a minimization problem corresponds to the largest negative number in the opportunity cost row. Accordingly, key column corresponds to $80 - 11M$. To locate the key row, we choose the smallest non-negative value from the ratio column just as we do in the case of a maximization problem. This being 50, the key row is also located and so is the key element at the intersection of the key row and the key column. It is 5. The table is thus, revised for subsequent iteration following the process of Table 19.8 and the resulting solution is shown in Table 19.12.

First iteration—Tableau: 1

	$C_j \rightarrow$		100	80	0	0	0	M	M	M	
	PM $\rightarrow$	Qty	P	Q	S_1	S_2	S_3	A_1	A_2	A_3	Ratio
M	A_1	100	2	1	−1	0	0	1	0	0	100
M	A_2	400	6	5	0	−1	0	0	1	0	80
M	A_3	250	3	5	0	0	−1	0	0	1	← 50 Key row
	Z_j		11M	11M	−M	−M	−M	M	M	M	
	$C_j - Z_j$		100 − 11M	80 − 11M	M	M	M	0	0	0	

↑ Key column

TABLE 19.12 Second iteration: Z_j and $C_j - Z_j$ are again computed as shown. Since values in the opportunity cost row are not all zero or positive, key row and key column are again ascertained as shown to determine the key element for subsequent revision of the solution. The revised table is as shown in Table 19.13.

Second iteration—Tableau: 2

C_j			100	80	0	0	0	M	M	M	
	PM	Qty	P	Q	S_1	S_2	S_3	A_1	A_2	A_3	Ratio
M	A_1	50	1.4	0	–1	0	0.2	1	0	–0.2	←250/7 Key-row
M	A_2	150	3	0	0	–1	1	0	1	–1	50
80	Q	50	0.6	1	0	0	–0.2	0	0	0.2	250/3
		Z_j	$48 + 4.4M$	80	$-M$	$-M$	$-16 + 1.2M$	M	M	$16 - 1.2M$	
		$C_j - Z_j$	$52 - 4.4M$	0	M	M	$16 - 1.2M$	0	0	$-16 + 2.2M$	

↑ Key column

TABLE 19.13 Third iteration: Z_j and $C_j - Z_j$ are again computed to ensure the optimality of the solution. As the opportunity cost row still contains some non-zero non-positive values, key row and key columns are again located and the key element is again determined for subsequent iterations. The solution is revised following the procedure of Table 19.8 and the resulting solution is as shown in Table 19.14.

Third iteration—Tableau: 3

C_j			100	80	0	0	0	M	M	M	
	PM	Qty	P	Q	S_1	S_2	S_3	A_1	A_2	A_3	Ratio
100	P	250/7	1	0	–5/7	0	1/7	5/7	0	–1/7	–50
M	A_2	300/7	0	0	15/7	–1	4/7	–15/7	1	–4/7	←20 Key row
80	Q	200/7	0	1	3/7	0	–2/7	–3/7	0	2/7	200/3
		Z_j	100	80	$(-260 + 15M)/7$	$-M$	$(-60 + 4M)/7$	$(260 - 15M)/7$	M	$(60 - 4M)/7$	
		$C_j - Z_j$	0	0	$(260 - 15M)/7$	M	$(60 - 4M)/7$	$(-260 + 22M)/7$	0	$(-140 + 11M)/7$	

↑ Key column

TABLE 19.14 **Fourth iteration:** Z_j and $C_j - Z_j$ are again computed to ensure the optimality of the solution. As the opportunity cost row still contains some non-zero non-positive values, key row and key columns are again located and key element is again determined for subsequent iterations. The solution is revised following the procedure of Table 19.8 and the result is shown in Table 19.15.

Fourth iteration—Tableau: 4

C_j			100	80	0	0	0	M	M	M	
	PM		P	Q	S_1	S_2	S_3	A_1	A_2	A_3	Ratio
		Qty									
100	P	50	1	0	0	−1/3	1/3	0	1/3	−1/3	150
0	S_1	20	0	0	1	−7/15	4/15	−1	7/15	−4/15	Key row ← 75
80	Q	20	0	1	0	1/5	−2/5	0	−1/5	2/5	−50
	Z_j		100	80	0	−52/3	4/3	0	52/3	−4/3	
	$C_j - Z_j$		0	0	0	52/3	−4/3	M	$M - 52/3$	$M + 4/3$	

Key column ↑

TABLE 19.15 **Fifth iteration:** Z_j and $C_j - Z_j$ are again computed to ensure the optimality of the solution. This time, the opportunity cost row contains no negative values. This shows that the optimal solution is reached and no further revision is called for. The optimal product mix comprises $P = 25$ and $Q = 50$. Just as the solution of the primal problem provided the solution of its dual, the solution of the dual (this solution) also provides the solution of its primal. The opportunity cost row contains entries **5, 15** and **0** under the columns S_1, S_2 and S_3. They give values of decision variables x, y and z of the primal problem. The biggest advantage of the simplex method, apart from its utility in solving multi-dimensional problems, is that the solution of the maximization problem gives the solution of the minimization problem and that of the minimization problem gives the solution of the maximization problem.

Fifth iteration—Tableau: 5

C_j			100	80	0	0	0	M	M	M	
	PM		P	Q	S_1	S_2	S_3	A_1	A_2	A_3	Ratio
		Qty									
100	P	25	1	0	−5/4	1/4	0	5/4	−1/4	0	
0	S_3	75	0	0	15/4	−7/4	1	−15/4	7/4	−1	
80	Q	50	0	1	3/2	−1/2	0	−3/2	1/2	0	
	Z_j		100	80	−5	−15	0	5	15	0	
	$C_j - Z_j$		0	0	5	15	0	$M - 5$	$M - 15$	M	

From the solutions of the primal and the dual problems by simplex method in this section, the following observations emerge:

1. If the maximization problem is treated as the primal problem, its minimization version is its dual and if the minimization problem is treated as the primal problem, its maximization version is its dual.
2. The solution of the primal problem by simplex method provides that of its dual as well and that of dual problem provides the solution of its primal problem as well.
3. In maximization problem, key column is the column corresponding to the largest positive value in the opportunity cost row while in the minimization problem, key column is the column corresponding to the largest negative value in the opportunity cost row.
4. The optimality of the solution in the maximization problem requires non-positive values in the opportunity cost row while that in the minimization problem, requires non-negative values in it.

Values in the opportunity cost row under the $S_1, S_2, S_3, ..., S_n$ columns in any simplex solution provide the solution of the corresponding dual problem.

A Maximization Case with Constraints '$\geq$', '=', and '$\leq$'

Many LP problems involve mixed constraints with '$\leq$', '$\geq$' and '=' signs. To demonstrate, let us consider the problem:

$$\text{Maximize: } \pi = 10x + 12y$$
$$\text{Subject to: } 2x + 2y = 10$$
$$x \geq 2$$
$$y \leq 4$$
$$x, y \geq 0$$

Graphical solution does not pose any problem here. Solution by simplex method, however, requires a little different treatment of the constraints. Using slack variables in '$\leq$' constraints, surplus and artificial variables in '$\geq$' constraints and artificial variables alone in '=' constraints, we can recast the model with '$-M$' (M being large) as the contribution of artificial variables in the objective function, as:

$$\text{Maximize: } \pi = 10x + 12y + 0S_1 + 0S_2 - MA_1 - MA_2$$
$$\text{Subject to: } 2x + 2y + 0S_1 + 0S_2 + A_1 + 0A_2 = 10$$
$$x - S_1 + 0S_2 + 0A_1 + A_2 = 2$$
$$y + 0S_1 + S_2 + 0A_1 + 0A_2 = 4$$
$$x, y \geq 0$$

Note that coefficients of artificial variables in the objective function are negative. This is so because of the maximization character of the problem. Had it been a minimization problem, the signs would have been positive as in case of the simplex solution (Tables 19.11 to 19.15) of dual problem [Equations (19.18) to (19.22)].

With this transformation of the model, the simplex method yields a solution $x = 2$ and $y = 3$. The case being a maximization case, the key column in each iteration would be the column corresponding to the largest positive value in the opportunity cost row. The reader may try the solution as an exercise (Q. 33 in the Exercise).

A Minimization Case with Constraints '$\geq$', '=', and '$\leq$'

Consider the problem

$$\text{Minimize: } C = 8x + 10y + 11z$$
$$\text{Subject to: } 2x + 2y + 2z = 20{,}000$$
$$x \leq 3{,}000$$
$$y \geq 1{,}500$$
$$z \geq 2000$$
$$x, y, z \geq 0$$

Restating the model with slack, surplus and artificial variables, we have:

$$\text{Minimize: } C = 8x + 10y + 11z + 0S_1 + 0S_2 + 0S_3 + M \cdot A_1 + M \cdot A_2 + M \cdot A_3$$
$$\text{Subject to: } 2x + 2y + 2z + 0S_1 + 0S_2 + 0S_3 + A_1 + 0 \cdot A_2 + 0 \cdot A_3 = 20{,}000$$
$$x + S_1 + 0S_2 + 0S_3 + 0 \cdot A_1 + 0 \cdot A_2 + 0 \cdot A_3 = 3{,}000$$
$$y + 0S_1 - S_2 + 0S_3 + 0 \cdot A_1 + A_2 + 0 \cdot A_3 = 1{,}500$$
$$z + 0S_1 + 0S_2 - S_3 + 0 \cdot A_1 + 0 \cdot A_2 + A_3 = 2000$$
$$x, y, z \geq 0$$

Note that the coefficients of the artificial variables in the objective function are positive for a minimization problem. With this transformation of the model, the simplex method yields a solution $x = 3{,}000$, $y = 5{,}000$ and $z = 2000$ (Q. 34 in the Exercise).

19.8 PROBLEM OF DEGENERACY IN LINEAR PROGRAMMING

While solving a linear programming problem through simplex method, one may encounter one or more zeroes in the quantity column or may come across two or more identical ratios in the ratio-column while selecting the key row. In the first case, it becomes difficult to continue with the iterative process for revision as the variable to be replaced is already zero. In the second case, a 'tie' emerges in between rows in terms of selection of the key row (Table 19.16). Both these situations give rise to a phenomenon called **degeneracy**. The problem of degeneracy in the second case can be tackled through arbitrary choice of any one of the tied rows as the key row. To demonstrate, let us consider the following model:

$$\text{Maximize: } \pi = 10x + 3y + 4z$$
$$\text{Subject to: } 8x + 2y + 3z \leq 200$$
$$8x + 6y + 0 \cdot z \leq 300$$
$$4x + 0 \cdot y + 2z \leq 100$$
$$x, y, z \geq 0$$

Employing the slack variables, the model can be expressed as:

$$\text{Maximize: } \pi = 10x + 3y + 4z + 0S_1 + 0S_2 + 0S_3$$
$$\text{Subject to: } 8x + 2y + 3z + S_1 + 0S_2 + 0S_3 = 200$$

$$8x + 6y + 0z + 0S_1 + S_2 + 0S_3 = 300$$
$$4x + 0y + 2z + 0S_1 + 0S_2 + S_3 = 100$$
$$x, y, z \geq 0$$

The initial iteration appears as in Table 19.16.

TABLE 19.16 Initial iteration: First and third rows are tied rows. Selecting any one of the two as the key row, we can proceed with the successive iterations. We choose the first row at random and continue.

Initial iteration—Tableau: 1

C_j →			10	3	4	0	0	0		
	PM →		x	y	z	S_1	S_2	S_3		
		Qty ↓							Ratio	
0	S_1	200	8	2	3	1	0	0	25	←
0	S_2	300	8	6	0	0	1	0	37.5	Tied rows
0	S_3	100	4	0	2	0	0	1	25	←
		Z_j	0	0	0	0	0	0		
		$C_j - Z_j$	10	3	4	0	0	0		

Key column

Subsequent iterations that follow (Tables 19.17 to 19.19) demonstrate the process of finding solutions to the degenerate problem in question.

TABLE 19.17 Second iteration: The quantity column contains a zero. The largest positive value in the opportunity cost row is ½. One of the ratios obtained is zero. While selecting the least positive ratio, it can be ignored on the grounds that it bears a negative sign. The least positive ratio, therefore, may be taken as 25. Key element, thus, is 4.

C_j →			10	3	4	0	0	0	
	PM →		x	y	z	S_1	S_2	S_3	
		Qty ↓							Ratio
10	x	25	1	1/4	3/8	1/8	0	0	100
0	S_2	100	0	4	−3	−1	1	0	← 25 Key row
0	S_3	0	0	−1	1/2	−1/2	0	1	−0
		Z_j	10	5/2	15/4	5/4	0	0	
		$C_j - Z_j$	0	1/2	1/4	−5/4	0	0	

Key column

TABLE 19.18 Third iteration: Existence of a positive value in the opportunity cost in the $C_j - Z_j$ row calls for further revision.

Third iteration—Tableau: 3

C_j →			10	3	4	0	0	0	
PM →			x	y	z	S_1	S_2	S_3	
		Qty ↓							Ratio
10	x	75/4	1	0	9/16	3/16	−1/16	0	← 100/3 Key row
3	y	25	0	1	−3/4	−1/4	1/4	0	−100/3
0	S_3	25	0	0	−1/4	−3/4	1/4	1	−100
		Z_j	10	3	27/8	9/8	1/8	0	
		$C_j - Z_j$	0	0	5/8	−9/8	−1/8	0	

Key column

TABLE 19.19 Fourth iteration: Opportunity cost row containing negative or zero values, the optimal solution is reached. No further iterations are called for. The optimal product mix consists of $x = 0$, $y = 50$, and $z = 100/3$. Had we chosen the other row as the key row in the initial iteration, we would have reached at the same solution.

Fourth iteration—Tableau: 4

C_j →			10	3	4	0	0	0	
PM →			x	y	z	S_1	S_2	S_3	
		Qty ↓							Ratio
4	z	100/3	16/9	0	1	1/3	−1/9	0	
3	y	50	4/3	1	0	−1/6	1/6	0	
0	S_3	100/3	4/9	0	0	−2/3	2/9	1	
		Z_j	100/9	3	4	5/6	1/18	0	
		$C_j - Z_j$	−100/9	0	0	−5/6	−1/18	0	

Key column

Such problems may arise even in the graphic method of solution. When more than two constraint lines, when graphed, pass through the same vertex of the feasible region, the problem of degeneracy is said to arise in the graphic method. To demonstrate, let us consider the situations graphed in Figures 19.11(a) and (b). Expressions such as basic or non-basic solutions, feasible and infeasible solutions, basic but infeasible solutions, non-basic but feasible solutions and optimal basic feasible solution appearing in the description of these figures are defined in the beginning of the next section.

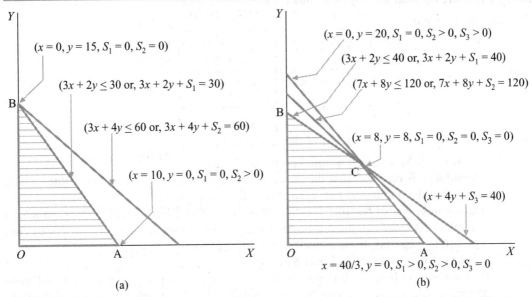

FIGURE 19.11 In the left panel, (a), three constraints ($x > 0$, $3x + 2y \leq 30$, and $3x + 4y \leq 60$) meet at point B. Clearly, $x = 0$, $y = 15$ and $S_1 = 0$, $S_2 = 0$ at this point. The number of non-zero-valued variables is one which is less than the number of the structural constraints. Point B is, thus, a degenerate extreme point, leading to a non-basic solution. On the other hand, point A provides a basic solution because the number of the non-zero-valued variables (whether slack or structural) is exactly equal to the number of constraints in the model. Even point O ($x = 0$, $y = 0$, $S_1 > 0$ and $S_2 > 0$) provides a basic solution as the number of structural constraints is exactly equal to the number of the non-zero-valued variables. Point B is the only degenerate extreme point in the feasible region, OAB. In the right panel, (b), the number of constraints is three. When graphed, they all pass through the vertex, C ($x = 8$, $y = 8$, $S_1 = 0$, $S_2 = 0$, $S_3 = 0$). The number of the non-zero-valued variables is 2 which is less than the number of the constraints in the model. The solution at point C is, thus, non-basic and hence, the point is a degenerate extreme point. At all other vertices of the feasible region (OACB), the number of non-zero-valued variables is just equal to the number of the structural constraints in the model. Even at point O ($x = 0$, $y = 0$, $S_1 > 0$, $S_2 > 0$ and $S_3 > 0$), the solution is basic. Hence, the solution at each of these vertices, O, A, and B, is basic. Point C is the only degenerate extreme point.

The problem of degeneracy in all such cases of graphic solution can be dealt with by introducing a tiny artificial variable into one of the constraints so that the constraint line does not exactly pass through the point of intersection of the other constraints.

Analysis of degeneracy calls for an understanding of basic and non-basic solutions. In the process, we come across a few more cases that need clarity at this point. Let us take them up in the next section.

19.9 SPECIAL CASES

In this section, we will discuss some special types of solutions, such as, feasible and infeasible solutions, basic and non-basic solutions, optimal and non-optimal solutions, bounded and unbounded solutions, and multiple and unique solutions, etc.

Basic, Feasible, Optimal and Optimal Basic Feasible Solutions

Consider the problem

$$\text{Maximize: } \pi = 2x + 4y + 0 \cdot S_1 + 0 \cdot S_2 + 0 \cdot S_3$$
$$\text{Subject to: } x + 4y + S_1 + 0 \cdot S_2 + 0 \cdot S_3 = 24$$
$$3x + y + 0 \cdot S_1 + S_2 + 0 \cdot S_3 = 21$$
$$x + y + 0 \cdot S_1 + 0 \cdot S_2 + S_3 = 9$$
$$x, y \geq 0$$

Now, consider the following solutions of the problem:

1. $x = 4, y = 5, S_1 = 0, S_2 = 4$ and $S_3 = 0$:

    The solution is **basic** because the number of the constraints in the problem is three which is equal to the number of **non-zero** slack/structural variables.

    The solution is also **feasible** because the **non-zero and non-negative** slack/structural variables in it satisfy all the constraints, including, of course, the non-negativity constraint. The solution is, thus, basic as well as feasible (BFS).

2. $x = 6, y = 0, S_1 = 18, S_2 = 3$ and $S_3 = 3$:

    The solution is **feasible but not basic**. It is *feasible* because the **non-zero and non-negative** slack/structural variables in it satisfy all the constraints, including the non-negativity constraint.

    The solution is, however, *not basic* because the number of constraints is less than the number of the **non-zero** slack/structural variables.

3. $x = 9, y = 0, S_1 = 15, S_2 = -6,$ and $S_3 = 0$:

    The solution is **basic but not feasible**. It is *basic* because the number of the constraints is equal to the number of the **non-zero** slack/structural variables.

    It is *not feasible* because the **non-zero and non-negative** slack/structural variables in it fail to satisfy all the constraints, including the non-negativity constraint.

Of the solutions given above, solution no. (1) is not only a basic and a feasible solution but also an optimal one. It is so because it is the only solution that optimises the objective function. Thus, it is an **Optimal Basic Feasible Solution (OBFS)**.

In graphic method, a basic solution occurs at a vertex of the **convex** polygon, a feasible solution occurs in the feasible region and an optimal solution occurs at a point on the periphery of the feasible polygon where the objective function is optimized. A convex polygon refers to a bounded region, joining any two points of which gives a straight line, no part of which lies outside the polygon (Figure 19.12).

An Infeasible Solution

In problems involving constraints with '=' or '≥' sign, artificial variables, such as, $A_1, A_2, ..., A_n$ are used. Despite heavy weights attached to them to prevent their entry into the final solution, one or more of them may enter into the final solution. In such cases, solution of the problem becomes infeasible.

Solution in Table 19.15 is feasible because none of the artificial variables is present in the final solution. Had there been any of them present, the solution would have been infeasible.

In graphical method, when the constraints are not satisfied simultaneously, the problem has no feasible solution (Figure 19.13).

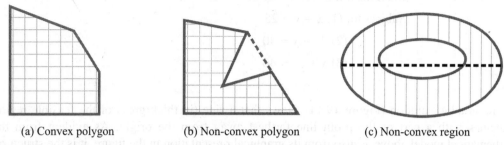

(a) Convex polygon (b) Non-convex polygon (c) Non-convex region

FIGURE 19.12 The points on the lines joining any two points of a convex polygon are all contained within the polygon (panel a). If some of the points on the lines fall outside the polygon, as in case of the dotted lines, the polygon is non-convex. Note that only the vertices of a convex polygon yield a basic solution.

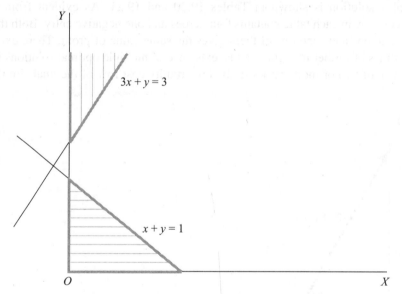

Figure 19.13 Constraints not satisfied simultaneously, no feasible solution exists.

Multiple Optimal Solutions

The presence of multiple optimal solutions in a linear programming model is indicated when one or more entries in the opportunity cost row of final simplex tableau are zero. The reason is obvious. If a variable having zero entry in the corresponding cell of opportunity cost row of final simplex tableau (Table 19.20) be entered in the objective function, the value of the objective function remains unaltered. This indicates existence of alternative optimal solution.

In graphic method, existence of multiple solutions is indicated when profit line coincides with one side of the feasible polygon (Figure 19.14).

Graphic and Simplex solutions worked out above, respectively in Figure 19.14 and Tables 19.20 and 19.21 relate to the LPP problem.

$$\text{Maximize: } \pi = 20x + 10y$$
$$\text{Subject to: (1) } x + y = 25$$
$$(2)\ 2x + y = 40$$
$$(3)\ x + 2y = 40$$
$$x, y \geq 0$$

Its graphic solution (Figure 19.14) shows that a side (in thick grey) of the feasible region coincides with a part of the profit line farthest away from the origin. As evident from the mathematical model above as also from its graphical presentation in the figure, it is the structural constraint (2) that overlaps a part of the profit line. The segment common to the two is a joint of points (20, 0) and (15, 10). Each point on this segment provides an optimal solution to the problem which, therefore, establishes existence of multiple optimal solutions.

Its simplex solution is shown in Tables 19.20 and 19.21. As evident from the tables, opportunity cost row in each table contains four zeroes and one negative entry. Both the solutions are optimal solutions and each one of them gives the same value of profit. There exist infinitely many possibilities of further iterations. Thus, existence of multiple optimal solutions is indicated by the existence of two or more zeroes in the opportunity cost row of the final simplex tableau.

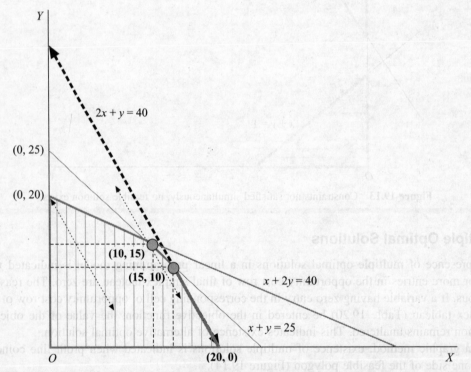

FIGURE 19.14 Infinitely many solutions exist when the profit function coincides with a side [thick grey side joining (20, 0) and (15, 10)] of the feasible polygon. Each point on this side yields the same value of profit (lying on the same profit function). They all constitute multiple or infinitely many solutions.

TABLE 19.20 Final simplex: Final simplex tableau, showing solution of LPP solved graphically in Figure 19.14. The solution comprises $x = 20$, and $y = 0$. Corresponding profit = **400**. Opportunity cost row $(C_j - Z_j)$ has zero opportunity costs in cells corresponding to columns x, y, S_1 and S_3. Of these, all but y constitute the solution of the problem. Admitting y-column as key row, we observe that S_1-row is the key row. Revising the solution, we obtain another solution comprising $x = 15$ and $y = 10$ as shown in Table 19.21. Again, profit = **400**.

Final Simplex Tableau: 1

C_j			20	10	0	0	0	
	PM		x	y	S_1	S_2	S_3	
		Qty						Ratio
0	S_1	5	0	1/2	1	−1/2	0	← 10
20	x	20	1	1/2	0	1/2	0	40
0	S_3	20	0	3/2	0	−1/2	1	40/3
		Z_j	20	10	0	10	0	
		$C_j - Z_j$	0	0	0	−10	0	

TABLE 19.21 Solution obtained by including y (not already a part of the solution set) in the programme comprises $x = 15$ and $y = 10$ which yields same profit as that produced earlier by the solution set $x = 20$ and $y = 0$ (Tableau 1). The opportunity cost row again contains four zeroes leaving room for further iterations. If performed, profit function will invariably have same value but variables x and y will have different values. Presence of one or more zeroes in the opportunity cost row of the final simplex tableau, thus, signifies existence of multiple optimal solutions.

Final Simplex Tableau: 2

C_j			20	10	0	0	0	
	PM		x	y	S_1	S_2	S_3	
		Qty						Ratio
10	y	10	0	1	2	−1	0	
20	x	15	1	0	−1	1	0	
0	S_3	5	0	0	−3	1	1	
		Z_j	20	10	0	10	0	
		$C_j - Z_j$	0	0	0	−10	0	

An Unbounded Optimal Solution

If the ratio column in the simplex method contains an infinitely large ratio, obtained when quantity column is divided by the corresponding entries in the key column, the problem has an unbounded optimal solution. This would happen when the key column contains zeroes.

In graphic method, when the feasible region is an unbounded polygon, extending infinitely on one or more sides, the value of the objective function varies from point to point in the feasible region. In such cases, an optimal solution does not exist (Figure 19.15, maximization problem). However, an unbounded solution may be had but the same may not be an optimal one also. An unbounded optimal solution is said to exist when the feasible region is not a closed polygon yet the objective function has unique optimum (minimum or maximum) at one of the vertices of the feasible region (Figure 19.15, minimization problem).

To demonstrate unbounded solution, consider the problem

$$\text{Maximize: } \pi = 8x + 5y$$
$$\text{Subject to: } x \geq 5$$
$$y \leq 10$$
$$x + 2y \geq 10$$

Figure 19.15 shows an unbounded solution.

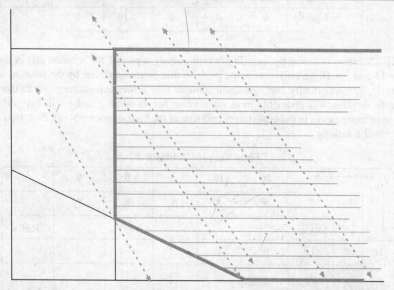

FIGURE 19.15 The value of the profit function is non-optimal at the vertices. The region being unbounded, optimal solution does not exist. An unbounded solution may be had anywhere in the feasible region. Had the problem been one of minimization, an unbounded optimal solution or simply an optimal solution would be a reality.

19.10 SENSITIVITY ANALYSIS

Solutions worked out by simplex method are based on an implicit assumption that the coefficients of the variables in the objective function remain unchanged over a long period of time. That is, the contributions made by the products remain fixed. In the real world, we know, this is rare. Product prices change frequently and so do the contributions (excess of price over cost) made by the products. This reduces the utility of the LP techniques unless the sensitivity of the solutions worked out to the changes in contributions is low. A highly sensitive solution has shorter life requiring frequent revisions or modifications. Analysis of sensitivity of the optimal solutions to such changes, thus, becomes important for the decision-maker as the solution itself.

To demonstrate, let us refer to Table 19.10. Table provides the optimal solution to the primal problem of Section 19.4 by simplex method. Variables x and y that appear in the solution of the problem are called the **solution variables** while variables z, S_1 and S_2 that don't form a part of the final solution are called the **non-solution variables**.

Let us start the sensitivity analysis with the non-solution variables first. For the purpose, let the contribution of z be increased by δ so that the new value is $250 + \delta$. Let us work out the entries in the opportunity cost row now. Table 19.22 shows the results. Sensitivity analysis conducted in Table 19.22 in respect of the non-solution variables z, S_1 and S_2 shows that the contributions of these variables may increase each to a maximum of 375, 25 and 50, respectively without affecting the optimality of the solution obtained in Table 19.10.

TABLE 19.22 To see how sensitive the solution of Table 19.10 is to changes in the coefficients of the objective function, suppose contribution made by one unit of z increases by δ with the result that it is ₹ $(250 + \delta)$ instead of ₹ 250. Entry in $(C_j - Z_j)$ row under z-column changes to $(\delta - 75)$ from (-75). For optimality of the solution all the entries in $(C_j - Z_j)$ row be 0 or negative. In the transformed row, all but $(\delta - 75)$ are 0 or negative. Thus, $(\delta - 75)$ too must be less than or equal to 0; i.e., $\delta < 75$. (Hence the solution worked out in Table 19.10 would continue to be optimal so long as the contribution of variable z does not increase beyond ₹ $(250 + 75)$ or ₹ 375. In the same way, the contribution of the non-solution variables S_1 and S_2 can be increased each from 0 to a maximum of $(0 + 25)$ and $(0 + 50)$, respectively without affecting the optimal solution of the problem.

C_j →			100	400	$250 + \delta$	0	0	
	PM →		x	y	z	S_1	S_2	
↓	↓	Qty ↓						Ratio
100	x	5	1	0	−3.75	1.25	−1.5	
400	y	15	0	1	1.75	−0.25	0.5	
		Z_j	100	400	325	25	50	
		$C_j - Z_j$	0	0	$(\delta - 75)$	−25	−50	

To test the sensitivity of the solution to changes in the solution variables x and y, let us increase their contributions of 100 and 400 by α and β respectively. Working out Z_j and $C_j - Z_j$ first under the increase in the contribution of x by α, Table 19.10 transforms to Table 19.23.

In the same way, increasing the contribution of y by β, it can be shown that $\beta = 100$. Thus, contribution can be increased from 400 to 500 without affecting the optimality of the solution in Table 19.10.

Sensitivity analysis helps decision-makers to investigate the strength and the weakness of a decision taken through LP techniques.

TABLE 19.23 Entries in $(C_j - Z_j)$ row have changed to $-\alpha$, 0, $(3.75\alpha - 75)$, $(-25 - 1.25\alpha)$, $-50 + 1.5\alpha$. For the optimal solution in Table 19.10 to remain unaffected, all these entries must be ≤ 0. Hence value of α must satisfy all of the following:

$$-\alpha \leq 0, \quad \text{(implying, } \alpha \geq 0\text{)}$$
$$3.75\alpha - 75 \leq 0, \quad \text{(implying, } \alpha \leq 20\text{)}$$
$$-1.25\alpha - 25 \leq 0, \quad \text{(implying, } \alpha \geq 20\text{), and}$$
$$-50 + 1.5\alpha \leq 0, \quad \text{(implying, } \alpha \leq 33.33\text{)}$$

Value of α satisfying all these inequalities is 20. Thus, contribution of x may be increased by 20 (that is from 100 to 120) without affecting the optimality of the solution in Table 19.10.

C_j →			100	400	250	0	0	
	PM →		x	y	z	S_1	S_2	
↓	↓	Qty ↓						Ratio
$100 + \alpha$	x	5	1	0	-3.75	1.25	-1.5	
400	y	15	0	1	1.75	-0.25	0.5	
		Z_j	$100 + \alpha$	400	$325 - 3.75\alpha$	$25 + 1.25\alpha$	$50 - 1.5\alpha$	
		$C_j - Z_j$	$-\alpha$	0	$-75 + 3.75\alpha$	$-25 - 1.25\alpha$	$-50 - 1.5\alpha$	

KEY TERMS AND CONCEPTS

Assumptions of LP model The most important assumption of the LPP-models is the *linearity* of the functions involved whether they refer to the objective function or to the constraints. The assumption requires constant coefficients of variables throughout the model. For instance, in a product mix model, constant input costs ensure linearity of constraints and constant product prices ensure linearity of the objective function. Constant return to scale ensure linearity of constraints and competitive market structure ensures linearity of the objective function.

Basic Solution It is the set of coordinates of vertices of a feasible convex polygon.

Convex Region It refers to a closed region which contains all the points on a straight line joining any pair of points of the region.

Degeneracy of LP Problem A LP problem is said to be degenerate if more than two of its constraints when graphed pass through the same vertex of the feasible polygon, or alternatively, a LPP is said to be degenerate when a tie between two or more rows arises in the iterative process of simplex solution or when one or more entries in the quantity column assume zero values in a simplex tableau.

Feasible Region It is the set of points satisfying the constraints in a LP model.

Feasible Solution It is a solution of LPP that satisfies the constraints.

Infeasible Region It refers to a set of points that fails to satisfy all the constraints in the LP problem simultaneously.

Linear Programming Linear programming (LP) refers to a technique of constrained optimization problems where the objective function is linear and there are one or more linear constraints.

Methods of solving the LP problems There are mainly three methods—graphic method, algebraic method and simplex method.

Multiple Optimal Solutions They refer to a set of points each of which satisfies the constraints, and at the same time, gives the same optimal value of the objective function.

Non-linear Programming Non-linear programming refers to a technique of constrained optimization problems where the objective function and/or one or more constraints are non-linear.

Non-negativity Constraints Non-negativity constraints restrain variables from assuming negative values.

Objective Function It is an algebraic expression of the objective intended to be achieved.

Optimal Basic Feasible Solution It refers to a solution of the LPP which is feasible as well as basic and which optimizes the objective function at the same time.

Optimal Solution It is a solution of the LPP that optimizes the objective function.

Primal and Dual Original LP problem is called the primal problem while its alternative version involving shadow prices is called its dual.

Sensitivity Analysis It refers to the sensitivity of an optimal solution to the changes in the coefficients (contributions) of the variables in a LPP.

Simplex Method Developed by George B. Dantzig in 1957, the Simplex Method is an iterative mathematical process employed to solve linear programming problems involving any number of unknown variables.

Structural Constraints Structural constraints refer to conditions that restrain attainment of an objective.

Unbounded Solution It refers to infinitely large set of points in the feasible region none of which gives an absolute optimal value of the objective function in a LPP.

EXERCISES

A. Short Answer Questions

Define the following: [1 through 16]
1. Linear programming
2. Structural constraints
3. Feasible region
4. Infeasible region
5. Basic solution
6. Optimal solution
7. Basic feasible solution
8. Optimal Basic Feasible Solution (OBFS)
9. Convex region
10. Degeneracy in linear programming problems
11. Primal and dual problems
12. Shadow prices
13. Multiple optimal solutions
14. Unbounded solution
15. Sensitivity analysis
16. Non-negativity constraints

17. What is the main assumption of the linear programming techniques?
18. Name three areas of decision making where the technique of linear programming is employed.
19. Can you guess one serious limitation of linear programming problems that defeats the entire exercise of resorting to it?

    [**Hint:** Think of a problem in which you have to determine the optimal product mix of two models of deluxe and a car and the solution involves fractional quantities]

B. Long Answer Questions

20. Explain the implications of the linearity assumption in linear programming problems.
21. Distinguish the following:
    (a) Linear and non-linear programming
    (b) Feasible and infeasible regions
    (c) Basic and non-basic solutions
    (d) Optimal and non-optimal solutions
    (e) Convex and non-convex regions
    (f) Primal and dual
    (g) Unique and multiple solutions
    (h) Bounded and unbounded solutions
    (i) Structural and non-negativity constraints
    (j) Slack and surplus variables
22. Explain the concept of shadow prices with the help of an illustration.
23. Write a short note on sensitivity analysis.
24. Write a short note on utility of linear programming techniques in decision making.
25. Consider the following LP model:

    $$\text{Maximize: } \pi = 2x + 4y$$
    $$\text{Subject to: } x + 4y \leq 24$$
    $$3x + y \leq 21$$
    $$x + y \leq 9$$
    $$x, y \geq 0$$

    Determine the optimal product mix using graphical method.
26. Recast the model in Q. 25 using slack/surplus variables and solve it by simplex method.
27. Transform the model in Q. 25 into its dual and solve it by simplex method. Interpret the solution.
28. Recast the model in Q. 25 using slack variables. Without actually solving it, label each of the following solutions as basic, feasible, basic but not feasible, feasible but not basic, or as optimal basic feasible solution:

    (i) $x = 4, y = 5, S_1 = 0, S_2 = 3$ and $S_3 = 0$
    (ii) $x = 6, y = 0, S_1 = 18, S_2 = 3$ and $S_3 = 3$
    (iii) $x = 9, y = 0, S_1 = 15, S_2 = -6,$ and $S_3 = 0$
    (iv) $x = 4, y = 5, S_1 = 0, S_2 = 3$ and $S_3 = 0$

    [**Ans.** (i) Basic, feasible, and optimal basic feasible solution (OBFS); (ii) Feasible but non-basic; (iii) Basic but non-feasible; (iv) Same as (i).]
29. Examine the solution in Q. 27. To what extent is it possible to alter the coefficients of the variables, slack or structural, without affecting the optimality of the solution?

C. Essay Type Questions

30. Consider the following model

$$\text{Maximize: } \pi = 80x + 60y$$
$$\text{Subject to: } x + y \le 60$$
$$x + 2y \le 100$$
$$2x + y \le 100$$
$$x, y \ge 0$$

(i) Solve the problem graphically.
(ii) Recast the model using slack variables and solve it by the simplex method. Do you get the same solution?
(iii) From the solution in part (ii), can you read the solution of the dual?
(iv) Transform the problem into its dual and solve it by simplex method. Is the solution same as that obtained in part (iii) above?
(v) From the solution in part (iv), can you read the solution of the primal? Is it the same as that obtained in part (i) or (ii)?
(vi) Conduct the sensitivity test of the solution obtained in part (ii) and determine the limits between which the coefficients of the variables can be changed without affecting the optimality of the solution.

[**Ans.** (i) $x = 40$, $y = 20$. (ii) Yes. (iii) Yes, it is $P = 40$, $Q = 0$, and $R = 20$. (iv) Yes. (v) Yes; yes, it is. (vi) S_1 and S_3 can be increased respectively by 40 and 20 at the maximum; contribution of y can be increased by values between 0 and 20 (both inclusive); contribution of x can be increased by values between 0 and 20 (both inclusive); contribution of S_2 can be increased by values between 0 and 40/3 (both inclusive).]

31. Consider the problem

$$\text{Minimize: } \pi = 6x + 5y$$
$$\text{Subject to: } 2x + y \ge 80$$
$$7x + 4y \le 560$$
$$3x + 8y \le 480$$
$$2x + 5y \ge 200$$
$$x, y \ge 0$$

Find the optimal product mix graphically as well as by simplex method.

[**Ans.** $x = 25$, $y = 30$]

32. Solve the problem by simplex method and verify the solution by graphic method.

$$\text{Maximize: } \pi = 10x + 12y$$
$$\text{Subject to: } 2x + 2y = 10$$
$$x \ge 2$$
$$y \le 4$$
$$x, y \ge 0$$

[**Ans.** $x = 2$ and $y = 3$]

33. Solve the problem by simplex method

$$\text{Minimize: } C = 8x + 10y + 11z$$
$$\text{Subject to: } 2x + 2y + 2z = 20{,}000$$
$$x \le 3{,}000$$
$$y \ge 1{,}500$$
$$z \ge 2{,}000$$
$$x, y, z \ge 0$$

[**Ans.** $x = 3{,}000$, $y = 5{,}000$ and $z = 2{,}000$]

34. Solve the problem by graphic/simplex method

$$\text{Maximize: } \pi = 8x + 5y$$
$$\text{Subject to: } x \geq 5$$
$$y \leq 10$$
$$x + 2y \geq 10$$

Does the problem possess a unique optimal solution? If not, why?

35. Solve the problem by graphic/simplex method

$$\text{Maximize: } \pi = 20x + 10y$$
$$\text{Subject to: (1) } x + y \leq 25$$
$$(2)\ 2x + y \leq 40$$
$$(3)\ x + 2y \leq 40$$
$$x, y \geq 0$$

Is the solution unique? If not, find an alternative solution as well.

[**Ans.** No; (1) $x = 20$, $y = 0$; (2) $x = 15$, $y = 10$]

20

Input–Output Analysis

CHAPTER OUTLINE

Introduction
- The Input–Output Model
- Open and Closed Input–Output Models
- Key Terms and Concepts
- Exercises

INTRODUCTION

Inputs of one industry are outputs of another. Cotton produced by farm industry is used as an input by textile industry and cloth produced by the textile industry is used as an input by ready-made-garments' industry. Industry from which an input originates (here, farm industry) is called the **industry of origin**. Inter industry flows of intermediate products such as these are much more complex in reality than they appear here. At times, industries sell their finished products to industries from which they buy their inputs. Apart from these inter-industry flows, there are simultaneous flows from each of these industries to the world of final consumers who don't use products bought for producing further goods or services. For instance, raw cotton is bought by the households for cushions, pillows and quilts. Also, cloth is bought by them for curtains, bed-covers, etc.

Prof. Wassily W. Leontief, the winner of 1973 Nobel Prize for Economics, invented in 1951, a technique known after him as **Leontief's Table**, for recording and analyzing inter industrial and extra inter industrial flows of products systematically. A commonly used version of the table is shown in Table 20.1.

TABLE 20.1 In the table, intakes or inputs are recorded column-wise and outputs, row-wise. Entry A_{ij} in the top-left quadrant represents input of jth industry from the ith industry. Entry P_i in the intermediate output column represents output of ith industry sold to the industries. Likewise, entries F_i and X_i respectively in the final demand and the output columns in the top-right quadrant represent, sale to final demand and total value output of ith industry. Thus, final demand for ith industry's product, $F_i = C_G + C_H + \text{GDFCF} + \Delta S + (X - M)$, where C_G is government's demand for final consumption, C_H is final demand for household consumption, GDFCF is gross domestic fixed capital formation, ΔS is change in stocks of inventories and $(X - M)$ is net investment abroad. Entries $I_j, D_j, T_j, V_j,$ and x_j in the bottom-left quadrant represent intermediate inputs, depreciations, net indirect taxes, values added and primary inputs, respectively of the jth industry ($j = 1, 2, 3$). Entries $\Sigma C_G, \Sigma C_H, \Sigma\text{GDFCF}, \Sigma\Delta S$, $\Sigma(X - M)$ represent total sales of all the industries to government final consumption, private final consumption, gross domestic capital formation, increase in inventories and net investment abroad, respectively.

GDP$_{MP}$ represents gross domestic product at market price which is the sum of $\Sigma C_G, \Sigma C_H, \Sigma\text{GDFCF}, \Sigma\Delta S$ and $\Sigma(X - M)$. Top-right quadrant, thus, accounts for GDP$_{MP}$ by expenditure method while bottom-left quadrant, $D + T + V + x$, in particular, accounts for GDP$_{MP}$ by income or value added method. Whatever the method, GDP$_{MP}$ is the same. *For all practical purposes, top-left, top-right and bottom-left quadrants, henceforth will be referred to as the input-output, final demand and the primary input quadrants.*

Input ↓ / Output →		1	2	3	Intermediate outputs	C_G	C_H	GDFCF	ΔS	$X - M$	Total FD	Total output
		INDUSTRY				**FINAL-DEMAND (FD)**						
INDUSTRY	1	A_{11}	A_{12}	A_{13}	P_1	$(C_G)_1$	$(C_H)_1$	$(\text{GDFCF})_1$	$(\Delta S)_1$	$(X-M)_1$	F_1	X_1
	2	A_{21}	A_{22}	A_{23}	P_2	$(C_G)_2$	$(C_H)_2$	$(\text{GDFCF})_2$	$(\Delta S)_2$	$(X-M)_2$	F_2	X_2
	3	A_{31}	A_{32}	A_{33}	P_3	$(C_G)_3$	$(C_H)_3$	$(\text{GDFCF})_3$	$(\Delta S)_3$	$(X-M)_3$	F_3	X_3
Intermediate inputs		I_1	I_2	I_3	$I = P$	ΣC_G	ΣC_H	ΣGDFCF	$\Sigma\Delta S$	$\Sigma(X-M)$	$F =$ GDP$_{MP}$	X
Depreciation D		D_1	D_2	D_3	D							D
N.I.T		T_1	T_2	T_3	T							T
NVA$_{FC}$		V_1	V_2	V_3	V							V
Primary inputs		x_1	x_2	x_3	x							x
Total inputs		X_1	X_2	X_3	X	ΣC_G	ΣC_H	ΣGDFCF	$\Sigma\Delta S$	$\Sigma(X-M)$	$F =$ GDP$_{MP}$	

It has four quadrants:

1. **Quadrant I (top-right)** – The final demand quadrant
2. **Quadrant II (top-left)** – The inter-industry flow quadrant
3. **Quadrant III (bottom-left)** – The primary-inputs-to-industry quadrant
4. **Quadrant IV (bottom-right)** – The primary-inputs-to-final-demand quadrant

Quadrant I, the final demand quadrant, records the end use of industrial products. It shows their final consumption by domestic entities such as government final consumption (C_G), private final consumption (C_H), gross domestic private investment (GDPI) also known as gross domestic capital formation (GDCF) comprising gross domestic fixed capital formation (GDFCF) and changes in stocks (ΔS) and finally, net investment abroad ($X - M$) from the industries. An aggregate of the four from all of them gives **gross domestic product at market price** (GDP$_{MP}$).

Quadrant II, the inter-industry flow quadrant, records industrial inputs from and outputs to the industries. Industries need inputs from other industries as well as from self for production of their outputs. In this quadrant, only those input transactions are recorded which remain confined as basic inputs intermediate products such as raw material and semi-finished goods to the industrial world called **producers' sector** separated from the households' sector by a hypothetical boundary called **production boundary**.

Quadrant III, the primary-inputs-to-industry quadrant, records components of **gross value added at market prices** (GVA$_{MP}$). The components comprise money value of productive services consumed in the process of value addition to basic inputs. To transform a basic input into the saleable output, an industry requires factors such as land-building, labour, capital and organizational services. Money value of consumption of real capital, compensation of employees including entrepreneurship, rentals of land-buildings, interest and dividends on financial capital, mixed incomes of the self-employed and professionals and net indirect taxes comprise value addition or factor incomes of the productive factors.

Quadrant IV, the primary-inputs-to-final-demand quadrant, is intended to record **direct purchases of primary factors for their final use**. Items recorded in this quadrant are assumed negligible for simplicity.

Table 20.1 shows the four quadrants and the entries therein.

20.1 THE INPUT–OUTPUT MODEL

For the sake of simplicity, the producers' sector is classified into three major heads: (a) the agriculture sector (b) the manufacturing sector and (c) the service sector. The sector outside the producers' sector is the final demand sector, which buys industrial outputs for final consumption. The sector comprises households, government and rest of the world sectors. The version presented here is designed to suit the needs of national income accounts as also those of producers who wish to know how sensitive their input needs are to the requirements of their outputs. Each industry uses a fixed proportion of its output to meet its input needs as also those of its fellow industries. The rest, it uses to satisfy the final demand. Proportion of its total output used by the jth industry as its input from the ith industry, written as a_{ij}, may be expressed as:

$$a_{ij} = \frac{A_{ij}}{X_j}$$

where, $A_{ij} \equiv$ inputs of the jth industry from the ith industry,

and, $X_j \equiv$ total output of the jth industry.

For instance, a_{12} is the proportion of A_{12} to X_2, representing the proportion of the second industry's output (X_2) which industry 2 uses as its inputs from industry 1 (A_{12}). Likewise, a_{23} represents the proportion to A_{23} to X_3, implying the proportion of its output (X_3) by which industry

3 uses industry 2's output (A_{23}) as its inputs. In simpler terms, a_{ij} is a fraction, $0 < a_{ij} < 1$, given by A_{ij}/X_j where X_j is the total output of industry 'j' and A_{ij} is the input bought by industry 'j' from industry 'i'.

Thus, industrial inputs can be expressed in terms of their outputs as:

$$A_{ij} = a_{ij} \cdot X_j; \quad [i = 1, 2, 3; j = 1, 2, 3] \tag{20.1}$$

From the table,

$$P_i + F_i = X_i; \quad i = 1, 2, 3 \tag{20.2}$$

or,

$$I_j + D_j + T_j + V_j + x_j = X_j; \quad j = 1, 2, 3 \tag{20.3}$$

Using the expanded notation, Eq. (20.2) can be expressed as:

$$\left.\begin{array}{l} P_1 + F_1 = X_1 \\ P_2 + F_2 = X_2 \\ P_3 + F_3 = X_3 \end{array}\right\} \tag{20.4}$$

Here,

$$\left.\begin{array}{l} P_1 = A_{11} + A_{12} + A_{13} \\ \quad = a_{11}.X_1 + a_{12}.X_2 + a_{13}.X_3 \\ P_2 = A_{21} + A_{22} + A_{23} \\ \quad = a_{21}.X_1 + a_{22}.X_2 + a_{23}.X_3 \\ P_3 = A_{31} + A_{32} + A_{33} \\ \quad = a_{31}.X_1 + a_{32}.X_2 + a_{33}.X_3 \end{array}\right\} \text{[from 20.1 for } A_{ij}\text{]} \tag{20.5}$$

From Eqs. (20.4) and (20.5), we have

$$\left.\begin{array}{l} a_{11}.X_1 + a_{12}.X_2 + a_{13}.X_3 + F_1 = X_1 \\ a_{21}.X_1 + a_{22}.X_2 + a_{23}.X_3 + F_2 = X_2 \\ a_{31}.X_1 + a_{32}.X_2 + a_{33}.X_3 + F_3 = X_3 \end{array}\right\} \tag{20.6}$$

In matrix notation*, Eq. (20.6) can be expressed as:

$$\begin{bmatrix} a_{11} & a_{12} & a_{13} \\ a_{21} & a_{22} & a_{23} \\ a_{31} & a_{32} & a_{33} \end{bmatrix} \begin{bmatrix} X_1 \\ X_2 \\ X_3 \end{bmatrix} + \begin{bmatrix} F_1 \\ F_2 \\ F_3 \end{bmatrix} = \begin{bmatrix} X_1 \\ X_2 \\ X_3 \end{bmatrix} \tag{20.7}$$

or,

$$AX + F = X \tag{20.8}$$

where,

$$\begin{bmatrix} a_{11} & a_{12} & a_{13} \\ a_{21} & a_{22} & a_{23} \\ a_{31} & a_{32} & a_{33} \end{bmatrix} = A; \quad \begin{bmatrix} F_1 \\ F_2 \\ F_3 \end{bmatrix} = F; \quad \begin{bmatrix} X_1 \\ X_2 \\ X_3 \end{bmatrix} = X$$

---

* An elementary knowledge of matrices and determinants is must to understand the rest of the chapter.

From Eq. (20.8), we have

$$X - AX = F$$
$$\Rightarrow \quad [I - A]X = F \quad (20.9)$$
$$\Rightarrow \quad X = [I - A]^{-1} \cdot F$$

where,

$$I = \begin{bmatrix} 1 & 0 & 0 \\ 0 & 1 & 0 \\ 0 & 0 & 1 \end{bmatrix}$$

and

$$I - A = \begin{bmatrix} 1 - a_{11} & -a_{12} & -a_{13} \\ -a_{21} & 1 - a_{22} & -a_{23} \\ -a_{31} & -a_{32} & 1 - a_{33} \end{bmatrix} \quad (20.10)$$

Equation (20.9) expresses outputs of different industries in terms of final demand faced by them and input–output coefficient matrix, A, also known as **technology matrix**. For the equation to possess a meaningful solution, matrix $(I - A)$, referred to at times as **transaction matrix** or even as **technology matrix,** must satisfy the following conditions called **Hawkins–Simon conditions:**

1. The determinant of the matrix must always be positive, i.e. $|I - A| > 0$; and
2. Each of the diagonal elements, namely, $(1 - a_{11})$, $(1 - a_{22})$ and $(1 - a_{33})$ must be positive. In other words, each of a_{11}, a_{22} and a_{33} must be less than 1.

Note that a_{11}, a_{22}, a_{33} are all zero when industries do not use own products as their inputs. Also, $[1 - (a_{11} + a_{21} + a_{31})]$, $[1 - (a_{12} + a_{22} + a_{32})]$ and $[1 - (a_{13} + a_{23} + a_{33})]$ represent **residual input coefficients** or **primary input coefficients** of industries 1, 2, and 3. These coefficients represent requirements of primary inputs per rupee value of their outputs by industries 1, 2, and 3 in that order.

Equation (20.9) can be solved through matrix inversion. Before demonstrating the process, let us briefly outline some of the assumptions on which input–output analysis is based.

Assumptions

1. Economy is made up of a finite number of sectors (industries) each of which produces only one homogeneous product. No two products are produced jointly. If at all the case arises, they are produced in fixed proportions.
2. Production in each sector is subject to constant returns to scale, that is, the production function of each industry is a linear homogeneous production function.
3. Input requirements per unit of output in each sector remain fixed and constant and output in each sector is uniquely determined by the quantities of inputs used.

ILLUSTRATION 20.1: Given the technology matrix and the final demand vector for an economy with sectors A_1, A_2 and A_3, find the respective outputs to meet the inter-sectoral and final demands.

$$A = \begin{bmatrix} 0.2 & 0.4 & 0.3 \\ 0.3 & 0.1 & 0.2 \\ 0.1 & 0.2 & 0.3 \end{bmatrix} ; \quad F = \begin{bmatrix} 100 \\ 60 \\ 80 \end{bmatrix}$$

Figures in final demand vector are in millions of rupees. How would your answer change if final demand increases by 50% for all the sectors? Also obtain the residual input coefficients and interpret them.

Solution: From Eq. 20.9,

$$X = [I - A]^{-1} \cdot F$$

$$[I - A]^{-1} = \begin{bmatrix} 1 - a_{11} & -a_{12} & -a_{13} \\ -a_{21} & 1 - a_{22} & -a_{23} \\ -a_{31} & -a_{32} & 1 - a_{33} \end{bmatrix}^{-1}$$

$$= \begin{bmatrix} 1 - 0.2 & -0.4 & -0.3 \\ -0.3 & 1 - 0.1 & -0.2 \\ -0.1 & -0.2 & 1 - 0.3 \end{bmatrix}^{-1}$$

$$= \begin{bmatrix} 0.8 & -0.4 & -0.3 \\ -0.3 & 0.9 & -0.2 \\ -0.1 & -0.2 & 0.7 \end{bmatrix}^{-1}$$

$$= \frac{\text{Adj. of} \begin{bmatrix} 0.8 & -0.4 & -0.3 \\ -0.3 & 0.9 & -0.2 \\ -0.1 & -0.2 & 0.7 \end{bmatrix}}{\text{Det. of} \begin{bmatrix} 0.8 & -0.4 & -0.3 \\ -0.3 & 0.9 & -0.2 \\ -0.1 & -0.2 & 0.7 \end{bmatrix}} \qquad (20.11)$$

$$\text{Det. of} \begin{bmatrix} 0.8 & -0.4 & -0.3 \\ -0.3 & 0.9 & -0.2 \\ -0.1 & -0.2 & 0.7 \end{bmatrix} = \begin{vmatrix} 0.8 & -0.4 & -0.3 \\ -0.3 & 0.9 & -0.2 \\ -0.1 & -0.2 & 0.7 \end{vmatrix}$$

$$= (0.8)\,[(0.9)(0.7) - (-0.2)(-0.2)] + (-1)(-0.4)[(-0.3)(0.7) - (-0.1)(-0.2)] + (+1)(-0.3)[(-0.3)(-0.2) - (-0.1)(0.9)]$$

$$= 0.472 - 0.092 - 0.045 \qquad \text{[Expanded by co-factor method]}$$

$$= 0.335 \qquad (20.12)$$

and,

$$\text{Adj. of} \begin{bmatrix} 0.8 & -0.4 & -0.3 \\ -0.3 & 0.9 & -0.2 \\ -0.1 & -0.2 & 0.7 \end{bmatrix}$$

$$= \begin{bmatrix} \begin{vmatrix} 0.9 & -0.2 \\ -0.2 & 0.7 \end{vmatrix} & (-)\begin{vmatrix} -0.3 & -0.2 \\ -0.1 & 0.7 \end{vmatrix} & \begin{vmatrix} -0.3 & 0.9 \\ -0.1 & -0.2 \end{vmatrix} \\ (-)\begin{vmatrix} -0.4 & -0.3 \\ -0.2 & 0.7 \end{vmatrix} & \begin{vmatrix} 0.8 & -0.3 \\ -0.1 & 0.7 \end{vmatrix} & (-)\begin{vmatrix} 0.8 & -0.4 \\ -0.1 & -0.2 \end{vmatrix} \\ \begin{vmatrix} -0.4 & -0.3 \\ 0.9 & -0.2 \end{vmatrix} & (-)\begin{vmatrix} 0.8 & -0.3 \\ -0.3 & -0.2 \end{vmatrix} & \begin{vmatrix} 0.8 & -0.4 \\ -0.3 & 0.9 \end{vmatrix} \end{bmatrix}^t$$

[Expanded as transpose of minors of the elements]

$$= \begin{bmatrix} 0.59 & 0.23 & 0.15 \\ 0.34 & 0.53 & 0.20 \\ 0.35 & 0.25 & 0.60 \end{bmatrix}^t \quad \text{[Transpose of determinates of minors]}$$

$$= \begin{bmatrix} 0.59 & 0.34 & 0.35 \\ 0.23 & 0.53 & 0.25 \\ 0.15 & 0.20 & 0.60 \end{bmatrix} \quad \text{[Matrix of the transpose]} \quad (20.13)$$

From Eqs. (20.11), (20.12), and (20.13), we have

$$(I-A)^{-1} = \frac{1}{0.335} \times \begin{bmatrix} 0.59 & 0.34 & 0.35 \\ 0.23 & 0.53 & 0.25 \\ 0.15 & 0.20 & 0.60 \end{bmatrix} \quad (20.14)$$

Substituting for $(I-A)^{-1}$ and F in Eq. (20.9), we have

$$X = \frac{1}{0.335} \times \begin{bmatrix} 0.59 & 0.34 & 0.35 \\ 0.23 & 0.53 & 0.25 \\ 0.15 & 0.20 & 0.60 \end{bmatrix} \times \begin{bmatrix} 100 \\ 60 \\ 80 \end{bmatrix}$$

$$= \frac{1}{0.335} \times \begin{bmatrix} 107.4 \\ 74.8 \\ 75.0 \end{bmatrix} \quad \text{[Using matrix multiplication]}$$

$$= \begin{bmatrix} 320.60 \\ 223.28 \\ 223.88 \end{bmatrix} \quad (20.15)$$

∴ $X_1 = \mathbf{320.60}$,

$X_2 = \mathbf{223.28}$, and

$X_3 = \mathbf{223.88}$

In case final demand for each sector increases by 50%, F changes to F', where,

$$F' = \begin{bmatrix} 150 \\ 90 \\ 120 \end{bmatrix}$$

$$X' = \frac{1}{0.335} \times \begin{bmatrix} 0.59 & 0.34 & 0.35 \\ 0.23 & 0.53 & 0.25 \\ 0.15 & 0.20 & 0.60 \end{bmatrix} \begin{bmatrix} 150 \\ 90 \\ 120 \end{bmatrix}$$

$$= \frac{1}{0.335} \times \begin{bmatrix} 161.11 \\ 112.20 \\ 112.50 \end{bmatrix}$$

$$= \begin{bmatrix} 480.93 \\ 334.93 \\ 335.82 \end{bmatrix} \qquad (20.16)$$

$\therefore \qquad X'_1 = 480.93,$

$X'_2 = 334.93,$ and

$X'_3 = 335.82.$

That is the utility of this analysis! It helps the industries to adjust their outputs directly to the changes in the final demand faced by them.

A more direct method for determining changes required in outputs of various sectors in response to changes in final demand can thus be obtained from Eq. (20.9) as:

$$\Delta X = (I - A)^{-1} \Delta F \qquad (20.17)$$

Equation in (20.17) can be detailed as:

$$\begin{bmatrix} \Delta X_1 \\ \Delta X_2 \\ \Delta X_3 \end{bmatrix} = (I - A)^{-1} \begin{bmatrix} \Delta F_1 \\ \Delta F_2 \\ \Delta F_3 \end{bmatrix} \qquad (20.18)$$

In the illustration above,

$\Delta F_1 = 150 - 100 = 50,$

$\Delta F_2 = 90 - 60 = 30,$ and

$\Delta F_3 = 120 - 80 = 40.$

Making substitutions in the right-hand side of Eq. (20.18), reader can verify that:

$\Delta X_1 = 160.68,$

$\Delta X_2 = 111.65,$ and

$\Delta X_3 = 111.94 \qquad (20.19)$

Adding desired changes ΔX_1, ΔX_2, and ΔX_3 as obtained in Eq. (20.19) to outputs of Eq. (20.15), we get the same outputs as in Eq. (20.16), which, as per our calculations, must be produced by the three sectors to meet 50% higher final demand.

$$\therefore \quad X_1' = X_1 + \Delta X_1 = 320.60 + 160.68 = 480.93,$$
$$X_2' = X_2 + \Delta X_2 = 223.28 + 111.65 = 334.93, \text{ and}$$
$$X_3' = X_3 + \Delta X_3 = 223.88 + 111.94 = 335.82$$

Residual Input Coefficients and their Significance

Column totals of matrix A in Illustration 20.1 are 0.6 (= 0.2 + 0.3 + 0.1), 0.7 (= 0.4 + 0.1 + 0.2) and 0.8 (= 0.3 + 0.2 + 0.3). Hence, residual input coefficients are 0.4 (= 1 − 0.6), 0.3 (= 1 − 0.7) and 0.2 (= 1 − 0.8) for industries 1, 2, and 3 per rupee value of their outputs, respectively. The amount of primary inputs needed to produce outputs X_1, X_2, and X_3 can be determined on the basis of residual input coefficients as 0.4 X_1, 0.3 X_2 and 0.2 X_3 for the three industries. When X_1 = 320.60, X_2 = 223.28, and, X_3 = 223.88; the respective quantities of primary inputs needed by the three are 128.24 (= 0.4 × 320.60), 66.98 (= 0.3 × 223.28) and 44.78 (= 0.2 × 223.88) and the total volume of primary inputs needed for the three products is 240 (= 128.24 + 66.98 + 44.78).

Lower left quadrant of Table 20.1 is the quadrant of value addition. It shows how industries add value to inputs through land-building, capital, labour and entrepreneurship. The third row of the quadrant shows expenditures incurred by respective industries on these factors as **'Net Value Added at Factor Cost (NVA_{FC})'**. The entries in this row record aggregated compensations made by the industries to their factors for the factor-services consumed in the process of value addition. Note, how gross and net estimates of value addition at factor cost and market price appear on the left-hand side of a GDP account (Table 20.2). The right-hand side of the same account records final demands (upper right quadrant of Table 20.1) faced by these industries.

TABLE 20.2 GDP account

GDP_{MP} (income approach)	GDP_{MP} (expenditure approach)
1. Depreciation = (D)	1. Government final consumption demand = (ΣC_G)
2. Net Indirect Taxes (NIT) = (T)	2. Private final consumption demand (C_H) = (ΣC_H)
3. NVA_{FC} = (V)	3. Gross domestic investment demand (GDCF) = $(\Sigma GDCF)$
+ Compensation of employees	= Gross domestic fixed capital formation ($\Sigma GDFCF$)
+ Rent	+ Changes in stocks ($\Sigma \Delta S$)
+ Interest	
+ Dividends	
+ Undistributed profits	
+ Mixed incomes of the self-employed	
4. Statistical discrepancy = (x)	4. Net investment demand abroad = $\Sigma(X - M)$
GDP_{MP} (income) = $D + T + V + x$	GDP_{MP} (expenditure) = $\Sigma C_G + \Sigma C_H + \Sigma GDCF + \Sigma(X - M)$

20.2 OPEN AND CLOSED INPUT–OUTPUT MODELS

The input–output table discussed above has two versions:
(i) The **Open Model**, and
(ii) The **Closed Model**.

20.2.1 The Open Model

The intput–output model of Table 20.1 is known as its open model. It has four distinct quadrants of which quadrant I (final demand quadrant) and quadrant III (primary input quadrant) are distinctly exogenous. The former (final demand sector of quadrant I) consumes a part of the output of industrial sector (quadrant II) without being a part of it (i.e., from outside) and the latter (primary input sector of quadrant III) feeds the industrial sector (quadrant II) with primary inputs such as labour and capital without being a part of it (i.e., from outside). Interestingly, each of the two involves the household sector. Such presence of exogenous sectors in an input–output model renders it the feature of an **open model** as outlined in Table 20.3 and detailed in Table 20.4.

TABLE 20.3 Outlines of open input–output model: An open input–output model has exogenous sectors such as quadrants I and III as also in Table 20.1.

Quadrant II Production Boundary (Industrial Sector)	Quadrant I Final Demand Sector (Household Sector)
Quadrant III Primary Input Sector (Household Sector)	Quadrant IV Primary Input to Final Demand Sector

The model of Table 20.3 can be detailed below as in Table 20.4 with specifications therein.

TABLE 20.4 Open input–output model with detailed specification: An open input–output model has exogenous sectors (quandrants I and III) comprising house holds, providing primary inputs labour and capital to industrial sector from outside (from quadrant III) and consuming a part of the industrial sector's output from outside (quadrant I)

Industries	Industries			Sub-total of outputs	Final demand (F)	Total outputs (X)
	1	2	3			
1	a_{11}	a_{12}	a_{13}	a_{1j}	F_1	X_1
2	a_{21}	a_{22}	a_{23}	a_{2j}	F_2	X_2
3	a_{31}	a_{32}	a_{33}	a_{3j}	F_3	X_3
Sub-total of inputs	Σa_{i1}	Σa_{i2}	Σa_{i3}	Σa_{ij} $i, j = 1, 2, 3$	ΣF_i $i = 1, 2, 3$	ΣX_i $i = 1, 2, 3$
Primary input (labour)	L_1	L_2	L_3	ΣL_j $j = 1, 2, 3$		ΣL_j $j = 1, 2, 3$
Total inputs	X_1	X_2	X_3	ΣX_{ij} $j = 1, 2, 3$	ΣF_i $i = 1, 2, 3$	$\Sigma X_j = \Sigma X_j$ $i, j = 1, 2, 3$

For clarification of the point, it becomes necessary to distinguish it from the closed model though the latter is taken up its requisite detail in the Sub-section 20.2.2 later. As against the open model, a closed model incorporates the household sector as fourth industry in the industrial sector producing primary inputs like the other three and consuming outputs like the other three as a part of the industrial sector within it (Table 20.5). In other words, there is only one sector, the industrial sector which contains quadrants I and III as endogenous sectors in quadrant II only.

Returning back to the open model, assuming, for simplicity, that labour is the only input provided by the households to industrial sector, we have,

$$L = L_1 + L_2 + L_3 \tag{20.20}$$

We have already seen how changes in final demands faced by the industries necessitate changes in their outputs, to produce which, changes in their input requirements become necessary. In other words, changes in input requirements are highly sensitive to changes in final demands or changes in outputs. In the same way, changes in factor requirements are sensitive to changes in value addition or changes in outputs.

Suppose an economy has two sectors. Each employs labour input for adding value to the basic inputs bought from the other sector. Suppose further that the outputs of the two sectors are X_1 and X_2 respectively, labour inputs employed by the two per rupee value of their outputs are f_{11} and f_{12} and total labour input employed is L. Evidently,

$$(L) = f_{11}X_1 + f_{12}X_2 \tag{20.21}$$

$$= (f_{11} \ f_{12}) \times \begin{bmatrix} X_1 \\ X_2 \end{bmatrix} \quad \text{(matrix notation)}$$

$$= (f_{11} \ f_{12}) \times (I - A)^{-1} \begin{bmatrix} F_1 \\ F_2 \end{bmatrix} \quad \text{(expressing outputs in terms of final demands)}$$

$$= (f_{11} \ f_{12}) \times (I - A)^{-1} F \tag{20.22}$$

$$= (f_{11} \ f_{12}) \times (X) \tag{20.23}$$

(Since, $(I - A)^{-1} F = X$)

where, $(X) = \begin{bmatrix} X_1 \\ X_2 \end{bmatrix}$, $(F) = \begin{bmatrix} F_1 \\ F_2 \end{bmatrix}$, $(I - A)^{-1} = \begin{bmatrix} 1 - a_{11} & -a_{12} \\ -a_{21} & 1 - a_{22} \end{bmatrix}^{-1}$

(for a two-sector economy)

In case industries employ two primary inputs, namely, labour(L) and capital (K), in Eq. (20.23) can be transformed as:

$$\begin{bmatrix} L \\ K \end{bmatrix} = \begin{bmatrix} f_{11} & f_{12} \\ f_{21} & f_{22} \end{bmatrix} \times \begin{bmatrix} X_1 \\ X_2 \end{bmatrix}$$

$$= \begin{bmatrix} f_{11} & f_{12} \\ f_{21} & f_{22} \end{bmatrix} (I - A)^{-1} (F)$$

$$= \begin{bmatrix} f_{11} & f_{12} \\ f_{21} & f_{22} \end{bmatrix} \times \begin{bmatrix} 1 - a_{11} & -a_{12} \\ -a_{21} & 1 - a_{22} \end{bmatrix}^{-1} \times \begin{bmatrix} F_1 \\ F_2 \end{bmatrix}$$

$$= (f)(I - A)^{-1}(F) \tag{20.24}$$

where, $(f) = \begin{bmatrix} f_{11} & f_{12} \\ f_{21} & f_{22} \end{bmatrix}$

f_{11} = proportion of labour input employed per unit of output X_1 of industry 1
f_{12} = proportion of labour input employed per unit of output X_2 of industry 2
f_{21} = proportion of capital input employed per unit of output X_1 of industry 1
f_{22} = proportion of capital input employed per unit of output X_2 of industry 2

Expression in Eq. (20.24) is called *factor demand vector*. Assuming competitive conditions in the product and factor markets, we can work out an expression for equilibrium level of product prices. Let these prices for the outputs X_1 and X_2 be P_1 and P_2, respectively. Further let there be only one factor, namely, labour, with competitive wage w. For competitive equilibrium with zero economic profit, total revenue = total cost for each industry. Total revenues for the two are $P_1 X_1$ and $P_2 X_2$. The total input cost of Industry 1 comprises (i) cost of its input from itself ($= a_{11} X_1$) at the rate of P_1 (i.e., $a_{11} X_1 P_1$), (ii) cost of its input from Industry 2 ($= a_{21} X_1$) at the rate of P_2 (i.e., $a_{21} X_1 P_2$) and (iii) cost of labour input ($= f_{11} X_1$) at the rate of 'w' (i.e., $f_{11} X_1 w$). It works out at $(a_{11} X_1 P_1 + a_{21} X_1 P_2 + f_{11} X_1 w)$.

Likewise, the total input cost of industry 2 works out at $(a_{12} X_2 P_1 + a_{22} X_2 P_2 + f_{12} X_2 w)$. In the steady state,

$$P_1 X_1 = a_{11} X_1 P_1 + a_{21} X_1 P_2 + f_{11} X_1 w$$
$$P_2 X_2 = a_{12} X_2 P_1 + a_{22} X_2 P_2 + f_{12} X_2 w$$

By cancellation of X_1 and X_2 from both the sides, we have:

$$P_1 = a_{11} P_1 + a_{21} P_2 + f_{11} w$$
$$P_2 = a_{12} P_1 + a_{22} P_2 + f_{12} w$$

Implying, $\begin{bmatrix} (1-a_{11}) & -a_{21} \\ -a_{12} & (1-a_{22}) \end{bmatrix} \begin{bmatrix} P_1 \\ P_2 \end{bmatrix} = \begin{bmatrix} f_{11} w \\ f_{12} w \end{bmatrix}$

Implying, $\begin{bmatrix} P_1 \\ P_2 \end{bmatrix} = \begin{bmatrix} (1-a_{11}) & -a_{21} \\ -a_{12} & (1-a_{22}) \end{bmatrix}^{-1} \begin{bmatrix} f_{11} w \\ f_{12} w \end{bmatrix}$

$$= [(I-A)^t]^{-1} V \qquad (20.25)$$

where, $V = \begin{bmatrix} f_{11} w \\ f_{12} w \end{bmatrix}$; $\begin{bmatrix} (1-a_{11}) & -a_{21} \\ -a_{12} & (1-a_{22}) \end{bmatrix} = \begin{bmatrix} (1-a_{11}) & -a_{12} \\ -a_{21} & (1-a_{22}) \end{bmatrix}^t = (I-A)^t$

If labour and capital are both employed by the two industries, the *value added vector*, V, changes to

$$V = \begin{bmatrix} f_{11} w + f_{21} r \\ f_{12} w + f_{22} r \end{bmatrix} = \begin{bmatrix} f_{11} & f_{21} \\ f_{12} & f_{22} \end{bmatrix} \begin{bmatrix} w \\ r \end{bmatrix} = \begin{bmatrix} f_{11} & f_{12} \\ f_{21} & f_{22} \end{bmatrix}^t \begin{bmatrix} w \\ r \end{bmatrix} = [f]^t \begin{bmatrix} w \\ r \end{bmatrix} \qquad (20.26)$$

Here, f_{ij} have same meaning as before and w and r are the competitive prices per unit of labour and capital employed. This follows from the steady state equations,

$$P_1 X_1 = a_{11} X_1 P_1 + a_{21} X_1 P_2 + f_{11} X_1 w + f_{21} X_1 r$$
$$P_2 X_2 = a_{12} X_1 P_1 + a_{22} X_2 P_2 + f_{12} X_2 w + f_{22} X_2 r$$

By cancellation of X_1 and X_2 from both the sides, we have

$$P_1 = a_{11} P_1 + a_{21} P_2 + f_{11}w + f_{21}r$$
$$P_2 = a_{12} P_1 + a_{22} P_2 + f_{12}w + f_{22}r$$

$$\Rightarrow \begin{bmatrix} P_1 \\ P_2 \end{bmatrix} = \begin{bmatrix} (1-a_{11}) & -a_{21} \\ -a_{12} & (1-a_{22}) \end{bmatrix}^{-1} \begin{bmatrix} f_{11} & f_{21} \\ f_{12} & f_{22} \end{bmatrix} \begin{bmatrix} w \\ r \end{bmatrix} = [(I-A)^t]^{-1} [f]^t \begin{bmatrix} w \\ r \end{bmatrix} \quad (20.27)$$

For an economy with n sectors, the expression can be generalized as:

$$\begin{bmatrix} P_1 \\ P_2 \\ \ldots \\ P_n \end{bmatrix} = \begin{bmatrix} (1-a_{11}) & -a_{12} & \ldots & -a_{1n} \\ -a_{21} & (1-a_{22}) & \ldots & -a_{2n} \\ \ldots & \ldots & \ldots & \ldots \\ -a_{n1} & -a_{n2} & \ldots & (1-a_{nn}) \end{bmatrix}^{t^{-1}} \begin{bmatrix} f_{11} & f_{21} \\ f_{12} & f_{22} \\ \ldots & \ldots \\ f_{1n} & f_{2n} \end{bmatrix} \begin{bmatrix} w \\ r \end{bmatrix}$$

$$= [(I-A)^t]^{-1} [f]^t \begin{bmatrix} w \\ r \end{bmatrix} \quad (20.28)$$

ILLUSTRATION 20.2: Industry 1 uses 20% and 10% of its output by way of its inputs from itself and from Industry 2 respectively. It faces a final demand, F_1. Industry 2, on the other hand, uses 30% and 40% of its output by way of its inputs from Industry 1 and from itself respectively and faces a final demand, F_2. Price per unit of the primary input, labour, is $w = 10$. The final demands, F_1 and F_2, faced by the two industries are 800 and 600 units, respectively. Determine outputs and product prices at equilibrium.

Solution: Information given above is presented in tabular form below:

Input \ Output	1	2	Final demand
1	0.2	0.4	$F_1 = 800$
2	0.1	0.3	$F_2 = 600$
Labour	0.7	0.3	

Here,

$$A = \begin{bmatrix} 0.2 & 0.4 \\ 0.1 & 0.3 \end{bmatrix}$$

$$I - A = \begin{bmatrix} 1 & 0 \\ 0 & 1 \end{bmatrix} - \begin{bmatrix} 0.2 & 0.4 \\ 0.1 & 0.3 \end{bmatrix}$$

$$= \begin{bmatrix} 0.8 & -0.4 \\ -0.1 & 0.7 \end{bmatrix}$$

$$(I - A)^{-1} = \frac{\text{Adj.of} \begin{bmatrix} 0.8 & -0.4 \\ -0.1 & 0.7 \end{bmatrix}}{\text{Det.of} \begin{bmatrix} 0.8 & -0.4 \\ -0.1 & 0.7 \end{bmatrix}}$$

$$= \frac{\begin{bmatrix} 0.7 & 0.1 \\ 0.4 & 0.8 \end{bmatrix}^t}{0.52}$$

$$= \frac{1}{0.52} \times \begin{bmatrix} 0.7 & 0.4 \\ 0.1 & 0.8 \end{bmatrix}$$

$$X = (I - A)^{-1} F$$

$$= \frac{1}{0.52} \times \begin{bmatrix} 0.7 & 0.4 \\ 0.1 & 0.8 \end{bmatrix} \begin{bmatrix} 800 \\ 600 \end{bmatrix}$$

$$= \begin{bmatrix} 1538.46 \\ 1076.92 \end{bmatrix}$$

Thus, $X_1 = 1538.46, X_2 = 1076.92$

From Eq. (20.21), $L = f_{11} X_1 + f_{12} X_2$

$$= 0.7 \times 1538.46 + 0.3 \times 1076.92$$

[Since, $f_{11} = (1 - a_{11} - a_{21}) = (1 - 0.1 - 0.2) = 0.7$ and $f_{12} = (1 - a_{12} - a_{22}) = 1 - 0.4 - 0.3 = 0.3$)]

$$= 1400$$

From Eq. (20.25), equilibrium prices of the products,

$$\begin{bmatrix} P_1 \\ P_2 \end{bmatrix} = [(I - A)^t]^{-1} \times \begin{bmatrix} f_{11} w \\ f_{12} w \end{bmatrix}$$

$$= \begin{bmatrix} \frac{1}{0.52} \end{bmatrix} \times \begin{bmatrix} 0.7 & 0.1 \\ -0.4 & 0.8 \end{bmatrix} \begin{bmatrix} 7 \\ 3 \end{bmatrix}$$

$$= \begin{bmatrix} 10.00 \\ 10.00 \end{bmatrix}$$

Thus, prices of the two products in equilibrium are $P_1 = P_2 = 10$.

ILLUSTRATION 20.3: In Illustration 20.2, if primary inputs are labour and capital both with respective coefficients (per rupee value of the outputs)

$$(f) = \begin{bmatrix} 0.4 & 0.2 \\ 0.3 & 0.1 \end{bmatrix},$$

and respective prices are $w = 10$ and $r = 20$, determine the outputs, quantities employed of labour and capital and the equilibrium prices of the outputs.

Solution: Information given can be represented below in the tabular form:

Input \ Output	1	2	Final demand
1	0.2	0.4	$F_1 = 800$
2	0.1	0.3	$F_2 = 600$
Labour	0.4	0.2	
Capital	0.3	0.1	

Outputs remain unchanged so long as technology matrix A is unchanged. Quantities of labour and capital can be determined from:

$$\begin{bmatrix} L \\ K \end{bmatrix} = (f)X$$

$$= (f)(I-A)^{-1}F$$

$$= \begin{bmatrix} 0.4 & 0.2 \\ 0.3 & 0.1 \end{bmatrix} \begin{bmatrix} 1538.46 \\ 1076.92 \end{bmatrix}$$

$$= \begin{bmatrix} 830.77 \\ 569.23 \end{bmatrix}$$

Product prices in equilibrium, from Eq. (20.27), are given as:

$$\begin{bmatrix} P_1 \\ P_2 \end{bmatrix} = \begin{bmatrix} (1-a_{11}) & -a_{21} \\ -a_{12} & (1-a_{22}) \end{bmatrix}^{-1} \begin{bmatrix} f_{11}w + f_{21}r \\ f_{12}w + f_{22}r \end{bmatrix}$$

$$= \begin{bmatrix} 0.8 & -0.1 \\ -0.4 & 0.7 \end{bmatrix}^{-1} \begin{bmatrix} 10.00 \\ 4.00 \end{bmatrix}$$

$$= \frac{\begin{bmatrix} 0.7 & 0.4 \\ 0.1 & 0.8 \end{bmatrix}^t \begin{bmatrix} 10.00 \\ 4.00 \end{bmatrix}}{0.52}$$

$$= \frac{\begin{bmatrix} 0.7 & 0.1 \\ 0.4 & 0.8 \end{bmatrix} \begin{bmatrix} 10.00 \\ 4.00 \end{bmatrix}}{0.52} = \begin{bmatrix} 14.42 \\ 15.38 \end{bmatrix}$$

Thus, $P_1 = 14.42$, $P_2 = 15.38$ are the equilibrium prices of the two products.

Total value added $= \begin{bmatrix} w & r \end{bmatrix} \begin{bmatrix} L \\ K \end{bmatrix} = \begin{bmatrix} 10 & 20 \end{bmatrix} \begin{bmatrix} 830.77 \\ 569.23 \end{bmatrix} = \mathbf{19692.30}$

20.2.2 The Closed Model

As against this, a **closed input–output model** is one that does not have an exogenous sector. All that is produced is consumed by the producing units. In Tables 20.2 or 20.1, if the household sector be absorbed in the production boundary as an additional industry, providing primary inputs such as labour and capital to the fellow industries and consuming in return from them portions of their outputs, we will have four industries instead of three in quadrant II. At the same time, all the exogenous sectors (Quadrants I and III) would disappear. The resulting model would be a **closed one** (Table 20.5).

TABLE 20.5 A closed input–output model has no exogenous sectors. All that is produced is exhausted by the producers.

Industries	Industries 0	1	2	3	Outputs
0	a_{00}	a_{01}	a_{02}	a_{03}	X_0
1	a_{10}	a_{11}	a_{12}	a_{13}	X_1
2	a_{20}	a_{21}	a_{22}	a_{23}	X_2
3	a_{30}	a_{31}	a_{32}	a_{33}	X_3
Inputs	X_0	X_1	X_2	X_3	

The number of industries in the production boundary in a closed model would, thus, be one higher than that in the open model. As such, we shall have $(n + 1)$ industries in the production boundary instead of n already in existence, each producing for the sake of satisfying the input needs of the existing industries, including itself. The new entrant may also be assumed to have its inputs as a fixed proportion of its output from all the industries including itself, much the same way as in the open model. The components of final consumption of the household sector from different industries in the open model are, thus, treated as inputs of the *household industry* in the closed model and the value of the factor services of the household sector in the open model is treated as the output of the household industry.

Would this transformation of the open model into a closed one affect our analysis and determination of the industry outputs? Let us see. Assume, as before, that the economy comprises these four industries (the newly added household industry serving as the fourth). Let the output of the new entrant be denoted by X_0. Expressing the outputs of the four in terms of their input coefficients, we have:

$$\left. \begin{array}{l} a_{00}.X_0 + a_{01}.X_1 + a_{02}.X_2 + a_{03}.X_3 = X_0 \\ a_{10}.X_0 + a_{11}.X_1 + a_{12}.X_2 + a_{13}.X_3 = X_1 \\ a_{20}.X_0 + a_{21}.X_1 + a_{22}.X_2 + a_{23}.X_3 = X_2 \\ a_{30}.X_0 + a_{31}.X_1 + a_{32}.X_2 + a_{33}.X_3 = X_3 \end{array} \right\} \quad (20.29)$$

Note that the final demand vector is just missing and that the system of equations has transformed into a homogeneous one. Representing it in matrix notation, we have

$$\begin{bmatrix} a_{00} & a_{01} & a_{02} & a_{03} \\ a_{10} & a_{11} & a_{12} & a_{13} \\ a_{20} & a_{21} & a_{22} & a_{23} \\ a_{30} & a_{31} & a_{32} & a_{33} \end{bmatrix} \begin{bmatrix} X_0 \\ X_1 \\ X_2 \\ X_3 \end{bmatrix} = \begin{bmatrix} X_0 \\ X_1 \\ X_2 \\ X_3 \end{bmatrix} \quad (20.30)$$

$$\Rightarrow \quad AX = X$$
$$\Rightarrow \quad (I - A)X = 0 \quad (20.31)$$

where,

$$I = \begin{bmatrix} 1 & 0 & 0 & 0 \\ 0 & 1 & 0 & 0 \\ 0 & 0 & 1 & 0 \\ 0 & 0 & 0 & 1 \end{bmatrix}, \quad A = \begin{bmatrix} a_{00} & a_{01} & a_{02} & a_{03} \\ a_{10} & a_{11} & a_{12} & a_{13} \\ a_{20} & a_{21} & a_{22} & a_{23} \\ a_{30} & a_{31} & a_{32} & a_{33} \end{bmatrix},$$

$$0 = \begin{bmatrix} 0 & 0 & 0 & 0 \\ 0 & 0 & 0 & 0 \\ 0 & 0 & 0 & 0 \\ 0 & 0 & 0 & 0 \end{bmatrix}, \quad X = \begin{bmatrix} X_0 \\ X_1 \\ X_2 \\ X_3 \end{bmatrix},$$

and,

$$(I - A) = \begin{bmatrix} (1 - a_{00}) & -a_{01} & -a_{02} & -a_{03} \\ -a_{10} & (1 - a_{11}) & -a_{12} & -a_{13} \\ -a_{20} & -a_{21} & (1 - a_{22}) & -a_{23} \\ -a_{30} & -a_{31} & -a_{32} & (1 - a_{33}) \end{bmatrix} \quad (20.32)$$

Equation (20.31) is a system of homogeneous equations. It possesses a solution $X_0 = X_1 = X_2 = X_3 = 0$ regardless of the values of the coefficients of X_0, X_1, X_2, X_3. A solution such as this is called a **trivial solution** since it provides no distinguishing information to characterize the system of equations. The necessary and sufficient condition for the system of equations to possess a **non-trivial solution** is that the determinant of its coefficients, $|I - A|$, must be zero. If the number of equations is less than the number of unknowns, the system always possesses a non-trivial solution. But when number of equations is the same as the number of unknowns in the system of homogeneous equations, the condition that $|I - A| = 0$ is necessary as well as sufficient.

The closed input–output model, therefore, possesses a trivial solution ($X_0 = X_1 = X_2 = X_3 = 0$) when $|I - A| \neq 0$ and non-trivial solutions including, of course, the trivial solution as one of them, when $|I - A| = 0$. In the former case, the solution is of little consequence as production of zero outputs by all the industries makes no sense. In the latter case, non-trivial solutions are non-unique and lead to infinitely many steady state (equilibria) situations. However, a little additional information about the household sector may make the closed input–output model and its solution even a more viable alternative than an open input–output model and its solution. To demonstrate, let us have a few illustrations.

ILLUSTRATION 20.4: Industry 1 uses 20% of its own output and 10% of the output of Industry 2 by way of its inputs. It faces a final demand, F_1. Industry 2, on the other hand, uses 30% of its own output and 40% of the output of Industry 1 by way of its inputs and it faces a final demand, F_2. Labour inputs per rupee value of outputs of industries 1 and 2 are ₹ 0.70 (f_{11}) and 0.30 (f_{12}), respectively. Given, for the two industries, the autonomous consumption levels as $C_1 = 100$ and $C_2 = 200$ and marginal propensities to consume as $b_1 = 0.50$ and $b_2 = 0.40$, respectively, determine the outputs of the two industries and the income of the household sector.

Solution: The information given can be presented below through the input–output table:

Input \ Output	1	2	Final demand
1	0.2	0.4	F_1
2	0.1	0.3	F_2
Labour	0.7	0.3	

Using Keynesian consumption function, F_1 and F_2 can be expressed in terms of marginal propensities b_1 and b_2 and autonomous consumption-levels, C_1 and C_2, as

$$F_1 = C_1 + b_1 Y$$
$$= 100 + 0.50 Y$$

and,
$$F_2 = C_2 + b_2 Y$$
$$= 200 + 0.40 Y$$

where, Y is household sector's income from labour.

The input–output system can thus be expressed as:

$$0.2 X_1 + 0.4 X_2 + F_1 = X_1,$$
$$0.1 X_1 + 0.3 X_2 + F_2 = X_2,$$

and,
$$0.70 X_1 + 0.30 X_2 = Y$$

where, X_1 and X_2 are outputs of the two industries. Note that labour inputs of the two industries cost them $0.70 X_1$ and $0.30 X_2$ respectively. The costs of the labour inputs to the industries form the household sector's income, Y.

Substituting for F_1 and F_2 in the input–output system and re-arranging the terms, we have

$$0.2 X_1 + 0.40 X_2 + 0.50 Y - X_1 = -100$$
$$0.10 X_1 + 0.30 X_2 + 0.40 Y - X_2 = -200$$

and,
$$0.7 X_1 + 0.3 X_2 - Y = 0$$

The system can also be expressed as

$$(1 - 0.20) X_1 - 0.40 X_2 - 0.50 Y = 100$$
$$-0.10 X_1 + (1 - 0.30) X_2 - 0.40 Y = 200$$
$$-0.7 X_1 - 0.30 X_2 + Y = 0$$

or, in the matrix notation, as

$$\begin{bmatrix} (1-0.20) & -0.40 & -0.50 \\ -0.10 & (1-0.30) & -0.40 \\ -0.70 & -0.30 & 1.00 \end{bmatrix} \begin{bmatrix} X_1 \\ X_2 \\ Y \end{bmatrix} = \begin{bmatrix} 100 \\ 200 \\ 0 \end{bmatrix}$$

$$\Rightarrow \begin{bmatrix} X_1 \\ X_2 \\ Y \end{bmatrix} = \begin{bmatrix} (1-0.20) & -0.40 & -0.50 \\ -0.10 & (1-0.30) & -0.40 \\ -0.70 & -0.30 & 1.00 \end{bmatrix}^{-1} \begin{bmatrix} 100 \\ 200 \\ 0 \end{bmatrix}$$

$$= \frac{1}{0.052} \times \begin{bmatrix} 0.58 & 0.38 & 0.52 \\ 0.55 & 0.45 & 0.52 \\ 0.51 & 0.37 & 0.52 \end{bmatrix}^t \begin{bmatrix} 100 \\ 200 \\ 0 \end{bmatrix}$$

$$= \frac{1}{0.052} \times \begin{bmatrix} 0.58 & 0.55 & 0.51 \\ 0.38 & 0.45 & 0.37 \\ 0.52 & 0.52 & 0.52 \end{bmatrix} \begin{bmatrix} 100 \\ 200 \\ 0 \end{bmatrix}$$

$$= \frac{1}{0.052} \times \begin{bmatrix} 168 \\ 128 \\ 156 \end{bmatrix}$$

$$= \begin{bmatrix} 3230.77 \\ 2461.54 \\ 3000.00 \end{bmatrix}$$

Thus, $X_1 = 3230.77$, $X_2 = 2461.54$ and $Y = 3000.00$.

(See how additional information about the household sector makes the closed model a viable alternative)

The general expression for the closed model with two sectors with consumption functions given works out as:

$$\begin{bmatrix} X_1 \\ X_2 \\ Y \end{bmatrix} = \begin{bmatrix} (1-a_{11}) & -a_{12} & -b_1 \\ -a_{21} & (1-a_{22}) & -b_2 \\ -f_{11} & -f_{12} & 1 \end{bmatrix}^{-1} \begin{bmatrix} C_1 \\ C_2 \\ 0 \end{bmatrix} \quad (20.33)$$

The symbols have their usual meanings. It can be extended to a model with three or more sectors on the same lines. Here is an expression for a closed economy with n sectors:

$$\begin{bmatrix} X_1 \\ X_2 \\ \ldots \\ X_n \\ Y \end{bmatrix} = \begin{bmatrix} (1-a_{11}) & -a_{12} & \ldots & -a_{1n} & -b_1 \\ -a_{21} & (1-a_{22}) & \ldots & -a_{2n} & -b_2 \\ \ldots & \ldots & \ldots & \ldots & \ldots \\ -a_{n1} & -a_{n2} & \ldots & (1-a_{nn}) & -b_n \\ -f_{11} & -f_{12} & \ldots & -f_{1n} & 1 \end{bmatrix}^{-1} \begin{bmatrix} C_1 \\ C_2 \\ \ldots \\ C_n \\ 0 \end{bmatrix} \quad (20.34)$$

ILLUSTRATION 20.5: A three sector input–output matrix $[I - A]$ is given as:

$$\begin{bmatrix} 1.0 & -0.5 & 0 \\ -0.2 & 1.0 & -0.5 \\ -0.4 & 0 & 1.0 \end{bmatrix}$$

The labour coefficients (per unit of output) are given as 0.4, 0.7 and 1.2 and the household-demands for the outputs of the three sectors are 1000, 5000 and 4000. Determine the level of employment and the volumes of outputs. If the wage rate per labour unit is 10, find the equilibrium prices and the total value added.

Solution: Outputs of the three industries are given by Eq. (20.9) as:

$$X = (I - A)^{-1} F$$

or,

$$\begin{bmatrix} X_1 \\ X_2 \\ X_3 \end{bmatrix} = \begin{bmatrix} 1 & -0.5 & 0 \\ -0.2 & 1 & -0.5 \\ -0.4 & 0 & 1 \end{bmatrix}^{-1} \begin{bmatrix} F_1 \\ F_2 \\ F_3 \end{bmatrix}$$

$$= \frac{1}{0.8} \begin{bmatrix} 1 & 0.40 & 0.40 \\ 0.50 & 1 & 0.20 \\ 0.25 & 0.50 & 0.90 \end{bmatrix}^t \begin{bmatrix} 1000 \\ 5000 \\ 4000 \end{bmatrix}$$

$$= \frac{1}{0.8} \begin{bmatrix} 1 & 0.50 & 0.25 \\ 0.40 & 1 & 0.50 \\ 0.40 & 0.20 & 0.90 \end{bmatrix} \begin{bmatrix} 1000 \\ 5000 \\ 4000 \end{bmatrix}$$

$$= \begin{bmatrix} 5625 \\ 9250 \\ 6250 \end{bmatrix}$$

Employment,

$$L = \begin{bmatrix} f_{11} & f_{12} & f_{13} \end{bmatrix} \begin{bmatrix} X_1 \\ X_2 \\ X_3 \end{bmatrix}$$

$$= \begin{bmatrix} 0.4 & 0.7 & 1.20 \end{bmatrix} \begin{bmatrix} 5625 \\ 9250 \\ 6250 \end{bmatrix}$$

$$= 2250 + 6475 + 7500$$

$$= 16225$$

From Eq. (20.27), equilibrium prices for a three-sector model are given as

$$\begin{bmatrix} P_1 \\ P_2 \\ P_3 \end{bmatrix} = \begin{bmatrix} (1-a_{11}) & -a_{12} & -a_{13} \\ -a_{21} & (1-a_{22}) & -a_{23} \\ -a_{31} & -a_{32} & (1-a_{33}) \end{bmatrix}^{t^{-1}} \begin{bmatrix} f_{11}w \\ f_{12}w \\ f_{13}w \end{bmatrix}$$

$$= \begin{bmatrix} 1 & -0.2 & -0.4 \\ -0.5 & 1 & 0 \\ 0 & -0.5 & 1 \end{bmatrix}^{-1} \begin{bmatrix} 4 \\ 7 \\ 12 \end{bmatrix}$$

$$= \frac{1}{0.8} \begin{bmatrix} 1 & 0.4 & 0.4 \\ 0.5 & 1 & 0.2 \\ 0.25 & 0.5 & 0.9 \end{bmatrix} \begin{bmatrix} 4 \\ 7 \\ 12 \end{bmatrix}$$

$$= \begin{bmatrix} 14.50 \\ 14.25 \\ 19.125 \end{bmatrix}$$

Value added $= [f_{11}w \quad f_{12}w \quad f_{13}w] \times \begin{bmatrix} X_1 \\ X_2 \\ X_3 \end{bmatrix}$

$$= [4 \quad 7 \quad 12] \times \begin{bmatrix} 5625 \\ 9250 \\ 6250 \end{bmatrix}$$

$$= 162250$$

ILLUSTRATION 20.6: Given the technology matrix as

$$\begin{bmatrix} 0.1 & 0.3 & 0.1 \\ 0.0 & 0.2 & 0.2 \\ 0.0 & 0.0 & 0.3 \end{bmatrix}$$

and the final demand functions as

$$F_1 = 0.1Y + C_1$$
$$F_2 = 0.3Y + C_2$$
$$F_3 = 0.4Y + C_3$$

Solution: Expressing the steady-state conditions for the three sectors, we have

$$a_{11} X_1 + a_{12} X_2 + a_{13} X_3 + F_1 = X_1$$
$$a_{21} X_1 + a_{22} X_2 + a_{23} X_3 + F_2 = X_2$$

$$a_{31} X_1 + a_{32} X_2 + a_{33} X_3 + F_3 = X_3$$
$$f_{11} X_1 + f_{12} X_2 + f_{13} X_3 - Y = 0$$

Implying,

$$(1 - a_{11}) X_1 - a_{12} X_2 - a_{13} X_3 - 0.1Y = C_1$$
$$-a_{21} X_1 + (1 - a_{22}) X_2 - a_{23} X_3 - 0.3Y = C_2$$
$$-a_{31} X_1 - a_{32} X_2 + (1 - a_{33}) X_3 - 0.4Y = C_3$$
$$-f_{11} X_1 - f_{12} X_2 - f_{13} X_3 + Y = 0$$

where, $f_{11} = 1 - (a_{11} + a_{21} + a_{31})$; $f_{12} = 1 - (a_{12} + a_{22} + a_{32})$ and $f_{13} = 1 - (a_{13} + a_{23} + a_{33})$.

$$\Rightarrow \begin{bmatrix} (1-a_{11}) & -a_{12} & -a_{13} & -0.1 \\ -a_{21} & (1-a_{22}) & -a_{23} & -0.3 \\ -a_{31} & -a_{32} & (1-a_{33}) & -0.4 \\ -f_{11} & -f_{12} & -f_{13} & +1.0 \end{bmatrix} \begin{bmatrix} X_1 \\ X_2 \\ X_3 \\ Y \end{bmatrix} = \begin{bmatrix} C_1 \\ C_2 \\ C_3 \\ 0 \end{bmatrix}$$

Here,

$$f_{11} = (1 - 0.1 - 0.0 - 0.0) = 0.9; \text{ as } a_{11} = 0.1, a_{21} = 0.0, a_{31} = 0.0$$
$$f_{12} = (1 - 0.3 - 0.2 - 0.0) = 0.5; \text{ as } a_{12} = 0.3, a_{22} = 0.2, a_{32} = 0.0$$
$$f_{13} = (1 - 0.1 - 0.2 - 0.3) = 0.4; \text{ as } a_{13} = 0.1, a_{23} = 0.2, a_{33} = 0.3$$

Substituting the data in the expression, we have

$$\begin{bmatrix} X_1 \\ X_2 \\ X_3 \\ Y \end{bmatrix} = \begin{bmatrix} 0.9 & -0.3 & -0.1 & -0.1 \\ 0.0 & 0.8 & -0.2 & -0.3 \\ 0.0 & 0.0 & 0.7 & -0.4 \\ 0.9 & 0.5 & 0.5 & +1.0 \end{bmatrix}^{-1} \begin{bmatrix} C_1 \\ C_2 \\ C_3 \\ 0 \end{bmatrix}$$

$$= \begin{bmatrix} 2.847 & 2.153 & 2.014 & 1.736 \\ 2.589 & 3.839 & 2.946 & 2.589 \\ 2.857 & 2.857 & 4.286 & 2.857 \\ 5.000 & 5.000 & 5.000 & 5.000 \end{bmatrix} \begin{bmatrix} 1000 \\ 2000 \\ 5000 \\ 0 \end{bmatrix}$$

(Substituting for C_1, C_2 and C_3 and simplifying)

$$= \begin{bmatrix} 17223 \\ 24997 \\ 30001 \\ 40000 \end{bmatrix}$$

KEY TERMS AND CONCEPTS

Assumptions of input–output analysis Some of the assumptions on which input–output analysis is based are:

1. Economy is made up of a finite number of sectors (industries) each of which produces only one homogeneous product. No two products are produced jointly. If at all the case arises, they are produced in fixed proportions.
2. Production in each sector is subject to constant returns to scale, that is, the production function of each industry is a linear homogeneous production function.
3. Input requirements per unit of output in each sector remain fixed and constant and output in each sector is uniquely determined by the quantities of inputs used.

Determination of required primary inputs, labour and capital for production of quantities $X_1, X_2, \ldots, X_n$ by n industries Suppose there are n industries in an economy which use primary inputs labour (L) and capital (K) apart from the use of basic inputs from each other. The general expression for the quantities of the two is:

$$\begin{bmatrix} L \\ K \end{bmatrix} = \begin{bmatrix} f_{11} & f_{12} & \cdots & f_{1n} \\ f_{21} & f_{22} & \cdots & f_{2n} \end{bmatrix} \times \begin{bmatrix} X_1 \\ X_2 \\ \cdots \\ X_n \end{bmatrix}$$

$$= \begin{bmatrix} f_{11} & f_{12} & \cdots & f_{1n} \\ f_{21} & f_{22} & \cdots & f_{2n} \end{bmatrix} \times (I-A)^{-1}(F)$$

$$= \begin{bmatrix} f_{11} & f_{12} & \cdots & f_{1n} \\ f_{21} & f_{22} & \cdots & f_{2n} \end{bmatrix} \times \begin{bmatrix} 1-a_{11} & -a_{12} & \cdots & -a_{1n} \\ -a_{21} & 1-a_{22} & \cdots & -a_{2n} \\ \cdots & \cdots & \cdots & \cdots \\ -a_{n1} & -a_{n2} & \cdots & (1-a_{nn}) \end{bmatrix}^{-1} \times \begin{bmatrix} F_1 \\ F_2 \\ \cdots \\ F_n \end{bmatrix}$$

$$= (f)\,(I-A)^{-1}\,(F)$$

If labour alone is employed, the second row in (f) vector will not be required.

Equilibrium prices of the products For a two sector model,

$$\begin{bmatrix} P_1 \\ P_2 \end{bmatrix} = \begin{bmatrix} (1-a_{11}) & -a_{21} \\ -a_{12} & (1-a_{22}) \end{bmatrix}^{-1} \begin{bmatrix} f_{11} & f_{21} \\ f_{12} & f_{22} \end{bmatrix} \begin{bmatrix} w \\ r \end{bmatrix} = [(I-A)^t]^{-1} [f]^t \begin{bmatrix} w \\ r \end{bmatrix}$$

Extended to n sector model, it transforms to

$$\begin{bmatrix} P_1 \\ P_2 \\ \cdots \\ P_n \end{bmatrix} = \left(\begin{bmatrix} (1-a_{11}) & -a_{12} & \cdots & -a_{1n} \\ -a_{21} & (1-a_{22}) & \cdots & -a_{2n} \\ \cdots & \cdots & \cdots & \cdots \\ -a_{n1} & -a_{n2} & \cdots & (1-a_{nn}) \end{bmatrix}^t \right)^{-1} \begin{bmatrix} f_{11} & f_{21} \\ f_{12} & f_{22} \\ \cdots & \cdots \\ f_{1n} & f_{2n} \end{bmatrix} \begin{bmatrix} w \\ r \end{bmatrix}$$

$$= [(I-A)^t]^{-1} [f]^t \begin{bmatrix} w \\ r \end{bmatrix}$$

Hawkins–Simon conditions For meaningful solution of an input–output model, the following two conditions, called the Hawkins-Simon conditions, must hold:

1. The determinant of the matrix must always be positive, i.e. $|I - A| > 0$; and,
2. Each of the diagonal elements, namely, $(1 - a_{11})$, $(1 - a_{22})$ and $(1 - a_{33})$ must be positive. In other words, each of a_{11}, a_{22} and a_{33} must be less than 1.

Leontief's closed model An input–output model with no exogenous sector for its outputs to sell in or for its inputs to buy from is termed as a closed input–output model. Outputs are consumed within and factor inputs are procured from within, that is, final demand and primary input sectors are absorbed in the production boundary as an additional industry by the name of the household industry producing factor inputs like other industries and consuming outputs like them. In absence of an exogenous sector, the accounting identity in a closed model transforms into a homogeneous one given by $(I - A) X = 0$. The emerging system of equations lacks a unique nontrivial solution, unless some additional information is provided.

Leontief's open model When industrial outputs are exogenously determined by the final demand sector, the input–output model is termed as an open model. That is, when industrial products crossover the producers' boundary to satisfy final demand and some of the industrial inputs are hailed from external sectors, the input–output model is an open model. It is characterized by $(I - A) X + F = X$; where X is the output vector, $(I - A)$ is the technology vector, and F the final demand vector.

Output and income in a closed model For a closed model with n sectors producing $X_1, X_2, X_3, ..., X_n$ outputs and having household sector as its $(n + 1)$th sector providing labour services to the industries with input coefficients $f_{11}, f_{12}, f_{13}, ..., f_{1n}$ and consuming $F_1, F_2, F_3, ..., F_n$ as its inputs from industries 1, 2, 3, ..., n respectively with descriptions:

$$F_1 = C_1 + b_1 Y$$
$$F_2 = C_2 + b_2 Y$$
$$F_3 = C_3 + b_3 Y$$
$$... \quad ... \quad ...$$
$$F_n = C_n + b_n Y$$

where, $C_1, C_2, C_3, ..., C_n$ stand for autonomous consumption by the households from the respective industries and $b_1, b_2, b_3, ..., b_n$ stand for propensities to consume their outputs; the industrial outputs and the national income are given as

$$\begin{bmatrix} X_1 \\ X_2 \\ ... \\ X_n \\ Y \end{bmatrix} = \begin{bmatrix} (1-a_{11}) & -a_{12} & ... & -a_{1n} & -b_1 \\ -a_{21} & (1-a_{22}) & ... & -a_{2n} & -b_2 \\ ... & ... & ... & ... & ... \\ -a_{n1} & -a_{n2} & ... & (1-a_{nn}) & -b_n \\ -f_{11} & -f_{12} & ... & -f_{1n} & 1 \end{bmatrix}^{-1} \begin{bmatrix} C_1 \\ C_2 \\ ... \\ C_n \\ 0 \end{bmatrix}$$

Residual or primary input coefficient Primary input of an industry expressed as a proportion of its output is known as primary input coefficient or residual coefficient. It can be determined by subtracting from 1 the sum of the inter-industry input–output coefficients of an industry. In a three sector model, the residual or primary input coefficient of industry 1 is given by $f_{11} = [1 - (a_{11} + a_{21} + a_{31})]$, that of Industry 2 as $f_{12} = [1 - (a_{12} + a_{22} + a_{32})]$ and that of industry 3 as $f_{13} = [1 - (a_{13} + a_{23} + a_{33})]$.

Technology matrix A matrix $A = [a_{ij}]$, a typical element a_{ij} of which represents industry j's input as a proportion of its output from industry i. In other words, it is input requirement of jth industry from the ith industry per rupee worth of output of jth industry.

Value added vector

$$V = \begin{bmatrix} f_{11}w + f_{21}r \\ f_{12}w + f_{22}r \end{bmatrix} = \begin{bmatrix} f_{11} & f_{21} \\ f_{12} & f_{22} \end{bmatrix} \begin{bmatrix} w \\ r \end{bmatrix} = \begin{bmatrix} f_{11} & f_{12} \\ f_{21} & f_{22} \end{bmatrix}^t \begin{bmatrix} w \\ r \end{bmatrix} = [f]^t \begin{bmatrix} w \\ r \end{bmatrix}$$

EXERCISES

A. Short Answer Questions

1. What is the main point of difference between open and closed input–output models?
2. How would you interpret an input–output coefficient?
3. Interpret a typical element of the technology matrix given below:

	I_1	I_2
I_1	0.3	0.2
I_2	0.4	0.5

   [**Ans.** Element $a_{ij} = \dfrac{\text{Input bought by industry } j \text{ from industry } i}{\text{Output of industry } j}$

   $a_{21} = 0.4$, which means industry 1 uses 40 paise worth of input from industry 2 to produce a rupee worth of output.

   $a_{12} = 0.2$, which means industry 2 uses 40 paise worth of input from industry 2 to produce a rupee worth of output.]

4. Obtain the transaction matrix $(I - A)$ for the technology matrix in Q. 3. Assuming final demand for X_1 and X_2 as 108 and 54, write down an expression for output matrix (X) in terms of final demand vector (F) and $(I - A)^{-1}$.

   [**Ans.** $(I - A) = \begin{bmatrix} 1 & 0 \\ 0 & 1 \end{bmatrix} - \begin{bmatrix} 0.3 & 0.2 \\ 0.4 & 0.5 \end{bmatrix} = \begin{bmatrix} 0.7 & -0.2 \\ -0.4 & 0.5 \end{bmatrix}$

   $\begin{bmatrix} X_1 \\ X_2 \end{bmatrix} = \begin{bmatrix} 0.7 & -0.2 \\ -0.4 & 0.5 \end{bmatrix}^{-1} \times \begin{bmatrix} 108 \\ 54 \end{bmatrix}$

5. Interpret a typical element of $(I - A)^{-1}$ obtained in Q. 4. For the information given in Questions 3 and 4, find the product-mix to satisfy the given levels of final demand.

   [**Ans.** A typical element b_{ij} in $(I - A)^{-1}$ represents amount of output of the ith industry required as its input by the jth industry to produce each unit of final demand for its output.

   $\begin{bmatrix} X_1 \\ X_2 \end{bmatrix} = \begin{bmatrix} 0.7 & -0.2 \\ -0.4 & 0.5 \end{bmatrix}^{-1} \begin{bmatrix} 108 \\ 54 \end{bmatrix} = \begin{bmatrix} 240 \\ 300 \end{bmatrix}$

6. Do the two industries referred to in Question 3 admit any primary inputs? If yes, find the primary input coefficients and interpret each assuming that the industries in question cannot admit any other primary input except labour.

   [**Ans.** Yes. Primary input coefficients for the two industries are 0.3 [1 − (0.3 + 0.4)] and 0.3 [1 − (0.2 + 0.5)]. This shows that each industry consumes labour worth 30% of its output, or, in money terms, it uses 30 paise worth of labour to produce one rupee worth of its output.]

7. Determine the magnitude of labour input required for the desired product-mix in Q. 6.

   [**Ans.** Labour required by industry 1 = 0.30 × 240 = 72. That required by industry 2 = 0.30 × 300 = 90.]

8. If one unit of labour costs ₹ 10, determine the equilibrium prices of the two products.

$$\text{Ans.} \begin{bmatrix} P_1 \\ P_2 \end{bmatrix} = [(I-A)^t]^{-1} \begin{bmatrix} f_{11}w \\ f_{12}w \end{bmatrix} = \begin{bmatrix} 0.7 & -0.4 \\ -0.2 & 0.5 \end{bmatrix}^{-1} \begin{bmatrix} 0.3 \times 10 \\ 0.3 \times 10 \end{bmatrix} = \begin{bmatrix} 10 \\ 10 \end{bmatrix}$$

9. If the household sector be treated as an industry producing labour as its output and admitting final consumption of X_1 and X_2 as its inputs for the data given in Questions 3, 4, 6 and 7, is a unique solution possible? Give reasons in support.

    [Ans. The system of equations, $(I-A)X = 0$ [Eq. (20.31)] being a homogeneous one and $|I-A| \neq 0$ for the data in Questions 3, 4, 6 and 7, a unique solution exists but it is a trivial one.]

10. Given that levels of autonomous consumption of X_1 and X_2 in Q. 9 are 50 and 20 while the marginal propensities to consume for the two are 0.3 and 0.2 respectively, find the product-mix and the income generated for the household sector.

$$\text{Ans.} \begin{bmatrix} X_1 \\ X_2 \\ Y \end{bmatrix} = \begin{bmatrix} (1-a_{11}) & -a_{12} & -b_1 \\ -a_{21} & (1-a_{22}) & -b_2 \\ -f_{11} & -f_{12} & 1 \end{bmatrix}^{-1} \begin{bmatrix} C_1 \\ C_2 \\ 0 \end{bmatrix} = \begin{bmatrix} 0.7 & -0.2 & -0.3 \\ -0.4 & 0.5 & -0.2 \\ -0.3 & -0.3 & 1 \end{bmatrix} \begin{bmatrix} 50 \\ 20 \\ 0 \end{bmatrix}$$

$$= \begin{bmatrix} 209.92 \\ 260.74 \\ 140 \end{bmatrix}$$

11. What is the condition for uniqueness of the solution in Q. 5? Is it satisfied? Explain.

    [Ans. The matrix to be inverted must be non-singular, i.e., its determinant must not be zero. The condition is satisfied, as can be the verified by evaluation of the determinant of the matrix.]

12. What are the conditions for the solution in Q. 5 to be meaningful? Are they satisfied? Explain.

    [Hint. Satisfy Hawkins–Simon conditions.]

13. State the Hawkins–Simon conditions.

14. What is a singular matrix? Give an example.

    [Hint. A matrix whose determinant is zero is a singular matrix.]

15. What is a non-singular matrix? Give an example.

16. Distinguish between the following:
    - trivial and nontrivial solutions
    - open and closed input–output models
    - a singular and a non-singular matrix

17. Given the following transactions for a two sector economy:

Input ↓ / Output →	Sector 1	Sector 2	FD	Output
Sector 1	4	3	13	20
Sector 2	5	4	3	12
Primary inputs	11	5		

(a) Write the technology matrix.
(b) Write the transaction equation.
(c) Rewrite the transaction equation when the final demand for the output of sector 1 increases to 23.

Ans. (a) $\begin{bmatrix} 0.2 & 0.25 \\ 0.25 & 0.333 \end{bmatrix}$ (b) $\begin{bmatrix} X_1 \\ X_2 \end{bmatrix} = (I-A)^{-1} \begin{bmatrix} F_1 \\ F_2 \end{bmatrix} = \begin{bmatrix} 0.8 & -0.25 \\ -0.25 & 0.667 \end{bmatrix}^{-1} \begin{bmatrix} 13 \\ 3 \end{bmatrix}$

(c) $\begin{bmatrix} X_1 \\ X_2 \end{bmatrix} = (I-A)^{-1} \begin{bmatrix} F_1 \\ F_2 \end{bmatrix} = \begin{bmatrix} 0.8 & -0.25 \\ -0.25 & 0.667 \end{bmatrix}^{-1} \begin{bmatrix} 23 \\ 3 \end{bmatrix}$

18. Given the technology matrix for an economy with two industries,

	Steel	Coal
Steel	0.2	0.2
Coal	0.4	0.1

write down the input–output table for the economy when the final demand targets are ₹ 100 and ₹ 20 crores.

[**Ans.**

	Steel	Coal	FD	Gross output
Steel	29.375	17.5	100	146.875
Coal	58.75	8.75	20	87.500.]

19. The following table gives the technology matrix for a two sector economy.

	Agriculture	Manufacturing
Agriculture:	0.10	0.50
Manufacturing:	0.20	0.25

The levels of final demand for the two industries are 300 and 100, respectively. Write down the input–output table for the economy. If the input coefficients for labour for the two industries are 0.7 and 0.25, respectively, calculate the quantity of labour required.

[**Ans.**

		FD	Gross output
47.826	130.44	300	478.26
95.652	65.22	100	260.87

Labour inputs required by the two are **334.78, 65.22.**]

20. In a two industry economy, it is known that industry 1 uses 0.1 unit worth of its own product and 0.6 unit the product of industry 2 to produce a unit worth of its output. Industry 2 uses none of its own product but uses 0.5 unit of the product of industry 1 to produce 1 unit of its output. Final demands for the products of the two industries are, respectively 1000 units and 2000 lac units.

(i) Write down the input matrix and the technology matrix for this economy.
(ii) If the input coefficients for labour for the two industries are 0.3 and 0.5 respectively, calculate the total requirement of labour in the economy.

[**Ans.** The technology matrix, $A = \begin{bmatrix} 0.1 & 0.5 \\ 0.6 & 0.0 \end{bmatrix}$

The output matrix, $X = (I-A)^{-1} F = \begin{bmatrix} 1666.7 \text{ lac} \\ 3000.01 \text{ lac} \end{bmatrix}$

The input matrix, $AX = \begin{bmatrix} 1666.675 \text{ lac} \\ 1000.020 \text{ lac} \end{bmatrix}$

Labour input required $= f_{11} X_1 + f_{12} X_2 =$ **(500.0025 + 500.010)** lac.]

21. In a two sector economy, it is known that industry 1 uses 10 paise worth of its own product and 60 paise worth of commodity 2 to produce a rupee worth of commodity 1; industry 2 uses 30 paise worth of its own product and 50 paise worth of commodity 1 to produce a rupee worth of commodity 2; and the final demands are ₹ 1100 billion worth of commodity 1, ₹ 2200 billion worth of commodity 2.

(i) Write down the input–output matrix for this economy.
(ii) Find the solution through matrix inversion.

(iii) Find the total primary input required to produce these outputs, given that the industries use only one non-durable primary input.

[**Ans.** (i) $A = \begin{bmatrix} 0.10 & 0.50 \\ 0.60 & 0.30 \end{bmatrix}$; (ii) $X = (I - A)^{-1} F = \begin{bmatrix} 5666.67 \\ 8000.00 \end{bmatrix}$

(iii) Primary input = $f_{11} X_1 + f_{12} X_2 = (0.3 \times 5666.67 + 0.2 \times 8000) = 1700 + 1600 = 3300$.]

22. The following gives the technology matrix for a two sector economy consisting of agriculture and manufacturing industries.

	Agr.	Mfg
Agr.	0.5	0.3
Mfg.	0.3	0.2
Lab.	0.5	0.33

Final demand for the two industries are 11 and 12, respectively. Write down the input–output matrix for the economy. Calculate the total labour required. If total labour available is 14; is the solution feasible?

[**Ans.** $X = (I - A)^{-1} F = \begin{bmatrix} 0.5 & -0.3 \\ -0.3 & 0.8 \end{bmatrix}^{-1} \begin{bmatrix} 11 \\ 12 \end{bmatrix} = \begin{bmatrix} 40 \\ 30 \end{bmatrix}$

The column totals are 1.3 and 0.83 instead of 1.00 each. Hence, outputs and inputs are not in monetary terms. Had it been so, the coefficients of the labour inputs to be used for a rupee worth of their outputs by the two industries would have been at most 0.2 (= 1 − 0.5 − 0.3) and 0.5 (= 1 − 0.3 − 0.2). In the steady state, therefore, labour requirements would have been 0.2 × 40 and 0.5 × 30 or 8 and 15, respectively and 23 in all. If labour available being only 14, the solution turns **infeasible**. As stated above, none of the column totals is 1.00, the technology matrix contains quantities of inputs used per unit of each output produced. Hence, labour requirements are 0.5 × 40 and 0.33 × 30 or 20 and 9.9, respectively or 29.9 in all. The solution again works out **infeasible** if total availability of labour is 14 units of it.]

23. An economy produces only coal and steel. The two commodities serve as intermediate inputs in each other's production. It is known that 0.4 tonne of steel and 0.8 tonne of coal are needed by the steel industry to produce 1 tonne of steel and 0.2 tonne of steel and 0.6 tonne of coal are needed by the coal industry to produce 1 tonne of coal. Labour inputs for producing a tonne of each commodity are 5 and 2 units, respectively. The economy requires 120 tonnes coal and 80 tonnes of steel. Calculate gross outputs of the two commodities and the labour requirements for the purpose.

[**Ans.** Technology matrix, $A = \begin{bmatrix} 0.4 & 0.2 \\ 0.8 & 0.6 \end{bmatrix}$

$$X = (I - A)^{-1} F = \begin{bmatrix} 0.6 & -0.2 \\ -0.8 & 0.4 \end{bmatrix}^{-1} \times \begin{bmatrix} 80 \\ 120 \end{bmatrix} = \begin{bmatrix} 700 \\ 1700 \end{bmatrix}$$

Requirement of labour to produce these quantities = $5 \times 700 + 2 \times 1700 = $ **6900**]

24. Outline the main assumptions of the input–output analysis.
25. Show that $(I - A) X = V$, where V is the gross value added vector (at market prices).
    [**Hint.** Value added by an industry is equal to its output less its inputs.]
26. Show that $(I - A) X = F$, where F is the final demand vector.

B. Long Answer Questions

27. The technology matrix (A) and the final demand (F) for an economy with three sectors are given below:

$$A = \begin{bmatrix} 0.3 & 0.4 & 0.2 \\ 0.2 & 0.0 & 0.5 \\ 0.1 & 0.3 & 0.1 \end{bmatrix}; F = \begin{bmatrix} 100 \\ 200 \\ 100 \end{bmatrix}$$

Interpret a typical element of the technology matrix (A). Obtain the transaction matrix ($I - A$) and its inverse $(I - A)^{-1}$. Interpret a typical element of $(I - A)^{-1}$. Determine the outputs of the three sectors and construct the input–output table for the economy. Does the economy use any primary inputs? If yes, what are the primary input coefficients?

[**Ans.** Let us take 0.4 ($i = 1, j = 2$). The element implies that 2nd sector uses 40 paise worth of inputs from the 1st sector for producing a rupee worth of its output.

$$(I - A)^{-1} = \frac{1}{0.401} \begin{bmatrix} 0.75 & 0.42 & 0.40 \\ 0.23 & 0.61 & 0.39 \\ 0.16 & 0.25 & 0.62 \end{bmatrix} = \begin{bmatrix} 1.87 & 1.05 & 1.00 \\ 0.57 & 1.52 & 0.97 \\ 0.40 & 0.62 & 1.55 \end{bmatrix}$$

Let us take 1.05 ($i = 1, j = 2$) in $(I - A)^{-1}$. The element implies that 2nd sector uses ₹ 1.05 worth of input from 1st sector to satisfy, apart from the industrial input needs, rupee 1 worth of final demand for its product $X = (I - A)^{-1}F$. Hence, $X_1 = 497$, $X_2 = 458$, $X_3 = 474$. The primary input coefficients are 0.4 (= 1 – 0.3 – 0.2 – 0.1), 0.3 (= 1 – 0.4 – 0.0 – 0.3) and 0.2 (= 1 – 0.2 – 0.5 – 0.1). Monetary value of the primary inputs works out at **198.8**; **137.4** and **94.8**. The input–output table, thus, can be presented as

Input / Output	Sector 1	Sector 2	Sector 3	FD	Output
Sector 1	149.1	183.2	94.8	100	**497**
Sector 2	99.4	0.0	237	200	**458**
Sector 3	49.7	137.4	47.4	100	**474**
Primary inputs	198.8	137.4	94.8		

28. Given the technology matrix,

$$A = \begin{bmatrix} 0.1 & 0.2 \\ 0.3 & 0.1 \end{bmatrix}$$

Show that

$$(I - A)^{-1} = \begin{bmatrix} 1.200 & 0.267 \\ 0.400 & 1.200 \end{bmatrix}$$

Now, summing up the first n terms of the geometric progression,

$$I, A, A^2, A^3, A^4, \ldots, A^{n-1}$$

where, $I = \begin{bmatrix} 1 & 0 \\ 0 & 1 \end{bmatrix}$

show that $S_n = \dfrac{I - A^n}{I - A} = (I - A)^{-1}(I - A^n)$

Find S_5 ($I + A + A^2 + A^3 + A^4$) for the technology matrix given and show that it is very close to the value of $(I - A)^{-1}$. Hence deduce that:

$$(I - A)^{-1} = S_n$$

as $n \to \infty$ [Given that each element a_{ij} in A ($i, j = 1, 2$) is less than 1].

[**Hint.** $S_n = I + A + A^2 + A^3 + A^4 + \ldots + A^{n-1}$]

∴ $AS_n = A + A^2 + A^3 + A^4 + \ldots + A^n$ (Multiplying both sides by A)

Subtracting, $(I - A) S_n = I - A^n$

or, $S_n = (I - A^n)/(I - A)$

$\Rightarrow$ $S_5 = I + A + A^2 + A^3 + A^4$

$= \begin{bmatrix} 1.1963 & 0.2636 \\ 0.399 & 1.208 \end{bmatrix}$

Comparing the result with the value of $(I - A)^{-1}$, we observe that the two are quite close to each other and it can be taken as a close approximation of $(I - A)^{-1}$.]

29. If the consumer output requirements are ₹80 million in steel, ₹20 million in coal and ₹55 million in railway transport, determine from the following matrix the final output goals of each industry

	Steel	Coal	Railway transport
Steel	0.2	0.2	0.3
Coal	0.4	0.1	0.3
Railway transport	0.1	0.3	0.3
Labour	0.3	0.4	0.1

Estimate the labour requirements for final outputs of the three industries

[*Calcutta, Applied Economics, 1966*]

[**Ans.** $X_1 = 188$, $X_2 = 149$, $X_3 = 131$; $L_1 = 56.6$, $L_2 = 59.6$, $L_3 = 39.3$]

30. From the following technological matrix and final consumer requirements determine gross levels of output of the three industries A, B, and C:

	A	B	C	Consumer requirements
A	0.2	0.4	0.5	₹ 70 million
B	0.5	0.1	0.1	₹ 60 million
C	0.1	0.2	0.1	₹ 90 million
Labour	0.2	0.3	0.3	–

What will be the total labour requirements? [*Calcutta, Applied Economics, 1968*]

[**Ans.** $X_1 = 360$, $X_2 = 289$, $X_3 = 204$; $L_1 = 72.0$, $L_2 = 86.7$, $L_3 = 61.2$]

31. From the following technological matrix and final consumer requirements determine gross levels of output of the three industries A, B and C:

	A	B	C	Consumer requirements
A	0.2	0.3	0.2	₹ 80 thousand
B	0.5	0.4	0.3	₹ 120 thousand
C	0.1	0.2	0.1	₹ 90 thousand
Labour	0.2	0.1	0.3	–

What will be the total labour requirements? [*Calcutta, Applied Economics, 1969*]

[**Ans.** $X_1 = 422$, $X_2 = 769$, $X_3 = 373$; $L_1 = 89.4$, $L_2 = 79.6$, $L_3 = 111.9$]

32. From the following matrix find the final output goals of each industry assuming that the consumer output targets are ₹ 85 million in steel, ₹ 25 million in coal, and ₹ 55 million in railway transport:

	Steel	Coal	Railway transport
Steel	0.4	0.1	0.2
Coal	0.2	0.2	0.4
Railway transport	0.2	0.3	0.3
Labour	0.2	0.4	0.1

Estimate the labour requirements for final outputs of the three industries.

[*Calcutta, Applied Economics, 1965*]

[**Ans.** $X_1 = 261$, $X_2 = 220$, $X_3 = 247$; $L_1 = 52.2$, $L_2 = 88.0$, $L_3 = 24.7$]

33. Consider the following triangular technology matrix:

$$A = \begin{bmatrix} 0.2 & 0.1 & 0.2 \\ 0.0 & 0.2 & 0.3 \\ 0.0 & 0.0 & 0.2 \end{bmatrix}$$

Find:
 (i) $(I - A)^{-1}$.
 (ii) Relationship between output and final demand vectors.
 (iii) Change in the levels of output of the three industries when final demand for each increases by 40%.

Comment on the nature of relationships in (ii) and (iii). Given the final demands for the three industries as 100, 200, and 400 respectively, find answers to (ii) and (iii). What are the primary input coefficients?

34. Find the final demand vector F consistent with output vector

$$X = \begin{bmatrix} 25 \\ 21 \\ 18 \end{bmatrix}$$

when input–output coefficient matrix is:

$$A = \begin{bmatrix} 0.2 & -0.3 & 0.2 \\ 0.4 & 0.1 & 0.2 \\ 0.1 & 0.3 & 0.2 \end{bmatrix}$$

Also compute the gross value added in each sector and show that total value added in each sector and total final demand are both equal to 21. [*Rajasthan, 1973*]

[**Ans.**

$$I - A = A = \begin{bmatrix} 0.2 & -0.3 & 0.2 \\ 0.4 & 0.1 & 0.2 \\ 0.1 & 0.3 & 0.2 \end{bmatrix}$$

$$F = (I - A) X$$

$$= \begin{bmatrix} 10.1 \\ 5.3 \\ 5.6 \end{bmatrix}$$

Total final demand = 10.1 + 5.3 + 5.6 = **21.00**

Primary input coefficients are 0.3 (= 1 − 0.2 − 0.4 − 0.1), 0.3 (= 1 − 0.3 − 0.1 − 0.3) and 0.4 (= 1 − 0.2 − 0.2 − 0.2 = 0.4). Gross value added = 0.3 × 25 + 0.3 × 21 + 0.4 × 18 = **21.00**.]

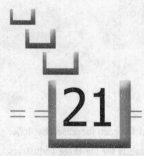

21

International Trade Factor Mobility and Comparative Advantage

CHAPTER OUTLINE

Introduction
- International versus Inter-regional Trade
- Theories of International Trade
- Modern Theory of International Trade
- A Comparative Analysis of Classical and the Modern Theories
- International or World Terms of Trade
- Factor Mobility and Factor Price Equalization
- Key Terms and Concepts
- Exercises

INTRODUCTION

International trade may be defined as an exchange of goods and services among different nations. Trade between two nations is known as **bilateral trade**. Under it, two countries exchange their products with each other on preferential basis generally under an agreement called **bilateral trade agreement**. As against this, trade agreements may take place among several nations to buy from and/or to sell to each other on preferential basis or a nation may be in agreement with two or more nations to buy from or to sell to the rest of the signatories either on preferential terms or on terms restricting trade among themselves. Trade agreements involving more than two nations are called **multilateral trade agreements** and trade resulting from such agreements is known as **multilateral trade**. Among the causes responsible for international trade, the most immediate one is people's desire to procure a good or service better in quality and/or cheaper, price-wise. For instance, a country producing cloth at ₹ 50 a metre would prefer to buy it from another producing the same quality of it at a price less than ₹ 50 a metre or a superior quality of it at a price of ₹ 50 a metre. It is a different matter why some countries can provide the same quality of certain products at lower prices or their superior quality at the same prices. There are a number of theories put forth from time to time by several schools of thought to explain issues such as these, as also those pertaining to the need and evolution of international trade. But the immediate cause of international trade remains intact. Price and quality differences cause international trade. Investigations into cause, need, evolution and mechanism of international trade constitute the subject matter of international economics. Before introducing it, let us have an idea of the background of the issues at the core of international trade.

Since the creation of universe, natural and human resources were not apportioned uniformly throughout. Some countries got abundant underground resources like petroleum deposits, while others got richness of surfacial resources such as fertile soil with abundant potential for cultivation. Nations, with abundant petroleum resources, concentrated on production of petroleum while those with abundant soil resources focussed on production of food. While petroleum producers needed food which they themselves could not produce, the food producers needed petroleum, production of which was inappropriate and costlier in their own lands. This initiated production of surpluses by the countries for exchanging them with the products they could not produce cheaper in price and better in quality than others.

Likewise, distribution and development of human resources and skills too was uneven or non-uniform. This created a wide gap in development of technology among the nation-states. While some nations resorted to capital intensive high-tech production, others continued with their labour-intensive primitive methods. While some were endowed to produce one product cheaper than others, the others were better poised to produce other products cheaper than the former ones, each specializing production of its speciality and raising of its surpluses. Surpluses of the specialized products paved the way for trading them with the surpluses of the rest of the products raised by the rest of nations. That way, each was to benefit from the other's specialization, as each was able to consume goods for production of which it suffered from inherent disadvantages in terms of costs due to non-availability of inputs, production techniques or technologies.

For thousands of years, particular kinds of goods have been hauled across the national boundaries from the territories of relative abundance to those of relative scarcity. The prehistoric mythology is full of fascinating accounts of man's adventures to distant lands in the quest of gold and other precious metals. The Greeks and Romans crossed the adjacent seas to procure wheat and other commodities that could not be availed of in their domestic territories in requisite amounts at affordable prices.

A number of factors, such as, localization of mineral deposits in certain regions, peculiarities of climate and soil as between different regions, differences in population densities in different geographical areas, non-uniformity in development and adaptation of improved technologies of production, have all made a significant contribution in promoting international trade.

The earliest known systematic treatment of international trade goes to accredit the classical economists such as Adam Smith, David Ricardo, J.S. Mill and others who formulated their theories in the background of the then dominant philosophy of economic liberalism, popularly known as **laissez-faire**, meaning free trade or trade without barriers across the border. Later, economists like Bertil Ohlin came up with what is known as the modern theory of international trade. For better understanding of these theories, let us first see in what respects does the international trade differ from the inter-regional trade.

21.1 INTERNATIONAL VERSUS INTER-REGIONAL TRADE

Bertil Ohlin* regarded 'international trade as a special case of inter-regional trade'. This means that the two are different on certain counts yet similar on others. Let us first see in what respects are the two similar. Both imply purchasing products costlier to produce by self and selling those costlier to purchase from others. Both require products bought from others or sold to others match the tastes and preferences of the buyers. Both involve costs of transportation as buyers and sellers are separated by distances—long or short. Both involve paying for products bought in the sellers currency. Both require absence of barriers because barriers restrict free flow of products from the sellers to the buyers, defeating the very purpose of trade.

As regards differences, the *first* and foremost difference relates to currency. International trade involves different currencies while inter-regional trade does not. As a result, acquiring seller's currency by the buyer is must in international trade while it is not in inter-regional trade as currencies of the two are the same. The *second* difference relates to suitability of the product to the customs, traditions, tastes and preferences of the buyer. For example, electrical appliances in US run on 110 volts while those in India run on 220 volts. An electric iron manufactured by one is unsuitable for the other unless modified to run on the buyer's voltage. Likewise, vehicles manufactured in US are unsuitable for Indians and those manufactured in India are unsuitable for Americans as those manufactured in India have driver's seat on the right side while those manufactured in US have it on the left side. The *third* difference relates to the tariff which is applicable in international trade but not in inter-regional trade. To protect domestic industries, many nations impose heavy tariff on imports so that foreign products to importers may turn costlier than the domestic products. The *fourth* difference between the two is the transportation cost which is generally higher in international trade than in inter-regional trade. But this need not always be true. The transportation costs from the southernmost tip of India to the extreme north is higher than that between a city in north India and another in Pakistan. Trade within the territory of India is inter-regional or domestic while that between a city in India and another in Pakistan is international. The *fifth* difference between the two relates to the economic policies which are generally same in case of inter-regional trade but different in case of international trade. For instance, policies of direct and indirect taxation are more or less same in the same country but different in different countries. The *sixth* difference relates to the mobility of factors which is high within a region but low between the countries. Low mobility of factors leads to high price-differences while high mobility to low price-differences. The *seventh* difference relates to the balance of payment problem that governs the international trade but not the inter-regional trade.

In summary, we can say that the two types of trades, despite certain similarities, are in fact different from each other. Can we then grant Prof. Ohlin his contention that international

---

*Bertil Ohlin was awarded the Nobel Prize for economics in 1977 by the Royal Swedish Academy for his contributions to the theory and policy of international trade in a way that has earned him a niche in the history of the economic theory of international trade. Professor Ohlin shared the Prize with Prof. James E. Meade whose contribution to the development of trade theory and policy is no less remarkable.

trade is a special case of inter-regional trade? If we view the two from the angle of economic motivation, we can but if we look at the two from the angle of its effects on those involved in it, we cannot.

21.2 THEORIES OF INTERNATIONAL TRADE

21.2.1 Mercantilist Doctrine

Excavations in various parts of the world in quest of knowledge reveal that some form of international trade existed even in the prehistoric periods. Lack of authenticity of information on various aspects of it, however, compels us to confine our analysis to the post-development of modern nation-states. In the first two centuries (the 17th and the 18th centuries) of the post-development period, the economic doctrine that governed the international trade was **mercantilism**. The doctrine possessed, at its core, several features on which modern nationalism rests. Well-being of a nation was, thus, of supreme importance in mercantilism. This, as believed, could be achieved through accumulation of wealth in the form of precious metals (gold and silver). While exports were favoured so long as they brought in gold, imports were viewed with apprehension. It was believed that imports caused a drain on stocks of gold and reduced the well-being of the nation.

21.2.2 Theory of Comparative Advantage

Mercantilist doctrine of international trade was replaced by the **classical theory of international trade**. Better known as the **theory of comparative advantage**, the classical theory was first formulated by David Ricardo around 1815 and was improvised by J.S. Mill, Cairns and Bastable, later. The best exposition of the theory is to be found in the works of Taussig and Haberler. The theory shifted emphasis from the goal of national well-being to that of the well-being of the individual. For Ricardo as also for Adam Smith, the supreme objective of all economics was the well-being of the consumer. In their view, nation was nothing more than the sum of its inhabitants.

Statement of the theory

In the language of David Ricardo, when a country enters into trade with another country, it has to export those commodities in which its production costs are comparatively less and import those commodities in which its production costs are comparatively higher. In other words, **each country will specialize in the production of those commodities for which it enjoys greater comparative advantage or lesser comparative disadvantage in production**. It will thus, export those commodities for which its comparative advantage in production is higher and will import those ones for which its comparative advantage in production is lower or its comparative disadvantage is higher.

Assumptions of the classical theory of international trade

The Ricardian theory of comparative cost advantage is based on the following assumptions:

1. There are two countries, say A and B, producing two goods, say X and Y through only one factor of production, labour.

2. All the labour units are homogeneous with fixed supply and fixed productivity in all the goods. They are perfectly mobile within the country and perfectly immobile beyond it. There exists full employment of labour in both the countries.
3. Tastes and preferences of the people are same in both the countries.
4. Production of commodities in the two countries takes place under constant cost conditions and unchanged technological know-how. Product prices depend on labour costs alone as transportation costs are assumed to be zero while trade is assumed to be free, without any barriers.
5. Trade between the two countries is based on barter and the exchange ratio for the two commodities is the same due to the existence of perfect competition in the international markets.

The reader can make a note that most of these assumptions are unrealistic and hence, attract severe criticism. Let us spare that for a later stage and proceed with what the Ricardian theory says about the emergence of international trade.

Costs differences

Given the assumptions, the theory of comparative cost advantage is explained by taking three types of cost differences:

1. Absolute cost difference
2. Equal cost difference
3. Comparative cost difference

To explain them, let us take the numerical example Ricardo himself used. Let the two countries be England and Portugal, both producing wine and cloth. Production costs in both are measured in labour hours. Further, let Table 21.1 presents the production costs of the two:

TABLE 21.1 Comparative Cost Difference (Opportunity Costs in Brackets)

Countries	Production costs in labour hours for	
	1 unit of wine	1 unit of cloth
Portugal	80 (80/90 = 0.89)	90 (90/80 = 1.125)
England	120 (120/100 = 1.20)	100 (100/120 = 0.83)

According to the model, Portugal has the absolute cost advantage in production of both the goods. The number of labour hours required to produce one unit of a product or what is called the **labour coefficient** is less in Portugal for both the commodities than what it is in England. One unit of wine costs 80 labour hours in Portugal while it costs 120 labour hours in England. In other words, the labour coefficient for wine in Portugal is less than what it is in England and hence production of wine is cheaper in Portugal than in England. Likewise, one unit of cloth in Portugal costs 90 labour hours while the same in England costs 100 labour hours. That is, labour coefficient for cloth is less in Portugal than in England and hence production of cloth also is cheaper in Portugal than in England, Portugal, thus, enjoys absolute cost advantage in production of both the goods. On the basis of the doctrine of absolute cost differences, Portugal would specialize production of both and the two nations would never enter in trade.

But, on the basis of the comparative cost differences, trade is very much possible between the two and is also gainful for both. We can show this either by the comparison of the opportunity costs or through the production possibility curves. Table 21.1 shows the opportunity cost of producing each of the two goods in both the countries. The opportunity cost of one unit of wine in Portugal is (80/90) or 0.89 units of cloth. This means that Portugal has to sacrifice production of 0.89 units of cloth in order to produce one unit of wine. Likewise, opportunity cost of one unit of wine in England is (120/100) or 1.2 units of cloth. Clearly, opportunity cost of wine in Portugal is less than what it is in England. This shows that Portugal has greater comparative cost advantage in production of wine over England. Likewise comparing the opportunity costs of producing one unit of cloth in the two nations, we observe that the opportunity cost of producing cloth is less in England (0.83) than what it is in Portugal (1.125). England, thus, has a greater comparative cost advantage in production of cloth over Portugal. On the basis of the doctrine of comparative cost differences, Portugal has a greater comparative cost advantage in production of wine while England has it in production of cloth. Accordingly, Portugal would specialize production of wine while England, that of cloth. Portugal would export wine to England and the latter would export cloth to Portugal. We will turn to gains from trade accruing to the trading partners as soon as we finish with the technique of the production possibility curves to demonstrate the comparative cost advantage of the two countries.

For this, assume that each of Portugal and England has 72,000 labour hours at its disposal. Under the assumption of full employment, Portugal can produce either 900 units of wine or 800 units of cloth or a combination of the two. The different production possibilities of wine and cloth in respect of Portugal are shown by the line *PP* in Figure 21.1. Likewise, England can produce either 600 units of wine or 720 units of cloth or a combination of the two. The production possibilities in respect of England are shown by the line *EE* in Figure 21.1. Note that PPCs of the two countries are linear. This is because of the assumption of constant cost conditions*. Note also that:

(i) When the PPCs are parallel, cost differences are equal and the nations do not enter in trade (Figure 21.2).
(ii) When the PPCs are non-parallel and non-intersecting, one nation has absolute cost advantage and the other, absolute cost disadvantage in production of both. On the basis of absolute cost advantage, no trade is possible between the two nations. But on the basis of comparative advantage or disadvantage, one nation specializes production of that good for which it has greater comparative cost advantage and the other nation specializes production of that good for which it has lesser comparative disadvantage. The trade is thus possible between the two nations on the basis of comparative cost advantage (Figure 21.1).

---

* Constant labour productivity in all products gives constant opportunity cost of labour. The ratio of the labour co-efficients for two goods is thus constant. Hence, marginal opportunity cost or the slope of the PPC is also constant. This gives linear PPCs. In reality, a PPC is concave to the origin.

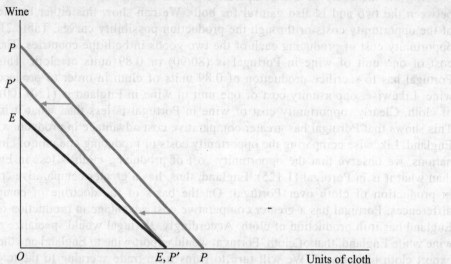

FIGURE 21.1 The straight lines *PP* and *EE* represent production possibilities of Portugal and England, respectively. Since *PP* is farther away from the origin than *EE*, Portugal has absolute advantage and England, absolute disadvantage in production of both. However, Portugal has comparatively **greater advantage** in production of wine than of cloth while England has comparatively **lower disadvantage** in production of cloth than of wine. In other words, Portugal has greater comparative cost advantage in production of wine while England has lesser comparative cost disadvantage in production of cloth. On the basis of absolute cost advantage, Portugal would produce both the goods, ruling out the possibility of trade between the two. But on the basis of comparative cost advantage, Portugal must specialize in production of wine while on the basis of lesser comparative cost disadvantage, England must specialize in production of cloth. Portugal will thus export wine to England and England will export cloth to Portugal. Portugal's excess advantage in production of wine = $P'E$. Had the PPCs of the two nations been parallel, the cost differences would have been equal and no trade would have taken place even on the basis of comparative cost advantage.

(iii) When the PPCs are non-parallel but intersecting (Figure 21.3), one nation has a greater absolute cost advantage in production of one good while the other nation has greater absolute cost advantage in production of the other good. The trade will take place between the two nations on the basis of their respective absolute cost advantages.

Table 21.2 shows the production costs of wine and cloth in labour hours in countries A and B. On the basis of absolute cost differences, no trade is possible between the two. On the basis of comparative cost differences too, no trade is possible between the two. The opportunity costs of production of wine and cloth are the same for the two. The production possibility curves for country A and B are parallel, leaving none of A and B with any comparative advantage or disadvantage (Figure 21.2).

TABLE 21.2 Equal Cost Difference (Opportunity Costs in Brackets)

Countries	Production costs in labour hours for	
	1 *unit of wine*	1 *unit of cloth*
A	80 (8/10 = 0.8)	100 (10/8 = 1.25)
B	100 (100/125 = 0.8)	125 (125/100 = 1.25)

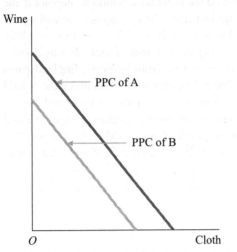
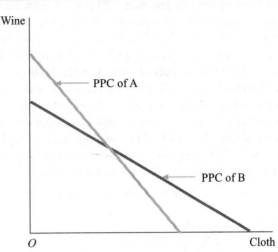

FIGURE 21.2 Parallel PPCs imply that the cost differences are equal. Hence, no trade is possible between the two countries.

FIGURE 21.3 Intersecting PPCs imply that country A has greater absolute cost advantage in production of wine while country B has greater absolute cost advantage in production of cloth. Country A specializes production of wine and exports it to B while B specializes that of cloth and exports it to A.

From Table 21.3, country A has absolute cost advantage in production of wine while country B has it in production of cloth. Country A should, therefore, specialize production of wine and country B that of cloth. Exactly same is the inference reached from comparative cost advantages. Country A has it in production of wine while country B, in production of cloth. Accordingly, country A specializes production of wine while country B that of cloth. Country A exports wine to country B and country B exports cloth to country A. Both gain from trade. Production possibility curves for the two countries intersect each other (Figure 21.3).

TABLE 21.3 Absolute Cost Difference (Opportunity Costs in Brackets)

Countries	Production costs in labour hours for	
	1 unit of wine	1 unit of cloth
A	80 (8/15 = 0.53)	150 (15/8 = 1.88)
B	120 (12/10 = 1.2)	100 (10/12 = 0.83)

Conclusions reached are the same even through the technique of production possibility curves.

Ricardo on gains from trade

To explain Ricardo's concept of gains from trade, suppose the two countries (Table 21.1) produce and consume in isolation. England spends 120 hours of labour on one unit of wine and 100 hours of it on one unit of cloth. Clearly, production of wine is more expensive than that of cloth in England. Production of 1 unit of wine costs England 1.2 units of cloth. Similarly, production of cloth is more expensive than that of wine in Portugal. One unit of wine costs Portugal 0.89 units of cloth. Let the two open up to a bilateral trade with England specializing production of cloth while Portugal, that of wine. England would import wine from Portugal and would be happier if she can get 1 unit of wine for less than 1.20 units of cloth. Portugal on the other hand would be happier if she can get more than 0.89 units of cloth for each unit of wine sacrificed. Now suppose England agrees to give away 1.05 units of cloth for 1 unit of wine. She thus saves 1.20 – 1.05 = 0.15 units of cloth. On the other hand, Portugal gets 1.05 units of cloth for giving away 1 unit of wine. Portugal gains 1.05 – 0.89 = 0.16 units of cloth. Clearly, both gain from trade than from isolation. England gains 0.15 units of cloth while Portugal gains 0.16 units of it. The exchange rate of cloth and wine is 1.05 units of English cloth per unit of Portuguese wine. Gains from trade are more or less equitable for both (0.15 ≈ 0.16). To split up total gains equitably, the rate of commodity exchange must be 1.045 units of English cloth for 1 unit of Portuguese wine. Each would then gain 0.155 units of cloth.

Ricardo's approach to gains from trade as explained by Prof. Ronald Findlay in his 'gains and specialization' (1970) is shown in Figure 21.4.

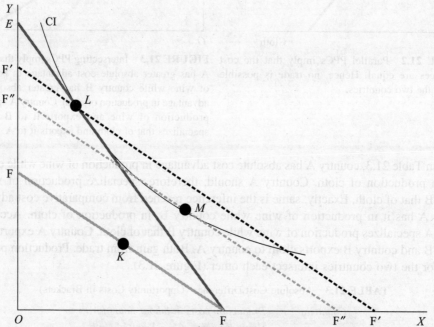

FIGURE 21.4 Let **FF** represent the linear production possibilities of goods X and Y in country **A:** In its pre-trade period, the country produces combination K on **FF**. Now suppose the country opens up to international trade. Slope of the price line (**FE**) gives the ratio of prices of X and Y in the international market. Suppose further that the country in question selects basket L for its consumption in the post-trade period and enjoys utility represented by the community indifference curve, **CI**. The country thus, produces basket K but consumes basket L in its post-trade period. If it were to produce basket L domestically, it would have to increase labour input sufficiently to shift its PPC up from **FF** to **F'F'**. Its gain from trade can thus, be measured by the ratio, **FF'/OF**. Country in question will export X and import Y. This gives Prof. Findlay's version of Ricardo's gains from trade. To Malthus, this measure of Ricardo's gains from trade was an overestimate of the gains. In his view, with the shift of the PPC to **F'F'**, point L should no longer be the equilibrium point. He argues that relative prices would turn more favourable to the exported commodity X with the shift and the equilibrium in consumption must shift to the right of point L on **F'F'**. Even Prof. Findlay modified Ricardo's measure of gains from trade. For this, he used the community indifference curve, **CI** and recommended increasing of the labour input only by as much as is needed to shift the country's PPC to **F"F"** so that **CI** may be tangential to the lowest possible PPC, as shown, at point M. The gains from trade accruing to the country in question would have a much smaller measure. It is given by **FF"/OF**.

Ricardo's version of gains from trade, as mentioned earlier is based on labour theory of value and the assumption of constant returns to scale. PPC is linear accordingly.

Ricardo's measure of gains from trade, FF'/OF, as demonstrated by Prof. Findlay, was an over-estimate of the gains, which Malthus too rejected as such. The true measure of gains from trade, as modified by Prof. Findlay with the help of community indifference curve (CI), is FF''/OF, which is less than FF'/OF. Malthus had advocated that equilibrium in consumption due to shifting of the PPC would fall on F'F', to the right of point L, while Prof. Findlay, showed with community indifference curve (CI) that it would fall to the right of point L, but on a PPC (F''F'') much lower than F'F'. The modern version of the gains from trade is provided in Figure 21.7 (Section 21.3) and the offer curve version, in Figure 21.10 (Section 21.5).

Criticism of the classical theory

The Classical Theory or the Theory of Comparative Cost Advantage has served as the basis of international trade for a little less than two centuries. All the criticism levelled against the theory in the intervening period could not go beyond the point of its modification or amplification. Despite its unrealistic assumptions, the basic content of the theory has remained intact. It would be interesting to quote Prof. Samuelson for his support to the theory, " If theories like girls could win beauty contests, comparative advantage would certainly rate high in that it is an elegantly logical structure."*

The theory, however, has met severe criticism at the hands of Bertil Ohlin and Frank D. Graham on the ground that it is based on unrealistic assumptions of:

1. Labour costs that remain unchanged.
2. Similar tastes.
3. Perfect internal mobility and external immobility of labour.
4. Absence of transportation costs.
5. Free trade.
6. Homogeneity of labour.
7. Barter as the basis of trade.
8. Two countries trading in two commodities.
9. Existence of perfect competition.

21.3 MODERN THEORY OF INTERNATIONAL TRADE

Bertil Ohlin in his famous work *Inter-regional and International Trade* (1933) criticized the classical theory of international trade and formulated his own theory known as the **Modern Theory of International Trade**. The theory, also known as **Heckscher–Ohlin Theorem**, is based on the framework of general equilibrium. In fact, it was Eli Heckscher, Ohlin's teacher, who first propounded the idea in 1919 that trade results from differences in factor endowments in different countries. Ohlin carried it forward to formulate the modern theory of international trade.

---

* P.A. Samuelson, Economics, 8th Edition, p. 656.

Statement of the Modern Theory

In essence, the immediate cause of international trade, according to the modern theory, is the price difference instead of the cost difference as advocated by the classical theory. The price difference, no doubt, is a consequence of cost difference, which in turn, is a consequence of the differences of factor endowments. The ultimate cause of international trade is thus, the difference of factor endowments between the trading partners. To elaborate, let us take the example of India and UK. India enjoys factor abundance for agricultural production which she can accomplish at costs much lower than the costs at which UK, lacking these factor endowments, can. India can therefore, provide agricultural products at prices much lower than the prices at which UK can. On the other hand, UK, better equipped with capital endowments than India, is better poised for production of capital intensive goods which she can provide at prices lower than the prices at which India, lacking capital endowments, can. As a result, India would specialize production of agricultural goods while UK would specialize production of capital intensive goods. The two would benefit by exchanging the surpluses of their specialities with each other. Ohlin's theory, in a nut-shell, states that a capital abundant country would export capital intensive goods and a labour abundant country would export labour intensive goods.

Note that in modern theory, immediate cause of international trade is price-difference caused by cost difference, which in turn, is caused by differences of factor endowments. In classical theory, immediate cause of international trade is cost difference. Compare the two and see for yourself how far the two theories deviate from each other.

The ultimate cause of international trade, the differences in factor endowments, as envisaged in modern theory, may be explained in terms of factor prices as also in physical terms*.

Factor abundance in terms of factor prices

If $(P_L/P_K)_A > (P_L/P_K)_B$, country A is relatively capital abundant or country B is relatively labour abundant. Here, P_K and P_L represent capital and labour prices, respectively. Subscripts A and B denote the names of the countries to which the price ratio belongs. Factor abundance through factor prices, as expressed above, can also be demonstrated through iso-quants and iso-costs as in Figure 21.5.

Factor abundance in physical terms

If $(C_A/L_A) > (C_B/L_B)$, country A is relatively capital abundant and Country B, relatively labour abundant. Here, C_A and L_A are capital and labour endowments in country A while C_B and L_B, those in country B. Factor abundance in physical terms, as expressed above, can also be demonstrated through PPCs and revenue lines as shown in Figure 21.6.

Assumptions of the modern theory

The modern theory of Ohlin is based on the following assumptions:

1. There are two countries (A and B), two commodities (X and Y) and two factors (L, K), involved.
2. Trade is free, with no transportation costs.
3. The factor and the product markets are competitive, with full employment of factors which are perfectly mobile within the country but immobile beyond it.

---

* Based on Bo Sodersten, *"International Economics"*, 2nd Edition, Macmillan, London, 1990, pp. 42–44.

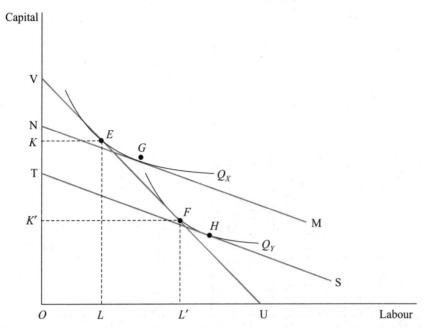

FIGURE 21.5 Q_X represents isoquant of commodity X (capital intensive) while Q_Y, that of commodity Y (labour intensive). For simplicity, suppose each isoquant represents 1 unit of the commodity. UV represents isocost curve of country A while MN and ST, those of country B. Slope of UV is $[(P_L/P_K)_A]$ and that of ST or MN is $[(P_L/P_K)_B]$. Let UV be steeper than either of MN or ST so that $[(P_L/P_K)_A] > [(P_L/P_K)_B]$. That is, either P_L in country A is higher than P_L in country B, given P_K as same in the two; or, P_K in country A is lower than P_K in country B, given P_L as same in the two; or, P_L in country A is higher than P_L in country B and, at the same time, P_K in country A is lower than P_K in country B. That is, labour is costlier in country A than in country B (implying that country B is relatively labour abundant while country A, relatively labour scarce) or capital is cheaper in country A than in country B (implying that country A is relatively capital abundant while country B, relatively capital scarce) or both (implying that country A is relatively capital abundant and country B relatively labour-abundant). That is why isoquant of commodity X is higher than that of commodity Y.

A capital rich country A produces $Q_X = 1$ unit at E employing OL labour and OK capital. KV units of its capital are equal to OL units of its labour. Hence, production cost of 1 unit of X in country A = OK units of capital + OL units of labour = OK units of capital +KV units of capital = OV units of capital. On the same lines, it can be shown that country B produces one unit of X at G employing ON units of capital. ON units of capital, though fewer than OV units of it in physical terms, they are costlier in country B than in country A when P_K in country A is lower than P_K in country B. Moreover, production of 1 unit of commodity Y requires OT units of capital in country B and OV units of capital in country A. OT being less than either of ON or OV, production of commodity Y is cheaper than that of X in country B and so is it, as compared to its cost in country A, (note that country A requires OV units of capital for 1 unit of Y at point F). Country B would therefore, specialize in production of Y which is labour intensive while country A would specialize production of X which is capital intensive. This owes its explanation to lower capital price (P_K) in country A due to its relative capital abundance and to lower labour price (P_L) in country B due to its relative labour abundance. This establishes Ohlin's theorem that a capital abundant country would export capital intensive goods while a labour abundant country would export labour intensive goods.

Thus, if $(P_L/P_K)_A > (P_L/P_K)_B$, *country A is capital abundant exporting capital intensive X while country B is labour abundant exporting labour intensive Y.*

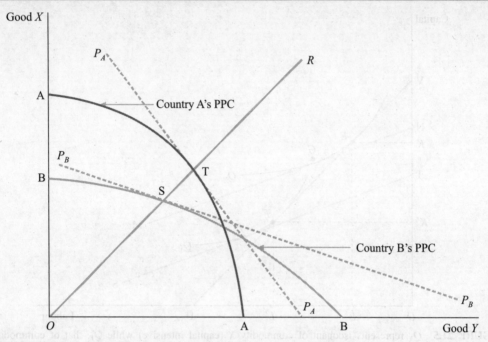

FIGURE 21.6 Let country A be relatively capital abundant and country B, relatively labour abundant. Further, let commodity X be capital intensive and commodity Y, labour intensive. PPC of country A (AA) would then show combinations of X and Y, for each of which, more of X would be associated with less of Y and that of country B (BB) would show those, for each of which, less of X would be associated with more of Y. Accordingly, AA would be steeper and BB, flatter. A ray, OR, is drawn through origin, depicting combinations of X and Y for each of which, $X = Y$. Such a ray would subtend an angle of $45°$ with the axes and would meet PPCs BB and AA at points S and T, respectively. A tangent, $P_B P_B$, drawn at S must therefore, be flatter than another, $P_A P_A$, drawn at T. That is, value of slope of $P_B P_B$, that is, $(P_Y/P_X)_B$ must be less than the value of slope of $P_A P_A$, that is, $(P_Y/P_X)_A$, implying, $(C_A/L_A) > (C_B/L_B)$. This shows factor abundance in physical terms. Conversely, if $(C_A/L_A) > (C_B/L_B)$, we have $(P_Y/P_X)_B < (P_Y/P_X)_A$. Thus, a capital abundant country would produce and export capital intensive X while a labour abundant country would produce and export labour intensive Y.

4. Production functions of the two commodities have different factor intensities, if one is labour intensive the other is capital intensive. But, for the same commodity, production functions are the same in both the countries. Production of both commodities in both countries takes place under constant returns to scale. Factor endowments in different countries are different quantitatively, but same qualitatively.
5. Technology remains unchanged and the consumer preferences and their demand patterns in the two countries are identical.

The modern theory was based on these assumptions, quite a few of which are the same as those incorporated in the classical theory. For example, assumptions 2, 3 and 5 are straight from the classical theory. Assumptions 1 and 4 differ due to the major deviation of the modern theory in respect of the productive factors. Ohlin's theory discards the assumption that labour is the only factor of production. Instead, it incorporates capital as a collaborating factor with labour.

Basic tenets of the theory and gains from trade accruing to the trading partners are explained through Figure 21.7.

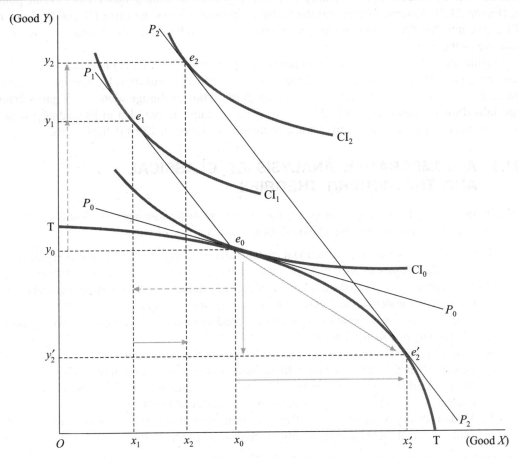

FIGURE 21.7 Under given technology and full employment, the country is producing and consuming (x_0, y_0) at point e_0 on the PPC, TT. Price line $P_0 P_0$ and the community indifference curve CI_0 are tangential to the PPC at e_0. Equation of the price line is $M = xP_X + yP_Y$, where, x and y are quantities of goods X and Y while P_X and P_Y are their market prices and M, the total value of the output. Value of the slope of the price line is therefore $|(-P_X/P_Y)|$, which is equal to the slopes of the PPC and the community indifference curve, CI_0, at e_0. The community indifference curve, also known as the **consumption possibility curve**, represents different combinations of the two goods X and Y that lead to the same utility to the community. Now suppose the country in question opens up to foreign trade. Let prices of goods X and Y in the international market be $P'_X (P'_X > P_X)$ and $P'_Y (P'_Y < P_Y)$. As a result, the price line becomes steeper ($e_0 P_1$) due to the increase of the value of the slope to $|(-P'_X/P'_Y)|$. The community moves to a higher indifference curve, CI_1 and is in equilibrium of consumption at $e_1 (x_1, y_1)$ basically by virtue of its exchange of $x_0 x_1$ of the costlier good X for $y_0 y_1$ of the cheaper good Y. Movement from CI_0 to CI_1 marks the **gain from exchange**. Since the country is fetching a higher price for its X in the international market, it would go for specialization in production of X. It will, therefore, shift the price line to $P_2 e'_2$ (parallel to $P_1 e_1$) to produce (x'_2, y'_2) at e'_2 and consume (x_2, y_2) at e_2. Movement from CI_1 to CI_2 (from e_1 to e_2) marks the **gain from specialization**. Gains from trade thus comprise **gain from exchange and that from specialization**.

Gains from trade

To understand the working of the theory and to have a feel of the gains accruing to the trading partners, let us assume that a country is producing and consuming under isolation at point e_0 (Figure 21.7). Assume further that the factor productivity is not the same for goods X and Y. TT represents the PPC of the country in question, which under diminishing returns to scale, is concave to the origin.

Figure 21.7 shows how a nation benefits by opening up to international trade rather than remaining closed to it. A closed and isolated economy is called an **autarky**. By opening to foreign trade, it may benefit substantially. It may reap **gains from exchange** along with **gains from specialization** as shown in Figure 21.7. Both types of gains accrue also to its trading partner. Measurement of partner's gains from trade is shown in Figure 16.12(b) (Chapter 16).

21.4 A COMPARATIVE ANALYSIS OF CLASSICAL AND THE MODERN THEORIES

Despite the fact that both the theories are based on unrealistic assumptions, Ohlin's theory is certainly an improvement over the classical theory in a number of ways:

1. Classical theory treats international trade totally different from the domestic trade while the modern theory treats it as a special case of the domestic or inter-regional trade.
2. Modern theory is cast in the framework of general equilibrium theory while classical theory is based on the defunct and unrealistic labour theory of value.
3. Modern theory of trade takes two factors of production into account while classical theory admits only one factor, labour.
4. Modern theory is superior to the classical theory in that it explains the cause of trade more logically than the classical theory. In the modern theory, the cause of the trade is the factor abundance due to which production costs and hence, product prices differ from country to country. Classical theory fails to explain why production costs differ.
5. Modern theory recognizes the differences in relative productivities of labour and capital while classical theory accounts only for the labour productivity.

That does not mean that all is absolutely fine with the modern theory. It suffers from a number of drawbacks some of which are of a more serious nature than those of the classical theory. One of them, in particular, deserves a special mention here. Empirical study conducted by Prof. Leontief falsifies the modern theory. The study shows how a capital abundant country resorts to export of labour intensive goods rather than of capital intensive ones as predicted by the modern theory. US provides the best example in support of Leontief's observation. The economy switched over to labour intensive production for some of its exports despite its capital abundance! Leontief's observation, known as **Leontief's paradox**, can be explained through a simple logic. When demand for capital shoots up high, so do prices of capital and capital intensive goods. Even a capital rich country like US that commands a high market share in the world trade reaches a stage in which its capital intensive exports suffer a loss of competitiveness in the international market. Observing its exports losing ground in the international market, such economies switch over to export of labour intensive goods if the same proves relatively cheaper. But if it does not, they resort to import of labour for the purpose from economies with surplus labour and labour intensive exports turn into a reality in a capital abundant country.

21.5 INTERNATIONAL OR WORLD TERMS OF TRADE

The international or the world terms of trade refer to the rate at which goods of one country are exchanged for goods of another. In Section 21.2, while demonstrating the comparative cost advantage theory through Ricardo's example, we demonstrated that the opportunity cost of a unit of wine in Portugal is 0.89 units of cloth and that in England is 1.2 units of cloth. Portugal's opportunity cost of cloth is 1.125 units of wine and that of England is 0.83 units of wine. From the comparison of the opportunity costs of wine and cloth, we had concluded that Portugal should specialize in production of wine while England in cloth and the two should exchange their specialities at a rate somewhere between 0.89 and 1.2 units of cloth per unit of wine. To have a feel of gains from accruing to the two nations from trade, we had assumed the rate of exchange as 1.05 units of cloth per unit of wine. At this rate, Portugal, we saw, gained by 0.16 units of cloth while England by 0.15 units of cloth. The two nations may decide mutually any other rate of exchange in between 0.89 and 1.20 units of cloth per unit of wine. The rate so determined would constitute the **terms of trade** between the two nations. Assuming only two nations in a two commodity world, the rate would constitute the **international or the world terms of trade**. Jacob Viner[1] and G.M. Meier[2] have discussed many types of terms of trade. Here, we will introduce them briefly for the benefit of the curious reader.

(i) Commodity or Net Barter terms of trade (T_c)

The Commodity or Net Barter Terms of Trade (T_c) refer to the ratio of prices of a country's exports to its imports. Symbolically,

$$T_c = P_X/P_M,$$

where, $T_c \equiv$ commodity terms of trade, P_X and $P_M \equiv$ export and import prices.

With the passage of time, export and import prices change and so do the commodity terms of trade. To measure the changes, the following expression is used:

$$T_c = \frac{(P_{X1}/P_{X0})}{(P_{M1}/P_{M0})}$$

where, subscripts 0 and 1 represent prices in the base and the current periods.

For instance, let India's export-import prices for 2007 (Base year: 2001) be given as 90 and 110 respectively, the change in India's terms of trade can be expressed as

$$T_c = \frac{(90/100)}{(110/100)}$$

$$= 81.82 \approx 82$$

This implies that India's terms of trade have declined by as much as 18% in 2007 as compared to 2001. In other words, India's terms of trade have worsened by that percentage.

---

[1] Viner, *op.cit.* pp. 558–70.
[2] G.M. Meier, *The International Economics of Development*, 1968, Ch. 3.

(ii) Gross barter terms of trade (T_g)

Introduced by F.W. Taussig[*1], the gross barter terms of trade refer to the ratio of the quantities of imports and exports of a country. Symbolically,

$$T_g = [Q_M / Q_X]$$

where $T_g \equiv$ gross barter terms of trade, Q_M and $Q_X \equiv$ quantities of imports and exports of a country. To measure changes in the gross barter terms of trade, the expression used is:

$$T_g = \frac{(Q_{M1}/Q_{M0})}{(Q_{X1}/Q_{X0})}$$

where, subscripts 0 and 1 represent quantities in the base and the current periods.

(iii) Income terms of trade (T_y)

It was Dorrance[*2] who improvised the net barter terms of trade (T_c) and formulated the income terms of trade. A rise in income terms of trade indicates an increase in the potential of a country's exports in buying its imports.

$$T_y = T_c \times Q_X, \text{ where, } T_c = (P_X/P_M)$$
$$= (P_X \times Q_X)/P_M$$

(iv) Single and double factoral term of trade (T_s and T_d)

Single factoral terms of trade (T_s) admit changes in domestic export sector so that productivity changes in the export sector may be incorporated in it through F_X, the productivity index of export industries.

$$T_s = T_c \times F_X$$
$$= (P_X \times F_X)/P_M$$

Double factoral terms of trade (T_d), on the other hand, admit productivity changes in domestic as well as foreign export sectors. Appart from F_X, as defined in single factoral terms of trade, F_M, the productivity changes in foreign export sector, is also incorporated.

$$T_d = (T_c) \times (F_X/F_M)$$
$$= (P_X \times F_X)/(P_M \times F_M)$$

(v) Real cost terms of trade (T_r)

Real cost terms of trade serve as a measure of real gains from trade and are given by

$$T_r = T_s \times R_X$$
$$= [(P_X \times F_X)/(P_M)] \times (R_X)$$

where, R_X is the index of the amount of disutility per unit of productive resource used in export production.

[*1] F.W. Taussig, *International Trade*, 1927.
[*2] G.S. Dorrance, *The Income Terms of Trade*, R.E.S., Vol. XVI, 1948–49.

Utility terms of trade (T_u)

Utility terms of trade refer to an index that measures changes in the disutility of producing a unit of exports and changes in the relative satisfaction yielded by imports. It is given as:

$$T_u = T_r \times u$$
$$= [(P_X \times F_X)/(P_M)] \times (R_X) \times u$$

where,
$$u = (U_{M1}/U_{a1})/(U_{M0}/U_{a0})$$

Here, u is defined as the index of relative utility of imports and domestically foregone commodities in export production by 'a'.

Terms of trade depend on several factors. They are changes in endowments, changes in technology, changes in tastes and preferences tariff and above all, reciprocal demand. The reciprocal demand may be defined as the strength and elasticity of a country's demand for another's product. We will study them later in this section.

21.5.1 Terms of Trade and Offer Curves

In response to changing international prices, quantities offered by trading countries for exchange also change. Such changes in quantities offered are depicted by offer curves. An **offer curve** can, therefore, be defined as the locus of different combinations of the quantities of a commodity offered (proposed export, say) for exchange by one country in lieu of the quantities of another commodity desired from the trading partner at changing prices of the two in the international market. In other words, an offer curve depicts changes in volumes of exports and imports of a country under changing prices of the commodities under export and import.

To derive an offer curve, suppose country A is producing and consuming at E in its pre-trade position with the price line PP depicting the ratio of prices of X and Y in its domestic territory. Now suppose it enters in trade with country B. Suppose further that country A's domestic price ratio settles down in country B as well with the result that country A switches its consumption to E' on the community indifference curve, CI. Clearly, country A exports hE of Y to country B and imports hh''' of X from it. In other words, country A offers hE of Y to country B for importing hh''' of X from it. Now suppose terms of trade between the two shift from PP to $P'P'$ with the result that country A produces at F and consumes at F', offering kF of Y to country B for kF' of X from it. Figure 21.8 demonstrates exchanges of Y by country A with X of country B under changing terms of trade.

Quantities offered by one country to another for quantities imported from the latter under changing terms of trade refer to the offer curve of the country in question. Offer curve for country A (Figure 21.8) can be obtained as in Figure 21.9 by joining points O, C, D and G smoothly; offer curve for country B can be obtained likewise.

Offer curves as derived above for the two trading countries are viewed as handy tools of analysis of gains from trade and their distribution between the trading partners, effects on terms of trade of changes in technology, tastes and preferences, endowments, tariffs and above all, effects on terms of trade of reciprocal demand. Here, we discuss some of such applications of offer curves.

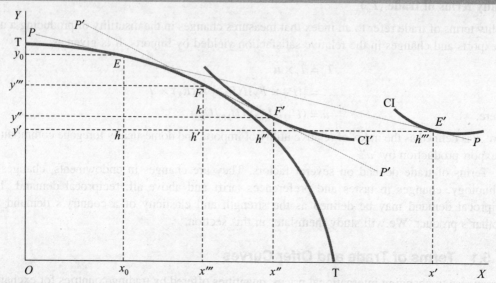

FIGURE 21.8 TT represents production possibilities of country A and PP, its domestic price line. Country A is initially producing and consuming x_0 of X and y_0 of Y at E. Now suppose country A enters in trade with country B with the result that price line in the two countries settles at PP with the result that country A switches its consumption to E' on the community indifference curve, CI. Clearly, country A exports hE of Y to country B and imports hh''' of X from it. Country A thus, produces at E and consumes at E' (x' of X and y' of Y), enjoying utility CI in its post-trade period. Now suppose terms of trade change to $P'P'$, indicating a rise in P_X and a fall in P_Y in the international market. Country A therefore, imports less of X (kF' or $h'h'' < hh'''$) from country B and also exports less of Y ($kF < hE$) to it. Thus,

Country A's initial imports of X from country B	= 0 (No trade position)
Country A's initial exports of Y to country B	= 0 (No trade position)
Country A's imports of X from country B in post-trade period with terms of trade given by PP	= hh'''
Country A's exports of Y to country B in post-trade period with terms of trade given by PP	= hE
Country A's imports of X from country B with terms of trade given by $P'P'$	= kF'
Country A's exports of Y to country B with terms of trade given by $P'P'$	= kF

Plotting changes in country A's imports and exports due to changes in terms of trade, we obtain country A's offer curve as shown in Figure 21.9.

21.5.2 Applications of Offer Curves

1. Gains from trade

J.S. Mill analysed gains from trade as well as their distribution between the trading partners in terms of the theory of reciprocal demand defined as the strength and elasticity of a country's demand for another's products. For instance, Germany's demand for England's cloth would be termed more intense (inelastic) if it remains more or less same whatever, the price.

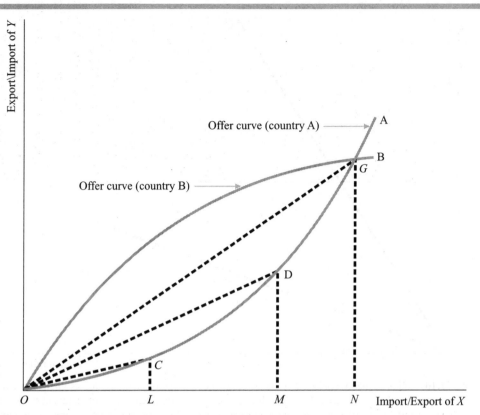

FIGURE 21.9 *(Not to Scale)* On the basis of discussions in Figure 21.8, represent import of X on x-axis and export of Y on y-axis for country A as shown. Plot points O (import of X = zero, export of Y = zero), C (import of $X = kF'$, export of $Y = kF$), D (import of $X = hh'''$, export of $Y = hE$) and so on. Join them by means of the smooth curve, OA. The curve so obtained gives country A's offer curve. Offer curve of country B can be obtained as shown by treating imports and exports of country A as exports and imports of country B, respectively and following the same procedure, thereafter. The curve so obtained would be OB. Point G where the offer curves of the two countries intersect gives the equilibrium position of trade between the two while the slope of ray OG determines equilibrium terms of trade between them. At G, ON of X is offered by country A for NG of Y from country B.

To illustrate, let the two countries be Germany and England, the former exporting linen to the latter for the latter's cloth and the latter exporting cloth for the former's linen. Measuring England's cloth on x-axis and Germany's linen on y-axis, draw the offer curves of the two countries as in Figure 21.10. If England's demand for Germany's linen is more intense (inelastic), the terms of trade will move in favour of Germany and against England. Germany stands to gain more from trade than England. On the contrary, if Germany's demand for England's cloth is more intense (inelastic), the terms of trade will move in favour of England rather than of Germany and the former would stand to gain more from trade than the latter. Distribution of gains from trade between the two trading nations is demonstrated in Figure 21.10.

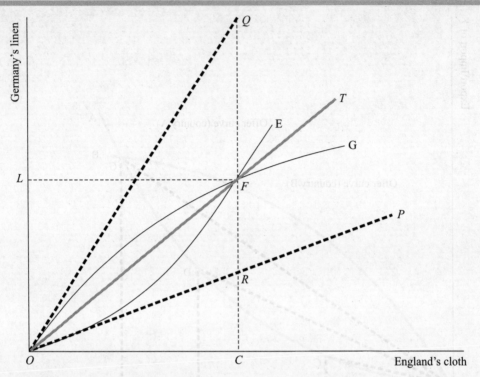

FIGURE 21.10 OE is England's offer curve for its cloth and OG that of Germany for its linen. The two offer curves intersect each other at F. Ray OT passing through the intersection determines the terms of trade between the two. Now let OP and OQ be the two rays representing fixed domestic cost ratios of producing cloth and linen in England and Germany. The two rays provide the limits within which the terms of trade between the two countries would fall. At F, cost ratio in England is CR units of linen: OC units of cloth while England getting CF units of linen through trade, gaining RF units of linen. Likewise, cost ratio in Germany at F is CQ units of linen: OC units of cloth but Germany imports OC units of cloth from England in exchange for its CF units of linen. Germany's gain in terms of linen therefore, is FQ units of linen. Offer curves thus, help in distribution of total gains from trade between the trading partners.

2. Changes in factor endowments

A change in factor endowments of a country affects its terms of trade by increasing or decreasing its exports. This may be explained with the help of offer curves (Figure 21.11). Continuing with the same example as in Figure 21.11, let the initial terms of trade be given by ray OT. England exports OC of cloth for OL of linen just before an increase in Germany's factor endowments. The factor endowments of England and the tastes and preferences of consumers in both the countries remaining unchanged, this would lead to an upward to left shift in Germany's offer curve, OG; implying more linen at its disposal to offer. The new offer curve, OG′, intersects England's offer curve at T'. Ray OT' gives the new terms of trade. Germany, as a result, would offer OL' of linen for OC' of English cloth.

Thus, as a result of an increase in Germany's factor endowments for production of linen, the terms of trade turn against Germany. It exports relatively more of linen (LL') for relatively less

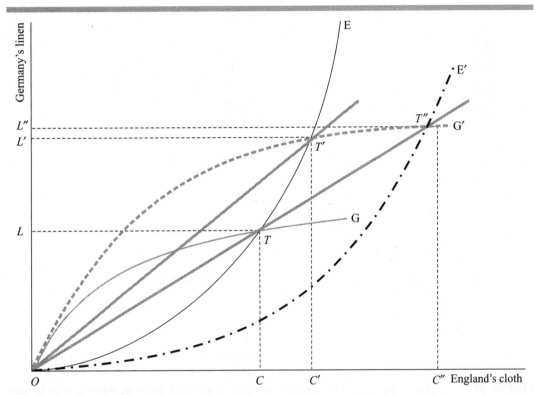

FIGURE 21.11 England (offer curve OE) and Germany (offer curve OG) are on equilibrium terms of trade at T on OT. England exports OC of cloth for OL of German linen. Now suppose Germany's factor endowments increase, leading to an upward to left shift in its offer curve (from OG to OG′). Other things remaining the same, the terms of trade between the two shift from OT to $OT′$. Germany now offers $OL′$ linen for $OC′$ of English cloth. Had the initial terms of trade (OT) continued, Germany would have offered $OL″$ of linen for $OC″$ of English cloth. But the same is not possible unless England increases production of cloth so that its offer curve (OE) shifts downwards to right (OE′) to meet OG′ at $T″$.

of English cloth ($CC′$). The beneficiary is England while for Germany, the terms of trade deteriorate. Had the initial terms of trade (OT) continued, Germany would have offered $OL″$ of linen for $OC″$ of English cloth. But the same is not possible unless England increases production of cloth so that its offer curve (OE) shifts downwards to right ($OE′$) to meet $OG′$ at $T″$. If England's endowments now increase leading to a downward to right shift in its offer curve, the overall terms of trade will go in favour of Germany which will then export $OL″$ of linen for $OC″$ of English cloth at $T‴$.

3. Changes in technology

Technological changes also affect a country's terms of trade much the same way as the changes in factor endowments do. Suppose that a technology improvement takes place in Germany while consumers' tastes and England's technology remain unchanged. If the technological change favours production of linen, the situation is much the same as that in Figure 21.11 but if it discourages production of linen, the situation is opposite, as depicted in Figure 21.12.

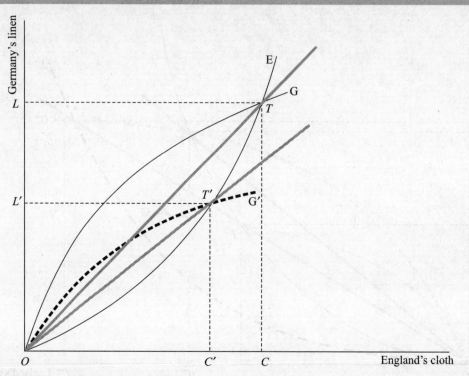

FIGURE 21.12 England (offer curve OE) and Germany (offer curve OG) are on equilibrium terms of trade at T on OT. England exports OC of cloth for OL of Germany's linen. Now suppose technology employed by Germany in production of its linen deteriorates with the result that linen output suffers and Germany's offer curve (OG) shifts downwards to right to OG'. With this, the terms of trade (OT) shift to the position OT', other things remaining the same. The terms of trade therefore, turn in favour of Germany which now offers much less linen (OL' << OL) for a little less of English cloth (OC'< OC). Technological deterioration thus, affects the terms of trade of the country in question favourably and those of its trading partner, adversely.

4. Changes in consumers' tastes

Changes in consumers' tastes and preferences also affect a country's terms of trade. At times, the affect results from their effect on reciprocal demand; at times, from their affect on direct demand but often, from their affect on both. For instance, suppose consumers' tastes and preferences in England move against the German linen. This affects reciprocal demand for linen in England. Suppose further that these changes in tastes and preferences of people in England move in favour of English cloth. The result is that reciprocal demand for German linen falls and direct demand for English cloth rises. In consequence, terms of trade turn against German linen but in favour of English cloth. The situation is explained in Figure 21.13. England offers less and less of cloth for German linen with the result that England's offer curve of cloth shifts upwards to left and so do the terms of trade, from OT to OT'.

Tariffs

An imposition of import tariff improves the terms of trade of the imposing country (Figure 21.14).

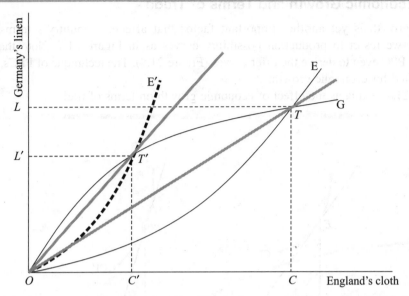

FIGURE 21.13 If tastes and preferences of people of England turn against German linen and in favour of their own cloth, the terms of trade also move against German linen and in favour of their own cloth. England's offer curve shifts upwards to left and so do the terms of trade, from OT to OT'. Before the change, England offered OC of cloth for OL of German linen. After the change, England offers OC' of cloth for OL' of German linen.

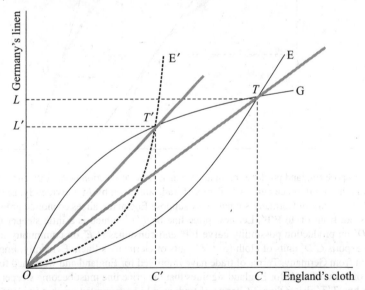

FIGURE 21.14 England (offer curve OE) and Germany (offer curve OG) are on equilibrium terms of trade at T on OT. England exports OC of cloth for OL of Germany's linen. Now suppose England imposes tariff on the imports of German linen. As a result, reciprocal demand for Germany's linen falls from OL to OL'. Corresponding exports of English cloth fall from OC to OC', implying an upward to left shift in England's offer curve of cloth, to OE'. Since fall in England's exports of cloth by CC' is much larger than the fall in imports of Germany's linen, the terms of trade have moved in favour of England's cloth and against Germany's linen.

21.5.3 Economic Growth and Terms of Trade

Economic growth is yet another important factor that affects a country's terms of trade. To explain, we resort to production possibility curves as in Figure 21.7. Note that, we had employed a PPC even to derive the offer curves (Figure 21.8). The technique of PPCs, we know, is better suited for economic growth.

Figure 21.15 explains the effect of economic growth on terms of trade.

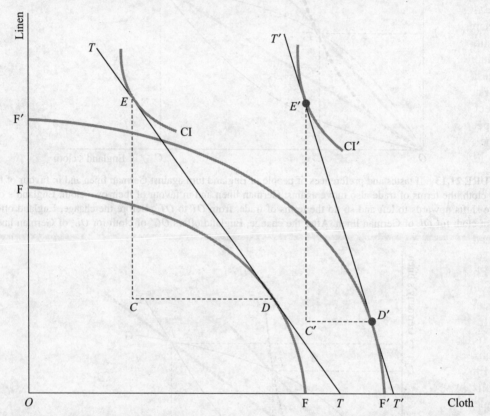

FIGURE 21.15 Suppose England produces cloth and linen at D on production possibility curve FF and consumes them at E on community indifference curve CI. Terms of trade are given by TT^*. Evidently, England is exporting CD units of cloth for CE units of Germany's linen. Now suppose England realizes economic growth with the result that its PPC blows out from FF to F'F'. Let new price line be $T'T'$, which is a little steeper than TT. England now produces at D' on production possibility curve F'F' and consumes at E' on community indifference curve CI'. England now exports $C'D'$ units of cloth for $C'E'$ units of Germany's linen. Evidently, England exports less cloth for more linen from Germany. Terms of trade have improved for England and worsened for Germany. Note that improvement of terms of trade for England signifies that the price line must become steeper than before. Had we chosen a price line $T'T'$ flatter than TT, terms of trade would have moved against England and in favour of Germany. Likewise, had $T'T'$ been parallel to TT, terms of trade would have remained unchanged. Growth may, thus, affect the terms of trade of a country in any way.

---

* TT is the price line. Its slope gives the price ratio, P_{cloth}/P_{linen}. If price of cloth (P_{CLOTH}) rises, price of linen (P_{LINEN}) remaining the same, the price line TT would turn steeper.

21.6 FACTOR MOBILITY AND FACTOR PRICE EQUALIZATION

Both the theories of trade, classical as well as modern, assume that factors of production are perfectly mobile domestically, but perfectly immobile internationally. Mobility of a factor refers to its movement from a low paying job to a high paying one. Factor-prices are low in factor abundant regions and high in factor deficient regions. Factors move from one job to another until the factor prices settle at the same level in both. In absence of perfect factor mobility, factor prices can never get equalized. The same is the case with production costs. They too cannot be same everywhere unless factor prices are same or factor mobility is perfect. If production costs are same, product prices too can be same. If product prices are same in all the countries, the question of international trade does not arise. Differences in factor prices lead to differences in production costs and hence in product prices. Differences in product prices lead to trade whether domestic or international.

Factor price equalization can exist under perfect factor mobility. But, can factor mobility be perfect in the days of specialization? Infact factor mobility can never be perfect in the presence of specialization. Prolonged work in a given position imparts a fair degree of specialization to the factor and it becomes difficult for the factor to quit the current job for a similar one in regions of deficient supply where higher rewards (prices) are available. This is true particularly in respect of skilled factors. (In case of the unskilled factors, free movement of factors from factor surplus regions to those factor deficient, is highly smooth, at least domestically.) Due to this reason, perfect equalization of factor and product prices is not possible even domestically. Mobility of factors, therefore, does not mean its simple movement from one place to another. Instead, it means movement to an identical job from a factor surplus region to a factor deficient one so that factor prices may get equalized everywhere.

Eli Heckscher* himself had suggested that under the assumption of the same technique in the two countries, trade would lead to complete factor price equalization but also admitted that the same is not possible because of the differences in productive techniques or technologies.

It was Samuelson,** who showed through his two articles in the Economic Journal, showed that free commodity trade under certain specified conditions will lead to complete factor price equalization. Samuelson's factor price equalization theorem has been severely criticized by Meade and Ellsworth on the basis of its highly restrictive assumptions. They argued that the factor price equalization can only be partial not complete. At slight deviation in any of its assumptions, Samuelson's theorem of factor price equalization collapses.

21.6.1 Samuelson's Factor Price Equalization Theorem

Professor Samuelson based his factor price equalization theorem on the following assumptions:

1. There are two countries (say, A and B) trading in two commodities (say, food and clothing) produced through two factors, land and labour, qualitatively identical in the two countries.
2. Production function of each commodity is homogeneous of degree one and hence subject to Euler's Theorem, showing constant returns to scale.
3. The factors are subject to the law of diminishing marginal productivity.

---

* Eli Heckscher, "The Effect of Foreign Trade and Distribution of Income," 1919 in *Readings in the Theory of International Trade*, 1950.
** P.A. Samuelson, "International Trade and Equalization of Factor Prices," E.J. June 1948, "International Factor Price Equalization Once Again," E.J. June 1949.

4. Factor intensities are different for different commodities. Thus, food is relatively land intensive and clothing is relatively labour intensive.
5. Quantities of the factors used in production are constant and factors are immobile between the countries.
6. The technical production function for each commodity is the same in the two countries.
7. There exists perfect competition with absence of tariffs and transportation costs.
8. Both countries produce both commodities with both factors of production. That is, no country goes as far as to specialize completely in one commodity.

On the basis of these assumptions, Prof. Samuelson provided the following intuitive proof of his factor price equalization theorem.
Due to existence of perfect competition,

$$\frac{P_F}{P_C} = \frac{MC_F}{MC_C}$$

P_F and P_C are prices of food and clothing while MC_F and MC_C are marginal costs of food and clothing.
Trade between the two countries being free, unrestricted and without transportation costs,

$$(P_F)_A = (P_F)_B = P_F$$

and,

$$(P_C)_A = (P_C)_B = P_C$$

implying,

$$(MC_F)_A = (MC_F)_B = MC_F$$

and,

$$(MC_C)_A = (MC_C)_B = MC_C$$

That is, prices of food and clothing would be the same in the two countries and so would be the marginal costs of production of the two commodities in the two countries.
Due to the assumption of identical production functions,

$$(MP_L)_A = (MP_L)_B$$

implying,

$$w_A = w_B$$

That is, marginal productivities of labour in the two countries would be same and so would be the wages in the two countries. The same would be the case with the other factor, land. As simple as that!

To test Samuelson's intuitive proof, let us refer to Figure 21.16*.

Criticism

As mentioned earlier, Samuelson's factor price equalization theorem has been criticized severely by Meade, Ellsworth and other economists due to its highly restrictive assumptions. They argue that factor price equalization can only be partial, not complete. Let us see their arguments in the following points:

1. Both the factors may not be available in both the countries. It is possible that only one factor is available in one country with the result that marginal productivities of the factor common to the two will differ and so will their prices.

---

* Based on Prof. Lerner's presentation, slightly modified.

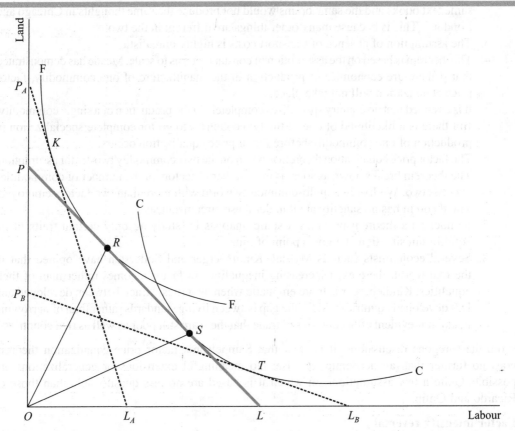

FIGURE 21.16 FF and CC are isoquants for food and clothing, PL is post-trade factor price line, $P_A L_A$ and $P_B L_B$ factor price lines in the pre-trade period.

At R on FF,
$$\frac{[MP_L]_F}{[MP_K]_F} = \frac{[P_L]_F}{[P_K]_F} \tag{21.1}$$

At S on CC,
$$\frac{[MP_L]_C}{[MP_K]_C} = \frac{[P_L]_C}{[P_K]_C} \tag{21.2}$$

From Eqs. (21.1) and (21.2), we have, by virtue of common tangent PL to isoquants FF and CC,

$$\frac{[P_L]_F}{[P_K]_F} = \frac{[P_L]_C}{[P_K]_C} \tag{21.3}$$

and

$$\frac{[MP_L]_F}{[MP_K]_F} = \frac{[MP_L]_C}{[MP_K]_C} \tag{21.4}$$

Since the isoquants refer to both the countries, factor prices will be the same in both.

2. Production functions can never be identical in the two countries. Even if resources be same in the two, they need not produce the same commodity as pointed out by Meade, "The

same text books and the same brains would not produce the same thoughts in Chicago and London." This is because many other things are different in the two.
3. The assumption of absence of transport costs is highly unrealistic.
4. The theorem is based on the assumption of constant returns to scale. Meade has demonstrated that if there are economies of production in the manufacture of one commodity, factor price equalization will not take place.
5. It is assumed that no country specializes completely in the production of a single commodity. But there is a likelihood of one of the two countries to go for complete specialization in production of one commodity before factor price equalization occurs.
6. The factor price equalization theorem is based on the two-commodity two-factor assumption. The theorem breaks down as soon as the number of factors or the number of commodities exceeds two. We live in a multi-commodity world with more than two factors employed. The theorem has no sanctity at all under these circumstances.
7. Samuelson's theorem provides a static analysis by studying only certain traits of an equilibrium situation at a given point of time.
8. Several economists such as Myrdal, Kindleberger and Sodersten have opined that in the real world, there exist increasing inequalities in factor incomes rather than of their equalities. Kindleberger is more emphatic when he writes, "trade between developed and less developed countries widens the gap between living standards rather than of narrowing it, and it is evident after centuries of trade that there are still poor as well as rich countries."

From the foregone discussions, it is clear that Samuelson's factor price equalization theorem goes no further than an academic exercise. No meaningful extensions or generalizations are possible. Quite a few assumptions on which it is based are no less questionable than those of Ricardo and Ohlin.

Factor intensity reversal

Samuelson's theorem assumes that the production functions differ in factor intensities. This implies that each production function can be identified as being relatively land-intensive or capital intensive at all relevant points on it. But it is possible that some point on a production function may be relatively land intensive and another, relatively labour intensive. This is the case of factor reversals where a one-to-one correspondence between factor prices and factor intensities is not possible.

This is explained in Figure 21.17. Two isoquants FF and CC intersect each other twice at points M and N. In between M and N, the two are intersected by a ray OR from origin at points T and S. It is only at T and S that parallel tangents are possible. Professor Lerner calls this ray, OR, as "radiant of tangency" as a sign of factor intensity reversal. That is, equilibrium points to its left or right on the two isoquants reveal factor intensity reversal.

Sir Roy Harrod looks upon Samuelson's theorem as a *curiosum* and not as a fundamental principle. Kindleberger admits that the theorem is not generally true but he regards it as more than an intellectual curiosity. We can conclude with Jagdish Bhagwati, "Although the subject is, therefore, both of historic interest and still continues to attract fresh minds, one cannot help feeling that too great a proportion of intellectual energy of trade theorists has been directed towards a question of limited utility."

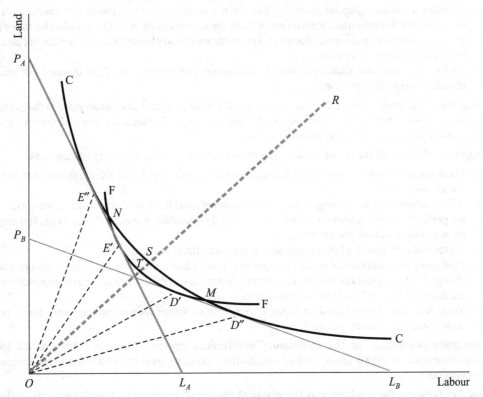

FIGURE 21.17 FF and CC are isoquants for food and clothing. The two intersect at points M and N. Ray OR cuts FF and CC at T and S, the points at which parallel tangents can be drawn to the two isoquants. $P_A L_A$ and $P_B L_B$ are factor price lines in countries A and B. Taking the price line $P_A L_A$, we observe from OE'' that clothing in country A is land intensive while food in it is relatively less land intensive as shown by OE' on isoquant FF. Likewise, taking factor price line $P_B L_B$, we observe that clothing is labour intensive in country B as shown by OD'' on isoquant CC while food in it is less labour intensive as shown by OD' on isoquant FF. Thus, we find that clothing is land intensive in country A but labour intensive in country B. Likewise, food in country A is land intensive but in country B it is labour intensive. This shows that clothing and food have different factor intensities in one country which get reversed for them in another country. Such factor intensity reversal leads the factor price equalization theorem to collapse.

KEY TERMS AND CONCEPTS

Autarky It is an economy which is closed to the foreign trade. It produces and consumes in isolation.

Assumptions of the modern theory The modern theory of Ohlin is based on the following assumptions:
1. There are two countries (A and B), two commodities (X and Y) and two factors (L, K).
2. Trade is free, with zero transportation costs.
3. The factor and the product markets are competitive with full employment of factors assumed perfectly mobile within the country and immobile beyond it.

4. Production functions of the two commodities have different factor intensities, that is, if one is labour intensive the other is capital intensive. But, for the same commodity, production functions are the same in both the countries. Production of both the commodities in both the countries takes place under constant returns to scale. Factor endowments are different quantitatively in different countries but same qualitatively in each.
5. Technology remains unchanged and the consumer preferences and their demand patterns are identical in both the countries.

Classical theory of trade   Also known as the theory of comparative cost advantage, it states that a country will export those commodities for which its production costs are comparatively less and import those for which its production costs are comparatively higher.

Assumptions of classical theory of trade   The theory is based on the following assumptions:

1. There are two countries, say A and B, producing two goods, say X and Y through only one factor of production, labour.
2. All the labour units are homogeneous with fixed supply and fixed productivity in all the goods. They are perfectly mobile within the country and perfectly immobile beyond it. There exists full employment of labour in both the countries.
3. Tastes and preferences of the people are same in both the countries.
4. Production of commodities in the two countries takes place under constant cost conditions and unchanged technological know-how. Product prices depend on labour costs alone as transportation costs are assumed zero and trade between the partners free.
5. Trade is assumed to be based on barter system with exchange ratio remaining same due to perfect competition in international markets.

Consumption possibilities or the community indifference curves   They are defined as the loci of different combinations of two goods each of which offers the same level of satisfaction to the community of the consumers.

Distinction between the modern and the classical theory of trade   The two differ in the following respects:

1. Classical theory treats international trade totally different from the domestic trade while the modern theory treats it as a special case of domestic or inter-regional trade.
2. Modern theory is cast in the framework of general equilibrium theory while classical theory is based on the defunct and unrealistic labour theory of value.
3. Modern theory of trade takes two factors of production into account while classical theory admits only one factor, labour.
4. Modern theory is superior to the classical theory in that it explains the cause of trade more logically than the classical theory. In the modern theory the cause of the trade is the factor abundance due to which production costs and, hence, product prices differ from country to country. Classical theory fails to explain why production costs differ.
5. Modern theory recognizes the differences in relative productivities of labour and capital while classical theory accounts only for the labour productivity.

Drawbacks of classical theory   The main drawbacks of the classical theory comprise its unrealistic assumptions listed below:

1. Labour costs that remain unchanged;
2. Similar tastes;
3. Perfect internal mobility and external immobility of labour;
4. Absence of transportation costs;
5. Free trade;
6. Homogeneity of labour;

7. Barter as the basis of trade;
8. Two countries trading in two commodities; and
9. Existence of perfect competition.

Drawbacks of the modern theory of trade Except for the merits that it is cast in the framework of the general equilibrium theory and that it admits two instead of one factor of production, the modern theory suffers from the same drawbacks of unrealistic assumptions as the classical theory suffers from.

Factor mobility It refers to smooth job hopping from low paying to high paying jobs. When a factor can switch from a job from factor-surplus regions to those of factor-deficient without facing any problem on account of differences in techniques and technologies, the mobility of the factors is referred to as perfect.

Factor price equalization It refers to a state of equilibrium in which factor prices get equalized ultimately due to perfect factor mobility. However, complete factor price equalization is impossible due to the difficulty of eliminating the differences in the techniques and technologies in between the regions or countries.

International trade International trade may be defined as exchange of goods and services among nations. People of one nation export their specialities to other nations and import specialities of other nation's themselves.

Inter-regional trade Inter-regional trade may be defined as trade between regions of the same country.

Distinction between inter-regional and international trade The domestic and international trade differ from each other in the following respects:

1. In international trade, currencies involved are different while this is not so in inter-regional trade.
2. In international trade, flow of goods and services need not be subject to the same rules regulations while in inter-regional trade, it generally is.
3. Labour is assumed to be perfectly mobile in inter-regional trade while perfectly immobile in international trade.
4. In international trade, problem of balance of payments serves as a constraint while in international trade, it does not.
5. Tastes, preferences and traditions of the trading partners need not be same in international trade while they are to a large extent same in the domestic trade.
6. In international trade, distances to be covered by the products are usually larger than those in inter-regional trade.
7. Political systems involved in international trade are different while they are generally not in inter-regional trade.

Labour coefficient It is defined as the number of labour units required to produce one unit of a product.

Leontief's paradox It refers to the trade practices adopted by certain economies in defiance to the tenets of the modern theory of international trade. When capital rich countries resort to export of labour intensive goods and import of capital intensive ones in defiance to the expected behaviour of exporting the capital intensive goods and importing the labour intensive ones, the practice demonstrates their paradoxical behaviour known as Leontief's paradox, after Prof. Leontief who first studied it.

Modern theory of international trade Also known as 'Heckscher–Ohlin theorem', the modern theory of international trade states that the immediate cause of trade is the difference of commodity prices. The difference is a consequence of the difference of production costs, which in turn, is a consequence of the difference of the factor endowments of the trading partners.

Terms of trade or world terms of trade or international terms of trade The world terms of trade or the international terms of trade refer to the rate at which the goods of one country are exchanged for the goods of another.

Gross barter terms of trade Introduced by F.W. Taussig, the gross barter terms of trade refer to the ratio of the quantities of imports and exports of a country.

Symbolically,

$$T_g = [Q_M / Q_X], \text{ where } T_g \equiv \text{gross barter terms of trade,}$$

$$Q_M \text{ and } Q_X \equiv \text{quantities of imports and exports of a country.}$$

Income terms of trade (T_y) It was Dorrance who improvised the net barter terms of trade (T_c) and formulated the income terms of trade. A rise in income terms of trade indicates an increase in the potential of a country's exports of buying its imports.

$$T_y = T_c \times Q_X, \text{ where, } T_c = (P_X/P_M)$$
$$= (P_X \times Q_X)/P_M$$

Net barter terms of trade Also known as commodity terms of trade, the net barter terms of trade refer to the ratio of prices of a country's exports to its imports.

Symbolically,

$$T_c = P_X/P_M,$$

where, $T_c \equiv$ commodity terms of trade, P_X and $P_M \equiv$ export and import prices.

Real cost terms of trade (T_r) Real cost terms of trade serve as a measure of real gains from trade and are given by

$$T_r = T_s \times R_X$$
$$= [(P_X \times F_X)/(P_M)] \times (R_X)$$

where, R_X is the index of the amount of disutility per unit of productive resource used in export production.

Single and double factoral terms of trade (T_s and T_d) Single factoral terms of trade (T_s) admit changes in domestic export sector so that productivity changes in the export sector may be incorporated in it through F_X, the productivity index of export industries.

$$T_s = T_c \times F_X$$
$$= (P_X \times F_X)/P_M$$

Double factoral terms of trade (T_d), on the other hand, admit productivity changes in domestic as well as foreign export sectors. Apart from F_X, as defined in single factoral terms of trade, F_M, the productivity changes in foreign export sector, is also incorporated.

$$T_d = (T_c) \times (F_X/F_M)$$
$$= (P_X \times F_X)/(P_M \times F_M)$$

Utility terms of trade (T_u) Utility terms of trade refer to an index that measures changes in the disutility of producing a unit of exports and changes in the relative satisfaction yielded by *a* unit of imports. It is given as:

$$T_u = T_r \times u$$
$$= [(P_X \times F_X)/(P_M)] \times (R_X) \times u$$

where,
$$u = (U_{M1}/U_{a1})/(U_{M0}/U_{a0}).$$

Here, u is defined as the index of relative utility of imports and domestically foregone commodities in export production by 'a'.

International Trade Factor Mobility and Comparative Advantage

EXERCISES

A. Short Answer Questions

Define the following (1 through 17):
1. International trade
2. Inter-regional trade
3. Consumption possibility curve or the community indifference curve
4. Autarky
5. World terms of trade or the international terms of trade
6. Commodity terms or net barter terms of trade
7. Gross barter terms of trade
8. Factor mobility
9. Factor price equalization
10. Leontief's paradox
11. Free trade
12. Income terms of trade
13. Real cost terms of trade
14. Utility terms of trade
15. Single factoral terms of trade
16. Double factoral terms of trade
17. Offer curves
18. Labour coefficient. State the essence of the classical theory of international trade.
19. Mention three important assumptions of the classical theory of international trade
20. Explain the absolute cost difference with the help of an example
21. Explain the equal cost difference with the help of an example
22. Explain the comparative cost difference with the help of an example
23. Name three important drawbacks of the classical theory of international trade
24. Briefly state the essence of the modern theory of international trade
25. Name three important assumptions of the modern theory of international trade
26. Name three important differences between the modern and classical theories of international trade
27. Name three important differences between international and inter-regional trade
28. Give an example of Leontief's paradox
29. What is the basis of the comparative advantage according to the Ricardian theory?
30. What according to the Modern theory is the immediate cause of international trade?
31. What according to the Modern theory is the ultimate cause of international trade?
32. With the help of examples differentiate between the capital intensive and the labour intensive goods.

B. Long Answer Questions

33. Explain the Ricardian concept of gains from trade.
34. Under what circumstances would trade between two nations fail according to the Ricardian theory? Support your answer with suitable examples.
35. In what respects is the modern theory of international trade superior to the classical theory?
36. Explain Leontief's paradox with an example.
37. Is perfect factor mobility possible? If yes, under what circumstances?
38. "Complete factor price equalization is impossible". Comment.
39. Assume two countries, A and B, producing two goods, X and Y. It costs country A 100 units of labour to produce 1 unit of X and 80 units of labour to produce 1 unit of Y. To country B, it costs 120 units of

labour to produce 1 unit of X and 100 units of labour to produce 1 unit of Y. Calculate the opportunity costs of producing 1 unit of each commodity by each country. Are the cost differences equal, absolute, or comparative? Give reasons and comment on the possibility of trade between the two.

[**Ans.** For A: 1.20, 0.8; For B: 1.20, 0.83; None.]

40. In Question 39, suppose it costs country A 120 units of labour to produce 1 unit of X and 90 units of labour to produce 1 unit of Y. To country B, suppose it costs 80 units of labour to produce 1 unit of good X and 60 units of labour to produce 1 unit of Y. What can you say about the nature of cost differences? Would the two countries enter trade? Explain using PPCs.

    [**Ans.** For A: 1.25, 0.80; For B: 0.80, 1.25; equal]

41. Suppose that the production costs of X and Y in country A are as given in Question 39 but those in country B change to 80 units of labour for 1 unit of X and 100 units of labour for 1 unit of Y. Comment on the nature of cost differences and determine whether the two countries would be able to establish trade ties. Explain opportunity cost method.

    [**Ans.** For A: 1.25, 0.80; For B: 0.80, 1.25; comparative]

42. Explain why the production possibility curves in the Ricardian theory of international trade are linear. What assumptions of the theory would you like to relax so that the production possibility curves may have the usual shape?
43. What is the condition of equilibrium of production and consumption in an autarky? Draw PPCs and the community indifference curves to demonstrate. What is the role of the price line?
44. What are the offer curves? How are they derived?
45. How can offer curves be employed to study gains from trade? Explain.
46. How are offer curves employed to study the affect of a change in technology on terms of trade? Explain.
47. How are offer curves used to demonstrate the affect of a change of tastes and preferences in terms of trade? Explain.
48. Explain the affect of a change in endowments in terms of trade.
49. Demonstrate the affect of tariffs in terms of trade. Explain.
50. How does economic growth affect the terms of trade? Explain.
51. State factor price equalization theorem. On what assumptions is it based?
52. Explain Samuelson's intuitive proof of factor price equalization.
53. How does factor intensity reversal lead to a collapse of factor price equalization theorem? Explain.
54. Employing isoquants establish Samuelson's factor price equalization theorem.
55. On what grounds is Samuelson's factor price equalization theorem criticized? Do you agree with the criticism?

D. Essay Type Questions

56. In each of Questions 39, 40 and 41, determine the terms of trade under which the two countries may benefit more or less equally from mutual trade.
57. "The classical and the modern theories of international trade are both based on unrealistic assumptions yet the modern theory is far superior to the classical theory." Discuss.
58. With the help of a suitable diagram, show that a country benefits substantially by opening itself up to foreign trade, one part of its gain arising from exchange and the other from specialization.
59. Critically evaluate Samuelson's factor price equalization theorem. Is complete factor price equalization possible?
60. Explain the concept of offer curves. Critically assess their utility in analysis terms of trade.
61. Explain the basic tenet of comparative cost advantage theory of international trade. Is it true to say that it is a timetested theory? Give reasons in support.
62. In what respects is Ohlin's theory superior to the classical theory of international trade? Give a comprehensive account.

Decision Theory

CHAPTER OUTLINE

Introduction
- Decisions under Certainty
- Decisions under Risk
- Decisions under Uncertainty
- Key Terms and Concepts
- Exercises

INTRODUCTION

The decision theory was barely introduced in Chapter 15. In Section 15.6, we made a mention of three categories of investors. In the first category, we included those who are risk-averse. For them, marginal utility of income diminishes with income. In the second category, we mentioned those who are risk neutral. For them, marginal utility of income is constant. And, in the third category, we referred to the risk-lovers for whom marginal utility of income increases with income. Panels (a), (b) and (c) of Figure 15.4 portrayed the three in that order. Risk-lovers believe in 'no pains, no gains' or in 'the higher the risk, the higher the return'. The risk neutral demonstrate indifference between the two, while the risk averse believe in safe play. For them, marginal utility of income has a monotonously diminishing trend. So far, so good. On what factors does their high or low risk preferences depend, apart from increasing, constant or decreasing marginal utilities of income? Is it their calculation, gutfeeling or the instinct of gambling that governs their behaviour? Gutfeeling depends on intution which may not be all that common. Gambling is unpopular amongst the risk-averse and calculation might serve the purpose of all. In sum, it is calculation on which a large number of investment decisions depend. In this chapter, we will discuss various types of calculations and criteria thereof that lend some rationality to risk preferences of various types. Such calculations and criteria relate, in main, to the three categories – *decisions under certainty*, *decisions under risk* and *decisions under uncertainty*.

We would confine our discussions to the most effective, popular and convenient methods of each here.

22.1 DECISION UNDER CERTAINTY

The reader may be wondering what a decision-maker has to do when everything is certain! For an answer, let us go through the problem of a multiplant firm.

The firm has three plants—Plant A, Plant B and Plant C, The plants operate in three metropolitan cities of India. They produce the same component for an engine in each plant. Production costs differ from plant to plant due to differences in input costs in different localities. The components has no substitutes, empowering absolute monopoly power to the multiplant firm. Price per unit of component is fixed at ₹ 5000. The firm follows high ethical values to care to change the price or to compromise the quality. The firm also believes in complete transparency. It wants to make it common knowledge to all the buyers of the component to direct their orders to the plants that can supply the quantities at specified price. What order size should be directed to which plant under the circumstances given the cost functions below for each?

Plant	Total Cost
A	$TC_A = 20,00,000 + 3000Q$
B	$TC_B = 30,00,000 + 2000Q$
C	$TC_C = 50,00,000 + 1000Q$

Considering the frequency of demand, if an order is assigned to a plant without any heed to its viability at that plant, the firm may either have to raise the price or to compromise the quality or to suffer loss none of which suits the ethical standards of the firm.

Here price, demand and costs are all given with certainty, but still a profit-maximizing assignment of lot sizes to the plants has to be decided with utmost precision. Let us see how we can help the decision in this regard. Refer to Figure 22.1 and to the Table 22.1 below for the purpose.

Figure 22.1 explains the process for general recommendations of assignment of orders to the plants. The criteria adhered to is to prefer plants that have lower cost of production. Price offered per unit is so far out of our consideration. Considering the price too, the final recommendations may be summarized as in Table 22.1.

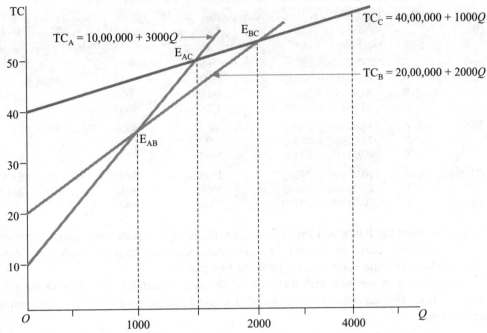

FIGURE 22.1 Decision under certainty: The figures, though not to scale, show that Plant A is most economic among the three when demand is less than 1000 units as $AC_A < AC_B < AC_C$, but as economic as Plant B when demand is exactly 1000 units at point E_{AB} as $AC_A = AC_B$ and as economic as Plant C when demand is 1500 units at point E_{AC} as $AC_A = AC_C$. Also, Plant A is more economic than Plant C when demand is between 0 and 1500 ($0 < Q < 1500$) units as $AC_A < AC_C$ and least economic among the three when demand is more than 1500 units ($Q > 1500$) as $AC_A > AC_B > AC_C$. That is, assignment of orders of lower size than 1000 units must be made to Plant A; those of exactly 1000 units may be assigned to Plant A or Plant B and of 1500 units to Plant A or Plant C, but no order of sizes higher than 1500 should be assigned to Plant A unless prices offered for the product by the buyers are high enough for break-even. A similar analysis of Plant B or Plant C with the rest of the plants in each case is left to the reader as an exercise and the end results can be tallied with those worked out in Table 22.1.

TABLE 22.1 Recommended Assignments to the Plants

Demand size(Q)	Plants	Total cost of order of size Q or at the mid-point of order range at A, B and C	Average cost (AC) of size Q or at the mid-point of order range at A, B and C	Price offered	Plant recommended for given size or at its mid-point
$0 < Q < 1000$	A	$10,00,000 + 3000Q$	5000.	5000	Plant A
	B	$20,00,000 + 2000Q$	6000	5000	
	C	$40,00,000 + 1000Q$	9000	5000	
$Q = 1000$	A	$10,00,000 + 3000Q$	4000.	5000	Plant A or Plant B
	B	$20,00,000 + 2000Q$	4000	5000	
	C	$40,00,000 + 1000Q$	5000	5000	

(Contd.)

TABLE 22.1 Recommended Assignments to the Plants (*Contd.*)

Demand size(Q)	Plants	Total cost of order of size Q or at the mid-point of order range at A, B and C	Average cost (AC) of size Q or at the mid-point of order range at A, B and C	Price offered	Plant recommended for given size or at its mid-point
1000 < Q < 1500	A	10,00,000 + 3000Q	3800.	5000	Plant B
	B	20,00,000 + 2000Q	3600	5000	
	C	40,00,000 + 1000Q	4200	5000	
Q = 1500	A	10,00,000 + 3000Q	3667.	5000	Plant B
	B	20,00,000 + 2000Q	3333	5000	
	C	40,00,000 + 1000Q	3667	5000	
Q = 2000	A	10,00,000 + 3000Q	3500.	5000	Plant B or Plant C
	B	20,00,000 + 2000Q	3000	5000	
	C	40,00,000 + 1000Q	3000	5000	

As evident from the figure and the table values, the least cost plants are assigned the order sizes as the most economic assignment. In case, such plants are busy, the order size can be assigned to relatively more economic of the other two plants.

It is not difficult to see how such decisions in the face of certainty may benefit the selling and buying firms. That answers the question that might have been occupying the attention of the keen reader.

22.2 DECISIONS UNDER RISK

When demand is uncertain, ordering perishable goods like fruits, vegetables, bread, etc. is a risky business. Still, many stores order them, store them and continue doing it every day. You would say, they know how much to order to avoid losses. You are right. Past sales guide them how much to order and when. They are traders, not agents, and the risk involved is theirs, not of any principal. At times, they may run into heavy losses too. But, if the number of times they suffer losses or the number of times they make profits prepares them for either, profits accumulated also make them a little carefree as well as optimistic each time they set their foot forward. If they made profits each time in the past, there is no reason to think they won't, this time too. Some of them harbour superstitious beliefs or even chant prayers to their diety to guard them against losses. If they sight a black cat crossing their path, they treat it as their diety's signal to watch out and not to stake funds that day. The same is the effect when some one sneezes in front of them when they set out. Some economists call reliance on omens and prayers to ward-off risks in business as a **Divine Theory or Faith Theory of decision-making**. One can dispose it off **as a subjective notion or a false paradigm.** Whatever the name you wish to assign it, it has no scientific or rational formulation though it is common among the traditional investors even today all over the world.

Complexities and competitiveness of business call for rational treatment to one's hard-earned money. Rising awareness of the fact among the traders and investors has led them to learn the tricks of the trade or seek opinions of consultants who possess knowledge and experience of making scientific decisions.

Business involving heavy stakes without justifications is a gamble. Rising competition makes things difficult for a raw hand in business just as buying and selling of shares in the stock markets even though they are not as perishable as fruits, vegetables and other food items, but not much different from them too in financial terms. Professional consultants can weigh pros and cons of every investment on the basis probabilities of loss or gain, success or failure and viability or non-viability of any venture estimated from data of past trends.

Probabilities quantify risks and uncertainties and lend rationality to decision-making.

Decision-theory prescribes the following four methods of making decisions under risk:

1. Expected Monetary Value (EMV) Method,
2. Incremental Analysis Method,
3. Marginal Analysis Method, and
4. Decision Tree Analysis Method.

Let us take them up in that order.

22.2.1 Expected Monetary Value Method

The method relies upon statistical probability $P(X_i)$ attached to monetary expectation X_i of ith outcome. Monetary Value (MV) of outcome X_i is the product of the two, that is, $X_i \times P(X_i)$ and Expected Monetary Value of the decision is the sum of all the monetary values of alternative outcomes of a decision. Thus,

$$\text{EMV} = \Sigma[X_i \times P(X_i)], \ (i = 1, 2, 3, \ldots, n), \ \Sigma P(X_i) = 1 \qquad (22.1)$$

Let us take a few illustrations to understand the application first.

ILLUSTRATION 22.1: An oil company has to decide whether to drill at a particular site for crude oil. Apart from their own estimates, the company hires a consultancy firm in the field for a second opinion. On the basis of data procured by the firm and the analysis conducted by it, the firm advises the company to drill. The drilling cost is ₹ 20,00,000; probability of success of finding enough crude oil as 0.3 and the likely revenue, ₹ 1,00,00,000. Should the oil company drill? Given that the fee of the consultancy company is ₹ 5,00,000.

Solution: There are two outcomes, success (X_1) and failure (X_2). Given that $P(X_1) = 0.3$, $P(X_2) = 1 - P(X_1) = 0.7$. In the event of success, the oil company may realize a profit of ₹ 75,00,000 [₹ 1,00,00,000 − 25,00,000] and in that of failure, it loses drilling cost and the fee of the consulting company.

Expected monetary value of the decision to drill,

$$\text{EMV} = \Sigma[X_i \times P(X_i)]$$
$$= X_1 \times P(X_1) + X_2 \times P(X_2)$$
$$= 75{,}00{,}000 \times 0.3 + (-25{,}00{,}000) \times 0.7$$

(*Note:* the negative sign indicates negative profit or loss.)

$$= 22{,}50{,}000 + (-17{,}50{,}000)$$
$$= ₹\ \mathbf{5{,}00{,}000}$$

As evident, the EMV bears a positive sign, indicating gain from drilling and justifying the decision. All these calculations lend rationality to decision, not the gurantee of its success.

Let us proceed to another illustration.

ILLUSTRATION 22.2: A bread manufacturer has invented a substitute of home cooked Indian *Chapatis* with digestive ingredients. The manufacturer has given it the name of ready *Rotis* which take a minute on the hot pan to be ready to eat. Package of 5 pieces costs the manufacture ₹ 20 inclusive of all the packaging costs and sells for ₹ 30 each if sold before the weekend and ₹ 15, if at the weekend but nothing thereafter. The market survey conducted by the marketing department of the manufacturer draws the following probability distribution of the weekly demand:

Number of packages Demanded per week (n):	1000	1100	1200	1300	1400	1500
Probability $P(n)$:	0.1	0.2	0.25	0.20	0.15	0.1

(i) Construct the pay-off Table to determine the optimal number of packages to be produced by the manufacturer as also the expected profit.

(ii) Calculate the Expected Value of Perfect Information (EVPI).

Solution:

TABLE 22.2 Pay-off matrix: When $n = m$, profit is $10n$; when $n < m$, profit is $10n - 5(m - n)$, and when $n > m$, profit is $10n$. For top left to right bottom, the entries in bold face along the diagonal show a profit of $10n$. All the entries downwards to left of this diagonal show a profit of $10n$ as $n > m$. All the entries upwards to right $10n - 5(m - n)$. If the producer produces the quantity demanded, profit is ₹ 10 per unit of demand, if the producer produces more than what is demanded, he loses ₹ 5 (20 – 15) per unit of the excess production from the profit of ₹ 10 per unit of **demand and if he produces less than what is demanded, he earns a profit of ₹ 10 per unit of demand.**

From the lowest row of table, maximum EMV, $\text{EMV}_{\text{max}} = 11{,}575$, which corresponds to production of **1300** packages.

Demand (n) \ Production (m)	1000	1100	1200	1300	1400	1500	Probability $P(n)$
1000	**10,000**	9,500	9,000	8,500	8,000	7,500	0.10
1100	10,000	**11,000**	10,500	10,000	9,500	9,000	0.20
1200	10,000	11,000	**12,000**	11,500	11,000	10,500	0.25
1300	10,000	11,000	12,000	**13,000**	12,500	12,000	0.20
1400	10,000	11,000	12,000	13,000	**14,000**	13,500	0.15
1500	10,000	11,000	12,000	13,000	14,000	**15,000**	0.10
EMV of Alternative Levels of Production	10,000	10,850	11,400	**11,575**	11,450	11,100	1.0

Calculation of EMV of production of m packages is done by running down the column of particular levels of m and multiplying each pay-off corresponding to each value of demand, n, by corresponding probability, $P(n)$ and summing up the products down the column for each m. That is, when $m = 1200$, EMV $= 9000 \times 0.1 + 10{,}500 \times 0.2 + 12000 \times 0.25 + 12{,}000 \times 0.2 + 12000 \times 0.15 + 12000 \times 0.1 = 11{,}400$ and when $m = 1300$, EMV $= 8500 \times 0.1 + 10{,}000 \times 0.2 + 11{,}500 \times 0.25 + 13{,}000 \times 0.2 + 13000 \times 0.15 + 13000 \times 0.1 = 11{,}575$ and so on. The highest EMV in last row of Table 22.2 is 11,575 corresponding to production of 1300 units [Table 22.2].

Now turning to the second part, let us first define what EVPI means. It is defined as the maximum amount a decision-maker would be willing to pay for perfect information. This is given as

$$\text{EVPI} = \text{EPPI} - \text{EMV}_{\max} \qquad (22.2)$$

Here, EPPI stands for Expected profit from Perfect Information and is given as a sum of the products of bold faced entries along the main diagonal, from top-left to bottom-right, with corresponding probabilities.

Thus,

EPPI $= 10{,}000 \times 0.1 + 11{,}000 \times 0.2 + 12{,}000 \times 0.25 + 13{,}000 \times 0.2 + 14{,}000 \times 0.15 + 15000 \times 0.1$

$= \mathbf{12{,}400}$

Therefore,

$$\text{EVPI} = \text{EPPI} - \text{EMV}_{\max}$$
$$= 12{,}400 - 11{,}575$$
$$= \mathbf{825}$$

This is the amount the decision-maker would be willing to pay for perfect information.

In this illustration, we computed the level of production that maximized the net profit under given probability distribution of demand.

In the next illustration, let us employ *Incremental Analysis* for the same problem in Illustration 22.2. The method is a little tedious than the earlier one. Nevertheless, it is found more compact and scientific by many decision-makers.

22.2.2 Incremental Analysis Method

Incremental profit refers to *additional profit generated from production/sale of additional quantity*. It is different from the *marginal profit,* which refers to *additional profit generated by an addional unit produced/sold.* If either of the two bears a negative sign, you may use the term 'loss' instead of 'profit' if you wish, but it is better to continue with the use of negative profit for all practical purposes. The notion of incremental profit as a criterion of decision-making is referred to as the **incremental analysis method**. The illustration below explains its utility as a more scientific and compact tool of decision making than the earlier one of analysis of pay-off matrices. But, the reader has the liberty to choose either one.

ILLUSTRATION 22.3: For the problem of Illustration 22.2, calculate net profit for each level of demand and determine the optimal quantity through incremental analysis the manufacturer must expect to produce. Table 22.3 summarizes the calculations.

Solution: Let X denote the number of packages stocked, as in the first column of Table 22.3. The second column gives the probability that the number of packages demanded is less than X. The third column gives the probability that the number of packages demanded is greater than or equal to X. The fourth column calculates the marginal profit when when demand is one unit less than the stock or one unit more than it as shown in the square brackets. It is multiplied by the difference in successive levels of demand in the given probability distribution to arrive at incremental profit. The incremental profit is added to the total profit from earlier level of stock/sale to arrive at the total profit at current level of stock/sale (Column 5). The method when applied to the current illustration is explained below and summarized in Table 22.3.

When stock is 1000 packages, the probability of less than 1000 packages being demanded and sold is 0.00 and that of 1000 or more being demanded or sold is $1 - 0.00$, that is 1.00. The marginal profit on one unit less than the stock or one unit more than it being demanded and sold is $[0.00 \times 0 + 1.00 \times 10]$, that is, ₹ 10. (Note that price being ₹ 30 per package and cost, ₹ 20 per package; profit per package is ₹ 10.). The total profit on 1000 packages stocked and sold is $[1000 \times 10]$, that is, ₹ 10,000 (Columns 4 and 5). When stock is 1100 packages, probability of less than 1100 packages being demanded and sold is 0.1 and that of 1100 or more being demanded and sold is is $1 - 0.1$, that is, 0.9. The marginal profit on one unit less than the stock or one unit more than it being demanded and sold is $[0.1 \times (-5) + 0.9 \times 10]$, that is, ₹ 8.50. The incremental profit to be added to that of the earlier level stocked/sold is ₹ 8.50×100 (current level differs from the earlier one by 100 packages), that is, ₹ 850.00. Total profit at the stock level of 1100 packages is thus ₹ 850.00 higher higher than that at at the earlier level of stock which was 1000 packages. It is therefore ₹ 10,850.00. Proceeding likewise, we can calculate total profits for all levels of stocks. We observe that they go on increasing every time stock increases by 100 units until it reaches 1300 units where it is ₹ 11,575.00. If stock is further increased by 100 units, that is, to 1400 units, the incremental profit is negative $[0.75 \times (-5) + 0.25 \times 10] \times 100$, that is, a loss of ₹ 125.00. The total profit at the stock level of 1400 units is ₹ 11,450.00, that is, ₹ 125 less than what it was at the stock level of 1300 units. This is so because $P[Dd < X]$ increases while $P[Dd \geq X]$ decreases everytime stock is increased as revealed by the probability distribution given in the question.

Table 22.3, summarizes the calculations.

TABLE 22.3 Calculations of net profits through incremental analysis [$Dd \equiv$ Demand]

Stock (X)	P(Dd < X)	P(Dd ≥ X)	Incremental Profit	Total Profit
1000	0.00	1.00	$[0.00 \times 0 + 1.0 \times 10] \times 1000 = 10{,}000$	**10,000**
1100	0.10	0.90	$[0.10 \times (-5) + 0.90 \times 10] \times 100 = 850$	$10{,}000 + 850 = \mathbf{10{,}850}$
1200	0.30	0.70	$[0.30 \times (-5) + 0.70 \times 10] \times 100 = 550$	$10{,}850 + 550 = \mathbf{11{,}400}$
1300	0.55	0.45	$[0.55 \times (-5) + 0.45 \times 10] \times 100 = 175$	$11{,}400 + 175 = \mathbf{11{,}575}$
1400	0.75	0.25	$[0.75 \times (-5) + 0.25 \times 10] \times 100 = -125$	$11{,}575 - 125 = \mathbf{11{,}450}$
1500	0.90	0.10	$[0.90 \times (-5) + 0.10 \times 10] \times 100 = -350$	$11{,}450 - 350 = \mathbf{11{,}100}$

The two methods yield the same results. $\text{EMV}_{\max} = \mathbf{11{,}575}$ and the optimal output is **1300**. The reader can use either whether it the optimal output to be determined by the producer or it is optimal size of the order placed by the outlets. Once a perishable item is produced, one of them or both have to face the consequences of loss if they behaved irrationally.

Expected Profit from *Perfect Information* is the profit arising when no demand is denied or no supply is rejected. In other words, perfect information means perfect knowledge of quantity demanded that is satisfied by what is produced or perfect knowledge of quantity produced that is sold out to the consumers. A glance at the diagonal running down from left to right with bold-faced entries in the Pay-off Table 22.2 would help you understand the point. These entries multiplied by the respective probabilities give EPPI, which is **12,400**, as calculated in the previous illustration. Thus, EVPI = EPPI − EMV$_{max}$ = 12400 − 11575 = **825**.

22.2.3 Marginal Analysis Method

When the alternatives to decide from are very large in number, the methods discussed in Subsections 22.2.1 and 22.2.2 prove quite time and effort consuming. In such cases *marginal analysis* comes as a very handy and effective tool of decision making.

The method is based on the principle that the level of demand or sale is the optimal level if the expected marginal loss is equal to the expected marginal profit. The equality refers to the *equilibrium level*.

We have already defined marginal profit and marginal loss. The former refers to addition of profit from an additional unit, while the later refers to negative profit from an additional unit stocked/sold. For example, marginal profit in respect of Illustration 22.2 is ₹ 10(30 − 20) and marginal loss is ₹ 5(20 − 15). Note that cost per unit is ₹ 20, while price per unit is ₹ 30 and the salvage value is ₹ 15. Now, let the equilibrium level of probability, P_e, given by $P(Dd \geq X)$, where Dd is demand and X is stock, represent the probability for marginal profit (MP), then $(1 − P_e)$ would represent that for marginal loss (ML) so that

$$P_e \times MP = (1 − P_e) \times ML$$

$$\Rightarrow (MP + ML) \times P_e = ML$$

$$\Rightarrow P_e = \frac{ML}{(MP + ML)} \quad (22.3)$$

$$\Rightarrow = \frac{5}{(10 + 5)} = \mathbf{0.3333}$$

(Substituting MP and ML as 10 and 5 respectively)

Now construct a 'greater than or equal to' cumulative probability distribution as given by columns 1, 2 and 3 of Table 22.3. Reproducing it here, we observe the desired probability distribution as in Column 4 of Table 22.4.

TABLE 22.4 Determination of Optimal X by Marginal Analysis: When demand is less than X where X is stock, loss will take place. When demand is greater than or equal to X, loss will not follow. The probability P_e at the equilibrium is 0.3333, which is greater than 0.25, but not equal to 0.25, (See last column). Hence the optimal level of demand is 1300 units, cumulative probability of which is 0.45.

X	P(X)	P(Dd < X)	P(Dd ≥ X)
1000	0.10	0.00	1.00
1100	0.20	0.10	0.90
1200	0.25	0.30	0.70
1300	0.20	0.55	**0.45**
1400	0.15	0.75	0.25
1500	0.10	0.90	0.10

(Dd represents Demand)

The example we discussed above is related to discrete data. Let us take one example of continuous probability distribution as well.

ILLUSTRATION 22.4 Demand for a certain input follows a normal distribution with mean, $m = 50$ kg and standard deviation, $\sigma = 10$ kg. The quantity of the input ordered by a plant has to be used the same day or else its potency falls. If it is used the same day, it generates a profit of ₹ 400 per kg; if not, it causes a loss of ₹ 100 per kg. What quantity should the plant buy?

Solution Since MP = ₹ 400 and ML = ₹ 100,

$$P_e = ML/(ML + MP)$$
$$= 100/(100 + 400)$$
$$= 0.25$$

Let X be the quantity of the input to be ordered. The value of Z corresponding to this X following the normal distribution, is

$$Z = \frac{X - m}{\sigma}$$

Given, $m = 50$ kg and $\sigma = 10$ kg, we have,

$$Z' = \frac{X - 50}{10}$$

Now, probability that X is greater than or equal to m,

$$P(X \geq m) = P(Z \geq Z')$$
$$= 0.50 - P(0 \leq Z \leq Z') \quad \text{[from Figure 22.2]}$$
$$= 0.25 \text{ [Given]}$$

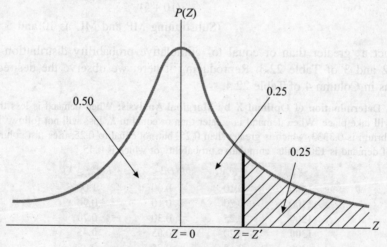

FIGURE 22.2 Areas under normal curve.

From the normal table,
$$Z' = 0.675$$

That is, $(X - 50)/10 = 0.675$
$$\Rightarrow \quad X = 50 + 0.675 \times 10$$
$$\Rightarrow \quad X = 56.75 \text{ kg}$$

The plant must therefore order **56.75 kg** of input.

22.2.4 Decision Tree Analysis Approach

A decision tree is a visual presentation of a decision process portraying various alternatives options with their respective probabilities and monetary consequences. In Chapter 12, we portrayed Bayesian decision rule (Figure 12.7) in context of oligopolistic games in which a firm matches its rival moves and the latter counters them. Each had its strategies and pay-offs, but wasn't certain about the strategy the first mover had to start with. That was the reason 'nature' was introduced in that game as the first mover to lend some certainty to the analysis and the game of *asymmetric, imperfect* and *incomplete information* was remodeled through **Harsanyi transformation**. The situation is not called for here as the case is not of rivalry between firms, but that of a firm choosing the course of action to lend rationally to risky decisions. We already know that such decisions are common as a vast number of investors believe in risk theory of returns. As mentioned in Section 15.6 and as pointed out in the introductory paragraph of this Chapter, 'no pains, no gains' is the motto of many of them. The purpose here is to impress upon the readers and investors to avoid blind risks as they may turn out suicidal. Instead, calculated risks, despite their slow pace, lead to stability, growth and prosperity. Note that 'one bird in hand is better than two in the bush' and 'fools rush in where angels fear to tread'.

Well, enough to remind you of the pitfalls of the **blind risks**. Let us see how can a decision-maker do that through decision tree analysis. Normally, we employ two types of decision trees—*first*, a **Simple Decision Tree** in which all the desired probabilities of alternative options are given, and *second*, **Bayesian Decision Tree**, in which some probabilities have to be calculated using *Bayes' Theorem*. Let us demonstrate each in that order with an illustration.

(A) A Simple Decision Tree

ILLUSTRATION 22.5 A decision-maker is facing a decision point whether or not to construct a model plant before staking huge investments on the real one. The model plant functions like the real one. The cost of the model plant is ₹ 10,000. He can proceed to build the real one once he is able to see the working of its model. Probability that the model plant works is 0.50 and the probability that the real plant works if its model does is 0.90. Also, the probability that the real plant works, if constructed despite the failure of its model to work, is 0.20, while the probability that the real plant works without the experiment of its model is 0.40.

If the main plant works, it means ₹ 200,000 to the decision-maker, but if it doesn't, it implies a loss of ₹ 150,000 to him. What would you do if you were in the shoes of the decision-maker?

Solution The flow chart in Figure 22.3 portrays how the simple decision tree depicting various alternatives, then probabilities and monetary consequences to the decision maker would look like. Expected monetary values of each are calculated by EMV method as below:

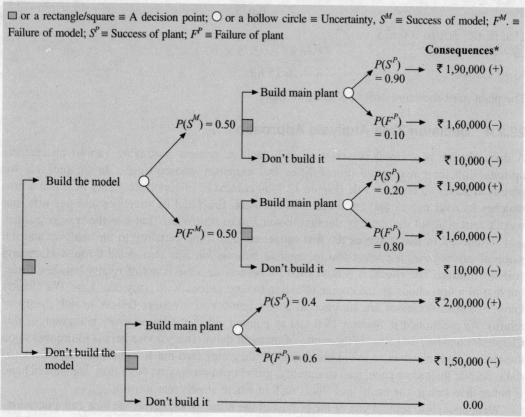

FIGURE 22.3 Simple Decision Tree: Monetary consequences of each outcome are presented in the extreme right column.

EMV of constructing the main plant when the model plant is a success = $1{,}90{,}000 \times 0.90 +$
$(-1{,}60{,}000) \times 0.1$
= ₹ **1,55,000**

EMV of constructing the main plant when the model plant is a failure = $1{,}90{,}000 \times 0.20 +$
$(-1{,}60{,}000) \times 0.8$
= $-$ ₹ **90,000**

EMV of building the main plant without the experiment of model plant = $2{,}00{,}000 \times 0.40 +$
$(-1{,}50{,}000) \times 0.6$
= $-$ ₹ **10,000**

EMV of building the main plant after the experiment of model plant = $1{,}55{,}000 \times 0.50 +$
$(-90{,}000) \times 0.50$
= ₹ **32,500**

Thus, the decision-maker must build the Main Plant after the experiment of the Model Plant.

---

* The sign '+' indicates gain in financial consequences while the sign '−' indicates loss in it.

(B) Bayesian Decision Tree

Refer back to Illustration 22.1, where, we mentioned drilling for crude petroleum in an oversimplified demonstration of EMVmethod. Let us take up the case in its proper perspective of Bayesian decision tree analysis in Illustration 22.5 below.

ILLUSTRATION 22.6 Consider the decision of drilling for crude petroleum in a certain region confronting the management of an oil exploratory company. According to the geologist report, chances of finding the crude in the said region are as high as 60%. The management has an allocation of ₹ 1,50,000. The consequences of drilling and getting oil and those of drilling and not getting it in terms of cash left with the company after the decision are ₹ 5,00,000 and and ₹ 40,000, respectively. The management, however, has the option of conducting a seismic test to ensure existence and extent of the crude in the region. The test costs them ₹ 5,000 only, but the benefit of the test is that the test will correctly predict the presence of oil on 90% of the times if it is actually there and 70% of the times if it is not.

What course of action would you recommend for the management?

Solution Figure 22.4 portrays Bayesian Decision Tree. It contains alternative options, their probabilities, and monetary consequences in terms of cash in hand left. Probabilities of some alternative options are explained and calculated below using Bayes' Theorem*:

EVENTS		DESCRIPTION
A	≡	Find oil
B	≡	Find no oil
C	≡	Seismic test says oil is there
D	≡	Seismic test says no oil is there

With these notations, we can identify and calculate probabilities $P(C)$, $P(D)$, $P(A/C)$, $P(A/D)$, $P(B/C)$ and $P(B/D)$. To arrive at the decision tree drawn above, let us identify first the given ones as below:

$P(A) = 0.6 \equiv$ Probability of finding oil

$P(B) = 0.4 \equiv$ Probability of not finding oil

$P(C/A) = 0.9 \equiv$ Probability that test predicts correctly when oil is actually there

$P(D/A) = 0.1 \equiv$ Probability that test predicts incorrectly when oil is actually there

$P(D/B) = 0.7 \equiv$ Probability that test predicts correctly when no oil is there

$P(C/B) = 0.3 \equiv$ Probability that test predicts incorrectly when actually there is no oil.

Now, let us find the desired probabilities from Bayes' theorem,

$$P(A/C) = \frac{P(A) \times P(C/A)}{P(A) \times P(C/A) + P(B) \times P(C/B)} = \frac{0.9 \times 0.6}{0.9 \times 0.6 + 0.3 \times 0.4} = \mathbf{0.818}$$

$$P(B/C) = \frac{P(B) \times P(C/B)}{P(A) \times P(C/A) + P(B) \times P(C/B)} = \frac{0.3 \times 0.4}{0.9 \times 0.6 + 0.3 \times 0.4} = \mathbf{0.182}$$

---

* The reader is expected to have workable knowledge of Bayes Theorem.

$$P(A/D) = \frac{P(A) \times P(D/A)}{P(A) \times P(D/A) + P(B) \times P(D/B)} = \frac{0.1 \times 0.6}{0.1 \times 0.6 + 0.7 \times 0.4} = \mathbf{0.176}$$

$$P(B/D) = \frac{P(B) \times P(D/B)}{P(A) \times P(D/A) + P(B) \times P(D/B)} = \frac{0.7 \times 0.4}{0.1 \times 0.6 + 0.7 \times 0.4} = \mathbf{0.824}$$

$$P(C) = P(A) \times P(C/A) + P(B) \times P(C/B) = 0.9 \times 0.6 + 0.3 \times 0.4 = \mathbf{0.66}$$

$$P(D) = P(A) \times P(D/A) + P(B) \times P(D/B) = 0.1 \times 0.6 + 0.7 \times 0.4 = \mathbf{0.34}$$

EMV of drilling when seismic test predicts presence of oil 66% of the times
$$= 0.66 \times [4{,}95{,}000 \times 0.818 + 35{,}000 \times 0.182]$$
$$= ₹\ \mathbf{2{,}71{,}444.80}$$

EMV of not drilling when seismic test predicts presence of oil 66% of the times
$$= ₹\ \mathbf{1{,}45{,}000}$$

Clearly drilling is a better option in this case.

EMV of drilling when seismic test predicts absence of oil 34% of the times
$$= 0.34 \times [4{,}95{,}000 \times 0.176 + 35{,}000 \times 0.828]$$
$$= ₹\ \mathbf{39{,}474}$$

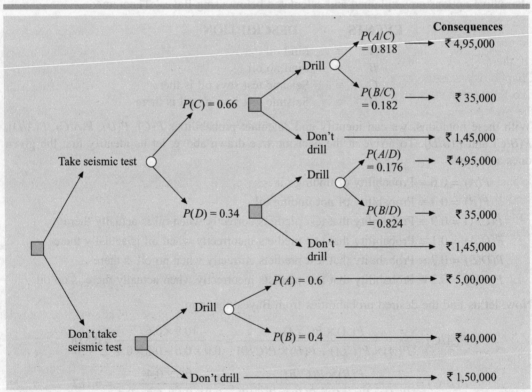

Figure 22.4 Bayesian Decision Tree: In the figure, ■ indicates decision point, ○ indicates uncertainty. Monetary consequences of each outcome are presented in the extreme right column. Some of the probabilities indicated at the uncertainty point are as calculated from the Bayes' theorem.

EMV of not drilling when seismic test predicts absence of oil 34% of the times
= ₹ **1,45,000**.
Clearly not drilling in this case is a better option.
Thus, EMV of taking a seismic test = ₹ **3,10,919** (= 2,71,445 + 39,474)
EMV of not taking a seismic test = 5,00,000 × 0.6 + 40,000 × 0.4 = ₹ **3,16,000**
Thus, proceeding without a seismic test is a better option.

22.3 DECISION UNDER UNCERTAINTY

Unlike decision making under risk in which probabilities of alternative options were known or could be known through statistical tools from those provided or those subjectively known, decision making under uncertainty rely on the following tools, which lend rationalty to decisions made without availability of any data on probabilities or even pay-offs. The methods in practice are the following ones:

1. Optimistic Approach (MaxiMax)
2. Pessimistic Approach (MaxiMin)
3. Hurwitz Approach
4. Laplace criteria of equal likelihood
5. MiniMax regret

Of these, methods listed against serial number 2 and 5 have already been discussed in Chapter 12. (Section 12.7, zero-sum pure strategy games). Yet we prefer to discuss all the five through same illustration here so that the reader may acquire better understanding in the present context Consider the following Illustration:

ILLUSTRATION 22.7 Consider the pay-off matrix of high, medium and low levels of demand of a certain washing powder with skin-friendly, neutral, skin-unfriendly but strong cleansing contents. Let us for the sake of simplicity name them as Brand A, Brand B, and Brand C. The matrix shows their demands, but due to cost-consideration and user consciousness of several types, we prefer to focus on pay-offs from each which form the decision criteria.

	Alternatives (Pay-offs., Lakhs of Rupees)		
Demands	Brand A (Skin-friendly)	Brand B (Skin neutral)	Brand C (Skin-unfriendly)
High	80	60	40
Medium	40	30	20
Low	10	15	5

Solution

TABLE 22.5 Decision under MaxiMax, MaxiMin, Hurwitz and Laplace Methods

Demands	Alternatives (Pay-offs, Lakhs of Rupees)		
	Brand A (Skin-friendly)	Brand B (Skin neutral)	Brand C (Skin-unfriendly)
High	80	60	40
Medium	40	30	20
Low	10	15	5
Max	80**	60	40
Min	10	15*	5
Hurwitz	45	37.5	22.5
Laplace	130/3 = 43.33	105/3 = 35.00	65/3 = 21.67

Maximum and minimum values of pay-offs for each brand are observed as shown in the lower half of the table. The *MaxiMax* (The Maximum of all the maximum pay-offs) is shown by two stars (**) and the *MaxiMin* (the maximum of all the minimum pay-offs), by one star (*). Under Maximax criterion, Brand A is chosen and under MaxiMin criterion, it is Brand B. Under Hurwitz criterion, coefficient of optimism, α, is determined first. It is between 0 and 1. According to Hurwitz, no person or producer can ever be perfectly optimistic (with $\alpha = 1$) nor perfectively pessimistic (with $\alpha = 0$). Optimum pay-off from a brand accordingly is given as $\alpha \times$ maximum pay-off from it + $(1 - \alpha) \times$ Minimum pay-off from it. For the sake of simplicity, taking α as 0.5, optimum pay-off from Brand A is 45 [= 0.5 × 80 + (1 – 0.5) × 10]; that from Brand B, 37.5 [= 0.5 × 60 + (1 – 0.5) × 15] and that from Brand C, 22.5 [= 0.5 × 40 + (1 – 0.5) × 5]. The maximum of these Hurwitzian pay-offs being 45 from Brand A, the method favours brand A. Thus, unlike MaxiMin criterion, Maxi-Max and Hurwitz criteria both recommend Brand A. Let us now turn to Laplace Criterion of equal likelihood. It assigns equal probability to each pay-off of a brand to determine the expected pay-offs of each of the three and decides in favour of the one that is highest. Accordingly, Brand A is favoured [See last row of Table 22.5]. As we see, Maxi-Max, Hurwitz and Laplace decide in favour of Brand A while MaxiMin, in favour of Brand B. On the basis of this analysis, one can choose Brand A because of 3:1 odds are in its favour.

Of the five, we still have to wait for the recommendation of the MiniMax Regret Criterion. The term 'Regret' may be defined as the loss due to incorrect decision. To demonstrate, suppose one decides in favour of any brand while the correct decision must be Brand A. under high demand (pay-off from Brand A being the highest, that is, 80). If one chooses Brand A, one looses nothing. In other words, one's regret is zero [=(80 – 80)]. If one chooses Brand B or Br and C, one's regret from choosing Brand B is 20 [=(80 – 60)] and that from choosing Brand C is 40 [=(80 – 40)]. Proceeding likewise for medium demand, the regrets are 0, 10, and 20 and for low demand, thry are 5, 0 and 10 for brands A, B and C, respectively. They are all shown in Table 22.6. Highest regret from choosing brands A, B and C, respectively are 5, 20 and 40 of which the least one is **5** corresponding to choice of Brand **A**. That is, the minimum of the maximum regrets, the MiniMax regrert, is **5** from choice of Brand **A**.

TABLE 22.6 MiniMax Regret

Brands / Demand	Brand A	Brand B	Brand C	Row maximum
High	80 – 80 = 0	80 – 60 = 20	80 – 40 = 40	80
Medium	40 – 40 = 0	40 – 30 = 10	40 – 20 = 20	40
Low	15 – 10 = 0	15 – 15 = 0	15 – 5 = 0	15
Maximum	5	20	40	

Clearly, the MiniMax regret criterion also sides with choice of brand A. Thus out of five methods, four point at Brand A and only one at Brand B. Siding with the majority, the decision maker must choose Brand A.

As you might recall, MiniMax regret criterion is the criterion discussed in Chapter 12 as Loss avoidance criterion.

Decision under complete uncertainty is a gamble but with aforesaid methods, it becomes a calculated gamble.

KEY TERMS AND CONCEPTS

Bayesian decision tree A decision tree in which some of the probabilities of some alternative courses are calculated from Bayes' theorem of inverse probability.

Expected Monetary Value (EMV) It is net expectation from all the alternative courses of action. Every course of action has a chance and monetary consequences. Hence, EMV = $\Sigma P(X_i) \times X_i = P(X_1) \times X_1 + P(X_2) \times X_2 + \cdots + P(X_n) \times X_n$.

Expected Monetary Value$_{MAX}$ Maximum of expected Monetary Values.

Expected Profit from Perfect Information (EPPI) Sum of products of profits and their respective probabilities from perfect information.

Expected Value of Perfect Information (EVPI) The excess of expected profit from perfect information over the maximum of the Expected Monetary Value (EMV)= EPPI – EMV$_{MAX}$.

Incremental loss Fall in profit from some additional units produced and sold.

Incremental profit Rise in profit from some additional units produced and sold.

Marginal analysis When expected marginal profit equals expected marginal loss, the probability of marginal profit, P_e, is called the equilibrium level of probability. The probability of demand/sales being more than or equal to the stock/production must be more than or equal to P_e in marginal analysis method of decision making.

Marginal loss Fall in profit from an additional unit produced and sold.

Marginal profit Rise in profit from an additional unit produced and sold.

Perfect information Knowledge of quantities of demand and supply and their probabilities that are common knowledge, leaving no room for loss or unsold stocks.

Risk It is calculated or quantified uncertainty.

Risk averse Those who refuse to take big risk. For them MU of income diminishes with income.

Risk lovers Those for whom MU of income has an increasing trend. They love risk as a resource of income. Risk theory of profit has great significance for them. 'The higher the risk, the higher the returns' they believe.

Risk neutral Those who are indifferent to risks and returns. MU of income is constant for them.

Simple decision tree It is a systematic flow chart portraying the given probabilities of all the alternative courses along with the monetary consequences of each for decision making.

Uncertainty A situation of decision making in which no past data or method is available for determining the probabilities of alternative courses of action for decision making. Decisions under uncertainty involve the following tools:

    MaxiMax (Optimistic) Choosing the maximum value from amongst the highest pay-offs of all the alternative actions.

    MaxiMin (pessimistic) Choosing the maximum value from amongst the lowest pay-offs of all the alternative actions.

    Hurwitz criterion The criterion that no individual or firm is perfectly optimistic (MaxiMax) or perfectly pessimistic (MaxiMin). Hurwitz coefficient, α, determines the level of optimism of the decision-maker. Taking, $\alpha = 1$ for perfect optimism, and $\alpha = 0$ for perfect pessimism. Hurwitz coefficient of optimism may be taken as 0.5, that is, half-way in-between. Thus, desired pay-off = $\alpha \times$ Maximum Pay-off + $(1 - \alpha) \times$ Minimum Pay-off.

    MiniMax regret It is defined as the excess of the maximum of the pay-offs of all the alternatives over that chosen. It is, in other words, the cost of the decision or the loss regretted by the decision-maker.

    Laplace criterion or equal likelihood criterion Assigning equal probabilities to all alternatives and getting the expected pay-off thereafter.

EXERCISES

A. Short Answer Questions

Define the following (1 through 23):

1. Certainty
2. Uncertainty
3. Risk
4. EMV
5. EPPI
6. EVPI
7. MaxiMax
8. MaxiMin
9. MiniMax regret
10. Simple decision tree
11. Bayesian decision tree
12. Decision point
13. EMV_{MAX}
14. Hurwitz criterion
15. Hurwitz coefficient of optimism
16. Laplace criterion or equal likelihood criterion
17. Marginal loss

18. Marginal profit
19. Incremental loss
20. Incremental profit
21. Marginal analysis
22. Pay-off matrix
23. Conditional probability
24. Which of the following offers the most appropriate description of the 'risk theory of profit' attached to the names of Hawley & Knight:
    (i) 'No pains, no gains'
    (ii) 'The higher the risk, the higher the profit'
    (iii) Gain don't accrue to those who don't take pains.
    (iv) Risk bearing is the necessary and sufficient condition of profit making.
    (v) All the above
    (vi) None of the above.
25. Does the notion of risk in Q. 24 refer to
    (i) Blind risk
    (ii) Calculated risk
    (iii) Quantified uncertainty
    (iv) Rational risk
26. MiniMax regret criterion suits the:
    (i) Risk-lover
    (ii) Risk-averse
    (iii) Risk-neutral
    (iv) None of the above
27. MiniMax loss avoidance criterion is
    (i) The same as MiniMax regret criterion
    (ii) Not the same as MiniMax regret criterion, but similar to it
    (iii) Exactly Opposite of MiniMax regret criterion
    (iv) Exactly opposite of Maximin criterion
28. Which of the following is true and which, false:
    (i) Incremental profit analysis and marginal analysis both lead to the same decision
    (ii) MiniMax loss avoidance refers to deciding in favour of an alternative that relates to the minimum of the maximum possible losses posed by various alternatives
    (iii) MiniMax regret criterion refers to deciding in favour of an alternative that relates to the least value of the sacrifices posed by various wrong alternatives if chosen by a decision-maker.
    (iv) A good decision is anytime better than a quick decision
    (v) A blind decision is a pure gamble
    (vi) Marginal analysis is based on the probability that makes expected marginal loss equal to the expected marginal profit
    (vii) The probability of equilibrium in marginal analysis, P_e, is given as $P_e = ML/(ML + MP)$, where ML denotes marginal loss and MP, marginal profit
    (viii) Expected profit from perfect information (EPPI) refers to the sum of monetary values of quantities of perishable goods precisely known to be demanded and supplied that cause no loss of revenue or good-will over stocking or understocking
    (ix) EMV_{MAX} is the highest value among the EMVs of all the alternative options
    (x) EVPI is the maximum amount a producer or stockist can pay for perfect information.
29. According to Hurwitz, no individual/firm is perfectly optimistic (MaxiMax criterion) nor perfectly pessimistic (MaxiMin criterion). Give an example from real world that supports the Hurwitz criterion.

B. Long Answer Questions

Distinguish between the following (31 through 40):

30. Marginal profit and incremental profit
31. Marginal loss and incremental loss
32. MaxiMax and MaxiMin criteria
33. MiniMax regret and MiniMax loss avoidance criteria
34. Expected Monetary Value (EMV) and Maximum Expected Monetary Value (EMV_{MAX})
35. Expected profit from perfect information and expected value of perfect information.
36. A simple decision tree and a Bayesian decision tree
37. Risk and uncertainty
38. Certainty and uncertainty
39. Hurwitz criterion and Laplanc equal likelihood criterion
40. Blind risk and calculated risk
41. The probability distribution of the likely daily demands of a newspaper in a locality is given as

The number demanded :	400	450	500	550	600
Probabilities:	0.15	0.20	0.30	0.20	0.15

    What number must a vendor order if it costs ₹ 1.50 and sells for ₹ 2.25 the same day and ₹ 0.50 ever after as scrap. Also, calculate the maximum fee to be paid to a consultant for perfect information.
    [Hint: See Illustration 22.3]
    [Ans: 500 papers; EMV_{MAX} = 331.25; EPPI = 375; EVPI = ₹ 44.75]

C. Essay/Project Type Questions

42. A multinational corporation has hired a consultancy firm to make recommendations on marketability of its user friendly android in a fast developing underdeveloped country. In absence of availability of past data, the consultancy firm conducts a market survey to feel the pulse of the likely users and concludes the following quantitative information to base its recommendations upon.

Demands	Pay-offs in Alternative Market Segments (Thousand Dollars)		
	Segment A	Segment B	Segment C
High	90	70	50
Medium	60	50	30
Low	30	20	10

    The corporation intends to introduce the android in one segment to start with. Assuming availability of no other information, what recommendation can the consultancy firm make in the best interests of the corporation? Give reasons in support.

43. According to Hawley's* *'Risk Theory of Profit,'** profit arose out of uninsured risk. Can we call it blind risk? If the capacity to bearing uninsured risk is the cause of profits, why do some firms suffer losses, while others with same stakes make huge profits in an industry? Give reasons in support.

44. How far are the uninsured risks responsible for the diversification of an investor's portfolio? Explain how an investor can optimize his portfolio through risk return indifference maps**?

---
* Hawley, *Risk theory of Profit,* The Quarterly Journal of Economics, Vol. 7, July 1, 1893. URL: https://archive.org/metadata/jstcor:1882285
** Refer to author's *'Microeconomics: Theory and Application*, Part I, 'Optimality in investor's portfolio management', Chapter 4, PHI Learning, Delhi, pp. 204–206.

23

Estimation of Functions in Economics—The Basics of Economics

CHAPTER OUTLINE
Introduction
- Stages of Econometric Estimation
- OLS-estimation of Functions
- Testing of Estimated Functions
- Problems with Regression Analysis
- Effect on R^2 of Additional Explanatory Variables
- Conclusion
- Key Terms and Concepts
- Exercises

INTRODUCTION

In earlier chapters, we saw how economic activities such as investment, production, distribution and consumption depend on market mechanism. Optimality of investor's portfolio management, efficiency in resource allocation, optimality in distributive justice, maximization of utility by a welfare state—all depend on quantitative statements of 'what exists' and 'how to make the most of it.' Such statements require precision of measurement. For instance, no production can proceed unless the producer has a precise idea of demand for his product at the going prices. This calls for demand forecasting, which in turn, necessitates functional relationship between demand and its determinants. The relationship is not as easy to ascertain as is one between pressure and volume of a gas at a given temperature or one, between increase in length of a metal-rod and rise in its temperature. The latter relate to physical sciences that deal with inanimate objects comprising atoms or molecules displaying a fixed pattern of behaviour. Such sciences are known as deterministic sciences therefore. As against them, the science of economics deals with living entities the behaviour patterns of whom are subject to unpredictable changes. A father may gift his son a very expensive smart phone in the first week of the month but may react disapprovingly of the carelessness of the son who misplaces it and asks him to provide a second one in the last week of the month. Had the son asked him at some other point of time, the father would have behaved less aggressively perhaps. Many of us experience unexpected behaviour from friends, relatives and family almost every day. No one can predict with utmost certainty whether a particular person will consume ice-creams in the coming summers in the town. May be he is out of station at the time or develops a bad throat or may be he no longer likes it. How can you then forecast demand for ice-creams? How can you ascertain multiple causes that influence one's consumption of the product? Human behaviour, being subject to multiplicity of causes, is therefore unpredictable. All sciences dealing with it are probabilitstic sciences. Forecasting demand appears an uphill task but not an impossible one if we look at it from another angle. It is of considering the behaviour of general people that counts, not that of an individual. If one doesn't, another one does. Mob behaviour is certainly different from that of an individual. What is not true of one, is generally true of groups. It is thus *inertia of large numbers* that makes demand forcasting and estimation of several other economic functions fairly realistic. This chapter is devoted to such estimations.

Let us cast a look at the functions of the deterministic sciences mentioned above and compare them with those mentioned above for probabilistic sciences. The functions in the first category were:

$$V = \frac{K}{P} \qquad (23.1)$$

where, $V \equiv$ volume of a gas, that varies inversely with the pressure, P, while temperature is held constant. K is a constant of proportionality, that is fixed for a particular gas. The observation refers to Boyle's law.

And,

$$\frac{(L_t - L_0)}{L_0} = \alpha \times t \qquad (23.2)$$

where, $L_t \equiv$ Length of the metal rod at t^0C, $L_0 \equiv$ its length at original temperature, and α, the constant of proportionality, is a trait of the material of which the rod is made up.

Variables on the left hand side of each equation are the dependent variables while those on the right ride hand side, independent variables.

The function mentioned in the second category of sciences was:

$$Q_D = a - b\, P_O + c\, Y + d\, P_R + T + u \qquad (23.3)$$

where, $Q_D \equiv$ demand; $P_O \equiv$ own price; $Y \equiv$ disposable income; $P_R \equiv$ price of related good (substitute/complement); $T \equiv$ qualitative variables such as tastes and preferences, etc.; while, $u \equiv$ the random disturbance or error term; $b,c,d \equiv$ coefficient parameters that vary from time to time but are fixed after their estimation in a given situation; and, $a \equiv$ initial level of demand.

As regards, T is dummy or qualitative variable, assuming the value 0 if tastes don't influence demand or 1, if they do. Negative sign ($-$) before the coefficient of P_O shows additively inverse variation of demand with product's own price (P_O), and positive sign (+) before the coefficient of Y or P_R shows direct variation of demand with income (Y) or price of related good (substitute/complement).

In case, inverse variation is multiplicative, as for own price (P_O), P_O appears in denominator while the sign of its coefficient, b, may be positive or negative. In fact, we may assign any sign to a coefficient to begin with as it seeks its own sign during its estimation The random disturbance term, u, is employed to account for uncertain variation of demand. For instance, *exogenous factors* like weather conditions are external ones as they don't figure in Equation 23.3, yet they can affect demand up or down to a marked extent due to high or low turn-up of buyers in the market.

Variable on the left hand side of Eq. 23.3, Q_D, is called *regressand* or explained variable while those on the right hand side, *regressors* or *explanatory variables*. This is so because they are estimated through regression method of Ordinary Least Squares (OLS).

If you compare Eq. 23.3 with Eqs. 23.1 and 23.2, you might think that the difference is only in the number of variables on the right hand side. This is not true. We may have multiple independent variables even in the deterministic sciences. The difference actually arises because of the random disturbance term, u.

Before we proceed further, let us have a workable definition of econometrics first.

Econometrics is a discipline that blends economics, mathematics and statistics to transform economic principles and observations into functional relationships in their truest possible forms for facilitating decisions in the face of uncertainty. It incorporates mathematics for their functional transformation and statistics for estimating the truest possible values of parameters involved by testing and revising their values through further research until they capture the trend as close as possible.

Quite comprehensive, isn't it? Don't bother much as you will be able to understand it very soon through illustrations. Before that let us outline various stages of econometric estimation.

23.1 STAGES OF ECONOMETRIC ESTIMATION

As some of you may guess by now, we pass through the following stages:

23.1.1 Stage 1: Specification of Variables

Identification of cause and effect is the first requisite of econometric estimation. Sort out the dependent and independent variables clearly. An error committed at this stage defeats the purpose of estimation. For instance, quantity demanded is a function of price and price that of quantity demanded. In the former case, price (P) is an independent variable while quantity demanded (Q_d), a dependent one, other things remaining the same. Here, quantity demanded varies inversely with price. In the latter case, quantity demanded is an independent variable and price, a depended one, other things remaining the same. Here, price varies directly with quantity demanded. Symbolically,

$$Q^d = f(P) \quad \text{[Inverse variation]} \tag{23.4}$$

$$P = f(Q_d) \quad \text{[Direct variation]} \tag{23.5}$$

Dependent or independent, the character of the variable depends on the objective of investigation. If demand is to be forecasted, price is independent (Eq. 23.4) and if best price is to be forecasted, demand is independent (Eq. 23.5). In a long-run forecast, assumption of other things remaining unchanged (*ceteris paribus*) is relaxed and income (Y), price (P_R) of related goods (substitute/complement) and tastes and preferences (T) along with product's own price (P_O) are all included in the functions which can now be expressed as in Eqs. 23.6 and 23.7.

$$Q_d = f(P_O, Y, P_R, T) \tag{23.6}$$
$$P_O = f(Q_d, Y, P_R, T) \tag{23.7}$$

Identification or specification of variables is of crucial importance. It requires their ascertainment for sure.

23.1.2 Stage 2: Assignment of Signs and Symbols to the Coefficients (Parameters)

Positive signs of parameters indicate positive correlation (direct variation), negative signs indicate negative correlation (additively inverse variation). If an independent variable is believed to be in a relation multiplicatively inverse with the dependent variable, the independent variable in question appears in denominator of the coefficient parameter. Even if the investigator is not very sure of positive or negative signs, he/she can proceed with positive sign because the estimation process of the parameters automatically seeks their true signs. On the contrary if the investigator is fully confident of the sign, he/she can deviate and use negative sign as in Eq. 23.3.

23.1.3 Stage 3: Formulation of Mathematical Model

Mathematical expression of the function with the random disturbance term u is called mathematical or econometric model. We have already introduced it in Eq. 23.3. The model is based on the following assumptions about the random disturbance term, u:

1. *It is a random variable.* That is, it can assume any value—negative, positive or zero at random. Each deviation or error e_i of the observed dependent variable from the estimated one, has a certain chance of being assumed by the uncertainty term, u, in a particular situation.
2. *The mean value of u is zero*, that is,
$$E(u) = 0 \tag{23.8}$$

   Make a note of the notation. It is so because u is a random variable not a discrete or continuous variable. In other words, the notation $E(u)$, the expected value of u, is the same as $\bar{u}$. Thus, $E(u) = \bar{u} = 0$.
3. The probability distribution of u is *homoscedastic*, that is, $\text{Var}(u) = \sigma_u^2$, a constant. Homoscedasticity implies same probability distribution of u for all observations of explanatory variable.
4. The probability distribution of u is a normal distribution, denoted as
$$u \sim N(0, \sigma_u^2) \tag{23.9}$$

   That is, $E(u) = 0$ and $\text{Var}(u) = \sigma_u^2$ (constant).
5. Random terms of different observations (u_i, u_j) are independent, that is,
$$\text{Cov}(u_i, u_j) = 0 \tag{23.10}$$

6. The random variable u is independent of the explanatory variables, that is,
$$\text{Cov}(X_i\ u_i) = 0 \tag{23.11}$$
Here, 'Var' ≡ Variance; 'Cov' ≡ Covariance.

23.1.4 Stage 4: Estimation of Functions

To estimate a function to fit the data best, the first requisite is to have a plot of data, if possible, to help in building the model. Often a rough sketch serves the purpose, but it is limited only to the two dimensional space. To introduce econometric technique, it is more than enough. At later stages, the reader will see that it is not of much significance. We therefore take up functions of one independent variable. Once the idea is home, we can extend our estimation to functions of several independent variables. As is not difficult to see, functions of one independent variable can take the following forms not all of them yield a linear trend. The simplest one of them is the linear one given by Eq. 23.12. The others involve a second degree trend or a parabolic trend given by Eq. 23.13, and exponential trends given by Eqs 23.14 and 23.15.

$$Q_i = a + bX \tag{23.12}$$
$$Q_i = a + bX + cX^2 \tag{23.13}$$
$$Q_i = ab^{X_i} \tag{23.14}$$
$$Q_i = a(X_i)^b \tag{23.15}$$

where, a, b and c are all constant–parameters to be determined and, $i = 1, 2,..., n$ for n observations.

Note that we have not involved any uncertainty or disturbance term to the functions but they can be assumed there in all the cases. As can be visualized from Figures 23.1 and 23.2, the best estimate of the function is one that is closest to all the points (X_i, Q_i), where X_i represent values of independent variable and Q_i those of the dependent variables. Some of the observations must fall above the function of the best fit while the rest, below it in such a way that the sum of the squares of negative and positive deviations of the observed data from the estimated data is least. Denoting those that fall above the curve of best fit as $(+e_i)$ and those below it as $(-e_i)$ and squaring each to get rid of the signs, the sum of the squares (E) of these deviations or errors can be written as

$$E = \Sigma e_i^2 \tag{23.16}$$

For the best fit of the function being estimated, E must be minimum possible. The method of minimizing E is called the method of Least Squares or more popularly that of Ordinary Least Squares (OLS) or even of Classical Least Squares (CLS).

To correlate OLS to what you have studied in statistics on regression analysis, let us mention simple and multiple regression here as closely linked to OLS. When the function under estimation involves only one independent or explanatory variable, its OLS estimation is called *simple regression* [Functions in Eqs. 23.12 to 23.15] and when the function under estimation involves more than one explanatory variables, as in case of estimation of *long-run demand* function (Eq. 23.3), its OLS estimation is called *multiple regression.*

Estimation of the functions of one explanatory variable is done in Sub-section 23.2.1 and that of functions of more than one explanatory variables is Sub-section 23.2.2.

23.1.5 Stage 5: Testing of the Estimated Functions

Testing of the estimated function is done through testing the estimated parameters through through first and second order tests for their significance. The *first order tests* refer to *statistical tests*. They include standard error test, t-test, z-test, F-test and the coefficient of determination, r^2. The first three are used to test the significance of parameters, while the last one, r^2, is used to test goodness of fit of the estimated function to the data or the explanatory or to forecasting power of the estimated function. The **second order tests** refer to econometric criteria for judging the goodness of the estimates. They include testing the plausibility of assumptions of the OLS. For our purpose here, we will confine to the first order tests only.

23.2 OLS ESTIMATION OF FUNCTIONS

In our analysis of OLS estimation of functions, we propose to use Q for the dependent variable (quantity supplied or demand) and X, Y, Z, etc. for the explanatory or independent variables (such as product's own price, or price of a related good or consumers' income).

23.2.1 OLS—Estimation of Functions of One Explanatory (Simple Regression)

In simple regression, a curve may be linear, such as one in Eq. (23.12) or non-linear, such as those in Eq. (23.13), [23.14(a)] and 23.15.

Let us attempt fitting a linear curve,

$$Q_i^* = a^* + b^*X$$

to the data (Figure 23.1) so that

$$Q_i = Q_i^* + e_i = a^* + b^*X_i + e_i$$

where, e_i is positive or negative distance of (X_i, Q_i) from the corresponding points on $Q^* = a^* + b^*X_i$.

The sum (E) of the squared distances of (X_i, Q_i) from the corresponding points on the line of best fit may be represented as

$$E = \Sigma(e_i)^2$$
$$= \Sigma[Q_i - Q_i^*]^2$$
$$= \Sigma[Q_i - a^* - b^*X_i]^2 \qquad (23.17)$$

This, when minimized under the method of least squares, yields two equations. Differentiating partially with respect to a^* and b^*, the parameters to be estimated, we have

$$\partial E/\partial a^* = -2\Sigma[Q_i - a^* - b^*X_i]$$
$$= 0 \qquad \text{(For minimization)}$$
$$\Rightarrow \quad \Sigma[Q_i - a^* - b^*X_i] = 0$$
$$\Rightarrow \quad \Sigma Q_i - na^* - b^*\Sigma X_i = 0$$
$$\Rightarrow \quad \Sigma Q_i = na^* + b^* \Sigma X_i \qquad (23.18)$$

and
$$\partial E/\partial b^* = -2\Sigma\,[Q_i - a^* - b^*\,X_i]X_i$$
$$= 0 \quad \text{(For minimization)}$$
$$\Rightarrow \quad \Sigma[Q_i - a^* - b^*X_i]\,X_i = 0$$
$$\Rightarrow \quad \Sigma X_i Q_i - a^*\Sigma X_i - b^*\Sigma X_i^2 = 0$$
$$\Rightarrow \quad \Sigma X_i Q_i = a^*\,\Sigma X_i + b^*\,\Sigma X_i^2 \tag{23.19}$$

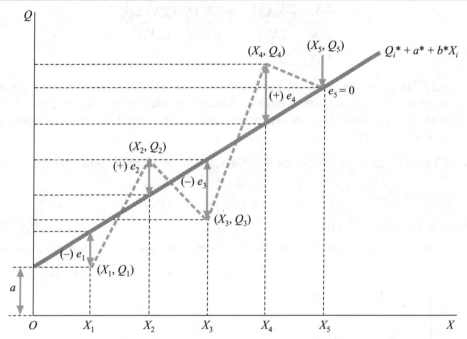

FIGURE 23.1 Representing independent variable (X) on the horizontal axis and dependent variable (Q) on the vertical axis, data obtained (X_i, Q_i) is plotted as shown. In order to fit a linear function, the line of best fit is taken as $Q_i^* = a^* + b^*X_i$. All points except (X_5, Q_5) fall above or below the line. For the line to be one of the best fit, the sum of the squared distances of points (X_i, Q_i) from it must be least under the method of least squares. Thus, $\Sigma(e_i)^2$, $i = 1, 2, 3, \ldots$, must be the least. Imposing the conditions of minimization on $\Sigma(e_i)^2$ leads to two normal equations, which give the estimates a^* and b^* of a and b on simultaneous solution.

Equations (23.18) and (23.19), (known as normal equations) follow from the first order condition of minimization of the sum of squares of distances of (X_i, Q_i) from the corresponding points on the line of best fit. Solving them for a^* and b^*, we get estimated values a^* and b^* and hence the equation of the line of best fit,

$$Q_i^* = a^* + b^*X_i \tag{23.20}$$

For the data provided or collected, ΣQ_i, $\Sigma X_i Q_i$, n, X_i and ΣX_i^2 are all known. Equations (23.18) and (23.19) can be solved simultaneously for a^* and b^* to yield the estimated function (23.20). Using Cramer's Rule, expressions for a^* and b^* can be laid down as below for the convenience of the reader.

$$a^* = \frac{\begin{vmatrix} \Sigma Q_i & \Sigma X_1 \\ \Sigma X_i Q_i & \Sigma X_1^2 \end{vmatrix}}{\begin{vmatrix} n & \Sigma X_i \\ \Sigma X_i & \Sigma X_i^2 \end{vmatrix}} = \frac{\Sigma Q_i \Sigma X_i^2 - \Sigma X_i \Sigma X_i Q_i}{n \Sigma X_i^2 - [\Sigma X_i]^2} \qquad (23.21)$$

$$b^* = \frac{\begin{vmatrix} n & \Sigma Q_i \\ \Sigma X_i & \Sigma X_i Q_i \end{vmatrix}}{\begin{vmatrix} n & \Sigma X_i \\ \Sigma X_i & \Sigma X_i^2 \end{vmatrix}} = \frac{n \Sigma X_i Q_i - \Sigma X_i \Sigma Q_i}{n \Sigma X_i^2 - [\Sigma X_i]^2} \qquad (23.22)$$

Equation (23.21) gives the intercept parameter and Eq. (23.22) gives the slope parameter. Readers familiar with statistics would have no difficulty in identifying the expression for b^* as the coefficient of regression (b_{QX}), of dependent variable, Q on the independent variable X. An illustration would help at this stage.

ILLUSTRATION 23.1: Consider the hypothetical data on quantity supplied (Q_i) at price (X_i)

X_i	1	2	3	4	5
Q_i	2	4	8	16	32

Estimate the line of best fit.

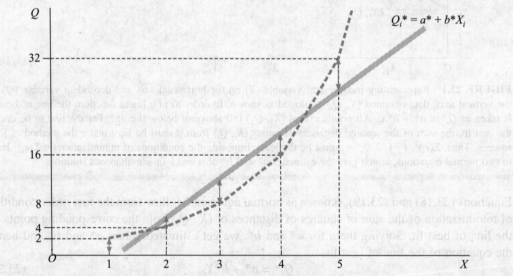

FIGURE 23.2 Dotted curve represents the data and the unbroken curve represents the line of the best fit ($Q_i^* = a^* + b^*X_i$).

To get the two normal equations for estimating the line of best fit, we need to compute ΣX_i, ΣQ_i, ΣX_i^2 and $\Sigma X_i Q_i$ from the data given. Table 23.1 shows the process of computation.

Estimation of Functions in Economics—The Basics of Econometrics

TABLE 23.1 Computations of ΣX_i, ΣQ_i, ΣX_i^2, $\Sigma X_i Q_i$, $\Sigma [Q - \bar{Q}]^2$ and $\Sigma [Q - Q^*]^2$ for fitting a linear function, which is $Q_i^* = -9.2 + 7.2 X_i$ with $a^* = -9.2$ and $b^* = +7.2$

X_i	1	2	3	4	5	$\Sigma X_i = 15$
Q_i	2	4	8	16	32	$\Sigma Q_i = 62$
X_i^2	1	4	9	16	25	$\Sigma X_i^2 = 55$
$X_i Q_i$	2	8	24	64	160	$\Sigma X_i Q_i = 258$
Q_i^*	-2	5.2	12.4	19.6	26.8	
$[Q_i - \bar{Q}]^2$	108.16	70.56	19.36	12.96	384.16	$\Sigma [Q - \bar{Q}]^2 = 595.2$
$[Q_i - Q_i^*]^2$	16.00	1.44	19.36	12.96	27.04	$\Sigma [Q - Q_i^*]^2 = 76.80$

Substituting for them in Eqs. (23.18) and (23.19), we have,

$$62 = 5a^* + 15b^*, \text{ and}$$
$$258 = 15a^* + 55b^*$$

A simultaneous solution for a^* and b^* yields

$$a^* = -9.2 \text{ and } b^* = +7.2$$

Substituting in Eq. (23.20), we have

$$Q_i^* = -9.2 + 7.2 X_i \qquad (23.23)$$

Estimated function (23.23) gives the line of best fit. It can be used to forecast Q corresponding to $X = 6, 7, \ldots$, etc. The extent to which forecasts based on the linear trend are reliable, can be investigated through the first order tests (Section 23.3) comprising coefficient of determination (r^2), standard error (S_{a^*}) of the estimate a^* and standard error (S_{b^*}) of the estimate b^* and t-test.

For the purpose of comparison, let us fit non-linear trends in Eqs. (23.13), (23.14) and (23.15) also to the data of Illustration 23.1. This would help to investigate which trend describes the data best, and hence, should be used in forecasting Q.

Let us begin with Eq. (23.13). The equation of best fit must take the form,

$$Q_i^* = a^* + b^* X_i + c^* X_i^2$$

so that
$$Q_i = Q_i^* + e_i$$
$$= a^* + b^* X_i + c^* X_i^2 + e_i$$

The sum (E) of the squared distances of (X_i, Q_i) from the corresponding points on the curve of best fit may be represented as

$$E = \Sigma(e_i)^2$$
$$= \Sigma[Q_i - Q_i^*]^2$$
$$= \Sigma[Q_i - a^* - b^* X_i - c^* X_i^2]^2 \qquad (23.24)$$

Differentiating partially with respect to a^*, b^* and c^*, we have

$$\partial E / \partial a^* = -2\Sigma [Q_i - a^* - b^* X_i - c^* X_i^2]$$
$$= 0 \qquad \text{(For minimization)}$$

$$\Rightarrow \quad \Sigma[Q_i - a^* - b^*X_i - c^*X_i^2] = 0$$
$$\Rightarrow \quad \Sigma Q_i - na^* - b^*\Sigma X_i - c^*\Sigma X_i^2 = 0$$

$$\Rightarrow \quad \Sigma Q_i = na^* + b^*\Sigma X_i + c^*\Sigma X_i^2 \qquad (23.25)$$

$$\partial E/\partial b^* = -2\Sigma[Q_i - a^* - b^*X_i - c^*X_i^2]X_i$$
$$= 0 \qquad \text{(For minimization)}$$
$$\Rightarrow \quad \Sigma[Q_i - a^* - b^*X_i - c^*X_i^2]X_i = 0$$
$$\Rightarrow \quad \Sigma X_i Q_i - a^*\Sigma X_i - b^*\Sigma X_i^2 + c^*\Sigma X_i^3 = 0$$

$$\Rightarrow \quad \Sigma X_i Q_i = a^*\Sigma X_i + b^*\Sigma X_i^2 + c^*\Sigma X_i^3 \qquad (23.26)$$

$$\partial E/\partial c^* = -2\Sigma[Q_i - a^* - b^*X_i - c^*X_i^2]X_i^2$$
$$= 0 \qquad \text{(For minimization)}$$
$$\Rightarrow \quad \Sigma X_i^2 Q_i - a^*\Sigma X_i^2 - b^*\Sigma X_i^3 + c^*\Sigma X_i^4 = 0$$

$$\Rightarrow \quad \Sigma X_i^2 Q_i = a^*\Sigma X_i^2 + b^*\Sigma X_i^3 + c^*\Sigma X_i^4 \qquad (23.27)$$

Solving Eqs. (23.25), (23.26) and (23.27) simultaneously, we have a^*, b^* and c^* as below:

$$a^* = \frac{\begin{vmatrix} \Sigma Q_i & \Sigma X_i & \Sigma X_i^2 \\ \Sigma X_i Q_i & \Sigma X_i^2 & \Sigma X_i^3 \\ \Sigma X_i^2 Q_i & \Sigma X_i^3 & \Sigma X_i^4 \end{vmatrix}}{\begin{vmatrix} n & \Sigma X_i & \Sigma X_i^2 \\ \Sigma X_i & \Sigma X_i^2 & \Sigma X_i^3 \\ \Sigma X_i^2 & \Sigma X_i^3 & \Sigma X_i^4 \end{vmatrix}} \qquad (23.28)$$

$$b^* = \frac{\begin{vmatrix} n & \Sigma Q_i & \Sigma X_i^2 \\ \Sigma X_i & \Sigma X_i Q_i & \Sigma X_i^3 \\ \Sigma X_i^2 & \Sigma X_i^2 Q_i & \Sigma X_i^4 \end{vmatrix}}{\begin{vmatrix} n & \Sigma X_i & \Sigma X_i^2 \\ \Sigma X_i & \Sigma X_i^2 & \Sigma X_i^3 \\ \Sigma X_i^2 & \Sigma X_i^3 & \Sigma X_i^4 \end{vmatrix}} \qquad (23.29)$$

$$c^* = \frac{\begin{vmatrix} n & \Sigma X_i & \Sigma Q_i \\ \Sigma X_i & \Sigma X_i^2 & \Sigma X_i Q_i \\ \Sigma X_i^2 & \Sigma X_i^3 & \Sigma X_i^2 Q_i \end{vmatrix}}{\begin{vmatrix} n & \Sigma X_i & \Sigma X_i^2 \\ \Sigma X_i & \Sigma X_i^2 & \Sigma X_i^3 \\ \Sigma X_i^2 & \Sigma X_i^3 & \Sigma X_i^4 \end{vmatrix}} \qquad (23.30)$$

To fit quadratic trend to the data of Illustration 23.1, we compute the required sums as in Table 23.2. Substituting them in the three normal Eqs. (23.25), (23.26), and (23.27) or directly in Eqs. (23.28), (23.29), and (23.30), parameters a^*, b^*, c^* can be easily determined. In the former case,

$$62 = 5a^* + 15b^* + 55c^*$$
$$258 = 15a^* + 55b^* + 225c^*$$
$$1146 = 55a^* + 225b^* + 979c^*$$

Simultaneously for a^*, b^*, and c^*, we have:
$$a^* = 6.9$$
$$b^* = -6.6$$
$$c^* = 2.3$$

Substituting the estimated values of the parameters in Eq. (23.9), the estimated equation of the curve of the best fit is given as

$$\Rightarrow \qquad Q_i^* = 6.9 - 6.6 X_i + 2.3 X_i^2 \qquad (23.31)$$

TABLE 23.2 Computations of ΣX_i, ΣQ_i, ΣX_i^2, $\Sigma X_i Q_i$, ΣX_i^3, ΣX_i^4, $\Sigma X_i^2 Q_i$, $\Sigma [Q_i - \bar{Q}]^2$ and $\Sigma [Q - Q^*]^2$ for fitting a non-linear second degree trend. The trend is $Q_i^* = 6.9 - 6.6 X_i + 2.3 X_i^2$ with parameters $a^* = 6.9$, $b^* = -6.6$, $c^* = +2.3$.

X_i	1	2	3	4	5	$\Sigma X_i = 15$
Q_i	2	4	8	16	32	$\Sigma Q_i = 62$
X_i^2	1	4	9	16	25	$\Sigma X_i^2 = 55$
$X_i Q$	2	8	24	64	160	$\Sigma X_i Q_i = 258$
$X_i^2 Q_i$	2	16	72	256	800	$\Sigma X_i^2 Q_i = 1146$
X_i^3	1	8	27	64	125	$\Sigma X_i^3 = 225$
X_i^4	1	16	81	256	625	$\Sigma X_i^4 = 979$
Q_i^*	2.57	2.93	7.87	17.39	31.49	
$[Q_i - \bar{Q}]^2$	108.16	70.56	19.36	12.96	384.16	$\Sigma [Q - \bar{Q}]^2 = 595.2$
$[Q_i - Q_i^*]^2$	0.325	1.145	0.017	1.932	0.26	$\Sigma [Q - Q_i^*]^2 = 3.660$

A simple comparison of the estimates of Q_i, (i.e., Q_i^*) as obtained from the linear trend [Eq. (23.12)] and the non-linear second degree trend [Eq. (23.13)] reveals that the latter provides a better fit to the data. Of the two, the latter if used for forecasting, would therefore, give better results. However, we will conduct the confirmatory tests later in Section 23.3 using the first order tests. Right now, we will proceed with the mechanism of fitting the exponential trends [(Eqs. (23.14) and (23.15)] as well to the data in question. Let us begin with Eq. (23.14) first.

Corresponding curve of best fit is

$$Q_i^* = a^* (b^*)^{X_i} \qquad (23.32)$$

Its logarithmic transformation yields

$$\log Q_i^* = \log a^* + X_i \log b^*$$
$$q_i = A^* + B^* X_i \qquad (23.33)$$

where, $q_i \equiv \log Q_i^*$, $A^* \equiv \log a^*$ and $B^* \equiv \log b^*$.

Equation (23.33) is called the *log-linear form* of the equation.

Following the process of the linear trend, the normal equations corresponding to the log-linear trend Eq. (23.33) can be expressed as:

$$\Sigma q_i = nA^* + B^* \Sigma X_i$$
$$\Sigma X_i q_i = A^* \Sigma X_i + B^* \Sigma X_i^2$$

Solving these equations for A^* and B^* for the data computed in Table 23.3, we observe that $A^* = 0.00$ and $B^* = 0.3010$. Antilogs of A^* and B^* yield the values of a^* and b^* as 1.00 and 2.00, respectively. When substituted in equation 23.32, the estimated exponential trend turns out as

$$Q_i^* = (1.00)(2.00)^{X_i} \qquad (23.34)$$

TABLE 23.3 Computations of Σq_i, $\Sigma X_i q_i$, ΣX_i and ΣX_i^2 for exponential trend (Equation A-1.14). $A^* = \log a^* = 0 \Rightarrow a^* = 1.00$. $B^* = \log b^* = 0.3010 \Rightarrow b^* = 2.00$. Exponential trend is $Q_i^* = (1.00)(2.00)^{X_i}$ and log-linear trend is $\log Q_i^* = 0.3010 X_i$.

X_i	1	2	3	4	5	$\Sigma X_i = 15$
Q_i	2	4	8	16	32	$\Sigma Q_i = 62$
X_i^2	1	4	9	16	25	$\Sigma X_i^2 = 55$
$(\log Q_i)$	0.3010	0.6020	0.9030	1.2040	1.5050	$\Sigma q_i = 4.5150$
$X_i q_i$	0.3010	1.2040	2.7090	4.8160	7.5250	$\Sigma X_i q_i = 16.5550$
Q_i^*	2	4	8	16	32	
$[Q_i - \bar{Q}]^2$	108.16	70.56	19.36	12.96	384.16	$\Sigma[Q - \bar{Q}]^2 = 595.2$
$[Q_i - Q_i^*]^2$	0.00	0.00	0.00	0.00	0.00	$\Sigma[Q - Q_i^*]^2 = 0.00$

Differentiating logarithmic transformation of Eq. (23.32) and multiplying the result by X_i gives **elasticity (e)** of the dependent variable with respect to the independent variable. Thus, $e = (X_i/Q_i)(dQ_i/dX_i) = \log b^*$ or B^*. This is **0.3010**, indicating low elasticity of Q_i with respect to X_i. Q_i and Q_i^* being the same (Table 23.3), the exponential trend appears the most perfect fit to the data.

Forecasts made on the basis of this trend are expected to be 100 percent accurate. A keen reader can verify the result through the first order tests suggested in Section 23.3.

Turning to the trend in Eq. 23.15, we have

$$Q_i^* = a^* (X_i)^{b^*} \qquad (23.35)$$

Logarithmic transformation yields

$$\log Q_i^* = \log a^* + b^* \log X_i \qquad (23.36)$$

Equation (23.30) gives a linear trend called *double-log-linear* trend. Coding $\log Q_i^*$ as q_i^*, $\log a^*$ as A^* and $\log X_i$ as x_i, we have

$$q_i^* = A^* + b^* x_i \qquad (23.37)$$

Corresponding normal equations as obtained from the method of least squares are

$$\Sigma q_i^* = nA^* + b^* \Sigma x_i \qquad (23.38)$$

and

$$\Sigma x_i q_i^* = A^* \Sigma x_i + b^* \Sigma x_i^2 \qquad (23.39)$$

Substituting data computed in Table 23.4 in the normal equations, we have

$$A^* = 0.2044$$

$\Rightarrow \qquad \log a^* = 0.2044$

$\Rightarrow \qquad a^* = 1.60$

and $\qquad b^* = 1.68$

Substituting for A^* and b^* in double log-linear form [Eq. (23.36)], we have

$$\text{Log } Q_i^* = 0.2044 + 1.68 \log X_i \qquad (23.40)$$

Estimated trend on substituting these values in Eq. (23.35) is given as

$$Q_i^* = (1.6)(X_i)^{1.68} \qquad (23.41)$$

TABLE 23.4 The exponential trend is $Q_i^* = (1.60)(X_i)^{1.68}$ and the double log linear form is $\log Q_i^* = 0.2044 + 1.68 \log X_i$. The trend is less efficient than the log-linear trend in its forecasting power. To make sure the reader is advised to turn to Section 23.3.

X_i	1	2	3	4	5	
$x_i = \log X_i$	0.0000	0.3010	0.4771	0.6020	0.6990	$\Sigma x_i = 2.0791$
Q_i	2	4	8	16	32	
$q_i = \log Q_i$	0.3010	0.6020	0.9030	1.2040	1.5050	$\Sigma q_i = 4.5150$
x_i^2	0.0000	0.0906	0.2276	0.3624	0.4886	$\Sigma x_i^2 = 1.1692$
$x_i q_i$	0.0000	0.1812	0.4308	0.7248	1.0520	$\Sigma x_i q_i = 2.3888$
Q_i^*	1.6042	5.1326	10.1352	16.4216	23.8881	
$(Q_i - \bar{Q})^2$:	108.16	70.56	19.36	12.96	384.16	$\Sigma[Q_i - \bar{Q}]^2 = 595.2$
$(Q_i - Q_i^*)^2$:	0.1567	1.2828	4.5591	0.1777	65.2029	$\Sigma[Q_i - Q_i^*]^2 = 71.49$

The linear and non-linear trends fitted so far to the data of Illustration 23.1 lead to the following observations:

1. The log-linear trend [Eq. (23.34)] provides the best fit to the data among all the trends attempted. The next in the line is the second degree (quadratic) trend [Eq. (23.31)], followed by the double log-linear trend [Eq. (23.41)] and the linear trend [Eq. (23.23)] thereafter. The conclusion follows from the sum of the residuals [$\Sigma(Q_i - Q_i^*)^2$], which is 0.00 for the log-linear trend, 3.66 for the second degree trend, 71.98 for the double log-linear trend and 76.80 for the linear trend.
2. The technique employed for fitting the trends to the data of Illustration 23.1 is the same (the method of least squares) for each trend. The sum of residuals is minimized in each case.

Why then different trends lead to different sums of residuals? The answer to the question rests in the implicit assumption that the trend being attempted in each case represents the actual relationship among the variables. The method of least squares provides the best fit, given in the relationship. Recall from the introduction of this chapter that specification of variables and identification of the true interrelationships among them is of crucial importance in estimation of functions.

23.2.2 OLS—Estimation of Functions of More than One Variables—Multiple Regression

Presence of more than one independent variable requires a multi-dimensional equation. Assume for simplicity that Q is a function of X and Y, so that

$$Q_i = a + bX_i + cY_i \tag{23.42}$$

The corresponding equation of the best fit may then be represented as:

$$Q_i^* = a^* + b^*X_i + c^*Y_i \tag{23.43}$$

so that

$$Q_i = Q_i^* + e_i$$
$$= a^* + b^*X_i + c^*Y_i + e_i \tag{23.44}$$

Equation (23.33) is a three-dimensional plane.

The sum (E) of the squared distances of (X_i, Y_i, Q_i) from the corresponding points on the plane of best fit may be given as

$$\begin{aligned} E &= \Sigma(e_i)^2 \\ &= \Sigma[Q_i - Q_i^*]^2 \\ &= \Sigma[Q_i - a^* - b^*X_i - c^*Y_i]^2 \end{aligned} \tag{23.45}$$

Following the method of least squares, differentiate Eq. (23.40) partially with respect to a^*, b^*, and c^* to have

$$\partial E/\partial a^* = -2\Sigma[Q_i - a^* - b^*X_i - c^*Y_i] = 0$$
$$\partial E/\partial b^* = -2\Sigma[Q_i - a^* - b^*X_i - c^*Y_i]X_i = 0$$
$$\partial E/\partial c^* = -2\Sigma[Q_i - a^* - b^*X_i - c^*Y_i]Y_i = 0$$

$$\Rightarrow \begin{bmatrix} \Sigma Q_i = na^* + b^*\Sigma X_i + c^*\Sigma Y_i, \\ \Sigma X_i Q_i = a^*\Sigma X_i + b^*\Sigma X_i^2 + c^*\Sigma X_i Y_i, \text{ and} \\ \Sigma Y_i Q_i = a^*\Sigma Y_i + b^*\Sigma Y_i X_i + c^*\Sigma Y_i^2 \end{bmatrix} \quad (23.46)$$

Set of Eq. (23.46) give three normal equations in a^*, b^* and c^*. Substituting for ΣQ_i, $\Sigma X_i Q_i$, $\Sigma Y_i Q_i$, ΣX_i, ΣY_i, ΣX_i^2, $\Sigma X_i Y_i$ and ΣY_i^2 from the data given/collected and solving the simultaneous equations for a^*, b^* and c^*, we get the regression plane of the best fit.

ILLUSTRATION 23.2 Estimate quantity demanded (Q_i) as a function of income (Y_i) and price (X_i), given

X_i:	4	3	2	1
Y_i:	3	3	4	5
Q_i:	10	20	40	100

Solution: Calculation (Table 23.5), substitutions in the three normal Eqs. 23.45, we have

$$170 = 4a^* + 10b^* + 15c^*$$
$$280 = 10a^* + 30b^* + 34c^*$$
$$750 = 15a^* + 34b^* + 59c^*$$

Solving them simultaneously for a^*, b^* and c^*, we have

$$a^* = -86.67$$
$$b^* = -3.33$$
$$c^* = +36.67$$

Substituting, a^*, b^* and c^* in the equation of the regression plane, we have

$$Q_i^* = -86.67 - 3.33X_i + 36.67Y_i \quad (23.47)$$

TABLE 23.5 Computation of normal equations for regression plane, $Q_i^* = a^* + b^*X_i + c^*Y_i$. The trend is $Q_i^* = -86.67 - 3.33X_i + 36.67Y_i$ with $a^* = -86.67$, $b^* = -3.34$ and $c^* = +36.67$

X_i	Y_i	Q_i	X_i^2	Y_i^2	X_iY_i	X_iQ_i	Y_iQ_i	Q_i^*	$(Q_i - Q_i^*)^2$	$(Q_i - \bar{Q})^2$
4	3	10	16	9	12	40	30	10.00	0.00	1806.25
3	3	20	9	9	9	60	60	13.33	44.36	506.25
2	4	40	4	16	8	80	160	53.33	177.69	6.25
1	5	100	1	25	5	100	500	93.33	44.36	3306.25
ΣX_i = 10	ΣY_i = 15	ΣQ_i = 170	ΣX_i^2 = 30	ΣY_i^2 = 59	ΣX_iY_i = 34	ΣX_iQ_i = 280	ΣY_iQ_i = 750	—	$\Sigma(Q_i - Q_i^*)^2$ = 266.41	$\Sigma(Q_i - \bar{Q})^2$ = 5625.00

Estimated Q_i^* is also shown in Table 23.5. Equation (23.47) shows that Q varies directly with Y and inversely with X.

We are now all set to test the goodness of fit of the estimated equations as also the significance of a^*, b^* and c^*.

23.3 TESTING THE ESTIMATED FUNCTIONS

In this section, we will test the estimations through the *statistical tests* or the *first order* tests as outlined below:

(a) Test for goodness of fit (the coefficients of determination)
(b) Standard error test
(c) Z-test and/or t-test
(d) F-test for regression

23.3.1 Test for Goodness of Fit—Coefficient of Determination

Coefficient of determination (r^2) is defined as a ratio of the total variations in the dependent variable (Q_i) explained by its estimated value (Q_i^*) to the total variations in its value from its mean, that is,

$$\text{Coefficient of determination } r^2 = \frac{\text{Explained variation}}{\text{Total variation}} = \frac{|\Sigma(Q_i^* - \bar{Q})^2|}{\Sigma|(Q_i - \bar{Q})^2|} \quad (23.48)$$

Total variations in Q_i from its mean, also called the **Total Sum of Squares (TSS)**, is defined as the sum of squares of the variations in Q_i from its mean, $\bar{Q}$ and is given as $\Sigma(Q_i - \bar{Q})^2$. A little manipulation yields

$$\Sigma(Q_i - \bar{Q})^2 = \Sigma(Q_i - Q_i^* + Q_i^* - \bar{Q})^2$$
$$= \Sigma(Q_i - Q_i^*)^2 + \Sigma(Q_i^* - \bar{Q})^2 + 2\Sigma(Q_i - Q_i^*)(Q_i^* - \bar{Q})$$

But, $\Sigma(Q_i - Q_i^*)(Q_i^* - \bar{Q}) = \Sigma(Q_i - \bar{Q} + \bar{Q} - Q_i^*)(a^* + b^*X_i - a^* - b^*\bar{X})$

(Since, $\bar{Q} = a^* + b^*X$)

$$= \Sigma[(Q_i - \bar{Q}) - (Q_i^* - \bar{Q})](b^*(X_i - \bar{X}))$$
$$= b^*\Sigma(Q_i - \bar{Q})(X_i - \bar{X}) - b^*\Sigma(Q_i^* - \bar{Q})(X_i - \bar{X})$$
$$= b^*\Sigma(Q_i - \bar{Q})(X_i - \bar{X}) - b^*\Sigma b^*(X_i - \bar{X})(X_i - \bar{X})$$

[Since, $(Q_i^* - \bar{Q}) = b^*(X_i - \bar{X})$]

$$= b^*\Sigma(Q_i - \bar{Q})(X_i - \bar{X}) - (b^*)^2\Sigma(X_i - \bar{X})^2$$
$$= b^*[\Sigma(Q_i - \bar{Q})(X_i - \bar{X}) - b^*\Sigma(X_i - \bar{X})^2]$$
$$= b^*[\Sigma(Q_i - \bar{Q})(X_i - \bar{X}) - \Sigma(Q_i - \bar{Q})(X_i - \bar{X})]$$

[Since, b^* = Coefficient of regression = $\Sigma(Q_i - \bar{Q})(X_i - \bar{X})/\Sigma(X_i - \bar{X})^2$]

$$= b^* \times 0$$
$$= 0$$

Therefore, $\Sigma(Q_i - \bar{Q})^2 = \Sigma(Q_i - Q_i^*)^2 + \Sigma(Q_i^* - \bar{Q})^2 + 2 \times 0$
$$= \Sigma(Q_i - Q_i^*)^2 + \Sigma(Q_i^* - \bar{Q})^2$$

$\Rightarrow$
$$1 = [\Sigma(Q_i - Q_i^*)^2/\Sigma(Q_i - \bar{Q})^2] + [\Sigma(Q_i^* - \bar{Q})^2/\Sigma(Q_i - \bar{Q})^2]$$

[Dividing on both the sides by $\Sigma(Q_i - \bar{Q})^2$

$$\Rightarrow \quad \frac{[\Sigma(Q_i^* - \bar{Q})^2]}{[\Sigma(Q_i - \bar{Q})^2]} = 1 - \frac{[\Sigma(Q_i - Q_i^*)^2]}{[\Sigma(Q_i - \bar{Q})^2]} \quad (23.49)$$

Left hand side of Eq. (23.49) is defined as *explained variation in Q expressed as a proportion of total variation* while expression subtracted from 1 on the right hand side is defined as *unexplained variation in Q expressed as a proportion of total variations in it*. Explained variation in Q is known as the *coefficient of determination*, r^2.

Thus,

$$r^2 = \frac{[\Sigma(Q_i^* - \bar{Q})^2]}{[\Sigma(Q_i - \bar{Q})^2]} = 1 - \frac{[\Sigma(Q_i - Q_i^*)^2]}{[\Sigma(Q_i - \bar{Q})^2]} \quad (23.50)$$

Note that:

$\Sigma(Q_i - \bar{Q})^2 \equiv$ Total variation in Q from its mean (TSS)
$\Sigma(Q_i - Q_i^*)^2 \equiv$ Variation in Q not explained by the curve of the best fit (ESS)
$\Sigma(Q_i^* - \bar{Q})^2 \equiv$ Variation in Q explained by the curve of the best fit (RSS)

where,
TSS $\equiv$ Total Sum of Squares,
ESS $\equiv$ Error Sum of Squares and
RSS $\equiv$ Regression Sum of Squares.

Substituting data from Table 23.2 for the linear trend [Eq. (23.23)], we have

$$r^2 = 1 - \frac{76.80}{595.2} \quad \text{(Table 23.2)}$$
$$= 1 - 0.129$$
$$= \mathbf{0.871 \text{ or } 87.1\%}$$

(Meaning, 87.1% of the total variation in Q_i is explained by the linear trend $Q^* = a^* + b^*X$), likewise, substituting data from Table 23.3 for the quadratic or second degree trend [Eq. (23.21)],

$$r^2 = 1 - \frac{3.66}{595.2} \quad \text{(Table 23.3)}$$
$$= 1 - 0.006$$
$$= \mathbf{0.994 \text{ or } 99.4\%}$$

(Meaning, 99.4% of the total variation in Q_i is explained by the quadratic trend, $Q^* = a^* + b^*X + c^*X^2$).

Substituting data from Table 23.4 for the log-linear trend [Eq. (23.34)], we have

$$r^2 = 1 - \frac{0.00}{595.2} \quad \text{(Table 23.4)}$$
$$= 1 - 0.00000$$
$$= \mathbf{1.00 \text{ or } 100\%}$$

[Meaning, 100% of the total variation in Q_i is explained by the log-linear trend, $Q^* = a^* + (b^*)^{X_i}$] and substituting data from Table 23.5 for the double log-linear trend [Eq. (23.41)], we have

$$r^2 = 1 - \frac{71.98}{595.2} \quad \text{(Table 23.5)}$$
$$= 1 - 0.1200$$
$$= 0.88 \text{ or } 88\%$$

[Meaning, 87.91 of the total variation in Q_i is explained by the double log-linear trend, $Q^* = a^* + (X_i)^{b^*}$].

The value of r^2 being the highest for the log-linear trend, it is the most perfect fit to the data. The second best is the quadratic trend, the third best, the double log-linear trend and fourth best is the linear trend.

The coefficient of determination is thus a measure of *goodness of fit* or *forecasting* or *explanatory power* of the *estimated function*.

Coefficient of determination for the regression plane of Eq. (23.42), as computed in Table 23.7, may be expressed as:

$$R^2 = 1 - \frac{\Sigma(Q_i - Q_i^*)^2}{\Sigma(Q_i - \bar{Q}_i)^2}$$
$$= 1 - \frac{266.41}{5625}$$
$$= 0.9526$$
$$= 95.26\%$$

That is, 95.26% of the total variations in the dependent variable are explained by the regression equation. Note that the notation is R^2 instead of r^2.

23.3.2 Tests for Significance of the Parameter Estimates

In order to test whether parameter estimates a^*, b^* and c^* are significant, one needs to investigate whether or not these least square estimates are significantly different from their expected values. For this, we must also conduct the rest of the statistical tests, that is, in particular, standard error test, t-test or Z-test, and F-test too to be sure. As a prelude to these tests, we introduce formulae for calculation of the expected values and variances of these parameters.

Expected values (Means) of parameters:

$$\left. \begin{array}{l} E(a^*) = a \\ E(b^*) = b, \text{ and} \\ E(c^*) = c \end{array} \right\} \quad [23.51]$$

For $\quad Q_i^* = a^* + b^* X_i,$

$$E(a^*) = E[\bar{Q} - b^* \bar{X}]$$
$$= E[Q_i/n] - \bar{X} E(b^*)$$
$$= E[Q_i/n] - \bar{X}\{\Sigma(X_i - \bar{X})(Q_i - \bar{Q})/\Sigma(X_i - \bar{X})^2\}$$

$$= E[Q_i/n] - \bar{X}\{\Sigma x_i(Q_i - \bar{Q})\}/\Sigma(x_i)^2, \text{ where } x_i = X_i - \bar{X}$$
$$= E[Q_i/n] - \bar{X}\{\Sigma x_i Q_i/\Sigma(x_i)^2 - \bar{Q}\,\Sigma x_i/\Sigma(x_i)^2\}$$
$$= E[Q_i/n] - \bar{X}\{\Sigma\{x_i/\Sigma(x_i)^2\}Q_i - \bar{Q} \times 0\,], \text{ as } \Sigma x_i = 0$$
$$= E[Q_i/n] - \bar{X}\{\Sigma k_i Q_i; \text{ where } k_i = \Sigma\{x_i/\Sigma(x_i)^2\} \quad (23.52)$$
$$= \Sigma\{1/n - \bar{X}k_i\}E(Q_i) \quad (23.53)$$
$$= \Sigma\{1/n - \bar{X}k_i\}(a + bX_i) \quad [\text{since, } E(Q_i) = (a + bX_i)]$$
$$= \Sigma(a/n) - a\bar{X}(\Sigma k_i) + b\Sigma X_i/n - b\bar{X}\Sigma k_i X_i)$$
$$= a - a\bar{X} \times 0 + b\bar{X} - b\bar{X} \times 1$$

$\Rightarrow \quad E(a^*) = a$

as, $\quad \Sigma k_i X_i = \Sigma k_i X_i$
$$= \Sigma x_i X_i/\Sigma(x_i)^2$$
$$= \Sigma(X_i - \bar{X})X_i/\Sigma(x)^2$$
$$= \Sigma(X_i)^2 - n(\bar{X})^2/\Sigma(x_i)^2$$
$$= 1. \quad [\text{since, } \Sigma(x_i)^2 = \Sigma(X_i)^2 - n(\bar{X})^2$$

Likewise,
$$E(b^*) = E\{\Sigma(X_i - \bar{X})(Q_i - \bar{Q})/\Sigma(X_i - \bar{X})^2\}$$
$$= E\{\Sigma(k_i\,Q_i)\} \qquad [\text{As above, Eq. (23.52)}]$$
$$= E\{\Sigma k_i\{a + bX_i + u\}, \qquad [\text{From assumption (1), } u = e]$$
$$= E[a \times \Sigma k_i + b\Sigma k_i X_i + \Sigma k_i u$$
$$= E[a \times 0 + b \times 1 + \Sigma x_i u/\Sigma x_i^2]$$
$$= E(b) + (\Sigma x_i/\Sigma x_i^2)E(u)$$
$$= E(b); \text{ as } E(u) = 0 \qquad [\text{From assumption (2), } E(u) = 0]$$
$$= b.$$

Likewise,
$$E(c^*) = c$$

Variance of parameters:

Substituting for a^* in Var (a^*) from Eq. (23.53), we have

$$\text{Var }(a^*) = \text{Var}[\Sigma(1/n - \bar{X}k_i)(Q_i)]$$
$$= \Sigma(1/n - \bar{X}k_i)^2 \text{Var}(Q_i) \qquad [\text{Since, Var } cQ = c^2 \text{ Var }(Q)]$$
$$= \Sigma(1/n - \bar{X}k_i)^2 \times \sigma_u^2$$
$$= \Sigma\{(1/n)^2 + (\bar{X})^2(\Sigma k_i)^2 - 2(\bar{X})\Sigma(k_i)/n\} \times \sigma_u^2$$
$$= \{1/n + (\bar{X})^2(\Sigma k_i^2) - 2(\bar{X})(\Sigma k_i)/n\} \times \sigma_u^2$$
$$= \{(1/n) + (\bar{X})^2(\Sigma x_i^2/\Sigma x_i^4) - 2(\bar{X})(\Sigma k_i)/n\} \times \sigma_u^2$$
$$= \{(1/n) + (\bar{X})^2(1/\Sigma x_i^2) - 2(\bar{X}) \times 0\} \times \sigma_u^2, \qquad [\text{Since, } \Sigma k_i = 0]$$
$$= \sigma_u^2 \times \{(\Sigma x_i^2) + n(\bar{X})^2\}/n(\Sigma x_i^2)$$
$$= \sigma_u^2 \times \{\Sigma X_i^2\}/n(\Sigma x_i^2), \quad [\text{Since, } (\Sigma x_i^2) = (\Sigma X_i - \bar{X})^2 = \Sigma X_i^2 - n(\bar{X})^2] \quad (23.54)$$

In Eq. (23.54), σ_u^2 is the variance of the random term u_i as also that of Q_i. But it is not possible to compute it as the values of the random term u_i are non-observable. However, an unbiased estimate of σ_u^2 can be obtained as

$$(\sigma_u^*)^2 = \Sigma e_i^2/(n-2)$$

where $n \equiv$ the sample size, $e_i \equiv (Q_i - Q^*) = Q_i - a^* - b^*X_i$, $(n-2) \equiv$ degrees of freedom, and $(\sigma_u^*) \equiv$ is an estimate of (σ_u). Hence variance of a^*,

$$\mathbf{Var}(a^*) = \frac{\Sigma e_i^2}{(n-2)} \times \frac{\Sigma X_i^2}{n(\Sigma x_i^2)} \tag{23.55}$$

Thus, the standard error of a^*, written as S_a^* may be given as

$$S_a^* = \sqrt{\frac{(\Sigma e_i^2) \times (\Sigma X_i^2)}{n(n-2) \times (\Sigma x_i^2)}} \tag{23.56}$$

With the help of Eq. (23.48), substituting for b^*, we have

$$\begin{aligned}\mathrm{Var}(b^*) &= \mathrm{Var}(\Sigma k_i Q_i) && \text{[From the results of Eq. (23.52)]}\\ &= (\Sigma k_i^2)\mathrm{Var}(Q_i)\\ &= (1/\Sigma x_i^2)(\sigma_u^2) && \text{[From the results of Eq. (23.54)]}\\ &= [\Sigma e_i^2]/[(n-2)(\Sigma x_i^2)]\end{aligned}$$

Thus
$$\mathbf{Var}(b^*) = \frac{\left|\Sigma e_i^2\right|}{\left|(n-2)\,\Sigma x_i^2\right|} \tag{23.57}$$

The standard error of b^*, given by its square root and denoted as S_b^*, may be given as

$$S_b^* = \sqrt{\frac{(\Sigma e_i^2)}{\left[(n-2)\,\Sigma x_i^2\right]}} \tag{23.58}$$

Standard Errors of the Dependent Variable

Standard error of the dependent variable, Q, can be obtained on the same lines as

$$\begin{aligned}S_{Q^*x} &= \sqrt{\frac{\text{Un-explained variation in } Q \text{ for given } X}{(n-k-1)}}\\ &= \sqrt{\frac{\Sigma(Q_i - Q^*)^2}{(n-k-1)}}\\ &= \sqrt{\frac{\Sigma q_i^2 - b^*\,\Sigma x_i q_i}{(n-k-1)}}\end{aligned} \tag{23.59}$$

Here, $q_i = (Q_i - \bar{Q})$, $x_i = (X_i - \bar{X})$, $(n-k-1)$ = **degrees of freedom**.

Alternatively, for simple numerical computations standard error of Q given X and standard error of X given Q can also be calculated from the expressions:

$$S_{QX} = \sigma_Q \times (1 - r^2)^{1/2}, \text{ and } S_{XQ} = \sigma_X \times (1 - r^2)^{1/2} \quad (23.60)$$

Here, $S_{QX} \equiv$ Standard error of Q given X; $S_{XQ} \equiv$ Standard error of X given Q; $r \equiv$ Coefficient of correlation between Q and X; $\sigma_Q \equiv$ Standard deviation of Q_i from $\bar{Q}$; and $\sigma_X \equiv$ Standard deviation of X from $\bar{X}$.

Note that the standard error refers to standard deviation of the sample. The latter (standard deviation) refers to population while the former refers to the sample. Degrees of freedom refer to the manipulative power of data in general. That is, a work shirking investigator can manipulate $(n - 1)$ observations while the nth one has to be the one that restricts the average of the data close to the true mean. If a work-shirker has to test whether average marks of the postgraduate students are 60% from 10 observations, he/she may manipulate 9 while the 10th has to be one that keeps the average close to 60%.

Let us now summarise the formulae in some what practicable for the benefit of the reader for direct calculations. The reader can work out the proofs for academic interest.

$$\left.\begin{array}{l} E(a^*) = a \\ E(b^*) = b \\ E(c^*) = c \\[6pt] \text{Var}(a^*) = \sigma_u^2 \times \left[\dfrac{1}{n} + \dfrac{\bar{X}^2 \Sigma y^2 + \bar{Y}^2 \Sigma x^2 - 2\bar{X}\bar{Y}\Sigma xy}{\Sigma x^2 \Sigma y^2 - (\Sigma xy)^2}\right] \\[10pt] \text{Var}(b^*) = \sigma_u^2 \times \left[\dfrac{\Sigma y^2}{\Sigma x^2 \Sigma y^2 - (\Sigma xy)^2}\right] \\[10pt] \text{Var}(c^*) = \sigma_u^2 \times \left[\dfrac{\Sigma x^2}{\Sigma x^2 \Sigma y^2 - (\Sigma xy)^2}\right] \end{array}\right\} \quad (23.61)$$

$\sigma_u^2 = \Sigma e^2/(n - k)$; $x = (X - \bar{X})$; $y = (Y - \bar{Y})$; n is the sample size while k is the number of parameters estimated.

For the quadratic trend,

$$Q^* = a^* + b^*X_i + c^*X_i^2$$

We rename X_i^2 as Y_i for the purpose of calculations of expected values and standard errors. With this, means and standard errors of a^*, b^* and c^* of the quadratic trend follow the same process as in multiple regression.

Formulae meant for multiple regression can be now applied to the quadratic equation too for testing its significance. Following the technique of substitution of expected values and variances of parameters in the exponential trends, a logarithmic transformation of

$$Q_i^* = a^*(b^*)X_i$$

As
$$\log Q_i^* = \log a^* + X_i \log b^*$$
or
$$q_i^* = A^* + B^* X_i$$
where $q_i^* \equiv \log Q_i^*$; $A^* \equiv \log a^*$; and $B^* \equiv \log b^*$.

Mean and variance of the parameter can be computed and interpreted in either form.

As soon as we recapitulate the estimated trends, and calculate the expected values and the standard errors of the parameters, we can proceed to test the significance of our estimates.

Linear (Eq. 23.23): $\quad Q_i^* = -9.2 + 7.2 X_i$
(SE): $\quad (5.31) \quad (1.6) \quad\quad r^2 = 87.1\%$
Quadratic (Eq. 23.31): $\quad Q_i^* = 6.9 - 6.6 X_i + 2.3 X_i^2$
or, $\quad Q_i^* = 6.9 - 6.6 X_i + 2.3 Y_i$
(SE): $\quad (2.36) \; (1.80) \; (0.293) \quad r^2 = 99.4\%$
log-linear (Eq. 23.34): $\quad Q_i^* = (1.00)(2.00)X_i,$
or, on logarithmic transformation,
$$\log Q_i^* = 0.00 + 0.3010 X_i$$
(SE): $\quad (0.0) \quad (0.0) \quad\quad r^2 = 100\%.$
Multiple regression (Eq. 23.47): $Q_i^* = -86.67 - 3.34 X_i + 36.67 Y_i$
(SE): $\quad (119.97) \; (16.06) \; (21.70) \quad R^2 = 95.3\%; \; \bar{R}^2 = 85.9\%$

Standard Error Test

Though not as accurate as t- and Z-tests, the standard error test is the traditional test of significance of parameters. The null and alternative hypotheses are:

$$H_0: \text{parameter} = 0,$$
and
$$H_1: \text{parameter} \neq 0$$

It is a two-tailed test mostly conducted at 5% level of significance. The criterion of the test is simple though somewhat arbitrary. Let us have a look at it.

If the standard error of a parameter is more than half the value of the parameter estimate, null hypothesis is accepted at 5% and if it is less than half the value of the parameter estimate, null hypothesis is rejected or alternative hypothesis accepted at 5%.

To demonstrate, let apply it to some of the models we have estimated so far.

1. *Consider the linear trend:* $Q_i^* = -9.2 \quad + 7.2 X_i$
   (SE): $\quad (5.3066) \quad (1.6)$

   Accordingly, H_0 must be accepted in respect of a^* and rejected in respect of b^* at 5% as the parameter a^* is statistically **insignificant** while b^*, statistically **significant** at this level of significance.

2. *Consider the multiple regression plane:* $Q_i^* = -86.67 \; - \; 3.34 X_i \; + \; 36.67 Y_i$
   (SE): $\quad (119.97) \quad (16.06) \quad (21.70)$

Here, H_0 must be accepted in respect of a^*, b^* and c^* at 5% and thus each one of them is statistically **insignificant** at this level. In other words, reliability of the estimated equation is doubtful.

3. *Consider the quadratic equation:* $Q_i^* = 6.9 - 6.6 X_i + 2.3 Y_i$ $[Y_i \equiv X_i^2]$
   (SE):   (2.36)   (1.80)   (0.2931)

   Here, H_0 must be rejected at 5% in respect of each of the three parameters. Hence each one of them is statistically **significant** at 5%. In other words, reliability of the model must be high.

4. *Consider the log-linear trend:* $\log Q_i^* = 0.00 + 0.3010 X_i$
   (SE):   (0.00)   (0.00)

   H_0 is rejected at 5% in respect of both the parameters and hence both are **significant**.

Student's t-test (when n < 30) or Z-test (when n > 30)

The "t" statistic is defined as

$$t = \left| \frac{X - \mu}{S} \right|; \text{ where, } S \text{ is standard error, } \mu \text{ is population mean and } X \text{ the sample mean.}$$

For a^*,
$$t = \left| \frac{a^* - a}{S_{a^*}} \right|,$$

For
$$Q_i^* = -9.2 + 7.2 X_i \text{ with } a^* = -9.2 \text{ and } b^* = +7.2,$$
(SE):   (5.3066)   (1.6)

$$H_0: a^* = 0 \;(\alpha = 0.05)$$
$$H_1: a^* \neq 0$$
$$t = |(-9.2 - 0)/5.3066|$$
$$= 1.7337$$

This is less than the critical value of t at 5% for 3 degrees of freedom. The degrees of freedom here are $(n - 2)$ with $n = 5$ [See Table 23.1]. The critical value of t from the t-tables is 3.182. H_0 is therefore accepted and the value of a^* is thus **insignificant**.

For b^*, likewise, $t = |(7.2 - 0)/1.6| = $ **4.50**. This being higher than the tabulated value (3.182) of t for 3 degrees of freedom at 5%, H_0 is rejected implying that b^* is statistically **significant**.

For,
$$Q_i^* = -86.67 - 3.34 X_i + 36.67 Y_i$$
(SE):   (119.97)   (16.06)   (21.70)

$$t_a^* = |(-86.67 - 0)/119.97| = \mathbf{0.57}$$

This is less than the critical value of t at 5% for $(n - K)$ or 1 degree of freedom. Hence, H_0 is accepted implying that a* is **insignificant**.

$$t_b^* = |(-3.34 - 0)/16.06| = \mathbf{0.35}$$
$$t_c^* = |(36.67 - 0)/21.70| = \mathbf{1.54}$$

That is even the other two parameters are **insignificant**. The reader can see that same conclusions are reached no matter which test of significance is used. The reader can as an exercise test the significance of the quadratic and the exponential trends.

23.4 PROBLEMS WITH REGRESSION ANALYSIS

OLS–estmation is an effective tool in estimating economic functions like those of demand, supply and cost. However, there exist a few potential threats posed by the following if handled carelessly. They are:

(i) Specification of mathematical model
(ii) Multicollinearity of variables, and
(iii) Identification problem.

23.4.1 Specification of Mathematical Model

Careful specification of mathematical model is crucial for econometric estimation. Clarity of cause and effect relationships, assignment of symbols and signs to the independent and dependent variables, projecting alternative possibilities of functional relationships all constitute mathematical formulation of model. For instance, omission of an explanatory variable or incorrect grasp of the relationship between explanatory and dependent variables may defeat the purpose of investigation. Quite often an investigator omits a crucial explanatory variable by sheer negligence. This leads to a very poor fit of the trend to the data. For instance, suppose an investigator believes that the annual match fee (M) of a cricketer varies inversely as the cricketer's failure rate (F) defined as a ratio of the number of failures to score 20 or more runs to the number of innings played in a year. Accordingly, he attempts a negatively sloped line of best fit to the data collected but ends up with a positively sloped one, as given below

$$M = -2.00 + 100F,$$
$$(Z): \quad (-5.25) \quad (2.50) \qquad (n = 33) \qquad (r^2 = 0.45)$$

Clearly, the explanatory power of 'F', the failure rate, is very weak ($r^2 = 45\%$) while estimated parameters ($a^* = -2.00$ and $b^* = 100$) are both highly significant at 5% ($|Z| > 1.96$). The sign of the coefficient of 'F' being positive and that of the intercept parameter being negative, the line of best fit leads to absurd conclusions. How can a batsman failing more often get a higher match fee or a batsman with zero failure rate earn a negative match fee! From the equation, match fees corresponding to failure rates ($100F$) = 30, 40, 50, 60, and 70 workout as 28, 38, 48, 58 and 68, which vary directly with the failure rates.

The reason for such absurdity is the mis-specification of the model. If the match fee is inversely related to the failure rate, it must be positively related to the total runs (T) scored by the cricketers during a year. Including T as another explanatory variable and regressing M on F and T, we have

$$M = 20.00 - 10.00 F + 112.00 T$$
$$(Z): \quad (3.50) \quad (3.00) \quad (12.60) \qquad (n = 33) \qquad (R^2 = 0.96)$$

The addition increases the explanatory power ($R^2 = 96\%$) of the independent variables. Note also that the sign of the coefficient of F changes to negative while all the estimated parameters are significant ($Z > 1.96$). Evidently, match fee must have more to do with runs scored than with the frequency of failure to score 20 or more runs.

Omission of variables may thus defeat the purpose of estimation.

23.4.2 Multicollinearity of Variables

Another problem with econometric estimation is multicollinearity. The problem crops up when the estimated equation involves too many explanatory variables, some of which, are highly correlated with each other. The remedy to the problem necessitates deletion of the superfluous variable or re-estimation of the equation without one of them and repeating the process as many times as is the number of the correlated variables until the estimated equation satisfies all the statistical tests and is usable in every respect.

Take, for example, the following equation estimated by a researcher to study the effect of the number of hours devoted by a student to study (H) and the number of pages (P) read by him/her on his/her grades points (G). The researcher for the purpose constructed a sample of 100 students.

$$G = 40 + 0.25H + 0.30P \qquad [R^2 = 84\%] \qquad (23.62)$$
$$(Z): \quad (2.64) \quad (0.60) \quad\quad (1.20)$$

The coefficient of determination (R^2) being as high as 84%, the equation estimated may be treated as a good estimator but for the values of the estimated slope parameters, 0.25 and 0.30, each of which being statistically insignificant at 5% even after the intercept parameter of 40 being statistically significant at 5%.

A closer look at the equation reveals that the number of hours (H) devoted to study and the number of pages (P) read are highly correlated, giving rise to the problem of *multicollinearity*. The problem can be resolved by dropping one of the correlated variables. Suppose the researcher drops H from the equation and estimates the relationship between G and P only and finds the estimated equation afresh as

$$G = 50 + 0.45P \qquad [R^2 = 81\%] \qquad (23.63)$$
$$(Z): \quad (2.50) \quad (2.70)$$

Clearly, the revised equation satisfies all the statistical tests of significance and is a much better estimate of the function despite a little lower value of r^2, which hardly matters.

The researcher may be advised to delete P instead of H to see if he can still improvise the explanatory power of the function.

Quite often, multicollinearity is easy to detect and to rectify. In an extreme case when two explanatory variables are perfectly correlated, regression analysis is difficult to perform. The most convenient way of detecting multicollinearity is to locate the correlated explanatory variables through reasoning and most convenient way of rectifying it is to delete one with smaller coefficient.

23.4.3 Identification Problem

Estimation of demand and supply functions often poses *identification problem in its process*. For instance, identification of quantity demanded may pose difficulty in its ascertainment due to simultaneity of demand and supply equations. Data pertaining to market price and quantity demanded at it relate to equilibrium at which quantity demanded is quantity supplied. Thus, at times, what appears as quantity demanded may in reality be quantity supplied and quantity supplied, quantity demanded. A change in market price leads to a change in quantity transacted, that is, quantity demanded as well as quantity supplied. An affect of a change in price on quantity demanded cannot, thus, be separated completely from its affect on quantity supplied. To understand, suppose determinants of demand, other than price, remain unchanged with the result that demand curve remains unchanged as in Figure 23.3(i). Suppose further that supply curve keeps shifting outwards due to changes in one of its determinants other than the product price. Initially, it shifts from S_1 to S_2 and finally, from S_2 to S_3. In a situation such as this, demand function can legitimately be determined or estimated without facing any problem of identification. Now suppose demand also shifts. Initially, it shifts from D_1 to D_2 and finally, from D_2 to D_3 [Figure 23.3(ii)] due to changes in any of its shift factors. The situation such as this poses the *problem of identification of demand or of supply.*

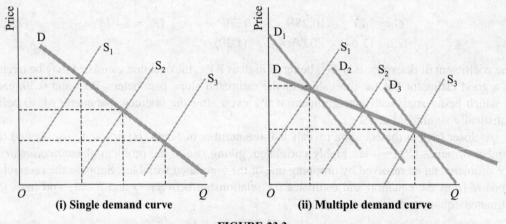

FIGURE 23.3

Demand estimation in Figure 23.3(i) poses no problem because demand function is stable; but in Figure 23.3(ii), it does because demand keeps shifting due to changes in one or more of its shift-factors. Supply shifts in both cases due to changes in its shift factors.

Let the demand and supply functions along with the condition of equilibrium be given as below:

$$Q^D = a + d_1 P_G$$
$$Q^S = b + s_1 P_G$$
and
$$Q^D = Q^S$$

where, $P_G \equiv$ price of petrol, $a, b, d_1, s_1 \equiv$ constant parameters, $Q^D \equiv$ quantity demanded and $Q^S \equiv$ quantity supplied.

Condition $Q^D = Q^S$ is imposed as the data relate to equilibrium prices and quantities. If demand is stable (no shift factor changes), demand function can be estimated given the possibility of shifts in the supply function [Figure 23.3(i)]. To make sure of demand as demand and of supply as supply, let us include a shift factor in each that influences the dependent variable of the equation to which it is added (without influencing the dependent variable of the other equation). Including income, for instance, on the right hand side of the demand equation and price of crude oil to the right hand side of the supply equation, we have

$$Q^D = a + d_1 P_G + d_2 I \qquad (23.64)$$
$$Q^S = b + s_1 P_G + s_2 P_C \qquad (23.65)$$
and
$$Q^D = Q^S \qquad (23.66)$$

Consumers' income included in the demand equation influences demand only and price of crude oil included in the supply equation influences supply only. The three equations so obtained are called the *structural equations*. Solving them for equilibrium, we have

$$a + d_1 P_G + d_2 I = b + s_1 P_G + s_2 P_C$$

$$\Rightarrow \qquad P_G = \frac{(b-a)}{(d_1 - s_1)} + \frac{s_2}{(d_1 - s_1)} P_C - \frac{d_2}{(d_1 - s_1)} I \qquad (23.67)$$

Substituting for P_G in demand Eq. (23.64), we have

$$Q^D = a + d_1 \frac{(b-a)}{(d_1 - s_1)} + \frac{d_1 s_2}{(d_1 - s_1)} P_C - \frac{d_2 s_1}{(d_1 - s_1)} I \qquad (23.68)$$

Equations (23.67) and (23.68) are called *reduced form equations*. Equation (23.68) can be expressed as

$$Q^D = A + B P_C + CI \qquad (23.69)$$

where, $\quad A \equiv a + d_1 \dfrac{(b-a)}{(d_1 - s_1)}, \; B \equiv \dfrac{d_1 s_2}{(d_1 - s_1)}, \;$ and $\; C \equiv -\dfrac{d_2 s_1}{(d_1 - s_1)}$

Equation (23.69) represents petrol demand as a function of price of the crude oil (P_C) and consumers' income (I). Parameters A, B and C can now be estimated through the technique of multiple regression and tested for significance through Z or t tests. One that tests highly insignificant would automatically have little influence on quantity demanded and may be dropped from the equation if desired. Fitting a multiple regression equation, thus, has an advantage. Note that price of petrol is treated as a dependent variable [Eq. (23.67)] due to simultaneity of demand and supply equations. If the simultaneity of demand and supply be ignored, the estimated equation will be less accurate but easier to determine.

23.5 EFFECT ON R^2 OF ADDITIONAL EXPLANATORY VARIABLES

What value of R^2 is significant or should we continue improvising by adding additional explanatory variables to multiple regression or improvising specification of the model until $R^2 = 100\%$? Would such additions or improvisations lead to more significant regression or yield a more significant R^2? To seek answers to these questions, let us take up Q. 66* of the exercises. The sample size (n) is 30 and the parameters (k) for estimation are 2 to begin with. The estimated equation of mileage (Y_i^*) over fuel-type (X_1) with the data given therein is

---

*Courtesy for data: A. Koutsoyiannis, *Theory of Econometrics* (2nd Edition), pp. 152–163.

$$Y_i^* = -84.50 + 1.30 X_1$$
$$(SE): \quad (9.3) \quad (0.1) \quad\quad R^2 = 86.4\% \quad\quad (23.70)$$

indicating that a^* and b^* are both **significant** as values of their SEs are less than half of each. The explanatory power of the model is 86.4%, which is not all that bad. The estimated function is a good forecaster therefore.

Let us conduct the F-test to confirm if it is so.

TABLE 23.6 ANOVA for regression [Q. 66 of Exercises]

Source of Variation	Sum of Squares	Degrees of Freedom	Mean Square	F^*
X_i	Σy_i^{*2} = ESS = 845	$k - 1 = 1$	845/1 = 845	F^* = 845/4.75 = 178
Residual	Σe_i^2 = RSS = 133	$n - k = 28$	133/28 = 4.75	$F_{0.05}(1, 28, 0.95) = 4.20$
Total	Σy_i^2 = TSS = 978	$n - 1 = 29$		[178 > 4.20]

Is the regression significant? Certainly, yes. $F^* > F_{0.05}$ [1, 28, 0.95]. F-test confirms our inference. But, is it possible to have a better estimate by adding an explanatory variable? Let us add another explanatory variable, weather condition (Rain index, X_2), which may have influenced mileage attained on driving the vehicle.

Regressing Y on X_1 and X_2 through OLS, we have:

$$Y_i^* = -36.9 + 1.00X_1 - 0.25X_2$$
$$(SE): \quad (19.5) \quad (0.12) \quad (0.24) \quad\quad R^2 = 89.3\% \quad\quad (23.71)$$

The SE of the intercept parameter a^* is greater than half of its value. Hence, H_0 is accepted implying a^* is **insignificant** but the SEs of b^* and c^* being less than half of their corresponding values are both therefore **significant** as H_0 is rejected. Moreover the sign of the weather conditions (X_2) being negative, Y_i varies inversely with X_2. R^2 too has gone up, implying higher forecasting power of the equation. But is it significant?

TABLE 23.7 ANOVA for regression [Q. 66 of Exercises]

Source of Variation	Sum of Squares	Degrees of Freedom	Mean Square	F^*
X_i	Σy_i^{*2} = ESS = 873	$k - 1 = 2$	873/2 = 436.50	F^* = 436.50/3.90 = 112.7
Residual	Σe_i^2 = RSS = 105	$n - k = 27$	105/27 = 3.90	$F_{0.05}(2, 27, 0.95) = 3.35$
Total	Σy_i^2 = TSS = 978	$n - 1 = 29$		[112.7 > 3.35]

$F^* > F_{0.05}$ [2, 27, 0.95], F-test confirms improvisation.

It is but natural now to continue the process to see if further improvisation is possible.

Let us add a third explanatory variable, the road-conditions (X_3) as another factor influencing mileage. Regressing Y on X_1, X_2 and X_3, we have

$$Y_i^* = -36.6 + 1.00X_1 - 0.25X_2 + 0.10X_3$$
$$(SE): \quad (19.9) \quad (0.12) \quad (0.09) \quad (0.7) \quad R^2 = 89.3\% \quad\quad (23.72)$$

Clearly, a^* (intercept term) and d^* (coefficient of X_3) are each greater than half the corresponding values of the parameters. They are thus **insignificant** but values of b^* and c^* are both **significant** as their SEs are less than half their values. The value of R^2 is 89.3%, which is the same as in case of Eq. (23.71). The results therefore remain unaltered by the addition of X_3.

One gets wary of adding additional explanatory variable one after another or of thinking which other variables are more appropriate to add for improvement. The exercise so far has ignored one significant factor that might be of great help in cutting our labour short, that is, adjusting R^2, for addition of an expanatory variable.

According to **Damodar N. Gujrati** and **Sangeeta***, adjusted R^2, denoted as $\bar{R}^2 < R^2$ whenever $k > 1$, where k is the number of the parameters estimated (including the intercept parameter) in the equation. Excerpts from the author's book, 'Basics of Econometrics' prove the fact as below:

Adjusted R^2, $\bar{R}^2 = 1 - \dfrac{\Sigma u_i^2 /(n-k)}{\Sigma y_i^2 /(n-1)}$, which is none other than $R^2 = 1 - \dfrac{\Sigma u_i^2}{\Sigma y_i^2}$, adjusted for the degrees of freedom. Note that u_i is our e_i in this chapter and y_i is $(Y_i - \bar{Y})$, the deviation of the dependent variable from its mean. Blending the two equations together, we have,

$$\bar{R}^2 = 1 - \frac{(n-1)}{(n-k)} \times (1 - R^2)$$

$$= 1 - (1 - R^2) \times \frac{(n-1)}{(n-k)} \quad (23.73)$$

$\Rightarrow \quad \bar{R}^2 < R^2$, whenever $k > 1$ and k is the number of parameters estimated in regression.

Clearly, this number, even in case of one explanatory variable, is 2 (one is the intercept parameter and the other, the slope parameter).

Given the values of R^2, n and k for the three values of R^2, calculated above in Eqs. (23.70), (23.71) and (23.72), we get the corresponding values of $\bar{R}^2$ as 85.9%, 88.5% and 88.06%, which proves their claim and also the fact that $\bar{R}^2$ falls when R^2 becomes constant at addition of an additional variable. This at least tells us where to stop or how to handle cases of small samples ($n \leq 30$). Also, when $n > 30$ (large samples) $\bar{R}^2 \cong R^2$.

CONCLUSION

The econometric techniques discussed so far relate to theoretical econometrics. It is linked to economic relationships, which relate to economic data are drawn from real life situations. Such data suffer from drawbacks of their limited availability, longer periodicity and exactness. The significance of econometric estimations through OLS are tested through first order tests called statistical tests. They are all based on the assumptions of the OLS method. If these assumptions get violated, the statistical tests prove inadequate.

The theoretical econometrics when applied to economic theory to study consumption, supply, demand, production and investment to evolve principles of economics to other fields of economic theory or to financial data, it is called *applied econometrics*. When theoretical econometrics is

---

* Damodar N. Gujrati and Sangeeta, *Basic Econometrics,* 4th ed., Tata McGraw-Hill Publishing Company, pp. 222–223.

applied to financial data whose periodicity of availability is very high and so is the possibility of multicollinearity, and *serial-* or *auto-correlation*. The latter term refers to existence of correlation between the values of the same variable at different points of time or in different situations. For example, when the value of the disturbance term 'u' (the random variable of uncertainty) depends on its value in the previous period, the phenomenon is called *serial-* or *auto-correlation*. When assumptions of the OLS methods get violated or when autocorrelation exists, the statistical tests of first order fail to work. Such situations arise usually in applied econometrics or in time series data. They require econometric criteria of testing the estimates called *second order tests*. Such tests call for testing plausibility of assumptions, autocorrelation, multicollinearity, errors in variable, time as a variable, qualitative variables also called *dummy variables*, *lagged variables*, and *distributed lagged variables*, and simultaneous equation models.

The purpose of including this chapter here was to provide the reader with the basic concepts of theoretical econometrics. Concepts of the applied econometrics are reserved for specialized fields where nature and the subject matter of the fields must dictate modifications in the tools of OLS.

KEY TERMS AND CONCEPTS

Adjusted coefficient of determination Presence of an additional explanatory variables in the function representing the regression plane, however, requires an adjustment of r^2 by the number of degrees of freedom. Adjusted coefficient of determination, thus is given as,

$$\bar{R}^2 = 1 - (1 - r^2) \times \frac{(n-1)}{(n-k)}$$

$$= 1 - \frac{\Sigma e^2 / (n-k)}{\Sigma q^2 / (n-1)}$$

where, $q = (Q_i - \bar{Q})$, $e = (Q_i - Q^*)$, n = sample-size or number of data-sets of Q, X and Y, K = number of variables.

If sample size n is large, $\bar{R}^2$ and R^2 would not differ much from each other.

Auto-correlation It refers to existence of correlation between the values of the same variable at different points of time or in different situations.

Auto-regression A relation such as $u_t = \sigma_t u_{t-1} + v_t$; where, u_t, u_{t-1} and v_t are random variables at point t, and $t - 1$, and σ_t is the auto-correlation coefficient. The equation marks the first order auto-regressive relation. If u_{t-1} is also dependent on u_{t-2}, so that $u_t = \sigma_t[\sigma_{t-1} u_{t-2} + v_{t-1}] + v_t$, the relationship is second order auto-regressive relation. The auto-regressive schemes may be of higher order too.

Coefficient of determination It is r^2, defined as the ratio of the explained variation to the total variations in the dependent variable from its mean. It may be given as

$$\text{Coefficient of determination, } r^2 = \frac{\text{Explained Variation}}{\text{Total Variation}} = \frac{\Sigma(Q_i^* - \bar{Q})^2}{\Sigma(Q_i - \bar{Q})^2} = 1 - \frac{\Sigma(Q_i - Q_i^*)^2}{\Sigma(Q_i - \bar{Q})^2}$$

Deterministic science A science in which behaviour of the subjects is fixed and accurately known.

Distributed lagged variables Distributed lagged variables include lagged values of the exogenous variables/lagged values of the dependent variables among the set of explanatory variables. For instance, $C_t = f [C_{t-1}, C_{t-2}, ..., Y_t, Y_{t-1}, ..., X_t, X_{t-1}, ..., ...,$ etc.)

Double-log linear model Logarithmic transformation of a mathematical model that yields a model linear in parameters yet involving logarithmic value of an explanatory variable along with that of the dependent variable as in log-linear model.

Dummy variables Qualitative variables such as favourable or unfavourable tastes and preferences are called dummy variables. They cannot take any values except 0 (for absence) or 1 (for presence of the attribute) in OLS – estimation.

Econometrics A scientific technique of converting economic principles into concrete functional relationships. It is a blend of three disciplines, namely, economics, mathematics and statistics.

Econometric tests Test for auto-correlation, auto-regressive schemes, multicollinearity, mis-specification of mathematical model, identification problems, etc. constitute econometric tests.

Heteroscedasticity It is opposite of homoscedasticity. It results when Var $(u_i) \neq \sigma_u^2$.

Homoscedasticity The term refers to same probability distribution of u for all observations of explanatory variables. The necessary condition for it is $\text{Var}(u) = \sigma_u^2$.

Identification problem The problem of identification of quantity transacted as quantity demanded or supplied at equilibrium, when supply and demand shift due to shift factors, is called the identification problem.

Lagged variables Lagged variables refer to the values of exogenously (endogenously) determined by explanatory variables over past-periods such as $Y_t = a + b_0 X_t + b_1 X_{t-1} + b_2 X_{t-2} + ..., ...,$ etc. For endogenously determined explanatory variables, $Y_t = a + b_0 X_t + b_0^2 X_{t-1} + b_0^3 X_{t-2} + ..., ...,$ etc.

Log-linear model Logarithmic transformation of the mathematical model that leads to a model linear in parameters.

Multicolleinearity When two or more explanatory variables are linearly correlated, the phenomenon is known as multicollinearity. It makes estimation of function a tough proposition but if they are perfectly correlated, the estimation of function becomes indeterminate.

Multiple regression OLS-estimation of a function of more than one explanatory variable.

Normal equations Equations involving the parameters [to be determined] through OLS. For instance to estimate linear equation $Q_i^* = a^* + b^* X_i$, the two normal equations for a^* and b^* obtained on minimization of the sum of squared errors are:

$$\Sigma Q_i = na^* + b^* \Sigma X_i \text{ and } \Sigma X_i Q_i = a^* \Sigma X_i + b^* \Sigma X_i^2$$

Here, ΣQ_i, ΣX_i and ΣX_i^2 are calculated from data collected.

Parameter Coefficients attached to the independent variables in an equation to assess its weightage in influencing the dependent variable.

Probabilistic science A science in which behaviour of the subjects is not fixed. It open to chance.

Properties of a random variable in econometric estimation assumes The random variable u is assumed to possess the following properties:

1. *It is a random variable.* That is, it can assume any value—negative, positive or zero at random. Each deviation or error e_i of the observed dependent variable from the curve of best fit, has a certain chance of being assumed by the uncertainty term, u, in a particular situation.
2. *The mean value of u is zero, that is,*
$$E(u) = 0$$
Make a note of the notation. It is so because u is a random variable not a discrete or continuous variable. In other words, the notation $E(u)$, the expected value of u, is the same as $\bar{u}$. Thus, $E(u) = \bar{u} = 0$.
3. *The probability distribution of u is homoscedastic, that is,* $\text{Var}(u) = \sigma_u^2$, a constant. Homoscedasticity implies same probability distribution of u for all observations of explanatory variable.
4. *The probability distribution of u is a normal distribution, denoted as*
$$u \sim N(0, \sigma_u^2)$$
That is, $E(u) = 0$ and $\text{Var}(u) = \sigma_u^2$ (constant).
5. *Random terms of different observations (u_i, u_j) are independent, that is,*
$$\text{Cov}(u_i, u_j) = 0$$
6. *The random variable u is independent of the explanatory variables, that is,*
$$\text{Cov}(X_i, u_i) = 0$$

Here, 'Var' $\equiv$ Variance; 'Cov' $\equiv$ Covariance.

Random disturbance term It refers to any of the positive or negative errors the random variable assumes in a situation or at a time.

Random variable It is a variable that assumes one value at random from the set of values open to it to select from. All the rest of the values become redundant once a value is assumed by the variable.

Risk When no outcome is certain but chance of each one is known.

Stages of econometric estimation Econometric estimation of functions has a sequence of stages to pass through. They are, specification of the variables, their signs, symbols, and nature of influence on the dependent variable.

Standard error Standard deviation of a sample is called standard error. It is related to the population standard deviation by the equation $\text{SE} = \sigma/\sqrt{(n-1)}$ if the sample size n is less than 30 (small sample) or by the equation, $\text{SE} = \sigma/\sqrt{(n)}$ if n is greater than 30 (large sample).

Standard error test If the standard error (SE) of a parameter is greater than half the numerical value of the parameter at 5% level, the parameter is insignificant and if less than it, it is significant.

Simple regression OLS-estimation of a function of one explanatory variable.

Specification and formulation of model Identification of the variables, their inter-relationship, signs and conditions under which it is to be estimated.

Statistical tests First order tests such as r^2, SE – test, t-test, Z-test are called the first order tests or statistical tests.

Uncertainty When no outcome is certain nor is its chance to happen known.

EXERCISES

A. Short Answer Questions

Define the following (1 through 30):

1. Econometrics
2. Applied econometrics
3. Deterministic science
4. Probabilistic science
5. Uncertainty
6. Risk
7. Parameters
8. Random variable
9. Random disturbance term
10. Homoscedasticity
11. Heteroscedasticity
12. Auto-correlation
13. Auto-regression
14. Simple regression
15. Multiple regression
16. Ordinary least square method
17. Multicollinearity
18. Standard error
19. Standard error test
20. First order tests
21. Coefficient of determination
22. Adjusted coefficient of determination
23. Normal equation
24. Lagged variables
25. Distributed lagged variables
26. Dummy variables
27. Identification problem
28. Second order tests
29. Statistical tests
30. Econometric tests
31. Which probability distribution is employed in econometric estimation? What are its mean and variance?
32. Name two very crucial assumptions of econometric estimation.
33. Why do we need to adjust the coefficient of determination?
34. What is the line of best fit?
35. When do we need a log-linear trend?
36. When do we need a double log-linear trend?
37. What are the conditions of the use of a student's t-test?
38. When do we use Z-test?
39. What do you understand by a significance level?
40. What is a confidence interval?
41. Give one example of multicollinearity.
42. Give one example of mis-specification.

B. Long Answer Questions

Distinguish between (43 through 63):

43. Theoretical econometrics and applied econometrics
44. Deterministic science and probability science
45. Statistical tests and econometric tests
46. Autocorrelation and auto-regression
47. Homoscedasticity and heteroscedasticity
48. Simple regression and multiple regression
49. First order tests and second order tests
50. Collinearity and multicollinearity
51. Log-linear trend and double log-linear trend
52. Coefficient of determination and adjusted coefficient of determination
53. t-test and Z-test
54. Standard deviation and standard error
55. Lagged variables and distributed lagged variables
56. Standard error and standard error test
57. Regressors and regressands
58. Forecasting power and goodness of fit
59. Exact sciences and inexact science
60. Significance level and confidence limit
61. Exogenous and endogenous variables
62. Explanatory variables and dependant variables
63. Linear trend and non-linear trend

C. Essay Type Questions/Long Answer Questions

64. (a) In what respects does the financial econometrics differ from theoretical econometrics?
    (b) State various assumptions of OLS estimation? What happens when the assumption of homoscedasticity is violated?
    (c) When is it appropriate to omit an explanatory variable from the OLS model and when it is appropriate to include it?
    (d) What is meant by identification problem? How can it be solved?

65. (a) Consider the time series data:

    Years (t):   2009   2010   2011   2012   2013
    Sales (Y_t): 2   4   8   16   32

    A researcher thinks that a linear model may capture the trend and help forecasting sales for 2014 and 2015. The line of best fit he gets is

    $$Y_t^* = -9.2 + 7.2t$$
    (SE):   (5.307)   (1.6)
    t: (1.734)   (4.5) $R^2 = 0.871$

    Table value of t at 5% for 3 degrees of freedom is 3.182. Comment on the strength of the model. Would the forecasts made on its basis be worth the effort?

    Fit in an exponential (log-linear) model instead and compare the results. Can we attribute the difference to the mis-specification of the model? Why? Why not?

66. Mileage per gallon (Y_i) of three types of fuels characterized as Octane 90, Octane 95 and Octane 100 each used for 10 days in a month, is regressed over octane ratings (X_i) through OLS for the data:

    Y_i: 32, 30, 35, 33, 35, 34, 29, 32, 36, 34, 35, 38, 37, 40, 41, 35, 37, 41, 36, 40, 44, 46, 47, 47, 46, 43, 47, 45, 48, 47.

    X_i: 90, 90, 90, 90, 90, 90, 90, 90, 90, 90, 95, 95, 95, 95, 95, 95, 95, 95, 95, 95, 100, 100, 100, 100, 100, 100, 100, 100, 100, 100.

    $$[\bar{X} = 95, \; \bar{Y} = 39]$$

The OLS estimation as obtained is:
$$Y_i^* = -84.5 + 1.30 X_i$$
$$(SE) = \quad (9.3) \quad\quad (0.1) \quad\quad R^2 = 0.864$$

Using the expressions:
(1) Variance of the random disturbance, $\sigma_u^2 = \Sigma e_i^2/(n-k)$, where, $\Sigma e_i^2 = \Sigma(Y_i - Y_i^*)^2 = ESS$
(2) Standard error of the estimate 1.30, given by $(SE_{1.30})^2 = \sigma_u^2 [1/\Sigma x_i^2]$
(3) Standard error of the estimate -84.5, given by $(SE_{-84.5})^2 = \sigma_u^2 [\{1/n\} + \bar{X}^2/\Sigma x_i^2]$
(4) $R^2 = 1 - [\Sigma e_i^2/\Sigma y_i^2]$, where, $\Sigma y_i^2 = \Sigma(Y_i - \bar{Y})^2 = TSS$
(5) $\Sigma y_i^{*2} = \Sigma(Y_i^* - \bar{Y})^2 = RSS$
(6) Adjusted R^2 (denoted as R_A^2) $= 1 - [\Sigma e_i^2/(n-k)]/[\Sigma y_i^2/(n-1)]$, if the number of the estimated parameters is k and n be the sample size.

(a) Complete the ANOVA table for regression by reporting values of α, β, γ, δ, λ, and μ.

Source of Variation	Sum of Squares	Degrees of Freedom	Mean Square	F*
X_i	$\Sigma y_i^{*2} = \alpha = ESS$	$k - 1 = \beta$	$\alpha/\beta = \lambda$	$F^* = \lambda/\mu = 178$
Residual	$\Sigma e_i^2 = \gamma = RSS$	$n - k = \delta$	$\gamma/\delta = \mu$	$F_{0.05}(1, 28) = 4.20$
Total	$\Sigma y_i^2 = TSS = 978$	$n - 1 = 29$		

(b) Is the regression significant? [That is, do the parameters, R^2 and F^* indicate their significance?]
(c) Can addition of another two explanatory variables, say, X_2 (Rain index) and X_3 (Road condition), if added, improve the fit? Given the respective rain indices as 100,104,102,104,96,96,110,105,103,102, 101,93,91,89,88,101,97,91,96,91,91,93,96,91,94,93,91,91,89,91 ($\bar{X}_2 = 96$) and corresponding road condition T as 0,0,0,0,0,1,1,1,1,1,0,0,0,0,0,1,1,1,1,1,0,0,0,0,0,1,1,1,1,1. ($\bar{X}_3 = 0.5$), T being a dummy variable assuming 0 if bad and 1 if good.
Proceeding with the assumption, and regressing Y on the three explanatory variables, we have:
$$Y_i^* = -36.88 + 1.05 X_1 - 0.25 X_2 + 0.10 X_3$$
$$SE: \quad (19.5) \quad (0.12) \quad (0.09) \quad (0.7) \quad\quad R^2 = 0.893$$

What inference can you draw from the signs of the explanatory variables as well as from the values of the parameters and their standard errors? R^2 has gone up significantly from 0.864 to 0.893, do you agree?

67. What are various limitations of OLS? How can they be corrected?
68. When do you need to adjust the coefficient of determination and with what results?
69. If the estimated function is a misfit, how will you improvise it and how will you test improvised model?
70. Quantity of a product demanded (Z) is a function of its price (X) and consumer's income (Y). Levels of demand at various levels of X and Y are given below:

   X: 4   3   2   1
   Y: 3   3   4   5
   Z: 10   20   40 100

Obtain Z as a function of X and Y and forecast demand when $X = 3$ and $Y = 5$.

71. Obtain expressions for expected mean and variance of estimated parameters a^* and b^* of a linear model. What role do they play in first order tests of OLS estimation?
72. Draw a schematic flow chart for econometric estimation of a function that has
   (1) Mis-specification of mathematical model,
   (2) Multicollinearity.

73. (i) What would happen to econometric estimation if one or more of the assumptions about the random disturbance term get violatedget violated? Outline the the most important ones and the consequences of their violation.
   (ii) Define correlation and covariance. How are they interrelated? Show with an example that two independent variables are uncorrelated but the converse is not true.
   [**Hint:** Coefficient of correlation,
   $$r_{yx} = \text{Cov}(x, y)/\sigma_x \sigma_y;$$
   $$\text{Cov}(x,y) = \Sigma(x - \bar{x})(y - \bar{y})/n$$
   $$= \Sigma(xy)/n - \bar{x} - \bar{y}.$$
   $$= E(xy) - \bar{x}\,\bar{y}$$
   If x and y are independent, $E(xy) = \bar{x}\,\bar{y}$ and $\text{Cov}(x, y) = 0$.
   Take the example,

x:	-4	-3	-2	-1	1	2	3	4
y:	16	9	4	1	1	4	9	16

   Calculate r_{yx} and $\text{Cov}(x, y)$. Here, x and y are not independent (why?), yet $r_{yx} = 0$, implying $\text{Cov}(x, y) = 0$. Hence, two independent variables are uncorrelated but if they are uncorrelated, they need not be independent.]

74. Consider the linear econometric model:
    $$Y_i = a + b X_i + u_i$$
    Show that
    (i) $E(u_i) = 0$, only when the point $(\bar{X}, \bar{Y})$ falls on thre estimated function which it always does.
    (ii) Random disturbance term u is independent of the explanatory variable, X.
    (iii) Random disturbance term u_i is independent of random disturbance term u_j when the two refer to different sets of observations.
    (iv) If u_i and u_j are independent, $\text{Cov}(u_i, u_j) = 0$; but if $\text{Cov}(u_i, u_j) = 0$, u_i and u_j are not necessarily be independent

75. Make a comprehensive case for the problem of identification of functions in econometric estimation identifying causes and suggesting a resolution of the problem

Pricing Policies in Practice

CHAPTER OUTLINE

Introduction
- A Brief Review of Pricing Policies
- Transfer Pricing
- Cartel Pricing
- Bundling
- Two-Part Tariff Pricing
- Suggestions of Prominent Study Groups on Pricing Policies
- Key Terms and Concepts
- Exercises

INTRODUCTION

Rising competition and interdependence have made business more dependent on calculation Supply no longer creates its own demand nor do gut feelings or business legacies ensure success in business. Product price plays the all important role in its sale or success of business. In Chapters 2, 3 and 4, we studied how market prices are determined and how consumer behaviour is governed by them. We know that a low price boosts sales but how low it can be made to avoid losses? This necessitates cutting costs, if possible, without compromising product quality. In Chapters 5 and 6, we studied how producers in private and public sectors allocate resources to minimize production cost of target or to maximize output under given resources. In Chapters 8, 9, 10 and 11, we saw how profit maximizing firms should in theory set price in different market forms. In Chapters 12, 13, 14, and 15 we studied how monopoly power can be reduced, how sales maximization can serve as an alternative option to profit maximization, how factors of production can be priced and employed and how investment decisions can be altered to maximize total returns. In Chapter 16 we studied general equilibrium and economic efficiency. In Chapters 17 and 18, we studied how externalities and asymmetric information disrupt market efficiency. In Chapters 19 and 20, we saw how we can optimize outputs with given inputs or resources through mathematical models of linear programming and input–output coefficients. In Chapter 21, we observed how foreign trade can clear over production and make goods available to us at competitive prices. Chapter 22 was devoted to decision-making in the face of uncertainty and risk while Chapter 23 was attributed to econometric tools to estimate economic functions for precision.

In this chapter, our endeavour is to show how pricing policies practiced by firms depend on theoretical premise.

24.1 A BRIEF REVIEW OF PRICING POLICIES

In this Chapter, we examine some of the pricing policies firms follow in the real world. The chapter reviews some of them to incorporate further research, if any, or to apprise all alike with the techniques of pricing their products not only in the interest of profit but also in the interest of Corporate Social Responsibility (CSR) of a modern business corporation or in the interest of the objective of social welfare maximization of a welfare state.

This will help to apprise the managers to assess the developments that prompted the theorists to incorporate the changes in the basic techniques and also to anticipate those that may be called for in future.

Pricing policies common in use in the real world may be outlined as follows:

1. Marginal cost pricing
2. Average cost pricing
3. Pricing with crowding costs
4. Inter-temporal pricing
5. Market skimming and market penetration pricing
6. Cost-plus pricing
7. Import-parity pricing
8. Retention pricing
9. Pricing with pollution costs
10. Transfer pricing
11. Cartel pricing
12. Bundling
13. Two-part tariff pricing

We will discuss them in their requisite detail in the subsequent sections of the chapter and wind it up with guidelines and recommendations of various administrative bodies, study groups and reform committees.

Pricing policies at (1) and (2), that is, *marginal cost pricing* and *average cost pricing* along with *profit maximizing pricing*, have already been discussed in Chapter 9 (Figure 9.9) as pricing policies common to the natural/regulated or state-owned monopolies. Profit maximizing price (P_M) is the highest and marginal cost price (P_{MC}) is the lowest. Average cost price lies somewhere in between and is intended to recover the total cost of production. Government monopolies, such as, state electricity boards, practise all the three simultaneously under price discrimination. The basis at times comprises consumption slabs. P_{MC} is applicable to essential consumption by masses, while P_{AC} and P_M to higher consumption levels of the rich or to commercial consumption by trading houses and industries. For detailed study, refer to Figure 9.9 (Chapter 9).

Pricing with crowding costs is an example of *peak load pricing*. Price is low during off-peak hours and high during peak hours of demand or consumption. For example, consider a subway or tunnel or a toll bridge, which is used heavily during peak hours and sparingly during off-peak hours. Mechanism of setting price in each case is explained in Chapter 9 (Figure 9.16).

Inter-temporal pricing is a discriminatory pricing policy. Market is segmented on the basis of demand elasticities before setting the price. The segment with low price elasticity is charged a high price and one with high price elasticity is charged a low price (Figure 9.15, Chapter 9). One of its variations is the *market skimming price*, which is very high at the introduction stage of a pioneering product. For instance, price of personal computers was very high at the introductory stage due to which, the product could not go beyond the rich and the business organizations. Later, price fell down significantly for the common consumer's segment when more players joined the field with *market penetrating price*. The new entrants employed improvised technology to set a much lower price to gain a foothold in the market. Even the pioneers had this in mind right from the start. They too slashed prices to reach out the common people's segment. Under inter-temporal pricing, the product is confined to the segment with low price elasticity (the segment of the rich) at the initial stages. It reaches the segments with higher price elasticities later. *Inter-temporal price discrimination* is practiced even in between the segments under one justification or another. It refers to charging of different prices from segregated segments. Market must be segmented into segregates submarkets each with a distinct price elasticity. Pricing for each segment is done accordingly as evident from Figure 9.15. To demonstrate, assume a constant cost industry producing a product at MC = 180. Further, let market have three segments— *first*, with a price elasticity of 1.5; *second*, with a price elasticity of 5.00; and *third*, with a price elasticity of 10.00. Profit maximizing prices to be set for the three are $P_1 = 540$, $P_2 = 225$ and $P_3 = 200$*.

Cost-plus pricing refers to a percent mark-up of cost to meet the profit intent. For instance, if production cost is 100 and if a profit margin desired is 20%, price to be set is 120. If cost increases to 125, price to be set is 150. The biggest disadvantage of this policy is that price increases by more than the increase in cost. Cost here refers to average cost.

Import-price parity pricing refers to the landed cost of comparable imports or imported substitutes. *Landed cost* includes custom duty and such other costs apart from the purchase cost of the close substitutes from abroad. Likewise, export price can be set equal to domestic price to restrict exports.

Retention pricing refers to a policy of setting a single price for products manufactured by industries with unequal production costs. The price so set is an average of the prices set individually by different industries through the policy of cost-plus pricing. Production costs vary from industry to industry due to production processes of varying capital vintages. The purpose is protection of high cost industries.

Pricing with pollution cost refers to a pricing policy which makes consumers to pay for pollution caused by production of a pollutant. Legislation these days requires firms causing

---

* For profit maximization, MC = MR while MR = AR $[1 - 1/|e|]$. Price, P (= AR) is thus given as:

$$P = \frac{MC}{[1 - 1/|e|]}$$ [Also see Eq. (9.53)]

pollution either to install equipment to abate pollution or to spend on relief measures to compensate the sufferers or to pay emission fee or *pollution tax* to government at a fixed rate per unit of emission. Paying compensation to the sufferers directly is highly inconvenient due to several reasons; paying pollution tax or installing equipment for abating emission of pollution are the only options before a polluting firm. If abatement of pollution is possible, firms incur expenditure called *abatement cost*, which they transfer to product price (Figure 24.1).

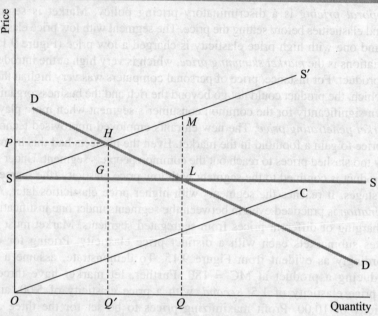

FIGURE 24.1 Pricing with pollution cost: DD represents demand for the product and SS its supply. Note that supply curve is perfectly elastic signifying unlimited supply at OS price. If pollution is ignored, quantity *OQ* is transacted at price OS. Now suppose the firm has to abate pollution. The marginal damage by pollution varies directly with quantity of pollutant produced, as shown by the curve OC. The supply curve with pollution cost is a vertical summation of OC and SS and is given as SS'. New equilibrium results at point *H*, where *OQ'* is transacted at a price OP. Price OP can be viewed as comprising OS and SP, where OS is private cost of production and *SP*, the cost of pollution. Thus, market price = production cost + pollution cost. Note that the presence of pollution cost has reduced sales by *QQ'*.

As regards pollution costs, polluting firms have a choice between abatement cost and emission fee. The latter is a pollution tax levied per unit of emission at a fixed rate. Abatement cost is the cost of equipment, that the polluting firms install to abate pollution. At low levels of emission, abatement cost per unit of emission is high just as average fixed cost is high at low level of output. As level of emission increases, abatement cost per unit of emission falls. The schedule of Marginal Cost of Abatement (MCA) thus varies inversely with the level of emission (Figure 18.4, Chapter 18). To determine the standard level of emission, a firm requires Marginal Social Cost (MSC) schedule as portrayed in Figure 18.4 (Figure 24.2, for ready reference). As expected, marginal social cost increases with increasing levels of emission. Equilibrium level of emission is determined at the intersection of the two schedules. Point *e*, therefore, gives the standard level of emission, OE^*, at, which MCA = MSC = *OF*.

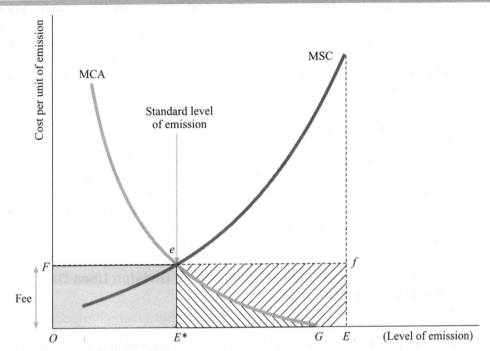

FIGURE 24.2 Choice between abatement and emission fee: The MSC and the MCA intersect each other at point e. At this point, the level of emission is OE^*, known as the **standard level of emission**. A firm emitting pollutants at level OE can, thus, be shown to benefit by paying an emission fee of E^*e upto an emission level of OE^* and by abating emission of pollution beyond this level. If the firm choose to pay the emission fee at the flat rate of E^*e per unit of emission, it pays a total fee given by the rectangle $O\ E f F$; if it chose to abate emission, it spends an amount given by the area under the MCA curve and if it chose to pay an emission fee of Ee^* per unit of emission for first OE^* units of emission and to abate emission thereafter, its total cost is an amount given by the sum of areas of the shaded rectangle ($OE^*e\ F$) and triangular region below the MCA curve ($E^*\ e\ G$). Of the three, clearly the last option of paying emission fee upto emission level OE^* and abating it beyond E^* is the cheapest option before the firm. Levy of emission fee or abating emission—both cost the polluting firm more dearly. This helps as a remedy for a negative externality.

The figure along with its description right underneath explains various alternative options before the firm and the cheapest one for the firm to choose. The reason of discussion is to facilitate comparison in between pricing with pollution, total abatement cost, or paying emission fee for the level of emission caused. A is evident from the figure, the best option is to pay emission tax at a fixed rate of OF per unit of the equilibrium level, OE^* and incur abatement cost thereafter, that is, area under that part of the MCA curve which lies to the right of OE^*. It is therefore, $OF \times OE^*$ + area of triangular region E^*eG (Figure 24.2).

Transfer pricing refers to a system of pricing through which intermediate inputs (parts, components, raw-materials, etc.) are sold by an upstream division of a firm to its downstream division. It is a system of internal pricing practiced by an integrated firm. For instance, suppose an automobile company produces engines, radiators, body-parts, and such other components in its upstream division and sells them to its downstream division assembling automobiles. The price charged by the upstream division from its downstream division is called the **transfer price**. It is equal to the marginal cost of the intermediate input.

The mechanism of transfer pricing requires an in-depth analysis, which follows in its requisite detail in Section 24.2.

Pricing by cartels, though discussed already in Section 11.7, requires a case study, which follows transfer pricing.

24.2 TRANSFER PRICING

As mentioned above, transfer pricing refers to a system of pricing through which intermediate inputs (parts, components, raw-materials, etc.) are sold by an upstream division of a firm to its downstream division. It is a system of internal pricing practiced by an integrated firm. The price charged by the upstream division from its downstream division is called the *transfer price*. It is equal to the marginal cost of the intermediate input. The mechanism of transfer pricing requires an in-depth analysis, which follows in its requisite detail here.

24.2.1 Transfer Pricing When the Downstream Division Uses One Intermediate Input

Case I: When No Outside Input Market Exists

To have a feel of how transfer pricing works, suppose an automobile company produces Q cars employing labour L, capital K and an equal number of engines which it procures from its upstream division at price P_E each. To determine P_E, the transfer price of an engine, suppose further that the company, the downstream division, has no other source of these engines except its own upstream division. Assuming that one engine is used in assembling one car, we have, $Q = Q_E$, where Q_E is the quantity of engines. Expressing profit function of the downstream division, we have

$$\pi(Q) = TR(Q) - TC_A(Q) - TC_E(Q_E)$$
$$= TR(Q) - TC_A(Q) - TC_E(Q) \qquad (Q_E = Q)$$

where, $TC_A(Q) \equiv$ total cost of assembling Q cars with the help of labour L and capital K; $TC_E(Q) \equiv$ cost of Q engines at the rate of P_E each.

Differentiating with respect to Q, we have

$$d\pi/dQ = MR - MC_A - MC_E$$
$$= 0 \qquad \text{(For maximization of profit)}$$
$$\Rightarrow \qquad MR - MC_A = MC_E$$
$$\Rightarrow \qquad NMR = MC_E \qquad (24.1)$$

Equation (24.1) provides the conditions of profit-maximization. Here, NMR = Net Marginal Revenue = $MR - MC_A$.

Let us have an illustration.

ILLUSTRATION 24.1: Suppose an automobile company faces the following demand for its cars:
$$P = 100{,}000 - Q$$
Its assembling cost is given by the function:
$$TC_A = 40{,}000 Q$$
while the total cost of Q_E engines procured by it from its upstream division given by
$$TC_E = 9 Q_E^2$$
Assuming one engine is used in assembling one car, determine:
1. Transfer price of an engine
2. Profit maximizing price of a car
3. Volume of profit earned by the company.

Solution

From the equation of demand for cars, we have
$$TR = 100{,}000\, Q - Q^2$$
$$\Rightarrow \quad MR = 100{,}000 - 2Q$$

From the equation of the assembling cost, we have
$$MC_A = 40{,}000$$
thus,
$$NMR = MR - MC_A$$
$$= 100{,}000 - 2Q - 40{,}000$$
$$= 60{,}000 - 2Q$$

From the equation of the total cost of engines, we have
$$MC_E = 18 Q_E$$
$$= 18 Q \qquad (Q_E = Q)$$

Since, $NMR = MC_E$, for profit maximization,
we have,
$$18Q = 60{,}000 - 2Q$$
$$\Rightarrow \quad Q = 3{,}000$$

Profit maximizing price of car,
$$P = 100{,}000 - Q$$
$$= 97{,}000$$

For joint profit maximization, the upstream division must treat MC_E as the transfer P_E of an engine. Thus,
$$P_E = MC_E$$
$$= 18 \times 3{,}000$$
$$= 54{,}000$$

Assembling cost of each car, $MC_A = 40{,}000$

Profit earned by the automobile company (Figure 24.3) is, thus, given by

$$\pi = TR - TC_A - TC_E$$
$$= 97{,}000 \times 3{,}000 - 40{,}000 \times 3{,}000 - 9(3{,}000)^2$$
$$= 291{,}000{,}000 - 120{,}000{,}000 - 81{,}000{,}000$$
$$= \mathbf{90{,}000{,}000}$$

To represent it all diagrammatically, we need AR and AC curves also apart from the NMR and MC_E curves. Let us obtain them from the given, equations:

$$AR = TR/Q = 100{,}000 - Q$$
$$AC = TC/Q = (TC_A + TC_E)/Q = 40{,}000 + 9Q$$

Figure 24.3 demonstrates the firm's equilibrium.

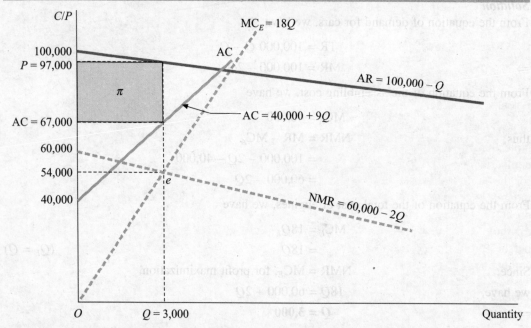

FIGURE 24.3 Illustration 24.1: MC_E = NMR at Q = 3,000. Average cost at this output is 67,000, while average revenue is 97,000. Profit per unit is 30,000 and the transfer price $P_E = MC_E$ = 54,000. Total profit of the firm (shaded) is 90,000,000. Point of equilibrium is e where NMR= MC_E. Note that the average cost function = $(40{,}000Q + 9Q^2)/Q = 40{,}000 + 9Q$.

Case II: When a Competitive Outside Input Market Exists

Now suppose the car engine in Illustration 24.1, is available in a competitive outside market at a price lower than the transfer price of ₹ 54,000. Let this price be ₹ 49,500. Then,

$$49{,}500 = NMR$$
$$= 60{,}000 - 2Q$$
$$\Rightarrow \qquad Q = \mathbf{5{,}250}$$

The firm now assembles more cars, which it can afford to sell at a lower price as well. Since all the 5250 engines needed for the profit maximizing quantity $Q = 5250$ will now be bought at ₹ 49,500 each, the firm will buy just that number of engines from its upstream division for which the transfer price (MC_E) is equal to ₹ 49,500. To see just how many it would buy from its upstream division, let us equate MC_E to 49,500; so that

$$18Q = 49,500$$
$$\Rightarrow Q = 2750$$

The rest, 2500 engines (5250 − 2750), it will buy from competitive outside market. The profit-maximizing price of the car is now given as

$$P = 100,000 - 5250$$
$$= \mathbf{94,750}$$

and the magnitude of profit,

$$\pi = TR - TC_A - TC_E$$
$$= 94,750 \times 5250 - 40,000 \times 5250 - 9(5025)^2$$
$$= 497,437,500 - 210,000,000 - 248,062,500$$
$$= \mathbf{39,375,000}$$

Average cost,

$$AC = \mathbf{87,250}$$

Note that firm's total profit and its profit margin (AR − AC) per car have both declined in comparison to their magnitudes in the earlier period in which no competitive outside market for the input existed. Nevertheless, its sales volume has gone up, which is strictly in line with the goal of a modern corporation, which has a bias for a higher turnover (TR) than for a higher profit. (To see how a modern corporation prefers maximization of sales with a reasonable profit for the shareholders, refer to Chapter 13 on goals of a modern corporation). In case the firm pursues profit maximization, it must purchase engines from its upstream division, not from the competitive outside market.

24.2.2 Transfer Pricing When the Firm Needs Two or More Inputs for Its Product

Case I: When No Outside Input Market Exists

Now suppose the downstream division uses two intermediate inputs which it buys from its two upstream divisions. Let the quantities of the inputs the firm needs for Q units of its product be Q_E and Q_W units so that Q is given as a function of L, K, Q_E and Q_W, as

$$Q = f(L, K, Q_E, Q_W)$$

Further let the product price be P so that total revenue realized from its sale is given by

$$TR = PQ$$

Also, let the assembling cost be given as

$$TC_A = g(Q)$$

and the input costs, as

$$TC_E(Q_E) = h(Q_E), \text{ and}$$
$$TC_W(Q_W) = m(Q_W)$$

respectively for inputs E and W.

[Note that the cost functions can be expressed each as a function of Q as

$$TC_E(Q_E) = k(Q)$$
and
$$TC_W(Q_W) = n(Q)$$

To demonstrate, suppose that the firm produces quantity Q of cars for which it needs Q_E engines and Q_W wheels. Clearly, $Q_E = Q$ and $Q_W = 5Q$, as one engine and 5 wheels are required for each car. The cost functions then reduce to

$$TC_E(Q_E) = h(Q_E) \Rightarrow TC_E(Q) = k(Q)$$
and
$$TC_W(Q_W) = m(Q_W) \Rightarrow TC_W(5Q) = n(Q)$$

The profit function of the downstream division can be spelled as

$$\pi(Q) = TR(Q) - TC_A(Q) - TC_E(Q_E) - TC_W(Q_W) \qquad (24.2)$$

Profit maximization by the downstream firm

Differentiating the profit function with respect to Q, we have

$d\pi/dQ = d[TR(Q)]/dQ - d[TC_A(Q)]/dQ - d[TC_E(Q_E)/dQ_E](dQ_E/dQ) - d[TC_W(Q)/dQ_W]$
$\qquad (dQ_W/dQ)$

$\qquad = MR - MC_A - [d\{TC_E(Q_E)\}/dQ_E](dQ_E/dQ) - [d\{TC_W(Q_W)\}/dQ_W](dQ_W/dQ)$

$\qquad = MR - MC_A - MC_E(Q_E) \times 1 - MC_W(Q_W) \times 5$

[Note that $dQ_E/dQ = 1$, as $Q_E = Q$ and $dQ_W/dQ = 5$, as $Q_W = 5Q$]

$\qquad = MR - MC_A - MC_E(Q_E) - 5MC_W(Q_W)$

$\qquad = MR - MC_A - MC_E(Q) - 5MC_W(5Q)$

$\qquad = 0 \qquad$ (for profit maximization)

$\Rightarrow \qquad [MR - MC_A] = MC_E(Q) + 5 MC_W(5Q)$
$\Rightarrow \qquad NMR_E = MC_E(Q) + 5 MC_W(5Q) \qquad (24.3)$

This sets the condition for maximization of profit by the downstream firm.

The net marginal revenue must therefore be equal to the weighted sum of the marginal costs of the inputs procured from the upstream divisions. Downstream firm's equilibrium vis-à-vis the upstream firms is shown in Figure 24.4.

Note that $AR = TR/Q$ and $AC = TC/Q$, where $TC = TC_A + TC_E + TC_W$

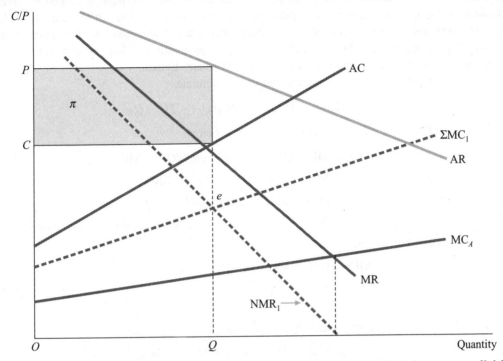

FIGURE 24.4 Equilibrium of the downstream division procuring two inputs from its upstream division (No outside market in existence for inputs): Equilibrium of downstream division vis-à-vis upstream divisions 1 and 2 takes place at e where firm's NMR curve cuts its aggregate MC [$\Sigma MC = MC_E(Q) + MC_W(Q)$]. The profit margin of the downstream firm is (AR − AC), while the total profit is the shaded region, π.

But, does that lead to maximization of the overall profit of all the units taken together? Or, does it imply that the upstream divisions too get their profits maximized simultaneously? Certainly not. Here the main concern of the downstream division is to maximize its own profits which implies maximization of its revenue and minimization of its costs. The latter is opposed to maximization of profits by the upstream divisions. To ensure maximization of the overall profits, the upstream divisions should not suffer losses, which if substantial, may offset the profits of the downstream division as well, leading to much lower overall profits to the integrated company.

Profit maximization by individual upstream divisions

We have seen above how the downstream firm determines its profit maximizing price and quantity. The question of transfer pricing has not figured explicitly in our discussions so far except to the reference to the total and the marginal costs of the inputs procured by the downstream division from its upstream divisions. Total input costs were estimated by the downstream division. Can marginal costs so obtained by the downstream division be treated as the transfer prices of the inputs?

Two things we have to bear in mind. The transfer prices must be such that not only exhaust the outputs of the upstream divisions, but also maximize the joint profits of all the divisions.

Marginal costs of the inputs of the profit maximizing downstream division if treated as given and taken as the transfer prices by the upstream divisions, the only thing left to be done by the upstream divisions is setting up of their quantities that just get exhausted by the downstream division. That is, given $P_E = MC_E$ and $P_W = MC_W$, the upstream divisions need to set Q_E and Q_W that get exhausted by the profit maximizing downstream division.

In order to determine such Q_E and Q_W, let us differentiate

$$\pi(Q) = TR(Q) - TC_A(Q) - TC_E(Q_E) - TC_W(Q_W)$$

with respect to Q_E and Q_W and equate each to zero as below:

$$\begin{aligned} d\pi/dQ_E &= MR\,(dQ/dQ_E) - MC_A\,(dQ/dQ_E) - MC_E \\ &= MR \times MP_E - MC_A \times MP_E - MC_E \\ &= [MR - MC_A] \times MP_E - MC_E \\ &= 0 \quad \text{(Necessary condition for maximization)} \end{aligned}$$

$$\Rightarrow \quad [MR - MC_A] \times MP_E = MC_E \quad (24.4)$$

$$\Rightarrow \quad MC_E = [MR - MC_A] \times MP_E$$

$$= NMR_E \quad (24.5)$$

Likewise,

$$\begin{aligned} d\pi/dQ_W &= MR(dQ/dQ_W) - MC_A\,(dQ/dQ_W) - MC_W \\ &= MR \times MP_W - MC_A \times MP_W - MC_W \\ &= [MR - MC_A] \times MP_W - MC_W \\ &= 0 \quad \text{(Necessary condition for maximization)} \end{aligned}$$

$$\Rightarrow \quad [MR - MC_A] \times MP_W = MC_W \quad (24.6)$$

$$\Rightarrow \quad MC_W = [MR - MC_A] \times MP_W$$

$$= NMR_W \quad (24.7)$$

From Eqs. (24.5) and (24.7), with $P_E = MC_E$ and $P_W = MC_W$, we have

$$P_E = MC_E = [MR - MC_A] \times MP_E = NMR_E \quad (24.8)$$

$$P_W = MC_W = [MR - MC_A] \times MP_W = NMR_W \quad (24.9)$$

Here, $MP_E \equiv$ marginal product of input E (Engine) and $MP_W \equiv$ marginal product of input W (Wheel). As mentioned earlier, if production of one car requires one engine and 5 wheels, $MP_E = 1$ and $MP_W = 5$.

Equations (24.8) and (24.9) provide conditions of profit maximization by each of the three divisions individually. Joint profits can also be maximized if the downstream division treats $P_E = MC_E$ and $P_W = MC_W$ as given and attempts determining the profit maximizing input requirements from the upstream divisions. The solution to the transfer pricing problem therefore, is a simple one, laid down in the following lines:

If the transfer prices, P_E and P_W of engines and wheels were set equal to their marginal costs, MC_E and MC_W, respectively, the number of engines and wheels, Q_E and Q_W, that the profit *maximizing downstream division would like to buy from its upstream divisions would be the same as that each of the profit maximizing upstream divisions would like to produce and supply.*

An illustration is highly called for at this stage.

ILLUSTRATION 24.2: A car manufacturing company buys engines from its upstream Division 1 and wheels from its upstream Division 2. To manufacture 1 car, it requires 1 engine and 5 wheels. Demand for cars is given by the function

$$P = 600 - Q$$

while the assembling cost of the company, by

$$TC_A = 120Q + Q^2$$

Cost functions of Q_E engines and Q_W wheels at Divisions 1 and 2 are respectively,

$$TC_E = 40\, Q_E + 2Q_E^2, \text{ and}$$
$$TC_W = (26/275)\, Q_W^2$$

Determine:
1. The profit maximizing number of cars and the price of a car,
2. Profits earned by each of the three divisions,
3. Transfer price of an engine and a wheel.

(All estimates are in thousands)

Solution: From the functions given,

$$TR = 600Q - Q^2$$
$$MR = 600 - 2Q$$
$$MC_A = 120 + 2Q$$
$$MC_E = 40 + 4Q_E$$
$$MC_W = (52/275)\, Q_W$$

Since one engine is required for one car, $Q = Q_E$. Hence,

$$MP_E = dQ/dQ_E = 1$$

and,
$$NMR_E = (MR - MC_A) \times MP_E$$
$$= (600 - 2Q - 120 - 2Q) \times 1$$
$$= 480 - 4Q$$

For profit maximizing, quantity of cars, Q, is given by

$$NMR_E = MC_E$$
$$480 - 4Q = 40 + 4Q_E$$
$$= 40 + 4Q \qquad\qquad \text{(Since, } Q = Q_E\text{)}$$

$$\Rightarrow \quad Q = 55$$
$$\Rightarrow \quad Q_E = 55$$

Thus, profit maximizing quantity of cars and engines is **55,000** each (Figure 24.5).

Profit maximizing price of a car,
$$P = 600 - Q$$
$$= 600 - 55$$
$$= 545$$

Thus, the profit maximizing price of a car is ₹ **545,000**.

Profit maximizing price of an engine, its transfer price,
$$P_E = MC_E$$
$$= 40 + 4 \times 55$$
$$= 260$$

Thus, profit maximizing transfer price of an engine is ₹ **260,000**.

Since five wheels are required for one car,
$$Q_W = 5Q$$
$$= 5 \times 55$$
$$= 275$$

The same is the value of Q_W when Eq. (24.8) is used. As $Q_W = 5Q$,
$$MP_W = dQ/dQ_W = 1/5$$
and,
$$NMR_W = (MR - MC_A) \times MP_W$$
$$= (600 - 2Q - 120 - 2Q) \times (1/5)$$
$$= 96 - 0.8Q$$

For profit maximizing quantity of wheels, Q_W,
$$NMR_W = MC_W$$
$$96 - 0.8Q = (52/275)\, Q_W$$
$$96 - 0.8Q = (52/275) \times 5Q \qquad \text{(Since, } Q_W = 5Q\text{)}$$
$$= (52/55) \times Q$$
$$\Rightarrow \quad (96/55)Q = 96$$
$$\Rightarrow \quad Q = 55$$
$$\Rightarrow \quad Q_W = 5Q = 275$$

Thus, profit maximizing quantity of wheels is **275,000**.

Profit maximizing price of wheels,
$$P_W = MC_W$$
$$= (52/275)\, Q_W$$
$$= 52$$

Thus, the transfer price of a wheel as set by the downstream division is ₹ **52,000**.

Profit earned by the downstream division (in thousand rupees)

$$\pi = TR - TC_A - TC_E - TC_W$$
$$= 600Q - Q^2 - 120Q - Q^2 - 40Q_E - 2Q_E^2 - (26/275)Q_W^2$$
$$= 4950 \quad \text{(Substituting for } Q, Q_E \text{ and } Q_W)$$

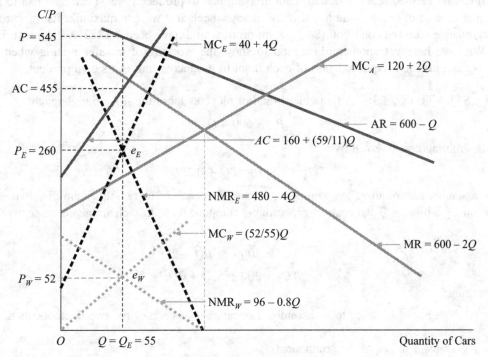

FIGURE 24.5 Illustration 24.2: Equilibrium of the downstream division vis-à-vis upstream divisions 1 and 2 is shown in the same figure with quantity of cars measured on the horizontal axis. Accordingly, MC_W and MC_E are expressed in Q, the quantity of cars, and so are NMR_E and NMR_W. Profit maximizing quantity of cars and engines is 55,000 each while that of wheels, $Q_W = 5Q = 275,000$. Profit maximizing price of a car is ₹ 545,000, transfer price of an engine is ₹ 260,000 and transfer price of a wheel is ₹ 52,000.

Profit earned by the upstream division 1 (in thousand rupees)

$$\pi_E = TR_E - TC_E$$
$$= P_E \times Q_E - TC_E$$
$$= 260 \times 55 - 40 \times 55 - 2(55)^2$$
$$= \mathbf{6050}$$

Profit earned by the upstream division 2 (in thousand rupees)

$$\pi_E = TR_W - TC_W$$
$$= P_W \times Q_W - TC_W$$

$$= 52 \times 275 - (26/275)(275)^2$$
$$= \mathbf{7150}.$$

Note that the transfer prices P_E and P_W are set at the levels of MC_E and MC_W. The upstream divisions set quantities Q_E and Q_W that maximize their individual profits. The downstream division exhausts these quantities. The joint profits are ₹ **18,150** (4950 + 6050 + 7150) **thousand**.

It can be verified that the downstream division had to produce (242/7) cars and had to buy an equal number of engines and five times as many wheels if it were to maximize its own profits in accordance with the condition (24.3). Joint profit would have been ₹ **12821.05 thousand**.

We have here yet another illustration to show the working of transfer pricing when the downstream division requires 1 unit of each input to produce 1 unit of its own product.

ILLUSTRATION 24.3: A particular brand of bicycles faces the following demand:

$$P = 6600 - Q$$

Its assembling cost is given by

$$TC_A = 2000 + 50Q + 0.25Q^2$$

The assembly unit requires two components, one from each of its two upstream divisions, for assembling a bicycle. Total costs of procuring Q components from each are given, respectively, by

$$TC_1 = 1000 + 50Q + 2Q^2$$
$$TC_2 = 200 + 50Q + 2Q^2$$

Determine:

(i) Number of bicycles to be assembled or number of each of the two components to be produced.
(ii) Transfer prices of the components.
(iii) Profit maximizing price of bicycle.
(iv) Total profit of the integrated firm.

Solution:
Since,
$$P = 6600 - Q,$$
$$TR = 6600Q - Q^2,$$
and,
$$MR = 6600 - 2Q$$

From the information given,

$$MC_A = 50 + 0.5Q,$$
$$MC_1 = 50 + 4Q$$
$$MC_2 = 50 + 4Q$$
$$NMR_1 = [MR - MC_A] \times MP_1$$
$$= [MR - MC_A]$$

($MP_1 = 1$, as 1 component is required for 1 bicycle)

$$= [6600 - 2Q - 50 - 0.5Q]$$
$$= [6550 - 2.5Q]$$

Transfer prices of the components being equal to their marginal costs or NMRs,

$$P_1 = MC_1$$
$$= NMR_1$$
$$\Rightarrow \quad 6550 - 2.5Q = 50 + 4Q$$
$$\Rightarrow \quad 6.5Q = 6500$$
$$\Rightarrow \quad Q = 1000$$

Profit maximizing price of a bicycle,

$$P = 6600 - Q$$
$$= 6600 - 1000$$
$$= 5600$$

Total profit of the integrated firm,

$\pi = TR - TC_A - TC_1 - TC_2$

$= 5600 \times 1000 - 2000 - 50 \times 1000 - 0.25 (1000)^2 - 1000 - 50 \times 1000 - 2 \times (1000)^2 - 200$
$\quad - 50 \times (1000) - 2 \times (1000)^2$ (Since, $Q = Q_1 = Q_2$)

$= 5{,}600{,}000 - 2000 - 50{,}000 - 250{,}000 - 1000 - 50{,}000 - 2{,}000{,}000 - 200 - 50{,}000 - 2{,}000{,}000$

$= 5{,}600{,}000 - 4{,}403{,}200$

$= \mathbf{1{,}196{,}800}.$

Transfer price of the first component,

$$P_1 = MC_1$$
$$= 50 + 4Q$$
$$= 50 + 4 \times 1000$$
$$= \mathbf{4050}$$

Transfer price of the second component,

$$P_2 = MC_2$$
$$= 50 + 4Q$$
$$= 50 + 4 \times 1000$$
$$= \mathbf{4050}$$

Note the difference between these illustrations. The latter is based on the assumption that $Q = Q_1 = Q_2$ (Figure 24.6) while the former is based on the assumption that $Q = Q_1 \neq Q_2$ (Figure 24.5).

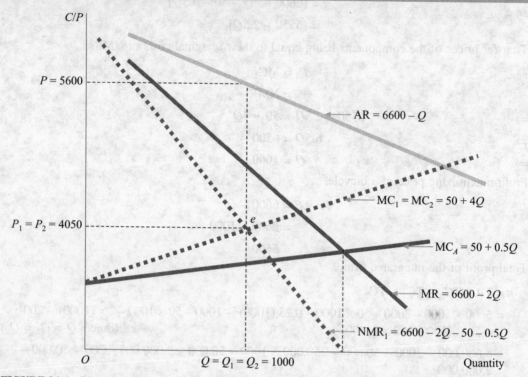

FIGURE 24.6 Diagrammatic representation of equilibrium of the downstream division (Illustration 24.3) vis-à-vis its upstream division: The downstream division uses one component from each one of its upstream divisions to assemble a bicycle. Marginal cost of each component being the same, their transfer prices are also same. Equilibrium outputs of the three divisions are 1000 each while profit maximizing price of a bicycle is ₹ 5600 and that of each component is ₹ 4050. Profit of the integrated firm is ₹ 1,196,800.

Case II: When an Outside Input Market Exists

Two situations emerge in this case:

1. When the competitive price lies below the point of intersection of MC_1 and NMR_1

Suppose, now that the intermediate inputs, so far procured by the downstream division from its upstream divisions, are available also in a competitive outside market at fixed prices. Let us assume, for simplicity, that the downstream division uses only one input, which is available with its upstream division at price P_1 (= MC_1) as also with a competitive outside market at a fixed price $\bar{P}$. Modifying Figure 24.4 to Figure 24.7, we observe that quantity OQ_1 of the input is bought from the upstream division because the transfer price P_1 (MC_1) is less than the competitive price $\bar{P}$ for this quantity and the rest, Q_1Q_2 ($OQ_2 - OQ_1$), is procured from the outside competitive market at price $\bar{P}$ which is less than the transfer price P_1 (MC_1) for all the units bought above OQ_1. Note that in the absence of an outside market the downstream division required quantity OQ from its upstream division, but ended buying OQ_2 instead due to its availability in the outside competitive market at a price $\bar{P}$ lower than that charged by its upstream division (Figure 24.7).

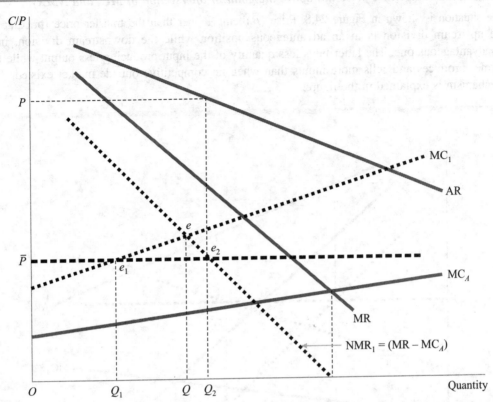

FIGURE 24.7 Transfer pricing when a competitive outside market exists with a price lower than the transfer price determined at the intersection of MC_1 and NMR_1: Transfer-price of the input, determined at e, is higher than the competitive price $\bar{P}$ in the outside market. The upstream division therefore, produces OQ_1 at e_1 instead of OQ at e. The downstream division buys OQ_2 a part of which, OQ_1(at e_1), it buys from its upstream division at P_1 (MC_1) $< \bar{P}$; and the rest, Q_1Q_2 (at e_2) it buys at $\bar{P}$, which is less than price P_1 (MC_1) charged by the upstream division. The downstream division thus buys more of the input and sells more of the output than when there existed no outside competitive market. The additional quantity of input it bought and output it sold is QQ_2. Upstream division is at its liberty to decide whether to discontinue production at Q_1 or to lower its price to the competitive level.

In case the firm employs more than one intermediate input, treatment for the other input follows the same mechanism. If both the inputs have same MCs, treatment of one applies to the other as well but if the MCs are different, separate treatments are required. They may be carried out in the same figure as in Figure 24.5 or in different figures following the mechanism of Figure 24.7.

Existence of an outside competitive market is advantageous for the downstream division as it gets more of the input at a lower price. As regards the upstream division, existence of an outside competitive market proves disadvantageous to it due to a restraint imposed on its output or a compulsion posed to slash price to the competitive level for all the units beyond OQ_1.

2. When the competitive price lies above the point of intersection of MC_1 and NMR_1

The situation is shown in Figure 24.8. Price ($\bar{P}$) being higher than the transfer price (price at e), the upstream division is in an advantageous position while the downstream division, in a disadvantageous one. The latter buys less quantity of the input producing less output while the former produces and sells more inputs than when no competitive outside market existed. The mechanism is explained in the figure.

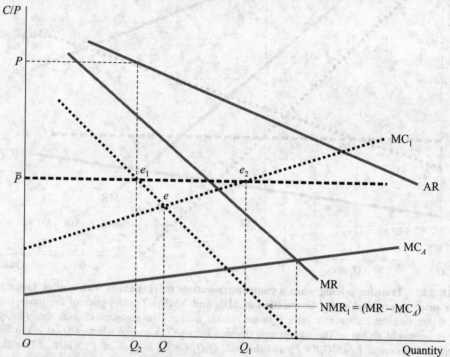

FIGURE 24.8 Transfer pricing when a competitive outside market exists with a price higher than the transfer price determined at the intersection of MC_1 and NMR_1: Transfer-price of the input, determined at e, is lower than the competitive price, $\bar{P}$ in the outside market. The upstream division, therefore, produces OQ_1 at e_2 instead of OQ at e. The downstream division buys OQ_2 at $\bar{P}$ instead of buying OQ which it did at the transfer price at e in the absence of the competitive outside market. The upstream division sells OQ_2 to the downstream division at $\bar{P}$ and the rest, $Q_2 Q_1$, equal to the difference of OQ_1 over OQ_2, it sells in the competitive outside market at the prevailing price.

24.2.3 Transfer Pricing When the Upstream Division is a Monopoly Supplier of Input to the Outside Market

In case, the upstream division is a monopoly supplier to the outside market, the **total net marginal revenue curve** of the input is the NMR_1^M curve (Figure 24.9, obtained through a horizontal summation of MR_1^M, the marginal revenue curve of the input sales of the upstream division to the outside market and NMR_1, the net marginal revenue curve of input sales by it to the downstream division. Equilibrium position of the upstream division is reached at E where MC_1 of the upstream division cuts the NMR_1^M curve. The upstream division, therefore, produces OQ_1 quantity of the input of which it supplies OQ_2 (at E'') to its downstream division at price OP_1 and the rest, OQ^M (= $Q_2Q_1 = OQ_1 - OQ_2$), to the outside market at price OP_1^M at E'.

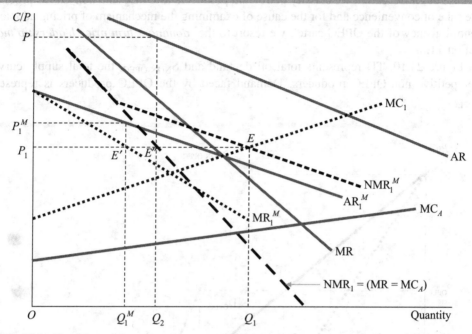

FIGURE 24.9 Transfer pricing when the upstream division is a monopoly supplier of input to the outside market: In contrast to the situation in Figure 24.7, the upstream division possesses a monopoly power with a downward sloping AR_1^M and MR_1^M. The total net marginal revenue curve (NMR_1^M) of the input is intersected by the MC_1 curve of the upstream division at E, signifying that quantity OQ_1 of inputs is produced and supplied by the upstream division of which, OQ_2 is sold by it at E'' to its downstream division at price OP_1 and the rest, OQ_1^M is sold by it at E' to the outside market at price OP_1^M. Note that $OQ_1^M = Q_2Q_1$ and that NMR_1^M is a horizontal summation of MR_1^M and NMR_1. Point E'' is the intersection of P_1E and NMR_1^M while point E', that of P_1E and MR_1^M.

Note that the upstream division gets a higher price in the outside market than the price offered by its downstream division. If the downstream division pays a price higher than OP_1, the upstream division would get prompted to produce more of the input raising thereby the marginal cost of the input much above the NMR_1 realized by the downstream division and if the price in the outside market be lowered, the marginal revenue realized by the upstream division from the outside market price in the outside market be lowered, the marginal revenue realized by the upstream division from the outside market would fall below its marginal cost curve. At prices OP_1 and OP_1^M, $MR_1^M = MC_1 = NMR_1 = (MR - MC_A)$.

24.3 CARTEL PRICING

In Section 11.7, we have studied cartel pricing in its theoretical premise. We saw how a central agency fixes price which the firms in the cartel follow. The mechanism adopted by the central agency for the purpose we could not discuss there in its requisite detail. Let us do it here in respect of two cartels – *one,* the OPEC cartel, which achieved considerable success in raising the price much above the competitive level; and *two,* the CIPEC* copper cartel, which failed in this respect.

In case of OPEC cartel, we classify petroleum producers as OPEC and non-OPEC producers. For the sake of convenience and for the cause of examining the mechanism of pricing adopted by the central agency of the OPEC cartel, we resort to the *'dominant firm price leadership model'* of Section 11.8.

In Figure 24.10, TD represents total oil demand and $S_{\text{NON-OPEC}}$, the total supply curve of the competitive non-OPEC producers. Demand faced by the OPEC producers is represented by D_{OPEC},

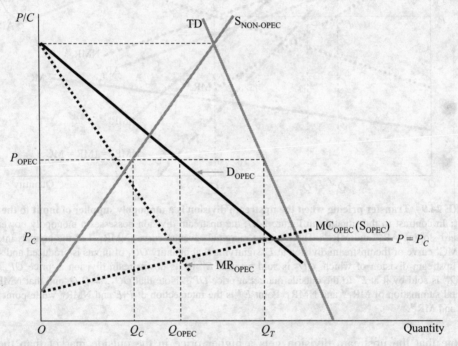

FIGURE 24.10 OPEC Pricing: The cartel succeeded in pegging the price up (P_{OPEC}) much above the competitive price (P_C) during seventies. It produced quantity Q_{OPEC}, which it sold at P_{OPEC}. The non-OPEC firms produced Q_C, which, they too sold at P_{OPEC}. In the figure, TD is total demand curve; D_{OPEC} is the demand curve faced by the OPEC cartel; MC_{OPEC} is its marginal cost curve and MR_{OPEC} is its marginal revenue curve. $S_{\text{NON-OPEC}}$ is the supply curve of the non-OPEC competitive firms. Q_T is total market demand at P_{OPEC}. $OQ_{\text{OPEC}} = Q_C Q_T$, implying, $OQ_C + Q_C Q_T = OQ_T$. The total demand is thus met by the OPEC and Non-OPEC suppliers at a price (P_{OPEC}) much higher than the competitive price (P_C).

their marginal revenue by MR_{OPEC} and marginal cost by MC_{OPEC}. The cartel determines its price and quantity at the point where its MC cuts its MR from below.

---

* CIPEC is the French acronym for International Council of Copper Exporting Countries.

The **OPEC cartel,** thus succeeds in pegging up its price much above the competitive price. The reason is the steepness of the supply curve in short-run (See also Figure 2.22). In the long-run, supply curve turns flatter (more elastic) and the cartel's power to raise price declines accordingly. Figure 24.10 shows how OPEC succeeded in hiking price during seventies, but later, during 1982–89, when the cartel's supply curve turned more elastic, its power to peg it up weakened. On the contrary, **CIPEC cartel** failed to achieve much even in short-run. Figure 24.11 explains why. The total demand, supply of the non-CIPEC producers, demand curve faced by CIPEC producers and the MC curve of the CIPEC producers are all elastic. The CIPEC cartel determines its price and output at the point where its MC curve cuts its MR curve from below. Cartel's output is Q_{CIPEC}, which it sells at P_{CIPEC}. At this price, supply of the non-CIPEC producers is Q_C, while total demand is Q_T. The price hike CIPEC cartel succeeds in realizing is only marginal.

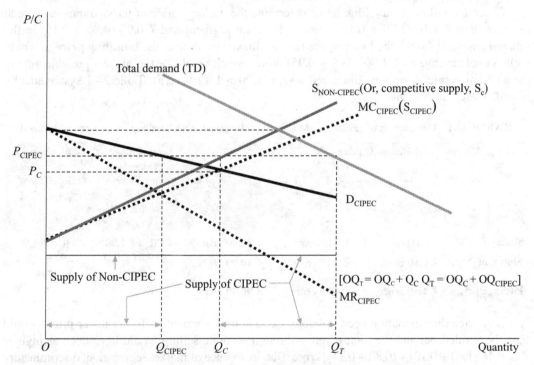

FIGURE 24.11 Only a marginal price hike was realized by the CIPEC-cartel due to its weak monopoly power (high elasticity of demand and supply). Quantity produced and supplied by CIPEC-cartel is OQ_{CIPEC} and at a price fixed is P_{CIPEC}. Competitive price P_C is determined at the intersection of MC_{CIPEC} (supply curve of CIPEC) and D_{CIPEC}. Clearly, $P_C < P_{CIPEC}$. Note that $Q_C = Q_T$, and OQ_C is competitive supply or supply of non-CIPEC firms while OQ_T is the demand at P_{CIPEC}. Thus, $OQ_T = OQ_C + OQ_{CIPEC}$.

24.4 BUNDLING

Selling two or more products as a package at a single price is known as **bundling**. The practice is common to attaching unpopular products with a highly popular one and pricing the package at a level that maximizes total revenue. To understand the mechanism, suppose a flop movie is bundled with an all time hit such as *Sholay*. Suppose, further that the market is split into two segments—the rural segment and the urban segment. In the rural segment, the flop movie fetches ₹ 10 lakh for its screening rights while *Sholay* fetches as high as ₹ 1.00 crore. In the urban segment, on the other hand, the flop movie fetches ₹ 15 lac while *Sholay* fetches ₹ 80 lakh. If *Sholay* is marketed at ₹ 1.00 crore, the urban segment offering ₹ 80 lakh gets excluded and the flop movie if marketed at ₹ 15 lakh, the rural market offering ₹ 10 lakh gets excluded. The total revenue realized is ₹ 1.15 (1.00 + 0.15) crore from separate selling. If each movie is sold at its lower price to avoid exclusion of any market segment, the total revenue realized would be ₹ 1.80 (0.80 × 2 + 0.10 × 2) crore from separate selling.

To see the utility of bundling, let us determine the package price of the two movies in each segment. It is ₹ 1.10 (1.00 + 0.10) crore in the rural segment and ₹ 0.95 (0.80 + 0.15) in the urban segment. If ₹ 0.95, the lower of the two, is allowed to serve as the **bundling price**, it would yield a total revenue of ₹ 1.90 (0.95 + 0.95) crore, which would be the highest possible among the alternative pricing options discussed above (1.90 > 1.80 > 1.15). Table 24.1 systematically records these calculations.

TABLE 24.1 Comparison of revenue from separate selling and from bundling under demand reversal

Market Product prices	Maximum price offer in		Price to be charged to avoid exclusion of the segments	Total revenue through separate selling at prices that avoid exclusion of the segments	Total revenue through bundling under demand reversal
	Rural segment	Urban segment			
Sholay	₹ 1.00 crore	₹ 0.80 crore	₹ 80.00 crore	TR = ₹ 1.80 (0.90 + 0.90) crore	TR = ₹ 1.90 (0.95 + 0.95) crore
Flop film	₹ 0.10 crore	₹ 0.15 crore	₹ 10.00 crore		
Package prices	₹ 1.10 crore	₹ 0.95 crore	₹ 90.00 crore		

Had price discrimination been possible, exclusion of segments offering lower prices would have been ruled out and the total revenue through separate selling would have been as high as ₹ 2.05 [= (1.00 + 0.10) + (0.80 + 0.15)] crore. But, in absence of market segregation, discriminatory policies can't be practiced. A single price for each movie is the only recourse. The price has to be the lower one of the two if the possibility of exclusion of the other segment is to be avoided. This would lead to a revenue of ₹ 1.80 crore from the two segments. Note that bundling generates a higher revenue only when demands for the two movies are negatively correlated, that is, when the segment offering a higher price for *Sholay* offers a lower price for the flop movie and the segment offering a lower price for *Sholay* offers a higher price for the flop movie. In the event of positively correlated demands for the two movies, that is, the segment offering a higher price for *Sholay* offers a higher price for the flop movie and the segment offering a lower price for

Sholay offers a lower price for the flop movie, bundling fails to serve its purpose as shown in Table 24.2. See how positively correlated demands for the two movies in the two segments make bundling ineffective. If the rural segment offers the higher of the two prices for both the movies while the urban segment offers the lower of the two prices for both, the package prices for the two segments would work out as ₹ 1.15 for the rural segment and ₹ 0.90 for the urban segment. Charging the lower one of the two package prices would yield only ₹ 1.80 crore, which is the same as that realized from separate selling at the lower of the two prices resorted with a view to avoid exclusion of market segments.

If the higher of the two prices be charged, the segments offering lower prices get excluded and the total revenue generated is only ₹ 1.15 (= 1.00 + 0.15). That explains why *bundling fails when demands are positively correlated, i.e., in absence of demand reversal.*

TABLE 24.2 Comparison of revenue from separate selling and from bundling under absence of demand reversal

Product prices	Market — Maximum price offer in		Price to be charged to avoid exclusion of the segments	Total revenue through separate selling at prices that avoid exclusion of the segments	Total revenue through bundling under demand reversal
	Rural segment	Urban segment			
Sholay	₹ 1.00 crore	₹ 0.80 crore	₹ 80.00 crore	TR = ₹ 1.80 (0.90 + 0.90) crore	TR = ₹ 1.80 (0.90 + 0.90) crore
Flop film	₹ 0.15 crore	₹ 0.10 crore	₹ 10.00 crore		
Package prices	₹ 1.15 crore	₹ 0.90 crore	₹ 90.00 crore		

To study effects of bundling when market segments are large or when a large number of consumers with distinct preferences make buying decisions, consider a firm selling two products—Product 1 and Product 2 at prices P_1 and P_2, respectively. Let consumer preferences be given in terms of their reservation prices r_1 and r_2. Reservation price is the maximum price a consumer is willing to pay for a product. It expresses consumer's preference for a product.

24.4.1 Bundling—Pure and Mixed

Under **pure bundling**, products are sold only as a package. If the product prices are $P_1 = 5.20$ and $P_2 = 4.00$, but the products are bundled at a package price of 8.00 ($P_B = 4 + 4 = 80$), consumer E (with the reservation price of 2.00 for product 1 and that of 4.00 for product 2) and consumer H (with the reservation price of 4.00 for product 1 and that of 2.00 for product 2) get excluded under pure bundling (Figure 24.12). Revenue generated by pure bundling is ₹ 56.00 (= 8 × 7). But, if the firm adopts **mixed bundling**, it can raise its revenue even further by adding ₹ 4.00 through selling product 2 to consumer E for a price of 4.00 (E's reservation price for product 2) to its total revenue of 56 generated by pure bundling. The total revenue realized would then be ₹ 60 (= 56 + 4). The term **mixed bundling** is used for the practice of selling two or more products as a package as well as individually. Mixed bundling may, thus, prove more beneficial than pure bundling.

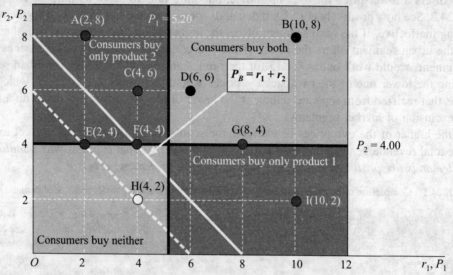

FIGURE 24.12 Reservation prices of 9 consumers for products 1 and 2 are graphed through dot-plot. The horizontal axis measures consumers reservation price (r_1) for product 1 while the vertical axis measures their reservation price (r_2) for product 2. Prices of the two products, P_1 and P_2, as fixed by the firm, are also shown on the x- and y-axes. Let $P_1 = ₹\,5.20$ and $P_2 = ₹\,4.00$. Consumers with the reservation prices less than the prices fixed by the firm can not buy the products. Consumer-preferences depicted by white dots are never bought by the consumers as their reservation prices are lower than the prices fixed by the firm; those with gray dots, are partially bought as the reservation price of only one of the two products is higher than or equal to the price fixed by the firm; and consumer preferences with black dots, are ones that are always bought by the consumers as their reservation prices are higher than or equal to the product-prices fixed by the firm. The upper-right and the lower-left quadrants (in gray setting) depict respectively the preferences that are always bought and never bought by the consumers for reasons explained while the upper-left and lower-right quadrants (in black setting) depict respectively the preferences partially bought, that is, only one of the two products is bought. Clearly, preferences marked with white dots represent consumers totally excluded and those marked with gray dots represent consumers partially excluded. Total revenue accruing to the firm without bundling can be verified as ₹ 48.80 [= 4(A) + 4(C) + 4(E) + 4(F) + 5.20(I) + 5.20(G) + 4(G) + 5.20(D) + 4(D) + 5.20(B) + 4(B)]. If the products were bundled with a package price of ₹ 8.00, only two consumers (E and H) get excluded with the result that the total revenue rises to ₹ 56.00 (= 7 × 8). Bundling (pure) thus proves beneficial even when there are multiple segments. Bundling price P_B is depicted by the price line sloping downwards in white. It is $P_B = r_1 + r_2$, where $r_1 = 4.00$ and $r_2 = 4.00$. Mixed bundling is even more beneficial. For instance, the firm can raise its revenue by ₹ 4.00 if it resorts to selling product 2 for ₹ 4.00 to consumer E.

Depending on production costs, it may be possible to raise the total revenue through a lower bundling price, as shown in Figure 24.12 by means of the broken price line in white. For instance, suppose it is possible to lower the bundling price from ₹ 8.00 to ₹ 6.00 (the dotted line in white) so that none of the consumers is excluded. The question that still remains to answer is whether such bundling leads to higher revenue or not. In the present case, the total revenue works out at ₹ 54.00 under the lower bundling price. It is higher than that realized (₹ 48.80) without bundling. Pure bundling of the products at a price of ₹ 8.00, yields ₹ 56.00 while mixed bundling yields ₹ 60.00. A simple comparison of revenues realized under various alternatives shows (Table 24.3) that mixed bundling proves better than pure bundling and pure bundling proves better than separate selling (without bundling). The analysis is based on the assumption that production costs are identical in all the alternatives.

TABLE 24.3 Comparison of revenues realized from separate selling, pure bundling and mixed bundling (under identical costs)

Options	Total revenue (₹)
Separate selling	48.80
Pure bundling (P_B = ₹ 8.00)	56.00
Pure bundling (P_B = ₹ 6.00)	54.00
Mixed bundling	**60.00**

If marginal cost of each product be ₹ 2.00 when less than 9 units of each be produced and zero when 9 units of each be produced, the basis of comparison shifts from the magnitude of revenue realized to the profit generated. Under separate selling, total cost is ₹ 22.00 [2 × 7 (for 7 units of product 2) + 2 × 4 (for 4 units of product 1)]; under pure bundling with a bundling price of ₹ 8.00, it is ₹ 28.00 (2 × 7 + 2 × 7), under pure bundling with a bundling price of ₹ 6.00, it is ₹ 0.00 (0 × 9 + 0 × 9) and under mixed bundling, it is ₹ 30 [2 × (7 × 2) + 2]. Profits generated in the respective alternatives work out as ₹ 26.80 (48.80 – 22.00), ₹ 28.00 (56.00 – 28.00), ₹ 54.00 (54.00 – 0.00) and ₹ 30.00 (60 – 30). Under these circumstances, pure bundling with a bundling price of ₹ 6.00 is the best option and mixed bundling, the next best (Table 24.4).

TABLE 24.4 Comparison of revenues realized from separate selling, pure bundling and mixed bundling (under non-identical costs)

Option	Total revenue (₹)	Total cost (₹)	Net revenue (Profit) (₹)
Separate selling	48.80	22.00	26.80
Pure bundling (P_B = ₹ 8.00)	56.00	28.00	28.00
Pure bundling (P_B = ₹ 6.00)	**54.00**	**0.00**	**54.00**
Mixed bundling	60.00	30.00	30.00

Evidently, pure bundling under the circumstances is the best option and mixed bundling, the next best. Net revenue (profit) replaces the revenue criterion when production costs vary with the size of outputs produced. Production of larger quantity often leads to scale economies. Recall that MC curve is horizontal at its bottom only when the firm possesses an inbuilt reserve capacity and is operating in it. Prior to reaching this capacity, the MC curve falls with output, and, after the reserve capacity is exhausted, the MC curve rises with output.

Different pricing policies in practice pose a common feature of real business. They cater to varying objectives of business firms and public sector undertakings.

24.5 TWO-PART TARIFF PRICING

Two-part tariff is a type of discriminatory practice providing a means to cut deeper into the consumer's surpluses. It comprises an initial or upfront payment by a consumer to acquire the right to buy a product followed by an additional fee or charge levied per unit of product the consumer wishes to consume. As an example, we can cite an initial entry fee charged to an amusement park followed by a charge of certain amount for each ride the visitor wished to enjoy. It remains for the owner of the amusement park to decide whether he must charge a higher entry fee followed by a lower charge per ride or to charge a lower entry fee followed by a higher charge per ride. Other examples are provided by several entertainment or sport clubs which charge an annual membership fee from each member and an additional charge for each use of a table, court or a round of golf. These days, even cyber cafes resort to two part tariff. They make a monthly charge for membership which allows the members to use internet free for first fifteen minutes. Thereafter, if the members so wish, they can extend their use of the facility by paying ₹ 10 per additional time-slot not exceeding fifteen minutes each. Even photographic laboratories make a fixed charge for processing the reels followed by an additional charge per photograph desired by the customer to be printed. For the sake of convenience, let call the initial charge as the entry fee and the subsequent charge per use of the facility as the usage fee.

Let us examine two cases—(a) the case of a single consumer, and (b) the case of two consumers with parallel demand curves. In the first case, price per usage is set equal to the marginal cost and the entry fee is set equal to the area below the demand curve that lies above the price set (the consumer surplus). The total charge comprises the sum of entry fee E and the cost U (Figure 24.13).

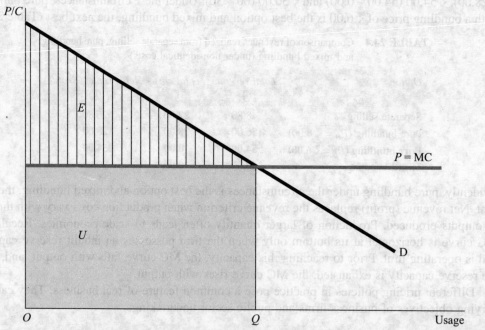

Figure 24.13 Two-part tariff with one consumer: The consumer with demand D uses OQ units of the facility for each of which he/she pays at the rate of $P = MC$. The total usage cost is U. The entry fee E is the area above the price P that lies below the demand curve D. The total revenue raised by the provider is equal to $R = E + U$. The resulting profit is equal to E.

In case of two identical consumers, one with smaller demand and the other with larger one, the usage fee set is higher than the marginal cost. This is equal to the price corresponding to the smaller demand for use of q units so that the provider may quote a uniform usage fee for both the consumers. In the same way, entry fee too is set equal to the consumer's surplus of the smaller consumer so that it is same for both of them (Figure 24.14).

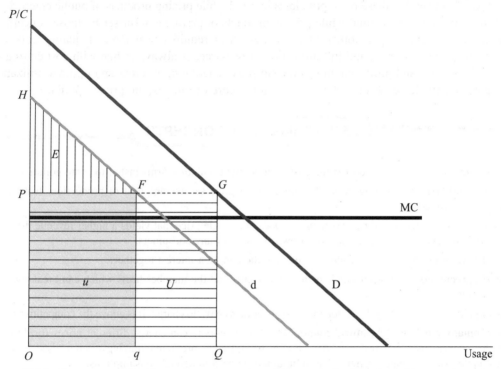

Figure 24.14 Two-part tariff with two consumers: An uniform entry fee E is charged from each, raising $2E$ worth of revenue from both by way of entry fee. Price charged per usage is then higher than the MC. Revenue raised from smaller user is $E + u$ and that from the larger user is $E + U$. The total revenue from both is $2E + u + U$ and the profit earned is $2E + (P - MC)(q + Q)$. Here, $u = OqFP$ and $U = OQGP$.

The criterion may be extended to many consumers case as well provided their demands are given. The provider has to ensure uniformity of both types of tariffs.

24.6 SUGGESTIONS OF PROMINENT STUDY GROUPS ON PRICING POLICIES

A UN study lays down several guidelines to be observed while formulating pricing policies of public enterprises. For instance, product price must cover operating costs, replacement cost of assets and contribution to the costs of the public services. A pricing policy must lead to generation of sufficient surpluses. The surpluses must be maximum in respect of amenity goods and minimum in respect of consumer goods. Detailed financial analysis should be conducted of the claims of the public enterprises on prices imposed in the line of the national goals. Financial targets must be set for each sector. Effects of proposed price changes must be analyzed in advance.

According to Administrative Reform Committee (ARC), pricing must serve three principal objectives—(1) the objective of rational resource allocation, (2) the objective of optimal utilization of inputs and (3) the objective of accelerating economic growth. In respect of public utilities and services, emphasis should be on output rather than on return on investment.

Apart from bearing these basic principles in mind while pricing products of public enterprises, they must also be kept in mind while pricing products of private enterprises by those concerned. For instance, social responsibility of a business firm requires provision of quality goods at reasonable prices. Efficient and full utilization of resources is always in line with cost cutting so essential for sales and profit maximization. Surplus generation, efficient and optimal utilization of inputs and stable economic growth-all form the core of most of the pricing policies.

KEY TERMS AND CONCEPTS

Abatement cost Abatement cost is the cost of equipment polluting firms install to abate pollution.

Average cost pricing Setting price at a point where price set average cost of production. It recovers total cost of production.

Bundling A practice of selling two or more goods at a single price that yields a higher revenue than that realized from separate selling. It must disallow exclusion of any consumers.

Cartel An informal group of producers pursuing the common interest together.

Cartel agreements Being informal, such cartels can't bind the member firms which can break-away at will from it.

Cartel pricing Price set by the cartel which member firms have to charge. It is above the competitive price.

Discriminatory pricing by natural monopoly The monopoly can charge different prices for different uses to recover costs. For instance, AC pricing, MC pricing, profit maximizing pricing, used based or consumption slab pricing, or pricing based on domestic or commercial consumptions.

Dominant pricing The low-cost firm in a group of firms dictates the price which being lowest is readily accepted by the rest. If they don't, they get ousted because of superior substitutes sold by the low-cost firm at lower price.

Downstream division The division of an integrated firm that uses intermediate products produced by its upstream division to process/assemble the final product.

Emission fee It is the pollution tax paid to government per unit of pollution emitted in production.

Entry fee Booking amount or amount required for right to buy.

Entry limiting pricing Price set below the point where price-elasticity of demand is unitary. The purpose is to restrict entry of new firms that can't survive at the price and seek exit or refuse to join in.

Export price parity pricing Export price set equal to or less than the domestic price to restrict exports.

Import price parity pricing Import price set equal to or above the domestic price to restrict imports.

Marginal cost pricing Setting price at a point where price equals marginal cost of production.

Market penetration pricing A price set to gain a foothold in the market when other sellers have captured it. It is usually a low price or a price with free gifts that may be withdrawn once the market gets penetrated.

Market signalling pricing A price that signal product quality. Normally, a higher price is taken as an indicator of higher quality and lower one, a lower quality from the same firm or from different ones. However, it may not always be the case necessarily.

Market skimming pricing Price setting by a pioneering firm to skim the cream of the market. The first movers do it before followers will appear with lower prices.

Mark-up pricing Price set after adding profit to the cost of production.

Mixed bundling The term is used for the practice of selling two or more products as a package as well as individually a higher revenue than that earned through pure bundling.

Natural monopoly A state monopoly or one regulated by state to which fresh entry is not possible at a price set by the natural monopoly. It can resort to discriminatory pricing, such as average cost pricing, marginal cost pricing and profit maximizing pricing. A natural monopoly alone can cater to the market demand efficiently.

Pricing with pollution Pricing with pollution cost refers to a pricing policy which makes consumers to pay for pollution caused by production of a product. Legislation these days requires firms causing pollution either to install equipment to abate pollution or to spend on relief measures to compensate sufferers or to pay emission fee or pollution tax to government at a fixed rate per unit of emission.

Profit maximizing pricing Price that maximizes profits, that is at the point on AR curve correspond to the point where MC cuts MR.

Pure bundling When two or more products are sold as a package at a price to raise a higher revenue. Pure bundling can exclude some consumers, but bundling can't.

Reasons of failure of CIPEC It was more elastic demand for the product.

Reasons of success of OPEC The main reason of success of OPEC—cartel was inelastic demand for its product.

Sales maximizing pricing A policy of pricing that maximizes sales rather than profits. The price set under it is less than the profit maximizing price.

Two-part tariff Two-part tariff is a type of discriminatory practice providing a means to cut deeper into the consumer's surpluses. It comprises an initial or upfront payment by a consumer to acquire the right to buy a product followed by an additional fee or charge levied per unit of product the consumer wishes to consume.

Upstream division The division of an integrated firm that supplies intermediate products to its downstream division. Components/parts are produced by the upstream division of a firm to be used by another division of the firm called the downstream division.

EXERCISES

A. Short Answer Questions

Define the following (1 through 36):

1. Market signalling price
2. Mark-up price
3. Downstream division
4. Upstream division
5. Cartel
6. Cartel agreements

7. Dominant pricing
8. Market skimming price
9. Entry limiting price
10. Market penetrating price
11. Sales maximizing price
12. Profit maximizing price
13. Natural monopoly
14. Discriminatory price
15. Average cost price
16. Marginal cost price
17. Inter-temporal price
18. Peak-load price
19. Entry fee
20. Abatement cost
21. Pricing with pollution
22. Emission price
23. Import-parity price
24. Bundling
25. Bundling price
26. Pure bundling
27. Mixed bundling
28. Two-part tariff
29. Pricing under pure bundling
30. Pricing under mixed bundling
31. Pricing under two-part tariff
32. Transfer pricing
33. Cost plus pricing
34. Retention pricing
35. Import price parity pricing
36. Export price parity pricing
37. What is the main objective of pricing with pollution?
38. What is the main objective of bundling?
39. What is the objective of two-part tariff?
40. What is the main objective of cartel pricing?
41. Why did OPEC cartel succeed in its objective?
42. Why did CIPEC cartel failed in its objective?
43. What is the objective of mixed bundling?
44. What is the main objective of pure bundling?
45. Why do firms follow transfer pricing?
46. Why is cartel so unstable?
47. What is the objective of retention pricing?
48. What is the main objective of import price parity pricing?
49. What is the main objective of export price parity pricing?
50. What is the main objective of price discrimination by natural monopoly?

B. Long Answer Questions

Distinguish between (51 through 61):

51. Formal and informal cartels
52. Pure bundling and mixed bundling
53. Average cost pricing and marginal cost pricing
54. Mark-up pricing and average cost pricing
55. Emission fee and entry fee
56. Pricing with and without pollution
57. Pricing with and without exclusion of market segments
58. Import price pairity pricing and export price parity pricing
59. Inter-temporal pricing and peakload pricing
60. OPEC cartel price and CIPEC cartel price
61. Mark-up pricing and marginal cost pricing.
62. Explain with examples the purpose and methodology of import-price parity pricing.
63. Explain with examples the purpose and methodology of export-price parity pricing.
64. Explain pricing policy with or without pollution with the help of examples.
65. Explain pricing method and its purpose under pure bundling with examples.
66. Explain pricing method and its purpose under mixed bundling with examples.
67. Explain survival of a natural monopoly with examples.
68. Show how a monopoly can afford to charge a higher price in less elastic and a lower one in more elastic market with examples.
69. Explain the notion of two-part tariff pricing and its purpose with examples.

C. Essay Type Questions

70. (a) The downstream division of a car company assembles cars with the help of components supplied by its upstream division. With the help of neat sketches show how the profit maximizing price, number of cars transacted and volume of profit if:
    (i) The upstream division is the only source of components.
    (ii) A competitive outside market exists for the components which sells them to the assembling unit at a lower price.
    (b) Suppose the company faces demand schedule,
    $$P = 100,000 - Q,$$
    the assembling cost of Q cars,
    $$TC_A = 34,000\ Q,$$
    and, the total cost of components for Q cars,
    $$TC_E = 10 Q_E^2$$
    Here, Q is the number of cars demanded at price P and Q_E is the number of sets of components for assembling 1 car, TC_A is the total assembling cost of Q cars and TC_E, the number of sets of components.

    Calculate:
    (i) Profit maximizing price of a car,
    (ii) Profit maximizing number of cars, and
    (iii) Volume of profit earned by the company.

(c) Recalculate the three when an outside competitive market for sets of components exists to supply the components at a price of ₹ 5800.

[Ans.: (b). $P = ₹\ 97,000$; $Q = 3,000$; $\pi = 99,000,000$; (c). $P = ₹\ 96,000$; $Q = 4,000$; $\pi = 88,000,000$]

71. A special vehicle is manufactured by an automobile company for secure transportation of VIPs. The company has three divisions—two to manufacture its components named engines and wheels called, respectively as 'Engine Division' and 'Wheel Division' and the third, to assemble them into the finished product. (The first two may be treated as its upstream divisions while the third, as its downstream division). The relevant estimated functions of demand and costs are as given below:

$$P = 520 - Q, \quad \text{(Demand function of vehicles)}$$
$$TC_A = 120Q + Q^2, \quad \text{(Assembling cost function)}$$
$$TC_E = 40Q_E + 2Q_E^2, \quad \text{(Cost function of engines)}$$
$$TC_W = (22/225)\ Q_W^2, \quad \text{(Cost function of wheels)}$$

where, $P \equiv$ Vehicle price in rupees thousand; $Q \equiv$ Quantity of vehicles demanded; $TC_A \equiv$ Total cost of assembling Q vehicles in rupees thousand; $TC_E \equiv$ Total cost of Q_E engines in rupees thousand, and $TC_W \equiv$ Total cost of Q_W wheels in rupees thousand.

Given that one vehicle requires one set of engine and five wheels, determine:
 (a) The profit maximizing number of vehicles and the price of a vehicle,
 (b) Profits earned by each of the three divisions,
 (c) Transfer prices of an engine and a wheel.
   (i) when each division maximizes its profit.
   (ii) profit maximizing number of vehicles produced, engines and wheels bought by the assembling unit if the assembling unit alone maximizes its profit. [Refer to Eqs. (24.2) and (24.3)].

[Ans.: (a) $Q = 45$ vehicles; $P = 475$ thousand rupees; (b) Profit of downstream div. = 18,225 thousand rupees; Profit of engine div. = 4050 thousand rupees; Profit of wheel div. = 4950 thousand rupees;
(c) (i) $P_E = 220$ thousand rupees; $P_W = 44$ thousand rupees;
   (ii) $Q = 810/29$; $Q_E = 810/29$; $Q_W = 4050/29$.]

72. Write comprehensive notes on any two:
 (a) Bundling
 (b) Two-part tariff
 (c) Transfer pricing

Statistical Tables

LOGARITHMS

	0	1	2	3	4	5	6	7	8	9	Mean Differences								
											1	2	3	4	5	6	7	8	9
10	00000	00432	00860	01284	01703						42	85	127	170	212	254	297	339	381
						02119	02531	02938	03342	03743	40	81	121	162	202	242	283	323	364
11	04139	04532	04922	05308	05690						37	77	116	154	193	232	270	309	348
						06070	06446	06819	07188	07555	37	74	111	148	185	222	259	296	333
12	07918	08279	08636	08991	09342						36	71	106	142	177	213	248	284	319
						09691	10037	10380	10721	11059	34	68	102	136	170	204	238	272	307
13	11394	11727	12057	12385	12710						33	66	98	131	164	197	229	262	295
						13033	13354	13672	13988	14301	32	63	95	126	158	190	221	253	284
14	14613	14922	15229	15534	15836						30	61	91	122	152	183	213	244	274
						16137	16435	16732	17026	17319	29	59	88	118	147	177	206	236	265
15	17609	17898	18184	18469	18752						28	57	85	114	142	171	199	228	256
						19033	19312	19590	19866	20140	28	55	83	110	138	165	193	221	248
16	20412	20683	20951	21219	21484						27	53	80	107	134	160	187	214	240
						21748	22011	22272	22531	22789	26	52	78	104	130	156	182	208	233
17	23045	23300	23553	23805	24055						26	50	76	101	126	151	176	201	227
						24304	24551	24797	25042	25285	25	49	73	98	122	147	171	196	220
18	25527	25768	26007	26245	26482						24	48	71	95	119	143	167	190	214
						26717	26951	27184	27416	27646	23	46	69	93	116	139	162	185	208
19	27875	28103	28330	28556	28780						23	45	68	90	113	135	158	180	203
						29003	29226	29447	29667	29885	22	44	66	88	110	132	154	176	198
20	30103	30320	30535	30750	30963	31175	31387	31597	31806	32015	21	43	64	85	106	127	148	170	190
21	32222	32428	32634	32838	33041	33244	33445	33646	33846	34044	20	41	61	81	101	121	141	162	182
22	34242	34439	34635	34830	35025	35218	35411	35603	35793	35984	20	39	58	77	97	116	135	154	174
23	36173	36361	36549	36736	36922	37107	37291	37475	37658	37840	19	37	56	74	93	111	130	148	167
24	38021	38202	38382	38561	38739	38917	39094	39270	39445	39620	18	35	53	71	89	106	124	142	159
25	39794	39967	40140	40312	40483	40654	40824	40993	41162	41330	17	34	51	68	85	102	119	136	153
26	41497	41664	41830	41996	42160	42325	42488	42651	42813	42975	16	33	49	66	82	98	115	131	148
27	43136	43297	43457	43616	43775	43933	44091	44248	44404	44560	16	32	47	63	79	95	111	126	142
28	44716	44871	45025	45179	45332	45484	45637	45788	45939	46090	15	30	46	61	76	91	107	122	137
29	46240	46389	46538	46687	46835	46982	47129	47276	47422	47567	15	29	44	59	74	88	103	118	132
30	47712	47857	48001	48144	48287	48430	48572	48714	48855	48996	14	29	43	57	72	86	100	114	129
31	49136	49276	49415	49554	49693	49831	49969	50106	50243	50379	14	28	41	55	69	83	97	110	124
32	50515	50650	50786	50920	51054	51188	51322	51455	51587	51720	13	27	40	54	67	80	94	107	121
33	51851	51983	52114	52244	52375	52504	52634	52763	52892	53020	13	26	39	52	65	78	91	104	117
34	53148	53275	53403	53529	53656	53782	53908	54033	54158	54283	13	25	38	50	63	76	88	101	113
35	54407	54531	54654	54777	54900	55023	55145	55267	55388	55509	12	24	37	49	61	73	85	98	110
36	55630	55751	55871	55991	56110	56229	56348	56467	56585	56703	12	24	36	48	60	71	83	95	107
37	56820	56937	57054	57171	57287	57403	57519	57634	57749	57864	12	23	35	46	58	70	81	93	104
38	57978	58092	58206	58320	58433	58546	58659	58771	58883	58995	11	23	34	45	57	68	79	90	102
39	59106	59218	59329	59439	59550	59660	59770	59879	59988	60097	11	22	33	44	55	66	77	88	99
40	60206	60314	60423	60531	60638	60746	60853	60959	61066	61172	11	21	32	43	54	64	75	86	97
41	61278	61384	61490	61595	61700	61805	61909	62014	62118	62221	10	21	31	42	53	63	74	84	95
42	62325	62428	62531	62634	62737	62839	62941	63043	63144	63246	10	20	31	41	51	61	71	82	92
43	63347	63448	63548	63649	63749	63849	63949	64048	64147	64246	10	20	30	40	50	60	70	80	90
44	64345	64444	64542	64640	64738	64836	64933	65031	65128	65225	10	20	29	39	49	59	68	78	88
45	65321	65418	65514	65610	65706	65801	65896	65992	66087	66181	10	19	29	38	48	57	67	76	86
46	66276	66370	66464	66558	66652	66745	66839	66932	67025	67117	9	19	28	37	47	56	65	74	84
47	67210	67302	67394	67486	67578	67669	67761	67852	67943	68034	9	18	27	36	46	55	64	73	82
48	68124	68215	68305	68395	68485	68574	68664	68753	68842	68931	9	18	27	36	45	53	63	72	81
49	69020	69108	69197	69285	69373	69461	69548	69636	69723	69810	9	18	26	35	44	53	62	70	79

(Contd.)

Logarithms (Contd.)

	0	1	2	3	4	5	6	7	8	9	Mean Differences								
											1	2	3	4	5	6	7	8	9
50	69897	69984	70070	70157	70243	70329	70415	70501	70586	70672	9	17	26	34	43	52	60	69	77
51	70757	70842	70927	71012	71096	71181	71265	71349	71433	71517	8	17	25	34	42	50	59	67	76
52	71600	71684	71767	71850	71933	72016	72099	72181	72263	72346	8	17	25	33	42	50	58	66	75
53	72428	72509	72591	72673	72754	72835	72916	72997	73078	73159	8	16	24	32	41	49	57	65	73
54	73239	73320	73400	73480	73560	73640	73719	73799	73878	73957	8	16	24	32	40	48	56	64	72
55	74036	74115	74194	74273	74351	74429	74507	74586	74663	74741	8	16	23	31	39	47	55	63	70
56	74819	74896	74974	75051	75128	75205	75282	75358	75435	75511	8	15	23	31	39	46	54	62	69
57	75587	75664	75740	75815	75891	75967	76042	76118	76193	76268	8	15	23	30	38	45	53	60	68
58	76343	76418	76492	76567	76641	76716	76790	76864	76938	77012	7	15	22	30	37	44	52	59	67
59	77085	77159	77232	77305	77379	77452	77525	77597	77670	77743	7	15	22	29	37	44	51	58	66
60	77815	77887	77960	78032	78104	78176	78247	78319	78390	78462	7	14	22	29	36	43	50	58	65
61	78533	78604	78675	78746	78817	78888	78958	79029	79099	79169	7	14	21	28	36	43	50	57	64
62	79239	79309	79379	79449	79518	79588	79657	79727	79796	79565	7	14	21	28	35	41	48	55	62
63	79934	80003	80072	80140	80209	80277	80346	80414	80482	80550	7	14	20	27	34	41	48	54	61
64	80618	80686	80754	80821	80889	80956	81023	81090	81158	81224	7	13	20	27	34	40	47	54	60
65	81291	81358	81425	81491	81558	81624	81690	81757	81823	81889	7	13	20	26	33	40	46	53	59
66	81954	82020	82086	82151	82217	82282	82347	82413	82478	82543	7	13	20	26	33	39	46	52	59
67	82607	82672	82737	82802	82866	82930	82995	83059	83123	83187	6	13	19	26	32	38	45	51	58
68	83251	83315	83378	83442	83506	83569	83632	83696	83759	83822	6	13	19	25	32	38	44	50	57
69	83885	83948	84011	84073	84136	84198	84261	84323	84386	84448	6	12	19	25	31	37	43	50	56
70	84510	84572	84634	84696	84757	84819	84880	84942	85003	85065	6	12	19	25	31	37	43	50	56
71	85126	85187	85248	85309	85370	85431	85491	85552	85612	85673	6	12	18	24	31	37	43	49	55
72	85733	85794	85854	85914	85974	86034	86094	86153	86213	86273	6	12	18	24	30	36	42	48	54
73	86332	86392	86451	86510	86570	86629	86688	86747	86806	86864	6	12	18	24	30	35	41	47	53
74	86923	86982	87040	87099	87157	87216	87274	87332	87390	87448	6	12	17	23	29	35	41	46	52
75	87506	87564	87622	87679	87737	87795	87852	87910	87967	88024	6	12	17	23	29	35	41	46	52
76	88081	88138	88195	88252	88309	88366	88423	88480	88536	88593	6	11	17	23	29	34	40	46	51
77	88649	88705	88762	88818	88874	88930	88986	89042	89098	89154	6	11	17	22	28	34	39	45	50
78	89209	89265	89321	89376	89432	89487	89542	89597	89653	89708	6	11	17	22	28	33	39	44	50
79	89763	89818	89873	89927	89982	90037	90091	90146	90200	90255	6	11	17	22	28	33	39	44	50
80	90309	90363	90417	90472	90526	90580	90634	90687	90741	90795	5	11	16	22	27	32	38	43	49
81	90848	90902	90956	91009	91062	91116	91169	91222	91275	91328	5	11	16	21	27	32	37	42	48
82	91381	91434	91487	91540	91593	91645	91698	91751	91803	91855	5	11	16	21	27	32	37	42	48
83	91908	91960	92012	97064	92117	92169	92221	92273	92324	92376	5	10	16	21	26	31	36	42	47
84	92428	92480	92531	92583	92634	92686	92737	92788	92840	92891	5	10	15	20	26	31	36	41	46
85	92942	92993	93044	93095	93146	93197	93247	93298	93349	93399	5	10	15	20	26	31	36	41	46
86	93450	93500	93551	93601	93651	93702	93752	93802	93852	93902	5	10	15	20	25	30	35	40	45
87	93952	94002	94052	94101	94151	94201	94250	94300	94349	94399	5	10	15	20	25	30	35	40	45
88	94448	94498	94547	94596	94645	94694	94743	94792	94841	94890	5	10	15	20	25	29	34	39	44
89	94939	94988	95036	95085	95134	95182	95231	95279	95328	95376	5	10	15	19	24	29	34	39	44
90	95424	95472	95521	95569	95617	95665	95713	95761	95809	95856	5	10	14	19	24	29	34	38	43
91	95904	95952	95999	96047	96095	96142	96190	96237	96284	96332	5	9	14	19	24	28	33	38	42
92	96379	96426	96473	96520	96567	96614	96661	96708	96755	96802	5	9	14	19	24	28	33	38	42
93	96848	96895	96942	96988	97035	97081	97128	97174	97220	97267	5	9	14	18	23	28	32	38	42
94	97313	97359	97405	97451	97497	97543	97589	97635	97681	97727	5	9	14	18	23	28	32	37	42
95	97772	97818	97864	97909	97955	98000	98046	98091	98137	98182	5	9	14	18	23	27	32	36	41
96	98227	98272	98318	98363	98408	98453	98498	98543	98588	98632	5	9	14	18	23	27	32	36	41
97	98677	98722	98767	98811	98856	98900	98945	98989	99034	99078	4	9	13	18	22	27	31	36	40
98	99123	99167	99211	99255	99300	99344	99388	99432	99476	99520	4	9	13	18	22	26	31	35	40
99	99564	99607	99651	99695	99739	99782	99826	99870	99913	99957	4	9	13	17	22	26	31	35	39

ANTILOGARITHMS

	0	1	2	3	4	5	6	7	8	9	\multicolumn{9}{c}{Mean Differences}
											1	2	3	4	5	6	7	8	9
0.00	10000	10023	10046	10069	10093	10116	10139	10162	10186	10209	2	5	7	9	12	14	16	19	21
0.01	10233	10257	10280	10304	10328	10351	10375	10399	10423	10447	2	5	7	10	12	14	17	19	21
0.02	10471	10495	10520	10544	10568	10593	10617	10641	10666	10691	2	5	7	10	12	15	17	20	22
0.03	10715	10740	10765	10789	10814	10839	10864	10889	10914	10940	3	5	8	10	13	15	18	20	23
0.04	10965	10990	11015	11041	11066	11092	11117	11143	11169	11194	3	5	8	10	13	15	18	20	23
0.05	11220	11246	11272	11298	11324	11350	11376	11402	11429	11455	3	5	8	11	13	16	18	21	24
0.06	11482	11508	11535	11561	11588	11614	11641	11668	11695	11722	3	5	8	11	13	16	19	21	24
0.07	11749	11776	11803	11830	11858	11885	11912	11940	11967	11995	3	5	8	11	14	16	19	22	25
0.08	12023	12050	12078	12106	12134	12162	12190	12218	12246	12274	3	6	8	11	14	17	20	22	25
0.09	12303	12331	12359	12388	12417	12445	12474	12503	12531	12560	3	6	9	11	14	17	20	23	26
0.10	12589	12618	12647	12677	12706	12735	12764	12794	12823	12853	3	6	9	12	15	18	21	24	26
0.11	12882	12912	12942	12972	13002	13032	13062	13092	13122	13152	3	6	9	12	15	18	21	24	27
0.12	13183	13213	13243	13274	13305	13335	13366	13397	13428	13459	3	6	9	12	15	18	21	25	28
0.13	13490	13521	13552	13583	13614	13646	13677	13709	13740	13772	3	6	9	13	16	19	22	25	28
0.14	13804	13836	13868	13900	13932	13964	13996	14028	14060	14093	3	6	10	13	16	19	22	26	29
0.15	14125	14158	14191	14223	14256	14289	14322	14355	14388	14421	3	7	10	13	16	20	23	26	30
0.16	14454	14488	14521	14555	14588	14622	14655	14689	14723	14757	3	7	10	13	17	20	24	27	30
0.17	14791	14825	14859	14894	14928	14962	14997	15031	15066	15101	3	7	10	14	17	21	24	28	31
0.18	15136	15171	15205	15241	15276	15311	15346	15382	15417	15453	4	7	11	14	18	21	25	28	32
0.19	15488	15524	15560	15596	15631	15668	15704	15740	15776	15812	4	7	11	14	18	22	25	29	32
0.20	15849	15885	15922	15959	15996	16032	16069	16106	16144	16181	4	7	11	15	18	22	26	30	33
0.21	16218	16255	16293	16331	16368	16406	16444	16482	16520	16558	4	8	11	15	19	23	26	30	34
0.22	16596	16634	16672	16711	16749	16788	16827	16866	16904	16943	4	8	12	15	19	23	27	31	35
0.23	16982	17022	17061	17100	17140	17179	17219	17258	17298	17338	4	8	12	16	20	24	28	32	36
0.24	17378	17418	17458	17498	17539	17579	17620	17660	17701	17742	4	8	12	16	20	24	28	32	36
0.25	17783	17824	17865	17906	17947	17989	18030	18072	18113	18155	4	8	12	17	21	25	29	33	37
0.26	18197	18239	18281	18323	18365	18408	18450	18493	18535	18578	4	8	13	17	21	25	30	34	38
0.27	18621	18664	18707	18750	18793	18836	18880	18923	18967	19011	4	9	13	17	22	26	30	35	39
0.28	19055	19099	19143	19187	19231	19275	19320	19364	19409	19454	4	9	13	18	22	26	31	35	40
0.29	19498	19543	19588	19634	19679	19724	19770	19815	19861	19907	5	9	14	18	23	27	32	36	41
0.30	19953	19999	20045	20091	20137	20184	20230	20277	20324	20370	5	9	14	19	23	28	32	37	42
0.31	20417	20464	20512	20559	20606	20654	20701	20749	20797	20845	5	10	14	19	24	29	33	38	43
0.32	20893	20941	20989	21038	21086	21135	21184	21232	21281	21330	5	10	15	19	24	29	34	39	44
0.33	21380	21429	21478	21528	21577	21627	21677	21727	21777	21827	5	10	15	20	25	30	35	40	45
0.34	21878	21928	21979	22029	22080	22131	22182	22233	22284	22336	5	10	15	20	25	31	36	41	46
0.35	22387	22439	22491	22542	22594	22646	22699	22751	22803	22856	5	10	16	21	26	31	37	42	47
0.36	22909	22961	23014	23067	23121	23174	23227	23281	23336	23388	5	11	16	21	27	32	37	43	48
0.37	23442	23496	23550	23605	23659	23714	23768	23823	23878	23933	5	11	16	22	27	33	38	44	49
0.38	23988	24044	24099	24155	24210	24266	24322	24378	24434	24491	6	11	17	22	28	34	39	45	50
0.39	24547	24604	24660	24717	24774	24831	24889	24946	25003	25061	6	11	17	23	29	34	40	46	51
0.40	25119	25177	25236	25293	25351	25410	25468	25527	25586	25645	6	12	18	23	29	35	41	47	53
0.41	25704	25763	25823	25882	25942	26002	26062	26122	26182	26242	6	12	18	24	30	36	42	48	54
0.42	26303	26363	26424	26485	26546	26607	26669	26730	26792	26853	6	12	18	24	31	37	43	49	55
0.43	26915	26977	27040	27102	27164	27227	27290	27353	27416	27479	6	13	19	25	31	38	44	50	56
0.44	27542	27606	27669	27733	27797	27861	27925	27990	28054	28119	6	13	19	26	32	39	45	51	58
0.45	28184	28249	28314	28379	28445	28510	28576	28642	28708	28774	7	13	20	26	33	39	46	52	59
0.46	28840	28907	28973	29040	29107	29174	29242	29309	29376	29444	7	13	20	27	34	40	47	54	60
0.47	29512	29580	29648	29717	29785	29854	29923	29992	30061	30130	7	14	21	28	34	41	48	55	62
0.48	30200	30269	30339	30409	30479	30549	30620	30690	30761	30832	7	14	21	28	35	42	49	56	63
0.49	30903	30974	31046	31117	31189	31261	31333	31405	31477	31550	7	14	22	29	36	43	50	58	65

(Contd.)

Antilogarithms (Contd.)

	0	1	2	3	4	5	6	7	8	9	\multicolumn{9}{c}{Mean Differences}
											1	2	3	4	5	6	7	8	9
0.50	31623	31696	31769	31842	31916	31989	32063	32137	32211	32285	7	15	22	29	37	44	52	59	66
0.51	32359	32434	32509	32584	32659	32735	32809	32885	32961	33037	8	15	23	30	38	45	53	60	68
0.52	33113	33189	33266	33343	33420	33497	33574	33651	33729	33806	8	15	23	31	39	46	54	62	69
0.53	33884	33963	34041	34119	34198	34277	34356	34435	34514	34594	8	16	24	32	40	47	55	63	71
0.54	34674	34754	34834	34914	34995	35075	35156	35237	35318	35400	8	16	24	32	40	48	56	65	73
0.55	35481	35563	35645	35727	35810	35892	35975	36058	36141	36224	8	16	25	33	41	50	58	66	74
0.56	36308	36392	36475	36559	36644	36728	36813	36898	36983	37068	8	17	25	34	42	51	59	68	76
0.57	37154	37239	37325	37411	37497	37584	37670	37757	37844	37931	9	17	26	35	43	52	61	69	78
0.58	38019	38107	38194	38282	38371	38459	38548	38637	38726	38815	9	18	27	35	44	53	62	71	80
0.59	38905	38994	39084	39174	39264	39355	39446	39537	39628	39719	9	18	27	36	45	54	63	72	82
0.60	39811	39902	39994	40087	40179	40272	40365	40458	40551	40644	9	19	28	37	46	56	65	74	83
0.61	40738	40832	40926	41020	41115	41210	41305	41400	41495	41591	9	19	28	38	47	57	66	76	85
0.62	41687	41783	41879	41976	42073	42170	42267	42364	42462	42560	10	19	29	39	49	58	68	78	87
0.63	42658	42756	42855	42954	43053	43152	43251	43351	43451	43551	10	20	30	40	50	60	70	80	89
0.64	43652	43752	43853	43954	44055	44157	44259	44361	44463	44566	10	20	30	41	51	61	71	81	91
0.65	44668	44771	44875	44978	45082	45186	45290	45394	45499	45604	10	21	31	42	52	62	73	83	94
0.66	45709	45814	45920	46026	46132	46238	46345	46452	46559	46666	11	21	32	43	53	64	75	85	96
0.67	46774	46881	46989	47098	47206	47315	47424	47534	47643	47753	11	22	33	44	54	65	76	87	98
0.68	47863	47973	48084	48195	48306	48417	48529	48641	48753	48865	11	22	33	45	56	67	78	89	100
0.69	48978	49091	49204	49317	49431	49545	49659	49774	49888	50003	11	23	34	46	57	68	80	91	103
0.70	50119	50234	50350	50466	50582	50699	50816	50933	51050	51168	12	23	35	47	58	70	82	93	105
0.71	51286	51404	51523	51642	51761	51880	52000	52119	52240	52360	12	24	36	48	60	72	84	96	108
0.72	52481	52602	52723	52845	52966	53088	53211	53333	53456	53580	12	24	37	49	61	73	85	98	110
0.73	53703	53827	53951	54075	54200	54325	54450	54576	54702	54828	13	25	38	50	63	75	88	100	113
0.74	54954	55081	55208	55336	55463	55590	55719	55847	55976	56105	13	26	38	51	64	77	90	102	115
0.75	56234	56364	56494	56624	56754	56885	57016	57148	57280	57412	13	26	39	52	66	79	92	105	118
0.76	57544	57677	57810	57943	58076	58210	58345	58479	58614	58749	13	27	40	54	67	80	94	107	121
0.77	58884	59020	59156	59293	59429	59566	59704	59841	59979	60117	14	27	41	55	69	82	96	110	123
0.78	60256	60395	60534	60674	60814	60954	61094	61235	61376	61518	14	28	42	56	70	84	98	112	126
0.79	61659	61802	61944	62087	62230	62373	62517	62661	62806	62951	14	29	43	58	72	86	101	115	130
0.80	63096	63241	63387	63533	63680	63826	63973	64121	64269	64417	15	29	44	59	74	88	103	118	132
0.81	64565	64714	64863	65013	65163	65313	65464	65615	65766	65917	15	30	45	60	75	90	105	120	135
0.82	66069	66222	66374	66527	66681	66834	66988	67143	67298	67453	15	31	46	62	77	92	108	123	139
0.83	67608	67764	67920	68077	68234	68391	68549	68707	68865	69024	16	32	47	63	79	95	110	126	142
0.84	69183	69343	69503	69663	69823	69984	70146	70307	70469	70632	16	32	48	64	81	97	113	129	145
0.85	70795	70958	71121	71285	71450	71614	71779	71945	72111	72277	17	33	50	66	83	99	116	132	149
0.86	72444	72611	72778	72946	73114	73282	73451	73621	73790	73961	17	34	51	68	85	101	118	135	152
0.87	74131	74302	74473	74645	74817	74989	75162	75336	75509	75683	17	35	52	69	87	104	121	138	156
0.88	75858	76033	76208	76384	76560	76736	76913	77090	77268	77446	18	35	53	71	89	107	125	142	159
0.89	77625	77804	77983	78163	78343	78524	78705	78886	79068	79250	18	36	54	72	91	109	127	145	163
0.90	79433	79616	79799	79983	80168	80353	80538	80724	80910	81096	19	37	56	74	93	111	130	148	167
0.91	81283	81470	81658	81846	82035	82224	82414	82604	82794	82985	19	38	57	76	95	113	132	151	170
0.92	83176	83368	83560	83753	83946	84140	84333	84528	84723	84918	19	39	58	78	97	116	136	155	175
0.93	85114	85310	85507	85704	85901	86099	86298	86497	86696	86896	20	40	60	79	99	119	139	158	178
0.94	87096	87297	87498	87700	87902	88105	88308	88512	88716	88920	20	41	61	81	102	122	142	162	183
0.95	89125	89331	89536	89743	89950	90157	90365	90573	90782	90991	21	42	62	83	104	125	146	166	187
0.96	91201	91411	91622	91833	92045	92257	92470	92683	92897	93111	21	42	64	85	106	127	149	170	191
0.97	93325	93541	93756	93972	94189	94406	94624	94842	95060	95280	22	43	65	87	109	130	152	174	195
0.98	95499	95719	95940	96161	96383	96605	96828	97051	97275	97499	22	44	67	89	111	133	155	178	200
0.99	97724	97949	98175	98401	98628	98855	99083	99312	99541	99770	23	46	68	91	114	137	160	182	205

Standard Normal Cumulative Probabilities: p-value = $P(Z \leq z)$

The following table shows cumulative probabilities for positive z. For $P(Z \geq z) = P(Z \leq -z)$ use $1 - P(Z \leq z)$

z	$P(Z \leq z)$	z	$P(Z \leq z)$	z	$P(Z \leq z)$	z	$P(Z \leq z)$	z	$P(Z \leq z)$	z	$P(Z \leq z)$
0.00	0.5000	0.35	0.6368	0.70	0.7580	1.05	0.8531	1.40	0.9192	1.75	0.9599
0.01	0.5040	0.36	0.6406	0.71	0.7611	1.06	0.8554	1.41	0.9207	1.76	0.9608
0.02	0.5080	0.37	0.6443	0.72	0.7642	1.07	0.8577	1.42	0.9222	1.77	0.9616
0.03	0.5120	0.38	0.6480	0.73	0.7673	1.08	0.8599	1.43	0.9236	1.78	0.9625
0.04	0.5160	0.39	0.6517	0.74	0.7704	1.09	0.8621	1.44	0.9251	1.79	0.9633
0.05	0.5199			0.75	0.7734			1.45	0.9265		
0.06	0.5239	0.40	0.6554	0.76	0.7764	1.10	0.8643	1.46	0.9279	1.80	0.9641
0.07	0.5279	0.41	0.6591	0.77	0.7794	1.11	0.8665	1.47	0.9292	1.81	0.9649
0.08	0.5319	0.42	0.6628	0.78	0.7823	1.12	0.8686	1.48	0.9306	1.82	0.9656
0.09	0.5359	0.43	0.6664	0.79	0.7852	1.13	0.8708	1.49	0.9319	1.83	0.9664
		0.44	0.6700			1.14	0.8729			1.84	0.9671
0.10	0.5398	0.45	0.6736	0.80	0.7881	1.15	0.8749	1.50	0.9332	1.85	0.9678
0.11	0.5438	0.46	0.6772	0.81	0.7910	1.16	0.8770	1.51	0.9345	1.86	0.9686
0.12	0.5478	0.47	0.6808	0.82	0.7939	1.17	0.8790	1.52	0.9357	1.87	0.9693
0.13	0.5517	0.48	0.6844	0.83	0.7967	1.18	0.881	1.53	0.9370	1.88	0.9699
0.14	0.5557	0.49	0.6879	0.84	0.7995	1.19	0.8830	1.54	0.9382	1.89	0.9706
0.15	0.5596			0.85	0.8023			1.55	0.9394		
0.16	0.5636	0.50	0.6915	0.86	0.8051	1.20	0.8849	1.56	0.9406	1.90	0.9713
0.17	0.5675	0.51	0.6950	0.87	0.8078	1.21	0.8869	1.57	0.9418	1.91	0.9719
0.18	0.5714	0.52	0.6985	0.88	0.8106	1.22	0.8888	1.58	0.9429	1.92	0.9726
0.19	0.5753	0.53	0.7019	0.89	0.8133	1.23	0.8907	1.59	0.9441	1.93	0.9732
		0.54	0.7054			1.24	0.8925			1.94	0.9738
0.20	0.5793	0.55	0.7088	0.90	0.8159	1.25	0.8944	1.60	0.9452	1.95	0.9744
0.21	0.5832	0.56	0.7123	0.91	0.8186	1.26	0.8962	1.61	0.9463	1.96	0.9750
0.22	0.5871	0.57	0.7157	0.92	0.8212	1.27	0.8980	1.62	0.9474	1.97	0.9756
0.23	0.5910	0.58	0.7190	0.93	0.8238	1.28	0.8997	1.63	0.9484	1.98	0.9761
0.24	0.5948	0.59	0.7224	0.94	0.8264	1.29	0.9015	1.64	0.9495	1.99	0.9767
0.25	0.5987			0.95	0.8289			1.65	0.9505		
0.26	0.6026	0.60	0.7257	0.96	0.8315	1.30	0.9032	1.66	0.9515	2.00	0.9772
0.27	0.6064	0.61	0.7291	0.97	0.8340	1.31	0.9049	1.67	0.9525	2.01	0.9778
0.28	0.6103	0.62	0.7324	0.98	0.8365	1.32	0.9066	1.68	0.9535	2.02	0.9783
0.29	0.6141	0.63	0.7357	0.99	0.8389	1.33	0.9082	1.69	0.9545	2.03	0.9788
		0.64	0.7389			1.34	0.9099			2.04	0.9793
0.30	0.6179	0.65	0.7422	1.00	0.8413	1.35	0.9115	1.70	0.9554	2.05	0.9798
0.31	0.6217	0.66	0.7454	1.01	0.8438	1.36	0.9131	1.71	0.9564	2.06	0.9803
0.32	0.6255	0.67	0.7486	1.02	0.8461	1.37	0.9147	1.72	0.9573	2.07	0.9808
0.33	0.6293	0.68	0.7517	1.03	0.8485	1.38	0.9162	1.73	0.9582	2.08	0.9812
0.34	0.6331	0.69	0.7549	1.04	0.8508	1.39	0.9177	1.74	0.9591	2.09	0.9817

Standard Normal Cumulative Probabilities: p-value = $P(Z \leq z)$

The following table shows cumulative probabilities for positive z. For $P(Z \geq z) = P(Z \leq -z)$ use $1 - P(Z \leq z)$

z	$P(Z \leq z)$	z	$P(Z \leq z)$	z	$P(Z \leq z)$	z	$P(Z \leq z)$	z	$P(Z \leq z)$	z	$P(Z \leq z)$
2.10	0.9821	2.35	0.9906	2.60	0.9953	2.85	0.9978	3.10	0.9990	3.35	0.9996
2.11	0.9826	2.36	0.9909	2.61	0.9955	2.86	0.9979	3.11	0.9991	3.36	0.9996
2.12	0.9830	2.37	0.9911	2.62	0.9956	2.87	0.9979	3.12	0.9991	3.37	0.9996
2.13	0.9834	2.38	0.9913	2.63	0.9957	2.88	0.9980	3.13	0.9991	3.38	0.9996
2.14	0.9838	2.39	0.9916	2.64	0.9959	2.89	0.9981	3.14	0.9992	3.39	0.9997
2.15	0.9842			2.65	0.9960			3.15	0.9992		
2.16	0.9846	2.40	0.9918	2.66	0.9961	2.90	0.9981	3.16	0.9992	3.40	0.9997
2.17	0.9850	2.41	0.9920	2.67	0.9962	2.91	0.9982	3.17	0.9992	3.41	0.9997
2.18	0.9854	2.42	0.9922	2.68	0.9963	2.92	0.9982	3.18	0.9993	3.42	0.9997
2.19	0.9857	2.43	0.9925	2.69	0.9964	2.93	0.9983	3.19	0.9993	3.43	0.9997
		2.44	0.9927			2.94	0.9984			3.44	0.9997
2.20	0.9861	2.45	0.9929	2.70	0.9965	2.95	0.9984	3.20	0.9993	3.45	0.9997
2.21	0.9864	2.46	0.9931	2.71	0.9966	2.96	0.9985	3.21	0.9993	3.46	0.9997
2.22	0.9868	2.47	0.9932	2.72	0.9967	2.97	0.9985	3.22	0.9994	3.47	0.9997
2.23	0.9871	2.48	0.9934	2.73	0.9968	2.98	0.9986	3.23	0.9994	3.48	0.9997
2.24	0.9875	2.49	0.9936	2.74	0.9969	2.99	0.9986	3.24	0.9994	3.49	0.9998
2.25	0.9878			2.75	0.9970			3.25	0.9994		
2.26	0.9881	2.50	0.9938	2.76	0.9971	3.00	0.9987	3.26	0.9994	3.50	0.9998
2.27	0.9884	2.51	0.9940	2.77	0.9972	3.01	0.9987	3.27	0.9995	3.51	0.9998
2.28	0.9887	2.52	0.9941	2.78	0.9973	3.02	0.9987	3.28	0.9995	3.52	0.9998
2.29	0.9890	2.53	0.9943	2.79	0.9974	3.03	0.9988	3.29	0.9995	3.53	0.9998
		2.54	0.9945			3.04	0.9988			3.54	0.9998
2.30	0.9893	2.55	0.9946	2.80	0.9974	3.05	0.9989	3.30	0.9995	3.55	0.9998
2.31	0.9896	2.56	0.9948	2.81	0.9975	3.06	0.9989	3.31	0.9995	3.56	0.9998
2.32	0.9898	2.57	0.9949	2.82	0.9976	3.07	0.9989	3.32	0.9995	3.57	0.9998
2.33	0.9901	2.58	0.9951	2.83	0.9977	3.08	0.9990	3.33	0.9996	3.58	0.9998
2.34	0.9904	2.59	0.9952	2.84	0.9977	3.09	0.9990	3.34	0.9996	3.59	0.9998

Critical Values of z for the selected values of alpha

α	z such that $P(Z \leq z) = \alpha$	z such that $P(Z \geq z) = \alpha$	z such that $P(Z \leq -z) + P(Z \geq z) = \alpha$
0.01	−2.3263	2.3263	2.5758
0.02	−2.0537	2.0537	2.3263
0.025	−1.96	1.96	2.2414
0.05	−1.6449	1.6449	1.96
0.1	−1.2816	1.2816	1.6449

Critical Values of t-Distribution

	For $P(T \geq t) =$				For $P(|T| \geq t) =$		
	0.01	0.05	0.1		0.01	0.05	0.1
DF	Critical t	Critical t	Critical t	DF	Critical t	Critical t	Critical t
1	31.8205	6.3138	3.0777	1	63.6567	12.7062	6.3138
2	6.9646	2.9200	1.8856	2	9.9248	4.3027	2.9200
3	4.5407	2.3534	1.6377	3	5.8409	3.1824	2.3534
4	3.7469	2.1318	1.5332	4	4.6041	2.7764	2.1318
5	3.3649	2.0150	1.4759	5	4.0321	2.5706	2.0150
6	3.1427	1.9432	1.4398	6	3.7074	2.4469	1.9432
7	2.9980	1.8946	1.4149	7	3.4995	2.3646	1.8946
8	2.8965	1.8595	1.3968	8	3.3554	2.306	1.8595
9	2.8214	1.8331	1.3830	9	3.2498	2.2622	1.8331
10	2.7638	1.8125	1.3722	10	3.1693	2.2281	1.8125
11	2.7181	1.7959	1.3634	11	3.1058	2.2010	1.7959
12	2.6810	1.7823	1.3562	12	3.0545	2.1788	1.7823
13	2.6503	1.7709	1.3502	13	3.0123	2.1604	1.7709
14	2.6245	1.7613	1.3450	14	2.9768	2.1448	1.7613
15	2.6025	1.7531	1.3406	15	2.9467	2.1314	1.7531
16	2.5835	1.7459	1.3368	16	2.9208	2.1199	1.7459
17	2.5669	1.7396	1.3334	17	2.8982	2.1098	1.7396
18	2.5524	1.7341	1.3304	18	2.8784	2.1009	1.7341
19	2.5395	1.7291	1.3277	19	2.8609	2.0930	1.7291
20	2.5280	1.7247	1.3253	20	2.8453	2.0860	1.7247
21	2.5176	1.7207	1.3232	21	2.8314	2.0796	1.7207
22	2.5083	1.7171	1.3212	22	2.8188	2.0739	1.7171
23	2.4999	1.7139	1.3195	23	2.8073	2.0687	1.7139
24	2.4922	1.7109	1.3178	24	2.7969	2.0639	1.7109
25	2.4851	1.7081	1.3163	25	2.7874	2.0595	1.7081
26	2.4786	1.7056	1.3150	26	2.7787	2.0555	1.7056
27	2.4727	1.7033	1.3137	27	2.7707	2.0518	1.7033
28	2.4671	1.7011	1.3125	28	2.7633	2.0484	1.7011
29	2.4620	1.6991	1.3114	29	2.7564	2.0452	1.6991
30	2.4573	1.6973	1.3104	30	2.7500	2.0423	1.6973
40	2.4233	1.6839	1.3031	40	2.7045	2.0211	1.6839
50	2.4033	1.6759	1.2987	50	2.6778	2.0086	1.6759
60	2.3901	1.6706	1.2958	60	2.6603	2.0003	1.6706
70	2.3808	1.6669	1.2938	70	2.6479	1.9944	1.6669
80	2.3739	1.6641	1.2922	80	2.6387	1.9901	1.6641
100	2.3642	1.6602	1.2901	100	2.6259	1.9840	1.6602
120	2.3578	1.6577	1.2886	120	2.6174	1.9799	1.6577

Critical Values of χ^2-Distribution

For $P(\chi^2 > \chi_c^2) =$

DF	0.99 Critical χ_c^2	0.95 Critical χ_c^2	0.90 Critical χ_c^2	0.10 Critical χ_c^2	0.05 Critical χ_c^2	0.01 Critical χ_c^2
1	0.0002	0.0039	0.0158	2.7055	3.8415	6.6349
2	0.0201	0.1026	0.2107	4.6052	5.9915	9.2103
3	0.1148	0.3518	0.5844	6.2514	7.8147	11.3449
4	0.2971	0.7107	1.0636	7.7794	9.4877	13.2767
5	0.5543	1.1455	1.6103	9.2364	11.0705	15.0863
6	0.8721	1.6354	2.2041	10.6446	12.5916	16.8119
7	1.2390	2.1673	2.8331	12.017	14.0671	18.4753
8	1.6465	2.7326	3.4895	13.3616	15.5073	20.0902
9	2.0879	3.3251	4.1682	14.6837	16.9190	21.6660
10	2.5582	3.9403	4.8652	15.9872	18.3070	23.2093
11	3.0535	4.5748	5.5778	17.275	19.6751	24.7250
12	3.5706	5.226	6.3038	18.5493	21.0261	26.2170
13	4.1069	5.8919	7.0415	19.8119	22.3620	27.6882
14	4.6604	6.5706	7.7895	21.0641	23.6848	29.1412
15	5.2293	7.2609	8.5468	22.3071	24.9958	30.5779
16	5.8122	7.9616	9.3122	23.5418	26.2962	31.9999
17	6.4078	8.6718	10.0852	24.7690	27.5871	33.4087
18	7.0149	9.3905	10.8649	25.9894	28.8693	34.8053
19	7.6327	10.1170	11.6509	27.2036	30.1435	36.1909
20	8.2604	10.8508	12.4426	28.4120	31.4104	37.5662
21	8.8972	11.5913	13.2396	29.6151	32.6706	38.9322
22	9.5425	12.3380	14.0415	30.8133	33.9244	40.2894
23	10.1957	13.0905	14.8480	32.0069	35.1725	41.6384
24	10.8564	13.8484	15.6587	33.1962	36.4150	42.9798
25	11.5240	14.6114	16.4734	34.3816	37.6525	44.3141
26	12.1981	15.3792	17.2919	35.5632	38.8851	45.6417
27	12.8785	16.1514	18.1139	36.7412	40.1133	46.9629
28	13.5647	16.9279	18.9392	37.9159	41.3371	48.2782
29	14.2565	17.7084	19.7677	39.0875	42.557	49.5879
30	14.9535	18.4927	20.5992	40.2560	43.7730	50.8922
40	22.1643	26.5093	29.0505	51.8051	55.7585	63.6907
50	29.7067	34.7643	37.6886	63.1671	67.5048	76.1539
60	37.4849	43.1880	46.4589	74.3970	79.0819	88.3794
80	53.5401	60.3915	64.2778	96.5782	101.8795	112.3288
100	70.0649	77.9295	82.3581	118.4980	124.3421	135.8067

Critical Values of F-Distribution. Crit. $F_{(v_1,v_2)}$ such that $P(F > F_{(v_1,v_2)}) = 0.01, 0.05$. v_1 = num DF, v_2 = deno DF

DF (v_1, v_2)	0.01 Crit. F	0.05 Crit. F	DF (v_1, v_2)	0.01 Crit. F	0.05 Crit. F	DF (v_1, v_2)	0.01 Crit. F	0.05 Crit. F	DF (v_1, v_2)	0.01 Crit. F	0.05 Crit. F	DF (v_1, v_2)	0.01 Crit. F	0.05 Crit. F
(1, 1)	4052	161.5	(2, 1)	4999	199.5	(3, 1)	5403	215.7	(4, 1)	5624	224.6	(5, 1)	5763	230.2
(1, 2)	98.50	18.51	(2, 2)	99.00	19.00	(3, 2)	99.17	19.16	(4, 2)	99.25	19.25	(5, 2)	99.30	19.30
(1, 3)	34.12	10.13	(2, 3)	30.82	9.552	(3, 3)	29.46	9.277	(4, 3)	28.71	9.117	(5, 3)	28.24	9.013
(1, 4)	21.20	7.709	(2, 4)	18.00	6.944	(3, 4)	16.69	6.591	(4, 4)	15.98	6.388	(5, 4)	15.52	6.256
(1, 5)	16.26	6.608	(2, 5)	13.27	5.786	(3, 5)	12.06	5.409	(4, 5)	11.39	5.192	(5, 5)	10.97	5.050
(1, 6)	13.75	5.987	(2, 6)	10.93	5.143	(3, 6)	9.780	4.757	(4, 6)	9.148	4.534	(5, 6)	8.746	4.387
(1, 7)	12.25	5.591	(2, 7)	9.547	4.737	(3, 7)	8.451	4.347	(4, 7)	7.847	4.120	(5, 7)	7.460	3.972
(1, 8)	11.26	5.318	(2, 8)	8.649	4.459	(3, 8)	7.591	4.066	(4, 8)	7.006	3.838	(5, 8)	6.632	3.687
(1, 9)	10.56	5.117	(2, 9)	8.022	4.256	(3, 9)	6.992	3.863	(4, 9)	6.422	3.633	(5, 9)	6.057	3.482
(1, 10)	10.04	4.965	(2, 10)	7.559	4.103	(3, 10)	6.552	3.708	(4, 10)	5.994	3.478	(5, 10)	5.636	3.326
(1, 11)	9.646	4.844	(2, 11)	7.206	3.982	(3, 11)	6.217	3.587	(4, 11)	5.668	3.357	(5, 11)	5.316	3.204
(1, 12)	9.330	4.747	(2, 12)	6.927	3.885	(3, 12)	5.953	3.490	(4, 12)	5.412	3.259	(5, 12)	5.064	3.106
(1, 13)	9.074	4.667	(2, 13)	6.701	3.806	(3, 13)	5.739	3.411	(4, 13)	5.205	3.179	(5, 13)	4.862	3.025
(1, 14)	8.862	4.600	(2, 14)	6.515	3.739	(3, 14)	5.564	3.344	(4, 14)	5.035	3.112	(5, 14)	4.695	2.958
(1, 15)	8.683	4.543	(2, 15)	6.359	3.682	(3, 15)	5.417	3.287	(4, 15)	4.893	3.056	(5, 15)	4.556	2.901
(1, 16)	8.531	4.494	(2, 16)	6.226	3.634	(3, 16)	5.292	3.239	(4, 16)	4.773	3.007	(5, 16)	4.437	2.852
(1, 17)	8.400	4.451	(2, 17)	6.112	3.592	(3, 17)	5.185	3.197	(4, 17)	4.669	2.965	(5, 17)	4.336	2.810
(1, 18)	8.285	4.414	(2, 18)	6.013	3.555	(3, 18)	5.092	3.160	(4, 18)	4.579	2.928	(5, 18)	4.248	2.773
(1, 19)	8.185	4.381	(2, 19)	5.926	3.522	(3, 19)	5.010	3.127	(4, 19)	4.500	2.895	(5, 19)	4.171	2.740
(1, 20)	8.096	4.351	(2, 20)	5.849	3.493	(3, 20)	4.938	3.098	(4, 20)	4.431	2.866	(5, 20)	4.103	2.711
(1, 21)	8.017	4.325	(2, 21)	5.780	3.467	(3, 21)	4.874	3.072	(4, 21)	4.369	2.840	(5, 21)	4.042	2.685
(1, 22)	7.945	4.301	(2, 22)	5.719	3.443	(3, 22)	4.817	3.049	(4, 22)	4.313	2.817	(5, 22)	3.988	2.661
(1, 23)	7.881	4.279	(2, 23)	5.664	3.422	(3, 23)	4.765	3.028	(4, 23)	4.264	2.796	(5, 23)	3.939	2.640
(1, 24)	7.823	4.260	(2, 24)	5.614	3.403	(3, 24)	4.718	3.009	(4, 24)	4.218	2.776	(5, 24)	3.895	2.621
(1, 25)	7.770	4.242	(2, 25)	5.568	3.385	(3, 25)	4.675	2.991	(4, 25)	4.177	2.759	(5, 25)	3.855	2.603
(1, 26)	7.721	4.225	(2, 26)	5.526	3.369	(3, 26)	4.637	2.975	(4, 26)	4.140	2.743	(5, 26)	3.818	2.587
(1, 27)	7.677	4.210	(2, 27)	5.488	3.354	(3, 27)	4.601	2.960	(4, 27)	4.106	2.728	(5, 27)	3.785	2.572
(1, 28)	7.636	4.196	(2, 28)	5.453	3.34	(3, 28)	4.568	2.947	(4, 28)	4.074	2.714	(5, 28)	3.754	2.558
(1, 29)	7.598	4.183	(2, 29)	5.420	3.328	(3, 29)	4.538	2.934	(4, 29)	4.045	2.701	(5, 29)	3.725	2.545
(1, 30)	7.562	4.171	(2, 30)	5.390	3.316	(3, 30)	4.510	2.922	(4, 30)	4.018	2.690	(5, 30)	3.699	2.534
(1, 40)	7.314	4.085	(2, 40)	5.179	3.232	(3, 40)	4.313	2.839	(4, 40)	3.828	2.606	(5, 40)	3.514	2.449
(1, 60)	7.077	4.001	(2, 60)	4.977	3.150	(3, 60)	4.126	2.758	(4, 60)	3.649	2.525	(5, 60)	3.339	2.368
(1, 80)	6.963	3.960	(2, 80)	4.881	3.111	(3, 80)	4.036	2.719	(4, 80)	3.563	2.486	(5, 80)	3.255	2.329
(1, 100)	6.895	3.936	(2, 100)	4.824	3.087	(3, 100)	3.984	2.696	(4, 100)	3.513	2.463	(5, 100)	3.206	2.305
(1, 120)	6.851	3.920	(2, 120)	4.787	3.072	(3, 120)	3.949	2.680	(4, 120)	3.480	2.447	(5, 120)	3.174	2.290

Critical Values of F-Distribution. Crit. $F_{(v_1,v_2)}$ such that $P(F > F_{(v_1,v_2)}) = 0.01, 0.05$. v_1 = num DF, v_2 = deno DF

DF (v_1, v_2)	0.01 Crit. F	0.05 Crit. F	DF (v_1, v_2)	0.01 Crit. F	0.05 Crit. F	DF (v_1, v_2)	0.01 Crit. F	0.05 Crit. F	DF (v_1, v_2)	0.01 Crit. F	0.05 Crit. F
(6, 1)	5859	234.0	(7, 1)	5928	236.8	(8, 1)	5981	238.9	(9, 1)	6022	240.5
(6, 2)	99.33	19.33	(7, 2)	99.36	19.35	(8, 2)	99.37	19.37	(9, 2)	99.39	19.39
(6, 3)	27.91	8.941	(7, 3)	27.67	8.887	(8, 3)	27.49	8.845	(9, 3)	27.35	8.812
(6, 4)	15.21	6.163	(7, 4)	14.98	6.094	(8, 4)	14.80	6.041	(9, 4)	14.66	5.999
(6, 5)	10.67	4.950	(7, 5)	10.46	4.876	(8, 5)	10.29	4.818	(9, 5)	10.16	4.772
(6, 6)	8.466	4.284	(7, 6)	8.260	4.207	(8, 6)	8.102	4.147	(9, 6)	7.976	4.099
(6, 7)	7.191	3.866	(7, 7)	6.993	3.787	(8, 7)	6.840	3.726	(9, 7)	6.719	3.677
(6, 8)	6.371	3.581	(7, 8)	6.178	3.500	(8, 8)	6.029	3.438	(9, 8)	5.911	3.388
(6, 9)	5.802	3.374	(7, 9)	5.613	3.293	(8, 9)	5.467	3.230	(9, 9)	5.351	3.179
(6, 10)	5.386	3.217	(7, 10)	5.200	3.135	(8, 10)	5.057	3.072	(9, 10)	4.942	3.020
(6, 11)	5.069	3.095	(7, 11)	4.886	3.012	(8, 11)	4.744	2.948	(9, 11)	4.632	2.896
(6, 12)	4.821	2.996	(7, 12)	4.640	2.913	(8, 12)	4.499	2.849	(9, 12)	4.388	2.796
(6, 13)	4.620	2.915	(7, 13)	4.441	2.832	(8, 13)	4.302	2.767	(9, 13)	4.191	2.714
(6, 14)	4.456	2.848	(7, 14)	4.278	2.764	(8, 14)	4.140	2.699	(9, 14)	4.030	2.646
(6, 15)	4.318	2.790	(7, 15)	4.142	2.707	(8, 15)	4.004	2.641	(9, 15)	3.895	2.588
(6, 16)	4.202	2.741	(7, 16)	4.026	2.657	(8, 16)	3.890	2.591	(9, 16)	3.780	2.538
(6, 17)	4.102	2.699	(7, 17)	3.927	2.614	(8, 17)	3.791	2.548	(9, 17)	3.682	2.494
(6, 18)	4.015	2.661	(7, 18)	3.841	2.577	(8, 18)	3.705	2.510	(9, 18)	3.597	2.456
(6, 19)	3.939	2.628	(7, 19)	3.765	2.544	(8, 19)	3.631	2.477	(9, 19)	3.523	2.423
(6, 20)	3.871	2.599	(7, 20)	3.699	2.514	(8, 20)	3.564	2.447	(9, 20)	3.457	2.393
(6, 21)	3.812	2.573	(7, 21)	3.640	2.488	(8, 21)	3.506	2.420	(9, 21)	3.398	2.366
(6, 22)	3.758	2.549	(7, 22)	3.587	2.464	(8, 22)	3.453	2.397	(9, 22)	3.346	2.342
(6, 23)	3.710	2.528	(7, 23)	3.539	2.442	(8, 23)	3.406	2.375	(9, 23)	3.299	2.320
(6, 24)	3.667	2.508	(7, 24)	3.496	2.423	(8, 24)	3.363	2.355	(9, 24)	3.256	2.300
(6, 25)	3.627	2.490	(7, 25)	3.457	2.405	(8, 25)	3.324	2.337	(9, 25)	3.217	2.282
(6, 26)	3.591	2.474	(7, 26)	3.421	2.388	(8, 26)	3.288	2.321	(9, 26)	3.182	2.265
(6, 27)	3.558	2.459	(7, 27)	3.388	2.373	(8, 27)	3.256	2.305	(9, 27)	3.149	2.250
(6, 28)	3.528	2.445	(7, 28)	3.358	2.359	(8, 28)	3.226	2.291	(9, 28)	3.120	2.236
(6, 29)	3.499	2.432	(7, 29)	3.330	2.346	(8, 29)	3.198	2.278	(9, 29)	3.092	2.223
(6, 30)	3.473	2.421	(7, 30)	3.304	2.334	(8, 30)	3.173	2.266	(9, 30)	3.067	2.211
(6, 40)	3.291	2.336	(7, 40)	3.124	2.249	(8, 40)	2.993	2.180	(9, 40)	2.888	2.124
(6, 60)	3.119	2.254	(7, 60)	2.953	2.167	(8, 60)	2.823	2.097	(9, 60)	2.718	2.040
(6, 80)	3.036	2.214	(7, 80)	2.871	2.126	(8, 80)	2.742	2.056	(9, 80)	2.637	1.999
(6, 100)	2.988	2.191	(7, 100)	2.823	2.103	(8, 100)	2.694	2.032	(9, 100)	2.590	1.975
(6, 120)	2.956	2.175	(7, 120)	2.792	2.087	(8, 120)	2.663	2.016	(9, 120)	2.559	1.959

DF (v_1, v_2)	0.01 Crit. F	0.05 Crit. F
(10, 1)	6056	241.9
(10, 2)	99.40	19.40
(10, 3)	27.23	8.786
(10, 4)	14.55	5.964
(10, 5)	10.05	4.735
(10, 6)	7.874	4.060
(10, 7)	6.620	3.637
(10, 8)	5.814	3.347
(10, 9)	5.257	3.137
(10, 10)	4.849	2.978
(10, 11)	4.539	2.854
(10, 12)	4.296	2.753
(10, 13)	4.100	2.671
(10, 14)	3.939	2.602
(10, 15)	3.805	2.544
(3, 16)	3.691	2.494
(10, 17)	3.593	2.450
(10, 18)	3.508	2.412
(10, 19)	3.434	2.378
(10, 20)	3.368	2.348
(10, 21)	3.310	2.321
(10, 22)	3.258	2.297
(10, 23)	3.211	2.275
(10, 24)	3.168	2.255
(10, 25)	3.129	2.236
(10, 26)	3.094	2.220
(10, 27)	3.062	2.204
(10, 28)	3.032	2.190
(10, 29)	3.005	2.177
(10, 30)	2.979	2.165
(10, 40)	2.801	2.077
(10, 60)	2.632	1.993
(10, 80)	2.551	1.951
(10, 100)	2.503	1.927
(10, 120)	2.472	1.910

Critical Values of F-Distribution. Crit. $F_{(v_1, v_2)}$ such that $P(F > F_{(v_1, v_2)}) = 0.01, 0.05$. v_1 = num DF, v_2 = deno DF

DF (v_1, v_2)	0.01 Crit. F	0.05 Crit. F	DF (v_1, v_2)	0.01 Crit. F	0.05 Crit. F	DF (v_1, v_2)	0.01 Crit. F	0.05 Crit. F	DF (v_1, v_2)	0.01 Crit. F	0.05 Crit. F
(12, 1)	6106	243.9	(15, 1)	6157	245.9	(20, 1)	6209	248.0	(24, 1)	6235	249.1
(12, 2)	99.42	19.41	(15, 2)	99.43	19.43	(20, 2)	99.45	19.45	(24, 2)	99.46	19.45
(12, 3)	27.05	8.745	(15, 3)	26.87	8.703	(20, 3)	26.69	8.66	(24, 3)	26.60	8.639
(12, 4)	14.37	5.912	(15, 4)	14.2	5.858	(20, 4)	14.02	5.803	(24, 4)	13.93	5.774
(12, 5)	9.888	4.678	(15, 5)	9.722	4.619	(20, 5)	9.553	4.558	(24, 5)	9.466	4.527
(12, 6)	7.718	4.000	(15, 6)	7.559	3.938	(20, 6)	7.396	3.874	(24, 6)	7.313	3.841
(12, 7)	6.469	3.575	(15, 7)	6.314	3.511	(20, 7)	6.155	3.445	(24, 7)	6.074	3.41
(12, 8)	5.667	3.284	(15, 8)	5.515	3.218	(20, 8)	5.359	3.15	(24, 8)	5.279	3.115
(12, 9)	5.111	3.073	(15, 9)	4.962	3.006	(20, 9)	4.808	2.936	(24, 9)	4.729	2.9
(12, 10)	4.706	2.913	(15, 10)	4.558	2.845	(20, 10)	4.405	2.774	(24, 10)	4.327	2.737
(12, 11)	4.397	2.788	(15, 11)	4.251	2.719	(20, 11)	4.099	2.646	(24, 11)	4.021	2.609
(12, 12)	4.155	2.687	(15, 12)	4.01	2.617	(20, 12)	3.858	2.544	(24, 12)	3.780	2.505
(12, 13)	3.960	2.604	(15, 13)	3.815	2.533	(20, 13)	3.665	2.459	(24, 13)	3.587	2.42
(12, 14)	3.800	2.534	(15, 14)	3.656	2.463	(20, 14)	3.505	2.388	(24, 14)	3.427	2.349
(12, 15)	3.666	2.475	(15, 15)	3.522	2.403	(20, 15)	3.372	2.328	(24, 15)	3.294	2.288
(12, 16)	3.553	2.425	(15, 16)	3.409	2.352	(20, 16)	3.259	2.276	(24, 16)	3.181	2.235
(12, 17)	3.455	2.381	(15, 17)	3.312	2.308	(20, 17)	3.162	2.23	(24, 17)	3.084	2.19
(12, 18)	3.371	2.342	(15, 18)	3.227	2.269	(20, 18)	3.077	2.191	(24, 18)	2.999	2.15
(12, 19)	3.297	2.308	(15, 19)	3.153	2.234	(20, 19)	3.003	2.155	(24, 19)	2.925	2.114
(12, 20)	3.231	2.278	(15, 20)	3.088	2.203	(20, 20)	2.938	2.124	(24, 20)	2.859	2.082
(12, 21)	3.173	2.25	(15, 21)	3.03	2.176	(20, 21)	2.88	2.096	(24, 21)	2.801	2.054
(12, 22)	3.121	2.226	(15, 22)	2.978	2.151	(20, 22)	2.827	2.071	(24, 22)	2.749	2.028
(12, 23)	3.074	2.204	(15, 23)	2.931	2.128	(20, 23)	2.781	2.048	(24, 23)	2.702	2.005
(12, 24)	3.032	2.183	(15, 24)	2.889	2.108	(20, 24)	2.738	2.027	(24, 24)	2.659	1.984
(12, 25)	2.993	2.165	(15, 25)	2.85	2.089	(20, 25)	2.699	2.007	(24, 25)	2.620	1.964
(12, 26)	2.958	2.148	(15, 26)	2.815	2.072	(20, 26)	2.664	1.99	(24, 26)	2.585	1.946
(12, 27)	2.926	2.132	(15, 27)	2.783	2.056	(20, 27)	2.632	1.974	(24, 27)	2.552	1.93
(12, 28)	2.896	2.118	(15, 28)	2.753	2.041	(20, 28)	2.602	1.959	(24, 28)	2.522	1.915
(12, 29)	2.868	2.104	(15, 29)	2.726	2.027	(20, 29)	2.574	1.945	(24, 29)	2.495	1.901
(12, 30)	2.843	2.092	(15, 30)	2.7	2.015	(20, 30)	2.549	1.932	(24, 30)	2.469	1.887
(12, 40)	2.665	2.003	(15, 40)	2.522	1.924	(20, 40)	2.369	1.839	(24, 40)	2.288	1.793
(12, 60)	2.496	1.917	(15, 60)	2.352	1.836	(20, 60)	2.198	1.748	(24, 60)	2.115	1.7
(12, 80)	2.415	1.875	(15, 80)	2.271	1.793	(20, 80)	2.115	1.703	(24, 80)	2.032	1.654
(12, 100)	2.368	1.85	(15, 100)	2.223	1.768	(20, 100)	2.067	1.676	(24, 100)	1.983	1.627
(12, 120)	2.336	1.834	(15, 120)	2.192	1.75	(20, 120)	2.035	1.659	(24, 120)	1.950	1.608

DF (v_1, v_2)	0.01 Crit. F	0.05 Crit. F
(30, 1)	6260	250.1
(30, 2)	99.47	19.46
(30, 3)	26.51	8.617
(30, 4)	13.84	5.746
(30, 5)	9.379	4.496
(30, 6)	7.229	3.808
(30, 7)	5.992	3.376
(30, 8)	5.198	3.079
(30, 9)	4.649	2.864
(30, 10)	4.247	2.7
(14, 11)	3.941	2.57
(30, 12)	3.701	2.466
(30, 13)	3.507	2.38
(30, 14)	3.348	2.308
(30, 15)	3.214	2.247
(30, 16)	3.101	2.194
(30, 17)	3.003	2.148
(30, 18)	2.919	2.107
(30, 19)	2.844	2.071
(30, 20)	2.778	2.039
(30, 21)	2.72	2.01
(30, 22)	2.667	1.984
(30, 23)	2.62	1.961
(30, 24)	2.577	1.939
(30, 25)	2.538	1.919
(30, 26)	2.503	1.901
(30, 27)	2.47	1.884
(30, 28)	2.44	1.869
(30, 29)	2.412	1.854
(30, 30)	2.386	1.841
(30, 40)	2.203	1.744
(30, 60)	2.028	1.649
(30, 80)	1.944	1.602
(30, 100)	1.893	1.573
(30, 120)	1.86	1.554

Critical Values of F-Distribution. Crit. $F_{(v_1, v_2)}$ such that $P(F > F_{(v_1, v_2)}) = 0.01, 0.05$. v_1 = num DF, v_2 = deno DF

DF (v_1, v_2)	0.01 Crit. F	0.05 Crit. F	DF (v_1, v_2)	0.01 Crit. F	0.05 Crit. F	DF (v_1, v_2)	0.01 Crit. F	0.05 Crit. F	DF (v_1, v_2)	0.01 Crit. F	0.05 Crit. F	DF (v_1, v_2)	0.01 Crit. F	0.05 Crit. F
(40, 1)	6286	251.1	(45, 1)	6295	251.5	(50, 1)	6302	251.8	(60, 1)	6313	252.2	(100, 1)	6334	253
(40, 2)	99.47	19.47	(45, 2)	99.48	19.47	(50, 2)	99.48	19.48	(60, 2)	99.48	19.48	(100, 2)	99.49	19.49
(40, 3)	26.41	8.594	(45, 3)	26.38	8.587	(50, 3)	26.35	8.581	(60, 3)	26.32	8.572	(100, 3)	26.24	8.554
(40, 4)	13.75	5.717	(45, 4)	13.71	5.707	(50, 4)	13.69	5.699	(60, 4)	13.65	5.688	(100, 4)	13.58	5.664
(40, 5)	9.291	4.464	(45, 5)	9.262	4.453	(50, 5)	9.238	4.444	(60, 5)	9.202	4.431	(100, 5)	9.13	4.405
(40, 6)	7.143	3.774	(45, 6)	7.115	3.763	(50, 6)	7.091	3.754	(60, 6)	7.057	3.74	(100, 6)	6.987	3.712
(40, 7)	5.908	3.34	(45, 7)	5.88	3.328	(50, 7)	5.858	3.319	(60, 7)	5.824	3.304	(100, 7)	5.755	3.275
(40, 8)	5.116	3.043	(45, 8)	5.088	3.03	(50, 8)	5.065	3.02	(60, 8)	5.032	3.005	(100, 8)	4.963	2.975
(40, 9)	4.567	2.826	(45, 9)	4.539	2.813	(50, 9)	4.517	2.803	(60, 9)	4.483	2.787	(100, 9)	4.415	2.756
(40, 10)	4.165	2.661	(45, 10)	4.138	2.648	(50, 10)	4.115	2.637	(60, 10)	4.082	2.621	(100, 10)	4.014	2.588
(40, 11)	3.86	2.531	(45, 11)	3.832	2.517	(50, 11)	3.81	2.507	(60, 11)	3.776	2.49	(100, 11)	3.708	2.457
(40, 12)	3.619	2.426	(45, 12)	3.592	2.412	(50, 12)	3.569	2.401	(60, 12)	3.535	2.384	(100, 12)	3.467	2.35
(40, 13)	3.425	2.339	(45, 13)	3.398	2.325	(50, 13)	3.375	2.314	(60, 13)	3.341	2.297	(100, 13)	3.272	2.261
(40, 14)	3.266	2.266	(45, 14)	3.238	2.252	(50, 14)	3.215	2.241	(60, 14)	3.181	2.223	(100, 14)	3.112	2.187
(40, 15)	3.132	2.204	(45, 15)	3.104	2.19	(50, 15)	3.081	2.178	(60, 15)	3.047	2.16	(100, 15)	2.977	2.123
(40, 16)	3.018	2.151	(45, 16)	2.99	2.136	(50, 16)	2.967	2.124	(60, 16)	2.933	2.106	(100, 16)	2.863	2.068
(40, 17)	2.92	2.104	(45, 17)	2.892	2.089	(50, 17)	2.869	2.077	(60, 17)	2.835	2.058	(100, 17)	2.764	2.02
(40, 18)	2.835	2.063	(45, 18)	2.807	2.048	(50, 18)	2.784	2.035	(60, 18)	2.749	2.017	(100, 18)	2.678	1.978
(40, 19)	2.761	2.026	(45, 19)	2.732	2.011	(50, 19)	2.709	1.999	(60, 19)	2.674	1.98	(100, 19)	2.602	1.94
(40, 20)	2.695	1.994	(45, 20)	2.666	1.978	(50, 20)	2.643	1.966	(60, 20)	2.608	1.946	(100, 20)	2.535	1.907
(40, 21)	2.636	1.965	(45, 21)	2.607	1.949	(50, 21)	2.584	1.936	(60, 21)	2.548	1.916	(100, 21)	2.475	1.876
(40, 22)	2.583	1.938	(45, 22)	2.554	1.922	(50, 22)	2.531	1.909	(60, 22)	2.495	1.889	(100, 22)	2.422	1.849
(40, 23)	2.535	1.914	(45, 23)	2.506	1.898	(50, 23)	2.483	1.885	(60, 23)	2.447	1.865	(100, 23)	2.373	1.823
(40, 24)	2.492	1.892	(45, 24)	2.463	1.876	(50, 24)	2.44	1.863	(60, 24)	2.403	1.842	(100, 24)	2.329	1.8
(40, 25)	2.453	1.872	(45, 25)	2.424	1.855	(50, 25)	2.4	1.842	(60, 25)	2.364	1.822	(100, 25)	2.289	1.779
(40, 26)	2.417	1.853	(45, 26)	2.388	1.837	(50, 26)	2.364	1.823	(60, 26)	2.327	1.803	(100, 26)	2.252	1.76
(40, 27)	2.384	1.836	(45, 27)	2.354	1.819	(50, 27)	2.33	1.806	(60, 27)	2.294	1.785	(100, 27)	2.218	1.742
(40, 28)	2.354	1.82	(45, 28)	2.324	1.803	(50, 28)	2.3	1.79	(60, 28)	2.263	1.769	(100, 28)	2.187	1.725
(40, 29)	2.325	1.806	(45, 29)	2.296	1.789	(50, 29)	2.271	1.775	(60, 29)	2.234	1.754	(100, 29)	2.158	1.71
(40, 30)	2.299	1.792	(45, 30)	2.269	1.775	(50, 30)	2.245	1.761	(60, 30)	2.208	1.74	(100, 30)	2.131	1.695
(40, 40)	2.114	1.693	(45, 40)	2.083	1.675	(50, 40)	2.058	1.66	(60, 40)	2.019	1.637	(100, 40)	1.938	1.589
(40, 60)	1.936	1.594	(45, 60)	1.904	1.575	(50, 60)	1.877	1.559	(60, 60)	1.836	1.534	(100, 60)	1.749	1.481
(40, 80)	1.849	1.545	(45, 80)	1.816	1.525	(50, 80)	1.788	1.508	(60, 80)	1.746	1.482	(100, 80)	1.655	1.426
(40, 100)	1.797	1.515	(45, 100)	1.763	1.494	(50, 100)	1.735	1.477	(60, 100)	1.692	1.45	(100, 100)	1.598	1.392
(40, 120)	1.763	1.495	(45, 120)	1.728	1.474	(50, 120)	1.7	1.457	(60, 120)	1.656	1.429	(100, 120)	1.559	1.369

CUMULATIVE BINOMIAL PROBABILITIES: $p\text{-value} = P(T \leq x) = \sum_{j=0}^{x} b(j; n, 0.5)$

n	x	p-value	n	x	p-value	n	x	p-value	n	x	p-value	n	x	p-value
1	0	0.5	8	5	0.8555	12	2	0.0193	14	14	1	17	5	0.0717
	1	1		6	0.9648		3	0.073	15	0	0		6	0.1662
2	0	0.25		7	0.9961		4	0.1938		1	0.0005		7	0.3145
	1	0.75		8	1		5	0.3872		2	0.0037		8	0.5
	2	1	9	0	0.002		6	0.6128		3	0.0176		9	0.6855
3	0	0.125		1	0.0195		7	0.8062		4	0.0592		10	0.8338
	1	0.5		2	0.0898		8	0.927		5	0.1509		11	0.9283
	2	0.875		3	0.2539		9	0.9807		6	0.3036		12	0.9755
	3	1		4	0.5		10	0.9968		7	0.5		13	0.9936
4	0	0.0625		5	0.7461		11	0.9998		8	0.6964		14	0.9988
	1	0.3125		6	0.9102		12	1		9	0.8491		15	0.9999
	2	0.6875		7	0.9805	13	0	0.0001		10	0.9408		16	1
	4	1		8	0.998		1	0.0017		11	0.9824		17	1
5	0	0.0313		9	1		2	0.0112		12	0.9963	18	0	0
	1	0.1875	10	0	0.001		3	0.0461		13	0.9995		1	0.0001
	2	0.5		1	0.0107		4	0.1334		14	1		2	0.0007
	3	0.8125		2	0.0547		5	0.2905		15	1		3	0.0038
	4	0.9688		3	0.1719		6	0.5	16	0	0		4	0.0154
	5	1		4	0.377		7	0.7095		1	0.0003		5	0.0481
6	0	0.0156		5	0.623		8	0.8666		2	0.0021		6	0.1189
	1	0.1094		6	0.8281		9	0.9539		3	0.0106		7	0.2403
	2	0.3438		7	0.9453		10	0.9888		4	0.0384		8	0.4073
	3	0.6563		8	0.9893		11	0.9983		5	0.1051		9	0.5927
	4	0.8906		9	0.999		12	0.9999		6	0.2272		10	0.7597
	5	0.9844		10	1		13	1		7	0.4018		11	0.8811
	6	1	11	0	0.0005	14	0	0.0001		8	0.5982		12	0.9519
7	0	0.0078		1	0.0059		1	0.0009		9	0.7728		13	0.9846
	1	0.0625		2	0.0327		2	0.0065		10	0.8949		14	0.9962
	2	0.2266		3	0.1133		3	0.0287		11	0.9616		15	0.9993
	3	0.5		4	0.2744		4	0.0898		12	0.9894		16	0.9999
	4	0.7734		5	0.5		5	0.212		13	0.9979		17	1
	5	0.9375		6	0.7256		6	0.3953		14	0.9997		18	1
	6	0.9922		7	0.8867		7	0.6047		15	1	19	0	0
	7	1		8	0.9673		8	0.788		16	1		1	0
8	0	0.0039		9	0.9941		9	0.9102	17	0	0		2	0.0004
	1	0.0352		10	0.9995		10	0.9713		1	0.0001		3	0.0022
	2	0.1445		11	1		11	0.9935		2	0.0012		4	0.0096
	3	0.3633	12	0	0.0002		12	0.9991		3	0.0064		5	0.0318
	4	0.6367		1	0.0032		13	0.9999		4	0.0245		6	0.0835

For $P(T \geq x)$, use $P(T \geq x) = 1 - P(T \leq x - 1) = \sum_{j=0}^{x-1} b(j; n, 0.5)$

CUMULATIVE BINOMIAL PROBABILITIES: $p\text{-value} = P(T \leq x) = \sum_{j=0}^{x} b(j; n, 0.5)$

n	x	p-value	n	x	p-value	n	x	p-value	n	x	p-value	n	x	p-value
19	7	0.1796	21	5	0.0133	22	22	1	24	14	0.8463	30	0	0
	8	0.3238		6	0.0392	23	0	0		15	0.9242		1	0
	9	0.5		7	0.0946		1	0		16	0.968		2	0
	10	0.6762		8	0.1917		2	0		17	0.9887		3	0
	11	0.8204		9	0.3318		3	0.0002		18	0.9967		4	0
	12	0.9165		10	0.5		4	0.0013		19	0.9992		5	0.0002
	13	0.9682		11	0.6682		5	0.0053		20	0.9999		6	0.0007
	14	0.9904		12	0.8083		6	0.0173		21	1		7	0.0026
	15	0.9978		13	0.9054		7	0.0466		22	1		8	0.0081
	16	0.9996		14	0.9608		8	0.105		23	1		9	0.0214
	17	1		15	0.9867		9	0.2024		24	1		10	0.0494
	18	1		16	0.9964		10	0.3388	25	0	0		11	0.1002
	19	1		17	0.9993		11	0.5		1	0		12	0.1808
20	0	0		18	0.9999		12	0.6612		2	0		13	0.2923
	1	0		19	1		13	0.7976		3	0.0001		14	0.4278
	2	0.0002		20	1		14	0.895		4	0.0005		15	0.5722
	3	0.0013		21	1		15	0.9534		5	0.002		16	0.7077
	4	0.0059	22	0	0		16	0.9827		6	0.0073		17	0.8192
	5	0.0207		1	0		17	0.9947		7	0.0216		18	0.8998
	6	0.0577		2	0.0001		18	0.9987		8	0.0539		19	0.9506
	7	0.1316		3	0.0004		19	0.9998		9	0.1148		20	0.9786
	8	0.2517		4	0.0022		20	1		10	0.2122		21	0.9919
	9	0.4119		5	0.0085		21	1		11	0.345		22	0.9974
	10	0.5881		6	0.0262		22	1		12	0.5		23	0.9993
	11	0.7483		7	0.0669		23	1		13	0.655		24	0.9998
	12	0.8684		8	0.1431	24	0	0		14	0.7878		25	1
	13	0.9423		9	0.2617		1	0		15	0.8852		26	1
	14	0.9793		10	0.4159		2	0		16	0.9461		27	1
	15	0.9941		11	0.5841		3	0.0001		17	0.9784		28	1
	16	0.9987		12	0.7383		4	0.0008		18	0.9927		29	1
	17	0.9998		13	0.8569		5	0.0033		19	0.998		30	1
	18	1		14	0.9331		6	0.0113		20	0.9995			
	19	1		15	0.9738		7	0.032		21	0.9999			
	20	1		16	0.9915		8	0.0758		22	1			
21	0	0		17	0.9978		9	0.1537		23	1			
	1	0		18	0.9996		10	0.2706		24	1			
	2	0.0001		19	0.9999		11	0.4194		25	1			
	3	0.0007		20	1		12	0.5806						
	4	0.0036		21	1		13	0.7294						

For $P(T \geq x)$, use $P(T \geq x) = 1 - P(T \leq x-1) = \sum_{j=0}^{x-1} b(j; n, 0.5)$

Index

Abatement cost, 910
Absence of excess capacity under price competition, 466
Accounting profit, 379
Additive inverse type, 35
Adjusted demand curve, 626
Administrative Reform Committee (ARC), 936
Adverse pricing, 719
Adverse selection, 718, 719
Adverse setting of interest rates, 720
Agent, 724
Aggregate excess demand, 705
Aggregative economics, 19
Applications of the PPCs, 11
Arc price elasticity, 104
Asset beta, 669
Asymmetric information, 716
Attainment of point of bliss, 704
Autarky, 830
Average cost (AC), 303
Average cost pricing, 908
Average expenditure curve of labour-buyer (AEB), 634
Average expenditure, AEL, 620
Average product, 261
Average revenue (AR), 333
Average revenue curve (ARs), 634
Average total cost (ATC), 303
Average wage (AW), 620

Backward bending supply curve, 218
Bad goods, 144
Bandwagon effect, 37
Bargaining power of the trade unions, 626, 636
Barometric price leadership, 515
Basic, 774
Baumol's dynamic model, 602
  of sales maximization, 606
Baumol's multi-product model without advertising, 601
Baumol's single product model of sales maximization, 592
Baumol's static models, 591
Bayes Nash equilibrium, 574
Bayes' theorem, 861
Bayesian decision rule, 574, 575, 861
Bayesian rationality, 574
Bayesianism, 574
Bergson's welfare contours, 703
Bertrand's model, 484
Bilateral monopoly, 633
Bilateral trade agreement, 816
Black market, 68
Blind risks, 861
Break-even analysis, 339
Budget constraint, 210
Bundling price, 930
Buyer's price, 75

Capital, 258
Capital Asset Pricing Model (CAPM), 670
Capital deepening technical progress, 289
Capitalist economies, 18
Cardinal utility approach, 133
Cartels maximizing joint profits, 499
Cash flows from investments, 669
Ceiling price, 68
Central problems, 3
Centrally planned, 18
Certainty, 574
Ceteris paribus, 19, 30, 32, 52, 121
Chamberlin's large group models of monopolistic competition, 459
Chamberlin's oligopoly model, 495, 496
Choice between abatement and emission fee, 735
CIPEC cartel, 929
Classical theory of
    international trade, 819
    rent, 644
Clearing-the-market equations, 53
Closed input–output model, 800
Cobb–Douglas indifference curves, 171
Cobb–Douglas preferences, 143, 171
Cobb–Douglas production, 286
    function, 285, 316
Cobweb theorem, 51, 58
Collisive oligopoly, 471
Colluding, 471
Collusive equilibrium, 538
Collusive oligopoly, 471
Commercial paper rate, 658
Compensation of employees, 300
Competitive, 707
    factor-market, 615
    firm versus monopolistic firm in the long term, 458
Complementary good, 30
Composite commodity theorem, 222, 223
Concave preferences, 145, 152, 153
Conditions, 415
Consistency and transitivity of choice, 138
Constant returns to scale, 265, 281
Consumer surplus (CS), 7
Consumer's bliss-point, 211
Consumer's demand, 30
Consumer's equilibrium, 134, 155

Consumer's indifference map, 158
Consumption externalities, 709
Contestable market theory, 516
Contraction of demand, 38
Contraction of supply, 45
Contractual rent, 644
Controlled price, 68
Convergent cobwebs, 60
Convex isoquants, 269
Convex preferences, 139, 215
Convexity of consumer preferences, 224
Cooperative game, 471, 538
Corporate bond rate, 658
Corporate social responsibility (CSR), 908
Cost of capital, 668
Cost of investment, 668
Costless entry and exit, 517
Cost–output elasticity, 329
Cost-plus pricing, 909
Cournot model with costless production, 472
Cournot's duopoly model, 473
Cournot's model, 484
Critique of Chamberlin's models, 464
Critique of indifference curve approach, 224
Cross-price elasticity, 102
Curve, 267

Dead weight loss, 399, 412
Decision tree analysis method, 855
Decisions under certainty, 679, 852
Decisions under risk, 679, 852
Decisions under uncertainty, 679, 852
Decrease in demand, 38, 39
Decrease in supply, 45
Decreasing returns to scale, 265, 281
Deductive method, 19
Degeneracy, 770
Degree of price elasticity, 112
Degree of scope economies, 330
Degrees of price discrimination, 418
Degrees of price elasticity of supply, 118
Demand curve, 31, 32, 35
Demand equation, 5, 31, 53
Demand function, 5, 31
Demand schedule, 31
Demonstration effect, 32
Depreciation allowance, 300

Derivation of grand utility possibility frontier, 704
Derivation of production possibility curve, 693
Determinants of demand, 32
    for factors of production, 614
Determinants of supply, 41
    of factors of production, 615
Determination of rate of interest, 657
Determination of sales-maximizing output under dyn, 606
Devine theory, 854
Direct intervention, 67
Discount rate, 658, 669
Discounting factor, 656
Discrete or integer preferences, 143
Discrete preferences, 143
Diseconomies of scale, 331
Distinction between micro and macro branches of economics, 19, 20
Divergent cobweb, 60, 61
Dominant strategy, 538, 578, 579
    equilibrium, 540
Double-log-linear, 883
Dual problem, 759, 761
Duopoly equilibrium Cournot' version, 482
Duopoly, 355, 471
Duopsony, 355
Dynamic equilibrium, 51
Dynamic model, 591

Economic activities, 2
Economic bad, 144
Economic problem, 1
Economic profits, 379
Economically viable, 288
Economic-rent, 639
Economies of scope, 330
Edgeworth box, 695
    of optimality of exchange of commodities, 696
Edgeworth contract, 692
Effective yield, 666
Effect of
    efficiency wage, 726
    increase in overheads on sales maximization, 594
    levy of indirect tax on oligopolistic, 498
    lump-sum tax, 429
    non-pivotal shift in AR on monopoly PR, 426

    non-pivotal shift in AR on price-output, 427
    pivotal shift accompanied by a change, 427
    pivotal shift in AR on price output decision, 426
    pivotal shift in demand on price-output, 498
    price discrimination, 419
    specific tax on price output decisions, 595
    unit tax on price-output of a monopoly, 429, 431
    taxation on price-output decisions of a monopoly, 428
Efficiency, 701
    of competitive equilibrium, 698
    in distribution of goods, 695
    parameter, 287, 288
    of resource allocation, 691
    wage theory, 725
Efficient provision of a public good, 739
Egalitarian society, 702
Elasticity of, 882
    demand, 100, 101
    factor substitution, 286
    supply, 115
EMI (equated monthly installment), 674
Endowments, 705
Engel curve, 169
Entrepreneur, 259
Equilibrium, 46, 47
    allocation, 707
    of duopolistic market (Bertrand's model), 484
    level of employment of a factor in competitive factor, 617
    of monopoly in short-run, 408
    of multiplant monopoly, 439
    of oligopolistic firms under indirect taxation, 497
Equity, 701
Excess capacity, 410, 467
Excess demands, 705
Existence of loss making monopoly through price discrimination, 424
Expansion of demand, 37
Expansion of supply, 44
Expansion path, 276
Expected monetary value (EMV) method, 855
Expected pay-off, 544
Expected profit from perfect information, 857
Explicit costs, 301

Extensive form of a game, 556
External benefits, 735
External costs, 301
External diseconomy, 731
External economies, 324
Externalities, 712, 731
    in consumption, 709, 734, 736
    in production, 734
    and market failure, 731

Factor costs, 299
Factor intensity, 287
Factor-market, 52, 613
Factor of production, 3
Factors affecting price elasticity of demand, 114
Fair allocation, 709, 710
Faith theory of decision-making, 854
False paradigm, 854
Feasible, 774
    region, 747, 748
Features of Cobb–Douglas production function, 286
Features of indifference curves, 146
Financial capital, 258
First-degree price discrimination, 419
First order tests, 876
First theorem of welfare economics, 707
Fixed costs, 302
Fixed utility curve, 139
Flow, 660
Flux's proportionality method, 113
Followers, 505
Free rider problem, 737
Free rider, 737
Free trade, 79
Full protection, 81
Future costs, 301

Gain from exchange, 699, 701, 830
Gain from specialization, 699, 701, 830
Gains from free trade, 699
Gains from trade, 700
Game theory, 535
General equilibrium, 19
    analysis, 686
Geographical discrimination, 365, 414

Giffen good, 32, 196
Government final consumption expenditure (CG), 787
Grant of subsidy, 76
Graphical or geometrical method, 113
Gross complements, 151
Gross domestic capital formation (GDCF), 787
Gross domestic fixed capital formation (GDFCF), 787
Gross domestic private investment (GDPI), 787
Gross domestic product at market price, 787
Gross profit, 379
Gross substitutes, 151
Gross value added at market prices (GVAMP), 787
Group equilibrium, 459

Harsanyi transformation, 575, 861
Hawkins–Simon conditions, 789
Heckscher–Ohlin theorem, 825
Heroic assumption, 459
Homogeneous, 568
    function, 285
Homothetic preferences, 143, 171
Hotelling rule, 676
Hurwitz approach, 865

Idle capacity, 746
Imperfect substitutes, 150
Implications of Baumol's static single-product mod, 592
Implications of the Prisoners' Dilemma, 519
Implicit costs, 301
Income consumption curve (ICC), 165
Income effect, 36
    component, 184
Income elasticity, 101
Income–demand, 32
Increase in demand, 37
Increase in supply, 44
Increasing returns to scale, 265, 281
Incremental analysis method, 855, 857
Indeterminacy of equilibrium of a bilateral monopoly, 633
Indifference curve, 138, 139
Indifference curve approach to analysis of demand, 137

Indirect intervention, 73, 361
Inductive method, 19
Industry of origin, 785
Infeasible solution, 774
Input-output isoquant, 269
Intangible service, 3
Interdependent, 471
Interest, 300
Interior optima, 162
Internal economies of scale, 324
Inter-plant economies of scale, 324
Inter-temporal discrimination, 364, 414
Inter-temporal price discrimination, 424, 425, 909
Inter-temporal pricing, 909
Inter-temporal production decisions, 675
Intra-plant economies of scale, 324
Investment decisions of consumers, 672
Inward shift, 39
Isocline, 280, 281
Isocost curve, 267
Isolated bundle, 141
Iso-present-value
    curve, 604
    function, 604
    map, 605
Isoprofit curve, 475
Isoprofit map, 475
Isoquant, 267

Job–shirking models, 725
Joint profit-maximizing Cartel, 500

Key column, 763
Key element, 763
Key row, 763
Kinked demand curve, 496
Kinked demand model of Sweezy, 496
Kinked isoquant, 269

Labour-capital ratio, 623
Labour coefficient, 820
Labour deepening technical progress, 289
Labour-force participation rate, 615
Lagrange's multiplier, 157
Laplace criteria of equal likelihood, 865

Law of demand, 5, 30, 32
Law of diminishing marginal productivity, 270
Law of diminishing marginal utility, 35, 136
Law of family expenditure, 169
Law of initial increasing returns, 263
Law of supply, 41
Learning by doing, 324
Learning curve, 324
Learning rate, 324, 328
Leisure–income indifference, 215
    curve, 214
Leisure-income trade-off line, 214
Leontief isoquant, 269
Leontief's paradox, 830
Leontief's table, 785
Less than unitary elastic, 112
Limit pricing, 557
Linear break-even, 336
Linear demand, 31
Linear isoquant, 269
Linear programming isoquant, 269
Linear programming problem (LPP-Model), 746
Linearity, 747
Load factor, 323
Log-linear form, 882
Long period supply, 50
Long-run average cost curve (LAC), 313
Long-run costs, 322
Long-run equilibrium, 48, 50
Long-run expansion path, 277
Long-run normal profit of a monopoly, 410
Long-run production, 261, 264
Long-run supply curve (LRS), 391
Loss-avoidance strategy, 547
Low cost price leader, firms with equal market
    share, 506
Low-cost price leader, firms with unequal market
    share, 507
Lumping method, 19
Lump-sum tax, 595

Macroeconomics, 18
Macro theory of distribution, 19
Macro-variables, 19
Managerial costs, 323
Managerial indivisibility, 266
Man-machine system, 324

Marginal analysis, 133, 859
  method, 855
Marginal conditions of Pareto optimality, 691
Marginal cost (MC), 304
Marginal cost curve (MCS), 634
Marginal cost of abatement (MCA), 734, 910
Marginal cost pricing, 908
Marginal efficiency of capital, 671
Marginal expenditure, 620
Marginal external benefit (MEB), 733, 735
Marginal external cost (MEC), 731
Marginal opportunity cost, 11
Marginal physical product, 627
Marginal physical product curve of labour (MPPL), 622
Marginal product of labour (MPL), 262
Marginal productivity theory of distribution, 628
Marginal rate of product transformation, 11
Marginal rate of substitution, 137
Marginal rate of technical, 267
Marginal rate of time preference, 199
Marginal revenue (MR), 333
Marginal revenue curve (MRS), 634
Marginal social benefit (MSB), 733
Marginal social cost (MSC), 731, 910
Marginal utility (MU), 35
Marginal Wage (MW), 620
Market, 354
Market behaviour, 100
Market demand, 39
Market economies, 18
Market failure and its sources, 711
Market-oriented economies, 17
Market-oriented producers, 29
Market-oriented society, 702
Market penetrating price, 909
Market power, 711
Market price, 62, 356
Market share curve, 460
Market share demand curve, 462
Market sharing cartels, 503
Market signalling, 720, 721
Market skimming price, 909
Market supply, 45
  curve, 45, 46
  and market demand of factors, 625
Mark-up price, 436
Marshall's total outlay method, 113

Maximin, 578
Maximin strategy, 548
Meaning of demand, 30
Measurement of monopoly power, 411
Measurement of price elasticity of demand, 113
Mercantilism, 819
Microeconomics, 18
Micro-variables, 19
Minimax, 578
Minimax regret, 865
Minimum optimal scale of plant, 323, 326
Minimum support price, 41, 67, 72
Mixed bundling, 931
Mixed economies, 18
Mixed strategy, 536, 542
Models with damped oscillations, 60
Models with explosive oscillations, 60
Models with perpetual oscillations, 60
Modern theory of costs, 319
Modern theory of international trade, 825
Money cost, 301
Money illusion, 658
Monopolistic competition, 355, 456
  and economic efficiency, 458
Monopolistic exploitation, 619
  of labour, 629
Monopolistic market, 355
Monopoly, 355, 633
  power, 411
  under dynamic changes, 426
  versus competitive firm, 441
Monopsonistic buyer firm versus labour union, 637
Monopsonistic exploitation, 620, 629
Monopsony, 355, 633
  and monopsony power, 442
  power and its sources, 444
Monotonic preference, 140
Moral hazard, 722
  and allocative efficiency, 723
More is better (MIB), 140, 146
More than unitary elastic, 112
MPPL or marginal physical product, 627
Multilateral trade agreements, 816
Multiplant monopoly, 437
Multiplant monopoly, 437
Multiple equilibrium, 51, 52
Multiple optimal solutions, 775
Multiplicative inverse type, 35

Nash equilibrium, 489, 517, 518, 519, 538
Natural monopoly, 415, 418
Nature's move, 574
Negative externality, 732
Negative network externalities, 39
Negative specific tax, 76
Neither perfectly specific nor perfectly non-specific factors, 642
Net benefit (NB), 442
Net demands, 705
Net present value (NPV), 659
Net present value criterion for capital investment, 668
Net value added at factor cost (NVAFC), 793
Neutral, 289
    equilibrium, 48
    good, 144, 151
    technical progress, 289
No excess capacity, 466
Nominal discount rate, 669
Non-collusive oligopoly, 471
Non-cooperative equilibrium, 517
Non-cooperative game, 471
Non-economic regions, 288
Non-exclusion, 736
Non-interior optima, 162
Non-linear demand, 31
Non-negativity constraint, 746
Non-pivotal shift, 426
Non-price competition and free entry-exit as sources, 467
Non-rival consumption, 737
Non-simultaneous, 544
Non-solution variables, 779
Non-trivial solution, 801
Non-zero-sum-game, 537, 549
Normal equations, 877
Normal goods, 35
Normative economics, 17
N-person or N-player game, 537

Objective function, 745
Objective of price discrimination, 417
Offer curve, 833
Oligopolistic market, 520
Oligopoly, 355, 470
Oligopsony, 355

OPEC Cartel, 929
Opportunity cost, 4, 300
Optimal basic feasible solution (OBFS), 774
Optimal product mix, 746
Optimality of resource allocation, 14
Optimistic approach (MaxiMax), 865
Output maximizing least cost employment of factors (OMLCEF), 278
Outward shift, 37

Pareto efficiency, 691
Pareto-efficient allocation, 707
Partial equilibrium, 51
    analysis, 19, 686
Partly market-oriented and partly planned, 18
Patent, 738
Patent life, 363, 738
Pay-off matrix, 518, 539
    for oligopolistic game, 518
Peak load pricing, 424, 425, 909
Pecuniary economies, 329, 333
Perceived excess capacity as social cost of variety, 465
Percent tax, 75
Perfect complements, 150, 151, 171
Perfect market, 354
Perfect mobility, 625
Perfect price discrimination, 420
Perfect substitutes, 150, 171
Perfectly elastic, 108, 112
Perfectly inelastic, 108, 112
Perfectly non-specific factors, 642
Perfectly specific factors, 642
Personal discrimination, 364, 414
Perspective buyer, 30
Pessimistic Approach (MaxiMin), 865
Pivotal element, 763
Planned economies, 18
Planning curves, 313
Point of satiation, 141
Point price elasticity, 105
Pollution tax, 910
Positive economics, 17
Positive externalities, 732
Positive network externalities, 38
Price ceiling, 68, 361
Price consumption curve (PCC), 165, 174

Price discrimination, 414, 418
Price-effect, 36
Price elasticity demand, 104
Price elasticity of supply, 117, 119
Price floor, 67
Price followers, 471, 505
Price leader, 471, 505
Price leadership by a dominant firm, 511, 512
Price leadership by a low-cost firm, 505
Price leadership models, 505
Price maker, 334
Price mechanism, 3, 18, 30
Price offer curve, 174
Price-output decisions of monopolistically competitve firm, 457
Price signaling, 520
Price taker, 333, 355
Pricing policies of state monopolies, 418
Pricing with crowding costs, 909
Pricing with pollution cost, 909
Primal problem, 761
Primal, 760
Primary input coefficients, 789
Prime rate, 658
Principal-agent problem, 723, 724
Principle of maximum social advantage, 3
Principles of equity and social justice, 3
Prisoners' dilemma, 517, 519, 538
Private cost, 301
Private final consumption expenditure (CH), 787
Problem of inefficiency, 4
Problem of resource allocation and reallocation, 14
Producer's equilibrium, 269
Producers' sector, 787
Producers' surplus, 68
Product curve, 280
Production, 258
    boundary, 787
    costs, 909
    function, 259
    possibility curve, 4, 10
    process, 258
Production possibility frontier (PPF), 10
Product line, 280
Product market, 52, 613
Profit and loss account, 379
Profit maximizing pricing, 908
Prospective buyer, 30

Public distribution system (PDS), 70
Public good, 712, 736
Purchasing power, 30
Pure bundling, 931
Pure competition, 356
Pure oligopoly, 499
Pure strategies, 541

Quality standardization, 721
Quality uncertainties, 717
Quality uncertainty as a source of market failure, 718
Quantity followers, 471
Quantity leader, 471
Quantity leadership, 489
Quasi-linear, 154
    preferences, 143, 171
Quasi-rent, 639, 645, 646

Rate of discount, 656
Rate of willingness, 199
Ration point constraint, 210
Rationing policy, 209
Rawlsian society, 702
Reaction curve approach, 475
    to duopoly equilibrium, 477
Real and nominal discount rates, 669
Real capital, 258
Real costs, 301
Real discount rate, 669
Real economies, 329, 333
Rectangular hyperbola, 67
Rectangular periphery cobwebs, 60
Regret, 866
Related goods, 32
Remedy to negative externality, 734
Rent, 646
    fertility difference, 644
    productivity difference, 644
Rent control in short- and long-run, 77
Reputation and standardization, 721
Reserve capacity, 319
Residual input coefficients, 789
Resource-gap, 1
Retention pricing, 909
Returns to scale, 265, 280

Returns to variable proportions, 263, 278
Revealed preference approach, 225
Revenue, 300, 332
Ricardo's concept of gains, 823
Risk-averse strategy, 547
Risk bearing, 720

SAC (short-run average cost), 384
Saddle point, 578
Sales growth function, 604
Saucer-shaped short-run average variable cost curve (Saucer-shaped SAVC), 319
SAVC (short-run average variable cost), 384
Scale, 265
Scale economies index, 329
Science of choice-making, 2
Second-degree price discrimination, 419
Second order tests, 876
Second theorem of welfare economics, 707
Self-adjustment process, 6
Seller's price, 75
Sequential game, 471
Shadow prices, 761
Shift-factors, 31
Shifts in demand, 357
Short period supply (SPS), 48
Short-run abnormal profit of monopoly, 408
Short-run average cost curve (SAC), 314, 409
Short-run costs, 319
Short-run equilibrium, 48
Short-run loss of a monopoly, 409
Short-run normal profit of a monopoly, 409
Short-run production, 260
Shutdown output, 385
Shutdown point, 385
Shutdown price, 385
Simple decision tree, 861
Simplex method, 759, 762
Simultaneous equilibrium of production and consumption, 697
Simultaneous game, 471, 544
Simultaneous quantity setting, 472
  under costless production, 473
Single buyer, 633
Single seller, 633
Singleton, 574
Slack variables, 765

Slicing method, 19
Slope of the indifference curve, 137
SMC (short-run marginal cost), 384
Social cost, 301
  of monopoly, 412
  of monopsony power, 445
  of variety, 466
Solution variables, 779
Sophisticated quantity leader, 492
Source of monopoly power, 411
Specific tax, 595
Specific unit tax, 73
Stabilization of producers' income, 81
Stable equilibrium, 48
Stackelberg model, 489
Stackelberg's disequilibrium, 490, 568
Stackelberg's duopoly model, 554
  of quantity leadership, 490
Standardization, 721
Static equilibrium, 50
Static model, 591
Static multi-product model with advertising, 600
Static multi-product model without advertising, 600
Static single product model with advertising, 595
Static single product model without advertising, 592
Steeper demand curve, 108
Stigler's model of open oligopoly, 557
Stock, 660
Structural constraints, 746
Subjective notion, 854
Substitution effect, 37
  component, 184
Success of price discrimination, 415
Sunk cost, 301
Supply, 40
  equation, 5
  function, 5
  schedule, 41
Supply curve, 41
  of a monopoly, 413
Surplus variables, 765
Swapped allocation, 710
Sweezy's kinked demand model of sticky price, 497
Sweezy's model, 499

Tangible commodity, 3
Technical indivisibility, 266
Technology matrix, 789
Theorems of welfare economics, 707
Theory of
    comparative advantage, 819
    distribution, 4, 364
    economic growth, 19
    employment, 4, 19
    growth and development, 4
    income, 19
    output, 19
    price, 3, 19
    production, 3
Third-degree price discrimination, 419
'tit-for-tat' strategy, 553
Total cost, 299, 304
Total fixed cost, 302, 303
Total net marginal revenue curve, 926
Total product of labour (TPL), 263
Total revenue, 300, 332, 645
Total sum of squares (TSS), 886
Total variable cost (TVC), 302, 303, 645
Trade protection, 79
Tragedy of commons, 712
Transaction matrix, 789
Transfer price, 911, 912
Transformation curves, 202
Treasury bill rate, 657
Treasury bond rate, 658
Trivial solution, 801
Two-person or two-player game, 537

Unavoidable costs, 301
Unbounded optimal solution, 777
Unique and multiple equilibrium, 51
Unitary elastic, 112
Unstable equilibrium, 48
User cost, 676
Util, 133
Utilitarian society, 702
Utility function, 220
Utility maximizing least cost basket (UMLCB), 165, 278

Value of marginal product (VMP), 629
Value of the game, 578
Variable cost, 302
Veblen effect, 32
Very long-run production, 261
Very short period supply (VSPS), 48
Very short-run production, 260

Walrasian adjustment process, 53
Walrasian equilibrium, 707
Walras' law, 705, 706
Weak Axiom of Revealed Preference (WARP), 226
Welfare economics, 4
Welfare function, 703
Willingness curve, 199, 220
Willingness to borrow, 199

Zero-sum game, 536, 580